# Handbook of Research on Sc
# Schooling, and Human Develo

Children spend more time in school than in any social institution outside the home and schools probably exert more influence on children's development and life chances than any environment beyond the home and neighborhood. The purpose of this book is to document some important ways schools influence children's development and to describe various models and methods for studying schooling effects. Key features include:

**Comprehensive Coverage**—This is the first book to provide a comprehensive review of what is known about schools as a context for human development. Topical coverage ranges from theoretical foundations to investigative methodologies and from classroom-level influences such as teacher–student relations to broader influences such as school organization and educational policies.

**Cross-Disciplinary**—This volume brings together the divergent perspectives, methods, and findings of scholars from a variety of disciplines, among them educational psychology, developmental psychology, school psychology, social psychology, psychiatry, sociology, and educational policy.

**Chapter Structure**—To insure continuity, chapter authors 1) describe how schooling influences are conceptualized, 2) identify their theoretical and methodological approaches, 3) discuss the strengths and weaknesses of existing research, and 4) highlight implications for future research, practice, and policy.

**Methodologies**—Chapters included in the text feature various methodologies including longitudinal studies, hierarchical linear models, experimental and quasi-experimental designs, and mixed methods.

**Judith L. Meece** (Ph.D., University of Michigan) is Professor and Chair of Human Development and Psychological Studies at the University of North Carolina–Chapel Hill. She has conducted research in school settings for over 25 years, and was the first scholar to write a child and adolescent textbook specifically aimed at educators. A Fellow of APA Division 15, Meece's research focuses on the role of classroom and school influences on the development of adolescents' academic motivation, future aspirations, and educational attainment.

**Jacquelynne S. Eccles** (Ph.D., University of California at Los Angeles) is McKeachie/Pintrich Distinguished University Professor of Psychology and Education at the University of Michigan. Her research focuses on gender-role socialization, school influences on academic motivation, and social development in the family and school context. Eccles has served as the president of the Society for Research on Adolescence, and has received numerous awards for her lifetime contributions to research on adolescence and human development.

# Handbook of Research on Schools, Schooling, and Human Development

Edited by

## Judith L. Meece

## Jacquelynne S. Eccles

Routledge
Taylor & Francis Group

NEW YORK AND LONDON

First published 2010
by Routledge
270 Madison Avenue, New York, NY 10016

Simultaneously published in the UK
by Routledge
2 Park Square, Milton Park, Abingdon, Oxon OX14 4RN

*Routledge is an imprint of the Taylor & Francis Group, an informa business*

© 2010 Taylor & Francis

Typeset in Times by EvS Communication Networx, Inc.
Printed and bound in the United States of America on acid-free paper by Sheridan Books, Inc.

*Library of Congress Cataloging in Publication Data*
Handbook of research on schools, schooling, and human development / edited by Judith L. Meece, Jacquelynne S. Eccles.
p. cm.
Includes bibliographical references and index.
1. Education, Primary—Research—Handbooks, manuals, etc. 2. Education, Secondary—Research—Handbooks, manuals, etc.
3. Educational achievemen—Research—Handbooks, manuals, etc. 4. Child development—Research—Handbooks, manuals, etc.
5. Adolescent development—Research—Handbooks, manuals, etc. I. Meece, Judith L. II. Eccles, Jacquelynne S.
LB1507.H255 2010
370.7'2—dc22
2009045554

ISBN 10: 0-8058-5948-9 (hbk)
ISBN 10: 0-8058-5949-7 (pbk)
ISBN 10: 0-203-87484-6 (ebk)

ISBN 13: 978-0-8058-5948-5 (hbk)
ISBN 13: 978-0-8058-5949-2 (pbk)
ISBN 13: 978-0-203-87484-4 (ebk)

*For our authors, students, and readers with gratitude
for advancing this field of inquiry.*

**Judith L. Meece**
**Jacquelynne S. Eccles**

# Contents

# List of Figures

# List of Tables

# Preface

Research on the school effects on children's development has greatly expanded over the last 30 years. Whereas early studies focused on school effectiveness in terms of standardized achievement, more recent studies have focused on a wider range of effects such as social and emotional development. Research now shows that the experiences and interactions of young people at school have a lasting influence on almost every aspect of development. Moreover, for many young people today, schools play an influential role in protecting them from the adverse effects of poverty, dangerous neighborhoods, or difficult home environments. At present, however, there is no single volume that brings together research and scholarship on schools as a context for children's development. This *Handbook* fills the gap by bringing together the research and scholarship of over 50 scholars in the fields of education, psychology, sociology, medicine and psychiatry, and educational policy.

We, the editors, have over 25 years of studying classroom and schooling effects on children's development. During this time the goals of schooling have shifted from addressing issues of desegregation and educational equity to increasing academic achievement, educational attainment, and workforce preparation for the global economy. In recent weeks, we have heard calls from the nation's highest office to increase the length of the school day and the school calendar. These requests come at a time of unprecedented school enrollments, student diversity, accountability pressures, teacher shortages, and declining school budgets. There is much we demand of educational practitioners today. Thus, in designing this *Handbook*, we wanted to produce a scholarly but practical discussion of research on schools, schooling, and development. The *Handbook* is intended as a resource for educational professionals, policymakers, scholars, and students. We anticipate that scholars and students from different fields of psychology (cognitive, developmental, educational, school, and social), education (educational leadership and administration, curriculum, teaching and learning, research methods, and school counseling), sociology, and public policy will find this *Handbook* useful and informative. In summary, the *Handbook* is intended for both consumers and producers of research with the overall goal of creating positive school environments for children and youth based on the best scholarly and empirical evidence available today.

# Acknowledgments

As coeditors we are grateful to each of the authors of this volume who understood the value of this *Handbook* and gave generously of their time to write and revise chapters. We also acknowledge the support these authors received from schools, students, and family members during their research and writing. We are also greatly indebted to Lane Akers and his staff at Lawrence Erlbaum Associates, now Routledge, Taylor & Francis Group, for understanding the importance of this volume and his unwavering support despite unexpected delays. We would also like to thank several external reviewers for their support on various chapters of the *Handbook:* Linda Baker, David Bergin, Peter Blatchford, David Bjorklund, Sara Rimm-Kaufman, Lisa Linnebrink-Garcia, Samuel Miller, Tamera Murdock, Scott Paris, Dale Schunk, Samuel Song, and Christopher Wolters. We also acknowledge the research and editing support of Karyl Askew, Katie Bouchard, Belinda Locke, Victoria Schaefer, and Meredith Walton at UNC-CH, as well as Lynn Goeller of EvS Communications, and Alexander Sharp of Routledge.

The editors have a long history of collaboration. We were very fortunate to share this history to together and to have other University of Michigan colleagues who made important contributions to this field of research. We wish to especially acknowledge the important early contributions of Phyllis Blumenfeld, Harold Stevenson, Janis Jacobs, Carol Kaczala, Martin Maehr, Carol Midgley, Paul Pintrich, Robert Roeser, Arnold Sameroff, and Allan Wigfield in assisting in the development of this field of inquiry. We also acknowledge the significant contributions of Victor Battistich to research on schooling and development. A contributing author, Victor, died unexpectedly in June 2008.

The final stages of this *Handbook* project were completed during a semester research leave to Judith Meece from the School of Education at UNC-CH in Spring 2009.

*Judith L. Meece*
*Jacquelynne S. Eccles*

# Part I

## Introduction

# 1

# Schools as a Context of Human Development

*Judith L. Meece and Victoria A. Schaefer*

Schools are one of the most influential contexts for children's development in our society. By the time they graduate from high school, children and adolescents will have spent more time in schools than any other social institution outside their home and community. Schools not only influence children's acquisition of knowledge and skills, but also provide an important context for their social and emotional growth. From the way schools are organized to the instructional and social processes that occur within and outside classrooms, children's daily experiences at school affect their behavior, beliefs, and well-being. Additionally, the cumulative effects of children's schooling experiences strongly contribute to their lives as adults, including future educational opportunities, career choices, and lifetime earnings.

The study of schooling experiences and children's development is a growing field of inquiry. Beginning with *Equality of Educational Opportunity* (Coleman et al., 1966), the field has expanded in terms of the theoretical perspectives and topics represented. As this edited volume demonstrates, children's schooling experiences have been examined through the lens of developmental, sociological, educational, and policy perspectives. Whereas early studies focused on school effectiveness in terms of achievement scores, more recent studies have examined the relation of school contexts to measures of social adjustment, identity development, and even mental health. Additionally, the development of new research methodologies has also contributed to the expansion of research on schools and development. Longitudinal studies have documented the long-term impact of school transitions, grade retention, curricular tracking, and other schooling experiences on children's development. Similarly, hierarchical linear modeling procedures provide methods for examining the ways in which individual, classroom, and school level characteristics interact in complex ways to influence children's development. The *Handbook of Research on Schools, Schooling, and Human Development* includes a diverse range of theoretical perspectives, developmental outcomes, and methodological approaches.

## Current Status of Youth in Schools

The focus of this edited volume is development during the elementary and secondary years when school attendance is compulsory in the United States. Although there are many excellent international and comparative studies of schooling experiences, this *Handbook* focuses on children's and adolescents' schooling experiences in American schools. Nearly 50 million students attend public elementary and secondary schools in the United States, and school enrollment is expected to reach a record of 54 million by 2017 (Planty et al., 2008). America's schools now serve a more diverse population of students than ever before. The number of racial or ethnic minorities in America's schools, 43% of the school population, has nearly tripled since the early 1970s, and the diversity of students extends beyond race and ethnicity. Approximately 10 million school-age children speak a language other than English at home, and an even larger proportion of America's students qualify for free or reduced lunch due to low family income status (Planty et al., 2008). Moreover, our students attend schools in diverse settings. Approximately, 35.4% and 30.4% of students attend schools in suburban or urban locations respectively, compared to 12.9% in towns and 21.3% in rural areas (Provansnik et al., 2007). Schools in these geographical regions must address different issues in meeting the needs of their children, such as teacher shortages, low parent education involvement, low tax revenues, high poverty rates, geographical isolation, and language diversity.

This edited volume draws together research on schooling experiences and children's development during a time of heightened scrutiny in public education from the highest level of government to local school boards regarding accountability and reform. Schools today are being asked to meet important challenges. International studies indicate that American students are routinely outperformed by other industrialized countries on standardized tests, especially in mathematics and science (Planty et al., 2008). The high school graduation rates of U.S. students are also among the lowest for industrialized countries (National Governor's Association, 2005). Despite school reform efforts over the last decades, significant differences in the academic achievement of White, Black, and Hispanic students remain, especially at the high school level (Planty et al., 2008). Lastly, data indicate that with the implementation of national accountability standards grade retention is on the rise, and it is a powerful predictor of school underachievement and drop out (Allensworth & Nagaoka, chapter 20 this volume).

While reports of school achievement and completion raise concerns about the status of America's children, reports of school violence and crime have shown some improvements. Over the last several years school violence has been declining but it has not yet returned to its lowest rate at the beginning of this decade (Planty et al., 2008). Large scale studies reveal that between 10 and 15% of students feel their schools are unsafe (DeVoe et al., 2003). One of young people's strongest fears is peer harassment in the form of bullying. In a study of over 15,000 adolescents (6th to 10th grade), nearly 30% of the participants indicated involvement in physical or verbal bullying, either as the bully or the victim (Nansel et al., 2001). Peer harassment at school has immediate consequences for school engagement and achievement, but it also has a long lasting impact on self-esteem, social isolation, and depression (Olweus, 1993).

Taken together, the reports on the status of children in America's schools reveal a number of important challenges facing primary and secondary education. While important gains have been made in achievement since the late 1970s, large achievement discrepancies remain related to ethnicity, family income, and geographical location. Moreover, a large proportion of America's youth report *not* feeling connected, engaged, or motivated to learn in school (National Research Council and Institutes of Medicine, 2004). By adolescence, poor achievement and disaffection combine such that far too many of America's youth leave school before earning a high school diploma. To address these issues, schools must implement practices, programs, and policies to foster the positive development of all its youth. There is now a wealth of research on schools, schooling, and human development to inform these efforts.

## Organization of *Handbook*

The purpose of this edited *Handbook* is to (1) document some important ways in which schools influence children's development; (2) describe various models for studying schooling effects; and (3) provide methods for studying schooling effects. The *Handbook* includes 30 chapters,

organized into seven sections. In chapter 2, Jacquelynne Eccles and Robert Roeser describe an ecological model for examining the influence of school contexts on adolescent development. This multilayered model of schooling hierarchically orders the effects of schools from the proximal influences of learning tasks and teacher–student interactions within classrooms to the more distal influences of district, state, and national educational policies outside of schools. Jacquelynne Eccles, Carol Midgley, Robert Roeser, and other colleagues at the University of Michigan were among the first researchers to identify ways in which certain aspects of the school environment can shape developmental trajectories in adolescence and beyond. This research played a significant role in shaping a new field of research on schooling and development. Eccles and Roeser's ecological model of school contexts guided the development and organization of the *Handbook*. Each chapter in this *Handbook* connects with the chapter in some important way.

Part II highlights research on the classroom context which has received the most attention from developmental and educational researchers thus far. Early classroom research focused on the effects of teacher management styles, classroom organization, nature of classroom work, student response opportunities, and so on. As demonstrated by the chapters in this section, classroom-level research has begun to focus more on the quality of instructional processes in terms of promoting academic and social development, as well as school engagement. This section leads off with a chapter, by Bridget Hamre and Robert Pianta (chapter 3), describing a methodology for examining classroom influences.

Part III examines school level processes. For the most part, developmental researchers and scholars have drawn on sociological studies to understand processes at the school level. Like Part II, this section deviates from previous traditions by examining the contributions of developmental theories to understanding the larger school context influences on development. All three chapters featured in this section draw on ecological theories to examine the influence of schools as developmental contexts on youths' social, moral, and civic development. In these chapters, we learn that schools have more than an instructional or academic attainment purpose; schools help to develop the citizens of tomorrow. This section leads off with a chapter, based on John Dewey's writing, written by Victor Battistich, a strong advocate for the positive role schools could play in developing the moral and civic attitudes of youth.

The effects of school transitions emerged as a field of developmental study in the late 1970s. By this time, federal funding was available to study the transition of Head Start students to elementary school. At the same time, national achievement data were suggesting that early benefits of Head Start could not be sustained. Also, due to the seminal work of Roberta Simmons and Robert Blyth (1987), many developmental and educational researchers began to focus on the effects of school transitions during the early adolescent years. For developmental scientists, these transitions represent a time when various developmental processes undergo significant change. Youth development is most challenged during these points of transition. For this reason, we feature four chapters on school transitions, and include one chapter by Melissa Roderick and Ginger Stoker (chapter 14), on the postsecondary transition, an understudied area of inquiry.

For the past 30 years, the editors of this volume have been strong advocates for educational equity. Most studies focused on educational equity and access have drawn on sociological theories or policy analyses. Of the various fields of schooling and development featured in this volume, this section needed to include a strong interdisciplinary focus. Five chapters are featured in this section, each of which is focused on a particular socioeconomic, ethnic, or racial group; however, there are common themes found across these chapters. In reading these chapters, it is clear that students' schooling experiences vary significantly depending on race, ethnicity, and gender; however, low family income and poverty are, by far, the most persistent barriers to attaining educational equity in American schools. Doris Entwisle, Karl Alexander, and Linda Olson (chapter 15) provide a 30-year analysis of the Beginning School Study of 1982 that focuses on the long-term impact of children's socioeconomic status.

Part VI features research on school organization and educational policy. In Eccles and Roeser's model of school contexts (chapter 2 this volume), the organization and policies of schools are distal influences which affect young people's development through shaping learning opportunities (e.g., class size, curricular tracking, retention and suspension policies, etc.), parent involvement programs, access to extracurricular activities, and school calendars. Part VI of the *Handbook* provides a wide sampling of research on these areas of schooling influences. Missing from this section are reviews of the effects of class size and curricular tracking; however, there are many excellent reviews of this research available.[1]

Part VII provides a description of five school-based interventions designed to improve a range of developmental outcomes, including school achievement, reading abilities, and social competence. The interventions draw on both quasi- and randomized controlled experiments. This section begins with James Comer's review (chapter 26) of the Yale Child Student Center School Development Program, which began in the late 1960s as one of the first comprehensive school reform efforts directed toward promoting children's development.

## Summary

Research on the influence of schools and schooling on human development is an emerging field of inquiry. This *Handbook* was intended to gather together important research in this area, to offer an interdisciplinary perspective, and to provide direction for future research. It is hoped that this field of inquiry will continue to grow and to expand over the next decades.

## Note

1. For an excellent review of research on class size, see Finn, Pannozzo, and Achilles (2003); Oakes (2005) provides a comprehensive overview of research on curricular tracking.

## References

Coleman, J. S., Campbell, E. Q., Hobson, C. J., McPartland, J., Mood, A. M., Weinfeld, F. D., et al. (1966). *Equality of educational opportunity.* Washington, DC: U.S. Department of Health, Education, and Welfare.

DeVoe, J. F., Katharin, P., Phillip, K., Ruddy, S. A., Miller, A. K., Planty, M., et al. (2003). *Indicators of school crime and safety* (6th ed.). Washington, DC: U.S. Department of Education, National Center for Education Statistics.

Finn, J. D., Pannozzo, G. M., & Achilles, C. M. (2003). The "whys" of class size: Student behavior in small classes. *Review of Educational Research, 73*(3), 321–368.

Nansel, T. R., Overpeck, M., Pilla, R. S., Ruan, W. J., Simons-Morton, B., & Scheidt, P. (2001). Bullying behaviors among U.S. youth: Prevalence and association with psychosocial adjustment. *Journal of the American Medical Association, 285,* 1094–2100.

National Governors Association. (2005). *2005 National educational summit on high schools.* Washington, DC: Author.

National Research Council and Institute of Medicine. (2004). *Engaging schools: Fostering high school students' motivation to learn.* Washington, DC: The National Academies Press.

Oakes, J. (2005). *Keeping track: How schools structure inequality* (2nd ed.). New Haven, CT: Yale University Press.

Olweus, D. (1993). Victimization by peers: Antecedents and long-term outcomes. In K. H. Rubin & J. B. Asendorpf (Eds.), *Social withdrawal, inhibition, and shyness in childhood* (pp. 315–341). Hillsdale, NJ: Erlbaum.

Planty, M., Hassar, W., Snyder, T., Kena, G., Dinkes, R., Kewal Ramani, A. J., et al. (2008). *The conditions of education 2008* (NCES 2008-31). Washington, DC: National Center for Educational Statistics, Institute of Education Sciences, U.S. Department of Education. Retrieved from http://nces.ed.gov.

Provansnik, S., Kewal Ramani, A., Coleman, M. M., Gilbertson, L., Herring, W., & Xie, Q. (2007). *Status of education in rural America* (NCES 2007-040). Washington, DC: U.S. Department of Education, National Center for Educational Statistics, Institute of Education Sciences. Retrieved from http://nces.ed.gov.

Simmons, R., & Blyth, D. (1987). *Moving into adolescence: The impact of pubertal change and school context.* Hawthorne, NY: Aldine de Guyter.

# 2

# An Ecological View of Schools and Development[1]

*Jacquelynne S. Eccles and Robert W. Roeser*

From the time individuals first enter school until they complete their formal schooling, children and adolescents spend more time in schools than in any other place outside their homes. In this chapter we discuss the ways in which schools influence adolescents' social-emotional and behavioral development through organizational, social, and instructional processes ranging from those based in the immediate, proximal relation between students and the tasks they are asked to perform to the role that principals and the school boards play in setting school-level and district-level policies, which in turn influence the social organization of the entire school community.

In 1999, we proposed a framework for thinking about school influences that conceptualized the school context into a series of hierarchically ordered, interdependent levels of organization beginning at the most basic level of the classroom and then moving up in complexity to the school as an organizational system embedded in a larger cultural system (see Eccles & Roeser, 1999). In adopting this heuristic, we assumed that (a) schools are *systems* characterized by multiple levels of analysis composed of various regulatory processes (organizational, interpersonal, and instructional in nature); (b) these processes are interrelated across levels of analysis; (c) such processes are usually dynamic in nature, sometimes being worked out each day between the various social actors (e.g., teachers and students); (d) these processes change as children move through different school levels (elementary, middle, and high school); and (e) these processes regulate children's and adolescents' cognitive, social-emotional, and behavioral development. In this chapter we focus on the interface between various theoretical frameworks that are consistent with these tenets of school influences. We begin with a summary of our multilevel description of school contexts.

In the late 1980s, Eccles and Midgley proposed a model of stage-environment fit to guide research on the impact of school transitions on adolescent development (see Eccles & Midgley, 1989; Eccles, Midgley, et al., 1993). They argued

that individuals have changing emotional, cognitive, and social needs and personal goals as they mature. Drawing on ideas related to person-environment fit and self-determination theory (Deci & Ryan, 2002; Hunt, 1975), as well as more general ideas regarding person-process-context models of human development (e.g., Bronfenbrenner, 1979), they argued that schools need to change in developmentally appropriate ways if they are to provide the kind of social context that will continue to motivate students' interest and engagement as the students mature. To the extent that this does not happen, they predicted that students would disengage first psychologically and then physically from school as they matured into and through adolescence. This should be particularly true as the adolescents acquired more incentives and more power to control their own behavior. We say more about both of these psychological perspectives on the impact of classroom experiences in the second half of this chapter.

## An Ecological View of Schools and Their Impact on Development during Adolescence

From the location of the school within macroregulatory systems characterized by national, state, and school district laws and educational policies to the miniregulatory systems that involve the minute-to-minute interactions between teachers and individual students, schools are systems of complex, multilevel, regulatory processes. Eccles and Roeser (1999) described these different levels of the school environment in terms of their hierarchical ordering— moving from the student in a classroom, to the school building itself, then to the school district, and finally to the larger communities in which school districts are located. Within each of these levels, we discussed those beliefs and practices that affect students' experiences on a daily basis. At the classroom level, we focused attention on teacher beliefs and instructional practices, teacher–student relationships, the nature and design of tasks and instruction, and the nature and structure of classroom activities and groups. At the level of the school building, we focused attention on organizational climate and such school-wide practices as academic tracking, school start time, and the provision of extracurricular activities. At the level of the school district, we focused on the between-school grade configurations that create particular school-transition experiences for students. Finally at the level of schools embedded in larger social systems, we discussed such issues as school resources, as well as the linkages of schools with parents and with the labor market. We draw heavily on this theoretical framing in the first section of this chapter.

## Level 1: Classrooms

***Teacher Beliefs*** Teacher beliefs have received much attention in educational psychology. In this section we focus on two types of beliefs: Teachers' general sense of their own teaching efficacy and teachers' expectations for specific students in their class.

*Teachers' General Sense of Efficacy* When teachers hold high general expectations for student achievement and students perceive these expectations, students learn more, experience a greater sense of self-worth and competence as learners, feel more connected to their teacher and their school, and resist involvement in problem behaviors (Lee & Smith, 2001; Wigfield, Eccles, Schiefele, Roeser, & Davis-Kean, 2006). Alternatively, when teachers lack confidence in their teaching efficacy, they can engage in behaviors that reinforce feelings of incompetence and alienation in their students, increasing the likelihood that their students will develop learned helpless responses to failure in the classroom (Roeser & Eccles, 2000). Unfortunately, the prevalence of teachers with a low sense of personal teaching efficacy is higher in junior high and middle schools than in elementary schools. Low teacher efficacy rates are also higher in schools that serve high proportions of ethnic minority and poor adolescents than in schools that serve more affluent and higher achieving adolescents (Darling-Hammond, 1997; Juvonen, Kaganoff, Augustine, & Constant, 2004).

*Differential Teacher Expectations* Equally important are the differential expectations teachers often hold for various individuals within the same classroom and the differential treatments that sometimes accompany these expectations. Many researchers have shown those differential expectations undermining teacher expectancy effects. Much of the work on teacher expectancy effects has focused on the negative effects of differential treatment related to gender, race-ethnic group, or social class (Ferguson, 1998; Wigfield, Eccles, & Davis-Kean, 2006). However, the magnitude of these negative effects depend on how teachers structure activities differently, as well as interact differently with, high- and low-expectancy students and on how the students perceive these differences (Brophy, 2004; Cooper, 1979;

Weinstein, 1989). Furthermore, even though these effects are typically quite small, Jussim, Eccles, and Madon (1996) found that young women, African American adolescents, and students from poorer homes are more subject to both the positive and negative effects of teacher expectancy effects than are other students.

Steele and Aronson (1995) have linked this form of differential treatment to school *disengagement* and *disidentification*. First applied to African Americans, Steele and Aronson argued that these students believe teachers and other adults have negative stereotypes of their academic abilities. This awareness, labeled *stereotype threat*, increases their anxieties, which in turn lead them to disidentify with the school context to protect their self-esteem. Interestingly, recent studies, using the same theoretical notions and experimental techniques, indicate that Asian students believe that teachers and adults expect them to perform very well, and these students perform better on tests when their ethnic identity is made salient (Shih, Pittinsky, & Ambady, 1999). Thus, the psychological processes associated with stereotype threat can either undermine or facilitate performance on standardized tests depending on the nature of commonly held stereotypes about the intellectual strengths and weaknesses of different social groups.

### General Classroom Climate

*Teacher–Student Relationships* The quality of teacher–student relationships is a key aspect of the classroom climate. Students fare best emotionally when they are in classrooms with teachers who trust, care about, and are respectful of students. More specifically, students fare best when teachers provide the social-emotional and intellectual scaffolding that students need to approach, engage, and persist on academic learning tasks; to develop positive achievement-related self-perceptions, values, and a sense of school belonging; and more generally to experience a sense of well-being when in school (Deci & Ryan, 2002; National Research Council, 2004; Wentzel, 2002; Wigfield et al., 2006).

*Classroom Management* Work related to classroom management has focused on two general issues: orderliness/predictability and control/autonomy. With regard to orderliness and predictability, the evidence is quite clear: Student achievement and conduct are enhanced when teachers establish smoothly running and efficient procedures for monitoring student progress, providing feedback, enforcing accountability for work completion, and organizing group activities. Unfortunately, such conditions are often absent, particularly in highly stressed and underfunded schools with inexperienced teachers (Darling-Hammond & Bransford, 2005; National Research Council, 2004).

Research on autonomy versus control is equally compelling. Classroom practices that support student autonomy are critical for fostering intrinsic motivation to learn and for supporting socioemotional development during childhood and adolescence (Deci & Ryan, 2002; Grolnick, Gurland,

Jacob, & DeCourcey, 2002). However, it is also critical that the teacher supports student autonomy in a context of adequate structure, orderliness, and relevance (Wigfield et al., 2006). This issue is complicated by the fact that the right balance between adult-guided structure and opportunities for student autonomy changes as the students mature: older students desire more opportunities for autonomy and less adult-controlled structure. To the extent that the students do not experience these changes in the balance between structure and opportunities for autonomy as they pass through the K-12 school years, their school motivation declines as they get older (Eccles et al., 1993).

*Motivational Climate*   In 1984, Rosenholtz and Simpson suggested a cluster of general teaching practices (e.g., individualized vs. whole-group instruction, ability grouping practices, and public presentation of feedback) that should affect motivation because the practices make ability differences in classrooms especially salient to students. They assumed that such practices affected the motivation of all students by increasing the salience of information about other students' abilities. The magnitude of the negative consequences of these shifts in instructional formats, however, should be greatest for low-performing students: As these students become more aware of their relative low standing, they are likely to adopt a variety of ego-protective strategies that unfortunately undermine learning and mastery (Covington & Dray, 2002).

Researchers interested in goal theory have proposed a similar set of classroom characteristics (Meece, Anderman, & Anderman, 2006; Midgley, 2002). Goal theorists propose two major achievement goal systems: mastery-oriented goals and performance-oriented goals. Students with mastery-oriented goals focus on learning the material and on their own improvement over time. Students with performance-oriented goals focus on doing better than other students in their class. Goal theorists further argue that a mastery orientation sustains school engagement and achievement better than does a performance orientation. Evidence is quite strong for the first prediction and more mixed for the second: The desire to do better than others often has positive rather than negative consequences, whereas the fear of failing (performance-avoidance goal orientation) undermines school performance (Midgley, 2002). The school-reform work of Midgley, Maehr, and their colleagues has shown that school reform efforts to reduce these types of classroom practices, particularly those associated with performance feedback, social comparative grading systems, and ego-focused, competitive motivational strategies have positive consequences for adolescents' academic motivation (Maehr & Midgley, 1996; see also National Research Council, 2004).

**The Nature of Academic Work**   Academic work is at the heart of the school experience. Two aspects of academic tasks are important: the content of the curriculum and the design of instruction. The nature of academic content has an important impact on students' attention, interest, and cognitive effort. Content that provides meaningful exploration is critical given that boredom in school, low interest, and perceived irrelevance of the curriculum are associated with poor attention, diminished achievement, disengagement, and alienation from school (Finn, 2006; National Research Council, 2004). Curricula that represent the voices, images, and historical experiences of traditionally underrepresented groups are also important (Valencia, 1991). Choosing materials that provide an appropriate level of challenge for a given class, designing learning activities that require diverse cognitive operations (e.g., opinion, following routines, memory, comprehension), structuring lessons so that they build on each other in a systematic fashion, using multiple representations of a given problem, and explicitly teaching students strategies that assist in learning are but a few of the design features that scaffold learning and promote effort investment, interest in learning, and achievement (Wigfield et al., 2006).

Unfortunately, American secondary schools have problems providing each of these types of educational experiences. Larson and his colleagues have documented the fact that adolescents are bored most of the time that they are in secondary school classrooms (Larson, 2000). Culturally meaningful learning experiences are rare in many American secondary schools (Graham & Taylor, 2002; Okagaki, 2001). The disconnection of traditional curricula from the experiences of these groups can explain the alienation of some group members from the educational process, sometimes eventuating in school dropout (Sheets & Hollins, 1999). Appropriately designed tasks that adequately scaffold learning are also rare in many inner-city and poor schools (Darling-Hammond, 1997).

***Experiences of Racial-Ethnic Discrimination***   Researchers interested in the relatively poor academic performance of adolescents from some ethnic-racial groups have suggested another classroom-based experience as critical for adolescent development, namely, experiences of racial-ethnic discrimination (Brody et al, 2006; Graham & Taylor, 2002; Harris-Britt, Valrie, Kurtz-Costes, & Rowley, 2007; Wong, Eccles, & Sameroff, 2003). Two types of discrimination have been discussed: (a) anticipation of future discrimination in the labor market, which might be seen as undermining the long-term benefits of education (Fordham & Ogbu, 1986), and (b) the impact of daily experiences of discrimination on one's mental health and academic motivation (Sellers, Caldwell, Schmeelk-Cine, & Zimmerman, 2003).

Both types have been shown to adversely affect the development of ethnic minority adolescents. On the one hand, anticipated future discrimination appears to motivate the African American youth to do well in school so that they would be maximally equipped to deal with future discrimination (Wong et al., 2003). In contrast, daily experiences of racial discrimination from their peers and teachers led to declines in school engagement and confidence in one's academic competence and grades, along with increases in depression and anger. Interestingly, evidence is beginning to show that a strong positive ethnic identity has protective effects against the aversive effects of daily experiences of racial and ethnic discrimination (Rowley, Kurtz-Costes, & Cooper, chapter 17 this volume; Sellers, Caldwell, Schmeelk-Cone, & Zimmerman, 2003; Wong et al., 2003).

***Summary of Classroom Level Effects*** The studies of classroom-level influences suggest that development is optimized when students are provided with challenging tasks in a mastery-oriented environment that also provides good emotional and cognitive support, meaningful and culturally diverse material to learn and master, and sufficient support for their own autonomy and initiative. Connell and Wellborn (1991) suggested that humans have three basic needs: to feel competent, to feel socially attached, and to have autonomous control in their lives. Further, they hypothesized that individuals develop best in contexts that provide opportunities for each of these needs to be met. Clearly, the types of classroom characteristics that emerge as important for intellectual, motivational, and socioemotional development would provide such opportunities.

## Level 2: School Buildings

As formal organizations schools have characteristics and features that are superordinate to classroom characteristics. These aspects of the whole school environment impact on adolescents' intellectual, social-emotional, and behavioral development. Important school-level organizational features include school climate and sense of community and the relationships among the students themselves. School organizational features also include such school-wide practices as curricular tracking, ability tracking, scheduling of instruction, and the availability of extracurricular activities.

***General School Climate*** Researchers suggest that variations in school climate and general expectations regarding student potential affect the development of both teachers and students (Darling-Hammond & Bransford, 2005; Jackson & Davis, 2000; National Research Council, 2004). For example, Bryk, Lee, and Holland (1993) concluded that the culture within Catholic schools is fundamentally different from the culture within most public schools in ways that positively affect the motivation of students, parents, and teachers. This culture (school climate) values academics, has high expectations that all students can learn, and affirms the belief that the business of school is learning. Similarly, Lee and Smith (2001) showed that between-school differences in teachers' sense of their own personal efficacy as well as their confidence in the general ability of the teachers at their school to teach all students accounted, in part, for between-school differences in adolescents' high school motivation and performance. Finally, Maehr, Midgley, and their colleagues argued that a school-level emphasis on different achievement goals creates a school-wide psychological environment that affects students' academic beliefs,

affects, and behaviors (Maehr & Midgley, 1996; Roeser, Midgley, & Urdan, 1996). For example, schools' use of public honor rolls and assemblies for the highest achieving students, class rankings on report cards, differential curricular offerings for students of various ability levels, and so on all emphasize relative ability, competition, and social comparison in the school and create a school-level ability rather than mastery/task focus. On the other hand, through the recognition of academic effort and improvement, rewards for different competencies that extend to all students, and through practices that emphasize learning and task mastery (block scheduling, interdisciplinary curricular teams, cooperative learning), schools can promote a school-level focus on discovery, effort and improvement, and academic mastery (Roeser et al., 1996). In support of these hypotheses, Roeser, Eccles, and Sameroff (1998) found that adolescent students' perceptions of their school as performance-oriented were related to diminished feelings of academic competence and valuing of school, increased feelings of emotional distress, and decreased grades over time; whereas perceived school task goal structures were associated with increased valuing of school and diminished emotional distress over time (Roeser et al., 1998). Using the same sample with person-centered techniques, they found that youth who were most engaged in school reported a cluster of positive school perceptions, including a mastery-oriented school climate and positive teacher–student relationships. In contrast, those who were most disengaged reported more of an ability-oriented school (Roeser, Eccles, & Sameroff, 2000).

The prevalence of violence is another aspect of school climate that is receiving a lot of attention. Ample evidence exists on the negative impact of school violence and harassment on the motivation and well-being of its victims (Nishina & Juvonen, 2005). Fear of being bullied drives students away from school and induces such high levels of anxiety that students cannot pay attention in their classes even when they do attend school. Until quite recently, researchers interested in aggression and violence have focused at the individual level—investigating the psychological causes of aggression and the psychological consequences of being a victim of aggression. Little attention has been placed on the role of the school setting in the prevalence of violence of school campuses. Over the last few years more attention is being placed on these setting characteristics. One group of scholars has shown that both the levels of school violence and students' concerns about their safety at school decrease as the social climate in the schools increases (Astor, Meyer, & Behre, 1999; Astor, Benbenbenishty, Zeora. & Vinokur, 2002; Astor, Meyer, & Behre, 1999; Benbenishty & Astor, 2007; Benbenishty, Astor, Zeira, & Vinokur, 2002). These same authors have studied the places at school in which students feel most unsafe; that is, the noninstructional space that adolescents move in and through before school, after school, and between classes (Astor, Meyer, et al., 1999). These spaces include the parking lots and the school grounds, the hallways and the bathrooms, the sports fields (if there are any), and the cafeteria(s). According to Astor and his colleagues, even though students may report feeling safe at school in general, many students still report strong fears in particular areas of the school or school grounds and at particular times of the day where and when violence is most likely to occur. Most violent events reported by students occur in what Astor and his colleagues call the "undefined public spaces" of the school, such as parking lots, bathrooms, particular hallways, and so on where no adults assumed supervisory jurisdiction. These spaces were undefined in terms of adult monitoring of behavior in them, and thus were the frequent sites for fights, unwanted sexual attention, and so forth (Astor, Meyer, et al., 1999).

Still other authors have looked at other aspects of the school context that appear to lead to escalating violence. For example, Fagan and Wilkinson (1998) reviewed theory and evidence that suggest several different functional goals that violence can serve for youth including the securing of high status among peers, acquisition of material goods, dominance of others and retribution for insults to the self, defiance of authority, and a form of "rough justice" in situations in which there is little legitimate adult authority. All of these goals likely reflect responses to the frustration or anticipated frustration of basic needs for autonomy and security in social situations characterized by a lack of adult supervision and an absence of opportunities for wholesome learning, work, and recreation. Thus, understanding the origins of school violence requires that we look at both the structural influences on school engagement and the personal benefits and costs of being a perpetrator or victim of violence. Furthermore, it is likely that general school climate and the prevalence of school violence are reciprocally related: as climate decreases, violence increases, and as violence and bullying increases, the general social climate in the school further deteriorates (Nishina & Juvonen, 2005).

***Academic Tracks and Curricular Differentiation*** There has been a long history of concern about the impact of academic tracking on student development (Oakes, 2005). Within-classroom ability tracking begins early in elementary school with reading groups. Such within class grouping practices often extend to mathematics by third grade. In the middle and high school years, between-class tracking becomes both more widespread and more broadly linked to the sequencing of specific courses for students bound for different postsecondary school trajectories (college preparation, general education, and vocational education). As curriculum differentiation practices intensify in public schools during secondary school, students of different ability levels get exposed to often very different kinds of academic work, classmates, teachers, and teaching methods (Eccles & Roeser, 1999; Oakes, 2005).

There is as yet no general consensus on the overall effects of both within class ability grouping and between class curriculum differentiation as an educational practice, particularly as these practices relate to low achieving and poor students (Eccles & Roeser, 1999). The basic rationale for such practices is based on a person–environment fit perspective: students will learn best if they are taught as near to their level of competence and interest as possible. Some research suggests that students who are placed in high tracks do evidence the kinds of educational benefits that one might expect based on this perspective. In contrast, most of the evidence on low ability placements suggests that students who are placed in low tracks placements fare worse academically than they would have if they had been placed in a mixed ability classroom (Hallinan & Kubitschek, 1999; Oakes, 2005). Differential teacher quality appears to explain some of these differential effects: Those students who are placed in lower tracks during secondary school are often exposed to teachers with less qualifications, experience less constructivist teaching practices, and are exposed to what amounts to watered-down curricula (e.g., Darling-Hammond, 1997; Oakes, 2005).

Lower-track students also report being labeled "dumb" by teachers and peers, feel less committed to school, and feel less successful academically (Oakes, 2005). In our own work, we have found that youth who were in lower track math, English, or English as a second language courses saw themselves as less scholastically competent, perceived school as less valuable, and felt less of a sense of school belonging than students in higher track math and English (Roeser, 2006; Roeser et al., 1998).

Finally, ability grouping has an impact on students' peer groups: Between-classroom ability grouping and curricular tracking increase the extent of contact among adolescents with similar levels of achievement and engagement with school. For those doing poorly in school, tracking is likely to facilitate friendships among students who are similarly alienated from school and are more likely to engage in risky or delinquent behaviors (Wigfield et al. 2006). Dishion, McCord, and Poulin (1999) showed how such collecting of alienated adolescents increases their involvement in problem behaviors. This collecting of adolescents with poor achievement or adjustment histories also places additional discipline burdens on the teachers who teach these classes (Oakes, 2005); making such classes unpopular with the teachers as well as the students and decreasing the likelihood that the teachers with the most experience will allow themselves to be assigned to these classes.

Given this accumulating evidence on the potential costs of tracking, educational scientists are now questioning the advisability of between class tracking. Concerns have also been raised about the ways in which students get placed in different classes and how difficult it is for students to change tracks once initial placements have been made. These issues are important both early in a child's school career (Entwisle & Alexander, 1993) and later in adolescence, when course placement is linked directly to the kinds of educational options that are available to the student after high school. Poor children, among whom African American, Latino, and Native American children are overrepresented, are more likely than their wealthier and European or Asian American peers to be placed in low ability classrooms and in vocational track courses during secondary school (Oakes, 2005). Even in integrated schools, minority students tend to receive poor access to teaching resources through tracking practices (Noguera & Wing, 2006). Furthermore, there is some evidence that students with limited English proficiency who are otherwise capable are placed in lower track classes (Fuligni, Eccles, & Barber, 1995). Finally, careful assessment of these types of track placements has shown that many of these youth are incorrectly assigned to these classes and tracks (Oakes, 2005). Such misassignment has long-term consequences for students' ability to go to college once they complete secondary school.

*School Size* In 1964, Barker and Gump proposed that smaller schools afford young people greater opportunities for close relationships, make it easier for students to be monitored by adults, and have a favorable roles-to-people ratio with respect to school extracurricular activities that allows for widespread student participation in the life of the school. In recent studies, support for the positive influence of small school size has grown. For example, Lee and Loeb (2000) found that elementary school size predicted both teacher beliefs and students' achievement gains. In the smaller schools (size <400 students), teachers took greater responsibility for fostering students' learning and students showed greater one-year gains in their mathematics test scores. Lee and Smith (1995) found a negative relation between school size and students' self-reported school engagement (e.g., positive attitudes toward classes, investing effort in school, feeling challenged) among eighth graders. Finally, Elder and Conger (2000) reported that school size was associated with adolescent developmental outcomes among high school students in rural Iowa during the 1990s. Across a variety of measures of academic and social functioning (e.g., grades, problem behavior), results showed that adolescents attending smaller schools, on average, did better than the adolescents attending larger schools after sociodemographic factors were controlled.

*Extracurricular Activities* There is growing interest in the role of extracurricular activities in adolescent development because increasing evidence suggests that there is a positive link between adolescents' extracurricular activities and their subsequent educational outcomes (e.g., high school completion, adult educational attainment, occupation, and income) and positive youth development (better mental health and lower rates of involvement in delinquent activities), even after controlling for social class and ability (Eccles & Templeton, 2002; Mahoney, Harris, & Eccles, 2006). In some studies, these relationships are particularly strong among low-achieving and poor students (Barber, Eccles, & Stone, 2001; Eccles & Barber, 1999; Mahoney, Harris, et al., 2006; Mahoney, Larson, et al., 2005). Similarly, participation in high school extracurricular and volunteer activities predicts high levels of adult participation in the political process and other types of volunteer activities, continued sport engagement, and better physical and mental health

(Youniss, McLellan, & Yates, 1997). Several researchers suggest that these associations are due to the following possible mediating mechanisms: participation increases the association with academically oriented peers and exposure to academic and prosocial values; participation can lead to enhanced self-esteem and generalization of a high sense of personal efficacy; participation can increase exposure to supportive adults and good mentoring, which, in turn can lead to superior career guidance and encouragement; participation can increase one's social networks and social capital; and finally participation can increase both soft skills and other skills needed for success in school and the transition to either college or the workplace.

What is important from a school-building perspective is that schools differ in the extent to which they provide positive extracurricular activities for their students. Researchers who study the advantages of small schools often point to the fact that more students get to participate in extracurricular activities in small schools because there are fewer bodies to fill all of the available slots (Elder & Conger, 2000). Large schools have an overabundance of students to fill all of the available activity slots. The situation is even worse in poor, large secondary schools that have had to cut extracurricular activities to stay within their budgets. Recently, federal and state initiatives have emerged to help increase the availability of after-school programs that are housed in school buildings. Unfortunately, most of this money is going to elementary school and middle school programs rather than high schools (Eccles & Gootman, 2001).

*Summary of School-Level Effects* In this section we reviewed the impact of several features of the whole school on adolescent development. These features included school climate, school size, curricular and ability tracking practices, the availability of extracurricular activities, and the use of noninstructional spaces. There is very strong evidence that each of these school-wide characteristics impacts adolescent development. Often, between-school variations on these characteristics result from school district policies or financial constraints that are beyond the control of the building's principal and staff. Reform efforts, however, have shown that changes can be created in each of these domains and that such changes can have a positive impact on the development of the adolescents attending the reformed school.

## Level 3: School District Level

Many school policies are implemented at the district level and affect all of the schools in the district. Such policies include standardized testing practices, the ways in which the grade levels are grouped together in different schools, when these various schools start and end their school days, when the whole district is in session, desegregation programs, busing practices, retention and expulsion policies, and the distribution of resources for various types of programs. In this section, we focus on just two of these school district policies: Time schedules and grade configurations.

***Time Schedules*** We discuss two aspects of timing scheduling: annual calendar and school start and stop times because they both have quite interesting implications for students' social and academic development.

*School Calendar* All districts must decide when the schools will be in session. Traditionally, schools are in session from September through mid-June and are closed during the summer months. Largely in response to economic issues, some districts have modified this calendar in various ways to increase the full year use of their facilities. Many high schools include a summer school session that can serve either a remedial or an acceleration function. Recently attention has refocused on the issue of summer school out of concern over the "summer learning gap." Recent work by Alexander, Entwisle, and their colleagues has shown that much of the social class differential in school achievement reflects differences that already exist when the students enter kindergarten and differences that accumulate over the elementary school years in learning over the summer vacations. On average, children living in poor families learn less and forget more over the summer vacation than children living in middle-class and upper-social class families, in part because these families are able to provide their children with a variety of structured learning experiences over the summer (Alexander, Entwisle, & Olson, 2007). When they compared the actual rate of learning over the course of the school year across social class lines in the Baltimore school district, Alexander and his colleagues found little if any social class difference; in contrast, they found a substantial difference over the summer time. Work on summer schools has shown that well designed summer school programs can help ameliorate this social class differential (Alexander et al., 2007).

Being in school during the summer months is likely to have other unintended consequences. For example, it will change the nature of children's activities and friendships during this period of time. It also changes the demands placed on working families during the summer when extra childcare arrangements need to made, as well as the demands placed on some teachers to find the supplementary work needed to pay their bills. These consequences of the nature of the school calendar are likely to influence the development and well-being of both the children and adults associated with schools. More research is needed on these types of unintended consequences of such school policies.

*School Start and Stop Time* Although it may not seem obvious at first, school start and stop time can affect students' social development, academic motivation, and learning. For example, an early start time can negatively affect adolescents' alertness and quality of sleep. As children progress through puberty they need more sleep and

their natural sleep cycles shift to a desire to go to sleep later in the evening and to wake up later in the morning (Carskadon, 1990). Unfortunately, secondary schools typically begin earlier in the morning than primary schools. In concert with other changes, such as the later hours at which adolescents go to bed, the earlier school start times of the middle and high school can both promote daytime sleepiness and undermine adolescents' ability to make it to school on time, alert, and ready to learn. A study of fifth grade students in Israel, for example, compared two groups of students: those who attended a school that started at 7:10 a.m. (early risers) and those in a school that started at 8:00 a.m. (regular risers). The early risers slept less, reported more daytime fatigue and sleepiness, and reported greater attention and concentration difficulties in school compared to their later rising counterparts (Epstein, Chillag, & Lavie, 1998). The time at which school ends also has implications for students' motivation to learn and their development. In communities where few structured opportunities for afterschool activities exist, especially impoverished communities, young people are more likely to be involved in high risk behaviors such as substance use, crime, violence, and sexual activity, and less likely to be engaged in productive or academically relevant activities during the period between 2:00 and 8:00 p.m. These patterns suggest that adolescents might be better served by schools that start later in the morning, end late in the afternoon, and provide well structured extracurricular activities to keep them engaged at school until early evening.

***School Grade Configurations and School Transitions*** School transitions are an excellent example of how the multiple levels of schools interact to affect adolescent development. All school districts must decide how they will group the grade levels within the various school buildings. One common arrangement is to group children in kindergarten through sixth grade in elementary schools, young adolescents in grades seven through nine in junior high schools, and older adolescents in grades 10 through 12 in senior high schools. Another common arrangement places the transitions after grades five and eight, creating elementary schools, middle schools, and senior high schools. The third popular arrangement groups young people in grades K–8 in one school and then grades 9–12 in a high school. In each of these arrangements the students typically move to a new and often larger building at each of the major transition points. These moves typically also involve increased busing and exposure to a much more diverse student body. In this section we discuss one of these transitions: the transition from elementary to middle or junior high school as an example of such research. Readers are encouraged to think about how similar arguments could be studied for other school transitions. Evidence is beginning to accumulate that similar effects are evident for the transition to high school leading to the currently high rates of high school drop out and school failure (Lee & Smith, 2001; Wigfield et al., 2006). More work in this area is badly needed.

*Middle School Transition*   There is substantial evidence of declines in academic motivation and achievement across the early adolescence and high school years (Eccles et al., 1993; Wigfield et al, 2006). These declines often coincide with the transition into either middle/junior high or high school. For example, there is a marked decline in some early adolescents' school grades as they move into junior high school (Simmons & Blyth, 1987). Similar declines occur for such motivational constructs as interest in school (Wigfield et al., 2006), intrinsic motivation (Gottfried, Fleming, & Gottfried, 2001), self-concepts/self-perceptions and confidence in one's intellectual abilities (Wigfield, Eccles, Mac Iver, Reuman, & Midgley, 1991), mastery goal orientation (E. M. Anderman & Midgley, 1997), and a sense of belonging at school (L. H. Anderman, 1999). There are also increases in test anxiety (Wigfield et al., 2006), focus on self-evaluation and performance rather than task mastery (E. M. Anderman & Midgley, 1997), and both truancy and school drop out (Rumberger & Thomas, 2000). Furthermore, increasing evidence indicates that these declines predict subsequent school drop out and high school failure (Finn, 2006; Wigfield et al., 2006). Several explanations have been offered for these seemingly negative changes in academic motivation: Some point to the intrapsychic upheaval associated with young adolescent development (Arnett, 1999). Others point to the simultaneous occurrence of several life changes. For example, Simmons and Blyth (1987) attributed these declines, particularly among females, to the coincidence of the junior high school transition with pubertal development. Still others point to the nature of the junior high school environment itself rather than the transition per se.

Extending person–environment fit theory into a developmental perspective (stage–environment fit theory), Eccles and Midgley (1989) proposed that these negative developmental changes result from the fact that traditional junior high schools do not provide developmentally appropriate educational environments for young adolescents. The authors suggested that different types of educational environments are needed for different age groups to meet developmental needs and foster continued developmental growth. Exposure to the developmentally appropriate environment would facilitate both motivation and continued growth; in contrast, exposure to developmentally inappropriate environments, especially developmentally regressive environments, should create a particularly poor person–environment fit, which should lead to declines in motivation as well as detachment from the goals of the institution. What is critical to this argument is that the transition itself is *not* the cause of the declines; instead, it is the nature of the school into which the students move. Within this framework, the right kinds of middle school reforms can be quite effective at reducing these declines.

Two approaches have been used to study the middle school transition: one focused on more global school-level characteristics such as school size, degree of departmentalization, and extent of bureaucratization and the other on more specific classroom and motivational dynamics. The first type is best exemplified by the work of Simmons and Blyth (1987). They pointed out that most junior high schools are substantially larger than elementary schools and that instruction is more likely to be organized departmentally. As a result, junior high school teachers typically teach several different groups of students, making it very difficult for students to form a close relationship with any school-affiliated adult precisely at the point in development when there is a great need for guidance and support from nonfamilial adults. Such changes in student–teacher relationships are also likely to undermine the sense of community and trust between students and teachers, leading to a lowered sense of efficacy among the teachers, an increased reliance on authoritarian control practices by the teachers, and an increased sense of alienation among the students. Finally, such changes are likely to decrease the probability that any particular student's difficulties will be noticed early enough to get the student necessary help, thus increasing the likelihood that students on the edge will be allowed to slip onto negative motivational and performance trajectories, leading to increased school failure and dropout.

The latter is best exemplified by the work of Eccles and Midgley and by the studies on middle school reform initiated by the Carnegie Foundation after their report *Turning Points* (Carnegie Council on Adolescent Development, 1989; Jackson & Davis, 2000). These scholars have looked at several specific aspects of the classroom and school environment and have shown that negative changes in these aspects of student' experiences at school as they make the middle or junior high school transition are linked to the declines in school motivation and engagement. They have also shown that changing these aspects of the middle school environment can be effective in reducing the declines in school engagement often associated with this school transition (E. M. Anderman, Maehr, & Midgley, 1999; Maehr & Midgley, 1996). We review the evidence for these claims in this section.

*Grade-Related Differences in Teacher Beliefs*   Differences in all types of teacher beliefs have been shown in studies comparing elementary and middle grades teachers. For example, junior high school teachers on average have lower confidence in their own teaching efficacy than do elementary school teachers (i.e., their ability to teach and influence all of the students in their classes; Feldlaufer, Midgley, & Eccles, 1988; Midgley, Feldlaufer, & Eccles, 1989). An equally troubling difference occurs for teachers' views of their roles in their students' lives. For example, Roeser and his colleagues found that with increasing grade level, middle school (6th to 8th grades) teachers are less likely to endorse the notion that students' mental health concerns are part of the teacher role (Roeser & Midgley, 1997; Roeser, Marachi, & Gehlbach, 2000). Thus, at a time when adolescents need academic and social-emotional guidance and support from both parents and nonparental adults (i.e., during early adolescence), teachers appear less likely to be able to provide such support given the number of students they teach, their educational training, and the size of secondary schools. This creates holes in the safety net available to adolescents at a time when they are in particularly acute need of adult support and guidance (Simmons & Blyth, 1987). It is not surprising that the most at-risk youth often fall through these holes.

*Grade-Related Differences in Authority Relationships*   Despite the increasing maturity of students, junior high school teachers place a greater emphasis on teacher control and discipline and provide fewer opportunities for student decision making, choice, and self-management than do elementary school teachers (Feldlaufer et al., 1988; Midgley & Feldlaufer, 1987). Both stage–environment fit theory (Eccles et al., 1993) and self-determination theory (Deci & Ryan, 2002) suggest that these practices will create a mismatch between young adolescents' desires for autonomy and control and their perceptions of the opportunities in their learning environments; this mismatch is predicted to lead to a decline in the adolescents' intrinsic motivation and interest in school. Evidence supports this prediction (Wigfield et al., 2006).

*Grade-Related Differences in Affective Relationships*   Junior high and middle school classrooms are often characterized by a less personal and positive teacher–student relationship than are elementary school classrooms (Feldlaufer et al., 1988; Midgley, Feldlaufer, & Eccles, 1988). Given the association of classroom climate and student motivation reviewed earlier, it should not be surprising that moving into a less supportive classroom leads to a decline in these young adolescents' interest in the subject matter being taught in that classroom, particularly among the low achieving students (Furrer & Skinner, 2003; L. H. Anderman, 1999; Midgley et al., 1988).

*Grade-Related Differences in Grading Practices*   There is no stronger predictor of students' self-confidence and efficacy than the grades they receive (Guay, Marsh, & Boivin, 2003). If academic marks decline with the junior high or middle school transition, then adolescents' self-perceptions and academic motivation should also decline. In fact, junior high school teachers do use stricter and more social comparison-based standards than do elementary school teachers to assess student competency and to evaluate student performance, leading to a drop in grades for many young adolescents as they make the transition to junior high school (Eccles & Midgley, 1989; Simmons & Blyth, 1987). Imagine what such a decline in grades might do to young adolescents' self-confidence and motivation. Several studies have shown that the magnitude of the grade drop following the transition into either junior high school or middle school is a major predictor of weak high school performance and leaving school early, even after controlling for a youth's performance prior to the school transition (Finn, 2006; Roderick, 1993; Roderick & Camburn, 1999; Simmons & Blyth, 1987).

*Grade-Related Differences in Motivational Goal Context*   Several of the changes just noted are linked together in goal theory. Classroom practices related to grading practices, support for autonomy, and instructional organization affect the relative salience of mastery versus performance goals that students adopt as they engage in the learning tasks at school. Given changes associated with these practices, it is not surprising that both teachers and students think that their school environment is becoming increasingly focused on competition, relative ability, and social comparison as the young adolescents progress from elementary to middle or junior high school (Midgley, Anderman, & Hicks, 1995). Midgley et al. (1995) found that both teachers and students indicated that performance-focused goals were more prevalent and task-focused goals were less prevalent in the middle school classrooms than in the elementary school classrooms. In addition, the elementary school teachers reported using task-focused instructional strategies more frequently than did the middle school teachers. Finally, at both grade levels the extent to which teachers were task-focused predicted the students' and the teachers' sense of personal efficacy. It is thus no surprise that personal efficacy was lower among the middle school participants than among the elementary school participants.

Extending this work, Roeser et al. (2002) looked at how elementary and middle school teachers' motivational practices and perceptions of the learning environment for teachers was related to their perceptions of their own work environments using both self-reports and principal reports. Results showed that teachers who were more performance-oriented based on self-reported instructional practices also (a) believed there was an emphasis on performance goals for students in the wider school environment; (b) worked in schools where their school principals reported greater use of performance-oriented practices and policies in the school as a whole; and (c) believed there was competition among staff and inequitable treatment of teachers by the administration (school performance goal structure for teachers). Similarly, teachers at both levels who reported a greater mastery orientation also (a) perceived a broader emphasis on such goals for students in the wider school culture and (b) perceived an emphasis on innovation and improvement for teachers among the staff and administration. These results suggest that the changing nature of the motivational climate for learning for students as they progress through school is paralleled by a changing motivational climate for teaching for teachers as well.

*Summary*   Changes such as those just reviewed are likely to have a negative effect on many children's motivational orientation toward school at any grade level. However, Eccles and Midgley (1989) argued that these types of school environmental changes are particularly harmful at early adolescence given what is known about psychological development during this stage of life. Evidence from a variety of sources suggests that early adolescent development is characterized by increases in desire for autonomy, peer orientation, self-focus and self-consciousness, salience of identity issues, concern over sexual relationships, and capacity for abstract cognitive activity (Eccles et al., 1993). Simmons and Blyth (1987) argued that adolescents need safe, intellectually challenging environments to adapt to these shifts. In light of these needs, the environmental changes often associated with the transition to junior high school are likely to be especially harmful in that they emphasize competition, social comparison, a performance-goal orientation rather than a mastery-goal orientation, and self-assessment of ability at a time of heightened self-focus; they decrease decision making and choice at a time when the desire for control is growing; and they disrupt the opportunity for a close relationship between students and teachers at a time when adolescents may be in special need of close adult relationships outside of the home. The nature of these environmental changes, coupled with the normal course of individual development, is likely to result in a developmental mismatch so that the fit between the young adolescent and the classroom environment is particularly poor, increasing the risk of negative motivational outcomes, especially for adolescents who are having difficulty succeeding academically in school.

## Level 4: Schools as Embedded Organizations in the Larger Community

The most distal aspect of school influence on adolescent development lies in the fact that schools are embedded in much larger social systems. Characteristics of the communities and the nations in which schools are placed influence everything about what goes on in the school building itself. Discussing all of the macroinfluences is beyond the scope of a single chapter. In this section we focus on two macrocharacteristics: private versus public schools and school resources. We do not discuss other possibilities such as the link between the schools and the labor market, the possible role of school vouchers, and the impact of the No Child Left Behind national policy. But we encourage the reader to consider how such macroprocesses and policies can affect human development through the various mechanisms discussed through this chapter.

***Public versus Private Schools*** The question of whether public vs. private schools do a better job motivating adolescent students and reducing achievement gaps between those from different social backgrounds is longstanding (Coleman et al., 1966). Because of their record with socially disadvantaged students in particular, various researchers have commented on the "religious schools effect" of Catholic schools in terms of student achievement and educational attainments, especially among adolescent non-Catholics, those of lower socioeconomic status, and African Americans and Latinos living in urban areas (Bryk, Lee, & Holland, 1993). In a meta-analysis of the effects of Catholic religious school attendance and personal religious commitment on academic achievement and school conduct, for instance,

Jeynes (2002) found that, after accounting for socioeconomic status and gender, the effect sizes for religious school attendance were between .20 and .25 of a standard deviation for both academic achievement and school conduct. These effects were particularly evident for Black and Hispanic secondary school students. Although some suggest these effects are due to Catholic schools selecting superior students, others have suggested that this claim is overdrawn and that the effects of a Catholic school education on achievement are quite robust (e.g., Bryk et al., 1993).

Three core features of the culture of these schools have been examined as instrumental in the reduction of inequality that are relevant here: a communal organization, a philosophy of human dignity, and a restricted range of curricular offerings (Bryk et al., 1993). First, Catholic secondary schools tend to be somewhat smaller than public secondary schools and have strong communal culture grounded in a rich array of rituals and activities outside of the classroom where teachers and students get to know one another beyond their school-related roles. This community environment provides a social basis for motivating school learning—a set of caring relationships and corresponding sense of community amongst faculty, staff, and students become major motivators of in-school behavior.

In addition, these secondary schools are characterized by a set of shared moral commitments and a spiritual ideology that emphasize the dignity of each individual and a corresponding ethic of care. These shared beliefs are grounded in a religious theology (Christian personalism) in which social justice and the desire to provide a humanistic education for all individuals are paramount, and in which the dignity of the individual as having moral worth is preeminent to a view in which worth is accorded to individuals based on relative social and academic statuses. Thus, the school culture is one that bridges two worlds for individuals—a moral-spiritual one in which the dignity of all individuals is recognized and acknowledged as primary; and a pragmatic one in which individuals are prepared for the demands of economic and civic life in a capitalist democracy. It is our view that this moral center and related humanistic approach to education that characterizes the culture of Catholic schools affords young people a non-status based foundation of worth and a sense of belonging and corresponding sense of dignity that disrupts pervasive negative images in the wider culture that may afflict ethnic minority youth and undermine their perceptions of themselves as successful students.

The final, related feature of Catholic secondary schools is their "delimited technical core" (Bryk et al., 1993, p. 297). Students in these schools have many required classes and less electives. Generally, all students are exposed to a common curriculum that the faculty expect them to learn. Although administrative sorting still occurs, there are less "tracks" and less differentiation of curricula by such tracks. The message to students is that every student is not only capable of, but is expected to, learn the core curriculum.

*School Resources* School resources in terms of adequate materials and continuity of teaching staff are often considered important for adolescents' learning and well-being. Early studies of school effects on adolescents' development and achievement were based on economic models in which the relation of so-called tangible school inputs (e.g., school resources or size) to student outputs (e.g., achievement and attainments) was the focus. Although the central question of how much school resources matter for raising achievement and reducing inequality in student outcomes is still being debated, school district-level variations in such school resources are likely a major contributor to the continuing inequity in educational outcomes for several minority groups in the United States.

Evidence does show that tangible physical plant of the school can affect students' behavioral conduct in school. In their study of 12 London area secondary schools, Rutter and colleagues (1979) found that although the age of the school buildings was not significantly related to achievement or behavioral outcomes in students, the cleanliness and use of plants, pictures, and other decorations inside the school buildings was a significant predictor of the level of behavioral misconduct students displayed in the school (after accounting for their social background). The more inhospitable and cold the school was, the greater the misconduct of students. This finding may reflect the "broken windows" theory (Wilson & Kelling, 1982) of delinquency and crime in relation to school physical environments. The basic thesis is that abandoned and dirty physical spaces connate a message of a lack of ownership and monitoring, and therefore become seedbeds for criminal activity and violence. It may be harder to value school and feel good about oneself as a learner in a broken down, leaky school building that communicates a serious lack of societal value for teachers and students. It also may be harder for an adolescent to be intrinsically motivated in a school environment in which poor lighting, crowding, noise, and debris are features that are as common as technology, books, and adequate desks and chairs.

Unfortunately, about 37% of African American youth and 32% of Latino youth, compared to 5% of European American and 22% of Asian youth, are enrolled in the 47 largest city school districts in this country; in addition, African American and Latino youth attend some of the poorest school districts in this country. In turn, 28% of the youth enrolled in city schools live in poverty, and 55% are eligible for free or reduced-cost lunch, suggesting that class may be as important as race (or more important) in the differences that emerge. Teachers in these schools report feeling less safe than do teachers in other school districts, dropout rates are highest, and achievement levels at all grades are the lowest (Council of the Great City Schools, 1992; United Way, 2008). Finally, schools that serve these populations are less likely than schools serving more advantaged populations to offer either high-quality remedial services or advanced courses and courses that facilitate the acquisition of higher order thinking skills and active learning strategies. Even

adolescents who are extremely motivated may find it difficult to perform well under these educational circumstances (United Way, 2008).

**Secondary School Reform Efforts**

We end our chapter with a discussion of several promising efforts at secondary school reforms because such reforms and interventions provide the opportunity to study changes in the types of practices we have discussed throughout this chapter. Given the focus on this book on education and social development and our mutual interest in the types of changes that commonly occur in students' motivation and social functioning as they move into and through secondary school, we discuss interventions and reforms aimed at this age group. We also focus on interventions that are aimed at social development as well as academic achievement.

Largely because of the kinds of negative developmental changes we discussed earlier that are linked to school transitions in early adolescence, in 1989, the Carnegie Foundation issued the report *Turning Reports* calling for the reform of education for early adolescents. Based in part on notions linked to stage environment fit as well as notions linked to the needs of early adolescent children, they made the following recommendations for middle grade school reform:

- Create small learning communities that will allow close relationships to emerge between teachers and students;
- Teach a core academic program to everyone that includes opportunities for service;
- Ensure success for all by eliminating tracking, using cooperative learning, providing flexible scheduling and adequate resources to meet the learning needs of all students;
- Empower teachers and administrators to take control of and responsibility for their schools;
- Staff schools with teachers who are trained to teach early adolescents;
- Foster health and fitness;
- Reengage families;
- Connect schools with communities.

Not surprisingly, the Carnegie Foundation report stimulated a major reassessment of schooling for early adolescents throughout the country and a cascade of middle school reform efforts. These efforts provided the opportunity to test the effectiveness of each of these recommendations. In 2000, Jackson and Davis summarized the findings of these many middle school reform efforts, concluding that the following middle grade school characteristics support both learning and positive youth development:

1. A curriculum grounded in rigorous academic standards and current knowledge about how students learn best and is relevant to the concerns of adolescents;
2. Instructional methods designed to prepare all students to achieve at the highest standards;

ional structures that support a climate of development and a caring community with ational goals;

ers who are trained experts at teaching young adolescents;

5. Ongoing professional development opportunities for the staff;
6. Democratic governance that involves both the adults and the adolescents;
7. Extensive involvement of parents and the community; and
8. High levels of safety and practices that support good health.

Similar conclusions were reached by Juvonen and her colleagues (Juvonen et al., 2004), and the National Research Council (2004) in their reviews of well-studied intervention and reform efforts focused on schools serving early adolescents. Juvonen et al. (2004) also argued that K-8 structures might be more successful at implementing the types of classroom characteristics and building level opportunities most supportive of continued academic engagement and positive youth development. Together, these findings fit very nicely with the stage–environment fit perspective we outlined earlier. They demonstrate that developmentally appropriate educational experiences can be created for early adolescent students and that these students do much better along several dimensions of social and academic functioning when they are given these types of educational experiences.

We want to illustrate these general findings with brief descriptions of three more targeted school programs and one whole school reform initiative. The first two demonstrate the power of providing youth with the opportunity to engage in meaningful volunteer activities within their communities as part of their school experiences. The third demonstrates the power of giving adolescents new visions for the future as part of their school experiences. We picked these three particular programs because they relate directly the developmental needs of adolescents and they demonstrate how experiences at school can influence a wide range of indicators of social development beyond just academic achievement. The final program illustrates how one can use the fundamental principles of motivation discussed throughout this chapter to successfully transform whole schools and school districts.

*The Coca-Cola Valued Youth Program* (CCVYP, www.idra.org) was designed to prevent high school students from dropping out. It took advantage of adolescents' desire to make a difference in their community and coupled it with specific experiences that would increase the adolescence sense of competence, belonging, and autonomy. The essence of the program was quite simple: it gave 7th to 12th grade students who were considered to be at risk for dropping out of school the opportunity to tutor elementary school students who were also identified as being at risk in terms of the reading ability. Although the adolescents themselves were only reading at the third to fourth grade level, they could read better than first graders and thus, with guidance could tutor first grade children in reading. The adolescent tutors were trained and supported by teacher coordinators. Thus, the program provided the adolescents with an opportunity to "matter" in their school community. By allowing them to tutor younger children, the program also provided academically challenged youth with an opportunity to feel good about their academic skills and their ability to help other children do well in school. Finally, it provided an unobtrusive and respectful means for the tutors' teachers to become their mentors. Thus, the program met several of adolescents' needs simultaneously. Not surprisingly, the program was very effective. Not only did participation in this program substantially reduce the likelihood of the vulnerable adolescents dropping out of high school, it also led to dramatic increases in the adolescents' own reading abilities and more general school achievement.

*The Teen Outreach Program (TOP)* was initially designed to reduce teenage pregnancy. But rather than focusing specifically on pregnancy, the program developers took a broader social developmental perspective and designed a program that would help adolescents understand and evaluate their future life options and develop life skills and autonomy in a context featuring strong social ties to adult mentors (Allen, Philliber, Herrling, & Kupermine, 1997). The developers concluded that the best way to prevent teenage pregnancy was to help the students create an alternative vision of themselves and their future—a vision that made staying in school and preparing for a bright possible future more salient than becoming a parent. The program had three components: 20 or more hours of supervised community service, classroom-based discussions of service experiences, and classroom-based discussions and activities related to social-developmental tasks of adolescence. The program designers assumed that such experiences would provide the students with a sense of mattering and agency in their communities, as well as making them feel more competent and engaged at school. Evaluations of the program found strong evidence that the program did succeed both in lowering teenage pregnancy rates and in increasing academic achievement (Allen, Kupermine, Philliber, & Herre, 1994; Allen, Philliber, et al., 1997). Furthermore, the evaluation studies found that the students who performed more volunteer service were at lower risk for course failure while they were involved in the program; they were also less likely to be suspended from school and to get pregnant. These evaluations suggest that the community service and the mentoring components are the most important program (Allen, Philliber, & Hoggson, 1990).

The intervention work by Oyserman and her colleagues (Oyserman, Gant, & Ager, 1995) is also based on the developmental needs of adolescents—in this case the importance of students' identities and future goals and imagined future "possible selves" for students' engagement in school. Oyserman, Gant, and Ager (1995) found that African American students are more motivated to invest time and energy in mastering school learning materials if they include academic success in their images of their future possible selves and if these African American adolescents included academic success in their view of what it means to be a successful African American (Oyserman et al., 1995). Subsequently, Oyserman and her colleagues developed and tested school-based interventions designed to increase the salience of academic achievement in both individuals' possible selves and ethnic identity. For example, using a randomized treatment intervention design, Oyserman, Terry, and Bybee (2002) provided a group of African American adolescents with a series of experiences designed to help them expand both their views of themselves in various future occupations and the means of obtaining these various occupational goals. These means included increased commitment to educational success. Those students who were part of the treatment reported greater bonding with school and greater concern with doing well in school than the controls. They also evidenced better school attendance.

We end this section with one final example of a whole school reform effort based on many of motivational principles discussed throughout this chapter. *The First Things First* school reform initiative, created by the Institute for Research and Reform in Education, entails three basic strategies: the creation of small learning communities, the creation of strong connections between family and school, and the provision of high quality instruction. These strategies were selected because they facilitate the following four experiences for students: (1) "continuity of care" and strong student–teacher relationships; (2) "flexible scheduling that allows for additional instructional time and attention to individual learning needs"; (3) "high, clear and fair standards for academics and conduct"; and (4) exposure to "enriched and diverse learning opportunities." To accomplish these goals, IRRE works with districts to provide the following three experiences for the teachers and staff: (1) "equip, empower, and expect staff to implement effective instructional practices"; (2) flexibility to redirect resources to meet emerging needs; and (3) "ensuring collective responsibility" (Institute for Research and Reform in Education [IRRE], 2004, pp. 6, 7). All three of these features require school districts to put together teams of teachers that work with the same students over time and across school years. These teams are provided with common planning time and with remedial curricular materials that can be used to help students succeed. The teams are also provided with resources for their own continued development as high quality teachers and mentors. All students are provided with a family advocate who works with 15 to 20 students and their families over time to help the students succeed. This reform has been implemented in many school districts across the country and has been carefully evaluated in the Kansas City, Kansas school district. The results of this evaluation are quite positive for both the middle and senior high school grades. The program both reduces high school drop out and increases academic performance, as well as closing the gap in academic performance between White and Black students.

## Summary and Conclusions

In this chapter, we outlined many ways in which schools affect the social and academic development of students. We stressed the need to take both a systems level and a developmental perspective on schools. We began by pointing out how the multiple levels of school organization interact to shape the day-to-day experiences of adolescents and teachers. We also stressed the interface of schools as complex changing institutions with the developmental trajectories of individuals. To understand how schools influence development, one needs to understand change at both the individual and the institutional level. Stage–environment fit theory provides an excellent example of the linking of these two developmental trajectories. Imagine two trajectories: one at the school level and one at the individual level. Schools change in many ways over the grade levels. The nature of these changes can be developmentally appropriate or inappropriate in terms of the extent to which they foster continued development toward the transition into adulthood and maturity. Youth travel through this changing context as they move from grade to grade and from school to school. Similarly, youth develop and change as they get older. They also have assumptions about their increasing maturity and the privileges it ought to afford them. Optimal development is most likely to take place when these two trajectories of change are in synchrony with each other; that is, when the changes in the context mesh well with, and perhaps even slightly precede the patterns of change occurring at the individual level. We also discussed the many ways in which experiences at school are influenced by the larger cultural and social milieu in which schools are nested. Culturally shared beliefs influence how we fund our schools, what and how we teach, and how we design school policy at all levels. These policies, in turn, influence the types of connections that schools have with families, communities, higher educational institutions, the labor market, and the daily experiences of youth in the schools they attend. On some levels, our schools are succeeding very well in supporting both learning and positive youth development for many groups of people. At other levels, schools are not supporting optimal learning or preparation for adult development for many young people. Adolescents of color, particularly African Americans, Latinos, and Native Americans, still perform less well than European Americans and some groups of Asian Americans (Steinberg, Dornbusch, & Brown, 1992; Suarez-Orozco & Suarez-Orozco, 2001; Valencia, 1991).

Finally, we discussed examples of school reform efforts that have made a difference in students' lives. We hope these examples provide readers with ideas about how one can use fundamental developmental and educational psychology theories and data to design effective interventions that improve students' lives. We also hope that these examples provide readers with ideas about how we need to study children and adolescents' experiences in schools if we are to fully understand human development. Children and adolescents spend more time in schools than in any other social context other than their homes and families. Extensive research exists on the ways in which experiences in the home influence human development. By comparison, we know relatively little about all the many ways in which experiences at school influence the course of human development. Studying social development in school contexts is a wonderful opportunity to add both to our basic understanding of the role that social contexts play in human development and to our ability to design effective school contexts for our children and adolescents.

## Note

1. This chapter is adapted from Eccles, J. S., & Roeser, R. (1999). School and community influences on human development. In M. Bornstein & M. Lamb (Eds.), *Developmental psychology: An advanced textbook* (4th ed., pp. 503–554). Mahwah, NJ: Erlbaum.

## References

Allen, J. P., Kuperminc, G., Philliber, S., & Herre, K. (1994). Programmatic prevention of adolescent problem behaviors: The role of autonomy, relatedness, and volunteer service in the Teen Outreach Program. *American Journal of Community Psychology, 22*(5), 617–638.

Allen, J. P., Philliber, S., Herrling, S., & Kuperminc, G. P. (1997). Preventing teen pregnancy and academic failure: Experimental evaluation of a developmentally based approach. *Child Development, 68*(4), 729–742.

Allen, J. P., Philliber, S., & Hoggson, N. (1990). School-based prevention of teen-age pregnancy and school dropout: Process evaluation of the national replication of the teen outreach program. *American Journal of Community Psychology, 18*(4), 505–524.

Alexander, K. L., Entwisle, D. R. & Olson, L. S. (2007). Lasting consequences of the summer learning gap. *Sociology of Education, 72,* 167–180.

Anderman, E. M., Maehr, M. L., & Midgley, C. (1999). Declining motivation after the transition to middle school: Schools can make a difference. *Journal of Research and Development in Education, 32,* 131–147.

Anderman, E. M., & Midgley, C. (1997). Changes in achievement goal orientation, perceived academic competence, and grades across the transition to middle level schools. *Contemporary Educational Psychology, 22,* 269–298.

Anderman, L. H. (1999). Classroom goal orientation, school belonging and social goals as predictors of students' positive and negative affect following the transition to middle school. *Journal of Research and Development in Education, 32,* 90–103.

Arnett, J. J., (1999). Adolescent storm and stress, reconsidered. *American Psychologist, 54,* 317–326.

Astor, R. A., Benbenishty, R., Zeira, A., & Vinokur, A. (2002). School climate, observed risky behaviors, and victimization as predictors of high school student fear and judgments of school violence as a problem. *Health Education & Behavior, 29,* 716–730.

Astor, R. A., Meyer, H. A., & Behre, W. J. (1999). Unowned places and times: Maps and interviews about violence in high schools. *American Educational Research Journal, 36,* 3–42.

Barber, B. L., Eccles, J. S., & Stone, M. R. (2001). Whatever happened to the Jock, the Brain, and the Princess? Young adult pathways linked to adolescent activity involvement and social identity. *Journal of Adolescent Research, 16,* 429–455.

Barker, R. G., & Gump, P. (1964). *Big school small school.* Stanford, CA: Stanford University Press.

Benbenishty, R., & Astor, R. A. (2007). Monitoring indicators of children's victimization in school: Linking national-, regional-, and site-level indicators. *Social Indicators Research, 84,* 333–348.

Benbenishty, R., Astor, R. A., Zeira, A., & Vinokur, A. D. (2002). Perceptions of violence and fear of school attendance among junior high school students in Israel. *Social Work Research, 2,* 71–87.

Brody, G. H., Chen, Y-F., Murry, V. M., Simons. R. L., Ge, X., Gibbons, F. X., et al. (2006). Perceived discrimination and the adjustment of African American youths: A five-year longitudinal analysis with contextual moderation effects. *Child Development, 77*(5), 1170–1189.

Bronfenbrenner, U. (1979). *The ecology of human development: Experiments by nature and design.* Cambridge, MA: Harvard University Press.

Brophy, J. E. (2004). *Motivating students to learn* (2nd ed.). Mahwah, NJ: Erlbaum.

Bryk, A. S., Lee, V. E., & Holland P. B. (1993). *Catholic schools and the common good.* Cambridge, MA: Harvard University Press.

Carnegie Council on Adolescent Development. (1989). *Turning points: Preparing American youth for the 21st century.* Washington, DC: Author.

Carskadon, M. A. (1990). Patterns of sleep and sleepiness in adolescents. *Pediatrician, 17,* 5–12.

Coleman, J. S., Campbell, E. Q., Hobson, C. J., McPartland, J., Mood, A. M., Weinfeld, F. D., et al. (1966). *Equality of educational opportunity.* Washington, DC: Department of Health, Education, and Welfare.

Connell, J. P., & Wellborn, J. G. (1991). Competence, autonomy, and relatedness: A motivational analysis of self-system processes. In R. Gunnar & L. A. Sroufe (Eds.), *Minnesota symposia on child psychology* (Vol. 23, pp. 43–77). Hillsdale, NJ: Erlbaum.

Cooper, H. M. (1979). Pygmalion grows up: A model for teacher expectation communication and performance influence. *Review of Educational Research, 49*(3), 389–410.

Council of the Great City Schools. (1992). *National urban education goals: Baseline indicators, 1990–91.* Washington, DC: Author.

Covington, M. V., & Dray, E. (2002). The developmental course of achievement motivation: A need-based approach. In A. Wigfield & J. S. Eccles (Eds.), *Development of achievement motivation* (pp. 33–56). San Diego, CA: Academic Press.

Darling-Hammond, L. (1997). *The right to learn: A blueprint for creating schools that work.* San Francisco, CA: Jossey-Bass.

Darling-Hammond, L., & Bransford, J. (Eds.). (2005). *Preparing teachers for a changing world: What teachers should learn and be able to do.* San Francisco, CA: Jossey-Bass.

Deci, E. L., & Ryan, R. M. (2002). Self-determination research: Reflections and future directions. In E. L. Deci & R. M. Ryan (Eds.), *Handbook of self-determination theory research* (pp. 431–441). Rochester, NY: University of Rochester Press.

Dishion, T. J., McCord, J., & Poulin, F. (1999). When interventions harm: Peer groups and problem behavior. *American Psychologist, 54*(9), 755–764.

Eccles, J. S., & Barber, B. L. (1999). Student council, volunteering, basketball, or marching band: What kind of extracurricular involvement matters? *Journal of Adolescent Research, 14,* 10–43.

Eccles, J. S., & Gootman, J. (2001). *Community programs to promote youth development.* Washington, DC: National Academy Press.

Eccles, J. S., & Midgley, C. (1989). Stage/environment fit: Developmentally appropriate classrooms for early adolescents. In R. Ames & C. Ames (Eds.), *Research on motivation in education* (Vol. 3, pp. 139–181). New York: Academic Press.

Eccles, J. S., Midgley, C., Wigfield, A., Buchanan, C. M., Reuman, D., Flanagan, C., et al. (1993). Development during adolescence: The impact of stage-environment fit on adolescents' experiences in schools and families. *American Psychologist, 48,* 90–101.

Eccles, J. S., & Roeser, R. (1999). School and community influences on human development. In M. Bornstein & M. Lamb (Eds.), *Developmental psychology: An advanced textbook* (4th ed., pp. 503–554). Mahwah, NJ: Erlbaum.

Eccles, J. S., & Templeton, J. (2002). Extracurricular and other after-school activities for youth. In W. S. Secada (Ed.), *Review of Educational Research* (Vol. 26, pp. 113–180). Washington DC: American Educational Research Association Press.

Elder, G. H., Jr., & Conger, R. D. (2000). *Children of the land*. Chicago, IL: University of Chicago Press.

Entwisle, D. R., & Alexander, K. L. (1993). Entry into school: The beginning school transition and educational stratification in the United States. *Annual Review of Sociology, 19*, 401–423.

Epstein, R., Chillag, N., & Lavie, P. (1998). Starting times of school: Effects on daytime functioning of fifth-grade children in Israel. *Sleep, 3*, 250–256.

Fagan, J., & Wilkinson, D. L. (1998). Guns, youth violence and social identity. In M. Tonry & M. H. Moore (Eds.), *Youth violence* (pp. 373–456). Chicago, IL: University of Chicago Press.

Feldlaufer, H., Midgley, C., & Eccles, J. S. (1988). Student, teacher, and observer perceptions of the classroom environment before and after the transition to junior high school. *Journal of Early Adolescence, 8*, 133–156.

Ferguson, R. F. (1998). Teachers' perceptions and expectations and the Black-White test score gap. In C. Jencks & M. Phillips (Eds.), *The Black-White test score gap* (pp. 273–317). Washington, DC: Brookings Institute Press.

Finn, J. D. (2006). *The adult lives of at-risk students: The roles of attainment and engagement in high school*. Report to National Center of Educational Statistics (NCES 2006-328). Washington DC: U. S. Department of Education.

Fordham, S., & Ogbu, J. U. (1986). Black students' school success: Coping with "the burden of 'acting white.'" *Urban Review, 18*, 176–206.

Fuligni, A. J., Eccles, J. S., & Barber, B. L. (1995). The long-term effects of seventh-grade ability grouping in mathematics. *Journal of Early Adolescence, 15*(1), 58–89.

Furrer, C., & Skinner, E. (2003). Sense of relatedness as a factor in children's academic engagement and performance. *Journal of Educational Psychology, 95*, 148–162.

Gottfried, A. E., Fleming, J. S., & Gottfried, A. W. (2001). Continuity of academic intrinsic motivation from childhood through late adolescence: A longitudinal study. *Journal of Educational Psychology, 93*, 3–13.

Graham, S., & Taylor, A. Z. (2002). Ethnicity, gender, and the development of achievement values. In A. Wigfield & J. S. Eccles (Eds.), *Development of achievement motivation* (pp. 123–146). San Diego, CA: Academic Press.

Grolnick, W. S., Gurland, S. T., Jacob, K. F., & DeCourcey, W. (2002). The development of self-determination in middle childhood and adolescence. In A. Wigfield & J. Eccles (Eds.), *Development of achievement motivation* (pp. 148–171). San Diego, CA: Academic Press.

Guay, F., Marsh, H. W., & Boivin, M. (2003). Academic self-concept and academic achievement: Developmental perspectives on their causal ordering. *Journal of Educational Psychology, 95*, 124–136.

Hallinan, M. T., & Kubitschek, W. N. (1999). Curriculum differentiation and high school achievement. *Social Psychology of Education, 3*, 41–62.

Harris-Britt, A., Valrie, C. R., Kurtz-Costes, B., & Rowley, S. J. (2007). Perceived racial discrimination and self-esteem in African American youth: Racial socialization as a protective factor. *Journal of Research on Adolescence, 17*(4), 669–682.

Hunt, D. E. (1975). Person-environment interaction: A challenge found wanting before it was tried. *Review of Educational Research, 57*, 437–466.

Institute for Research and Reform in Education. (2004). *First things first*. Philadelphia, PA: Author. Internal working document.

Jackson, A. W., & Davis, G. A. (2000). *Turning points 2000: Educating adolescents in the 21st century*. New York: Teachers College Press.

Jeynes, W. H. (2002). A meta-analysis of the effects of attending religious schools and religiosity on Black and Hispanic academic achievement. *Education and Urban Society, 35*(1), 27–49.

Jussim, L., Eccles, J. S., & Madon, S. (1996). Social perception, social stereotypes, and teacher expectations: Accuracy and the quest for the powerful self-fulfilling prophecy. In L. Berkowitz (Ed.), *Advances in experimental social psychology* (pp. 281–388). New York: Academic Press.

Juvonen, J., Le, V. N., Kaganoff, T., Augustine, C., & Constant, L. (2004). *Focus on the wonder years: Challenges facing the American middle school*. Santa Monica, CA: RAND.

Larson, R. W. (2000). Toward a psychology of positive youth development. *American Psychologist, 55*, 170–183.

Lee, V. E., & Loeb, S. (2000). School size in Chicago elementary schools: Effects on teacher attitudes and student achievement. *American Educational Research Journal, 37*, 3–31.

Lee, V. E., & Smith, J. B. (1993). Effects of school restructuring on the achievement and engagement of middle-grade students. *Sociology of Education, 66*, 164–187.

Lee, V. E., & Smith, J. B. (1995). Effects of high school restructuring and size on early gains in achievement and engagement. *Sociology of Education, 68*(4), 241–270.

Lee, V. E., & Smith, J. B. (1997). High school size: Which works best, and for whom? *Educational Evaluation and Policy Analysis, 19*(3), 205–227.

Lee, V. E., & Smith, J. (2001). *Restructuring high schools for equity and excellence: What works*. New York: Teacher's College Press.

Maehr, M. L., & Midgley, C. (1996). *Transforming school cultures to enhance student motivation and learning*. Boulder, CO: Westview Press.

Mahoney, J. L., Harris, A. L., & Eccles, J. S. (2006). Organized activity participation, positive youth development, and the over-scheduling hypothesis. *Social Policy Report, 20*, 1–30.

Mahoney, J. L., Larson, R. W., & Eccles. J. S. (Eds.). (2005). *Organized activities as contexts of development: Extracurricular activities, after-school and community programs*. Mahwah, NJ: Erlbaum.

Meece, J. L., Anderman, E. M., & Anderman, L. H. (2005). Classroom goal structure, student motivation, and academic achievement. *Annual Review of Psychology, 5*, 487–503.

Midgley, C. (2002). *Goals, goal structures, and patterns of adaptive learning*. Mahwah, NJ: Erlbaum.

Midgley, C., Anderman, E., & Hicks, L. (1995). Differences between elementary and middle school teachers and students: A goal theory approach. *Journal of Early Adolescence, 15*, 90–113.

Midgley, C., & Feldlaufer, H. (1987). Students' and teachers' decision-making fit before and after the transition to junior high school. *Journal of Early Adolescence, 7*, 225–241.

Midgley, C., Feldlaufer, H., & Eccles, J. S. (1988). The transition to junior high school: Beliefs of pre- and post-transition teachers. *Journal of Youth and Adolescence, 17*, 543–562.

Midgley, C., Feldlaufer, H., & Eccles, J. S. (1989). Changes in teacher efficacy and student self- and task-related beliefs during the transition to junior high school. *Journal of Educational Psychology, 81*, 247–258.

National Research Council. (2004). *Engaging schools: Fostering high school students' motivation to learn*. Washington, DC: National Academies Press.

Nishina, A., & Juvonen, J. (2005). Sticks and stones may break my bones but words will make me feel sick: the psychosocial, somatic, and scholastic consequences of peer harassment. *Journal of Clinical Child and Adolescent Psychology, 34*(1), 37–48.

Noguera, P. A., & Wing, J. Y. (Eds.). (2006). *Unfinished business: Closing the achievement in our schools*. San Francisco, CA: Jossey-Bass.

Oakes, J. (2005). *Keeping track: How schools structure inequality* (2nd ed.). New Haven, CT: Yale University Press.

Ogbu, J. (1992). Understanding cultural diversity and learning. *Educational Researcher, 21*, 5–14.

Okagaki, L. (2001). Triarchic model of minority children's school achievement. *Educational Psychologist, 36*, 9–20.

Oyserman, D., Gant, L., & Ager, J. (1995). A socially contextualized model of African American identity: Possible selves and school persistence. *Journal of Personality and Social Psychology, 69*, 1216–1232.

Oyserman, D., Terry, K., & Bybee, D., (2002). A possible selves intervention to enhance school involvement. *Journal of Adolescence, 24*, 313–326.

Roderick, M. (1993). *The path to dropping out: Evidence for intervention.* Westport, CT: Auburn House.

Roderick, M., & Camburn, E. (1999). Risk and recovery from course failure in the early years of high school. *American Educational Research Journal, 36*, 303–344.

Roeser, R. W., & Eccles, J. S., (2000). Schooling and mental health. In A. J. Sameroff, M. Lewis, & S. M. Miller (Eds.), *Handbook of developmental psychopathology* (2nd ed., pp. 135–156). New York: Plenum.

Roeser, R. W., Eccles, J. S., & Sameroff, J. (1998). Academic and emotional functioning in early adolescence: Longitudinal relations, patterns, and prediction by experience in middle school. *Development and Psychopathology, 10*, 321–352.

Roeser, R. W., Marachi, R., & Gelhbach, H. (2002). A goal theory perspective on teachers' professional identities and the contexts of teaching. In C. M. Midgley (Ed.), *Goals, goal structures, and patterns of adaptive learning* (pp. 205–241). Mahwah, NJ: Erlbaum.

Roeser, R. W., & Midgley, C. M. (1997). Teachers' views of aspects of student mental health. *Elementary School Journal, 98*(2), 115–133.

Roeser, R. W., Midgley, C. M., & Urdan, T. C. (1996). Perceptions of the school psychological environment and early adolescents' psychological and behavioral functioning in school: The mediating role of goals and belonging. *Journal of Educational Psychology, 88*, 408–422.

Rosenholtz, S. J., & Simpson, C. (1984). The formation of ability conceptions: Developmental trend or social construction? *Review of Educational Research, 54*, 31–63.

Rumberger, R. W., & Thomas, S. L. (2000). The distribution of dropout and turnover rates among urban and suburban high schools. *Sociology of Education, 73*, 39–67.

Rutter, M., Maughan, B., Mortimore, P., & Ouston, J. (1979). *Fifteen thousand hours: Secondary schools and their effects on children.* Cambridge, MA: Harvard University Press.

Sellers, R. M., Caldwell, C. H., Schmeelk-Cone, K. H., & Zimmerman, M. A. (2003). Racial identity, racial discrimination, perceived stress, and psychological distress among African American young adults. *Journal of Health and Social Behavior, 44*(3), 302–317.

Sheets, R. H., & Hollins, E. R. (Eds.). (1999). *Racial and ethnic identity in school practices: Aspects of human development.* Mahwah, NJ: Erlbaum.

Shih, M., Pittinsky, T. L., & Ambady, N. (1999). Stereotype susceptibility: Identity salience and shifts in quantitative performance. *Psychological Science, 10*, 80–83.

Simmons, R. G., & Blyth, D. A. (1987). *Moving into adolescence: The impact of pubertal change and school context.* Hawthorn, NY: Aldine de Gruyter.

Slavin, R. E. (1995). *Cooperative learning* (2nd ed.). Boston: Allyn & Bacon.

Steele, C. M., & Aronson, J. (1995). Stereotype threat and the intellectual test performance of African-Americans. *Journal of Personality and Social Psychology, 69*, 797–811.

Steinberg, L., Dornbusch, S., & Brown, B. (1992). Ethnic differences in adolescents' achievements: An ecological perspective. *American Psychologist, 47*, 723–729.

Suarez-Orozco, C., & Suarez-Orozco, M. (2001). *Children of immigration.* Cambridge, MA: Harvard University Press.

United Way. (2008). *Seizing the middle ground: Why middle school creates the pathway to college and the workforce.* Los Angeles: United Way of Greater Los Angeles.

Valencia, R. R. (Ed.). (1991). *Chicano school failure and success: Research and policy agendas for the 1990s.* London: Falmer Press.

Weinstein, R. (1989). Perceptions of classroom processes and student motivation: Children's views of self-fulfilling prophecies. In C. Ames & R. Ames (Eds.), *Research on motivation in education: Vol. 3. Goals and cognitions* (pp. 13–44). New York: Academic Press.

Wentzel, K. (2002). Are effective teachers like good parents? Teaching styles and student adjustment in early adolescence. *Child Development, 73*, 287–301.

Wigfield, A., Eccles, J. S., Mac Iver, D., Reuman, D., & Midgley, C. (1991). Transitions at early adolescence: Changes in children's domain-specific self-perceptions and general self-esteem across the transition to junior high school. *Developmental Psychology, 27*, 552–565.

Wigfield, A., Eccles, J. S., Schiefele, U., Roeser, R., & Davis-Kean, P. (2006). Motivation. In N. Eisenberg (Ed.), *Handbook of child psychology: Vol. 3. Social, emotional, and personality development* (6th ed., pp. 933–1002). New York: Wiley.

Wilson, J. Q., & Kelling, G. L. (1982, March). Broken windows. *Atlantic Monthly, 249*, 29–38.

Wong, C. A., Eccles, J. S., & Sameroff, A. J. (2003). The influence of ethnic discrimination and ethnic identification on African-Americans adolescents' school and socioemotional adjustment. *Journal of Personality, 71*, 1197–1232.

Youniss, J., McLellan, J. A., & Yates, M. (1997). What we know about engendering civic identity. *American Behavioral Scientist, 40*, 619–630.

# Part II

## Classroom Contexts

# 3

# Classroom Environments and Developmental Processes

## *Conceptualization and Measurement*

*BRIDGET K. HAMRE AND ROBERT C. PIANTA*

Children on average spend at least 15,000 hours in class-rooms from the age of 4 or 5 until they leave high school. Indeed, there are few places in which they spend more time. Within classrooms, children and adolescents are exposed to critical developmental experiences—they learn to read, write, and think critically, they make friends and have to face the inevitable issues with peer relationships, and they are challenged to become productive, independent members of a larger society. Driven in part by the rise of contextualism in developmental science (Cicchetti & Aber, 1998; Lerner, 1998), several seminal programs of research have illuminated the powerful effect classroom experiences can have on children's development (e.g., Alexander & Entwisle, 1988; Ladd & Burgess, 1999; Morrison & Connor, 2002; National Institute of Child Health and Human Development, Early Childcare Research Network [NICHD, ECCRN], 2002, 2003a; Roeser, Eccles, & Sameroff, 2000; Skinner & Belmont, 1993). Notwithstanding the contributions of these research programs, such examples are exceptions in developmental science, which has drawn much more intensively on the study of home environments and their effects to develop theories of how social settings influence development (Eccles & Roeser, 2005).

Recently, however, there has been a significant increase in research activity devoted to examining the nature of students' experiences in classrooms and the ways in which these experiences uniquely contribute to social, cognitive, and academic development. This increase in research has been driven by several factors. First, educational accountability reform in general, and the No Child Left Behind Act (NCLB) in particular, have placed individual schools and teachers in the spotlight by requiring evidence of their ability to produce student achievement. No Child Left Behind has required policymakers and school administrators to produce evidence that classroom experiences are causes of student outcomes. Second, the well-documented achievement gaps related to culture, race, and income (National Center for Education Statistics, 2003; West, Denton, & Germino-Hausken, 2000), have drawn attention to ways schools need to modify curriculum, school culture, and staffing in attempts to close this gap. Finally, new investments of funds, and even the creation of new research societies, are aimed at producing evidence of the effectiveness of education interventions. One could plausibly argue that the United States is paying more attention to what happens in classrooms than ever before.

The increased interest in the classroom has led to the development of new theoretical models and methodologies for classroom-based research and has emphasized the importance of integrating developmental research with educational science. Pianta (2006) argues that the study of development in classrooms offers as much for developmental theory as it does for educational practice. In an effort to spur continued interest in this intersection, this chapter: (1) provides a rationale for studying classrooms as a unique developmental context; (2) describes a conceptual framework for the study of classrooms that organizes and integrates findings across developmental and educational sciences; (3) summarizes issues in the measurement of classroom environments; and (4) discusses implications for future research.

## Classrooms as a Unique Developmental Context

Schools are multilevel organizations—districts, school buildings, grade levels, classrooms, social groups are all identifiable levels that could be a legitimate focus for understanding the connection between schooling and development. But classrooms, rather than other levels of schooling, are the unit of focus within this chapter.

*Why Focus on Classrooms?* First, evidence from developmental science strongly indicates that effects of social settings on children's development are driven by proximal processes (Bronfenbrenner & Morris, 1998), the interactions that children have on a daily basis with adults, peers, organizational structures, and materials. When examining schooling effects, children's experiences in classrooms constitute the majority of their day and thus constitute the majority of school-based proximal processes. Furthermore, it is classroom level experiences that appear to be most closely associated with student outcomes (Nye, Konstantopoulos, & Hedges, 2004). School-level effects, such as school climate and culture, are important aspects of students' experiences. However, these effects are more distal from students' developmental progress and are largely mediated through or moderated by classroom processes (Hamre & Pianta, 2007).

Another reason to consider classrooms, discussed by Pianta (2006), is the recognition that classroom interactions are not simply applications of practices that are only of interest to educators, but rather reflect processes that should be of as much interest to developmental scientists as are interactions children have with parents and peers, if only for the reason that they are intended to produce developmental change. Researchers who have applied developmental theories to classrooms have discovered that classrooms offer an incredibly rich context in which to study basic developmental processes. Unlike in families, in which only a few children are exposed to a given familial context, in classrooms there are many children who are exposed to that environment over time. This allows for modeling aspects of bio-ecological theory (Bronfenbrenner & Morris, 1998), such as the potential for differential responsiveness to different features of a social setting. For example, work by Connor, Morrison, and colleagues (Connor, 2005; Connor, Morrison, & Petrella, 2004; Morrison & Connor, 2002) provides consistent evidence that children coming into classrooms with varying levels of reading ability benefit from very different instructional practices. Their studies have shown that children at risk of reading difficulties benefit from high levels of teacher-directed explicit language instruction but that this type of instruction makes no difference in decoding skills for children with already high skills on this dimension upon school entry. Highly skilled children, in contrast, make the strongest gains in classrooms with more child-led literacy-related activities.

A final reason for a focus on classrooms is that, with increasing focus on the design, implementation, and evaluation of prevention and intervention programs through experimental contrasts, classrooms are very often a location in which these programs are implemented (Greenberg, Domitrovich, & Bumbarger, 2001). It is our contention that such programs will not be entirely successful nor will they be theoretically informative without the full recognition, conceptually and methodologically, that everyday classroom interactions are the medium through which such programs will ultimately produce change. There is consistent evidence that the effects of school-based interventions rise and fall with how they are implemented within schools (Greenberg et al., 2001; Rones & Hoagwood, 2000). Due in part to early failures of some school-based intervention approaches, prevention science has increasingly focused on

ways in which to conceptualize and measure classroom level implementation variables as critical to the success of any program of research in this area (Hamre et al., in press; Han & Weiss, 2005; Kam, Greenberg, & Walls, 2003; Valente, Unger, Ritt-Olson, Cen, & Johnson, 2006). These efforts are critical to the successful adaptation of developmental theory into educational interventions.

***Current Developmental Theory and Educational Processes—Confluence and Deviations*** As more developmental scientists move to study classrooms, there is a need for conceptual models that integrate decades of research on children's development in home and peer contexts, with educational research. There are two basic approaches to this task, one which highlights the commonalities between developmental processes elucidated through the study of families and peers and their classroom equivalents and one which seeks to understand classrooms as a unique developmental context. Both approaches have made important contributions to our understanding of the role of classroom environments in children's development.

The first approach views classrooms primarily as extensions of home environments. Thus, developmental processes known to be important causal agents in home settings, such as parent–child interactions, are transferred to the classroom environment. This view draws from ideas that there are underlying mechanisms driving development (Pianta, 2006). Much of the developmentally informed research conducted to date on classroom effects has taken this approach. For example, just as maternal sensitivity is a key mechanism of young children's development (Ijzendoorn & Bakermans-Kranenburg, 2004; NICHD, ECCRN, 2005), teacher sensitivity has been shown to uniquely contribute to gains in students' performance (Rimm-Kaufman, Early, & Cox, 2002). Effective classroom teachers have also been shown to share many of the same characteristics of Baumrind's (1991) description of effective parents (Wentzel, 2002). Our own work (e.g., Hamre & Pianta, 2001; Pianta, 1999) and the work of others (Birch & Ladd, 1996, 1998; Silver, Measelle, Essex, & Armstrong, 2005; Van Ijzendoorn, Sagi, & Lambermon, 1992; Wentzel, chapter 6 this volume) has similarly focused attention on the ways student–teacher relationships mirror child–parent relationships, both in conceptualization and effects.

An approach assuming some underlying mechanism or contextual isomorphism as accounting for classroom effects and experiences is, however, insufficient to explain the entirety of classroom effects. The approach fails to recognize that classrooms and families are often oriented around very different goals and thus similar processes may function in different ways across home and school environments. For example, because teachers and administrators typically view their primary goal as producing academic gains rather than social, personal, or moral development, strategies for managing students' behavior take on different meanings from the way behavior is managed within families. In classrooms, behavioral control serves primarily as a tool to help get as much instruction accomplished as possible. In contrast, families may use these practices with much broader goals in mind, such as helping children develop important self-regulatory skills. The consequences for children who challenge behavioral regulation or control strategies are also different. Teachers have options such as sending the child out of the classroom or, ultimately, out of the school, that are not available to or desirable for most families. Thus, although the broad concept of behavioral control may be similar across schools and families, the specific interactions, goals, and outcomes associated with this concept are likely to differ. The larger point here is that interactions in classrooms are likely to serve goals that are different from interaction systems in families even when they both draw upon phenotypically similar behavioral domains.

Beyond different goals, the classroom context itself and the interactions that occur within it can be very different from those within families. As just one example, Hughes, Cavell, and Wilson (2001) suggest that classrooms are a unique context in the development of peer relationships, in part, because teacher–student interactions serve as a potent and frequent source of information about other students that can figure prominently in children's preferences and beliefs about others. Another set of differences between classrooms and families involves constraints on adult–child interaction. Unlike in families, physical contact and comforting is not a feature of teacher–student interactions in third grade or beyond, and although students often voice the importance of supportive relationships with teachers (Resnick et al., 1997), teachers themselves receive very little in the way of training or knowledge about forming such relationships. Another feature that differentiates classrooms and home settings in relation to developmental processes is the absence of genetic mediation in the interactions between people: in families the qualities of a parent's behavior and a child's response are linked in part by shared genetic substrates; in classrooms the common genetic mechanisms are not present and so the extent of a teacher's interactions having an influence on child outcomes is somewhat different in terms of the nature of the mechanism explaining these effects.

A final distinction between home and classroom environments relates to the ways in which these environments change over time. Family environments are much more stable than classrooms. Within the United States, children typically change classrooms, teachers, and peer groups each year and go through major shifts as they move from preschool to elementary school to middle school and high school (Anderman & Anderman, 1999; Eccles & Midgley, 1989; La Paro et al., 2009; Midgley, 2002; Wigfield, Eccles, MacIver, Reuman, & Midgley, 1991). This lack of continuity offers both a challenge and opportunity to developmental scientists and can be an important entry point for links between developmental science and educational practices; Eccles's work on middle school transition is one example (Eccles, 2004). Another opportunity is the case of "looping," a practice involving students staying with the same peers and teacher for more than one year, rather than moving

from year to year. There is almost no empirical research on looping (see Hampton, Mumford, & Bond, 1997 for an exception), but it offers a unique opportunity to examine the consequences of an educational practice with significant implications for understanding the role of relationships, both with peers and with teachers, in children's development. Thus again, the changing nature of classroom contexts offers opportunities for developmentally informed research that exploits the natural variation present in these changes (e.g., looping or not; tracked classes and nontracked classes; having fewer or more teachers in a given grade).

In each of the examples cited above, there is a need to move beyond theories and measures developed in home contexts to ensure that the developmental contexts and processes most salient to the classroom environment are adequately captured. It is these adaptations and integrations of developmental theory and educational research that are a focus of this chapter. The examples cited above offer a glimpse of what could be learned through a more systematic exploitation and exploration of this "seam" between home and classroom and the processes that operate to promote children's gains in and across both settings. The extent to which further research contributes to understanding development in educational settings is in part predicated on further specification of the nature and dimensions of classroom processes as unique in their own right and not a derivative of the literature on families. The next section provides a conceptual framework for understanding classroom environments that integrates years of research from developmental scientists and educational researchers.

## Defining and Understanding Classroom Environments

Educational and developmental researchers have often approached the study of classrooms in fairly distinct ways, with educational research much more focused on the instructional context and developmental research concentrating on the social dynamics of classrooms. Although there are conceptual models that stress the relative salience of a variety of different features of classrooms (e.g., Eccles & Roeser, 1999), they tend to be the exception. Consistent with developmental theories emphasizing the role of proximal process on development (Bronfenbrenner & Morris, 1998), this chapter takes the view that the most critical ingredients of any classroom environment are the interactions among adults and students. This view of classroom environments excludes a focus on some aspects of classrooms that have been the focus of research, such as the availability of furnishings, materials, and curricula. However, it also provides a broad, holistic view of the classroom environment that includes all types of interactions—those that are social, organizational, and instructional in nature. As such, this view of classroom environments is inclusive of research focused on more discrete aspects of classrooms such as quality or effective teaching, learning environments, and student–teacher and peer relationships.

To help organize the diverse literatures that inform class-room environments, we proposed a system for organizing the wide range of interactions in classrooms, referred to as the Classroom Assessment Scoring System (CLASS) Framework (Hamre & Pianta, 2007; Pianta, Hamre, Spekman, Mintz, & La Paro, 2006; Pianta, La Paro, & Hamre, 2007). The CLASS Framework is a theoretically driven and empirically supported conceptualization of class-room interactions organized into three major domains: Emo-tional Supports, Classroom Organization, and Instructional Supports. Within each domain are a set of more specific dimensions of classroom interactions that are presumed to be important to students' academic or social development (see Figure 3.1). The CLASS Framework is consistent with several other descriptions of classroom environments or quality teaching put forth in the educational and devel-opmental literatures (e.g., Brophy, 1999; Brophy & Good, 1986; Eccles & Roeser, 1999; Gage, 1978; Pressley et al., 2003; Soar & Soar, 1978).

The CLASS Framework draws heavily from theoretical and empirical work on classrooms advanced within edu-cational literatures, but it also relies on a developmentally informed analysis of the features of classroom settings salient for producing developmental change (see Pianta & Allen, 2008). There are several additional conceptual and methodological distinctions between the CLASS Framework and other frameworks for studying classrooms. One distinction is that although most educational research has relied on studies of discrete behavioral indicators of putatively effective teaching (e.g., time allocations, pres-ence of advanced organizers, number of instructional cues, etc.), the model proposed by Hamre and Pianta (2007) describes a *latent* structure for organizing teachers'

behaviors. Importantly, this three-domain latent structure (emotional supports, organizational supports, instructional supports) emanates from an analysis of classroom set-tings predicated on identifying proximal processes that developmental theory would suggest to be important for growth in academic and social outcomes (Pianta, 2006). This identification of a latent structure for developmentally salient proximal processes in classrooms is similar to the model proposed by Eccles and Roeser (1999); however, the CLASS Framework extends this earlier work by in-cluding a more thorough description of the developmental processes underlying each broad domain. For example, as shown in Figure 3.1, the latent domain of Emotional Sup-ports includes several key dimensions: Classroom Climate, Teacher Sensitivity, and Regard for Student Perspective that have empirical support for effects related to child outcomes. Within each dimension, specific behaviors and interactions are also identified and provide indications of classrooms that may be high or low on the dimension (see Table 3.1). Classroom Climate includes observable behavioral indictors such as the frequency and quality of teacher affective communications with students (smiles, positive verbal feedback) as well as the degree to which students appear to enjoy spending time with one another. This detailed conceptualization of levels of classroom environments, moving from broad theoretically based domains to very specific behavioral indicators, facilitates the integration of a wide range of educational and devel-opmental literatures.

Another key distinction between the CLASS Framework and others is recent empirical support for this organiza-tion of classroom processes derived from observational studies of actual classrooms (Hamre, Pianta, Mashburn, &

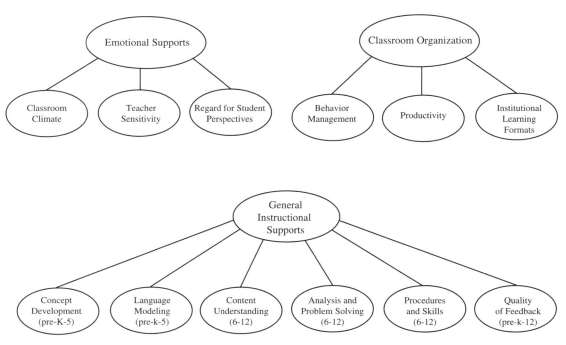

**Figure 3.1** Classroom Assessment Scoring System (CLASS) Framework.

**TABLE 3.1**
**Description of CLASS Framework Dimensions**

| Dimension | Description |
|---|---|
| **Emotional Support** | |
| Classroom climate | Reflects the overall emotional tone of the classroom and the connection between teachers and students. Considers the warmth and respect displayed in teachers and students interactions with one another as well as the degree to which they display enjoyment and enthusiasm during learning activities. |
| Teacher sensitivity | Encompasses teachers' responsivity to students' needs and awareness of students' level of academic and emotional functioning. The highly sensitive teacher helps students see adults as a resource and creates an environment in which students feel safe and free to explore and learn. |
| Regard for student perspectives | The degree to which the teacher's interactions with students and classroom activities place an emphasis on students' interests, motivations, and points of view, rather than being very teacher driven. This may be demonstrated by teachers' flexibility within activities and respect for students' autonomy to participate in and initiate activities. |
| **Classroom Organization** | |
| Behavior management | Encompasses teachers' ability to use effective methods to prevent and redirect misbehavior, by presenting clear behavioral expectations and minimizing time spent on behavioral issues. |
| Productivity | Considers how well teachers manage instructional time and routines so that students have the maximum number of opportunities to learn. Not related to the quality of instruction, but rather teachers efficiency. |
| Instructional learning formats | The degree to which teachers maximize students' engagement and ability to learn by providing interesting activities, instruction, centers, and materials. Considers the manner in which the teacher facilitates activities so that students have opportunities to experience, perceive, explore, and utilize materials. |
| **Instructional Support (General)** | |
| Concept development* | The degree to which instructional discussions and activities promote students' higher order thinking skills versus focus on rote and fact-based learning. |
| Quality of feedback | Considers teachers' provision of feedback focused on expanding learning and understanding (formative evaluation), not correctness or the end product (summative evaluation). |
| Language modeling (pre-k to 3rd) | The quality and amount of teachers' use of language-stimulation and language-facilitation techniques during individual, small-group, and large-group interactions with children. Components of high-quality language modeling include self and parallel talk, open-ended questions, repetition, expansion/extension, and use of advanced language. |
| Content understanding (6th to 12th) | Refers to the emphasis and approaches the teacher uses to help students understand both the broad framework and key ideas in an academic discipline. This is viewed in part as a continuum ranging from an isolated set of facts, vocabulary definitions, etc. to an integrated understanding of key concepts and principles. |
| Analysis and problem solving (6th to 12th) | Reflects the emphasis and approaches the teacher uses to help students engage in higher order thinking skills. Emphasis is on analysis, integration, and application of knowledge and skills through problem solving, reasoning, and experimentation. Opportunities for demonstrating metacognition; that is, thinking about thinking, are also included. |
| Procedures and skills (6th to 12th) | Measures the degree to which the teacher presents explicit learning opportunities that enhance the students' ability to remember how and when to utilize procedures, algorithms, and skills. |

*Concept Development is relevant across grades, but it is differentiated within secondary settings to include both Content Understanding and Analysis and Problem Solving.

Downer, 2009). Drawing from a sample of over just under 4,000 preschool to fifth grade classrooms that were a part of several large, national and regional studies, Hamre and colleagues (2009) first examined the different observational instruments used in these studies and sorted observed dimensions of classroom process into the domains described by the CLASS Framework. They then used confirmatory factor analysis to examine the extent to which the three-latent domain organization of classroom interactions was consistent with actual observations in large numbers of classroom settings across grades and samples. Results indicated adequate fit of the three-factor model across variations in grade or sample, and in each instance the fit of this model was superior to a one- or two-factor model. Such findings provide evidence that the three-domain structure suggested by the CLASS Framework provides a reasonably good fit

to the natural variation in proximal processes observed in classrooms from preschool to fifth grade.

A final distinction between the CLASS Framework and other conceptualizations of classrooms is that the focus on a latent structure of proximal processes was conceptualized to apply to classroom contexts across all grades, from preschool to high school; thus the three-domain latent structure is hypothesized as grade-invariant. Yet, although latent structure is hypothesized as invariant, the CLASS Framework does allow for variation in the specific dimensions of teaching that could vary from preschool to high school (see Figure 3.1) both in terms of added or different dimensions and the specific behavioral indicators that might be organized within dimensions. Nonetheless, the overall structure for classroom interactions in three broad domains is assumed to remain constant.

*The CLASS Framework* In the next section we review the three major domains of classroom environment described in the CLASS Framework, including a discussion of the relevance of the domain to educational practice and the developmental theories on which they are based. Within each broad domain, we review literature on specific classroom dimensions with empirically supported links to child and adolescent outcomes. It is beyond the scope of this chapter to provide an exhaustive review of research in each domain; however, the literature cited provides examples of relevant work from educational and developmental research.

*Emotional Supports* As a behavioral setting, classrooms run on interactions between and among participants: relationships between students and teachers and relationships of students with one another. It is not an overstatement to suggest that most children and adolescents *live* for their social relationships (Collins & Repinski, 1994). Students who are more motivated and connected to teachers and peers demonstrate positive trajectories of development in both social and academic domains (Buhs, Ladd, & Herald, 2006; Gregory & Weinstein, 2004; Hamre & Pianta, 2001; Harter, 1996; Ladd, Birch, & Buhs, 1999; Pianta, Steinberg, & Rollins 1995; Resnick et al., 1997; Roeser et al., 2000; Ryan, Stiller, & Lynch, 1994; Silver et al., 2005; Wentzel, 1999). Students' social and emotional functioning in the classroom is embedded in teachers' and students' views of what constitutes school success (Blair, 2002; Denham & Weissberg, 2004; Raver, 2004) and even has been advanced as a student outcome that might be governed by a set of standards similar to those for academic achievement (Illinois State Board of Education, 2004). Yet, the ways in which classrooms provide emotional supports to students or encourage the development of social and emotional knowledge and skills are frequently afterthoughts in battles over curricula and testing.

Two broad areas of developmental theory guide much of the work on emotional support in classrooms, specifically attachment theory (Ainsworth, Blehar, Waters, & Wall, 1978; Bowlby, 1969; Pianta, 1999) and self-determination theory (Connell & Wellborn, 1991; Ryan & Deci, 2000; Skinner & Belmont, 1993). Attachment theory (Ainsworth et al., 1978; Bowlby, 1969) has been broadly applied to and validated in school environments in research demonstrating the value of the child–teacher relationship to developmental outcomes and self-reliant classroom behavior (Birch & Ladd, 1998; Hamre & Pianta, 2001; Howes, Hamilton, & Matheson, 1994; Lynch & Cicchetti, 1992; Pianta, 1999). Self-determination (or self-systems) theory (Connell & Wellborn, 1991; Ryan & Deci, 2000; Skinner & Belmont, 1993) suggests that the quality of emotional supports available to children affects child outcomes as a function of motivation; children are most motivated to learn when adults support their need to feel competent, positively related to others, and autonomous (Eccles & Roeser, 1998). Related work by Wentzel (1999, 2002) suggests that students who see teachers as supportive are more likely to pursue goals valued by teachers, such as engagement in academic activities.

Building from these two theoretical backgrounds, the CLASS Framework posits three dimensions of emotional support in the classroom: Classroom Climate, Teacher Sensitivity, and teachers' Regard for Student Perspectives, each of which reflects a different feature of interactions and classroom processes in relation to the overall emotional supportiveness in the classroom setting. These dimensions and associated indicators are described below.

*Classroom climate* encompasses the emotional qualities of relationships and interactions within the classroom, including student–teacher and peer relationships. The dimension focuses on the emotional tone of interactions, expressions of emotional experiences, and signaling of emotional states both in terms of valence (positive or negative) and intensity. Students with more positive and less conflictual relationships with teachers display greater peer competencies and show more positive academic development (Birch & Ladd, 1996, 1998; Bryk & Driscoll, 1988; Connell & Wellborn, 1991; Crosnoe, Johnson, & Elder, 2004; Hamre & Pianta, 2001; Ladd et al., 1999; Pianta et al., 1995; Roeser et al., 2000; Silver et al., 2005; van Ijzendoorn et al., 1992). These relationships with adults may be particularly critical during middle and high school as a way to enhance student motivation and academic success in school and emotional functioning outside of school (Gregory & Weinstein, 2004; Resnick et al., 1997; Roeser et al., 1998; Skinner, Zimmer-Gembeck, & Connell, 1998).

Peer relations are also fundamental to any description of classroom climate. Children who experience peer rejection or victimization in the early years of schooling are likely to have continued problems as they mature, including social difficulties and academic failure (Asher, Parkhurst, Hymel, & Williams, 1990; Buhs & Ladd, 2001; Buhs et al., 2006; Cassidy & Asher, 1992; Ladd, Kochenderfer, & Coleman, 1997; Ladd & Troop-Gordon, 2003). Being in a classroom characterized by high levels of peer aggression appears to be particularly problematic for boys who start school with high levels of aggression (Kellam, Ling, Merisca, Brown, & Ialongo, 1998). On the more positive side, adolescents who feel support from classroom peers feel more positive and interested in school (Hamm & Faircloth, 2005) and pursue more prosocial goals (Wentzel, 1999).

*Teacher sensitivity* is another key dimension of the degree of emotional support provided in classrooms. Sensitive teachers monitor all children in the room, are attuned and responsive to the individual cues and needs of students in their classrooms and, through their consistent and responsive interactions, help students see adults as a resource and create environments in which students feel safe and free to explore and learn (Pianta et al., 2007). Students in classrooms with sensitive teachers are more engaged and self-reliant in the classroom and have lower levels of mother-reported internalizing problems than do those with less sensitive teachers (NICHD, ECCRN, 2003b; Rimm-Kaufman et al., 2002). Sensitive teaching is not only important to social outcomes, but to academic outcomes as well. For example, among a group of preschoolers, those who experienced more responsive teacher interactions in preschool displayed stronger vocabulary and decoding skills at the end of first grade (Connor, Son, & Hindman, 2005) and highly sensitive teaching has also been shown to be related to closing achievement gaps for young students at risk of poor performance (Hamre & Pianta, 2005).

A final dimension of emotional support is the degree to which classrooms and interactions are structured around the interests and motivations of the teacher, versus those of the students, referred to within the CLASS Framework as *Regard for Student Perspectives*. This dimension is often studied within the developmental literature under the construct of autonomy support (e.g., Anderman & Midgley, 1998; Skinner & Belmont, 1993). In classrooms high on this dimension teachers frequently ask for students' ideas and thoughts, follow students' lead, and provide opportunities for students to have a *formative* role in the classroom. Young children report more positive feelings about school, display more motivation, and are more engaged when they experience more child-focused and autonomy supportive instruction (de Kruif, McWilliam, Ridley, & Wakely, 2000; Gutman & Sulzby, 2000; Pianta, La Paro, Payne, Cox, & Bradley, 2002; Valeski & Stipek, 2001), while children in more teacher-directed classrooms have higher levels of internalizing problems (NICHD, ECCRN, 2003b). Similarly, adolescents are engaged by challenges that are within reach and that provide a sense of self-efficacy and control: experiences that offer challenges viewed as adultlike but for which appropriate scaffolding and support are provided (Bandura, Barbaranelli, Caprara, & Pastorelli, 1996; Eccles, Midgley et al., 1993). When teachers do this well, adolescents report being more motivated to learn, more engaged, and happier with the school environment (Deci, Vallerand, Pelletier, & Ryan, 1991; Eccles & Midgley, 1989; Reeve, Jang, Carrell, Jeon, & Barch, 2004; Roeser et al., 2000).

*Classroom Organization and Management*    In the education literature focused on teaching and teacher training perhaps no other aspect of classroom practice receives as much attention as classroom management and organization. Management of time and of students is an area of great concern to new and experienced teachers. On the student side, self-regulatory skills show strong links to success in all areas of schooling and are highly valued as an outcome (Raver, 2004). Thus, the extent to which classrooms are organized and managed has relevance in a number of ways: as an indicator of teacher competence, as a focus of teachers' concerns, as a source of input to the development of self-regulatory skills, and ultimately as a foundation for learning academic skills.

From a developmental standpoint the theoretical underpinnings of this domain include work by psychologists interested in children's self-regulatory skills (Blair, 2002; Paris & Paris, 2001; Raver, 2004; Tobin & Graziano, 2006). These self-regulatory skills include the development of memory, attention, planning, and inhibitory control, all of which have clear relevance to success in school environments. Children's self-regulatory behaviors are multidetermined, with family processes and individual differences (e.g., temperament, personality) contributing to children's ability to self-regulate in home, school, and laboratory environments (e.g., Blair, 2002; Connell & Wellborn, 1991; Grolnick & Ryan, 1989; Rimm-Kaufman et al., 2002; Rubin, Coplan, Fox, & Calkins, 1995; Tobin & Graziano, 2006). Recent advancements in developmental neuroscience, suggesting rapid growth and changes in brain areas associated with self-regulation during early childhood years, have placed particular emphasis on the role of preschool and elementary classrooms in developing these skills (Blair, 2002). Surprisingly, despite the clear need for research in this area, few studies have examined how specific classroom processes intersect with the *development* of self-regulatory skills (see Arnold, McWilliams, & Arnold, 1998; Cameron, Connor, Morrison, 2005 for exceptions) with most research instead focused more simply on correlations between the provision of organization and management to more positive classroom attention and behavior.

In the CLASS Framework, classroom organization is a broad domain of classroom processes related to the organization and management of students' *behavior*, *time*, and *attention* in the classroom (Emmer & Strough, 2001). The framework suggests three dimensions of this classroom-level regulation: Behavior Management, Productivity, and Instructional Learning Formats, each of which contributes to aspects of the classroom as a predictable, consistent, engaging setting.

*Behavior management* is a term that is often applied to a broad spectrum of classroom management strategies, including teachers' abilities to engage students and make constructive use of time. Within the CLASS Framework, behavior management is defined more narrowly as practices intended to *promote positive behavior* and *prevent or terminate misbehavior* in the classroom. There is general consensus around a set of practices associated with more positive student behavior including: (1) providing clear and consistent behavioral expectations; (2) monitoring the classroom for potential problems and proactively preventing problems rather than being reactive; (3) efficiently redirecting minor misbehavior before it escalates; (4) using positive, proactive strategies such as praising positive behavior rather than calling attention to misbehavior; and (5) spending a minimal amount of time on behavior management issues (Emmer & Strough, 2001).

Most of the research on behavior management was conducted by educational researchers in the 1970s and 1980s; these studies indicated that elementary and middle classrooms with positive behavior management tend to have students who make greater academic progress (Good & Grouws, 1977; Soar & Soar, 1978). Furthermore, teachers who adopt these types of practices after training are more likely than teachers in control groups to have students who are engaged and learning (Emmer & Strough, 2001;

Evertson, Emmer, Sanford, & Clements, 1983; Evertson & Harris, 1999; Gottfredson, Gottfredson, & Hybl, 1993). More recent school and classroom intervention programs have found similar results (Tingstrom, Sterling-Turner, & Wilczynski, 2006).

In *productive* classrooms teachers are not only effective managers of behavior, but are well-organized, spend a minimal amount of time on basic management activities such as taking attendance or passing out and collecting homework, and are prepared for instructional activities so that little time is lost in transition. Highly productive classrooms may resemble a "well-oiled machine" in which everyone in the classroom seems to know what is expected of them and how to go about doing it (Pianta et al., 2008). Productivity serves as a measure of the "dosage" of schooling students receive on a daily basis. Students are most engaged in productive classrooms and this engagement, in turn, is directly associated with student learning (Brophy & Evertson, 1976; Cameron et al., 2005; Coker, Medley, & Soar, 1980; Good & Grouws, 1977; Stallings, 1975; Stallings, Cory, Fairweather, & Needels, 1978).

For students to learn, they must have more than something to do; they must also be effectively engaged and interested in the instructional activities provided to them, a dimension of classrooms referred to within the CLASS Framework as *Instructional Learning Formats*. As stated by Yair (2000), "Highly engaging instructional settings encourage students to immerse themselves in learning, buffering their consciousness from external intrusions, and hence maximize the use of opportunities to learn" (p. 249). Consistent with constructivist theories of learning (Bowman & Stott, 1994; Bruner, 1996; Rogoff, 1990; Vygotsky, 1978), when teachers provide high quality learning formats, students are not just *passively* engaged in learning, but are *active* participants in it.

Some of the most novel work on the ways classroom environments may stimulate or alienate students' attention comes from researchers using experience sampling method (ESM) to capture students' perceptions of engagement and external factors that may influence engagement at randomly sampled periods throughout the school day (Csikszentmihalyi & Larson, 1987; Yair, 2000). In one study of 6th through 12th grade students, Yair (2000) found that levels of student reported engagement were highest when students were participating in more active methods such as labs and groups and lowest during lectures. Unfortunately, these more active methods were infrequent, occurring only 3% of the sampled time, with lectures occurring much more frequently, a finding corroborated in recent observational studies of elementary school classrooms nationwide (Pianta, Belsky, Houts, Morrison, & the NICHD Early Child Care Research Network, 2006).

*Instructional Supports*   The previous sections discussed the ways in which classrooms' provision of nurturing and supportive emotional environments and clear and consistent organizational systems may provide students with

opportunities to learn, promote self-regulation, and foster emotional development and motivation. These two broad areas set the stage for what most consider the main goal of schooling—to educate children. The conceptualization of effective classroom environments requires attending to the nature and quality of instructional interactions in the classroom. Instructional methods have been put in the spotlight in recent years as more emphasis has been placed on the translation of cognitive science, learning, and developmental research to educational environments (Carver & Klahr, 2001). The exemplary work of the National Research Councils series, *How Students Learn* (Donovan & Bransford, 2005) summarizes research across disciplines to emphasize how specific teaching strategies can enhance students' learning (Bransford et al., 2000).

The theoretical foundation for the conceptualization of instructional supports in the CLASS Framework comes primarily from research on children's cognitive and language development (e.g., Carver & Klahr, 2001; Catts, Fey, Zhang, & Tomblin, 2001; Fujiki, Brinton, & Clarke, 2002; Romberg, Carpenter, & Dremlock, 2005; Taylor, Pearson, Peterson, & Rodriguez, 2003; Vygotsky, 1991; Wharton-McDonald, Pressley, & Hampston, 1998). This literature highlights the distinction between simply learning facts and gaining "usable knowledge" which is built upon learning how facts are interconnected, organized, and conditioned upon one another (Bransford et al., 2000; Mayer, 2002). A student's cognitive and language development is contingent on the opportunities adults provide to express existing skills and scaffold more complex ones (Davis & Miyake, 2004; Skibbe, Behnke, & Justice, 2004; Vygotsky, 1991). The development of "metacognitive" skills, or the awareness and understanding of one's thinking processes, is also critical to children's academic development (Veenman, Kok, & Blöte, 2005; Williams, Blythe, & White, 2002).

Because of the significant shifts in classroom goals and students' cognitive abilities as children mature, the individual dimensions described as a part of Instructional Supports vary more by grade level than do those in the Emotional Support or Classroom Organization domains. The instructional dimensions become more differentiated in middle and high school as a greater emphasis is placed on content (Figure 3.1). So, for example, while Concept Development is a dimension of relevance for younger children, this dimension is broken down into Content Understanding and Analysis and Problem Solving for middle and high school classrooms. In addition, there is an explicit focus on increasing general language skills as children enter elementary school, while learning specific procedures and skills becomes more important as students mature. For the purposes of this chapter, we focus on reviewing literature for the dimensions of Concept Development and Quality of Feedback, which are relevant across the grade levels.

*Concept development* describes the instructional behaviors, conversations, and activities that teachers use to help stimulate students' higher order thinking skills, cognitions, and understanding of content (Pianta et al., 2008). Learning requires not only the acquisition of knowledge (retention), but the ability to access and apply this knowledge in new situations (transfer). Teachers can facilitate this transfer process by providing students with opportunities to: *understand*—build connections between new and previous knowledge; *apply*—use procedures and knowledge to help solve new problems; *analyze*—divide information into meaningful parts; *evaluate*—make conclusions based on criteria or standards; and *create*—put pieces of knowledge together to produce new ideas (Mayer, 2002). Teachers who use concept development practices tend to have students who make greater achievement gains (Romberg et al., 2005; Taylor, et al., 2003; Wharton-McDonald et al., 1998). As noted by Brophy and Good (1986), this does not require that all of a teacher's questions are "higher level" questions, but that there is a balance in which teachers use higher level questions to help focus student attention on the process of learning rather than solely on the product.

Another major part of effective concept development is making content and instruction relevant and meaningful to students, because there is a direct link between relevance and understanding of information (Barron, Schwartz, & Vye., 1998). Engaging high school students in this type of instruction can have powerful effects. For example, involving students in significant, real-world, voluntary community service and then discussing it within the classroom in an ongoing way, has been found to reduce failure rates by 50%, in randomly controlled trials, with similarly profound effects upon other behaviors in youths' lives as well (Allen, Philliber, Herrling, & Kuperminc, 1997). Thus, the extent to which teachers make opportunities for problem and project-based learning available to students is a key part of the ability of classrooms to stimulate higher order thinking skills and cognition (Barron et al., 1998).

In order to get the most benefit from the instructional opportunities described above, students need feedback about their learning. *Feedback* is a term used in education to refer to a broad range of teachers' interactions with students in which the teacher provides some information back to the student about his or her performance or effort. Research on feedback has typically focused on praise (Brophy & Everton, 1976; Stallings, 1975) or attributional feedback, in which teachers make statements to students attributing their performance to either ability (e.g., "You did this well because you are a good reader") or effort (e.g., "You did this well because you worked hard") (Burnett, 2003; Dohrn & Bryan, 1994). Although the CLASS Framework definition includes these forms of feedback, the focus is on "instructional feedback" or feedback that provides students with specific information about the content or process of learning.

High quality feedback is described as communications from teachers that provide students with specific information about not only whether or not they are correct (Brophy & Good, 1986), but about how they might get to the correct answer. Teachers providing high quality feedback provide frequent feedback loops, or back and forth exchanges in which a teacher responds to an initial student comment by engaging with the student, or group of students, in a sustained effort to reach deeper understanding (Pianta et al., 2008). Educational researchers have referred to this type of feedback interaction as scaffolded instruction (Many, 2002). Classrooms offering higher quality feedback, have students who display greater gains in literacy and language across the preschool and kindergarten years (Howes et al., 2008; Mashburn et al., 2008) and appear to contribute to a closing of the achievement gap among first grade students coming from disadvantaged backgrounds (Hamre & Pianta, 2005). In one study of fourth and fifth grade classrooms, teachers who used these strategies as a part of instructional conversations had students who showed greater improvements in the quality of their essays than did students in a control condition who did not receive these supports (Saunders & Goldenberg, 1999).

## Measuring Classroom Environments

For the science of classroom environments to move forward, there is a need for measurement tools that reliably assess the types of classroom environments described by the CLASS Framework. There has been considerable progress in measurement of classroom environments over the past 10 years, particularly in the area of standardized observations. In the next section we summarize research on the two most common types of measures: observations and questionnaires.

***Classroom Observations*** There is a long history of classroom observation in educational research, although the extent to which classroom processes can be reliably and validly assessed has been a subject of great debate within educational research community for the past 30 years (Gage & Needels, 1989). Until recently, most standardized observations of classrooms were conducted as a part of research referred to as "process-product" research. Process-product research relied heavily on gathering frequency data on specific types of classroom interactions and occurrences and linking these to student outcomes. Brophy and Good (1986) offer a thorough summary of this research. Within the educational research community, this research was criticized for, among other things, reliance on decontextualized, discrete observations that did not accurately portray the complexity of classroom environments (Gage, 1989; Gage & Needels, 1989). The result of these criticisms was that very few educational researchers used standardized methods of observation during the 1990s, relying instead on qualitative observational methods.

More recently, developmental scientists have used their experiences in observation in home settings to create new observational measures of classroom environments that address some of the early critiques. Much of this work was stimulated by the NICHD Study of Early Childhood and Youth Development (SECCYD; NICHD, ECCRN, 2003a) which followed a cohort of children from birth through early adolescence. As children entered school settings, researchers realized a need to develop new observational tools. The measures used in the NICHD SECCYD proved successful in capturing a wide range of features of the classroom environment that were related to students' social and academic development across childhood and early adolescence (Gazelle, 2006; Hamre & Pianta, 2005; NICHD, ECCRN, 2002, 2005; Pianta et al., 2006; Rimm-Kaufman et al., 2002). These measures extended previous work by measuring more complex patterns of interactions than can be captured with frequency counts of behavior. Other researchers have developed similar observational measures, some of which are specific to one domain of the classroom environment (e.g., Howes, 2000; Morrison & Conner, 2002; Patrick et al., 1997; Taylor et al., 2003) and others that are more global (Pianta et al., 2007; Pianta, Hamre et al., 2006; Pressley, Gaskins, Solic, & Collins, 2006; Stipek & Byler, 2004).

Researchers interested in conducting classroom observations are faced with a variety of measurement decisions which have important implications for resulting data. One of the issues that arises most frequently is the extent to which measures capture the *frequency* or *quality* of behaviors. Examples of behaviors assessed by frequency measures include: time spent on literacy instruction, the number of times teachers ask questions during instructional conversations, and the number of negative comments made by peers to one another. Quality measures may instead rate the degree to which literacy instruction in a classroom matches a description of evidence-based practices, how much instructional conversations stimulate children's higher-order thinking skills, and the extent to which classroom interactions contain a high degree of negativity between teachers and students and among peers.

Frequency measures typically rely on time sampling methods while quality is assessed using rating systems; however, this distinction can sometimes be blurred. For instance, some measures that rely on assessing the presence of certain behaviors or interactions can focus on behaviors that have a quality component to them (e.g., Morrison & Conner, 2002). Thus, rather than measuring simply the number of questions a teacher asks, researchers interested in the cognitive demands of instructional conversations could, for example, count the number of closed questions (e.g., "What are the three parts of an insect's body called?") versus open questions that require higher levels of cognition (e.g., "Tell me two similarities and two differences between a spider and an insect?"). Similarly, many quality measures take into account the frequency of a group of behaviors in making the quality rating. For example, several measures make ratings based on the frequency with which a set of quality indicators are observed across a time period (NICHD, ECCRN, 2002; Pianta et al., 2007). So, for example, a teacher who has one brief interaction with a student constituting a high degree of teacher sensitivity, but who is quite insensitive for the rest of the observation period receives a lower score than does a teacher who is consistently sensitive across time and students.

There are advantages to each type of system. Quality measures assess higher order organizations of behaviors in ways that may be more meaningful that looking at the discrete behaviors in isolation and tend to parse the behavioral stream into more contextually and situationally sensitive "chunks." For example, teachers' positive affect and smiling can have different meanings and may be interpreted differently depending on the ways in which this affect is responded to by students in the classroom. In some classrooms teachers are exceptionally cheerful, but their affect appears very disconnected from that of the students. In other classrooms teachers are more subdued in their positive affect but there is a clear match between this affect and those of their students. A measure that simply counted the number of times a teacher smiled at students would miss these more nuanced interpretations. Another indication of the potential importance of observational measures focused on quality is that similar measures were critical to advancement in other areas of human behavior, such as the development of attachment theory (Ainsworth et al., 1978; Bowlby, 1969) and understanding antisocial behavior in youth (Dishion, Spracklen, Brown, & Haas, 1999).

One distinct advantage to using frequency measures, specifically when they are time-coded is the ability to conduct sequential and contingency analyses, thus allowing for studies of the complex interdependence and flow of interactions (Bakeman & Gnisci, 2006). Among the few researchers who have used this methodology in work on classrooms are those focused on the study of children with emotional and behavioral disorders. For example, Sutherland, Wehby, and Yoder (2002) examined the time-sequenced relationship between teacher praise and the provision of opportunities to respond among a group of children with problem behavior. Erickson, Stage, and Nelson (2006) examined the extent to which they could identify reliable antecedent and consequent events related to inappropriate behavior for children with ADHD diagnoses. Future work using these methods may help paint a more vivid picture of the complex interpersonal interactions among teachers and peers in their everyday interactions with one another.

***Student and Teacher Questionnaires***  The ultimate effect of any observable classroom process on student outcomes is largely mediated by the ways in which individual students make meaning of and respond to it. Therefore, a complete understanding of these environments requires gaining access to the participants' perceptions of these environments. Questionnaires designed to assess the classroom environment have been used in educational research for over 30 years. Fraser (1998) provides a helpful review of the most commonly used classroom environment instruments. Four major issues related to the use of questionnaire data on classroom environments are: the domains of classroom environment on which they focus; whether the reporter is the teacher or students; the age of student reporters; and the extent to which they measure students' personal or classroom level perceptions of the environment.

Notable among questionnaires on the classroom environment is that they focus almost exclusively on the emotional and organizational aspects of classrooms, with few if any examples of measures providing data on students' perceptions of availability and quality of instructional supports. For example, the most commonly used measure, the Classroom Environment Scale (CES: Moos & Trickett, 1987), has scales measuring involvement, affiliation, teacher support, task orientation, order and organization, and rule clarity. One exception comes from work by Midgley and colleagues (1996) using the Patterns of Adaptive Learning Survey. Several items on this survey assess the degree to which teachers report using strategies that encourage understanding, rather than rote knowledge (Deemer, 2004).

Issues related to the reporter on questionnaires include differences between teacher and student report and the age of students. Most classroom environment questionnaires include both teacher and student report versions; however, research examining relations between teacher and student report have found low to moderate associations (Feldlaufer, Midgley, & Eccles, 1988; Fraser & O'Brien, 1985). In general, teachers report more positive environments than do students (Fisher & Fraser, 1983; Fraser & O'Brien, 1985), so capturing student report data allows for researchers to document the range of students' experiences within the classroom.

Questionnaire methods are much more common in research on middle and secondary classrooms than on elementary classrooms. This is not surprising given the challenges of reliably assessing young children's perceptions; however, there is growing evidence of effective practices for obtaining self-reports from children as young as 5 (Daniels, Kalkman, & McCombs, 2001; Measelle, John, Ablow, Cowan, & Cowan, 2005). One of the few examples of work on young children's perceptions of classroom environments comes from Daniels, Kalkman, and McCombs (2001) who used an interview technique with cartoonlike depictions of classroom situations to elicit kindergarten through second grade students' feelings about their classroom. This measure was validated against external judgments about the classroom with evidence of some agreement, but clearly there is a great need for more work in this area.

One final distinction of relevance for those selecting questionnaires to assess the classroom environment is the extent to which they assess students' personal or classroom experiences (Fisher & Fraser, 1983; Fraser, Giddings, & McRobbie, 1995; Fraser & Tobin, 1991). Many classroom environment measures have both types of versions. Personal versions ask students questions specifically about their experiences in the classroom (e.g., "My teacher treats me fairly"), while classroom versions of measures ask questions about students' perceptions of classroom level processes (e.g., "The teacher tends to treat students fairly"). A direct comparison of these two types of measures offers several important distinctions (Fraser et al., 1995). For example,

there are greater gender differences when using the personal versions of the measures and students report more favorable environments using the classroom as compared to the personal version. However, each version accounts for independent variance in student outcomes, suggesting they both may be important aspects of the classroom environment to assess (Fraser & McRobbie, 1995).

## Implications and Future Directions for Classroom Environment Research

The literature reviewed above provides strong evidence that emotional, organizational, and instructional processes in classrooms are a key feature accounting for direct and indirect links to children and adolescents' social, emotional, and academic outcomes. There is, however, much about classrooms and their significance for development that is not well-understood. Continued efforts to integrate developmental and educational sciences will produce research that can further our understanding of basic developmental processes as well as inform important educational questions. Below we discuss several limitations of current work that provide direction for future research on classroom environments.

One key weakness of current work is that the vast majority of research on classroom environments and child outcomes is correlational, and thus conclusions about effects are qualified by the lack of rigor in methods and design. Even though there is a growing body of experimental work on school-based interventions (Greenberg, Weissberg, & O'Brien, 2003), until recently few of these studies included observational measures of classroom environments; thus even when these interventions yield strong inferences about effects, we know little about the specific types of classroom interactions (i.e., the mechanisms) that resulted in these positive effects. There are some exceptions, including early work by process-product researchers on behavior management (Emmer & Strough, 2001; Evertson et al., 1983; Evertson & Harris, 1999) as well as several programs of research on school-based intervention, such as the Child Development Project (CDP: Battistich, Solomon, Watson, & Schaps, 1997) and the School Transitional Environment Project (Felner et al., 2001). The increased use of experimental designs within classroom research, along with the inclusion of observational methods, may provide evidence meeting the dual goals of informing developmental science and providing useful information to educational practitioners.

Measurement is also a key challenge, with one of the primary limitations of research to date being the use of different methodologies among research on early childhood, elementary, middle, and high school classrooms. There is a dire need for research in middle and high school classrooms that focuses more closely on measurement and methodological issues in the use of observations. In addition, we know too little about how to improve assessments that rely on young students' report about classroom environments.

Finding a way to more coherently bridge literatures that were developed using these different methodologies will be critical to the understanding of the nature of classroom experiences across the preschool to high school period.

In addition, the thoughtful integration of new developmentally salient constructs could help revolution the science of classroom environments in much the same way as they did for research in other areas of development (e.g., Gottman & Notarius, 2002). For example, the inclusion of measures of cortisol levels in classroom-based research (Gunnar, Sebanc, & Tout, 2003; Tout, de Haan, Campbell, & Gunnar, 1998) has produced some intriguing findings such as the fact that within child care, cortisol levels rise over the course of the day (in contrast to typical patterns in which cortisol levels decrease from morning to afternoon) and that this rise is associated with higher levels of internalizing behavior for boys (Tout et al., 1998). Linking cortisol and other physiological measures directly to classroom processes would enhance our understanding of the ways in which classroom environments exert their influence on children's development.

A final challenge concerns the ability of developmental scientists to successfully bridge the lab with the classroom. This has happened more successfully in some areas of developmental science than in others. Carver and Klahr (2001) discuss the many challenges inherent in conducting research on children's cognitive development that is relevant to classroom settings. They suggest that the current separation between basic cognitive research and classroom research prohibits the effective use of research in classroom settings. Two remedies to this problem include the provision of a conceptual framework for classifying cognitive research in ways that are meaningful to educators as well as encouraging the development, implementation, and evaluation of specific instructional materials and approaches. The CLASS Framework is one approach to the first remedy. As outlined above, each dimension described by the CLASS is well established as a relevant aspect of classrooms, about which teachers, administrators, and policymakers are concerned. Future research may use the CLASS Framework, or other similar frameworks, as a starting place for approaching the second remedy—designing, implementing, and testing specific classroom strategies hypothesized to have a direct effect on students' social, regulatory, and cognitive functioning. The key here is that this research must be conducted in real classrooms and must make an active effort to model and measure *normative* classroom practices, rather than focusing solely on some manipulated process identified in lab-based research.

As work on classroom environments continues, it is essential to remember that, consistent with the tenets of bio-ecological theory (Bronfenbrenner & Morris, 1998), the ultimate results of any processes, such as those present in classroom environments, are dependent upon a complex interaction of those processes with characteristics of the people involved, the setting or context, and time. It would be inconsistent with the principles upon which the CLASS Framework is based to assume that the classroom environments described above operate in the same way for all students, teachers, or classrooms. Rather, they describe general classroom processes involved in children's development, and thereby form the basis of numerous examinations of this complex process-person-context-time model (Bronfenbrenner & Morris, 1998) as applied to classroom and school settings. For example, it will be important for future research to examine the extent to which child characteristics may moderate the ultimate effect of process on children's development (e.g., Hamre & Pianta, 2005; Rimm-Kaufman et al., 2002), ways in which culture can influence the meaning of observed behaviors (Inagaki, Morita, & Hatano, 1999; Rogoff, 2003), and the extent to which these basic classroom processes may change as children move from preschool through high school. Further explorations of the complicated nature of classrooms will offer insights into larger developmental theories (Pianta, 2006) and have many potential implications for the ways in which findings on classroom processes are translated into practice.

## References

Ainsworth, M. D., Blehar, M. C., Waters, E., & Wall, D. (1978). *Patterns of attachment: A psychological study of the strange situation.* Hillsdale, NJ: Erlbaum.

Alexander, K. L., & Entwisle, D. R. (1988). Achievement in the first 2 years of school: Patterns and processes. *Monographs of the Society for Research in Child Development, 53*(2), 157.

Allen, J. P., Philliber, S., Herrling, S., & Kuperminc, G. P. (1997). Preventing teen pregnancy and academic failure: Experimental evaluation of a developmentally based approach. *Child Development, 68*(4), 729–742.

Anderman, L. H., & Anderman, E. M. (1999). Social predictors of changes in students' achievement goal orientations. *Contemporary Educational Psychology, 25*, 21–37.

Anderman, L. H., & Midgley, C. (1998). Motivation and middle school students. *ERIC Digest, EDO-PS-98-5*.

Arnold, D. H., McWilliams, L., & Arnold, E. H. (1998). Teacher discipline and child misbehavior in day care: Untangling causality with correlational data. *Developmental Psychology, 34*, 276–287.

Asher, S. R., Parkhurst, J. T., Hymel, S., & Williams, G. A. (1990). Peer rejection and loneliness in childhood. In S. R. Asher & J. D. Coie (Eds.), *Peer rejection in childhood* (pp. 253–273). New York: Cambridge University Press.

Bakeman, R., & Gnisci, A. (2006). Sequential observation methods. In M. Eid & E. Diener (Eds.), *Handbook of multimethod measurement in psychology* (pp. 127–140). Washington, DC: American Psychological Association.

Bandura, A., Barbaranelli, C., Caprara, G. V., & Pastorelli, C. (1996). Multifaceted impact of self-efficacy beliefs on academic functioning. *Child Development, 67*(3), 1206–1222.

Barron, B. J. S., Schwartz, D. L., Vye, N. J., & Cognition & Technology Group, Vanderbilt University, Learning Technology Center. (1998). Doing with understanding: Lessons from research on problem-and project based learning. *Journal of the Learning Sciences, 7*(3–4).

Barron, B., Schwartz, D., Vye, N., Moore, A., Petrosino, A., Zech, L., Bransford, J., & Cognition and Technology Group, Vanderbilt University. (1998). Doing with understanding: Lessons from research on problem- and project-based learning. *Journal of the Learning Sciences, 7*, 271–312.

Battisch, V., Solomon, D., Watson, M., & Schaps, E. (1997). Caring school communities. *Educational Psychologist, 32*(3), 137–151.

Baumrind, D. (1991) The influence of parenting style on adolescent competence and substance use. [Special issue]. *Journal of Early Adolescence*, *11*(1), 56–95.

Birch, S. H., & Ladd, G. W. (1996). Interpersonal relationships in the school environment and children's early school adjustment. In K. Wentzel & J. Juvonen (Eds.), *Social motivation: Understanding children's school adjustment* (pp. 199–225). New York: Cambridge University Press.

Birch, S. H., & Ladd, G. W. (1998). Children's interpersonal behaviors and the teacher–child relationship. *Developmental Psychology, 34*, 934–946.

Blair, C. (2002). School readiness: Integrating cognition and emotion in a neurobiological conceptualization of children's functioning at school entry. *American Psychologist, 57*(2), 111–127.

Bowlby, J. (1969). *Attachment and loss: Vol. 1. Attachment.* New York: Basic Books.

Bowman, B., & Stott, F. (1994). Understanding development in a cultural context: The challenge for teachers. In B. Mallory & R. New (Eds.), *Diversity and developmentally appropriate practices: Challenges for early childhood education* (pp. 19–34). New York: Teachers College Press.

Bransford, J. D., Brown, A. L., & Cocking, R. R. (2000). *How people learn: Brain, mind, experience, and school: Expanded edition.* Washington, D.C.: National Academy Press.

Bronfenbrenner, U., & Morris, P. A. (1998). The ecology of developmental processes. In W. Damon & R. M. Lerner (Eds.), *Handbook of child psychology: Vol. 1. Theoretical models of human development* (5th ed., pp. 993–1029). New York: Wiley.

Brophy, J. (1999). Teaching (Educational Practices Series No. 1). Geneva: International Bureau of Education. Retrieved January 20, 2010, from http://www.ibe.unesco.org/International/Publications/EducationalPractices/prachome.htm

Brophy, J., & Evertson, C. (1976). *Learning from teaching: A developmental perspective.* Boston, MA: Allyn & Bacon.

Brophy, J., & Good, T. L. (1986). Teacher behavior and student achievement. In M. C. Wittrock (Ed.), *Handbook of research on teaching* (3rd ed., pp. 328–375). New York: Macmillan.

Bruner, J. (1996). *The culture of education.* Cambridge, MA: Harvard University Press.

Bryk, A. S., & Driscoll, M. (1988). *The high school as a community: Contextual influences and consequences for teachers.* Madison, WI: University of Wisconsin, National Center on Effective Secondary Schools.

Buhs, E. , & Ladd, G. W. (2001). Peer rejection as antecedent of young children's school adjustment: An examination of mediating processes. *Developmental Psychology, 37*, 550–560.

Buhs, E., Ladd, G., & Herald, S. (2006). Peer exclusion and victimization: Processes that mediate the relation between peer group rejection and children's classroom engagement and achievement? *Journal of Educational Psychology, 98*(1), 1–13.

Burnett, P. C. (2003). The impact of teacher feedback on student self-talk and self-concept in reading and mathematics. *Journal of Classroom Interaction, 38*(1), 11–16.

Cameron, C. E., Connor, C. M., & Morrison, F. J. (2005). Effects of variation in teacher organization on classroom functioning. *Journal of School Psychology, 43*(1), 61–85.

Carver, S. M., & Klahr, D. (2001). *Cognition and instruction: Twenty-five years of progress.* Mahwah, NJ: Erlbaum.

Cassidy, J. & Asher, S. R. (1992). Loneliness and peer relations in young children. *Child Development*, *63*, 350–365.

Catts, H. W., Fey, M. E., Zhang, X., & Tomblin, J. B. (1999). Language basis of reading and reading disabilities: Evidence from a longitudinal investigation. *Scientific Studies of Reading, 3*(4), 331–361.

Catts, H., Fey, M. E., Zhang, X., & Tomblin, J. B. (2001). Estimating risk for future reading difficulties in kindergarten children: A research-based model and its clinical implications. *Language, Speech, and Hearing Services in Schools, 32*, 38–50.

Cicchetti, D., & Aber, J. L. (1998). Editorial: Contextualism and developmental psychopathology. *Development and Psychopathology*, *10*(2), 137–141.

Coker, H., Medley, D. M., & Soar, R. S. (1980). How valid are expert opinions about effective teaching? *Phi Delta Kappan*, *62*(2), 131–134, 149.

Collins, W. A., & Repinski, D. J. (1994). Relationships during adolescence: Continuity and change in interpersonal perspective. In R. Montemayor, G. Adams, & T. P. Gullotta (Eds.), *Personal relationships during adolescence* (pp. 7–36). San Francisco, CA: Sage.

Connell, J. P., & Wellborn, J. G. (1991). Competence, autonomy, and relatedness: A motivational analysis of self-system processes. In R. Gunnar & L. A. Sroufe (Eds.), *Minnesota Symposia on child psychology* (Vol. 23, pp. 43–77). Hillsdale, NJ: Erlbaum.

Connor, C. M. (2005). *Individual students' differences in response to preschool literacy instruction: Effects on vocabulary, alphabet and letter-word recognition skill growth.* A presentation made at the Society for the Scientific Study of Reading, Toronto, Canada.

Connor, C. M., Morrison, F. J., & Petrella, J. (2004). Effective reading comprehension instruction: Examining child x instruction interactions. *Journal of Educational Psychology, 96*(4), 682–698.

Connor, C. M., Son, S., & Hindman, A. H. (2005). Teacher qualifications, classroom practices, family characteristics, and preschool experience: Complex effects on first graders' vocabulary and early reading outcomes. *Journal of School Psychology, 43*(4), 343–375.

Crosnoe, R., Johnson, M. K., & Elder, G. H., Jr. (2004). Intergenerational bonding in school: The behavioral and contextual correlates of student–teacher relationships. *Sociology of Education, 77*(1), 60–81.

Csikszentmihalyi, M., & Larson, R. (1987). Validity and reliability of the experience-sampling method. *The Journal of Nervous and Mental Disease, 175,* 526–536.

Daniels, D. H., Kalkman, D. L., & McCombs, B. L. (2001). Young children's perspectives on learning and teacher practices in different classroom contexts: Implications for motivation. *Early Education and Development, 12*(2), 253–273.

Davis, E. A., & Miyake, N. (2004). Explorations of scaffolding in complex classroom systems. *Journal of the Learning Sciences, 13*(3), 265–272.

Deci, E. L., Vallerand, R. J., Pelletier, L. G., & Ryan, R. M. (1991). Motivation and education: The self-determination perspective. *The Educational Psychologist, 26*, 325–346.

Deemer, S. A. (2004). Classroom goal orientation in high school classrooms: Revealing links between teacher beliefs and classroom environments. *Educational Research, 46*(1), 73–90.

de Kruif, R. E. L., McWilliam, R. A., Ridley, S. M., & Wakeley, M. B. (2000). Classification of teachers' interaction behaviors in early childhood classrooms. *Early Childhood Research Quarterly, 15*(2), 247–268.

Denham, S. A., & Weissberg, R. P. (2004). Social-emotional learning in early childhood: What we know and where to go from here. In E. Chesebrough, P. King, T. P. Gullotta, & M. Bloom (Eds.), *A blueprint for the promotion of prosocial behavior in early childhood* (pp. 13–50). New York: Kluwer Academic/Plenum.

Dishion, T. J., Li, F., Spracklen, K. M., Brown, G., & Haas, E. (1999). The measurement of parenting practices in research on adolescent problem behavior: A multimethod and multitrait analysis. In R. S. Ashery (Ed.), *Research meeting on drug abuse prevention through family interventions* (NIDA Research Monograph 177, pp. 260–293). Bethesda, MD: National Institute on Drug Abuse.

Dohrn, E., & Bryan, T. (1994). Attribution instruction. *Teaching Exceptional Children, 26*(4), 61–63.

Donovan, S., & Bransford, J. (2005). *How students learn: History, mathematics, and science in the classroom.* Washington, DC: National Academy Press.

Eccles, J. S. (2004). Schools, academic motivation, and stage-environment fit. In R. M. Lerner & L. Steinberg (Eds.), *Handbook of adolescent psychology* (2nd ed., pp. 125–153). Hoboken, NJ: Wiley.

Eccles, J. S., & Midgley, C. M. (1989). Stage-environment fit: Developmentally appropriate classrooms for young adolescents. In C. Ames & R. Ames (Eds.), *Research on motivation in education* (Vol. 3, pp. 139–186). San Diego, CA: Academic Press.

Eccles, J. S., Midgley, C., Wigfield, A., Buchanan, C. M., Reuman, D., Flanagan, C., et al. (1993). Development during adolescence: The impact of stage-environment fit on young adolescents' experiences in schools and in families. *American Psychologist, 48*(2), 90–101.

Eccles, J. & Roeser, R. (1998). School and community influences on human development. In M. H. Bornstein & M. E. Lamb (Eds.), *Developmental psychology: An advanced textbook* (4th ed., pp. 503–554). Mahwah, NJ: Erlbaum.

Eccles, J. S., & Roeser, R. W. (1999). Adolescents' perceptions of middle school: Relation to longitudinal changes in academic and psychological adjustment. *Journal of Research on Adolescence, 8*(1), 123–158.

Eccles, J. S., & Roeser. R. W. (2005). School and community influences on human development. In M. H. Bornstein & M. E. Lamb (Eds.), *Developmental science: An advanced textbook* (5th ed., 513–556). Mahwah, NJ: Erlbaum.

Emmer, E. T., & Strough, L. (2001). Classroom management: A critical part of educational psychology, with implications for teacher education. *Educational Psychologist, 36*(2), 103–112.

Erickson, M. J., Stage, S. A., & Nelson, J. R. (2006). Naturalistic study of the behavior of students with EBD referred for functional behavioral assessment. *Journal of Emotional and Behavioral Disorders, 14*(1), 31–40.

Evertson, C., Emmer, E., Sanford, J., & Clements, B. (1983). Improving classroom management: An experiment in elementary classrooms. *Elementary School Journal, 84,* 173–188.

Evertson, C. M., & Harris, A. H. (1999). Support for managing learning centered classrooms: The classroom organization and management program. In H. J. Freiberg (Ed.), *Beyond behaviorism: Changing the classroom management paradigm* (pp. 57–73). Boston, MA: Allyn & Bacon.

Feldlaufer, H., Midgley, C., & Eccles, J. (1988). Student, teacher, and observer perceptions of the classroom before and after the transition to junior high school. *Journal of Early Adolescence, 8*(2), 133–156.

Felner, R., Favazza, A., Shim, M., Brand, S., Gu, K., & Noonan, N. (2001). Whole school improvement and restructuring as prevention and promotion: Lessons from project STEP and the project on high performance learning communities. *Journal of School Psychology, 39,* 177–202.

Fisher, D. L., & Fraser, B. J. (1983, January). A comparison of actual and preferred classroom environments as perceived by science teachers and students. *Journal of Research in Science Teaching, 20*(1), 55–61.

Fraser, B. J. (1998). Classroom environment instruments: Development, validity and applications. *Learning Environment Research, 1,* 7–33.

Fraser, B. J., Giddings, G. J., & McRobbie, C. J. (1995). Evolution and validation of a personal form of an instrument for assessing science laboratory classroom environments. *Journal of Research in Science Teaching, 32,* 399–422.

Fraser, B. J. & McRobbie, C. J. (1995). Science laboratory classroom environments at schools and universities: A cross-national study. *Educational Research and Evaluation, 1,* 289–317.

Fraser, B. J., & O'Brien, P. (1985). Student and teacher perceptions of the environment of elementary school classrooms. *Elementary School Journal, 85,* 567–580.

Fraser, B. J. & Tobin, K. (1991). Combining qualitative and quantitative methods in classroom environment research. In B. J. Fraser & H. J. Walberg (Eds.), *Educational environments: Evaluation, antecedents and consequences* (pp. 271–292). London: Pergamon.

Fujiki, M., Brinton, B., & Clarke, D. (2002). Emotion regulation in children with specific language impairment. *Language, Speech, and Hearing Services in Schools, 33*(2), 102–111.

Gage, N.L. (1978). *The scientific basis of the art of teaching,* New York: Teachers College Press.

Gage, N. L. (1989). The paradigm wars and their aftermath: A "historical" sketch of research on teaching since 1989. *Educational Researcher, 18*(7), 4–10.

Gage, N. L., & Needels, M. C. (1989). Process-product research on teaching: A review of criticisms. *Elementary School Journal, 89*(3), 253–300.

Gazelle, H. (2006). Class climate moderates peer relations and emotional adjustment in children with an early childhood history of anxious solitude: A child-by-environment model. *Developmental Psychology, 42,* 1179–1192.

Good, T., & Grouws, D. (1977). Teaching effects: A process-product study of fourth grade mathematics classrooms. *Journal of Teacher Education, 28,* 49–54.

Gottfredson, D. C., Gottfredson, G. D., & Hybl, L. G. (1993). Managing adolescent behavior: A mulityear, mulitschool study. *American Educational Research Journal, 30*(1). 179–215.

Gottman, J. M., & Notarius. C. I. (2002). Marital research in the 20th century and a research agenda for the 21st century. *Family Process, 41,* 159–197.

Greenberg, M. T., Domitrovich, C., & Bumbarger, B. (2001). The prevention of mental disorders in school-aged children: Current state of the field [Special issue]. *Prevention and Treatment, 4,* 1–62.

Greenberg, M. T., Weissberg, R. P., & O'Brien, M. U. (2003). Enhancing school-based prevention and youth development through coordinated social, emotional, and academic learning. *American Psychologist, 58*(6–7), 466–474.

Gregory, A., & Weinstein, R. S. (2004). Connection and regulation at home and in school: Predicting growth in achievement for adolescents. *Journal of Adolescent Research, 19*(4), 405–417.

Grolnick, W. S., & Ryan, R.M. (1989). Parent styles associated with children's self-regulation and competence in school. *Journal of Educational Psychology, 81*(2), 143–154.

Gunnar, M. R., Sebanc, A, M., & Tout, K. (2003). Peer rejection, temperament, and cortisol activity in preschoolers. *Developmental Psychobiology, 43*(4), 346–358.

Gutman, L. M., & Sulzby, E. (2000). The role of autonomy-support versus control in the emergent writing behaviors of African-American kindergarten children. *Reading Research & Instruction, 39*(2), 170–183.

Hamm, J. V., & Faircloth, B. S. (2005). Peer context of mathematics classroom belonging in early adolescence. *Journal of Early Adolescence, 25*(3), 345–366.

Hampton, F., Mumford, D., & Bond, L. (1997). *Enhancing urban student achievement through family oriented school practices.*

Paper presented at the Annual Meeting of the American Educational Research Association, Chicago, IL.

Hamre, B. K., Justice, L., Pianta, R. C., Kilday, C., Sweeny, B., Downer, J., et al. (in press). Implementation fidelity of the MyTeachingPartner literacy and language activities: Associations with preschoolers' language and literacy growth. *Early Childhood Research Quarterly.*

Hamre, B. K., & Pianta, R. C. (2001). Early teacher–child relationships and the trajectory of children's school outcomes through eighth grade. *Child Development, 72*(2), 625–638.

Hamre, B. K., & Pianta, R. C. (2005). Can instructional and emotional support in the first grade classroom make a difference for children at risk of school failure? *Child Development, 76*(5), 949–967.

Hamre, B. K. & Pianta, R. C. (2007). Learning opportunities in preschool and early elementary classrooms. In R. C. Pianta, M. J. Cox, & K Snow (Eds.), *School readiness and the transition to school* (pp. 49–84). Baltimore: Brookes.

Hamre, B. K., Pianta, R. C., Mashburn, A. J., & Downer, J. T. (2009). *Measuring good teaching in early education: Testing the CLASS Framework in over 4,000 U.S. early childhood and elementary classrooms.* Manuscript submitted for publication.

Han, S. S., & Weiss, B. (2005). Sustainability of teacher implementation of school-based mental health programs. *Journal of Abnormal Child Psychology, 33*(6), 665–679.

Harter, S. (1996). Teacher and classmate influences on scholastic motivation, self-esteem, and level of voice in adolescents. In J. Juvonen & K. Wentzel (Eds.), *Social motivation: Understanding children's school adjustment* (pp. 11–42). New York: Cambridge University Press.

Howes, C. (2000). Social-emotional classroom climate in child care, child-teacher relationships and children's second grade peer relations. *Social Development, 9,* 191–204.

Howes, C., Burchinal, M., Pianta, R., Bryant, D., Early, D., Clifford, R., & Barbarin, O. (2008). Ready to learn? children's pre-academic achievement in pre-kindergarten programs. *Early Childhood Research Quarterly, 23,* 27–50.

Howes, C., Hamilton, C. E., & Matheson, C. C. (1994). Children's relationships with peers: Differential associations with aspects of the teacher–child relationship. *Child Development, 65,* 253–263.

Hughes, J. N., Cavell, T. A., & Willson, V. (2001). Further evidence for the developmental significance of teacher–student relationships: Peers' perceptions of support and conflict in teacher–student relationships. *Journal of School Psychology, 39,* 289–301.

Illinois State Board of Education. (2004). Illinois learning standards—social/emotional learning (SEL). Retrieved from http://www.isbe.net/ils/social_emotional/standards.htm

Inagaki, K., Morita, E., & Hatano, G. (1999). Teaching-learning of evaluative criteria for mathematical arguments through classroom discourse: A cross-national study. *Mathematical Thinking and Learning, 1*(2), 93–111.

Kam, C., Greenberg, M. T., & Walls, C. T. (2003). Examining the role of implementation quality in school-based prevention using the PATHS curriculum. *Prevention Science, 4*(1), 55–63.

Kellam, S. G., Ling, X., Merisca, R., Brown, C., & Ialongo, N. (1998). The effect of the level of aggression in the first grade classroom on the course and malleability of aggressive behavior into middle school. *Development and Psychopathology, 10*(2), 165–185.

Ladd, G. W., Birch, S. H., & Buhs, E. S. (1999). Children's social and scholastic lives in kindergarten: Related spheres of influence? *Child Development, 70,* 1373–1400.

Ladd, G. W., & Burgess, K. B. (1999). Charting the relationship trajectories of aggressive, withdrawn, and aggressive/withdrawn children during early grade school. *Child Development, 70,* 910–929.

Ladd, G. W., Kochenderfer, B. J., & Coleman, C. C. (1997). Classroom peer acceptance, friendship, and victimization: Distinct relational systems that contribute uniquely to children's school adjustment? *Child Development, 68,* 1181–1197.

Ladd, G. W., & Troop-Gordon, W. (2003). The role of chronic peer difficulties in the development of children's psychological adjustment problems. *Child Development, 74,* 1325–1348.

La Paro, K. M., Hamre, B. K., Locasale-Crouch, J., Pianta, R. C., et al. (2009). Quality in kindergarten classrooms: Observational evidence for the need to increase children's learning opportunities in early education classrooms. *Early Education and Development, 20,* 657–692.

Lerner, R. M. (1998). Theories of human development: Contemporary perspectives. In W. Damon & R. M. Lerner (Eds.), *Handbook of child psychology (5th ed.): Theoretical models of human development* (pp. 1–24). New York: Wiley.

Lynch, M., & Cicchetti, D. (1992). Maltreated children's reports of relatedness to their teachers. In R. C. Pianta (Ed.), *Relationships between children and non-parental adults: New directions in child development* (pp. 81–108). San Francisco, CA: Jossey-Bass.

Many, J. E. (2002). An exhibition and analysis of verbal tapestries: Understanding how scaffolding is woven into the fabric of instructional conversations. *Reading Research Quarterly, 37*(4), 376–407.

Mashburn, A. J., Pianta, R. C., Hamre, B. K., Downer, J. T., Barbarin, O., Bryant, D., et al. (2008). Pre-k program standards and children's development of academic, language, and social skills. *Child Development, 79,* 732–749.

Mayer, R. E. (2002). Rote versus meaningful learning. *Theory into Practice, 41,* 226–233.

Measelle, J., John, O., Ablow, J., Cowan, P., & Cowan, C. (2005). Can children provide coherent, stable, and valid self-reports on the big five dimensions? A longitudinal study from ages 5 to 7. *Journal of Personality & Social Psychology, 89*(1), 90–106.

Midgley, C. (Ed.). (2002). Achievement goals and goal structures. *Goals, goal structures, and patterns of adaptive learning.* Mahwah, NJ: Erlbaum.

Midgley, C., Maehr, M., Hicks, L., Roeser, R., Urdan, T., Anderman, E., et al. (1996). *Patterns of Adaptive Learning Survey* (PALS). Ann Arbor: The University of Michigan.

Moos, R. H., & Trickett, E. J. (1987). *Classroom environment scale manual* (2nd ed.). Palo Alto, CA: Consulting Psychologists Press.

Morrison, F. J., & Connor, C. M. (2002). Understanding schooling effects on early literacy: A working research strategy. *Journal of School Psychology, 40,* 493–500.

National Center for Education Statistics. (2003). *The condition of education 2003.* Washington, DC: U.S. Department of Education, Institute of Education Sciences.

National Institute of Child Health and Human Development (NICHD), Early Child Care Research Network (ECRN). (2002). The relation of global first-grade classroom environment to structural classroom features and teacher and student behaviors. *The Elementary School Journal, 102*(5), 367–387.

National Institute of Child Health and Human Development (NICHD), Early Child Care Research Network (ECCRN). (2003a).The NICHD study of early child care: Contexts of development and developmental outcomes over the first seven years of life. In J. Brooks-Gunn, A.S. Fuligni, & L. J. Berlin (Eds.), *Early child development in the 21st century* (pp. 181–201). New York: Teachers College Press.

National Institute of Child Health and Human Development ( NICHD), Early Child Care Research Network (ECCRN). (2003b). Social functioning in first grade: Prediction from home, child care and concurrent school experience. *Child Development, 74,* 1639–1662.

National Institute of Child Health and Human Development (NICHD), Early Child Care Research Network (ECCRN). (2005). A day in third grade: A large-scale study of classroom quality and teacher and student behavior. *The Elementary School Journal, 105,* 305–323.

Nye, B., Konstantopoulos, S., & Hedges, L. (2004). How large are teacher effects? *Educational Evaluation and Policy Analysis, 26,* 237–257.

Paris, S. G., & Paris, A. H. (2001). Classroom applications of research on self-regulated learning. *Educational Psychologist, 36,* 89–101.

Patrick, H., Ryan, A. M., Anderman, L. H., Middleton, M., Linnenbrink, L., Hruda, L. Z., et al. (1997). *Manual for observing patterns of adaptive learning (OPAL): A protocol for classroom observations.* Ann Arbor, MI: University of Michigan.

Pianta, R. C. (1999). *Enhancing relationships between children and teachers.* Washington, DC: American Psychological Association.

Pianta, R. C. (2006). Schools, schooling, and developmental psychopathology. In D. Cicchetti & D. Cohen (Eds.), *Developmental psychopathology: Vol. 1. Theory and method* (pp. 494–529). Hoboken, NJ: Wiley.

Pianta, R. C. & Allen, J. P. (2008). Building capacity for positive youth development in secondary school classrooms: Changing teachers' interactions with students. In M. Shinn & H. Yoshikawa (Eds.), *Toward positive youth development: transforming schools and community programs* (pp. 21–39). New York: Oxford University Press.

Pianta, R.C., Belsky, J., Houts, R., Morrison, F., & NICHD ECCRN. (2007). Opportunities to learn in America's elementary classrooms. *Science, 315,* 1795-1796

Pianta, R. C., Hamre, B. K., Spekman, N. J., Mintz, S., & La Paro, K. M. (2006). *Classroom Assessment Scoring System [CLASS]—Secondary version.* Unpublished measure, University of Virginia.

Pianta, R. C., La Paro, K., & Hamre, B. K. (2008). *Classroom Assessment Scoring System.* Baltimore, MD: Brookes.

Pianta, R. C., La Paro, K. M., Payne, C., Cox, M. J., & Bradley, R. (2002). The relation of kindergarten classroom environment to teacher, family, and school characteristics and child outcomes. *Elementary School Journal, 102*(3), 225–238.

Pianta, R. C., Steinberg, M. S., & Rollins, K. B. (1995). The first two years of school: Teacher–child relationships and deflections in children's classroom adjustment. *Development and Psychopathology, 7,* 295–312.

Pressley, M., Gaskins, I. W., Solic, K., & Collins, S. (2006). A portrait of Benchmark School: How a school produces high achievement in students who previously failed. *Journal of Educational Psychology, 98*(2), 282–306.

Pressley, M., Roehrig, A., Raphael, L., Dolezal, S., Bohn, K., Mohan, L., et al. (2003). Teaching processes in elementary and secondary education. In W. M. Reynolds & G. E. Miller (Eds.), *Comprehensive handbook of psychology: Vol. 7. Educational psychology* (pp. 153–175). New York: Wiley.

Raver, C. C. (2004). Placing emotional self-regulation in sociocultural and socioeconomic contexts. *Child Development, 75*(2), 346–353.

Reeve, J., Jang, H., Carrell, D., Jeon, S., & Barch, J. (2004). Enhancing students' engagement by increasing autonomy support. *Motivation & Emotion, 28,* 147–169.

Resnick, M. D., Bearman, P. S., Blum, R. W., Bauman, K., Harris, K. M., Jones, J., Tabor, J., et al. (1997). Protecting adolescents from harm: Findings from the National Longitudinal Study of Adolescent Health. *Journal of the American Medical Association, 278,* 823–832.

Rimm-Kaufman, S. E., Early, D. M., & Cox, M. J. (2002). Early

behavioral attributes and teachers' sensitivity as predictors of competent behavior in the kindergarten classroom. *Journal of Applied Developmental Psychology, 23*(4), 451–470.

Roeser, R. W., Eccles, J. S., & Sameroff, A. J. (2000). School as a context of early adolescents' academic and social-emotional development: A summary of research findings. *The Elementary School Journal, 100,* 443–471.

Rogoff, B. (1990). *Apprenticeship in thinking: Cognitive development in social context.* New York: Oxford University Press.

Rogoff, B. (2003). *The cultural nature of human development.* New York: Oxford University Press.

Romberg, T. A., Carpenter, T. P., & Dremock, F. (2005). *Understanding mathematics and science matters.* Mahwah, NJ: Erlbaum.

Rones, M., & Hoagwood, K. (2000). School-based mental health services: A research review. *Clinical Child and Family Psychology Review, 3*(4), 223–241.

Rubin, K. H., Coplan, R. J., Fox, N. A., & Calkins, S. D. (1995). Emotionality, emotion regulation, and preschoolers' social adaptation. *Development and Psychopathology, 7,* 49–62.

Ryan, R. M., & Deci, E. L. (2000). Self-determination theory and the facilitation of intrinsic motivation, social development, and well-being. *American Psychologist, 55,* 68–78.

Ryan, R. M., Stiller, J. D., & Lynch, J. H. (1994). Representations of relationships to teachers, parents, and friends as predictors of academic motivation and self-esteem. *Journal of Early Adolescence, 14*(2), 226–249.

Saunders, W. M., & Goldenberg, C. (1999). Effects of instructional conversations and literature logs on limited- and fluent-English-proficient students' story comprehension and thematic understanding. *Elementary School Journal, 99*(4), 277–301.

Silver, R. B., Measelle, J., Essex, M., & Armstrong, J. M. (2005). Trajectories of externalizing behavior problems in the classroom: Contributions of child characteristics, family characteristics, and the teacher–child relationship during the school transition. *Journal of School Psychology, 43,* 39–60.

Skibbe, L., Behnke, M., & Justice, L. M. (2004). Parental scaffolding of children's phonological awareness skills: Interactions between mothers and their preschoolers with language difficulties. *Communication Disorders Quarterly, 25*(4), 189–203.

Skinner, E. A., & Belmont, M. J. (1993). Motivation in the classroom: Reciprocal effects of teacher behavior and student engagement across the school year. *Journal of Educational Psychology, 85,* 571–581.

Skinner, E. A., Zimmer-Gembeck, M. J., & Connell, J. P. (1998). Individual differences and the development of perceived control. *Monographs of the Society for Research in Child Development, 63*(2–3), v–220.

Soar, R. S., & Soar, R. M. (1978) Emotional climate and management. In P. L. Peterson & H. J. Walberg (Eds.), *Research on teaching: Concepts, findings and implications* (pp. 97–119). Berkeley, CA: McCutchin.

Stallings, J. (1975). Implementation and child effects of teaching practices in follow through classrooms. *Monographs of the Society for Research in Child Development, 40* (7–8, Serial No. 163).

Stallings, J., Cory, R., Fairweather, J., & Needels, M. (1978). *Early childhood education classroom evaluation.* Menlo Park, CA: SRI International.

Stipek, D., & Byler, P. (2004). The early childhood classroom observation measure. *Early Childhood Research Quarterly, 19*(3), 375–397.

Sutherland, K.S., Wehby, J. H., & Yoder, P. J. (2002). Examination of the relationship between teacher praise and opportunities for students with EBD to respond to academic requests. *Journal of Emotional and Behavioral Disorders, 10*(1), 5–13.

Taylor, B. M., Pearson, P. D., Peterson, D. S., & Rodriguez, M. C. (2003). Reading growth in high-poverty classrooms: The influence of teacher practices that encourage cognitive engagement in literacy learning. *The Elementary School Journal. 104*, 3–28.

Tingstrom, D., Sterling-Turner, H., & Wilczynski, S. (2006). The good behavior game: 1969–2002. *Behavior Modification, 30*(2), 225–253.

Tobin, R. M., & Graziano, W. G. (2006). Development of regulatory processes through adolescence. In D. K. Mroczek & T. D. Little (Eds.), *Handbook of personality development* (pp. 263–283). Mahwah, NJ: Erlbaum.

Tout, K., de Haan, M., Campbell, E., & Gunnar, M. (1998). Social behavior correlates of cortisol activity in child care: Gender differences and time-of-day effects. *Child Development, 69*(5), 1247–1262.

Valente, T., Unger, J., Ritt-Olson, A., Cen, S., & Johnson, C. (2006). The interaction of curriculum type and implementation method on 1-year smoking outcomes in a school-based prevention program. *Health Education Research, 21*(3), 315–324.

Valeski, T., & Stipek, D. (2001). Young children's feelings about school. *Child Development, 72*(4), 1198–1213.

Van Ijzendoorn, M., & Bakermans-Kranenburg, M. (2004). Maternal sensitivity and infant temperament in the formation of attachment. In G. Bremner & A. Slater (Eds.), *Theories of infant development* (pp. 233–257). Malden, MA: Blackwell.

Van Ijzendoorn, M. H., Sagi, A., & Lambermon, M. W. E. (1992). The multiple caretaker paradox: Some data from Holland and Israel. In R. E. Pianta (Ed.), *New directions in child development: Vol. 57. Relationships between children and non-parental adults* (pp. 5–24). San Francisco, CA: Jossey-Bass.

Veenman, M. V. J., Kok, R., & Blöte, A. W. (2005). The relation between intellectual and metacognitive skills in early adolescence. *Instructional Science, 33*(3), 193–211.

Vygotsky, L .S. (1978). *Mind and society: The development of higher mental processes.* Cambridge, MA: Harvard University Press.

Vygotsky, L. S. (1991). Genesis of the higher mental functions. In P. Light, S. Sheldon, & M. Woodhead (Eds.), *Learning to think* (pp. 32–41). Florence, KY: Routledge.

Wentzel, K. R. (1999). Social-motivational processes and interpersonal relationships: Implications for understanding motivation at school. *Journal of Educational Psychology, 91*, 76–97.

Wentzel, K. R. (2002). Are effective teachers like good parents? Teaching styles and student adjustment in early adolescence. *Child Development, 73*(1), 287–301.

West, J., Denton, K., & Germino-Hausken, E. (2000) America's kindergartners: Findings from the early childhood longitudinal study, kindergarten class of 1998–99. *Education Statistics Quarterly, 2*(1), 7–13.

Wharton-McDonald, R., Pressley, M., & Hampston, J. M. (1998). Literacy instruction in nine first-grade classrooms: Teacher characteristics and student achievement. *Elementary School Journal, 99*(2), 101–128.

Wigfield, A., Eccles, J., MacIver, D., Reuman, D., & Midgley, C. (1991). Transitions during early adolescence: Changes in children's domain-specific self-perceptions and general self-esteem across the transition to junior high school. *Developmental Psychology, 27*(4), 552–565.

Williams, W. M., Blythe, T., & White, N. (2002). Practical intelligence for school: Developing metacognitive sources of achievement in adolescence. *Developmental Review, 22*(2), 162–210.

Yair, G. (2000). Educational battlefields in America: The tug-of-war over students' engagement with instruction. *Sociology of Education, 73*, 247–269.

# 4

# Linking the Classroom Context and the Development of Children's Memory Skills

PETER ORNSTEIN, JENNIFER COFFMAN, JENNIE GRAMMER,
PRISCILLA SAN SOUCI, AND LAURA McCALL

Over the course of the elementary school years, children become increasingly facile users of an impressive array of strategies for remembering (Schneider & Pressley, 1997). Indeed, there are dramatic age-related changes in the use of deliberate techniques such as rehearsal, organization, and elaboration that influence the encoding, storage, and retrieval of information (Schneider & Bjorklund, 1998). Much has been learned about this progression in skill, but less attention has been devoted to the task of exploring the forces that affect the development of these important cognitive abilities (Ornstein & Haden 2001; Ornstein, Haden, & San Souci, 2008). Yet, it has been suggested that these skills typically develop in the context of children's experiences in settings such as school in which remembering is both expected and valued (Cole, 1992; Rogoff & Mistry, 1990; Wagner, 1981). As such, the perspective adopted here stems from the assumption that aspects of the elementary school classroom may serve as mediators of developmental changes in children's skills for remembering. Moreover, given that social-communicative interactions among parents and their preschoolers have been implicated in the development of young children's abilities to talk about their prior experiences (e.g., Reese, Haden, & Fivush, 1993), emphasis is placed here on the nature of the memory-relevant language used by teachers in the course of everyday instruction.

In this chapter, we draw upon a number of intersecting bodies of work to articulate our view of the importance of the classroom context for the development of children's memory skills. First, to understand age-related changes in children's deliberate skills in remembering, we sample from the large literature on cross-sectional studies of age-related changes in the use of strategies such as rehearsal and organization (e.g., Lange, 1978; Ornstein & Naus, 1978), as well as the small collection of longitudinal (e.g., Guttentag, Ornstein, & Siemens, 1987; Lehmann & Hasselhorn, 2007; Schneider, Kron, Hünnerkopf, & Krajewski, 2004; Weinert

& Schneider, 1999) and microgenetic (e.g., Schlagmüller & Schneider, 2002) studies of children's deliberate memory. Second, to make an initial case for the importance of school, we draw upon comparative-cultural explorations of children's cognition that identify formal schooling as a critical context for development (e.g., Wagner, 1978), as well as cross-national explorations of schooling in different countries (e.g., Carr, Kurtz, Schneider, Turner, & Borkowski, 1989) and work focused on the timing of school entry (Morrison, Smith, & Dow-Ehrensberger, 1995). Third, after exploring a number of aspects of the classroom context that may be associated with the emergence and refinement of children's mnemonic skills, we focus on the potential importance of adult–child social interactions, and to build the case for these interactions, we summarize studies of mother–child talk about the past and as events unfold (e.g., Haden, Ornstein, Eckerman, & Didow, 2001; Reese et al., 1993). Finally, in an effort to link the classroom with children's developing mnemonic skills, we examine the few studies that explore memory development in the classroom context (Coffman, Ornstein, McCall, & Curran, 2008; Moely et al., 1992).

## Children's Use of Strategies in the Preschool Years

Although the focus of this chapter is on the development of children's strategic repertoire during the elementary school years, these abilities build on a foundation of cognitive skills that are evident long before school entry. In this regard, a considerable body of research documents the surprising mnemonic competence of preschoolers (e.g., Baker-Ward, Ornstein, & Holden, 1984; Wellman, 1988), at least under supportive conditions. However, the literature also confirms the presence of substantial age differences in many aspects of memory performance. Thus, for example, across the preschool years, young children evidence increases in their abilities to report previously experienced events (Reese et al., 1993) and to make use of deliberate techniques for remembering (Ornstein, Baker-Ward, & Naus, 1988).

Concerning the use of deliberate strategies, it is now clear that 3- and 4-year-olds have a basic understanding of the need to "do something" when confronted with the task of remembering a set of materials (Baker-Ward et al., 1984; Wellman, 1988). Consider, for example, a study by Baker-Ward et al. (1984) in which 4-, 5-, and 6-year-olds were placed in a setting in which they could interact with a set of common objects and toys for a 2-minute period. Although all children were told that they could play with the items, some of them received specific memorization instructions, as well. Examination of the children's video-taped interactions with the materials revealed that even at age 4, the participants who had been instructed to remember behaved differently from those simply told to play. For example, spontaneous labeling or naming occurred almost exclusively among the children who had been instructed to remember, and these children also played less than the others. Instructions in remembering also resulted in increased levels of visual inspection and what seemed to be reflection and self-testing. However, even though the memory instructions were associated with a "studious" approach to the task by the 4-, 5-, and 6-year-olds alike, only among the older children were the strategic behaviors associated with the facilitation of memory.

Findings such as those reported by Baker-Ward et al. (see also DeLoache, Cassidy, & Brown, 1985; Wellman, 1988) indicate that under some conditions preschoolers may approach memory tasks in a focused and deliberate manner that suggests an understanding of the need to engage in specific behaviors in response to memory requests. As such, at one level these data contradict a long-accepted view of young children as being nonstrategic in cognitive endeavors (e.g., Myers & Perlmutter, 1978). However, at another level, it must be emphasized that the strategic efforts of the 4- and 5-year-olds in Baker-Ward et al.'s investigation did not facilitate remembering. Moreover, the developmental literature is now replete with comparable demonstrations of this failure of young children's strategies to affect recall performance. For example, Wellman (1988) has used the term *faulty strategies* to characterize these early efforts, but he has also emphasized their importance for understanding the developmental course of children's mnemonic activities. Moreover, at a more general level, researchers (e.g., Bjorklund, Miller, Coyle, & Slawinski, 1997) have used the term *utilization deficiencies* to refer to situations in which mnemonic strategies may be generated spontaneously or after training in response to memory demands but nonetheless are not associated with changes in the amount recalled.

Why should young children's strategic activities fail to be associated with increments in remembering? If, for example, Baker-Ward et al.'s 4- and 5-year-olds engaged in the same strategic behaviors as did their 6-year-olds, why did only the efforts of the 6-year-olds have a positive effect on their recall? On the one hand, it is possible that there were subtle differences in the strategies produced by the three groups of children. That is, even though the observable behaviors (e.g., naming, visual inspection) of the 4-, 5-, and 6-year-olds were similar, they may have been the external manifestation of quite different underlying strategies. As such, the similarity across age may be illusory with, for example, the children of different ages combining the observable behaviors into qualitatively different strategies, and higher order coding schemes might capture these age-related changes in the coordination of different mnemonic behaviors. On the other hand, it is possible that these fine-grained analyses will leave open questions about the conditions under which children's use of strategies may and may not impact remembering. Indeed, there are other factors such as age related changes in underlying knowledge (Bjorklund, 1985), speed of processing (Kail, 1991), and the effort requirements of strategy usage (Case, 1985; Guttentag, 1984), that may influence whether or not a given strategy impacts remembering.

This very brief discussion of early strategies that do not "work" should serve to emphasize the fact that *intentionality* is only one aspect of strategic behavior. Although the data indicate clearly that young children can behave in an intentional manner, it is essential to consider two other features of strategy application—*effectiveness* and *consistency*—that are particularly important in any account of the development of children's mastery of mnemonic skills across the elementary school years. Concerning effectiveness, research on utilization deficiencies, mentioned above, indicates that the strategic efforts of young children often do not facilitate remembering. Further, even when strategies influence recall, younger children may derive less benefit than do older children (Folds, Footo, Guttentag, & Ornstein, 1990; Ornstein et al., 1988; Wellman, 1988). Moreover, in terms of consistency, novice strategy users have a limited group of techniques at their disposal, and the application of any given procedure is often quite context specific. To illustrate, when young children are able to demonstrate "sophisticated" strategy use, they typically do so only in highly supportive and salient settings (Ornstein & Myers, 1996; Ornstein et al., 1988). In contrast, children who are skilled strategy users come to have command over a broad set of mnemonic techniques (e.g., rehearsal, organization, elaboration, and later, study skills) and can apply them adeptly in many situations that call for remembering (Ornstein et al., 1988; Schneider & Pressley, 1997). In effect, across the elementary school years, changes are observed in the ways in which children more flexibly select strategies to meet the needs of the task at hand. They also become better able to monitor the success of their efforts, and make adjustments as needed in the techniques that they use. This cognitive orientation, as characterized by effective, consistent, and flexible strategy use, has been described as "good strategy use" (Pressley, Borkowski, & Schneider, 1987) or "good information processing" (Pressley, Borkowski, & Schneider, 1989).

## Children's Strategy Use in the Elementary School Years

The intentional, but ineffective early strategic behavior of preschoolers changes over time such that elementary school children's use of mnemonic techniques becomes more effective and consistent. Thus, with increases in age, strategy use becomes more strongly correlated with recall performance (Bjorklund, 1987; Schneider & Pressley, 1997), and by the time children make the transition to middle school, they typically behave quite strategically in a wide range of memory tasks. To illustrate the course of this development, we turn to studies in which a progression from "passive" to "active" memorization styles has been demonstrated (Ornstein et al., 1988; Ornstein, Grammer, & Coffman, 2010).

Age-related changes in a number of different strategies have been examined extensively—rehearsal (e.g., Ornstein & Naus, 1978), organization (e.g., Lange, 1978), and elaboration (e.g., Rohwer, 1973). In the context of tasks that involve the deliberate memorization of sets of words or pictures, across the school years there is a very systematic transition from relatively inactive to more active techniques of remembering. For example, when given a list of words to remember and prompted to "talk aloud" as the items are being presented, younger children tend to rehearse each to-be-remembered item alone as it is displayed, whereas older subjects rehearse each one with several previously presented stimuli (Ornstein, Naus, & Liberty, 1975). To illustrate, if the first three items on a to-be-remembered list are *table*, *car*, and *flower*, older children are apt to rehearse *table*, *table*, *table*, when *table* is presented; *table*, *car*, *table*, *car*, when *car* is presented; and *table*, *car*, *flower*, when *flower* is displayed. In contrast, younger children typically rehearse *table*, *table*, *table*, when the first word is shown; *car*, *car*, *car*, when the second word is presented; and *flower*, *flower*, *flower*, when the third word is shown. Moreover, training studies in which rehearsal instructions are manipulated—sometimes in combination with the provision of information-processing supports—have indicated that these differences in rehearsal style are causally linked to recall success. For example, providing young children with instructions to rehearse several items together leads to elevated recall, especially of the early list items (i.e., those in the initial sections of the serial position curve), and these effects are magnified when the demands of retrieving previously presented words for rehearsal are reduced (e.g., Ornstein, Medlin, Stone, & Naus, 1985; Ornstein, Naus, & Stone, 1977).

A comparable picture of strategy development emerges in the organizational and elaboration literatures (Ornstein & Corsale, 1979; Pressley, 1982), one that is paralleled later in development in children's use of study skills (Brown & Smiley, 1978; Brown, Day, & Jones 1983). For example, in a sort-recall task with interleaved study and recall trials in which children are given a set of relatively low-associated (i.e., essentially unrelated) words and asked to form groups

that will help them remember, the sorting of older children is rather semantically constrained, in contrast to what seems to be the random sorting of younger children. Inspection of the sorting patterns suggests that older children (e.g., seventh graders) search actively for meaningful relations among the stimuli (even with relatively unstructured lists), whereas younger children (e.g., even third graders) do not do this (e.g., Bjorklund, Ornstein, & Haig, 1977; Liberty & Ornstein, 1973). However, it can be shown that the young children do in fact have the knowledge that would permit them to sort in a manner similar to that of the older children and their performance can be improved when they are prompted to use that knowledge. For example, by using a "yoking" procedure, young children can be required to learn the sorting patterns of older children, and when they do so, their recall is facilitated (Liberty & Ornstein, 1973). Similar effects are obtained with instructional manipulations. Thus, by telling young children to form groups of words that "go together" or are "similar in some way," as opposed to groups that will "help you remember," we can observe a major change in sorting style and recall performance (Bjorklund et al., 1977; Corsale & Ornstein, 1980). Facilitation can also be observed by providing young children with experience in sorting highly organized categorical materials before presenting them with low-associated to-be-remembered words (Best & Ornstein, 1986).

The findings outlined above indicate that children of elementary-school age differ markedly from preschoolers in terms of the effectiveness of their strategic efforts and suggest further that the "mnemonic payoff" of their strategies increases across the school years. Indeed, the experimental manipulations mentioned briefly (e.g., Bjorklund et al., 1977; Ornstein et al., 1977) demonstrate clear linkages between children's changing rehearsal and organizational strategies and corresponding age-related increases in remembering. However, it must be emphasized that there often are limits to the success of these interventions, as can be seen in Ornstein et al.'s (1977) attempt to instruct second graders in the use of an active rehearsal strategy in which several to-be-remembered items are rehearsed together. This instructional manipulation did result in more active rehearsal and improved recall, but it certainly did not bring the second graders to the level of the sixth graders. Why should this be the case? What can be learned from the limited success of this instructional manipulation that will inform our understanding of additional factors that influence the effectiveness of children's strategic efforts?

This failure to eliminate age differences in performance most likely reflects at least in part age-related differences in the effort demands of active rehearsal strategies. To illustrate, in explorations of children's rehearsal, each item is typically displayed for several seconds and then removed as the next one is presented. As a consequence of this mode of presentation, rehearsing several items together requires that one must remember words that are no longer visible, and this retrieval process can be quite demanding, especially for young children. Indeed, assessments of the effort requirements of mnemonic strategies indicate that young children must commit more of their attentional resources when they use an active rehearsal strategy than do older children (Guttentag, 1984), but when the effort demands of the task are reduced, by keeping items visible after they have been presented, the performance of young children can be considerably enhanced. As such, if instructions to rehearse several items together are combined with continued visual access to each item after it has been displayed, second graders are better able to rehearse actively, and there is a dramatic improvement in their recall performance (Ornstein et al., 1985). Importantly, under these conditions of presentation, even without instructions in active rehearsal, approximately a third of the third graders studied by Guttentag et al. (1987) spontaneously rehearsed several items together, whereas two thirds of the sample rehearsed in a passive fashion. Moreover, a year later, the children who had rehearsed actively in the "scaffolded" condition were more likely than their peers to rehearse actively as fourth graders, even under the typical item-by-item mode of presentation.

Several other factors may contribute to children's developing abilities to produce effective strategies for remembering: their increasing "prior" knowledge of the materials being remembered, their developing metacognitive understanding of the operation of the memory system, and the increasing automaticity of their cognitive processes. Regarding prior knowledge, there is a considerable amount of evidence to indicate that changes with age in both the content and structure of children's underlying knowledge in permanent memory can influence strategy selection and implementation (Bjorklund, 1985; Folds et al., 1990; Ornstein & Naus, 1985; Ornstein et al., 1988). Indeed, what a child knows about the materials to be remembered may impact dramatically just what can be done with those materials. Increases with age in the articulation of the knowledge system may facilitate the retrieval of stored information and thereby reduce the effort involved in carrying out the various subcomponents of memory strategies. Within the context of active rehearsal techniques, the increasingly stronger interitem associations in permanent memory that accompany increases in age may make it easier for a child to execute strategies that call for the joint rehearsal of several to-be-remembered items. Similarly, changes with age in the underlying knowledge system may affect children's use of organizational techniques; simply put, even with intent to use a sorting or clustering strategy it is difficult to group on the basis of meaning if a child has an imperfect understanding of the structure linking materials being remembered.

The growth of children's knowledge is paralleled by corresponding changes in their understanding of the demands of tasks that require remembering and, in general, the operation of the memory system (Cavanaugh & Perlmutter, 1982; Flavell & Wellman, 1977; Schneider, 1985). This understanding, "metamemory," in turn figures prominently in accounts of the development of memory (e.g., Cavanaugh

& Borkowski, 1980; Schneider, 1985), but it must be emphasized that the evidence to support claims of metamnemonic awareness orchestrating strategy selection and implementation has been quite limited. Indeed, the results of correlational investigations in which both metamemory and memory performance have been assessed have been mixed. In addition to potential measurement problems, consider two of the difficulties that have been encountered in generating support for a metamemory–memory linkage. First, under some conditions, children have been shown to articulate awareness of a particular mnemonic strategy but nonetheless fail to make use of it in practice (Sodian, Schneider, & Perlmutter, 1986). Second, other situations have been documented in which children appear to be using a deliberate strategy (e.g., clustering in free recall), but fail to demonstrate any corresponding metamnemonic understanding (Bjorklund & Zeman, 1982). On the other hand, the importance of metamemory can be seen in the key role it plays in training children to use strategies that they do not deploy spontaneously; indeed, supplementing strategy instruction with the provision of metamnemonic information has been shown to facilitate children's performance (e.g., Paris, Newman, & McVey, 1982). In addition, more recent studies involving improved techniques for assessing young children's understanding (e.g., Schlagmüller & Schneider, 2002; Schneider, Schagmüller, & Vise, 1998) have also generated convincing support for a linkage between metamemory and memory development.

Although the focus in this chapter is on the ways in which the school context may contribute to the development of children's *deliberate* memory strategies over the course of the elementary school years, it is necessary to discuss seemingly *automatic* contributions to the operation of these skills. Indeed, the impact of prior knowledge on children's deployment of mnemonic techniques, discussed above, may to some extent reflect the operation of automatic processes, as strong interitem associations are activated without full strategic awareness. Thus, young children appear to be more "strategic" with some sets of materials than others, largely because highly organized or salient stimulus items seem to elicit strategies at a point in development at which they might not otherwise be operative (Bjorklund, 1985; Lange, 1973, 1978; Ornstein & Naus, 1985). For example, Lange (1973, 1978) pointed out that the variation in the findings of studies exploring category clustering in the recall of kindergarten-age children most likely reflects whether the categorical materials being remembered did or did not also contain strong interitem associations: when such associations are present, the category structure is reflected in the children's recall protocols (e.g., Rossi, 1964), but when they are absent, category clustering is not observed (e.g., Lange, 1973). These findings led Lange to suggest that much of what had previously been viewed as the application of a deliberate strategy might be viewed more parsimoniously as reflecting the more-or-less automatic activation of strong interitem associations in the knowledge base. More generally, it is clear that a considerable amount of evidence indicates that the use of highly associated stimulus materials can facilitate the early execution of active rehearsal and sorting strategies (Ornstein & Naus, 1985). In addition to these materials-driven contributions to the deployment of strategies, practice in the use of mnemonic techniques contributes to the automatization of skill. Indeed, with practice and experience, as well as increases in the speed of processing (Kail, 1991), strategies that were at one time somewhat difficult to perform may later be carried out with relative ease because they come to be less demanding of effort (Bjorklund & Harnishfeger, 1987; Footo, Guttentag, Ornstein 1988; Guttentag, 1984). This increased automaticity no doubt contributes to the greater effectiveness of older children's strategic efforts.

These different factors come together as we consider again one aspect of strategy use that was mentioned above, namely, consistency. Older children clearly have command over various strategies that can be used flexibly and effectively in a range of situations that require remembering. In contrast, the strategic repertoire of younger children, even third graders, is much more limited in scope and dependent on the specifics of the context in which memory is requested. Simply put, our "diagnosis" of the extent to which a child is strategic will vary considerably as a function of instructions, effort demands, and information processing supports, as well as knowledge and the associative characteristics of the to-be-remembered materials (Folds et al., 1990; Ornstein & Myers, 1996). Putting these different factors together, Ornstein et al. (1988, p. 38) proposed a "continuum of mnemonic effectiveness" to characterize the growth of mnemonic skill from the initial tentative applications of strategies in certain highly supportive contexts to their later efficient use in many settings.

This picture of an age-related progression in children's acquisition and utilization of mnemonic skills must be qualified because it is based largely on the results of cross-sectional studies in which the performance of groups of children of different ages is contrasted. As such, these studies can provide little information about the course of developmental change within individual children. Cross-sectional work provides us with very useful accounts of the average level of performance on particular tasks at specified age levels, but the resulting impression that one derives is that of a smooth developmental trajectory. However, in order to make statements about developmental changes in the individual, it is important to consider findings from alternative methodologies, such as longitudinal and microgenetic designs, that can complement the picture painted by cross-sectional work.

Although there have been relatively few longitudinal studies of the development of mnemonic skills, two recent investigations provide insights into developmental change that contrast with some impressions drawn from the cross-sectional literature. Indeed, Schneider and Sodian (1997) suggested that cross-sectional findings provide a picture of change that is actually a reflection of average strategy use and does not capture the marked variability

in children's individual trajectories. This variability was documented in the findings of the Munich Longitudinal Study on Individual Development (LOGIC) (Weinert & Schneider, 1999). Included in this large-scale investigation was an assessment of children's organizational strategies every 2 years between ages 4 and 12 (Sodian & Schneider, 1999). Although strategic behavior increased on average across the 2-year intervals, over the same period of time test-retest correlations revealed that individual children's use of organized sorting was not stable from one point of measurement to the next. The researchers concluded that this lack of stability revealed the individual variability of children's patterns of strategy acquisition. Although the assessments were widely spaced across childhood, further analyses indicated that the majority of children tested revealed an all-or-nothing transition from nonuse of the organizational strategy to complete use, and they did so at different ages. In a follow-up to this project, the Würzburg Longitudinal Memory Study, Schneider and his colleagues (2004) made use of more frequent assessments of children's skills so as to better understand the nature of changes over time in their use of strategies for remembering. Schneider et al. were able to confirm the earlier longitudinal findings in that when viewed at the level of the individual child, the acquisition of a strategic sorting strategy was much less gradual and more rapid than was implied by earlier cross-sectional findings. Indeed, the improvements with age in strategy use that the children evidenced reflect a picture of dramatic leaps in performance and not gradual increases in sophistication over time.

Important information about the development of strategic competence is also derived from microgenetic studies (Siegler, 2006) in which children are assessed repeatedly over relatively restricted periods of time. This methodology is closely linked, and often informed by a longitudinal approach, but the emphasis is placed on making focused, in-depth observations at times in which the skills being examined are undergoing change. Interestingly, the results of these studies lead to important conclusions about the nature of developmental change in strategy use. First, microgenetic studies of children's acquisition of a categorization strategy (Schlagmüller & Schneider, 2002) have confirmed the basic findings from the longitudinal literature that indicate that children do not routinely transition from rudimentary to complex strategies in a gradual fashion. Indeed, children who came to use the organizational strategy did so at different times, but in an all-or-none fashion as evidenced by nearly complete categorical sorting of the to-be-remembered materials and corresponding increases in recall as a benefit of the improved strategy use; importantly, the children's organizational efforts invariably followed metamnemonic insights concerning the soon-to-be deployed strategy and led to immediate gains in recall. Second, microgenetic explorations of a variety of cognitive strategies suggest that children may often employ several strategies simultaneously; indeed, they may use less effective techniques at the same time that they produce recently acquired more efficient strategies (Siegler, 2006). These findings have led Siegler (e.g., 1996) to propose an overlapping-wave description of strategy development such that at any one point in elementary school, children are seen as having mastery over a mix of strategies, with cognitive growth being expressed in terms of changes in the composition of this strategy mix. Lehman and Hasselhorn (2007) observed similar patterns of multiple strategy use and change in their longitudinal exploration of the development of rehearsal strategies.

## School as a Potential Mediator of Developmental Change

The extensive literature on children's developing facility with mnemonic techniques indicates substantial age-related changes in the ability to make effective and consistent use of a range of memory strategies. However, what is missing in the literature is a clear indication of the experiential factors that are associated with this developing mnemonic sophistication. Nonetheless, a number of studies lead to the suggestion that these important changes in skill are not linked to age per se, but rather to experiences in a formal classroom setting. Indeed, it seems likely that techniques for remembering may emerge and become articulated in institutions such as schools in which remembering is valued and rewarded.

Several lines of research point to the potential impact of formal schooling on the development of memory strategies. In this chapter we examine cross-cultural investigations in which schooled and nonschooled children have been contrasted, cross-national explorations of the impact of different educational practices, and "natural experiments" in which children of essentially the same age are enrolled in different elementary school grades.

*Attending School* In the 1970s and early 1980s, several groups of investigators (e.g., Cole, Gay, Glick, & Sharp, 1971; Rogoff, 1981; Wagner, 1974, 1978) launched research programs on the impact of formal schooling on children's cognitive development. Set mostly in developing countries in which there was no universal public education at the time, these researchers examined the performance of "schooled" versus "nonschooled" children (i.e., those who did versus those who did not attend a formal Western-style school) on a range of cognitive measures including categorization, reasoning, and remembering. In these quasi-experimental studies, enrollment in a formal school program was governed not only by proximity but by decision making within the family. As such, it was necessary for the researchers to consider characteristics of the children (e.g., intelligence) and the families (e.g., socioeconomic status; beliefs about modernity) that could be confounded with school attendance. Although these factors may be associated with aspects of the children's performance on various cognitive assessments, it also seems to be the case that they cannot account for the impact of schooling. Indeed, schooling appears to have an independent effect on performance, over

and above the influence of family background (Rogoff, 1981).

The contrast between schooled and nonschooled children in terms of their memory skills is informative because in the formal school setting children encounter strong expectations for remembering and face tasks that are similar in many respects to those used to assess mnemonic skill. Indeed, Rogoff (1981; see also Cole, 2006) observed that the majority of tasks used to assess mnemonic strategy use in cross-cultural research were very similar to the types of tasks children most encounter everyday in school, but are dissimilar to the types of tasks that children face outside of the school context. For example, Cole (1992) indicated that copying and memorizing lists of information was an important part of early "Western" style formal schools and pointed out that in modern schools children are still expected to memorize lists of information (such as spelling lists, the names of presidents) as a part of routine classroom activities.

To illustrate the comparative-cultural approach, consider first work by Wagner (1978) that was motivated by an interest in determining those aspects of memory performance that might be influenced by culture and experience, as opposed to those that are more-or-less universal. Wagner worked within the context of models of memory (e.g., Atkinson & Shiffrin, 1968) that differentiated between *control processes* that could affect the flow of information within the memory system, and *structural features* such as the capacity of various memory stores (e.g., sensory register; short-term memory) and rates of information loss over time from these stores. Applications of these models to questions of developmental change suggested that the structural features of the memory system were more-or-less constant across a broad age range (Ornstein et al., 1975), whereas control processes such as rehearsal and category clustering in recall increased with age (Cole, Frankel, & Sharp, 1971; Ornstein et al., 1975). Given that the use of control processes increased with age, Wagner wanted to examine the extent to which children's early experiences, as in school, contributed to their development and utilization. In addition, assuming that the structural features were in fact universal, Wagner predicted that different experiences in childhood would not influence these aspects of the memory system.

Wagner's (1978) studies in Morocco were designed to examine the separate and combined effects on memory of school attendance and living environment on memory performance, factors that were confounded in an earlier study carried out in Mexico (Wagner, 1974). In one of these studies, Wagner explored the mnemonic skills of Moroccan males who ranged from 6 to 22 years of age and who differed in terms of enrollment in school (schooled or nonschooled) and locale (urban or rural). Assessment involved presenting each participant with several sets of pictures and then probing primarily for the location of a specific picture in each series. On every trial, seven cards (each containing an animal and a household object) were presented in the following fashion: each item was first displayed briefly, and then placed face down in a row in front of the participant. Following the presentation of each series, a card containing one of the animals (objects) was displayed and the participant's task was to indicate the location of the picture being probed. Over the series of trials, each animal (object) and each location were probed twice.

Wagner (1978) was interested in overall recall, as measured by the number of correct responses, and in recall as a function of serial position, as measured by the number of correct responses for each position in the set (i.e., the first, the second, and so on to the seventh). The patterns of performance were complex such that memory performance increased with age, but only in the context of an urban environment or attendance in school. Indeed, the rural nonschooled participants consistently performed below the level of the other three groups and evidenced essentially no improvement with age. With regard to the primacy effect—taken to reflect the operation of control processes such as verbal rehearsal—both schooling and to a lesser extent residence in an urban environment were associated with enhanced memory and with age-related changes in remembering. The impact of an urban environment was particularly salient for the younger children, whereas the impact of schooling was seen especially with the older participants. Wagner (1978) also found that the recency effect did not vary markedly as a function of age, school experience, and living environment, suggesting again that structural features of memory may be universal.

The impact of Western-style schooling is also shown in the use of organizational strategies, specifically clustering in free recall according to the category structure of a list of to-be-remembered items. Consider, for example, Cole et al.'s (1971) work with various Kpelle groups in Liberia who were presented with sets of 20 objects that were drawn from four taxonomic categories and asked to remember these items in any order. Cole and his colleagues found that recall patterns reflecting the category structure of the items and overall level of recall both varied as a function of amount of experience in school. Although Kpelle children with a few years of schooling, like their nonschooled counterparts, did not structure their recall output according to the taxonomic categories represented on the list being remembered, older individuals with 4 to 6 years of schooling evidenced clustering and enhanced recall in comparison to nonliterate Kpelle of the same age. A linkage between amount of exposure to formal schooling and recall and clustering was also observed by Sharp, Cole, and Lave (1979) in their work with indigenous Mayans from the Yucatán. Moreover, in a review of these and other cross-cultural studies of the impact of school on developing cognitive skills, Rogoff (1981) concluded that nonschooled children generally:

> …are unlikely to engage spontaneously in strategies that provide greater organization for unrelated items…. Since differences do not generally appear until the schooled sample has received several years of schooling, it seems that some experience at school influences learning of organizational strategies. (p. 245)

*Cross-National Studies* The impact on memory performance of school as an institution has also been observed in cross-national studies in which children who have experienced comparable amounts of schooling, but in different school contexts, have been contrasted. For example, Carr, Kurtz, and their colleagues (e.g., Carr et al., 1989; Kurtz, Schneider, Carr, Borkowski, & Rellinger, 1990; Schneider, Borkowski, Kurtz, & Kerwin, 1986) have suggested that differences in both teacher and parental instructional strategies in Germany and the United States may be associated with comparable differences in the use of strategies for remembering. To illustrate, Carr et al. (1989) asked parents to report on study skill instruction that they provided in the home to assist their second and third grade children with school work, as well as the extent to which they played strategy-related games with their children. These investigators found that German parents indicated that they gave their children more direct instruction in the use of strategies for remembering than did American parents of children in comparable grades, and that they more often played games with their children that required strategic thinking. In addition, Kurtz et al. (1990) modified Carr et al.'s (1989) survey for use with teachers, asking specifically about strategy instruction and the ways in which they might help their students develop the types of skills that would make them "good strategy" users (see, e.g., Pressley et al., 1987). Kurtz and her colleagues indicated that German teachers reported more direct strategy instruction than did American teachers. Overall, however, it must be emphasized that teachers from both countries reported relatively little metacognitive and direct strategy instruction.

Against this background of cross-national differences in parent and teacher behaviors that may impact children's skills in remembering, consider Carr et al.'s (1989) exploration of German and American second and third graders' use of organizational techniques in a sort-recall and training task. On an initial baseline trial, the children were asked "to work to remember" 20 pictures of common objects that could be grouped into 4 sets of 5 pictures on a sort board. After a 3-minute period in which they were free to move the pictures around on the board, the children were given 2 minutes to study the items prior to a request for written recall. Carr et al. reported that the German students evidenced higher levels of categorical sorting during study and clustering in recall than did their peers in American schools. After baseline assessment, the children were instructed to group the to-be-remembered items categorically, to rehearse the pictures in groups, to name the categories, and to cluster according to the semantic structure during recall. Importantly, there were no differences in the performance of the American and German children after this organizational and rehearsal training. Moreover, inspection of the data indicated that the training did not affect the performance of the German students because they were already using the techniques on which they were instructed, but that it did have a substantial impact on the American children.

*A "Natural" Experiment* Additional information concerning the impact of school on strategies for remembering comes from Morrison et al.'s (1995) use of a "natural experiment" to explore the development of skill across the kindergarten and first grade years. Taking advantage of the fact that all school systems establish cut-offs for school entry, Morrison and his colleagues developed an ingenious procedure for studying children who "just made" the mandated date for entry into first grade (a "young" first grade group) and those who "just missed" the date (an "old" kindergarten group). Thus, the resulting groups were essentially matched in terms of age but nonetheless differed in their formal school experiences, thereby permitting an assessment of the impact of these 2 years of school on children's memory skills. The performance of these two groups was assessed at the beginning and end of the school year on a picture recall task.

Morrison et al. (1995) reported that the two groups of children did not differ in the number of items recalled at the start of the school year (kindergarten for the group that missed the cut-off, and first grade for the group that made the cut-off date), but that substantial differences were observed at the end of the year. Interestingly, the children who missed the cut-off and spent the year in kindergarten evidenced no improvement in recall at all, whereas their same-aged peers who made the cut-off and entered the first grade showed considerable improvement. As would be expected, the old kindergartners improved and caught up with their peers the next year, when they had the opportunity to attend first grade. It should be noted that these group differences in overall recall were paralleled by comparable differences in terms of the primacy section of the serial position curve. More specifically, at the pretest assessment, there were no group differences in the primacy effect, but clear differences in favor of the young first graders were evidenced at the end of the year. Interpreting the primacy effect as reflecting the operation of active rehearsal strategies, Morrison and his colleagues suggested that there was something in the first grade context that supported the development and expression of mnemonic techniques.

## Accounting for the Effects of Schooling

How can we account for the effects of formal schooling observed in the three types of studies—comparative-cultural, cross-national, and the "natural experiment"—discussed above? What is it about the school context that influences the development of children's repertoire of mnemonic skills? We consider here three possible aspects of the classroom that may impact children's performance: the emphasis on the importance of remembering; the exposure to a highly structured instructional environment; and the memory-relevant language in the home and school.

*The Emphasis on the Importance of Remembering* Consider first the comparisons of schooled versus nonschooled individuals, as seen in the work of Cole, Rogoff, and Wagner.

To begin, it is important to emphasize that demonstrations of the impact of formal schooling do not in any way imply that schooled individuals outperform their nonschooled peers on everyday memory tasks that are embedded in activities central to their culture. Nonetheless, they do suggest that something in the school context most likely is related to the emergence of skills that are important for success on tasks that involve deliberate memorization. One possibility might be that attendance at school carries with it an expectation that remembering per se is valued, and as students move through the school years they are clearly required to commit large amounts of information to memory in the service of future learning. An emphasis on remembering can, of course, contribute to the effects observed in these studies of the impact of formal schooling, but a cautionary note is sounded by the performance of a Moroccan comparison group assessed by Wagner (1978). In addition to the groups defined by age, attendance in school, and locale, Wagner recruited a group of students from a traditional school of Koranic scholarship because these students were assumed to have special mnemonic skills, given that much of their day is spent studying and memorizing verses of the Koran. As it turned out, however, the performance of these adult students was much like the nonschooled participants in the study, and thus there was little evidence for the use of rehearsal techniques. Of course, as Wagner (1978) points out, it is possible that the Koranic scholars acquired specific skills that were relevant for the memorization of text but could not be applied to the serial probe task used in his research, but the general point is that experience with memory demands would seem to be insufficient to account for the results discussed above.

*Exposure to a Highly Structured Instructional Environment* To what extent does exposure to structured material in the school context contribute to the emergence and subsequent refinement of mnemonic techniques? Much of the material that students are expected to remember in the school is certainly ordered and structured in ways that are rarely found outside of school. In this regard, Cole (1992) has suggested that the learning that takes place in school has:

> …no clear connection to everyday activities outside of school… this information is structured according to category systems that are a part of the tradition that created modern science and bureaucratic institutions. It privileges the taxonomic/paradigmatic form of organization over the thematic/syntagmatic…. This aspect of the context of schooling appears, in my opinion, to be sufficient to explain most of the tested results comparing schooled and nonschooled children on memory and classification tasks. (p. 104)

Best and Ornstein (1986) also thought that the structures of the classroom most likely had an impact on children's developing mnemonic skills and carried out a laboratory-based "simulation" of certain features of the classroom setting within the context of a sort-recall task in which semantic grouping was known to facilitate recall (e.g., Bjorklund et al., 1977). Based on their understanding of the implications of the comparative-cultural literature, Best and Ornstein (1986) observed in elementary-school classrooms and talked with teachers about memory and strategy development. They found that there was little direct instruction in strategy use in the early elementary school years, but thought that the salient organizational structures of the classroom might impact the development of children's strategies for remembering. More specifically, Best and Ornstein suggested that exposure to highly structured bodies of knowledge might facilitate the discovery and application of organizational strategies. To explore these notions of strategy discovery and deployment, they examined the extent to which third graders could be led to induce the operation of semantically constrained sorting strategies without even being given the "sort-for-meaning" instructions that had been used successfully in "training studies" by Bjorklund et al. (1977) and Corsale and Ornstein (1980).

Best and Ornstein (1986) based their study on Corsale's (1978) work showing that even though third graders would not form semantically based groups when asked to remember low-associated words in a sort-recall task, they would nonetheless group on the basis of meaning when given highly salient categorically related items. Corsale's finding suggested that the strong organizational properties of highly salient categories were difficult to ignore, leading children to sort meaningfully in a more-or-less automatic fashion. Best and Ornstein, in turn, felt that young children might make inferences about the benefits of meaning-based grouping as a result of exposure to highly structured to-be-remembered materials and designed a transfer study to examine the degree to which experience with categorically-organized materials would lead to organized sorting on a subsequent task with low-associated items. Consistent with this perspective, they found that third graders who had been given several sort-recall trials with taxonomically organized materials evidenced organized sorting when presented with low-associated items to remember, whereas peers in a control condition who had experienced repeated trials with low-associated materials continued to group in a non-semantic manner. In essence, Best and Ornstein used the exposure to the categorically related words as an approximation of experiences in the classroom environment they presumed to be relevant to the use of categorization and suggested that exposure to formal educational settings and to materials that are presented in an organized manner might work in a similar fashion.

***Memory Relevant Language in the Home and School***  To what extent could memory-relevant conversation in the home and at school play a role in the development of children's memory? This possibility is consistent with research on parental influences on cognitive development. For example, as indicated above, Kurtz et al. (1990) reported that German children whose parents provided higher levels of strategy instruction at home were more likely to spon-

taneously employ memory strategies than their American counterparts. In addition, there is an extensive literature on linkages between the ways in which mothers of preschoolers structure conversations about both ongoing and prior events and the abilities of their children to remember those experiences (e.g., Fivush & Fromhoff, 1988; Haden et al., 2001; Reese et al., 1993). Indeed, the issue of adults' involvement in the facilitation of children's cognitive development is central to studies that focus on mother–child conversation as a mediator of young children's memory performance (Farrant & Reese, 2000; Fivush, Reese, & Haden, 2006; Ornstein, Haden, & Hedrick, 2004).

The focus of research on parent–child reminiscing has been on variability in the "reminiscing styles" used by parents to structure their conversations about past events with their young children (see Fivush et al., 2006). For example, Fivush and her colleagues have shown that children's memory is facilitated by mothers' elaborative style of interaction with their children in conversations about their prior experiences. More specifically, Reese et al. (1993) observed two styles of conversation when mothers reminisced with their 40-month-old children. To illustrate, they found that young children of "high elaborative" mothers—who were asked more *wh-* questions and evaluated more positively for their contributions to conversation—recalled more of the events that were discussed than those of "low elaborative" mothers. Furthermore, it seemed that the children of high elaborative mothers acquired some general skills for remembering, given that maternal elaboration was also related to children's independent memory reports 1½ and 2½ years later. These findings have been replicated widely, both in the United States and cross-nationally (e.g., Bauer & Burch, 2004; Farrant & Reese, 2000; Leichtman, Pillemer, Wang, Koreishi, & Han, 2000; Peterson, Jesso, & McCabe, 1999), and Peterson et al. (1999) were able to bring conversational style under experimental control, finding that the children of mothers who were trained to use elaborative techniques while reminiscing with their children produced more detailed memory reports than children of mothers who did not receive such training. It thus seems clear that mothers who are highly elaborative in their early conversations about the past with their preschoolers foster their children's abilities to report their past experiences.

Complementing this corpus of research, an emerging literature also makes it clear that language-based interactions as an event is being experienced can be of considerable importance in guiding encoding and establishing a representation in memory (Haden et al., 2001; Hedrick, Haden, & Ornstein, 2009; McGuigan & Salmon, 2004; Ornstein et al., 2004; Tessler & Nelson, 1994). To illustrate, Haden et al. (2001) carried out a short-term longitudinal study in which young children interacted with their mothers while taking part in three specifically constructed events: at 30 months, a camping trip; at 36 months, a bird-watching adventure; at 42 months, the opening of an ice-cream shop. These "adventures" took place within the confines of each family's living room and were videotaped, thus creating a record of the ways in which each dyad interacted with the various component features of each event (e.g., in the camping activity: hotdogs, backpack, sleeping bag) as it unfolded. Haden and her colleagues observed that both mothers and their children handled most of the features (i.e., props) of the activities, and with this demonstration of joint attention they could then ask if recall of the components varied as a function of type of "talk" that was directed to them during the events. In this regard, they reported that the children's reports differed as a function of the amount of "joint talk." That is, those features that were discussed jointly by mother and child were better remembered than those features that were commented on only by mothers, which in turn were better remembered than those components that were not discussed at all. Follow-up analyses suggested that joint talk that involved contingent responding, for example, with children responding to specific questions that were posed by their mothers, was particularly supportive of recall (Ornstein et al., 2004). The findings of this study suggest that mother–child interaction as an event unfolds influences encoding and subsequent remembering. In addition, experiments in which adults are trained in the use of an elaborative style of engaging with children prior to these jointly experienced "adventures" also support this conclusion (Boland, Haden, & Ornstein, 2003; Hedrick et al., 2009).

In sum, the findings from longitudinal and experimental studies converge to indicate that social-communicative exchanges can have a dramatic influence on children's memory performance. Although the mechanisms underlying these effects have not been explored critically, it seems as though elaborative parent–child conversations may influence the encoding and representation of information in memory on the one hand, as well as search, retrieval, and reporting operations, on the other. For example, conversations as events unfold enable parents to direct children's attention to salient features of the activity so as to facilitate comprehension, thus impacting the ways events are encoded and represented in memory (Ornstein et al., 2004). Similar benefits of elaborative conversation may result from opportunities to reminisce with an adult about previously experienced events (e.g., Fivush et al., 2006; Reese et al., 1993). Indeed, it seems likely that an elaborative conversational style in reminiscing may provide opportunities for children to practice searching and retrieving information from memory and experience in using narrative conventions to provide accounts of their experiences.

Given that exposure to elaborative conversational styles at home facilitates young children's reports of their experiences—perhaps by influencing comprehension, encoding, and storage, and perhaps by affecting search, retrieval, and reporting—it seems possible that exposure to certain types of conversation in the school context may impact children's later developing deliberate memory skills. Indeed, teacher–child "talk" in the early elementary school classroom has the potential to foster the development of memory strategies by enabling children to discover on their own techniques that are helpful for remembering. More

specifically, paralleling the parent–child conversational literature, perhaps teacher–child dialogue during an ongoing lesson and conversations after it had taken place can serve to facilitate the discovery and articulation of techniques such as rehearsal, organization, and elaboration. Thus, not only do teachers present information in the course of their lessons that they hope that children will remember, they may often do so in ways that may facilitate the establishment of elaborated representations in memory. In addition, they may facilitate memory search and retrieval by the ways in which they ask children to report information that has already been learned. This is certainly an area that remains ripe for investigation, with only a series of studies by Moely and her colleagues (e.g., Moely et al., 1986; Moely, Hart, et al., 1992) and several studies by Ornstein and his collaborators (e.g., Coffman et al., 2008; Ornstein, Coffman, & Grammer, 2009; Ornstein, Grammer, & Coffman, 2010) serving to provide some information about aspects of the classroom environment that may be important for children's strategic development.

## What Is It About the School Context that Is Important?

With multiple lines of research identifying school as a potential mediator of developmental changes in mnemonic skill, it becomes essential to consider seriously just what it is about the classroom context that is important for bringing about this cognitive growth. To our knowledge, only the Moely and Ornstein groups have made in-depth observations in elementary school classrooms and explored linkages to children's memory performance. In this section, we provide a description of the elementary school classroom that had been outlined in these projects, discuss the identification of contrasting teaching styles, and illustrate the ways in which aspects of the classroom have been associated with children's memory performance.

***Characterizations of Elementary School Classrooms***  The first detailed exploration of the elementary school context was Moely et al.'s (1992) cross-sectional study of classrooms from kindergarten through the sixth grade. In an effort to catalog teachers' memory-relevant behaviors that might support children's developing skills, as well as changes across the elementary school years in these behaviors, Moely and her colleagues made detailed observations of instruction in a range of subjects. To do so, they developed a coding system to catalog many aspects of the teaching process, and based upon their observations used factor analytic techniques to identify four distinct factors: (a) teachers' responses to error, (b) cognitive processes and strategies, (c) positive interactive teaching, and (d) communicating task-related information (see Table 4.1 for a complete description of the behavioral categories subsumed by each factor). Moely et al. then focused specifically on cognitive processes and strategies, a factor that included instances in which a teacher gives suggestions about

**TABLE 4.1**
**Description of Moely's Coding System**

| Factor Name | Observational Categories |
|---|---|
| *Teachers' Responses to Error* | Asking for information |
| | Providing feedback |
| | Telling the correct answer |
| | Explaining an answer |
| | Providing a hint or rephrasing a question |
| | Encouraging child's effort after an error |
| *Cognitive Processes and Strategies* | Describing or suggesting cognitive processes |
| | Suggesting a strategy |
| | Giving rationale or feedback for strategy use |
| | Suppressing a strategy |
| | Requesting a child's inquiry |
| | Warning or stating a memory goal |
| *Positive Interactive Teaching* | Asking questions |
| | Providing positive feedback during lessons |
| | Acknowledging a correct response |
| | Praising a child's efforts |
| | Communicating content specific information |
| *Communicating Task-Related Information* | Setting a lesson in context of previous work |
| | Stating goals or objectives |
| | Instructing children to remember |

studying or learning such as providing information about ways to approach the task at hand, describing or suggesting the use of specific task strategies, or providing rationales or feedback for strategy use.

Moely and her colleagues (1992) used this instrument to make observations in 69 elementary school classrooms. Over the course of 5 days in each classroom, the teachers were observed during either language arts or during both language arts and mathematics lessons, for an average of 294 30-second observational intervals per teacher. When collapsed across domain, grade, and classroom, the data revealed that the most commonly coded teacher behaviors involved rather traditional teaching activities, as can be seen in the fact that 32.3% of the observational intervals included requests for answers to questions, and 27.1% involved the provision of specific information that was relevant for the ongoing lesson. In contrast, instruction that called for children to engage in cognitive processing and strategy use occurred rather infrequently, being observed in only 9.5% of the intervals. Moreover, strategy suggestions were documented in only 2.3% of the coded intervals, with 10% of the 69 teachers offering no strategy suggestions at all during the observations.

These data paint a picture of the classroom in which teachers are not often involved in direct strategy instruction and therefore raise anew the question of how children come to develop a repertoire of strategies in the context of school if they are not taught to use these techniques. This question becomes all the more salient because in conversations with interviewers, teachers routinely articulate the importance of memory skills for children's success in school, both in terms of learning new information and of relating an ongoing lesson to previously learned material (see Coffman et al., 2008; Ornstein et al., 2009). But with teachers suggesting that memory is important and observational work

(Moely et al., 1992) indicating that there is little strategy instruction in the classroom, what else is there in the setting that enables children to discover strategies that are effective for remembering? To explore this issue, Ornstein and his colleagues (e.g., Coffman et al., 2008; Ornstein et al., 2009, 2010) carried out a longitudinal investigation in which they focused on the memory "talk" that teachers use during the course of instruction and the mnemonic goals that are expressed in their lessons.

In their classroom memory study, Ornstein et al. followed students over the course of the elementary school years, while simultaneously making detailed observations in their classrooms. In the first year of this project, the researchers observed in 14 first-grade classrooms, using a coding instrument, the *Taxonomy of Teacher Behaviors*, that built upon Moely et al.'s (1992) cognitive processes and strategies factor, but focused in greater detail on teachers' language that is relevant to memory and on the provision of metacognitive information.

Over the course of several visits, two researchers observed in each class for a total of one hour of instruction in each of two subject areas, language arts and mathematics. Using this multilevel coding system, one observer employed the *Taxonomy* to make coding decisions every 30 seconds (for a total of 120 intervals in each of mathematics and language arts), while simultaneously a second observer prepared a detailed contextual narrative of each lesson as it was taught. The *Taxonomy* is composed of four main categories of teacher "talk" including: (a) instructional activities, (b) cognitive structuring activities, (c) memory requests, and (d) metacognitive information, and enables the coding of teacher language concerning the nature and extent of various instructional memory-related strategies. In addition, the coding of the contextual narratives enabled later inferences about the nature of the memory goals or demands (either expressed or implied) being communicated by the teacher (see Table 4.2 and Coffman et al., [2008] for a description of the *Taxonomy* and narrative codes).

As can be seen in Table 4.2, the teachers focused their efforts in the classroom largely on instructional activities, with 78.2% of observational intervals containing some form of instruction. Consistent with Moely et al.'s (1992) findings in the context of these lessons, direct instruction in the use of strategies was a rare event, with only 4.9% of the intervals containing a suggestion for the use of a specific technique. In contrast, however, the coding system employed by Ornstein and his colleagues enabled them to observe that there actually was a good deal of memory "talk" in the classroom. Indeed, 52.6% of the intervals included some memory-related request of the children, as for example: "What is 5 plus 3?" and "What book did we read yesterday?" Moreover, the use of the narratives permitted a further characterization of the intervals in which the teachers made these memory-related requests, distinguishing between the relatively rare occasions (5.4% of the intervals) in which memory demands were explicitly stated with words such as *remember* and the more common situations (47.3%) in which the demand

**TABLE 4.2**
**Overall Categories in Ornstein's Taxonomy of Teacher Relevant "Talk"**

| Behavioral Categories | Examples | Mean Percent Occurrence (Range) |
|---|---|---|
| *Instructional Activities* | Book reading, information giving, task instruction | **78.2%** *(66.7% – 85.4%)* |
| *Cognitive Structuring* | Regulating attention, drawing inferences, making connections | **42.6%** *(26.3% – 62.5%)* |
| *Memory Requests* | Retrieval of facts, ideas, or previously experienced events | **52.6%** *(42.5% – 61.3%)* |
| *Metacognitive Information* | Strategy suggestion or replacement, metacognitive questioning | **9.5%** *(2.5% – 19.2%)* |
| **Nature of Memory Demand** | **Definitions** | |
| *Expressed Deliberate* | Direct requests for deliberate remembering such as "remember" or "don't forget" | **5.4%** *(2.1% – 10.4%)* |
| *Implied Deliberate* | Requests for information that do not specifically reference memory (e.g., Who is the president?) | **47.3%** *(36.7% – 56.3%)* |

for the use of memory were implicit without an expressed prompt to remember or not to forget.

Collectively, Moely and Ornstein's characterizations of the classroom context provide a description of an environment in which there is very little in the way of explicit conversations either about the use of specific strategies or remembering in general. Moreover, the findings of Ornstein and his colleagues highlight the fact that memory still permeates the language of the classroom, with over half of the observational intervals containing some form of a deliberate memory request. However, it should also be emphasized that both research groups observed marked variability across classrooms in the teachers' use of strategy suggestions and memory demands, and sought to link these naturally occurring differences in teachers' instructional "styles" to their students' memory performance.

***Linking Contrasting Teacher Styles to Children's Memory Performance*** To explore these associations, Moely et al. (1992) identified 13 first-, second-, and third-grade teachers who were essentially equal in other instructional behaviors, such as the provision of content information and positive feedback to the children, but who differed in the amount of information that they provided about strategies. They then divided this set of teachers into "high" and "low strategy" groups that differed considerably in their provision of (a) suggestions for cognitive processes, or information about how to study or approach a learning task; (b) memory-specific strategies; and (c) rationales for strategy use. Moreover, to examine the consequences of being taught by these two groups of teachers, the memory performance of 64 children drawn from the first, second, and third-grade classrooms of these teachers was contrasted on a variation of the typical sort-recall task that was developed by Moely et al. (1992). With this task, the children were presented with 16 picture cards with line drawings that were taken from four conceptual categories, allowing for the assessment of organizational strategies at both input (e.g., sorting or grouping) and output (e.g., categorical clustering). On the baseline trial, the children were told to do whatever they could to remember the pictures, and their organizational efforts were seen in the extent to which the pictures were

moved into groups of related items during the study phase of the task and the degree to which the categorical structure of the materials was reflected in their recall output. On the following training trial, the children were given explicit instructions on how to use categorization during study (sorting) and recall (clustering) as aids to remembering, and on the final trial new categorical items were presented to assess generalization of the trained strategies.

To examine the children's organizational skills, Moely and her colleagues (1992) focused primarily on their use of clustering in recall as a function of age and classroom styles of the teachers. In this cross-sectional study, there was the expected age-related increase in clustering in recall. More importantly, however, the impact of the classroom environment was seen in the children's response to organizational training, such that children in classrooms taught by "high strategy" teachers were more likely to take advantage of the training than were their peers who were taught by "low strategy" teachers. This contrast was most striking for first graders, such that children with high strategy teachers showed greater use of categorical clustering on the generalization trial than did their peers whose teachers were low in strategy suggestion, indicating that experiences in the first grade may have a unique impact on children's memory performance. Similarly, Moely and her colleagues documented classroom differences in the children's metacognitive knowledge of organizational strategies. Indeed, children from the high-strategy classrooms were more likely to understand the utility of organization than were students drawn from the low-strategy classrooms.

Moving beyond Moely's (1992) focus on teachers' process-oriented instruction and strategy suggestions, Ornstein and his colleagues (e.g., Coffman et al., 2008) emphasized other aspects of teachers' memory "talk" in the classroom, including the memory demands or goals that teachers weave into their lessons. Drawing on their *Taxonomy* as well as the detailed contextual narratives that they obtained, these researchers developed a measure of *mnemonic style*, or the extent to which teachers focused on remembering in their instructional activities. This measure is based upon two simultaneous judgments, those concerning relevant teacher behaviors, as captured by the *Taxonomy* coding, and those reflecting implied or expressed memory demands, as inferred from the classroom narratives. Moreover, the index of mnemonic style reflects the beliefs of Ornstein and his colleagues that general memory demands would likely be of particular importance when teachers (a) engage in instructional activities; (b) provide metacognitive information (such as suggestions or rationales); and (c) encourage children to interact with information in ways that are known to facilitate encoding, storage, and subsequent retrieval (e.g., categorizing, attending, or making links to previous experiences).

Importantly, from the perspective of measuring mnemonic style and examining associations between this characterization of the classroom context and the children's performance, there was considerable variability among the participating teachers in the extent to which remembering was emphasized in their classrooms. For example, the 14 first grade teachers studied by Coffman et al. (2008) varied substantially not only in the instructional techniques that were observed but also in the extent to which these behaviors co-occurred with the imposition of specific memory demands. The provision of *strategy suggestions* across the classrooms varied between 0.8% and 13.8%, and the degree to which the teachers posed *metacognitive questions* ranged from 0.8% to 9.6%. In addition, substantial differences across the classrooms were also seen in the co-occurrence of *deliberate memory demands* and either *instructional activities* (25.8% to 50%), *cognitive structuring activities* (10% to 35.4%), or *metacognitive information* (1.3% to 12.1%). Using the naturally occurring variability across classrooms of these codes, Coffman et al. classified the participating teachers into contrasting high versus low mnemonic style group, based on a median split of the average standard score that was calculated across these multiple codes.

Ornstein (e.g., Coffman et al., 2008; Ornstein, Coffman, et al., 2009; Ornstein, Grammer, et al., 2010) then examined the performance of children nested into each type of first-grade classroom. Importantly, the children drawn from high versus low mnemonic classrooms did not differ on measures of basic memory capacity. This equivalence notwithstanding, by the end of the first-grade year the children in classes taught by teachers with the contrasting mnemonic orientations differed in their use of memory strategies and in the amount of information recalled on a range of tasks. Consider, for example, the performance of the children on the same sort-recall task described above in the discussion of Moely et al.'s (1992) study. Each child received three trials at the first assessment point in the fall of grade 1, baseline, training, and generalization, whereas at each subsequent assessment in the winter and spring only noninstructed generalization trials were administered. Similarly, when the children were in Grade 2, three assessments with noninstructed generalization trials were carried out, one each in the fall, winter, and spring. At all points, performance measures included the number of items recalled and use of categorical sorting and clustering during the study and recall phases of each trial, respectively, as

indexed by the Adjusted Ratio of Clustering (ARC) scores (Roenker, Thompson, & Brown, 1971), which range from −1 (below chance organization), to 0 (chance), to 1 (complete categorization).

Coffman et al. (2008) identified linkages between the classroom context and children's mnemonic skills in Grade 1, and Ornstein, Coffman, et al. (2009; Ornstein, Grammer, et al., 2010) described the continuing influence of the mnemonic style of the first grade teacher on the children's performance in later years. As can be seen in the top and middle panels of Figure 4.1, there were pronounced differences between the groups of children taught by high and low mnemonic teachers, with those assigned to high-mnemonic teachers outperforming their peers with lower mnemonic instructors. Indeed, these patterns of diverging skill in terms of sorting on the basis of meaning and clustering in recall emerged as early as the winter of the first grade, and were

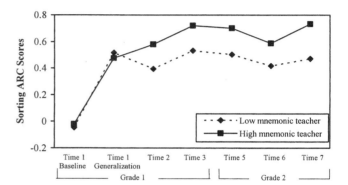

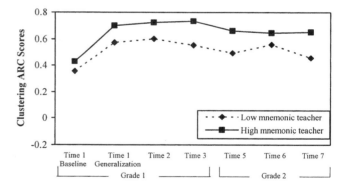

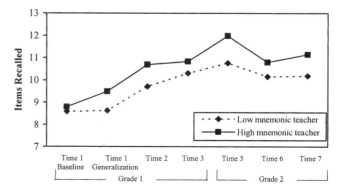

**Figure 4.1** Sorting, clustering, and recall scores as a function of first-grade teacher mnemonic orientation.

maintained across grades 1 and 2. Thus, not only did the mnemonic orientation of the first-grade teachers have an impact on the performance of the children in their classes, but it also evidenced a sustained impact even when the children were being taught by other teachers. Similar but less dramatic patterns are seen in the children's recall performance, illustrated in the bottom panel of Figure 4.1.

***Exploring the Interplay of the Classroom Context, Academic Achievement, and Children's Memory Performance*** In addition to examining the impact of the classroom context on children's mnemonic skill, both Moely and Ornstein and their colleagues also explored child-level factors that may moderate the influence of teachers' mnemonic style. One such factor is academic achievement, and it seems that exposure to a classroom in which remembering is emphasized may be especially important for children who are low achieving.

When Moely et al. (1992) divided their sample into groups of children with high, moderate, and low levels of academic achievement, they found that the classroom context was of particular importance for children with low and moderate levels of achievement, and less critical for those with high levels of achievement. This finding was especially evident in Grade 1, where Moely and her colleagues grouped children on the basis of their scores on the Comprehensive Tests of Basic Skills (1975) into high, moderate, and low achievement groups. They then were able to demonstrate that low- and moderate-achieving students benefited more from exposure to high-strategy classrooms than did high-achieving students. More specifically, first-grade children with low or moderate achievement levels who were also taught by high-strategy teachers increased their use of organization dramatically, from no meaning-based sorting of the to-be-remembered materials at the pretest to high levels of organized sorting on the posttest. Although the high-achieving students with low-strategy

teachers made similar gains from pre- to posttest in their sorting, the low- and moderate-achieving students in the same low-strategy classrooms did not evidence this level of improvement.

Overall, Moely et al.'s (1992) findings suggest that high-achieving students demonstrated elevated levels of strategy use regardless of teacher style, whereas average- and low-achieving students whose teachers were high in strategy suggestions were more likely than their peers with low-strategy teachers to benefit from the strategy instruction, to use organization during recall, to recall more items, and to organize items during study. Moely and her colleagues demonstrated these striking differences at the end of the first-grade year, after the children had been in either a high- or low-strategy classroom for an entire academic year, but were unable to discuss how those children may have performed at the beginning of the year or changed over time from fall to spring. Given the longitudinal nature of their study, Ornstein and his colleagues could track over time the memory skills of groups of children who were identified as higher or lower in academic achievement and were taught by either high- or low-mnemonic first-grade teachers. Consider, for example, findings reported by Ornstein et al. (2009), in which children's sorting performance was presented as a function of their academic achievement level, as assessed by the Woodcock Johnson (WJ-III) (Woodcock, McGrew, & Mather, 2001). The children were categorized as either high or low in their academic achievement, based on a median split of their Broad Reading and Broad Math Clusters percentile ranks, thus establishing a higher-achieving group and lower-achieving group. As can be seen in Figure 4.2, the higher achieving students had elevated patterns of sorting regardless of their first-grade teachers' mnemonic orientation, but the performance of the lower-achieving participants was strongly linked to their teachers' mnemonic style. Most interestingly, by the end of the first grade lower-achieving students who were in high

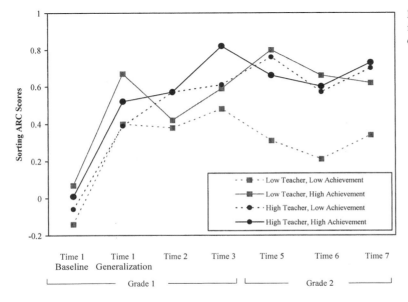

**Figure 4.2** Sorting scores as a function of first-grade teacher mnemonic orientation and children's academic achievement.

mnemonic classrooms were indistinguishable from their higher-rated peers. In contrast, lower-achieving children who had teachers with low-mnemonic orientations showed lower levels of sorting. Moreover, the interplay of first-grade teacher orientation and children's academic achievement learning persisted through the second grade.

## Summary and Concluding Remarks

With increased age, children become more skilled in a wide range of strategies that affect the flow of information within the developing memory system. Mnemonic techniques such as rehearsal and organized sorting influence the encoding of information and the establishment of representations in memory storage, whereas other strategies such as clustering influence retrieval and reporting. Even preschoolers evidence some competence in deliberate memory, often producing simple protostrategies such as focused visual attention and naming when instructed to remember sets of materials. These strategic efforts are typically not associated with gains in remembering, but they nonetheless do indicate that even young children have some genuine metacognitive awareness of the need to "do something" when confronted with tasks requiring remembering. These findings suggest that an understanding of *intentionality* may be an important foundational skill but also indicate that it does not guarantee success in remembering. Additional research, however, demonstrates that strategy *effectiveness* and *consistency* both increase dramatically over the elementary school years and contribute to children's developing strategy repertoire (Folds et al., 1990).

Although the general outlines of an age-related progression in children's skills across the elementary school years are well documented, it is nonetheless the case that most researchers have employed cross-sectional designs and as a result relatively little is known about the course of memory development within individuals (Ornstein & Haden, 2001). Thus, for example, one could ask about the ways in which the initial protostrategies of preschoolers (e.g., naming) are transformed over time into the more sophisticated mnemonic efforts (e.g., active rehearsal) of older children. Although the literature is silent with regard to these types of developmental sequences, recent longitudinal and microgenetic work has shed light on the course of development of specific skills such as organized sorting over limited periods of time (e.g., Schlagmüller & Schneider, 2002; Schneider et al., 2004). Indeed, these studies both confirm the general outline suggested by the cross-sectional literature but also add important qualifications concerning the course of strategy development. In contrast to the impressions of a gradual increase with age in strategic competence that are derived from cross-sectional studies, the longitudinal work indicates that the acquisition of a particular technique is more often than not an abrupt transition, with individual children making this transition at different points in time.

Not only is strategy acquisition less gradual than was initially thought, it also turns out that it is less universal. Indeed, a number of lines of evidence suggest that the development of a repertoire of deliberate memory skills tends to occur primarily in the context of structured environments, such as the elementary school classroom, in which remembering is both expected and valued (e.g., Cole, 1992; Rogoff & Mistry, 1990; Wagner, 1981). But if formal schooling is important for the growth of children's strategic competence, what particular features of the classroom context are linked to skill acquisition? One plausible hypothesis—that teachers provide direct instruction in strategy use—has been ruled out by recent explorations of the classroom, as teachers do not devote much of their teaching time to strategy instruction (Moely et al., 1992; Ornstein et al., 2009). This negative finding, when taken in conjunction with the fact that teachers appear to want their students to develop memory skills, raises many questions about the ways in which children acquire a repertoire of strategies that can be effectively deployed in many settings (Ornstein et al., 2009).

In their explorations of the classroom-based origins of children's mnemonic skills, Moely and her colleagues (1992) and Ornstein and his collaborators (Coffman et al., 2008; Ornstein, Coffman, et al., 2009; Ornstein, Grammer, et al., 2010) chose to examine aspects of the memory-relevant language that teachers use in the course of instruction. In this regard, both research groups observed that the inclusion of memory-related language during instruction was associated with the acquisition of mnemonic techniques. Further, both research groups demonstrated that academic achievement may serve to moderate the impact of the classroom on students' mnemonic skills. Of course, much remains to be learned about these associations between the language of instruction and the development of memory. Consider three sets of interrelated issues—*measurement*, *mechanisms*, and *application*—that need to be addressed in the next wave of research on the impact of the classroom on children's memory development.

In terms of *measurement,* how should teachers' memory talk be characterized? In the research to date, mnemonic style was treated as a dichotomous fashion, but it certainly is more likely a continuous variable, one that can be measured more precisely. Moreover, at the level of mechanisms that underlie *skill acquisition*, just how does exposure to a high mnemonic first grade teacher influence a child's ability to use mnemonic techniques? For example, is it the case that being exposed to the memory language of a high mnemonic teacher permits children to discover strategies on their own, or is some form of generalization operating—say, from lessons in mathematics? Further, at the level of *application*, how can causal statements linking instructional style and child outcomes be made? The data provided by the Moely and Ornstein research groups are based on observational investigations and thus are correlational in nature. Before these findings can be applied in the school context, it is essential to carry out investigations in which instructional style is brought under experimental control.

In closing, it seems clear that with (a) improved measurement of teachers' memory-relevant talk; (b) a better understanding of the principles by which strategies develop in the context of mnemonically rich classrooms; and (c) successful experimental manipulations of teachers' language, this body of knowledge can be readily applied in the service of children's learning. Indeed, it should be possible to instruct teachers in how to present lessons in ways that facilitate the development of children's skills for remembering. In this way, teachers will be able to benefit from basic research in cognitive development and, in the process, affect directly the mnemonic skills of the students in their classes.

# References

Atkinson, R. C., & Shiffrin, R. M. (1968). Human memory: A proposed system and its control processes. In K. W. Spence & J. T. Spence (Eds.), *The psychology of learning and motivation* (Vol. 2, pp. 89–195). New York: Academic Press.

Baker-Ward, L. E., Ornstein, P. A., & Holden, D. J. (1984). The expression of memorization in early childhood. *Journal of Experimental Child Psychology, 37*, 555–575.

Bauer, P. J., & Burch, M. M. (2004). Developments in early memory: Multiple mediators of foundational processes. In J. M. Lucariello, J. A. Hudson, R. Fivush, & P. J. Bauer (Eds.), *The development of the mediated mind* (pp. 101–125). Mahwah, NJ: Erlbaum.

Best, D. L., & Ornstein, P. A. (1986). Children's generation and communication of mnemonic organizational strategies. *Developmental Psychology, 22*, 845–853.

Bjorklund, D. F. (1985). The development of conceptual knowledge in the development of organization in children's memory. In C. J. Brainerd & M. Pressley (Eds.), *Basic processes in memory development: Progress in cognitive development research* (pp. 103–142). New York: Springer-Verlag.

Bjorklund, D. F. (1987). How age changes in knowledge base contribute to the development of children's memory: An interpretive review. *Developmental Review, 7*, 93–130.

Bjorklund, D. F., & Harnishfeger, K. K. (1987). Developmental differences in the mental effort requirements for the use of an organizational strategy in free recall. *Journal of Experimental Child Psychology, 44*, 109–125.

Bjorklund, D. F., Miller, P. H., Coyle, T. R., & Slawinski, J. L. (1997). Instructing children to use memory strategies: Evidence of utilization deficiencies in memory training studies. *Developmental Review, 17*, 411–441.

Bjorklund, D. F., Ornstein, P. A., & Haig, J. R. (1977). Developmental differences in organization and recall: Training in the use of organizational techniques. *Developmental Psychology, 3*, 175–183.

Bjorklund, D. F., & Zeman, B. R. (1982). Children's organization and metamemory awareness in the recall of familiar information. *Child Development, 53*, 799–810.

Boland, A. M., Haden, C. A., & Ornstein, P. A. (2003). Boosting children's memory by training mothers in the use of an elaborative conversational style as an event unfolds. *Journal of Cognition and Development, 4*, 39–65.

Brown, A. L., Day, J. D., & Jones, R. S. (1983). The development of plans for summarizing texts. *Child Development, 54*, 968–979.

Brown, A. L., & Smiley, S. S. (1978). The development of strategies for studying text. *Child Development, 49*, 1076–1088.

Carr, M., Kurtz, B. E., Schneider, W., Turner, L., & Borkowski, J. G. (1989). Strategy acquisition and transfer among American and German children: Environmental influences on metacognitive development. *Developmental Psychology, 25*, 765–771.

Case, R. (1985). *Intellectual development: Birth to adulthood*. New York: Academic Press.

Cavanaugh, J. C., & Borkowski, J. G. (1980). Searching for metamemory-memory connections: A developmental study. *Developmental Psychology, 16*, 441–453.

Cavanaugh, J. C., & Perlmutter, M. (1982). Metamemory: A critical examination. *Child Development, 53*, 11–28.

Coffman, J. L., Ornstein, P. A., McCall, L. E., & Curran, P. J. (2008). Linking teachers' memory-relevant language and the development of children's memory skills. *Developmental Psychology, 44*, 1640–1654.

Cole, M. (1992). Cognitive development and formal schooling: The evidence from cross-cultural research. In L. C. Moll (Ed.), *Vygotsky and education: Instructional implications and applications of sociohistorical psychology* (pp. 89–110). New York: Cambridge University Press.

Cole, M. (2006). Culture and cognitive development in phylogenetic, historical, and ontogenetic perspective. In W. Damon & R. M. Lerner (Series Eds.) & D. Kuhn & R. S. Siegler (Vol. Eds.), *Handbook of child psychology: Vol. 2. Cognition, perception, and language* (6th ed., pp. 636–683). Hoboken, NJ: Wiley.

Cole, M., Frankel, F., & Sharp, D. (1971). Development of free recall learning in children. *Developmental Psychology, 4*, 109–123.

Cole, M., Gay, J., Glick, J., & Sharp, D. W. (1971). *The cultural context of learning and thinking: An exploration in experimental anthropology*. New York: Basic Books.

Corsale, K. (1978). *Factors affecting children's use of organization in recall*. Unpublished doctoral dissertation, University of North Carolina at Chapel Hill.

Corsale, K., & Ornstein, P. A. (1980). Developmental changes in children's use of semantic information in recall. *Journal of Experimental Child Psychology, 30*, 231–245.

DeLoache, J. S., Cassidy, D. J., & Brown, A. L. (1985). Precursors of mnemonic strategies in very young children. *Child Development, 56*, 125–137.

Farrant, K., & Reese, E. (2000). Maternal style and children's participation in reminiscing: Stepping stones in autobiographical memory development. *Journal of Cognition and Development, 1*, 193–225.

Fivush, R., & Fromhoff, F. A. (1988). Style and structure in mother–child conversations about the past. *Discourse Processes, 11*, 337–355.

Fivush, R., Reese, E., & Haden, C. A. (2006). Elaborating on elaborations: Role of maternal reminiscing style in cognitive and socioemotional development. *Child Development, 77*, 1568–1588.

Flavell, J. H., & Wellman, H. M. (1977). Metamemory. In R. V. Kail & J. W. Hagen (Eds.), *Perspectives on the development of memory and cognition* (pp. 3–33). Hillsdale, NJ: Erlbaum.

Folds, T. H., Footo, M., Guttentag, R. E., & Ornstein, P. A. (1990). When children mean to remember: Issues of context specificity, strategy effectiveness, and intentionality in the development of memory. In D. F. Bjorklund (Ed.), *Children's strategies: Contemporary views of cognitive development* (pp. 67–91). Hillsdale, NJ: Erlbaum.

Footo, M., Guttentag, R., & Ornstein, P. A. (1988, April). Capacity demands of strategy execution: Effects of training and practice. In F. Dempster (Chair), *Attentional and capacity constraints on strategy utilization*. Paper presented at the annual meeting of the American Educational Research Association, New Orleans.

Guttentag, R. E. (1984). The mental effort requirements of cumulative rehearsal: A developmental study. *Journal of Experimental Child Psychology, 37*, 92–106.

Guttentag, R. E., Ornstein, P. A., & Siemens, L. (1987). Children's spontaneous rehearsal: Transitions in strategy acquisition. *Cognitive Development, 2*, 307–326.

Haden, C. A., Ornstein, P. A., Eckerman, C. O., & Didow, S. M. (2001). Mother–child conversational interactions as events unfold: Linkages to subsequent remembering. *Child Development, 72*, 1016–1032.

Hedrick, A. M., Haden, C. A., & Ornstein, P. A. (2009). Elaborative talk during and after an event: Conversational style influences children's memory reports. *Journal of Cognition and Development, 10*, 188–209.

Kail, R. (1991). Developmental change in speed of processing during childhood and adolescence. *Psychological Bulletin, 109*, 490–501.

Kurtz, B. E., Schneider, W., Carr, M., Borkowski, J. G., & Rellinger, E. (1990). Strategy instruction and attributional beliefs in West Germany and the United States: Do teachers foster metacognitive development? *Contemporary Educational Psychology, 15,* 268–283.

Lange, G. (1973). The development of conceptual and rote recall skills among school age children. *Journal of Experimental Child Psychology, 15,* 394–406.

Lange, G. (1978). Organization-related processes in children's recall. In P. A. Ornstein (Ed.), *Memory development in children* (pp. 101–128). Hillsdale, NJ: Erlbaum.

Lehmann, M., & Hasselhorn, M. (2007). Variable memory strategy use in children's adaptive intratask learning behavior: Developmental changes and working memory influences in free recall. *Child Development, 78,* 1068–1082.

Leichtman, M. D., Pillemer, D. B., Wang, Q., Koreishi, A., & Han, J. J. (2000). When Baby Maisy came to school: Mothers' interview styles and preschoolers' event memories. *Cognitive Development, 15,* 99–114.

Liberty, C., & Ornstein, P. A. (1973). Age differences in organization and recall: The effects of training in categorization. *Journal of Experimental Child Psychology, 15,* 169–186.

McGuigan, F., & Salmon, K. (2004). The time to talk: The influence of the timing of adult–child talk on children's event memory. *Child Development, 75,* 669–686.

Moely, B. E., Hart, S. S., Leal, L., Santulli, K. A., Rao, N., Johnson, T., et al. (1992). The teacher's role in facilitating memory and study strategy development in the elementary school classroom. *Child Development, 63,* 653–672.

Moely, B. E., Hart, S. S., Santulli, K. A., Leal, L., Johnson, T., Rao, N., et al. (1986). How do teachers teach memory skills? *Educational Psychologist, 21,* 55–71.

Morrison, F. J., Smith, L., & Dow-Ehrensberger, M. (1995). Education and cognitive development: A natural experiment. *Developmental Psychology, 31,* 789–799.

Myers, N. A., & Perlmutter, M. (1978). Memory in the years two to five. In P. A. Ornstein (Ed.), *Memory development in children* (pp. 191–218). Hillsdale, NJ: Erlbaum.

Ornstein, P. A., Baker-Ward, L., & Naus, M. J. (1988). The development of mnemonic skill. In F. E. Weinert & M. Perlmutter (Eds.), *Memory development: Universal changes and individual differences* (pp. 31–49). Hillsdale, NJ: Erlbaum.

Ornstein, P. A., Coffman, J. L., & Grammer, J. K. (2009). Teacher and parent influences on children's use of memory strategies. In O. A. Barbarin & B. H. Wasik (Eds.), *Handbook of child development and early education: Research to practice* (pp. 103–122). New York: Guilford.

Ornstein, P. A., & Corsale, K. (1979). Organizational factors in children's memory. In C. R. Puff (Ed.), *Memory structure and organization* (pp. 219–257). New York: Academic Press.

Ornstein, P., Grammer, J., & Coffman, J. (2010). Teachers' "mnemonic style" and the development of skilled memory. In H. S. Waters & W. Schneider (Eds.), *Metacognition, strategy use, and instruction* (pp. 23–53). New York: Guilford.

Ornstein, P. A., & Haden, C. A. (2001). Memory development or the development of memory? *Current Directions in Psychological Science, 10,* 202–205.

Ornstein, P. A., Haden, C. A., & Hedrick, A. M. (2004). Learning to remember: Social-communicative exchanges and the development of children's memory skills. *Developmental Review, 24,* 374–395.

Ornstein, P. A., Haden, C. A., & San Souci, P. P. (2008). The development of skilled remembering in children. In J. H. E. Byrne (Ed.) & H. Roediger, III (Vol. Ed.), *Learning and memory: A comprehensive reference: Vol. 4. Cognitive psychology of memory* (pp. 715–744). Oxford, England: Elsevier.

Ornstein, P. A., Medlin, R. G., Stone, B. P., & Naus, M. J. (1985). Retrieving for rehearsal: An analysis of active research in children's memory. *Developmental Psychology, 21,* 633–641.

Ornstein, P. A., & Myers, J. T. (1996). Contextual influences on children's

remembering. In K. Pezdek & W. Banks (Eds.), *The recovered memory/false memory debate* (pp. 211–223). New York: Academic Press.

Ornstein, P. A., & Naus, M. J. (1978). Rehearsal processes in children's memory. In P. A. Ornstein (Ed.), *Memory development in children* (pp. 69–99). Hillsdale, NJ: Erlbaum.

Ornstein, P. A., & Naus, M. J. (1985). Effects of the knowledge base on children's memory strategies. In H. W. Reese (Ed.), *Advances in child development and behavior* (Vol. 19, pp. 113–148). New York: Academic Press.

Ornstein, P. A., Naus, M. J., & Liberty, C. (1975). Rehearsal and organizational processes in children's memory. *Child Development, 46,* 818–830.

Ornstein, P. A., Naus, M. J., & Stone, B. P. (1977). Rehearsal training and developmental differences in memory. *Developmental Psychology, 13,* 15–24.

Paris, S. G., Newman, R. S., & McVey, K. A. (1982). Learning the functional significance of mnemonic actions: A microgenetic study of strategic acquisition. *Journal of Experimental Child Psychology, 34,* 490–509.

Peterson, C., Jesso, B., & McCabe, A. (1999). Encouraging narratives in preschoolers: An intervention study. *Journal of Child Language, 26,* 49–67.

Pressley, M. (1982). Elaboration and memory development. *Child Development, 53,* 296–309.

Pressley, M., Borkowski, J. G., & Schneider, W. (1987). Cognitive strategies: Good strategy users coordinate metacognition and knowledge. In R. Vasta & G. Whilehurst (Eds.), *Annals of child development* (Vol. 4, pp. 80–129). Greenwich, CT: JAI Press.

Pressley, M., Borkowski, J. G., & Schneider, W. (1989). Good information processing: What it is and how education can promote it. *International Journal of Educational Research, 13,* 857–897.

Reese, E., Haden, C. A., & Fivush, R. (1993). Mother–child conversations about the past: Relationships of style and memory over time. *Cognitive Development, 8,* 403–430.

Roenker, D., Thompson, C., & Brown, S. (1971). Comparisons of measures for the estimation of clustering in free recall. *Psychological Bulletin, 76,* 45–48.

Rogoff, B. (1981). Schooling and the development of cognitive skills. In H. C. Triandis & A. Heron (Eds.), *Handbook of cross-cultural psychology* (Vol. 4, pp. 233–294). Boston: Allyn & Bacon.

Rogoff, B., & Mistry, J. (1990). The social and functional context of children's remembering. In R. Fivush & J. A. Hudson (Eds.), *Knowing and remembering in young children* (pp. 197–222). New York: Cambridge University Press.

Rohwer, W. D. (1973). Elaboration and learning in childhood and adolescence. In H. W. Reese (Ed.), *Advances in child development and behavior* (Vol. 8, pp. 1–57). New York: Academic Press.

Rossi, E. (1964). Development of classificatory behavior. *Child Development, 35,* 137–142.

Schlagmüller, M., & Schneider, W. (2002). The development of organizational strategies in children: Evidence from a microgenetic longitudinal study. *Journal of Experimental Child Psychology, 81,* 298–319.

Schneider, W. (1985). Developmental trends in the metamemory—Memory behavior relationship: An integrative review. In D. L. Forrest-Pressley, G. E. MacKinnon, & T. G. Waller (Eds.), *Metacognition, cognition, and human performance* (Vol.1, pp. 57–109). New York: Springer-Verlag.

Schneider, W., & Bjorklund, D. F. (1998). Memory. In W. Damon, R. S. Siegler, & D. Kuhn (Eds.), *Handbook of child psychology* (Vol. 2, pp. 467–521). New York: Wiley.

Schneider, W., Borkowski, J. G., Kurtz, B., & Kerwin, K. (1986). Metamemory and motivation: A comparison of strategy use and performance in German and American children. *Journal of Cross-Cultural Psychology, 17,* 315–336.

Schneider, W., Kron, V., Hunnerkopf, M., & Krajewski, K. (2004). The development of young children's memory strategies: First findings from the Würzburg longitudinal memory study. *Journal of Experimental Child Psychology, 88,* 193–209.

Schneider, W., & Pressley, M. (1997). *Memory development between 2 and 20*. New York: Springer-Verlag.

Schneider, W., Schlagmüller, M., & Vise, M. (1998). The impact of metamemory and domain specific knowledge on memory performance. *European Journal of Psychology of Education, 13*, 91–103.

Schneider, W., & Sodian, B. (1997). Memory strategy development: Lessons from longitudinal research. *Developmental Review, 17*, 442–461.

Sharp, D., Cole, M., & Lave, C. (1979). Education and cognitive development: The evidence from experimental research. *Monographs of the Society for Research in Child Development, 44* (1–2, Serial No.178).

Siegler, R. S. (1996). *Emerging minds: The process of change in children's thinking*. New York: Oxford University Press.

Siegler, R. S. (2006). Microgenetic analyses of learning. In W. Damon & R. M. Lerner (Series Eds.) & D. Kuhn & R. S. Siegler (Vol. Eds.), *Handbook of child psychology: Vol. 2. Cognition, perception, and language* (6th ed., pp. 464–510). Hoboken, NJ: Wiley.

Sodian, B., & Schneider, W. (1999). Memory strategy development: Gradual increase, sudden insight, or roller-coaster? In F. E. Weinert & W. Schneider (Eds.), *Individual development from 3 to 12: Findings from the Munich Longitudinal Study* (pp. 61–77). Cambridge, England: Cambridge University Press.

Sodian, B., Schneider, W., & Perlmutter, M. (1986). Recall, clustering, and metamemory in young children. *Journal of Experimental Child Psychology, 41*, 395–410.

Tessler, M., & Nelson, K. (1994). Making memories: The influence of joint encoding on later recall by young children. *Consciousness and Cognition, 3*, 307–326.

Wagner, D. A. (1974). The development of short-term and incidental memory: A cross-cultural study. *Child Development, 45*, 389–396.

Wagner, D. A. (1978). Memories of Morocco: The influence of age, schooling, and environment on memory. *Cognitive Development, 45*, 389–396.

Wagner, D. A. (1981). Culture and memory development. In H. Triandis & A. Heron (Eds.), *Handbook of cross-cultural psychology* (Vol. 4, pp. 187–232). Boston: Allyn & Bacon.

Weinert, F. E., & Schneider, W. (Eds.). (1999). *Individual development from 3 to 12*. Cambridge, MA: Cambridge University Press.

Wellman, H. (1988). The early development of memory strategies. In F. E. Weinert & M. Perlmutter (Eds.), *Memory development: Universal changes and individual differences* (pp. 3–29). Hillsdale, NJ: Erlbaum.

Woodcock, R. W., McGrew, K. S., & Mather, N. (2001). *Woodcock-Johnson III*. Itasca, IL: Riverside.

# 5

# Learner-Centered Practices

*Providing the Context for Positive Learner Development, Motivation, and Achievement*

B<small>ARBARA</small> M<small>C</small>C<small>OMBS</small>

## Introduction

For decades educators have grappled with how schools can provide not only for the academic achievement of students but also promote their positive social and emotional development. Schools provide a vital social context for overall student development as well as for equipping them with the knowledge and skills to be productive citizens in a democratic society. The ways in which schools can provide this positive social context have been studied extensively over the last century. One consensus is emerging about practices that can achieve these educational goals, in the form of research-validated principles distributed by the American Psychological Association (APA, 1997); for example, *The Learner-Centered Psychological Principles: A Framework for School Reform and Redesign.* These principles continue to be validated in current research and provide a foundation for learner-centered practices at all levels of schooling. They also provide a framework for addressing the needs of teachers as learners.

### From Learner-Centered Principles and Practices to Teacher Professional Development

As I explore the evidence for how the APA Learner-Centered Principles (LCPs) and their associated practices provide a context for positive learner development, motivation, and achievement, I will focus on our work using the LCPs to guide the professional development of teachers. In this work we have discovered that there are a number of evidence-based tools teachers can use to address their needs as learners. These tools help them learn about what their students need and what impact their own teaching practices are having on student learning and motivation. Teachers learn to self-assess their beliefs, essential teacher characteristics, and perceptions of their own teaching practices. They also learn how to reflect deeply on ways in which their perceptions of teaching practices differ from those of their students

and what changes they could make to more positively impact desired academic and nonacademic student outcomes.

### Overview of the Chapter

This chapter is organized to first provide the research base for the LCPs. This research base comes from over a century of research on learning, motivation, development, and individual differences. The chapter then moves to a discussion of the distinctions between learner-centered practices derived from the LCPs and what have been called child- and person-centered approaches in earlier periods of educational reform. Next, the chapter links learner-centered principles and practices to recent reports and research summaries showing parallels between characteristics of engaging schools and the key qualities of learner-centered classrooms and schools that our research has uncovered. The remaining parts of the chapter describe our research on translating the LCPs to classroom and school practice and how best to use the LCPs to guide teacher professional development, followed by implications of this research for new learner-centered directions in school reform.

### The Research and Theory Base for the LCPs

To determine the contributions of research-validated "learner-centered" practices to positive classroom contexts and, in turn, enhanced student learning and motivational outcomes, it is necessary to first understand what has been learned in a century of research.

*The APA Learner-Centered Psychological Principles (LCPs)* The LCPs, shown in Table 5.1, serve as the foundation for the Learner Centered Model (LCM) that colleagues and I developed over the past decade (McCombs, 1999, 2003a, 2003b, 2004a; McCombs & Lauer, 1997; McCombs & Miller, 2007, 2008; McCombs & Whisler, 1997). Based on years of research, the LCPs were adopted by the APA

**TABLE 5.1**
**The Learner-Centered Psychological Principles**

| Principle | Description |
|---|---|
| **Cognitive and Metacognitive Factors** | |
| Nature of the learning process | The learning of complex subject matter is most effective when it is an intentional process of constructing meaning from information and experience. |
| Goals of the learning process | The successful learner, over time and with support and instructional guidance, can create meaningful, coherent representations of knowledge. |
| Construction of knowledge | The successful learner can link new information with existing knowledge in meaningful ways. |
| Strategic thinking | The successful learner can create and use a repertoire of thinking and reasoning strategies to achieve complex learning goals. |
| Thinking about thinking | Higher order strategies for selecting and monitoring mental operations facilitate creative and critical thinking. |
| Context of learning | Learning is influenced by environmental factors, including culture, technology, and instructional practices. |
| **Motivational and Affective Factors** | |
| Motivational and emotional influences on learning | What and how much is learned is influenced by the learner's motivation. Motivation to learn, in turn, is influenced by the individual's emotional states, beliefs, interests and goals, and habits of thinking. |
| Intrinsic motivation to learn | The learner's creativity, higher order thinking, and natural curiosity all contribute to motivation to learn. Intrinsic motivation is stimulated by tasks of optimal novelty and difficulty, relevant to personal interests, and providing for personal choice and control. |
| Effects of motivation on effort | Acquisition of complex knowledge and skills requires extended learner effort and guided practice. Without learners' motivation to learn, the willingness to exert this effort is unlikely without coercion. |
| Developmental and social factors | |
| Developmental influence on learning | As individuals develop, they encounter different opportunities and experience different constraints for learning. Learning is most effective when differential development within and across physical, intellectual, emotional, and social domains is taken into account. |
| Social influences on learning | Learning is influenced by social interactions, interpersonal relations, and communication with others. |
| **Individual Differences Factors** | |
| Individual differences in learning | Learners have different strategies, approaches, and capabilities for learning that are a function of prior experience and heredity. |
| Learning and diversity | Learning is most effective when differences in learners' linguistic, cultural, and social backgrounds are taken into account. |
| Standards and assessment | Setting appropriately high and challenging standards and assessing the learner and learning progress—including diagnostic, process, and outcome assessment—are integral parts of the learning process. |

*Note.* Summarized from the APA Work Group of the Board of Educational Affairs (1997, November). *Learner-centered psychological principles: Guidelines for school reform and redesign.* Washington, DC: American Psychological Association.

(1997) as a definition of the psychological principles with the greatest positive effect on learners and learning. The 14 Learner Centered Principles, organized into four categories or domains, define much of what is known about learning and learners as a result of research into both. Many of these principles are consistent with recent discoveries from psychology relating to positive youth development and prevention interventions (e.g., Blum, McNeely, & Rinehart, 2002; Catalano, Haggerty, Oesterle, Flemming, & Hawkins, 2004; Libbey, 2004; Seligman & Csikszentmihalyi, 2000).

### Background and History
The American Psychological Association (APA) adopted the Learner-Centered Psychological Principles (LCPs) in 1993 largely as a response to what the APA considered

ill-informed decisions being made based on *A Nation at Risk* that had been published in 1983.[1] *A Nation at Risk* concluded that student achievement in the United States showed an alarming decline, especially in comparison with other countries such as Japan. As a consequence, political leaders began responding with a call for greater accountability and higher standards for education. The APA was concerned that the push toward testing and accountability was not informed by evidence regarding what best supports and fosters learning. Members of the APA Task Force working on the LCPs believed that psychology, as a scientific field that has studied learning for over 100 years, had a responsibility to clearly present to educators and policymakers its accumulated and research-validated knowledge base about learning and learners.[2]

In 1989, the National Governors' Association was asked to meet with presidential committees to formulate the National Education Goals, which later became Goals 2000[3] and then the America 2000 national education goals. Discussions began about the need for national standards in all academic disciplines, with increased debates about the need for national and state assessments that could provide greater levels of accountability for student achievement of rigorous academic standards. Members of the Task Force were committed to exploring how school reform could be informed by contributions of psychology in understanding the learner in different learning contexts.

When work on the LCPs began, no one knew what the final product would look like or what it would be called. The Task Force saw it as a "living document" that would be revised and reissued as more was learned about learning, motivation, development, and individual differences that must be addressed to achieve optimal learning for all (APA, 1993). The LCP document is now in its second iteration and continues to be widely disseminated to educators and researchers in this country and abroad (APA, 1997).

***The LCPs and their Domains Addressing Learners and Learning***   Taken together, the four domains of the LCPs offer a holistic way of looking at how individual principles combine and interact to influence learners and learning. Research findings on which the LCPs are based confirm the four domains as follows (McCombs, 2004a, 2007):

- *Cognitive and metacognitive*—what the intellectual capacities of learners are and how they facilitate the learning process.
- *Motivational and affective*—the roles played by motivation and emotions in learning.
- *Developmental and social*—the influence of various diverse aspects of learner development and the importance of interpersonal interactions in learning and change.
- *Individual differences*—how individual differences influence learning, how teachers, students, and administrators adapt to learning diversity, and how standards and assessment can best support individual differences in learners.

Each of the four domains affects each learner in a unique way, as does the synergy resulting from the interaction of the domains.

***Empirical Studies Supporting the LCP Domains***   When the original LCP document was being developed, the process and studies that were reviewed to arrive at the principles and their domains were summarized (McCombs, 1994). In the more than a decade since the original LCPs were developed, studies continue to confirm the validity and usefulness of the four domains. The following sections cite some of the more important recent sources of support.

*Cognitive and Metacognitive Principles*   The six principles in this domain address the nature of the learning process as an intentional process of constructing meaning, which requires instructional support and guidance for learners to acquire and retain knowledge. It is a process in which learners link new information with existing knowledge, that is facilitated by a variety of thinking and reasoning strategies for thinking critically about the subject matter. It is also facilitated by higher order metacognitive strategies for monitoring and regulating the learning process, as well as by a variety of contextual factors in the classroom, school, and community environments that include technology and innovative instructional practices. These six principles have been supported by a variety of researchers, most recently Bransford, Brown, and Cocking (1999) and a variety of reports from the National Research Council (1999, 2000, 2001, 2002) related to research on how people learn.

*Motivational and Affective Principles*   The three principles in this domain acknowledge the role of motivation, curiosity, and emotion in learning, including emotional states, self-beliefs, interests and goals, and habits of thinking. The nature and importance of intrinsic motivation to creativity and higher order thinking, and the conditions that stimulate intrinsic motivation (e.g., novelty, relevance, optimal difficulty, choice and control), are summarized. Finally, the role of motivation in stimulating effort in learning is explained. These three principles continue to be supported in the research of a variety of motivation researchers, including Ames (1992), Bandura (1997), Brophy (1998), Deci and Ryan (2002), Dweck (1999), Eccles, Wigfield, and Schiefele (1998), Kanfer and McCombs (2000), Maehr and Midley (1991), Meece (1991), Oldfather and McLaughlin (1993), and Zimmerman and Schunk (2001).

*Developmental and Social Principles*   The two principles in this domain focus first on the development process across physical, intellectual, emotional, and social areas and how this process uniquely unfolds within and across individuals, thereby influencing learning in ways that educators need to be knowledgeable about. The second principle focuses on the broad area of social influences on learning, including the social interactions, interpersonal relationships, and communication with others in the educational environment, home environment, and broader community. Again, research has continued to verify the importance of developmental and social influences on learning, including the work of Daniels and Perry (2003), Dweck (1999), Flock, Repetti, and Ullman (2005), Eccles and Wigfield (1992), Harter (1999), Meece (2002, 2003), Pianta (1999), and Ryan and Deci (2000).

*Individual Differences Principles*   The three principles in the domain cover the general topics of the range of individual differences learners bring to learning situations, including those that are a function of prior experience and those that are a function of heredity. The need to adapt to these diverse differences that also include linguistic, cultural, and social backgrounds is highlighted. Finally, it is recommended that individual differences be addressed by setting appropriately high and challenging standards and assessing the learner and learning process with a variety of formative and summative assessment methodologies. Current research confirms these principles and further refines what is known about addressing individual differences in ways that maximize learning and motivation. This includes the work of Amrein and Berliner (2003), Darling-Hammond (1997), Gordon (2004), Graham, Taylor, and Hudley (1998), Klem and Connell (2004), Moses and Chang (2006), the National Study Group for the Affirmative Development of Academic Ability (2004), Neill (2003), Stiggins (1996), and Wiggins (1993).

## Defining Learner-Centered Practices

The term *learner-centered* often connotes specific images for both researchers and practitioners. For some, it means individualizing instruction for every learner; for others, it means focusing on affective, motivational, and social-emotional needs. From a research-validated perspective, however, the definition of "learner-centered" is both straightforward and complex (McCombs & Miller, 2006). On the one hand, it describes the processes individuals engage in during learning, resulting from the unique combination of factors they bring to any learning situation: heredity; temperament; experiential history; beliefs, values, and perspectives; talents; interests; capacities; and prior learning experiences and needs.

On the other hand, "learner-centered" is a focus on the "best available knowledge about learning and how it occurs and about teaching practices that are most effective in promoting the highest levels of motivation and achievement" (McCombs & Whisler, 1997, p. 9). This includes research evidence showing that the most highly motivated learning of all, self-motivated learning, occurs only when learners possess (1) choice and control about how, what, and when to learn; and (2) choice and control over what they want to achieve (cf. Connell & Wellborn, 1991; Deci & Ryan, 1985, 1991; Deci, Vallerand, Pelletier, & Ryan, 1991; Kanfer & McCombs, 2000; Zimmerman & Schunk, 2001).

Putting both parts of the concept together, "learner centered" can be understood as the combination of a focus on individual learners with a focus on the best available knowledge we have about learning and the teaching practices that support learning for all—teachers and students alike.

### *Distinctions between Learner- and Child-Centered Classrooms* From the broad perspective of a century of research, not only are all people individual learners but they are also learners for life. Although this isn't always evident, particularly in some school settings, the same basic principles of learning, motivation, development, and individual differences apply to all of us. In the progressive and child-centered movements that gained popularity in the last half of the 20th century, educators and researchers focused on the child or student. In the vision of progressive education (Dewey, 1938), the distinctive talents of individual children were recognized and environments were created

to actualize those potentialities. This vision also meant that teachers designed experiences that allow students to respond not just in cognitive ways, but also emotionally, imaginatively, and socially. Assessment focused on more than academic outcomes and also included more formative measures of what is best to nourish the positive learning and development of the whole child.

The basic argument for the education of the whole child (or whole person) is that in human organisms, there are no independent parts—all are interconnected. Those favoring child- and person-centered approaches argued for motivationally and emotionally supportive learning contexts and putting the needs of the child above even academic concerns (e.g., Combs, 1986, 1991; Fielding, 2000; Lambert & McCombs, 1998; Rogers & Freiberg, 1994). For some researchers and educators, this approach was too soft, too "touchy-feely" and it began to be replaced with a more rigorous focus on learning. There was a lack of integration between those approaches focused on the child, student, person, or learner and those focused on the learning process and the strategies that could deepen and challenge the quality of learning.

A review of alternative educational models examined learner-centered, progressive, and holistic education (Martin, 2002). The growing numbers of diverse alternative schools are in keeping with social values that include pluralism and diversity, a more sustainable world, and a just democracy (e.g., democratic and free schools, folk education, Quaker schools, homeschools, Krishnamurti schools, Montessori education, open schools, Waldorf schools). Similarly, in discussing results with his School Development Program, Comer (2005) maintains that the key to improving academic achievement is to link it to child and adolescent development. From Comer's work, school cultures that promote positive growth in physical, social, ethical, emotional, linguistic, and cognitive ways remove the brain's response to threat by the "fight or flight" phenomenon. Cultures that promote belonging provide for comfort, confidence, competence, and motivation to learn—findings also verified in the research of Deci and Ryan (1991, 2002) and others (Harde & Reeve, 2003; Klem & Connell, 2004; Legault, Green-Demers, & Pelletier, 2006; Osterman, 2000).

For these types of school cultures to be created requires that the resistance to accepting child and adolescent development, or psychological principles in general, be overcome through strategies that allow teachers to be involved in collecting their own data and evaluating the outcomes. It is then that educators will see, as did those who implemented Comer's School Development Program, that new learner-centered practices yield quick gains in a host of student outcomes (Comer, 2005). Models such as these address needs of the whole child in balance with the needs of the community and society at large (e.g., Caring School Community project described by Battistich, Soloman, Watson, & Schaps, 1997; findings from the Social Development Research Group described by Catalano et al., 2004). They hold in common a respect for diversity and different philosophical beliefs about what it means to live, learn, love, and grow in today's society.

***Letting Research and Theory Guide the Definition*** Another issue in the debate over the years about what defines "learner-centered" was the lack of sound research evidence for person- or learner-centered approaches. As that evidence began to accumulate and more integrative perspectives were applied, a new theoretical perspective supported by the research began to surface. This theoretical perspective focused on both the learner and the learning process (e.g., Alexander & Murphy, 1998; Bransford et al., 1999; Marshall, 1992, 1996; McCombs, 1995, 1999, 2001, 2003b). The emerging consensus is that a focus on both learners and learning is vital in producing the broad range of academic and nonacademic outcomes valued from the experience of schooling (e.g., Cornelius-White, 2007; Klem & Connell, 2004; Zins, Weissberg, Wang, & Walberg, 2004). I turn next to a look at how learner-centered principles and practices are linked to current research reports on characteristics of schools that establish positive classroom contexts for promoting learning and motivation.

## What the LCPs Imply for School and Classroom Contexts: Links with Current Research

In national studies conducted by the National Research Council (2003) and the Just for the Kids (2003) organization, current research is continuing to verify the importance of practices that are consistent with the LCPs. Among the many recommendations coming out of these studies, the first key is to focus on the student, followed by high-quality teaching and research-based instructional practices. Teachers must also be given the materials, training, and support they need and the time to plan together, discuss student progress, and reflect on best practices. In one such high performance school in Los Angeles, teachers work together to help students take risks so that they develop character and the skills to succeed in life (Mathews, 2004, January 20). As with the Central Park East program, students were taught to develop their minds by weighing evidence, seeing other ways of looking at the same data or situation, comparing and contrasting, seeking patterns, conjecturing and arguing (Meier, 2002). This type of transformational learner-centered paradigm can help students develop into the creative and critical thinkers, self-directed learners, problem solvers, time managers, and lifelong learners needed in our complex society.

***Addressing the Learning Needs of the Whole Learner*** Another strong link with current national studies (e.g., National Research Council, 2003) is in keeping with the implication of the LCPs that education must address the whole learner. This is certainly not a new idea (e.g., Combs, 1986, 1991; Noddings, 1988, 2005). The evidence base for this approach was less clear in earlier years than now, making a stronger case for positive outcomes that extend beyond

academic achievement. William Glasser (1990), author of choice theory and Quality Schools, has maintained that students will be more motivated to work harder and learn more, or have lower dropout rates, when we create more need-satisfying schools. These new schools will provide environments where students can really get to know their peers and teachers and develop a sense of trust, potentially also avoiding school violence issues. It is essential that students have an opportunity to study real world problems and learn for understanding in self-directed ways. In the new school paradigm, Patterson (2003) argues that decisions will be made based on what makes educational and personal sense for students. Combining this model with general education that contributes to the development of citizenship in a democratic society increases the usefulness and long-term impact of this model. All of these new paradigms combine academic and social-emotional curricula in ways that address the whole learner (Zins et al., 2004).

Addressing the whole learner also includes teachers as learners. Although it is unlikely that policymakers will stop mandating change and reducing external pressures anytime soon, Adelman and Walking-Eagle (1997) stress the importance of communicating research that demonstrates the efficacy of reform efforts that acknowledge teachers' needs as learners. Networks and expanded relationships as support systems are also vital. Lieberman and Grolnick (1997) see these as ongoing learning tools for teachers that can foster learning and a deepening understanding of the ingredients of learning that are needed for themselves and their students—a wide array of learning opportunities, inquiry methods, access to real problems to solve, acknowledgment of the importance of building on prior experiences, and the opportunities to work with, collaborate, and be mentored by others.

The needs of learners, including teachers as learners, are also changing. Learner alienation is becoming an issue of concern, given its relationships to problems such as school dropout and teacher departures from the profession. Ryan and Deci (2000) maintain that alienation in any age population is caused by failing to provide supports for competence, autonomy, and relatedness. Preparing teachers to meet these needs for themselves and their students is essential to healthy development and to creating contexts that engender individual commitment, effort, and high-quality performance. Unfortunately, there are too many examples in the current educational reform agenda of coercive and punitive consequences for students, teachers, and administrators when students fail to achieve educational standards on state and national tests. The time has come for a research-based model that addresses these learner needs while also addressing rigorous and high standards of performance for all learners.

***Building Practices on Research-Validated Principles*** There are many principles validated by research that have both theoretical and practical significance. For example, it has long been recognized that humans have a need and tendency to form social connections (e.g., Deci & Ryan, 1985; McCombs, 2007). Humans also have common qualities such as empathy, kindness, compassion, love, friendship, and hope that represent their spirituality. Sociality is foundational to these qualities in the sense that in social relationships these qualities emerge and/or are developed. Many researchers emphasize these more complex metaphors in describing the human mind and behavior. They move us away from the mechanical or solitary computer metaphors that do not do justice to the interconnectivity of humans (e.g., Cacioppo, Hawkley, Rickett, & Masi, 2005).

The fundamental cause of current imbalances in our educational models and philosophies can be clarified by situating human learning principles within the larger framework of human and systems functioning. The "industrial paradigm" that characterizes most 21st century organizations, including schools and school systems, reflects the mismatch between principles of nature and human functioning, and institutions. Wielkiewicz and Stelzner (2005) argue that the industrial paradigm be replaced with an ecological paradigm. Principles that define ecological systems include: interdependence (components with bidirectional influences, such as subgroups within the organization, families, communities); open systems and feedback loops (dependence on inflow of materials, resources, and information from internal and external systems such as the economic, political, social, and environmental systems that surround the organization); cycling of resources (making multiple uses of resources such as human talents without relying on a single individual); and adaptation (providing structures and processes for adaptive learning to meet challenges and changes in technology, economics, student populations, etc.). In the ecological perspective from Wielkiewicz and Stelzner's (2005) view, leadership is an emergent process in keeping with learner-centered principles and practices that share leadership among all learners. Others present similar ecological views that see the school as a series of networks and overlapping systems of interaction, ideally structured to support goal-directed and engaged learning behaviors as part of the individual–environment relations at the multiple levels of individuals, classroom, schools, school districts, and the larger surrounding community (Barab & Roth, 2006; Eccles & Roeser, 1999). In Eccles and Roeser's (1999) view, there are a number of classroom and school practices that impact students' learning experiences, including teacher beliefs, teacher–student relationships, school climate, and schoolwide practices such as academic tracking and the quality of school resources.

Addressing the mismatch between learning principles and education systems brings into focus a range of pressing issues schools face today. One big issue is that as many as 33% of new teachers leave within 3 years and another 46% leave in the first 5 years (Rubalcava, 2005). Many teachers go into teaching because they want to connect with students as individuals, create a sense of community, and help students develop their personal creativity and talents—goals that are very different from teaching realities.

Although new teachers pick self-actualization and socialization goals, current school policies focus on economic efficiency, testing, accountability, and predetermined content objectives (Kim & Sunderman, 2005). In learner-centered environments, however, Rubalcava (2005) found teachers are able to balance current policies with nurturing students' emotional health and creativity. They engage students in critical thinking and creative expression, using strategies such as cultural exchanges, environmental projects, story writing, integrated physical education, and inquiry based collaborative learning. Helping new teachers connect meaningfully with their students is the key to the success of any of these strategies.

***Producing Positive Development, Motivation, and Achievement across the School-Age Years*** Decades of research have confirmed the importance of student–teacher relationships in impacting student motivation, social outcomes, and classroom learning (e.g., Davis, 2006; Deci et al., 1991; Klem & Connell, 2004; Pianta, 1999; Pianta, La Paro, Payne, Cox, & Bradley, 2002; Pianta & Stuhlman, 2004; Wentzel, 1997, 2002). Low levels of conflict and high levels of closeness and support define good relationships. Through a good relationship with teachers, students experience their academic work as meaningful, personal, complementing their goals, and promoting their understanding. This is in contrast with poor relationships where students see their academic work as coercive, repetitive, isolated, irrelevant, and contrary to their social and academic goals. Positive teacher–student relationships teach students how to regulate their behavior and affect as well as develop social competence (Ryan & Deci, 2000).

In a meta-analysis of person- and learner-centered education models, Cornelius-White (2007) found these models are associated with large increases in student participation and initiation ($r = .55$), satisfaction ($r = .44$), and motivation to learn ($r = .32$), indicating high levels of engagement in learner-centered classrooms. Cornelius-White (2007) credits Carl Rogers as being the founder of the person-centered approach, which focuses in education on the goal of facilitating the whole and fully functioning person (e.g., Rogers, 1983; Rogers & Freiberg, 1994). There were also positive effects on self-esteem ($r = .35$) and social connections and skills ($r = .32$) and reductions in dropout ($r = .35$), disruptive behavior ($r = .25$) and absences ($r = .25$). This meta-analysis also found support for the importance of student perspectives as predictors of student success relative to teacher perspectives. The major teacher variables associated with positive student outcomes include positive relationships, nondirectivity, empathy, warmth, and encouraging thinking and learning skills. Cornelius-White (2007) also found that learner-centered practices may work better with minority teachers and learners, suggesting that these universal variables are particularly important for students who traditionally do not receive this level of support.

The foregoing findings and their underlying principles apply to all learners across economic, social, and cultural lines. A recent national study of low SES and minority elementary students indicated that the most powerful school characteristics for promoting resiliency (academic success) included a supportive school environment model that was safe and orderly and promoted positive student–teacher relationships (Borman & Overman, 2004). Students in these environments also display greater engagement in academic activities, a stronger sense of math efficacy, higher self-esteem, and a more positive outlook toward school (Phillips, 1997). This is particularly needed in today's culture with fewer stable family and social institutions to promote resilience.

In spite of clear evidence about the effectiveness of learner-centered teaching, the use of evidence-based, learner-centered principles and practices is not yet widespread. Instead, the well-publicized focus of current efforts has been on cognitive outcomes and the academic achievement of content standards. However, this focus has not led to desired increases in student achievement in the majority of American schools, nor has it stemmed the ever-increasing dropout rates endemic to many schools (e.g., Amrein & Berliner, 2003; Barton, 2006). Further, engagement in school learning and academic achievement are declining for large numbers of school-age children (National Research Council, 2003). Social problems, including school dropout, are on the rise, along with associated problems of absenteeism, disruptive behaviors, and even school violence (Blum, 2005). As currently structured, the educational system is obviously out of balance. Encouraging the widespread use of learner-centered practices can restore faith in schools as places where people are encouraged to learn meaningful and relevant skills that will serve them well as active participants in society.

***Defining Classroom and School Contexts from Learner Perspectives*** Our experience has been that putting the learner centered model into practice results in increased motivation, learning, and academic achievement for a much larger number of students, including many who are currently underachieving or dropping out (McCombs & Miller, 2007). Utilizing the learner centered model in the classroom means that teachers discover the unique learner perspectives and characteristics of their students. In addition, they discover the teaching and learning characteristics of teachers who are the most successful in providing the learning contexts and experiences that motivate their students to the highest achievement levels and the pursuit of learning beyond school and throughout their lifetimes.

As a strategy to help reduce rising dropout rates, Cushman (2006) presents the voices of students who speak out for a meaningful curriculum. Compared with students in suburban schools, urban students had far fewer opportunities to participate in challenging and interesting courses. They also had fewer opportunities to participate in extracurricular activities and as a result, they found school to be boring. To help get them interested in school again, many urban students express that they would like a voice

in determining what courses are offered, respect for their nonacademic interests, inspiring role models, and opportunities to connect with the community. In Cushman's study, students were not trying to avoid academic challenge but they were asking for schoolwork that builds on what they know and care about. They want schoolwork that stretches their thinking and relates to their interests. They want teachers who respect them and their needs, relate to them as partners and colearners, and provide role models that foster their interest in school and academic subjects. As motivation experts have long posited, students need a sense of agency, purpose, and meaning that will help them with the major task of adolescence, which is to form a personal identity and sense of purpose (cf. Deci & Ryan, 2002; Dweck, 1999; Harter, 2006).

## How Positive Learner Development, Motivation, and Achievement Are Addressed

Williams (2003) argues persuasively that both student input and decades of research into human resilience document the power of caring teachers and schools to develop young people who can successfully overcome risks and challenges. These teachers convey high expectations and provide opportunities for students to be active participants in their own learning process. Caring teachers provide not only opportunities for students to achieve academic skills but also present a confident and positive model for character development. Caring teachers are compassionate, interested in, actively listen to, and get to know the gifts and talents of individual students (Noddings, 2005; Wentzel, 1997, 2002; Williams, 2003). They hold strong beliefs in all students' innate resilience and capacity to learn. They are, according to Williams (2003), student-centered and understand that successful learning means engaging the whole child. They connect learning to students' lives, culture, and strengths. They give students a voice and opportunities to make choices as well as opportunities to work with and help others through strategies such as reciprocal peer tutoring and service-learning. The fundamental characteristic of schools that can make the difference between risk and resilience is the quality of relationships between teachers and students—a hallmark and foundation of the learner-centered classroom and school. With a focus on relationships, they also build small learning communities where the need to belong is met—findings confirmed in the National Research Council (2003) report on characteristics of engaging schools.

In urban schools, in particular, Corbett, Wilson, and Williams (2005) argue that great teachers believe it is their job to make sure that all students succeed. These teachers use a variety of best practices—cooperative groups, checking for understanding, hands-on activities, connecting new content to prior knowledge, and other strategies consistent with the LCPs—but it was their attitudes that really made the difference in helping students succeed, according to results of a 3-year study of teachers in two urban school districts by Corbett et al. (2005). When kids were asked about these teachers, they liked the strict approaches and high expectations because they know these teachers care and want them to have a good education. These teachers also give students a lot of responsibility to make choices and participate in meaningful activities. Thus, this study supports what we consistently find with LC practices: it isn't about the practices alone; it's also about the beliefs, attitudes, and characteristics of teachers that provide the support for all students to succeed.

The Caring Schools Community Project is a prime example of a program consistent with the LCPs that has been rigorously evaluated for over 20 years (Battistich et al., 1997; Developmental Studies Center, 2005). In a study of 14,000 socioeconomically diverse students in 12 program and 12 comparison schools in six school districts across the United States, students in the program schools exhibited greater liking for school, stronger academic motivation, higher sense of efficacy, stronger commitment to democratic values, more frequent reading of books outside of school, more concern for others, and less alcohol and marijuana use. Follow-up studies with students in the high implementing schools showed that students continued to have higher grades in core academic classes, higher achievement test scores, a greater sense of community, higher educational aspirations, more liking for school, greater trust in and respect for teachers, and less misconduct and delinquent behavior. All these findings are consistent with those we have found in schools that meet our learner-centered rubric, the next major topic of this chapter.

***Researching Learner-Centered Principles and Practices in School Contexts***  In our work with research-validated learner-centered principles, we have learned that learner-centered practices do not look the same from school to school, classroom to classroom, day to day, or even moment to moment within the same classroom. When teachers are attentive to learners and their learning needs, and understand basic principles of human learning, motivation, development, and individual differences, they "go with the flow" and create innovative environments that are flexible and dynamic. The most learner-centered teachers we have studied are not afraid to share power and control with students in a collaborative learning partnership (McCombs & Miller, 2007). The learner-centered framework adds a constant reminder that the human element cannot be left out of even the most advanced educational systems, including technology-supported networked learning communities (cf. McCombs & Vakili, 2005).

***Understanding the LCPs as a Framework for Practice at all Levels of Schooling***  The LCPs define domains of factors that impact learning, motivation, and development across the lifespan. In school settings, they are reflected in the beliefs, characteristics, dispositions, and practices of teachers. Although programs and practices at school and classroom levels do not need to have a particular form or look a particular way, there are a number of qualities that

define learner-centeredness from the students' perspectives as well as their maximum levels of learning and motivation (McCombs, 2004b; McCombs & Lauer, 1997). Learners are included in these practices in educational decision making, their diverse perspectives are respected and encouraged, their individual developmental differences are adapted to, and they are treated as partners in the teaching and learning process.

***Defining the Learner-Centered Model (LCM) and Its Components***  When translating the LCPs into practice, the LCM consists of a variety of materials, guided reflection, and assessment tools that support teacher effectiveness and change at the individual and school levels. Staff development workshops and videos exemplify learner-centered practices in diverse school settings. As an additional support for teachers changing their practices, my colleagues and I (McCombs, 1999, 2001, 2003a; McCombs & Lauer, 1997, 1998; McCombs & Whisler, 1997) developed a set of self-assessment and reflection tools for K–20 teachers, called the Assessment of Learner-Centered Practices (ALCP). The ACLP includes surveys for teachers, students, and administrators that facilitate reflection and a willingness to change instructional practices. The teacher surveys offer an opportunity for reflection on how personal beliefs about learners, learning, and teaching coincide with the knowledge base underlying the LCPs. More importantly, they allow teachers to become aware of their students' perceptions about the frequency of their teacher's learner-centered practices.

***Development and Validation of the ALCP Teacher and Student Surveys***  A major impetus for the development of the ALCP teacher and student surveys was to provide teachers with tools for self-assessment and reflection. The emphasis of this work has been to identify profiles of effective beliefs, practices, and discrepancies between teacher and student perspectives as a tool for assisting teachers to reflect on and to change their practices. The process has focused on desired student learning and motivational outcomes and on those teacher beliefs and practices that most contribute to maximizing these outcomes.

*Development and Validation Process*  The development of teacher and student surveys began in 1994 with the generation of a pool of approximately 180 items per survey, developed by a team of educators and researchers (McCombs & Lauer, 1997). Items were generated to assess teachers' beliefs and assumptions about learning, learners, and teaching that were consistent with the LCPs as well as those that were reflective of a more traditional teacher-centered perspective. Similarly, items to assess teachers' perceptions of classroom practices were developed based on evidence-based practices representative of the five domains represented by the LCPs. This was followed by the generation of parallel classroom practice items from the students' perspectives. Ongoing data collection from over

35,000 students and their teachers in kindergarten through graduate school have now been collected with the ALCP surveys (McCombs, 1999, 2001; McCombs & Lauer, 1997; McCombs & Pierce, 1999; McCombs & Quiat, 2002) to validate developmentally appropriate versions of the ALCP surveys. The goal of this validation process was to identify empirically those teacher qualities and classroom practices that enhance the teaching and learning process. Validated versions of the student and teacher ALCP surveys now exist for grades K–3, 4–8, 9–12, and college levels.

In our more than 10 years of research with the LCM and its associated tools, we have verified the benefits of learner-centered practices at the school and classroom levels. Specific teacher and student scales have been identified along with a validated rubric defining the range of scores on these scales that define learner-centered practice. Research with the ALCP self-assessment surveys for teachers and students confirms that "learner-centeredness" is not solely a function of particular instructional practices or programs. Rather, learner-centeredness is a complex interaction of the programs, practices, policies, and people as perceived by the individual learners.

***Summary of Research with ALCP Self-Assessment Tool*** Results with the ALCP teacher and student surveys on samples of over 35,000 students and their teachers across the elementary and postsecondary levels continue to substantiate that (1) student perceptions of their teacher's instructional practices are significantly related to their motivation, learning, and achievement; and (2) student perceptions of a positive learning environment and relationship with the teacher are the most important practices for enhancing student motivation and achievement. Thus, at all levels of the educational system, teachers can be helped to change toward more learner-centered practices by attending to what students are perceiving and creating positive climates and relationships—critical connections for personal and system learning and change (McCombs, 2001; Weinberger & McCombs, 2003).

In our research (McCombs, 2004a, 2004b), qualities related to being perceived by students as engaging in high levels of learner-centered practice in domains most related to high achievement and motivation include: high learner-centered beliefs (consistent with the APA principles) and low non-learner-centered beliefs (more traditional), high levels of self-efficacy about their ability to reach and teach diverse learners, high reflective self-awareness, and high degrees of autonomy support. In schools and districts where the LCPs have been widely shared, teaching practices are achieving a more balanced approach that encourages high student learning and achievement while also promoting learner-centered approaches.

***Grades K–3 Results*** The most important finding with K–3 teachers and students is that even young children can reliably and validly assess the degree to which their teachers engage in learner-centered practices. For young children,

there are three validated domains that most relate to positive learning and motivation outcomes: (1) creates positive interpersonal relationships/climate; (2) provides motivational support for learning; and (3) facilitates thinking and learning. Results indicated that when students perceived more learner-centered teacher practices, they had higher academic achievement and also reported greater interest in and liking of school and academic subjects (McCombs, Perry, & Daniels, 2008).

***Grades 4–8 Results*** With upper elementary and middle school students, learner-centered practices begin to have stronger impacts on learning and motivation. Four domains of practice have been validated to most impact learning, motivational, and behavior outcomes: (1) creating positive relationships; (2) honoring student voice; (3) supporting higher order thinking and learning skills; and (4) adapting to individual differences (McCombs, 2004b; McCombs & Quiat, 2002; Meece, Herman, & McCombs, 2003). At this developmental stage, students' perceptions of classroom practices are more strongly related to valued outcomes than teachers' perceptions.

***Grades 9–12 Results*** For high school students, the importance of learner-centered practices continues to increase. At this level, although there are different items from the grades 4-8 level, the same four domains of practice exist (McCombs, 2004b). The findings show that students' perceptions that their teachers frequently perform the four learner-centered domains of classroom practice are significantly correlated with all motivation variables, and are particularly highly related to student self-efficacy, epistemic (knowledge-seeking) curiosity, active learning strategies, and task mastery goals. In addition, students' perceptions that their teachers significantly perform these four domains of practice are positively correlated with classroom achievement and negatively correlated with classroom absences.

## How the LCPs Were Used to Guide Teacher Professional Development

As we have learned in our research and as Fullan (1997) has noted, when successful school reform efforts are analyzed, the critical differences are in (1) *how* these practices are implemented and in (2) whether there is explicit and shared attention given to individual learners and their unique cognitive, social, and emotional learning needs. We have learned that using the ALCP self-assessment and reflection tools to encourage the development of learner-centered teacher dispositions can help balance this focus on learners with a focus on challenging academic content and standards and attention to social and emotional development.

***The Concept of Teacher as Learner*** To guide teacher professional development, the LCPs provided key concepts, notably a recognition that the principles apply to teachers as learners. Licklider (1997) argues for a model of continuing professional development in which teachers take responsibility for their own growth and learning. She sees professional development as a person-centered model based on participant needs, structured in ways that encourage inquiry, collaboration with others, and opportunities for mentoring and practice. In our work with the *Learner-Centered Psychological Principles* as they apply to teacher education, we believe this model applies to both teacher preparation programs and higher education faculty (Lambert & McCombs, 1998; McCombs & Whisler, 1997). The process needs to begin with teachers articulating their beliefs and assumptions and building an awareness of the need for change, followed by modeling of effective strategies, and then application with the support of mentors and the larger learning community. Finally, teachers' expertise and experience needs to be honored.

One of the most powerful implications of the LCPs translated into practice is the confirmation that in the school setting, teachers, students, parents, and administrators are continually in the process of learning with and from each other. Research underlying the LCPs validates that learning is nonlinear, recursive, continuous, complex, relational, and natural in humans. The key processes in developing learner-centered practices for teachers are:

- building ways to meet teacher needs for interpersonal relationships and connections;
- finding strategies that acknowledge individual differences and the diversity of teacher needs, abilities, and interests;
- tailoring strategies to differing teacher needs for personal control and choice; and
- assessing the efficacy of instructional practices to meet diverse and emerging individual teacher and learning community needs.

As an overriding principle, when teachers experience the LCPs in practice in their own learning and change process, the "truth" of these principles for students becomes clear. The benefits of faculty and students sharing academic goals and working together have been recognized at all educational levels (Summers, Beretvas, Svinicki, & Gorin, 2005). They lead to the development of a sense of community, which has been shown to have a number of positive benefits, including reduced high school dropout rates and increased student retention at the college level, as well as meeting basic human needs for connectedness.

***The Self-Assessment and Guided Reflection Process*** A shift in assessment practices to support such a learning culture is advocated by Shepard (2000). She argues that it is essential to move the current paradigm to one that blends current ideas from cognitive, constructivist, and sociocultural theories to prevent the corruption of the standards movement into a heavy-handed system of rewards and punishments. Dynamic, ongoing assessments that can

help determine what a student is able to do independently and with adult guidance are needed to guide optimal development. By placing learners in communities of practice, individuals can become increasingly adept and competent while developing robust understandings of concepts. Good assessments, Shepard argues, are those that help students rethink old understandings, draw new connections, and create new applications. Self-assessments that help students monitor their own progress also help them share responsibility for learning with teachers while developing increased ownership of their own learning. The evaluation of teaching should include helping teachers make their own investigations and reflections visible to students as part of the teaching and learning dialogue. For these changes to occur, however, teacher development must include an understanding of motivation and how to develop classroom cultures where learning and learners are at the center. Attention to helping teachers reflect on their beliefs is required in order to undergo a personal change process.

Using the ALCP teacher and student surveys, K–20 teachers can be assisted in reflecting on individual and class discrepancies in perceptions of classroom practice and in changing practices to meet student needs (McCombs, 2001). Our research with the ALCP has confirmed that teachers and instructors can be helped to improve instructional practices and change toward more learner-centered practices. Reflection on ALCP feedback helps teachers become aware of students' perceptions. It raises their consciousness of the importance of spending time creating positive climates and relationships as well as supporting meaningful learning—critical connections so important to personal and system learning and change.

We also found that teachers who are more learner-centered are more successful in engaging all students in an effective learning process, and are, themselves, more effective learners and happier with their jobs (McCombs, 2000, 2001). Furthermore, teachers report that the process of self-assessment and reflection helps them identify areas in which they might change their practices to be more effective in reaching more students. This is an important finding that relates to the "how" of transformation. Helping teachers to engage in a process of self-assessment and reflection—particularly about the impact of their beliefs and practices on individual students and their learning and motivation—a respectful and nonjudgmental impetus to change is provided. Combining the opportunity for teacher self-assessment of and reflection on their beliefs and practices (and the impact of these practices on individual students) with skill training and dialogue about how to create learner-centered K–20 schools and classrooms can help make the transformation complete.

Our ongoing research has also revealed that teachers are not absolutely learner-centered or completely non-learner-centered (e.g., McCombs, 2001, 2004a, 2004b; Weinberger & McCombs, 2001). Different learner-centered teachers have different but overlapping beliefs. At the same time, however, specific *beliefs or teaching practices* can be classified as learner-centered (likely to enhance motivation, learning, and success) or non-learner-centered (likely to hinder motivation, learning, and success). We have established a research-validated learner-centered rubric that defines the score ranges for teachers who have the highest motivated and highest achieving students at grades K–3, 4–8, 9–12, and the college level. Learner-centered teachers see each student as unique and capable of learning, have a perspective that focuses on the learner (knowing that this promotes learning), understand basic principles defining learners and learning, and honor and accept the student's point of view. As a result, the student's natural inclinations to learn, master the environment, and grow in positive ways are enhanced.

In our current work, we define "seamless professional development" as a process in which self-assessment and reflection on the knowledge base about learners and learning are connected to self-evaluations of practice from the learners' perspectives at all levels of the K–20 system (McCombs, 1999, 2001, 2004a). The ALCP surveys provide tools at the college level that instructors take to assess and reflect on their practices relative to their students, and preservice teacher education students also use the K–12 ALCP surveys to evaluate themselves during their field experiences. Practicing K–12 teachers use the tools to continually assess and improve their practices, and the information is fed back to higher education to refine courses and methods in teacher preparation and other departments. Hence, "seamless professional development" refers to the continual cycle of assessment, reflection, refinement, learning, and improvement.

## Implications for School Redesign and Reform

In discussing why school reform efforts have often failed, Rich (2005) argues that they were based on mistaken and misleading assumptions. They include the assumption that schools are the primary source of education, test scores are the best measures of student achievement, punishment works to help students learn, raising standards means students will meet them, and better teaching in schools can close the achievement gap. In line with the message of the LCPs, Rich (2005) contends that the impact of school reform initiatives depends on the positive attitudes, behaviors, and habits that students bring into the classroom as well as the ones they learn in classrooms and schools. Recognizing the importance of these social and emotional factors in addition to more academic factors is what Rich considers the most critical lever in effective school reform.

A number of researchers (Amrein & Berliner, 2003; Neill, 2003) are increasingly arguing that high-stakes testing will not improve schools. Rather, just the opposite seems to be the case. Research is consistently showing that a focus on high-stakes testing narrows curriculum and "dumbs down" instruction. As a result, students disengage, and many drop out mentally, emotionally, or physically. Worse, many schools are induced to push students out, increase grade retention, force many teachers to leave, and

impede real and needed improvements. The bottom line is that those students most in need of quality schools are those who are the most hurt.

In over a decade of research, evidence shows that those states without high-stakes tests had (a) more improvement in average scores on the National Assessment of Educational Progress (NAEP) than states with such tests; (b) improvement at a faster rate on a variety of standardized tests; and (c) higher motivation and lower dropout rates (Amrein & Berliner, 2003). In fact, researchers have found that the stakes attached to performance on these tests lead to less intrinsic motivation to learn and lower levels of critical thinking (Neill, 2003). In environments where the focus is on student performance on high-stakes tests, teachers are less inclined to encourage students to explore concepts and subjects of interest to them, thus obstructing students' paths to becoming lifelong, self-directed learners. Further, high-stakes testing does not adequately deal with low income and non-English speaking students and can lead to teaching to the test and inflated or misleading test scores. More effective approaches include engaging students in self-evaluation and meaningful feedback in the form of formative assessment that provides them with information on their learning progress, all of which is of particular benefit to low achievers.

Darling-Hammond and Ifill-Lynch (2006) cite that by ninth grade, 40% of urban students fail multiple classes and that 50% or more leave school without graduating. Of those who enter high school, many lack the learning and study skills they need to be good students (e.g., knowing how to take notes, study on their own, engage in classwork, and finish their homework). Consistent with research by motivation researchers (e.g., Covington & Teel, 1996; Dweck, 1999; Meece, Herman, & McCombs, 2003), to protect their self-esteem, many adolescents maintain they don't care about school and the boring or "stupid" work they have to do. Darling-Hammond and Ifill-Lynch (2006) contend that an effective approach to engaging students with their schoolwork is to create a strong academic culture that changes students' beliefs and behaviors. A big part of this culture is work that students find relevant, meaningful, and authentic such as inquiry- and project-based learning based on successful approaches such as reported by Deborah Meier (2002) at Central Park East. Involving students and making them part of the solution is also very effective, along with meeting alone or in teams with students to emphasize their strengths and areas where they have been successful, using collaboration as a key strategy where students and their teachers can work together, as well as helping those students who work to get credit with work-based learning plans. In short, Darling-Hammond and Ifill-Lynch (2006) propose learner-centered approaches that recognize the learning and life needs of struggling students.

*A New Model: The Learner-Centered Educational System as an Intellectual Supply Chain* A number of colleagues and I have been working over the past 2 years to develop the Center for Innovation Competencies (CIC).[4] Our work is driven by the vision of creating and implementing a transformed learner-centered educational systems model. To this end, we have developed a framework called the intellectual supply chain (ISC). The ISC supports the LCPs and is a system for integrating all key stakeholders in education and the workplace so that each has input at every level. The major goal of the ISC is the alignment of all functions, content, and processes across the educational system and the workplace in order to nurture and further develop the natural human capacities of collaboration, learning, and creativity (CLC). Together, these capacities form a meta-competency necessary for a positive and productive life in all aspects of the personal, interpersonal, life work, and broader social-economic system levels. The end result of the ISC is an educational system that will be more responsive to technological changes and the need for innovation in the global economy.

Our vision for the CIC grew out of our shared understanding and concern over the fundamentally flawed current public education system and the policies surrounding its operation. We observed that the public education system is presently incapable of developing the intellectual capital and innovation that will drive the economy in the 21st century. We reviewed empirical evidence showing that schools willing to step outside the narrow testing and accountability agenda and implement practices consistent with research-validated principles of human learning, motivation, development, and individual differences are achieving higher levels of student learning across academic and social-emotional domains. Thus, we verified that the balance of high achievement and positive personal development is possible.

The challenge is to capture these best practice principles into a new educational systems design that prepares all learners (students and adults alike) to be lifelong learners and innovators in the workplace and in life. The positive outcomes at an individual level can transfer to the ultimate establishment of new human social, economic, and political systems on a global scale. These new systems further promise a more competent, more productive, more collaborative, and more creative world. The long-range goal of the CEI is to create a transformed view of educational systems that transfers to enlightened corporate settings. These systems must be grounded in an understanding of nature's natural sorting system and principles of human learning, motivation, development, and individual differences.

***The Alignment of Processes and Structures to Balance Learning and Accountability*** For schools and districts with whom the LCPs have been widely shared, teaching practices are achieving a more balanced approach that encourages high student learning and achievement while also promoting learner-centered approaches. These learner-centered approaches, recognized in many of the nation's most excellent schools, reflect both conventional and scientific wisdom that can lead to effective schooling and

to positive mental health and productivity of our nation's children, their teachers, and the systems that serve them. They create a new vision of schooling.

A further vision is created by adding the new metacompetency and ISC, implemented in keeping with the LCPs and the LCM. This transformed educational system is based on learner-centered, organic, and ecological principles. It trusts human capacity to deal with complex and ill-defined problems of learning and life. It builds upon, yet goes beyond, currently known collaborative processes that allow the system to evolve and emerge. It follows from and expands upon existing research that is already moving us in exciting directions and that can balance concerns with higher levels of learning and accountability.

## Summary and Conclusions

This chapter examined what defines "learner-centered" from historical, theoretical, and empirical perspectives. It also looked at what learner-centered practices contribute to positive classroom and school contexts, including how the LCPs can be used to guide teacher professional development. In keeping with the purpose of this *Handbook*, it is clear from our research and that of others that the learner-centered model and its self-assessment assessment tools provide a useful way to study the effects of schooling. Based on the research-validated learner-centered psychological principles, the research base demonstrates how the provision of classroom practices in keeping with the principles clearly has a positive effect on student learning and motivation. An important future step is to conduct rigorous longitudinal studies of how these learner-centered practices impact students' development throughout the school years. From what we have learned in our research, I would predict that more attention to the principles and practices that define "learner-centeredness" throughout the school years can contribute greatly to the overall positive academic, emotional, and social development of our children and adolescents.

## Notes.

1. U.S. Department of Education. (April 1983). *Nation at risk: the imperative for educational reform.* Retrieved from http://www.ed.gov/pubs/NatAtRisk/index.html.
2. The research that is summarized in the APA *Principles* derives from many fields, including psychology, education, sociology, and brain research. Research documentation can be found in Alexander and Murphy (1998), Combs, Miser, and Whitaker (1999); Kanfer and McCombs (2000); Lambert and McCombs (1998); McCombs (2000, 2001, 2004a); McCombs and Miller (2007); McCombs and Whisler (1997); and Perry and Weinstein (1998). Copies of the *Principles* may be downloaded from http://www.education@apa.org.
3. H.R. 1804. Goals 2000: Educate America Act. Retrieved from http://www.ed.gov/legislation/GOALS2000/TheAct/
4. Michael Beyerlein and Susan Beyerlein, University of North Texas; Jill Nemiro, Cal Poly Pomona; Marty Bink and Ann Rinn, Western Kentucky University; Barbara McCombs, University of Denver.

## References

Adelman, N. E., & Walking-Eagle, K. P. (1997). Teachers, time, and school reform. In A. Hargreaves (Ed.), *Rethinking educational change with heart and mind: 1997 ASCD Yearbook* (pp. 92–110). Alexandria, VA: Association for Supervision and Curriculum Development.

Alexander, P. A., & Murphy, P. K. (1998). The research base for APA's learner-centered psychological principles. In N. Lambert & B. L. McCombs (Eds.), *How students learn: Reforming schools through learner-centered education* (pp. 287–308). Washington, DC: American Psychological Association.

Ames, C. (1992). Classrooms, goals, structures, and student motivation. *Journal of Educational Psychology, 84*, 261–271.

Amrein, A. L., & Berliner, D. C. (2003). The effects of high-stakes testing on student motivation and learning. *Educational Leadership, 60*(5), 32–38.

APA Task Force on Psychology in Education. (1993, January). *Learner-centered psychological principles: Guidelines for school redesign and reform.* Washington, DC: American Psychological Association and Mid-Continent Regional Educational Laboratory.

APA Work Group of the Board of Educational Affairs. (1997, November). *Learner-centered psychological principles: A framework for school reform and redesign.* Washington, DC: American Psychological Association.

Bandura, A. (1997). *Self-efficacy: The exercise of control.* New York: Freeman.

Barab, S. A., & Roth, W. M. (2006). Curriculum-based ecosystems: Supporting knowing from an ecological perspective. *Educational Researcher, 35*(5), 3–13.

Barton, P. E. (2006). The dropout problem: Losing ground. *Educational Leadership, 63*(5), 14–18.

Battistich, V., Soloman, D., Watson, M., Schaps, E. (1997). Caring school communities. *Educational Psychologist, 32*(3), 137–151.

Blum, R. W. (2005). A case for school connectedness. *Educational Leadership, 62*(7), 16–20.

Blum, R. W., McNeeley, C. A., & Rinehart, P. M. (2002). *The untapped power of schools to improve the health of teens.* Minneapolis, MN: Center for Adolescent Health and Development, University of Minnesota.

Borman, G. D., & Overman, L. T. (2004). Academic resilience in mathematics among poor and minority students. *Elementary School Journal, 104*, 177–195.

Bransford, J., Brown, A., & Cocking, R. (Eds.). (1999). *How people learn: Brain, mind, experience, and school* (Committee on Developments in the Science of Learning Commission on Behavioral and Social Sciences and Education National Research Council). Washington, DC: National Academy Press.

Brophy, J. (1998). *Motivating students to learn.* Boston, MA: McGraw-Hill.

Cacioppo, J. T., Hawkley, L. C., Rickett, E. M., & Masi, C. M. (2005). Sociality, spirituality, and meaning making: Chicago health, aging, and social relations study. *Review of General Psychology, 9*(2), 143–155.

Catalano, R. F., Haggerty, K. P., Oesterle, S., Flemming, C. B., & Hawkins, J. D. (September, 2004). The importance of bonding to school for healthy development: Findings from the Social Development Research Group. *Journal of School Health, 74*(7), 252–261.

Combs, A. W. (1986). What makes a good helper? A person-centered approach. *Person-Centered Review, 1*(1), 51–61.

Combs, A. W. (1991). *The schools we need: New assumptions for educational reform.* Lanham, MD: University Press of America.

Combs, A. W., Miser, A. B., & Whitaker, K. S. (1999). *On becoming a school leader: A person-centered challenge.* Alexandria, VA: Association for Supervision and Curriculum Development.

Comer, J. P. (2005). Child and adolescent development: The critical missing focus in school reform. *Phi Delta Kappan, 86*(10), 757–763.

Connell, J. P., & Wellborn, J. G. (1991). Competence, autonomy, and relatedness: A motivational analysis of self-system processes. In M. R. Gunnar & L. A. Sroufe (Eds.), *Self-processes in development: Minnesota Symposium on Child Psychology* (Vol. 23, pp. 43–77). Chicago, IL: University of Chicago Press.

Corbett, D., Wilson, B., & Williams, B. (2005). No choice but success. *Educational Leadership, 62*(6), 8–12.

Cornelius-White, J. (2007). Learner-centered teacher-student relationships are effective: A meta-analysis. *Review of Educational Research, 77*(1), 113–143.

Covington, M. V., & Teel, K. M. (1996). *Overcoming student failure: Changing motives and incentives for learning.* Washington, DC: APA Books.

Cushman, K. (2006). Help us care enough to learn. *Educational Leadership, 63*(5), 34–37.

Daniels, D. H., & Perry, K. E. (2003). "Learner-centered" according to children. *Theory into Practice, 42*(2), 102–108.

Darling-Hammond, L. (1997). *The right to learn: A blueprint for creating schools that work.* San Francisco, CA: Jossey-Bass.

Darling-Hammond, L., & Ifill-Lynch, O. (2006). If they'd only do their work! *Educational Leadership, 63*(5), 8–13.

Davis, H. A. (2006). Exploring the contexts of relationship quality between middle school students and teachers. *Elementary School Journal: Special Issue on the Interpersonal Contexts of Motivtion and Learning, 206*, 193–223.

Deci, E. L., & Ryan, R. M. (1985). *Intrinsic motivation and self-determination in human behavior.* New York: Plenum.

Deci, E. L., & Ryan, R. M. (1991). A motivational approach to self: Integration in personality. In R. Dienstbier (Ed.), *Nebraska symposium on motivation: Vol. 38. Perspectives on motivation* (pp. 237–288). Lincoln: University of Nebraska Press.

Deci, E. L., & Ryan, R. M. (2002). Overview of self-determination theory: An organismic dialectical perspective. In E. L. Deci & R. M. Ryan (Eds.), *Handbook of self-determination research* (pp. 3–33). Rochester, NY: University of Rochester Press.

Deci, E. L., Vallerand, R. J., Pelletier, L. G., & Ryan, R. M. (1991). Motivation and education: The self-determination perspective. *Educational Psychologist, 26*(3 & 4), 325–346.

Developmental Studies Center. (2005). Summary of evaluation findings on the Child Development Project. Retrieved from http://www.devstu.org/cdp/pdfs/cdp_eval_summary.pdf (The Caring School Community Project was previously known as the Child Development Project)

Dewey, J. (1938). *Experience and education.* New York: Macmillan.

Dweck, C. S. (1999). *Self-theories: Their role in motivation, personality and development.* Philadelphia, PA: Psychology Press.

Eccles, J. S., & Roeser, R. (1999). School and community influences on human development. In M. Bornstein & M. Lamb (Eds.), *Developmental psychology: An advanced textbook* (4th ed., pp. 503–554). Mahwah, NJ: Erlbaum.

Eccles, J. S., & Wigfield, A. (1992). The development of achievement-task values: A theoretical analysis. *Developmental Review, 12*, 265–310.

Eccles, J. S., Wigfield, A., & Schiefele, U. (1998). Motivation to succeed. In N. Eisenberg (Ed.), *Social, emotional, and personality development handbook of child psychology* (Vol. 3, pp. 1017–1096). New York: Wiley.

Fielding, M. (2000). The person centered school. *Forum, 42*(2), 51–54.

Flock, L., Repetti, R., & Ullman, J. (2005). Classroom social experiences as predictors of academic performance. *Developmental Psychology, 41*(2), 319–327.

Fullan, M. (1997). Emotion and hope: Constructive concepts for complex times. In A. Hargreaves (Ed.), *Rethinking educational change with heart and mind: ASCD Yearbook* (pp. 216–223). Alexandria, VA: Association for Supervision and Curriculum Development.

Glasser, W. (1990). *The quality school: Managing students without coercion.* New York: Harper Perennial.

Gordon, E. W. (2004). Closing the gap: High achievement for students of color. *Research Points, 2*(3), 1–4.

Graham, S., Taylor, A. Z., & Hudley, C. (1998). Exploring achievement values among ethnic and minority early adolescents. *Journal of Educational Psychology, 90*, 606–620.

Harde, P. L., & Reeve, J. (2003). A motivational model of rural students' intentions to persist in, versus drop out of, high school. *Journal of Educational Psychology, 95*(2), 347–356.

Harter, S. (2006). *The cognitive and social construction of the developing self.* New York: Guilford.

Just for Kids. (2003). *Texas get results.* Austin, TX: Author.

Kanfer, R., & McCombs, B. L. (2000). Motivation: Applying current theory to critical issues in training. In S. Tobias & D. T. Fletcher (Eds.), *Handbook of training* (pp. 85–108). New York: Macmillan.

Kim, J. S., & Sunderman, G. L. (2005). Measuring academic proficiency under the No Child Left Behind act: Implications for educational equity. *Educational Researcher, 34*(8), 3–13.

Klem, A. M., & Connell, J. P. (2004). Relationships matter: Linking teacher support to student engagement and achievement. *Journal of School Health, 74*(7), 262–273.

Lambert, N., & McCombs, B. L. (Eds.). (1998). *How students learn: Reforming schools through learner-centered education.* Washington, DC: APA Books.

Legault, L., Green-Demers, I., & Pelletier, L. (2006). Why do high school students lack motivation in the classroom? Toward an understanding of academic motivation and the role of social support. *Journal of Educational Psychology, 98*(3), 567–582.

Libbey, H. P. (2004, September). Measuring student relationships to school: Attachment, bonding, connectedness and engagement. *Journal of School Health, 74*(7), 274–283.

Licklider, B. L. (1997). Breaking ranks: Changing the inservice institution. *NASSP Bulletin, 81*(585), 9–22.

Lieberman, A., & Grolnick, M. (1997). Networks, reform, and the professional development of teachers. In A. Hargreaves (Ed.), *Rethinking educational change with heart and mind: 1997 ASCD Yearbook* (pp. 192–215). Alexandria, VA: Association for Supervision and Curriculum Development.

Maehr, M. L., & Midgley, C. (1991). Enhancing student motivation: A schoolwide approach. *Educational Psychologist, 26,* 399–428.

Marshall, H. H. (1992). *Redefining student learning: Roots of educational change.* Norwood, NJ: Ablex.

Marshall, H. H. (1996). Implications of differentiating and understanding constructivist approaches. *Educational Psychologist, 31*(3/4), 235–240.

Martin, R. A. (2002, April). *Alternatives in education: An exploration of learner-centered, progressive, and holistic education.* Paper presented at the Annual Meeting of the American Educational Research Association, New Orleans.

Mathews, J. (2004, January 20). Turning strife into success. *Washington Post.*

McCombs, B. L. (1994). *Development and validation of the learner-centered psychological principles.* Aurora, CO: Mid-Continent Regional Educational Laboratory.

McCombs, B. L. (1995). Putting the learner and learning in learner-centered classrooms: The learner-centered model as a framework [Special Issue]. *Michigan ASCD Focus, 17,* 17–12.

McCombs, B. L. (1999). *The assessment of learner-centered practices (ALCP): Tools for teacher reflection, learning, and change.* Denver, CO: University of Denver Research Institute.

McCombs, B. L. (2000). Reducing the achievement gap. *Society, 37*(5), 29–36.

McCombs, B. L. (2001). Self-regulated learning and academic achievement: A phenomenological view. In B. J. Zimmerman & D. H. Schunk (Eds.), *Self-regulated learning and academic achievement: Theory, research, and practice* (2nd. ed., pp. 67–123). Mahwah, NJ: Erlbaum.

McCombs, B. L. (2003a). Applying educational psychology's knowledge base in educational reform: From research to application to policy In W. M. Reynolds & G. E. Miller (Eds.), *Comprehensive handbook of psychology: Vol. 7. Educational psychology* (pp. 583–607). New York: Wiley.

McCombs, B. L. (2003b). Providing a framework for the redesign of K-12 education in the context of current educational reform issues [Special issue]. *Theory into Practice, 42*(2), 93–101.

McCombs, B. L. (2004a). The learner-centered psychological principles: A framework for balancing a focus on academic achievement with a focus on social and emotional learning needs. In J. E. Zins, R. P. Weissberg, M. C. Wang, & H. J. Walberg (Eds.), *Building academic success on social and emotional learning: What does the research say?* (pp. 23–39). New York: Teachers College Press.

McCombs, B. L. (2004b, April). *The case for learner-centered practices.* Paper presented as part of the interactive symposium, "The Case for Learner-Centered Practices Across the K-12 and College Levels," presented at the annual meeting of the American Educational Research Association, San Diego.

McCombs, B. L. (2007). Balancing accountability demands with research-validated, learner-centered teaching and learning practices. In C. E. Sleeter (Ed.), *Educating for democracy and equity in an era of accountability* (pp. 41–60). New York: Teachers College Press.

McCombs, B. L. & Kanfer, R. (2000). Motivation. In H. F. O'Neil, Jr., & S. Tobias (Eds.), *Handbook on training* (pp. 85–108). New York: Macmillan.

McCombs, B. L., & Lauer, P. A. (1997). Development and validation of the learner-centered battery: Self-assessment tools for teacher reflection and professional development. *The Professional Educator, 20*(1), 1–21.

McCombs, B. L., & Lauer, P. A. (1998, July). *The learner-centered framework model of seamless professional development: Implications for practice and policy changes in higher education.* Paper presented at the 23rd International Conference on Improving University Teaching, Dublin.

McCombs, B. L., & Miller, L. (2007). *Learner-centered classroom practices and assessments: Maximizing student motivation, learning, and achievement.* Thousand Oaks, CA: Corwin Press.

McCombs, B. L., & Miller, L. (2008). *The school leader's guide to learner-centered education: From complexity to simplicity.* Thousand Oaks, CA: Corwin Press.

McCombs, B. L., Perry, K. E., & Daniels, D. H. (2008). Understanding children's and teachers' perceptions of learner centered practices: Implications for early schooling. *Elementary School Journal, 109*(1), 16–35.

McCombs, B. L., & Pierce, J. W. (1999). *The college level assessment of learner-centered practices (ALCP): Tools for teacher reflection, learning, and change.* Denver, CO: University of Denver Research Institute.

McCombs, B. L., & Quiat, M. A. (2002). What makes a comprehensive school reform model learner-centered? *Urban Education, 37*(4), 476–496.

McCombs, B. L., & Vakili, D. (2005). A learner-centered framework for e-learning. *Teachers College Record, 107*(8), 1582–1600.

McCombs, B. L., & Whisler, J. S. (1997). *The learner-centered classroom and school: Strategies for increasing student motivation and achievement.* San Francisco, CA: Jossey-Bass.

Meece, J. L. (1991). The classroom context and students' motivational goals. In M. Maehr and P. Pintrich (Eds.), *Advances in motivation and achievement* (Vol. 7, pp. 261–286). Greenwich, CT: JAI Press.

Meece, J. L. (2002). *Child and adolescent development for educators* (2nd ed.). New York: McGraw-Hill.

Meece, J. L. (2003). Applying learner-centered principles to middle school education. *Theory into Practice, 42,* 109–116.

Meece, J. L., Herman, P., & McCombs, B. L. (2003). Relations of learner-centered teaching practices to adolescents' achievement goals. *International Journal of Educational Research, 39*(4–5), 457–475.

Meier, D. (2002). Standardization versus standards. *Phi Delta Kappan, 84*(3), 190–198.

Moses, M. S., & Chang, M. J. (2006). Toward a deeper understanding of the diversity rationale. *Educational Researcher, 35*(1), 6–11.

National Commission on Excellence in Education. (2010, January 12). A Nation at Risk: The Imperative of Education Reform, April 1983, retrieved from www.ed.gov/pubs/NatAtRisk/risk.html

National Research Council. (1999). How children learn. In J. D. Bransford, A. L. Brown, & R. R. Cocking (Eds.), Committee on Developments in the Science of Learning, Committee on Learning Research and Educational Practice, Commission on Behavioral and Social Sciences and Education. *How people learn: Brain, mind, experience, and school* (pp. 67–101). Washington, DC: National Academy Press.

National Research Council. (2000). *How people learn: Brain, mind, experience, and school* (rev. ed.). J. D. Bransford, A. L. Brown, & R. R. Cocking (Eds.), Committee on Developments in the Science of Learning, Committee on Learning Research and Educational Practice, Commission on Behavioral and Social Sciences and Education. Washington, DC: National Academy Press.

National Research Council. (2001). *Adding it up: How children learn mathematics. Mathematics Learning Study Committee.* J. Kilpatrick, J. Wafford, & B. Findell (Eds.), Center for Education, Division of Behavioral and Social Sciences and Education. Washington, DC: National Academy Press.

National Research Council. (2002). *Scientific research in education. Committee on Scientific Principles for Education Research,* R. J. Shavelson & L. Towne (Eds.), Center for Education, Division of Behavioral and Social Sciences and Education. Washington, DC: National Academy Press.

National Research Council. (2003). *Engaging schools: Fostering high school students' motivation to learn.* Board on Children, Youth, and Families, Division of Behavioral and Social Sciences and Education. Washington, DC: National Academy Press.

National Study Group for the Affirmative Development of Academic Ability. (2004). *All students reaching the top: Strategies for closing academic achievement gaps.* Naperville, IL: Learning Point Associates.

Neill, M. (2003). The dangers of testing. *Educational Leadership, 60*(5), 43–46.

Noddings, N. (1988). An ethic of caring and its implications for instructional arrangements. *American Journal of Education, 96*(2), 215–231.

Noddings, N. (2005). What does it mean to educate the whole child? *Educational Leadership, 63*(1), 8–13.

Oldfather, P., & McLaughlin, H. J. (1993). Gaining and losing voice: A longitudinal study of students' continuing impulse to learn across elementary and middle level contexts. *Research in Middle Education, 17*(1), 1–25.

Osterman, K. F. (2000, Fall). Students' need for belonging in the school community. *Review of Educational Research, 70*(3), 323–367.

Patterson, W. (2003). Breaking out of our boxes. *Phi Delta Kappan, 84*(8), 569–574.

Perry, K. E., & Weinstein, R. S. (1998). The social context of early schooling and children's school adjustment. *Educational Psychologist, 33*(4), 177–194.

Pianta, R. (1999). *Enhancing relationships between children and teachers.* Washington, DC: American Psychological Association.

Pianta, R., La Paro, K., Payne, C., Cox, M., & Bradley, R. (2002). The relations of kindergarten classroom environment to teacher, family, and school characteristics and child outcomes. *The Elementary School Journal, 3,* 225–238.

Pianta, R., & Stuhlman, M. (2004). Teacher–child relationships and children's success in the first years of school. *School Psychology Review, 2004, 33*(3), 444–458.

Phillips, M. (1997). What makes schools effective? A comparison of the relationships of communitarian climate and academic climate to mathematics achievement and attendance during middle school. *American Educational Research Journal, 34,* 543–578.

Rich, D. (2005). What educators need to explain to the public. *Phi Delta Kappan, 87*(2), 154–158.

Rogers, C. R., (1983). *Freedom to learn for the 80's.* Columbus, OH: Charles E. Merrill.

Rogers, C. R., & Freiberg, H. J. (1994). *Freedom to learn* (3rd ed.). New York: Merrill.

Rubalcava, M. (2005). Let kids come first. *Educational Leadership, 62*(8), 70–72.

Ryan, R. M., & Deci, E. L. (2000). Self-determination theory and the facilitation of intrinsic motivation, social development, and well-being. *American Psychologist, 55*(1), 68–78.

Seligman, M. E. P., & Csikszentmihalyi. M. (2000). Positive psychology: An introduction. *American Psychologist, 55*(1), 5–14.

Shepard, L. A. (2000). The role of assessment in a learning culture. *Educational Researcher, 29*(7), 4–14.

Stiggins, R. J. (1996). *Student-centered classroom assessment* (2nd ed.). Columbus, OH: Merrill.

Summers, J. J., Beretvas, S. N., Svinicki, M. D., & Gorin, J. S. (2005). Evaluating collaborative learning and community. *Journal of Experimental Education, 73*(3), 165–188.

Tomlinson, J. (1999). *Globalization and culture.* Chicago, IL: University of Chicago Press.

Wentzel, K. (1997). Student motivation in middle school: The role of perceived pedagogical caring. *Journal of Educational Psychology, 89,* 411–419.

Wentzel, K. (2002). Are effective teachers like good parents? Teaching styles and student adjustment in early adolescence. *Child Development, 73,* 287–301.

Wielkiewicz, R. M., & Stelzner, S P. (2005). An ecological perspective on leadership theory, research, and practice. *Review of General Psychology, 9*(4), 326–341.

Weinberger, E., & McCombs, B. L. (2001, April). *The impact of learner-centered practices on the academic and non-academic outcomes of upper elementary and middle school students.* Paper presented in the Symposium, "Integrating What We Know About Learners and Learning: A foundation for Transforming PreK-20 Practices," at the annual meeting of the American Educational Research Association, Seattle.

Weinberger, E., & McCombs, B. L. (2003). Applying the LCPs to high school education. *Theory Into Practice, 42*(2), 117–126.

Wiggins, G. T. (1993). *Assessing student performance: Exploring the purpose and limits of testing.* San Francisco, CA: Jossey-Bass.

Williams, B. (2003). *Closing the achievement gap: A vision for changing beliefs and practices* (2nd ed.). Alexandria, VA: Association for Supervision and Curriculum Development.

Zimmerman, B. & Schunk, D. H. (Eds.) (2001). *Self-regulated learning and academic achievement: Theory, research, and practice* (2nd ed.). Mahwah, NJ: Erlbaum.

Zins, J. E. Weissberg, R. P. Wang, M. C., & Walberg, H. J. (Eds.). (2004). *Building academic success on social and emotional learning: What does the research say?* New York: Teachers College Press.

# 6

# Students' Relationships with Teachers

*Kathryn R. Wentzel*

There is growing consensus that the nature and quality of children's relationships with their teachers play a critical and central role in motivating and engaging students to learn, and teaching them what they need to know to become knowledgeable and productive citizens (Becker & Luthar, 2002; Pianta, Hamre, & Stuhlman, 2003; Stipek, 2004). Effective teachers are typically described as those who create relationships with students that are emotionally close, safe, and trusting, that facilitate provisions of instrumental help and communication of positive and high expectations for performance, and that foster a more general ethos of community and caring in their classrooms. Many researchers interested in children's relationships with teachers have focused exclusively on the affective nature and quality of these relationships. In this regard, principles of attachment theory (Bowlby, 1969; Bretherton, 1987), self-determination theory (R. M. Ryan & Deci, 2000), and social support perspectives have guided research on teacher–student relationships at all levels of schooling and with respect to a broad range of student outcomes. Broader socialization perspectives that take into account multiple provisions of teacher–student relationships also have contributed to this literature (Wentzel, 2004). In each case, however, these relationship qualities are believed to support the development of students' emotional well-being and positive sense of self, motivational orientations for social and academic outcomes, and actual social and academic skills. In support of these notions is a growing body of evidence that the affective nature and qualities of teacher–student relationships are related significantly to a broad range of positive student outcomes.

In light of this interest in the causal nature of teachers' relationships with students, a central question addressed in this chapter is how and why students' relationships with teachers might be related to their social and academic functioning at school. Indeed, are student competencies that contribute positively to their social and academic successes at school simply those that also lead to the development of positive relationships with teachers? Similarly, is it the case that teacher–student relationships influence the development of students' social and academic competencies at school or, are the positive outcomes associated with these relationships the product of other relationships that students have with parents and peers? Toward this end, this chapter is organized around issues relevant for understanding the role that teacher–student relationships play in students' lives. First, the various theoretical perspectives that guide work in the field are described. Despite their common focus on the nature and functions of teachers' relationships with students, each of these perspectives provides the field with unique insights into the role of teachers in promoting students' competence at school. Next, research on teacher–student relationships that informs questions of causal influence is reviewed. Measurement and design issues associated with this research also are raised. Finally, directions for future work in this area are offered.

## Theoretical Perspectives on Teacher–Student Relationships

Researchers have documented significant relations between students' academic and social accomplishments at school and their positive interactions and relationships with teachers. Why then, might students' competent interactions with teachers influence or be related to other school-related outcomes? At the simplest level, it is possible that the nature of students' relationships with teachers and their social and academic accomplishments are correlated but not causally related outcomes, and reflect the fact that many students who are highly competent in one domain of functioning also display high levels of functioning in other domains. Similarly, students' competent interactions with teachers might not influence their other accomplishments, but functioning in multiple domains might be linked by way of underlying behavioral styles or self-regulatory processes that contribute to positive outcomes in each. Finally, assuming that a causal relation does exist, two explanations are possible. First, it is reasonable to expect that positive relationships with teachers support the development of students' self processes that contribute to positive social and academic outcomes as well as the development of specific social and academic skills. Conversely, it is also reasonable to assume that students' social and academic achievements can elicit social approval and corresponding positive interactions with teachers.

Theoretical perspectives that guide work in this area typically adopt a causal approach. The prevailing models describe the function of teacher–student relationships as promoting student competence primarily through the affective quality of relationships. An additional approach has been to adopt a broader socialization perspective, focusing on additional functions of teacher–student relationships including the communication of expectations for social and academic performance, provisions of help and instrumental aid, and provisions of safety. In the following section, each of these approaches will be described, followed by a discussion of ways in which student characteristics might contribute to the formation of positive relationships with teachers and influence the benefits that might ensue.

## The Affective Quality of Relationships

Central to several theoretical perspectives on teacher–student relationships is the notion that the affective quality of teacher–student relationships is a critical motivator of student adjustment. Research on this aspect of teacher–student relationships has been based on a number of perspectives, including attachment theory (Bowlby, 1969; Bretherton, 1987), self-determination theory (Connell & Wellborn, 1991; Ryan & Deci, 2000), and models of social support (e.g., Sarason, Sarason, & Pierce, 1990). In this section, each of these theoretical perspectives will be described, followed by a review of empirical research.

*Theoretical Perspectives* Attachment theory has provided the strongest impetus for work on teachers' relationships with young children. According to this perspective, the dyadic relationship between a child and caregiver (usually the mother) is a system in which children experience various levels of positive affect and responsiveness to their basic needs, with predictable and sensitive responses being associated with secure attachments, and more arbitrary and insensitive responses leading to insecure attachments (Bowlby, 1969). Attachment theorists hypothesize qualitatively different outcomes associated with secure and insecure attachment systems. Secure relationships are believed to foster children's curiosity and exploration of the environment, positive coping skills, and a mental representation of one's self as being worthy of love and of others as being trustworthy. In contrast, insecure attachments are believed to result in either wary or inappropriately risky exploratory behavior, difficulty in regulating stress in new settings, and negative self-concepts.

A basic tenet of attachment theory is that the primary attachment relationship results in children's mental representations of self and others, which is then used as a basis to interpret and judge the underlying intentions, reliability, and trustworthiness of others' actions in new relationships (Bretherton, 1987). Depending on the nature of primary attachments, children will expect new relationships to generate interactions marked by positive affect and trust, by conflict and rejection, or as anxiety-producing, overly dependent, or enmeshed. Given its central focus on the quality of interpersonal relationships, attachment theory has provided a useful framework for generating predictions concerning children's relationships with their teachers. Indeed, although teacher–student relationships are not typically viewed as primary attachment relationships, attachment theory principles would suggest that they would be fairly concordant with the quality of parent–child attachments and therefore, related to children's sense of self and emotional well-being. In turn, these intrapersonal outcomes are believed to contribute to the development of positive social and cognitive skills at school.

Self-determination theory (Ryan & Deci, 2000) posits that students will engage positively in the social and academic tasks of the classroom when their needs for relatedness, competence, and autonomy are met. Contextual supports in the form of interpersonal involvement, structure, and provisions of autonomy are believed to be essential to this process, with teacher involvement and students' corresponding sense of relatedness being most frequently associated with the study of teacher–student relationships. According to self-determination theory, involvement is expressed through teachers' demonstrations of interest in their students' personal well-being and provisions of emotional support. Students' sense of relatedness at school reflects feelings of emotional security and being socially connected to others and in line with attachment theory, experiencing a positive sense of self and of others as trustworthy. Feelings of relatedness are believed to facilitate the adoption of goals and interests valued by teachers, and to encourage desires to contribute in positive ways to the overall functioning of the social group. In this regard, feeling related to teachers has been studied most often in relation to students' motivation and engagement in the social and academic life of the classroom (e.g., Connell & Wellborn, 1991; Skinner & Belmont, 1993).

Finally, social support perspectives on teacher–student relationships reflect the notion that students' subjective appraisals of teachers' emotional support have implications for their subsequent adjustment to school. Similar to attachment theory, social support perspectives (Sarason et al., 1990) focus on students' mental representations of relationships, with perceived support serving as a buffer from stress and anxiety (Cohen & Wills, 1985). Therefore, perceptions of positive emotional support are believed to result in outcomes related to security of attachments, such as perceived competence, social skills, and coping (Saronson et al., 1990). However, whereas attachment theory focuses on interpersonal relationships reflecting dyadic systems with fairly stable histories of interactions, social support perspectives typically consider relationships as personal resources that can range from highly familiar and stable (e.g., a parent) to relatively impersonal and fleeting (e.g., a semester-long instructor).

***Correlates of Emotionally Supportive Relationships*** Levels of emotional closeness and security associated with close relationships are believed to support the development of a range of positive social and academic outcomes in children. Although most of the research is correlational, research based on each theoretical perspective supports this general conclusion. In work on young children, teacher–student relationships typically are assessed by asking teachers about the quality of their relationships with students. This research indicates that preschool children who enjoy emotionally secure relationships with their teachers are more likely to demonstrate prosocial, gregarious, and complex play and less likely to show hostile aggression and withdrawn behavior toward their peers (e.g., Howes & Hamilton, 1993). Close, secure teacher–child relationships also have been related positively to school readiness scores, whereas teacher–child conflict has been related negatively to positive work habits and readiness scores (Pianta, Nimetz, & Bennett, 1997). Researchers who have followed children over time report that teacher–child closeness in preschool is associated positively with children's language skills, sociability, and attention in kindergarten and first grade (Peisner-Feinberg et al. 2001) and negatively with internalizing (Pianta & Stuhlman, 2004) and problem behavior (Peisner-Feinberg et al., 2001).

In kindergarten, teacher–student relationships marked by emotional closeness have been related positively to academic functioning, school liking, and socially competent and self-directed behavior (Birch & Ladd, 1997), and negatively to aggressive behavior (Ladd & Burgess, 2001; Silver, Measelle, Armstrong, & Essex, 2005) and peer rejection (Ladd & Burgess, 2001). In contrast, relationships marked by conflict have been related positively to children's aggressive and socially incompetent behavior (Birch & Ladd, 1997; Ladd & Burgess, 2001) and peer rejection (Ladd & Burgess, 2001), and negatively to school liking, self-directed behavior (Birch & Ladd, 2001), academic grades, and test scores (Hamre & Pianta, 2001). Longitudinal studies have documented that qualities of teacher–student relationships in kindergarten predict similar social-emotional outcomes in first and second grade (Birch & Ladd, 1998; Ladd & Burgess, 1999; Peisner-Feinberg et al., 2001; Pianta & Stuhlman, 2004; Silver et al.). Significant relations with academic outcomes also have been reported (Hamre & Pianta; Peisner-Feinberg et al., 2001) but not as consistently (cf., Ladd & Burgess, 2001; Pianta & Stuhlman, 2004). Following children from kindergarten through eighth grade, Hamre and Pianta (2001) found kindergartners' relationships with teachers marked by conflict and dependency predicted not only lower grades and standardized test scores, but fewer positive work habits and increased numbers of disciplinary infractions through eighth grade, especially for boys.

Attachment theory and self-determination theory both specifically predict that the affective quality of teacher–student relationships also should be related to students' sense of self and emotional well-being. Although rarely the focus of research on young children, in late elementary school, students' reports of negative relationships with teachers also have been related to anxiety and depression (Murray & Greenberg, 2000); secure relationships with teachers have been related to students' identification with teachers' values and positive social self-concept (Davis, 2001). Similarly, reports of teacher involvement are strong predictors of students' emotional functioning and engagement over time, especially when reports of relatedness and student functioning come from the same informant (student or teacher; Furrer, & Skinner, 2003). Finally, in middle school samples the affective quality of relationships with teachers has been related to a range of self-processes including perceived autonomy, perceived control, and self-esteem (R. M. Ryan, Stiller, & Lynch, 1994).

Studies of perceived social support from teachers also have examined academic as well as social outcomes. Students' perceived support from teachers has been related to classroom grades (Crosnoe, Johnson, & Elder, 2004; Faircloth & Hamm, 2005; Felner, Aber, Primavera, & Cauce, 1985; Isakson & Jarvis, 1999; A. M. Ryan & Patrick, 2001; Wentzel, 1997, 1998) and dropping out of school (Rumberger, 1995), as well as to motivational outcomes such as goal orientations (A. M. Ryan & Patrick, 2001; Wentzel, 1997, 1998), values, interest, and self-efficacy (Goodenow, 1993; Ibanez, Kuperminc, Jurkovic, & Perilla, 2004; Midgley, Feldlaufer & Eccles, 1989; Mitchell-Copeland, Denham, & DeMulder, 1997; Murdock & Miller, 2003; Roeser, Midgley, & Urdan, 1996; Sanchez, Colon, & Esparza, 2005; Valeski & Stipek, 2001; Wentzel, 1997, 1998, 2003). Eccles and her colleagues (e.g., Midgley et al., 1989) found that young adolescents report declines in the nurturant qualities of teacher–student relationships after the transition to middle school, that correspond to declines in academic motivation and achievement.

Students' appraisals of teacher support also have been related to social outcomes including pursuit of social goals (Wentzel, 1994, 1997, 1998, 2003), prosocial actions (Blankemeyer, Flannery, & Vazsonyi, 2002; Wentzel, 1994, 1997), and aggressive, delinquent behavior (Blankemeyer et al., 2002; Chang, 2003; Crosnoe et al., 2004; Hughes et al., 2006; Isakson & Jarvis, 1999; Murdock, Miller, & Kohlhardt, 2004). In support of a basic tenet of social support paradigms, perceiving positive support from teachers also has been related to emotional well-being (Wentzel, 1997, 1998), whereas a lack of perceived support has been related to internalizing problems such as depression and emotional distress (Mitchell-Copeland et al., 1997; Reddy, Rhodes, & Mulhall, 2003; Wentzel, 1997).

***Summary*** Researchers have adopted multiple theoretical perspectives to study the affective nature and qualities of teacher–student relationships. In general, these models assume that aspects of teacher–student relationships have a causal effect on children's school-related competence, primarily by promoting a positive sense of self and emotional well-being. In line with attachment theory principles, evidence from correlational studies confirms that secure and close relationships with teachers are related positively to young children's cognitive and social competence at school. Similarly, work based on self-determination theory and social support perspectives supports an association between the affective quality of teacher–student relationships and older students' school-related competencies.

A second approach to the study of teacher–student relationships has been to consider positive student–teacher relationships as serving a broader range of relationship functions that contribute to students' competence at school. For the most part, researchers adopting this approach have focused on teachers as socialization agents who create interpersonal contexts for students that influence levels and quality of motivation and engagement (Wentzel, 2004). Although the quality of dyadic relationships are not always the explicit focus of discussion, researchers assume that ongoing student–teacher interactions reflect a form of social reciprocity that provides students with opportunities to pursue their own goals but also to learn about and then actively pursue those social and academic goals that are valued by others at school. In the following section, this perspective is described.

## Teacher–Student Relationships as Socialization Contexts

Models of socialization suggest several mechanisms whereby social interactions might influence goal-directed behavior. First, ongoing social interactions teach children what they need to do to become accepted and competent members of their social worlds. In addition, the quality of social interactions informs children about the degree to which they are valued and accepted by others. For example, children who enjoy interpersonal relationships with adults that are nurturant and supportive are more likely to adopt and internalize the expectations and goals that are valued by these adults than if their relationships are harsh and critical (see Grusec & Goodnow, 1994; R. M. Ryan, 1993). In general, these mechanisms correspond to parenting dimensions characterized by consistent enforcement of rules, expectations for self-reliance and self-control, solicitation of opinions and feelings, and concern for emotional and physical well-being (Wentzel, 2002).

When applied to the social worlds of the classroom, these dimensions are reflected in opportunities for learning as reflected in teachers' communications of rules and expectations for behavior and performance, direct instruction, and instrumental help. These practices can be viewed as ways in which teachers scaffold students to take ownership of the social and academic agenda of the classroom. Models of socialization also imply that teachers are likely to have motivational significance for students if they create

contexts in which children feel emotionally supported and safe (Connell & Wellborn, 1991; Grolnick, Kurowski, & Gurland, 1999). This includes establishing relationships that are emotionally secure and safe, as described in the previous section, but also creating a climate free of threats to students' emotional and physical well-being.

Wentzel (2004) describes how teacher–student interactions along these dimensions can promote student motivation and subsequent performance. Derived from theoretical perspectives on person–environment fit and personal goal setting (e.g., Bronfenbrenner, 1989; Eccles & Midgley, 1989), she argues that school-related competence is achieved to the extent that students are able to accomplish goals that have personal as well as social value, in a manner that supports continued psychological and emotional well-being. The ability to accomplish these goals, however, is contingent on opportunities and affordances of the school context that allow students to pursue their multiple goals. Applying this perspective more specifically to the study of teacher–student relationships, Wentzel further suggests that students will come to value and subsequently pursue academic and social goals valued by teachers when they perceive their interactions and relationships with them as providing clear direction concerning goals that should be achieved; as facilitating the achievement of their goals by providing help, advice, and instruction; as being safe and responsive to their goal strivings; and as being emotionally supportive and nurturing (see also Ford, 1992). In this manner, students' school-based competencies are a product of social reciprocity between teachers and students. Students must behave in ways that meet teachers' expectations, and teachers must provide support for the achievement of students' goals. Students' motivation to achieve academic and social goals that are personally as well as socially valued should then serve as mediators between opportunities afforded by positive interactions with teachers and their academic and social accomplishments.

***Correlates of Contextual Supports*** Empirical evidence supports the notion that positive interactions with teachers along these dimensions are related to various aspects of academic and social motivation at school. In the following sections, evidence suggesting that these dimensions of support can promote social and academic accomplishments by motivating students to display positive forms of social behavior and to engage in academic activities is reviewed. Dimensions are categorized in terms of teachers' communication of expectations, provisions of help and instrumental aid, and of emotional support and safety. Evidence supporting the multidimensional nature of teacher supports and their influence on student outcomes is described last.

*Teacher Communications and Expectations* It is reasonable to assume that the degree to which students pursue goals valued by teachers is dependent on whether teachers communicate clearly their values and expectations concerning classroom behavior and performance.

Researchers rarely have asked teachers directly about their specific goals for students. However, teachers' expectations for students can be gleaned from research on the characteristics of students that teachers tend to like. For example, Auffrey and Wentzel (2000) report that middle school teachers' descriptions of "ideal" students reflect three general types of desired outcomes: social outcomes such as sharing, being helpful to others, and being responsive to rules; motivational qualities related to learning such as being persistent, hard-working, inquisitive, and intrinsically interested; and performance outcomes such as getting good grades and completing assignments. Similarly, elementary-school teachers have consistently reported preferences for students who are cooperative, conforming, cautious, and responsible (e.g., Brophy & Good, 1974). Researchers have documented that teachers continuously communicate these ideals directly to their students, regardless of their instructional goals, teaching styles, and ethnicity (Hargreaves, Hester, & Mellor, 1975).

Teachers also structure learning environments in ways that make certain goals more salient to students than others. For example, cooperative learning structures can be designed to promote the pursuit of social goals to be responsible to the group and to achieve common objectives (e.g., Slavin, Hurley, & Chamberlain, 2003; Solomon, Schaps, Watson, & Battistich, 1992); students report stronger levels of social satisfaction when given the opportunity to learn within cooperative learning settings (Slavin et al., 2003). In addition, teachers provide students with evaluation criteria and design tasks in ways that can focus attention on goals to learn and develop skills (task-related and intellectual goals) or to demonstrate ability to others (performance goals; see Ames, 1992). Teachers who provide students with a diverse set of tasks that are challenging, personally relevant, and promote skill development are likely to foster pursuit of mastery goals; teachers who use normative and comparative evaluation criteria and who provide students with controlling, noncontingent extrinsic rewards are likely to promote pursuit of performance goals (e.g., Midgley, 2002).

Beyond communicating values and expectations for behavior and achievement at the classroom level, teachers also convey expectations about ability and performance to individual students. Weinstein (2002) describes these communications as part of a process of influence whereby teachers' expectations result in their differential treatment of students. These communications most often reflect beliefs that students are able to achieve more than previously demonstrated or negative expectations reflecting underestimations of student ability. Teachers' negative expectations are often targeted toward minority students, with expectations for competent behavior and academic performance being lower for them than for other students (e.g., Oates, 2003; Weinstein, Gregory, & Strambler, 2004).

Teachers' false expectations can become self-fulfilling prophecies, with student performance changing to conform to teacher expectations (see Weinstein, 2002), especially as students get older (Valeski & Stipek, 2001). Although the ef-

fects of these negative expectations appear to be fairly weak (e.g., Jussim, 1991; Jussim & Eccles, 1995), and short-lived (Jussim & Harber, 2005), self-fulfilling prophecies tend to have stronger effects on African American students, students from low socioeconomic backgrounds, and low achievers (Smith, Jussim, & Eccles, 1999). In addition, however, teachers' overestimations of ability seem to have a somewhat stronger effect in raising levels of achievement than teachers' underestimates have on lowering achievement, especially for low performing students (Madon, Jussim, & Eccles, 1997). Therefore, teachers who communicate high expectations for individual students can bring about positive changes in academic accomplishments.

*Providing Help, Advice, and Instruction* In the classroom, teachers play the central pedagogical function of transmitting knowledge and training students in academic subject areas. In doing so, teachers routinely provide children with resources that promote the development of social and academic competencies. These resources can take the form of information and advice, modeled behavior, or specific experiences that facilitate learning. Children's willingness to seek help from teachers is related to several factors, including their ability level, academic goals, and self-efficacy, and the availability of emotional support, structure, and autonomy (Newman, 2000). Less is known about teacher characteristics that predict their willingness to help students. However, Brophy and Good (1974) documented the relevance of teachers' attachments to students for gaining access to academic resources. The teachers observed in their research reported that they were more appreciative and positive toward students who were cooperative and persistent (i.e., behaviorally competent) than toward students who were less cooperative but displayed high levels of creativity and achievement. Teachers also responded with help and encouragement to students about whom they were concerned when these students sought them out for help. In contrast, students toward whom they felt rejection were treated most often with criticism and typically were refused help.

*Emotional Support and Safety* In addition to providing clear expectations, and help, teachers also create contexts characterized by levels of emotional support and personal safety (Connell & Wellborn, 1991; Grolnick et al., 1999; Isakson & Jarvis, 1999). As evidenced by the work on affective qualities of teacher–student relationships, emotionally supportive interactions have the potential to provide strong incentives for students to engage in valued classroom activities. Of additional interest are findings that students are more likely to establish affectively positive relationships with teachers when they feel safe at school (Crosnoe et al., 2004). Most frequently, issues of safety are discussed with regard to peer interactions. National surveys indicate that large numbers of students are the targets of classmate aggression and take active measures to avoid being harmed physically as well as psychologically by peers (National

Center for Educational Statistics [NCES], 1995). Although this literature implies that peers might be the primary source of threats to students' physical safety and well-being, of central importance to understanding this process is that teachers can play a central role in creating classrooms that are free of peer harassment and in alleviating the negative effects of harassment once it has occurred (Olweus, 1993).

***Research on Multiple Dimensions of Support*** Describing teachers' relationships with students along multiple dimensions to include not only emotional support but also communication of expectations, instrumental help, and safety provides a more comprehensive picture of ways in which teachers can promote students' social and academic adjustment at school. This broader perspective is supported by students' and teachers' qualitative descriptions of caring and supportive teachers, and from studies relating multiple types of support to student outcomes. Qualitative approaches have identified multiple types of teacher support by asking students and teachers what a supportive or caring teacher is like (Hoy & Weinstein, 2006). For example, when asked to characterize teachers who care, middle school students describe teachers who demonstrate democratic and egalitarian communication styles designed to elicit student participation and input, who develop expectations for student behavior and performance in light of individual differences and abilities, who model a "caring" attitude and interest in their instruction and interpersonal dealings with students, and who provide constructive rather than harsh and critical feedback. Moreover, students who perceive their teachers to display high levels of these characteristics also tend to pursue appropriate social and academic classroom goals more frequently than students who do not (Wentzel, 2002).

Others have documented differences in middle school students' characterizations of supportive teachers as a function of student ability, with students from high ability tracks valuing teachers who challenge them, encourage class participation, and who express educational goals similar to theirs. In contrast, students from low ability tracks tend to value teachers who treat them with kindness, who are fair, explain subject matter clearly, and maintain control in the classroom (Daniels & Arapostathis, 2005). Ethnographic studies document that academically successful inner-city ethnic minority adolescents value instrumental help from teachers but also warmth and acceptance coupled with high academic expectations (Smokowski, Reyonolds, & Bezrucko, 2000). Racially mixed groups of middle school students highlight the importance of teachers who are responsive to individual differences and needs, who provide students with autonomy and choice (Oldfather, 1993), who show interest in students as individuals, help with academics, encourage students to work up to their potential, and who teach well and make subject matter interesting (Hayes, Ryan, & Zseller, 1994).

Research on teachers' notions of what it means to be supportive and caring has been infrequent. However, C. S.

Weinstein (1998) asked prospective elementary and secondary teachers about specific things they could do to demonstrate caring to their students. Almost two thirds of teachers' responses referred to affective qualities of interpersonal interactions such as establishing positive rapport, creating a climate of trust and respect, and fostering self-esteem, whereas specific teaching and classroom management strategies were mentioned less often. Ethnographic work also has documented teacher beliefs concerning the importance of making interpersonal connections, establishing rapport and creating a classroom atmosphere of mutual respect and trust as important aspects of classroom instructional support (Moje, 1996). Similarly, in the middle school grades, teachers have described their "ideal" students as sharing, helpful, responsive to rules, persistent, intrinsically interested, and as earning high grades (Wentzel, 2003).

Additional support for multiple dimensions of teacher–student relationships is provided in studies where multiple dimensions have been assessed simultaneously. This work has documented differential effects as a function of dimension and the outcome being studied (Isakson & Jarvis, 1999; Marchant, Paulson, & Rothlisberg, 2001; Skinner & Belmont, 1993; Wentzel, 2002; Wentzel, Battle, Russell & Looney, 2010). For example, Wentzel and her colleagues (Wentzel et al., 2010) documented unique relations of teachers' provisions of clear expectations, classroom safety, instrumental help, and nurturance to students' interest in class and efforts to behave appropriately. Skinner and Belmont also documented significant relations between teachers' provisions of involvement and structure (e.g., clear expectations, instrumental help) and students' engagement in class.

***Summary*** Models that examine the multiple functions of student–teacher relationships provide a more complex and complete picture of the supports that teachers provide their students than those that focus exclusively on the affective quality of teacher–student relationships. Dimensions reflecting the communication of expectations and values, provisions of help, and safety complement that of emotional support in explaining the potential influence of teachers on student accomplishments. Additional dimensions of support might also provide insights into the functions of teacher–student relationships. For instance, provisions of autonomy, as expressed in opportunities for choice and egalitarian decision making are likely to have a direct impact on students' own perceptions of autonomy and self-regulation (Grolnick, Gurland, Jacob, & Decourcey, 2001). In general, teacher provisions of autonomy along with structure and guidance have been related to a range of positive, motivational outcomes including students' perceptions of competence, self-determination, and relatedness to teachers (e.g., Grolnick & Ryan, 1989; Skinner & Belmont, 1993).

Additional pathways of influence also need further consideration. In the following section, ways in which students and their various accomplishments at school might influence the quality of their relationships with teachers are discussed.

## Student–Teacher Relationships and Student Characteristics

Aside from models that posit a direction of causal influence from teacher to student, the notion that establishing positive relationships with teachers is the result of student characteristics has rarely been the focus of theoretical discussions. Indeed, the effects that students might have on the nature of teacher–student relationships have not been the focus of empirical study (cf., Skinner & Belmont, 1993). However, social-cognitive processes in the form of attributions of teacher intent (Wyatt & Haskett, 2001), social self-efficacy (Patrick, Hicks, & Ryan, 1997), beliefs about control (Wentzel, 1997), and accuracy of social-cognitive processing (O'Connor & Hirsch, 1999) explain at least in part their perceptions of teacher support and the degree to which they can be socialized by teachers. Finally, other aspects of social-cognitive processing such as selective attention, attributions, and social biases and stereotypes (Lemerise & Arsenio, 2000), can influence students' interpretations of social communications as well as teacher reactions to their behavior. Individual characteristics such as racial identity (Graham, Taylor, & Hudley, 1998), perceived discrimination, and the extent that students are oriented toward gaining social approval (Goetz & Dweck, 1980) are also likely to influence the degree to which they are open to forming relationships with teachers.

Metacognitive and self-regulatory processes also are likely to contribute to positive relationships with teachers as well as to social and academic accomplishments. Several theorists have posited goal-setting skills, emotion regulation, self-monitoring, attributions and means–end thinking, and other basic information-processing skills as factors that contribute to the ability to implement behavior that contributes to the formation of positive relationships (Lemerise & Arsenio, 2000). From a motivational perspective, goal networks and hierarchies based on students' beliefs about cause–effect relations also are likely to link the quality of relationships with teachers to performance in other domains. For instance, students might try to demonstrate academic competence to gain social approval from teachers or, they might behave in socially competent ways to earn the positive regard of their teachers (Wentzel, Filisetti, & Looney, in press). In any case, the possibility that students' social and academic competencies contribute to the quality of their relationships with teachers and that forming positive relationships with teachers is an important competency in and of itself, should not be ignored in conceptualizations of teacher–student relationships.

In addition, research indicates that characteristics of students might enhance or detract from their tendency to establish supportive relationships with teachers. For example, in the elementary-school years, relations between close and secure teacher–student relationships and student adjustment tend to be stronger for ethnic minority and at-risk students than for European American students (Burchinal, Peisner-Feinberg, Pianta, & Howes, 2002;

Meehan, Hughes, & Cavell, 2003; cf., Ladd & Burgess, 2001). Relatedness with teachers also tends to be associated with student outcomes more strongly for special education students than for regular students (Little & Kobak, 2003) and for boys than girls (Furrer & Skinner, 2003). Research on perceived emotional support also suggests that supportive relationships might be more important for some students than for others. In particular, relations between perceived emotional support from teachers and student adjustment are moderated by SES and race such that students from lower SES backgrounds (Dornbusch, Erickson, Laird, & Wong, 2001) and members of minority groups (Certo, Cauley, & Chafin, 2003; Crosnoe et al., 2004) tend to benefit more from close relationships with teachers than do other students; school-level factors such as safety, racial homogeneity, SES of the student body (Crosnoe et al., 2004), and composition of instructional teams (Murdock & Miller, 2003) also appear to moderate relations between perceived teacher support and student outcomes. Finally, relatedness with teachers appears to differ as a function of students' age, with more elementary grade students reporting optimal or adequate relationships than middle school students (Lynch & Cicchetti, 1997).

*Summary* Researchers have documented significant relations between positive aspects of teacher–student relationships and students' social and academic functioning at school. At a general level, the theoretical perspectives used to guide this work are based on notions of causal influence, with the nature of teacher–student relationships resulting in student outcomes. In this regard, each acknowledges the importance of emotionally supportive relationships with teachers for students' success at school. Secure and emotionally supportive relationships and interactions are believed to result in a sense of belongingness and relatedness in children that in turn, support a positive sense of self, the adoption of socially desirable goals and values, and the development of social and academic competencies. Socialization perspectives based on the notion of person–environment fit complement this work by focusing on additional dimensions of teacher–student interactions, highlighting their independent contributions to student outcomes. A distinguishing characteristic of this approach is an exclusive focus on social provisions that are central to the educative process, such as resources that contribute directly to learning and to physical and emotional safety in the classroom.

In contrast to assumptions that teacher–student relationships have causal influence, the possibility that student competencies determine the nature and quality of teacher–student relationships or that significant correlations between qualities of teacher–student relationships and student outcomes are merely spurious, raises the important question as to whether these relationships really matter when other factors are taken into account. In the following section, evidence that addresses this question is reviewed.

## Do Students' Relationships with Teachers Really Matter?

For the most part, when children rate the importance of their relationships with mothers, fathers, siblings, teachers, and friends, they typically report being very satisfied with their relationships with their teachers, and rank teachers as most important for providing instrumental aid and informational support at levels comparable to instrumental help from mothers and fathers (Lempers & Clark-Lempers, 1992). In contrast, on dimensions such as intimacy, companionship, nurturance, and admiration, teachers are routinely ranked by children as the least likely source of support when compared to parents and peers (Furman & Buhrmester, 1985; Lempers & Clark-Lempers, 1992; Reid, Landesman, Treder, & Jaccard, 1989). Moreover, although these relative rankings remain stable from childhood into adolescence (Furman & Buhrmester, 1985), the overall importance of teachers in students' lives appears to decline with age (Lempers & Clark-Lempers, 1992).

Given these findings, it is important to ask if teachers have a meaningful impact on students when other sources of support are taken into account. Indeed, most conclusions concerning the importance of teacher–student relationships and interactions are based on studies that have not taken into account the contribution of other relationships that might contribute to students' adjustment to school. Understanding the impact of teacher–student relationships on student functioning also is constrained by methodological challenges. In this section, each of these issues will be considered, beginning with a review of studies that address the impact of teacher–student relationships on student outcomes when other interpersonal relationships are considered, followed by a discussion of measurement and design issues.

### Teacher versus Parental Influence

One of the enduring issues with respect to the influence of teacher–student relationships on student adjustment concerns the possibility that the quality of students' interactions with teachers simply duplicates the quality of their relationships at home. If so, then assessments of teacher–student relationships are merely proxies for parent–child relationships, with supports and continuity across home and school settings explaining student outcomes more so than students' experiences that are unique to teachers. Research that addresses this issue has been conducted from multiple perspectives. Attachment theory predicts that at least in young children, internal representations of the self and others established in the context of the primary attachment relationship should result in relationship qualities that are similar across parents and teachers. In support of this notion are findings indicating that mother–child attachment classifications at 54 months predict the quality of teacher–child relationships in kindergarten and first grade (O'Connor & McCartney, 2006). In studies of preschool and early elementary school children, attachment classifications for mother–child and teacher–child relationships are fairly concordant, with 69% of relationships showing the same classification (Howes & Hamilton, 1992).

Similar levels of concordance have been reported in studies of elementary-aged and middle school children's emotional relatedness with mothers and teachers. Lynch and Cicchetti (1992) demonstrated moderate levels of concordance between elementary-aged maltreated and nonmaltreated children's reports of relatedness to teachers and to their mothers, although 37% could not be classified into a relatedness category. Maltreated children had less positive patterns of emotional quality and proximity seeking with teachers than those not maltreated by their parents. Finally, the degree and intensity of conflict that children experience with parents and siblings tends to predict later relationships with teachers marked by conflict (Ingoldsby, Shaw, & Garcia, 2001)

If the quality of a child's relationships remains fairly stable across caregivers, however, an important question is whether the affective quality of teacher–student relationships are important for understanding children's functioning at school when the quality of the parent–child relationship is taken into account. Research that addresses this question has had mixed results, depending on the age of the child and the outcomes being studied. In some observational studies of caregiver–child relationships in preschool and kindergarten, emotionally supportive interactions with nonparental caregivers have not been related significantly to child outcomes when family and child characteristics (e.g., child sex, maternal sensitivity) were taken into account (National Institute of Child Health and Development [NICHD], 2003a, 2003b).

Other researchers, however, have documented significant relations between affective qualities of teacher–child relationships (i.e., closeness and conflict) and student outcomes when controlling for family characteristics and observed classroom climate (Peisner-Feinberg et al., 2001). For example, mothers' education and parenting styles have been found to moderate relations between teacher–child closeness and children's problem behavior (Peisner-Feinberg et al., 2001), and between teacher–child closeness and changes in academic performance over time (Burchinal et al., 2002), such that children with high risk backgrounds tend to benefit more from positive relationships with teachers than do other children. Secure and emotionally close relationships with teachers also appear to have some positive compensatory effects on the prosocial behavior of preschool children who are insecurely attached to their mothers (Mitchell-Copeland et al., 1997). Finally, grade retention has been related to teacher reports of supportive teacher–student relationships but not to parental involvement in first-grade children's schooling (Willson & Hughes, 2006).

In studies of elementary-aged children, results based on assessments of teacher involvement and students' sense of relatedness (Connell & Wellborn, 1991) also are mixed. For example, Furrer and Skinner (2003) reported that student–teacher relatedness predicts classroom engagement and emotional functioning over and above relatedness with parents and peers. Teachers also appeared to play a compensatory role in that children who enjoyed high levels of relatedness to parents and peers but not to teachers demonstrated lower levels of school adjustment than did children who enjoyed high levels of relatedness across all three relationships. In addition, students who experienced low levels of relatedness in relationships with parents and peers but high levels in relationships with teachers also reported higher levels of positive engagement and emotion than did students who reported low levels of relatedness in all three relationships. In contrast, R. M. Ryan et al. (1994) reported that associations between teacher–student relationships and adolescent outcomes are fairly weak and inconsistent when parental attachment dimensions are included in analyses.

The question of whether the quality of teacher–student relationships makes a meaningful difference in students' lives has also been addressed in research on students' subjective appraisals of emotional support from teachers. For instance, nonsignificant relations between teacher support and problem behavior at school when support from peers and parents is taken into account have been reported (Dubow, Tisak, Causey, Hryshko, & Reid, 1991). In other studies, however, parenting styles have moderated the relation between perceived support and behavior such that highly aggressive students with rejecting parents seem to benefit more from positive teacher support than children experiencing more positive interactions with parents (Hughes, Cavell, & Jackson, 1999).

In addition, research on multiple sources of emotional support suggests that perceived teacher support is a significant predictor of academic motivation in the form of self-efficacy, intrinsic value, and academic aspirations (Ibanez et al., 2004; Murdock, & Miller, 2003) when support from parents and peers also is considered. Middle school students' perceptions of teacher emotional support have been related positively to students' perceived academic competence, and to values and interest in academics, over and above the influence of perceived parental support (Marchant et al., 2001). Finally, in a study of perceived emotional support from teachers, parents, and peers, perceived support from teachers was unique in its relation to students' interest in class and pursuit of goals to adhere to classroom rules and norms; in contrast, perceived support from parents was related to students' motivational orientations toward achievement, and support from peers was related to students' pursuit of goals to be helpful and cooperative (Wentzel, 1998).

In summary, evidence that the effects of students' relationships with teachers on their functioning at school can be explained by the quality of parent–child relationship is mixed. As evidenced by research on the concordance of students' attachment relationships with parents and teachers, continuity across contexts is not always evident, and aspects of teacher–student relationships often predict student outcomes over and above similar aspects of parent–child relationships (e.g., Brody, Dorsey, Forehand, & Armistead,

2002). The effects of teacher–student relationships on student outcomes appear to be strongest when parent–child relationships are less positive than teacher–student relationships. Findings on perceived social support also suggest that the effects of emotional support from teachers are likely to be domain specific, with teacher support being related most strongly to those outcomes to which teachers contribute most, such as academic interest and classroom behavior.

## Teacher versus Peer Influence

Researchers also have examined the relative contribution of student–teacher relationships and student–peer relationships to adjustment at school. The notion that peers can serve as potentially powerful motivators of academic engagement is generally supported in the empirical literature. For example, the positive academic and social effects of emotional support from peers are well-documented (Wentzel, 2005). Students communicate academic and social expectations to each other on an ongoing basis (Wentzel & Looney, 2006). In addition, enjoying positive relationships with peers also can lead directly to resources and information that help students learn (Guay, Boivin, & Hodges, 1999). Few of the studies on the quality of students' peer interactions and supports have also included assessments of the quality of teacher–student relationships. Indeed, positive peer relationships often are considered to be an outcome of positive relationships with teachers (e.g., Howes & Hamilton, 1993).

In support of a conclusion that teacher–student relationships have unique influence relative to peer relationships, Ladd and Burgess (2001) reported teacher–child conflict and closeness to predict aspects of children's behavioral, psychological, and academic adjustment when taking into account levels of peer rejection and acceptance. A study of middle school students without friends (Wentzel & Asher, 1995) supports this finding in that students who had few friends and were neither well-liked or disliked by their peers (sociometrically neglected children), were the most well-liked by their teachers, the most highly motivated students, and were equally self-confident when compared to their average status peers. In contrast, Wentzel et al. (2007) reported that perceived peer expectations for positive social behavior but not teachers' expectations in that regard predicted middle school students' prosocial behavior. However, teacher and peer expectations both predicted students' reasons for behaving prosocially, with peer expectations predicting internal reasons (e.g., it's important) and teachers' expectations predicting internal as well as external reasons (e.g. to stay out of trouble) for behavior.

## Measurement and Design Issues

It is clear that drawing conclusions about the effects of teacher–student relationships on student outcomes must take into account the contributions of parents and peers in students' lives. Measurement issues associated with various assessments of teacher–student relationships also are important to consider. In this section, issues associated with the measurement of the affective quality of teacher–student relationships and more general issues of methods and design are discussed.

***Measuring the Affective Quality of Teacher–Student Relationships*** Most researchers who study the affective quality of teacher–student relationships typically assess attachment-related constructs of emotional closeness and security, conflict, and overdependency (e.g., Pianta et al., 2003), or levels of psychological proximity and affective qualities of relationships (e.g., Wellborn & Connell, 1987). Operationalizations of these constructs generally reflect their focus on the affective quality of relationships. However, assessment strategies differ with respect to the source of information about the relationship. The most widely used measure, the Student–Teacher Relationship Scale (STRS; Pianta & Steinberg, 1992), was developed from items in the parent–child attachment Q-Set (Waters & Deane, 1985) to tap teachers' representations of their relationships with students (Lynch & Cicchetti, 1992). Initial scale development identified four factors reflecting teachers' reports of the quality of affect and involvement in a specific teacher–child relationship: warm/close, dependent, troubled/closed, and conflicted/angry. Most researchers have used a revised form of the STRS that includes three dimensions, closeness, conflict, and dependency, with dependency and conflict often collapsed into a single dimension (e.g., Ladd & Burgess, 1999). The STRS has been used primarily to study the affective quality of teacher–child relationships in the preschool and early elementary school years.

A consideration of the psychometric properties of the STRS is essential for understanding the literature on teachers' relationships with young children. On a positive note, scale scores for this measure are reliable, with acceptable levels of internal consistency. Conflict and closeness tend to be stable across the preschool, kindergarten, and first grade years (Birch & Ladd, 1998; Ladd & Burgess, 1999; Peisner-Feinberg et al., 2001; Pianta & Stuhlman, 2004), even when controlling for child behavior (Birch & Ladd, 1998); reports of teacher–child dependency tend to be less stable (Ladd & Burgess, 1998). The STRS also has demonstrated good predictive validity. Pianta and Steinberg (1992) report low to moderate correlations between STRS subscales and mothers' reports of child behavior, with teacher–child conflict related positively to acting out and negatively to competent behavior, and teacher–child closeness related positively to competent behavior. Positive affective qualities of observed mother–child interactions (Pianta et al., 1997) but not harsh and restrictive childrearing (Silver, Measelle, Armstrong, & Essex, 2005) also have been related to secure teacher–student relationships. However, observations of classroom climate and instruction tend to be more predictive of achievement outcomes than STRS scores over time (Hamre & Pianta, 2005; Peisner-Feinberg et al., 2001), and children's reports of the emotional qual-

ity of their relationships with teachers tend to be related to externalizing behavior and with observed teacher–student interactions more strongly than STRS scores (Henricsson & Rydell, 2004).

Finally, in studies of elementary-aged students, researchers also have provided evidence of convergent validity in that teacher reports of conflict but not closeness are related to child reports of emotional dissatisfaction with teachers (Henricsson & Rydell, 2004), and reports of closeness are related to child reports of teacher warmth (Mantzicopoulos & Neuharth-Pritchett, 2003) and caring (Valeski & Stipek, 2001). Teacher-reported conflict also has been related positively to observations of mutual anger and teachers' use of corrective behavior (Henricsson & Rydell, 2004). In contrast, observational scores of positive teacher–student interactions have not been related positively to teacher–child closeness in preschool samples (Henricsson & Rydell, 2004), and at this age, child and teacher reports of warmth and conflict tend to be unrelated (Mantzicopoulos, 2005). In studies of older children, teacher and child reports of teacher–student relationships also tend to have low levels of concordance. Elementary school teachers' reports of their involvement (i.e., relatedness with students) are related only weakly to students' reports of teacher involvement (Furrer & Skinner, 2003).

The general lack of concordance between teacher and student reports of the quality of teacher–student relationships is especially important to note in that most studies use teachers' reports to assess the quality of teacher–student relationships. A sole reliance on information from teachers is problematic in several respects. First, teacher ratings of closeness and warmth tend to differ for boys and girls (e.g., Birch & Ladd, 1998; Hamre & Pianta, 2001; Silver et al., 2005) and for minority and majority children (Ladd & Burgess, 2001), with teachers reporting closer and less conflictual relationships with girls and majority (European American) children. Moreover, teacher ethnicity and mismatch between the race/ethnicity of teachers and students is related to conflict and dependency in teacher–student relationships (E. O'Connor & McCartney, 2006; Saft & Pianta, 2001). These findings suggest that the role of specific teacher characteristics in creating biased reports cannot be discounted. Second, teachers also tend to be the source of information about student outcomes (e.g., Birch & Ladd, 1997; Hughes & Kwok, 2006). Therefore, relationship quality and student adjustment scores rarely are independent; significant findings are likely to be inflated. Finally, the teachers who participate in these studies are female; it is unknown if male teachers would yield similar findings.

In studies of older students, researchers have typically employed student reports to assess the quality of teacher–student relationships. Early versions of the Relatedness scale from the Rochester Assessment Package for Schools (RAPS, 1998; Wellborn & Connell, 1987), assessed both the emotional quality of relationships, (e.g., "When I'm with my teacher I feel…relaxed, ignored, happy, mad, bored, important, unhappy, scared, safe and sad"), and psychological proximity (e.g., "I wish my teacher paid more attention to me"), typically yielding five patterns of relatedness: optimal, disengaged, average, confused, deprived. More recently, the RAPS relatedness scale was redesigned to assess felt emotional security (RAPS, 1998). Students' perceptions of teachers are tapped by the Inventory of Adolescent Attachments (IAA; Murray & Greenberg, 2000) regarding emotional security, emotional utilization (reliance in emotionally charged situations), school utilization (help with school problems), and emulation (identification with).

Most of the research on subjective appraisals of emotionally supportive teachers can be characterized by the assessment of students' general perceptions that teachers care about them, facilitate their emotional well-being, and demonstrate appreciation of them as individuals. A number of measures have been employed to measure perceptions of social support, although items are highly similar across the various instruments. Most research in this area has targeted middle school (e.g., Mitchell-Copeland et al., 1997; Murdock & Miller, 2003; Reddy et al., 2003; A.M. Ryan, Patrick, & Shim, 2005), and high school (e.g., Crosnoe et al., 2004; Faircloth & Hamm, 2005; Felner et al., 1985; Sanchez et al., 2005) samples (see Blankemeyer et al., 2002; Hughes et al., 1999; Valeski & Stipek, 2001, for studies of younger children). Students and schools representing all levels of the socioeconomic spectrum, and diverse racial and ethnic groups are represented in this research (Certo et al., 2003; Ibanez et al., 2004; Mitchell-Copeland et al., 1997; Sanchez et al.; Seidman, Allen, Aber, Mitchell, & Feinman, 1994; Valeski & Stipek, 2001).

Measurement issues also should inform interpretations of the research based on student reports. First, findings tend to differ depending on the characteristics of student informants. For example, students' perceptions of teacher support tend to decline with age and across school transitions (Blankemeyer et al., 2002; Reddy et al., 2003; Seidman et al., 1994), and are typically stronger for girls than for boys (Blankemeyer et al.; Wentzel, 2002) and for European American than for ethnic minority students (Wentzel). The degree to which these findings reflect differences in actual support received, or differences in the interpretation or relevance of items across different groups of students within different educational contexts remains an empirical question.

An additional issue regarding the use of students' subjective appraisals of teacher support is that, as with any self-report data, results might be explained by other self-processes related to perceived support. For example, significant and often moderate to strong correlations between perceived support and emotional stress, depression, or low feelings of self-worth (e.g., Wentzel, 1997, 1998) suggest that conclusions concerning perceived social support be made with caution. Research designs that control for the potentially confounding effects of other self-processes and that assess the impact of perceived support over time and contexts are essential for determining the unique impact of perceived support on student functioning.

Finally, few studies have examined the correspondence between teacher and student reports of a teacher's emotional support. Hughes et al. (1999) report nonsignificant relations between the two reports. However, students' perceptions of social and academic support from teachers have been related to teacher reports that they enjoy having students in their class (Wentzel, 1994). Teacher reports of liking students have been related to students' perceptions of teaching styles characterized by warmth, clear communication, and democratic interactions (Chang et al., 2004) as well as observed instructional practices characterized by warmth (Stipek & Byler, 2004). Hughes, Zhang, and Hill (2006) report a weak but significant correlation between teacher support as assessed by peers and student responses to a school belonging scale that includes questions about teacher support.

A small number of researchers have assessed teacher support from the perspective of teachers, asking them how much they like individual students personally or like having them in their classrooms. Results of these studies correspond closely to those obtained from researchers using student reports. Teacher reports have been related positively to young adolescents' prosocial behavior and peer acceptance, and negatively to antisocial behavior and peer rejection (Chang et al., 2004; Wentzel, 1994; Wentzel & Asher, 1995). Being well-liked by teachers also has been related positively to grades (e.g., Wentzel, 1993; Wentzel & Asher, 1995) and test scores (Wentzel, 1993).

***Design Issues*** Most conclusions concerning the importance of teacher–student relationships and interactions are based on correlational data. Correlational strategies have resulted in a wealth of data that can serve as a strong foundation for further theory building and research. Qualitative designs also have been useful for developing profiles of relationships that competent students enjoy. In addition, longitudinal studies of perceived support have documented the predictive strength of students' perceptions over time. For the most part, these studies suggest that students' beliefs about relationships with teachers are highly stable or are likely to have lasting effects on behavior.

In contrast, studies of change in student outcomes as a result of changes in relationships with teachers are rare. Some researchers have documented that an increase in perceived teacher support can lead to improvements in behavior and academic performance (Mitchell-Copeland et al., 1997) as well as in efforts to learn and behave appropriately (Wentzel, 1997) from one year to the next. Experimental studies designed to change the nature of teacher–student relationships are rare. However, when teachers are taught to provide students with warmth and support, clear expectations for behavior, and developmentally appropriate autonomy, their students develop a stronger sense of community, increase displays of socially competent behavior, and show academic gains (Schaps, Battistich, & Solomon, 1993; Watson, Solomon, Battistich, Schaps, & Solomon, 1989). Many comprehensive school reform models also incorporate an explicit focus on teacher–student relationships as a strategy for improving student engagement and learning (Stipek, 2004). However, few of these efforts have documented the unique impact of these relationships on student improvements.

It is clear that establishing causal connections requires assessments of change in student outcomes as a function of changing perceptions of teachers from one year to the next (Wentzel, Williams, & Tomback, 2005), of changing perceptions and outcomes across multiple classrooms, or of interventions designed to change the quality of support from a particular teacher (see Pianta et al., 2003). These strategies also are useful for determining the influence of teacher–student relationships on student outcomes relative to parent–child relationships. Assuming that parent–child relationships remain fairly constant, significant changes in child outcomes could then be attributed to new relationships with teachers. In this regard, changes in the quality of child–teacher attachments during the preschool years as children move to new childcare settings have been related to changes in their social functioning (Howes & Hamilton, 1993).

An additional issue with respect to research design concerns the unit of analysis, and whether support is assessed at the level of the individual student, classroom, or school (Fraser & Fisher, 1982). Studies that relate individual students' perceptions of support to student outcomes yield important information about the psychological impact of social support. For the most part, however, researchers that focus on individual differences typically disregard the fact that teacher or classroom effects might also explain student outcomes. These studies could profit from an examination of between-classroom effects by gathering information on a larger number of classrooms. More complex designs that take into consideration the nested quality of social support at the level of student, classroom, and school are needed in this regard.

*Summary* Although research is mixed, there is some indication that students might form relationships with teachers that are different from those with parents and peers, and that these relationships can motivate positive student outcomes over and above other social influences. However, identifying specific ways in which these relationships can actively and directly promote the development of positive motivational orientations toward learning and academic competencies, independently of other relationship supports from parents and peers, remains a challenge for researchers in this area. Measurement and design issues also need to inform future work on students' relationships with teachers. In this regard, the influence of students' and teachers' sex, race, and other background characteristics on perceptions of teacher–student relationships requires further examination. Developmental issues also require greater focus. Ideally, studies should be designed so that multiple and independent sources inform assessments; work in this area also could benefit from more experimental approaches and observational techniques that capture supportive aspects of teachers' instructional practice.

## Conclusions and Future Directions for the Field

I began this chapter by posing the question of how and why students' relationships with teachers might be related to their social and academic functioning at school. Several hypotheses have been put forward, including directional influences in which teachers influence students' social and academic adjustment, and student competencies promote the development of positive relationships with teachers. In general, the affective quality of teacher–student relationships has been related to children's social and academic competencies as well as to motivational and affective functioning from the preschool years through adolescence. Although many of these findings are based on concurrent assessments of relationship quality and student outcomes, longitudinal findings document that the effects of teacher–student relationships often persist over time. The significance of the teacher–student relationship as a causal predictor of student adjustment is not yet clear. Although some evidence for causal influence has been reported, experimental work is rare.

Regardless of causal directions, the research described in this chapter has established clear associations between the nature and quality of teacher–student relationships and students' social and academic motivation, behavioral competencies, and academic performance at school. These findings appear to be robust regardless of theoretical perspective, type of assessments, and age of the student. Throughout this chapter, issues pertinent to the interpretation of research on this area have been raised. In addition, progress toward understanding the developmental significance of students' relationships with teachers requires more systematic attention to the development of more complex theoretical models, further consideration of what might develop in students as a result of teacher–student relationships, and identification of individual differences in teachers that contribute to the nature and quality of teacher–student relationships.

As noted at the beginning of this chapter, the predominant approach to the study of teacher–student relationships is to assume a causal connection such that the nature and quality of relationships and interactions influence student outcomes. A consideration of alternative pathways, however, would add critical and important insights to the discussion of these relationships. For instance, given the broad range of social and academic skills that students demonstrate at school, it is likely that the influence of student characteristics on the development of teacher–student relationships is as powerful as the reverse. Therefore, models that address the potential impact of children on teachers' behavior and that identify child characteristics that lead to receptive as opposed to rejecting or neglectful behavior on the part of teachers need to be developed to inform this area of research. Similarly, models that identify factors that serve to maintain the cohesion and integrity of teacher–student relationships over time need to be developed. It also is important to consider the possibility that lack of concordance between teacher and student reports of supportive relationships does not always reflect methodological imprecision but rather the fact that relationships often function at a psychological level that is not necessarily reflected in reality. Therefore, examination of various ways in which students interpret teachers' behavior and of the degree to which they attribute their own successes and failures to this behavior is a critical next step in this area of research.

A final issue with respect to model development is that although progress is being made, much of our current understanding of teacher–student relationships is based on studies of White middle-class children. Therefore, models that take into account the diversity of student backgrounds also are needed in this area of research. Although it is likely that the underlying psychological processes that contribute to school adjustment are similar for all students regardless of race, ethnicity, gender, or other contextual and demographic variables, the degree to which these latter factors interact with psychological processes to influence adjustment is not known. To illustrate, self-regulation skills, such as planning, monitoring, and regulation of behavior that support the achievement of classroom goals might be more important for the adjustment of children from minority backgrounds than for children who come from families and communities whose goals and expectations are similar to those of the educational establishment (e.g., Fordham & Ogbu, 1986). Similarly, beliefs about how to characterize supportive interpersonal interactions and relationships are likely to vary as a function of race, gender, neighborhood, or family background. Achieving a better understanding of such interactions deserves our full attention. Models of teacher–student relationships that focus on the impact of multiple interacting systems on child functioning (e.g., Bronfenbrenner, 1989; Patterson & Bank, 1989; Pianta et al., 2003) are likely to provide important insights for future work in this area.

Assuming that teacher–student relationships have a causal influence on student adjustment, what is it that develops or is changed on the part of students as a function of their relationships and interactions with teachers? It is clear that responsive and warm teacher–student relationships are related to a student's sense of emotional well-being and corresponding desires to contribute to the smooth functioning of classroom activities. In this regard, teachers' communication of expectations might be particularly important for understanding students' reasons for pursuing classroom-specific goals (Wentzel et al., 2007), and values for academic and social outcomes (Wigfield & Eccles, 2000). Teachers' provisions of help and instrumental aid are likely to be especially influential in promoting students' sense of efficacy for academic and social tasks (Bandura, 1986). In turn, these motivational outcomes are likely to influence students' school-related outcomes (Wentzel, 2004). It also is possible that supportive relationships with teachers might be especially critical at certain ages and transition points when rules and student roles are renegotiated. Teachers are the most proximal source of support during transitions

and therefore, have the potential to play a significant role of sustaining children's self-perceptions and motivation to engage in positive social and academic tasks as they adapt to new school settings (Eccles & Midgley, 1989).

Also important for understanding "what develops" is a focus on the cumulative effects of having positive relationships with many teachers over time, and their contribution to a student's sense of school community and belongingness. School belongingness measures assess in part students' perceptions of the quality of relationships with all of their teachers as a group (see Goodenow, 1993; Roeser & Eccles, 1998). The power of these overall effects is evidenced by positive relations of school belongingness to students' behavioral (Battistich et al., 1995; Brand, Felner, Shim, Seitsinger, & Dumas, 2003) and academic (Anderman, 2002; Brand et al., 2003) outcomes, with effects often being moderated by students' sex, race (e.g., Kuperminc, Leadbetter, Emmons, & Blatt, 1997), school size (Anderman, 2002), and poverty levels of the schools' community (Battistich et al., 1995). The extent to which these more global beliefs develop out of interactions and relationships with single or multiple teachers, reflect a student's ongoing history of relationships or a single but salient recent relationship, or explain positive student outcomes over and above relationships with single teachers are important remaining questions to address in this area of work.

If teachers have influence by way of the relationships and interactions they have with students, it also becomes essential to understand those factors that contribute to teachers' ability and willingness to engage in these positive forms of social interaction. Research is relatively rare that examines factors that foster supportiveness and caring on the part of teachers. However, teacher stress appears to contribute to the number of negative relationships that elementary school teachers report having with their students (Yoon, 2002), depression has been related to the sensitivity and responsiveness of preschool teachers (Hamre & Pianta, 2005), and a secure attachment style has been related to positive as opposed to conflictual interactions of elementary school teachers with their students (Morris-Rothschild & Brassard, 2006). Teachers' sense of efficacy with regard to classroom management also has been related to positive relationships and interactions with elementary-aged students (Morris-Rothschild & Brassard, 2006; Yoon, 2002). Therefore, the potential impact of teacher characteristics on their assessments of relationships with students needs to be taken into account when drawing inferences from this work.

Research on characteristics of parents that predict effective parenting (see Grusec & Goodnow, 1994) might also be informative for understanding effective teachers. For example, it is clear that teachers communicate their expectations and goals to students on a daily basis. However, less is known about the nature of these communications that might predispose students to accept or reject them. The family socialization literature suggests that parental messages are more likely to be perceived accurately by children if they are clear and consistent, are framed in ways that are meaningful to the child, require decoding and processing, are perceived by the child to be of clear importance to the parent, and as being conveyed with positive intentions (Grusec & Goodnow, 1994). Adapting this work to the realm of the classroom might provide important insights into effective forms of teacher communication that lead to students' adoption of socially valued goals.

Finally, school-level factors are likely to influence teachers' ability to create supportive classroom environments for their students. For example, job satisfaction, over and above gender, teacher education, and classroom management skills, has been related to high school teachers' provisions of instrumental help and challenge, especially with low ability students (Opdenakker & Van Damme, 2006). Other factors such as the quality of feedback given to teachers from administrators, teacher autonomy, and participation in school decision making, opportunities for collaboration and development of positive relationships with peers, and instructional help and resources are likely to contribute to teachers' ability and willingness to provide similar kinds of supports for their students (Firestone & Pennell, 1993). Indeed, if provisions of positive supports contribute to students' successful functioning at school, provisions of similar supports to teachers are likely to improve their practice as well.

## References

Auffrey, A., & Wentzel, K. R. (2000, March). *Teachers as caregivers: Their beliefs in relation to student outcomes.* Poster presented at the Biennial meeting of the Society for Research on Adolescence, Chicago.

Ames, C. (1992). Classrooms: Goals, structures, and student motivation. *Journal of Educational Psychology, 84,* 261–271.

Anderman, E. M. (2002). School effects on psychological outcomes during adolescence. *Journal of Educational Psychology, 94,* 795–780.

Bandura, A. (1986). *Social foundations of thought and action: A social cognitive theory.* Englewood Cliffs, NJ: Prentice-Hall.

Battistich, V., Solomon, D., Kim, D., Watson, M., & Schaps, E. (1995). Schools as communities, poverty levels of student populations, and students' attitudes, motives, and performance: A multilevel analysis. *American Educational Research Journal, 32,* 627–658.

Becker, B. E., & Luthar, S. S. (2002). Social-emotional factors affecting achievement outcomes among disadvantaged students: Closing the achievement gap. *Educationalist Psychologist, 37,* 197–214.

Birch, S. H., & Ladd, G. W. (1997). The teacher–child relationship and children's early school adjustment. *Journal of School Psychology, 35,* 61–79.

Birch, S. H., & Ladd, G. W. (1998). Children's interpersonal behaviors and the teacher-child relationship. *Developmental Psychology, 34,* 934–946.

Blankemeyer, M., Flannery, D. J., & Vazsonyi, A.T. (2002). The role of aggression and social competence in children's perceptions of the child-teacher relationship. *Psychology in the Schools, 39,* 293–304.

Bowlby, J. (1969). *Attachment and loss: Vol. 1. Attachment.* New York: Basic Books.

Brand, S., Felner, R., Shim, M., Seitsinger, A., & Dumas, T. (2003). Middle school improvement and reform: Development and validation of a school-level assessment of climate, cultural pluralism and school safety. *Journal of Educational Psychology, 95,* 570–588.

Bretherton, I. (1987). New perspectives on attachment relations: Security, communication and internal working models. In J. Osofsky (Ed.), *Handbook of infant development* (pp. 1061–1100). New York: Wiley.

Brody, G. H., Dorsey, S., Forehand, R., & Armistead, L. (2002). Unique and protective contributions of parenting and classroom processes to the adjustment of African American children living in single-parent families. *Child Development, 73,* 274–286.

Bronfenbrenner, U. (1989). Ecological systems theory. In R. Vasta (Ed.), *Annals of child development* (Vol. 6, pp. 187–250). Greenwich, CT: JAI.

Brophy, J. E., & Good, T. L. (1974). *Teacher–student relationships: Causes and consequences.* New York: Holt, Rinehart & Winston.

Burchinal, M. R., Peisner-Feinberg, E., Pianta, R., & Howes, C. (2002). Development of academic skills from preschool through second grade: Family and classroom predictors of developmental trajectories. *Journal of School Psychology, 40,* 415–436.

Certo, J. L., Cauley, K. M., & Chafin, C. (2003). Students' perspectives on their high school experience. *Adolescence, 38,* 705–724.

Chang, L. (2003). Variable effects of children's aggression, social withdrawal, and prosocial leadership as functions of teacher beliefs and behaviors. *Child Development, 74,* 535–548.

Chang, L., Liu, H. Y., Wen, Z. L., Fung, K. Y., Wang, Y., & Xu, Y. Y. (2004). Mediating teacher liking and moderating authoritative teachering on Chinese adolescents' perceptions of antisocial and prosocial behaviors. *Journal of Educational Psychology, 96,* 369–380..

Cohen, S., & Wills, T. A. (1985). Stress, social support, and the buffering hypothesis. *Psychological Bulletin, 98,* 310–357.

Connell, J. P., & Wellborn, J. G. (1991). Competence, autonomy, and relatedness: A motivational analysis of self-system processes. In M. R. Gunnar & L. A. Sroufe (Eds.), *Self processes and development: The Minnesota symposia on child development* (Vol. 23, pp. 43–78). Hillsdale, NJ: Erlbaum.

Crosnoe, R., Johnson, M. K., & Elder, G. H., Jr. (2004). Intergenerational bonding in school: The behavioral and contextual correlates of student–teacher relationships. *Sociology of Education, 77,* 60–81.

Daniels, E., & Arapostathis, M. (2005). What do they really want? Student voices and motivation research. *Urban Education, 40,* 34–59.

Davis, H. A. (2001). The quality and impact of relationships between elementary school students and teachers. *Contemporary Educational Psychology, 26,* 421–453.

Dornbusch, S. M., Erickson, K. G., Laird, J., & Wong, C. A. (2001). The relation of family and school attachment to adolescent deviance in diverse groups and communities. *Journal of Adolescent Research, 16,* 396–422.

Dubow, E. F., Tisak, J., Causey, D., Hryshko, A., & Reid, G. (1991). A two-year longitudinal study of stressful life events, social support, and social problem-solving skills: Contributions to children's behavioral and academic adjustment. *Child Development, 62,* 583–599.

Eccles, J. S., & Midgley, C. (1989). Stage-environment fit: Developmentally appropriate classrooms for young adolescents. In C. Ames & R. Ames (Eds.), *Research on motivation in education* (Vol. 3, pp. 139–186). New York: Academic Press.

Faircloth, B. S., & Hamm, J. V. (2005). Sense of belonging among high school students representing 4 ethnic groups. *Journal of Youth and Adolescence, 34,* 293–309.

Felner, R. D., Aber, M. S., Primavera, J., & Cauce, A. M. (1985). Adaptation and vulnerability in high-risk adolescents: An examination of environmental mediators. *American Journal of Community Psychology, 13,* 365–379.

Firestone, W. A., & Pennell, J. R. (1993). Teacher commitment, working conditions, and differential incentive policies. *Review of Educational Research, 63,* 498–525.

Ford, M. E. (1992). *Motivating humans: Goals, emotions, and personal agency beliefs.* Newbury Park, CA: Sage.

Fordham, S., & Ogbu, J. U. (1986). Black students' school success: Coping with "the burden of 'acting white'." *The Urban Review, 18,* 176–206.

Fraser, B. J., & Fisher, D. L. (1982). Predicting students' outcomes from their perceptions of classroom psychosocial environment. *American Educational Research Journal, 19,* 498–518.

Furman, W., & Buhrmester, D. (1985). Children's perceptions of the personal relationships in their social networks. *Developmental Psychology, 21*, 1016–1024.

Furrer, C., & Skinner, E. (2003). Sense of relatedness as a factor in children's academic engagement and performance. *Journal of Educational Psychology, 95*, 148–162.

Goetz, T. S., & Dweck, C. S. (1980). Learned helplessness in social situations. *Journal of Personality and Social Psychology, 39*, 246–255.

Goodenow, C. (1993). The psychological sense of school membership among adolescents—Scale development and educational correlates. *Psychology in the Schools, 30*, 79–90.

Graham, S., Taylor, A., & Hudley, C. (1998). Exploring achievement values among ethnic minority early adolescents. *Journal of Educational Psychology, 90*, 606–620.

Grolnick, W. S., Gurland, S. T., Jacob, K. F., & Decourcey, W. (2001). The development of self-determination in middle childhood and adolescence. In A. Wigfield & J. Eccles (Eds.), *Development of achievement motivation* (pp. 148–174). Academic Press.

Grolnick, W. S., Kurowski, C. O., & Gurland, S. T. (1999). Family processes and the development of children's self-regulation. *Educational Psychologist, 34*, 3–14.

Grolnick, W. S., & Ryan, R. M. (1989). Parent styles associated with children's self-regulation and competence in school. *Journal of Educational Psychology, 81*, 143–154.

Grusec, J. E., & Goodnow, J. J. (1994). Impact of parental discipline methods on the child's internalization of values: A reconceptualization of current points of view. *Developmental Psychology, 30*, 4–19.

Guay, F., Boivin, M., & Hodges, E. V. E. (1999). Predicting change in academic achievement: A model of peer experiences and self-system processes. *Journal of Educational Psychology, 91*, 105–115.

Hamre, B. K., & Pianta, R. C. (2001). Early teacher–child relationships and the trajectory of children's school outcomes through eighth grade. *Child Development, 72*, 625–638.

Hamre, B. K., & Pianta, R. C. (2005). Can instructional and emotional support in the first-grade classroom make a difference for children at risk of school failure? *Child Development, 76*, 949–967.

Hargreaves, D. H., Hester, S. K., & Mellor, F. J. (1975). *Deviance in classrooms*. London: Routledge & Kegan Paul.

Hayes, C. B., Ryan, A., & Zseller, E. B. (1994). The middle school child's perceptions of caring teachers. *American Journal of Education, 103*, 1–19.

Henricsson, L., & Rydell, A. M. (2004). Elementary school children with behavior problems: Teacher–child relations and self-perception. A prospective study. *Merrill-Palmer Quarterly—Journal of Developmental Psychology, 50*, 111–138.

Howes, C., & Hamilton, C. E. (1992). Children's relationships with caregivers—Mothers and child-care teachers. *Child Development, 63*, 859–866.

Howes, C., & Hamilton, C. E. (1993). The changing experience of child care: Changes in teachers and in teacher–child relationships and children's social competence with peers. *Early Childhood Research Quarterly, 8*, 15–32.

Hoy, A. W., & Weinstein, C. S. (2006). Student and teacher perspectives on classroom management. In C. Evertson & C. Weinstein (Eds.), *Handbook of classroom management—Research, practice, and contemporary issues* (pp. 181–219). Mahwah, NJ: Erlbaum.

Hughes, J. N., Cavell, T. A., & Jackson, T. (1999). Influence of the teacher–student relationship on childhood conduct problems: A prospective study. *Journal of Clinical Child Psychology, 28*, 173–184.

Hughes, J. N., & Kwok, O. M. (2006). Classroom engagement mediates the effect of teacher–student support on elementary students' peer acceptance: A prospective analysis. *Journal of School Psychology, 43*, 465–480.

Hughes, J. N., Zhang, D., & Hill, C. R. (2006). Peer assessments of nonnative and individual teacher–student support predict social acceptance and engagement among low-achieving children. *Journal of School Psychology, 43*, 447–463.

Ibanez, G. E., Kuperminc, G. P., Jurkovic, G., & Perilla, J. (2004). Cultural attributes and adaptations linked to achievement motivation among Latino adolescents. *Journal of Youth and Adolescence, 33*, 559–568.

Ingoldsby, E. M., Shaw, D. S., & Garcia, M. M. (2001). Intrafamily conflict in relation to boys' adjustment at school. *Development and Psychopathology, 13*, 35–52.

Isakson, K., & Jarvis, P. (1999). The adjustment of adolescents during the transition into high school: A short-term longitudinal study. *Journal of Youth and Adolescence, 28*, 1–26.

Jussim, L. (1991). Social perception and social reality: A reflection-construction model. *Psychological Review, 98*, 9–34.

Jussim, L., & Eccles, J. (1995). Naturalistic studies of interpersonal expectancies. *Psychology, 63*, 947–961.

Jussim, L., & Harber, K. D. (2005). Teacher expectations and self-fulfilling prophecies: Knowns and unknowns, resolved, and unresolved controversies. *Personality and Social Psychology Review, 9*, 131–155.

Kuperminc, G. P., Leadbetter, B. J., Emmons, C., & Blatt, S. J. (1997). Perceived school climate and difficulties in the social adjustment of middle school students. *Applied Developmental Psychology, 1*, 76–88.

Ladd, G. W., & Burgess, K. B. (1999). Charting the relationship trajectories of aggressive, withdrawn, and aggressive/withdrawn children during early grade school. *Child Development, 70*, 910–929.

Ladd, G. W., & Burgess, K. B. (2001). Do relational risks and protective factors moderate the linkages between childhood aggression and early psychological and school adjustment? *Child Development, 72*, 1579–1601.

Lemerise, E. A., & Arsenio, W. F. (2000). An integrated model of emotion processes and cognition in social information processing. *Child Development, 71*, 107–118.

Lempers, J. D., & Clark-Lempers, D. S. (1992). Young, middle and late adolescents' comparisons of the functional importance of five significant relationships. *Journal of Youth and Adolescence, 21*, 53–96.

Little, M., & Kobak, R. (2003). Emotional security with teachers and children's stress reactivity: A comparison of special-education and regular-education classrooms. *Journal of Clinical Child and Adolescent Psychology, 32*, 127–138.

Lynch, M., & Cicchetti, D. (1997). Children's relationships with adults and peers: An examination of elementary and junior high school students. *Journal of School Psychology, 35*, 81–99.

Madon, S., Jussim, L., & Eccles, J. (1997). In search of self-fulfilling prophecy. *Journal of Personality and Social Psychology, 72*, 791–809.

Mantzicopoulos, P. (2005). Conflictual relationships between kindergarten children and their teachers: Associations with child and classroom context variables. *Journal of School Psychology, 43*, 425–442.

Mantzicopoulos, P., & Neuharth-Pritchett, S. (2003). Development and validation of a measure to assess head start children's appraisals of teacher support. *Journal of School Psychology, 41*, 431–451.

Marchant, G. J., Paulson, S. E., & Rothlisberg, B. A. (2001). Relations of middle school students' perceptions of family and school contexts with academic achievement. *Psychology in the Schools, 38*, 505–519.

Meehan, B. T., Hughes, J. N., & Cavell, T. A. (2003). Teacher–student relationships as compensatory resources for aggressive children. *Child Development, 74*, 1145–1157.

Midgley, C. (2002). *Goals, goal structures, and patterns of adaptive learning*. Mahwah, NJ: Erlbaum.

Midgley, C., Feldlaufer, H., & Eccles, J. (1989). Student/teacher relations and attitudes toward mathematics before and after the transition to junior high school. *Child Development, 60*, 981–992.

Mitchell-Copeland, J., Denham, S. A., & DeMulder, E. K. (1997). Q-sort assessment of child–teacher attachment relationships and social competence in the preschool. *Early Education and Development, 8*, 27–39.

Moje, E. B. (1996). "I teach students, not subjects": Teacher–student relationships as contexts for secondary literacy. *Reading Research Quarterly, 31*, 172–195.

Morris-Rothschild, B. K., & Brassard, M. R. (2006). Teachers' conflict management styles: The role of attachment styles and classroom management efficacy. *Journal of School Psychology, 44*, 105–121.

Murdock, T. B., & Miller, A. (2003). Teachers as sources of middle school students' motivational identity: Variable-centered and person-centered analytic approaches. *Elementary School Journal, 103*, 383–399.

Murdock, T. B., Miller, A., & Kohlhardt, J. (2004). Effects of classroom context variables on high school students' judgments of the acceptability and likelihood of cheating. *Journal of Educational Psychology, 96*, 765–777.

Murray, C., & Greenberg, M. T. (2000). Children's relationship with teachers and bonds with school an investigation of patterns and correlates in middle childhood. *Journal of School Psychology, 38*, 423–445.

National Center for Educational Statistics (1995). *Student strategies to avoid harm at school* (NCES Publication No. NCES 95-203). Washington, DC: U.S. Government Printing Office.

National Institute of Child Health and Development (NICHD), Early Child Care Research Network. (2003a). Social functioning in first grade: Associations with earlier home and child care predictors and with current classroom experiences. *Child Development, 74*, 1639–1662.

National Institute of Child Health and Development (NICHD), Early Child Care Research Network. (2003b). Does quality of child care affect child outcomes at age 4½? *Developmental Psychology, 39*, 451–469.

Newman, R. S. (2000). Social influences on the development of children's adaptive hold seeking: The role of parents, teachers, and peers. *Developmental Review, 20*, 350–404.

O'Connor, E., & McCartney, K. (2006). Testing associations between young children's relationships with mothers and teachers. *Journal of Educational Psychology, 98*, 87–98.

O'Connor, T. G., & Hirsch, N. (1999). Intra-individual differences and relationship-specificity of mentalising in early adolescence. *Social Development, 8*, 256–274.

Oates, G. L. (2003). Teacher–student racial congruence, teacher perceptions, and test performance. *Social Science Quarterly, 84*, 508–525.

Oldfather, P. (1993). What students say about motivating experiences in a whole language classroom. *The Reading Teacher, 46*, 672–681.

Olweus, D. (1993). Victimization by peers: Antecedents and long-term outcomes. In K. Rubin & J. B. Asendorf (Eds.), *Social withdrawal, inhibition, and shyness in childhood* (pp. 315–341). Chicago, IL: University of Chicago Press.

Opdenakker, M. C., & Van Damme, J. (2006). Teacher characteristics and teaching styles as effectiveness enhancing factors or classroom practice. *Teaching and Teacher Education, 22*, 1–21.

Patterson, G. R., & Bank, C. L. (1989). Some amplifying mechanisms for pathologic processes in families. In M. R. Gunnar & E. Thelan (Eds.) *Systems and development: The Minnesota symposia on child psychology* (Vol. 22, pp. 167–210). Hillsdale, NJ: Erlbaum.

Patrick, H., Hicks, L., & Ryan, A. M. (1997). Relations of perceived social efficacy and social goal pursuit to self-efficacy for academic work. *Journal of Early Adolescence, 17*, 109–128.

Peisner-Feinberg, E. S., Burchinal, M. R., Clifford, R. M., Culkin, M. L., Howes, C., Kagan, S. L., et al. (2001). The relation of preschool child-care quality to children's cognitive and social developmental trajectories through second grade. *Child Development, 72*, 1534–1553.

Pianta, R. C., Hamre, B., & Stuhlman, M. (2003). Relationships between teachers and children. In W. Reynolds & G. Miller (Eds.), *Handbook of psychology: Vol. 7. Educational psychology* (pp. 199–234). New York: Wiley.

Pianta, R. C., Nimetz, S. L., & Bennett, E. (1997). Mother–child relationships, teacher–child relationships, and school outcomes in preschool and kindergarten. *Early Childhood Research Quarterly, 12*, 263–280.

Pianta, R. C., & Steinberg, M. (1992). Teacher–child relationships and the process of adjusting to school. In W. Damon (Series Ed.) & R. C. Pianta (Vol. Ed.), *New directions for child development: Vol. 57. Beyond the parent: The role of other adults in children's lives* (pp. 61–80). San Francisco, CA: Jossey-Bass.

Pianta, R. C., & Stuhlman, M. W. (2004). Teacher–child relationships and children's success in the first years of school. *School Psychology Review, 33*, 444–458.

Reddy, R., Rhodes, J. E., & Mulhall, P. (2003). The influence of teacher support on student adjustment in the middle school years: A latent growth curve study. *Development and Psychopathology, 15*, 119–138.

Reid, M., Landesman, S., Treder, R., & Jaccard, J. (1989). "My family and friends": Six-to twelve-year-old children's perceptions of social support. *Child Development, 60*, 896–910.

Rochester Assessment Package for Schools (RAPS). (1998). Retrieved from http://www.irre.org/publications/pdfs/RAPS_manual_entire_1998.pdf

Roeser, R. W., & Eccles, J. S. (1998). Adolescents' perceptions of middle school: Relation to longitudinal changes in academic and psychological adjustment. *Journal of Research on Adolescence, 8*, 123–158.

Roeser, R. W., Midgley, C., & Urdan, T. C. (1996). Perceptions of the school psychological environment and early adolescents' psychological and behavioral functioning in school: The mediating role of goals and belonging. *Journal of Educational Psychology, 88*, 408–422.

Rumberger, R. W. (1995). Dropping out of middle school: A multilevel analysis of students and schools. *American Educational Research Journal, 32*, 583–625.

Ryan, A. M., & Patrick, H. (2001). The classroom social environment and changes in adolescents' motivation and engagement during middle school. *American Educational Research Journal, 38*, 437–460.

Ryan, A. M., Patrick, H., & Shim, S. O. (2005). Differential profiles of students identified by their teacher as having avoidant, appropriate, or dependent help-seeking tendencies in the classroom. *Journal of Educational Psychology, 97*, 275–285.

Ryan, R. M. (1993). Agency and organization: Intrinsic motivation, autonomy, and the self in psychological development. In J. Jacobs (Ed.), *Nebraska symposium on motivation* (Vol. 40, pp. 1–56). Lincoln: University of Nebraska Press.

Ryan, R. M., & Deci, E. L. (2000). Self-determination theory and the facilitation of intrinsic motivation, social development, and well-being. *American Psychologist, 55*, 68–78.

Ryan, R. M., Stiller, J. D., & Lynch, J. H. (1994). Representations of relationships to teachers, parents, and friends as predictors of academic motivation and self-esteem. *Journal of Early Adolescence, 14*, 226–249.

Saft, E. W., & Pianta, R. C. (2001). Teachers' perceptions of their relationships with students: Effects of child age, gender, and ethnicity of teachers and children. *School Psychology Quarterly, 16*, 125–141.

Sanchez, B., Colon, Y., & Esparza, P. (2005). The role of sense of school belonging and gender in the academic adjustment of Latino adolescents. *Journal of Youth and Adolescence, 34*, 619–628.

Sarason, B. R., Sarason, I. G., & Pierce, G. R. (1990). Traditional views of social support and their impact on assessment. In B. R. Sarason, I. G. Sarason, & G. R. Sarason (Eds.), *Social support: An interactional view* (pp. 9–25). New York: Wiley.

Schaps, E., Battistich, V., & Solomon, D. (1997). School as a caring community: A key to character education. In A. Molnar (Ed.), *Ninety-sixth yearbook of the National Society for the Study of Education* (pp. 127–139). Chicago, IL: University of Chicago Press.

Seidman, E., Allen, L., Aber, J. L., Mitchell, C., & Feinman, J. (1994). The impact of school transitions in early adolescence on the self-esteem and perceived social context of poor urban youth. *Child Development, 65*, 507–522.

Silver, R. B., Measelle, J. R., Armstrong, J. M., & Essex, M. J. (2005). Trajectories of classroom externalizing behavior: Contributions of child characteristics, family characteristics, and the teacher–child relationship during the school transition. *Journal of School Psychology, 43*, 39–60.

Skinner, E. A., & Belmont, M. J. (1993). Motivation in the classroom: Reciprocal effects of teacher behavior and student engagement across the school year. *Journal of Educational Psychology, 85*, 571–581.

Slavin, R. E., Hurley, E. A., & Chamberlain, A. (2003). Cooperative learning and achievement: Theory and research. In W. Reynolds & G. Miller (Eds.), *Handbook of psychology: Vol. 7. Educational psychology* (pp. 177–198). New York: Wiley.

Smith, A. E., Jussim, L., & Eccles, J. (1999). Do self-fulfilling prophecies accumulate, dissipate, or remain stable over time? *Journal of Personality and Social Psychology, 77*, 548–565.

Smokowski, P. R., Reynolds, A. J., & Bezrucko, N. (2000). Resilience and protective factors in adolescence: An autobiographical perspective from disadvantaged youth. *Journal of School Psychology, 37*, 425–448.

Solomon, D., Schaps, E., Watson, M., & Battistich, V. (1992). Creating caring school and classroom communities for all students. In R. Villa, J. Thousand, W. Stainback, & S. Stainback (Eds.), *Restructuring for caring and effective education: An administrative guide to creating heterogeneous schools* (pp. 41–60). Baltimore, MD: Brookes.

Stipek, D. (2004). *Engaging in schools: Fostering high school students' motivation to learn.* Committee on Increasing High School Students' Engagement and Motivation to Learn. Division of Behavioral and Social Sciences and Education. Washington, DC: National Academy Press.

Stipek, D., & Byler, P. (2004). The early childhood observation measure. *Early Childhood Quarterly, 19,* 375–397.

Valeski, T. N., & Stipek, D. J. (2001). Young children's feelings about school. *Child Development, 72,* 1198–1213.

Waters, E., & Deane, K. E. (1985). Defining and assessing individual differences in attachment relationships—Q-methodology and the organization of behavior in infancy and early childhood. *Monographs of the Society for Research in Child Development, 50*(1–2), 41–65.

Watson, M., Solomon, D., Battistich, V., Schaps, E., & Solomon, J. (1989). The child development project: Combining traditional and developmental approaches to values education. In L. Nucci (Ed.), *Moral development and character education: A dialogue* (pp. 51–92). Berkeley: McCutchan.

Weinstein, C. S. (1998). "I want to be nice, but I have to be mean": Exploring prospective teachers' conceptions of caring and order. *Teaching and Teacher Education, 14,* 153–163.

Weinstein, R. S. (2002). *Reaching higher: The power of expectations in schooling.* Cambridge, MA: Harvard University Press.

Weinstein, R. S., Gregory, A., & Strambler, M. J. (2004). Intractable self-fulfilling prophecies: Brown v. Board of Education. *American Psychologist, 59,* 511–520.

Wellborn, J. G., & Connell, J. P. (1987). *A manual for the Rochester Assessment Package for schools.* Unpublished manuscript, University of Rochester.

Wentzel, K. R. (1994). Relations of social goal pursuit to social acceptance, classroom behavior, and perceived social support. *Journal of Educational Psychology, 86,* 173–182.

Wentzel, K. R. (1997). Student motivation in middle school: The role of perceived pedagogical caring. *Journal of Educational Psychology, 89,* 411–419.

Wentzel, K. R. (1998). Social support and adjustment in middle school: The role of parents, teachers, and peers. *Journal of Educational Psychology, 90,* 202–209.

Wentzel, K. R. (2002). Are effective teachers like good parents? Interpersonal predictors of school adjustment in early adolescence. *Child Development, 73,* 287–301.

Wentzel, K. R. (2003). School adjustment. In W. Reynolds & G. Miller (Eds.), *Handbook of psychology: Vol. 7. Educational psychology* (pp. 235–258). New York: Wiley.

Wentzel, K. R. (2004). Understanding classroom competence: The role of social-motivational and self-processes. In R. Kail (Ed.), *Advances in child development and behavior* (Vol. 32, pp. 213–241). New York: Elsevier.

Wentzel, K. R. (2005). Peer relationships, motivation, and academic performance at school. In A. Elliot & C. Dweck (Eds.), *Handbook of competence and motivation* (pp. 279–296). New York, NY: Guilford.

Wentzel, K. R., & Asher, S. R. (1995). Academic lives of neglected, rejected, popular, and controversial children. *Child Development, 66,* 754–763.

Wentzel, K. R., Battle, A., Russell, S., & Looney, L. (2010). *Teacher and peer contributions to classroom climate in middle school.* Unpublished manuscript.

Wentzel, K. R., Filisetti, L., & Looney, L. (2007). Adolescent prosocial behavior: The role of self-processes and contextual cues. *Child Development, 78,* 895–910.

Wentzel, K. R., & Looney, L. (2006). Socialization in school settings. In J. Grusec & P. Hastings (Eds.), *Handbook of social development* (pp. 382–403). New York: Guilford.

Wentzel, K. R., Williams, A. Y., & Tomback, R. M. (2005, April). *Relations of teacher and peer support to classroom behavior in middle school.* Paper presented at the annual meeting of the American Educational Research Association, Montreal, QC.

Wigfield, A., & Eccles, J. S. (2002). The development of competence beliefs and values from childhood through adolescence. In A. Wigfield & J. S. Eccles (Eds.), *Development of achievement motivation* (pp. 92–120). San Diego, CA: Academic Press.

Willson, V. L., & Hughes, J. N. (2006). Retention of Hispanic/Latino students in first grade: Child, parent, teacher, school, and peer predictors. *Journal of School Psychology, 44,* 31–49.

Wyatt, L. W., & Haskett, M. E. (2001). Aggressive and nonaggressive young adolescents' attributions of intent in teacher/student interactions. *Journal of Early Adolescence, 21,* 425–446.

Yoon, J. S. (2002). Teacher characteristics as predictors of teacher–student relationships: Stress, negative affect, and self-efficacy. *Social Behavior and Personality, 30,* 485–493.

# 7

# The Challenges and Promise of Research on Classroom Goal Structures

*Tim Urdan*

Achievement goal theory is one of the dominant frameworks for research on motivation, in part because of its emphasis on the contextual influences on achievement goals. Goal researchers have always argued that features of the achievement situation, including performance feedback (E. S. Elliott & Dweck, 1988), grouping and reward structures in the classroom (Ames & Felker, 1979), and even cultural values (Maehr & Nicholls, 1980) affect the goals that people pursue. This early research and speculation was followed by the development of theory and research regarding the specific policies and practices of educators that can create *classroom goal structures* (Ames, 1992; Ames & Archer, 1988; Maehr & Midgley, 1991). Classroom goal structures are defined as the policies, practices, and perhaps shared beliefs or norms among students in a classroom that make mastery or performance goals salient.

Although research on personal goals (i.e., the goals that individuals pursue) haa received most of the attention among goal theory researchers, research on classroom goal structures has been conducted continuously since the 1980s and has increasingly been the focus of research attention. To date, however, there is not yet consensus about how goal structures are defined (either conceptually or operationally), how they function, where they come from, and how important they are in the daily experience of students. The purpose of this chapter is to define what classroom goal structures are, to summarize existing research on classroom goal structures, and to discuss a number of the questions that remain about the definition and effects of classroom goal structures. The chapter concludes with a discussion of future directions in research on classroom goal structures.

## Classroom Goal Structures: Definitions and Assumptions

To understand how classroom goal structures have been defined, it is helpful to first consider the meaning of *personal goals* (or *personal goal orientations*).

***Personal Achievement Goals: Definition and Measurement Issues*** The term *personal goals* refer to the specific goals that individuals strive to achieve in achievement contexts, such as school. Most research has examined two types of goals: mastery (also called learning or task) and performance (also called ability, relative ability, or ego). Mastery goals represent a concern with *developing* competence and skills, and are generally considered to be evaluated against internal norms (i.e., Have I learned? Have I improved?). Performance goals represent the individual's concern with *demonstrating* competence by appearing able or outperforming others and are usually evaluated using interpersonal norms (i.e., Did I do better than other students in the class? Do others think I'm smart?). Mastery and performance goals each have been divided into approach and avoidance components, with the approach component representing an outcome to be attained (e.g., mastering a concept, outperforming peers) and the avoidance component representing an outcome to be avoided (i.e., failing to learn the information, being outperformed by peers; A. J. Elliot, 1997; Pintrich, 2000).

Research examining personal achievement goals has found a generally positive constellation of correlates with mastery-approach goals, a negative pattern of motivational beliefs and behaviors associated with performance-avoidance and mastery-avoidance goals, and a mixed (and controversial) pattern of results associated with performance-approach goals (for reviews see Elliot, 2005; Hulleman & Senko, in press; Roeser, 2004). Mastery goals are positively correlated with interest and deep cognitive processing whereas the opposite is true when pursuing avoidance goals. Interestingly, researchers have often failed to find a correlation between mastery-approach goals and achievement, but have often found a positive association between achievement and performance-approach goals (Hulleman & Senko, in press). This pattern of results has led to a heated debate regarding the relative merits, and potential costs, of pursuing mastery or performance goals in achievement contexts such as school (e.g., Harackie-wicz, Barron, Pintrich, Elliot, & Thrash, 2002; Midgley, Kaplan, & Middleton, 2001). As I discuss later, this debate has direct implications for the research on classroom goal structures.

It is important to note that there is not yet a consensual definition of personal achievement goals. Both mastery and performance goals have been assessed with a remarkable level of variation across researchers, leading to contradic-tory and confusing results (Hulleman & Senko, in press). One of the remaining questions regarding the definition of performance goals is whether these goals should focus exclusively on social comparison or whether appearance concerns (i.e., wanting to appear smart) are also part of these goals (Elliot, 1999). Similarly, mastery-approach goals have been operationally defined as including a prefer-ence for challenging work by some researchers, but not all (Hulleman & Senko, in press). A second question about the definition of performance goals is whether there are really separate approach and avoidance dimensions of these goals in students' phenomenological experience. Although these separate dimensions appear in laboratory manipulations (e.g., Elliot & Harackiewicz, 1996), some researchers have had trouble finding this distinction when using surveys (e.g., Wolters, 2004) and others have questioned the relevance to students of this distinction (Brophy, 2005; Roeser, 2004). Finally, researchers differ in whether they conceptualize achievement goals as situation-specific cognitions about desired outcomes (Elliot, 2005) or broader constructs that encompass cognitions, beliefs, and affective reactions in the achievement context (Kaplan & Maehr, 2007). All of these definitional issues have implications for the definition and measurement of classroom goal structures.

***Classroom Goal Structures: Definitional Issues*** In ad-dition to personal goals, there are also *goal structures*, a term which refers to messages in the environment (e.g., experimental situation, classroom, school) that make certain goals salient. Such goal-related messages can come from a variety of sources in the achievement context, including how the purposes or definitions of success are presented, the types of tasks that are assigned, how much time stu-dents are given to complete the task, and how students are recognized and rewarded in the classroom or school. For example, it is common in experimental manipulations of goals to provide research participants with instructions that make one type of goal salient, and these instructions constitute the goal structure for that situation. Similarly, in a classroom, teachers can emphasize ability differences between students (performance goal structure) by grading on a curve or emphasize the development of competence by using portfolio assessment to chart the progress of each student over time (mastery goal structure). Although any achievement situation can have a goal structure, in this chapter I focus primarily on classroom goal structures.

Although goal structures are easily defined in broad terms (i.e., messages that make mastery and performance

goals salient), consistent operational definitions of goal structures are elusive. Part of this difficulty is attribut-able to the imprecise definition of personal goals, as de-scribed above. The difficulty in clearly defining personal performance goals foreshadows a similar difficulty that researchers have encountered when trying to operation-ally define classroom goal structures. For example, it is unclear whether the classroom performance goal structure can be divided into approach and avoidance components, as Midgley and her colleagues attempted (Midgley et al., 2000) or if a classroom performance goal structure is a unitary construct (Urdan, 2004a, 2004b). Urdan (2004a) has argued that students may not perceive a distinction between approach and avoidance performance goal messages in the classroom. Rather, they may perceive an emphasis on rela-tive ability and social comparison and then interpret these messages as either approach or avoidance goals, depending on a variety of factors such as their personal achievement history, perceived competence, and perhaps cultural or personality factors.

In addition to definitional issues that are directly related to ongoing discussions about how to define performance goals, the definition and assessment of classroom goal structures poses challenges unique to classroom-level as-sessments. First among these is where the goal structures "live." Are classroom goal structures primarily the objective perceptions of the students in the classroom, as some have argued (Ames & Archer, 1988; Kaplan, Middleton, Urdan, & Midgley, 2002)? Or is there a more *objective* classroom goal structure that is independent of student perceptions? Whereas experimental manipulations suggest that goal structures are objective and components of the achievement context that can be manipulated, attempts to assess the objective classroom goal structure have generally provided more ambiguous results than have experimental manipula-tions. These attempts have taken two forms: observational research and hierarchical linear modeling (HLM) studies, each of which is described in more detail later in the chapter. For now, suffice it to say that the evidence regarding the existence of objective goal structures in real classrooms is far from definitive (Urdan, 2004c).

Another question regarding the operational definition of classroom goal structures is where goal structures come from. Most of the existing research on classroom goal structures assumes that teachers create the goal structure through their words and practices (Ames, 1992; Maehr & Midgley, 1991). Survey measures of classroom goal structures typically ask students about teacher behaviors (Church, Elliot & Gable, 2001; Greene, Miller, Crowson, Duke, & Akey, 2004; Midgley et al., 2000). Similarly, obser-vational studies generally examined teacher behaviors and their relation to student perceptions of the classroom goal structure (Meece, 1991; Urdan, Kneisel, & Mason, 1999). More recent research has focused on the shared values of students in the classroom that may emphasize mastery or performance goals (e.g., Urdan, 2004a). Despite recent advances in the conceptualization and measurement of classroom goal structures, questions remain about the exact definition of goal structures, their strength as an objective component of the classroom, and the factors that create and influence the goal structures in classrooms.

***Assumptions about Classroom Goal Structures***  Research on classroom goal structures is guided by a set of assumptions, either explicitly or implicitly. First, there is the assumption that classroom goal structures exist. As alluded to earlier, what a classroom goal structure is and where it resides (the "subjective" vs. "objective" distinction) are issues that are still being debated. Those who have examined classroom goal structures have assumed that mastery and performance goal structures exist in each classroom to varying degrees. A second assumption about classroom goal structures is that they matter. Classroom goal structures are believed to exert some influence on the students in those classrooms, either indirectly through their influence on the personal goals that students pursue in those settings or directly onto various outcomes (Ames, 1992). A third assumption is that some goal structures are better than others. This assumption has involved a favoring of mastery goal structures and a devaluing of performance goal structures (Maehr & Midgley, 1996), which arose mostly from research on personal goals that suggested more benefits of pursuing mastery than performance goals. Finally, there is the assumption that classroom goal structures can be altered. This assumption is most readily found in the writings that present suggestions and strategies for promoting a mastery goal structure in the classroom (Ames, 1992) or school (Maehr & Midgley, 1991, 1996).

Although these assumptions may seem obvious, they should not go unchallenged. Evidence that classroom goal structures exist, are important, are differentially beneficial for students, and can be modified is not yet fully established. Some of this lack of evidence is attributable to imprecise conceptual and operational definitions of classroom goal structures. Other reasons to question these assumptions include a pattern of weak and contradictory associations between classroom goal structures and a variety of outcomes, a lack of longitudinal research that has controlled for prior personal goal orientations, and a lack of experimental and quasi-experimental research conducted in classrooms with the specific aim of altering classroom goal structures. Because research on classroom goal structures is still a fairly recent endeavor, it is not surprising that it contains gaps. My goal here is not to criticize previous research efforts as much as it is to identify some of the gaps in the knowledge about classroom goal structures so that future research might fill them.

***Summary***  As research examining classroom goal structures gains momentum, it is important to develop consensus among researchers regarding their definition and measurement. Because there are still questions about the exact definition of achievement goals (particularly performance goals), and it is not yet clear whether goal structures are objective or subjective or where they come from, a considerable amount of work remains before a clear and consensual definition of classroom goal structures can be attained.

## Summary of Research on Classroom Goal Structures

In this section of the chapter I review much of the research on classroom goal structures that has been conducted to date. This section is divided into three subsections: Survey methods (including subsections for HLM research and longitudinal designs), experimental and quasi-experimental research, and qualitative research. The purposes of this review are to determine what existing research reveals about classroom goal structures and to consider some of the limitations of the existing research.

***Survey (Questionnaire) Research***  Most of the research examining classroom goal structures has employed survey methodology. Typically, students are asked a series of questions on a survey to assess their perceptions of teacher practices or shared student beliefs that reflect either mastery goals (i.e., an emphasis on learning and developing skills) or performance goals (i.e., an emphasis on competition and social comparison in the classroom). These student perceptions of the mastery and performance goal structures in the classroom are then correlated with motivational and behavior variables, such as self-efficacy, achievement, self-handicapping, and so on. In a few instances, teacher reports of their instructional practices believed to reflect mastery and performance goals have been assessed. Survey data have been reported as single-time assessments of student perceptions, in HLM studies, and in multiwave longitudinal research.

In general, the pattern of results reported in survey research has indicated that students' perceptions of a mastery goal structure in the classroom are positively associated with achievement, self-efficacy, value, cognitive and metacognitive strategy use, adaptive help seeking, and positive affect in school and either negatively related or unrelated to less favorable outcomes such as negative affect, maladaptive help-seeking, self-handicapping and cheating (Ames & Archer, 1988; Anderman & Midgley, 2004; Green et al., 2004; Karabenick, 2004; Midgley & Urdan, 2001; Urdan & Midgley, 2003). Students' perceptions of a performance goal structure in the classroom are generally associated with less adaptive motivational and behavioral outcomes, such as cheating, procrastination, self-handicapping, lack of persistence, and lower academic achievement (Nolen, 2003; Urdan & Midgley, 2003; Wolters, 2004). Research using teacher reports of their instructional practices that reflect mastery and performance goal structures has typically produced similar patterns of results, with teacher-reported performance goal practices associated with self-handicapping (Urdan, Midgley, & Anderman, 1998) and reduced valuing of mathematics over time (Anderman, Eccles, et al., 2001).

The survey research examining classroom goal structures

has a number of important limitations. First, as with all survey research, the results are correlational and therefore make it difficult to ascertain the causal effects of classroom goal structures. Survey research has generally not controlled for other variables that might influence perceptions of the classroom goal structure (e.g., personal goal orientations, prior achievement, cultural factors; see Miller & Murdock, 2007; Urdan, 2004a, for exceptions). Therefore, survey research has not yet adequately determined the cause–effect association between classroom goal structures and these other variables, most notably preexisting personal goal orientations. When personal achievement goals have been controlled, little additional variance is explained by classroom goal structure variables (Urdan, 2004a, 2007).

A second concern about survey assessments is that they have varied widely in their operational definition of goal structures. The most widely used measure is the PALS (Midgely et al., 2000). This measure includes items in the mastery goal structure scale that seem to tap into perceptions that the teacher is caring (e.g., the teacher wants students to learn new things and enjoy learning) whereas the performance goal structure measure includes items that imply the teacher is unfair, or plays favorites (e.g., gives special privileges to higher achievers, points out high achievers to the rest of the class). Such items may invite students to report their perceptions that the teacher is nice and caring or unfair rather than simply differentiating between mastery and performance goal messages. A study of college students by Church et al. (2001) used a measure that may have a similar problem because it asks students to rate whether they find the lectures interesting and engaging and to report on the professor's use of "harsh" grading practices. Again, such items may allow students to differentiate between "good" and "bad" instruction or fun teachers vs. mean teachers, rather than focusing simply on the mastery-performance distinction. Greene et al. (2004) focused exclusively on assessing perceptions of three components of the mastery goal structure: motivating tasks, autonomy support, and mastery evaluation practices. The original survey measure of classroom goal structures, developed by Ames and Archer (1988), combined items assessing personal goals and perceived classroom goals. Items such as "In this class, I work hard to learn" and "In this class, I really don't like to make mistakes" appear to be more indicative of personal goals. All of these measures of classroom goal structures include items that may assess more than simply perceived emphases on mastery or performance goals in the classroom.

*Single-Time Survey Administrations* A number of studies have examined students' perceptions of the classroom goal structure, and the effects of these perceptions, using single-administration surveys. The first to do this were Ames and Archer (1988). Examining a sample of 176 high-achieving middle school students, they found that students' perceptions of an emphasis on mastery goals in the classroom were positively related to liking of class, using strategies that promote learning, preferring challenging tasks, and attributing success to effort, strategy use, and the teacher doing a good job. A perceived classroom emphasis on performance goals was weakly related or unrelated to most outcomes except for the attribution that success is due to using good strategies (a positive correlation) and attributing failure to lack of ability, task difficulty, or failure to use appropriate strategies. They also found no relationship between perceiving a performance goal structure in the classroom and the use of learning strategies, preference for challenging tasks, or how much students liked the class, suggesting a lack of negative consequences of a perceived performance goal structure. As mentioned earlier, their measure of goal structures included a combination of personal goal items and perceived goal structure items, thereby limiting the utility of this measure for assessing classroom goal structure effects.

A study by Green and her colleagues (2004) examined high school students' perceptions of classroom mastery goal structures, personal goals, and several additional motivational, self-regulatory, and achievement variables. Although these data were not collected during a single survey administration, the design was not exactly longitudinal either (data were collected during three survey administrations over a 3-month period). Using path analysis, Greene and her colleagues found that perceptions of the classroom mastery goal structure were related to cognitive strategy use and achievement not directly, but through their effects on self-efficacy, personal mastery goals, and perceived instrumentality of the work in the class.

Wolters (2004) gave surveys to 525 middle school students to examine how personal goals and perceived classroom goal structures predicted motivational engagement, learning strategies, and achievement. When controlling for prior achievement, gender, and personal mastery and performance goals, Wolters found weak associations between classroom goal structures and his dependent variables. For example, neither mastery nor performance goal structure significantly predicted choice, effort, or course grade. Perceived classroom mastery goal structure was not significantly related to persistence or procrastination, and perceived classroom performance goal structure was not related to the use of cognitive or metacognitive strategies. Classroom performance goal structure was negatively related to persistence and positively related to procrastination whereas classroom mastery goal structure was positively related to the use of cognitive and metacognitive strategies. These relationships were generally quite weak (significant standardized regression coefficients ranged from .15 to .22 in magnitude). Overall, Wolters's results suggest that, when examined simultaneously, personal goal orientations have stronger associations with these outcomes than do perceived classroom goal orientations.

The Wolters (2004) study included two other results worth noting. First, he tried to distinguish between classroom performance-approach and classroom performance-avoidance goal structures. This attempt failed to produce an internally reliable performance-avoidance goal structure scale.[1] Wolters also mentioned that although his intention had been to perform an HLM analysis, he found too little between-classroom variability in the outcomes included in this study. Moreover, the little between-classroom variability that did exist in the outcome variables was not well explained by between-classroom variability in perceived classroom goal structures.

These single-time survey administration studies have revealed that students' perceptions of the classroom mastery and performance goal structures are associated with a variety of motivational, cognitive, and achievement outcomes, but the pattern and strength of these associations vary depending on the way classroom goal structures were assessed, how other variables were controlled, and the outcomes examined. Because perceptions of the classroom goal structures are nested within classrooms and their effects are complex, researchers have often used more sophisticated research designs and analytic strategies to analyze them, such as HLM and longitudinal research designs. This research is summarized next.

***HLM Studies*** Although there are often fairly strong (by social science standards) correlations between perceived classroom goal structures and several motivational and behavioral outcomes, it is not clear how much of the strength of the associations is due to such factors as lack of control for other variables and inflated correlations caused by the similarity of items across constructs (e.g., self-efficacy items and classroom mastery goal structure items used in some surveys). Therefore, it is important to find additional evidence that survey measures of classroom goal structures assess a genuine phenomenon in real classrooms. One method researchers have used to demonstrate such a phenomenon is to use HLM.

Several studies have used hierarchical linear modeling (HLM) to examine classroom goal structures. The primary benefit of this methodology is that it allows the researcher to partition the variance of particular variables into individual-level and classroom-level components. This allows researchers to determine whether students within different classrooms differ from students in other classrooms in their perceptions of the classroom goal structure. Classroom-level distinctions in teacher-reported behaviors believed to reflect mastery and performance goals have also been examined. Across this set of HLM studies, three patterns emerged. First, between-classroom variation in the perceived classroom goal structures was fairly weak. A second, related pattern was that there was more variability in the individual-level student perceptions of the classroom goal structure than in the classroom-level perceptions, and when compared, the individual-level perceptions of the classroom goal structures were the stronger predictors of outcomes. Finally, the pattern of associations between classroom goal structures and outcomes was not consistent across studies, perhaps because of differences in design and measurement. Each of these patterns will be discussed in turn.

*Between-Classroom Variability*   Researchers who have used HLM to examine students' perceptions of the classroom goal structures have generally found that between-classroom variation accounts for about 15% or less of the total variability in these student perceptions (Anderman & Young, 1994; Karabenick, 2004; Nolen, 2003; Urdan, 2004b). Some have reported finding too little between-classroom variation to even conduct HLM analyses (Wolters, 2004) or used HLM to examine the association between perceived classroom variables and personal goals within the classroom but not testing for differences in classroom goal structures between classrooms due to a lack of between-classroom variability (Church et al., 2001). These percentages reveal that most of the variability (about 85% or more) in the perceived classroom mastery and performance goal structures exists *within* classrooms. Such results may indicate that classroom goal structures are primarily a subjective construction rather than an objective reality in the classroom. As Miller and Murdock (2007) noted in a recent analysis of classroom goal structure effects, estimates of between-classroom variability in perceived classroom goal structures have often failed to account for the number of students per classroom or the reliability (i.e., similarity) of the perceptions of students within classrooms. They caution that researchers using HLM to examine classroom-level effects must consider intraclass reliability and sample sizes within classrooms when using aggregated student reports of the classroom goal structure.

*Comparisons of Predictive Power*   Urdan (2004b) used HLM to compare the predictive power of high school students' perceptions of the classroom goal structure assessed at both the individual level and the aggregated class level in their English classrooms. He found that individual-level perceptions of the mastery and performance goal structures were stronger predictors of personal mastery and performance goals, self-handicapping, and valuing of academic work than were perceptions of the classroom goal structure aggregated to the classroom level. Classroom-level perceptions of the mastery goal structure were a stronger predictor of self-efficacy than were individual-level perceptions of classroom goal structures, and the individual-level perception of the classroom performance goal structure was about as strong a predictor (negative) as the classroom level mastery goal structure (positive) of students' English grades. For most outcomes, individual perceptions of the classroom goal structures were stronger predictors than were classroom goal structure perceptions aggregated to the classroom level.

Karabenick (2004) used HLM to examine within-and-between classroom variation in help-seeking among college students. He found that between-class variability in perceived classroom goal structures was unrelated to students' reported approach tendencies toward seeking help when they needed it. But he also found that the avoidance of help seeking was predicted by between-classroom variation in students' perceptions of a classroom performance-avoidance goal structure. This effect was quite weak, but Karabenick did control for students' personal achievement goals, aggregated at the classroom level.

*Variation in Research Design and Measures*   The examination of classroom goal structures using HLM has employed a variety of designs and measures and sometimes produced contradictory results. Two studies have used teacher-reported use of instructional practices hypothesized to promote mastery and performance goals in the classroom as well as student-reported perceptions of the classroom goal structure. In one study, Urdan and his colleagues (1998) used HLM to examine individual and classroom level predictors of self-handicapping among a sample of fifth grade students. They found that students reported engaging in self-handicapping behavior more in some classrooms than in others. Urdan et al. found, after controlling for achievement and perceived competence (individual-level predictors), that the between-classroom variability in self-handicapping was predicted by teacher-reported use of instructional practices that reflect a performance goal orientation and, more strongly, by students' perceptions of an emphasis on performance goals in the classroom.

Ryan, Gheen, and Midgley (1998) also found that teacher-reported instructional practices believed to promote mastery and performance goals (i.e., the "objective" goal structure) were weaker predictors than student perceptions of the classroom goal structure in mathematics classrooms. Specifically, among a sample of sixth grade middle school students in 63 math classrooms, they found that students' avoidance of help-seeking varied across classrooms, and that students avoided seeking help more in classrooms with a stronger perceived performance goal structure and less in classrooms with a stronger perceived mastery goal structure. Teacher-reported goal practices were unrelated to avoidance of help-seeking.

A third study using only teacher-reported instructional practices believed (by the researchers) to promote mastery or performance goal messages in the classroom examined changes in students' valuing of math and reading over two successive spring semesters (Anderman et al., 2001). Using HLM, these researchers found that teacher-reported use of performance-goal-oriented instructional strategies was associated with a decrease in students' valuing of both math and English. There was no significant association between teachers' reported use of mastery instructional strategies and change in valuing of either mathematics or reading.

Across these three studies, the association between teacher practices that emphasized either mastery or performance goals in the classroom and the various outcomes studied were quite weak, and in two of the studies were weaker than the student-level perceptions of the classroom goal structures. These results suggest that differences between classrooms in the perceived classroom goal structures may be due in part to different characteristics of the students in those classrooms, such as those created by separating students into different academic tracks (Nolen, 2003) and

pre-existing differences in the personal goal orientations of the students in the classrooms (Urdan, 2004a).

Perhaps as a consequence of differing methodologies and measures, research using HLM has also produced some apparently contradictory results. For example, whereas Urdan et al. (1998) found that a perceived classroom performance goal structure, but not mastery goal structure, was associated with students' use of self-handicapping strategies, Turner and her colleagues (2002) found the opposite pattern: Among a sample of sixth grade students in middle school, perceived classroom mastery goal structure, but not performance goal structure, predicted (negatively) the use of self-handicapping strategies. Such contradictory results may be attributable to the analysis design employed. Urdan et al. (1998) controlled for students' perceptions of their competence and teacher-reported instructional practices, variables that may have suppressed the effects of perceived mastery goals on self-handicapping reported by Turner et al. (2002).

Similarly, the study by Anderman and his colleagues (2001) found that changes in students' valuing of mathematics and reading were weakly, negatively related to teacher reports of performance-oriented instructional strategies, but unrelated to teacher reports of mastery-oriented instructional strategies. These findings seem to contradict the results in the Urdan (2004b) HLM study, which reported positive associations between students' valuing of English and both individual-level and classroom-level perceptions of the classroom mastery goal structure, but neither individual- or classroom-level performance goal structures predicted valuing. Whether the difference in predictors of valuing between the two studies was caused by grade level (elementary and middle vs. high school), or measure (teacher reports vs. student reports) cannot be determined, but such contradictions in research findings regarding the effects of classroom goal structures need to be better understood.

HLM studies of classroom goal structures, as has much of the research using survey methods, have also defined classroom goal structures differently, possibly producing some of the contradictory and confusing results. For example, Church and her colleagues (2001) operationally defined classroom goal structures as perceptions of engaging lectures, an emphasis on evaluation, and harsh grading practices. In contrast, the PALS measure developed by Midgley and her colleagues (2000) defined goal structures more broadly as an emphasis on learning and understanding (mastery) or making ability differences among students salient (performance). Nolen (2003) offered a third operational definition, combining students' perceptions of the classroom climate (cooperative and competitive) with their perceptions of the teachers' emphasis on mastery or achievement goals. These three measurement approaches have all yielded somewhat different results. The PALS measure, like Nolen's, has generally shown that an emphasis on social comparison is associated with lower levels of engagement and sometimes with lower levels of achievement and higher avoidance behaviors. Church and her colleagues found that personal mastery goals were associated with a perception that lectures were engaging, but performance-approach goals were associated with a perceived emphasis on evaluation. Performance-avoidance goals were linked with perceptions of harsh grading practices.

The research on classroom goal structures that has employed HLM techniques has produced an interesting and confusing pattern of results. For the most part, this research indicates that the between-classroom variability in perceptions of the classroom goal structures is small, yet is sometimes able to explain variability in motivational and achievement outcomes. Because within-classroom variation tends to be much larger than between-classroom variation in perceived classroom goal structures, associations between teacher-reported and student-reported goal structures have been weak (when assessed), and important student characteristics that may contribute to students' perceptions of the classroom goal structures have rarely been controlled (see Miller & Murdock, 2007; Urdan, 2004c), the real between- and within-classroom effects of classroom goal structures have been difficult to determine. Differences across research programs in the definition and assessment of goal-structure constructs, as well as differences in samples, controls, and designs, contribute to the difficulty in drawing definitive conclusions about classroom goal structures from HLM research. As Miller and Murdock (2007) argue, HLM is a promising strategy for examining classroom goal structure effects, but more work is needed before a clear picture of these effects can emerge.

***Longitudinal Research*** In addition to the two longitudinal studies that employed HLM methods (Anderman et al., 2001; Nolen, 2003, both reviewed in the previous section), a number of longitudinal studies have been conducted that examined the perceptions and effects of goal structures. The aims of these longitudinal studies generally have been to examine the consequences of shifting goal structure perceptions as students move from one class to another in successive academic years and to test for mediation effects in causal models.

Anderman and Midgley (1997) collected survey data from a sample of students twice, in the spring of their fifth grade year (in elementary school) and again in the fall of the sixth grade year, after they made the transition to middle school. They found that, in both math and English, students perceived weaker mastery and stronger performance goal structures after the transition to middle school. Kaplan and Midgley (1999) extended this research to examine the reciprocal associations between perceived classroom goal structures, coping strategies, and affect across the transition and during middle school. Using surveys, they collected data across four waves (fall and spring of fifth grade, fall and spring of sixth grade) and analyzed the associations among the variables using structural equation modeling (SEM). They found that a perceived emphasis on mastery goals predicted positive coping strategies, which in turn predicted positive affect. In contrast, a perceived performance

goal structure predicted denial and projective coping, and these predicted subsequent negative affect. Interestingly, when they examined these associations from the beginning of sixth grade to the end of sixth grade (i.e., fall to spring semesters in middle school), they found that later perceptions of classroom mastery goal structure were predicted by positive coping and affect at the beginning of the academic year, whereas perceptions of a performance goal structure at the end of the year were predicted by noncoping earlier in the year. These results suggest that whereas perceptions of the classroom goal structure may influence coping and affect, coping and affect may in turn influence perceptions of the classroom goal structure.

In an examination of high school girls in Korea, Bong (2005) found that student perceptions of the classroom mastery goal structure declined from one semester to the next in two of the four domains tested (general school and English), but not in math or Korean classes. Students also perceived an increase in the classroom performance goal structure from the first to the second semester across all four domains. Bong noted that the effect sizes for the changing perceptions of the classroom goal were generally small, but they did explain some of the variance in the changes across students' motivational variables. She also found that within-year changes in the perceived mastery goal structure were generally smaller than were changes in the perceived performance goal structure across academic domains.

Urdan and Midgley (2003) collected three waves of survey data from a sample of students: in the spring semesters of fifth grade (elementary school), sixth grade, and seventh grade (both in middle school). Students were classified into three groups based on changes in their perceptions of the classroom goal structures from one grade to the next: (a) a decrease in the goal structure, (b) little change, and (c) an increase in the goal structure. This was done separately for mastery and performance goal structures and for each year (i.e., fifth to sixth grade, sixth to seventh grade). Next, repeated-measures analysis of variance were conducted on a series of dependent variables (e.g., personal achievement goals, self-efficacy, affect, and grade point average) to determine whether the pattern of changes in these dependent variables varied across the three goal-structure-change groups. Urdan and Midgley found that when students perceived a decline in the classroom mastery goal structure from one year to the next, they experienced a decline in their pursuit of personal mastery goals, self-efficacy, positive affect, and achievement, and an increase in negative affect. This negative pattern was found when students moved from fifth grade to sixth grade (i.e., across the transition to middle school) and again from sixth grade to seventh grade (during middle school). Students who perceived an increase in the mastery goal structure were not significantly higher achieving, efficacious, or happy from one year to the next, but they also did not report any declines in these dependent variables. The pattern of change in the dependent variables that was associated with changes in the perceived performance goal structure was generally much weaker than those found for the mastery goal structure, with only personal performance goals and negative affect increasing significantly among students who perceived a stronger classroom performance goal structure over time.

A similar study that examined the effects of changes in the perceived classroom goal structure was conducted by Anderman and Midgley (2004). With survey data collected over three waves, they used growth curve analysis to examine self-reported cheating in mathematics class as the dependent variable and followed students as they moved from middle school to high school. Anderman and Midgley found that self-reported cheating did not increase from the beginning to the end of eighth grade, but increased after students made the transition to high school. Further analysis revealed that when students moved from eighth to ninth grade into classrooms that they perceived as either weaker in mastery goal emphasis or stronger in performance goal emphasis, self-reported cheating increased. But self-reported cheating behavior declined when students moved into ninth grade classrooms that they perceived to have a stronger mastery goal structure than did their eighth grade mathematics classroom.

One of the difficult questions involving classroom goal structures is how much individual differences in other variables (e.g., achievement level, perceived competence, personal goal orientations) shape perceptions of the classroom goal structure. Most research examining classroom goal structures has either relied on single-time data collection or has assumed that classroom goal structures belong at the beginning of the model and exert influence on all variables that come after without trying to control for antecedents to classroom goal structure perceptions. There is some evidence that calls this assumption into question. For example, as previously noted, Kaplan and Midgley (1999) found that coping strategies and affect measured in the fall semester predicted perceived classroom goal structures in the following spring semester. In addition, single-time measures of achievement goals and classroom goal structures reveal moderate correlations between them. Most have assumed that this correlation is caused by the influence of perceived goal structures on personal goals (e.g., Kaplan et al., 2002). But it is also possible that personal goals influence perceptions of the classroom goal structure (see Figure 7.1 for a model of possible antecedents and consequences of classroom goal structures).

Urdan (2004a) used survey data collected from high school students over two academic years (spring semester at Time 1, fall semester of the following academic year at Time 2) to examine the associations between personal performance goals, perceptions of the classroom performance goal structure, achievement, and self-handicapping among high school students. Using SEM analyses, he found that personal performance-approach and performance-avoidance goals, as well as academic achievement, measured at Time 1 all significantly predicted perceptions of the classroom performance goal structure at Time 2. Because students moved to a new classroom from one year to the next, these results suggest that their early perceptions of the new classroom performance goal structure were influenced by their preexisting personal performance goals, as well as prior academic achievement. Urdan (2004a) was then able to determine that the perceived classroom performance goal structure was related to concurrent personal performance goals, and to self-handicapping, after controlling for prior achievement and prior personal performance goals. These associations were statistically significant, but the effect sizes were quite small.

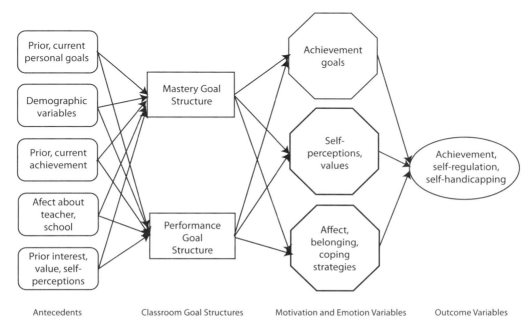

**Figure 7.1** A model of potential classroom goal structure antecedents and effects.

There is not enough longitudinal research examining classroom goal structures to reach firm conclusions about the nature of changes in perceived classroom goal structures over time. However, taken as a whole, there are a few tentative conclusions suggested by the existing longitudinal research. First, although some students experienced quite dramatic changes in their perceptions of the classroom goal structures from one year to the next (Urdan & Midgley, 2003), on average the changes were modest (Bong, 2005). In addition, in the two studies that included predictors *of* perceived classroom goal structures, it was clear that perceptions of the classroom goal structures are associated with variables believed to be more intrapersonal and less contextual, such as coping strategies (Kaplan & Midgley, 1999), prior achievement, and personal achievement goals (Urdan, 2004a). Research examining the association between perceived classroom goal structures and motivational and achievement outcomes that does not control for such potential influences on perceived classroom goal structures make it difficult to determine the causal nature of these associations. Some research indicates that the correlations between personal achievement goals and classroom goal structures are of comparable magnitude when assessed within an academic year as they are when assessed across two academic years, using personal achievement goals in year 1 to predict perceived classroom goal structures in year 2, even though students have changed classrooms and teachers (Urdan, 2007). Such results suggest that the moderate association often found between personal goals and classroom goal structures may be caused more by the influence of stable personal goal orientations on perceived classroom goal structures than vice versa. Clearly, more longitudinal research examining the causal associations among goal structures, motivational variables, and achievement is needed.

***Experimental Research*** Since the beginning of research on achievement goals, researchers have attempted to experimentally manipulate goal message in the learning environment with the intention of influencing the goals, behaviors, and achievement of individuals in those achievement situations. Most of this research has been conducted in laboratory settings, and therefore is not technically representative of classroom goal structure manipulation or research. In typical experimental manipulations of goals, individuals are tested one at a time and are provided with a single, clear goal-related message to induce either a mastery or a performance goal orientation among experiment participants. Real classrooms, in contrast, are collections of dozens of students who differ in ability levels, attitudes about school, and motivational orientations. In addition, real classrooms contain multiple goal-related messages simultaneously, as well as a host of other factors that might influence student motivation (e.g., teacher beliefs, peer pressures, student beliefs about the personal characteristics of the teacher, etc.). Moreover, the tasks participants work on in experimental studies are often low-stakes, such as games and puzzles: there are no real-world consequences for performing poorly on them. Therefore, there are serious questions about the applicability of laboratory-based goal manipulations to actual classrooms and schools (see Urdan & Turner, 2005 for a more thorough consideration of these limitations). But because this lab research operates on the same general principles as classroom goal structures (i.e., contextual messages about the purposes of achievement), it will be reviewed briefly.

Elliott and Dweck (1988) attempted to induce a performance (relative ability) goal orientation by telling fifth grade children in their experiment that their performance on a task would be filmed and judged normatively. To induce a mastery learning goal orientation, children were not told that they would be filmed. Instead, they were told "that the learning task might be a big help in school, because it 'sharpens the mind' and learning to do it well could help their studies" (p. 7). They found that children in the mastery and performance goal conditions performed similarly under success conditions (i.e., solving a number of problems correctly) but individuals in the performance-goal condition developed a helpless pattern after several failed attempts to solve problems.

Ames and Felker (1979) read stories to students across grades 1 through 5 about fictional children that were working on puzzles and would be rewarded for either solving more puzzles than others (competitive reward structure), solving five puzzles on their own (individualistic reward structure), or working with a partner and solving seven puzzles combined (cooperative reward structure). Ames and Felker found that children in the competitive and individualistic structures had very similar patterns of attributions (i.e., a tendency to attribute outcomes to ability levels) whereas students in the cooperative reward structure were less likely to attribute outcomes to ability level.

With two samples of college students, Elliot and Harackiewicz (1996) tested three experimental goal conditions to determine whether participants in the different conditions varied in their intrinsic motivation and performance on a puzzle-solving task. In the performance-approach goal orientation, participants were told that the purpose of the experiment was to try to solve more puzzles than other students whereas in the performance-avoidance goal condition participants were instructed to try to avoid solving fewer puzzles. Participants in the mastery goal condition were told to try to solve as many puzzles as they could and that they would be given nonnormative feedback about their performance at the end of the task. They found that participants in the mastery-goal condition were more intrinsically interested in the task but participants in the performance-approach condition performed better. Participants in the performance-avoidance condition were neither intrinsically motivated nor high performers.

In a study of the effects of congruence and incongruence between personal goals and contextual goal structures, Newman (1998) found that fourth- and fifth-grade students with performance goal orientations (as assessed by surveys) were less likely to avoid seeking help when the experimental context was manipulated to promote mastery goals than they were when in contexts that promoted performance goals. Graham and Golan (1991) conducted two experiments with fifth- and sixth-grade students in which they manipulated the goal message. In the task (i.e., mastery) goal condition, they told participants to focus on enjoying the task and viewing it as a challenge; in the ego (i.e., performance) goal condition, they told participants that the upcoming task was the type that indicates whether one is good at such tasks or not, relative to others their age. In both experiments, they found the students in the performance-goal condition remembered fewer words at the deep-processing level than did the students in the mastery condition.

This section contains just a small sampling of the research involving the experimental manipulation of goals. Additional research has generally supported the experimental research reviewed here indicating that even fairly subtle messages about the purposes of achievement in specific task contexts can produce significant motivational and behavioral differences among individuals of various ages. Current experimental research is aimed at discovering the specific mechanisms by which goals influence motivation and achievement (e.g., Senko & Miles, 2008). Despite important questions about the generalizability of lab-based experimental research to real classrooms, this research continues to produce important insights into the nature and functioning of goals, and the contextual cues that influence them.

***Quasi-Experimental Research*** A few researchers have conducted quasi-experiments in real classrooms and schools. In an unpublished study, Ames (1990) worked with a group of 36 elementary teachers to develop and implement strategies teachers could use to promote a mastery goal structure in their classrooms. There were also 30 teachers and their students that served as the control group. The experimental group implemented the strategies to promote classroom mastery goal structures at least 12 times over the course of the semester in their classes. At the end of the intervention, students in the 36 intervention classrooms identified as "at-risk" by their teachers were compared with at-risk students from the control group. Ames found that students in the treatment classrooms did not decline over the course of the intervention in their self-reported use of learning strategies, intrinsic motivation, attitudes toward math, reading, and school, or perceptions of competence. Their self-concept of ability increased. In contrast, at-risk students in the control classrooms experienced declines in intrinsic motivation, use of learning strategies, attitudes toward reading and school, and perceived competence. At the end of the intervention, at-risk students in the treatment classrooms also perceived their classes as more mastery oriented than did students in the control classrooms.

More recently, Linnenbrink (2005) conducted an experimental manipulation of the goal structures in 10 upper-elementary school classrooms during a 5-week mathematics

unit. She discussed achievement goal theory with the five participating teachers and then assigned teachers to one of three conditions: mastery, performance, or combined mastery and performance. Linnenbrink gave teachers a set of strategies they could use to promote the appropriate goal or combination of goals and then observed them to see if they faithfully implemented strategies to promote the appropriate goal emphasis. She also used surveys to assess students motivation (self-efficacy, interest value, and utility value), emotional well-being (positive affect, negative affect, and test anxiety), cognitive engagement (the quantity and quality of self-regulatory strategy use), and help-seeking behavior before the unit began and again immediately upon its conclusion. An end-of-unit achievement test was also administered pre- and postintervention. Linnenbrink found that scores on the unit test improved the most (from pretest to posttest) among students in the performance and combined performance-mastery conditions relative to the mastery goal condition. This difference between the groups decreased by the time of the follow-up test administered 5 weeks after the conclusion of the math unit. She also found that students in the performance-approach condition increased their use of expedient help-seeking (i.e., just asking for someone to give them the correct answer) whereas students in the other two groups decreased slightly in their expedient help-seeking behavior from pre- to posttest. There were no goal-structure-group differences, either in mean level or change over time, for motivation, emotional well-being, cognitive engagement, or adaptive or avoidance help-seeking. Parenthetically, Linnenbrink noted that teachers did not always enact strategies consistent with their assigned goal condition and sometimes engaged in practices associated with a different goal condition.

In a quasi-experimental attempt to alter the goal structure at the school level, Maehr and Midgley (1996) tried to alter the goal structure of one middle school and one elementary school over a 2-year period. Meetings with teachers and administrators in the treatment schools were conducted weekly during the first year (less frequently the second year) to discuss achievement goal theory and to develop and implement strategies for promoting mastery goals and deemphasizing performance goals in the classrooms and the schools. Data were collected from students in the two treatment schools and two matched comparison schools several times for the duration of the intervention project. The primary findings from the project were (a) attempts to change the goal structure proceeded more smoothly in the elementary school than the middle school, in part because of the smaller size of the elementary school; (b) efforts at school-wide reform were very difficult to enact and were actively opposed by some teachers, particularly at the middle school; and (c) students in the two experimental schools did perceive and endorse mastery goals more and performance goals less than did students at the comparison schools (Anderman, Maehr, & Midgley, 1999), but these results were quite weak.

The few attempts to actually manipulate classroom and

school goal structures have produced mixed results. The Ames (1990) study suggests that mastery goal structures can be created in classrooms with resulting motivational benefits for students. These results were limited to students identified as "at-risk" by teachers, so it is not clear whether the results would generalize to higher-achieving populations. In addition, there was little information about what teachers actually did in the treatment classrooms to create mastery goal structures, how faithfully they implemented the strategies, or what other, non-goal-related changes may have occurred in the classrooms. After all, the teachers in the experimental group had the opportunity to meet regularly with other teachers and researchers to discuss, and reflect upon, teaching. Teachers rarely have an opportunity to do this, and the teachers in the Ames study may have experienced increased feelings of support and enthusiasm as a result of engaging in the study. These factors, rather than the promotion of mastery goal messages, may account for some of the differences between the students in the experimental and control groups. The results of the Linnenbrink (2005) and Maehr and Midgley (1996) studies, which produced much less consistent results regarding the effects of classroom goal structures, or the ability to meaningfully alter them, suggest that manipulating goal structures in real classrooms and schools is difficult, and can produce unpredictable results.

***Observational Research*** A few researchers have conducted observations in classrooms with the intention of identifying classroom procedures and instructional practices that might convey mastery or performance goal messages. This research has revealed the complexity of the process through which teachers make mastery and performance goals salient in the classroom, how students respond to these messages, and the effects of goal-related messages on student motivation and behavior. Some of this research has also contradicted results found using survey or experimental methods.

Meece (1991) found that teachers in classrooms containing students with relatively high personal mastery goal orientations (as assessed with student surveys) tended to use activities with clearer procedures than did teachers in classrooms containing less mastery oriented students. Yet she also reported that high and low mastery classrooms were not distinguished by the grouping structures used in the classroom or the cognitive complexity of the tasks assigned, two features of the classroom believed to influence the mastery goal structure (Ames, 1992).

Anderman, Patrick, Hruda, and Linnenbrink (2002; see also Patrick, Anderman, Ryan, Edlin, & Midgley, 2001) found that teachers in classrooms where students perceived a relatively weak classroom mastery goal structure (as assessed with student surveys) tended to emphasize the importance of following rules and procedures more than did teachers in classrooms with a stronger perceived mastery goal structure, according to the researchers' observations. Such an emphasis on rules and procedures, as opposed to

autonomous exploration and skill development, is consistent with the lower perceptions of a mastery goal structure in these classrooms. Yet these researchers also found that high-perceived and low-perceived mastery and high- and low-perceived performance classrooms were not distinguished by the frequency of classroom practices believed to increase students' performance goal orientations.

Turner, Meyer, Midgley, and Patrick (2003) used surveys to determine that some elementary classrooms were distinguished by having higher-than-average perceived mastery goal structures and lower-than-average use of avoidance strategies (i.e., self-handicapping, avoidance of help-seeking) among students. Observations of teaching practices revealed that teachers in those classrooms provided both *instructional* and *motivational* support for students. More specifically, these teachers combined an emphasis on learning, understanding, and transferring the responsibility for learning gradually to students with frequent motivational messages encouraging students to persist and to view mistakes as part of the learning process. These practices are all consistent with a mastery goal focus (Ames, 1992). But Turner and her colleagues also found that teachers in high-perceived-mastery and low-perceived-mastery classrooms did not necessarily differ on key variables thought to promote a mastery goal structure, such as the percentage of time teachers spent scaffolding learning (i.e., negotiation and transfer of responsibility).

Urdan, Kneisel, and Mason (1999) videotaped four classroom sessions in each of four different classrooms (one elementary and three middle school). In each classroom, they videotaped class sessions that involved the teacher introducing a new topic, having students work on some task during class, assessing student learning, and recognizing students for some accomplishment. They then selected segments of the videotaped sessions that they believed most clearly reflected either mastery or performance goal messages and used these clips for stimulated recall interviews with six target students in each classroom. They found that the teacher with the most consistent messages of concern for student input and personal relevance of the material had students that perceived the most mastery goal messages in the classroom. However, Urdan and his colleagues also found that students often did not interpret teacher behaviors in ways the researchers would have predicted. For example, when students in the elementary classroom were asked about their teachers' behavior of recognizing some students for high academic achievement and others for helping to clean up the classroom (a practice predicted to convey powerful messages about ability differences in the classroom), the students reported that the recognition itself was more important than the behavior that was being recognized. Some students in the eighth-grade classroom appeared to be more sensitive to their teacher's practice of listing students' test scores on the chalkboard for all to see, but only the lower-achieving students in this class identified the practice as potentially reducing student motivation.

Taken together, these observational studies suggest that there are observable differences between classrooms that students perceive as relatively strong or weak in their emphasis on mastery goals. But this research has also raised questions about just what constitutes a classroom goal structure and how predictive the observed goal structure is of student attitudes and behaviors. These observational studies suggest that the associations between classroom goal messages and student motivation are complex, depending in part on how students perceive teacher practices and policies and on other, non-goal-related messages in the classroom. Using observational methods to find the specific mechanisms through which classroom goal structures influence students' motivation and behavior will be a difficult endeavor.

***Conclusions about Existing Research*** Important questions remain about the exact definition of classroom goal structures, the combination of teacher practices, classroom policies, and student attitudes that create the classroom goal structure, the modifiability of classroom goal structures, and the strength of the associations, or influence, of classroom goal structures on motivational, affective, behavioral, and achievement outcomes. Although the existing research suggests that students' perceptions about the purposes of achievement can be influenced by the goal-related messages in the learning context, it also appears that the influence of classroom goal structures on these outcomes is not particularly strong or consistent across studies. More work is clearly needed to determine how, and how much, classroom goal structures influence student engagement and achievement.

## Remaining Questions about Classroom Goal Structures

In this section, I consider some of the questions about classroom goal structures that have not yet received adequate attention. The first of these remaining questions concerns the relative importance of classroom goal structures. The existing research raises questions about their importance because the associations between goal structures and outcomes, when controlling for personal goals or when examining between-classroom variability in goal structures, are generally quite weak. One reason for these weak associations may be that other factors, both inside and outside the classroom, have important influences on student engagement and achievement.

***The Influence of Other Contextual Variables*** Research suggests that social relationships with teachers and peers in schools and classrooms have important consequences for student motivation and achievement (Coleman, 1961; Wentzel, 1989). Wanting to please teachers, gain or maintain social status with friends, and having the social and emotional support of teachers are all potentially important, in-class influences of motivation and achievement that are not captured by either mastery or performance goal defini-

tions. Research examining classroom goal structures has occasionally included measures of social relational variables and found them to have stronger effects than either mastery or performance classroom goal structures. For example, Ryan and her colleagues (1998) found that appropriate help-seeking behavior was promoted in classrooms where teachers reported that it was important to attend to students' social and emotional needs. Several observational studies have found that in classrooms where teachers promoted interaction and respect among students, and supported students' social and emotional needs, students in the class and the researchers judged the classrooms to have the stronger mastery goal structures than were classrooms with teachers who did not attend to support these needs (Patrick et al., 2001; Turner et al., 2002; Urdan et al., 1999).

Based largely on the evidence from these studies, Patrick (2004) argued that the definition of mastery goal structures should perhaps be expanded to include an emphasis on, and support for the development of the social and emotional welfare of students. Although it certainly appears that there is a correlation between classroom mastery goal structures and the social-emotional dimension of the classroom, it may be a mistake to merge the two into a single construct. The definition of mastery goals is the development of competence, and it appears that students may perceive that the development of competence is enhanced in caring, respectful, and supportive environments. But that does not mean mastery goals and support for social and emotional development are equivalent. Indeed, the strong association between mastery goal structures and social-emotional dimensions of the classroom may reveal a problem with the assessment of classroom mastery goal structures: Perhaps students have a difficult time distinguishing between teacher caring about the development of their academic competence and teacher caring about their social and emotional development. Commonly used survey measures of classroom goal structures may invite students to confound a general liking of the teacher with an emphasis on mastery goals in the classroom and a perception of the teacher as unfair or displaying favoritism with emphasizing performance goals in the classroom (see Urdan, 2004c for a more thorough consideration of this issue).

There also is a long tradition of research outside of the goal theory framework indicating the importance of contextual variables in the classroom besides goal structures. For example, self-determination theory research has demonstrated that student motivation differs in classrooms where student autonomy is supported (Ryan & Grolnick, 1986). Similarly, research examining such constructs as teacher expectancies (Weinstein, 2002), interest (Hidi, 2000), and the broader classroom climate (Fraser, 1989) all reveal how many and complicated are the classroom factors that can influence student motivation and achievement.

Several variables outside of the classroom may be important to consider as well. For example, school-wide policies such as academic tracking, pressure for teachers to cover a large amount of content to prepare students for the next grade level, and the curricular materials used in the school all may influence student motivation in ways that complement, or supercede, mastery and performance goal structures. Beyond the school level, there are policies and practices at the district, state, and federal levels that can influence student motivation in important ways. The recent emphasis on testing, accountability, and comparisons of student test scores across schools, districts, states, and nations, provide powerful messages about the social-comparative nature of schooling. Given the multiple messages at the classroom, school, and societal levels about the purposes of academic achievement, and the multitude of contextual influences on student motivation and achievement, it should not be surprising that students' perceptions of the mastery and performance goal structures in their classrooms explain little of the variance in most motivational and behavioral outcomes examined. It is important to develop an understanding of how classroom goal structures are influenced by, and combine with, these other contextual variables to affect student engagement and achievement.

***Domain and Developmental Differences***  Classroom goal structures may operate differently for students at different developmental stages and in different academic domains. Although a few studies have considered these issues, much remains unknown about these potentially important factors. Most of the research on classroom goal structures has been conducted with students in late-elementary and middle grades. Midgley and her colleagues found that across the transition to middle schools, students reported a perception that mastery goals were emphasized less, and performance goals more, in their classrooms (Anderman & Midgley, 1997; Urdan & Midgley, 2003). Some research has been conducted at the high school level (Bong, 2005; Urdan, 2004a, 2004b) and some has focused exclusively on the late elementary school level, specifically fifth grade (Urdan et al., 1998). Although several of these studies employed longitudinal designs (e.g., Anderman & Midgley, 1997; Bong, 2005; Kaplan & Midgley, 1999; Urdan, 2004a; Urdan & Midgley, 2003), they were generally only one or two years long and did not specifically examine whether students at different developmental stages might perceive and respond to classroom goal structures in different ways. As described earlier, Urdan and his colleagues (1999) found limited evidence that younger students may perceive and respond to classroom goal messages differently than older students. Specifically, whereas the elementary school students rarely perceived teacher practices in social-comparative terms, some of the students in the eighth-grade classroom did discuss some teacher practices in social-comparative terms. These results hint at a potentially important question: Might the benefits and costs of classroom mastery and performance goal structures vary across developmental levels? Certainly, early adolescence may be a heightened period of susceptibility to the influence of social comparison information, thereby potentially making the effects of per-

formance goal structures stronger during early adolescence. But early adolescence is also a time of heightened concern with social relationships with peers and nonparental adults. Might these concerns with social relationships outweigh the effects of classroom goal structures or modify the way they operate? Similarly, as students approach the end of high school and consider applying to colleges, might a healthy concern with outperforming others be adaptive, thereby creating new benefits of classroom performance goal structures for some students? To date, little is known about the association between developmental level and classroom goal structures.

Similarly, little research has examined domain differences in the prevalence and function of classroom mastery and performance goal structures. There may be reason to suspect that students differ in their perceptions of the work in different academic areas, and these perceptions can shape their personal achievement goals as well as their perceptions of the classroom goal structures. For example, mathematics is often viewed as a subject with clear correct and incorrect answers, making it easier than subjects like English and history to engage in social comparisons. In addition, students may be more likely to view mathematics as a subject that requires innate ability. Whereas just about anyone can learn history, given enough effort and interest, there is a perception that some people are simply "math people" and others are not. If students view mathematics as a subject that one either has a talent for or not, they may be more inclined to adopt an "entity" view of ability in math, leading to the adoption of performance goals (Dweck & Leggett, 1988). Such a view of mathematics may also lead students to view their mathematics classrooms, more so than they English or social studies classrooms, as having strong performance goal structures.

A few studies have examined classroom goal structures in multiple academic domains. Anderman and Midgley (1997) reported that students perceived declines in the mastery goal structures and increasing emphasis on performance goals in both mathematics and English classrooms after the transition to middle school. Bong (2005) found, with a sample of high school girls in Korea, that perceptions of the mastery goal structure declined during the academic year in English but no other academic subjects, whereas their perceptions of the performance goal structure increased across all academic domains. In two separate studies, Anderman and his colleagues report results for the domain of mathematics that differ markedly from the results Urdan reported in English. Anderman and his colleagues found that teacher-reported use of instructional practices that emphasized performance goals were associated with declines in mathematics valuing over time whereas there was no association between mastery-goal-oriented instructional practices and changes in valuing in mathematics (Anderman et al., 2004). In contrast, Urdan (2004b) found relatively strong associations between classroom mastery goal structures and valuing in English, but no association between performance goal structures and valuing in English.

The existing research examining domain differences in classroom goal structures is too sparse and varied to allow for reliable conclusions. Some evidence indicates that classroom goal structures operate differently in mathematics and English, but this research was conducted with different samples and examined different research questions (i.e., change over time in the Anderman et al. and Bong studies, single-time associations in the Urdan, 2004b study). Because students have quite different beliefs about the relevance, ease, and causes of success in different domains, it is reasonable to hypothesize differences in the strength and effects of classroom goal structures in various domains. Sound research is needed to determine whether such differences exist.

***Patterns of Classroom Goal Structures*** How do classroom goal structures combine to influence motivation and achievement? In real classrooms both mastery and performance goal messages are always present to varying degrees. In just about any classroom, teachers will encourage students to develop their understanding of the material and their skills *and* present social comparison information to students, either explicitly via normative grading or more subtly through differential feedback or task assignments to students at different levels of achievement. Achievement goal theory researchers have found that students often pursue multiple goals simultaneously (Barron & Harackiewicz, 2001), and recently developed survey measures of classroom goal structures also reveal weak-to-null associations between perceived mastery and performance goal structures (Urdan, 2004b). Mastery and performance goal structures undoubtedly combine to influence motivation and achievement. Yet very little research has been conducted to date examining how combinations of perceived classroom goal structures influence student engagement and achievement.

Linnenbrink (2005) found that fifth-grade students test scores on an end-of-unit test improved the most in classrooms where teachers emphasized performance goals or a combination of mastery and performance goals compared to students in the classrooms where the teacher emphasized mastery goals. But she reported no significant differences between these three classroom types on her measures of motivation, emotional well-being, cognitive engagement, or adaptive or avoidance help-seeking, and the group differences in achievement test scores diminished significantly by the time of the 5-week follow-up. These results suggest that mastery and performance goal structures in the classroom may combine to influence engagement and achievement, but these effects may be weak. Clearly, more research examining the effects of various classroom goal structure patterns is needed.

## Future Directions in Research on Classroom Goal Structures

At this point, there are more questions than answers regarding classroom goal structures and their effects, so future research might profitably be pursued in any number of directions. In my view, the three most important areas for future research in this field are these: (a) How does one determine the importance of classroom goal structures for student motivation and achievement independent of other factors, such as students' feelings about the teacher, their level of comfort in the classroom, and the other goals that concern them besides mastery and performance goals? (b) What methods must researchers employ to capture the complex and dynamic realities of classroom life? (c) If classroom goal structures are important, what can and should teachers do to promote the goal structure, or combinations of goal structures, most likely to enhance student motivation?

***Determining the Importance of Classroom Goal Structures*** Researchers must separate the effects of goal structures from other variables (such as teacher caring or general feelings students have about the teacher) and to determine the cause–effect relationship among the variables. It may be very difficult for students in real classrooms to distinguish between the defining features of mastery goals and the larger collection of teacher practices that simply represent good instructional practice: being well organized, presenting information in a clear way, selecting and assigning interesting tasks and assignments. If a teacher has a good sense of humor and is able to engage students in the lecture using humor, does that represent a mastery goal structure, or just good instructional practice? Similarly, if teachers are caring and fair with students, should these teacher skills and practices be considered part of the mastery goal structure?

The difficulty researchers face is in separating goal-related messages from the many other sources of information in the classroom that might influence motivation but may not be specifically part of the definition of achievement goals. Separating mastery and performance goal messages from other variables, such as student interest in the topic, students' feeling about the teacher, and generally effective instructional practices that are neither mastery or performance goal focused, is necessary before the unique effects of mastery and performance goal structures can be determined. Further complicating matters, these nongoal variables may influence students' perceptions of the classroom goal structures. For example, students who like their teachers and perceive them as fair and caring may be more likely to perceive that there is a strong classroom mastery goal structure. Conversely, students who dislike the subject matter and their teacher may be more likely to perceive a strong classroom performance goal structure, even if the teacher does not promote social comparison among students. Because most of the existing research examining classroom goal structures has relied on correlational data, isolating the effects of mastery and performance goal structures has been difficult.

***Methods of Studying Classroom Goal Structures*** Attempts to study the classroom goal structure are ambitious undertakings. The individuals in any classroom vary, and the classroom experience is dynamic and changing from hour to hour and from day to day. Experimental manipulations of goal messages tend to simplify the goal messages in a way that may not accurately represent the complexity of classroom life. Observations of classrooms tend to provide infrequent "snapshots" and are unable to determine how individuals in the classroom vary in their interpretations of goal messages. Survey measures of classroom goal structures treat the classroom as static, as if the goal structure assessed on a given day is stable and unchanging. In addition, survey research tends to focus on means, providing a picture of the average perceptions of students in the classroom without much consideration of the variability among students.

To gain a more accurate picture of how messages in the learning situation intersect with individual differences in perceptions, values, and culture, a number of scholars have suggested a movement toward a sociocultural approach to motivation research (Hickey, 2003; Turner & Patrick, 2006). These researchers argue most current theories of motivation, including achievement goal theory, overemphasize the cognitive aspect of motivation, placing most of the motivational process within the minds and perceptions of individuals. In contrast, the sociocultural view argues that motivation is situated in specific activities and contexts, and that motivation is often socially constructed through the interactions of people (e.g., students and teachers) in specific situations. Hickey (2003) argues strongly that motivation must be examined at the level of the situation (i.e., while a student interacts with a teacher or another student on a specific task) rather than at the more general level typically assessed by surveys. Turner and Patrick (2006), using Rogoff's framework of multiple planes, argue that an accurate appraisal of motivation processes can only be gained when the different planes of experience (the individual level, the contextual level, and the societal level) are all considered. When a ninth-grade Latina student in California is working on an algebra problem in her math class, for example, her motivation may be influenced by personal-level factors (e.g., her self-efficacy, her achievement goal, her valuing of mathematics achievement, her future educational aspirations), contextual factors (e.g., the instructional support she gets from her teacher, messages from her teacher about the value of the work, distractions and help from other students in the class), and the societal level (e.g., stereotypes about Latinas regarding math achievement, value placed on math achievement by the popular culture). The influence of these planes shifts across individuals, domains, and across situations within domains. Given the complexity of classroom life, the variety of factors that contribute to classroom goal structures (including intraindividual, interindividual, and cultural), and the limitations of existing research on classroom goal structures, sociocultural approaches to the study of goal structures represent a promising future direction for research in this field.

*Applying Research to Practice* If research reveals motivational and achievement benefits associated with a mastery goal structure, it follows that such structures should be promoted in classrooms. But the research-to-practice link can be a difficult one to create (Blumenfeld, 1992; Urdan & Turner, 2005). There is currently very little research examining how teachers can promote mastery goal structures in the classroom, weaken performance goal structures, and sustain these changes over time and without support. There are a few studies that have examined classroom process that influence students' perceptions of the classroom goal structure (e.g., Turner et al., 2002; Urdan et al., 1999), but such research is rare and a number of questions remain.

Future research aimed at discovering how to create or reduce particular goal structures in the classroom is needed. Such research might profitably focus on a series of questions: (a) What are the classroom processes most directly responsible for creating mastery and performance goal structures? (b) What kinds of support do teachers need to alter their instructional practices in ways that will make mastery and performance goal structures more or less salient in their classrooms? (c) What are some of the obstacles (e.g., lack of training, lack of support from the school, resistance from students, etc.) that teachers need to overcome to create the desired goal structures in their classrooms? (d) How does the process of classroom goal structure change unfold? Those who have attempted to alter the classroom motivational climate report that it is a difficult process producing uneven results (e.g., Maehr & Midgley, 1996; Miller & Meece, 1997). Although such research is daunting, it is necessary if research on classroom goal structures is to have a meaningful effect on teachers and students in real classrooms.

## Conclusion

Compared to the scores of studies examining personal achievement goals, classroom goal structures have been relatively understudied. With increasing calls for research on contextual influences on motivation (Hickey, 2003; Turner & Patrick, 2006), examinations of classroom goal structures have increased, a trend that will likely continue. To date, research on classroom goal structures has revealed interesting correlates, antecedents, and potential consequences of mastery and performance goal emphases in the classroom. Yet a number of interesting, important, and confounding questions remain. Gaining a clear understanding of how classroom goal structures are created and how they affect motivation and achievement holds great promise for altering instruction in a manner that enhances student motivation. For such promise to be realized, however, additional research is needed that sharpens the definition of classroom goal structures and employs methodologies capable of incorporating the multiple and dynamic features of classroom life that make these systems so complex.

## Note

1. Wolters used the PALS measure to assess classroom goal structures; the measure did not include several new items for assessing both the approach and avoidance components of classroom performance goal structure.

## References

Ames, C. A. (1990, April). *The relationship of achievement goals to student motivation in classroom settings.* Paper presented at the meeting of the American Educational Research Association, Boston.

Ames, C. A. (1992). Classrooms: Goals, structures, and student motivation. *Journal of Educational Psychology, 84,* 261–271.

Ames, C., & Archer, J. (1988). Achievement goals in the classroom: Students' learning strategies and motivation processes. *Journal of Educational Psychology, 80,* 260–267.

Ames, C., & Felker, D. (1979). An examination of children's attributions and achievement-related evaluations in competitive, cooperative, and individualistic reward structures. *Journal of Educational Psychology, 71,* 413–420.

Anderman, E. A., Eccles, J. S., Yoon, K. S., Roeser, R., Wigfield, A., & Blumenfeld, P. (2001). Learning to value mathematics and reading: Relations to mastery and performance-oriented instructional practices. *Contemporary Educational Psychology, 26,* 76–95.

Anderman, E. M., Maehr, M. L., & Midgley, C. (1999). Declining motivation after the transition to middle school: Schools can make a difference. *Journal of Research and Development in Education, 32,* 131–147.

Anderman, E. M., & Midgley, C. (1997). Changes in personal achievement goals and the perceived classroom goal structures across the transition to middle level schools. *Contemporary Educational Psychology, 22,* 269–298.

Anderman, E. A., & Midgley, C. (2004). Changes in self-reported academic cheating across the transition from middle school to high school. *Contemporary Educational Psychology, 29,* 499–517.

Anderman, L. H., Patrick, H., Hruda, L. Z., & Linnenbrink, E. A. (2002). Observing goal structures to clarify and expand goal theory. In C. Midgley (Ed.), *Goals, goal structures, and patterns of adaptive learning* (pp. 243–278). Mahwah, NJ: Erlbaum.

Anderman, E. A., & Young, A. J. (1994). Motivation and strategy use in science: Individual differences and classroom effects. *Journal of Research in Science Teaching, 31,* 811–831.

Barron, K. E., & Harackiewicz, J. M. (2001). Achievement goals and optimal motivation: Testing multiple goal models. *Journal of Personality and Social Psychology, 80,* 706–722.

Blumenfeld, P. C. (1992). Classroom learning and motivation: Clarifying and expanding goal theory. *Journal of Educational Psychology, 84,* 272–281.

Bong, M. (2005). Within-grade changes in Korean girls' motivation and perceptions of the learning environment across domains and achievement levels. *Journal of Educational Psychology, 97,* 656–672.

Brophy, J. (2005). Goal theorists should move on from performance goals. *Educational Psychologist, 40,* 167–176.

Church, M. A., Elliot, A. J., & Gable, S. L. (2001). Perceptions of classroom environment, achievement goals, and achievement outcomes. *Journal of Educational Psychology, 93,* 43–54.

Coleman, J. (1961). *The adolescent society.* Glencoe, IL: Free Press.

Dweck, C. S., & Leggett, E. L. (1988). A social-cognitive approach to motivation and personality. *Psychological Review, 95,* 256–273.

Elliot, A. J. (2005). A conceptual history of the achievement goal construct. In A. J. Elliot & C. S. Dweck (Eds.), *Handbook of competence and motivation* (pp. 52–72). New York: Guilford.

Elliot, A. J. (1997). Integrating the "classic" and the "contemporary" approaches to achievement motivation: A hierarchical model of approach and avoidance achievement motivation. In M. L. Maehr & P. R. Pintrich (Eds.), *Advances in motivation and achievement* (Vol. 10, pp. 143–179). Greenwich, CT: JAI Press.

Elliot, A. J. (1999). Approach and avoidance motivation and achievement goals. *Educational Psychologist, 34,* 169–189.

Elliot, A. J., & Harackiewicz, J. M. (1996). Approach and avoidance achievement goals and intrinsic motivation: A mediational analysis. *Journal of Personality and Social Psychology, 70,* 461–475.

Elliott, E. S., & Dweck, C. S. (1988). Goals: an approach to motivation and achievement. *Journal of Personality and Social Psychology, 54,* 5–12.

Fraser, B. J. (1989). 20 years of classroom climate work: Progress and prospect. *Journal of Curriculum Studies, 21,* 307–27.

Graham, S., & Golan, S. (1991). Motivational influences on cognition: Task involvement, ego involvement, and depth of information processing. *Journal of Educational Psychology, 83,* 187–194.

Greene, B. A., Miller, R. B., Crowson, H. M., Duke, B. L., & Akey, K. L. (2004). Predicting high school students' cognitive engagement and achievement: Contributions of classroom perceptions and motivation. *Contemporary Educational Psychology, 29,* 462–482.

Harackiewicz, J. M., Barron, K. E., Pintrich, P. R., Elliot, A. J., & Thrash, T. M. (2002). Revision of achievement goal theory: Necessary and illuminating. *Journal of Educational Psychology, 94,* 638–645.

Hickey, D. T. (2003). Engaged participation versus marginal nonparticipation: A stridently sociocultural approach to achievement motivation. *Elementary School Journal, 103,* 401–429.

Hidi, S. (2000). An interest researcher's perspective: The effects of extrinsic and intrinsic factors on motivation. *Intrinsic and extrinsic motivation: The search for optimal motivation and performance* (pp. 309–339). New York: Academic Press.

Hulleman, C. S., & Senko, C. (in press). Up around the bend: Forecasts for achievement goal theory and research in 2020. In T. Urdan & S. Karabenick (Eds.), *Advances in motivation and achievement: Vol. 16: The decade ahead.*

Kaplan, A., & Maehr, M. L. (2007). The contributions and prospects of goal orientation theory. *Educational Psychology Review, 19,* 141–184.

Kaplan, A., & Midgley, C. (1999). The relationship between perceptions of the classroom goal structure and early adolescents' affect in school: The mediating role of coping strategies. *Learning and Individual Differences, 11,* 187–212.

Kaplan, A., Middleton, M. J., Urdan, T., & Midgley, C. (2002). Achievement goals and goal structures. In C. Midgley (Ed.), *Goals, goal structures, and patterns of adaptive learning* (pp. 21–54). Mahwah, NJ: Erlbaum.

Karabenick, S. A. (2004). Perceived achievement goal structure and college student help seeking. *Journal of Educational Psychology, 96,* 569–581.

Linnenbrink, E. A. (2005). The dilemma of performance-approach goals: The use of multiple goal contexts to promote students' motivation and learning. *Journal of Educational Psychology, 97,* 197–213.

Maehr, M. L., & Midgley, C. (1991). Enhancing student motivation: A school-wide approach. *Educational Psychologist, 26,* 399–427.

Maehr, M. L., & Midgley, C. (1996). *Transforming school cultures.* Boulder, CO: Westview Press.

Maehr, M. L., & Nicholls, J. G. (1980). Culture and achievement motivation: A second look. In N. Warren (Ed.), *Studies in cross-cultural psychology* (Vol. 2, pp. 221–267). New York: Academic Press.

Meece, J. L. (1991). The classroom context and students' motivational goals. In M. L. Maehr & P. R. Pintrich (Eds.), *Advances in motivation and achievement: Vol. 7. Goals and self-regulatory processes* (pp. 261–285). Greenwich, CT: JAI Press.

Midgley, C., Kaplan, A., & Middleton, M. (2001). Performance-approach goals: Good for what, for whom, under what circumstances, and at what costs? *Journal of Educational Psychology, 93,* 77–86.

Midgley, C., Maehr, M. L., Hruda, L. Z., Anderman, E., Anderman, L., Freeman, K. E., Gheen, M., Kaplan, A., Kumar, R., Middleton, M. J., Nelson, J., Roeser, R., & Urdan, T. (2000). *Manual for the patterns of adaptive learning scales (PALS).* Ann Arbor: University of Michigan.

Midgley, C., & Urdan, T. (2001). Academic self-handicapping and performance goals: A further examination. *Contemporary Educational Psychology, 26,* 61–75.

Miller, A. D., & Murdock, T. B. (2007). Modeling latent true scores to determine the utility of aggregate student perceptions as classroom indicators in HLM: The case of classroom goal structures. *Contemporary Educational Psychology, 32,* 83–104.

Miller, S. D., & Meece, J. L. (1997). Enhancing elementary students' motivation to read and write: A classroom intervention study. *Journal of Educational Research, 90,* 286–299.

Newman, R. (1998). Students' help-seeking during problem solving: Influences of personal and contextual achievement goals. *Journal of Educational Psychology, 90,* 644–658.

Nolen, S. B. (2003). Learning environment, motivation, and achievement in high school science. *Journal of Research in Science Teaching, 40,* 347–368.

Patrick, H. (2004). Re-examining classroom mastery goal structure. In P. R. Pintrich & M. L. Maehr (Eds.), *Advances in motivation and achievement: Vol. 13. Motivating students, improving schools: The legacy of Carol Midgley* (pp. 233–264). Oxford, England: Elsevier.

Patrick, H., Anderman, L. H., Ryan, A. M., Edelin, K., & Midgley, C. (2001). Teachers' communication of goal orientations in four fifth-grade classrooms. *Elementary School Journal, 102*(1), 35–58.

Pintrich, P. R. (2000). Multiple goals, multiple pathways: The role of goal orientation in learning and achievement. *Journal of Educational Psychology, 92,* 544–555.

Pintrich, P. R., & Garcia, T. (1991). Student goal orientation and self-regulation in the college classroom. In M. L. Maehr & P. R. Pintrich (Eds.), *Advances in motivation and achievement: Vol. 7. Goals and self-regulatory processes* (pp. 371–402). Greenwich, CT: JAI Press.

Roeser, R. W. (2004). Competing schools of thought in achievement goal theory? In P. R. Pintrich & M. L. Maehr (Eds.), *Advances in motivation and achievement: Vol. 13. Motivating students, improving schools: The legacy of Carol Midgley* (pp. 265–300). Oxford, England: Elsevier.

Roeser, R. W., Midgley, C., & Urdan, T. (1996). Perceptions of the school psychological environment and early adolescents' self appraisals and academic engagement: The mediating role of goals and belonging. *Journal of Educational Psychology, 88,* 408–422.

Ryan, A. M., Gheen, M. H., & Midgley, C. (1998). Why do some students avoid asking for help? An examination of the interplay among students' academic efficacy, teachers' social-emotional role, and the classroom goal structure. *Journal of Educational Psychology, 88,* 1–8.

Ryan, R. M., & Grolnick, W. S. (1986). Origins and pawns in the classroom: self-report and projective assessments of individual differences in children's perspectives. *Journal of Personality and Social Psychology, 50,* 550–558.

Senko, C., & Miles, K. M. (2008). Pursuing their own learning agenda: How mastery-oriented students jeopardize their class performance. *Contemporary Educational Psychology, 33,* 561–583.

Turner, J. C., Meyer, D. K., Midgley, C., & Patrick, H. (2003). Teacher discourse and sixth graders' reported affect and achievement behaviors in two high-mastery/high performance mathematics classrooms. *Elementary School Journal, 103,* 359–382.

Turner, J. C., Midgley, C., Meyer, D. K., Gheen, M., Anderman, A. M., Kang, Y., & Patrick, H. (2002). The classroom environment and students' reports of avoidance strategies in mathematics: A multimethod study. *Journal of Educational Psychology, 94,* 88–106.

Turner, J. C., & Patrick, H. (2006). How does motivation develop and why does it change? Reframing motivation research. *Educational Psychologist, 43,* 119–131.

Urdan, T. (2004a). Predictors of academic self-handicapping and achievement: Examining achievement goals, classroom goal structures, and culture. *Journal of Educational Psychology, 96,* 251–264.

Urdan, T. (2004b). Using multiple methods to assess students' perceptions of classroom goal structures. *European Psychologist, 4,* 222–231.

Urdan, T. (2004c). Can achievement goal theory guide school reform? In P. R. Pintrich & M. L. Maehr (Eds.), *Advances in motivation and achievement* (Vol. 13, pp. 361–392). Stamford, CT: Elsevier.

Urdan, T. (2007, April). *What are classroom goal structures and how much do they matter?* Paper presented at the annual meetings of the American Educational Research Association, Chicago, IL.

Urdan, T., Kneisel, L., & Mason, V. (1999). Interpreting messages about motivation in the classroom: Examining the effects of achievement goal structures. In T. Urdan (Ed.), *Advances in motivation and achievement* (Vol. 11, pp. 123–158). Stamford, CT: JAI Press.

Urdan, T., & Mestas, M. (2006). The goals behind performance goals. *Journal of Educational Psychology, 98,* 354–365.

Urdan, T., & Midgley, C. (2003). Changes in the perceived classroom goal structure and pattern of adaptive learning during early adolescence. *Contemporary Educational Psychology, 28,* 524–551

Urdan, T., Midgley, C., & Anderman, E. (1998). The role of classroom goal structure in students' use of self-handicapping strategies. *American Educational Research Journal, 35,* 101–122.

Urdan, T., & Turner, J. C. (2005). Competence motivation in the classroom. In A. E. Elliot & C. Dweck (Eds.), *Handbook of competence motivation* (pp. 297–317). New York: Guilford.

Weinstein. R. S. (2002). *Reaching higher: The power of expectations in schooling.* Cambridge, MA: Harvard University Press.

Wentzel, K. R. (1989). Adolescent classroom goals, standards for performance, and academic achievement: An interactionist perspective. *Journal of Educational Psychology, 81,* 131–142.

Wolters, C. A. (2004). Advancing achievement goal theory: Using goal structures, and goal orientations, to predict students' motivation, cognition, and achievement. *Journal of Educational Psychology, 96,* 216–235.

# Part III

**Schools as Social Context for Development**

# 8

# School Contexts that Promote Students' Positive Development

*Victor Battistich*

This chapter examines schools as environmental contexts and considers how characteristics of the school setting influence students' development. Curiously, despite the voluminous body of research on schools, relatively little of this research has focused specifically on the school as a developmental context. Most educational research has focused on particular teaching practices and characteristics of teachers and students. It is almost as if the environment of the school is seen as having little to do with the outcomes of schooling; that a school is simply a building, a convenient physical location in which students gather with teachers to engage in formal teaching and learning processes. Yet, attributes of the environment in which activities occur undoubtedly influence the experiences of individuals in those settings (Barker, 1968). The "same" lesson or extracurricular activity can have widely varying effects on students as a function of differences in the physical setting (e.g., light, temperature, noise level, seating arrangements) and, especially, the social situation (e.g., goals, organization, interpersonal relationships) in which it occurs. Consequently, while it is certainly important to understand the formal educational practices that occur in schools, it is equally important to consider the context in which these activities take place if we are to adequately understand how schools influence students (Eccles & Roeser, 2003).

It is not especially surprising that educational research has tended to pay more attention to the attributes of teachers and students than the nature of the context in which they interact. Despite the longstanding recognition that human behavior and development is jointly determined by characteristics of both the individual and the environment (e.g., Lewin, 1951; Murray, 1938), there has been a widespread tendency in the behavioral and social sciences to focus on individual-level causal explanations (Earls & Carlson, 2001). Even within this general emphasis on the individual, educational research has tended to be even more narrowly concerned with only one aspect of students' development.

That is, it has emphasized the academic outcomes of schooling (students' acquisition of basic literacy and numeracy skills, and mastery of disciplinary content knowledge) and paid much less attention to the effects of schooling on nonacademic outcomes. Yet, it is indisputable that students' experiences in school not only influence the development of their intellectual capacities, but have widespread effects on their personal, interpersonal, and moral development as well (Battistich, Schaps, Solomon, & Watson, 1991; Solomon, Watson, & Battistich, 2001). Moreover, as will be detailed below, the explicit goals of schooling have always included more than the acquisition of academic knowledge and skills. Indeed, these social goals of schooling are arguably of even greater importance to contemporary society than the academic goals with which policy makers seem so preoccupied.

This chapter, then, adopts a broader perspective on schools and the outcomes of schooling than is typical of most educational research. Specifically, it considers schools as primary contexts of and for the development of children and adolescents. Indeed, outside of the home, schools are the most sustained and significant developmental context for youth (Eccles & Roeser, 2003). Moreover, schools are formally and intentionally designed to influence the course of development (Pianta, 2006). As such, schools are not just institutional settings where formal teaching and learning take place, but social environments where youth spend much of their time during the critical developmental period between early childhood and early adulthood, when they are developing their basic understandings of themselves, human society, and their place in it.

Consistent with the recent emergence of "positive psychology" (Seligman & Csikszentmihalyi, 2000) and current theory and research on child and adolescent development more generally (Smetana, Campione-Barr, & Metzger, 2006), the emphasis of this chapter is on the contextual characteristics of schools that are likely to effectively promote the positive development of youth (Larsen, 2000). This is not to say that the traditional academic outcomes of schooling will be ignored. Mastery of subject matter knowledge and disciplinary skills certainly are important outcomes of schooling, and successful completion of elementary and secondary school and, increasingly, postsecondary education, are important developmental milestones. Effects on academic outcomes will thus be considered as one of the effects of schooling, but not as the sole or even primary outcome.

A general theoretical perspective on contexts and development will be described in the next section, including general issues in conceptualizing contextual influences, measuring characteristics of contexts, and estimating context effects. This section will be followed by discussion of the goals and outcomes of schooling. Building on the seminal ideas of John Dewey and drawing upon related theory and research in child development and socialization, a general conceptual model of school contexts that should facilitate positive youth development will be described and relevant empirical research will be reviewed. Finally, the implications of this perspective for future research and school improvement efforts, including some fundamental issues in conceptualizing and investigating school contexts, will be discussed.

## Contexts and the Ecology of Human Development

In common with other chapters in this volume, the perspective adopted here is consistent with Bronfenbrenner's ecological model of human development (Bronfenbrenner & Morris, 1998). Development from this perspective is seen as occurring within multiple environmental contexts and interrelated levels of organization (e.g., biological, psychological, social), and to involve interaction and reciprocal causation among these levels. This perspective encompasses context as broadly defined, including the physical, psychological, social, institutional, cultural, and historical aspects of settings, as well as the characteristics of persons within them. Development is seen as occurring simultaneously in multiple contexts, with the effects of distal contexts generally being mediated by more proximal contextual influences. Developmental processes, then, consist of complex transactions between the person and the environment that are the critical determinants of developmental outcomes (Masten & Coatsworth, 1998), and it is the "person-in-setting" (i.e., the individual's interaction with the setting) that is of primary concern.

Although theoretically compelling, application of the ecological perspective in research has been hindered by significant methodological problems. The recent prevalence of empirical studies of contextual influences, such as a peer group, school, or neighborhood, is largely attributable to the development of better statistical methods, particularly multilevel regression (Goldstein, 2003; Raudenbush & Bryk, 2002) and structural equations approaches to modeling growth processes (e.g., MacCallum, Kim, Malarkey, &

Kiecolt-Glaser, 1997; Raudenbush, 2001). These improvements have satisfactorily addressed the basic problem of bias in statistical estimation due to the nonindependence of observations of individuals within contexts. Nevertheless, there remain important issues in the conceptualization, measurement, and estimation of context effects that have yet to be satisfactorily resolved. These will be briefly addressed below.

***Conceptualizing, Measuring, and Estimating Context Effects*** A "context effect" is typically defined as the effect of an environment, such as a school or neighborhood, on the individuals within that setting that is not reducible to individual-level characteristics (Leventhal & Brooks-Gunn, 2003; Osgood & Anderson, 2004; Sampson, Morenoff, & Gannon-Rowley, 2002). For example, studies have found that schools differ in average student achievement even when student "input" characteristics (e.g., ability or prior achievement, socioeconomic status) are controlled (e.g., Everson & Millsap, 2004; Hofman, Hofman, & Guldemond, 2002), and that neighborhood differences in crime rates cannot be fully accounted for by characteristics of the individuals and families that inhabit them (e.g., Browning, Feinberg, & Dietz, 2004). A primary problem in identifying context effects, of course, is assuring that all individual-level causal influences have, in fact, been accounted for; a condition which is quite difficult to achieve in practice because individual and contextual characteristics are almost always confounded (Duncan, Connell, & Klebanov, 1997; Duncan & Raudenbush, 1999; Raudenbush & Willms, 1995).

One reason for the confounding of individual and contextual characteristics in research is because contextual variables are commonly defined in terms of aggregate characteristics of the individuals who inhabit them. In such compositional models, people are hypothesized to be influenced by the aggregate demographic characteristics of the group. For example, much of the research on both neighborhood and school contexts has focused on socioeconomic composition, and has shown that there are differences in the outcomes of individuals who inhabit neighborhoods or schools that differ in average socioeconomic status (SES) after individual-level SES is controlled (e.g., Hallinger, Bickman, & Davis, 1996; Leventhal & Brooks-Gunn, 2000).

Use of multilevel regression appropriately accounts for the nonindependence of observations within contexts and adequately controls for individual-level scores in estimating context effects (Raudenbush & Bryk, 2002). It also addresses potential issues of aggregation bias and heterogeneity of regression slopes when analyzing data from individuals who are nested within contexts. However, the use of multilevel statistical procedures is not a panacea for problems in investigating context effects. It is important that all significant individual-level characteristics have been included in the statistical model. The omission of any important variables will result in statistical bias and cross-level misspecification (Duncan et al., 1997). Even when all important individual-level variables are included in the statistical model, measurement error can introduce bias in the estimates of context effects (Hutchison, 2004). More importantly, approaches that address the confounding of individual and context characteristics by statistically controlling for individual characteristics attribute all shared variance in the outcome to the individual variable, and thus may either under- or overestimate the actual effect of context depending upon the quality of the measurement model and the nature of the causal relationship between person and context (Duncan et al., 1997).

Recent research on neighborhoods provides an excellent example of these issues in estimating context effects. There has been considerable correlational research on relationships between the socioeconomic composition of neighborhoods and developmental outcomes of youth (see Leventhal & Brooks-Gunn, 2000). Living in a poor neighborhood has consistently been found to be associated with a variety of negative outcomes, including violence, alcohol and drug abuse, and criminal behavior. After controlling for individual and family characteristics, neighborhood context usually has been estimated to account for about 5% of the variance in these outcomes. However, in a rare experimental study where randomly selected low-income Black families were moved to more affluent neighborhoods Rosenbaum (1991; Rubinowitz & Rosenbaum, 2000) found much larger effects of neighborhood context, suggesting that the statistical adjustments for individual and family characteristics in the correlational studies underestimated the actual effects of neighborhood context (Leventhal & Brooks-Gunn, 2003).

Another substantive issue with using compositional indicators of contextual influences is the "reflection problem" (Manski, 1993). This occurs when the observed relationship between contextual characteristics and individual outcomes reflects nothing more than the artifactual correlation between an aggregate measure and the individual-level characteristics that comprise it. The reflection problem is potentially a common one in cross-sectional studies of compositional context effects. For example, if "negative peer influences" in a school is operationalized as the aggregate of individual student reports of engaging in antisocial behaviors, then this measure of school context will necessarily be positively correlated with the likelihood of antisocial behavior on the part of any individual student within the school. This relationship can hardly be considered a causal one. Longitudinal data can help to resolve this problem by measuring the compositional contextual variable prior to measuring the individual variable which it is hypothesized to affect (Duncan & Raudenbush, 1999).

A more serious and pervasive confounding problem that applies to both compositional and noncompositional definitions of contexts is that people generally do not come to inhabit particular settings through random processes. These "selection effects" may result from intentional or accidental processes, but whether the result of choice or circumstance, they confound individual- and setting-level influences.

For example, the generally higher student achievement at private, selective schools may result because they admit students of higher ability (a compositional characteristic), or because the practices at such schools are more effective at fostering learning than those at public schools (a noncompositional characteristic), or both (Shinn & Toohey, 2003). Similar considerations apply when trying to disentangle the influences that contribute to apparent effects of neighborhoods. In both cases, because individuals with different characteristics tend to inhabit different contexts, it is almost impossible to make a valid causal inference about context effects in observational studies and very difficult to do so in quasi-experiments. Moreover, even in an experimental study of school effects where individuals are randomly assigned to schools (which would control for compositional differences resulting from selection), it is unlikely that differences in noncompositional contextual characteristics (e.g., organizational structure, curriculum, teaching practices) would be randomly distributed in the sample of schools (Raudenbush & Willms, 1995). This is another type of "selection effect" in that the practices used in a school are likely to be influenced by the larger context in which the school operates (an example of multilevel, interrelated contextual influences), making a causal inference about the unique effects of school practices difficult.

One conclusion to be drawn from these formidable issues in conceptualizing context effects and implementing particular research designs to investigate them is that, given our current understanding of contextual influences and the methodological tools available, no single type of study is adequate or even preferable for understanding the effects of school or other contexts on development. Rather, what is required is a systematic program of research utilizing a variety of methodological approaches, each of which will have some serious flaws but, collectively, can provide a body of complementary findings sufficient to improve our understanding of contextual influences (Raudenbush & Willms, 1995).

*Measurement Issues* Understanding of contextual influences also has been hampered by problems in adequately measuring contextual characteristics. Consistent with the historical emphasis on studying attributes of individuals rather than environments, there is a scarcity of theoretically relevant, psychometrically sound measures of characteristics of social contexts (Shinn & Toohey, 2003; William T. Grant Foundation, 2006). Consequently, much of the research on contextual effects has relied upon compositional indices of demographic characteristics or other setting variables that are readily available (or computable) from existing data sources, such as the census, school records, or large-scale surveys conducted for other purposes. As a result, the contextual variables examined in research are often more determined by what measures are available than their theoretical significance and, even if theoretically derived, are often poorly operationalized. When using census data, for example, variables often are combined into compositional indices that have little relation to theory, and are combined in different ways across studies, making integration of findings quite difficult (Leventhal & Brooks-Gunn, 2000; Shinn & Toohey, 2003).

In addition to constructing indicators from sociodemographic measures available in public records and other existing data sources, researchers have used a variety of approaches to measuring contextual characteristics directly (Linney, 2000). The most common is to utilize aggregate indices based on individual perceptions of the social qualities of environments. For example, Moos (2002) has done extensive research on the social climate of settings, including schools. His measures (Moos, 1994) are representative of those used in this area and characterize settings in terms of relationships (e.g., amount and quality of interpersonal interaction, social cohesion, supportiveness), opportunities for personal growth (e.g., support for autonomy, skill development, participation), and "system maintenance and change" (e.g., social structure, organization, norms). Studies of school climate are by far the most prevalent type of research on school contexts, and have consistently found significant associations between the perceived dimensions of the social environment of schools and a wide variety of individual outcome variables (e.g., Griffith, 1999; Loukas & Robinson, 2004; McEvoy & Welker, 2000).

Although a convenient and widely used methodology, questions remain about whether perceptions of environments reflect perceiver characteristics, setting characteristics, or both (Shinn & Toohey, 2003). To argue that these measures reflect contextual characteristics, it must be shown that: (a) individuals within the settings generally agree with one another about these attributes; (b) contexts differ reliably from one another when measured along these dimensions; and (c) the aggregate contextual-level measures demonstrate theoretically meaningful relationships with other variables (with individual-level scores controlled). Even where such conditions have been demonstrated in studies (e.g., Battistich & Hom, 1997; Battistich, Solomon, Kim, Watson, & Schaps, 1995), there remain issues with using participant reports about setting qualities when these same participants provide data about other predictor or outcome variables. When the setting-level measure is simply an aggregation of individual-level reports of an outcome variable, the "reflection problem" described above is of concern. Even when the measured contextual and individual outcome variables are conceptually distinct, however, errors of measurement will be correlated to some degree for measures collected from the same group of informants. It also is plausible in many circumstances that individuals' perceptions of contextual characteristics hypothesized to influence outcome variables will be influenced by their own outcomes in those settings (Duncan & Raudenbush, 1999). For these reasons, it is preferable to utilize different samples of informants for assessing contextual and outcome variables (see Sampson, Morenoff, & Gannon-Rowley, 2002).

As with conceptualization and design, there clearly are important measurement issues to be addressed in conducting research on context effects. The prominence of theoretical and empirical work on contextual influences, especially with respect to the impacts of neighborhoods on the developmental outcomes of youth (e.g., Jencks & Mayer, 1990; Leventhal & Brooks-Gunn, 2000; Sampson et al., 1997; Wandersman & Nation, 1998), is bringing much-needed attention toward the resolution of these challenges. Indeed, at least one major foundation has recently made improving understanding of contextual influences, including work toward conceptualizing contexts, measuring characteristics of settings, and improving the design of studies of contexts and setting-level interventions, among its top research priorities (William T. Grant Foundation, 2006).

## The Need for Theory

The apparent complexity of contextual influences and the substantial issues and problems in investigating them are a prime example of the wisdom of Kurt Lewin's famous statement that there is nothing so practical as a good theory. Although there is ample empirical evidence to suggest that school environments have widespread effects on the developmental outcomes of students (e.g., Everson & Millsap, 2004; Gottfredson, Gottfredson, Payne, & Gottfredson, 2005; Haynes, Emmons, & Ben-Avie, 1997; Loukas & Robinson, 2004; McEvoy & Welker, 2000; Rutter, Maughan, Mortimore, & Ouston, 1979), the causal mechanisms that produce these contextual effects are as yet poorly understood. Adequate specification of a context effect requires identification of both the sources of between-context variation and the processes within contexts that produce (mediate) the context-level effect (Alwin, 1976; Alwin & Otto, 1977); in short, the theoretical nature of the processes that underlie observed context effects must be specified.

One reason that there has been more recent progress in understanding the effects of neighborhood than school contexts is that neighborhood research has drawn on the extensive body of theoretical arguments in sociology in general, and the study of criminology and deviant behavior in particular, about how group processes and environmental conditions affect individual behavior. For example, from a social disorganization perspective (Shaw & McKay, 1969), structural factors such as poverty and residential instability reduce the social factors in neighborhoods that regulate crime, such as the strength of social networks, attachments to neighbors, and shared norms, resulting in between-neighborhood differences in the prevalence of criminal behaviors. This perspective has been elaborated in recent research on neighborhoods, drawing particularly upon Coleman's concept of social capital (Coleman, 1990) and collective efficacy theory (e.g., Sampson et al., 1997). This contemporary research (e.g., Buka, Stichick, Birdthistle, & Earls, 2001; Leventhal & Brooks-Gunn, 2003; Wandersman & Nation, 1998) has found significant relationships between characteristics of the social organization of neighborhoods (e.g., the extent of informal social control) and not only rates of criminal and delinquent behaviors, but also the physical and mental health, cognitive abilities, and academic achievement of youth.

In contrast to the variety of theoretical models and mechanisms that have been proposed to explain the effects of neighborhood contexts on development (Jencks & Mayer, 1990), there are few models of the effects of school contexts. Undoubtedly, some of what has been learned about neighborhood contexts will have applicability to schools (Duncan & Raudenbush, 1999). Like neighborhoods, schools are social networks that can be characterized in terms of their norms, cohesion, and social organization. But schools are not neighborhoods. Schools are formal institutions with distinct social purposes and functions that differ substantially from those of informal collectivities such as neighborhoods. Schools as contexts must be understood in terms of their unique characteristics, and if we are to understand the types of school contexts that positively influence students' development, it is necessary to have a theory of how a school's practices and processes impact students (cf. Raudenbush & Willms, 1995).

One good place to start developing such a theory is to consider the explicit purposes and formal goals of schooling, and how the organization, practices, and social regularities of schools facilitate (or impede) attainment of these goals. Examination of the social organization of schools, in turn, should help reveal the tacit, perhaps even unintended influences of school environments on the people who inhabit them.

***Goals and Effects of Schooling***   Although with the publicity following reports like A Nation at Risk (National Commission on Excellence in Education, 1983) and resultant more recent legislation like the No Child Left Behind Act (2002) it might easily seem otherwise, education has always been about more than simply the development of students' basic academic knowledge and skills. From its beginning, formal education has been fundamentally a means of socialization of youth (Nash, 1968). Schools serve as a necessary bridge between the small, intimate world of family and friends and the broader, impersonal world of society. That is, one very important function of schooling is to effectively communicate to each generation the fundamental principles and values upon which the society is based, and the laws, norms, and conventions that regulate social behavior to assure the common good.

Even were we to wish to restrict formal education to teaching children the "three Rs" we could not do so. For most children, entry into school marks the initial encounter with large and complex social organizations, with their attendant rules, norms, and procedures; where most people are strangers (at least initially); and where relationships are based largely on social roles and pursuit of common goals rather than affective bonds. These circumstances pose some formidable developmental tasks (e.g., making new friends, understanding formal social relationships and authority structures), and it is inevitable that children will learn much about the nature of social living and their

place in the larger society, however much of this knowledge is or is not included in academic subject matter. Indeed, much of what children will learn about social living is not covered in the formal curriculum, but in the "hidden curriculum"—the tacit knowledge that is embodied in the normative structures, organizational processes, and nature of interpersonal relationships that characterize the school as a social organization (Hansen, 1993; Jackson, Boostom, & Hansen, 1993). The question then is not whether such lessons will be "taught" to students, but how they will be conveyed. Concentrating narrowly on the academic goals of schooling relegates influences of the school on students' social, emotional, and moral development to the unexamined realm of the hidden curriculum and risks either failing to teach students important principles of social living, or "teaching" them the "wrong" lessons. Fortunately, the formal, explicit goals of schooling do include the social and moral development of students, even if these nonacademic goals have not received nearly as much attention recently as the goal of promoting students' academic achievement.

In the United States, the idea that an essential goal of schooling is to develop in students the traits of character necessary for citizenship in a democracy goes back to the founding of the country (McClellan, 1999). Thomas Jefferson argued strongly that schools must foster democratic values and skills if the fledging democracy was to survive (Gilreath, 1999; Tozer, Violas, & Senese, 1995), and because public education was a common experience, the framers of the U.S. Constitution saw it as a primary vehicle for supporting a democratic society. This view of education was widespread in early America, and became solidified by Horace Mann and the institution of the public school in the 1830s. A central goal of mass education was the development of a "properly trained" and socialized citizenry. Therefore, all children should receive sufficient education to enable them to participate fully as citizens and workers in adulthood (Dornbusch, Glasgow, & I-Chun, 1996). Even with the current emphasis on academic achievement, it is still widely recognized among educators that schools can and should play a critical role developing in students the knowledge, skills, motives, and values necessary for them to be active and effective citizens (Becker & Couto, 1996; Cohen, 2006; Giroux, 1989), and the last two U.S. administrations have explicitly made "character education" a national educational priority. Equally important, this sentiment is widely shared among the general public: since its inception over 30 years ago, the annual Phi Delta Kappa/Gallup poll has consistently found that Americans regard preparing students to be responsible citizens as the most important purpose of public education (Rose & Gallup, 2000).

The view of schools as institutions whose principal purpose is to prepare students for democratic life was most clearly and strongly articulated by John Dewey (1899, 1900). In distinct contrast to the current emphasis in educational policy and practice on academics, Dewey's approach gave primacy to the social goals of education (Shutz,

2001). He argued that schools needed to be microcosms of the democratic society they are intended to promote, and therefore emphasized joint planning, inquiry, and problem solving as mechanisms for students to develop their individual capabilities through group efforts. However, Dewey's approach to education was not entirely pragmatic. He saw the function of schooling as not merely preparing students for the workforce and participation in a democratic form of government, but as helping them to understand the purposes of what they are asked to do in school. Dewey believed that real learning only results from purposeful activity; that unless students understand the purpose of what they are asked to do in school, they will lack motivation to engage in activity and their schoolwork will simply be mechanical routine (Dewey, 1916). It was therefore essential to Dewey to promote connections between the world of the school and the world of society. Schools, he argued, must help students develop their capacity to respond to the world, to control their own lives, and to contribute to society.

Dewey (1916) insisted that democratic ideals and competencies can only be attained through democratic means: "Democracy is more than a form of government; it is primarily a mode of associated living, of conjoint communicated experience" (p. 87). He therefore argued that schools should be democratic communities, which he defined as including three essential characteristics: (a) association and social interaction; (b) collaborative action (i.e., action directed toward shared goals); and (c) common values (Campbell, 1995; Shutz, 2001). Dewey's vision was thus of schools as microcosms of the larger society, both because such an environment would optimally promote development of the personal and interpersonal attitudes, skills, and values necessary for full participation in the larger society, and because students would more readily apprehend the purposes of their learning activities (i.e., how these activities were instrumental to accomplishing common goals and preparing oneself for adulthood) in such an environment. This model of the school as a democratic community provides a theoretical perspective on the type of school context that is likely to promote the positive development of students as defined here—to promote not only their intellectual development and academic achievement, but also the development of their interpersonal competencies, positive social attitudes, prosocial behavior, and moral values.

***Schools as Communities*** Despite Dewey's widespread influence on educational theory and practice[1] with the exception of the period from 1896 to 1904 when he created and directed the Laboratory School at the University of Chicago, attempts at democratic schooling in the United States have been limited and not notably successful (Apple & Benne, 1995). The progressive education movement, which was derived from Dewey's work (although Dewey himself felt that progressive educators had misunderstood critical elements of his view of democratic education; see Campbell, 1995; Shutz, 2001), was considered largely defunct by the 1950s (Cremin, 1961) and most reviewers have

concluded that progressive schools were not more effective than traditional schools (e.g., Horwitz, 1979; Minuchin, Biber, Shapiro, & Zimiles, 1969). This conclusion, however, was based primarily upon consideration of the academic achievement of students. Comparisons of progressive and traditional schools generally found that progressive schools had a more positive impact on students' social attitudes, interpersonal skills, and moral reasoning and values (Solomon & Kendall, 1976; Solomon et al., 2001). Thus, it appears that progressive schools were about as effective as traditional schools at promoting students' academic achievement, but at the same time were more effective at promoting their social and moral development.

Although not often linked directly to Dewey, there has recently been a renewed interest in schools as communities. Part of the impetus for recent empirical work in this area was Coleman's influential study of secondary schools (Coleman & Hoffer, 1987), in which it was argued that the greater success of Catholic and private schools than public schools, particularly with respect to educating disadvantaged students, was due to their being functional communities. Subsequent research that directly measured the contextual characteristics of high schools relevant to community (e.g., collegial relationships, shared decision making, and common values among faculty) and examined relationships between a communal school organization and student outcomes, particularly academic achievement, provided evidence consistent with Coleman's hypothesis (e.g., Bryk & Driscoll, 1988; Bryk, Lee, & Holland, 1993). Since the 1990s, the importance of schools as communities for improving academic achievement has received increasing attention in education, particularly with respect to the education of economically disadvantaged and academically underperforming students (e.g., Shouse, 1996; Wehlage, Rutter, Smith, Lesko, & Fernandez, 1989).

A second source of current interest in schools as communities comes from research on the prevention of drug abuse and other problem behaviors among youth (e.g., Battistich & Hom, 1997; Battistich, Schaps, Watson, Solomon, & Lewis, 2000; Gottfredson et al., 2005). Students' perceptions of their school as a community have been found to be strongly associated with their affective bonding to the school (e.g., Battistich et al., 1995; Payne et al., 2003; Solomon, Battistich, Watson, Schaps, & Lewis, 2000), and bonding to school has repeatedly been shown to be related to reduced risk of drug use and delinquent behavior among youth (e.g., Hawkins, Catalano, Kosterman, Abbott, & Hill, 1999; Hawkins, Lishner, Catalano, & Howard, 1986). In particular, a recent series of influential articles describing findings from the National Longitudinal Study of Adolescent Health have focused considerable attention on students' attachment or "connectedness" to school as a key factor in preventing a wide range of adverse health and academic outcomes in youth (McNeely, Nonnemaker, & Blum, 2002; Resnick, Ireland, & Borowsky, 2004).

Finally, the importance of communal characteristics of school contexts for promoting the positive development of youth has been supported by work in the area of character education during the last two decades. Indeed, there is now widespread agreement in this field that creating schools that are "caring communities" is an essential element of effective character education programs (Berkowitz, 2002; Berkowitz & Bier, 2005a, 2005b; Lapsley & Narvaez, 2006; Schaps, Battistich, & Solomon, 1997).

This diverse body of research has provided considerable evidence consistent with the general hypothesis that a communal school context has positive effects on students. However, in addition to suffering from various methodological weaknesses described above, these studies have largely focused on the effects of emotional connections and sense of belonging or membership in a school community. Other key elements of community, such as shared values, member influence, and collaborative work toward common goals (Battistich, Solomon, Watson, & Schaps, 1997; Bryk & Driscoll, 1988; Dewey, 1916; Strike, 2000), typically have not been examined in the same studies. In addition, few of these studies have adequately distinguished between community as a school-level characteristic and its individual-level psychological counterpart, students' sense of the school as a community (cf. Payne et al., 2003; Shinn & Toohey, 2003). This research, then, provides mostly partial and indirect support for the hypothesized effects of democratic school communities on students' development.

Although quite limited, some research has provided more direct evidence of the positive effects of a democratic school environment on students' social and moral development, as well as on academic outcomes. The most extensive evidence comes from research on two intervention programs, one for elementary schools (the Child Development Project) and one for secondary schools (the Just Community), both of which involve restructuring the school to become a more participatory and democratic community. The programs and research findings for these two interventions will be described next, followed by a summary of related research on school communities.

*The Child Development Project*   The Child Development Project (CDP) was a comprehensive, whole school reform effort for elementary schools that focused on helping the school to become a "caring community of learners" (Battistich et al., 1997; Solomon, Watson, Battistich, Schaps, & Delucchi, 1992).[2] The program has been implemented in a large number of elementary schools across the United States and evaluated in two longitudinal quasi-experimental studies. The program and its effects have been extensively described elsewhere (Battistich, 2003; Battistich, Schaps, Watson, & Solomon, 1996; Battistich et al., 2000; Battistich, Schaps, & Wilson, 2004; Battistich, Solomon, Watson, Solomon, & Schaps, 1989; Solomon, Battistich, Kim, & Watson, 1997; Solomon, Battistich, Watson, et al., 2000; Solomon, Watson Battistich, et al., 1992; Solomon, Watson, Battistich, Schaps, et al., 1985; Solomon, Watson, Delucchi, Schaps, & Battistich, 1988; Watson, Battistich, & Solomon,

1997) and only the most relevant aspects of this work will be briefly reviewed here.

The CDP intervention program was initially developed to promote students' prosocial development (Solomon, Watson, Battistich, Schaps et al., 1985). Theoretically, the program combines Dewey's educational philosophy with attachment theory (Ainsworth, Blehar, Waters, & Wall, 1978; Bowlby, 1968), theory and research on motivation (Ames, 1992; deCharms, 1976; Deci & Ryan, 1985; Ryan & Deci, 2000), and constructivist developmental psychology (Watson & Ecken, 2003). The program's classroom and school-wide practices (e.g., collaborative learning, active involvement of students in norm-setting and decision-making through class meetings, discipline practices that focus on developing self-control and intrinsic motivation for prosocial behavior, moral discourse around values of fairness, concern for others, and social responsibility) are intended to produce a supportive and democratic elementary school environment. Membership in such a caring school community is hypothesized to satisfy students' fundamental psychological needs for belonging, autonomy, and competence (Connell & Wellborn, 1991; Deci & Ryan, 1985) which, in turn, is expected to promote their attachment to the school community and commitment to its norms and values (Strike, 2000; Watson & Battistich, 2006).

Comparative evaluations of CDP consistently found that the program had positive effects on students' academic, social, emotional, and ethical development, including: their attitudes toward school and teachers, learning motivation, academic achievement, interpersonal skills, concern for others, commitment to democratic values, and social behavior (increased prosocial behavior and decreased drug use and antisocial behavior) (for a summary of the findings from the most recent, large-scale evaluation of CDP, see Solomon et al., 2000). Moreover, these effects persisted at follow-up in middle school (Battistich et al., 2004), suggesting that caring and participatory elementary school environments may have lasting positive effects on students' development (also see Watson, 2006).

Perhaps of most importance here, the research on CDP utilized longitudinal, quasi-experimental designs that included comprehensive assessments of the environments at both program and comparison schools. These designs allowed for explicit testing of the underlying program theory and provided a basis for assessment of the causal influences of school environment on student development. This body of research showed that: (a) there were large differences between program and comparison schools in use of CDP program practices; that is, practices characteristic of a democratic, caring, and supportive school community (Solomon, Battistich, Watson, Schaps, et al., 2000; Solomon, Watson, Delucchi et al., 1988); (b) use of these practices by teachers was associated with an increased sense of community among students (Solomon, Battistich, Kim, et al., 1997); so that (c) students' sense of their school as a community (an environment characterized by caring and supportive interpersonal relationships, and student autonomy and influence) was consistently and significantly higher among program than comparison students (Battistich et al., 1997; Solomon, Battistich, Watson, Schaps, et al., 2000); (d) there are reliable differences between schools in sense of community and these school context differences are significantly related to differences in student outcomes, controlling for both student-level sense of community and outcome scores (Battistich & Hom, 1997; Battistich, Solomon, Kim et al., 1995); and (e) program effects on student outcome variables were mediated by effects on sense of school community (Battistich & Hong, 2002; Battistich, Solomon, Watson, & Schaps, 1997; Solomon, Battistich, Watson, Schaps, et al., 2000). Although clearly in need of replication and refinement by future research on school contexts, this work provides considerable empirical support for the hypothesized positive effects of a democratic and supportive school environment on the development of students.

*The Just Community*   Lawrence Kohlberg and his colleagues developed the Just Community intervention to promote high school students' moral development and commitment to a democratic society (Kohlberg, 1975, 1985; Power, 1988). Based on an integration of the perspectives of Piaget (1932/1965) and Durkheim (1925/1961) on moral development (Kohlberg & Higgins, 1987), the Just Community program utilizes moral discourse around salient community issues within the context of a participatory democracy to influence the collective norms and moral atmosphere of the school in order to promote students' moral reasoning and behavior. Like the Child Development Project, the Just Community has been extensively described elsewhere (Kohlberg, 1985; Kohlberg & Higgins, 1987; Kohlberg, Lieberman, Powers, Higgins, & Codding, 1981; Lickona, 2001; Lind & Althof, 1992; McDonough, 2005; Power, Higgins, & Kohlberg, 1989; Wasserman & Garrod, 1983) and its program and outcomes will only be briefly summarized here.

In a Just Community school, all community members (both faculty and students) are involved in establishing and maintaining community norms. The primary mechanisms of the Just Community are regular meetings of both small advisory groups (one teacher and 10–15 students) and the entire school community where problems, issues, and policies are discussed and decisions are made. To promote active participation by all, it is desirable that the community be relatively small. In large schools this is accomplished by creating "schools within schools" or dividing the school into "clusters" of 60 to 100 students and four or five teachers. The advisory groups also serve to promote active participation by providing a smaller group setting for discussion, and help to prepare members and provide structure for the meetings of the whole school community. The program also includes a student-run disciplinary committee that determines fair punishments for students who have violated community rules, mediates disputes, and counsels students with disciplinary problems.

Although faculty make decisions regarding curriculum in Just Community schools, and the school obviously must follow applicable regulations, law, and mandated educational policies, all other aspects of school life are decided by the community as a participatory democracy—on a one-person, one-vote basis, whether faculty or student. Although teachers and administrators clearly have some special authority because of their formal roles, they act as equal members of the community and exercise authority on the basis of knowledge, experience, and expertise rather than their position in the school. Adult members of the community act as facilitators of democratic processes by encouraging perspective-taking, raising issues of fairness and morality, articulating "higher-stage" reasoning, helping to ensure full participation, and advocating positions that help develop group expectations of and commitment to justice and community. In effect, the Just Community approach relies on the teacher to aid in establishing in the community an atmosphere of mutual respect, democratic processes, and "the constitutive rules of a fair morality" (Kohlberg & Higgins, 1987, p.121).

Evaluations of the Just Community high school interventions have not assessed the broad range of outcomes examined in CDP research, but have focused on the development of school norms and moral atmosphere, and on students' moral reasoning. The findings have consistently indicated positive effects in these areas (Higgins, 1991, 1995; Kohlberg et al., 1981): students in Just Community schools report greater commitment to values of democracy, fairness, and community than students at comparison schools, are more likely to see norms and values as collectively shared, and score higher on measures of moral reasoning than comparison students.

A version of the Just Community approach modified for elementary schools and students (Althof, 2003) has been implemented and evaluated in Germany. Findings from this project (Lind & Althof, 1992; Oser, 1992a, 1992b) indicated that, like the high school interventions, the program increased students' perception of the school as a community and their moral reasoning. There is limited but consistent evidence, then, that the Just Community is effective at creating a democratic community context in K-12 schools, and that this type of school environment positively influences students' moral development. As with CDP, these findings are in need of replication. Future research on the Just Community also would benefit greatly from stronger research designs and assessment of a broader range of outcome variables, including students' academic performance.

***Related Research on School Communities***   The evaluations of the Child Development Project and Just Community schools appear to be the principal comparative intervention research on school communities generally or democratic school communities in particular. There also are a few cross-sectional studies that have examined relationships between characteristics of a communal school context and student outcomes. For example, Bryk and Driscoll (1988) found positive relationships between the communal characteristics of high schools and students' academic achievement in a large study utilizing measures available in the High School and Beyond data. However, because this investigation relied on measures from an existing data set, it was not possible to include measures of all elements of school community. Moreover, the measures utilized were based almost exclusively on structural characteristics (e.g., school size) and teacher or administrator reports of school context, with very little information provided by students. Most other research on democratic schools has been descriptive. For example, Print, Ørnstrøm, and Neilson (2002) describe a wide range of positive differences in social and civic attitudes between students in democratic schools in Europe compared to those in traditional (i.e., nondemocratic) schools in the United States, and there have been a number of case studies of democratic schools that suggest positive effects on students (Beatty, 2004; Lewis, 1999; Wallin, 2003).

As indicated above, most other research on schools as communities has focused on only one element of a community, the sense of belonging or membership in the community, and has examined this characteristic almost exclusively as a characteristic of individual students, rather than as a contextual variable. Although these studies have reported widespread positive relationships between belonging or "connectedness" to school and the academic, social, and moral characteristics of students, they do not address the fundamental question of whether the psychological sense of community reflects a school contextual characteristic or merely a characteristic of individual students (Shinn & Toohey, 2003). As Payne et al. (2003) have correctly pointed out, a communal school context refers to social organizational characteristics (e.g., social support, collaboration, decision-making processes, common values), whereas the sense of belonging refers to an individual psychological characteristic (i.e., affective attachment to the school).

Two recent studies have directly measured school contextual characteristics and examined relationships between a communal school organization and student bonding or sense of community. In a study of a large, nationally representative sample of public high schools, Payne et al. (2003) found that a communal school organization (measured as collaborative and supportive relations among school staff and common school goals and norms) was strongly associated with higher student bonding to school (measured as attachment, belief in the legitimacy of school norms, and commitment to schoolwork). Moreover, similar to the findings from research on CDP, this study found that relationships between school organization and student delinquent behavior were mediated by effects on student bonding. Similarly, a study conducted with a large sample of schools in Italy provides evidence of the relationship between a democratic school climate and students' sense of community. Vieno, Perkins, Smith, and Santinello (2005) assessed student perceptions of democratic school practices (e.g., participation in making rules and organizing events, freedom of expression)

and their sense of community (defined as membership and emotional connection) among 6th, 8th, and 10th grade students from 134 schools. Using hierarchical regression, they demonstrated that measures of both democratic climate and sense of community (controlling for individual-level perceptions) varied significantly between classrooms and schools (and thus could be considered contextual characteristics), and that democratic climate at the classroom and school levels was strongly predictive of school sense of community, controlling for individual (e.g., gender, socioeconomic status, parenting practices), classroom (e.g., grade level), and school characteristics (e.g., size, public vs. private).

*Summary* Overall, there is moderately strong evidence to support the general hypothesis that schools that can be characterized as communities are contexts that effectively promote the positive development of students. Using a variety of designs and methodologies, studies have consistently found that schools that are experienced as caring and supportive environments in which students are actively involved are associated with positive effects on students' general psychological, social, and moral development, as well as on their attitudes toward school and education, learning motivation, and academic achievement. Less often examined than interpersonal support, engagement, and sense of belonging, but showing similarly positive effects, are studies of explicitly democratic practices and school organization, and those demonstrating significant relationships between a democratic school environment and sense of school community. Least often conducted but most persuasive are comparative intervention studies showing that changes in school environments that make them more communal and democratic result in the kinds of positive effects on students consistently found in correlational research on school environments.

## Problems, Issues, and Prospects for Research on Democratic School Communities

Although the research findings to date appear very promising, there are a number of important issues related to conceptualizing schools as communities in general, and democratic communities in particular, that need to be addressed to improve understanding of how such school contexts influence the development of youth. One set of issues involves the basic definition of a school community, including the nature and locus of community values, and the importance of student autonomy, participation, and influence. These issues are related to concerns about the proper role of public education in a democratic and pluralistic society, and whether it is desirable (or even possible) for schools to be organized and operated as the kind of participatory democracy that Dewey envisioned. Another issue concerns the mechanisms through which communities influence their members: that is, what are the social and psychological processes linking the contextual characteristics of school communities and the developmental outcomes of individual students? A final, broader set of issues concerns how to best conceptualize schools as developmental contexts, and the implications of this contextual perspective for research on the effects of schooling.

***The Constituents of School Community***  The term community has been variously used to refer to primary interpersonal groups (e.g., families, neighbors), groups or organizations with common interests and activities, and geographical and political units (e.g., McLeroy, Bibeau, Steckler, & Glanz, 1988). The most important distinctions between types of communities in terms of how they influence their members are those related to the quality of interpersonal relationships (O'Donnell, Tharp, & Wilson, 1993; Pedersen et al., 2005). This is clearly represented in Tönnies' (1887/1988) classic description of two types of community: Gemeinshaft, or the community of family, neighborhood, and intimate relationships, and Gessellschaft or society, the community of strangers, the public life, and instrumental relationships. Although schools (particularly secondary schools) have been described as bureaucratic environments where interpersonal relationships are formal and impersonal (e.g., Powell, Farrar, & Cohen, 1985; Wise, 1979), this depiction is generally used as a contrast to schools that are organized as communities.

In actuality, as Bryk and Driscoll (1988) point out, a school community involves characteristics of both Gemeinshaft and Gessellschaft. That is, schools are places where people associate and work together to achieve common goals, and where they are emotionally connected to one another by personal relationships, common traditions, and shared values. In addition to the characteristics of association, collaboration, and common values identified by Dewey (1916), Bryk and Driscoll include an "ethic of caring" (Noddings, 1988, 1992), a pattern of warm and supportive interpersonal relationships, as a defining element of a school community. Psychologically, participating in a school community should result in students experiencing a sense of membership or belonging, of participation and influence, and of common purpose and shared values (cf. McMillan & Chavis, 1986).

*Membership*  One essential characteristic of a school community is that students feel that they are members of the group. As discussed above, much of the research on schools as communities has focused on this quality of belonging. Although variously described as attachment, belonging, bonding, or connectedness to the school, and assessed using a variety of different measures (Libbey, 2004), the basic element is an emotional connection to the group. Students in a school community feel accepted and valued by other community members (e.g., teachers and fellow students), which should satisfy their basic need to belong (Baumeister & Leary, 1995). Satisfaction of the need to belong, in turn, results in attachment or bonding to the group (Battistich et al., 1997).

The sense of belonging to the school community is important because it is considered essential to norm acquisition. Acceptance of community norms is a requirement for membership in the group, and members experience negative affective consequences (and, perhaps, physical or material consequences as well) as a result of normative violations, either on the part of themselves or other community members (Strike, 2000). It is presumably this acceptance of the school's prosocial norms that accounts for the associations between bonding or connectedness to school and the positive student academic, social, and moral outcomes described above. Conversely, alienation and disengagement from traditional social institutions like the school is commonly invoked to explain adolescents' involvement in antisocial behaviors (Hawkins & Weis, 1985; Jenkins, 1997; Liska & Reed, 1985).

*Influence*  In contrast to belonging, student influence has received much less attention in research on school community. Part of this relative neglect stems from concerns about whether member influence is a necessary characteristic of the experience of community, particularly when considering youth and schools as communities (Chipuer & Pretty, 1999; Fisher & Sonn, 2002; Vieno et al., 2005). Member influence is, of course, a necessary component of a democratic school community. However, even when explicitly democratic decision-making processes are not characteristic of a school, there is evidence to suggest that opportunities for student influence in school are strongly related to their attachment and sense of school community (Battistich et al., 1997; Whitlock, 2006). Student influence therefore does seem to be an important characteristic of any school community. The issue, then, is not so much whether students in a school community should have opportunities for influence, but rather the nature of these activities.

Certainly there are legitimate differences in authority between students and teachers, and hence in their relative influence in schools. Even in Just Community schools, where students and teachers have equal influence in making decisions about community issues, decisions about curriculum and related academic issues are reserved for teachers and administrators. Moreover, student influence does not require that decisions be made through formal democratic processes. Rather, what seems most important is that students have opportunities in school to express their opinions about community life, actively participate in shared activities, and experience a sense of self-determination (Prilleltensky, Nelson, & Peirson, 2001). Like belonging, people appear to have basic psychological needs to experience themselves as autonomous and competent (Connell & Wellborn, 1991; Deci & Ryan, 1985; Ryan & Deci, 2000). Opportunities for influence in school should contribute to students' sense of membership or belonging, and hence to their acquisition of school norms. In addition to fostering attachment to school, active participation in developing the norms of the community and discussing why these norms are desirable or necessary should itself contribute to students' personal commitment to them (Maccoby & Martin, 1983; Oser, 1986).

The nature and extent of student influence in the school community may be particularly important for moral development. In most schools, virtually all authority and decision-making power is vested in the teacher (Goodlad, 1984), and students have no influence over either the nature of school rules and norms or their enforcement. Such circumstances represent a heteronomous moral system in which acceptable conduct in the school community is defined by those in authority and enforced through extrinsic controls. In contrast, in a school community where students actively participate in the development of norms, acceptable conduct is consensually defined on the basis of moral discourse and justified by intrinsic moral values rather than external authority. If attachment to the community promotes acquisition of community norms and values, such differences in community context should result in different ways of reasoning about why one should avoid violating community norms.

Although only rarely examined in research to date, there is some evidence to suggest that differences between schools in authority structures and, specifically, student autonomy and influence, affect students' moral reasoning. For example, the Child Development Project research found that students' belonging or attachment to school had differential effects on moral reasoning in program than comparison schools. Increased belonging was associated with moral justifications based on reference to values and concerns for the rights and needs of others among program students, but with justifications based on social disapproval or punishment among comparison students (Battistich et al., 1997). Similarly, Weinstock, Broida, and Assor (2006) found that students at democratic schools in Israel (similar to Just Community schools) gave more principled reasons for behavior than students at traditional schools on a test of moral judgment.

The more general point is that if attachment to a school community promotes acceptance of community norms, then the nature of these norms (and their underlying values) is of critical importance. Conceptions of community that focus on its affective components (e.g., Noddings, 1988, 1992) without giving adequate consideration to the common aims and values of the community run the risk of promoting antisocial rather than prosocial attitudes and behaviors (cf. McMillan & Chavis, 1986; Strike, 1999).

*Common Values*    The question of "which values" should be instilled by schools has long been a contentious one. Prior to the establishment of universal compulsory education in the United States in the mid-19th century, schools were closely tied to their local communities and teachers shared responsibility with the family and church for socializing children in the norms and values of the community (Mead, 1951). With the increased urbanization and immigration brought about by the industrial revolution came increased ethnic, cultural, and religious diversity, and ac-

commodating this pluralism required public schools to shift from emphasizing the sectarian values of specific communities to more secular values (Johnson, 1987). In particular, concerns about increasing social diversity contributed to public schools becoming deliberate instruments of social policy, with the explicit goal of instilling in all students the fundamental values necessary to a democratic society: justice, equality, tolerance, respect for individual rights, and social responsibility (Ryan & Lickona, 1987).

Through the mid-20th century, social consensus for moral or values education in the United States declined as the increasing emphasis on individual rights supported the view that values were matters of personal preference and not the legitimate concern of schools. Various ethnic and religious groups rejected secular values and asserted their rights to raise their children within their own sectarian value systems (Prakash, 1987), and public schools increasingly withdrew from the explicit teaching of values, whether democratic or otherwise. However, beginning in the mid-1950s and continuing through the present day, concerns over declining academic achievement and increasing discipline problems in schools, as well as evidence of general declines in social responsibility and increases in a variety of problematic behaviors among youth (e.g., drug use, violence, delinquency) led to increasing calls for public schools to once again take responsibility for instilling fundamental social and moral values in students (Damon, 2002; Grant, 1989; Lapsley & Narvaez, 2006).

Public schools are thus once again called upon to actively socialize all students in the fundamental values of a democratic society. At the same time, however, concerns about schools respecting cultural diversity continue to raise the question of "which values," and pose a challenge for the model of schools as communities.

***Schools as Democratic Communities***    A fundamental problem facing schools that seek to be communities is one of inclusion (Strike, 1999). This stems from the fact that attachments among community members are based on the shared practices and common values that define membership in the community, and thus are, to some extent, exclusionary.

This is not problematic for private schools because membership is selective and based on free-association. Public schools, on the other hand, are obligated to educate students from all of the diverse groups represented in the society and cannot exclude students simply because their personal beliefs and values differ from those of the majority.

One possible approach to making schools inclusive is to essentially reject the idea that they should be communities and argue that education should be neutral with respect to questions of personal values. This is generally the approach that has been taken with respect to public education in recent decades. In this "liberal instrumentalist" conception (Strike, 2000), the role of the school is to provide students with the knowledge and skills that are instrumental to achieving their personal goals and aspirations. Education in this conception is seen as a means to economic ends (i.e., jobs and income), and knowledge as a commodity that teachers provide and students consume. Although such a view of schools is arguably value neutral, it has some negative implications. Schools under this conception will tend to be bureaucratic and hierarchically organized, and teachers and students will be motivated by extrinsic incentives (e.g., test scores, income). Because learning is valued for its instrumental purposes, it is it likely to be seen as a scarce commodity that is normatively evaluated (i.e., each student's success is judged relative to the attainment of other students). The resulting competition among students (and between teachers and schools, as well) undermines concern for others and any sense of common purpose, and inherently creates winners and losers in the educational "marketplace." In addition, concerns about justice and equality in such schools tend to be reduced to matters of fair competition, and democracy and democratic citizenship are likely to be addressed only in the "thinnest" sense: as political structures and procedures that regulate competing interests in a fair manner (e.g., voting).

The alternative approach is Dewey's view of the school as a democratic community. Schools that function as participatory democracies can be broadly inclusive because attachments among members are based upon their active participation and influence in the consensual pursuits of the group, and community is created through shared participation in democratic practices (Strike, 2000). Although democratic values form the basis of the community, and thus their acceptance is a condition of membership, these values are inherently inclusive, and other goals and commitments of the school are established through democratic processes, as in the Just Community schools. Rather than being bureaucratic and having a hierarchical authority structure, democratic schools emphasize active involvement among all community members, deliberation among alternative viewpoints, and decision making by consensus. Influence is not based on social position per se (e.g., whether one is a teacher or a student), but rather on differences in relevant knowledge, competencies, and responsibilities. Because members have shared goals and are concerned for one another's welfare, learning is a collaborative rather than an individual matter, and success is defined (at least to a significant degree) in terms of the aggregate performance of the group rather than the relative performance of individuals. Rather than extrinsic incentives, teachers and students in a democratic school community are motivated by the intrinsic value of participation in a joint enterprise, successful attainment of common goals, and the caring and supportive relationships among community members.

It is important to emphasize that the inclusiveness of democratic school communities rests on their commitment to being participatory rather than simply representative, and on the substantive rather than the procedural elements of democratic life (Dewey, 1916; Shutz, 2001; Strike, 2000). Dewey rejected both the "melting pot" metaphor of social integration and the self-isolation of groups from "mainstream" society. Rather, he believed in promoting cultural diversity through the democratic process, by coordinating the differences between social groups and promoting the development of a sense of self that integrates the diverse roles people play in the different social groups they are involved in. He therefore saw diversity as serving an important function in society as long as individuals and groups were responsive to the larger whole (Dewey, 1916).

Dewey's model of schools as democratic communities thus appears to be sufficiently inclusive to be consistent with the view of schools as socializing institutions whose primary goal is to that prepare students from diverse backgrounds for full and active participation in a democratic society. In support of this perspective, the research reviewed in this chapter suggests that the characteristics of a democratic school context are associated with widespread positive effects on students' social, ethical, and academic development. However, while Dewey's model of schooling identifies the organizational characteristics and value commitments of schools as democratic communities, and embodies a set of pedagogical practices, it does not specify the psychological mechanisms through which schools influence the development of students.

***Schools as Democratic Communities and Positive Youth Development: Person–Environment Fit*** Why should a school that functions as a democratic community be particularly effective at promoting the positive development of youth? The general answer suggested here is fundamentally a motivational one: that a democratic school community is a context that meets students' psychological needs for belonging, autonomy, and competence (Connell & Wellborn, 1991). All human beings appear to have basic needs for caring and supportive relationships with others (Baumeister & Leary, 1995; Bowlby, 1968), and to experience themselves as self-directing and in control of their own lives (deCharms, 1968; R. M. Ryan & Deci, 2000), and as competent or effective (Connell, 1990). Correspondingly, environments differ in the extent to which they provide opportunities for satisfaction of these needs, and people's patterns of engagement or disengagement with particular settings will be determined in large part by the degree to which the setting fulfills their needs (Connell, 1990; Deci & Ryan, 1985). By providing students with opportunities to actively and effectively participate in a cohesive and caring group to accomplish shared goals, a school community fulfills students' basic needs, which enhances their motivation to remain in the community, adopt its norms and values, and acquire the knowledge and skills that are valued by the community (Battistich et al., 1997). When the school community functions democratically, the attitudes, values, knowledge and skills necessary for full participation in the school community include not only those incorporated in academic subject matter, but also those necessary for democratic citizenship.

The hypothesis of a "mismatch" between the developmental needs of students and the environmental affordances provided by typical middle schools has been invoked to explain the increase in the number youth who experience declining grades and academic motivation and increased psychological and behavioral problems during early adolescence (Eccles & Midgley, 1989; Eccles et al., 1993). More specifically, building upon the theoretical model proposed by Connell and Wellborn (1991), Roeser, Eccles, and Sameroff (2000) have conceptualized this issue of person–environment fit specifically in terms of student needs for autonomy, competence, and belonging, and argued that viewing contexts according to the affordances they provide for fulfilling these needs provides a very useful framework that applies across both a variety of important social settings and developmental periods (also see Pianta, 2006).

## Implications for Research of Viewing Schools as Developmental Contexts

The research reviewed in this chapter clearly suggests that the social contexts of the schools that children and youth attend have important and widespread influences not only on their development of academic and intellectual knowledge and skills, but on their self-concepts, social attitudes, interpersonal competencies, and moral values as well. However, contextual influences and the possible mechanisms that underlie their observed effects have been only sparsely investigated to date. Improving our understanding of school and other contextual influences on development will require considerable additional conceptual and empirical work. In part, this will require improvements in the methodological tools necessary to investigate contextual influences, including the development of more comprehensive and psychometrically sound measures of contextual characteristics, as noted earlier. However, perhaps the most important and fundamental requirement is a conceptual one: that we begin to seriously consider contexts as units of causal influence and possible intervention, as dynamic systems that function and change over time, much as individuals develop and change (cf. William T. Grant Foundation, 2006).

The research on schools as communities illustrates the work needed in this area. It currently is quite common to describe a sense of community as a critical element of an effective school environment. However, while descriptions of school community share many elements (Watson & Battistich, 2006), there also are important differences between them in descriptions of the nature and role of community in schools (e.g., Battistich et al., 1997; DeVries & Zan, 1994; Freiberg, 1999; Kohlberg, 1985; Rogoff, 1994; Wolk, 1998). Virtually none of these differences in type of community have been examined in empirical research. Rather, as indicated in the review of research presented earlier in this chapter, a number of studies have examined particular elements of dimensions of community (e.g., sense of belonging, provision for student autonomy), but studies examining community as a context are rare. As a result, much of the evidence of the effects of school community on students' development is piecemeal and fragmented.

Extant research on school community also has been focused much more on classrooms than schools. With the exception of the Child Development Project and the Just Community, and some conceptually related work in preschools (DeVries & Zan, 1994), programs focused on building community in schools are almost exclusively classroom-focused interventions (Freiberg, 1999; Putnam, 1995; Rogoff, 1994; Wolk, 1998). Although, as noted earlier, classroom characteristics are more proximal influences on students than school-level characteristics, and thus arguably have larger immediate effects on students' development, they nevertheless are determined to some degree by the larger school context. Moreover, it is unlikely that experiencing an individual classroom or two that functions as a community among other decidedly noncommunal classrooms in the course of one's schooling will have the same positive effects on development as attending a school that is a community. Indeed, it is possible that such an incoherent school environment may have negative effects on students. For example, the numerous positive effects of the Child Development Project on students were only observed in elementary schools where program practices were widespread throughout the school. In schools where the program was only implemented by isolated teachers, no such widespread positive effects of the program were found, and there were some indications that students at these program schools had poorer outcomes in some areas of development than students at comparison schools (see Battistich et al., 2000; Solomon et al., 2000). Such findings underscore the point that if we are to improve our understanding of how school contexts influence students' development, we need to consider the school as a coherent environment, as the unit of investigation and change, rather than as an amalgam of individual classrooms.

## Summary, Conclusions, and Future Directions

This chapter has considered the school as a primary developmental context and reviewed theory and research on the types of school contexts that are likely to promote the positive development of children and youth. Although there are still substantial issues to be addressed in adequately conceptualizing and operationalizing schools and other developmental contexts and estimating their effects, it was argued that there is sufficient evidence to suggest that schools that can be characterized as communities, and particularly democratic communities, are contexts that should have widespread positive effects on students' academic social, emotional, and moral development. The extant research, however, has largely focused on examining the effects of individual aspects or elements of community in isolation, and very few studies have examined the effects of a communal school context. Thus, while promising, the available evidence is far from conclusive. Improving our understanding of the effects of a communal school context, and of school contexts more generally, on the development of students will require research that focuses on the school as the unit of investigation and intervention. Undertaking such research will necessarily involve addressing and improving the conceptual and methodological inadequacies that currently characterize the study of contextual influences on development.

## Notes

1. It is noteworthy that Dewey's views on education, while written more than a century ago (Dewey, 1897), are remarkably contemporary. For example, his theory of learning was thoroughly "constructivist," and his pedagogy was infused with such "modern" methods as cooperative and problem-based learning.
2. The Child Development Project as described here is no longer being disseminated by its developers. A less comprehensive program was derived from the elements of CDP in an effort to improve ease of program implementation. Information on this revised program, called Caring School Community, is available from the Developmental Studies Center (http://www.devstu.org).

## References

Ainsworth, M. D., Blehar, M. C., Waters, E., & Wall, S. (1978). *Patterns of attachment.* Hillsdale, NJ: Erlbaum.

Althof, W. (2003). Implementing "just and caring communities" in elementary schools: A Dewian perspective. In W. Veuglers & F. K. Oser (Eds.), *Teaching in moral and democratic education* (pp. 153–172). Bern, Switzerland: Lang.

Alwin, D. F. (1976). Assessing school effects: Some identities. *Sociology of Education, 49,* 294–303.

Alwin, D. F., & Otto, L. B. (1977). High school context effects on aspirations. *Sociology of Education, 50,* 259–273.

Ames, C. (1992). Classrooms: Goals, structures, and student motivation. *Journal of Educational Psychology, 84,* 261–271.

Apple, M., & Benne, J. (Eds.). (1995). *Democratic schools.* Alexandria, VA: Association for Staff and Curriculum Development.

Barker, R. G. (1968). *Ecological psychology: Concepts and methods for studying the environment of human behavior.* Stanford, CA: Stanford University Press.

Battistich, V. (2003). Effects of a school-based program to enhance prosocial development on children's peer relations and social adjustment. *Journal of Research in Character Education, 1,* 1–16.

Battistich, V., & Hom, A. (1997). The relationship between students' sense of their school as a community and their involvement in problem behaviors. *American Journal of Public Health, 87,* 1997–2001.

Battistich, V., & Hong, S. (2002, May). *Follow-up effects of the Child Development Project: Second-order latent linear growth modeling of students' "connectedness" to school, academic performance, and social adjustment during middle school.* Paper presented at the Society for Prevention Research, Seattle, WA.

Battistich, V., Schaps, E., Solomon, D., & Watson, M. (1991). The role of the school in prosocial development. In H. E. Fitzgerald, B. M. Lester, & M. W. Yogman (Eds.), *Theory and research in behavioral pediatrics* (Vol. 5, pp. 89–127). New York: Plenum.

Battistich, V., Schaps, E., Watson, M., & Solomon, D. (1996). Prevention effects of the Child Development Project: Early findings from an ongoing multisite demonstration trial. *Journal of Adolescent Research, 11,* 12–35.

Battistich, V., Schaps, E., Watson, M., Solomon, D., & Lewis, C. (2000). Effects of the Child Development Project on students' drug use and other problem behaviors. *Journal of Primary Prevention, 21,* 75–99.

Battistich, V., Schaps, E., & Wilson, N. (2004). Effects of an elementary school intervention on students' "connectedness" to school and social adjustment during middle school. *Journal of Primary Prevention, 24,* 243–262.

Battistich, V., Solomon, D., Kim, D., Watson, M., & Schaps, E. (1995). Schools as communities, poverty levels of student populations, and students' attitudes, motives, and performance: A multilevel analysis. *American Educational Research Journal, 32,* 627–658.

Battistich, V., Solomon, D., Watson, M., & Schaps, E. (1997). Caring school communities. *Educational Psychologist, 32,* 137–151.

Battistich, V., Solomon, D., Watson, M., Solomon, J., & Schaps, E. (1989). Effects of an elementary school program to enhance prosocial behavior on children's social problem-solving skills and strategies. *Journal of Applied Developmental Psychology, 10,* 147–169.

Baumeister, R. F., & Leary, M. R. (1995). The need to belong: Desire for interpersonal attachments as a fundamental human motivation. *Psychological Bulletin, 117,* 497–529.

Beatty, E. E. (2004). Creating a laboratory for democracy. *Educational Leadership, 61,* 75–78.

Becker, T., & Couto, R. (1996). *Teaching democracy by being democratic.* Westport, CT: Praeger.

Berkowitz, M. W. (2002). The science of character education. In W. Damon (Ed.), *Bringing in a new era in character education* (pp. 43–63). Stanford, CA: Hoover Institution Press.

Berkowitz, M. W., & Bier, M. (2005a). The interpersonal roots of character education. In D. K. Lapsley & F. C. Power (Eds.), *Character psychology and character education* (pp. 269–285). Notre Dame, IN: University of Notre Dame Press.

Berkowitz, M. W., & Bier, M. (2005b). *What works in character education: A research-driven agenda for educators.* Washington, DC: Character Education Partnership.

Bowlby, J. (1968). *Attachment and loss: Vol. 1. Attachment.* New York: Basic Books.

Bronfenbrenner, U., & Morris, P. A. (1998). The ecology of developmental processes. In W. Damon & R. M. Lerner (Eds.), *Handbook of child psychology: Vol. 1. Theoretical models of human development* (5th ed., pp. 993–1028). New York: Wiley.

Browning, C. R., Feinberg, S. L., & Dietz, R. D. (2004). The paradox of social organization: Networks, collective efficacy, and violent crime in urban neighborhoods. *Social Forces, 83,* 503–534.

Bryk, A. S., & Driscoll, M. E. (1988). *The school as community: Theoretical foundations, contextual influences, and consequences for students and teachers.* Madison: National Center on Effective Secondary Schools, University of Wisconsin.

Bryk, A. S., Lee, V. E., & Holland, P. B. (1993). *Catholic schools and the common good.* Cambridge, MA: Harvard University Press.

Buka, S. L., Stichick, T. L., Birdthistle, I., & Earls, F. J. (2001). Youth exposure to violence: Prevalence, risks and consequences. *American Journal of Orthopsychiatry, 71,* 298–310.

Campbell, J. (1995). *Understanding John Dewey.* Chicago: Open Court.

Chipuer, H. M., & Pretty, G. M. H. (1999). A review of the Sense of Community Index: Current issues, factor structure, reliability, and further development. *Journal of Community Psychology, 27,* 643–658.

Cohen, J. (2006). Social, emotional, ethical, and academic education: Creating a climate for learning, participation in democracy, and well-being. *Harvard Educational Review, 72,* 201–237.

Coleman, J. S. (1990). *Foundations of social theory.* Cambridge, MA: Harvard University Press.

Coleman, J. S., & Hoffer, T. (1987). *Public and private high schools: The impact of communities.* New York: Basic Books.

Connell, J. P. (1990). Context, self, and action: A motivational analysis of self-system processes across the life span. In D. Ciccheti & M. Beeghly (Eds.), *The self in transition: Infancy to childhood* (pp. 61–97). Chicago, IL: University of Chicago Press.

Connell, J. P., & Wellborn, J. G. (1991). Competence, autonomy, and relatedness: A motivational analysis of self-system processes. In M. Gunnar & A. Sroufe (Eds.), *Minnesota symposium on child psychology* (Vol. 22, pp. 43–77). Hillsdale, NJ: Erlbaum.

Cremin, L. A. (1961). *The transformation of the school.* New York: Knopf.

Damon, W. (2002). *Bringing in a new era in character education.* Stanford, CA: Hoover Institution Press.

deCharms, R. (1968). *Personal causation: The internal affective determinants of behavior.* New York: Academic.

deCharms, R. (1976). *Enhancing motivation: Change in the classroom.* New York: Irvington.

Deci, E. L., & Ryan, R. M. (1985). *Intrinsic motivation and self-determination in human behavior.* New York: Plenum.

DeVries, R., & Zan, B. (1994). *Moral classrooms, moral children: Creating a constructivist atmosphere in early education.* New York: Teachers College Press.

Dewey, J. (1897). My pedagogic creed. *The School Journal, 54,* 77–80.

Dewey, J. (1899). *The school and society.* Chicago: University of Chicago Press.

Dewey, J. (1900). *The child and the curriculum and the school and society.* Chicago: University of Chicago Press.

Dewey, J. (1916). *Democracy and education.* New York: Macmillan.

Dornbusch, S. M., Glasgow, K. L., & I-Chun, L. (1996). The social structure of schooling. *Annual Review of Psychology, 47,* 401–429.

Duncan, G. J., Connell, J. P., & Klebanov, P. K. (1997). Conceptual and methodological issues in estimating causal effects of neighborhoods and family conditions on individual development. In J. Brooks-Gunn, G. J. Duncan, & J. L. Aber (Eds.), *Neighborhood poverty: Vol. 1. Context and consequences for children* (pp. 219–250). New York: Russell Sage Foundation.

Duncan, G. J., & Raudenbush, S. W. (1999). *Assessing the effects of context in studies of child and youth development.* Educational Psychologist, 34, 29–41.

Durkheim, E. (1961). *Moral education: A study in the theory and application of the sociology of education.* New York: Free Press. (Original work published 1925)

Earls, F., & Carlson, M. (2001). The social ecology of child health and well-being. *Annual Review of Public Health, 22,* 143–166.

Eccles, J. S., & Midgley, C. (1989). Stage–environment fit: Developmentally appropriate classrooms for young adolescents. In C. Ames & R. Ames (Eds.), *Research on motivation in education: Goals and cognitions* (Vol. 3, pp. 13–44). New York: Academic.

Eccles, J. S., Midgley, C., Wigfield, A., Buchanan, C. M., Reuman, D., Flanagan, C., et al. (1993). Development during adolescence: The impact of stage-environment fit on young adolescents' experiences in schools and in families. *American Psychologist, 48,* 90–101.

Eccles, J. S., & Roeser, R. W. (2003). Schools as developmental contexts. In G. Adams & M. D. Berzonsky (Eds.), *Blackwell handbook of adolescence* (pp. 129–148). Malden, MA: Blackwell.

Everson, H. T., & Millsap, R. E. (2004). Beyond individual differences: Exploring school effects on SAT scores. *Educational Psychologist, 39,* 157–172.

Fisher, A. T., & Sonn, C. C. (2002). Psychological sense of community in Australia and the challenges of change. *Journal of Community Psychology, 30,* 597–610.

Freiberg, H. J. (1999). Consistency management and cooperative discipline: From tourists to citizens in the classroom. In H. J. Freiberg (Ed.), *Beyond behaviorism: Changing the classroom management paradigm* (pp. 75–97). Boston: Allyn & Bacon.

Gilreath, J. (Ed.). (1999). *Thomas Jefferson and the education of a citizen.* Washington, DC: Library of Congress.

Giroux, H. (1989). *Schooling for democracy.* London: Routledge, & Kegan Paul.

Goldstein, H. (2003). *Multilevel statistical models* (3rd ed.). London: Arnold.

Goodlad, J. (1984). *A place called school: Prospects for the future.* New York: McGraw-Hill.

Gottfredson, G. D., Gottfredson, D. C., Payne, A. A., & Gottfredson, N. C. (2005). School climate predictors of school disorder: Results from a national study of delinquency prevention in schools. *Journal of Research in Crime and Delinquency, 42,* 412–444.

Grant, G. (1989, January). Bringing the "moral" back in. *NEA Today,* 54–59.

Griffith, J. (1999). School climate as "social order" and "social action": A multi-level analysis of public elementary school student perceptions. *Social Psychology of Education, 2,* 339–369.

Hallinger, P., Bickman, L., & Davis, K. (1996). School context, principal leadership, and student reading achievement. *Elementary School Journal, 96,* 527–549.

Hansen, D. T. (1993). From role to person: The moral layeredness of classroom teaching. *American Educational Research Journal, 30,* 651–674.

Hawkins, J. D., Catalano, R. F., Kosterman, R., Abbott, R., & Hill, K. G. (1999). Preventing adolescent health-risk behaviors by strengthening protection during childhood. *Archives of Pediatric and Adolescent Medicine, 153,* 226–234.

Hawkins, J. D., Lishner, D. M., Catalano, R. F., & Howard, M. O. (1986). Childhood predictors of adolescent substance abuse: Toward an empirically grounded theory. *Journal of Children in Contemporary Society, 18,* 11–48.

Hawkins, J. D., & Weis, J. G. (1985). The social development model: An integrated approach to delinquency prevention. *Journal of Primary Prevention, 6,* 73–79.

Haynes, N. M., Emmons, C., & Ben-Avie, M. (1997). School climate as a factor in student adjustment and achievement. *Journal of Educational & Psychological Consultation, 8,* 321–329.

Higgins, A. (1991). The Just Community approach to moral education: Evolution of the idea and recent findings. In W. M. Kurtines & J. L. Gewirtz (Eds.), *Handbook of moral behavior and development. Vol. 3: Application* (pp. 111–141). New York: Wiley.

Higgins, A. (1995). Educating for justice and community. In W. M. Kurtines & J. L. Gewirtz (Eds.), *Moral development: An introduction* (pp. 49–81). Toronto, Canada: Allyn & Bacon.

Hofman, R. H., Hofman, W. H. A., & Guldemond, H. (2002). School governance, culture, and student achievement. *International Journal of Leadership in Education, 5,* 249–272.

Horwitz, R. (1979). Psychological effects of the "open classroom." *Review of Educational Research, 49,* 71–86.

Hutchison, D. (2004). The effect of measurement errors on apparent group level effects in educational progress. *Quality & Quantity, 38,* 407–424.

Jackson, P. W., Boostrom, R. E., & Hansen, D. T. (1993). *The moral life of schools.* San Francisco, CA: Jossey-Bass.

Jencks, C., & Mayer, S. E. (1990). The social consequences of growing up in a poor neighborhood. In L. E. Lynn & M. F. H. McGeary (Eds.), *Inner city poverty in the United States* (pp. 111–186). Washington, DC: National Academy Press.

Jenkins, P. (1997). School delinquency and the school social bond. *Journal of Research in Crime and Delinquency, 34,* 337–368.

Johnson, H. C., Jr. (1987). Society, culture, and character development. In K. Ryan & G. F. McLean (Eds.), *Character development in schools and beyond* (pp. 49–76). New York: Praeger.

Kohlberg, L. (1975). The Just Community School: The theory and the Cambridge Cluster School experiment. In *Collected papers from the Center for Moral Education* (pp. 1–77). (ERIC Document Reproduction Service No. ED 223 511)

Kohlberg, L. (1985). The Just Community approach to moral education in theory and practice. In M. Berkowitz & F. Oser (Eds.), *Moral education* (pp. 27–87). Hillsdale, NJ: Erlbaum.

Kohlberg, L., & Higgins, A. (1987). School democracy and social interaction. In W. M. Kurtines & J. L. Gewirtz (Eds.), *Moral development through social interaction* (pp. 102–128). New York: Wiley.

Kohlberg, L., Lieberman, M., Powers, F. C., Higgins, A., & Codding, J. (1981). Evaluating Scarsdale's "Just Community School" and its curriculum: Implications for the future. *Moral Education Forum, 6,* 31–42.

Lapsley, D. K., & Narvaez, D. (2006). Character education. In A. Renninger & I. Siegel (Eds.), *Handbook of child psychology* (Vol. 4, pp. 248–296). New York: Wiley.

Larsen, R. W. (2000). Toward a psychology of positive youth development. *American Psychologist, 55,* 170–183.

Leventhal, T., & Brooks-Gunn, J. (2000). The neighborhoods they live in: The effects of neighborhood residence on child and adolescent outcomes. *Psychological Bulletin, 126,* 309–337.

Leventhal, T., & Brooks-Gunn, J. (2003). Children and youth in neighborhood contexts. *Current Directions in Psychological Science, 12,* 27–31.

Lewin, K. (1951). *Field theory in the social sciences: Selected theoretical papers.* New York: Harper.

Lewis, R. (1999). Preparing students for democratic citizenship: Codes of conduct in Victoria's "Schools of the Future." *Educational Research & Evaluation, 5,* 41–61.

Libbey, H. P. (2004). Measuring student relationships to school: Attachment, bonding, connectedness, and engagement. *Journal of School Health, 74,* 274–283.

Lickona, T. (2001). Creating the Just Community with children. *Theory Into Practice, 16,* 97–104.

Lind, G., & Althof, W. (1992). Does the Just Community experience make a difference? Measuring and evaluating the effect of the DES project. *Moral Education Forum, 17,* 19–28.

Linney, J. A. (2000). Assessing ecological constructs and community context. In J. Rappaport & E. Seidman (Eds.), *Handbook of community psychology* (pp. 647–668). New York: Kluwer Academic/Plenum.

Liska, A., & Reed, M. (1985). Ties to conventional institutions and delinquency: Estimating reciprocal effects. *American Sociological Review, 50,* 547–560.

Loukas, A., & Robinson, S. (2004). Examining the moderating role of perceived school climate in early adolescent adjustment. *Journal of Research on Adolescence, 14,* 209–233.

MacCallum, R. C., Kim, C., Malarkey, W. B., & Kiecolt-Glaser, J. K. (1997). Studying multivariate change using multilevel models and latent growth curve models. *Multivariate Behavioral Research, 32,* 215–254.

Maccoby, E. E., & Martin, J. A. (1983). Socialization in the context of the family: Parent–child interaction. In P. H. Mussen (Ed.), *Handbook of child psychology: Vol 4. Socialization, personality, and social development* (pp. 1–101). New York: Wiley.

Manski, C. (1993). Identification of endogenous social effects: The reflection problem. *Review of Economic Studies, 60,* 531–542.

Masten, A. S., & Coatsworth, J. D. (1998). The development of competence in favorable and unfavorable environments. *American Psychologist, 53,* 205–220.

McClellan, B. E. (1999). *Moral education in America: Schools and the shaping of character from colonial times to the present.* New York: Teachers College Press.

McDonough, G. P. (2005). Moral maturity and autonomy: Appreciating the significance of Lawrence Kohlberg's Just Community. *Journal of Moral Education, 34,* 199–213.

McEvoy, A., & Welker, R. (2000). Antisocial behavior, academic failure, and school climate: A critical review. *Journal of Emotional and Behavioral Disorders, 8,* 130–140.

McLeroy, K. R., Bibeau, D., Steckler, A., & Glanz, K. (1988). An ecological perspective on health promotion programs. *Health Education Quarterly, 15,* 351–378.

McMillan, D. W., & Chavis, D. M. (1986). Sense of community: A definition and theory. *Journal of Community Psychology, 14,* 6–23.

McNeely, C. A., Nonnemaker, J. M., & Blum, R. W. (2002). Promoting student connectedness to school: Evidence from the National Longitudinal Study of Adolescent Health. *Journal of School Health, 72,* 138–146.

Mead, M. (1951). *The school in American culture.* Cambridge, MA: Harvard University Press.

Minuchin, P., Biber, B., Shapiro, E., & Zimiles, H. (1969). *The psychological impact of school experiences.* New York: Basic Books.

Moos, R. H. (1994). *The Social Climate Scales: A user's guide* (2nd ed.). Palo Alto, CA: Consulting Psychologists Press.

Moos, R. H. (2002). The mystery of human context and coping: An unraveling of clues. *American Journal of Community Psychology, 30,* 67–88.

Murray, H. A. (1938). *Explorations in personality.* New York: Oxford University Press.

Nash, P. (1968). *Models of man: Explorations in the western educational tradition.* Malabar, FL: Krieger.

National Commission on Excellence in Education. (1983). *A nation at risk: The imperative for educational reform.* Washington, DC: U.S. Government Printing Office.

Noddings, N. (1988). An ethic of caring and its implications for instructional arrangements. *American Journal of Education, 96,* 215–230.

No Child Left Behind Act. (2002, January 8). Pub.L. 107-110, 115 Stat. 1425.

Noddings, N. (1992). *The challenge to care in schools: An alternative approach to education.* New York: Teachers College.

O'Donnell, C. R., Tharp, R. G., & Wilson, K. (1993). Activity settings as the unit of analysis: A theoretical basis for community intervention and development. *American Journal of Community Psychology, 21,* 501–520.

Oser, F. K. (1986). Moral education and values education: The discourse perspective. In M. C. Wittrock (Ed.), *Handbook of research on teaching* (3rd ed., pp. 917–941). New York: Macmillan.

Oser, F. K. (1992a). The pilot project "Democracy and Education in the School" (DES) in Northrine-Westphalia. *Moral Education Forum, 17,* 1–4.

Oser, F. K. (1992b). Three paths toward a Just Community: Process and transformation. *Moral Education Forum, 17,* 18, 35–36.

Osgood, D. W., & Anderson, A. L. (2004). Unstructured socializing and rates of delinquency. *Criminology, 42,* 516–549.

Payne, A. A., Gottfredson, D. C., & Gottfredson, G. D. (2003). Schools as communities: The relationships among communal school organization, student bonding, and school disorder. *Criminology, 41,* 749–777.

Pedersen, S., Seidman, E., Yoshikawa, H., Rivera, A. C., Allen, L., & Aber, J. L. (2005). Contextual competence: Multiple manifestations among urban adolescents. *American Journal of Community Psychology, 35,* 65–82.

Piaget, J. (1965). *The moral judgment of the child.* New York: Free Press. (Original work published 1932)

Pianta, R. C. (2006). Schools, schooling, and developmental psychopathology. In D. Cicchetti & D. J. Cohen (Eds.), *Developmental psychopathology: Vol. 1. Theory and method* (2nd ed., pp. 494–529). Hoboken, NJ: Wiley.

Powell, A. G., Farrar, E., & Cohen, D. K. (1985). *The shopping mall high school: Winners and losers in the educational marketplace.* New York: Houghton Mifflin.

Power, F. C. (1988). The Just Community approach to moral education. *Journal of Moral Education, 17,* 195–208.

Power, F. C., Higgins, A., & Kohlberg, L. (1989). *Lawrence Kohlberg's approach to moral education.* New York: Columbia University Press.

Prakash, M. S. (1987). Partners in moral education: Communities and their public schools. In K. Ryan & G. F. McLean (Eds.), *Character development in schools and beyond* (pp. 97–116). New York: Praeger.

Prilleltensky, I., Nelson, G., & Peirson, L. (2001). The role of power and control in children's lives: An ecological analysis of pathways toward wellness, resilience and problems. *Journal of Community and Applied Social Psychology, 11,* 143–158.

Print, M., Ørnstrøm, S., & Neilson, H. S. (2002). Education for democratic processes in schools and classrooms. *European Journal of Education, 37,* 193–210.

Putnam, R. D. (1995). Bowling alone: America's declining social capital. *Journal of Democracy, 6,* 65–78.

Raudenbush, S. W. (2001). Toward a coherent framework for comparing trajectories of individual change. In L. M. Collins & A. G. Sayer (Eds.), *New methods for the analysis of change* (pp. 33–64). Washington, DC: American Psychological Association.

Raudenbush, S. W., & Bryk, A. S. (2002). *Hierarchical linear models: Applications and data analysis methods* (2nd ed.). Thousand Oaks, CA: Sage.

Raudenbush, S. W., & Willms, J. D. (1995). The estimation of school effects. *Journal of Educational and Behavioral Statistics, 20,* 307–335.

Resnick, M. D., Ireland, M., & Borowsky, I. (2004). Youth violence perpetration: What protects? What predicts? Findings from the National Longitudinal Study of Adolescent Health. *Journal of School Health, 35,* 424.

Roeser, R. W., Eccles, J. S., & Sameroff, A. J. (2000). School as a context of early adolescents' academic and social-emotional development: A summary of research findings. *The Elementary School Journal, 100*, 443–471.

Rogoff, B. (1994). Developing understanding of the idea of communities of learners. *Mind, Culture, and Activity, 1*, 209–229.

Rose, L. C., & Gallup, A. M. (2000). The 32nd annual Phi Delta Kappa/Gallup poll of the public's attitudes toward the public schools. *Phi Delta Kappan, 82*, 41–57.

Rosenbaum, J. E. (1991). Black pioneers—Do their moves to the suburbs increase economic opportunity for mothers and children? *Housing Policy Debate, 2*, 1179–1213.

Rubinowitz, L. S., & Rosenbaum, J. E. (2000). *Crossing the class and color lines: From public housing to white suburbia.* Chicago, IL: University of Chicago Press.

Rutter, M., Maughan, B., Mortimore, P., & Ouston, J. (1979). *Fifteen thousand hours: Secondary schools and their effects on children.* Cambridge, MA: Harvard University Press.

Ryan, K., & Lickona, T. (1987). Character development: The challenge and the model. In K. Ryan & G. F. McLean (Eds.), *Character development in schools and beyond* (pp. 3–116). New York: Praeger.

Ryan, R. M., & Deci, E. L. (2000). Self-determination theory and the facilitation of intrinsic motivation, social development, and well being. *American Psychologist, 55*, 68–78.

Sampson, R. J., Morenoff, J. D., & Gannon-Rowley, T. (2002). Assessing neighborhood effects: Social processes and new directions in research. *Annual Review of Sociology, 28*, 433–478.

Sampson, R. J., Raudenbush, S. W., & Earls, F. (1997). Neighborhoods and violent crime: A multilevel study of collective efficacy. *Science, 277*, 918–924.

Schaps, E., Battistich, V., & Solomon, D. (1997). School as a caring community: A key to character. In A. Molnar (Ed.), *The construction of children's character. Ninety-sixth yearbook of the National Society for the Study of Education* (pp. 127–139). Chicago: National Society for the Study of Education.

Seligman, M. E. P., & Csikszentmihalyi, M. (2000). Positive psychology: An introduction. *American Psychologist, 55*, 1–14.

Shaw, C. R., & McKay, H. D. (1969). *Juvenile delinquency in urban areas* (Rev. ed.). Chicago: University of Chicago Press.

Shinn, M., & Toohey, S. M. (2003). Community contexts of human welfare. *Annual Review of Psychology, 54*, 427–459.

Shouse, R. C. (1996). Academic press and sense of community: Conflict, congruence, and implications for student achievement. *Social Psychology of Education, 1*, 47–68.

Shutz, A. (2001). John Dewey's conundrum: Can democratic schools empower? *Teachers College Record, 103*, 267–302.

Smetana, J. G., Campione-Barr, N., & Metzger, A. (2006). Adolescent development in interpersonal and societal contexts. *Annual Review of Psychology, 57*, 255–284.

Solomon, D., Battistich, V., Kim, D., & Watson, M. (1997). Teacher practices associated with students' sense of the classroom as a community. *Social Psychology of Education, 1*, 235–267.

Solomon, D., Battistich, V., Watson, M., Schaps, E., & Lewis, C. (2000). A six-district study of educational change: Direct and mediated effects of the child development project. *Social Psychology of Education, 4*, 3–51.

Solomon, D., & Kendall, A. J. (1976). Individual characteristics and children's performance in "open" and "traditional" classroom settings. *Journal of Educational Psychology, 68*, 613–625.

Solomon, D., Watson, M., & Battistich, V. (2001). Teaching and schooling effects on moral/prosocial development. In V. Richardson (Ed.), *Handbook of research on teaching* (4th ed., pp. 566–603). Washington, DC: American Educational Research Association.

Solomon, D., Watson, M., Battistich, V., Schaps, E., & Delucchi, K. (1992). Creating a caring community: Educational practices that promote children's prosocial development. In F. K. Oser, A. Dick, & J.-L. Patry (Eds.), *Effective and responsible teaching: The new synthesis* (pp. 383–396). San Francisco, CA: Jossey-Bass.

Solomon, D., Watson, M., Battistich, V., Schaps, E., Tuck, P., Solomon, J., Cooper, C., & Ritchey, W. (1985). A program to promote interpersonal consideration and cooperation in children. In R. Slavin, S. Sharan, S. Kagan, R. Hertz-Lazarowitz, C. Webb, & R. Schmuck (Eds.), *Learning to cooperate, cooperating to learn* (pp. 371–401). New York: Plenum.

Solomon, D., Watson, M., Delucchi, K., Schaps, E., & Battistich, V. (1988). Enhancing children's prosocial behavior in the classroom. *American Educational Research Journal, 25*, 527–554.

Strike, K. A. (1999). Can schools be communities? The tension between shared values and inclusion. *Educational Administration Quarterly, 35*, 46–70.

Strike, K. A. (2000). Schools as communities: Four metaphors, three models, and a dilemma or two. *Journal of Philosophy of Education, 34*, 617–642.

Tönnies, F. (1988). *Community and society.* New Brunswick, NJ: Transaction Books. (Original work published 1887)

Tozer, S. E., Violas, P. C., & Senese, G. B. (1995). *School and society: Historical and contemporary perspectives.* New York: McGraw-Hill.

Vieno, A., Perkins, D. D., Smith, T. M., & Santinello, M. (2005). Democratic school climate and sense of community in schools: A multilevel analysis. *American Journal of Community Psychology, 36*, 327–341.

Wallin, D. (2003). Student leadership and democratic schools: A case study. *NASSP Bulletin, 87*, 55–78.

Wandersman, A., & Nation, M. (1998). Urban neighborhoods and mental health: Psychological contributions to understanding toxicity, resilience, and interventions. *American Psychologist, 53*, 647–656.

Wasserman, E., & Garrod, A. (1983). Application of Kohlberg's theory to curricula in democratic schools. *Educational Analysis, 5*, 17–36.

Watson, M. S. (2006, April). *Elementary moral education can make a long-term difference: High-school students reflect.* Paper presented at the American Educational Research Association, San Francisco.

Watson, M. S., & Battistich, V. (2006). Building and sustaining caring communities. In C. M. Evertson & C. S. Weinstein (Eds.), *Handbook of classroom management:* (pp. 253–279). Mahwah, NJ: Erlbaum.

Watson, M. S., Battistich, V., & Solomon, D. (1997). Enhancing students' social and ethical development in schools: An intervention program and its effects. *International Journal of Educational Research, 27*, 571–586.

Watson, M. S., & Ecken, L. (2003). *Learning to trust: Transforming difficult elementary classrooms through developmental discipline.* San Francisco, CA: Jossey-Bass.

Wehlage, G. G., Rutter, R. A., Smith, G. A., Lesko, N., & Fernandez, R. R. (1989). *Reducing the risk: Schools as communities of support.* New York: Falmer.

Weinstock, M., Broida, G., & Assor, A. (2006, April). *Type of school and the autonomy factor in moral development.* Paper presented at the American Educational Research Association, San Francisco, CA.

Whitlock, J. L. (2006). Youth perceptions of life in school: Contextual correlates of school connectedness in adolescence. *Applied Developmental Science, 10*, 13–19.

William T. Grant Foundation. (2006). *Report and resource guide 2005–2006.* New York: Author.

Wise, A. (1979). *Legislated learning: The bureaucratization of the American classroom.* Berkeley: University of California Press.

Wolk, S. (1998). *A democratic classroom.* Portsmouth, NH: Heinemann.

# 9

# School Contexts and the Development of Adolescents' Peer Relations

*Jill V. Hamm and Lei Zhang*

Peer relations have long been recognized as one of the central developmental issues of adolescence. For decades, scholars from diverse fields have demonstrated how various types and features of adolescents' peer relations predict key developmental outcomes, including academic achievement, problem behavior, and schooling adjustment. Researchers have tapped into peer relations within the school setting, using methodologies such as classroom-based peer nominations and classroom/school observations, to identify and measure specific peer relations. Research participants are often asked to limit their identification of peers to class- or schoolmates; so that, the determination of adolescents' status, reputation, or relationships, is fully dependent on the school context in which it was measured. Such efforts rightly recognize the significance of the school context to adolescents' peer relations, but surprisingly, there is little acknowledgment that these peer relations might be in part influenced by features of the very school settings in which they are defined and measured.

The school context of peer relations is of further significance given that educators and curriculum developers depend on peer relations as a vehicle to student learning. Popular instructional methods such as peer collaboration, cooperative learning, and reciprocal teaching rely on positive peer relations, yet there has been little attention to the features or nature of the peer relations that are required to support such methods. Understanding how schools and classrooms contribute to peer relations can help to optimize the educational value of peer relations to student learning. The purpose of this chapter is to review research on the extent to which, and the ways in which, schools shape peer relations for adolescents, as well as to provide direction for future research on this topic.

## Conceptualizing Adolescent Peer Relations

By the time individuals reach adolescence, which for purposes of this review involves the period of life that spans ages roughly 11 to 18 and middle and high school, their peer relations have expanded considerably from those of childhood. Brown (1999) conceptualized three facets of relationships: structure, or how relationships are organized, such as friendships, social networks, or peer crowds; content, or features and qualities of relationships across relationship structures; and process, which addresses how adolescents shape and are shaped by their peer environments; for instance, through peer socialization and selection. Most research on peer relationships in schools has focused on friendship, social networks, and social status and acceptance.

Distinctions across the structure, content, and processes of relationships are important to investigate, as each potentially relates differently to specific adolescent outcomes (Ladd, Kochenderfer, & Coleman, 1997; Wentzel & Caldwell, 1997). Furthermore, these different facets may themselves be differentially shaped by schooling effects; school effects on interaction-based relationships (e.g., friendships) may differ from school effects on social status (e.g., popularity), although researchers have not compared directly the schooling effects on different types of relationships.

Within this larger framework of peer relations, our review is circumscribed in several ways. First, representation of studies varies across the relationship facets. The relationship structure that has garnered by far the most research attention is friendship. This may be because many studies of schooling effects on peer relations draw samples from national, large-scale data sets, such as the High School and Beyond (HSB) of 1980 and the National Longitudinal Study of Adolescent Health (Add Health) of 1995 to 2008 which includes significant numbers of schools and school-level variables. With regard to relationship content, the primary focus has been the ethnic composition of relationships (generally friendships), nearly to the neglect of other features or qualities of relationships. Finally, only a small number of studies have focused on the effects of schooling on relationship processes.

Second, we focused on naturally occurring, rather than teacher-occasioned peer relations. Certain teacher- or school-occasioned peer interactions, such as cooperative learning and extracurricular activities, are considered to be schooling effects.

Third, we excluded relationship structures that have received little attention in relation to schooling effects. Although they increase in significance across the adolescent period (Furman, Brown, & Feiring, 1999), there is little research on schooling effects on romantic relations. And, although bullying and victimization remain, regrettably, part of the adolescent peer experience, this relationship structure is addressed in another chapter of this *Handbook* (Espelage, Holt, & Poteat, chapter 10 this volume).

## Conceptualizing Schools as a Context of Peer Relations

In fitting with the overarching theme of this *Handbook*, we drew on an ecological framework to understand ways in which peer relations can be shaped by schooling contexts. Bronfenbrenner (1979) partitioned the context of human development into nested layers, from proximal to distal influences on development. Microsystems, the most proximal influences on development, involve relations between the developing adolescent and his or her immediate settings, such as the family, classroom, or peers. Mesosystems involve the interrelationships among microsettings, such as linkages between the family, classroom, and peer groups. Exosystems involve social structures that do not directly include the developing adolescent, such as school boards, but which affect the immediate settings of the adolescent. Macrosystems represent cultural values and beliefs that shape all the other ecological systems, and the chronosystem encompasses elements of time that impinge on the contexts that affect the developing child.

Much of the research relevant to this review involves a conceptualization of the structure, content, and processes of adolescents' peer relations as developmental outcomes, shaped by features of the microsettings in which they develop, such as classrooms and schools. The majority of these studies, albeit not necessarily based explicitly in an ecological framework, fall under a "main effects" perspective, in which researchers have assessed the association of particular features of schools with peer relational structure, content, or process. However, some developmental researchers have conceptualized peer relationships themselves as a microsystem or context of adolescent adjustment (e.g., Collins & Laursen, 1999). One research possibility is to investigate how peer relational content and processes account for, or mediate, schooling effects on adolescent adjustment: If schooling features shape facets of peer relations, and facets of peer relations shape adolescent adjustment, then understanding the extent to which peer relations explain or account for schooling effects follows as a point of inquiry. From a different mesosystemic perspective, researchers can incorporate nonschool contexts such as neighborhood into analyses, to consider how features of school and nonschool settings work together to shape peer relations within the school. Finally, from an ecological standpoint, research should focus on the roles, activities, and relationships that adolescents experience within schooling microsystems; according to Bronfenbrenner (1979), these are the key processes within settings that promote development.

Based in Bronfenbrenner's ecological perspective, social scientists have defined schools as embedded contexts characterized both objectively and subjectively (e.g., student perceptions) along multiple levels and dimensions, for their effects on development. The following categories, differentiated first by their location at the school or classroom, capture some of the ways in which researchers have investigated schooling effects on peer relations.

*School-Level Microsystemic Effects* Demographic features of schools include aspects of the student body, such as racial/ethnic and socioeconomic distributions, and school size. Structural/ organizational features address the organization of schools for learning, including curricular and extracurricular activity structures. Cultural features of schools encompass affective and relational dimensions of schooling. School cultures establish what is valued, emphasized, and acceptable within the school setting, which can contribute to relationship structures as well as to content and processes of relationships (Epstein & Karweit, 1983).

*Classroom-Level Microsystemic Effects* The classroom is among the most proximal or immediate levels of the schooling context to students' adjustment (Talbert & McLaughlin, 1999). In addition to involving the dimensions identified at the school level, classrooms feature specific instructional dimensions such as instructional formats, tasks, reward structures, and participatory formats. Despite their potential significance, there are fewer studies of classroom than school of context in part due to use of large-scale data sets sampled at the school rather than classroom level.

*Beyond Microsystemic Effects* Although an ecological perspective provides a conceptual rationale for investigating school effects beyond the immediate setting, few researchers have moved beyond a focus on schools as a microsystem of peer relations. We have separated works that transcend a microsystemic approach because they are substantively different from the rest of the literature either in their positioning of schools (as a setting shaped by other contexts) or in their focus on peer relational content or processes as a context of schooling effects on adjustment. It is rare for researchers to incorporate distal variables, such as exo- or macrosystemic, or temporal contexts into the study of schooling effects on peer relations.

*Theoretical Perspectives within an Ecological Framework* An ecological framework provides a multilevel conceptualization of the study of schooling effects on peer relations, and allows for integration of research findings across diverse disciplines and theoretical approaches. Within this broad framework, dominant theoretical approaches to the study of schooling effects on peer relations derive primarily from social psychology and sociology; such approaches consider forces that generate and sustain relationships within the schooling context. It is generally accepted that relationships are shaped by basic dynamics of contact, similarity, and propinquity (Gifford-Smith & Brownell, 2003). Social psychological and sociological views support the premise that schools provide opportunity for contact, and through various structural and organizational means, locate students in proximity to one another. Furthermore, school structural features are theorized to create pockets of opportunity for relationships to form, while school culture sets norms and conditions which contribute further to relational content and process (Epstein & Karweit, 1983). Although much of the literature draws explicitly or implicitly on these propositions, other theoretical rationales are used, and are explained in relation to specific studies.

## Research on Schools as a Developmental Context for Peer Relations

Across diverse disciplines, a substantial literature addresses the school context of peer relations; two overlapping literatures exist. One focuses on school effects on the structure, content, and processes of peer relations in general; the other focuses on school effects on specific relational content: cross-ethnic relations. The study of school effects on intergroup relations was fueled by early studies of desegregated schools that indicated that when schools desegregated, students did not integrate socially (e.g., Epstein, 1985).

These two literatures have developed to a large degree as distinct lines of research. There is theoretical overlap in that the literature on intergroup relations often draws on general tenets of interpersonal attraction and contact. However, we separate findings on the schooling context of intergroup relations from general findings regarding the schooling context of peer relations. To some degree, the literature on schooling effects on intergroup relations is the more extensive of the two, likely because educational policies focused attention on schools as a primary setting of intergroup relations, and created an obvious and socially significant research opportunity. However, interest in intergroup relations has dwindled significantly over the past decade. Because important insights can be gained from the interdisciplinary literature on schooling effects on intergroup relations, and because peer relations in contemporary American schools naturally involve cross-ethnic relations and are a normative experience for many adolescents, we present those research findings first, followed by research on school effects on general peer relations.

## Schooling Context of Intergroup Relations

Qualitative and quantitative studies alike document school variability in patterns and qualities of intergroup relations.

Metz (1983) described "strikingly positive" (p. 202) relations between African American and European American youth in a desegregated middle school; Peshkin (1991) described ethnic "mingling" that pervaded relationships from casual interaction to close friendship in an ethnically diverse school in southern California. Yet others portray less positive images. Lee's (1996) study of an academically elite and ethnically diverse public high school depicted avoidance and tension between Asian-descent and African American students as they jockeyed for status in the school's social hierarchy. Numerous large-scale quantitative studies confirm racial/ethnic segregation in students' as a normative pattern in adolescents' relationships in ethnically diverse schools. In a cross-sectional study of a Southern community in the early 1980s, Shrum, Cheek, and Hunter (1988) documented grade-level differences in racial/ethnic similarity of friendship nominations from elementary school through high school. Nearly complete racial/ethnic segregation in friendship was evident during the middle school years. More recent studies that have incorporated hierarchical linear modeling (HLM) affirm the conclusion from ethnographic works of school differences in patterns of intergroup relations, by demonstrating significant school-level variability in intergroup friendship nomination (e.g., Hamm, Brown, & Heck, 2005) and in ethnic minority students' affiliations with reputation- (e.g., Jocks, Populars) versus ethnic-based peer groups (Brown, Herman, Hamm, & Heck, 2008). Findings also reveal that patterns of intergroup relations do not reflect patterns of relationship that would be expected to occur given the ethnic distribution of students in the school and the number of friends nominated (e.g., Hamm et al., 2005; Joyner & Kao, 2000). Much of the research on classroom variability in patterns of intergroup relations predates the use of HLM to partition variance associated with differences between classrooms; thus, information regarding classroom differences in intergroup relationship formation is not available as it is at the school-level. Collectively, these studies document school differences in intergroup friendship, and suggest differences in the quality of student intergroup relations. A handful of theoretical views have been the basis of investigations of the contribution of schools to these differences.

***Theoretical Perspectives*** One is hard-pressed to locate psychologically or sociologically based studies of intergroup relations that do not draw on social contact theory. Allport (1954) argued that contact alone will not yield positive intergroup relations; three features of the contact situation influence the quality of relations that ensue: equal status of the groups, cooperation between the groups, and institutional support for positive relations between the groups. Application of this theory to intergroup relations in schools has been discussed at length (e.g., Schofield, 1991). Other researchers have applied tenets of interpersonal attraction to understand schooling effects on intergroup relations, but often integrate features of social contact theory. A handful of studies have applied theoretical perspectives that are variations of Ogbu's (1988) cultural ecological theory. Most do not focus directly on intergroup relations, but through investigating topics such as ethnic minority student achievement, findings include attention to intergroup relations in schools.

### School-Level Effects

*Demographic Characteristics*   A clear finding from a number of studies is that school ethnic composition is a factor in intergroup friendships that form and are sustained in schools. The focus is on the proportion of students from one's own group relative to other groups. Argued from an opportunity perspective, the fewer students available from one's own group, the more likely students are to seek friends from outside their ethnic group. In a study based on the Add Health data set, Joyner and Kao (2000) reported that for African American, Asian-descent, Latino, Native American, and European American students, the likelihood of nominating a cross-ethnic friend increased as the proportion of students of one's ethnic group decreased. Using a data set of seven ethnically diverse high schools, Hamm et al. (2005) created a variable that reflected students' likelihood of nominating a cross-ethnic friend, given school ethnic diversity and number of friends nominated; for African American, Asian-descent, Latino, and European American students this variable was positively associated with students' listing of at least one cross-ethnic peer among the friends they nominated. Moody (2001) drew on sociological contact theory to predict that within-ethnic group friendship nomination would increase as the ethnic heterogeneity of a setting increased. Findings from the Add Health data set, after controlling for the school ethnic distribution and individual, dyadic, and social network factors indicated that the most pronounced increases to friendship segregation occurred for moderate levels of school ethnic heterogeneity; friendship segregation decreased at the highest levels of heterogeneity. Results of a different study conducted with the Add Health data set revealed a statistically significant intensification of same-ethnic friendship nomination when adolescents were in schools with very small (less than 10%) concentrations of members of their own ethnic group (Quillian & Campbell, 2003). Although these findings could be interpreted as an opportunity for contact and availability of same-ethnic peers, empirical study of substantive features of schools detailed below suggest a more complex interpretation. School-level distributions of racial/ethnic groups rarely reflect students' experiences, given school organizational and structural practices such as tracking (Oakes, 2005) and selective sorting into extracurricular activities (e.g., Quiroz, Flores-Gonzalez, & Frank, 1996) that resegregate students within schools. Other research (e.g., Peshkin, 1991) suggests that the numerical balance of different ethnic groups within a school contributes to the social culture to shape intergroup relations.

From a social contact theoretical perspective, school-level status differentials should relate to intergroup relations because unequal status between groups can provoke con-

flict and promote tension, making intergroup interactions and relationship formation undesirable (Pettigrew, 1975). Peshkin (1991) proposed that interethnic social mingling resulted from the lack of numerical dominance of any ethnic group in the school, generally comparable (and low) SES backgrounds, and small achievement disparities across the ethnic groups. In contrast, other ethnographers have attributed interethnic avoidance and ethnically segregated friendship networks that they observed to pronounced status differences between European American and ethnic minority (e.g., Dehyle, 1986; Schofield, 1989) and Asian-descent, European American, and African American students (Lee, 1996). However, these findings were based in single-school studies. Hamm et al. (2005) tested for effects of school effects of achievement and SES differentials by ethnic group in a sample of seven high schools, and found that for both Asian-descent and European American students, students were more likely to nominate cross-ethnic friends in schools in which their ethnic group was more comparable academically to the rest of the student body. Furthermore, while European American students whose parental education was more comparable to that of the remaining student body were more likely to nominate cross-ethnic friends, Latino students were more likely to nominate cross-ethnic friends when their parental educational attainment collectively was higher than that of the other ethnic groups in the school. These school-level effects were evident after accounting for numerous student-level variables.

Demographic factors are not sufficient to explain schooling effects on intergroup relations. The ways in which school practices create contact opportunities, emphasize similarities and differences between ethnic groups, foster a social culture more or less conducive to intergroup relations, both within classrooms and at the school level, must be considered as well.

*School Structure and Organization*   In reviewing sociological and social psychological empirical literatures, Khmelkov and Hallinan (1999) concluded that school organizational practices circumscribe the pool of peers available for relationship formation, thus affecting contact among students. In particular, curricular tracking practices shape students' daily schedules in academic and nonacademic settings, which influence the pool of students for peer relationships. Studies of the effects of curricular tracking have focused primarily on intergroup friendship. Using the High School and Beyond (HSB) data set, Hallinan and Williams (1989) found that when African American and European American students were in the same curricular track, their likelihood of cross-ethnic friendship nomination increased. Broadening the literature to include African American, Asian-descent, Latino, and European American students attending seven high schools, Hamm et al. (2005) found that Latino students in college-bound tracks were more likely than Latino students not in college-bound tracks, to nominate at least one friend of a different ethnic group. Using the larger Add Health data set, Moody (2001) reported greater ethnic-based heterogeneity in friendship nomination in schools where racial mixing within tracks was greater. Two longitudinal studies offer insight into the impact of tracking on intergroup relations over time. Schofield and Sagar (1977) investigated racial homogeneity in lunchroom seating patterns among seventh grade students without tracking experience, compared to tracked eighth graders at the same school. Across the school year, cafeteria seating decreased in racial homogeneity among the seventh graders but increased in homogeneity among the eighth graders. In a follow-up study (Schofield, 1979) of the original cohort of seventh graders as they progressed from nontracked classes in seventh grade through the tracked eighth grade, students interacted more across racial lines than did the previous cohort of tracked eighth graders, but still declined significantly in integration of their seating patterns as they experienced the tracked system.

School-level structure/organization contributes to intergroup relations through extracurricular activities; findings demonstrate benefits to the nomination of ethnically diverse friends (Khmelkov & Hallinan, 1999). For instance, from Educational Testing Service data from 10th graders in 48 schools, Slavin and Madden (1979) reported that students on sports teams identified more cross-ethnic friends and more positive intergroup attitudes than their peers not on sports teams. Patchen (1982) found participation in cooperative extracurricular activities to be a strong predictor of cross-ethnic friendship. For early adolescents, cross-race friend nomination was greater when African American and European American students shared participation in at least one extracurricular activity (Hallinan & Teixeira, 1987b). Similarly, Moody (2001) found that friendship ethnic segregation diminished in schools with greater ethnic integration within extracurricular activities even after adjusting for dyadic similarity factors and school-level controls.

Research on extracurricular experiences has evolved over the past decade, beyond simple attention to participation in the activities, to the qualities of experiences, and leadership and relationship opportunities within extracurricular experiences (e.g., Mahoney, Larson, Eccles, & Lord, 2005). These new directions should be applied to understand the nature and development of intergroup relations. A word of caution about the extracurricular context of intergroup relations is its potential to perpetuate relationship ethnic homophily. Differential participation rates by ethnic group (e.g., Darling, 2005; Quiroz et al., 1996) may mean that students segregate through self-selection into different activities (Hamm, 1998).

*Summary of Structural/Organization School-Level Effects*  Many studies document that intergroup relations develop within the school context as a function of both the ethnic diversity of the student body as a whole, and also in relation to school organization and structure. The most consistent findings for school structural effects involve curricular tracking. Extra curricular activities appear to foster positive intergroup relations but have received less

attention. Beyond these two dimensions, only a handful of school structural and organizational features have been addressed, and only in isolated studies (e.g., cross-grade mixing, Moody, 2001).

Several issues emerge from the more recent research in this area. First, it is important to distinguish schooling effects from individual or dyadic effects. Researchers have successfully accomplished this through defining dependent variables of friendship segregation that are adjusted for non-schooling effects (e.g., Moody, 2001); more widespread use of multilevel statistical modeling may facilitate such efforts further, for instance, by supporting attention to cross-level (student characteristic by school variables) interactive effects (Pettigrew, 1998). Second, the literature thus far is primarily cross-sectional in design, with researchers investigating track and extracurricular activities concurrent with friendship nomination, and is limited to intergroup friendships. Although cross-sectional findings contribute to the literature, it is necessary to consider the longer-term as well as cumulative effects of school structure and organization on students' intergroup relations. Many research design and methodological issues can be addressed within contemporary, large-scale data sets (e.g., Add Health) as well as through researchers' development of data sets that are smaller in scope.

Research has evolved from simple consideration of academic tracking, or extracurricular activity participation, to more detailed consideration, such as ethnic mixing within these structures or coexperiences of the school structure. Beyond these examples, however, an ecological approach advocates for greater attention to the nature of students' experiences within these settings—to the roles, relationships, and activities that take place for students of different ethnic backgrounds, and how these experiences within tracks, extracurricular activities, and other schooling structures, contribute to intergroup relationship structure, content, and process.

Many researchers, drawing on social contact theory, have argued that part of structural/organizational effects arise from differential status when ethnic group differences in achievement and other factors are accentuated. Insight into how these status differentials take form and affect intergroup relations can be found in studies on school cultural effects.

*School Culture*  Ethnographers interpret the quality and nature of intergroup relations in terms of school relational and affective dimensions. Ethnically diverse schools can develop social norms regulating intergroup relations; Peshkin (1991) articulated a "code" of ethnic relations (p. 221) gleaned from a year-long study of one high school. Norms, such as not making decisions about others based on racial/ethnic group membership, or feeling good about your own ethnic group, supported frequent cross-ethnic friendships and general cross-ethnic mingling in the school. Whether or not schools characterized by avoidant intergroup relations in other studies have social norms sanctioning cross-ethnic interaction is not clear. Several studies reveal school social cultures in which European American students assume the role of "model" and "good" student while ethnic or racial minority students (e.g., African American, Native American) students are relegated to roles of "troublemaker" and "non-student" (e.g., Dehyle, 1986; Schofield, 1981). Lee's (1996) study added the model minority stereotype of Asian-descent students to this ethnic minority-majority dichotomized relationship. These ethnographers have concluded that schools with conflicting social identities across ethnic groups, inhibit and undermine positive interactions and relationship development. As noted previously, actual academic status differentials are related to cross-ethnic friend nomination (e.g., Hamm et al., 2005); the social identities imposed on students in relation to their ethnicity typically have some grounding in actual economic or academic disparities which then become infused into the student social hierarchy (e.g., Dehyle, 1986; Lee, 1996; Schofield, 1989).

These ethnographers have argued that group differentials and their ensuing effects on intergroup relations, result from the ways in which schools structure and organize the academic heterogeneity of their student body through practices such as tracking. For instance, in regards to a school comprising Korean, Asian American-identified, Asian-identified, Asian New Wavers, African American, and European American students, Lee's (1996) interpretation was that through its highly competitive environment and endorsement of meritocratic ideals, the school positioned African American and Asian-descent students to compete with one another for status in the school. This emphasized that ethnic groups in the school were not equal in status, which encouraged tensions among ethnic minority students, but overall resulted in very little intergroup mingling across any ethnic group. A study of European American, Ute, and Navajo students in a school bordering a reservation revealed a similar tale, though in a setting that was not academically elite. Dehyle (1986) partially attributed this school's avoidant intergroup relations to academic disparities embedded within a structure that segregated students and perpetuated negative stereotypes. In her ethnographic study, Schofield (1989) emphasized how a faculty culture of "colorblindness," or unwillingness to treat race as a legitimate identity and relational element, meant that teachers avoided the role of race and did little to undermine the social identities of each groups, resulting in little support to work through their intergroup experiences.

In Lee's, Dehyle's and Schofield's schools, there were pronounced academic and socioeconomic differences across the ethnic groups attending the school. Other ethnographers have argued that ethnic group-based social identities do not have to become polarized, even when actual disparities are present. Metz (1983) studied a magnet middle school with academic disparities between African American and European American students and attributed the uncharacteristically positive intergroup relations, including intergroup mixing in formal and informal school settings and positive intergroup attitudes and dispositions toward intergroup re-

lations, in part to an absence of formal curricular tracking and instruction, and assessment. She concluded that behind these positive intergroup dynamics was a faculty culture that endorsed the school's structural practices and exemplified to the students a belief that all can learn. Peshkin (1991), too, credited school personnel's social culture of interaction across ethnic lines, as well as overt efforts to treat students equally across ethnic groups, toward the positive intergroup relations he observed among students.

Some of the most direct evidence for the role of teachers in the student social culture comes from Fine, Weis, and Powell (1997), who juxtaposed their ethnographic research findings from three distinct, ethnically diverse secondary school settings to demonstrate how school cultures functioned as "desegregated spaces" that both reflected and contributed to intergroup relations. First portrayed was an urban school (Weis) that was rife with intergroup hostility. Weis attributed students' conflict-laden intergroup relations in part to the unwillingness of school personnel to undermine the dominant European American masculine culture. A different school (Powell) evidenced potential for positive intergroup relations but lacked school personnel who overtly undermined intergroup tensions or promoted positive intergroup relations. In a third study of detracked English classes in a school social culture characterized by intergroup tension and avoidance, Fine demonstrated how teachers' instructional practices and perseverance could promote student understanding of race and ethnicity, social class and power, and correspondingly engender more positive intergroup dynamics and relations.

*Summary of Cultural Effects of Schooling*    The extent to which organizational features of schools, such as tracking, create dynamics within schools such as unequal status across groups, and their impact on intergroup relations, appear to be affected by how school personnel and students understand and respond to student race and ethnicity. Findings imply that polarizing social identities in the school social culture, while not originating solely within schools, can be exacerbated and perpetuated both by school practices and by teachers' implementation of those practices. Furthermore, school social climates do not need to evolve in this way, even when ethnic group disparities are present, and when formal structural practices such as tracking are in place. Research that addresses the school cultural context of intergroup relations is nearly exclusively ethnographic in methodology. True to their methods, researchers have not measured the association of dimensions of school social cultures with formally defined peer relations. Large-scale studies focused on social culture indicators could expand and lend generalizability to these findings, as well as begin to address the nesting of classroom social cultures within the larger culture of the school. Furthermore, longitudinal research is noticeably absent, but necessary, to track long-term effects of school social cultures on intergroup relations. School-level social norms that define students by their ethnic group membership cannot be divorced from the student relationships that take shape within the school environment; these norms evolve in response to relationships that students forge (Peshkin, 1991). From an ecological standpoint, this is an area for which there is potential to demonstrate how individuals and their actions shape the environment which, in turn, shapes their development. Studies to date suggest important hypotheses worthy of systematic investigation.

***Classroom-Level Effects*** Few researchers have investigated classroom effects on intergroup relations among adolescents. At the middle and secondary levels of schooling, perhaps this is not surprising, as students cycle in and out of multiple classes with different collections of classmates, different teachers, and correspondingly, vastly different social environments.

*Demographic Factors* Two variables have received attention: racial composition and class size. The limited evidence available suggests that in classrooms of African American and European American students, the greater the proportion of African American students in the class, the more likely the European American students are to nominate an African American friend (Hallinan & Smith, 1985; Hallinan & Teixeira, 1987a, 1987b). In subsequent work, Hallinan and Williams (1987) found that for European American students only, cross-race friend nominations were more stable in classrooms with a greater proportion of African American students. The authors suggest that this finding implies that a greater proportion of African American classmates increases the pool of compatible peers of a different race.

*Classroom Structures and Organization* The majority of studies within this domain have involved instructional use of cooperative learning techniques. Slavin is a scholar prominently associated with this instructional method and its effects on relationships, authoring numerous reviews of the effects of cooperative learning. The most recent (Slavin & Cooper, 1999) is the primary basis for the findings reported here. Since the late 1990s there has been little empirical study of the effects of cooperative learning on intergroup relations.

Slavin has argued that cooperative learning groups approximate Allport's (1954) social contact theory conditions. Groups engage in cooperative activity and have institutional support through teacher endorsement; group members are accorded equal status through distribution of workload and a shared emphasis on all members' successful learning. Ethnic diversity in groups and shared workload further minimizes the extent to which any single ethnic group commands the role of good student.

Studies report that, when conducted under experimental conditions, including implementation that adheres to guidelines for formal cooperative learning practices, African American, Mexican-descent, and European American adolescents who have experienced cooperative learning-based instruction, compared with students in control classrooms who have experienced traditional, teacher-led instruction, nominate more cross-ethnic friends, in some cases at levels that reflect the ethnic diversity of the classroom (Slavin & Cooper, 1999). Cooperative learning experiences also improve students' intergroup acceptance and attitudes (Slavin & Cooper, 1999), and sustain intergroup friendship (Hansell, 1984; Hansell & Slavin, 1981). It is important to note that these effects have been obtained under experimental conditions, and the results may not apply to more informal instructional applications of "small groups" that do not meet the criteria for cooperative learning. Moreover, with only a few exceptions, researchers have utilized classroom-based friendship nomination, which does not reveal the extent to which student behaviors transcend that particular classroom setting. Classrooms in which formal cooperative learning practices are in place may be isolated within a larger context of teacher-led instruction, which may affect students' actions with peers in other classes and in the larger social context.

In a handful of studies, researchers have investigated the relationship between ability grouping and cross-race friend nomination. Similar to the effects of curricular tracking practices, being in the same ability group within a classroom is related to greater cross-ethnic friend nomination, particular with respect to European American students' nomination of an African American friend (Khmelkov & Hallinan, 1999). Evidence also suggests that intergroup relations are strengthened when common group goals and rewards are instituted versus competition among groups (Khmelkov & Hallinan, 1999).

Drawing on tenets of social contact theory and principles of interpersonal attraction, researchers have argued that if teachers deemphasize achievement differentials in classroom, they can alter African American and European American students' appeal to one another as nominated friends (Cohen, Lotan, Scarloss, & Arellano 1999; Hallinan & Teixeira, 1987a; Hallinan & Williams, 1987). For example, European American early adolescents were more likely to nominate African American classmates as friends in classrooms in which instruction placed less emphasis on achievement, as well as mastery of skills and of the curriculum. Among African American students, however, nomination of European American classmates as friends was associated with teachers' greater emphasis on skills and mastery of the curriculum, as well as emphasis on student initiative and enjoyment of the class material (Hallinan & Teixeira, 1987a).

Much of the research available on classroom-level effects on intergroup relations has been conducted using large data sets of classrooms of early adolescents, particularly those in K-8 schooling configurations rather than middle schools and was published in the 1980s. More recent work that reflects contemporary instructional practices (e.g., reform-based practices across academic content areas), and classroom experiences within middle schools, is necessary to more fully understand the role of classroom structure in intergroup relations.

*Conclusions about Schooling Effects on Intergroup Relations* Ethnographers have focused primarily on relationship structure and content with some inferences about relationship qualities among members of different ethnic groups. Such studies, using exploratory methodologies, yield findings that suggest systematic investigation. With few exceptions (e.g., Schofield's findings of cafeteria seating), quantitative research on intergroup relations has focused predominantly on friendship nomination, likely attributable to reliance on large-scale national data sets such as HSB and Add Health. These data sets offer large numbers and diversity of schools and students sampled, and school- and student-level variables measured. However, conclusions that can be drawn about schooling effects on intergroup relations are not necessarily generalizable to relationship structures beyond friendship nomination. Other relationship structures may afford adolescents the experience of a supportive social network. Peer group affiliations can provide affirmation and a sense of belonging within ethnically diverse school contexts (Hamm & Faircloth, 2005). Measures of social acceptance and rejection also can signify from a group (e.g., classroom) perspective how well a child is viewed as fitting in with different racial and ethnic groups (Kistner, Metzler, Gatlin, & Risi, 1993).

One strength of the literature on the effects of schooling on intergroup relations (largely friendship) has been an adherence to theory, primarily to social psychological views. However, theoretical views on intergroup relations have evolved and should be used to guide future work. Large-scale data sets and advanced statistical analytic techniques such as HLM make available the potential to act on such recommendations. Moreover, much of the theoretically driven work to date has focused on structural and organizational dimensions of schools, with less attention to dimensions of school culture. Such variables are not represented in large data sets that afford cross-school comparisons. As we elaborate in subsequent sections, researchers who have studied the school context of non-inter-group relations have found creative ways to apply existing theory in novel ways, and to define school and classroom culture in ways that enables a deeper consideration of students' experiences of the school context in interaction with student characteristics. Much of this work is at the classroom level and for late elementary and middle school participants; recruitment of multiple classrooms may be a less onerous task than recruitment of numerous schools.

## Schooling Context of General Peer Relations

A growing body of literature addresses the schooling context of peer relations in general. Although earlier work on this topic focused on basic aspects of relationship structure (e.g., whether or not teens are friends) and paralleled aspects of quantitative studies of intergroup friendship, researchers have sought recently to explain relationship content (e.g., features and qualities) and processes (e.g., relational dynamics) in relation to the schooling context, though no-

tably, without regard to the racial or ethnic content of the particular relationships under study.

In further parallel to quantitative research on intergroup relations, researchers have historically grounded their work in social psychological tenets of interpersonal attraction. As described in this section, contemporary researchers have incorporated a developmental perspective, conceptualizing peer relations as contexts of children's adjustment, in relation to the study of schooling effects. Additionally, attention to a broad array of school contextual features has advanced, reflecting researchers' application of social psychological theories that consider individuals functioning in groups, and congruence of norms and behavior across individual, group, and larger settings such as classrooms. Similar to research on intergroup relations, schooling effects have been described at school and classroom levels, and within these levels, with respect to structural and cultural features.

### School-Level Effects

*Structural/Organizational* Structural and organizational effects on peer relations in general include some of the same variables as for the intergroup relations literature; curricular tracking, in particular, has received significant attention. Unlike intergroup relations, researchers have focused not only on the structure of relationships (e.g., friendship formation) but also on relational processes (e.g., peer socialization) taking place within relationship structures. Findings regarding relational processes are explained in a subsequent section on mesosystemic analyses.

Students are more likely to nominate a schoolmate as a friend if they attend the same track (e.g., Hallinan & Williams, 1989; Karweit, 1983). Using the HSB data set, Kubitschek and Hallinan (1998) investigated why tracking organizes friendships, drawing on social psychological principles of interpersonal attraction: propinquity, similarity, and status. School size, used as an indicator of propinquity, differentiated how curricular tracking related to friend nominations. Within the largest high schools, track similarity was a significant predictor of friendship nominations likely because tracking pervaded not only the scheduling of the tracked classes but all aspects of the school day (e.g., lunchtime). In contrast, among the smallest schools in the sample (e.g., schools with 100 sophomores), shared curricular track was no more predictive of friendship nominations than was similarity in academic aspirations and academic status. Such findings suggest that school organizational practices not only create opportunities for and constrain friendship nomination through segregating and resegregating students, they affect the operation of dimensions of interpersonal attraction.

Sociologists have argued that while curricular track placement restricts student choice in relationships, participation in extracurricular activities potentially counters tracking effects. Using large-scale data sets including HSB, Karweit (1983) demonstrated that the more extracurricular activities in which students engaged, the more friendships they identified outside their own curricular track. Karweit

(1983) suggested that friendship nominations were extended because extracurricular activity participation reduced status differentials between students across tracks.

*Summary of Structural/Organizational Effects*  As with intergroup friendship, school organizational and structural practices are associated with friendship nominations of adolescents within schools. Researchers have indicated that school structuring creates opportunities for contact, as well as social status of students. These studies are subject to many of the same criticisms identified for studies of intergroup friendship. Specifically, individual characteristics and dyadic similarity have not been accounted for in statistical models. As Moody's (2001) analyses of school structural effects on cross-ethnic friendship nomination revealed, effects attributed to structure can reflect dyadic similarity and personal characteristics related to placement of students within those structures.

*School Culture*  Several researchers have addressed cultural features of schools; unlike intergroup relations these studies are quantitative in nature. Moreover, several of these studies focus not simply on predicting friendship nomination, but on the features and qualities of friendship. These studies are aligned with Epstein's (1983) view that the school culture undergirds the qualities of school-based friendship. Epstein proposed that negative affective qualities of schools, such as discrimination, competition, and low expectations, breed isolation and distrust among students, which infiltrates the quality of friendships and other peer relations. In contrast, when positive affective features of schools, such as equity, opportunities for participation, and high expectations are present, students experience acceptance and support, which promotes positive qualities in their own relationships based in that setting. Epstein examined these propositions in a longitudinal sample of over 4,000 adolescents, grades 5 to 12. Based on opportunities for interaction, decision making, and self-reliance among students, schools were classified as high versus low participatory. Students in the high, compared with low participatory settings developed friendship networks that included students outside their own classes; their networks also had more diverse representation with respect to ethnicity, SES, and achievement.

Epstein's work is unique in its objective measurement of the school culture; recent work in this area has defined school culture by student perceptions. Additionally, the focus has been exclusively on ethnic minority adolescents. In a study of African American early adolescents from a full range of socioeconomic backgrounds, Wong, Eccles, and Sameroff (2003) investigated students' reports of the achievement and effort orientations of their friends in relation to their perceptions of school-based ethnic discrimination. After controlling for numerous seventh-grade background factors, results indicated that eighth graders with stronger self-reported experiences of discrimination from teachers and peers were more likely to report having

friends who devalued school. Results from a study of peer group affiliations lend additional support to a relationship between perceptions of ethnic-based discrimination at school and peer relational content. Latino adolescents who perceived greater levels of school-based ethnic discrimination were both more likely to identify an ethnic-based crowd affiliation for themselves as well as to be identified by peers as belonging to an ethnic-based peer group. Among Asian-descent adolescents, however, greater perceptions of ethnic-based discrimination were associated with a lower likelihood for these youth to be seen by peers as affiliated with an ethnic-based peer group. The authors speculated that the different direction of findings within each ethnic group reflected differences in how ethnic-based crowds functioned for each ethnic group, specifically, that because of the social status of their ethnic group, Latino adolescents used Latino-oriented crowds to buffer against the negative social context of school (Brown et al., 2008). Way and colleagues reported longitudinal findings spanning one to multiple years, of the relationship between the school climate perceptions of urban, poor, ethnic minority teens in a single high school, and their ratings of their friendship quality (ratings of social support from friends). In one study, increases in perceived general friendship support across a single school-year period were predicted by students' overall rating of the school climate at the beginning of the time period (Way & Paul, 2001). Results from a subsequent study of the same students across four consecutive years of high school (Way & Greene, 2006) further suggest a relationship between perceptions of school climate and support perceived from friends. Using HLM growth curve analyses, the authors demonstrated that perceptions of general friendship support increased within individuals across the high school years. Improvements to friendship support ratings across time were predicted by improvements in their ratings of student/teacher relations at their school, suggesting that within-student growth in peer relations occurs in relation to simultaneous changes in perception of school climate. These findings highlight that both overall perceptions of school climate across one's high school career, as well as perceptions at any single time during schooling experiences, can relate to friendship quality.

The legitimacy and value of student perceptions of classrooms and schools has been discussed (e.g., Schunk & Meece, 1992). Individual perceptions of discrimination appear to align with objective ratings in experimentally based research (Ruggiero & Taylor, 1997). However, conclusions about students' perceptions of dimensions of school culture as schooling effects are not possible based on the studies' research designs. Specifically, in none of the studies cited was the extent to which perceptions of school discrimination or other aspects of school culture shared among students within schools evaluated, and, in the studies that involved multiple schools (Brown et al., 2008; Wong et al., 2003), school differences in student perceptions of culture were not addressed. Future researchers must address how student perceptions function as school effects through aggregating perceptions and differentiating between schools based on this aggregation. Recent studies in this area suggest compelling possibilities but research designs limit our ability to interpret these results as schooling effects.

### Classroom-Level Effects

*Structural/Organizational*   Similar to intergroup friendship, older studies investigated several classroom-level structural and organizational factors in relation to friendship nomination. Hallinan (1976) documented an association between instructional practices that promote interaction and less hierarchical status differentials, as well as less mutuality in friendship. Later work documented an association between shared ability group membership and friendship nomination (Hallinan & Sorenson, 1985). Much of the research on this topic was on structural features of classrooms; interpretations of effects involved cultural aspects of classrooms. For instance, "open" versus "traditional" classrooms differ by structural features, but are distinguished further by underlying cultural differences relevant to friendship characteristics (Hallinan, 1976). Research on the classroom context of peer relations over the past decade has moved toward cultural dimensions, and also toward mesosystemic analyses of classroom effects on peer socialization (described in a subsequent section).

*Cultural*   Chang and his colleagues offer new classroom contextual perspectives on peer acceptance within classrooms. Intrigued by significant variability across studies in the strength of relationship between student behaviors and peer acceptance, the results of their studies emphasize the need for researchers to investigate classroom variability in culture as a meaningful context of peer relations rather than downplaying classroom differences through statistical means. Chang (2004) applied social-psychological theories on group behavioral norms to propose that classroom-level means of particular behaviors (signifying classroom behavioral norms), were associated with the relationship between Chinese students' behavior and their peer acceptance within the classroom. Results from HLM indicated that negative relations between aggression and peer acceptance, as well as between withdrawn behavior and peer acceptance, were weakened in classrooms in which these behaviors were normative; the positive relation between prosocial behavior and peer acceptance was strengthened in classrooms in which prosocial behavior was behaviorally normative. Such findings underscore the role of the classroom behavioral context in defining behaviors that lead to acceptance. Chang's (2004) study followed from a recent line of work on classroom behavioral culture; several studies have focused either on peer relations not covered within the scope of this chapter (e.g., peer victimization; Bellmore, Witkow, Graham, & Juvonen, 2004) or on peer relations of elementary school-aged youth (e.g., Barth, Dunlap, Bane, Lochman & Wells, 2004). In resurrecting existing theories of group dynamics and taking advantage of recent statistical advances in nested contexts (students in classrooms in schools), re-

search on the classroom behavioral context represents a new generation of conceptualizations of the classroom context that can be applied to specific peer relations.

In a different study, Chang et al. (2004) investigated, using structural equations modeling, teacher variables that both mediated and moderated the relationship between Chinese early adolescents' behaviors (antisocial and prosocial) and their peer acceptance. Teachers' ratings of their liking of students were predicted to mediate the student behavior–peer acceptance relationship. Results indicated that the relationship between antisocial disruptive behaviors and peer acceptance was moderated in several ways by teacher variables. For instance, peer acceptance was related less significantly to aggression when teacher ratings of students were included in the model. Similar patterns of mediating and moderating effects of teacher variables on the relationship between prosocial behavior and acceptance were evident. A theoretical contribution of this study is a diversification of classroom effects into teacher behavior versus teacher style, derived from and parallel to parent socialization theory (e.g., Darling & Steinberg, 1993), in which the behaviors of individuals (be they students or teachers) within a classroom regarding peer acceptance depend on the broader affective context occasioned by teachers through their responsivity, warmth, and egalitarian treatment of students. Further, this study lends support to a growing body of research on elementary schools, that demonstrates that behaviors associated with peer acceptance are contextually defined (e.g., Meisinger, Blake, & Lease, 2007; Stormshak et al., 1999).

## Beyond the School as a Microsystem of Peer Relations

The research described thus far has conceptualized schools as microsystems of the structure and, to a lesser degree, the content of peer relations. Relations between schooling and peer relationships are treated as unidirectional with a focus on the main effects of schools on peer relations. Researchers are gradually working toward a deeper consideration of schools as a microsystem; that is, exploring student experiences within school structures in terms of relationships, activities, and roles of students and school personnel, and linking structural dimensions to the emergence of cultural dimensions, rather than simply considering how structural features organize students' contact. However, conceptualizing school settings as microsystems of peer relations, scratches only the surface of ecological ways to investigate school–peer relations connections. At a level beyond the microsystem is the mesosystem, which entails interrelations between two or more developmental contexts for their impact on developmental outcomes (Bronfenbrenner, 1979). Two categories of studies are mesosystemic in nature. First are efforts that conceptualize schools and peer relationships (e.g., friendship) as microsystems, and assess features of schools as contexts in which the effects of peer relational processes on adolescent school-based adjustment play out. Second are efforts that extend to nonschool settings as contexts of schooling effects on adolescent peer relations (i.e., schools and community/neighborhood/family are microsystems that operate conjointly to contribute to peer relations).

### School Context of the Effects of Peer Relations on Adolescent Behavior

Recent sociologically based studies have advanced conceptualizations of both the school context and the peer context of adjustment while simultaneously taking advantage of advanced statistical modeling techniques for nested data. This work is mesosystemic in its focus on joint effects of school and peer contexts on adolescent adjustment. The primary aspect of relationships of interest is relational processes (e.g., peer socialization), and schools as a context of these processes in relation to both school structural and cultural dimensions.

Crosnoe and colleagues published three studies, drawing on ecological theory, combining developmental perspectives on friendship and sociological perspectives on schools from a longitudinal standpoint. Crosnoe (2002) investigated school-based tracking as a context of friend socialization of delinquency. In non-college-preparatory tracks, students became more similar to their friends in their level of delinquency; friends' level of delinquency was a positive and significant predictor of students' delinquency a year later. In addition, Crosnoe (2002) compared students' ratings of their orientations toward adults and school/schooling activities across tracks; teens in non-college-bound tracks evidenced less positive feelings toward adults, less favorable orientations toward school, and less inclination to counter friends' expectations. Taken together, the findings suggest that adolescents in non-college-bound tracks were more vulnerable to the negative influences of their friends in relation to their greater disaffection toward schooling processes.

Focusing on adolescents' development of problem behavior, Crosnoe and Needham (2004) investigated the school context of peer influence both through specific friends' characteristics and a holistic friendship network profile. Relationships between friends' and the target student's problem behavior were moderated by the larger school culture; school-level academic press intensified both positive and negative peer socializing effects. Behavioral problems were evident among teens whose friends engaged in problematic behavior, even coincident with positive behavior, when they attended schools with a strong academic press. The authors interpreted this as social redundancy; when friends reinforced the culture through their own behavior, adolescents were buffered against problem behavior. Teens in schools with a stronger academic press, with friends' behavior and group characteristics that were misaligned with the school culture, were at increased risk to evidence behavioral problems.

In a third study, Crosnoe, Cavanaugh, and Elder (2003) combined developmental views of friendship with sociological perspectives of social resources and social capital, to investigate academic adjustment as a function of friend socialization of European American and African American youth in schools that differed by size, socioeconomic composition, and achievement level. Over a year's time, White, but not African American friends' higher achievement and greater school belonging predicted more optimal academic adjustment, indicated by achievement, completion of homework, and grade retention. High achieving friends were less protective for African American youth in large rather than small schools. By investigating institutional and demographic contexts of friendship, it is evident that the extent to which friendship operates as a resource may be context-specific.

One additional sociological study exemplifies a mesosystemic approach. Again, operating at the school level, Cleveland and Wiebe (2003) focused on adolescents' substance use in relation to the intersection of school culture and peer influence, testing if the effects of friends' substance use was conditioned on a school culture of substance use. Findings indicated that the greater the school's drug usage, the stronger the association of friends' usage on individuals' own subsequent usage.

The studies described in this section have investigated school-level contextual effects and expand Epstein's (1983) notion that aspects of school culture not only undergird the quality of relations that form within the school setting, by demonstrating that they also operate as contexts of adjustment. However, classrooms represent a significant proximal context within which to study adjustment (Talbert & McLaughlin, 1999). In a classroom-level mesosystemic approach, McFarland (2001) argued that classroom-based defiance resulted from an intersection of academic content, instructional format and classroom-based social network processes. In a study of 36 mathematics, science, English, and social studies high school classrooms, McFarland demonstrated how at different time points of the year, classrooms characterized by teachers' use of student-centered, compared to teacher-centered instruction, were vulnerable to acts of defiance. Significantly greater acts of defiance were evident among students in networks of higher density in classrooms in which student-centered tasks were in use, whereas in classrooms in which teacher-centered tasks were dominant, the density of the network did not differentiate defiant behavior. These findings suggest that instructional decisions by teachers contribute to social networks and status, and that instruction and peer dynamics together can occasion student misbehavior. In summary, recent studies of school–peer linkages to adolescent adjustment provide theoretically derived empirical evidence that dimensions of school and classroom structure and culture potentiate differential peer socialization effects. A focus of these works has been on peer socialization of problem behavior, which perhaps reflects a history and literature of understanding adolescent problem behavior in relation to peer dynamics as well as a rich sociological theoretical background on which to base studies. Although most of the research available from this approach is based in large-scale survey data sets, McFarland's (2001) study illustrates how this approach can be enacted by the design of studies by individual researchers.

***Nonschool Context Effects on Schooling Effects on Peer Relations***  A different way to conceptualize a mesosystemic relationship is to analyze how schools act in concert with other contexts to shape peer relations. With one exception, the research described in this section is based on ethnographic methodology. Findings highlight the interconnectedness of adolescents' experiences across multiple contexts and counter research on schooling effects that decontextualizes schools from their broader communities, and neglects adolescents' experiences outside the school setting.

Eckert (1989) maintained that social stratifications in high school peer relations have origins in elementary school contexts, and reflect SES socialization differences, as well as early extracurricular activity participation. Children develop different relational dispositions, interests, implicit goals and purposes for their peer relations through experiencing differential activities related to their family socialization. Early on, Eckert (1989) argued, students who became Jocks in high school were socialized by teachers and school personnel to experience greater visibility and status in school than their lower SES peers who became Burnouts in high school. School context was more discernable beginning in middle school/junior high, and operated in full force in high school. Eckert (1989) argued further that Jocks, more so than Burnouts, had been socialized from family, extracurricular, and schooling experiences to endorse and participate in school-based activities. High school teachers and school personnel maintained different relationships with Jocks versus Burnouts, in response to the different school orientations of these groups. Differential treatment and access to participation cemented the polarization of Jocks and Burnouts, and perpetuated group-based reputations. Thus, social segregation and resulting peer affiliations had origins outside the school context, but continued and were perhaps reinforced by structural and cultural forces in the high school (Eckert, 1989; see also Brantlinger, 1993).

Another study was a retrospective historical analysis of the community context of schooling effects on adolescents' intergroup relations. Peshkin (1991) situated the present school structure and culture within a community that had experienced a decade of ethnic-related and school-based rioting, ethnic-related political changes, and extensive European American flight. Peshkin incorporated historical time into his analysis of current schooling effects on intergroup relations in relation to past and evolving community dispositions toward ethnic diversity.

Research on multicontextual correlates of peer relations offers intriguing considerations to understanding schooling effects on social group-based segregation. These ethnographers conclude that the behaviors and dispositions of high school students have developed across previous schooling, neighborhood, family, and community experiences. These studies highlight the potential for schools to perpetuate or intensify nonschooling effects. Studies of nonschool contexts of schooling effects on peer relations suggest that information about feeder schools or neighborhoods bear

consideration. However, microsystemic studies do reveal school practices that offset tendencies toward segregated relationships. For instance, Moody's (2001) findings for extracurricular activity effects on cross-ethnic friendship found school effects above and beyond student and dyadic characteristics effects, which ethnographers have attributed to family and neighborhood socialization. Fine et al. (1997; see also Metz, 1983; Peshkin, 1991) suggested that teachers can dismantle deep-seated student hostilities toward other groups.

One unique quantitative study bears inclusion in this section, though it fits neatly in neither category of mesosystemic studies. Cook, Herman, Phillips, and Settersten (2002) examined how school, family, neighborhood, and peer contexts combined in relation to early adolescent adjustment. Drawing survey and census-tract data from a large-scale, longitudinal study of adolescent development, the researchers created contextual indexes defined by multiattribute qualities: Friend context (e.g., orientations to friends, friends' positive and negative values and behaviors); School context (e.g., parental involvement, academic press, and demographics); Family context (e.g., decision making, monitoring, and parent–child relations); Neighborhood context (e.g., tract-level index of structural and affective qualities and demographics). The authors used advanced statistical modeling techniques to determine how these four contexts conjointly influenced adjustment over a 19-month period of early adolescence. After appropriate statistical controls, only an additive combination of the four contexts together resulted in a significant change in adjustment. No multiplicative effects of any contexts were evident. The work contributes, beyond the specific findings, to conceptualizing, analyzing, and interpreting the joint effects of contexts that include schools and peers, and offers insight into ways to expand mesosystemic research.

Collectively, these studies encourage greater attention both to how schools and peer groups operate together to shape adjustment, and how schools may operate with other contexts to affect peer relations. These examples attempt to understand the dynamic nature of student experiences within the organization and structure of schools; they tend to be longitudinal, spanning at least an academic year of school. Future researchers interested in mesosystemic approaches should draw on and expand to multiple sites and models that incorporate school, neighborhood, and family conjoint influences on adolescent schooling adjustment in general (e.g., Furstenburg, Cook, Eccles, Elder, & Sameroff, 1999). Additionally, widespread access to U.S. Census and GPS data increases researchers' opportunity to consider mesosystemic relations on a scale larger than what is possible with ethnographic work.

***Reconsidering the Nature of Peer Relationships in Ethnically Diverse Schools***  We conclude this section on research findings with comments regarding the future of peer relationships in contemporary American schools. For a period of time, research on schooling effects on intergroup relations and on peer relations in general developed in parallel; both traditions shared a focus on structural aspects of schooling and a social psychological theoretical perspective. These research traditions have diverged over the past decade. Research on the schooling context of peer relations in general has moved toward a stronger and larger-scale focus on school culture and peer relational processes; researchers have taken advantage of new methodological approaches and have introduced novel theoretical approaches to advance this work. In contrast, research on positive cross-ethnic relations has stagnated. A recommendation for researchers interested in intergroup relations is to apply advances from the literature on peer relations generally to inform future study. In particular, research that moves to studying schooling influences on qualities and processes of intergroup relationships is sorely needed.

An early impetus to distinguish intergroup from non-inter-group relations arose from policies that made intergroup relations a novelty in adolescents' school and peer experiences. Intergroup dynamics are a ubiquitous feature of peer ecology of many American adolescents. Although research highlights that intergroup relations in schools do not reflect patterns that would be expected, the majority of teens do report ethnic diversity in their relationships, including friendship networks (e.g., Hamm et al., 2005; Joyner & Kao, 2000; Quillian & Campbell, 2003), even in spite of structural and cultural forces of schools that promote segregation. We question what is served by continuing to study intergroup relations as distinct from peer relations in general, or perhaps more to the point, to analyze peer relations in ethnically diverse schools without attention to the ethnic diversity inherent in the relationships under investigation. Recent studies of the schooling context of peer relations do attend to race/ethnicity as variables in school–peer linkages. Given the ethnic composition of the samples used by contemporary researchers, it is probable that significant proportions of the relationships analyzed were intergroup in nature.

Issues of relationship content and process are no less significant to intergroup relationships than to ethnically homogeneous relationships. Analyses that address, in relation to the schooling context, the quality of socialization processes in homogeneous versus heterogeneous relationships, are essential to understanding how schooling contributes to peer relations, and would be likely to inform our understanding of adjustment outcomes such as academic achievement or ethnic identity. We miss a critical component of peer relationships, as they are experienced by adolescents, if we neglect the experience of ethnic and racial diversity within their relationships.

## Challenging but Promising Conceptual and Methodological Issues

Designing, conducting, and interpreting research on the schooling contexts of peer relations from an ecological perspective is neither simple nor straightforward. The studies reviewed illustrate various ways in which scholars have become increasingly sophisticated in conceptual and methodological approaches. Future directions pose new challenges; we identify and discuss the status of and, where possible, suggest responses to a handful of contemporary challenges that arise in ecological study of the schooling context of peer relations.

***The Complexity of Schools and Peer Relations as Contexts*** Researchers have typically addressed a narrowly focused set of components of schooling, in relation to a single aspect of peer relations. Yet during the school day, adolescents cycle in and out of numerous school microsettings, and simultaneously experience multiple relationship structures. An important step in research is to learn how different levels and dimensions of schools fit together to contribute to multiple types of peer relations. Age segregation, curricular tracking, extracurricular opportunities, and many more social organizations of schooling create numerous microsettings that pervade or coexist with contexts such as classrooms and lunchrooms, all situated within the broader school context with social and cultural dimensions. Adolescents integrate, interpret, and respond to the expectations, values, and opportunities that arise in the diverse contexts, and forge positive relations within and across social contexts. Research suggests ways in which structural and cultural aspects of schools are intertwined; systematic analyses of such possibilities are necessary. Moreover, an understanding of particular levels and dimensions of schools that make the most significant contributions to structural, content, and process features of peer relations is not yet possible. Nor is an understanding of the implications of consistency and inconsistency across settings of the school environment.

Regarding the overlapping nature of contexts within schools, a conceptualization that has been applied primarily to the study of schooling effects on student learning and achievement is that of coherence across policy, structural, and cultural decisions, enacted at the classroom and larger school levels (Newman, Smith, Allensworth, & Bryk, 2001). Schooling effects are intensified when multiple levels and dimensions of the schooling process are aligned toward coherent, or shared goals; they are attenuated when there is incoherence within the schooling process. Schooling effects may be desirable or undesirable, depending on the nature of the shared goals, but the combined effect of within-school processes must be considered. The notion of coherence may be useful in considering the impact of localized settings within the school, such as individual classrooms, that counter the coherence of the larger school setting (e.g., Fine et al., 1997), raising questions such as whether or not adolescents' experiences in such settings compel them to respond differently in the larger school setting. Coherence may also be useful for interpreting why a school like Wexford Middle School (Schofield, 1989), that was developed to promote positive intergroup relations, and had policies and practices in place to accomplish this, fell short of its intended mark on intergroup relations. Dimensions of schools likely vary in their power to challenge the coherence of the larger school setting, be it favorable or not toward desired relationship outcomes.

***Schools and Peer Relations as Nested Data*** A primary issue for researchers is to identify and to focus analyses on appropriate analytic levels with respect both to peer relations and school settings. Once those are defined, addressing the nested nature of students within these various levels is challenging analytically. Due to shared experiences (e.g., attending the same school; affiliation with the same social network), observations about individuals are often not independent. Previous efforts to address the dependence issue have involved disaggregating higher-level variables to the individual-level (e.g., assigning school characteristics to students), which results in incorrect estimation of standard errors. Aggregation of individual-level data to, and analysis at, the higher level results in a loss of within-group information and potentially distorts relations between aggregated variables (Raudenbush & Bryk, 2002). For instance, school-level SES aggregated from students' SES serves as social context, not simply a reflection of student demographics (Alexander, McDill, Febbessey, & D'Amico, 1979; Hamm et al., 2005).

Peer contexts also represent nested data structures, conceptualized at different levels such as group-based and dyadic peer interactions (Gifford-Smith & Brownell, 2003). Regardless of the level under investigation, researchers have typically taken individual participants as the unit of analysis. Peer networks as units of analysis are largely neglected, despite consensus that group and individual dynamics constitute distinctly different effects, and that group-level effects are of particular significance in adolescence (Cairns & Cairns, 1994). Concerns about stability of peer networks and overlapping memberships in groups raise issues for treating peer groups as a level of analysis. Stable group membership is greater over shorter time periods and lower over longer intervals (e.g., Cairns, Leung, Buchanan, & Cairns, 1995), but stability in group orientations is feasible (Kindermann, 1993). Because peer group members evidence a tendency toward similarity, peer group profiles can be formed to represent certain group features (e.g., Farmer et al., 2003; Kindermann, 1993).

Quantitative studies of schooling effects on peer relations require models that provide for the exploration of hierarchical relationships, with partitioning of variance and covariance across levels of data, improved estimation of individual effects, and cross-level effects testing (Raudenbush & Bryk, 2002). A discussion of the benefits and challenges inherent in the use of HLM for research on schooling effects on peer relations is beyond the scope of this chapter. Here we note some measurement issues inherent in the identification of optimal and accurate higher order units for analysis when nested data effects are modeled. A recommendation is to locate objective indicators from sources (e.g., teachers) other than the focal participants in

the study (Duncan & Raudenbush, 1999). This approach is sensible conceptually for research questions related to demographic or structural contexts of schools, or even to cultural indicators that do not involve student culture (e.g., Epstein, 1983). Data are often available from nonstudent sources. A challenge arises when student perceptions are of interest. They can be aggregated at the school or classroom level, but they tend to correlate with participants' self-report behaviors or attitudes, causing disturbance terms to be correlated across predictor variables and outcome variables (Duncan & Raudenbush, 1999). Furthermore, student perceptions may be so diverse that aggregation fails to create a legitimate contextual indicator. A point that must be addressed in future research is the extent to which student perceptions of dimensions of culture are shared to actually reflect a classroom- or school-level effect. Raudenbush, Rowan, & Kang (1991) offer recommendations for making determinations about aggregating data from lower to higher levels of analytic units, using HLM.

Context-based measurement issues also pervade the operationalization of variables in studies of contextual norms. Classroom behavioral norms have been defined as the extent to which group members share a behavior (Chang, 2004), typically calculated as a classroom/group mean (e.g., Bellmore et al., 2004), or as median (e.g., Stormshak et al., 1999) of student behaviors. Class mean (i.e., arithmetic mean) is independent of the actual distribution of the measure of behavior; one large outlier may affect the magnitude of the mean. Class median is not affected by outliers, and is independent of the actual distribution of the behavior, but a large concentration of zero nominations (e.g., when most of students receive no nominations for a behavior) can result in a median of zero, which is meaningless (Chang, 2004). Chang applied a weighted geometric mean to calculate behavioral norms; based on the actual distribution of nominations, a weighting factor was applied that accounted for a large number of zero nominations. However, classroom behavioral norm score often use the same instrument as that used to collect individuals' scores, potentially creating within-classroom linear dependency between the classroom mean and students' scores (Henry et al., 2000). Alternative strategies include constructing context-level measures, for example, students evaluating characteristics of their classroom as a whole (e.g., Henry et al., 2000), or obtaining an independent sample of raters (e.g., teachers) and using their reports as context-level measures (Raudenbush et al., 1991).

***The Impact of School Contexts over Time*** Wachs (1999) outlined additional ways in which time (i.e., the chronosystem) pervades development within contexts such as schools. We highlight two: changes associated with age/schooling transitions, and the accumulation of schooling experiences across multiple years.

*Change Associated with Transitions* Dramatic structural and cultural changes across adolescents' schooling transitions are well known (e.g., Eccles, Midgley, Wigfield, Buchanan et al., 1993). Researchers have also documented how peer relational structures such as friendships, social network affiliations, and social status, are disrupted during school transitions, particularly between elementary and middle school (Hardy, Bukowski, & Sippola, 2002). Farmer et al. (2006) proposed that relational processes within peer groups change following school transitions, becoming more aggressive as adolescents respond to the disruption of their relationships and the increased heterogeneity of their schools. The relationship of school structure and culture to the peer relational structure, content, and process that settles out in this transition, have not been addressed. An important question for future research involves the extent to which school structural and cultural dimensions can help to ease the transition through supporting positive peer relations and positive peer processes.

*Continuous and Cumulative Effects* Adolescents have experienced numerous years of classroom and school contexts when they reach middle and high school, but we know little about the continuing and cumulative influence of prior experiences. Schofield (1979) investigated the effects of a curricular structural change on intergroup cafeteria seating patterns across seventh and eighth grade patterns among students who had experienced a detracked seventh grade versus a tracked seventh grade, finding that a lingering effect of the tracking experience could be detected in the subsequent year. This is an area with rich potential for investigation given the limited attention it has received thus far and published models are now available for analyzing cumulative schooling effects. Research on student achievement points to the significance of cumulative schooling effects: where there is continuity, schooling effects can be intensified. Furthermore, the impact of continuity presents a significant challenge to be overcome by any single, discontinuous contextual effect (e.g., Smith, Jussim, & Eccles, 1999). Wachs (1999) asserted that while the strongest contextual impact occurs when setting aspects are repeated over time, environmental stability is not desirable if it undermines positive peer relations. Limited models for multiyear effects are available in research on elementary schools or nonpeer relational outcomes. For instance, long-term impact of past contexts were found in a study of the influence of first grade classroom aggression on changes in children's behavior in sixth grade (Kellam et al., 1998). Schools and teachers were randomly assigned to intervention/control conditions; children were assigned to classrooms alphabetically. Analysis of the control group revealed that children rated as aggressive in first grade and in highly aggressive classrooms, were more likely to be severely aggressive in middle school, compared with less aggressive children in highly aggressive classrooms, or children rated as individually aggressive but in low aggression classrooms. However, no evidence was found for the contribution of cumulative schooling effects (classroom- or school-level) by Barth et al. (2004). Thus, concurrent influence of fifth grade classroom

norms on the change in individual peer relations was significant, but the fourth grade classroom environment did not have long-lasting impact on fifth grade individual behaviors. The discrepant findings may be attributable to the 1- versus 6-year window between the two studies; this disparity raises an important issue with inclusion and omission of classrooms over time. In Kellam et al. (1998), cumulative effects of being aggressive may have been confounded with classroom environments, exacerbating the risk of being severely aggressive. Because the children were reassigned to classrooms after second grade, those who displayed a high level of aggression in the first 2 years might have been placed to the same classroom; a high concentration of aggressive children in a classroom may have reinforced their aggressive behavior in later grades. Such circumstances make it difficult to disentangle the effects of the first grade classroom environment, later-grade classroom environment and individual characteristics. Researchers focused on the adolescent context stand to learn from these studies, both from the approaches that assess continuity and change in accumulated schooling experiences relevant to peer relations, and from the limitations that might be addressed through improved designs and measures.

*Changing Individuals in Changing Contexts* An additional temporal issue involves individual growth in peer relational experiences over time, with respect to changes in individuals and contexts. With the use of growth curve modeling, it becomes possible to investigate changes in student and school characteristics in relation to changes in adolescents' peer relations across time. Beyond this level of analysis, interindividual differences can be assessed to reveal heterogeneity in change across individuals and to investigate relationships between individual and contextual predictors, and each person's individual trajectory (Singer & Willett, 2003). Growth curve analyses of this type work well even when the number of higher-level units (e.g., classrooms or social networks) is small, so long as the data are relatively balanced across higher-level units (Raudenbush & Bryk, 2002). Growth curve analysis affords study of outcomes that monotonically increase or decrease over time, or more complex trajectories, such as plateaus or reversals (Singer & Willet, 2003). In our review of research linking school contexts and peer relations, we could not locate any studies that involved multiple school or classroom contexts, and changes in students over time in relation to their changing school context.

A final issue to consider under this section involves conceptualizing the nature of the relationship between schools and peer contexts. The focus of this chapter, reflecting the primary focus of research, has been that schools influence adolescents' peer relations. However, from an ecological standpoint, students' behavior and their peer relations also affect the school context; thus, there is likely a bidirectional influence between schools and peer relations. Researchers have paid little attention to how schools react and respond to changes brought by students' relationship structures, content, and processes. Longitudinal ethnographic research suggests that school social climates evolve, and that student peer relations contribute to those changes (e.g., Peshkin, 1991; Schofield, 1989). Most existing studies regard schooling effects as static and use mean values of school effect variables (e.g., averaged over time or at a single point in time) to represent context-level factors. We could not locate studies that inform selection of analytic models best suited to capturing the reciprocal relationship between school effects and peer relations, while also accounting for nested data structures.

## Conclusions

It is well-documented that peer relations are foundational to adolescent adjustment. The literature reviewed in this chapter demonstrates that features of the schooling context are foundational to the peer relations that develop within school settings. An ecological framework facilitates the integration of research on the schooling context of peer relations across diverse disciplines and theoretical perspectives, and reveals new directions to explore these richly intertwined contexts more fully, for the role they play in adolescent development.

## References

Alexander, K. L., McDill, E. L., Febbessey, J., & D'Amico, R. J. (1979). School SES influences: Composition or context? *Sociology of Education, 52,* 222–237.

Allport, G. W. (1954). *The nature of prejudice.* Reading, MA: Addison-Wesley.

Barth, J. M., Dunlap, S. T., Dane, H., Lochman, J. E., & Wells, K. C. (2004). Classroom environment influences on aggression, peer relations, and academic focus. *Journal of School Psychology, 42,* 115–133.

Bellmore, A. D., Witkow, M., Graham, S., & Juvonen, J. (2004). Beyond the individual: The impact of ethnic context and classroom behavioral norms on victims' adjustment. *Journal of Educational Psychology, 40,* 1159–1172.

Brantlinger, E. A. (1993). *The politics of social class in secondary school.* New York: Teachers College Press.

Bronfenbrenner, U. (1979). *The ecology of human development: Experiments by nature and design.* Cambridge, MA: Harvard University Press.

Brown, B. B. (1999). Measuring the peer environment of American adolescents. In S. Friedman & T. Wachs (Eds.), *Measuring environment across the lifespan* (pp. 59–90). Washington DC: American Psychological Association.

Brown, B. B., Herman, M., Hamm, J. V., & Heck, D. J. (2008). Ethnicity and image: Correlates of crowd affiliation among ethnic minority youth. *Child Development, 79,* 529–546.

Cairns R. B., & Cairns, B. D., (1994). *Lifelines and risks: Pathways of youth in our time.* Cambridge, England: Cambridge University Press.

Cairns, R. B., Leung, M-C., Buchanan, L. D., & Bairns, B. D. (1995). Friendships and social networks in childhood and adolescence: Fluidity, reliability, and interrelations. *Child Development, 66,* 1330–1345.

Chang, L. (2004). The role of classroom norms in contextualizing the relations of children's social behaviors to peer acceptance. *Developmental Psychology, 40,* 691–702.

Chang, L., Liu, H. Y., Wen, Z. L., Fung, K. Y., Wang, Y., & Xu, Y. Y. (2004). Mediating teacher liking and moderating authoritative teaching on Chinese adolescents' perceptions of antisocial and prosocial behaviors. *Journal of Educational Psychology, 96,* 369–380.

Cleveland, H. H., & Wiebe, R. P. (2003). The moderation of adolescent-

to-peer similarity in tobacco use by school levels of substance use. *Child Development, 74,* 279–291.

Cohen, E., Lotan, R., Scarloss, B. A., Arellano, A. (1999). Complex instruction: Equity in cooperative learning classrooms. *Theory into Practice, 38,* 80–86.

Collins, W. A. & Laursen, B. (1999). *Relationships as developmental contexts.* Mahwah, NJ: Erlbaum.

Cook, T. D., Herman, M., Phillips, M., & Settersten, M., Jr. (2002). Some ways in which neighborhoods, nuclear families, friendship groups, and schools jointly affect changes in early adolescent development. *Child Development, 73,* 1283–1309.

Crosnoe, R. (2002). High school curriculum track and adolescent association with delinquent friends. *Journal of Adolescent Research, 17,* 143–167.

Crosnoe, R., Cavanaugh, S., & Elder, G. (2003). Adolescent friendships as academic resources: The intersection of friendship, race, and school disadvantage. *Sociological Perspectives, 46,* 331–352.

Crosnoe, R., & Needham, B. (2004). Holism, contextual variability, and the study of friendships in adolescent development. *Child Development, 75,* 264–279.

Darling, N. (2005). Participation in extracurricular activities and adolescent adjustment: Cross-sectional and longitudinal findings. *Journal of Youth & Adolescence, 34,* 493–505.

Darling, N., & Steinberg, L. (1993). Parenting style as context: An integrative model. *Psychological Bulletin, 113*(3), 487–496.

Dehyle, D. (1986). Break dancing and breaking out: Anglos, Utes and Navajos in a border reservation high school. *Anthropology and Education Quarterly, 17,* 111–127.

Duncan, G. J., & Raudenbush, S. W. (1999). Assessing the effects of context in studies of child and youth development. *Educational Psychologist, 34,* 29–41.

Eccles, J., Midgely, C., Wigfield, A., Buchanan, C. M., Reuman, D., Flanagan, C., et al. (1993). Development during adolescence: The impact of stage–environment fit on young adolescents' experiences in schools and families. *American Psychologist, 48,* 90–101.

Eckert, P. (1989). *Jocks and burnouts: Social categories and identity in the high school.* New York: Teachers College Press.

Epstein, J. L. (1983). Selection of friends in differently organized schools and classrooms. In J. L. Epstein & N. Karweit (Eds.), *Friends in school* (pp. 167–182). New York: Academic Press.

Epstein, J. (1985). After the bus arrives: Resegregation in desegregated schools. *Journal of Social Issues, 41,* 23–43.

Epstein, J. L., & Karweit, N. (1983). *Friends in school.* New York: Academic Press.

Farmer, T. W., Estell, D. B., Leung, M., Trott, H., Bishop, J., & Cairns, B. D. (2003). Individual characteristics, early adolescent peer affiliations, and school dropout: An examination of aggressive and popular and group types. *Journal of School Psychology, 41,* 217–232.

Farmer, T. W., Irvin, M. J., Thompson, J. H., Hutchins, B. C., & Leung, M.-C. (2006). School adjustment and the academic success of rural African American early adolescents in the Deep South. *Journal of Research in Rural Education, 21,* 1–14.

Fine, M., Weis, L. M., & Powell, L. (1997). Communities of difference: A critical look at desegregated spaces created for and by youth. *Harvard Educational Review, 67,* 247–284.

Furman, W., Brown, B. B., & Feiring, C. (1999). *The development of romantic relations in adolescence.* New York: Cambridge University Press.

Furstenburg, F. F., Cook, T. D., Eccles, J., Elder, G. H., & Sameroff, A. (1999). *Managing to make it.* Chicago, IL: University of Chicago Press.

Gifford-Smith, M. E., & Brownell, C. A. (2003). Childhood peer relationships: Social acceptance, friendships, and peer networks. *Journal of School Psychology, 41,* 235–284.

Hallinan, M. T. (1976). Friendship patterns in open and traditional classrooms. *Sociology of Education, 49,* 254–265.

Hallinan, M. T., & Smith, S. S. (1985). The effects of classroom racial composition on students' interracial friendliness. *Social Psychology Quarterly, 48,* 3–16.

Hallinan, M. T., & Sorensen, A. B. (1985). Ability grouping and student friendships. *American Educational Research Journal, 22*, 485–499.

Hallinan, M. T., & Teixeira, R. A. (1987a). Opportunities and constraints: Black–white differences in the formation of interracial friendships. *Child Development, 58*, 1358–1371.

Hallinan, M. T. & Teixeira, R. A. (1987b). Students' interracial friendships: Individual characteristics, structural effects, and racial differences. *American Journal of Education, 95*, 563–583.

Hallinan, M. T., & Williams, R. A. (1987). The stability of students' interracial friendships. *American Sociological Review, 52*, 653–664.

Hallinan, M., & Williams, R. (1989). Interracial friendship choice in secondary schools. *American Sociological Review, 54*, 67–78.

Hamm, J. V. (1998). Negotiating the maze: Adolescents' cross-ethnic peer relations in ethnically diverse schools. In L. H. Meyer, H. S. Park, M. Grenot-Schuyer, I. S. Schwartz, & B. Harry (Eds.), *Making friends: The influences of culture and development* (pp. 225–242). Baltimore, MD: Brookes.

Hamm, J. V., Brown, B. B., & Heck, D. J. (2005). Bridging the ethnic divide: Student and school characteristics in African American, Asian-descent, Latino, and White adolescents' cross-ethnic friend nominations. *Journal of Research on Adolescence, 15*, 21–46.

Hamm, J. V., & Faircloth, B. S. (2005). Peer context of mathematics classroom belonging in early adolescence. *Journal of Early Adolescence, 25*, 345–366.

Hansell, S. (1984). Cooperative groups, weak ties, and the integration of peer friendships. *Social Psychology Quarterly, 47*, 316–328.

Hansell, S., & Slavin, R. E. (1981). Cooperative learning and the structure of interracial friendships. *Sociology of Education, 54*, 98–106.

Hardy, C. L., Bukowski, W. M., & Sippola, L. K. (2002). Stability and change in peer relationships during the transition to middle-level school. *Journal of Early Adolescence, 22*, 117–142.

Henry, D., & Guerra, N. (2000). Normative influences on aggression in urban elementary school classrooms. *American Journal of Community Psychology*, 59–82.

Joyner, K., & Kao, G. (2000). School racial composition and adolescent racial homophily. *Social Science Quarterly, 81*, 810–825.

Karweit, N. (1983). Extracurricular activities and friendship selection. In J. L. Epstein & N. Karweit (Eds.), *Friends in school* (pp. 206–228). New York: Academic Press.

Kellam, S. G., Ling, X., Mersica, R., Brown, C. H., & Ialongo, N. (1998). The effect of the level of aggression in the first grade classroom on the course and malleability of aggressive behavior into middle school. *Development and Psychopathology, 10*, 165–185.

Khmelkov, V. & Hallinan, M. T. (1999). Organizational effects on race relations in schools. *Journal of Social Issues, 55*, 627–645.

Kindermann, T. (1993). Natural peer groups as contexts for individual development: The case of children's motivation in school. *Developmental Psychology, 29*, 970–977.

Kistner, J., Metzler, A., Gatlin, D., & Risi, S. (1993). Classroom racial proportions and children's peer relations: Race and gender effects. *Journal of Educational Psychology, 85*, 446–452.

Kubitschek, W., & Hallinan, M. (1998). Tracking and student's friendships. *Social Psychology Quarterly, 61*, 1–15.

Ladd, G. W., Kochenderfer, B. J., & Coleman, C. C. (1997). Classroom peer acceptance, friendship, and victimization: Distinct relational systems that contribute uniquely to children's school adjustment. *Child Development, 68*, 1181–1197.

Lee, A. E., Jussim, L., & Eccles, J. (1999). Do self-fulfilling prophecies accumulate, dissipate, or remain stable over time? *Journal of Social and Personality Psychology, 77*, 548–565.

Lee, S. J. (1996). *Unraveling the "model minority" stereotype.* New York: Teachers College Press.

McFarland, D. (2001). Student resistance: How the formal and informal organization of classrooms facilitate everyday forms of student defiance. *American Journal of Sociology, 107*, 612–678.

Mahoney, J., Larson, R., Eccles, J., & Lord, H. (2005). Organized activities as developmental contexts for children and adolescents. In J. Mahoney, R. Larson, & J. Eccles (Eds.), *Organized activities as contexts of development* (pp. 3–22). Mahwah, NJ: LEA.

Meisinger, E. B., Blake, J. J, & Lease, A. M. (2007). Variant and invariant predictors of popularity across majority Black and majority White classrooms. *Journal of School Psychology, 45*, 21–44.

Metz, M. H. (1983). Sources of constructive social relationships in an urban magnet school. *American Journal of Education, 91*, 203–241.

Moody, J. (2001). Race, school integration, and friendship segregation in America. *American Journal of Sociology, 107*, 679–716.

Newmann, F. M., Smith, B., Allensworth, E., & Bryk, A. S. (2001). Instructional program coherence: What it is and why it should guide school improvement policy. *Educational Evaluation and Policy Analysis, 23*, 297–321.

Oakes, J. (2005). *Keeping track: How schools structure inequality* (2nd ed.). New Haven, CT: Yale University Press.

Ogbu, J. U. (1988). Black education: A cultural–ecological perspective. In H. P. MccAdoo (Ed.), *Black families.* Thousand Oaks, CA: Sage.

Patchen, M. (1982). *Black–White contact in schools: Its social and academic effects.* West Lafayette, IN: Purdue University Press.

Peshkin, A. (1991). *The color of strangers, the color of friends.* Chicago, IL: University of Chicago Press.

Pettigrew, T. (1975). Power, racism, and privilege—Race-relations in theoretical and sociohistorical perspectives. *Social Forces, 54*, 291–292.

Pettigrew, T. (1998). Intergroup contact theory. *Annual Review of Psychology, 49*, 65–85.

Quillian, L., & Campbell, M. E. (2003). Beyond black and white: The present and future of multiracial friendship segregation. *American Sociological Review, 68*, 540–566.

Quiroz, P., Flores-Gonzales, N. F., & Frank, K. (1996). Carving a niche in the high school social structure: Formal and informal constraints on participation in the extracurriculum. *Research in Sociology of Education and Socialization, 11*, 93–120.

Raudenbush, A. S., & Bryk, S. W. (2002). *Hierarchical linear models: Application and data analysis methods.* Thousand Oaks, CA: Sage.

Raudenbush, S. W., Rowan, B., & Kang, S. J. (1991). A multilevel, multivariate model for studying school climate in secondary schools with estimation via the EM algorithm. *Journal of Educational Statistics, 16*, 295–330.

Raudenbush, S. W., & Sampson, R. (1999). Assessing direct and indirect effects in multilevel designs with latent variables. *Sociological Methods and Research, 28*, 123–153.

Ruggiero, K. M. & Taylor, D. M. (1997). Why minority group members perceive or do not perceive the discrimination that confronts them. *Journal of Personality and Social Psychology, 72*, 373–392.

Schofield, J. W. & Sagar, H. A. (1977). Peer interaction patterns in an integrated middle school. *Sociometry, 40*, 130–138.

Schofield, J. W. (1979). The impact of positively structured contact on intergroup behavior: Does it last under adverse conditions? *Social Psychology Quarterly, 42*, 280–284.

Schofield, J. W. (1981). Complementary and conflicting identities: Images and interaction in an interracial school. In S. R. Asher & J. M. Gottman (Eds.), *The development of children's friendships* (pp. 53–90). New York: Cambridge University Press.

Schofield, J. W. (1989). *Black and white in school: Trust, tension, or tolerance?* New York: Teachers College Press.

Schofield, J. W. (1991). School desegregation and intergroup relations: A review of the literature. *Review of Research in Education, 17*, 335–419.

Schunk, D. & Meece, J. L. (1992). *Student perceptions in the classroom.* Hillsdale, NJ: LEA.

Shrum, W., Cheek, N. R., & Hunter, S. M. (1988). Friendship in school: Gender and racial homophily. *Sociology of Education, 61*, 227–239.

Singer, J. D., & Willett, J. B. (2003). *Applied longitudinal data analysis: Modeling change and event occurrence.* New York: Oxford University Press.

Slavin, R. E., & Cooper, R. (1999). Improving intergroup relations: Lessons learned from cooperative learning programs. *Journal of Social Issues, 55*, 647–663.

Slavin, R. E., & Madden, N. A. (1979). School practices that improve race relations. *American Educational Research Journal, 16*, 169–180.

Smith, A. E., Jussim, L., & Eccles, J. (1999). Do self-fulfilling prophecies accumulate, dissipate, or remain stable over time? *Journal of Personality and Social Psychology, 77,* 548–565.

Stormshak, E. A., Bierman, K. L., Bruschi, C., Dodge, K. A., Coie, J., & the Conduct Problems Prevention Research Group. (1999). The relation between behavior problems and peer preference in different classroom contexts. *Child Development, 70,* 169–182.

Talbert, J. E., & McLaughlin, M. W. (1999). Assessing the school environment: Embedded contexts and bottom-up research strategies. In S. Friedman & T. Wachs (Eds.), *Measuring environment across the lifespan* (pp. 197–227). Washington, DC: APA.

Wachs, T. D. (1999). Celebrating complexity: Conceptualization and assessment of the environment. In S. Friedman & T. Wachs (Eds.), *Measuring environment across the lifespan* (pp. 197–227). Washington, DC: APA.

Way, N., & Greene, M. (2006). Trajectories of perceived friendship quality during adolescence: The patterns and contextual predictors. *Journal of Research on Adolescence, 16,* 293–320.

Way, N., & Paul, K. (2001). Individual and contextual predictors of perceived friendship quality among ethnic minority, low-income adolescents. *Journal of Research on Adolescence, 11,* 325–349.

Wentzel, K. R., & Caldwell, K. (1997). Friendships, peer acceptance, and group membership: Relations to academic achievement in middle school. *Child Development, 68,* 1198–1209.

Willett, J. B., Singer, J. D., & Martin, N. C. (1998). The design and analysis of longitudinal studies of development and psychopathology in context: Statistical models and methodological recommendations. *Development and Psychopathology, 10,* 395–426.

Wong, C. A., Eccles, J. S., & Sameroff, A. (2003). The influence of ethnic discrimination and ethnic identification on African American adolescents' school and socioemotional adjustment. *Journal of Personality, 71,* 1197–1232.

# 10

# Individual and Contextual Influences on Bullying

*Perpetration and Victimization*

Dorothy L. Espelage, Melissa K. Holt, and V. Paul Poteat

Bullying is recognized as one of the major problems facing schools today, as evidenced by the documented deleterious effects it has on the psychological and social functioning and academic performance of students and its broader negative effects on the overall climate of schools (Hodges & Perry, 1999; Kasen, Berenson, Cohen, & Johnson, 2004; Schwartz, Gorman, Nakamoto, & Toblin, 2005). The seriousness and difficulty of this problem is further indicated by the absence of data showing any overall decrease in bullying since researchers first began studying this behavior within schools. However, research has provided a more critical understanding of this behavior. Specifically, this research has included a better characterization of individuals who are bullies, victims, and individuals who adopt other roles in bullying episodes, the identification of immediate and long-term effects associated with bullying involvement, the identification of individual and social factors that contribute to the development and perpetuation of this behavior, documentation of where and when bullying behavior is more likely to occur, and more recently, the identification of longitudinal developmental trajectories of bullies and victims that have assisted in better predicting the progression of bullying behavior and victimization for certain groups of individuals.

In this chapter, we provide a general overview and discussion of the current bullying literature, and highlight the current state of research within this area of study. We begin with a general definition of bullying and also specify various forms of bullying that have been identified and studied in research. We then elaborate on the various factors that have been found to be associated with bullying and victimization. From this, we provide further characterization of individuals identified as bullies and victims. We also include information on bully-victims, or individuals who report bullying other students and also being bullied themselves. After providing information on bullying from an individual perspective, we broaden our discussion of bullying to incorporate several social environments that have more recently been studied in relation to bullying, including the family, peer, and school context. We also include an overview of some emerging longitudinal research, including research examining bullying over the transition from elementary school to middle school. Finally, we review several bullying prevention and intervention models and programming that have been used in schools.

## Defining and Assessing Bullying Behavior

Dan Olweus was one of the first scholars to systematically research bullying, which began when he spearheaded a multination Scandinavian campaign against bullying in the 1970s. Olweus proposed the following definition of bullying, which remains current today: "A student is being bullied or victimized when he or she is exposed, repeatedly and over time, to negative actions on the part of one or more students" (Olweus, 1993b, p. 3). The preceding definition highlights (a) the aggressive component of bullying, (b) the associated inherent power imbalance, and (c) its repetitive nature. It is also important to distinguish bullying from other more extreme forms of maladaptive and deviant behavior, such as conduct disorder or oppositional defiant disorder (American Psychiatric Association, 2000). Although a significant level of aggression is often displayed by individuals diagnosed with these conditions, the prevalence rate of individuals meeting classification criteria for these categories is significantly less than individuals typically identified as bullies. In addition, significant distinctions exist in developmental trajectories, prognoses, and outcomes for individuals identified as bullies and individuals classified in these more extreme categories.

In recent years scholars have recognized the wide range of behaviors consistent with bullying, including physical, verbal, and relational manifestations (Coie & Dodge, 1998; Crick, 1996; Crick & Bigbee, 1998; Ladd & Burgess, 2001;

Smith & Sharp, 1994; Swearer & Doll, 2001). Physical bullying consists of overt physical acts directed toward peers, such as hitting or shoving. Verbal bullying includes behaviors such as calling someone else names or making derogatory remarks about someone else. Actions designed to damage or manipulate relationships, such as spreading rumors or excluding an individual from group activities, are considered to be forms of relational bullying. Finally, bullying research has also begun to examine Internet-based and electronically related forms of bullying (Raskauskas & Stoltz, 2007; Ybarra, Alexander, & Mitchell, 2005). These studies have explored how some children and adolescents have started to use personal WebPages, e-mail, text-messaging, and other electronic forms of communication to post threats, rumors, or embarrassing pictures of an individual as a way in which to bully the targeted person. Preliminary findings suggest this to increasingly be an outlet used for bullying, and one that poses more complex and difficult challenges for researchers and school administrators.

*Assessment of Bullying* A variety of methodologies have been used by researchers to assess bullying and identify bullies, victims, and other individuals involved during bullying episodes. These methods include the use of self-report to document levels of bullying and victimization (e.g., Espelage & Holt, 2001), self- and peer-nominations of bullies and victims by participating students (e.g., Kochenderfer & Ladd, 1996; Rodkin, Farmer, Pearl, & Van Acker, 2000; Xie, Cairns, & Cairns, 1999), observational documentation of bullying and victimization by researchers (e.g., Pepler & Craig, 1995), and laboratory and experimental examination of bullying among dyads and groups of students (e.g., Dodge, Coie, Pettit, & Price, 1990; Hubbard, Dodge, Cillessen, Coie, & Schwartz, 2001). Self-reported levels of bullying and victimization have been assessed through various empirically validated scales, and can be helpful in examining the frequency of bullying and victimization along a continuum. Nomination methods reflect a sociometric approach to assessing bullying behavior, and have generally been found to converge with self-report data, where individuals self-reporting higher levels of bullying and victimization also receive a higher number of peer-nominations for being a bully or victim, respectively (Espelage & Holt, 2001). At the same time, research has documented that differences between peer-nominated and self-reported victimization can reflect different psychological and social adjustment issues faced by these students (Graham, Bellmore, & Juvonen, 2003). Observational methods have included naturalistic observations with researchers physically present to document the behavior as it occurs, and also more technologically advanced observational methods through the use of video recordings. Laboratory and experimental methods have allowed researchers greater control over the social environment, and usually involve observation within a laboratory setting, where children are brought in to interact with one another for a specified amount of time or to complete a particular activity given to them by the researchers.

The use of a multimethod approach to studying bullying has enabled researchers to test the convergence, agreement, and forms of validity of each method, and to address unique limitations in the use of each method.

*Prevalence of Bullying* Current estimates suggest that nearly 30% of American students are involved in bullying (Nansel et al., 2001). Specifically, findings from this nationally representative sample indicated that among 6th to 10th graders, 13% had bullied others, 11% had been bullied, and 6% had both bullied others and been bullied. Other smaller-scale studies within the United States and abroad have also reported similar findings. For example, Boulton and Smith (1994) found that approximately 13% of British students were nominated by their peers as bullies. Similarly, in the United States, Espelage and Holt (2001) classified 15% of students as bullies based on self-report data. When examining the entirety of students' experiences at school, a majority of students have reported experiencing victimization, ranging from 58% (Eslea & Rees, 2001) through 77% (Hoover, Oliver, & Hazler, 1992). Bullying prevalence rates vary based on a number of factors, however, including the type of bullying under consideration and the sex and age of youth. For instance, verbal bullying is much more common than physical bullying (Benbenishty & Astor, 2005), with one study finding that verbal aggression was twice as frequent as physical aggression among children aged 7 to 11 (Tapper & Boulton, 2005). Boys are also more often identified in studies as both bullies and as victims (Espelage & Holt, 2001; Kumpulainen, Rasanen, & Henttonen, 1998), although other studies have identified girls as experiencing more frequent forms of relational aggression and victimization than boys (Crick, 1996). With respect to age trends, bullying tends to decrease from childhood through adolescence (Nansel et al., 2001) although research is somewhat mixed in this regard; some studies have found high rates of bullying around the beginning of high school (Pelligrini & Long, 2002; Pepler, Craig, Connolly et al., 2005). In this sense, research suggests that the frequency with which students engage in bullying behavior does not follow a strictly linear path (i.e., progressively increasing or decreasing); rather, the increase and decrease in bullying can correspond with particular experiences or major social changes, such as the transition from elementary to middle school, or middle school to high school. This latter finding is particularly relevant. It suggests that the school context may play an important role in eliciting or supporting bullying behavior.

Bullying occurs along a continuum, with students assuming roles including bully, victim, bully-victim, and bystander (Espelage, Bosworth, & Simon, 2000; Unnever, 2005). Bullies are characterized as perpetrators of aggression but those who do not experience significant victimization by peers. Conversely, victims are often targets of aggression by peers but are not frequent perpetrators of aggressive acts. Bully-victims are youth who are both perpetrators of and are victimized by high levels of bullying behavior, and may react aggressively to victimization (and therefore are at times labeled "provocative victims"). Finally, it is important to consider the experiences of bystanders as well, students who do not participate actively in bullying episodes but whose involvement (e.g., through supporting the bully) nonetheless influences bullying dynamics (Salmivalli, Lagerspetz, Björkqvist, Osterman, & Kaukianinen, 1996). Examining bullying and victimization along a continuum and from a social framework has enabled researchers to expand beyond the more basic and limited dyadic labeling of students as either bullies or victims, and to better capture the multiple roles of individuals during bullying episodes and the experiences of different types of victims.

## Correlates of Bullying Involvement

Victims, bullies, and bully-victims often report adverse psychological effects and poor school adjustment as a result of their involvement in bullying (Juvonen, Nishina, & Graham, 2000; Nansel, Haynie, & Simons-Morton, 2003). For example, targets of bullying reveal more loneliness, greater school avoidance, more suicidal ideation, and less self-esteem than their nonbullied peers (Hawker & Boulton, 2000; Kochenderfer & Ladd, 1996; Olweus, 1992; Rigby, 2001). Depression also has been found to be a common mental health symptom experienced by male and female victims of bullying (Kaltiala-Heino, Rimpelae, & Rantanen, 2000; Neary & Joseph, 1994). Further, being victimized is associated with physical health problems, such as headaches and stomachaches (Srabstein, McCarter, Shao, & Huang, 2006). Victims are also often characterized as more insecure, anxious, and quiet than their peers (Olweus, 1995a). Victimization and academic performance have also received increased attention. Victimized children receive lower grades than individuals not identified as bullies or victims (Graham, Bellmore, & Mize, 2006), and frequent victimization by students has been shown to predict poor academic performance over time (Schwartz et al., 2005). The effects of bullying victimization are not necessarily transitory in nature. As discussed by Olweus (1995b), results from his longitudinal work indicate that at age 23, individuals who had been chronically victimized in their youth had lower self-esteem and were more depressed than nonvictimized members of their cohort.

Whereas victims tend to report more internalizing behaviors (e.g., depression), bullies are more likely than their peers to engage in externalizing behaviors such as experiencing conduct problems, to report lower levels of school belonging, and to engage in delinquent behavior (Espelage & Holt, 2001; Haynie, Nansel, & Eitel, 2001; Nansel et al., 2001). As is the case with victims of bullying, perpetrators of bullying are more likely than uninvolved youth to experience physical health problems (Srabstein et al., 2006). Also, long-term outcomes for bullies can be serious; compared to their peers, bullies are more likely to be convicted of crimes in adulthood (Olweus, 1993a). One study conducted in the United States revealed that youth

identified as bullies in school had a 1 in 4 chance of having a criminal record by age 30 (Eron, Huesmann, Dubow, Romanoff, & Yarnel, 1987).

Finally, considerable research has documented that the most at-risk group of youth is bully-victims. For instance, bully-victims demonstrate more externalizing behaviors, are more hyperactive, and have a greater probability of being referred for psychiatric consultation than their peers (Kumpulainean et al., 1998; Nansel, Haynie, et al., 2003; Nansel, Overpeck et al., 2001). Bully-victims have also been found to report higher levels of depression compared to both bullies and victims (Austin & Joseph, 1996; Swearer, Song, Cary, Eagle, & Mickelson, 2001). Similarly, bully-victims have been found to have lower grades than both bullies and victims and were reported by teachers to be the least engaged of their students (Graham et al., 2006).

## Individual and Contextual Influences on Bullying Involvement

As set forth by Bronfenbrenner's classic ecological theory (Bronfenbrenner, 1979), there is a complex interplay between the individual and the multiple environments in which she or he is embedded. This theoretical framework has been applied to the conceptualization of bullying perpetration and victimization (Espelage & Swearer, 2003; Garbarino & DeLara, 2002; Swearer & Doll, 2001). In particular, in recent years there has been an increasing recognition that to understand and to prevent bullying it is necessary to consider how both individual and contextual factors (e.g., characteristics of families, schools, peer groups, and communities) exert influence on youth bullying involvement. Some of the research findings to date in both of those domains are discussed below.

*Individual Characteristics*   Differences in the rates of victimization have been identified based on several individual demographic characteristics, including sex, race, and age. With respect to sex, boys are more often victimized than girls (Espelage & Holt, 2001; Kumpulainen et al., 1998), although this depends somewhat on the form of victimization. Boys are more likely to experience physical bullying victimization (e.g., being hit; Grunbaum et al., 2004). However, much debate remains about whether girls are more likely to be targets of indirect, relational forms of victimization than boys (e.g., social exclusion; Crick & Grotpeter, 1995; Prinstein, Boergers, & Vernberg, 2001; Tomada & Schneider, 1997). In terms of racial/ethnic differences in bullying rates, there is more limited information. One study addressing racial differences found that Black students reported less victimization than White or Hispanic youth (Nansel et al., 2001); however, two other studies found that Black students were more likely to be classified as victims than Hispanic youth (Juvonen, Graham, & Schuster, 2003; Peskin, Tortolero, & Markham, 2006). Increased levels of victimization have also been documented among other marginalized groups of students, including students characterized as not "fitting in" (Hoover, Oliver, & Thomson, 1993), obese students (Lagerspetz, 1982), students enrolled in remedial education (Byrne, 1994), students with developmental disabilities (Marini, Fairbairn, & Zuber, 2001), lesbian, gay, bisexual, and transgender students (Kosciw, 2004), and students engaging in gender nonconforming behavior (Young & Sweeting, 2004).

Differences in rates of bullying have also been identified based on individual demographic characteristics. Boys are more likely than girls to bully their peers (Kumpulainen et al., 1998); however, comparable to victimization, sex differences in relational forms of bullying perpetration are inconsistent (Crick & Grotpeter, 1995; Prinstein et al., 2001). In contrast, differences between boys and girls on the development of various forms of aggression have been documented. For example, Murray-Close, Ostrov, and Crick (2007) found that relational aggression among girls in elementary school steadily increased over the course of a year, although a similar pattern did not emerge among boys. Other research has found that girls, but not boys, who are associated with relationally aggressive peers also became more relationally aggressive over time, although this held for physical forms of aggression for both boys and girls (Werner & Crick, 2004). In a comprehensive and longitudinal study, Broidy and colleagues (2003) found that childhood physical aggression predicted violent behavior of boys, but not girls, when they entered adolescence.

In terms of race, Juvonen and colleagues (2003) found that Black middle school youth were more likely to be categorized as bullies and bully-victims than White students, and Peskin and colleagues (2006) found that Black students were more likely to be classified as bullies and bully-victims than Hispanic students (Peskin et al., 2006). Conversely, another study found that Hispanic students reported somewhat more bullying than Black and White youth (Nansel et al., 2001). However, studies have also found that aggression is related to social and economic factors and therefore cannot be directly attributed directly to ethnic minority status (Gibbs, 1988). In addition, individuals with behavioral, emotional, or learning problems are more likely to engage in bullying than their peers (Kaukiainen, Salmivalli, & Lagerspetz, 2002). Furthermore, bullies, particularly male bullies, tend to be physically stronger than their peers (Tremblay et al., 1998). A lack of empathy also is associated with bullying perpetration (Borg, 1998). In relation to this, bullying individuals also report higher levels of support for violence and are more likely to believe that bullying is to be expected and a part of the social experience (Bentley & Li, 1995; Pellegrini, 2002).

***General Developmental Trajectories*** An important contextual variable to consider when examining bullying and peer victimization is age. Findings have been mixed about the stability of bullying (and more broadly, aggression) and victimization over time. In one study, bullying and victimization at age 8 were related to bullying and victimization at age 16, with particularly strong associations emerging

for victimization patterns and for the experiences of boys (Sourander, Helstela, Helenius, & Piha, 2000). Similarly, in another study, girls and boys classified as victims in Grade 4 were significantly more likely than their peers to be identified as victims in Grade 7 (Paul & Cillesen, 2003). However, other studies have shown that bullying behaviors tend to diminish as youth mature (Nansel et al., 2001). Still other researchers have documented increases in bullying that correspond with transitional changes from elementary school to middle school, which were then followed by decreases in bullying (Pellegrini & Bartini, 2001; Pellegrini & Long, 2002). A partial explanation for differences in these findings could be based on the possibility that different forms of bullying behavior follow different developmental trajectories. Some research has indicated that although physical forms of aggression tend to decrease over time, other forms can increase (Björkqvist, Lagerspetz, & Kaukiainen, 1992). In response to the use of correlation analyses, some researchers (Loeber & Stouthame-Loeber, 1998) have argued that it is erroneous to conclude that a high correlation coefficient between aggressive behaviors at two time points necessarily indicates stability of these behaviors; rather, it is critical to assess more systematically which groups of youth (e.g., highly aggressive boys) remain on aggressive trajectories and which youth desist in these behaviors over time.

Recently, more advanced methodological and statistical techniques, such as multilevel modeling and latent growth curve analysis, have been employed to examine individual developmental trajectories over extended periods of time, and have enabled a more accurate and complex analysis and documentation of the stability and change in bullying and victimization. During childhood, heterogeneity in victimization trajectories have been documented, with some children increasing and others decreasing in victimization (Snyder et al., 2003). Later in development, research has found that preadolescents gradually begin to perceive their peers as more hostile (Troop-Gordon & Ladd, 2005). Research among young adolescents has also documented that experiences of victimization predict later psychological maladjustment, although current victimization was a stronger predictor than earlier victimization (Juvonen et al., 2000). Other researchers have argued for the need to distinguish between individuals who experience periodic victimization and individuals who experience persistent and chronic victimization (Juvonen et al., 2000; Kochenderfer-Ladd & Wardrop, 2001). When examining students over a 4-year period, Kochenderfer-Ladd and Wardrop (2001) found that while many students did experience some victimization, most did not experience chronic and persistent victimization over this period of time.

***Contextual Factors*** As research continues to expand the examination of bullying behavior, an increased emphasis has been placed on examining individuals within their social environment and to approach the study of bullying from a social framework. A social ecological framework has been applied to studying bullying in several ways, including the examination of specific bullying episodes from a more dynamic and interpersonal perspective, and identifying the way in which contextual factors and social environments contribute to the development and perpetuation of bullying, and how they promote or discourage bullying behavior. Several social contexts receiving attention in the literature include the school, peer, and family environments.

*The School Context*   Social control theory is a dominant theory in the literature to explain the development of both prosocial and antisocial behavior (Hirschi, 1969). This theory postulates that as individuals establish connections with conventional institutions within society (e.g., schools, churches, community organizations), they are less prone to wrongdoing and more likely to internalize norms of appropriate conduct. A conventional institution that is experienced by most children at a young age is school. Positive school bonding has been associated with lowered risk of student substance abuse, truancy, and other acts of misconduct (Hawkins, Catalano, & Miller, 1992). However, considerable debate has emerged over many decades about what aspects of the school environment make a difference in buffering any negative family or community factors that children are exposed to. Early research focused on tangible, physical aspects of the school environment, including teacher–student ratio, population, budget, etc (Griffith, 1996; Huber, 1983; Rutter, Maughan, Mortimore, Ouston, & Smith, 1979), with inconsistent associations with these factors and academic outcomes for students.

More recent research has focused on expanding school influence investigations to include boarder constructs such as school policies, teacher attitudes, and the general ethos of a school as potential predictors of children's academic, social, and psychological development. Kasen and colleagues have produced the vast majority of the research in the past 17 years on the relation between school climate factors (Kasen, Berenson, et al., 2004; Kasen, Cohen, & Brook, 1998; Kasen, Johnson, & Cohen, 1990). In their earliest work, Kasen and colleagues (1990) found students (ages 6 through 16 years old) who went to schools with high rates of student–student and teacher–student conflict had significantly greater increases in oppositional, attentional, and conduct problems, while students from "well-organized, harmonious schools" that emphasized learning reported decreases in these outcomes. A follow-up study involving this sample found that students from the high-conflictual schools were at an increased risk for alcohol abuse and a criminal conviction 6 years later (Kasen, Cohen, et al., 1998).

Kasen and colleagues' 1994 study is perhaps the most comprehensive examination of impact of school climate on changes in verbal and physical aggression, anger, and school problem indices. In this study, 500 children (and their mothers) across 250 schools were surveyed at the age of 13.5 and 16 years across a 2½ year interval. A 45-item school climate survey included multiple scales assessing social and emotional features of the school environment, including a conflict scale (classroom control, teacher-student conflict), learning focus scale, social facilitation scale, and student authority scale (student has say in politics and planning) as predictors. Outcome measures included a wide range of scales, including school problems, deviance, rebelliousness, anger, physical and verbal aggression, and bullying. School context can influence engagement in bullying and more positive social interactions. Results found that students in high conflict schools had an increase in verbal and physical aggression, after controlling for baseline aggression. In contrast, attendance at schools that emphasized learning resulted in a decrease in aggression and other school-related problems. Of particular interest was the finding that schools high in informal relations had increases in bullying perpetration over the 2½ year interval and schools with high conflict and high informality combined had the highest increase in bullying over time.

School climate is a particularly important variable to consider because adult supervision decreases from elementary to middle school. In turn, less structure and supervision are associated with concomitant increases in bullying rates among middle school students, in particular at locations such as playgrounds and lunchrooms (Craig & Pepler, 1997) and in the hallways between classes (American Association of University Women, 2001) where students often report feeling unsafe and afraid (Astor, Meyer, & Pitner, 2001). Astor and colleagues (2001) offer additional insights into how students and teachers in both elementary and middle schools perceive public spaces in their schools as violence-prone locations. In that study, these authors drew upon theories of territoriality and undefined public spaces to argue that bullying and other violent acts are more likely to occur in undefined public spaces (e.g., hallways, stairwells) than those places that are more defined as being someone's territory (e.g., classrooms). Students in five elementary schools and two middle schools in grades 2, 4, 6, and 8 were presented with maps of their school and asked to identify places that they feel are unsafe or dangerous.

Qualitative and quantitative analyses yielded supported early work, but also provided some new information that has direct prevention implications for school administrators. It was not surprising that students in all schools perceived places lacking in adult supervision and monitoring as unsafe. Crowding and bullying were consistently mentioned as reasons for feeling unsafe. Middle school students reported feeling less safe than elementary school students and were not certain which adults they could turn to for help. Similarly, middle school teachers reported greater conflict in their role in monitoring public spaces. Although middle school students reported feeling unsafe in most undefined public spaces, elementary school students reported feeling less safe on playgrounds than middle school students. These results suggest that bullying could be decreased in schools by first understanding where bullying is happening through Astor and colleagues' mapping procedure. These data could then be used to develop an increase in monitoring of the high frequency areas.

Bullying also occurs within the confines of the classroom. As such, it is clear that classroom practices and teachers' attitudes are also salient components of school climate that contribute to bullying prevalence. Aggression varies from classroom to classroom, and in some instances aggression is supported. For example, researchers have found levels of aggression in elementary school to significantly differ across classrooms (Henry et al., 2000; Kellam, Ling, Merisca, Brown, & Ialongo, 1998), and those aggressive students in classrooms with norms supportive of aggression become more aggressive over time compared to students in less aggressive classrooms. Bullying tends to be less prevalent in classrooms in which most children are included in activities (Newman, Murray, & Lussier, 2001), teachers display warmth and responsiveness to children (Olweus & Limber, 1999), and teachers respond quickly and effectively to bullying incidents (Olweus, 1993b). Furthermore, Hoover and Hazler (1994) note that when school personnel tolerate, ignore, or dismiss bullying behaviors they are conveying implicit messages about values that victimized students internalize.

*Transition from Elementary to Middle School*   Theorists and researchers have long recognized the transition from elementary school to middle or junior high school as a potential stressor for students (Blyth, Simmons, & Carlton-Ford, 1983; Feldlaufer, Midgley, & Eccles, 1988; Hirsch & Rapkin, 1987; Midgley, Anderman, & Hicks, 1995; Seidman, Allen, Aber, Mitchell, & Feinman, 1994; Wigfield, Eccles, Mac Iver, Reuman, & Midgley, 1991). For many years, Eccles and colleagues (Eccles, 2004; Eccles & Midgley, 1989; Eccles et al., 2003; Eccles & Roeser, 1999) have proposed and tested a model of stage–environment fit to guide research on the impact of school transitions on social and emotional development among adolescents. Here, stage–environment fit refers to the appropriateness of the environment to meet the needs of individuals at their particular stage of development, and is not synonymous with person–environment fit, which refers to the interaction between individual/personality characteristics with environmental factors. The transition can be conceptualized as a stressor given that it demands an adjustment to a new classroom environment and school culture, and as such reflects a disruption in daily functioning. Adjustments to changes in the classroom environment and school culture, in turn, have been associated with outcomes indicative of a negative emotional and psychological process for some students (e.g., a decrease in self-esteem, an increase in symptoms of depression) (Hankin et al., 1998). Further, transitioning from elementary to middle school also necessitates changes in peer groups, a shift that also can result in stress, especially when the schools do not adjust to the developmental needs of adolescents (Eccles, 2004).

However, to date, limited research has been conducted on the transition to middle school in relation to aggression, despite evidence that fifth graders identify bullying as one of their primary concerns about starting sixth grade (Akos,

2002; Pellegrini, 2002). It might be that fears of increased involvement in aggression as perpetrators exacerbate stress incurred as a result of the elementary–middle school transition. In a recent study examining factors that predicted bullying across the transition from elementary school to middle school, Espelage, Poteat, Holt, and VanBoven (2006) found that teacher attachment in fifth grade was a strong predictor of lower levels of bullying for students during their sixth grade year, even after controlling for their level of bullying during their fifth grade year. Furthermore, teacher attachment was the strongest predictor of lower levels of bullying, whereas other factors (e.g., parental attachment, social acceptance, and psychological functioning) were nonsignificant predictors after controlling for previous levels of bullying behavior. This finding provides additional support for the importance of the social context and students' interactions with not only their peers but their teachers in accounting for and predicting their engagement in bullying behavior over a transitional period that can be difficult for many students.

*The Peer Context*   The peer context is another salient contributor to bullying behaviors. Several theories dominate the literature, including the homophily hypothesis (Cairns & Cairns, 1994; Espelage, Holt, & Henkel, 2003), attraction theory (Bukowski, Sippola, & Newcomb, 2000), and dominance theory (Pellegrini, 2002). According to the homophily hypothesis, individuals within the same group are likely to report similar attitudes and engagement in similar forms of behavior as a result of either self-selection, peer socialization, or the combined effects of both factors (Kandel, 1978). Self-selection refers to individuals selecting to be friends with others who already hold similar attitudes or participate in similar behaviors. Socialization refers to the process by which individuals within the group influence each other and internalize the norms that are established by the group (Eder & Nenga, 2003; McPerson, Smith-Lovin, & Cook, 2001). Support for the homophily hypothesis has been documented in the bullying literature, which has found that individuals within the same friendship group tend to report engaging in similar levels of bullying behaviors (Espelage et al., 2003; Espelage, Green, & Wasserman, 2007). In addition, bullying levels within the peer group are predictive of adolescents' bullying behavior over time, even after controlling for individuals' own baseline levels of bullying, a finding that holds true for both males and females. The documented social influence of the group, in addition to self-selection, suggests a more active role of peer group members in accounting for individuals' own bullying behavior, than would be suggested based on self-selection alone. This documented effect might in part be due to deviancy training, a process by which values supportive of aggression are fostered, and youth ultimately engage in problematic behaviors such as substance use and delinquency (Dishion & Owen, 2002). In contrast, peer groups can also have a positive influence on individuals. For example, students who perceive greater peer social support tend to be uninvolved in bullying (Demaray & Malecki, 2002), and in one study, peer victimization was not linked to internalizing and externalizing behavior problems for those youth with sufficient social support (Hodges & Perry, 1999). Further, peers can promote positive social functioning among youth; adolescents with low levels of prosocial behaviors in sixth grade relative to their friends demonstrated improved prosocial behaviors at the end of eighth grade (Wentzel & Caldwell, 1997). As such, just as the homophily hypothesis can explain similarities in aggression within the peer group, it also can explain similarities in prosocial interactions.

Attention to the peer context has also led researchers to identify the various roles that can be ascribed to peers during bullying episodes. In most cases, individuals are not victimized by a single individual. Rather, many bullying episodes involve the active and passive participation of multiple individuals. The work of Salmivalli and colleagues (Salmivalli et al., 1996; Salmivalli & Voeten, 2004) has identified several additional ways in which individuals participate in bullying episodes. In relation to the bully, other students can be classified as either assisting or reinforcing the bully. Students assisting the bully may engage in actions such as chasing or holding down the victim for the bully. Students reinforcing the bully may engage in actions such as encouraging the bully to continue aggressive behavior toward the victim, or by further teasing the victim. Alternately, other students provide support for the victimized individual, such as attempting to stop the bully, finding help for the victim, or providing psychological support for the victim after the bullying episode is over. Finally, other students might be classified as outsiders, such that they are not usually involved in bullying episodes, or attempt to leave the situation when the bullying episode begins (Salmivalli et al., 1996).

In addition to the homophily hypothesis, several researchers have used the concept of dominance as an organizational framework to understand individuals' engagement in bullying behavior. From this perspective, bullying is a means by which to establish dominance hierarchies among peers, such that certain individuals eventually attain a higher status, more access to resources, and greater control or influence over other peers (Bjorklund & Pellegrini, 2002; Boulton, 1992; Pellegrini & Long, 2002). Although dominance status can be attained through either affiliative (e.g., leadership) or antagonistic (e.g., bullying) methods (Hawley, 1999; Lease, Musgrove, & Axelrod, 2002), research suggests that dominance is initially established through antagonistic methods late in elementary school, followed by affiliative methods later in middle school or further into the establishment of the peer group (Pellegrini & Long, 2002). In addition to offering an explanation for individuals' bullying behavior, dominance and the establishment of dominance hierarchies also posits an explanation for the relative increase in bullying behavior during certain time points. Specifically, the establishment of dominance hierarchies could explain why bullying behavior typically increases during transition periods, such as from elemen-

tary school to middle school (Pellegrini & Bartini, 2001; Pellegrini & Long, 2002). Because this transition often involves the introduction of and interaction with a new set peers and within a new social context, the increase in bullying behavior could reflect the attempt by some students to assert their dominance or establish a dominant position within a new, and often times larger, social context and cohort of students.

The social-information-processing model (see Coie & Dodge, 1998 for a review) has also been used to explain individuals' aggressive behavior. From this perspective, individuals' aggressive behavior can be explained based on past experiences, their intake and interpretation of social cues, and on their generation of possible reactions. Research suggests that aggressive individuals are more likely to attribute hostile intentions to ambiguously antagonistic actions, focus more on aggressive cues, and are more likely to generate and act on aggressive responses (Coie & Dodge, 1998; Gouze, 1987). Several possible explanations for these differences in cognitive attributions have been proposed (Dodge, Bates, & Pettit, 1990; Hubbard et al., 2001), including past negative experiences of abuse or conflict within the family, or deficits in social interaction skills for other children.

The way in which bullying is viewed by peers can also further contribute to a characterization of bullying individuals. Although the study of popularity represents an entire area of focus in the adolescent empirical literature itself, several studies have explored the association between popularity and bullying. This research suggests that boys who are bullies and aggressive are not always viewed negatively by their peers. Rather, these individuals can be nominated as popular by their peers in elementary school (Rodkin et al., 2000), and associate with individuals rated similarly in popularity and aggression (Farmer, Estell, Bishop, O'Neil, & Cairns, 2003; Farmer, Leung, et al., 2002). Among middle school students, aggressive and tough boys have also been nominated as cool by other aggressive boys and by some girls (Rodkin, Farmer, et al., 2006).

*The Family Context*  With respect to the family context, bullies, as a group, report that their parents are more authoritarian, condone "fighting back," and use physical punishment (Baldry & Farrington, 2000; Loeber & Dishion, 1984; Olweus, 1995b). Families of bullies have also been described as lacking warmth and structure (Oliver, Oaks, & Hoover, 1994; Olweus, 1993b), having low family cohesion (Bowers, Smith, & Binney, 1994; Stevens, De Bourdeaudhuji, & Van Oost, 2002), and being high in conflict (Stevens et al., 2002). Parent–child attachment patterns are also related to bullying. Specifically, children who had insecure, anxious-avoidant, or anxious-resistant attachment styles when 18 months old were more likely than children with secure attachments to become involved in bullying at ages 4 and 5 (Troy & Sroufe, 1987). McFadyen-Ketchum and colleagues (McFadyen-Ketchum, Bates, Dodge, & Pettit, 1996) found that parents also can contribute to decreases in children's aggression over time; aggressive children who experienced affectionate mother–child relationships showed significant decreases in aggressive–disruptive behaviors. Parental social support is another factor related to bullying involvement; middle school students classified as bullies and bully-victims indicated receiving substantially less social support from parents than students in the uninvolved group (Demaray & Malecki, 2003). There have been mixed findings with respect to family structure and bullying, with some studies showing a heightened risk for youth in nonintact families (Flouri & Buchanan, 2003) and others finding no association (Espelage et al., 2000). Finally, witnessing domestic violence and experiencing child maltreatment are associated with bullying perpetration (Baldry, 2003; Shields & Cicchetti, 2001).

A unique set of family characteristics exist for victims of bullying. Families of victims often have high levels of cohesion (Bowers et al., 1994). Further, victims are more likely to have less authoritative parents (Smith & Myron-Wilson, 1998) and live in families in which there are low levels of negotiation (Oliver et al., 1994) and high levels of conflict (Baldry & Farrington, 2005; Mohr, 2006). Some evidence suggests that family structure and income are associated with being victimized by peers. In particular, in a study of Nordic children, both living in a single-parent home and having a low SES family were associated with increased odds of being bullied (Nordhagen, Nielsen, Stigum, & Kohler, 2005). Further, as summarized by Duncan (2004) there appear to be some family characteristics of victims that vary by the child's gender. For instance, whereas male victims often have overly close relationships with their mothers, female victims are more likely to have mothers who withdraw love. Finally, peer victimization is associated with greater victimization in other domains, such as child maltreatment (Holt, Finkelhor, & Kaufman-Kantor, 2007).

Less research has focused on family environments of bully-victims, although evidence suggests that parents of bully-victims tend to be less warm and more overprotective than parents of uninvolved youth, and provide inconsistent discipline and monitoring (Schwartz, Dodge, Pettit, & Bates, 1997; Smith, Bowers, Binney, & Cowie, 1993). In addition, families of bully-victims are characterized by low levels of cohesion, although not as low as cohesion levels in families of bullies (Bowers et al., 1994).

A growing body of literature has assessed the influence of sibling aggression. Duncan (1999) surveyed 375 middle school students, 336 of whom had siblings. Results indicated that 42% reported that they often bullied their siblings, 24% reported they often pushed or hit their brothers and sisters, and 11% stated that they often beat up their siblings. A smaller group (30%) reported that siblings frequently victimized them, with 22% stating they were often hit or pushed around and 8% reporting they were often beaten up by a sibling. What is most pertinent to the discussion is the finding that 57% of bullies and 77% of bully-victims reported also bullying their siblings. A previous study by Bowers et al. (1994) detected a similar pattern of relations, finding that bullies reported negative and ambivalent relationships with siblings and viewed their siblings as more powerful than themselves. The opposite was found for victims, who reported enmeshed and positive relationships with their siblings (Bowers et al., 1994).

***Interactions among Contexts*** Demographic characteristics and developmental transitions all interact together to impact children's and adolescents' social development. These contexts are not mutually exclusive, but are nested contextual systems that can have multiplicative influences on a child or adolescent's social development (Bronfenbrenner, 1979). Peers, parents, and schools are referred to as microsystems. Interrelations among these microsystems are mesosystems. Indeed, a recurrent challenge within developmental research is examining how contexts (e.g., family, peers) interact together to predict problematic attitudes and behavior. Research progress in some ways has been slowed with the lack of user-friendly statistical models that could handle nested data. However, there has been recognition for some time, that the contexts need to be examined simultaneously. As noted by Bronfenbrenner (1977), "environmental structures, and the processes taking place within and between them, must be viewed as interdependent and must be analyzed in systems terms" (p. 518). Recent advancements by Raudenbush and Bryk (2002) in the development of Hierarchical Linear Modeling (HLM) have changed the way in which developmental researchers conduct research and analyze their data. HLM and other statistical software can be used to model how variation in school climate, discipline practices among school administrators, and teacher classroom management skills affect student behavior. In addition, future research on bullying and peer victimization needs to consider this methodology to examine how these microsystems influence each other, such as in how teacher practices at the classroom level might buffer a potentially conflictual school environment.

One area of emerging research connected with bullying that nicely demonstrates the advances that can be made by expanding from a primarily individual focus to a broader and more dynamic framework with attention to the interaction between multiple systems is research on homophobic behavior (Kimmel & Mahler, 2003; Phoenix, Frosh, & Pattman, 2003; Poteat, Espelage, & Green, 2007; Russell, McGuire, Laub, & Manke, 2006). Rates of victimization of gay and lesbian students have remained high across several decades of research (D'Augelli, 2002; Gross, Aurand, & Adessa, 1988; Pilkington & D'Augelli, 1995), with more recent research indicating that heterosexual students can also experience victimization that is homophobic in nature (Phoenix et al., 2003; Poteat & Espelage, 2005). Homophobic behavior can include teasing, threats, harassment, and physical or sexual assault. Recent research from a broader social ecological perspective has documented a number of findings, including: LGBT harassment at the school level predicts higher truancy rates for LGBT individuals over and above individual experiences of harassment (Birkett, Espelage, & Poteat, 2007); lesbian and gay students are often bullied by groups of students rather than by a single individual (Rivers, 2001); students questioning their sexual orientation and who rated their school climate as caring reported lower rates of depression and drug use than questioning students who did not feel that teachers cared about them (Espelage, Aragon, Birkett, & Koenig, 2008); substantial similarity in rates of homophobic behavior exists within peer groups (Poteat, 2007); the presence of gay-straight alliances at school and LGBT-inclusive curriculum contributes to increased perceived safety at school (Russell et al., 2006); the homophobic climate of peer groups moderates individuals' engagement in homophobic banter (Poteat, 2007), peers can influence individuals' engagement in homophobic behavior toward other students over time (Poteat, 2008); and knowledge of the social climate of peer groups contributes to a more accurate prediction of individuals' homophobic attitudes (Poteat et al., 2007). Expansion of the focus of research on homophobic attitudes and behavior has since led to a more complex and accurate understanding of this pervasive social behavioral concern, informed the development of intervention programming, and strengthened the argument for passing protective school policies.

## Bullying Prevention and Intervention Programs

Given that bullying perpetration and victimization develops and is maintained through a number of contexts, prevention and intervention efforts should intervene at multiple levels. Indeed, school preventative interventions for bullying have slowly been introduced over the last several decades and include some parental and peer related components. Programs began following the introduction of the Norway-based *Olweus Bullying Prevention Program* (OBPP; Olweus, Limber, & Mihalic, 2000), which will be discussed more completely later. Since the introduction of this program in 1993, the U.S. Department of Health and Human Services launched its *Stop Bullying Now: Take a Stand, Lend a Hand* and provided schools and administrators with information on best practices in bullying prevention and intervention, which is available from their web site (www.stopbullyingnow.hrsa.gov).

Programs to address bullying perpetration and victimization use two primary approaches: universal and targeted. A universal approach is one that is provided to all people involved in the school, and is used as a means of providing the skills necessary to avoid developing problems. A targeted intervention, on the other hand, involves specific groups of students identified as having a particular problem. Children identified as bullies, for example, would be targeted/selected for a more intensive intervention. However, there is considerable debate in relation to the effectiveness of school-wide bullying prevention and intervention efforts. Although some evaluation efforts have offered promising findings, results of a recent meta-analytic study of 14 whole-school antibullying programs provide a more modest assessment (Smith, Schneider, Smith, & Ananidou, 2004). This study included the OBPP, the Peaceful Schools Project, and the Steps to Respect program. Results indicated that only moderate effect sizes emerged on self-reported bullying victimization and small to negligible effects were found for self-reported bullying perpetration. The authors concluded that significant caution should be observed when implementing school-wide programs. At the same time, several programs have demonstrated positive impact and future research is needed to identify the characteristics of those programs that have greater effects in order to build upon their strengths. A few of these programs are briefly summarized below.

*Olweus Bullying Prevention Program (OBPP)* The OBPP is a universal prevention program that is widely cited. There are now six large-scale evaluations of over 30,000 Norwegian students of the effects of the OBPP (for a review, see Olweus, 2005). In the majority of these evaluations, what is usually called a "selection cohort" or "age cohort design" has been used. One of the evaluation studies has used a more traditional control group design. Data supporting this program's effectiveness include the Olweus et al. (2000) report that bullying is reduced by as much as 50% in one year of school program implementation in Norway. Partial replications of (adapted versions) of the program in other countries including the United States and Britain have provided positive but somewhat weaker results (Olweus & Limber, 1999). This comprehensive program aims to reduce bullying among elementary and middle school students by reducing opportunities to engage in bullying and the rewards that maintain bullying behavior. Consistent with data from the extant literature, teachers are trained to improve peer relations and create a positive school climate for all students. The intervention focuses on increasing awareness among students, teachers, and parents, highlighting the need for clear and consistent guidelines or rules against bullying, and protecting victims. Program ingredients are delivered at school, classroom, and individual levels.

*Bully Busters: A Teacher's Manual for Helping Bullies, Victims, and Bystanders* Although Olweus' program is a comprehensive approach to bully prevention programming, many schools might not have the personnel or finances to implement this program. Counselors, psychologists, and teachers often ask for a more focused and affordable approach. Bully Busters (Newman, Horne, & Bartolomucci, 2000) is a program that schools with fewer resources might be able to implement. Two versions are available, one for youth in grades k through 5, and one for youth in grades 6 through 8. Broadly, the goal of Bully Busters is to modify the school environment and all its constituents such that bullying no longer occurs (Horne, Orpinas, Newman-Carlson, & Bartolomucci, 2004). Data support this program. For example, teachers who take part in the training program reported significantly higher levels of self-efficacy for managing bullying behavior, demonstrated greater knowledge of classroom behavior management, and had fewer classroom behavior problems and office referrals than comparison teachers (Newman-Carlson & Horne, 2004).

*Steps to Respect: A Bullying Prevention Program* This program was developed by the Committee for Children (www.cfchildren.org) and has empirical data suggesting promising outcomes (Frey et al., 2005). For example, a fairly minimal intervention included having peers step in to tell bullies to stop the bullying and in more than 50% of the time it stopped within a few seconds. The foundation of this program includes creating a "safe, caring, and respectful" culture and targets students at three levels (grades 3 and 4, 4 and 5, and 5 and 6). In the first phase, a school-wide framework is established before the curriculum is implemented. A program guide details the role of the principal or administrator as a supportive leader of the implementation and program evaluation. A steering committee is formed to facilitate this process, including teachers, administrators, and others who encounter students during the school day (e.g., bus drivers, nurses, secretaries). Steps of implementation are outlined and worksheets are used to guide the steering committee in their planning to increase the efficacy and sustainability of the program. The second phase involves training of all staff, curriculum orientation for classroom teachers, and then booster training for staff and faculty. The third phase of the program is implementation in classrooms and throughout the school environment. All staff involved in the school participates in having the school become totally immersed in the antibullying campaign. The bully prevention lessons are incorporated into academic lessons so that learning of subject matter and skills development are complementary.

*Promoting Alternative Thinking Strategies (PATHS; Kusché & Greenberg, 1994)* The PATHS program, designed for children in kindergarten through sixth grade, was designated a Blueprints model program by the Office of Juvenile Justice and Delinquency Prevention. Following the universal prevention model, PATHS was developed to integrate into existing curricula. Goals of the program include enhancing social and emotional competence and reducing aggression. Some program components are targeted at parents, but most are delivered by classroom teachers who are initially trained by PATHS project staff. Three randomized trials of PATHS have indicated positive outcomes including a reduction in aggressive solutions to problems and increases in prosocial behaviors (Greenberg, Kusché, & Mihalic, 1998). Further, the curriculum recently was modified for the preschool population and initial results are promising (Domitrovich, Cortes, & Greenberg, 2007). Finally, the PATHS curriculum was selected as a universal prevention for use in Fast Track project, a multifaceted longitudinal project that targets youth at risk for conduct disorders. Findings for first graders showed positive results including a reduction in peer ratings of aggression (Conduct Problems Prevention Research Group, 1999).

## Conclusions

In summary, much research has been conducted in the United States and internationally on the phenomenon of bullying in schools. It is clear that bullying is prevalent among children and young adolescents and has serious detrimental consequences for bullies, victims, bully-victims, and bystanders. The onset of bullying is best understood from a social-ecological perspective in which individual characteristics of children interact with environmental factors to promote teasing and harassment. Children and adolescents experience bullying victimization and perpetrate bullying most often while at school. Research demonstrates that the prevalence of these behaviors varies across schools and these fluctuations are attributable to tangible and less tangible aspects of schools. For example, in this chapter, research found that students feel unsafe, and fear being bullied, in unsupervised locations of their schools, including hallways, stairwells, cafeterias, bathrooms, and playgrounds. In addition, school climate (e.g., perceived safety, support from other students and teachers) are associated with better academic and social outcomes for students. Conflict among students and teachers is associated with an increase in bullying perpetration, but schools that place an importance on learning report a decrease in bullying. An informal environment appears to be related with increases in bullying perpetration, especially in high conflict schools. These studies suggest that school-based bullying prevention programs should include an assessment (mapping) of where students feel unsafe at school and then supervision needs to be increased in these locations. Supervision should foster positive relations among students and teachers rather than simply appearing as a strictly security measure. Finally, it is evident that a positive school climate plays an important role in decreasing bullying, but much work needs to be conducted to understand how school climate buffers the relation between risk factors in other contexts (e.g., family, peers, and media) and bullying perpetration/victimization at school.

## References

Akos, P. (2002). Student perceptions of the transition to middle school. *Professional School Counseling, 5*, 339–345.

American Association of University Women. (2001). *Hostile hallways: Bullying, teasing, and sexual harassment in schools*. Washington, DC: Author.

American Psychiatric Association. (2000). *Diagnostic and statistical manual of mental disorders* (4th ed., text revision). Washington, DC: Author.

Astor, R. A., Meyer, H. A., & Pitner, R. O. (2001). Elementary and middle school students' perceptions of violence-prone school subcontexts. *Elementary School Journal, 101*, 511–528.

Austin, S., & Joseph, S. (1996). Assessment of bully/victim problems in 8- to 11-year-olds. *British Journal of Educational Psychology, 66*, 447–456.

Baldry, A. C. (2003). Bullying in schools and exposure to domestic violence. *Child Abuse & Neglect, 27*, 713–732.

Baldry, A. C., & Farrington, D. P. (2000). Bullies and delinquents: Personal characteristics and parental styles. *Journal of Community and Applied Social Psychology, 10*, 17–31.

Benbenishty, R., & Astor, R. A. (2005). *School violence in context: Culture, neighborhood, family, school, and gender*. New York: Oxford University Press.

Bentley, K. M., & Li, A. K. F. (1995). Bully and victim problems in elementary schools and students' beliefs about aggression. *Canadian Journal of School Psychology, 11*, 153–165.

Birkett, M.A., Espelage, D. L., & Poteat, V. P. (2007, August). *Effects of school-level LGBT harassment on truancy*. Symposium conducted at the 115th Annual Convention of the American Psychological Association, San Francisco, California.

Bjorklund, D. F., & Pellegrini, A. D. (2002). *The origins of human nature*. Washington, DC: American Psychological Association.

Bjorkqvist, K., Lagerspetz, K., & Kaukiainen, A. (1992). Do girls manipulate and boys fight? Developmental trends in regard to direct and indirect aggression. *Aggressive Behavior, 18*, 815–823.

Blyth, D. A., Simmons, R. G., & Carlton-Ford, S. (1983). The adjustment of early adolescents to school transitions. *Journal of Early Adolescence, 3*, 105–120.

Borg, M. G. (1998). The emotional reactions of school bullies and their victims. *Educational Psychology, 18*, 433–443.

Boulton, M. J. (1992). Rough physical play in adolescents: Does it serve a dominance function? *Early Education and Development, 3*, 312–333.

Boulton, M. J., & Smith, P. K. (1994). Bully/victim problems in middle school children: Stability, self-perceived competence, peer perceptions and peer acceptance. *British Journal of Developmental Psychology, 12*, 315–329.

Bowers, L., Smith, P. K., & Binney, V. (1994). Perceived family relationships of bullies, victims, and bully/victims in middle childhood. *Journal of Social and Personal Relationships, 11*, 215–232.

Broidy, L. M., Nagin, D. S., Tremblay, R. E., Bates, J. E., Brame, B., Dodge, K., et al. (2003). Developmental trajectories of childhood disruptive behaviors and adolescent delinquency: A six-site, cross-national study. *Developmental Psychology, 39*, 222–245.

Bronfenbrenner (1977). Toward an experimental ecology of human development. *American Psychologist, 32*, 513–531.

Bronfenbrenner, U. (1979). *The ecology of human development*. Cambridge, MA: Harvard University Press.

Bukowski, W. M., Sippola, L. K., & Newcomb, A. F. (2000). Variations in patterns of attraction to same- and other-sex peers during early adolescence. *Developmental Psychology, 36*, 147–154.

Byrne, B. (1994). Bullies and victims in a school setting with reference to some Dublin schools. *The Irish Journal of Psychology, 15*, 574–586.

Cairns, R. B., & Cairns, B. D. (1994). *Lifelines and risks: Pathways of youth in our time*. Cambridge, England: Cambridge University Press.

Coie, J. D., & Dodge, K. A. (1998). Aggression and antisocial behavior. In W. Damon & N. Eisenberg (Eds.), *Handbook of child psychology: Vol. 3. Social, emotional, and personality development* (5th ed., pp. 779–862). Hoboken, NJ: Wiley.

Conduct Problems Prevention Research Group. (1999). Initial impact of the Fast Track prevention trial for conduct problems: II. Classroom effects. *Journal of Consulting and Clinical Psychology, 67*, 648–657.

Craig, W. M., & Pepler, D. J. (1997). Observations of bullying and victimization in the school yard. *Canadian Journal of School Psychology, 13*(2), 41–59.

Crick, N. R. (1996). The role of relational aggression, overt aggression, and prosocial behavior in the prediction of children's future social adjustment. *Child Development, 67*, 2317–2327.

Crick, N. R., & Bigbee, M. A. (1998). Relational and overt forms of peer victimization: A multiinformant approach. *Journal of Consulting and Clinical Psychology, 66*, 337–347.

Crick, N. R., & Grotpeter, J. K. (1995). Relational aggression, gender, and social-psychological adjustment. *Child Development, 66*, 710–722.

D'Augelli, A. R. (2002). The cutting edges of lesbian and gay psychology. In A. Coyle & C. Kitzinger (Eds.), *Lesbian and gay psychology: New perspectives* (pp. xiii–xvi). London: British Psychological Society/Blackwell.

Demaray, M. K., & Malecki, C. K. (2001). Importance ratings of socially supportive behaviors by children and adolescents. *School Psychology Review, 32*, 108–131.

Demaray, M. K., & Malecki, C. K. (2002). The relationship between perceived social support and maladjustment for students at risk. *Psychology in the Schools, 39*, 305–316.

Demaray, M. K., & Malecki, C. K. (2003). Perceptions of the frequency and importance of social support by students classified as victims, bullies, and bully/victims in an urban middle school. *School Psychology Review, 32*, 471–489.

Dishion, T., & Owen, L. D. (2002). A longitudinal analysis of friendships and substance use: Bidirectional influence from adolescence to adulthood. *Developmental Psychology, 38*, 480–491.

Dodge, K. A., Bates, J. E., & Pettit, G. S. (1990). Mechanisms in the cycle of violence. *Science, 250*, 1678–1683.

Dodge, K. A., Coie, J. D., Pettit, G. S., & Price, J. M. (1990). Peer status and aggression in boys' groups: Developmental and contextual analyses. *Child Development, 61*, 1289–1309.

Domitrovich, C. E., Cortes, R., & Greenberg, M. T. (2007). Improving young children's social and emotional competence: A randomized trial of the preschool "PATHS" curriculum. *Journal of Primary Prevention, 28*, 67–91.

Duncan, R. D. (1999). Maltreatment by parents and peers: The relationship between child abuse, bullying victimization, and psychological distress. *Child Maltreatment, 4*, 45–55.

Duncan, R. D. (2004). The impact of family relationships on school bullies and their victims. In D. L. Espelage & S. M., Swearer (Eds.), *Bullying in American schools: A social-ecological perspective on prevention and intervention* (pp. 227–244). Mahwah, NJ: Erlbaum.

Eccles, J. S. (2004). Schools, academic motivation, and stage-environment fit. In R. M. Lerner & L. Sternberg, *Handbook of adolescent psychology* (2nd ed., pp. 125–153). Hoboken, NJ: Wiley.

Eccles, J. S., & Midgley, C. (1989). Stage/environment fit: Developmentally appropriate classrooms for early adolescents. In R. Ames & C. Ames (Eds.), *Research on motivation in education* (Vol. 3, pp. 139–181). New York: Academic Press.

Eccles, J. S., Midgley, C., Wigfield, A., Miller-Buchanan, C., Reuman, D., Flanagan, C., et al. (2003). Development during adolescence: The impact of stage-environment fit on young adolescents' experiences in schools and in families. *American Psychologist, 48*, 90–101.

Eccles, J. S., & Roeser, R. (1999). School and community influences on human development. In M. Bornstein & M. Lamb (Eds.), *Developmental psychology: An advanced textbook* (4th ed., pp. 503–554). Mahwah, NJ: Erlbaum.

Eder, D., & Nenga, S. K. (2003). Socialization in adolescence. In J. Delamater (Ed.), *Handbook of social psychology* (pp. 157–182). New York: Kluwer Academic.

Eron, L. D., Huesmann, L. R., Dubow, E., Romanoff, R., & Yarnel, P. W. (1987). Aggression and its correlates over 22 years. In D. H. Crowell & I. M. Evans (Eds.), *Childhood aggression and violence: Sources of influence, prevention, and control* (pp. 249–262). New York: Plenum.

Eslea, M., & Rees, J. (2001). At what age are children most likely to be bullied at school? *Aggressive Behavior, 27*, 419–429.

Espelage, D. L., Aragon, S. R., Birkett, M., & Koenig, B. W. (in press). Psychological adjustment and sexual orientation during adolescents: Do parents and teachers help? In D. L. Espelage & S. M. Swearer (Eds.), *Sexual orientation, homophobia, bullying, and psychological adjustment during adolescence* [Special issue]. *School Psychology Review*.

Espelage, D. L., Bosworth, K., & Simon, T. R. (2000). Examining the social context of bullying behaviors in early adolescence. *Journal of Counseling and Development, 78*, 326–333.

Espelage, D. L., Green, H., & Wasserman, S. (2007). Friendship ties of preadolescent bullies, victims, and bully-victims. In L. Hanish & P. Rodkin (Eds.), *Peer Social Networks, New Directions for Child and Adolescent Development, 118*, 61–75.

Espelage, D. L., & Holt, M. K. (2001). Bullying and victimization during early adolescence: Peer influences and psychosocial correlates. In R. Geffner & M. Loring (Eds.), *Bullying behaviors: Current is-*

sues, research, and interventions (pp. 123–142). Binghamton, NY: Haworth Press.

Espelage, D. L., Holt, M. K., & Henkel, R. R. (2003). Examination of peer-group contextual effects on aggression during early adolescence. *Child Development, 74*, 205–220.

Espelage, D. L., Mebane, S., & VanBoven (2006, August). Contextual influences on bullying trajectories across the elementary–middle school transition. In M. Holt & D. Espelage (Co-Chairs), *New Directions in Bullying Research,* Symposium conducted at the annual meeting of the American Psychological Association, New Orleans, LA.

Espelage, D. L., & Swearer, S. M. (2003). Research on school bullying and victimization: What have we learned and where do we go from here? *School Psychology Review, 32*, 365–383.

Farmer, T. W., Estell, D. B., Bishop, J. L., O'Neil, K. K., & Cairns, B. D. (2003). Rejected bullies or popular leaders? The social relations of aggressive subtypes of African American early adolescents. *Developmental Psychology, 39*, 992–1004.

Farmer, T. W., Leung, M. C., Pearl, R., Rodkin, P. C., Cadwallader, T. W., & Van Acker, R. (2002). Deviant or diverse peer groups? The peer affiliations of aggressive elementary students. *Journal of Educational Psychology, 94*, 611–620.

Feldlaufer, H., Midgley, C., & Eccles, J. S. (1988). Student, teacher, and observer perceptions of the classroom environment before and after the transition to junior high school. *Journal of Early Adolescence, 8*, 133–156.

Flouri, E., & Buchanan, A. (2003). The role of mother involvement and father involvement in adolescent bullying behavior. *Journal of Interpersonal Violence, 18*, 634–644.

Frey, K. S., Hirschstein, M. K., Snell, J. L., Van Schoiack-Edstrom, L., MacKenzie, E. P., & Broderick, C. J. (2005). Reducing playground bullying and supporting beliefs: An experimental trial of the *Steps to Respect* program. *Developmental Psychology, 41*, 479–491.

Garbarino, J., & DeLara, E. (2002). *And words can hurt forever: How to protect adolescents from bullying, harassment, and emotional violence.* New York: Free Press.

Gibbs, J. (1988). *Young, black, and male in America: An endangered species.* Dover, MA: Auburn House.

Gouze, K. R. (1987). Attention and social problem solving as correlates of aggression in pre-school males. *Journal of Abnormal Child Psychology, 15*, 181–197.

Graham, S., Bellmore, A., & Juvonen, J. (2003). Peer victimization in middle school: When self- and peer views diverge. *Journal of Applied School Psychology, 19*, 117–137.

Graham, S., Bellmore, A. D., & Mize, J. (2006). Peer victimization, aggression, and their co-occurrence in middle school: Pathways to adjustment problems. *Journal of Abnormal Child Psychology, 34*, 363–378.

Greenberg, M. T., Kusché, C., & Mihalic, S. F. (1998). *Blueprints for violence prevention, book ten: Promoting alternative thinking strategies (PATHS).* Boulder, CO: Center for the Study and Prevention of Violence.

Griffith, J. (1996). Relation of parental involvement, empowerment, and school traits to student academic performance. *Journal of Educational Research, 90*, 33–41.

Gross, L., Aurand, S., & Adessa, R. (1988). *Violence and discrimination against lesbian and gay people in Philadelphia and the Commonwealth of Pennsylvania.* Unpublished report, Philadelphia Lesbian and Gay Task Force.

Grunbaum, J. A., Kann, L., Kinchen, S., Ross, J. G., Lowry, R., Harris, W. A., et al. (2004). Youth risk behavior surveillance—United States, 2003. MMWR 2004;53(SS-2):1–100. Retrieved from http//:www.cdc.gov/mmwr/preview/mmwrhtml/ss5302a1.htm

Hankin, B. L., Abramson, L. Y., Moffitt, T. E., Silva, P. A., McGee, R., & Angell, K. E. (1998). Development of depression from preadolescence to young adulthood: Emerging gender differences in a 10-year longitudinal study. *Journal of Abnormal Psychology, 107*(1), 128–140.

Hawker, D. S. J., & Boulton, M. J. (2000). Twenty years' research on peer victimization and psychosocial maladjustment: A meta-analytic review of cross-sectional studies. *Journal of Child Psychology and Psychiatry and Allied Disciplines, 41*, 441–455.

Hawkins, J. D., Catalano, R. F., & Miller, J. Y. (1992). Risk and protective factors for alcohol and other drug problems in adolescence and early adulthood: Implications for substance abuse prevention. *Psychological Bulletin, 112*, 64–105.

Hawley, P. H. (1999). The ontogenesis of social dominance: A strategy-based evolutionary perspective. *Developmental Review, 19*, 97–132.

Haynie, D. L., Nansel, T., & Eitel, P. (2001). Bullies, victims, and bully/victims: Distinct groups of at-risk youth. *Journal of Early Adolescence, 21*, 29–49.

Henry, D., Guerra, N., Huesmann, R., Tolan, P., Van Acker, R., & Eron, L. (2000). Normative influences on aggression in urban elementary school classrooms. *American Journal of Community Psychology, 28*, 59–81.

Hirsch, B. J., & Rapkin, B. D. (1987). The transition to junior high school: A longitudinal study of self esteem, psychological symptomatology, school life, and social support. *Child Development, 58*, 1235–1243.

Hirschi, T. (1969). *Causes of delinquency.* Berkeley: University of California Press.

Hodges, E. V. E., & Perry, D. G. (1999). Personal and interpersonal antecedents and consequences of victimization by peers. *Journal of Personality and Social Psychology, 76*, 677–685.

Holt, M. K., Finkelhor, D., & Kaufman Kantor, G. (2007). Hidden victimization in bullying assessment. *School Psychology Review, 36*, 345–360.

Hoover, J. H., & Hazler, R. J. (1994). Bullies and victims. *Elementary School Guidance and Counseling, 25*, 212–220.

Hoover, J. H., Oliver, R., & Hazler, R. J. (1992). Bullying: Perceptions of adolescent victims in the Midwestern USA. *School Psychology International, 13*, 5–16.

Hoover, J. H., Oliver, R., & Thomson, K. (1993). Perceived victimization by school bullies: New research and future directions. *Journal of Humanistic Education and Development, 32*, 76–84.

Horne, A., Orpinas, P., Newman-Carlson, D., & Bartolomucci, C. (2004). Elementary school bully busters program: Understanding why children bully and what to do about it. In D. L. Espelage & S. M. Swearer (Eds.), *Bullying in American schools* (pp. 297–326). Mahwah, NJ: Erlbaum.

Hubbard, J. A., Dodge, K. A., Cillessen, A. H. N., Coie, J. D., & Schwartz, D. (2001). The dyadic nature of social information processing in boys' reactive and proactive aggression. *Journal of Personality and Social Psychology, 80*, 268–280.

Huber, J. D. (1983) Comparison of disciplinary concerns in small and large schools. *Small School Forum, 4*, 7–9.

Juvonen, J., Graham, S., & Schuster, M.A. (2003). Bullying among young adolescents: The strong, the weak, and the troubled. *Pediatrics, 112*, 1231–1237.

Juvoven, J., Nishina, A., & Graham, S. (2000). Self-views versus peer perceptions of victim status among early adolescents. In J. Juvonen & S. Graham (Eds.), *Peer harassment in schools: The plight of the vulnerable and victimized* (pp. 105–124). New York: Guilford.

Juvonen, J., Nishina, A., & Graham, S. (2006). Ethnic diversity and perceptions of safety in urban middle schools. *Psychological Science, 17*, 393–400.

Kaltiala-Heino, R., Rimpelae, M., & Rantanen, P. (2001). Bullying at school: An indicator for adolescents at risk for mental disorders. *Journal of Adolescence, 23*, 661–674.

Kandel, D. B. (1978). Homophily, selection, and socialization in adolescent friendships. *American Journal of Sociology, 84*, 427–436.

Kasen, S., Berenson, K., Cohen, P., & Johnson, J. (2004). The effects of school climate on changes in aggressive and other behaviors related to bullying. In D. L. Espelage & S. M. Swearer (Eds.), *Bullying in American schools: A social-ecological perspective on prevention and intervention* (pp. 187–210). Mahwah, NJ: Erlbaum.

Kasen, S., Cohen, P., & Brook, J. S. (1998). Adolescent school experiences and dropout, adolescent pregnancy, and young adult deviant behavior. *Journal of Adolescent Research, 13*, 49–72.

Kasen, S., Johnson, J., & Cohen, P. (1990). The impact of school emotional climate on student psychopathology. *Journal of Abnormal Child Psychology, 18*, 165–177.

Kaukiainen, A., Salmivalli, C., & Lagerspetz, K. (2002). Learning difficulties, social intelligence, and self-concept: Connections to bully-victim problems. *Scandinavian Journal of Psychology, 43*, 269–278.

Kellam, S. G., Ling, X., Merisca, R., Brown, H. C., & Ialongo, N. (1998). The effect of the level of aggression in the first grade classroom on the course and malleability of aggressive behavior into middle school. *Development and Psychopathology, 10*, 165–185.

Kimmel, M. S., & Mahler, M. (2003). Adolescent masculinity, homophobia, and violence. *American Behavioral Scientist, 465*, 1439–1458.

Kochenderfer, B. J., & Ladd, G. W. (1996). Peer victimization: Cause or consequence of school maladjustment? *Child Development, 67*, 1305–1317.

Kochenderfer-Ladd, B., & Wardrop, J. L. (2001). Chronicity and instability of children's peer victimization experiences as predictors of loneliness and social satisfaction trajectories. *Child Development, 72*, 134–151.

Kosciw, J. G. (2004). *The 2003 national school climate survey: The school-related experiences of our nation's lesbian, gay, bisexual, and transgender youth.* New York: GLSEN.

Kumpulainen, K., Rasanen, E., & Henttonen, I. (1998). Children involved in bullying: Psychological disturbance and the persistence of the involvement. *Child Abuse & Neglect, 23*, 1253–1262.

Kusché, C. A., & Greenberg, M. T. (1994). *The PATHS curriculum.* South Deerfield, MA: Channing-Bete.

Ladd, G. W., & Burgess, K. B. (2001). Do relational risks and protective factors moderate the linkages between childhood aggression and early psychological and school adjustment? *Child Development, 72*, 1579–1601.

Lagerspetz, K. M. (1982). Group aggression among school children in three schools. *Scandinavian Journal of Psychology, 23*, 45–52.

Lease, M. L., Musgrove, K. T., & Axelrod, J. L. (2002). Dimensions of social status in preadolescent peer groups: Likeability, perceived popularity, and social dominance. *Social Development, 11*, 508–533.

Loeber, R., & Dishion, T. (1984). Boys who fight at home and school: Family conditions influencing cross-setting consistency. *Journal of Consulting & Clinical Psychology, 52*, 759–768.

Loeber, R., & Stouthame-Loeber, M. (1998). Development of juvenile aggression and violence: Some common misconceptions and controversies. *American Psychologist, 53*, 242–259.

Marini, Z., Fairbairn, L., & Zuber, R. (2001). Peer harassment in individuals with developmental disabilities: Towards the development of a multidimensional bullying identification model. *Developmental Disabilities Bulletin, 29*, 170–195.

McFadyen-Ketchum, S. A., Bates, J. E., Dodge, K. A., & Pettit, G. S. (1996). Patterns of change in early childhood aggressive-disruptive behavior: Gender differences in predictions from early coercive and affectionate mother-child interactions. *Child Development, 67*, 2417–2433.

McPerson, M., Smith-Lovin, L., & Cook, J. M. (2001). Birds of a feather: Homophily in social networks. *Annual Review of Sociology, 27*, 415–444.

Midgley, C., Anderman, E., & Hicks, L. (1995). Differences between elementary and middle school teachers and students: A goal theory approach. *Journal of Early Adolescence, 15*, 90–113.

Mohr, A. (2006). Family variables associated with peer victimization: Does family violence enhance the probability of being victimized by peers? *Swiss Journal of Psychology, 65*, 107–116.

Murray-Close, D., Ostrov, J. M., & Crick, N. R. (2007). A short-term longitudinal study of growth of relational aggression during middle childhood: Associations with gender, friendship intimacy, and internalizing problems. *Development and Psychopathology, 19*, 187–203.

Nansel, T. R., Haynie, D. L., & Simons-Morton, B. G. (2003). The association of bullying and victimization with middle school adjustment. *Journal of Applied School Psychology, 19*, 45–61.

Nansel, T. R., Overpeck, M., Pilla, R. S., Ruan, W. J., Simons-Morton, B. G., & Scheidt, P. (2001). Bullying behaviors among US youth: Prevalence and association with psychosocial adjustment. *Journal of the American Medical Association, 285*, 2094–2100.

Neary, A., & Joseph, S. (1994). Peer victimization and its relationship to self-concept and depression among schoolgirls. *Personality and Individual Differences, 16*, 183–186.

Newman-Carlson, D., & Horne, A. (2004). Bully-Busters: A psychoeducational intervention for reducing bullying behavior in middle school students. *Journal of Counseling and Development, 82*, 259–267.

Newman, D. A., Horne, A. M., & Bartolomucci, C. L. (2000). *Bully busters: A teacher's manual for helping bullies, victims, and bystanders.* Champaign, IL: Research Press.

Newman, R. S., Murray, B., & Lussier, C. (2001). Confrontation with aggressive peers at school: Students' reluctance to seek help from the teacher. *Journal of Educational Psychology, 93*, 398–410.

Nordhagen, R., Nielson, A., Stigum, H., & Kohler, L. (2005). Parental reported bullying among Nordic children: A population-based study. *Child: Care, Health and Development, 31*, 693–701.

Oliver, R., Oaks, I. N., & Hoover, J. H. (1994). Family issues and interventions in bully and victim relationships. *School Counselor, 41*, 199–202.

Olweus, D. (1992). Bullying among schoolchildren: Intervention and prevention. In R. D. Peters, R. J. McMahon, & V. L. Quinse (Eds.), *Aggression and violence throughout the life span* (pp. 100–125). London: Sage.

Olweus, D. (1993a). Bully/victim problems among schoolchildren: Long-term consequences and an effective intervention program. In S. Hodgins (Ed.), *Mental disorder and crime* (pp. 317–349). Thousand Oaks, CA: Sage.

Olweus, D. (1993b). *Bullying at school: What we know and what we can do.* Oxford, UK: Blackwell.

Olweus, D. (1995a). Bullying or peer abuse at school: Facts and interventions. *Current Directions in Psychological Science, 4*(6), 196–200.

Olweus, D. (1995b). Bullying or peer abuse at school: Intervention and prevention. In G. Davies & S. Lloyd-Bostock (Eds.), *Psychology, law, and criminal justice: International developments in research and practice* (pp. 220–224). Oxford, England: Walter De Gruyter.

Olweus, D. (2005). A useful evaluation design and effects of the Olweus Bullying Prevention Program. *Psychology, Crime & Law, 11*, 389–402.

Olweus, D., & Limber, S. (1999). *The bullying-prevention program: Blueprints for violence prevention.* Boulder, CO: Center for the Study and Prevention of Violence.

Olweus, D., Limber, S. P., & Mihalic, S. (2000). *The bullying prevention program: Blueprints for violence prevention* (Vol. 10). Boulder, CO: Center for the Study and Prevention of Violence.

Paul, J., & Cillesen, A. H. N. (2003). Dynamics of peer victimization in early adolescence: Results from a four-year longitudinal study. *Journal of Applied School Psychology, 19*, 25–43.

Pellegrini, A. D. (2002). Bullying, victimization, and sexual harassment during the transition to middle school. *Educational Psychologist, 37*, 151–163.

Pellegrini, A.D., & Bartini, M. (2001). Dominance in early adolescent boys: Affiliative and aggressive dimensions and possible functions. *Merrill-Palmer Quarterly, 47*, 142–163.

Pellegrini, A. D., & Long, J. (2002). A longitudinal study of bullying, dominance, and victimization during the transition from primary to secondary school. *British Journal of Developmental Psychology, 20*, 259–280.

Pepler, D. J., & Craig, W. M. (1995). A peek behind the fence: Naturalistic observations of aggressive children with remote audiovisual recording. *Developmental Psychology, 31*, 548–553.

Pepler, D. J., Craig, W. M., Connolly, J. A., Yuile, A., McMaster, L., & Jiang, D. (2005). A developmental perspective on bullying. *Aggressive Behavior, 32*, 376–384.

Peskin, M. F., Tortolero, S. R., & Markham, C. M. (2006). Bullying and victimization among Black and Hispanic adolescents. *Adolescence, 41*, 467–484.

Phoenix, A., Frosh, S., & Pattman, R. (2003). Producing contradictory masculine subject positions: Narratives of threat, homophobia, and bullying in 11–14 year old boys. *Journal of Social Issues, 59*, 179–195.

Pilkington, N. W., & D'Augelli, A. R. (1995). Victimization of lesbian, gay, and bisexual youth in community settings. *Journal of Community Psychology, 23*, 34–56.

Plummer, D. C. (2001). The quest for modern manhood: Masculine stereotypes, peer culture and the social significance of homophobia. *Journal of Adolescence, 24*, 15–23.

Poteat, V. P. (2007). Peer group socialization of homophobic attitudes and behavior during adolescence. *Child Development, 78*, 1830–1842.

Poteat, V. P. (2008). Contextual and moderating effects of the peer group climate on use of homophobic epithets. *School Psychology Review, 37*, 188–201.

Poteat, V. P., & Espelage, D. L. (2005). Exploring the relation between bullying and homophobic verbal content: The Homophobic Content Agent Target (HCAT) Scale. *Violence and Victims, 20*(5), 513–528.

Poteat, V. P., Espelage, D. L., & Green, H. D., Jr. (2007). The socialization of dominance: Peer group contextual effects on homophobic and dominance attitudes. *Journal of Personality and Social Psychology, 92*, 1040–1050.

Prinstein, M. J., Boergers, J., & Vernberg, E. M. (2001). Overt and relational aggression in adolescents: Social-psychological adjustment of aggressors and victims. *Journal of Clinical Child Psychology, 30*, 479–491.

Raskauskas, J., & Stoltz, A. D. (2007). Involvement in traditional and electronic bullying among adolescents. *Developmental Psychology, 43*, 564–575.

Raydenbush, S. W., & Bryk, A. S. (2002). *Hierarchical linear models* (2nd ed.). Newbury Park, CA: Sage.

Rigby, K. (2001). Health consequences of bullying and its prevention in schools. In J. Juvonen & S. Graham (Eds.), *Peer harassment in school: The plight of the vulnerable and victimized* (pp. 310–331). New York: Guilford.

Rivers, I. (2001). The bullying of sexual minorities at school: Its nature and long-term correlates. *Educational and Child Psychology, 18*, 32–46.

Rodkin, R. C., Farmer, T. W., Pearl, R., & Van Acker, R. (2000). Heterogeneity of popular boys: Antisocial and prosocial configurations. *Developmental Psychology, 36*, 14–24.

Rodkin, R. C., Farmer, T. W., Pearl, R., & Van Acker, R. (2006). They're cool: Social status and peer group supports for aggressive boys and girls. *Social Development, 15*, 175–204.

Rodkin, P. C., & Hodges, E. V. (2003). Bullies and victims in the peer ecology: Four questions for psychologists and school professionals. *School Psychology Review, 32*, 384–400.

Russell, S. T., Kostroski, O., McGuire, J. K., Laub, C., & Manke, E. (2006). *LGBT issues in the curriculum promote school safety* (California Safe Schools Coalition Research Brief No. 4). San Francisco, CA: California Safe Schools Coalition.

Rutter, M., Maughan, B., Mortimore, P., Ouston, J., & Smith, A. (1979). *Fifteen thousand hours: Secondary schools and their effects on children.* Cambridge, MA: Harvard University Press.

Salmivalli, C., Lagerspetz, K., Björkqvist, K., Österman, K., & Kaukiainen, A. (1996). Bullying as a group process: Participant roles and their relations to social status within the group. *Aggressive Behavior, 22*, 1–15.

Salmivalli, C., & Voeten, M. (2004). Connections between attitudes, group norms, and behaviour in bullying situations. *International Journal of Behavioral Development, 28*, 246–258.

Schwartz, D., Dodge, K. A., Pettit, G. S., & Bates, J. E. (1997). The early socialization of aggressive victims of bullying. *Child Development, 68*, 665–675.

Schwartz, D., Gorman, A. H., Nakamoto, J., & Toblin, R. L. (2005). Victimization in the peer group and children's academic functioning. *Journal of Educational Psychology, 97*, 425–435.

Seidman, E., Allen, L., Aber, J. L., Mitchell, C., & Feinman, J. (1994). The impact of school transitions in early adolescence on the self-system and perceived social context of poor urban youth. *Child Development, 65*, 507–522.

Shields, A., & Cicchetti, D. (2001). Parental maltreatment and emotion dysregulation as risk factors for bullying and victimization in middle childhood. *Journal of Clinical Child Psychology, 30*, 349–363.

Smith, J. D., Schneider, B. H., Smith, P. K., & Ananiadou, K. (2004). The effectiveness of whole-school antibullying programs: A synthesis of evaluation research. *School Psychology Review, 33*, 547–560.

Smith, P. K., Bowers, L., Binney, V., & Cowie, H. (1993). Relationships of children involved in bully/victim problems at school. In S. Duck (Ed.), *Learning about relationships, understanding relationship processes* (pp. 184–212). London: Sage.

Smith, P. K., & Myron-Wilson, R. (1998). Parenting and school bullying. *Child Psychology and Psychiatry, 3*, 405–417.

Smith, P. K., & Sharp, S. (1994). *School bullying: Insights and perspectives.* London: Routledge.

Snyder, J., Brooker, M., Patrick, M. R., Snyder, A., Schrepferman, L., & Stoolmiller, M. (2003). Observed peer victimization during early elementary school: Continuity, growth, and relation to risk for child antisocial and depressive behavior. *Child Development, 74*, 1881–1898.

Sourander, A., Helstela, L., Helenius, H., & Piha, J. (2000). Persistence of bullying from childhood to adolescence—A longitudinal 8-year follow-up study. *Child Abuse & Neglect, 24*, 873–881.

Srabstein, J. C., McCarter, R. J., Shao, C., & Huang, Z. J. (2006). Morbidities associated with bullying behaviors in adolescents: School based study of American adolescents. *International Journal of Adolescent Medicine and Health, 18*, 587–596.

Stevens, V., De Bourdeaudhuji, I., & Van Oost, P. (2002). Relationship of the family environment to children's involvement in bully/victim problems at school. *Journal of Youth and Adolescence, 31*, 419–428.

Swearer, S. M., & Doll, B. (2001). Bullying in schools: An ecological framework. *Journal of Emotional Abuse, 2*, 7–23.

Swearer, S. M., Song, S. Y., Cary, P. T., Eagle, J. W., & Mickelson, W. T. (2001). Psychosocial correlates in bullying and victimization: The relationship between depression, anxiety, and bully/victim status. *Journal of Emotional Abuse, 2*, 95–121.

Tapper, K., & Boulton, M. J. (2005). Victim and peer group responses to different forms of aggression among primary school children. *Aggressive Behavior, 31*, 238–253.

Tomada, G., & Schneider, B. H. (1997). Relational aggression, gender, and peer acceptance: Invariance across culture, stability over time, and concordance among informants. *Developmental Psychology, 33*, 601–609.

Tremblay, R. E., Schaal, B., Boulerice, B., Arseneault, L., Soussignan, R. G., Paquette, D., et al. (1998). Testosterone, physical aggression, dominance, and physical development in early adolescence. *International Journal of Behavioral Development, 22*, 753–777.

Troop-Gordon, W., & Ladd, G. W. (2005). Trajectories of peer victimization and perceptions of the self and schoolmates: Precursors to internalizing and externalizing problems. *Child Development, 76*, 1072–1091.

Troy, M., & Sroufe, L. A. (1987). Victimization among preschoolers: Role of attachment relationship history. *Journal of the American Academy of Child and Adolescent Psychiatry, 26*, 166–172.

Unnever, J. D. (2005). Bullies, aggressive victims, and victims: Are they distinct groups? *Aggressive Behavior, 31*, 153–171.

Wentzel, K. R., & Caldwell, K. A. (1997). Friendships, peer acceptance, and group membership: Relations to academic achievement in middle school. *Child Development, 68*, 1198–1209.

Werner, N. E., & Crick, N. R. (2004). Maladaptive peer relationships and the development of relational and physical aggression during middle childhood. *Social Development, 13*, 495–514.

Wigfield, A., Eccles, J. S., Mac Iver, D., Reuman, D., & Midgley, C. (1991). Transitions during early adolescence: Changes in children's domain-specific self-perceptions and general self-esteem across the transition to junior high school. *Developmental Psychology, 27*, 552–565.

Xie, H., Cairns, R. B., & Cairns, B. D. (1999). Social networks and configurations in inner-city schools: Aggression, popularity, and implications for students with EBD. *Journal of Emotional and Behavioral Disorders, 7*, 147–155.

Ybarra, M. L., Alexander, C., & Mitchell, K. J. (2005). Depressive symptomatology, youth internet use, and online interactions: A national survey. *Journal of Adolescent Health, 36*, 9–18.

Young, R., & Sweeting, H. (2004). Adolescent bullying, relationships, psychological well-being, and gender-atypical behavior: A gender diagnosticity approach. *Sex Roles, 50*, 525–537.

# Part IV

**Developmental Effects of School Transitions**

# 11

# The Transition to School in Rural America

## *A Focus on Literacy*

LYNNE VERNON-FEAGANS, KATHLEEN C. GALLAGHER, AND KIRSTEN KAINZ

## Introduction

One of the most important transition points for children during childhood is the transition to formal schooling. Studies have shown that these early school years set the trajectory for children's academic performance throughout their schooling, especially in the area of reading (Alexander & Entwisle, 1988; Juel, 1988; Morrison & Connor, chapter 12 this volume; Vernon-Feagans, 1996; Vernon-Feagans & Blair, 2006). These studies have shown that children who do not progress quickly in reading in the early school years, have a difficult time catching up in the later elementary years. For instance, Juel (1988) found that "the probability that a child would remain a poor reader at the end of fourth grade if the child was a poor reader at the end of first grade was .88%" (p. 440).

A number of important current research studies implicate three specific processes in early elementary school classrooms that set children on their academic trajectory in reading. These processes include: (1) positive relationships between teachers and children in the classroom (Hamre & Pianta, 2001; Mashburn & Pianta, 2006); (2) implementation by teachers of a comprehensive research based literacy instruction in the context of an organized classroom environment (Kainz & Vernon-Feagans, 2007; Lonigan, 2006; Torgesen, 2002); and (3) use of teaching strategies in the classroom that match the instructional level of the child (Juel, 1991; Morrison, 2005; Connor, Morrison, & Slominski, 2006).

While these classroom processes have been identified as critical for early learning and particularly for early literacy, little research addresses how these factors may operate in settings for children in rural schools because so little research has been specifically targeted to address education in rural settings. Rural children constitute about 43% of school age children in America and live on 80% of the country's land mass (Rural School and Community Trust,

2005). Rural children, a largely understudied population in the research literature, are likely to have unique risk and protective factors as they enter school.

This chapter will draw upon the research on rural places and rural education to help underscore the importance of the possible differences between urban and rural places. It will note how these differences might have an impact on how children make a successful transition to school. We begin by defining the term *rural* and describing characteristics of many rural places in the United States. We will then present our conceptual framework that will guide the literature review. We will use this framework to explore the different links among the characteristics of communities, schools, families, and children as they relate to children's successful transition to school. We will emphasize the importance of the proximal processes and relationships within families and classrooms that could be important mediators in understanding children's transition to school in rural places. Finally, we will describe a current rural school intervention project during the transition to school that incorporates critical aspects of our model of early literacy development while being sensitive to the specific context of rural children.

## Defining What Is Rural

A major challenge in understanding rural life and the ways in which it differs from urban/suburban life is how to define *rural*. Both qualitative and quantitative studies have tried to capture the essence of rural life. We will try to summarize some of these data in the next two sections in defining rural life and its relationship to rural education.

***Quantitative Definition of Rural*** In a report by Mathematica (Strong, Del Gross, Burwick, Jethwani, & Ponza, 2005), commissioned by the U.S. Department of Health and Human Services to examine the human services needs in rural areas of the United States, the authors struggled

with the definition of rural. They listed six definitions that
have been used by U.S. federal agencies as a way to give
background for their analysis, while at the same time acknowledging that no common definition was accepted by
everyone. Given the diversity of the definitions, it would
take up much of this chapter to describe and discuss the
merits of each of them. Yet, it is important to understand
the range of definitions of rural, as a way to understand
the research about rural places. To give some sense of
this diversity, two definitions will be described that are
widely used and originate with the National Center for
Educational Statistics (NCES) and the U.S. Census Bureau.
These definitions generally encompass the scope of what
is rural as reported in most of the research mentioned in
this chapter. For more in-depth information, see http://nces.
ed.gov/surveys/ruraled/Definitions.asp as well as the recent
Mathematica report (Strong et al., 2005).

The U.S. Census Bureau and the Office of Management
and Budget (OMB) have used variations of the rural/urban
continuum codes in categorizing counties as either metro
or nonzero (rural). There are three categories of metro from
large to rather small urban areas of 50,000 or more people.
The nonmetro counties are classified into six categories, by
population size and adjacency to metro areas. The Census
Bureau currently uses census tracts rather than counties as
their basic geographic unit. This newer definition is similar
to the older one but with a smaller unit of analysis in use at
the census tract level.

The U.S. Department of Education has updated its
guidelines to reflect advances in technology and research in
defining rural in order to better classify schools as located
in an urban or rural setting, without using census tracts or
counties as the geographic unit. The new 12 locale code
system includes four major categories: city, suburban, town,
and rural. Rural places may be fringe, distant, or remote,
depending on the distance from an urbanized area of greater
than 50,000 people or an urban cluster of between 25,000
and 50,000 people. The advantages of this new system are
that it does not rely on county boundaries, it has a small
city designation, it better identifies suburban areas and
towns, and it has a more differentiated classification of
rural areas.

Even though these two definitions of rural and nonmetro
differ, there are two central tenets that they both endorse.
First, they both capture areas of the country outside of
large urban areas and their suburbs. Second, they generally
include only areas/counties that have towns with fewer than
50,000 people, in addition to being located far from urban/
suburban areas. Data presented in this chapter include reports and research that use a range of definitions but generally fall within the scope of these two broad definitions.

### Qualitative Definitions of Rural and Rural Education   In
reviewing a number of the qualitative/ethnographic studies of rural places (i.e., Coles, 2003; Duncan, 1999; Stack,
1996), there is a consensus on common characteristics that
describe more of the intangible aspects of rural life that are

important in understanding the character of the people living
there. Although these qualitative studies describe family
life as well as education, it is important to understand these
aspects in relation to rural education. Taking these intan-
gibles and combining them with aspects of rural education
has resulted in some consensus as to what makes rural
education differ from urban education (Vernon-Feagans, in
press). There are generally six areas of agreement that help
to better describe rural education, with the recognition that
there is enormous diversity in rural areas, which include
wealthy farming areas in the Midwest as well as some of
the poorest areas in the country, such as the Mississippi
Delta. However, in general, rural education facilities have
these general characteristics: (1) They are located in a small
town or village  at a distance from a large urban area and
in an environment that has historical roots in an agrarian
culture. There may be recent decreases in ties to agriculture because of out-migration and lower levels of farming.
(2) Such areas have access to fewer resources than larger
urban or suburban areas because of distance to resources
and higher poverty rates. There is less ability in these areas
to attract and retain highly qualified teachers, less access to
state-of-the-art professional development opportunities, and
poorer quality educational buildings. (3) Smaller communities may have smaller community based schools, although
there are current trends toward large consolidated schools.
(4) Schools in rural communities may be ready to meet
community needs through cooperation with other sectors
of the local economy, such as support for agrarian life, but
with a need for children to attend school. (5) Rural schools
are grounded in a "sense of place" and are rooted in the lives
of the families whose children attend them.

### The Theoretical Framework that Organizes the
### Transition to School in Rural America

Although people in urban places often envy the pastoral life
in rural America, with farms and small friendly communities, this portrait of rural America is less accurate than it
was 50 years ago. We will describe some of the challenges
faced by people who live in rural America in the early 21st
century, and the advantages of the physical, economic,
and social context of living in rural places in describing
the transition to school. This framework draws from both
an ecological perspective and from a risk perspective in
understanding the factors that enhance and hinder children's
transition to school in rural areas.

The ecological perspective as developed by Bronfenbrenner and colleagues (Bronfenbrenner & Crouter, 1983;
Bronfenbrenner & Evans, 2000) emphasizes both the distal
contextual factors and the proximal relationship factors that
affect children's development. They argue that although the
larger distal contextual factors like poverty, education, and
jobs are important in understanding children's development,
the proximal relationship factors that develop in various
microsystem settings where the child interacts with others might be most important in understanding children's

development. For instance, parent–child relationships and teacher–child relationships may involve critical proximal processes within the home and the school that drive development, beyond the more distal factors. In addition, each ecological setting contains risk and promotive factors that can either enhance or hinder children's development (Bronfenbrenner & Morris, 1998; Sameroff & Fiese, 2000). Furthermore, the accumulation of risk factors leads to an exponential increase in poor outcomes for children (Rutter, 1979; Sameroff, Seifer, Barocas, Zax, & Greenspan, 1987; Sameroff, Seifer, Baldwin, & Baldwin, 1993). For instance, Rutter (1979) found that zero or one risk was related to a 2% rate of psychiatric disorders while four or more risks were related to a 20% rate of psychiatric disorder. Sameroff and colleagues have shown that it is not merely the kind of risk but the number of risks that are most related to poor child outcomes. The accumulation of risks can increase poor child outcomes geometrically, especially with regard to child IQ early and later in childhood.

This review will link this theoretical framework to literature on rural children and the transition to school, despite the dearth of theoretical and empirical work on factors affecting children's transition to school in rural communities. A framework has emerged from our theoretical model that will guide this review and facilitate consideration of risk and promotive factors for the early education of rural children and contexts. Our model considers economic and social factors of the community, school, and family, as well as the individual child's characteristics that affect the transition to school (these influences are indicated by the solid black lines in Figure 11.1). However, we believe that family and classroom processes/relationships may be important mediators of children's successful transition to school, indicated by the dotted lines in Figure 11.1.

Throughout the chapter, major headings will elaborate on the constructs in the model, underscoring the unique aspects of rural life that affect children's transition to school.

## The Rural Economic and Social Community Context

Many of the social and economic shifts since the late 1950s have had profound implications for children and their families who live in nonurban areas of the United States. Farming related occupations now constitute a very small percentage of jobs in rural America, as mechanization of agriculture has increased with a concomitant increase in large corporate farms and the demise of the small family farm (O'Hare & Johnson, 2004). There has been an out-migration of talented young adults to urban areas, leaving behind an elderly population and a smaller but less educated young adult population (O'Hare & Johnson, 2004; Weber, Jensen, Miller, Mosley & Fisher, 2005). This out-migration of talented young adults has been exacerbated by the decrease in small farms and a dramatic decrease in manufacturing jobs in the textile and furniture industries that have moved their operations overseas (O'Hare & Johnson, 2004). This out-migration has been further fueled by the increasingly greater educational and job opportunities in urban and suburban communities (Weber, Duncan, & Whitener, 2002). Education data for rural adults suggests that talented young adults move to more urban areas; only 18% of young adults in rural areas have a bachelor's degree, compared with 30% of young adults in urban areas (Johnson, 2002).

Rural areas did not gain from the economic boom of the 1990s because most rural areas did not participate in the technology revolution that centered on more urban areas, leaving them even more vulnerable to economic losses in the 21st century. These shifts in rural economics have been

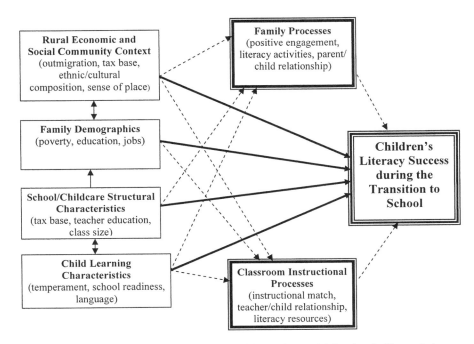

**Figure 11.1** The transition to school in rural America: An ecological and risk/promotion model. Reprinted with permission.

qualitatively and quantitatively different from the shifts that have taken place in urban areas (Regional Educational Laboratory Network, 2004). One of the consequences of these shifts in jobs and people has been an increase in child poverty and an increasing gap between child poverty in urban versus nonurban areas, especially in relation to the gap in the 1990s. Over half the children in rural areas live below 200% of poverty compared to 37% in urban areas (Rivers, 2005). As discussed later, this greater poverty has implications for the resources in young children's homes and the consequently poorer preparedness of children as they enter formal schooling

When one examines families living below 200% of the federal poverty level in rural and urban areas a fairly devastating picture of rural family economics is revealed, even though 80% of rural families have an adult who is working full time. Summers (1997) reported that two thirds of rural poor families who had at least one family member with a full-time job were living below the poverty level. In addition, one quarter of rural poor families had two or more household members with jobs and still the family was living in poverty. These data suggest that available jobs in rural areas are often low wage, which puts stress on families that can lead to adverse consequences, particularly for children (Lichter, Roscigno, & Condron, 2003).

## Family Demographics in Rural America

These economic changes in rural life have implications for children's access to social capital in the family, an element that is especially important as children make the transition to school. Family structural characteristics, such as parental education, poverty status, marital status, and parental mental health, are all associated with children's academic and social competence in the transition to formal schooling (Burchinal, Peisner-Feinberg, Pianta, & Howes, 2002; Entwisle & Alexander, 1999). For example, when parents have more education, their children demonstrate better academic skills over the early school years (Bickel & Spatig, 1999; Burchinal et al., 2002). Rural families have both risks and benefits with respect to these demographic characteristics.

Rural parents work more hours and still earn less than their urban counterparts, which allows them to spend less time with their children. One recent trend among rural families has been an increase in nonstandard work hours and an increase in multiple jobs (Mather & Scopilitti, 2004). These irregular work hours by mothers early in the child's life have been linked to poorer language and cognitive skills at 36 months of age (Han, 2005). In addition, rural families have to commute longer distances to work, school, and services, and only 40% of rural areas have access to public transportation (Friedman, 2003). These trends reflect the changing economics of a service economy in rural areas that have implications for the time parents can spend with their children and the conflict between work hours and parent participation and support of school activities. Parents who

work long hours or have to commute further, have less time to talk with their children about school and be involved in their children's school. This parent participation may be particularly important during the transition to school when children are learning critical skills like reading. Even if these work factors are not relevant for some families, the distance to schools, especially consolidated schools, can be a barrier to parents' participation in school, especially when the school is not community based (Rural School and Community Trust, 2005).

Although rural children are more likely than are urban children to live in two-parent families with at least one employed parent, 59.9% of rural poor children live in single-parent families with rates that are becoming more comparable with urban areas (Dill, 1999). The poverty rates of single-mother headed families have always been greater in rural than in urban areas. Although overall poverty rates declined for female-headed households after the welfare reform in 1996, single rural mothers continued to experience higher rates of poverty than do similar urban mothers, despite the fact that these rural mothers were working more than did their urban counterparts (Lichter & Jensen, 2001). The aggregate data on single mothers mask the large racial differences in rural areas, where African American children are much more likely to live in a female-headed household and twice as likely to be poor in comparison to other children (Graefe & Lichter, 2002). Although African American women with children are much less likely to be married in comparison to their non-African American counterparts, even Black childless women have much lower marriage rates than non-African American women (Graefe & Lichter, 2002). Graefe and Lichter speculate that the low marriage rates for African American women are in large part due to "factors such as cultural attitudes and values or the shortage of economically attractive men" (p. 290). Nevertheless, a one-parent family structure often provides children with a smaller economic base and less access to parental time and resources. The marginal economic position of rural single mothers often is immune to traditional antipoverty strategies that stress job growth (Lichter & McLaughlin, 1995). Rural women, especially poor single mothers, continue to face serious barriers that restrict access to rural employment. For many single mothers, the lack of employer-provided health benefits also is an additional barrier to employment in rural areas.

Children of single mothers in rural areas may be at even greater risk than are children of single mothers in urban areas. As children make the transition to school, single mothers will have even more barriers to overcome with respect to transportation to school, time for their child, and time to develop a relationship to the school. This may be an even greater challenge for minority single mothers because they are much poorer than are nonminority single mothers.

On the other hand, rural life may yield some benefits for early experiences, such as the tendency for rural mothers (more so than urban mothers) to be married at the birth of their first child (Atkinson, 1994) and for children to grow up in a two-parent family. The population density, accompanied by more families living in single-family homes and owning their homes than is the case with urban families, may also mean that children have greater access to nature and larger play areas around their homes (Jaure, Rapoza & Swesnik, 2003; Kannapel & DeYoung, 1999). In addition, people in rural places are also exposed to almost 4 times less violent crime compared to urban places (Donnermeyer, 1994), which means neighborhoods for children are safer and more secure in rural areas. There is now a strong movement among people in rural areas to preserve the "sense of place" and to capitalize on the safer spaces for rearing children and the fact that most live in homes owned by their families (Weber & Jensen, 2004).

Unfortunately, no strong research base exists that examines how the rural family structural and job characteristics discussed above might affect children's transition to school. In a later section we will link these distal structural characteristics to family processes that may exert stronger influences on children's development.

## School Structural Characteristics and Resources in Rural America: Risk and Promotive Factors in Rural Schools

Rural schools present both challenges and benefits to children as they enter school. On the one hand, lower population density is associated with many positive aspects for families and their children; however, it can also render rural schools less competitive for federal funding (Beeson, 2003), and increase education costs associated with busing children long distances to school (Reeves, 2003). The frequent relocation of talented young adults to more urban areas leaves the less skilled workers who remain to support an aging population. What emerges from this trend are rural school districts that are poorer than urban/suburban districts with respect to school resources and community capital. Rural school districts have 66% more children eligible for free/reduced lunch than children in urban schools (27% versus 18%) and per pupil expenditure is about 25% lower in rural than in urban areas (Rural School & Community Trust, 2005).

Schools in rural areas often are geographically isolated resulting in fewer students per school compared to urban and suburban schools (Reeves, 2003). In some cases a single school that serves kindergarten through 12th grade students forms a rural school district. The loss of a tax base to support schools and the loss of population has led to pressure for consolidation of schools across large geographic areas, a process that removes essential education and employment resources from small communities (Lichter et al., 2003). This push toward consolidation since the late 1970s has not improved the schooling of nonurban children. In fact, there is new evidence that nonurban children who attend smaller community schools have higher achievement than nonurban children who attend consolidated larger schools (Rural School and Community Trust, 2005). Although

consolidated schools were supposed to be a cost saving device that could boost the performance of rural schools, this has not happened.

The school bus is a highly salient factor in rural schools. Bus route roads are less developed in rural locations, and bus supervisors are less common. Children who attend consolidated schools in rural areas spend long periods of time on school buses, up to 2 hours each day, without adult supervision (Howley, Howley & Shambelen, 2001; Zars, 1998). These bus rides often include children of very different ages. This age disparity on rural buses with little adult monitoring has been linked to more bullying and antisocial behavior on the buses. These long bus rides may contribute to the poorer academic and social development of rural children, although there are no definitive studies that have investigated these effects.

Smaller and less affluent communities also pose challenges for the quality of schooling children receive. Lee and Burkam (2003) found that although the best schools were in suburban areas and the worst schools were in urban areas as expected, "low-quality schools—as defined by many measures we investigated here—also typify educational institutions in small towns and rural areas" (Lee & Burkam, 2002, p. 77).

Rural school districts struggle to recruit highly qualified teachers (Collins, 1999; Reeves, 2003). They also have less access to professional development for teachers, and poorer physical facilities (Beach, 1997). Research on kindergartens across the United States indicates that rural kindergarten teachers have been on the job longer and with less preparation than is the case with their colleagues in urban/suburban areas (Lee & Burkam, 2002; Zill, 1999). In addition, rural kindergarten teachers rate the level of professional community within their schools lower than do suburban teachers (Lee & Burkam, 2002). A combination of rundown facilities, inadequate preparation, and a poor professional climate in schools may diminish their capacity to be ready to support children's successful transition to kindergarten. These statistics regarding teachers are probably closely associated with teacher salaries. While the general population gained income in the 1990s, teaching professionals in nonurban communities did not (Huang, 1999). On average, the pay of nonurban teachers was 80% of their urban counterparts' remuneration and they were less likely to receive medical benefits (National Education Association, 1998).

To counterbalance these challenges rural schooling offers some benefits that may offset risks for the transition to school, including smaller schools, a more stable teacher workforce, and a more positive view of the schools by parents (Beach, 1997; Loveless, 2003). Rural school communities are often close-knit. For instance, students in rural locations may receive strong teacher support and attention (Ballou & Podgursky, 1995). In addition, students in rural locations may be more likely to connect with teachers and community members, participate in extracurricular activities, and graduate from 12th grade (Khattri, Riley, &

Kane, 1997; Reeves, 2003). In addition, students in rural locations experience smaller class sizes (Khattri, Riley, & Kane 1997), even in kindergarten (Lee & Burkam, 2002). These aspects of rural communities could act as buffers, supporting children's successful transition into school even in the presence of considerable challenges. Unfortunately, there is no research available on the combination of these risk and protective factors related to rural schools.

***School Demographic and Teacher Characteristics*** The transition to school represents a critical opportunity for children to develop and demonstrate academic and social skills that will serve as a foundation for subsequent academic development (Entwisle & Alexander, 1993, 1998). Children attending rural schools develop within unique transition ecologies associated with rural locations described earlier in this chapter. Given the small number of studies on these ecologies and their implications for academic development, we will try to review the data available and suggest some areas for future research.

Kindergarten students in rural schools begin school with academic skills and family economic resources that are lower on average than kindergarteners who attend suburban schools (Lee & Burkam, 2002). Although student characteristics in rural locations might increase the likelihood of difficult school transitions, teachers in rural compared to nonrural locations are more likely to report that their students transitioned to kindergarten with virtually no problems (Zill, 1999). This may be due to school transition practices because teachers in rural locations also report a higher frequency of transition activities, such as outreach to parents and home visits, than is the case with teachers in nonrural locations (Lee & Burkam, 2002; Zill, 1999). In addition, smaller class sizes associated with rural schools could facilitate student–teacher relationships, thereby supporting students' successful transition experiences. Overall, these findings from national surveys suggest that rural school practices support children during the critical transition to school, even though the children's initial academic skills may be lower than those of children in more urban settings. They also allude to the fact that perhaps classroom processes, more so than school structural characteristics, account for children's transition experiences (see Hamre & Pianta, chapter 3 this volume).

Most children, regardless of their background, begin school eager to learn (Morrison, Bachman, & Connor, 2005; Vernon-Feagans, 1996). Studies suggest that most poor children (rural, urban, and minority) come to school with great hopes for success and have families who value education and have high aspirations for their children's educational future (Fitzgerald, Spiegel, & Cunningham, 1991; Vernon-Feagans, 1996). Yet, many economically disadvantaged children do not do well in school for a variety of reasons that may be linked to the failure of schools to address the needs of children from poor and diverse backgrounds. Alexander and Entwisle (1988) found that children with similar backgrounds and skills who did not do well in the first few years

of formal schooling in an urban context were very likely to do poorly throughout their schooling. In addition, it was unusual for children to change that trajectory over the school years. Vernon-Feagans (1996) reported that even children who had an excellent preschool experience but were low income, African American, and lived in a small town grew increasingly behind their nonpoor peers in achievement throughout the elementary school years. From observations in the classroom and analysis of instructional lessons, she found that low-income African American children in the lowest ability groups in school were on task and attentive as much as were their higher ability group counterparts. Yet, an analysis of the instructional context revealed that the teachers were less organized, more redundant, and less clear in working with low ability group children. Although this is just one study, teachers in more rural settings may have challenges in adapting teaching strategies for struggling learners in early elementary classrooms.

Since the first few years of school are important for all children, it is problematic that rural children are behind their urban counterparts in reading and math achievement during elementary school. Pigott and Israel (2005), in an analysis of the ECLS-K data, found that children in suburban schools scored 20% higher in reading and 10% higher in math in the early school years in comparison to children in rural schools. Pigott and Israel (2005) suggest that the lower scores of rural children were due to less skilled teaching. Lower parent involvement due to the long distances between home and school may also account for lower scores. Finally, lower teacher pay may also be an important factor for recruiting and retaining excellent teachers in rural areas (U.S. Government Accountability Office [GAO], 2004), now being addressed somewhat in some specific programs in rural schools, which are discussed in the next section of this chapter.

***The National Programs that Provide Support for Rural Schools*** American schools all over this country have come under increasing scrutiny, in large part because of evidence suggesting that many children are not acquiring the skills they need to succeed in the larger culture (Grissmer, Flanagan, Kawata, & Williamson, 2000). This is particularly evident in rural schools where achievement scores are lower than in more urban areas and where the rates of postsecondary education are much lower for young rural adults. With the advent of No Child Left Behind (NCLB) Act of 2001 all schools now publicly report their achievement levels and gains from year to year. The disaggregated data mandated by NCLB revealed differences in achievement for minority and low-SES groups compared to nonminority children (National Center for Education Statistics [NCES], 2003). No Child Left Behind expects all students to achieve on grade level and make adequate growth across a year by 2014, but many schools lack resources they need to meet this mandate. This is especially true in rural areas where geographic isolation and decreasing populations make recruiting highly qualified teachers more difficult. A GAO report in 2004 examined the extra help that rural schools might need to meet the demands of NCLB by 2014. Interviews with rural school officials revealed that rural schools reported more challenges with economically disadvantaged students, less access to resources, more geographic isolation, limited access to teacher training, and less consistent access to the Internet.

Recent legislation has been successful in supporting rural schools through the Rural Education Achievement Program (REAP) (http://www.ed.gov/nclb/freedom/local/reap), which provides two special grant programs to help small and low income rural schools meet the NCLB goals. These include The Small Rural School Grant Program (CDFA # 84.358A) and The Rural and Low-Income School Program (CDFA # 84.358B). Another program that has been implemented is Reading First (http://www.ed.gov/programs/readingfirst/index.html) designated for low wealth schools whose Annual Yearly Progress also needs improvement if it is to meet the goals of NCLB. Most schools that receive these monies are located in urban or rural areas. Each school that receives Reading First monies must develop a plan that focuses on the enhancement of early literacy in the five areas identified by the National Reading Panel (2000) and endorsed by Reading First. They are phonological awareness, phonics (decoding and word identification), fluency, vocabulary, and comprehension. Reading First provides intensive training and on site literacy consultants to facilitate teacher effectiveness in the teaching of reading. The implementation study documented some advantages to Reading First with respect to resources in the classrooms, having a literacy consultant, and focusing more instruction on literacy. Reading First, along with other rural enhancement programs may help rural schools, but only if these policies intensively target the specific range of challenges faced by rural schools as they attempt to provide an excellent education for all students in the face of limited resources, geographic isolation, and dwindling community populations.

***Childcare/Preschool Programs before School Entry*** Although public schools provide the learning context for children from kindergarten through 12th grade, the preschool/childcare context is an important educational one for children prior to school entry. Thus, it is valuable to understand what is known about the preschool experiences of rural children since we know that they come to school with skills below those of their urban and suburban counterparts.

Nearly half of the nation's children enter childcare before their third birthday; nearly 60% have childcare experience before formal school entry (Singer, Fuller, Keiley, & Wolf, 1998). While childcare use among rural families is less than in urban areas (Beach, 1997), formal childcare use is even less common. Rural families tend to have their children cared for by informal "kith and kin" arrangements with someone they know and trust. This may provide some benefits for children (Strong et al., 2005). A study with low-

income minority kindergarteners reported that early entry to childcare predicted higher kindergarten social skills, while more time in a childcare setting predicted lower kindergarten social skills (Connell & Prinz, 2002). While numerous studies have documented the benefits of childcare for children's academic and social development, benefits are found only when high quality structure and processes characterize childcare. Children who participate in high quality childcare in early childhood demonstrate higher language, cognitive, and social skills in the transition to school (National Institute of Child Health and Development [NICHD], 2003a). These effects are stronger for children who live in poverty (Christian, Morrison, & Bryant, 1998).

While some research suggests that patterns of childcare use do not vary by geographic location (Singer et al., 1998), a limited body of research suggests that patterns of childcare use in rural communities are different from those in urban and suburban communities (Atkinson, 1994; Katras, Zulker, & Bauer, 2004). These differences, which include access, affordability, and cultural considerations, may contribute to challenges for children, families, and teachers in the transition to formal school. Atkinson (1994) described rural and urban families' use of childcare, examining issues related to accessibility and family preferences. In rural communities, regulated childcare arrangements were less available and affordable than in urban communities. With limited accessibility and affordability, rural families were more likely to use relative care than urban families, but had fewer caregivers for longer periods, than their urban counterparts (Atkinson, 1994).

Childcare information and referral services, designed to help families find and evaluate childcare, are less accessible in rural areas. Instead, rural families use family and community social networks. In the wake of welfare reform, rural families combined resources to secure childcare to support their employment, creating a network of family and community relationships (Katras et al., 2004). Despite the creation of a "private safety net," rural families still often face challenges with maintaining consistent, affordable childcare for their children. Evidence suggests that access to consistent, high quality childcare may be limited in rural communities, and may influence families' economic burden and workforce issues, as well as constrain children's preparedness in the transition to school.

***Head Start in Rural America*** For children in poverty, those who participate in Head Start programs have an academic and social advantage over nonparticipants in the transition to school (C. T. Ramey & Ramey, 2006; S. L. Ramey, 1999). In particular, programs with strong family connections benefit children the most (Peters, Bolin, & Murphy, 1991). Early Head Start, a program serving infants to 3 years, has been successful at helping families prepare children for school. In a randomized trial of 3001 children, researchers found that children enrolled in Early Head Start performed better in cognitive and language development, had more sustained attention with objects, were more engaged with parents, and had less aggressive behavior than children who had not been in a Head Start program (Love et al., 2005). Additionally, parents of program children provided more language and learning stimulation, read more to their children, and spanked less than did parents of children not enrolled in Early Head Start.

Participation in Early Head Start and Head Start are associated with better adjustment to school, but only a percentage of children who qualify for Head Start programs are able to attend. Rural children are more likely than nonrural children to attend Head Start programs, but are less likely to attend prekindergarten programs overall (Zaslow, Brown, & Aufseeser, 2005). Rural children's greater representation in Head Start programs is most likely due to the greater prevalence of poverty in rural communities. Furthermore, due to distance and transportation issues, many rural children participate in programs using a home visiting model, which may have different benefits, in terms of preparation for formal schooling, from those found in a center-based program. Research is needed that examines rural contexts of early intervention programs to elucidate benefits and challenges of these programs for rural children and families in the transition to school.

Therefore, although there is a great need for more and better research on rural schools, particularly during the critical transition to schooling, this brief review suggests that the structural features of rural schools and childcare are complex and provide both risks and buffers for students as they transition to school. The exact nature of the effects of these structural features of rural schools remains unknown and they would be important to understand in relationship to the processes within schools that may affect children's transition to school.

## Characteristics of Children and Early School Success

All schools, even rural ones (Rosenkoetter, 2001), expect children to demonstrate linguistic, organizational, and regulatory competencies by the start of kindergarten. Children's individual characteristics, such as approaches to learning, social skills, and language and literacy "readiness" all play pivotal roles in their preparation for the transition to school. To illustrate, one study revealed that child differences on academic and social indicators of school adjustment accounted for 83.5% of the variance in school adjustment, while class and school membership accounted for 10.3% and 6.2% of the variance, respectively (van den Oord & Van Rossem, 2002). Since most research on individual differences in children's functioning in early schooling has failed to consider rural populations, this section addresses important characteristics for children's successful school transitions, in general, highlighting a few studies with rural populations.

Vernon-Feagans (1996) reported the literacy trajectories of poor small town children who had attended an early intervention program over the early school years. Their entry skills were at the 40th percentile in literacy at school entry compared to their more mainstream middle class counterparts who started school at about the 75th percentile. Schooling did not compensate for their lower entry skills; in fact, the gap between poor and nonpoor children increased throughout elementary school, suggesting the importance of these entry skills for later achievement. Alexander and Entwisle (1988, 1998) found similar trajectories for children in a more urban setting. In studies of the transition to school, using the The Early Childhood Longitudinal Study, Kindergarten Class of 1998-99 ECLS-K data set, children from rural areas entered school with poorer readiness skills in literacy and related school behaviors than children in suburban settings (Lee & Burkam, 2002). However, Kainz and Vernon-Feagans (2007) found that entry level skills of children living in poverty, regardless of geographic location, were important in predicting reading growth of early elementary school although school quality and racial composition also influenced growth.

A constellation of behavioral characteristics associated with early school success is referred to as children's *approaches to learning*. Combining temperament and school-related dispositions, approaches to learning include attention, behavioral and emotional regulation, and affective and motivational characteristics associated with learning (Hair, Hulle, Terry-Humen, Lavelle, & Calkins, 2006). In studies with children from a variety of geographical areas, some temperamental approaches to learning appear to disadvantage children in the transition to school. For example, children prone to shyness may experience difficulty with the multiple novelties of entering a new classroom environment (Early et al., 2002) and very active children are subject to poorer academic scores in first grade (Bramlett, Scott, & Rowell, 2000). On the other hand, children who are more adaptable when approaching new situations fare better socially and academically in preschool and in the transitions to kindergarten and first grade (Mendez, Fantuzzo, & Cicchetti, 2002). Fish and Pinkerman (2003) reported several temperamental correlates of children's language skills in the transition to school with a poor, rural sample. Poorer language skills were associated with less cooperative temperament and lack of initiative, while relatively better language skills were associated with more temperamental cooperation and persistence.

Attention and behavior problems have also been implicated in poorer performance in school (Feagans & McKinney, 1991; Feagans & Merriwether, 1990; Vernon-Feagans & Blair, 2006). For example, children who have trouble attending during classroom instruction, as rated by their teachers or through observation, do more poorly in reading during the early elementary years (Feagans & McKinney, 1991; McKinney & Feagans, 1987). One study with a rural sample reported poorer cognitive functioning and more behavior problems for kindergarten boys identified by teachers as having attention difficulties (McGlamery, Ball, Henley, & Besozzi, 2007). Faced with stringent progress goals and unprepared learners, teachers explained that they often referred children with challenging behaviors to outside sources, in order to stay on task in the classroom.

Research suggests that problems with aggression are more prevalent in urban than rural schools (Thomas & Bierman, 2006). However, rural children are as likely to require mental health services as children in nonrural settings (Walrath et al., 2003). While teachers cite behavior problems as impeding children's ability to learn, there is evidence that children's cognitive and self-regulation skills develop independently. This suggests that both may play an important role (Konold & Pianta, 2005) in early school success. A particular challenge is the dearth of mental health resources available to support rural schools and families in their efforts to help children with behavior problems (Walrath et al., 2003).

Another important skill in the transition to formal schooling is language abilities. Hart and Risley (1995) found that low-income children came to school with poorer vocabulary than more advantaged children and this gap in vocabulary began in early childhood and increased over the preschool years. They argued that the maternal vocabulary input experienced by these children in their homes contributed to the child's vocabulary, suggesting that mothers in poverty provided much fewer individual words to their children than more economically advantaged mothers over the preschool period. The children's vocabulary at school entry related to their later reading performance in elementary school. In research that used the Abecedarian study of low-income African American children, children's initial abilities to answer questions about stories, paraphrase stories, as well as teacher ratings of their oral language in the classroom were very predictive of children's later reading achievement (Feagans & Farran, 1994; Feagans, Farran, & Fendt, 1995; Feagans & Fendt, 1991). In a more recent study, toddlers living in rural Appalachia had language abilities similar to their nonrural peers; however, by kindergarten the rural children's language abilities were much lower than their nonrural peers (Fish & Pinkerman, 2003). Children in rural areas are poorer than are children in urban or suburban settings, and their poorer readiness skills and later achievement are probably due in part to poverty and the related factors already discussed in this chapter.

Ecological features associated with rurality may interact with children's individual characteristics in limiting (or supporting) their success in the transition to school. These ecological features include race, immigration status, poverty, and access to resources, and may exacerbate the school challenges posed for children who are less socially and academically ready for the demands of formal schooling. In studies rating kindergarten and first grade adjustment among nonrural children, teachers reported more behavior problems and lower social competence for African American as compared to European American children (Sbarra & Pianta, 2001). Additionally, teachers reported decreased task orientation and frustration tolerance from kindergarten to first grade for African American, but not for European American children. Boys were more likely to experience

difficulty in the transition to school, possibly due to poorer approaches than girls to learning and self-regulation (Zill, 1999). Children from minority families, except Asian, performed more poorly at school entry on a wide range of school readiness measures (Lee & Burkam, 2002), but the gap identified between White and Black entry skills was largely accounted for by SES differences, suggesting that SES may be the most pervasive influence on school readiness skills.

In conclusion, teachers report that 16% of children experience serious difficulty in the transition to kindergarten (Rimm-Kaufman, Pianta, & Cox, 2000), and higher percentages of children with difficult transitions are reported in schools with more minorities and higher poverty (Zill, 1999), both of which are prevalent in many rural schools. However, one study documents that associations between family characteristics and children's readiness for the transition to school were mediated by child attention (National Institute of Child Health and Development [NICHD], 2003a), suggesting that individual differences in child characteristics may account for children's early school success, regardless of family characteristics. This finding supports the notion that, regardless of children's early experiences and cultural influences, schools need to be "ready" for children. Much more research is needed to examine how children's individual characteristics influence and are influenced by rural classroom contexts in the transition to school, and how rural schools can be more "ready" for rural children and families. Additionally, more process-oriented research is required if we are to understand the fit between child, family, and school instructional characteristics. For example, there is evidence that low-income rural elementary school children are exposed to a greater variety of physical and psychosocial stressors than are middle-income children. In one study comparing children of different socioeconomic levels within rural samples, children from lower income families demonstrated and reported more psychological distress and more self-regulating and physiological symptoms of stress (Evans & English, 2002).

## Family Processes in the Home as a Mediator of Children's Transition to School

The most consistent predictor of school success has consistently been the quality of the home, including parenting (Cummings, Davies & Campbell, 2000; NICHD Early Childcare Network, 2001, 2003a, 2003b; Shonkoff & Phillips, 2000). Children's early experiences in families shape their preparation for the transition to formal schooling. For example, children's early relationships with parents are associated with social adjustment to kindergarten (Schmidt, Demulder, & Denham, 2002). Among a sample of nonrural African American children, family structure, cohesion, and beliefs were associated with children's academic, social, and behavioral competence (Smith, Prinz, Dumas, & Laughlin, 2001).

Research has documented structural and demographic

differences between urban and rural families, but it has yet to elaborate the processes within rural families that differ from those found in urban and suburban families and that may be implicated in child outcomes. The bottom line for children beginning school is that being poor or living with a single or less-educated parent is associated with at least some element of risk for a successful transition and early school experience (Entwisle & Alexander, 1999). But risk is not reality, and several other factors impact a child's success in the transition to school, including parental attitudes and beliefs, parenting processes, and family literacy practices that have generally been considered the proximal processes that mediate early learning (Vernon-Feagans, Head-Reeves, & Kainz, 2004; Vernon-Feagans, Odom, Pancsofar, & Kainz, 2007).

Parental attitudes and beliefs, particularly about children's development and education, are associated with children's success in the transition to school. Mothers' higher educational expectations for their children are associated with higher achievement and teachers' ratings of cognitive competence (Mantzicopoulos, 1997). Furthermore, when parents have more progressive parenting beliefs, defined as promoting independence and curiosity, children demonstrate better academic skills in the transition to formal schooling (Burchinal, Peisner-Feinberg, Pianta, & Howes, 2002). Research is needed on rural families' attitudes toward and beliefs about their children's education and development, and how those views impact children's success in the transition to formal schooling.

Family processes, in particular parenting styles, are associated with children's success in early schooling. Generally, children of parents who are sensitive and responsive to their children's needs (NICHD Early Child Care Research Network, 2001), supportive of their learning (Mantzicopoulos, 1997), and independence (Brody, Stoneman, & McCoy, 1994), demonstrate better academic and social adjustment in the transition to school. The Study of Child Care and Youth Development (SECCYD) found that, the quality of the home was the most influential predictor of outcomes for early language, social and cognitive outcomes for children (NICHD, Early Childhood Research Network [ECCRN], 2002). In their most recent evidence of school outcomes through third grade, the NICHD, ECCRN (2005) found that persistent poverty was the greatest predictor of child achievement through third grade, but that less positive parenting partially mediated these relationships.

Other studies have found similar relationships with parenting as an important mediator between risk (poverty, poor parental education, dangerous neighborhoods, and maternal depression) and child achievement in school (Burchinal, Roberts, Zeisel, Hennon & Hooper, 2006; Greenberg, Lengua, Coie, & Pinderhughes, 1999). Furthermore, the impact of poverty on children may be mediated, at least in part, by poverty's negative impact on parenting (Brody & Flor, 1998; Burchinal et al., 2006; Evans, 2004; Krishnakumar & Black, 2003; Liver, Brooks-Gunn, & Kohen, 2002; NICHD, ECCRN, 2005). For example, in one study fewer economic resources in female single-parent households were associated with parents feeling less efficacy in their discipline and parental affection, and subsequently associated with teachers reporting poorer social and behavioral outcomes for elementary school children (Mistry, Vandewater, Huston, & McLoyd, 2002).

Analyses of the ECLS-K data suggest that rural parents are more likely than nonrural parents to report higher warmth in their parenting style and less likely to report parental aggravation (Zaslow et al., 2005). This study suggests that there may be compensatory processes in the home that can benefit children in rural homes. Yet, in the same analyses, rural parents reported using less positive discipline with their children. This seeming inconsistent finding needs to be investigated more carefully but may be related to rural families' reliance on more authoritarian child rearing in the context of a loving family environment.

Studies also suggest that parental language input may be a critical component of parenting that may serve as a mediator of children's later achievement. Studies of both African American and non-African American families note that parental language input is related both to children's later language use and to their later achievement in school (Bornstein, Haynes, Painter, & Genevro, 2000; Dickinson & Tabors, 2001; Hart & Risley, 1995; Roberts et al., 1995, 1998; Pancsofar & Vernon-Feagans, 2006). Parents who read to their children and talk in sentences that are more complex and use more words have children who perform better on language and literacy measures both early and later in childhood.

Children learn the purposes and uses of literacy through those in their immediate environment, so their literacy development is also shaped, in part, by the home literacy environment (cf. Hammer, Miccio, & Wagstaff, 2003; Hardman & Jones 1999; Heath, 1983; Vernon-Feagans, Head-Reeves, & Kainz, 2004). Family literacy activities and shared reading, including book reading, are associated with better language outcomes in the early school years (Neuman, 1997; Payne, Whitehurst, & Angell, 1994). Book reading interactions enhance children's vocabularies (Ninio, 1983; Senechal, LeFevre, Hudson, & Lawson, 1996), provide them with knowledge of language in books and talk about books, expose them to print and literacy conventions (Dickinson, De Temple, Hirschler, & Smith, 1992; Snow & Ninio, 1986), and stimulate metalinguistic awareness (Bus, van Ijzendorn, & Pelligrini, 1995). Parents often set up joint routines when reading to their young children (Ninio & Bruner, 1978). They may ask many questions (Anderson-Yockel & Haynes, 1994), adjust their teaching strategies as their children become more proficient in participating in the interactions (Ninio & Bruner, 1978; van Kleeck, Gillam, Hamilton, & McGrath, 1997), and produce more abstract utterances and questions as their children reach preschool age (Pelligrini, Perlmutter, Galda, & Brody, 1990; van Kleeck et al., 1997). There is little information about how these book-reading interactions might be different in rural families as compared to urban/suburban families because of the dearth of research in this area. Lee and Burkam (2002) reported that parents in rural areas read to their children less often and had fewer books in the home than suburban families. It is likely that these findings are related to the greater poverty in rural areas but may also be related to parents having less access to libraries and other literacy related materials than they would in urban/suburban areas. In future research it will be important to understand how the proximal processes in the home during book reading and other home literacy experiences are related to children's success in reading in rural areas.

## Classroom Instructional Processes: Characteristics that Make a Difference for Children

*Classroom Processes* Although home processes are important in understanding children's early literacy, the classroom instructional environment is also critical to children's learning, especially for children who are at risk because of poverty and related factors. There is some controversy over specific classroom instructional strategies that promote the most growth in literacy and math (Bredekamp & Copple, 1997; Maxwell, McWilliam, Hemmeter, Ault, & Schuster, 2001). However, there is also consensus about the general attributes of good teaching in the early grades that should apply across both the rural and urban context (Morrison et al., 2005; Morrison & Connor, chapter 12 this volume; Hamre & Pianta, chapter 3 this volume; Snow, Burns, & Griffin, 1998). These include at least three important processes that occur in early elementary classrooms, which were mentioned at the beginning of the chapter.

The development of a positive teacher–child relationship helps children feel valued and successful as learners in the classroom. So clearly, this is the first, and especially important process to take place in the early elementary school classroom (Hamre & Pianta, 2005, chapter 3 this volume; Peisner-Fineberg et al., 2001; Pianta & Stuhlman, 2004). Second, teachers need to implement a comprehensive research based instruction within the context of an organized classroom environment (Kainz & Vernon-Feagans, 2007). The third process is the instructional match in the classroom, suggesting that teachers need to develop instructional strategies that match the strengths and weaknesses of individual learners (Connor, Morrison, Fishman, Schatschneider, & Underwood, 2007; Foorman & Torgesen, 2001; Morrison, 2005). Even though there is agreement on these characteristics, there is not good evidence in urban or rural schools that these attributes are often observed in classrooms. For instance an article from the NICHD Study of Early Childcare (Pianta, LaParo, Payne, Cox, & Bradley, 2002) found that first graders spent most of their time in teacher directed activities, including one class during which they spent all their time on work sheets. In another recent study of first grade children, the amount of time spent in nonacademic activities during instructional time varied from 40 to 90 minutes, suggesting considerable variability in instructional time for children (Connor, Morrison, & Katch, 2004). These

are characteristics of classroom instruction that need to be improved in most classrooms, both urban and rural. We will look at these three individual processes and how they might be important for enhancing early literacy development in rural schools.

*Teacher–Child Relationships* Although teacher–child relationships have been a focus of much research, only recently has there been consistent evidence of the importance of this relationship in predicting early literacy during the first years of formal schooling; and virtually no research has addressed these issues with children in rural settings. Hamre and Pianta (2005) reported that gaps in reading achievement growth in first grade narrowed when first grade teachers displayed both sensitive behaviors toward children and implemented specific instructional supports, used conceptually complex language, and gave appropriate feedback to students on their work. Teachers who had good relationships with their students in conjunction with appropriate instruction helped their struggling children make gains. Teachers also rated children's achievement higher when they had a closer relationship with the child (Pianta & Stuhlman, 2004). In addition, there is evidence that even students' perceptions of teacher–child relationships in elementary school predict child outcomes (Hughes, Cavell, & Wilson, 2001).

In rural areas where teachers are more likely to know the families of the children they teach and more likely to see the families in a nonschool context, there is more opportunity for a good teacher/child/family relationship. However, there is some risk of stereotyping nonmainstream or poor families that have a reputation in the community that could hinder teacher–child relationships. A recent study highlights the complexity of teacher–student relationships in rural settings. Kindergarten and first grade teachers reported increasing relational conflict over the course of the school year with boys and African American children. More frequent behavior problems accounted for the increasing conflict with boys; however, conflict was associated with increasing relationship conflict for African American children, regardless of a myriad of child, teacher, and family variables (Gallagher, Kainz, Mayer, & Vernon-Feagans, in press).

*Comprehensive Literacy Instruction* The second characteristic that is linked to progress in literacy is the actual instruction that the teacher employs in the classroom. The ECLS-K data set has been instructive to this issue. Kainz and Vernon-Feagans (2007) found that a comprehensive literacy instruction by teachers, that included the important aspects of research based practice, was important in understanding the literacy growth of children who lived in poverty. Especially important has been the research on the measurement and importance of early phonological abilities in young children (Juel, Griffith, & Gough, 1986; Lonigan, 2006; Lonigan, Burgess, Anthony, & Barker, 1998; Wagner, Torgesen & Rashotte, 1994), including phonemic awareness and sensitivity to rhyme and alliteration. Lonigan and colleagues have linked poor preschool abilities in phonological processing and vocabulary skills to growing up in poverty (Lonigan, 2006; Lonigan et al., 1998). Snow et al. (1998), in their national consensus report on early reading concluded that most of children's reading problems could be prevented by increasing their skills in eight domains of oral language and vocabulary, print knowledge, and processing of phonological information. The National Reading Panel (2000) focused on these eight domains and reduced the number of areas to five critical ones. These domains range from the most basic to the most complex aspects of reading: phonemic awareness, phonics, fluency, vocabulary, and reading comprehension. The first three are critical to word identification, while the last two are linked to the comprehension of the text material. In the next few paragraphs, we will elaborate briefly on these skills.

*Phonemic Awareness, Phonics, and Fluency*  Phonemic awareness, phonics, and fluency are central to word recognition (Torgesen, Rashotte, Alexander, Alexander, & MacPhee, 2003). The National Reading Panel (2000) determined that effective instruction includes teaching children to hear the sounds in words and to understand that words are made up of sounds (phonemic awareness). Phonics is the process of linking sounds with letters and combining these into words. Young readers must first recognize the relation between alphabetic symbols and spoken language at several levels (words, syllables, and phonemes) (Adams, 1990; Lyon, 1996). The basic task of the beginning reader is to learn that graphemes represent phonemes. Most studies that include children from a range of economic backgrounds demonstrate very clearly that low-income children perform more poorly than do their more advantaged peers. Low-income children's normative developmental progression is slower than that of their more affluent peers; and their ultimate competence with regard to literacy outcomes may be highly dependent upon intense, direct instruction in these very skills (Lonigan et al., 1998; Raz & Bryant, 1990; Vernon-Feagans, Miccio, Manlove, & Hammer, 2001).

Early problems with phonemic awareness and phonics have cumulative, adverse effects and can lead to reading disability and underachievement in literacy and literacy-dependent content areas (Lyon, 1995; MacDonald & Cornwall, 1995; Mann, 1993; Stanovich, 1987). Prereaders with the poorest phoneme segmentation skills are most likely to become the poorest readers (Ball & Blachman, 1988). Children who from the beginning are behind in phonemic awareness tend to fall further behind (Connor, Morrison, & Slominski, 2006; Stanovich, 1987). In a meta-analysis of 61 studies, Scarborough (1998) found letter identification and print concepts at school entry were highly correlated with reading ability 1 or 2 years later. Putting these skills together in recognizing and pronouncing words easily also involves fluency in reading. This takes practice in oral reading using passages with words that are initially familiar to children so they learn to read efficiently and

effectively. There is a dearth of information about whether rural teachers are more or less proficient in using these strategies but since rural children perform more poorly on reading achievement than children from urban/suburban areas, it is likely that rural teachers may not have access to the best practices and professional development. More process related classroom research is essential if we are to understand the current reading practices of rural elementary teachers.

*Vocabulary, Narrative Skills, and Reading Comprehension*  Vocabulary skills and oral language provide the foundation for reading comprehension (NICHD ECCRN, 2005; Stork & Whitehurst, 2002; Whitehurst & Lonigan, 1998). The diversity of vocabulary has been found to be especially important (Neuman & Dickinson, 2002) in laying the foundation for reading comprehension (NICHD ECCRN, 2005; Scarborough, 2001; Sénéchal & LeFevre, 2002; Whitehurst & Lonigan, 2001). Children of the poor are at risk for academic failure, in part, because they are more likely to come to school with a paucity of vocabulary (Brody & Flor, 1998; Burchinal et al., 2006). For example, Hart and Risley (1995) examined the vocabulary input of urban Black low-income children versus more advantaged children. They found that the children's exposure to diverse vocabulary was much greater in the advantaged families and that the gap between the groups increased over time (Hart & Risley, 1995). These differences were related to the children's language use and their later achievement in school.

Other studies have also documented language use and other oral language differences by social class, ethnicity, and geographic location (Blank, Rose, & Berlin, 1978; Heath, 1983; Tizard & Hughes, 1984,) but have found some interesting cultural and ethnic differences that may have implications for teaching children from different backgrounds. Two of these studies focus on nonurban African American children in the South (Feagans & Farran, 1981; Heath, 1983; Vernon-Feagans, 1996). These studies of poor African American children found elaborated language skills in young children, especially the boys. In fact, the rural African American boys (Vernon-Feagans, 1996) had superior narrative and storytelling skills relative to the middle-class White children in the naturalistic environment, but these skills did not translate into better performance in school (Feagans & Haskins, 1986; Vernon-Feagans, 1996). The 5-year-old African American boys, who, in their neighborhoods told the best narratives and used the most words, were rated by their teachers as having the worst language ability in school. Heath also reported that these rural Black children had extensive storytelling skills, and that Black boys as young as 2 years of age were encouraged to tell stories. Heath (1983) reported, that African American adults rarely asked questions of children, especially ones where the answer was known to the adults. These results suggest the importance of examining the cultural and ethnic differences among children who are living in rural areas and helping teachers to understand how these differences may have an impact on children's language and literacy skills.

***Instructional Match between Teacher and Child***  Finally, it is particularly important to understand whether teacher instructional activities are appropriate for the individual characteristics of children. Although programs like Reading First have endorsed individualized instruction that meets the needs of different children, most reading instructional programs do not offer specific strategies that match the level of the child's literacy skills. This match between skills and instruction may be particularly important for struggling readers who come to school without the preliteracy skills that allow them to profit from many general reading programs. Foorman and Torgesen (2001) propose that struggling readers need the same set of skills as other children but they will need more effective and more intensive instruction. Accordingly, they argue,

> Risk for reading failure always involves the interaction of a particular set of child characteristics with specific characteristics of the instructional environment. Risk status in not entirely inherent in the child, but always involves a "mismatch" between child characteristics and the instruction that is provided. (p. 206)

They stress that children who do not profit from regular classroom instruction require more explicit and comprehensive, more intensive, and more supportive teaching, which should be done synergistically by the classroom teacher. Instruction for these children needs to be in a small group or one-on-one sessions where instruction is initially very explicit, sequenced, and phonics-based. In addition, the instruction needs to be supportive in both emotional and cognitive terms. Helping struggling learners to develop a good relationship with the teacher is important, but it is also important for the teacher to help scaffold learning so that the child feels success at the end of each learning session. This approach, which is suggested by Foorman and Torgesen (2001), is not appropriate for all learners. Juel and Minden-Cupp (1998) observed that children with better reading skills made more progress in classrooms that used a meaning based approach (instruction that helps children extract and construct meaning from text), while children with weaker skills seemed to gain more from classrooms with a code based emphasis (instruction that helps children become proficient in phonological decoding and word reading skills). Similarly, Connor, Morrison, and Katch (2004) note that children who entered first grade with low letter–word reading progressed most when they received explicit code managed instruction, while students with higher letter–word skills did better with less code managed instruction. Children with higher entry vocabulary scores progressed most in literacy with meaning managed instruction while children with lower vocabulary scores progressed most with code managed instruction at the beginning of the school year and meaning managed instruction near the end of the year. In a follow-up study when children were in third grade, Connor, Morrison, and Petrella (2004) found that children with average to low reading comprehension achieved greater growth in classrooms that spent more time on code managed instruction but demonstrated less growth in classrooms when more time was spent on meaning focused instruction. In their most recent study, they examined the effect of software developed to individualize instruction based on the assessed skills of children. Similar to their other work, they examined the effect of this A2i software that helped teachers decide on whether to use code managed instruction or to use child focused meaning focused instruction. The teachers in the experimental schools who were trained to use the A2i software to individualize instruction had children who progressed more in literacy than the control teachers who did not have access to such software and training. Additionally, those teachers who implemented the A2i the most had children who gained the most in literacy over the school year.

No studies have been conducted in rural areas at the time of writing to examine the match between the child's level of language/literacy and classroom instruction. There is a study, however, that examined teacher strategies as a function of the cultural–ethnic background of children in rural America. The study demonstrated the possible mismatch between teacher and children that could lead to poorer child learning. Using the children from the Abecedarian early intervention project as they were entering school (Feagans & Fendt, 1991) children were presented with a story task to act out with toys and then to paraphrase. After children successfully paraphrased a story, they were asked a series of concrete and abstract questions. Findings suggested that the rural poor African American children and middle class European American children were more similar in their ability to answer abstract questions about a story but they were more different in the kind of incorrect answers they gave to these questions. Middle class European American children were more likely to say, "I don't know" or were silent when they were asked a question they could not answer. On the other hand, the African American poor children were much more likely to answer a question they could not answer with a category mistake (an answer that could not possibly be the answer to that kind of question). For instance, they might give a "place" answer to a "why" question or the name of a person as the answer to a "how" question. Although on the surface, these answers are all incorrect, there were implications for the kind of feedback and strategies that teachers used in response to these different kinds of errors.

In a follow-up to this story task, the classroom teachers of these children were asked to go through a wordless picture book in kindergarten and second grade and ask concrete and difficult abstract questions about the story while looking through the book with each child. There were no group differences on correct answers between the African American poor children and the middle class European American children. Again, there were differences between the groups in the kind of incorrect answers. For children who said "I don't know" or were silent, teachers were able to give appropriate feedback to get the child to understand the right answer through restructuring the question or prodding the child to think again. On the other hand, when children gave a category mistake, teachers were much less likely to use facilitating strategies. Instead, teachers more often ignored the child's answer and went on to the next question or actually reinforced positively the category mistake answer, even though it was incorrect. This finding suggests that a mismatch between children and their teachers' strategies may negatively affect children's learning because of the poorer feedback children received when they provided certain incorrect responses.

Although this study took place in a rural area, this same mismatch is to be found in other geographic areas. Most of the studies that examined cultural/ethnic differences in rural children's classroom processes used very small sample sizes, yet these studies do suggest that not all poor children are alike and that the pathways to school readiness may be different for poor children in urban versus rural contexts and for African American versus non-African American children in rural contexts. This differentiated instruction for individual learners may be particularly important in the rural context where there are more struggling readers and where African American children are much poorer than are their urban counterparts. It might also be the case if this individualized instruction were taught to teachers, it could be most effective in rural areas where there are generally smaller schools, smaller class size, and teachers who are more familiar with children's families and backgrounds than is the case in urban/suburban schools. Clearly, there needs to be much more research to understand the parameters of individualized instruction in rural education.

***Family Involvement and Connections to School***  Families' involvement in children's education is a critical piece of children's early school success. Specifically, when the home environment and relationships regularly include learning activities, and when communication with the school is established and sustained, children have fewer behavioral and academic difficulties in the transition to school and subsequent years (Taylor & Machida, 1994). During the preschool years, families and teachers typically communicate frequently, and collaboratively support children's development. After children begin kindergarten, however, home–school communication and parental involvement decrease with the passing years (Izzo, Weissberg, Kasprow, & Fendrich, 1999).

In one of the few large scale studies of nonurban children that examined processes related to schooling (Brody, Dorsey, Forehand, & Armistead, 2002; Brody, Stoneman, Flor, McCrary, Hastings, & Conyers, 1994), lack of financial resources in two-parent Black families in the South was related to greater parental depression, marital strain, and parenting conflicts among adolescent children. These factors were later related to poorer outcomes for adolescents in reading and math as well as child behavior problems and poorer mental health. There does not appear to be any current research on young rural children that is similar to the Brody and colleagues' studies that would help us to understand the confluence of factors that are associated with good academic trajectories in early elementary school.

Family–school connections during the transition to formal schooling typically take place after the school year has started (Early, Pianta, Taylor, & Cox, 2001), despite evidence that activities to involve families before the transition to school facilitate positive family relationships and fewer child difficulties during the early months of school. Programs that assist families during children's early school years facilitate better parent and child outcomes (Root & Levant, 1984).

Teachers report that family attitudes predict children's success in early schooling more than families' actual involvement (Rimm-Kaufman, Pianta, Cox, & Bradley, 2003); however, other studies suggest that educational activities in the home are associated with academic achievement in early schooling (Izzo et al., 1999). Rural contexts provide some opportunities for family involvement, including social relationships that are more personal, a stronger sense of community and traditional values, and smaller school enrollment, which allows the individual needs of students to be addressed (Prater, Bermudez, & Owens, 1997). However, in Prater et al.'s study comparing rural, urban, and suburban families, rural families were less likely than urban and rural families to discuss school with their children, participate in school meetings, and interact with their children's teachers. Due to the unique qualities of rural life, much more information must be gathered about how rural families, schools, and communities connect in children's transition to formal schooling.

## The Targeted Reading Intervention (TRI)

***The TRI for Rural Schools***  Because there is such a dearth of research on rural teachers and schools, the Institute for Educational Sciences funded a large center dedicated to rural education. This center, The National Research Center on Rural Education Support (NRCRES), has launched several major studies (Farmer, Vernon-Feagans, & Hannum, in press), one of which focuses on literacy development for struggling readers in the early elementary grades. Known as the targeted reading intervention (TRI), this initiative draws on research described in this chapter to develop effective assessment based teacher strategies to help struggling readers in kindergarten and first grade. The TRI is designed to provide specific strategies that teachers can use in one-on-one instruction with children who do not profit from regular literacy instruction (Farmer, Vernon-Feagans, & Hannum, in press). It is geared to teachers in low wealth rural school districts that have many children in poverty and many children who come to school with lower preliteracy skills.

The TRI is not a curriculum but a set of assessment based literacy strategies that match the child's level of literacy to appropriate teaching strategies. This means that schools adopting this model do not need to change their reading curriculum but can use TRI to supplement their instruction for struggling readers. Our model is based on the five areas described as critical for reading instruction by the National Reading Panel (2000) and endorsed by Reading First. It includes all these five areas but in addition, stresses the importance for motivation and engagement as critical for the success of struggling readers. The model is implemented with the classroom teacher who begins the TRI process with intensive one-on-one instruction, using assess based strategies. Teachers work initially with one child 15 minutes per day in an individualized one-on-one instructional session that builds teacher efficacy as well as child motivation and engagement.

As can be seen in Figure 11.2, the targeted reading intervention focuses on word identification as a starting point for most struggling readers but always in the context of also emphasizing the other areas. Word identification includes phonological awareness and phonics but also includes decoding and the learning of sight words. These initial skills are taught explicitly from the outset in the context of words and text in order to help these struggling readers understand the purpose of phonological and decoding skills. Rereading for fluency is emphasized as the outcome of good word identification strategies as children practice with words and passages they are familiar with each day. Vocabulary is clearly important and it is incorporated into our word identification strategies through a picture vocabulary for particular words children are trying to read. Unique words are highlighted by the teacher and if necessary defined during guided oral reading. Comprehension is the goal of reading instruction so asking questions of children during guided oral reading and having them paraphrase stories is important to make sure that each child truly comprehends the text. Finally, motivation and engagement are critical for

any kind of learning. The focus on individualized one-on-one instruction with one child is an extremely motivating experience for almost all children and it maximizes the child's engagement with the material (Foorman & Torgesen, 2001). Choosing topics of interest to the child as a starting point for reading can be very important for struggling readers' motivation and engagement in reading. Making sure there is an instructional match between the teacher and child ensures that the reading material is not too easy and not too hard for the child, again maximizing motivation and engagement. The model, displayed in Figure 11.2, shows the integration of all these elements for a successful reader.

***The LEEP Model of Consultation***  The TRI strategies are delivered through a collaborative consultation model, known as Listening, Empathizing, Empowering, and Problem Solving (LEEP). This LEEP model (see Figure 11.3) is geared to understanding the challenges of teachers in rural areas who have access to limited resources and with a significant proportion of children at risk for developing reading difficulties.

The collaborative consultation model emphasizes the cycle of diagnostic teaching in daily interactions with struggling readers. The LEEP model helps our TRI consultants be more effective with teachers by employing several research-based consultation practices (Buysse & Wesley, in press). Our LEEP model of collaboration with teachers has been adapted for rural teachers but has many of the elements described in the early childhood literature in the Community of Practice and Lesson Study described by Buysse and Wesley (in press). They describe evidence-based practices that are effective in empowering all professionals to work together and to share expertise in teaching children. Our model is also a collaborative model, which emphasizes collaboration among professionals in the schools and the TRI team in helping individual children succeed in reading. In addition, TRI uses many of the elements of *Lesson Study* (Stigler & Hiebert, 1999). *Lesson Study* is a professional development process used by Japanese teachers to examine their classroom instructional practices. *Lesson Study* has now been adapted for use in the United States. Teachers work collaboratively on particular lessons, often focusing on the instruction for a particularly challenging child. Working on these study lessons involves participants in planning, teaching, observing, and critiquing each others' lessons. Data are collected and examined carefully in a problem solving approach that gives teachers feedback about the efficacy of their instructional methods.

Specifically our LEEP model integrates the important elements of previous professional development models with aspects that we believe are critical for rural teachers. The model includes four important process elements that are particularly salient when working with rural schools and teachers if change is to be adopted and sustained. First, it is important for TRI consultants to *listen* to teachers talk about their understanding of the challenges of teaching struggling readers in the rural context. The TRI is introduced at focus

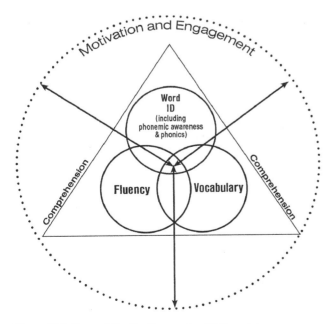

**FIgure 11.2** Targeted Reading Intervention (TRI) model.

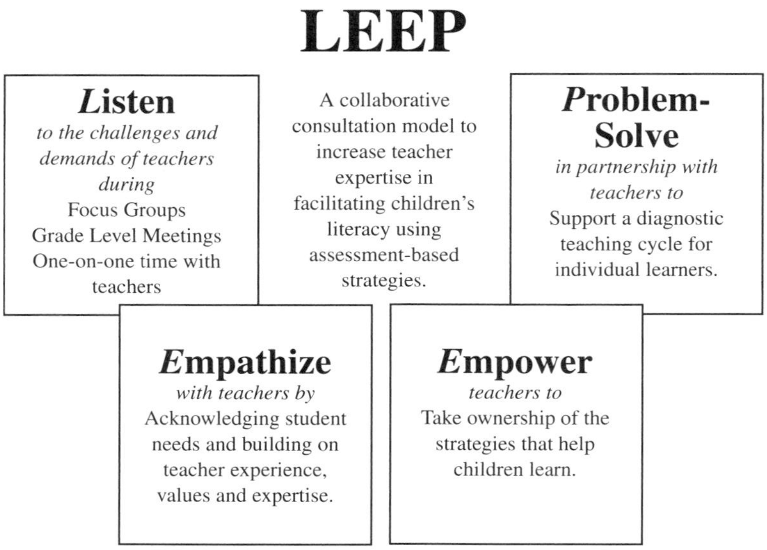

# LEEP

**Listen**
*to the challenges and demands of teachers during*
Focus Groups
Grade Level Meetings
One-on-one time with teachers

A collaborative consultation model to increase teacher expertise in facilitating children's literacy using assessment-based strategies.

**Problem-Solve**
*in partnership with teachers to*
Support a diagnostic teaching cycle for individual learners.

**Empathize**
*with teachers by*
Acknowledging student needs and building on teacher experience, values and expertise.

**Empower**
*teachers to*
Take ownership of the strategies that help children learn.

Figure 11.3 The LEEP model.

group sessions with teachers and other professionals, which helps us understand how these professionals describe the skills and behaviors of their struggling readers as well as the perceived causes for these children's failure within the culture of the particular community setting. For instance, teachers need to be heard when they must work with a class composed of mostly struggling readers yet do not have the classroom aide they were promised. They also need to be heard when they tell us about the behavior problems of the children or family background of the struggling readers that may contribute to their poorer learning ability. This input from teachers can help us by incorporating their comments into our rationale for why the TRI can be successful in their classrooms. It also allows the TRI staff to be cognizant of the barriers and constraints that teachers perceive in teaching these struggling readers.

Second, TRI consultants also need to *empathize* with teachers who often come from a very different perspective about the reasons that children are struggling with reading and about the use of different approaches to teaching. This empathic approach goes beyond listening. Our TRI consultants must try to take the teachers' perspective and the challenges they face in teaching. For instance, it is critically important for our consultants to put themselves in the teacher's position with respect to attitudes, values, and skills that reflect the rural sense of place and sense of tradition in the schools. The TRI consultants are trained to respect and consider carefully the perspective of the teachers, children, and families in these communities. Our identification with teachers, children, and families helps to break down the barriers so that TRI fits into the school culture of child learning. Third, TRI consultants empower teachers by encouraging them to see that rapid progress for these struggling readers is possible without interfering with the reading programs already in use in the classroom. Although there is much comfort for teachers in doing what they have always done, the TRI consultant empowers teachers to take ownership

of the changes in their instructional strategies to help their struggling learners.

Last and critically important to the TRI process, consultants need to *problem solve* with teachers in grade level meetings or individually to develop effective assessment based teaching strategies for particular children. The literacy consultants do this on an ongoing cycle of diagnosis teaching, through classroom consultations, phone calls, and e-mail so that assessment is built into teaching, thus helping teachers gauge the success of the strategies for each individual struggling reader. Grade or across grade meetings of all teachers are strongly encouraged as a way to jointly problem solve. This LEEP collaborative process ensures that teachers are equal partners in their own professional development and that their concerns are incorporated into our literacy strategies for each individual child.

***The TRI Cluster Randomized Trial*** The effectiveness of the TRI is being evaluated through a cluster randomized trial of treatment and control schools in low wealth counties around the country. In the first year of the clinical trial, we were located in a low wealth county in the South. The county was a persistently poor rural county where well over 90% of the children were eligible for free and reduced lunch. The county had few aides in the classrooms and few support teachers. There were no on site school counselors, reading specialists, or special educators to help classroom teachers support children with special needs. Based on demographic information, schools with similar demographic profiles with respect to race and SES were paired; one was randomly assigned to the TRI group and the other to the control group. Due to a change in administration, one TRI school withdrew, leaving one experimental and two control schools.

From our first year in delivering the intervention, data have been collected on the teachers and the students. It was clear from our first year that our teachers had more experience than most teachers in other contexts, with an average of 26 years teaching in this county, far more than reported in more urban contexts. Despite their experience, only 20% of these rural teachers had a master's degree in comparison to the national average of 40%. This difference is even more dramatic if the number of years in teaching is factored into the data. Sixty percent of teachers with at least 20 years of experience have master's degrees nationally (NCES, 2005), over three times the rate of the teachers in our study. This rather lower percentage for teachers with a master's degree is probably due to less access to higher education in this relatively remote county. The struggling learners identified by the teachers appeared to be low on all five areas of Reading First. After one year, the TRI students in our experimental school gained more on the Letter/Word Identification subtests of the Woodcock Johnson Tests of Achievement in comparison to the children in the control schools, with moderate effect sizes (Vernon-Feagans, Gallagher, Ginsberg & Amendum, 2007). In addition, the teachers who implemented the most and with the most fidelity had children who gained 15 points more on the Woodcock Johnson than did children with low-implementation teachers.

In the next few years, effectiveness will be assessed through a technology system that has been successfully tested through pilot work and is being implemented in rural Texas and New Mexico. Each experimental classroom has been provided with a laptop and a webcam. Our literacy consultants in their offices at the University of North Carolina can thereby see, hear, and communicate with the classroom teachers and children in these rural schools as the teachers deliver the TRI to individual children in real time. This allows collaborative conversation and consultation in the regular classroom in real time that has the potential to change the way that effective professional development is delivered, and in a cost effective way, to isolated schools almost anywhere in the United States.

## Conclusions

The transition to school for children in rural America is both similar and different from the experience of children in other areas. The skills that children need to acquire are the same in every part of the country as they enter school, but child entry-level characteristics, the experience and expertise of teachers, and family economics and structure can all impact how well a child learns during those first few years of school. We know that children in rural areas are poorer than are children in more urban/suburban areas and come to school with skills that are lower than those of children in urban/suburban areas, making them at higher risk for a poor transition to school. They also have families that work more nonstandard work hours, live further from school, and with less access to public transportation than is the case in more densely populated areas. This presents barriers for families' involvement in their child's school. We still know very little about the processes that occur within rural families, especially those that might be related to children's successful transition to school and might mediate the relationship between risk factors and early reading.

Teachers in rural areas are less educated and have less access to resources, including professional development opportunities than those in urban/suburban areas. With all these risk factors, there are also buffers for rural children. They have teachers who have more experience and more knowledge of individual families than is the case in urban/suburban areas. Families rate the teachers as better than in urban schools and they believe their children are safer in these schools than they would be in urban schools. Yet, we do not have detailed information about the instructional processes that occur in classrooms that help children, and especially at risk children, make progress in literacy. Projects like Targeted Reading Intervention (TRI) should help us to move forward in understanding what might be effective in helping teachers promote rapid learning in struggling readers. We still need to know much more about how the within family processes and the within classroom processes might work together in promoting the best learning for all children to be successful learners.

## References

Adams, M. J. (1990). *Beginning to read: Thinking and learning about print.* Cambridge, MA: MIT Press.

Alexander, K. L., & Entwisle, D. R. (1988). Achievement in the first 2 years of school: Patterns and processes. *Monographs of the Society for Research in Child Development, 53,* 1–157.

Anderson-Yockel, J., & Haynes, W. O. (1994). Joint book-reading strategies in working-class African American and white mother-toddler dyads. *Journal of Speech & Hearing Research, 37,* 583–593.

Atkinson, A. M. (1994). Rural and urban families' use of child care. *Family Relations, 43,* 16–22.

Ballou, D., & Podgursky, M. (1995). Rural schools: Fewer highly trained teachers and special programs, but better learning environment. *Rural Development Perspectives, 10,* 6–16.

Beach, B. (1997). *Perspectives on rural child care.* Charleston, WV: Clearinghouse on Rural Education and Small Schools, Appalachia Educational Laboratory.

Beeson, E. (2003). *Why rural matters.* Washington, D.C.: Rural School and Community Trust.

Bickel, R., & Spatig, L. (1999). Early achievement gains and poverty-linked social distress: The case of post-head start transition. *Journal of Social Distress & the Homeless, 8,* 241–254.

Blank, M., Rose, S. A., & Berlin, L. J. (1978). *The language of learning: The preschool years.* New York: Grune & Stratton.

Bornstein, M. H., Haynes, O. M., Painter, K. M., & Genevro, J. L. (2000). Child language with mother and with stranger at home and in the laboratory: A methodological study. *Journal of Child Language, 27,* 407–420.

Bramlett, R. K., Scott, P., & Rowell, R. K. (2000). A comparison of temperament and social skills in predicting academic performance in first graders. *Special Services in the Schools, 16,* 147–158.

Bredekamp, S., & Copple, C. (1997). *Developmentally appropriate practices in early childhood programs*: Revised edition. Washington, DC: National Association for the Education of Young Children.

Brody, G. H., Dorsey, S., Forehand, R., & Armistead, L. (2002). Unique and protective contributions of parenting and classroom processes to the adjustment of African American children living in single-parent families. *Child Development, 73,* 274–286.

Brody, H. B., & Flor, D. L. (1998). Maternal resources, parenting practices, and child competence in rural, single-parent African American families. *Child Development, 69*, 803–816.

Brody, G. H., Stoneman, Z., Flor, D., McCrary, C., Hastings, L., & Conyers, O. (1994). Financial resources, parent psychological functioning, parent co-caregiving, and early adolescent competence in rural two-parent African-American families. *Child Development, 65*, 590–605.

Brody, G. H., Stoneman, Z., & McCoy, J. K. (1994). Contributions of protective and risk factors to literacy and socioemotional competency in former head start children attending kindergarten. *Early Childhood Research Quarterly, 9*, 407–425.

Bronfenbrenner, U., & Crouter, A. C. (1983). The evolution of environmental models in developmental research. In W. Kessen (Ed.), *History, theories and methods* (Vol. 1, pp. 357–414). New York: Wiley.

Bronfenbrenner, U., & Evans, G. W. (2000). Developmental science in the 21st Century: Emerging theoretical models, research designs, and empirical findings. *Social Development, 9*, 115–125.

Bronfenbrenner, U., & Morris, P. A. (1998). The ecology of developmental processes. In W. Damon & R. M. Lerner (Eds.), *Handbook of child psychology (5th ed.): Theoretical models of human development* (pp. 993–1028). New York: Wiley.

Burchinal, M. R., Peisner-Feinberg, E., Pianta, R., & Howes, C. (2002). Development of academic skills from preschool through second grade: Family and classroom predictors of developmental trajectories. *Journal of School Psychology, 40*, 415–436.

Burchinal, M., Roberts, J.E., Zeisel, S.A., Hennon, E.A., & Hooper, S. (2006). Risk and resiliency: Protective factors in early elementary school years. *Parenting: Science and Practice, 6*, 79–113.

Bus, A.G., van Ijzendoorn, M. H., & Pellegrini, A. D. (1995). Joint book reading makes for success in learning to read: A meta-analysis on intergenerational transmission of literacy. *Review of Educational Research, 65*, 1–21.

Christian, K., Morrison, F. J., & Bryant, F. B. (1998). Predicting kindergarten academic skills: Interactions among child care, maternal education, and family literacy environments. *Early Childhood Research Quarterly, 13*, 501–521.

Coles, R. (2003). *Children of crisis: Selections from the Pulitzer Prize-winning five-volume Children of crisis series.* Boston: Little, Brown.

Collins, T. (1999). *Attracting and retaining teachers in rural areas.* Charleston, WV: ERIC Clearinghouse on Rural and Small Schools.

Connell, C. M., & Prinz, R. J. (2002). The impact of childcare and parent-child interactions on school readiness and social skills development for low-income African American children. *Journal of School Psychology, 40*(2), 177–193.

Connor, C. M., Morrison, F. J., Fishman, B. J., Schatschneider, C., & Underwood, P. (2007). The early year: Algorithm-guided individualized reading instruction. *Science, 315*(5811), 464–465.

Connor, C. M., Morrison, F. J., & Katch, L. E. (2004). Beyond the reading wars: Exploring the effect of child-instruction interactions on growth in early reading. *Scientific Studies of Reading, 8*(4), 305–336.

Connor, C. M., Morrison, F. J., & Petrella, J. N. (2004). Effective reading comprehension instruction: Examining child x instruction interactions. *Journal of Educational Psychology, 96*, 682–698.

Connor C. M., Morrison, F. J., & Slominski, L. (2006). Preschool instruction and children's emergent literacy growth. *Journal of Educational Psychology, 98*(4), 665–689.

Dickinson, D. K., DeTemple, J., Hischler, J., & Smith, M. (1992). Book reading with preschoolers. *Early Childhood Research Quarterly, 7*, 323–346.

Dill, B.T. (1999). *Poverty in the rural U.S.: Implications for children, families, and communities.* Literature review prepared for The Annie E. Casey Foundation.

Donnermeyer, J. F. (1994). Crime and violence in rural communities. In S. M. Blaser, J. Blaser, & K. Pantoja, (Eds.), *Perspectives on violence and substance use in rural America.* (pp. 27–63). Oak Brook, IL: Midwest Regional Center for Drug-Free Schools and Communities.

Duncan, C. M. (1999). *Worlds apart: Why poverty persists in rural America.* New Haven, CT: Yale University Press

Early, D. M., Pianta, R. C., Taylor, L. C., & Cox, M. J. (2001). Transition practices: Findings from a national survey of kindergarten teachers. *Early Childhood Education Journal, 28*, 199–206.

Early, D. M., Rimm-Kaufman, S. E., Cox, M. J., Saluja, G., Pianta, R. C., Bradley, R. H., et al. (2002). Maternal sensitivity and child wariness in the transition to kindergarten. *Parenting: Science and Practice, 2*(4), 355–377.

Entwisle, D. R., & Alexander, K. L. (1993). Entry into school: Beginning school transition and educational stratification in the United States. *Annual Review of Sociology, 19*, 401–423.

Entwisle, D. R., & Alexander, K. L. (1998). Facilitating the transition to first grade: The nature of transition and research on factors affecting it. *The Elementary School Journal, 98*, 351–364

Entwisle, D. R., & Alexander, K. L. (1999). Early schooling and social stratification. In R. Pianta, S. Rimm-Kaufman, & M. Cox (Eds.), *The transition to kindergarten* (pp. 13–38). Baltimore, MD: Brookes.

Evans, G. W., & English, K. (2002). The environment of poverty: Multiple stressor exposure, psychophysiological stress, and socioemotional adjustment. *Child Development, 73*, 1238–1248.

Farmer, T., Vernon-Feagans, L., & Hannum, W. (In press). Educational issues in diverse rural communities: The research agenda of the National Research Center on Rural Education Support. *Journal of Research in Rural Education.*

Feagans, L., & Farran, D. C. (1981). How demonstrated comprehension can get muddled in production. *Developmental Psychology, 17*, 718–727.

Feagans, L. V., & Fendt, K. (1991). The effects of intervention and social class on children's answers to concrete and abstract questions. *Journal of Applied Developmental Psychology, 12*, 115–130.

Feagans, L. V., Fendt, K., & Farran, D. C. (1995). The effects of day care intervention on teacher's ratings of the elementary school discourse skills in disadvantaged children. *International Journal of Behavioral Development, 18*, 243–261.

Feagans, L., & Haskins, R. (1986). Neighborhood dialogues of black and white 5-year-olds. *Journal of Applied Developmental Psychology, 7*, 181–200.

Feagans, L. V., & McKinney, J. D. (1991). Subtypes of learning disabilities: A review. In L. V. Feagans, E. J. Short, & L. Meltzer (Eds.), *Subtypes of learning disabilities* (pp. 3–31). Hillsdale, NJ: Erlbaum.

Feagans, L. V., & Merriwether, A. (1990). Visual discrimination of letter-like forms and its relationship to achievement over time in children with learning disabilities. *Journal of Learning Disabilities, 23*, 417–425.

Fitzgerald, J., Spiegel, D., & Cunningham, J. (1991). The relationship between parental literacy level and perceptions of emergent literacy. *Journal of Reading Behavior, 23*, 191–213.

Fish, M., & Pinkerman, B. (2003). Language skills in low-SES rural Appalachian children: Normative development and individual differences, infancy to preschool. *Applied Developmental Psychology, 23*, 539–565.

Foorman, B. R., & Torgesen, J. K. (2001). Critical elements of classroom and small-group instruction promote reading success in all children. *Learning Disabilities Research & Practice, 16*, 202–211.

Friedman, P. *Meeting the Challenge of Social Service Delivery in Rural Areas.* Welfare Information Network: Issue Note, vol. 7, No. 2, March 2003.

Gallagher, K. C., Kainz, K., Mayer, K. L., & Vernon-Feagans, L. (in press) Development of teacher–child relationships in rural kindergarten and first grade classrooms. *Early Childhood Research Quarterly.*

Graefe, D. R., & Lichter, D. T. (2002). Marriage Among Unwed Mothers: Whites, Blacks and Hispanics compared. *Perspectives on Sexual and Reproductive Health, 34*, 286–293.

Greenberg, M. T., Lengua, L. J., Coie, J. D., & Pinderhughes, E. E. (1999). Predicting developmental outcomes at school entry using a multiple-risk model: Four American communities. *Developmental Psychology, 35*, 403–417.

Grissmer, D.W., Flanagan, A., Kawata, J., & Williamson, S. (2000). *Improving student achievement: What NAEP state test scores tell us.* Santa Monica, CA: Rand Corporation.

Hair, E., Hulle, T., Terry-Humen, T., Lavelle, P., & Calkins, J. (2006).

Children's school readiness in the ECLS-K: Predictions to academic, health, and social outcomes in first grade. *Early Childhood Research Quarterly, 4,* 431–454.

Hammer, C. S., Miccio, A. W., & Wagstaff, D. A. (2003). Home literacy experiences and their relationship to bilingual preschoolers' developing English literacy abilities: An initial investigation. *Language, Speech, & Hearing Services in Schools, 34,* 20–30.

Hamre, B. K., & Pianta, R. C. (2001). Early teacher-child relationships and the trajectory of children's school outcomes through eighth grade. *Child Development, 72,* 625–638.

Hamre, B. K., & Pianta, R. C. (2005). Can instructional and emotional support in the first-grade classroom make a difference for children at risk of school failure? *Child Development, 76,* 949–967.

Han, W.J. (2005). Maternal nonstandard work schedules and child cognitive outcomes. *Child Development, 76,* 137–154.

Hardman, M., & Jones, L. (1999). Sharing books with babies: Evaluation of an early literacy intervention. *Educational Review, 51,* 221–229.

Hart, B., & Risley, T. R. (1995). *Meaningful differences in the everyday experience of young American children.* Baltimore, MD: Brookes.

Heath, S. B. (1983). *Ways with words: Language, life, and work in communities and classrooms.* New York: McGraw-Hill; Oxford University Press.

Howley, C. B., Howley, A. A., & Shamblen, S. (2001). Riding the school bus: A comparison of rural and suburban experience in five states. *Journal of Research in Rural Education, 17,* 41–63.

Huang, G. G. (1999). *Sociodemographic changes: Promise and problems for rural education.* Charleston, WV: ERIC Clearinghouse on Rural Education and Small Schools. (ERIC Document Reproduction Services No. ED425048).

Hughes, J. N., Cavell, T. A., & Willson, V. (2001). Further support for the developmental significance of the quality of the teacher–student relationship. *Journal of School Psychology, 39,* 289–301.

Izzo, C. V., Weissberg, R. P., Kasprow, W. J., & Fendrich, M. (1999). A longitudinal assessment of teacher perceptions of parent involvement in children's education and school performance. *American Journal of Community Psychology, 27,* 871–839.

Jaure, R., Rapoza, R. A. & Swesnik, D. (2003). *Opening Doors to Rural Homeownership: Outcomes from the National Rural Housing Coalition Rural Homeownership Symposium.* Washington. DC: National Rural Housing Coalition.

Johnson, R. (2002). *Using data to close the achievement gap: How to measure equity in our schools.* Thousand Oaks, CA: Corwin.

Juel, C. (1988). Learning to read and write: A longitudinal study of 54 children from first through fourth grades. *Journal of Educational Psychology, 80,* 437–447.

Juel, C. (1991). Cross-age tutoring between student athletes and at-risk children. *The Reading Teacher, 45,* 178–186.

Juel, C., Griffith, P. L., & Gough, P. B. (1986). Acquisition of literacy: A longitudinal study of children in first and second grade. *Journal of Educational Psychology, 78,* 243–255.

Juel, C., & Minden-Cupp, C. (1998). *Learning to read words: Linguistic units and strategies.* Ann Arbor, MI: Center for the Improvement of Early Reading Achievement.

Kainz, K., & Vernon-Feagans, L. (2007). The ecology of early reading development for children in poverty. *Elementary School Journal, 107,* 407–427.

Kannapel, P. J., & DeYoung, A. J. (1999). The rural school problem in 1999: A review and critique of the literature. *Journal of Research in Rural Education, 15,* 67–79.

Katras, M. J., Zulker, V. S., & Bauer, J. W. (2004). Private safety net: Childcare resources from the perspective of rural low-income families. *Family relations, 53*(2), 201–209.

Khattri, N., Riley, K. W., & Kane, M. B. (1997). Students at risk in poor, rural areas: A review of the research. *Journal of Research in Rural Education, 13,* 79 100.

Konold, T. R., & Pianta, R. C. (2005). Empirically-derived, person-oriented patterns of school readiness in typically-developing children: Description and prediction to first-grade achievement. *Applied Developmental Science, 9,* 174–187.

Krishnakumar, A., & Black, M. M. (2003). Family processes within three-generation households an adolescent mothers' satisfaction with father involvement. *Journal of Family Psychology, 17,* 488–498.

Lee, V., & Burkam, D. (2002). *Inequality at the starting gate: Social background differences in achievement as children begin school.* Washington, DC: Economic Policy Institute.

Lee, V., & Burkam, D. (2003). Dropping out of high school: The role of school organization and structure. *American Educational Research Journal, 40,* 353–393.

Lichter D., & Jensen L. (2001). Poverty and welfare among rural female-headed families: Before and after PRWORA. *Rural America, 16,* 28–35.

Lichter, D., & McLaughlin, D. (1995). Changing economic opportunities, family structure, and poverty in rural areas. *Rural Sociology, 60,* 688–706.

Lichter, D., Roscigno, V., & Condron, D. (2003). Rural children and youth at risk. In D. Brown & L. E. Swanson (Eds.), *Challenges for rural America in the twenty-first century* (pp. 97–108). University Park, PA: The Pennsylvania State University Press.

Liver, M. R., Brooks-Gunn, J., & Kohen, D. E. (2002). Family processes as pathways from income to young development. *Developmental Psychology, 38,* 719–734.

Lonigan, C. J. (2006). Development, assessment, and promotion of pre-literacy skills. *Early Education and Development, Special Issue on School Readiness, 17,* 91–114.

Lonigan, C. J., Burgess, S. R., Anthony, J. L. & Barker, T. A., (1998). Development of phonological sensitivity in two- to five-year-old children. *Journal of Educational Psychology, 90,* 294–311.

Love, J. M., Kisker, E. E., Ross, C., Raikes, H., Constantine, J., Boller, K., et al. (2005). The effectiveness of early head start for 3-year-old children and their parents: Lessons for policy and programs. *Developmental Psychology, 41,* 885–901.

Loveless, T. (2003). *The 2003 brown center report on american education how well are american students learning? With special sections on homework, charter schools, and ruralschoolachievement.* Retrieved from: http://www.brookings.edu/gs/brown/bc%5Freport/2003/2003report.htm

Lyon, G. R. (1995). Toward a definition of dyslexia. *Annals of dyslexia, 45,* 3–27.

Lyon, G. R. (1996). Learning disabilities. *Future of children, 6,* 54–76.

MacDonald, G.W., & Cornwall, A. (1995). The relationship between phonological awareness and reading and spelling achievement eleven years later. *Journal of Learning Disabilities, 28,* 523–527.

Mann, V. (1993). Phoneme awareness and future reading ability. *Journal of Learning Disabilities, 26,* 259–269.

Mantzicopoulos, P. Y. (1997). The relationship of family variables to head start children's preacademic competence. *Early Education and Development, 8,* 357–375.

Mashburn, A. J., & Pianta, R. C. (2006). Social relationships and school readiness *early education and development, special issue on school readiness, 17,* 151–176.

Mather, M., & Scopilitti, M. (2004, September). *Multiple jobholding rates higher in rural America.* Washington, DC: Rural Family Data Center: Popualtion Reference Bureau.

Maxwell, K. L., McWilliam, R. A., Hemmeter, M. L., Ault, M. J., & Schuster, J. W. (2001). Predictors of developmentally appropriate classroom practices in kindergarten through third-grade. *Early Childhood Research Quarterly, 16,* 431–452.

McGlamery, M. E., Ball, S. E., Henley, T. B., & Besozzi, M. (2007). Theory of mind, attention, and executive function in kindergarten boys. *Emotional & behavioural difficulties, 12,* 29–47.

McKinney, J. D., & Feagans, L. (1987). Current issues in research and services for learning disabled children in the United States. *Padoperise, 1,* 91–107

Mendez, J. L., Fantuzzo, J., & Cicchetti, D. (2002). Profiles of social competence among low-income African American preschool children. *Child Development, 73,* 1085–1100.

Mistry, R. S., Vandewater, E. A., Huston, A. C., & McLoyd, V. C. (2002). Economic well-being and children's social adjustment: The role of family process in an ethnically diverse low-income sample. *Child Development, 73,* 935–951.

Morrison, B. (2005). Evaluating learning gain in a self-access language learning centre. *Language Teaching Research, 9,* 267–293.

Morrison, F. J., Bachman, H. J., & Connor, C. M. (2005). *Improving literacy in America: Guidelines from research.* New Haven, CT: Yale University Press .

National Center for Education Statistics. (2003). *The nation's report card: Fourth-grade reading 2003.* From: http://nces.ed.gov/nationsreport-card/reading/results2003/

National Center for Education Statistics [NCES]. (2005). *Digest of Education Statistics: 2005.* Retrieved from: http://nces.ed.gov/programs/digest/d05/tables/dt05_067.asp

National Education Association. (1998). *Status of public education in rural areas and small towns—a comparative analysis.*

National Institute of Child Health and Development [NICHD], Early Child Care Research Network [ECCRN]. (2001). Nonmaternal care and family factors in early development: An overview of the NICHD study of early child care. *Journal of Applied Developmental Psychology, 22,* 457–492.

National Institute of Child Health and Development [NICHD], Early Child Care Research Network [ECCRN]. (2002). Early child care and children's development prior to school entry: Results from NICHD study of early child care. *American Educational Research Journal, 39,* 133–164.

National Institute of Child Health and Development [NICHD], Early Child Care Research Network [ECCRN]. (2003a). Do children's attention processes mediate the link between family predictors and school readiness? *Developmental Psychology, 39,* 581–593.

National Institute of Child Health and Development [NICHD], Early Child Care Research Network [ECCRN]. (2003b). Social functioning in first grade: Associations with earlier home and child care predictors and with current classroom experiences. *Child development, 74,* 1639–1662.

National Institute of Child Health and Development [NICHD], Early Child Care Research Network [ECCRN]. (2005). Duration and developmental timing of poverty and children's cognitive and social development from birth through third grade. *Child Development, 76,* 795–810.

National Institute of Child Health and Development [NICHD], Early Child Care Research Network [ECCRN]. (2005). Pathways to reading: The role of oral language in the transition to reading. *Developmental Psychology, 41,* 428–442.

National Reading Panel. (2000). *Teaching children to read: An evidence-based assessment of the scientific research literature on reading and its implications for reading instruction.* Bethesda, MD: National Reading Panel.

Neuman, S.B. (1997) Guiding young children's participation in early literacy development: A family literacy program for adolescent mothers. *Early Child Development and Care, 127/128,* 119–129.

Ninio, A. (1983). Joint bookreading as a multiple vocabulary acquisition device. *Developmental Psychology, 19,* 445–451.

Ninio, A., & Bruner, J. (1978). The achievement and antecedents of labeling. *Journal of Child Language, 5,* 1–15.

O'Hare, W. P., & Johnson, K. M. (2004). *Child poverty in rural America.* Washington, DC: Population Reference Bureau: Reports on America, 4.

Pancsofar, N., & Vernon-Feagans, L. (2006). Mother and father language input to young children: Contributions to later language development. *Journal of Applied Developmental Psychology, 27,* 571–587.

Payne, A. C., Whitehurst, G. J., & Angell, A. L. (1994). The role of home literacy environment in the development of language ability in preschool children from low-income families. *Early Childhood Research Quarterly, 9,* 427–440.

Peisner-Fineberg, E. S., Burchinal, M. R., Clifford, R. M., Culkin, M. L., Howes, C., Kagan, S. L., & Yazejian, N. (2001). The relation of preschool child-care quality to children's cognitive and social developmental trajectories through second grade. *Child Development, 72,* 1534–1553.

Pellegrini, A. D., Perlmutter, J. C., Galda, L., & Brody, G. H. (1990). Joint reading between black Head Start children and their mothers. *Child Development, 61,* 443–453.

Peters, D. L., Bollin, G. G., & Murphy, R. E. (Eds.). (1991). *Head start's influence on parental competence and child competence.* New York: Elsevier Science/JAI Press.

Pianta, R.C., La Paro, K., Payne, C., Cox, M. J., & Bradley, R. (2002). The relation of kindergarten classroom environment to teacher, family, and school characteristics and child outcomes. *Elementary School Journal, 102,* 225–238.

Pianta, R. C., & Stuhlman, M. W. (2004). Teacher-child relationships and children's success in the first years of school. *School Psychology Review, 33,* 444–458.

Pigott, T. D., & Israel, M. S. (2005). Head start children's transition to kindergarten: Evidence from the early childhood longitudinal study. *Journal of Early Childhood Research, 3,* 77–104.

Prater, D. L., Bermudez, A. B., & Owens, E. (1997). Examining parental involvement in rural, urban, and suburban schools. *Journal of Research in Rural Education, 13,* 72–75.

Ramey, C. T., & Ramey, S. L. (Eds.). (2006). *Early learning and school readiness: Can early intervention make a difference?* Westport, CT: Praeger.

Ramey, S. L. (1999). Head start and preschool education: Toward continued improvement. *American Psychologist, 54,* 344–346.

Raz, R. S., & Bryant, P. (1990) Social background, phonological awareness, and children's reading. *British Journal of Developmental Psychology, 8,* 209–225.

Reeves, C. (2003). *Implementing the No Child Left Behind Act: Implications for rural schools and districts.* Napperville, IL: North Central Regional Educational Library.

Regional Educational Laboratory Network. (2004). *Responding to Regional Needs & National Priorities. Annual Report.* Jessup, MD: US Department of Education. (ERIC Document Reproduction Service No. ED485196)

Rimm-Kaufman, S. E., Pianta, R. C., & Cox, M. J. (2000). Teachers' judgments of problems in the transition to kindergarten. *Early Childhood Research Quarterly, 15,* 147–166.

Rimm-Kaufman, S. E., Pianta, R. C., Cox, M. J., & Bradley, R. H. (2003). Teacher-rated family involvement and children's social and academic outcomes in kindergarten. *Early Education and Development, 14,* 179–198.

Rivers, K. (2005, February). *Rural southern children falling behind in well-being indicators.* (Population Reference Bureau Brief). Retrieved October 1, 2006, from http://www.prb.org/Template.cfm?Section=PRB&template=/ContentManagement/ContentDisplay.cfm&ContentID=12124

Roberts, J. E., Burchinal, M.R., Medley, L. P., Zeisel, S. A., Mundy, M., Roush, J., et al. (1995). Otitis media, hearing sensitivity, and maternal responsiveness in relation to language during infancy. *Journal of Pediatrics, 126,* 481–489.

Roberts, J. E., Burchinal, M. R., Zeisel, S. A., Neebe, E. C., Hooper, S. R., Roush, J., et al. (1998). Otitis media, the caregiving environment, and language and cognitive outcomes at 2 years. *Pediatrics, 102,* 346–353.

Root, R. W., & Levant, R. F. (1984). An evaluation of parent effectiveness training for rural parents. *Journal of Rural Community Psychology, 5,* 45–54.

Rosenkoetter, S. E. (2001). Lessons for preschool language socialization from the vantage point of the first day of kindergarten. *Early Education and Development, 12,* 325–342.

Rural School and Community Trust: Annual Report. (2005). *Addressing the Crucial Relationship between Good Schools and Thriving Rural Communities.*

Rutter, M. (1979). Protective factors in children's responses to stress and disadvantage. In M. W. Kent & E. J. Rolf (Eds.), *Primary prevention of psychopathology: Vol. 3. Social competence in children* (pp. 49–74). Hanover, NH: University of New England Press.

Sameroff, A. J., & Fiese, B. H. (2000). Models of development and developmental risk. In C. H. Zeanah (Ed.), *Handbook of infant mental health* (2nd ed. pp. 3–19). New York: Guilford.

Sameroff, A. J., Seifer, R,, Baldwin, A., & Baldwin, C. (1993). Stability of intelligence from preschool to adolescence: The influence of social and family risk factors. *Child Development, 64,* 80–97.

Sameroff, A. J., Seifer, R., Barocas, R., Zax, M., & Greenspan, S. (1987). Intelligence quotient scores of 4-yr.old children: Social-environmental risk factors. *Pediatrics, 79,* 343–350.

Sbarra, D. A., & Pianta, R. C. (2001). Teacher ratings of behavior among African American and Caucasian children during the first two years of school. *Psychology in the Schools, 38,* 229–238.

Scarborough, H. S. (1998). Early identification of children at risk for reading disabilities: Phonological awareness and some promising predictors. In B. K. Shapiro, P. J. Pasquale, & A. J. Capute (Eds.), *Specific reading disability: A view of the spectrum* (pp. 75–119). Timonium, MD: York.

Scarborough, H. (2001). Connecting early language and literacy to later reading (dis)abilities: Evidence, theory, and practice. In S. B. Neuman & D. K. Dickinson (Eds.), *Handbook of early literacy research* (pp. 97–110). New York: Guilford.

Schmidt, M. E., Demulder, E. K., & Denham, S. A. (2002). Kindergarten social-emotional competence: Developmental predictors and psychosocial implications. *Early Child Development and Care, 172,* 451–462.

Sénéchal, M., & LeFevre, J. (2002). Parental involvement in the development of children's reading skill: A five-year longitudinal study. *Child Development, 73,* 445–460.

Sénéchal, M., LeFevre, J., Hudson, E., & Lawson, E. P. (1996). Knowledge of storybooks as a predictor of young children's vocabulary. *Journal of Educational Psychology, 88,* 520–536.

Singer, J. D., Fuller, B., Keiley, M. K., & Wolf, A. (1998). Early child-care selection: Variation by geographic location, maternal characteristics, and family structure. *Developmental Psychology, 34,* 1129–1144.

Smith, E. P., Prinz, R. J., Dumas, J. E., & Laughlin, J. (2001). Latent models of family processes in African American families: Relationships to child competence, achievement, and problem behavior. *Journal of Marriage and Family, 63,* 967–980.

Snow, C. E., Burns, M. S., & Griffin, P. (1998). *Preventing reading difficulties in young children.* Washington, DC: National Academy Press.

Snow, C. E., & Ninio, A. (1986). The contracts of literacy: What children learn from learning to read books. In W. H. Teale & E. Sulzby (Eds.), *Emergent literacy: Writing and reading* (pp. 116–138). Norwood, NJ: Ablex.

Stack, C. B. (1996). *Call to home.* New York: Basic Books.

Stanovich, K. E. (1987). Introduction: Children's reading and the development of phonological awareness. *Merrill-Palmer Quarterly, 33,* 251–254.

Stigler, J. W., & Hiebert, J. (1999). The teaching gap: Best ideas from the world's teachers for improving education in the classroom. New York: Free Press.

Strong, D. A., Del Gross, P., Burwick, A., Jethwani, V., & Ponza, M. (Eds.). (2005). *Rural research needs and data sources for selected human services topics.* Princeton, NJ: Mathematica Policy Research, Inc.

Stork, S. A., & Whitehurst, G. J. (2002). Oral language and code-related precursors to reading: Evidence from a longitudinal structural model. *Developmental Psychology, 38,* 934–947.

Summers, G. F. (Ed.). (1997). *Working together for a change: Creating pathways from poverty.* Bellingham, WA: Western Washington State University, Rural Sociological Society.

Taylor, A. R., & Machida, S. (1994). The contribution of parent and peer support to head start children's early school adjustment. *Early Childhood Research Quarterly, 9,* 387–405.

Thomas, D. E., & Bierman, K. L. (2006). The impact of classroom aggression on the development of aggressive behavior problems in children. *Development and Psychopathology, 18,* 471–487.

Tizard, B., & Hughes, M. (1984). *Young children learning.* Cambridge, MA: Harvard University Press.

Torgesen, J. (2002). The prevention of reading difficulties, *Journal of School Psychology, 40,* 7–26.

Torgesen, J. K., Rashotte, C., Alexander, A., Alexander, J., & MacPhee, K. (2003). Progress towards understanding the instructional conditions necessary for remediating reading difficulties in older children. In B. Foorman (Ed.), *Preventing and remediating reading difficulties: Bringing science to scale* (pp. 275–298). Baltimore, MD: York.

Unites States Government Accountability Office. (2004, September 23). *No Child Left Behind Act: Additional assistance and research on effective strategies would help small rural districts,* GAO-04-909. Washington, DC: U.S.. Government Printing Office.

van den Oord, E. J. C. G., & Van Rossem, R. (2002). Differences in first graders' school adjustment: The role of classroom characteristics and social structure of the group. *Journal of School Psychology, 40,* 369–394.

van Kleeck, A., Gillam, R. B., Hamilton, L., & McGrath, C. (1997). The relationship between middle-class parents' book-sharing discussion and their preschoolers' abstract language development. *Journal of Speech, Language, and Hearing, 40,* 1261–1271.

Vernon-Feagans, L. V. (1996). *Children's talk in communities and classrooms.* Cambridge, MA: Blackwell.

Vernon-Feagans, L. (in press). Rural Education. In D. Crook & G. McCulloch (Eds.), *The Encyclopedia of Education.* London: Routledge.

Vernon-Feagans, L., & Blair, C. (2006). Measurement of School Readiness: Introduction to a Special Issue of Early Education and Development. *Early Education and Development, 17,* 1–5.

Vernon-Feagans, L., Gallagher, K., Ginsberg, M. C., & Amendum, S. (2007, June). *The Targeted Reading Intervention: A clinical trial to test the effectiveness of a collaborative professional development program to help classroom teachers assess and teach struggling learners in early elementary school.* Poster Presentation at the 2007 Institute for Educational Sciences Conference. Washington, D.C.

Vernon-Feagans, L., Head-Reeves, D., & Kainz, K. (2004). An eco-cultural perspective on early literacy: Avoiding the perils of school for non-mainstream children. In B. Wasik (Ed.), *Handbook of family literacy* (pp. 427–448). Mahwah, NJ: Erlbaum.

Vernon-Feagans, L., Miccio, A.W., Manlove, E. E., & Hammer, C. J. (2001). Early language and literacy skills in low-income African American and Hispanic children. In S. Neuman & D. Dickinson (Eds.), *Handbook of early literacy research* (pp. 192–210). New York: Guilford.

Vernon-Feagans, L. V., Odom, E., Pancsofar, N,. & Kainz, K. (2007). A transactional/ecological model of readiness and inequality. In A. Booth & A. C. Crouter (Eds.), *Disparities in school readiness: How families contribute to transitions into school* (pp. 61–78). Mahwah, NJ: Erlbaum.

Wagner, R. K., Torgesen, J. K., & Rashotte, C. A. (1994). Development of reading-related phonological processing abilities: New evidence of a bidirectional causality from a latent variable. *Developmental Psychology, 30,* 73–87.

Walrath, C., Miech, R., Holden, E. W., Mantueffel, B., Santiago, R., & Leaf, P. (2003). Child functioning in rural and nonrural areas: How does it compare when using the service program site as the level of analysis? *The Journal of Behavioral Health Services and Research, 30,* 452–461.

Weber, B.A., Duncan, G.J., & Whitener, L.A. (2002). *Rural dimensions of welfare reform.* Kalamazoo, MI: W.E. Upjohn Institute for Employment Research.

Weber, B., & Jensen, L. (2004). *Poverty and place: A critical review of rural Poverty literature.* Rural Poverty Research Center. Retrieved from http://www.rprconline.org/

Weber, B. L., Jensen, K., Miller, J., Mosley, & Fisher, M. (2005). A critical review of rural poverty literature: Is there truly a rural effect? *International Regional Science Review, 28,* 381–414.

Whitehurst, G. J., & Lonigan, C. J. (1998). Child development and emergent literacy. *Child Development, 69,* 848–872.

Whitehurst, G. J., & Lonigan, C. J. (2001). Emergent literacy: Development from prereaders to readers. In S. B. Neuman & D. K. Dickinson (Eds.), *Handbook of early literacy research* (pp. 11–29). Cambridge, MA: Guilford.

Zars, B. (1998). *Long rides, tough hides: Enduring long school bus rides.* Randolph, VT: Rural School and Community Trust Policy Program.

Zaslow, M., Brown, B., & Aufseeser, D. (2005). *Preliminary rural analy-ses of the early childhood longitudinal study—kindergarten cohort.* Mississippi State, MS: National Center for Rural Early Childhood Learning Initiatives.

Zill, N. (1999). Promoting educational equity and excellence in kindergar-ten. In R. Pianta, S. Rimm-Kaufman, & M. Cox (Eds.), *The transition to kindergarten* (pp. 67–105). Baltimore, MD: Brookes.

# 12

# Literacy Development in the Transition to School

## *An Integrative Framework*

FREDERICK J. MORRISON AND CAROL MCDONALD CONNOR

Several recent trends in contemporary research on literacy have converged on the process of school transition. First, it is now clear that meaningful individual differences in important language, cognitive, literacy, and social skills appear before children begin formal schooling in kindergarten or first grade (Morrison, Bachman, & Connor, 2005; Shonkoff & Phillips, 2000). Second, children's success or failure is influenced by a number of factors in the child, family, preschool, and larger sociocultural context (National Institute of Child Health and Development [NICHD] Early Childcare Research Network [ECCRN], 2004). Third, these influences do not operate independently, but interact to shape children's variable trajectories (Storch & Whitehurst, 2002). Finally, the early schooling experiences of American children are also highly variable, in some cases magnifying the differences in skills found among children prior to school entry (NICHD-ECCRN, 2002b, 2005; Pianta, Paro, Payne, Cox, & Bradley, 2002). The cumulative impact of these ongoing trends has been to focus attention on the process of school transition as a unique and important milestone in the academic development of children and as a foundational experience for early school success.

In the present chapter we will first outline a working conceptualization of children's literacy development across the school transition period, from roughly 3 years of age to third grade. As we shall illustrate, full understanding of literacy growth during school transition involves consideration of a variety of factors. The bulk of our discussion, however, will focus on the impact of schooling on children's academic development.

## Conceptualizing School Transition

Working from an ecological perspective (Bronfenbrenner, 1986), scientists have attempted to develop a coherent conceptualization of the process of school transition. Figure 12.1 depicts a working model of the major factors impinging

on children's literacy development and their independent and combined influences over the school transition period (Morrison et al., 2005). Four features should be noted. First the model distinguishes processes active prior to school entry from those operative once school begins. At the same time, where appropriate, the model highlights continuity of influences (e.g., from parenting) across the two periods.

Second, the conceptualization strives to portray the interplay of distal (more remote) and proximal (more immediate) factors shaping children's literacy trajectories. In Bronfenbrenner's scheme, these factors would distinguish micro- and mesosystems from more remote exo- and macrosystems. Concretely, the causal links between proximal factors and distal factors leading to literacy outcomes is depicted. Hence, in the preschool period, the contribution of more distal sociocultural factors, like parental education or income, is shown as operating through their effect on more proximal parenting or preschool influences. Likewise, during early schooling the impact of teacher education or experience manifests itself primarily through the ongoing instructional activities of the teacher in the classroom.

Third, the model highlights salient components within each of the larger factors. For parenting, research has highlighted the unique influence of the learning environment, parental warmth/responsivity, and control/discipline.

Finally the model depicts important interactions among these factors, reflecting the emerging consensus that these factors do not operate in isolation. For example, the home learning environment contributes directly to children's literacy growth but not to their self-regulation skills (Morrison & Cooney, 2002). Yet self-regulation and related social skills are shaped by parental control/discipline strategies and in turn contribute to literacy growth. On a broader plane accumulating evidence increasingly highlights the need to capture the complex interplay of forces shaping children's literacy trajectories across the school transition period.

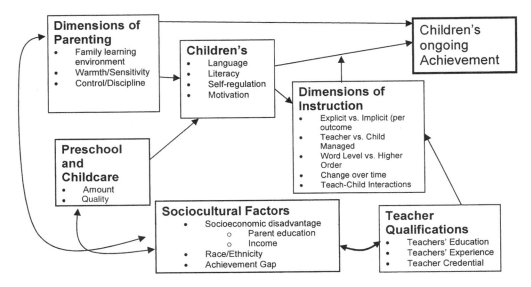

**Figure 12.1** Working model (Morrison et al., 2005).

### Prior to School Entry

***Sociocultural Factors*** The link between a family's socio-economic status (SES), measured via income, education, or occupational status, and a child's academic success has been well documented (see Entwisle, Alexander, & Olson, chapter 15 this volume). Likewise, accumulating evidence has established links between race/ethnicity and school success, particularly the persistently poorer performance of African American students compared to their European American peers. These factors are obviously linked, since the poverty rate among Black and Hispanic families in America is three times higher than it is for White families (Federal Interagency Forum on Child and Family Statistics, 2005). Clearly, the challenge for scientists has been to disentangle the independent and combined impact of social, economic, and racial/ethnic influences on academic development.

***Socioeconomic Factors and Academic Achievement*** The National Assessment of Educational Progress (2007) reports that 9-, 13-, and 17-year-old students from families with less than high school education scored lower on tests of reading, math, and science than did children whose parents completed some education after high school. More significant, there is documentation that children from low SES families start school behind their more affluent peers and progress more slowly through the early years of elementary school (Alexander & Entwisle, 1988; Stipek & Ryan, 1997). Recent work has unearthed additional SES-related differences in language and emergent literacy skills (Raviv, Kessenich, & Morrison, 2004). In a pioneering study, Hart and Risley (1995) found that preschool children from welfare families had smaller vocabularies compared to children from working class and professional families as early as 3 years of age. Moreover, their rates of vocabulary acquisition were much slower over the ensuing preschool years.

Notwithstanding the clear association of socioeconomic disadvantage and poor school performance, it is not obvious how SES factors operate to shape children's academic trajectories, especially in the preschool years. In their efforts to probe more deeply into the mechanisms underlying the SES–performance connection, scientists have distinguished between direct and mediated pathways of influence (Morrison et al., 2005).

Direct pathways reflect influences that operate directly on the child to affect academic performance. Yet, increasingly, scientists are describing the impact of SES as operating through more immediate influences in the child's environment. For instance, mothers living in poverty are less likely to receive adequate prenatal care, which could contribute, in part, to the connection between SES and prematurity. Researchers describe these as *mediated pathways*, where SES is viewed as a distal variable that exerts its influence through a more immediate or proximal variable. The whole process is described as a *mediated relation*. Scientists are beginning to pinpoint how the effects of SES are mediated through more proximal factors, like parenting. Parents living in poverty may be less likely to talk to their preschool children; they frequently communicate with a more limited vocabulary, offer fewer questions or descriptive statements to them, and are often more repetitive than are professional or working class parents (Hart & Risley, 1995; Hoff-Ginsberg, 1991). In general, parents with fewer economic or educational resources are often less likely to provide the stimulating home environments children require to be maximally ready for school (Barbarin et al., 2006; Wasik & Bond, 2001). The important insight gained from seeing SES in this mediated fashion is that improving a family's economic circumstances alone may not translate into improved parenting, the more immediate causal agent shaping the child's development.

High concentrated poverty in schools and neighborhoods contributes even more to the cognitive and behavioral differences observed in children living in poverty when compared to their more affluent peers. Results of an investigation by Rauh et al. (Rauh, Parker, Garfinkel, Perry, & Andrews, 2003) supported previous findings (Duncan & Raudenbush, 2001), which suggested that aside from the home environment, school and neighborhood are among the most important settings for school-age children. Unfortunately, in many cases, children from low-SES families reside in neighborhoods that are less likely to promote academic competence. Often in poor neighborhoods, children not only live in substandard housing, but must also cope with the presence of drugs, violence, and neighborhood crime. Such stressful conditions often are associated with the onset of behavioral and developmental deficits (Cowen, Wyman, & Work, 1996; Garbarino, 2001; Leadbeater & Bishop, 1994). Additionally, in impoverished neighborhoods where most residents' employment has little to do with their education, children may be less likely to see the benefits of education in career outcomes; these children may see few instances of success related to participation in formal education. At the same time, the presence of more affluent neighbors is related to better school outcomes (Garmezy, Masten, & Tellegen, 1984; Loesel & Bliesener, 1990). According to Brooks-Gunn and colleagues (Brooks-Gunn, Duncan, Klebanov, & Sealand, 1993), successful life conditions, a positive environment, and the presence of affluent neighbors, can serve as protective factors for children otherwise at risk for behavioral and developmental problems (Brooks-Gunn et al., 1993; Rauh et al., 2003). Living in a neighborhood with high levels of concentrated poverty is also harmful to students in other ways. In high poverty schools, a large number of students needing special education services may exhaust already taxed school resources (Ansalone, 2001). Moreover, high poverty schools are less likely to attract the most qualified teachers (Connor, Son, Hindman, & Morrison, 2005)

In addition to differences in home literacy environment, a less stimulating home environment during the summer may also account for disparities seen in children from lower SES homes. Several studies have revealed that the achievement gap between these students and those from higher SES homes increases more over the summer, when school is not in session, than during the academic year (Alexander, Entwisle, & Olson, 2001; Cooper, Nye, Charlton, Lindsay, & Greathouse, 1996; Jencks & Phillips, 1998). This theory, known as the "faucet theory," holds that "summer effects" take place as, generally, those with less income and education are less able to provide academically enriching home environments during the summer months (Ansalone, 2001; Cooper et al., 1996; Entwisle, Alexander, & Olson, 1997; McCoach, O'Connell, Reis, & Levitt, 2006).

Poverty is associated with the way in which parents interact with their children. A lack of energy, weakened self-confidence, stress, and feeling of loss of control over their lives due to the circumstances of poverty, is often associated with less responsive parenting practices, resulting in lack of parental support needed to help foster cognitive ability within children (McLoyd, 1990). While the reasons for these differences in parenting are not clearly understood, and there are many distal factors that are implicated (Morrison et al., 2005), the focus on parenting and related proximal causes is yielding a clearer, more comprehensive picture of the complex forces contributing to the continued underperformance of children living in poverty.

***Race, Ethnicity, and Academic Achievement*** Parallel issues emerge in efforts to explain disparities across racial and ethnic groups in academic attainment. Clearly, race or ethnicity qualifies as a distal variable whose influence on academic trajectories is mediated by more proximal factors. Since most progress in understanding these complex relations comes from the study of differences between African American and European American students, we will focus on this issue here (for discussion of other ethnic groups, see Morrison et al., 2005).

Broadly, African American children do not perform as well academically as their European American counterparts (National Assessment of Educational Progress, 2007). While some variation has been noted over the last three decades, sizable differences have persisted throughout the period in which scientists have been tracking children's performance.

Common interpretations for "the gap" have leaned on socioeconomic and other sociocultural factors (Jencks & Phillips, 1998). For example, the higher rate of poverty among African American families presents itself as an obvious cause for poorer performance in Black children. Likewise, the legacy of racial discrimination, which limits opportunities for Black children, surfaces as a likely contributor to lower academic aspirations and accomplishment.

Perhaps the most salient and controversial proximal factor implicated in the Black–White test score gap is the home environment. Much disparity arises even before birth. Because African American women are more likely to experience higher levels of stress than European American women, and, if living in poverty, have less access to nutritional diets before and after pregnancy, and to be exposed to more harmful health behaviors, they are also more likely to deliver prematurely and have children with low birth weight (McLoyd, 1998). In a study that examined birth weight, in relation to later cognitive performance, Goldberg, McLaughlin, Grossi, Tytun, and Blum (1992) found that low birth weight consistently predicted children's use of special education services (Rauh et al., 2003). A great deal of research indicates that children born with low birth weight exhibit more problems than those who are born at normal weight (Andrews, Goldberg, Wellen, Pittman, & Struening, 1995; Rauh et al., 2003). In addition to the physical health problems related to birth status (i.e., prematurity) and malnutrition, which place children at greater risk for behavior problems and academic failure, poverty itself compounds that risk. Poor nutrition, as is often the reality for those people who are living in poverty, limited access to adequate health care, and exposure to dangerous environments, further exacerbate cognitive functioning problems. Because those living in poverty often have less access to adequate health care and other such services, which could minimize the effects of physical problems, children living in poverty are at greater risk than their high-SES counterparts for developing developmental impairment (McLoyd, 1998).

While these factors clearly play some role in the gap, two recent empirical discoveries have caused scientists to reassess the nature and sources of the "Black-White test score gap." First, the gap is not limited to lower SES groups (Phillips, Crouse, & Ralph, 1998). Black, middle SES children are generally performing more poorly than their White peers. Second, the gap in academic skills emerges before children begin school (Phillips et al., 1998). These two findings have caused researchers to look more deeply into the proximal environments of Black families for a more comprehensive understanding of the roots of academic problems. For example, studies have found that infant mortality rates are higher in Black families (Centers for Disease Control and Prevention, 2000), and more significantly, this difference occurs independently of SES (Schoendorf, Hogue, Kleinman, & Rowley, 1992).

## Preschool and Early Child Care

The majority of America's preschoolers (approximately 20 million) will spend some time in alternate care (Smith, 2002). Hence, scientists have become increasingly concerned about the psychological consequences of child care for children under 5 years of age as well as its impact on school transition and later school functioning. In addition, for children most at risk for school failure, intensive interventions during the preschool years have attempted to help children at risk for academic failure (e.g., children living in poverty) catch up to their peers and be equally ready for school.

*Is Day Care Good or Bad for Children?* While phrased dramatically, the above question succinctly captures the essence of the debate on the impact of early child care for preschool children. The importance of this question can be appreciated by realizing that the Federal government funded a major national study of the nature and consequences of early child care in the late 1980s. The NICHD Study of Early Childcare, as well as others, has yielded valuable insights on the impact of child care experiences on children's development and school performance.

Closer examination reveals that two variables—quality and quantity of care—are crucial to understanding the role of child care in children's lives. In broad terms, higher quality childcare produces positive effects on children's cognitive, language, and literacy skills (NICHD-ECCRN, 2002a) while high quantities of care (defined as more that 30 hours per week) have been associated with slightly poorer social outcomes (Brooks-Gunn, Han, & Waldfogel, 2002). Even these conclusions do not capture the complexity of

the role of childcare. As active agents in choosing care for their child, more educated mothers have been shown to be more sensitive and responsive to their children than mothers with less education (NICHD-ECCRN, 2002a). Consequently, the more educated and responsive mothers are more proactive in seeking out higher quality childcare, can afford to pay for it, and monitor it more closely. In fact when direct comparisons have been made between parenting and childcare environments, the impact of the quality of parenting was three to four times greater than that of childcare on children's language and social skills (NICHD-ECCRN, 2004). Nevertheless there is early evidence that, independent of quality, children who spend more than 30 hours per week in center-based care may be less socially competent and somewhat more disruptive to other children and teachers (NICHD-ECCRN, 2003), though whether there is any long-term impact of these early experiences is less obvious at present.

In summary, in answer to our original question, day care, per se, is neither good nor bad for preschool children. High quality care promotes cognitive growth, while high amounts of childcare per week may put children at risk for slightly poorer social outcomes.

*Are Early Intervention Programs for At-Risk Students Effective?* High quality interventions can significantly enhance development, while poor quality programs can impede children's progress (S. W. Barnett, 1995). High quality preschool interventions have been shown to significantly improve children's prospects for academic success (S. W. Barnett, 1995), to promote stronger language and literacy development (Dickinson & Tabors, 2001) and yield significant return on investment over children's lifetimes (Reynolds, Temple, Robertson, & Mann, 2003).

A number of interventions have been attempted for at-risk children. The most visible (and controversial) is Head Start, the mixed outcomes of which illustrate the crucial importance of ensuring high quality programs for producing consistently positive effects (see Morrison et al., 2005, for a more in-depth review). Some of the more prominent and successful model programs include the Perry Preschool Project (S. W. Barnett, 1995), the Abecedarian Project (Campbell & Ramey, 1994), the School Development Program (Haynes, Comer, & Hamilton-Lee, 1988), and the Chicago Title 1 Child–Parent Centers (Reynolds et al., 2003). Across programs, children receiving these interventions showed significantly stronger academic and social skill development compared to equally at-risk children not enrolled in the program. Moreover, high quality preschool interventions have been shown to reduce referral to special education and to enhance overall educational attainment (S. W. Barnett, 1995; Conyers, Reynolds, & Ou, 2003; Nelson, Benner, & Gonzalez, 2003; Reynolds & Ou, 2004).

On balance then, there is growing consensus that both high quality childcare and interventions for children at-risk for academic underachievement significantly improve the psychological well-being of preschool children, enhance school readiness, and facilitate more successful school transition.

What constitutes high quality care? There are at least five salient elements (Morrison et al., 2005):

1. Strong support for parents. Successful programs coupled intensive intervention with home visits, parent education, and parent involvement.
2. Intensity. Programs that were more available to children all day, 5 days a week, like the Abecedarian project, tended to produce stronger, more durable outcomes for children.
3. Starting earlier. Programs that yielded greater cost–benefit ratios (e.g., Abecedarian and Chicago Title 1) began their interventions when participants were infants.
4. Well-qualified teachers. Programs with more teachers who were certified produced more consistently positive effects than those with fewer teachers who were certified.
5. Rich linguistic and literacy environment. Perhaps most fundamental to success was an explicit focus on improving the language and literacy skills needed for early school success. Included were emphases on vocabulary, syntax, world knowledge, phonology, alphabet knowledge, and elementary word decoding.

However, there is substantial variability in classroom practices and resulting child outcomes across programs and studies (S. W. Barnett, 1995; Nelson et al., 2003) and research seeks to understand how specific types of preschool classroom experiences relate to child outcomes. Teachers' sensitivity and responsiveness (NICHD-ECCRN studies), their use of cognitively challenging talk and rare words (e.g., Dickinson & Tabors, 2001), and their styles of book reading including Dialogic Reading (Whitehurst et al., 1994), as well as child initiated practices (Schweinhart & Weikart, 1988), for example, are related to positive child outcomes and these findings have been consistent in multiple settings (Conyers et al., 2003; NICHD-ECCRN, 2002a).

Until lately, there has been less research and evidence that a focus on academic skills provides consistently stronger child outcomes (Graue, Clements, Reynolds & Niles, 2004; Stipek, Feiler, Byler, et al., 1998; Stipek, Feiler, Daniels, & Milburn, 1995). However, recent studies are showing that appropriate attention to children's emergent literacy skills is associated with stronger academic outcomes later on. Emergent literacy "involves the skills, knowledge, and attitudes that are developmental precursors to conventional forms of reading and writing. These skills are the basic building blocks for how students learn to read and write" (Connor & Tiedemann, 2005, p. 1). In contrast to a reading readiness perspective, an emergent literacy perspective holds that learning to read begins well before formal school-based reading instruction. There is no boundary between what is considered to be the conventional reading that students learn in school and everything that comes before. Rather,

the emergent literacy perspective views literacy-related behaviors that occur in the preschool period as legitimate and important features on a developmental continuum of literacy (Bowman, Donovan, & Burns, 2001; Shonkoff & Phillips, 2000; Teale & Sulzby, 1986).

Studies that focus on the explicit instruction of emergent literacy in preschool have mixed findings (Graue et al., 2004). For example, preschoolers in programs that provided explicit instruction in basic reading skills showed stronger skills but less positive feelings about themselves and less motivation than did students in child-centered programs, which encouraged children's learning through play (Stipek et al., 1995). In still another study, preschoolers in classrooms that focused on basic skills demonstrated weaker cognitive and motivation outcomes than did preschoolers in classrooms that deemphasized basic skills and had more positive social climates (Stipek, Feiler, Byler et al., 1998). However, more recent evidence, using teacher report, suggests that curricula that were high in teacher-directed instruction with specific content and simultaneously high in child initiated/teacher responsive approaches yielded more positive short- and long-term educational and social outcomes for preschoolers than did programs that emphasized one over the other or neither (Graue et al., 2004). Another study investigated preschoolers' classroom language and literacy experiences, defined across multiple dimensions, and their vocabulary and emergent literacy development (Connor, Morrison, & Slominski, 2006). Videotaped classroom observations revealed substantial variability in amount and types of language and emergent literacy activities, across classrooms and for individual children within classrooms. Generally, more time in emergent code-focused activities was associated with preschoolers' alphabet and letter–word recognition growth while more time in meaning-focused activities (e.g., book reading) was related to vocabulary growth. This specificity (code-focused instruction predicts code-related skills and language related instruction predicts language development) has been observed by other researchers for parenting as well (Senechal, 2006; Senechal & LeFevre, 2001a, 2001b, 2002).

## Parenting

Throughout the previous sections we have referred to parenting as a critical mediator of the effects of SES, as well as being inextricably linked to the influences of child care. But, as our original conceptualization implied, parenting plays a complex interactive role with several other factors. For example, recent work on the genetic bases of development has challenged the once dominant position of parental socialization as the shaper of human nature. Further, efforts to improve parenting in at-risk families have proven surprisingly unsuccessful. We are gradually coming to the realization that, though parenting is a critical source of children's development we need to broaden our perspective on parenting in order to appreciate its full sweep and power.

***Does Parenting Matter?*** Until about 20 years ago, most developmental theories accorded parents primacy over genetics, peers, and other contextual influences (Collins, Maccoby, Steinberg, Hetherington, & Bornstein, 2000; Cowan & Cowan, 2002). Nevertheless, in the past two decades behavior-geneticists and others have challenged this simple view (Plomin, 1990; Rowe, Vazsonyi, & Flannery, 1994). Utilizing twin and related research methods designed to separate genetic from environmental influences, researchers have found that: (1) children's development can withstand substantial variability in parenting practices and emerge intact; and (2) other socializing forces, particularly peers, can exert long-term influence on selected personality traits (Harris, 1995; Rowe et al., 1994).

This work has had the salutary effect of yielding a more balanced view of the complex forces shaping human development. More recent work has attempted to gauge the complex interplay across children's development as affected by parenting along with genetic and other factors (Collins et al., 2000). As an example, in a French study of late-adopted children (3–5 years old) with below average IQs, the children that were adopted in higher SES families exhibited substantially greater IQ gains (19 points) by 11 to 18 years of age than did children adopted into lower SES households (8 points). This finding neatly demonstrates that children with similar genetic characteristics make differential progress depending on the SES of the family in which they are reared; this difference is, presumably, mediated in part by differing parenting practices.

***How Malleable Is Parenting?*** One way to examine the power of parenting is to conduct intervention studies to examine whether programs actually improve parenting skills and whether there are corresponding increases in children's literacy skills. Two strategies have been adopted: (1) family-focused early childhood education (ECE) coupled with home-based services; and (2) exclusively parent-focused home visiting programs. Reviews have concluded that home-based interventions alone, without a center-based child-intervention component were surprisingly ineffective in improving children's cognitive skills (see Morrison et al., 2005 for an overview).

Many of these adult-based efforts did not substantially increase parental outcomes (e.g., educational attainment), which, in part, may explain why their children's cognitive performance did not improve (Magnusson & Duncan, 2004).

If parenting is so important to a child's development, then why haven't the interventions been more powerful? Actually, there are several reasons these efforts may have fallen short. First, as the authors themselves noted, case managers in these studies quickly found that they needed to deal with a number of family crises and chronic adversities, like inadequate housing, lack of food, and heat and legal problems and that it was difficult to move beyond crisis intervention to work on parenting for literacy (St. Pierre & Layzer, 1999). In addition, there were sizable differences across families in

the uptake of services or the "dosage" effect. Specifically, since participation in these interventions was, ultimately, voluntary, parental participation varied widely, with about half the scheduled visits actually taking place (Gomby, Culross, & Behrman, 1999). Significantly, when eligible families were split by their participation level, children in families with more involvement made greater gains than did their peers whose families participated less. Finally, it should be noted that smaller, more focused interventions (e.g., around book reading) have yielded measurable gains in children's oral language skills (Lonigan & Whitehurst, 1998; Payne, Whitehurst, & Angell, 1994; Reese & Cox, 1999; Senechal & LeFevre, 2001b, 2002).

## Child Characteristics

Since the late 1980s, scientists have better appreciated that there are important child characteristics that influence how children interact with their parents and teachers, and the resilience they bring to situations, such as poverty, that operate outside the family's control. Although many child characteristics might be considered, in this chapter we focus on three: language, literacy, and self-regulation, because of their demonstrated relevance to children's early literacy development.

***Language Skills*** Accumulating research strongly indicates that children's language skills are absolutely critical in predicting how well or poorly they will achieve proficient reading skills and school success overall (Catts, 1993; Catts, Fey, Zhang, & Tomblin, 1999; Connor & Tiedemann, 2005; Scarborough, 1990, 1998, 2001; Storch & Whitehurst, 2002). Early language skills hold long term consequences for the likelihood that children will be retained a grade, be referred to special education, or drop out of high school (Reynolds & Ou, 2004). Indeed, the single best predictors of how quickly children's academic skills will develop are the language and literacy skills with which they enter school (Connor et al., 2005; Dickinson & Neuman, 2006; Neuman & Dickinson, 2001; NICHD-ECCRN, 2004; Reynolds & Ou, 2004) and children living in poverty are less likely to enter school with large vocabularies (Hart & Risley, 1995).

Research also indicates that children's language skills have an important effect on the types of instruction that will be effective for them (Connor, Morrison, Fishman, Schatschneider, & Underwood, 2007; Connor, Morrison, & Katch, 2004; Connor, Morrison, & Petrella, 2004; Connor, Morrison, & Slominski, 2006). For example, in preschool, children with stronger vocabulary skills were able to gain emergent literacy skills from a broader range of types of learning activities than were children with weaker vocabulary skills (Connor, Morrison, & Slominski, 2006). This suggests that children with strong language skills will automatically have more opportunities to learn than will children with weaker skills even when they share the same classroom.

While much of research has focused on vocabulary, other aspects of language appear to be critical for literacy development. These include morphosyntactic, semantic, and pragmatic knowledge and metalinguistic awareness (Carlisle, 2000; Charity, Scarborough, & Griffin, 2004; Snow & Tabors, 1993). Typically phonological awareness has been considered a literacy skill but it may also be considered a language skill that falls within the family of metalinguistic awareness. It constitutes a salient link between oral and written language and represents a fundamental stumbling block for children experiencing difficulties learning to read (Scarborough, 1998; Storch & Whitehurst, 2002; Torgesen, Burgess, Wagner, & Rashotte, 1994; Vellutino et al., 1996). It is strongly related to vocabulary and reading development and most current models of reading conceive this to be a reciprocal relation (Perfetti, Beck, Bell, & Hughes, 1987). Strong language skills support metalinguistic awareness (Storch & Whitehurst, 2002) because words are made up of sounds that correspond to the letters in the alphabet. Letter name knowledge contributes to this understanding as do developing decoding skills (Ehri & Roberts, 2006). In fact, this notion of letter–sound correspondence becomes so ingrained that many literate adults will say that the word *box* has three sounds when it actually has four, /b/ /a/ /k/ /s/. There is evidence that phonological awareness is highly heritable but also that, for the majority of children, explicit instruction facilitates growth of phonological awareness (Bradley & Bryant, 1983; Ehri & Roberts, 2006; Rayner, Foorman, Perfetti, Pesetsky, & Seidenberg, 2001; Torgesen et al., 2001). What seems to vary across children is the amount and intensity of instruction needed for children to grasp the alphabetic principle and crack the code.

*Self-Regulation* Children may begin school with strong language and literacy skills and still be unsuccessful in their transition. An emerging construct, behavioral self-regulation, appears to contribute to children's learning in the classroom (Connor, Ponitz, et al., 2010; McClelland et al., 2007). The definition of this construct is still under debate, but for this chapter, we will use the increasingly accepted idea that self-regulation relates to the ability to focus attention, to inhibit inappropriate behavior, to switch tasks when needed, and to ignore distractions. Self-regulation may also relate to components of executive function including attention, working memory, and inhibitory control (Bronson, 2000; Ponitz, McClelland, Jewkes, et al., 2007; Müller, Zelazo, Hood, Leone, & Rohrer, 2004). In general, children with good attention are able to focus on a task or problem, access working memory, and carry out the task without being distracted by what is going on around them. Working memory too, is related to aspects of self-regulation such as problem solving, children's ability to remember and follow directions, and to problem solve (Gathercole & Pickering, 2000). Inhibitory control is another aspect of self-regulation (Rennie, Bull, & Diamond, 2004) wherein children can stop incorrect actions and carry out more adaptive responses (Dowsett & Livesey, 2000). All of the

aspects of behavioral self-regulation contribute to successful learning overall, not just to literacy development.

In summary, it has become clear from accumulating research over the last 20 years that significant developmental changes in important literacy skills occur during the formative years before children enter formal schooling. Equally striking has been the realization from the evidence that large individual differences in a host of important cognitive, language, and social skills emerge by at least 3 years of age. Factors in the more proximal child and parenting environment contribute to this variability, as do more distal sociocultural influences. These facts form a foundational context in which the influences of schooling must be viewed.

## Schooling and Literacy Development

*Preschool Experiences* As our model depicts, the years from preschool to the beginning of formal schooling are increasingly seen as a continuous system. This is reflected in new efforts to offer high quality preschool to all children, such as the voluntary PK programs emerging in states across the country, as well as in efforts to study and enhance the transition from home to preschool to kindergarten. These trends in programming and research are important because child development does not recognize an artificial break between preschool, kindergarten, and first grade. Rather, using an emergent literacy paradigm, skills critical for literacy are developing well before children walk in the school door (Connor & Tiedemann, 2005). Formal preschool experiences that deliberately build children's language and emergent literacy skills make a lifelong difference in children's success in school (Barnett, Frede, Mobasher, & Mohr, 1987; Reynolds & Ou, 2004; Reynolds et al., 2003). Research suggests that these early formal schooling experiences operate through at least two pathways—one primarily academic and the other social (NICHD-ECCRN, 2004; Reynolds & Ou, 2004).

We are starting to understand the true complexity of providing preschool experiences that will make a meaningful contribution to children's success in school. The effect of particular preschool activities on students' emergent literacy depends on the vocabulary and emergent literacy skills they bring to the classroom (Connor, Morrison, & Slominski, 2006). For example, new research reveals that opportunities to play, specifically symbolic play, are important for language development (Roskos & Christie, 2000). Play is symbolic when, for example, a child is pretending that a block is a car going down an imaginary road, or role-playing a scientist who is examining how chicks hatch from eggs. In our study of preschoolers we found that the more time children spent in these kinds of play opportunities predicted greater vocabulary growth (Connor, Morrison, & Slominski, 2006). However, this finding was true only for children who began the preschool year with relatively weak vocabulary skills. Play had no meaningful effect on vocabulary growth for children who already had relatively larger vocabularies.

Rather, opportunities to read and discuss books and learn letter names and sounds were associated with vocabulary growth for children who started preschool with strong vocabulary skills.

It is unfortunate that in many states, preschool teachers are not required to have a bachelor's degree. In some programs, three college credits and 45 hours of training are considered sufficient (e.g., https://training01-dcf.myflorida. gov/dcf/cct/cdaetraining.html). It is hard to see how underpaid and underprepared teachers are going to be able to plan and implement the kind of individualized instruction new research suggests will be critical to preparing all children for the transition to school. On the other hand, research also suggests that increasing educational requirements and credentials may be necessary but are not sufficient to obtain stronger student outcomes (Early, Bryant, et al., 2006; Early, Maxwell, et al., 2007).

*Early Elementary School Experiences* Just as preschool experiences make an important contribution to students' learning, so do their experiences in elementary classrooms (Morrison, Griffith, & Alberts, 1997; Morrison, Smith, & Dow-Ehrensberger, 1995). Moreover, we are beginning to understand that the learning experiences at each grade are cumulative. Consistently effective instruction through second grade (Connor, Morrison, & Underwood, 2007) and beyond (Sanders & Horn, 1998) will predict much stronger student literacy than inconsistently effective instruction. It is not necessarily the case that a good teacher can make up for lost opportunities following ineffective instruction.

*Providing Effective Instruction* Research evidence over the last decade cautions us that providing effective instruction is not easy. Classroom instruction has multiple dimensions and the impact of any particular strategy for any given child significantly depends on the child's language and literacy skills (Morrison et al., 2005). What is effective for a child who reads proficiently, may not be effective for a child still struggling with basic decoding skills. These child-by-instruction interactions have been found in different samples of children from Michigan to Florida and from preschool through third grade (Connor, Jakobsons, Crowe, & Meadows, 2009; Connor, Morrison, Fishman et al., 2007; Connor, Morrison, & Katch, 2004; Connor, Morrison, & Petrella, 2004; Connor, Morrison, Slominski, 2006; Foorman, Francis, Fletcher, Schatschneider, & Mehta, 1998; Juel & Minden-Cupp, 2000).

*Multiple Dimensions of Teaching* Just as the construct of literacy has multiple components, effective teaching also appears to be multidimensional. Teachers who are warm and responsive in their interactions with their students tend to be more effective than more detached teachers (Connor et al., 2005; NICHD-ECCRN, 2002b). Teachers' ability to organize their classrooms and impart classroom rules and routines, and explain activities clearly is more effective that unorganized teachers (Brophy, 1979; Cameron, Connor, &

Morrison, 2005). Moreover, within the overall dimension of instruction there are also multiple dimensions that capture the nature of interactions between the teacher and student (e.g., teacher-, teacher/child-, child- and peer-managed interactions), the content of the instructional activity (e.g., reading, science, social studies, and within reading specifically, code- versus meaning-focused or explicit versus implicit), and on the context (e.g., whole class, small group, pairs, individual). These dimensions operate simultaneously so that any instructional activity across the content areas (e.g., Connor, Morrison, Fishman, et al., 2007) can be described multidimensionally.

Comparing across studies, a pattern seems to be emerging that suggests a new theory of literacy teaching and learning. For children with weaker initial language and literacy skills, more time in teacher/child-managed instruction explicitly focused on the skill to be learned appears to lead to stronger learning of that skill, whereas for children with stronger language and literacy skills, more implicit instruction appears to be associated stronger reading outcome growth. For example, a study of third grade reading comprehension demonstrated that children who begin the year with weaker to average reading comprehension skills demonstrate greater growth, on average, when they are in classrooms where more time is spent on instruction that explicitly focuses on reading comprehension, including comprehension strategies (e.g., graphic planners, summarizing, inferring, etc), discussions about books read, and vocabulary activities. In contrast, asking these same children to spend substantial amounts of time reading independently is associated with less reading comprehension skill growth for them. Overall, these kinds of activities have little overall effect on reading comprehension growth for students who begin the year with very strong reading comprehension skills (Connor, Morrison, & Petrella, 2004).

Plus there are surprises in the literature. It has been generally assumed that second graders need substantially less time in explicit code-focused instruction (Foorman et al., 2006). However, in two recent studies with very different groups of children (one in an affluent northern community, and the other in a state-wide study of Reading First), greater amounts of teacher-managed explicit code-focused instruction in second grade predicted greater letter–word reading (Connor, Morrison, & Underwood, 2007) and reading comprehension skill growth (Connor, Jakobsons, et al., 2009.

## Individualizing Student Instruction

Providing effective instruction is highly complex. While rigorous research has revealed that school and curriculum-based innovations can contribute to student learning overall, unless the individual child is considered, some children will fail to learn. But individualizing instruction for each child in the classroom is difficult, especially when abilities vary widely among the students in the class. One encouraging development is the Individualizing Student Instruction

Project. This study, conducted initially with first readers, uses a web-based software program called Assessment-to-Instruction (A2i), to help teachers provide effective instruction to all the children in their classroom (Connor, Piasta et al., 2009). The software uses algorithms, based on research showing child-by-instruction interactions, to recommend specific amounts and types of instruction for each child in the classroom using each student's assessed language and literacy skills. After only 4 months, children demonstrated significantly stronger growth in letter–word skills when their teachers individualized instruction (i.e., used small groups with appropriate learning goals and planned instruction using A2i) compared to a control group and to children whose teachers had access to the software but did not use it consistently. By the end of the school year, children in the treatment group achieved stronger reading comprehension skill growth, overall, than did children in the control classrooms.

Additionally, classroom observation results were analyzed for each individual child. With the exception of teacher/child-managed meaning-focused instruction, the total amount of time a child spent in a particular type of instruction did not predict their reading skill gains. However, the closer to the recommended amount of instruction each child received of either teacher/child-managed code focused or child-managed meaning focused instruction, the stronger were their reading skill gains (Connor, Piasta, et al., 2009). In general, the more teacher/child-managed meaning-focused instruction children received, the stronger was their reading comprehension skill growth. Thus, it appears that we can predict with some precision the amounts and types of instruction that will promote stronger reading achievement for children as long as we know their language and literacy skills.

However, individualizing instruction was challenging for fully 40% of the teachers. Many of these teachers complained that the planning took too much time. Others had difficulty managing the classroom organization aspects of individualizing instruction. Orchestrating small groups of children engaged in substantially different learning activities is difficult, no doubt about it. For others, whole class instruction was their preferred method of instruction based on their philosophy of teaching. They felt it was detrimental to children to be placed in homogeneous skill-based groups. For others still, planning whole class instruction was much easier than planning for the different instructional needs of each child in the classroom. Additionally, in some schools, teachers were expected to be on the same page of the core curriculum for all of the children in the classroom rather than considering whether or not, for example, a group of proficient readers really needed to learn again how to blend sounds to make words.

For all of the teachers, using assessment results to tailor instruction was difficult. When they used A2i, teachers stated that using assessment to guide instruction was much easier for them. Still, some teachers never used the assessment information provided. These teachers, in particular,

had a higher proportion of children who failed to achieve grade expectations by the end of first grade.

***Variability in Teacher Quality*** Our finding that some teachers were more effective than others in teaching their students how to read proficiently is not a unique finding. For example, some embraced the opportunity to learn new methods to improve student achievement and others did not. The professional development literature and the literature on teacher qualifications make clear that the quality of teachers in the classroom is highly variable (Connor et al., 2005; Gersten, Baker, Haager, & Graves, 2005; Palmaffy, 1999; Piasta, Connor, Fishman, & Morrison, 2007; Walsh, Glaser, & Wilcox, 2006). Why might this be? While many reasons are offered—teachers are underpaid and under appreciated, they are poorly trained and unprepared for the challenges of today's classrooms, or the field is not attracting the caliber of person required to teach effectively (Berry, Hoke, & Hirsch, 2004; Leigh & Mead, 2005; Steiner, 2003; U.S. Department of Education & Office of Postsecondary Education, 2004). Most likely, all of these issues as well as others contribute to the variability in teacher quality.

We contend, however, that focusing on practice in the classroom and teachers' knowledge of research-based concepts and practice, rather than more distal variables, such as years of education or teaching credentials, will be more informative as we strive to understand what makes teachers effective (Connor et al., 2005; Morrison et al., 2005; Piasta et al., 2009). This calls for a focus on teacher preparation before teachers enter the classroom and providing professional development once they are there. Unfortunately, as the National Council on Teacher Quality reveals (Walsh et al., 2006), only 11% of the randomly selected teacher education programs included the five components of reading identified in the National Reading Panel report (2000). This leaves new teachers sadly unprepared to teach reading effectively.

If teachers are entering the classroom largely unprepared to teach, then professional development becomes increasingly important. Unfortunately, the literature on professional development is filled with assertions with little research to back up these assertions. What research does reveal is not encouraging. Generally, the field consensus is that it takes 2 to 3 years of intensive work to change teachers' beliefs and practices (Fishman, Marx, Best, & Tal, 2003; Klingner, Vaughn, Arguelles, Hughes, & Leftwich, 2004; Sadoski & Willson, 2006). This leaves the field in a very real quandary and shows, increasingly, that preparing preservice teachers well before they enter the classroom and supporting them appropriately throughout their career is crucial.

## Summary and Conclusions

The last two decades have witnessed major shifts in our understanding of the nature and sources of literacy growth in children and the implications for improving literacy in America. Children begin to diverge on a host of educationally important skills well before their formal school years. The experiences they receive at home, in pre-school, and other social contexts all contribute in complex, interacting fashion to shape those widening trajectories. One clear lesson that we have learned over the past decade is that we cannot simply treat the preschool period as an inexorable unfolding of maturationally driven competencies. Efforts to intervene and improve early skill development during the preschool years must be a national priority.

Over the same period, we have gradually come to realize that instructional efforts that do not incorporate the wide variability among children will miss the mark in attempting to provide effective instruction. The call for individualized (or differentiated or personalized) instruction represents a bold attempt to move beyond the "one size fits all" mentality and focus attention on the individual child learner and not the curriculum.

Individualizing instruction is a challenging goal to achieve and one that teachers may not at present be prepared to master. It will likely require a major national effort to provide stronger preservice training for the next generation of teachers, as well as intensive professional development for existing teachers, to support implementation of these ideas.

In this chapter we have attempted to portray the richness and complexity that characterize the current scientific study of early school transition and literacy development. Clearly, the effort is seen as crucial to understanding the larger questions of the nature of literacy development in American children and how we might endeavor to improve the nation's literacy profile. Over two decades of research have solidified our conviction that meaningful variation in important literacy, language, and social skills surface early in life and solidify, without major intervention to help. Parents, teachers, and the larger society all play a role in contributing to and, ultimately, in dealing with, these early differences. Elsewhere (Morrison et al., 2005) we have offered concrete suggestions for improving literacy in America. For our purposes here, it is sufficient to emphasize that deeper understanding of the complex, interacting forces (proximal and distal) that shape early development will significantly inform our efforts to provide each one of our children with the experiences they need to grow optimally.

## Author Note

Preparation of the chapter was supported in part by grants from National Institute for Child and Human Development (NICHD) (27176-13) to Frederick J. Morrison and by grants from NICHD (R01HD48539) and the U.S. Department of Education, Institute for Education Sciences (R305H04013 and R305B070074) to Carol M. Connor.

## References

Alexander, K., & Entwisle, D. (1988). Achievement in the first 2 years of school: Patterns and processes. *Monographs of the Society for Research in Child Development, 53*(2).

Alexander, K. L., Entwisle, D. R., & Olson, L. S. (2001). Schools, achievement, and inequality: A seasonal perspective. *Educational Evaluation and Policy Analysis, 23*, 171–191.

Andrews, H., Goldberg, D., Wellen, N., Pittman, B., & Struening, E. (1995). Prediction of special education placement from birth certificate data. *American Journal of Preventive Medicine (Amsterdam), 11*, 55–61.

Ansalone, G. (2001). Schooling, tracking, and inequality. *Journal of Children and Poverty, 7*(1), 33–47.

Barbarin, O., Bryant, D., McCandies, T., Burchinal, M., Early, D., Clifford, R., et al. (2006). Children enrolled in public pre-K: The relation of family life, neighborhood quality, and socioeconomic resources to early competence. *American Journal of Orthopsychiatry, 76*, 265–276.

Barnett, S. W. (1995). Long-term effects of early childhood programs on cognitive and school outcomes. *Future of Children, 5*(3), 25–50.

Barnett, W. S., Frede, E. C., Mobasher, F. H., & Mohr, P. (1987). The efficacy of public preschool programs and the relationship of program quality to efficacy. *Education Evaluation and Policy Analysis, 10*(1), 37–49.

Berry, B., Hoke, M., & Hirsch, E. (2004). NCLB: Highly qualified teachers. The search for highly qualified teachers. *Phi Delta Kappan, 85*, 684.

Bowman, B. T., Donovan, S., & Burns, M. S. (2001). *Eager to learn: Educating our preschoolers*. Washington DC: National Academy Press.

Bradley, L., & Bryant, P. E. (1983). Categorizing sounds and learning to read—A causal connection. *Nature, 301*(3), 419–421.

Bronfenbrenner, U. (1986). Ecology of the family as a context for human development: Research perspectives. *Developmental Psychology, 22*, 723–742.

Bronson, M. B. (2000). *Self-regulation in early childhood: Nature and nurture*. New York: Guilford.

Brooks-Gunn, J., Duncan, G. J., Klebanov, P. K., & Sealand, N. (1993). Do neighborhoods influence child and adolescent development? *American Journal of Sociology, 99*, 353–395.

Brooks-Gunn, J., Han, W.-J., & Waldfogel, J. (2002). Maternal employment and child cognitive outcomes in the first three years of life: NICHD study of early child care. *Child Development, 73*(4), 1052–1072.

Brophy, J. E. (1979). Teacher behavior and its effects. *Journal of Educational Psychology, 71*(6), 733–750.

Cameron, C. E., Connor, C. M., & Morrison, F. J. (2005). Effects of variation in teacher organization on classroom functioning. *Journal of School Psychology, 43*(1), 61–85.

Campbell, F. A., & Ramey, C. T. (1994). Effects of early intervention on intellectual and academic achievement: A follow-up study of children from low income families. *Child Development, 65*, 684–698.

Carlisle, J. F. (2000). Awareness of the structure and meaning of morphologically complex words: Impact on reading. *Reading & Writing, 12*(3–4), 169–190.

Catts, H. W. (1993). The relationship between speech–language impairments and reading disabilities. *Journal of Speech and Hearing Research, 36*, 948–958.

Catts, H. W., Fey, M., Zhang, X., & Tomblin, B. (1999). Language basis of reading and reading disabilities: Evidence from a longitudinal investigation. *Scientific Studies of Reading, 3*(4), 331–361.

Centers for Disease Control and Prevention. (2000). *CDC fact book 2000/2001*. Department of Health and Human Services. Atlanta, GA: Author.

Charity, A. H., Scarborough, H. S., & Griffin, D. (2004). Familiarity with "School English" in African-American children and its relation to early reading achievement. *Child Development, 75*, 1340–1356.

Collins, W. A., Maccoby, E., Steinberg, L., Hetherington, E. M., & Bornstein, M. H. (2000). Contemporary research on parenting: The case for nature and nurture. *American Psychologist, 55*, 218–232.

Connor, C. M., Jakobsons, L. J., Crowe, E., & Meadows, J. (2009). Instruction, differentiation, and student engagement in Reading First classrooms. *Elementary School Journal, 109*(3), 221–250.

Connor, C. M., Morrison, F. J., Fishman, B. J., Schatschneider, C., & Underwood, P. (2007). The early years: Algorithm-guided individualized reading instruction. *Science, 315*(5811), 464–465.

Connor, C. M., Morrison, F. J., & Katch, E. L. (2004). Beyond the reading wars: The effect of classroom instruction by child interactions on early reading. *Scientific Studies of Reading, 8*(4), 305–336.

Connor, C. M., Morrison, F. J., & Petrella, J. N. (2004). Effective reading comprehension instruction: Examining child by instruction interactions. *Journal of Educational Psychology, 96*(4), 682–698.

Connor, C. M., Morrison, F. J., & Slominski, L. (2006). Preschool instruction and children's literacy skill growth. *Journal of Educational Psychology, 98*(4), 665–689.

Connor, C. M., Morrison, F. J., & Underwood, P. (2007). A second chance in second grade? The independent and cumulative impact of first and second grade reading instruction and students' letter–word reading skill growth. *Scientific Studies of Reading, 11*(3), 199–233.

Connor, C. M., Piasta, S. B., Fishman, B., Glasney, S., Schatschneider, C., Crowe, E., et al. (2009). Individualizing student instruction precisely: Effects of child by instruction interactions on first graders' literacy development. *Child Development, 80*(1), 77–100.

Connor, C. M., Ponitz, C. E. C, Phillips, B., Travis, Q. M., Glasney, S., & Morrison, F. J. (in press). Teachers' participation in an individualized instruction intervention and children's literacy and behavioral regulation growth. *Journal of School Psychology.*

Connor, C. M., Son, S., Hindman, A. H., & Morrison, F. J. (2005). Teacher qualifications, classroom practices, family characteristics, and preschool experience: Complex effects on first graders' vocabulary and early reading outcomes. *Journal of School Psychology, 43,* 343–375.

Connor, C. M., & Tiedemann, P. (2005). *IRA/NICHD conference on early childhood literacy: Research summary.* Washington DC: International Reading Association and the National Institute on Child Health and Human Development. Retrieved from http://www.reading.org/Libraries/Reports_and_Standards/092005IRA-NICHD_summary.sflb.ashx

Conyers, L. M., Reynolds, A. J., & Ou, S.-R. (2003). The effect of early childhood intervention and subsequent special education services: Findings for the Chicago Child-Parent Centers. *Educational Evaluation and Policy Analysis, 25*(1), 75–95.

Cooper, H., Nye, B., Charlton, K., Lindsay, J., & Greathouse, S. (1996). The effects of summer vacation on achievement test scores: A narrative and meta analytic review. *Review of Educational Research, 66*(3), 227–268.

Cowan, P. A., & Cowan, C. P. (2002). What an intervention design reveals about how parents affect their children's academic achievement and behavior problems. In J. G. Borkowski, S. L. Ramey, & M. Bristol-Power (Eds.), *Parenting and the child's world: Influences on academic, intellectual, and social-emotional development* (pp. 75–97). Mahwah, NJ: Erlbaum.

Cowen, E. L., Wyman, P. A., & Work, W. C. (1996). Resilience in highly stressed urban children: Concepts and findings. *Bulletin of the New York Academy of Medicine, 73*(2), 267–284.

Dickinson, D. K., & Neuman, S. B. (Eds.). (2006). *Handbook of early literacy research* (Vol. 2). New York: Guilford.

Dickinson, D. K., & Tabors, P. O. (2001). *Beginning literacy with language.* Baltimore, MD: Brookes.

Dowsett, S. M., & Livesey, D. J. (2000). The development of inhibitory control in preschool children: Effects of "executive skills" training. *Developmental Psychobiology, 36*(2), 161–174.

Duncan, G. J., & Raudenbush, S. W. (2001). The well-being of children and families: Research and data needs. In A. Thornton (Ed.), *The well-being of children and families: Research and data needs.*(pp. 356–383). Ann Arbor, MI: University of Michigan Press.

Early, D. M., Bryant, D. M., Pianta, R. C., Clifford, R. M., Burchinal, M. R., Ritchie, S., et al. (2006). Are teachers' education, major, and credentials related to classroom quality and children's academic gains in pre-kindergarten? *Early Childhood Research Quarterly, 21,* 174–195.

Early, D. M., Maxwell, K. L., Burchinal, M., Bender, R. H., Ebanks, C., Henry, G. T., et al. (2007). Teachers' education, classroom quality, and young children's academic skills: Results from seven studies of preschool programs. *Child Development, 78,* 558–580.

Ehri, L. C., & Roberts, T. (2006). The roots of learning to read and write: acquisition of letters and phonological awareness. In D. K. Dickinson & S. B. Neuman (Eds.), *Handbook of early literacy research* (Vol. 2, pp. 113–131). New York: Guilford.

Entwisle, D. R., Alexander, K. L., & Olson, L. S. (1997). *Children, schools, and inequality.* Boulder, CO: Westview.

Federal Interagency Forum on Child and Family Statistics. (2005). *America's children: Key national indicators of well being, 2005.* Washington, DC: U.S. Government Printing Office.

Fishman, B. J., Marx, R. W., Best, S., & Tal, R. (2003). Linking teacher and student learning to improve professional development in systemic reform. *Teacher and Teacher Education, 19*(6), 643–658.

Foorman, B. R., Francis, D. J., Fletcher, J. M., Schatschneider, C., & Mehta, P. (1998). The role of instruction in learning to read: Preventing reading failure in at risk children. *Journal of Educational Psychology, 90,* 37–55.

Foorman, B. R., Schatschneider, C., Eakin, M. N., Fletcher, J. M., Moats, L. C., & Francis, D. J. (2006). The impact of instructional practices in grades 1 and 2 on reading and spelling achievement in high poverty schools. *Contemporary Educational Psychology, 31,* 1–29.

Garbarino, J. (2001). An ecological perspective on the effects of violence on children. *Journal of Community Psychology, 29,* 361–378.

Garmezy, N., Masten, A. S., & Tellegen, A. (1984). The study of stress and competence in children: A building block for developmental psychopathology. *Child Development, 55*(1), 97–111.

Gathercole, S. E., & Baddeley, A. D. (1989). Evaluation of the role of phonological STM in the development of vocabulary in children: A longitudinal study. *Journal of Memory and Language, 28,* 200–213.

Gathercole, S. E., & Pickering, S. J. (2000). Working memory deficits in children with low achievements in the national curriculum at seven years of age. *British Journal of Educational Psychology Review, 70,* 177–194.

Gersten, R., Baker, S. K., Haager, D., & Graves, A. W. (2005). Exploring the role of teacher quality in predicting reading outcomes for first-grade English learners. *Remedial and Special Education, 26*(4), 197–206.

Goldberg, D., McLaughlin, M., Grossi, M., Tytun, A., & Blum, S. (1992). Which newborns in New York City are at risk for special education placement? *American Journal of Public Health, 82,* 438–440.

Gomby, D. S., Culross, P. L., & Behrman, R. E. (1999). Home visiting: Recent program evaluations—Analysis and recommendations. *Future of Children, 9,* 4–26.

Graue, E., Clements, M. A., Reynolds, A. J., & Niles, M. D. (2004). More than teacher directed or child initiated: Preschool curriculum type, parent involvement, and children's outcomes in the Child-Parent Centers. *Education Policy Analysis Archives, 12*(72), 1–40.

Harris, J. R. (1995). Where is the child's environment? A group socialization theory of development. *Psychological Review, 102,* 458–489.

Hart, B., & Risley, T. R. (1995). *Meaningful differences in the everyday experience of young American children.* Baltimore, MD: Brookes.

Haynes, N. M., Comer, J., & Hamilton-Lee, M. (1988). The School Development Program: A model for school improvement. *Journal of Negro Education, 57*(1), 11–21.

Hoff-Ginsberg, E. (1991). Mother–child conversation in different social classes and communicative settings. *Child Development, 62,* 782–796.

Jencks, C., & Phillips, M. (1998). *The Black-White test score gap.* Washington, DC: Brookings Institute.

Juel, C., & Minden-Cupp, C. (2000). Learning to read words: Linguistic units and instructional strategies. *Reading Research Quarterly, 35*(4), 458–492.

Klingner, J. K., Vaughn, S., Arguelles, M. E., Hughes, M. T., & Leftwich, S. A. (2004). Collaborative strategic reading: "Real-world" lessons from classroom teachers. *Remedial and Special Education, 25*(5), 291–302.

Leadbeater, B. J., & Bishop, S. J. (1994). Predictors of behavior problems in preschool children of inner-city Afro-American and Puerto Rican adolescent mothers. *Child Development, 65,* 638–648.

Leigh, A., & Mead, S. (2005, April). Lifting teacher performance. Retrieved from http://www.ppionline.org/ppi_ci.cfm?knlgAreaID=1 10&subsecid=135&contentid=253286

Loesel, F., & Bliesener, T. (1990). Resilience in adolescence: A study on the generalizability of protective factors. In K. Hurrelmann & F. Loesel (Eds.), *Health hazards in adolescence: Prevention and intervention in childhood and adolescence* (pp. 299–320). Berlin: Walter De Gruyter.

Lonigan, C. J., & Whitehurst, G. J. (1998). Relative efficacy of parent and teacher involvement in a shared book-reading intervention for preschool children from low income backgrounds. *Early Childhood Research Quarterly, 13*(2), 263–290.

Magnusson, K., & Duncan, G. (2004). Parent versus child-based intervention strategies for promoting children's well-being. In A. Kalil & T. DeLeire (Eds.), *Family investments in children's potential* (pp. 209–236). Mahwah, NJ: Erlbaum.

McClelland, M. M., Cameron, C. E., Connor, C. M., Farris, C. L., Jewkes, A. M., & Morrison, F. J. (2007). Links between behavioral regulation and preschoolers' literacy, vocabulary, and math skills. *Developmental Psychology, 43*(4), 947–459.

McCoach, B., O'Connell, A. A., Reis, S. M., & Levitt, H. A. (2006). Growing readers: A hierarchical linear model of children's reading growth during the first 2 years of school. *Journal of Educational Psychology, 98*(1), 14–28.

McLoyd, V. C. (1990). The impact of economic hardship on black families and children: Psychological distress, parenting, and socioemotional development. *Child Development, 61*, 311–346.

McLoyd, V. C. (1998). Socioeconomic disadvantage and child development. *American Psychologist, 53*(2), 185–204.

Morrison, F. J., Bachman, H. J., & Connor, C. M. (2005). *Improving literacy in America: Guidelines from research*. New Haven, CT: Yale University Press.

Morrison, F. J., & Cooney, R. (2002). Parenting and academic achievement: Multiple paths to early literacy. In J. Borkowski, S. Ramey Landesman, & M. Bristol-Power (Eds.), *Parenting and the child's world: Influences on academic, intellectual, and social-emotional development* (pp. 141–160). Mahwah, NJ: Erlbaum.

Morrison, F. J., Griffith, E. M., & Alberts, D. M. (1997). Nature–nurture in the classroom: Entrance age, school readiness, and learning in children. *Developmental Psychology, 33*(2), 254–262.

Morrison, F. J., Smith, L., & Dow-Ehrensberger, M. (1995). Education and cognitive development: A natural experiment. *Developmental Psychology, 31*(5), 789–799.

Müller, U., Zelazo, P. D., Hood, S., Leone, T., & Rohrer, L. (2004). Inference control in a new rule use task: Age-related changes, labeling and attention. *Child Development, 75*, 1594–1609.

National Assessment of Educational Progress. (2007). *The nation's report card*. Washington, DC: U.S. Department of Education, National Center for Educational Statistics. Retrieved from http://nces.ed.gov/nationsreportcard/

National Institute of Child Health and Development (NICHD), Early Child Care Research Network (ECCRN). (2002a). Child-care structure—process—outcome: Direct and indirect effects of child-care quality on young children's development. *Psychological Science, 13*(2), 199–206.

National Institute of Child Health and Development (NICHD), Early Child Care Research Network (ECCRN). (2002b). The relation of global first grade classroom environment to structural classroom features and teacher and student behaviors. *Elementary School Journal, 102*(5), 367–387.

National Institute of Child Health and Development (NICHD), Early Child Care Research Network (ECCRN). (2003). Does amount of time spent in child care predict socioemotional adjustment during the transition to kindergarten? *Child Development, 74*(4), 969–1226.

National Institute of Child Health and Development (NICHD), Early Child Care Research Network (ECCRN). (2004). Multiple pathways to early academic achievement. *Harvard Educational Review, 74*(1), 1–29.

National Institute of Child Health and Development (NICHD), Early Child Care Research Network (ECCRN). (2005). Pathways to reading: The role of oral language in the transition to reading. *Developmental Psychology, 41*(2), 428–442.

National Reading Panel. (2000). *Teaching children to read: An evidence-based assessment of the scientific research literature on reading and its implications for reading instruction* (No. NIH Pub. No. 00-4769). Washington DC: U.S. Department of Health and Human Services, Public Health Service, National Institutes of Health, National Institute of Child Health and Human Development. from http://www.nichd.nih.gov/publications/nrp/report.cfm

Nelson, J. R., Benner, G. J., & Gonzalez, J. (2003). Learner characteristics that influence treatment effectiveness of early literacy interventions: A meta-analytic review. *Learning Disabilities Research and Practice, 18*(4), 255–267.

Neuman, S. B., & Dickinson, D. K. (2001). *Handbook of early literacy research*. New York: Guilford.

Palmaffy, T. (1999). Measuring the teacher quality problem. In M. Kanstoroom & C. E. Finn (Eds.), *Better teachers, better schools* (pp. 21–22). Washington, DC: Thomas B. Fordham Foundation.

Payne, A. C., Whitehurst, G. J., & Angell, A. L. (1994). The role of home literacy environment in the development of language ability in preschool children from low-income families. *Early Childhood Research Quarterly, 9*, 427–440.

Perfetti, C. A., Beck, I., Bell, L. C., & Hughes, C. (1987). Phonemic knowledge and learning to read are reciprocal: A longitudinal study of first grade children. *Merrill-Palmer Quarterly, 33*(3), 283–319.

Phillips, M., Crouse, J., & Ralph, J. (1998). Does the black-white test score gap widen after children enter school? In C. Jencks & M. Phillips (Eds.), *The Black-White test score gap* (pp. 229–272). Washington, DC: Brookings Institution Press.

Pianta, R. C., Paro, L., Payne, K., Cox, C., & Bradley, R. H. (2002). The relation of kindergarten classroom environment to teacher, family and school characteristics and child outcomes. *Elementary School Journal, 102*(3), 225–238.

Piasta, S. B., Connor, C. M., Fishman, B., & Morrison, F. J. (in press). Teachers' knowledge of literacy, classroom practices, and student reading growth. *Scientific Studies of Reading*.

Plomin, R. (1990). *Nature and nurture: An introduction to human behavioral genetics*. Pacific Grove, CA: Brooks/Cole.

Ponitz, C. E., McClelland, M. M., Jewkes, A. M., Connor, C. M., Farris, C. L., & Morrison, F. J. (2008). Touch your toes! Developing a behavioral measure of preschool self-regulation. *Early Childhood Research Quarterly, 23*, 141–158.

Rauh, V. A., Parker, F. L., Garfinkel, R. S., Perry, J., & Andrews, H. F. (2003). Biological, social, and community influences on third-grade reading levels of minority head start children: A multilevel approach. *Journal of Community Psychology, 31*, 255–278.

Raviv, T., Kessenich, M., & Morrison, F. J. (2004). A mediational model of the association between socioeconomic status and preschool language abilities. *Early Childhood Research Quarterly, 19*(4), 528-547.

Rayner, K., Foorman, B. R., Perfetti, C. A., Pesetsky, D., & Seidenberg, M. S. (2001). How psychological science informs the teaching of reading. *Psychological Science in the Public Interest, 2*(2), 31–74.

Reese, E., & Cox, A. (1999). Quality of adult book reading affects children's emergent literacy. *Developmental Psychology, 35*, 20–28.

Rennie, D. A. C., Bull, R., & Diamond, A. (2004). Executive functioning in preschoolers: Reducing the inhibitory demands of the Dimensional Change Card Sort Task. *Developmental Neuropsychology, 26*(1), 423–443.

Reynolds, A. J., & Ou, S.-R. (2004). Alterable predictors of child well-being in the Chicago longitudinal study. *Children and Youth Services Review, 26*, 1–14.

Reynolds, A. J., Temple, J. A., Robertson, D. L., & Mann, E. A. (2003). Age 21 cost-benefit analysis of the Title I Chicago child–parent centers. *Educational Evaluation and Policy Analysis, 24*(4), 267–303.

Roskos, K. A., & Christie, J. F. (Eds.). (2000). *Play and literacy in early childhood*. Mahwah, NJ: Erlbaum.

Rowe, D., Vazsonyi, A., & Flannery, D. (1994). No more than skin deep:

Ethnic and racial similarity in developmental process. *Psychological Review, 101*, 396–413.

Sadoski, M., & Willson, V. L. (2006). Effects of a theoretically based larege-scale reading intervention in a multicultural urban school district. *American Educational Research Journal, 43*(1), 137–154.

Sanders, W. L., & Horn, S. P. (1998). Research findings from the Tennessee value-added assessment system (TVAAS) database: Implications for educational evaluation and research. *Journal of Personnel Evaluation in Education, 12*(3), 247–256.

Scarborough, H. S. (1990). Very early language deficits in dyslexic children. *Child Development, 61*, 1728–1743.

Scarborough, H. S. (1998). Early identification of children at risk for reading disabilities: Phonological awareness and some other promising predictors. In B. K. Shapiro, P. J. Accardo, & A. J. Capute (Eds.), *Specific reading disability: A view of the spectrum* (pp. 75–119). Timonium, MD: York Press.

Scarborough, H. S. (2001). Connecting early language and literacy to later reading (dis)abilities: Evidence, theory, and practice. In S. B. Neuman & D. K. Dickinson (Eds.), *Handbook of early literacy research* (pp. 97–110). New York: Guilford.

Schoendorf, K., Hogue, C., Kleinman, J., & Rowley, D. (1992). Mortality among infants of black as compared with white college-educated parents. *The New England Journal of Medicine, 326*(23), 1522–1526.

Schweinhart, L. J., & Weikart, D. P. (1988). Education for young children living in poverty: Child-initiated learning or teacher-directed instruction. *Elementary School Journal, 89*(2), 213–225.

Senechal, M. (2006). Testing the home literacy model: Parent involvement in kindergarten is differentially related to grade 4 reading comprehension, fluency, spelling, and reading for pleasure. *Scientific Studies of Reading, 10*(1), 59–87

Senechal, M., & LeFevre, J.-A. (2001a). On refining theoretical models of emergent literacy: The role of empirical evidence. *Journal of School Psychology, 39*(5), 439–460.

Senechal, M., & LeFevre, J.-A. (2002). Parental involvement in the development of children's reading skill: A five-year longitudinal study. *Child Development, 73*(2), 445–460.

Senechal, M., & LeFevre, J. (2001b). Storybook reading and parent teaching: Links to language and literacy development. In P. R. Britto & J. Brooks-Gunn (Eds.), *New directions in child development: No. 92. The role of family literacy environments in promoting young children's emerging literacy* (pp. 39–52). San Francisco, CA: Jossey-Bass.

Shonkoff, J. P., & Phillips, D. A. (Eds.). (2000). *From neurons to neighborhoods: The science of early childhood development.* Washington DC: National Academy Press.

Smith, K. (2002). *Who's minding the kids? Child care arrangements: Spring 1997.* Washington, DC: U.S. Census Bureau.

Snow, C. E., & Tabors, P. (1993). Language skills that relate to literacy development. In B. Spodek & O. N. Saracho (Eds.), *Yearbook in early childhood education* (pp. 1–14). New York: Teachers College Press.

Steiner, D. (2003, October 23–24). *Preparing teachers: Are American schools of education up to the task?* Paper presented at the A Qualified Teacher in Every Classroom: Appraising Old Answers and New

Ideas ECF Education Briefs. Retrieved from http://www.education-consumers.org/briefpdfs/3.11-preparing_teachers.pdf

Stipek, D., Feiler, R., Byler, P., Ryan, R., Milburn, S., & Salmon, J. M. (1998). Good beginnings: What differences does the program make in preparing young children for school? *Journal of Applied Developmental Psychology, 19*(1), 41–66.

Stipek, D., Feiler, R., Daniels, D., & Milburn, S. (1995). Effects of different instructional approaches on young children's achievement and motivation. *Child Development, 66*(1), 209–223.

Stipek, D., & Ryan, R. (1997). Economically disadvantaged preschoolers: Ready to learn but further to go. *Developmental Psychology, 33*(4), 711–723.

Storch, S. A., & Whitehurst, G. J. (2002). Oral language and code-related precursors to reading: Evidence from a longitudinal structural model. *Developmental Psychology, 38*(6), 934–947.

St. Pierre, R. G., & Layzer, J. I. (1999). Using home visits for multiple purposes: The Comprehensive Child Development Program. *Future of Children, 9*, 134–151.

Teale, W. H., & Sulzby, E. (Eds.). (1986). *Emergent literacy: Writing and reading.* Norwood, NJ: Ablex.

Torgesen, J. K., Alexander, A. W., Wagner, R. K., Rashotte, C. A., Voelier, K. K. S., & Conway, T. (2001). Intensive remedial instruction for children with severe reading disabilities: Immediate and long-term outcomes from two instructional approaches. *Journal of Learning Disabilities, 34*(1), 33–58.

Torgesen, J. K., Burgess, S., Wagner, R. K., & Rashotte, C. A. (1994). Longitudinal studies of phonological processing and reading. *Journal of Learning Disabilities, 27*, 276–286.

U.S. Department of Education & Office of Postsecondary Education. (2004). *Meeting the highly qualified teachers challenge: The Secretary's third annual report on teacher quality.* Washington, DC. Retrieved from http://www.ed.gov/about/reports/annual/teachprep/2004Title2-Report.pdf

Vellutino, F. R., Scanlon, D. M., Sipay, E. R., Small, S. G., Pratt, A., Chen, R. et al. (1996). Cognitive profiles of difficult to remediate and readily remediated poor readers: Early intervention as a vehicle for distinguishing between cognitive and experiential deficits as basic causes of specific reading disability. *Journal of Educational Psychology, 88*(4), 601–638.

Walsh, K., Glaser, D., & Wilcox, D. D. (2006). *What education schools aren't teaching about reading and what elementary teachers aren't learning.* Washington DC: National Council on Teacher Quality. Retrieved from http://www.nctq.org/nctq/images/nctq_reading_study_exec_summ.pdf

Wasik, B. A., & Bond, M. A. (2001). Beyond the pages of a book: Interactive book reading and language development in preschool classrooms. *Journal of Educational Psychology, 9*(2), 243–250.

Whitehurst, G. J., Arnold, D. S., Epstein, J. N., Angell, A. L., Smith, M., & Fischel, J. E. (1994). A picture book reading intervention in day care and home for children from low-income families. *Developmental Psychology, 30*(5), 679–689.

# 13

# Middle School Transitions and Adolescent Development

*ERIC M. ANDERMAN AND CHRISTIAN E. MUELLER*

Adolescence is a period of enormous change. The transformations that occur during adolescence emanate both from within the developing child (i.e., physiological and biological development), and in the social worlds in which adolescents interact (i.e., their schools, families, and social networks). Although the changes that occur during adolescence are often portrayed by the media as being troublesome and difficult, research actually indicates that unpleasant experiences are not inevitable outcomes during adolescence (Eccles, Midgley, et al., 1993; R. Epstein, 2007; Midgley, 1993; Simmons & Blyth, 1987). One of the most prominent experiences during early adolescence is the transition from elementary to middle school. Whereas this transition is not universal, it is quite common across a variety of cultures, and it often coincides with the simultaneous pubertal changes occurring during that time.

Although historically researchers and educators have believed that many of the problems encountered by adolescents are due to pubertal changes (Hall, 1904), more recent research on school transitions clearly indicates that school environments can foster either beneficial or problematic developmental changes for adolescents (E. M. Anderman & Maehr, 1994). In the present chapter, we specifically examine a variety of programs of research that have examined school transitions that occur during the early adolescent years. Most of these studies are framed by an array of motivational theories, and examine changes in students' motivation and achievement across the middle school transition.

Specifically, we examine studies of changes in academic and psychological variables as students transition from elementary schools into middle or junior high schools. We examine this research via the different theoretical frameworks that have guided various research programs. Most, although not all, of these programs have been rooted in theories of academic motivation. In addition, we also examine some of the methodological concerns and advances that have

accompanied this research. Finally, we offer suggestions for future study.

The examination of school transitions is particularly useful in research on the effects of schooling on development. The transition from one school building to another represents a formidable shift in social and instructional contexts for many students. This shift in learning environments in some ways represents a naturally occurring quasi-experimental design for examining the relations of such environmental changes to student outcomes. As early adolescents move from elementary schools into junior high or middle schools, both observable changes in the facets of learning environments, and students' perceptions of these changes, can be studied in relation to students' motivation, achievement, adjustment, and behavior.

## The Simmons and Blyth Studies

Some of the most important and influential studies of school transitions were conducted by Roberta Simmons, Dale Blyth, and their colleagues in the 1970s and 1980s. It is important to note that Simmons and Blyth studied the transition from elementary school into junior high school, which in their research occurred between the sixth and seventh grades. This study stands in contrast with many of the studies which will be described later in this chapter, which occurred across the transition from elementary school into middle school (i.e., often between the fifth and sixth grades).

### The Simmons and Blyth Studies in a Historical Perspective
Historically, junior high schools emerged in the United States in the early 1900s, in order to meet the needs of early adolescents (Clark & Clark, 1993). In the 1960s, debates emerged regarding the education of adolescents in junior high schools, which were similar to high schools in structure (usually housing students in grades 7 through 8 or 9),

and middle schools (for students in the range of grades 5 through 8), which focused more directly on the developmental needs of early adolescents. In the 1980s, the voices of educators and developmental psychologists were heard, and middle school reform focused more specifically on the developmental needs of early adolescents (Carnegie Council on Adolescent Development, 1989; Lipsitz, 1997).

***Two Influential Studies*** Simmons and her colleagues conducted two important studies: one in Baltimore during the late 1960s, and another in Milwaukee in the mid- to late 1970s. Both studies (Simmons & Blyth, 1987; Simmons, Rosenberg, & Rosenberg, 1973) highlighted the importance of changing biological and contextual processes and many aspects of early adolescent development, including the development of a healthy self-image. Prior to their work, researchers often assumed that pubertal and school factors operated independently during the transition from childhood to adulthood. Since the time of Hall, struggles with identity (Erikson, 1963), changes in cognitive functioning (Elkind, 1976; Piaget, 1952, 1954), and hormonal changes caused by the onset of puberty were thought to make the adolescent period a time of "storm and stress" (Hall, 1904). With the work of Simmons and Blyth, however, researchers gained a better understanding of how gender, biology, ethnicity, and school contexts interact to influence adolescent development.

Simmons et al. (1973) first demonstrated that entry into early adolescence was sometimes characterized by problematic disturbances in the development of a healthy self-image. As compared to late childhood (ages 8–11), Simmons et al. showed that early adolescents often experienced unpleasant periods, including

> heightened self-consciousness, greater instability of the self-image, slightly lower global self-esteem, lower opinions of themselves with regard to specific qualities they valued, and a reduced conviction that their parents, teachers, and peers of the same sex held favorable opinions of them. (Simmons & Blyth, 1987, p. 5)

These same adolescents also exhibited more depressed affect as compared to the younger children. For many, especially girls, these negative trends continued through junior high and into the high school years.

Whereas the Baltimore study was instrumental in helping researchers differentiate biological and contextual influences on adolescent development, it was also plagued with methodological problems that limited Simmons and her colleagues from drawing more definitive conclusions. Simmons and Blyth (1987) summarized the main limitations of the study as having a cross-sectional design, lacking an adequate measure of pubertal development, and erroneously assuming that all of the sixth graders in their study had moved into the same middle school configuration. With the undertaking of the second study in Milwaukee, however, many of these limitations were addressed. What emerged was a much clearer understanding of how gender, puberty,

and changing school contexts influence development as children move into early adolescence.

Using a longitudinal design in the follow-up study allowed Simmons and Blyth to test for cohort effects, as well as to follow the developmental trajectories of each child. Second, the follow-up study contained more thorough measures of pubertal development, which allowed for more accurate assessments and more precise conclusions. Lastly, the Milwaukee study utilized a quasi-experimental design in which two different school configurations (K-6 and K-8) allowed for testing of differences between middle school contexts. By addressing some of the limitations found in the earlier study, Simmons and Blyth were able to more carefully examine the unique and interactive impacts of gender, ethnicity, puberty, and school transitions on many aspects of adolescent development.

In the new study, Simmons and Blyth (1987) expanded the outcomes examined in their previous research. In addition to self-image, Simmons and Blyth became interested in how gender, pubertal timing, and changes in the middle school context influenced (a) peer relationships; (b) the process of establishing independence; (c) planning for the future; and (d) dealing with adolescent deviance versus adult conformity issues. In addition, Simmons and Blyth were able to further disentangle pubertal effects from timing effects by including stricter measures of pubertal development, as well as including different middle school configurations (i.e., K-6/7-8 versus K-8). This quasi-experimental design allowed for testing of unique influences of both pubertal changes, as well as effects of timing on the expanded outcomes included in the study.

Simmons and Blyth (1987) suggested that when children are thrust too quickly into the developmental period of early adolescence, where they undergo fundamental sociopsychological changes, many will experience problems with identity development, peer relationships, and academic achievement. In what they referred to as the "developmental readiness hypothesis," Simmons and Blyth found that timing was instrumental in determining how many of the children in their study coped with the transition between sixth and seventh grade. For example, they found that students who moved into a large, impersonal junior high school during the transition were more likely to experience negative outcomes (e.g. reduced participation in extracurricular activities) than those students who did not experience a transition until ninth grade with the move into high school.

In relation to pubertal development, Simmons and Blyth also found that timing was important. In what they labeled as "on-time" versus "off-time," Simmons and Blyth found that timing of development, in relation to peers, was an important indicator of negative or positive outcomes. For instance, they found that in general, early developing boys fared better in overall psychosocial adjustment than did early developing girls. Conversely, later developing girls often fared better in the long run than later developing boys, with the difference being in how each group was treated based on stereotyped expectations (i.e., boys should be "strong," so late muscularity development would not match this societal expectation).

In addition, Simmons and Blyth found that the timing of the transition is important. For the most part, students who attended K-8 schools and did not move into a new building until the ninth grade typically fared better than the students who underwent earlier school transitions. For those students transitioning during the seventh grade, declines in functioning were found for both boys and girls, including reduced participation in extracurricular activities, and lower GPAs and math achievement scores. Further, declines in self-esteem were found for girls making the transition, whereas boys were more likely to show higher levels of victimization. They also found that girls who transitioned into traditional junior high schools experienced declines in self-esteem, compared to girls who were in K-8 schools.

The Milwaukee study confirmed earlier findings from Simmons et al. (1973) indicating that the transition into adolescence often is much more volatile and difficult for girls than for boys. Specifically, results indicated that females experienced greater difficulties across many domains, with the exception of engagement in deviant behaviors. For example, Simmons and Blyth found that gender was a significant predictor of differences on all of the outcomes measured in the 1987 study. First, females reported lower overall self-image, including self-esteem and especially body image; second, girls (preadolescent and adolescent) placed higher emphasis on same-sex popularity, with boys being less concerned with how they were perceived by others; third, boys were encouraged to become independent earlier than were girls; fourth, boys were more likely than girls to have long range career plans, with only a small portion of the girls expressing the desire to work continuously through adulthood; and fifth, boys were much more likely than girls to rebel and become involved in deviant behaviors, and earned lower GPAs and verbal test scores than did the girls.

Finally, Simmons and her colleagues also compared African American and White students making the transition from elementary to junior high school (Simmons, Black, & Zhou, 1991). Although there were no ethnic differences noted on most variables (e.g., perceptions of parents' and teachers' evaluations, self-esteem, self-concept of ability), Simmons et al. did find that African American students' grade point averages decreased over the transition more than did the GPAs of White students. In addition, African American students reported liking school less than did White students. Simmons et al. also noted some trends that were unique to African American males: they reported higher levels of body-image, and they were more involved in school problem behaviors than were African American females or White students. These findings for male African American adolescents are somewhat similar to data reported by Graham, Taylor, and Hudley (1998), who found that male ethnic minority middle school students do not value high-achieving male students. Simmons and her colleagues suggest that the preexisting differences between African

American and White students continue to exist after the transition.

In summary, the studies conducted by Simmons and her colleagues clearly indicated that the transition from elementary school into junior high school is problematic for many youth. Their results indicated that students do experience difficulties in traditional junior high schools, and that these difficulties may be particularly salient for females and for minority students. These studies laid the groundwork for future studies further examining the relationship between gender, pubertal timing, and middle school transitions.

## Expectancy-Value Studies of School Transitions

The expectancy-value theory of academic motivation has guided many studies of school transitions during the adolescent years. This framework has proven to be particularly useful in the study of school transitions; expectancy-value theory in particular has allowed researchers to examine predictors of both learning (i.e., academic achievement) and behaviors (i.e., future choices to enroll in certain courses or programs of study) (Eccles & Wigfield, 2002; Wigfield & Eccles, 1992).

*Current Expectancy-Value Model* Although the study of expectancies and values in education and psychology can be traced to early work by Lewin (1935) and later work by Atkinson (1957, 1964), studies of school transitions during adolescence using an expectancy-value framework are primarily based on the current expectancy-value model developed by Jacquelyne Eccles, Alan Wigfield, and their colleagues.

Although a thorough review of the entire model is beyond the scope of this chapter, it is important to note some of the highlights of Eccles and Wigfield's model, in order to better frame the transition studies that have been based on this framework. Briefly, Eccles and colleagues demonstrated that the inverse relation between expectancies and values proposed by Atkinson was invalid, and that in actuality, expectancies and values covary positively (Eccles, Adler, et al., 1983; Meece, Wigfield, & Eccles, 1990; Wigfield & Eccles, 1992). Consequently, a student who holds high expectations for success in a given subject area is also likely to value that subject area.

According to the theory, expectancies refer to students' beliefs about whether or not they can successfully complete a task, as well as their beliefs about their future potential at being successful at a task or within a given domain (Eccles, Adler, et al., 1983). In contrast, academic task values break down into four distinct types: *attainment value* (i.e., how important a task is to a student), *utility value* (i.e., how useful the task is to a student, in terms of reaching future goals), *intrinsic value* (i.e., how enjoyable the task is to a student), and *cost* (i.e., whether or not it is worth a student's time to engage in a particular task) (Eccles & Wigfield, 1995; Wigfield & Eccles, 1992).

Eccles and her colleagues have conducted extensive studies on expectancies and values. Variables measured in these studies have included students' self-perceptions of ability in specific subject areas (e.g., English and math), students' liking of subject areas, self-esteem (Eccles, Wigfield, Midgley, & Reuman, 1993; Wigfield, Eccles, Mac Iver, Reuman, & Midgley, 1991) and students' general valuing of subject domains (E. M. Anderman et al., 2001). In addition, some of these studies also included teacher reports of students' abilities in specific domains (Wigfield et al., 1991). Some of the major findings indicate that expectancies tend on average to decrease as students move into higher grades in school (Eccles & Midgley, 1989; Eccles, Wigfield, & Schiefele, 1998). In terms of values, research indicates that young elementary school children (below the fifth grade) generally do not distinguish well between the constructs of attainment value, utility value, and intrinsic value (Eccles & Wigfield, 1995; Wigfield & Eccles, 1992); however, research indicates that overall, achievement values decline as students get older (Eccles & Midgley, 1989; Fredricks & Eccles, 2002; Jacobs, Lanza, Osgood, Eccles, & Wigfield, 2002; Wigfield & Eccles, 1992).

***Empirical Studies of School Transitions*** Eccles and her colleagues have conducted several longitudinal studies examining the transition from elementary school into the middle school grades. This work emanated from an early study of student motivation in mathematics and English, which revealed that discontinuities in students' values and beliefs were particularly prominent when students made the transition from sixth grade elementary classrooms into seventh grade middle school classrooms (Eccles, 1983).

In one of the seminal junior high school transition studies, Wigfield, Eccles, MacIver, Reuman, and Midgley (1991) examined changes in expectancies (which they referred to as *self-concept of ability* in this study) and intrinsic value across the transition from sixth grade elementary school classes into seventh grade junior high school classes. Measures were collected twice per year both before and after the transition, in the domains of mathematics, English, athletics, and social activities. Social activities were operationalized in terms of students' expectancies and values related to making friends and self-perceptions of popularity.

Results indicated that expectancies declined in both math and English over the transition, although differences were only significant for English. In the social and athletic domains, expectancies also declined after the transition. It also is important to note that social and athletic expectancies did improve somewhat across the seventh grade. Students' reports of liking math and athletics declined across all four waves of data collection, with particularly noteworthy declines emerging after the transition into junior high school. However, there again was a trend for students' reported liking of English and social activities to rise somewhat during the seventh grade.

Susan Harter and her colleagues also examined changes in beliefs rooted in expectancy-value theory across school transitions during early adolescence. In one study, Harter

and her colleagues (Harter, Whitesell, & Kowalski, 1992) examined longitudinally changes in students' motivational beliefs before and after the transition from elementary school into middle school. In some schools, students made the transition between grades 5 and 6, whereas in other schools, the transition occurred between grades 6 and 7; in addition, some students remained in the same school, whereas others physically moved to a new building across the transition. Students completed measures of perceived competence, and intrinsic/extrinsic motivation. Results indicated that overall, those students who experienced declines in expectancies (referred to as *perceived competence* in this study) also experienced declines in intrinsic motivation; those whose expectancies remained unchanged showed stability in intrinsic motivation; and those who evidenced increases in expectancies for success experienced increases in intrinsic motivation (Harter et al., 1992). Harter et al. also included measures of anxiety in this study; they found that in particular, students with lower expectancies for success and lower levels of intrinsic motivation experienced anxiety about academic work when they transitioned into a new building and had to cope with a new learning environment; these patterns were not evident in the students who remained in the same building at the transition.

Feldlaufer, Midgley, and Eccles (1988) examined changes in students' perceptions of how mathematics teachers communicated the value of mathematics before and after the transition. Results indicated that students perceived their elementary school math teachers as talking more about intrinsic reasons for studying mathematics than did their junior high school math teachers. These findings from student survey data were supported by classroom observation data indicating that elementary school teachers emphasized intrinsic reasons for studying math more than did junior high math teachers.

In a more recent study, Gutman and Midgley (2000) studied the middle school transition in a sample of 62 African American families living in poverty. Results indicated that students' grades declined over the transition, although feelings of efficacy were related to higher grades after the transition. Interestingly, students who experienced *both* parental involvement and perceived teacher support received higher grades after the transition than did other students.

***Developmental Studies of Expectancies and Values Over Longer Periods of Time*** Several longitudinal studies have examined changes in expectancies and values across longer time periods, which have included the period during which the middle school or junior high school transition occurs. These studies suggest that declines in expectancies and values that occur across the middle school transition are part of a broader developmental trend, indicating declines in both expectancies and values across childhood and adolescence (Fredricks & Eccles, 2002; Jacobs et al., 2002).

In an early study examining students' beliefs about the quality of life in school, J. L. Epstein and McPartland (1976) included measures of students' interest in their schoolwork.

Although this study was not designed to measure transition effects, they did compare data for students in elementary and secondary schools. Results indicated that students in secondary schools (who presumably had made a transition) reported lower levels of interest than did students in elementary schools (J. L. Epstein & McPartland, 1976).

In a longitudinal study examining changes in children's and adolescent's expectancies and values in math and athletics from first through 12th grades, Fredricks and Eccles (2002) found that both expectancies and values declined throughout the school years. They suggest that since declines in expectancies and values occur both before and after the transition, the declines observed across the transition are consistent with the overall patterns of decline noted throughout childhood and adolescence. Declines in expectancies may be related to developmental changes in the standards that children use to determine their academic standing, and to the use of more competitively based instructional practices as students progress through the grades. The decline in values may be related to students receiving declining grades: students may value certain activities less in order to protect their self-esteem (Fredricks & Eccles, 2002).

In another study, Jacobs et al. (2002) examined changes in expectancies and values between grades 1 through 12 in mathematics, language arts, and athletics. Results again indicated general declines in both expectancies and values, although actual rates of decline varied depending on subject domain. For example, the rate of change in expectancies declined during elementary school, but remained relatively stable after grades 7 and 8; expectancies in mathematics, although initially higher for boys than for girls, declined more rapidly for boys than for girls, resulting in approximately equivalent expectancies by the end of high school.

In summary, transition studies emanating from an expectancy-value framework indicate that students' expectancies for success and valuing of academic domains do tend to decrease across the transition. Although some research indicates that these declines in motivation are particularly prominent at the transition, studies conducted over longer periods of time indicate that the decline in motivation observed at the transition is part of a larger trend for expectancies and values to generally decline throughout childhood and adolescence.

## Studies Examining Intrinsic Motivation

Students are intrinsically motivated to participate in an academic task when they participate in the activity for its own sake; whether or not the student is going to receive some type of external reward (i.e., a grade) is irrelevant. There is an abundance of research on the topic of intrinsic motivation, much of which is rooted in Deci and Ryan's Cognitive Evaluation Theory (Deci & Ryan, 1985).

It is important to note that there is some theoretical and substantive overlap between intrinsic motivation and other related constructs. For example, intrinsic motivation is similar to the aforementioned concept of intrinsic value

from expectancy-value theory (Wigfield & Eccles, 1992); intrinsic motivation also is similar to a mastery orientation as described by goal orientation theorists (Ames, 1992a; Dweck & Leggett, 1988; Maehr & E. M. Anderman, 1993; Nicholls, 1989). When a student holds mastery goals for a particular academic task, the student's primary goal is to truly learn about and master that specific task.

There have been some studies that have examined changes in students' intrinsic motivation across school transitions during early adolescence. Harter (1981) examined intrinsic and extrinsic motivation in five measures that she developed to examine motivation. Although the transition itself was not a focus of the study, Harter did document clear developmental patterns: students became less intrinsically motivated and more extrinsically motivated in terms of seeking challenge, expressing interest/curiosity, and independently trying to master tasks; in contrast, students became less extrinsic and more intrinsic in terms of making independent judgments and using internal criteria in making self-judgments about performance (as opposed to relying on information from external sources, such as the teacher).

Bronstein and her colleagues (Bronstein, Ginsburg, & Herrera, 2005) examined the relations between parenting styles and changes in intrinsic motivation across the transition. Data were collected during the fifth grade, and again during the seventh grade (after the transition). Results indicated that students whose parents used many external types of control (e.g., the use of rewards, pressure, coercion) and who offered little guidance during the fifth grade were less intrinsically motivated during the seventh grade; in contrast, when parents listened to children's voices and included them in making important family decisions, intrinsic motivation increased after the transition.

Gottfried and her colleagues (Gottfried, Fleming, & Gottfried, 2001) examined changes in intrinsic motivation in longitudinal samples, from the middle elementary years through high school. Their results indicated that students' prior intrinsic motivation is highly predictive of subsequent intrinsic motivation. Results also indicated that over time, intrinsic motivation declined in math, science, and reading, but not in the domain of social studies (although a slight increase in intrinsic motivation was found from the ages of 16 to 17). Gottfried et al., explain these findings in terms of changes in curricula across grade levels. They argue that declines in intrinsic motivation are not inevitable, but rather, are related to changes in instructional practices that occur as students move into junior and then senior high school.

In a related study, Gottfried and her colleagues examined the relations of home environments to changes in academic intrinsic motivation at the time of the middle school transition (Gottfried, Fleming, & Gottfried, 1998). Students completed survey measures at ages 9, 10, and 13. Direct observations were obtained by researchers in the students' homes and from mothers. Results indicated that students who experienced a cognitively stimulating home environment experienced increases in intrinsic motivation. Although direct effects of school transitions on intrinsic motivation were not assessed, results suggest that cognitively stimulating home environments may ameliorate some of the negative effects associated with the transition. Other research also indicates that home environments are related to school adjustment during early adolescence (e.g., DuBois, Eitel, & Felner, 1994).

In summary, research examining changes in intrinsic motivation across the transition indicates that intrinsic motivation does tend to decline across the transition. Nevertheless, this decline is not inevitable; indeed, students whose parents provide opportunities for autonomy and provide cognitively enriching experiences may experience less of a decline in intrinsic motivation than do other students. In addition, higher levels of perceived competence may buffer decrements in intrinsic motivation (e.g., Losier & Vallerand, 1994; Wigfield & Eccles, 2002). Thus although declines in intrinsic motivation occur often, educational settings that enhance perceptions of competence in children and early adolescents may lessen this decline.

## Studies Examining Person–Environment Fit

One of the most influential developments in research on school transitions concerns the observation that typical junior high school or middle school environments often do not meet the developmental needs of early adolescents (E. M. Anderman & Maehr, 1994; Eccles & Midgley, 1989; Eccles, Midgley, et al., 1993).

Eccles, Midgley, and their colleagues identified and described this phenomenon in the early 1990s, and subsequent research has confirmed that there is indeed a "mismatch" between the needs of adolescent learners and many of the instructional practices used in schools serving early adolescents. This mismatch is related to some of the observed declines in motivation across the transition.

*Person–environment fit* theories suggest that individuals' behaviors are related to individual differences associated with the person, *and* to characteristics of the social context (Hunt, 1975). In terms of schools and learning, when students' learning needs are met by the context of the classroom, then students are more likely to achieve at high levels and to be motivated to learn; in contrast, when students' needs are not met in the classroom they are likely to become disengaged, and less learning may occur.

Eccles and Midgley (1989) refer to this phenomenon as *stage–environment fit*. Specifically, Eccles and Midgley have argued that the stage of development of the adolescent learner and the environment provided by the classroom must be a good "fit." If the classroom environment does not provide the appropriate context for learning for a specific student, then that student's achievement and motivation will likely suffer. From this perspective, motivation often declines at the transition from elementary to middle school because students move from the elementary school environment (which fits well with elementary students' cognitive and social development) to middle schools, which often are less congruent with the developmental needs of early

adolescents (Eccles & Midgley, 1989; Eccles, Midgley, et al., 1993).

***The Developmental Mismatch*** From a developmental perspective, adolescents are changing both physiologically and psychologically. It is the psychological changes in particular that often are not in sync with the learning environments provided by many schools serving early adolescents. Eccles and Midgley have referred to this as a "developmental mismatch." More specifically, Eccles and Midgley proposed that the environments provided by many middle schools are antithetical to the developmental needs of early adolescents. Although middle schools have changed somewhat to meet the needs of early adolescents (e.g., Juvonen, Le, Kaganoff, Augustine, & Constant, 2004), there is still much empirical evidence to support this hypothesis.

*The Need for Autonomy* First, adolescents want to be autonomous; they want to be able to make their own decisions, and to separate themselves from their parents (Steinberg, 1990). This need for autonomy can be expressed by adolescents in a variety of ways. For example, as a result of continuing cognitive development, adolescents are more able to make complex and sophisticated decisions than are younger children (Lewis, 1981). This improved ability to make decisions leads many adolescents to want to be able to make such decisions while they are at school. Thus optimal middle school environments should provide students with opportunities to be autonomous and to be able to make decisions during the school day (see also Ryan & Deci, 2006).

However, there is evidence that often adolescents are not provided with opportunities to be autonomous and make meaningful decisions in middle and junior high schools (Brophy & Everston, 1978). This situation is problematic, because learning environments that promote autonomy and choice should benefit learners of all ages (Deci & Ryan, 1994; Stefanou, Perencevich, DiCintio, & Turner, 2004). Research dating back to the 1960s suggests that junior high school teachers are highly focused on issues of control (Hoy, 1969)—many teachers of early adolescents feel that behavioral problems are likely to arise with adolescent populations; therefore, there is a rampant belief that educating early adolescents in tightly controlled environments will lead to better behavior management. Nevertheless, this viewpoint sharply contrasts with adolescents' needs for autonomy. In a large-scale study involving teacher, observer, and student data in elementary and junior high classrooms, Feldlaufer and her colleagues found that students experienced less autonomy in math classrooms (i.e., fewer opportunities to provide input and fewer opportunities to make decisions about academic tasks) after the transition to junior high school than before (Feldlaufer, Midgley, & Eccles, 1988).

*The Need for Positive and Productive Relationships with Teachers* Early adolescents need to maintain positive relationships with adults (Lynch & Ciccheti, 1997), including parents (Allen, Hauser, Bell, & O'Connor, 1994) and teachers (Davis, 2003; Lee, 2007). The relationships between teachers and students in particular are extremely important, as these relationships can be very influential in terms of the long-term trajectories of success for at-risk students (Pianta, 1999). For example, research indicates that students who experience positive school environments during adolescence (which includes good relationships with teachers) engage in fewer risky behaviors during adolescence (Resnick et al., 1997); other research indicates that perceiving one's teacher as caring is related to increased motivation to learn (Murdock & Miller, 2003).

However, the relationships between students and teachers are often qualitatively different before and after the transition. Students do not either physically or socially change much over the summer between the end of elementary school and the start of middle school; nevertheless, the types of relationships that they experience with teachers often change dramatically before and after the transition. Research indicates that the relationships between teachers and students often become negative and confrontational after the transition from elementary to middle school. Midgley and her colleagues have conducted several studies that indicate that relationships between teachers and students are markedly different before and after the transition. In one study, Midgley and her colleagues examined the beliefs of elementary and middle school math teachers. Their analyses indicated that middle school teachers reported trusting their students less, and believing more in the importance of controlling students than did elementary school math teachers (Midgley, Feldlaufer, & Eccles, 1988).

In another study examining students, Midgley and her colleagues examined the relations between students' perceptions of their relationships with their teachers and changes in motivation toward mathematics before and after the transition. Results indicated that the valuing of mathematics increased for students who moved from less supportive to more supportive teachers across the transition. In contrast, when students moved from highly supportive elementary teachers into classrooms with less supportive middle school teachers, both students' intrinsic valuing of math and perceived usefulness of math declined (Midgley, Feldlaufer, & Eccles, 1989b).

Feldlaufer et al. (1988) used teacher data, student data, and classroom observational data to examine changes in relationships before and after the transition. Both student-reported data and data from classroom observations indicated that teachers were perceived as less caring, supportive, and friendly after the transition than before. All three data sources indicated that students had fewer opportunities to make choices and to provide input (i.e., students had less control) in posttransition math classrooms than in pretransition math classrooms (Feldlaufer et al., 1988).

Seidman and colleagues (Seidman, Allen, Aber, Mitchell, & Feinman, 1994) examined changes in perceived support from teachers across the transition, using a large and highly diverse sample of urban early adolescents (30% African American and 41% Latino). Results again indicated that after the transition, students reported less support from teachers than they did in elementary school. In addition, results also indicated that self-esteem, class preparation, and GPA declined after the transition.

In the United States, the changing roles of teachers under the No Child Left Behind legislation (NCLB; 2002), which holds teachers and schools highly accountable for student performance, may further constrain relationships between middle school teachers and adolescent students. For example, research on elementary students and teachers already indicates that teachers' workloads have increased quite dramatically due to NCLB, and that this increased workload has negatively affected their relationships with students (Valli & Buese, 2007).

Although the quality of relationships between teachers and students clearly seems to deteriorate after the transition, and although recent studies indicate that middle school reform efforts have not gone far enough in improving teacher–student relationships in early adolescence (Juvonen et al., 2004), there is some hope that this can change. In the late 1990s, several researchers reported improvements in the quality of relationships between middle school teachers and students (Felner et al., 1997a; Lipsitz, 1997). One suggestion often made for improving student–teacher relationships after the middle school transition is to reduce class sizes and teacher to student ratios. Nevertheless, it is important to realize that a reduction in class size will not automatically lead to improved relationships. Indeed, professional development is necessary for teachers, so that they can learn how to alter instructional practices to better suit smaller, more personal classes (Graue, Hatch, Rao, & Oen, 2007).

*The Need for Cognitively Demanding Academic Tasks* Early adolescents are ready and often eager to engage in cognitively demanding academic tasks. From a Piagetian perspective, early adolescents are entering the period of formal operations, when they are capable of thinking about complex, abstract issues (Piaget, 1952, 1972). According to the stage–environment fit model, middle school students should be presented with increasingly challenging, yet interesting, academic tasks.

Nevertheless, some research indicates that the types of academic tasks that early adolescents are asked to do in school often are cognitively undemanding, and in some cases even less cognitively complex than tasks that they were asked to do in elementary school. For example, in an early study examining students' beliefs about the cognitive demand of academic tasks, students reported that throughout the middle school years, academic tasks became less cognitively demanding; this trend continued through the high school years as well (Walberg, House, & Steele, 1973). Eccles and her colleagues (Eccles, Midgley, & Adler, 1984) report the results of a study by Rounds and Osaki (1982), which compared academic tasks in sixth grade classrooms (prior to the transition) and seventh grade classrooms (after the transition); results indicated that tasks in the junior high classrooms generally required cognitively undemanding strategies (e.g., memory and recall), compared to the more cognitively complex tasks afforded to the students during the sixth grade

More recently, NCLB legislation clearly has affected the types of curricular materials that teachers use. As noted by Mathis (2005), the legislation in the United States has constrained many teachers' choices of curricula and tasks; teachers are likely to choose curricula that will lead to high test scores during an era of accountability, which may lead some teachers to avoid cognitively challenging tasks that will be interesting and developmentally appropriate for early adolescents; instead, teachers may choose the types of materials that will lead to mastery of material likely to be on examinations used for accountability purposes.

On a positive note, research demonstrates that middle school students can successfully learn from and achieve at high levels when they are confronted with cognitively demanding academic work, as long as teachers are well trained in the presentation of such curricula. Marx, Blumenfeld, and their colleagues (Marx et al., 2004) examined the infusion of such curricula in science in the Detroit public schools. Results indicated that teachers were able to successfully instruct students, and that students demonstrated noticeable achievement gains. This research indicates that early adolescents even in underperforming urban middle schools can successfully learn complex, challenging material when teachers receive appropriate professional development in the use of such materials.

In summary, stage–environment fit theory suggests that students' motivation will decline if the environments of schools do not meet the developmental needs of students. Much empirical research indicates that there is indeed a mismatch between the instructional practices used in middle schools, and student outcomes. Research indicates that students' opportunities for autonomy, their relationships with their teachers, and engagement in cognitively demanding academic tasks, often worsen after the transition. This stands in sharp contrast to what adolescents desire during this phase of cognitive, social, and physical development.

## Studies Involving Goal Orientation Theory

Much of the more recent research on the middle school transition has been framed in terms of achievement goal theory, which we first introduced in the earlier discussion of studies of intrinsic motivation. This theoretical framework posits that students approach academic tasks with several underlying goals; these "goals" represent students' beliefs about *why* they are engaging with specific academic tasks (Ames & Archer, 1988; Dweck & Leggett, 1988; Kaplan, Middleton, Urdan, & Midgley, 2002; Maehr & Midgley, 1991, 1996; Nicholls, 1989).

Although a variety of terms are used in the literature, broadly these goals break down into two classes of goals:

*mastery goals*, wherein the student's goal is to truly learn and master the task, and *performance goals*, wherein the student's goal is to demonstrate his or her ability relative to others. Several researchers have argued that there are also both approach and avoid dimensions to mastery and performance goals (Elliot & Church, 1997; Elliot & Harackiewicz, 1996; Middleton & Midgley, 1997). In this 2 × 2 framework, there are four distinct classes of achievement goals: *mastery approach goals*, wherein the goal is to master a task; *mastery avoid goals*, wherein the goal is to avoid misunderstanding the task; *performance approach goals*, wherein the goal is to demonstrate one's superior ability relative to others; and *performance avoid goals*, wherein the goal is to avoid appearing inferior or "dumb." Researchers for the most part argue that schools should emphasize mastery goals in order to facilitate positive outcomes for students (Ames, 1992a, 1992b; Meece, Blumenfeld, & Hoyle, 1988; Meece, Herman, & McCombs, 2003; Midgley, 2002; Urdan, Ryan, Anderman, & Gheen, 2002), particularly in middle schools (E. M. Anderman & Maehr, 1994; Maehr & Anderman, 1993). Research generally indicates that mastery approach goals are related to the use of adaptive learning strategies (Meece & Miller, 2001; Miller, Greene, Montalvo, Ravindran, & Nichols, 1996; Nolen, 1988), although not often related directly to enhanced achievement (Harackiewicz, Barron, Pintrich, Elliot, & Thrash, 2002). There is debate about the benefits of performance approach goals (e.g., Brophy, 2005; Harackiewicz et al., 2002; Midgley, Kaplan, & Middleton, 2001). For example, some studies indicate positive relations of approach goals to persistence and effort (J. Elliot, McGregor, & Gable, 1999), whereas others reveal no such relations (Wolters, 2004). Research generally indicates that performance avoid goals are unrelated to any beneficial educational outcomes (J. Elliot et al., 1999; Middleton & Midgley, 1997; Wolters, 2004). Research on the relations of mastery-avoid goals to outcomes is still nascent (see E. M. Anderman & Wolters, 2006, for a review).

Although most studies focus on students' individual goals, it is important to note that achievement goals have been operationalized in other ways. For example, researchers also examine perceived stresses on goals in learning environments. These include, perceived classroom goal structures (i.e., whether or not the classroom as a whole is perceived as focusing on mastery or performance; Ames, 1992b; Ames & Ames, 1984; Kaplan et al., 2002) and perceived school goal stresses (i.e., whether or not the schools' overall policies and practices are perceived as focusing on mastery or performance; E. M. Anderman & Maehr, 1994; Maehr & Buck, 1992).

Nevertheless, research evidence indicates that middle schools are more focused on grading and ability than are elementary schools (Eccles, Lord, & Midgley, 1991; Eccles & Midgley, 1989; Eccles, Midgley et al., 1993; Maehr & Anderman, 1993; Midgley, 1993). Middle school teachers talk more about tests, and rely more heavily on testing and on grades as determinants of students' abilities; thus the stress on the importance of grades and relative ability increases during the middle grades years. Consequently, in recent years, several transition researchers have adopted a goal orientation theory framework; this framework has been particularly useful, since the main constructs in the theory (mastery and performance goals) relate directly to variables that are perceived as changing across the transition (e.g., stress on grades and test scores, the purpose of engaging in academic work, etc.). In addition, the fact that goal orientation theory allows researchers to examine students' personal goals, as well as perceptions of school and classroom goal structures, has allowed researchers to examine changes in mastery and performance goals across a variety of contexts.

Some transition studies have focused on changes in students' personal goal orientations. In a longitudinal study examining changes in achievement goals across the transition, E. M. Anderman and Midgley (1997) followed 341 students across the middle school transition. Measures were assessed for both mathematics and English. Results indicated that after the transition, students endorsed personal mastery goals less than in elementary school. No change over the transition was found for personal performance goals; however, students reported that the mastery goal structure was lower in middle school than in elementary school, and that the performance goal structure was higher in middle school.

In another longitudinal study of changes in achievement goals across the transition, L. Anderman and E. Anderman found that personal mastery goals declined and personal performance goals increased across the transition (L. H. Anderman & E. M. Anderman, 1999). Results also indicated that perceiving a high sense of school belonging and holding personal responsibility goals (i.e., trying to follow rules) were related to increases in personal mastery goals across the transition, whereas holding personal relationship goals (i.e., wanting to get to know friends well) and social status goals (i.e., wanting to be popular) were related to increases in personal performance goals.

Other studies have focused on differences in perceived goal structures across the transition. In a cross-sectional study comparing data from elementary school students and teachers to middle school students and teachers, Midgley, Anderman, and Hicks (1995) found that both middle school teachers and students perceived that middle schools stressed performance goals more and mastery goals less than did elementary school teachers and students. Middle school teachers also reported emphasizing performance goals to students more than did elementary teachers. Middle school students reported greater endorsement of performance goals and lesser endorsement of mastery than did elementary students.

There is some evidence that the reform of middle level schools has changed the nature of personal goals and perceptions of goal structures somewhat in middle schools. In one study, Midgley and her colleagues examined changes in perceptions of goal structures across the middle school tran-

sition. Interestingly, results did not indicate that a perceived emphasis on performance goals increased across the transition (Midgley, Maehr, et al., 1998). Midgley et al. note that these results may reflect reforms in middle-level education deemphasizing ability differences and performance goals in classrooms serving early adolescents (Midgley, Middleton, Gheen, & Kumar, 2002). However, although some structural changes have occurred in some middle schools (i.e., creating schools within schools, providing advisors for students), the overall emphasis on mastery goals is low in many American middle schools (Midgley & Edelin, 1998).

More often than not, middle school environments are focused on grades and relative comparisons of ability; therefore, it is not surprising that after the transition, middle school students often report being more performance-oriented and less mastery-oriented than in elementary school. Nevertheless, research indicates that classroom and school goal structures can be changed, and that middle schools can be reformed to place more emphasis on mastery goals (E. M. Anderman, Maehr, & Midgley, 1999; Maehr & Midgley, 1996).

## Teacher and Student Relationships across the Transition

Many of the studies reviewed thus far are rooted in one of several motivation theories. Nevertheless, there are some important studies of the middle school/junior high transition that are not based in motivation theory, but nevertheless have examined psychological and educational outcomes. These studies have made important and unique contributions to our understanding of adolescent learning during the middle school years.

In particular, we examine transition studies involving teacher efficacy and peer relationships. We have chosen these areas for two reasons. First, there is a fair amount of research that has been conducted in each of these domains; thus they continue to be areas of interest for researchers and educators. Second, these broad areas have important implications for our understanding of the effects of schooling on development. Transition studies involving teachers' sense of efficacy and peer relationships inform the knowledge base related to how schooling affects educational and psychological growth and change.

***Studies Examining Teacher Efficacy*** Teacher efficacy refers to teachers' beliefs about their abilities to affect learning in their students (Ashton & Webb, 1986; Guskey & Passaro, 1994; Tschannen-Moran, Woolfolk Hoy, & Hoy, 1998). Research indicates that positive efficacy beliefs among teachers are related to higher achievement in students (Tschannen-Moran et al., 1998). Several studies have examined differences in efficacy beliefs among elementary and middle school teachers.

Midgley et al. (1995) compared teacher efficacy in elementary and middle school teachers, and found that elementary teachers reported higher levels of efficacy than did middle school teachers. Regression analyses predicting teacher efficacy indicated that after controlling for school-level (elementary or middle school), teacher efficacy was most strongly related to perceiving that the entire school was mastery-oriented (i.e., a mastery school culture), and the use of mastery-oriented instructional practices (e.g., encouraging students to take academic risks in classes). In another study, Midgley and her colleagues (Midgley et al., 1988) compared a sample of elementary math teachers to junior high school math teachers, who taught the same students before and after the transition. Results indicated that the elementary math teachers reported higher teaching efficacy than did the junior high teachers.

In a longitudinal study of both students and teachers, Midgley and her colleagues examined the effects of teacher efficacy on changes in students' beliefs before and after the junior high transition (Midgley, Feldlaufer, & Eccles, 1989a). Results indicated that students who transitioned from high efficacy math teachers in elementary school to low efficacy math teachers after the transition experienced declines in expectancies for success in math and perceived performance in math; those students also reported high perceptions of task difficulty in mathematics after the transition.

In summary, the results of studies examining teacher efficacy before and after the transition generally indicate that middle school teachers report feeling somewhat less efficacious than do elementary school teachers. These lower feelings of efficacy are related to some negative educational outcomes for early adolescents.

***Studies Examining Relationships with Peers***   The relationships that students have with their peers are related to important academic and psychological outcomes during early adolescence (Berndt, 1999). As children become adolescents, they spend more time with peers, and less time with adults; this is particularly true for females (Larson & Richards, 1991; Larson, Richards, & Sims, 2001). In addition, adolescents tend to associate with peers who share similar interests to themselves (Crosnoe, 2002; Wentzel & Caldwell, 1997).

The transition from elementary school to middle school certainly affects the nature of the relationships that students have with each other. Both the structure of the school day and actual cohorts of students are strikingly different after the transition. Whereas many students spent most of their day with the same group of students for the entire academic year prior to the transition, in middle school students often experience different peer groups across their various classes throughout the day. In addition, many districts are organized such that many elementary schools feed into fewer large middle schools—thus the student population in middle school often is larger than that of the elementary school.

Several studies have examined the relations of school transitions to peer-related variables. Research generally indicates that the nature of peer groups changes across the transition from elementary to middle school (Berndt,

1989, 1992). For example, Seidman et al. (1994) found that participation in extracurricular activities decreases over the transition from elementary to middle school; thus students may not spend as much time with certain peer groups after the transition than they did before. Simmons and Blyth (1987) compared students who made the transition from K-6 to 7-9 schools to students who stayed in K-8 schools. Sixth graders attending K-6 type schools rated themselves as more popular with their same-sex peers than did sixth graders in K-8 schools. However, once the K-6 sixth graders moved into seventh grade in traditional middle schools, this advantage disappeared, and did not reemerge.

Cantin and Boivin (2004) examined stability in early adolescents' social networks across the transition from elementary to middle school. Their findings indicated the number of supportive peers in students' social networks declined immediately following the transition into middle school, but subsequently increased. Although they found that students' reports of companionship declined across the middle school transition and throughout the first 2 years of middle school, students' reports of peer support (instrumental, informational, and emotional) increased across the transition.

Thus research indicates that moving from elementary school into middle school often is associated with increased concerns with peer relationships, and initially with less social support from peers. These findings, coupled with research indicating that bullying and victimization are quite prevalent after the middle school transition (E. M. Anderman & Kimweli, 1997; Pellegrini, 2002), are causes of concern for middle grades educators. In particular, it will be important for teacher training programs to better prepare educators to be aware of these important issues in the lives of adolescents.

## Discussion

The research that we have reviewed clearly indicates that the transition to middle school is problematic for many youth. Whereas many recommendations have been made regarding appropriate learning environments for early adolescents (e.g., Carnegie Council on Adolescent Development, 1989, 1995), problems still persist in middle schools for many students. For example, a recent report on the status of middle school education in New York City indicated that "elementary and high school students in New York City have experienced improved academic outcomes, but middle-grade students continue to lag behind, with only slight increases in student performance" (New York City Council Middle School Task Force, 2007, p. 6).

As we noted at the start of this chapter, the study of school transitions is a particularly useful means of examining the effects of schooling on development. As various programs of research have successfully examined the relations between student characteristics and school learning environments (E. M. Anderman & Midgley, 1997; Wigfield et al., 1991), researchers have been able to better understand the specific ways that school environments and instructional practices affect student outcomes across the transition.

In the final sections of this chapter, we suggest several ways to broaden this research base in the future. We review some encouraging research suggesting that middle grades education can be improved, so that the transition does not have to be a traumatic experience for youth. In addition, we examine some of the methodological issues inherent in previous transition studies, and we discuss some promising new avenues for future research.

## Is the Middle School Transition Inevitably a Negative Experience?

Although there is abundant literature indicating that the transition from elementary school into middle school is traumatic for many adolescents, this transition does not have to be a negative experience. Most individuals can identify early adolescents who have experienced positive changes across this transition; in addition, many middle school educators will readily speak of students who have adjusted exceedingly well to middle school.

*Preexisting Individual Differences* Some research indicates that there are certain individual difference variables that either exacerbate problems or facilitate the transition for a variety of outcomes. For example, Harter and her colleagues (1992) found that students' prior perceived academic competence is related to the types of experiences that students have after the transition into middle school. Specifically, students with low self-perceptions of ability prior to the transition experience poorer outcomes after the transition than do students with higher self-perceptions of ability. Thus children's experiences in elementary school, which shape their self-perceptions, are related to posttransition experiences.

In a study of African American students making the transition, Gutman and Midgley (2000) found that minority students who felt more academically efficacious received higher grades after the transition than did students who felt less efficacious. In addition, results indicated that students who perceived high levels of teacher support *and* parental involvement received higher grades after the transition than did students who perceived only one or neither of these factors. Thus the presence of these factors prior to the transition may help to buffer some of the potential negative effects of the transition.

Research clearly indicates that some types of middle school environments are more developmentally appropriate than are others (E. M. Anderman & Maehr, 1994; Eccles & Midgley, 1989; Eccles, Midgley, et al., 1993). In addition, research indicates that some educational and psychological factors are related to positive outcomes for students after the transition. For example, Roeser and colleagues examined predictors of adjustment after the transition to middle school (Roeser, Eccles, & Sameroff, 2000). Their findings indicated that adolescents who are academically and so-

cially successful in middle school tend to feel competent at learning, to value what they are learning, and to not be emotionally distressed (e.g., feeling angry, sad, or hopeless). In summary, some individual characteristics of students help protect early adolescents during transitions into new school settings.

*Programmatic Efforts to Reform Middle Schools* Some studies also indicate that intervention programs aimed at reforming the instructional practices of middle schools to be in line with current research may improve student outcomes after the transition. Felner and his colleagues (Felner et al., 1993) examined the results of the School Transition Environmental Project (STEP) on student outcomes. This project was designed to ease school transitions during early adolescence by providing increased supports for students after the transition, and to increase students' sense of connectedness with school after the transition. Results indicated that students who transitioned into STEP middle schools had more positive school experiences, even after controlling for background/demographic differences. Specifically, STEP students reported less stress, higher self-esteem, less depression and delinquency, and higher academic expectations. Teacher data also indicated that STEP students displayed adaptive classroom behaviors. In addition, attendance patterns and grades were better for STEP students than for non-STEP students.

Maehr, Midgley, and their colleagues worked with a middle school in the early 1990s, in order to change the culture of the school to be more conducive to early adolescents' developmental needs (Maehr & Midgley, 1996). This work was rooted in goal orientation theory (Ames, 1992a, 1992b; Ames & Archer, 1988; Dweck & Leggett, 1988; A. J. Elliot & Harackiewicz, 1996; Elliott & Dweck, 1988; Nicholls, 1989). Maehr, Midgley, et al. worked with school personnel to try to develop a school-wide culture that focused on mastery and improvement, rather than on performance and relative ability (Maehr & Midgley, 1991). Specifically, they worked with two neighboring middle schools in a working-class neighborhood in the Midwestern United States. One school worked with the university team for approximately 3 years, whereas the other school served as a comparison site. A university team consisting of faculty and graduate students (including several former classroom teachers) met weekly with a team of teachers, administrators, and parents at the middle school. The specific policies and practices of the school, and the relations of those practices to student learning and motivation, were critically analyzed by this collaborative group over the three years.

Results after 3 years of collaborative work and longitudinal analysis indicated that although there were no differences in students' motivational beliefs prior to the transition to middle school, students who moved to the comparison school (as compared to the school working to change its school culture) exhibited higher mean levels of personal performance goals and extrinsic goals (E. M. Anderman et al., 1999). Thus although students' motivational profiles were unrelated to school attendance prior to the transition, those profiles did reflect the cultures of middle schools after students had made the transition. If most middle schools do utilize developmentally inappropriate practices, we can logically expect decrements in student motivation after the transition; however, the aforementioned intervention work by Maehr, Midgley, and their colleagues indicates that when middle schools do engage in theoretically based and developmentally appropriate reform efforts, at least some of the negative effects of the transition can be avoided (Maehr & Midgley, 1996).

In summary, although the middle school transition is related to the onset and continuation of serious educational and psychological problems for some youth, the negative effects of the transition can be ameliorated. Reform efforts that are designed to create developmentally appropriate school environments for early adolescents can lead to increased motivation and improved achievement (Carnegie Council on Adolescent Development, 1995). The aforementioned studies and other school-based research (E. M. Anderman, 1998; Barber & Olsen, 2004) indicate that even high-risk students can experience positive outcomes across the transition when the learning environment is appropriate.

## Methodological Issues in the Study of School Transitions

Transition researchers have had to contend with a number of complex methodological issues. The very nature of a school "transition" implies that the same individuals move from one social context into another social context; thus the transition is not simply a reflection of individual differences; rather, the transition reflects the effects of changing social environments on subsequent changes in individual differences (Eccles & Midgley, 1989).

*Longitudinal verses Cross-Sectional Studies* Clearly one of the most important methodological issues has to do with the nature of the data that are collected. Whereas longitudinal data clearly are better suited to school transition studies, longitudinal studies also are fraught with complexities and difficulties, such as attrition of participants, expense (i.e., longitudinal studies are costly), and finding subjects who are still eligible for participation but have moved out of the study area. Nevertheless, longitudinal studies allow for the examination of simultaneous changes of individuals nested within contexts. In contrast, cross-sectional studies are certainly less expensive and less complex in nature, but such studies are problematic in terms of internal and external validity. In particular, cross-sectional studies, which compare students in elementary school to different samples of students in middle schools, do not easily allow for examinations of specific cohort effects (i.e., one particular cohort of students may have unique experiences).

Studies of the middle school transition have used both longitudinal and cross-sectional designs. As an example of a cross-sectional study, Midgley et al. (1995) administered similar measures to elementary and middle school students, and compared results across the two samples. However, the majority of studies on the middle school transition have used longitudinal designs. Clearly the work of Eccles and her colleagues has been influential in this area (Eccles, Wigfield, et al., 1993; Wigfield & Eccles, 1994; Wigfield et al., 1991). Nevertheless, a number of other researchers also have examined the middle school transition using longitudinal designs (E. M. Anderman & Midgley, 1997; L. H. Anderman & Anderman, 1999; Felner et al., 1993; Harter et al., 1992; Simmons, Blyth, VanCleave, & Bush, 1979). Whereas some studies have only used two time points (e.g., E. M. Anderman & Midgley, 1997), others have included multiple time points (e.g., Wigfield et al., 1991). The use of multiple time points is particularly informative, since such studies allow for examinations of both within-grade and between-grade change.

*Student Samples verses Other Samples* Since teachers, students, and parents all are players in the middle school transition, studies utilizing multiple sources of data are important. Nevertheless, most studies utilize only one of these populations at a time. The most obvious source for data for transition studies is the students themselves. It is the student who is experiencing the transition, and therefore, students' beliefs and experiences during this transition are crucial in understanding the effects of the transition. This has been particularly important in person-centered approaches, which examine clusters of various student profiles (e.g., Roeser et al., 2000).

However, other sources of data have been used in some studies. In particular, a number of researchers have used teachers as a source of data (Feldlaufer et al., 1988; Midgley, Anderman, & Hicks, 1995; Midgley et al., 1988). Many of these studies have used survey instruments to compare the beliefs and practices of pre- and posttransition teachers. Other sources of data have included data reported by classroom observers (Feldlaufer et al., 1988), data from case studies (Turner & Patrick, 2004), and data collected directly from parents (Gutman & Midgley, 2000). Some particularly rich studies have combined both student and teacher data, to examine their mutual effects (Midgley et al., 1989a).

*Data Analytic Challenges* The study of middle school transitions poses some particularly interesting issues regarding quantitative analyses of data. Most studies of this nature are highly complex, in that students are nested in multiple environments. This is further complicated by the fact that in longitudinal studies, multiple observations are made on the same individuals.

Most longitudinal studies incorporated traditional ANOVA-type designs, prior to the mid 1990s (e.g., Wigfield et al., 1991). However, with the advent of multilevel regression techniques such as HLM (Bryk & Raudenbush, 1992; Raudenbush & Bryk, 2002), it has become possible to disaggregate unique sources of variance, and to thus

more carefully examine contextually based school influences on development. Several studies have been conducted
in recent years that have utilized multilevel techniques to
examine transition effects on student outcomes (E. M.
Anderman, 1998; E. M. Anderman et al., 2001; Meece,
Herman, & McCombs, 2003). These studies indicate that
the types of environments that are manifested in middle
schools explain unique proportions of variance in student
outcomes. For example, Anderman et al. (2001) used HLM
in a study including both elementary and middle school
students to demonstrate that students' valuing of certain
subject areas decreased when teachers indicated that they
used performance-oriented instructional practices.

## Areas for Future Research

At this point, research indicates that the middle school
transition often is problematic for youth, but the transition does not have to be a negative experience if schools
are designed to meet the needs of early adolescents (E.
M. Anderman et al., 1999; Eccles, Midgley, et al., 1993;
Felner et al., 1993). We believe that there are several areas
that will be particularly fruitful in future research on the
middle school transition.

*Studies Examining Effects of Interventions* First and
foremost, additional intervention research is sorely needed.
Whereas much descriptive research has been conducted on
the transition, only a few large-scale intervention studies
have been designed specifically to make the transition a
more positive experience for youth (Felner et al., 1993;
Maehr & Midgley, 1996). In particular, interventions that
are aimed both at comprehensive school-wide reforms,
as well as changes in specific classroom practices, are
needed.

The recommendations set forth in major publications
produced by Carnegie (1989, 1995) clearly indicate that
the reform of middle schools is necessary and important.
However, as noted by Felner and colleagues (Felner et al.,
1997b), for such reform efforts to be successful, research-
based recommendations need to be implemented *comprehensively*; piecemeal programs that attempt to change
one or two aspects of the middle school environment at a
time probably will not be successful at improving learning
environments for early adolescents.

Whereas experimental studies with true randomization would serve as the strongest empirical test of such
interventions, such work is often difficult to accomplish
in educational settings. Nevertheless, quasi-experimental
studies with matched comparison schools, such as the
work conducted in the 1990s by Maehr, Midgley, and
their colleagues (Maehr & Midgley, 1996), serves as a
potential model for the study of large-scale school-level
interventions.

*Studies Examining Students' Experiences Immediately
after the Transition* Another area for future research

involves how schooling is handled immediately after the
transition. Students' initial experiences during their first
days in middle school may have long-lasting impacts on
their future performance in the middle school environment.
If a student has unpleasant experiences during those first
days, those events may negatively affect students' later
experiences in middle school.

Research with sixth graders enrolled in K-6 elementary
schools indicates that the first days of school are indeed
very important. Patrick and her colleagues (Patrick, Turner,
Meyer, & Midgley, 2003) conducted observations in eight
sixth-grade mathematics classrooms, and found that when
teachers created positive learning environments at the
beginning of the school year (i.e., emphasizing the value
of mathematics, being willing to offer help to students,
expressing the belief that all students can and will learn
math, being respectful, and creating an enjoyable/pleasant
environment in the classroom), students were less likely to
report engaging in avoidance behaviors in mathematics later
in the academic year. Although this study was conducted
in elementary school classrooms, results suggest that the
instructional techniques used during the first days of school
may have an important impact on learning when students
are in middle school.

*Studies Examining Concurrent Biological Changes* Research examining the interrelations of biological development and school transitions is nascent, but may lead to
a more comprehensive understanding of how to create
appropriate schools for early adolescents. Two issues in
particular that are worthy of further inquire include (a) the
impact of pubertal timing on adolescent development, and
(b) new discoveries in the area of neuropsychology about
brain development during adolescence (Spear, 2000).

*Pubertal Timing and the Transition to Middle
School* Simmons and her colleagues (e.g. Simmons &
Blyth, 1987; Simmons, Blyth, Van Cleave, & Bush, 1979)
have conducted the most extensive research examining the
interactions between school context, puberty, and adolescent development. Simmons and Blyth characterized most
of the research examining the impact of pubertal timing on
adolescent development as having to do with the timing
(early, middle, or late) of pubertal changes, or about the
extremes (early or late development). Summarizing many
of the findings in this area, Simmons and Blyth concluded
that, in general, there are gender differences between boys
and girls, regardless of whether they develop early or late.
Furthermore, they concluded that on average, boys tend to
have more favorable self- and body images than do girls; in
addition, boys are less concerned about same-sex popularity
than are girls. Simmons and Blyth (1987) concluded that
school transitions may be more difficult for early versus
later maturing adolescents.

Other researchers continue to argue that our understanding of middle school transitions still can be enhanced from
additional studies of physiological development. Wigfield,

Lutz, and Wagner (2005) proposed that there are several important differences in how boys and girls develop during puberty that may impact their ability to handle successfully the transition from elementary to middle school. For example, girls tend to enter puberty approximately 18 months before boys do, thereby developing physically much faster than boys. Simmons, Blyth, and McKinney (1983) suggested that noticeable physical changes that occur in girls who experience early puberty can sometimes have a negative impact on their self- or body image. Furthermore, and given the increased concern over same-sex relationships with peers (Eccles & Roeser, 1999), some girls may experience increased self-consciousness as a result of some of these physiological changes (Ruble & Brooks-Gunn, 1982). These feelings of self-consciousness may be exacerbated when there is teasing involved by other peers. Given these findings, it is easy to see how physical changes as a result of early puberty might make this transition more difficult for early developing girls. Thus future intervention studies aimed specifically at helping female adolescents at the transition may be particularly illuminating.

*Social Relationships and Puberty*   Another important area that is impacted by timing of puberty is in the area of social relationships during early adolescence (Wigfield et al., 2005). On average, it seems that early physical development may be more facilitative for boys than for girls (Simmons & Blyth, 1987). Wigfield and his colleagues (2005) suggest that early developing boys tend to gain preferred status among their peers and adults, especially if they participate or excel in some sport or activity. Furthermore, Simmons, Blyth, and Bulcroft (1987) noted that early increases in height and muscular development may make boys more physically attractive to members of the opposite sex, thereby increasing their overall self- and body-image. It is also interesting to note that Simmons et al. (1983) found that early developing girls tended to date earlier than their later developing peers. Thus males and females become more attractive to their opposite-sex peers when they are physically more mature than others of the same age. Nevertheless, additional studies examining the effects of pubertal development on social relationships after the transition are needed.

Another important area for future research concerns the relation between early physical development, and within-classroom social interactions. For example, Eccles et al. (1993) found that female adolescents who were more physically developed than their same-sex peers reported fewer opportunities to participate in classroom decision making, resulting in reduced motivation to learn. Whereas there do appear to be some advantages for early developing boys as compared to early developing girls in many areas of psychosocial development, there is clearly a need for additional research examining the complex interactions among pubertal timing, adolescent psychological and physiological development, and changes in school or classroom environments.

*Brain Growth during Early Adolescence*   In addition to differences in the onset of pubertal development, there are also important changes occurring in the human brain that may affect students' reactions to the middle school transition; also, it is possible that negative experience at the middle school transition may adversely affect continued brain development during early adolescence. There is a need for additional research in these areas; virtually no research to date has examined these phenomena concurrently with the middle school transition.

Contrary to the popular notion that the human brain stops developing in early childhood at around age 6, the emerging field of neuroscience has clearly demonstrated that the brain continues to develop well into late adolescence and early adulthood. Through the use of longitudinal research designs and neuroimaging technology (e.g., MRI), researchers are now able to track developmental changes over time in the human brain. By taking multiple pictures of the same brain over many years, researchers have been able to track changes that occur in areas of the frontal lobe that control executive functions (Giedd, 2003), increases or decreases in synaptic growth (Giedd), areas that control language function and associative thinking (Thompson et al., 2000), and other areas of cognitive functioning (Rivkin, 2000). Giedd and his colleagues (e.g., Giedd, Blumenthal, et al., 1999; Giedd, Rumsey, et al., 1996; Lange, Giedd, Castellanos, & Rapoport, 1997) at the Child Psychiatry Branch of the National Institute of Mental Health (NIMH) have been at the forefront of this research, collecting almost 3,000 brain scans on approximately 1,500 children and adolescents.

Giedd (2003) has found that traumatic events (e.g., childhood neglect for boys and sexual abuse for girls) can affect the corpus callosum, which integrates activity across the right and left hemispheres of the brain. Whereas the trauma and stress associated with sexual abuse and neglect are qualitatively different from the stresses associated with the middle school transition, this emerging research does suggest that experiences that occur during early adolescence can affect brain development. Consequently, future studies that examine the effects of particularly traumatic middle school transitions on brain development will be extremely informative.

Caskey and Ruben (2003) have suggested that the emerging field of neuropsychology can also have important implications for the ways that teachers teach and treat adolescents in their classrooms. Specifically, they suggest that certain classroom practices and teacher–student interactions can actually aid and enhance healthy brain development during this period. Comer (2005) further suggests that actions taken at the school- and district-wide levels can have significant impacts on student learning and development. Comer suggests, in line with other educational researchers (Eccles, 2004; Eccles & Roeser, 1999; Simmons & Blyth, 1987), that schools play an essential role in many areas of adolescent development, including the brain.

## Conclusion

The transition to middle school is a complex and important period in the lives of early adolescents. Indeed, the middle school experience is an important determinant of students' academic achievements in the future. Positive experiences in school during early adolescence can be extraordinarily beneficial, but adverse experiences can have deleterious effects on students' continuing motivation to learn.

Although the transition to middle school is difficult for many students, unpleasant experiences are not inevitable. Research to date has clearly identified what does "not" work in middle schools for early adolescents; consequently, prescriptions for school reform can be easily made. Future intervention studies that fully consider the theoretical, biological, and social variables associated with the transition will enhance our ability to develop effective schools that truly promote motivation and achievement throughout early adolescence, and continuing throughout the lifespan. In addition, advances in both social science methodologies and in neuropsychology will further enhance our understanding of this crucial developmental period.

## References

Allen, J., Hauser, S., Bell, K., & O'Connor, T. (1994). Longitudinal assessment of autonomy and relatedness in adolescent-family interactions as predictors of adolescent ego development and self-esteem. *Child Development, 65*, 179–194.

Ames, C. (1992a). Achievement goals and the classroom motivational climate. In D. H. Schunk & J. L. Meece (Eds.), *Student perceptions in the classroom* (pp. 327–348). Hillsdale, NJ: Erlbaum.

Ames, C. (1992b). Classrooms: Goals, structures, and student motivation. *Journal of Educational Psychology, 84*(3), 261–271.

Ames, C., & Ames, R. E. (1984). Goal structures and motivation. *Elementary School Journal, 85*(1), 39–52.

Ames, C., & Archer, J. (1988). Achievement goals in the classroom: Students' learning strategies and motivation processes. *Journal of Educational Psychology, 80*(3), 260–267.

Anderman, E. M. (1998). The middle school experience: effects on the math and science achievement of adolescents with LD. *Journal of Learning Disabilities, 31*(2), 128–138.

Anderman, E. M., Eccles, J. S., Yoon, K. S., Roeser, R. W., Wigfield, A., & Blumenfeld, P. (2001). Learning to value math and reading: Individual differences and classroom effects. *Contemporary Educational Psychology, 26*, 76–95.

Anderman, E. M., & Kimweli, D. M. S. (1997). Victimization and safety in schools serving early adolescents. *Journal of Early Adolescence, 17*(4), 408–438.

Anderman, E. M., & Maehr, M. L. (1994). Motivation and schooling in the middle grades. *Review of Educational Research, 64*(2), 287–309.

Anderman, E. M., Maehr, M. L., & Midgley, C. (1999). Declining motivation after the transition to middle school: Schools can make a difference. *Journal of Research and Development in Education, 32*, 131–147.

Anderman, E. M., & Midgley, C. (1997). Changes in achievement goal orientations, perceived academic competence, and grades across the transition to middle-level schools. *Contemporary Educational Psychology, 22*(3), 269–298.

Anderman, E. M., & Wolters, C. A. (2006). Goals, values, and affect: Influences on student motivation. In P. A. Alexander & P. H. Winne (Eds.), *Handbook of educational psychology* (pp. 369–389). Mahwah, NJ: Erlbaum.

Anderman, L. H., & Anderman, E. M. (1999). Social predictors of changes in students' achievement goal orientations. *Contemporary Educational Psychology, 25*, 21–37.

Ashton, P. T., & Webb, R. B. (1986). *Making a difference: Teachers' sense of efficacy and student achievement.* New York: Longman.

Atkinson, J. W. (1957). Motivational determinants of risk-taking behavior. *Psychological Review, 64*(6), 359–372.

Atkinson, J. W. (1964). An introduction to motivation. Oxford, England: Van Nostrand.

Barber, B. K., & Olsen, J. A. (2004). Assessing the transitions to middle and high school. *Journal of Adolescent Research, 19*(1), 3–30.

Berndt, T. J. (1989). Obtaining support from friends during childhood and adolescence. In D. Belle (Ed.), *Children's social networks and social supports* (pp. 308–331). New York: Wiley.

Berndt, T. J. (1999). Friends' influence on students' adjustment to school. *Educational Psychologist, 34*, 15–29.

Bronstein, P., Ginsburg, G. S., & Herrera, I. S. (2005). Parental predictors of motivational orientation in early adolescence: A longitudinal study. *Journal of Youth and Adolescence, 34*(6), 559–575.

Brophy, J. (2005). Goal theorists should move on from performance goals. *Educational Psychologist, 40*, 167–176.

Brophy, J., & Everston, C. M. (1978). Context variables in teaching. *Educational Psychologist, 12*, 310–316.

Bryk, A. S., & Raudenbush, S. W. (1992). *Hierarchical linear models: Applications and data analysis methods.* Newbury Park, CA: Sage.

Cantin, S., & Boivin, M. (2004). Change and stability in children's social network and self-perceptions during transition from elementary to junior high school. *International Journal of Behavioral Development, 28*, 561–570.

Carnegie Council on Adolescent Development. (1989). *Turning points: Preparing youth for the 21st century.* New York: Carnegie Corporation.

Carnegie Council on Adolescent Development. (1995). *Great transitions: Preparing adolescents for a new century.* New York: Carnegie Corporation.

Caskey, M. M., & Ruben, B. (2003). Research for awakening adolescent learning. *Middle Matters, 12*, 36–38.

Clark, S. N., & Clark, D. C. (1993). Middle level school reform: The rhetoric and the reality. *Elementary School Journal, 93*(5), 447–460.

Comer, J. P. (2005). Child and adolescent development: The critical missing focus in school reform. *Phi Delta Kappan, 86*(10), 757–763.

Crosnoe, R. (2002). High school curriculum track and adolescent association with delinquent friends. *Journal of Adolescent Research, 17*(2), 143–167.

Davis, H. A. (2003). Exploring the contexts of relationship quality between middle school students and teachers. *Elementary School Journal, 106*(3), 193–221.

Deci, E., & Ryan, R. M. (1985). *Intrinsic motivation and self-determination in human behavior.* New York: Plenum.

Deci, E., & Ryan, R. M. (1994). Promoting self-determined education. *Scandinavian Journal of Educational Research, 38*(1), 3–14.

DuBois, D. L., Eitel, S. K., & Felner, R. D. (1994). Effects of family environment and parent-child relationships on school adjustment during the transition to early adolescence. *Journal of Marriage and the Family, 56*, 405–414.

Dweck, C. S., & Leggett, E. L. (1988). A social-cognitive approach to motivation and personality. *Psychological Review, 95*(2), 256–273.

Eccles, J. (2004). Schools, academic motivation, and stage-environment fit. *Handbook of adolescent psychology* (2nd ed., pp. 125–153). Hoboken, NJ: Wiley.

Eccles, J., Adler, T. F., Futterman, R., Goff, S. B., Kaczala, C. M., Meece, J. L., et al. (1983). Expectancies, values, and academic behaviors. In J. T. Spence (Ed.), *Achievement and achievement motivation* (pp. 75–146). San Francisco, CA: Freeman.

Eccles, J. S., Lord, S., & Midgley, C. (1991). What are we doing to early adolescents? The impact of educational contexts on early adolescents. *American Journal of Education, 99*(4), 521–542.

Eccles, J. S., & Midgley, C. (1989). Stage-environment fit: Developmentally appropriate classrooms for young adolescents. In C. Ames & R.

Ames (Eds.), *Research on motivation in education: Goals and cognitions* (Vol. 3, pp. 139–186). New York: Academic.

Eccles, J. S., Midgley, C., & Adler, T. F. (1984). Grade-related changes in the school environment: Effects on achievement motivation. In J. G. Nicholls & M. L. Maehr (Eds.), *Advances in motivation and achievement: The development of achievement motivation* (pp. 283–331). Greenwich: JAI.

Eccles, J. S., Midgley, C., Wigfield, A., Miller-Buchanan, C. M., Reuman, D., Flanagan, C., et al. (1993). Development during adolescence: The impact of stage-environment fit on young adolescents' experiences in schools and in families. *American Psychologist, 48*(2), 90–101.

Eccles, J. S., & Roeser, R. W. (1999). School and community influences on human development. In M. Borstein & M. Lamb (Eds.), *Developmental psychology: An advanced textbook* (4th ed., pp. 503–554). Mahwah, NJ: Erlbaum.

Eccles, J. S., & Wigfield, A. (1995). In the mind of the actor: The structure of adolescents' achievement task values and expectancy-related beliefs. *Personality and Social Psychology Bulletin, 21*(3), 215–225.

Eccles, J. S., & Wigfield, A. (2002). Motivational beliefs, values, and goals. *Annual Review of Psychology, 53*(1), 109–132.

Eccles, J. S., Wigfield, A., Midgley, C., & Reuman, D. (1993). Negative effects of traditional middle schools on students' motivation. *Elementary School Journal, 93*(5), 553–574.

Eccles, J. S., Wigfield, A., & Schiefele, U. (1998). Motivation to succeed. In N. Eisenberg (Ed.), *Handbook of child psychology: Social, emotional, and personality development* (5th ed., Vol. 3, pp. 1017–1095). New York: Wiley.

Elkind, D. (1976). *Child development and education: A Piagetian perspective.* New York: Oxford University Press.

Elliot, A. J., & Church, M. A. (1997). A hierarchical model of approach and avoidance achievement motivation. *Journal of Personality and Social Psychology, 72*(1), 218–232.

Elliot, A. J., & Harackiewicz, J. M. (1996). Approach and avoidance achievement goals and intrinsic motivation: A mediational analysis. *Journal of Personality and Social Psychology, 70*(3), 461–475.

Elliot, J., McGregor, H. A., & Gable, S. (1999). Achievement goals, study strategies, and exam performance: A mediational analysis. *Journal of Educational Psychology, 91*(3), 549–563.

Elliott, E. S., & Dweck, C. S. (1988). Goals: An approach to motivation and achievement. *Journal of Personality and Social Psychology, 54*(1), 5–12.

Epstein, J. L., & McPartland, J. M. (1976). The concept and measurement of the quality of school life. *American Educational Research Journal, 31*(1), 15–30.

Epstein, R. (2007). *The case against adolescence: Rediscovering the adult in every teen.* Sanger, CA: Quill Driver.

Erikson, E. H. (1963). *Childhood and society* (2nd ed.). New York: Norton.

Feldlaufer, H., Midgley, C., & Eccles, J. S. (1988). Student, teacher, and observer perceptions of the classroom environment before and after the transition to junior high school. *Journal of Early Adolescence, 8*(2), 133–156.

Felner, R. D., Brand, S., Adan, A. M., Mullhall, P. F., Flowers, N., Sartain, B., et al. (1993). Restructuring the ecology of the school as an approach to prevention during school transitions: Longitudinal follow-ups and extensions of the School Transitional Environment Project (STEP). In L. A. Jason, K. E. Danner, & K. S. Kurasaki (Eds.), *Prevention and school transitions* (pp. 103–136). Binghamton, NY: Haworth Press.

Felner, R. D., Jackson, A. J., Kasak, D., Mulhall, P., Brand, S., & Flowers, N. (1997a). The impact of school reform for the middle years: Longitudinal study of a network engaged in Turning Points-based comprehensive school transformation. *Phi Delta Kappan, 78*, 528–532, 541–550.

Felner, R. D., Jackson, A. W., Kasak, D., Mulhall, P., Brand, S., & Flowers, N. (1997b). *The impact of school reform for the middle grades: A longitudinal study of a network engaged in Turning Points-based comprehensive school transformation.* New York: Cambridge University Press.

Fredricks, J. A., & Eccles, J. S. (2002). Children's competence and value beliefs from childhood through adolescence: Growth trajectories in two male-sex-typed domains. *Developmental Psychology, 38*(4), 519–533.

Giedd, J. N. (2003). The anatomy of mentalization: A view from developmental neuroimaging. *Bulletin of the Menninger Clinic, 67*(2), 132–142.

Giedd, J. N., Blumenthal, J., Jeffries, N. O., Castellanos, F. X., Liu, H., Zijdenbos, A., et al. (1999). Brain development during childhood and adolescence: A longitudinal MRI study. *Nature Neuroscience, 2*, 861–863.

Giedd, J. N., Rumsey, J. M., Castellanos, F. X., Rajapakse, J. C., Kaysen, D., Vaituzis, A. C., et al. (1996). A quantitative MRI study of the corpus callosum in children and adolescents. *Developmental Brain Research, 91*, 274–280.

Gottfried, A. E., Fleming, J. S., & Gottfried, A. W. (1998). Role of cognitively stimulating home environment in children's academic intrinsic motivation: A longitudinal study. *Child Development, 69*(5), 1448–1460.

Gottfried, A. E., Fleming, J. S., & Gottfried, A. W. (2001). Continuity of academic intrinsic motivation from childhood through late adolescence: A longitudinal study. *Journal of Educational Psychology, 93*(1), 3–13.

Graham, S., Taylor, A. Z., & Hudley, C. (1998). Exploring achievement values among ethnic minority early adolescents. *Journal of Educational Psychology, 90*(4), 606–620.

Graue, E., Hatch, K., Rao, K., & Oen, D. (2007). The wisdom of class-size reduction. *American Educational Research Journal, 44*(3), 670–700.

Guskey, T. R., & Passaro, P. D. (1994). Teacher efficacy: A study of construct dimensions. *American Educational Research Journal, 31*(3), 627–643.

Gutman, L. M., & Midgley, C. (2000). The role of protective factors in supporting the academic achievement of poor African American students during the middle school transition. *Journal of Youth and Adolescence, 29*, 223–248.

Hall, G. S. (1904). *Adolescence: Its psychology and its relation to physiology, anthropology, sociology, sex, crime, religion, and education* (Vols. 1, 2). Englewood Cliffs, NJ: Prentice-Hall.

Harackiewicz, J. M., Barron, K. E., Pintrich, P. R., Elliot, A. J., & Thrash, T. M. (2002). Revision of achievement goal theory: Necessary and illuminating. *Journal of Educational Psychology, 94*(3), 638–645.

Harter, S. (1981). A new self-report scale of intrinsic versus extrinsic orientation in the classroom: Motivational and informational components. *Developmental Psychology, 17*(3), 300–312.

Harter, S., Whitesell, N. R., & Kowalski, P. S. (1992). Individual differences in the effects of educational transitions on young adolescents' perceptions of competence and motivational orientation. *American Educational Research Journal, 29*(4), 777–807.

Hoy, W. K. (1969). Pupil control ideology and organizational socialization: A further examination of the influence of experience on the beginning teacher. *American Journal of Education, 77*, 257–265.

Hunt, D. E. (1975). Person-environment interaction: A challenge found wanting before it was tried. *Review of Educational Research, 45*, 209–230.

Jacobs, J. E., Lanza, S., Osgood, D.W., Eccles, J. S., & Wigfield, A. (2002). Changes in children's self-competence and values: Gender and domain differences across grades one through twelve. *Child Development, 73*, 509–527.

Juvonen, J., Le, V. N., Kaganoff, T., Augustine, C., & Constant, L. (2004). *Focus on the wonder years: Challenges facing the American middle school.* Santa Monica, CA: RAND.

Kaplan, A., Middleton, M. J., Urdan, T., & Midgley, C. (2002). Achievement goals and goal structures. In C. Midgley (Ed.), *Goals, goal structures, and patterns of adaptive learning* (pp. 21–53). Mahwah, NJ: Erlbaum.

Lange, N., Giedd, J. N., Castellanos, F. X., & Rappaport, J. L. (1997). Variability of human brain structure size: Ages 4–20. *Psychiatry Research: Neuroimaging, 74*, 1–12.

Eric M. Anderman and Christian E. Mueller

Larson, R., & Richards, M. (1991). Daily companionship in late childhood and early adolescence: Changing developmental contexts. *Child Development, 62,* 284–300.

Larson, R., Richards, M., & Sims, B. D., J. (2001). How urban African American young adults spend their time: Time budgets for locations, activities, and companionship. *American Journal of Community Psychology, 29,* 565–597.

Lee, S.-J. (2007). The relations between the student–teacher trust relationship and school success in the case of Korean middle schools. *Educational Studies, 33*(2), 209–216.

Lewin, K. (1935). *A dynamic theory of personality.* New York: McGraw-Hill.

Lewis, C. (1981). How adolescents approach decisions: Changes over grades seven to twelve and policy implications. *Child Development, 52,* 538–544.

Lipsitz, J. (1997). Middle grades improvement program. *Phi Delta Kappan, 78,* 555.

Losier, G. A., & Vallerand, R. J. (1994). The temporal relationship between perceived competence and self-determined motivation. *Journal of Social Psychology, 134,* 793–801.

Lynch, M., & Ciccheti, D. (1997). Children's relationships with adults and peers: An examination of elementary and junior high students. *Journal of School Psychology, 35,* 81–99.

Maehr, M. L., & Anderman, E. M. (1993). Reinventing schools for early adolescents: Emphasizing task goals. *Elementary School Journal, 93*(5), 593–610.

Maehr, M. L., & Buck, R. (1992). Transforming school culture. In M. Sashkin & H. J. Walberg (Eds.), *Educational leadership and school culture* (pp. 40–57). Berkeley, CA: McCutchan.

Maehr, M. L., & Midgley, C. (1991). Enhancing student motivation: A school-wide approach. *Educational Psychologist, 26,* 399–427.

Maehr, M. L., & Midgley, C. (1996). *Transforming school cultures.* Boulder, CO: Westview.

Marx, R. W., Blumenfeld, P., Krajcik, J. S., Fishman, B., Soloway, E., Geier, R., et al. (2004). Inquiry-based science in the middle grades: Assessment of learning in urban systemic reform. *Journal of Research in Science Teaching, 41*(10), 1063–1080.

Mathis, W. J. (2005). The cost of implementing the no child left behind act: Different assumptions, different answers [Special issue]. *Peabody Journal of Education, 80*(2), 90–110.

Meece, J. L., Blumenfeld, P. C., & Hoyle, R. H. (1988). Students' goal orientations and cognitive engagement in classroom activities. *Journal of Educational Psychology, 80,* 514–523.

Meece, J., Herman, P., & McCombs, B. L. (2003). Relations of learner-centered teaching practices to adolescents' achievement goals. *International Journal of Educational Research, 39,* 457–475.

Meece, J. L., & Miller, S. D. (2001). A longitudinal analysis of elementary school students' achievement goals in literacy activities. *Contemporary Educational Psychology, 26*(4), 454–480.

Meece, J. L., Wigfield, A., & Eccles, J. S. (1990). Predictors of math anxiety and its influence on young adolescents' course enrollment intentions and performance in mathematics. *Journal of Educational Psychology, 82*(1), 60–70.

Middleton, M. J., & Midgley, C. (1997). Avoiding the demonstration of lack of ability: An underexplored aspect of goal theory. *Journal of Educational Psychology, 89*(4), 710–718.

Midgley, C. (1993). Motivation and middle level schools. In M. L. Maehr & P. R. Pintrich (Eds.), *Advances in motivation and achievement: Motivation in the adolescent years* (Vol. 8, pp. 219–276). Greenwich, CT: JAI.

Midgley, C. (Ed.). (2002). *Goals, goal structures, and patterns of adaptive learning.* Mahwah, NJ: Erlbaum.

Midgley, C., Anderman, E. M., & Hicks, L. H. (1995). Differences between elementary and middle school teachers and students: A goal theory approach. *Journal of Early Adolescence, 15*(1), 90–113.

Midgley, C., & Edelin, K. C. (1998). Middle school reform and early adolescent well-being: The good news and the bad. *Educational Psychologist, 33*(4), 195–206.

Midgley, C., Feldlaufer, H., & Eccles, J. S. (1988). The transition to junior high school: Beliefs of pre- and posttransition teachers. *Journal of Youth and Adolescence, 17*(6), 543–562.

Midgley, C., Feldlaufer, H., & Eccles, J. S. (1989a). Change in teacher efficacy and student self- and task-related beliefs in mathematics during the transition to junior high school. *Journal of Educational Psychology, 81*(2), 247–258.

Midgley, C., Feldlaufer, H., & Eccles, J. S. (1989b). Student/teacher relations and attitudes toward mathematics before and after the transition to junior high school. *Child Development, 60*(4), 981–992.

Midgley, C., Kaplan, A., & Middleton, M. (2001). Performance-approach goals: Good for what, for whom, under what circumstances, and at what cost? *Journal of Educational Psychology, 93,* 77–86.

Midgley, C., Maehr, M. L., Gheen, M. H., Hruda, L. Z., Middleton, M. J., & Nelson, J. (1998). *The Michigan middle school study: Report to participating schools and districts.* Ann Arbor: University of Michigan.

Midgley, C., Middleton, M. J., Gheen, M. H., & Kumar, R. (2002). Stage-environment fit revisited: A goal theory approach to examining school transitions. In C. Midgley (Ed.), *Goals, goal structures, and patterns of adaptive learning* (pp. 109–142). Mahwah, NJ: Erlbaum.

Miller, R. B., Greene, B. A., Montalvo, G. P., Ravindran, B., & Nichols, J. D. (1996). Engagement in academic work: The role of learning goals, future consequences, pleasing others, and perceived ability. *Contemporary Educational Psychology, 21*(4), 388–422.

Murdock, T. B., & Miller, A. (2003). Teachers as sources of middle school students' motivational identity: Variable-centered and person-centered analytic approaches. *The Elementary School Journal, 103*(4), 383–399.

New York City Council Middle School Task Force. (2007, August). *Report of the New York City Council middle school task force.* New York: Pedro Noguera.

Nicholls, J. G. (1989). *The competitive ethos and democratic education.* Cambridge, MA: Harvard University Press.

No Child Left Behind Act. (2002). Pub. L. No. 107–110, 115 Stat. 1425.

Nolen, S. B. (1988). Reasons for studying: Motivational orientations and study strategies. *Cognition and Instruction, 5,* 269–287.

Patrick, H., Turner, J. C., Meyer, D. K., & Midgley, C. (2003). How teachers establish psychological environments during the first days of school: Associations with avoidance behaviors in mathematics. *Teachers College Record, 105*(8), 1521–1558.

Pellegrini, A. D. (2002). Bullying, victimization, and sexual harassment during the transition to middle school. *Educational Psychologist, 37*(3), 151–163.

Piaget, J. (1952). *The origin of intelligence in children.* New York: International Universities Press.

Piaget, J. (1954). *The construction of reality in the child.* New York: Basic Books.

Piaget, J. (1972). Intellectual evolution from adolescence to adulthood. *Human Development, 15,* 1–12.

Pianta, R. C. (1999). *Enhancing relationships between children and teachers.* Washington, DC: American Psychological Association.

Raudenbush, S. W., & Bryk, A. S. (2002). *Hierarchical linear models: Applications and data analysis methods* (2nd ed.). Thousand Oaks, CA: Sage.

Resnick, M. D., Bearman, P. S., Blum, R. W., Bauman, K. E., Harris, K. M., Jones, J., et al. (1997). Protecting adolescents from harm: Findings from the National Longitudinal Study on Adolescent Health. *Journal of the American Medical Association, 278,* 823–832.

Rivkin, M. J. (2000). Developmental neuroimaging of children using magnetic resonance techniques. *Mental Retardation and Developmental Disabilities Research Reviews, 6,* 68–80.

Roeser, R. W., Eccles, J. S., & Sameroff, A. J. (2000). School as a context of early adolescents' academic and social-emotional development: A summary of research findings. *Elementary School Journal, 100*(5), 443–471.

Ruble, D. N., & Brooks-Gunn, J. (1982). The experience of menarche. *Child Development, 53,* 1557–1566.

Ryan, R. M., & Deci, E. L. (2006). Self-regulation and the problem of human autonomy: Does psychology need choice, self-determination, and will? *Journal of Personality, 74*, 1557–1585.

Seidman, E., Allen, L., Aber, J. L., Mitchell, C., & Feinman, J. (1994). The impact of school transitions in early adolescence on the self-system and perceived social context of poor urban youth. *Child Development, 65*, 507–522.

Simmons, R. G., Black, A., & Zhou, Y. (1991). African American versus white children and the transition into junior high school. *American Journal of Education, 99*(4), 481–520.

Simmons, R. G., & Blyth, D. A. (Eds.). (1987). *Moving into adolescence: The impact of pubertal change and school context.* Hawthorne, NY: Aldine de Gruyter.

Simmons, R. G., Blyth, D. A., & Bulcroft, R. A. (1987). The social-psychological effects of puberty on White males. In R. G. Simmons & D. A. Blyth (Eds.), *Moving into adolescence: The impact of pubertal change and school context* (pp. 137–158). Hawthorne, NY: Aldine de Gruyter.

Simmons, R. G., Blyth, D. A., & McKinney, K. L. (1983). The social and psychological effects of puberty on white females. In J. Brooks-Gunn & A. C. Petersen (Eds.), *Girls at puberty: Biological and psychosocial perspectives* (pp. 229–272). New York: Plenum.

Simmons, R. G., Blyth, D. A., VanCleave, E. F., & Bush, D. (1979). Entry into early adolescence: The impact of school structure, puberty, and early dating on self-esteem. *American Sociological Review, 44*, 948–967.

Simmons, R. G., Rosenberg, M., & Rosenberg, F. (1973). Disturbance in the self-image at adolescence. *American Sociological Review, 39*(5), 553–568.

Spear, L. P. (2000). Neurobehavioral changes in adolescence. *Current Directions in Psychological Science, 9*(4), 111–114.

Stefanou, C. R., Perencevich, K. C., DiCintio, M., & Turner, J. C. (2004). Supporting autonomy in the classroom: Ways teachers encourage student decision making and ownership. *Educational Psychologist, 39*(2), 97–110.

Steinberg, L. (1990). Autonomy, conflict, and harmony in the family relationship. In S. S. Feldman & G. R. Elliott (Eds.), *At the threshold: The developing adolescent* (pp. 255–278). Cambridge, MA: Harvard University Press.

Thompson, P. M., Giedd, J. N., Woods, R. P., MacDonald, D., Evans, A. C., & Toga, A. W. (2000). Growth patterns in the developing brain detected by using continuum mechanical tensor maps. *Nature, 404*, 190–193.

Tschannen-Moran, M., Woolfolk Hoy, A., & Hoy, W. K. (1998). Teacher efficacy: Its meaning and measure. *Review of Educational Research, 68*(2), 202–248.

Turner, J. C., & Patrick, H. (2004). Motivational influences on student participation in classroom learning activities. *Teachers College Record, 106*(9), 1759–1785.

Urdan, T., Ryan, A. M., Anderman, E. M., & Gheen, M. (2002). Goals, goal structures, and avoidance behaviors. In C. Midgley (Ed.), *Goals, goal structures, and patterns of adaptive learning* (pp. 55–83). Mahwah, NJ: Erlbaum.

Valli, L., & Buese, D. (2007). The changing role of teachers in an era of high-stakes accountability. *American Educational Research Journal, 44*(3), 519–558.

Walberg, H. J., House, E. R., & Steele, J. M. (1973). Grade level, cognition, and affect: A cross-section of classroom perceptions. *Journal of Educational Psychology, 64*(2), 142–146.

Wentzel, K. R., & Caldwell, K. (1997). Friendships, peer acceptance, and group membership: Relations to academic achievement in middle school. *Child Development, 68*, 1198–1209).

Wigfield, A., & Eccles, J. S. (1992). The development of achievement task values: A theoretical analysis. *Developmental Review, 12*(3), 265–310.

Wigfield, A., & Eccles, J. S. (1994). Children's competence beliefs, achievement values, and general self-esteem: Change across elementary and middle school. *Journal of Early Adolescence, 14*(2), 107–138.

Wigfield, A., & Eccles, J. S. (2002). The development of competence beliefs, expectancies for success, and achievement values from childhood through adolescence. In A. Wigfield & J. S. Eccles (Eds.), *Development of achievement motivation* (pp. 91–120). San Diego, CA: Academic.

Wigfield, A., Eccles, J. S., Mac Iver, D., Reuman, D. A., & Midgely, C. (1991). Transitions during early adolescence: Changes in children's domain-specific self-perceptions and general self-esteem across the transition to junior high school. *Developmental Psychology, 27*(4), 552–565.

Wigfield, A., Lutz, S. L., & Wagner, L. A. (2005). Early adolescents' development across the middle school years: Implications for school counselors [Special issue]. *Professional School Counseling, 9*(2), 112–119.

Wolters, C. A. (2004). Advancing achievement goal theory: Using goal structures and goal orientations to predict students' motivation, cognition, and achievement. *Journal of Educational Psychology, 96*, 236–250.

# 14

# Bringing Rigor to the Study of Rigor

*Are Advanced Placement Courses a Useful Approach to Increasing College Access and Success for Urban and Minority Youths?*

Melissa Roderick and Ginger Stoker

## Introduction

In his 2006 State of the Union Address, President Bush announced a new initiative to train 70,000 high school teachers to teach Advanced Placement (AP) mathematics and science courses.[1] This initiative reflects the growing consensus that high schools must provide more students with the rigorous coursework they will need to gain access to and be prepared for college. It also reflects the transformation of AP from a program aimed at offering an elite group of students the opportunity to earn advanced standing in college to a program used by students and high schools to increase college preparedness and gain advantage in college admissions. From 1981 to 2004, the number of students taking AP examinations increased from 178,000 to over 1.1 million (The College Board, 2005). More recently, as reflected in former President Bush's pledge, the AP program is being advanced as a policy strategy for addressing the minority achievement gap (National Governors Association, 2005a). Many states have already adopted policies to support the expansion of AP for low-income students, including providing start-up AP grants to districts, supplementing AP examination fees, and even requiring that every high school offer AP courses (American Diploma Project, 2004; Education Commission of the States, 2000; Klopfenstein, 2004; National Governors Association, 2005b).

These policy initiatives stand, however, on a relatively weak research base. Proponents of expanding course offerings point to research evidence that students who take more rigorous coursework perform higher on standardized tests, do better in college, and ultimately are more likely to graduate from college (ACT, 2005; Adelman, 1999; Berkner, He, Cataldi, & Knepper, 2002; Horn & Carroll, 2001; Pallas & Alexander, 1983; Rose & Betts, 2001; Warburton, Bugarin, & Nuñez, 2001). The central question is not, however, whether moving to more rigorous coursework makes sense. The question is whether offering AP courses is a more effective strategy than other approaches, such as requiring that students take more upper level mathematics and science courses, or working to align content and instruction in high school courses with college standards. In 2002, the National Research Council conducted a review of the AP and International Baccalaureate (IB) programs and concluded that there was little evidence to evaluate the effects of AP courses (National Research Council, 2002). The review issued a call for more rigorous research, and since then, several studies have investigated whether AP participation is associated with improved college performance (Adelman, 2006; Dougherty, Mellor, & Jian, 2005; Geiser & Santelices, 2004; Klopfenstein & Thomas, 2006). These new studies have surprisingly found little evidence that taking AP courses is associated with greater persistence in college, higher college grades, or increases in the likelihood of graduation. There is some evidence that AP test performance is predictive of college performance (Dougherty et al., 2005; Geiser & Santelices, 2004). Recent studies, however, are analyzing the effect of AP participation in samples where there is very limited AP participation among racial and ethnic minority students. Thus, while these studies question the efficacy of the growth in AP in the 1990s, which was largely concentrated among nonminority students in more advantaged schools, we do not know the extent to which these results generalize to the current policy debate.

The expansion of AP and its transformation into a policy strategy for low-income students is an important example of where policy and practice have advanced with little research guidance and little rigorous evidence. It is also an example of how methodologically complicated it is for researchers to confidently identify the potential effects of a specific strategy. This chapter uses AP as a case study to illustrate the range of methodological issues that arise when trying to evaluate the efficacy of policy approaches to improving minority achievement, particularly when students and schools are selecting into programs and when program estimates will be influenced by general school quality effects. We

216

begin with a general discussion of why issues of advanced coursework have become so central to current high school reform debates and the central role that curriculum debates have played in the study of "school effects." We then turn to the case of AP and outline the "case" for investments in expansion of AP as a means of improving college access for low-income and urban youth. We focus on two questions. First, why would AP be viewed as a preferable policy option to improving college access and college performance, particularly in urban school systems? And, second, is there any evidence that AP participation improves college access and college performance, particularly for minority and low-income students?

The remainder of this chapter focuses on methodology. We discuss the range of methodological issues that researchers must contend with in both evaluating current research and in moving forward to fill in gaps in knowledge. We then present the results of a recent study of the effects of AP on 4-year college enrollment from a study of Chicago Public Schools (CPS) to demonstrate approaches to addressing these problems. The conclusion discusses potential future areas for research.

***The Policy Context*** Over the past several years, high school reform has moved to the top of the policy agenda at the national, state, and local levels. There is an emerging consensus that high schools, particularly in urban areas, are plagued by high dropout rates and low student engagement and performance, and that few high schools are developing in students the skills they will need to gain access to and do well once they are in college. The contention that high schools should be judged by whether their students are prepared for college and postsecondary training is a relatively new expectation. It reflects a recognition that the new economy is demanding higher skills and that high school graduates who do not go to college face declining economic prospects (Kirsch, Braun, Yamamoto, & Sum, 2007). It also reflects the rising aspirations of today's youth. From 1980 to 2002, the percentage of 10th graders in the United States who hoped to complete a bachelor's degree or higher doubled, from 40 to 80% (U.S. Department of Education, 2004a). Increases in aspirations have been observed across racial and ethnic groups, with the largest increases occurring among students from low income families.

The problem, however, is that too often students' aspirations are not translating into college success. Among students who plan to attend a 4-year college, minority students are much more likely to end up attending a 2-year college or not attending college at all (Berkner, Chavez, & Carroll, 1997). Once in college, racial/ethnic minority and first-generation college students are much more likely to be placed in remedial courses that do not count for college credit (Warburton, Bugarin, & Nunez, 2001). Most importantly, rising college enrollment is not translating into concomitant increases in degree attainment. From 1990 to 2004, the percentage of African Americans aged 25 to 29 who report that they have attended some college increased

by 16% so that, by 2004, more than half of African Americans in this age group had attended some college (U.S. Department of Education, 2004b). However, only 17% of these African American young adults had graduated from a 4-year college, an increase of only 4% since 1990. Lack of progress in college participation is particularly dire for Latino/a students who lag in both college attendance and completion. In 2004, less than one third of Latino/a young adults had attended some college, and only 11% of Latino/a young adults had completed a bachelor's degree or higher, rates only slightly higher than 15 years earlier.

Addressing this aspirations-attainment gap is one of the most vexing problems in education today. How do we translate rising aspirations into college success and completion? What does it mean to support students in gaining access to 4-year colleges, in being prepared for college, and in making successful transitions? While there are many factors that shape whether a student who hopes to go to college will be able to enroll and be successful, one of the most important is whether the student has the skills and credentials they need to gain access and participate successfully once there. Minority and low-income students are much less likely to leave high school with the qualifications (such as test scores, grades, and coursework) that give them access to postsecondary education, particularly to 4-year colleges, and which have proven critical in determining college performance and persistence (Adelman, 1999; Berkner et al., 1997; Roderick et. al., 2006). For example Greene and Winters (2005), using transcript data from that National Assessment of Educational Progress, estimated that in 2002 only one quarter of African American and 20% of Latino/a high school seniors compared to 40% of White seniors graduated with the coursework and test scores that would have given them access to a 4-year college with minimal admissions criteria.

## Addressing the Aspirations-Achievement Gap: The Role of Curriculum

Many policymakers and educators looking at the poor qualifications of minority, low-income, and urban high school students come to the conclusion that a central culprit driving low school achievement and college access is the high school curriculum. Advocates of expanding AP offerings argue that AP is not just about "adding qualifications" to the high school transcripts of those students who already have the grades and test scores to qualify them for admittance to a 4-year selective college. Rather, AP is increasingly being advanced as a key strategy for engaging more students in more rigorous coursework and raising standards throughout the high school curriculum (The College Board, 2006). To those familiar with the history of the American high school, the fact that the high school curriculum has emerged as an important policy solution to the need to improve college access would not be surprising. In many ways, the historical development of the American high school has been marked by dramatic shifts and debates over what students should take and what they need for success after high school (Angus & Mirel, 1999).

In this respect, a chapter on the high school curriculum has an important place in an edited volume on "school effects." Research on the high school curriculum has played a central role in "school effects" research as investigators sought to develop methods to identify the processes by which high schools may work to increase or ameliorate inequality. In the 1980s and 1990s, researchers initiated a new era in education research when they began developing empirical approaches to studying "school effects" and when new national data sets, particularly the High School and Beyond (HS&B) study, which followed a group of 1980 high school sophomores, and the National Longitudinal Educational Study of 1988 (U.S, Department of Education, 2003), which followed eighth graders into high school, began to allow for comparison of differences in student performance across schools in large samples (Bryk, Lee, & Holland, 1993; Lee & Smith, 1995; Lee, Smith, & Croninger, 1995; McPartland & Schneider, 1996).

This research on "effective schools" has two thematic lines of analysis. One line of inquiry seeks to identify aspects of school climate, such as the expectations of teachers, parent involvement, learning climates, or working conditions within schools that are associated with higher or more equitable student achievement (Lee, Smith, Perry, & Smylie, 1999; Pallas, 1988; Purkey & Smith, 1983; Rutter, Maughan, Mortimore, & Ouston, 1979; Shouse, 1996). A second line of inquiry, particularly for those studying high schools, focuses on identifying aspects of school policy, practice, and organization that distinguishes schools with above average performance (Lee & Bryk, 1988; Lee & Smith, 1995). This second line of inquiry posits that high school organization and policy, such as curriculum requirements, shape student achievement in two ways. First, the organization of schools (i.e. small versus large) shapes student achievement indirectly by creating conditions that promote behaviors found in effective schools such as high expectations, positive adult–student and peer relationships, and parent involvement.

Second, the organization of learning shapes achievement directly by structuring opportunity to learn: whether students have been exposed to material (e.g. whether they have taken the course), the quality of that exposure (the quality of teaching and content within that course), and the accessibility of that exposure (whether the course material is conveyed in a way that give students access to material and promotes understanding) (Kilgore & Pendleton, 1993; Stevenson et al., 1994). Thus, the concept of "opportunity to learn" suggests that school effects arise from the extent to which schools structure learning so that students are given the opportunity to be exposed to new material and participate in a demanding curriculum (Dougherty, 1996; Kilgore & Pendleton, 1993; McPartland & Schneider, 1996). A central finding of this research was that schools in which students took more rigorous coursework and where there was less variability in course taking produced higher overall levels of achievement, and reduced the gap in achievement outcomes among students of varying socioeconomic status and race/ethnicities (Alexander & Pallas, 1984; Lee, Burkham, Chow-Hoy, Smerdon & Geverdt, 1998; Lee & Bryk, 1998; Lee, Smith, & Croninger, 1995; McPartland & Schneider, 1996; Sebring, 1987; Walberg & Shanahan, 1983).

In the 1990s, the availability of post-high school longitudinal data from these same databases allowed researchers to extend the analysis to examine the link between students' high school coursework and their subsequent college access and performance. Perhaps the best known study in this area is Clifford Adelman's *Answers in the Tool Box* (1999). Adelman drew on transcript data from the U.S. Department of Education's high school longitudinal studies to examine the link between a student's high school GPA, achievement test scores, coursework, and the likelihood of college graduation. The most important findings were in the area of coursework. The rigor of a student's coursework, which included measures of the total number of Carnegie units in core subjects and participation in AP, was significantly associated with the likelihood of college graduation, with benefits being significantly larger for minority students. Other studies have similarly documented strong associations between the level of coursework students take, particularly participation in advanced mathematics, and performance on college admission tests, college performance, and the likelihood of college graduation (ACT, 2004; Berkner et al., 2002; Chen, 2005; Horn & Carroll, 2001; Pallas & Alexander, 1983; Rose & Betts, 2001; Tai, Sadler, & Loehr, 2005; Warburton, Bugarin, & Nuñez, 2001).

Most of this research on the effects of coursework is cross-sectional and, although researchers statistically adjust for differences in prior achievement and background characteristics, studies have not yet controlled adequately for selection into coursework. As a result, the benefits of advanced coursework may be overstated because studies are comparing the college performance of those students who are selecting into advanced courses, and thus may be more oriented toward college, with those who are not. Even with this caveat, coursework as a mechanism to shape achievement makes sense. In the opportunity to learn framework, students who take higher level courses are exposed to more advanced material. They stay on task longer, which may be particularly important in mathematics where the lack of 4th year mathematics means that students enter college having been off task for over a year. Coursework participation is also the area identified by the school effects research that is the most easily influenced by policy.

***Why is Advanced Placement Preferable to Other Forms of Advanced Coursework?*** If there is evidence that moving more students into rigorous coursework may be an important approach to raising achievement and improving college readiness, why is AP a better option than other forms of advanced coursework? In this section, we outline four arguments for why AP may be viewed as having advantages in urban school systems over simply raising graduation requirements or offering more upper level courses: (a) equity concerns, (b) feasibility, (c) efficacy, and (d) student effort.

The first argument for AP is that if colleges use AP in making admissions decisions, there is concern that urban and particularly low-income students are being left behind by not having access to AP courses. The growth of the AP program parallels the rising aspiration of today's students and the increasing scramble for college. The AP program began in 1955 as a small advanced standing program intended to give an academically select group of students the opportunity to place out of introductory college classes by demonstrating proficiency while in high school (Lichten, 2000). Beginning in the 1980s and 1990s the AP program was transformed as many students and schools, largely in suburban areas, began using AP courses as a mechanism to gain a step up in the increasingly competitive college admissions process. Colleges began considering participation in AP coursework (rather than AP examination scores) in decisions about admissions and many high schools began giving students extra "GPA credits" for taking AP courses. Thus, AP began to have an advantage over non-AP coursework because colleges and high schools started enacting policies that explicitly advantaged the program.

Geiser and Santelices (2004) note that the University of California's initial rationale for giving extra points for AP courses was that colleges wanted an indicator of the seriousness of a student's interest and ambitions. Thus, AP participation was viewed as a marker of an individual student's motivation. Advanced Placement participation and AP course offerings are, however, increasingly being used by colleges and the general public as a marker of high school and coursework quality. The College Board now reports increases in AP enrollments as an indicator of a state's progress in improving college readiness (College Board, 2005). *Newsweek* magazine publishes a yearly list of the "top 100 high schools," identified primarily by the percentage of their students taking AP or International Baccalaureate (IB) courses (Matthews, 2006). Not surprisingly, students, parents, and educators responded to these signals. From 1981 to 2004, the number of students who took an AP exam increased from 178,000 to over 1.1 million (College Board, 2005). By 2003, nearly one third (30%) of high school seniors had taken at least one AP or IB course; but since the expansion occurred primarily in more advantaged districts, marked disparities in participation by socioeconomic status and race/ethnicity became apparent (Planty, Bozick, & Ingels, 2006). In 2004, national estimates suggest that graduates from high SES backgrounds were over three times more like (50.9 versus 16.3%) to have taken an AP course than students from low SES backgrounds (Planty et al. 2006). Only 16% of African American students versus one quarter of Latino/a students and 33% of Whites had taken an AP course. Given these wide disparities and the "validation" of the program among upper income students, it is not surprising that AP has become popular among

policymakers because it is seen as an attempt to advance higher standards while promoting equity in access for urban students using a "validated," publicly popular strategy (Education Commission of the States, 2000).

A second argument is that implementing AP courses provides a feasible means of moving to more rigorous coursework. In most states and large districts, new AP course offerings come with additional fiscal resources and external supports unavailable to schools that develop their own courses. The College Board, while not providing an explicit day-by-day curriculum, does provide a basic structure through its AP program materials and provides teachers with opportunities to participate in professional development.

As a result, a third related argument is that AP courses may be a more effective approach than simply adding regular high school courses designed by teachers because the use of external assessments and the core program materials are more likely to promote higher standards. One of the most important policy concerns in moving to higher coursework requirements is that high schools will add advanced courses with little attention to whether content meets standards (ACT, 2004). Adding AP courses seems a way out of this problem. The use of external exams may make it more likely that teachers will explicitly focus on standards based material that will prepare students for college, set high expectations for performance, and, ultimately, as the College Board argues, begin to increase the rigor of lower level courses to prepare students for AP (Camera, Dorans, Morgan, & Myford, 2000; College Board, 2006). Thus, the argument is that AP courses will lead to higher performance because alignment with AP examinations and the press to increase students' ability to do well on those exams will raise standards for students both in and prior to their AP courses.

The expansion of AP and the efforts of the College Board to promote the program as a means of moving to more college oriented curricula are not without controversy. Several researchers have argued that the College Board has placed too much emphasis on expanding participation without quality control. They cite dramatically different passing rates by race/ethnicity and income as evidence that adding AP courses in urban schools may not really address the problem of ensuring that courses are comparable across high schools or school systems (Dougherty et al., 2006; Lichten, 2000).

A final argument is that, by providing real payoffs for students, the program addresses a central concern in high schools: low levels of student motivation and engagement in course work (Bishop, 1990; Powell, 1996). Arthur Powell (1996) argues that the AP program has special advantages because the curriculum goals are clearly linked to outcomes that matter to students (college preparation), because students receive a direct incentive or reward for doing well, and because external assessments provide for colleges clear markers of students' capacities. Because students garner external rewards for performance, it is an approach that signals to teachers and students that mastering course content matters, increasing student motivation.

The argument that AP increases performance through motivational effects makes sense if students are applying to colleges that give them rewards for AP participation. An important question is whether expansion of AP reduces or increases inequities within high schools. Most of the evidence for coursework effects, as discussed above, was that equity in course taking and high expectations for students of all ability levels contributed to higher overall achievement and less variation in achievement. But, AP is seen as an elite program that students select into, committing themselves to greater work effort and higher expectations. This may have benefits to those students who have the abilities and motivation to participate, but it may have other costs in not offering an alternative to those who don't have the capacity or motivation to take AP but who may be highly at risk of problems in the transition to college. An equally important question is whether participation in AP will have positive payoffs to students with weaker academic skills. Is AP out of reach for these students who are the most in need of increasing their college readiness? And, is the skills focus in AP, which is aligned with content coverage at 4-year more selective universities, a good match for students who need to increase their basic levels of college readiness? Resolving these questions requires that we understand how AP participation shapes college participation and performance among urban and minority students of varying achievement levels, how those effects differ from the effect of upper level non-AP courses, and how those effects differ by both the characteristics of students and the high schools and colleges they attend.

***Evidence for Advanced Placement*** The previous section focused on the question: Why would expansion of AP participation be a preferable policy strategy for moving to higher standards than other policy approaches such as raising high school graduation requirements? There remains the question: Is there any evidence that offering AP courses is a more effective strategy for increasing college readiness and college outcomes for students? The above discussion suggests two primary mechanisms by which participation in AP courses could influence students' college outcomes. First, students who take AP may have access to more selective colleges—an access effect. And, second, students who take AP may be better prepared for college and do better in college—a preparation effect.

*Access Effects* Most suburban students are attracted to AP courses because they hope that AP participation will make it more likely they will get into their college of choice and, most often, into more highly selective colleges. Thus, AP for students already oriented toward college, may not shape the likelihood of attending college but may influence the types of college students attend. Advanced Placement may have this effect because, as discussed previously, colleges explicitly give students extra points for AP courses and

are advantaging AP in college admissions. Advanced Placement participation could also improve students' college access by influencing their qualifications (e.g. grade point averages and college entrance examination test scores). In many school systems, students receive additional GPA points for taking honors and AP courses and thus will have higher GPAs to report to colleges. Thus, AP may indirectly shape students' college access if students have higher skills and higher grades that increase their college qualifications. For many urban students, these effects on college access might not be negligible and may extend to shaping access to 4-year colleges. Advanced Placement courses may also have important effects for urban students by providing them with an academically oriented peer group, greater access to support for college from teachers and counselors, and confidence in their ability to do college level work.

*College-Preparation Effects* A second way that AP participation could shape college performance is if students leave high school with higher levels of precollegiate preparation that would lead them to do better once they are enrolled in college. In the opportunity to learn framework, students who take AP courses may do better than students in courses of comparable content that are not AP because teachers are more likely to align their content with precollegiate material in AP courses. Advanced Placement courses may also increase college readiness if teachers are more likely to emphasize core precollegiate skills such as writing, research, oral communication, problem solving, and analytic thinking skills that are highly valued by colleges and are the areas most often cited by college professors and students as the weakest areas of preparation in high school (Achieve, 2005). Unfortunately, there is a scarcity of research on the effects of AP in shaping college access. There is also little evidence to test the claim that AP leads to higher quality curriculum and greater levels of precollegiate preparation. In one of the most promising studies to date, Tai, Sadler, and Loehr (2005) are using surveys of students in introductory college physics and chemistry courses to examine the association between aspects of a student's high school performance, instructional experiences and prior curricula, and performance in introductory science classes (Sadler & Tai, 2001; Tai et al., 2005). Their findings suggest that students who take AP level courses, particularly AP calculus, do better in their introductory college courses partly because of differences in the activities and instruction they received (Sadler & Tai, 2001). In one analysis, Sadler and Tai (2001) concluded that most of the positive effect of taking an AP or honors physics course in high school could be explained by the fact that students in these courses were more likely than students who had taken a regular level physics class to report that their high school teachers taught in ways that were associated with better college performance in physics—such as covering fewer topics in greater depth, explaining problems in multiple ways, and relying less on or not using a text. This research in science suggests that AP courses may make it more likely that teachers will emphasize instructional practices that lead to improved readiness for college level work.

Regardless of specific content effects, the bottom line question is: Does AP participation lead students to do better overall in college? Until recently, there has been little evidence to address this question. Early research on AP conducted by the College Board focused on validating the practice of allowing students who scored high on AP examinations to gain advanced standing. These studies examined the college performance of those AP participants who scored high enough on examinations to pass out of introductory courses, a very select group, and generally found that AP students who passed out of introductory courses did as well or better in their higher level coursework (as measured by grades) than students who took introductory courses (Breland & Oltman, 2001; Casserly, 1986; Morgan & Ramist, 1998).

More recently, researchers have begun to tap state level data sets to examine whether AP participation and AP test performance, regardless of whether students obtain advanced standing, are associated with improved college performance, graduation and retention (Dougherty et al., 2005; Geiser & Santelices, 2004; Klopfenstein & Thomas, 2006). In one of the first studies that looked at the impact of AP participation on college performance, Saul Geiser and Veronica Santelices (2004) used data from the University of California at Berkeley to examine whether the University of California's practice of giving students who took AP courses extra credit in the college application pool could be supported by evidence of better college outcomes among AP course takers who received that advantage. These researchers found that AP and honors coursework in high school was not associated with an increase in the likelihood of persistence in the first or second year of college, once they had accounted for variables that would traditionally be used in college admission (unweighted high school GPA and SAT scores), as well as measures of family background (parental education) and high school quality (the school's average test scores). Students who took AP courses received higher grades in their freshman year, though this effect was moderate and was not sustained once the researchers included measures of AP test scores. A student's AP examination score was, however, positively associated with course performance across college majors. While the College Board (2006) has cited this study as evidence that getting high scores on AP exams improves college performance, Geiser and Santelices (2004) point out that AP examination scores may simply be a better measure than SAT scores in predicting performance within college majors—an effect that may have occurred if any measure of content knowledge were used.

Two studies in Texas focused specifically on the question of whether the expansion of AP participation in that state led students to do better in college (Dougherty et al., 2005; Klopfenstein & Thomas, 2006). These studies found that students in Texas who took AP courses were more likely to graduate from a Texas public university, to

receive higher grades in college, and to persist in their first year of college. These effects, however, do not hold up in more rigorous analysis once researchers control for both selection into AP coursework (Dougherty et al., 2005) and students' overall course taking patterns (Klopfenstein & Thomas, 2006).

Dougherty, Mellor, and Jian (2005) examined the effect of AP participation and AP test scores on the likelihood of graduating from a Texas public university. These authors looked separately at the college performance of students who: (a) took an AP course but did not take the examination, (b) took the examination but did not pass, and (c) took an AP course and passed the exam. Analyses were run separately for White, African American, and Hispanic students and for low-income and non-low-income students. Controlling for pre-high school test scores, high school GPA, and high school characteristics, Dougherty and his colleagues found that each of the AP groups outperformed students who had not taken AP coursework in high school. For example, controlling for high school performance and high school characteristics, African American students who took an AP course but did not take an AP exam were 16% more likely to graduate from a Texas public university than students who had not taken an AP course. Taking an AP course and taking but not passing the exam was associated with a 22% increase in the likelihood of college graduation for African American students and taking an AP courses and passing the exam was associated with a fully 28% increase in the likelihood of graduation compared to African American students who did not participate in AP. In general, the effects of AP were slightly larger for White and non-low-income students. These researchers conclude, however, that most of these impressive positive effects of AP course participation can be attributed to the fact that students who were in AP courses were a select group who would have done better in college regardless. At the high school level, the percentage of students taking but not passing AP examinations was not associated with higher average college graduation rates for Latino/a and White students, although some positive effects were found African American students.

Like Geiser and Santelices (2004), Dougherty and his colleagues did find a positive effect of passing AP examinations. The percentage of students in a student's high school who passed the AP exam was associated with an increase in the likelihood of an individual student graduating from college after adjusting for the average skill level of students entering that high school (as measured by 8th grade test scores), the demographic characteristics of the student body, and the average level of non-AP advanced course taking in the school. As we will discuss in greater detail later in this chapter, it is unclear what the association between a high school's AP passing rates and the college graduation rates of students from that high school means. It could mean that AP courses do not proffer benefits to students unless students demonstrate mastery of the material. The average AP test scores of a high school, however, could also serve as a proxy variable for the overall quality of that school.

Klopfenstein and Thomas (2006), using similar Texas data, also found a positive association between participation in AP courses in high school and freshman college GPA as well as first year college retention. The authors looked separately at the effects of the number of AP courses taken for Whites, African American, and Hispanics and, unlike the previous study, used a fixed effects methodology to adjust for college effects. The number of AP courses a student took in high school was positively associated with college GPA and the likelihood of retention even after controlling for demographic characteristics, SAT scores, high school GPA, class rank, measures of family background and financial need, and the college the student attended. The effects were most dramatic for African American and Hispanic students. Klopfenstein and Thomas conclude, however, that much of the positive association between AP coursework and college performance reflects the fact that students who took AP courses were also more likely to take a more rigorous sequence of courses in high school. Consistent with previous findings, Klopfenstein and Thomas (2006) find that students who took higher level mathematics and science courses in high school did significantly better in college. Participation in AP courses, particularly taking only one or two AP courses, offered little additional benefit for White and African American students once a student's overall course taking was accounted for. This was not true among Hispanic students in science.[2]

Klopfenstein and Thomas's (2006) research was directly aimed at Clifford Adelman's (1999) finding that AP was a strong predictor of college performance. Adelman's *Answers in a Toolbox* (1999) is perhaps the most widely cited study supporting the benefits of AP participation. But, as Klopfenstein and Thomas (2006) point out, Adelman included the number of AP courses a student took as part of an overall measure of the academic intensity of the student's high school curriculum—a curriculum measure that combined AP participation with the number of advanced mathematics, science courses, and foreign language courses students took. Partly in reaction to this new research, Adelman (2006) revisited his findings, taking apart his index to look separately at the effect of the participation in AP, advanced foreign language, and advanced science and mathematics courses. He concluded that most of the strength of his original index came from the strong effects of participation in advanced mathematics and science in predicting college performance. Like Klopfenstein and Thomas, Adelman's reanalysis suggests that once a student's upper level non-AP courses are controlled for, AP participation is not associated with an increase in the likelihood of college graduation.

The results of these new studies are disappointing. Despite the rapid expansion of AP courses in American high schools and the increasing public investment in expanding AP courses for low-income and minority students, there is little concrete evidence that even the most advantaged students benefit from simply taking AP courses if those benefits are measured by their grades in college, persistence, and

likelihood of graduation. These results may not derail the AP train. As discussed previously, expanding participation in Advanced Placement is seen as a means of opening access to college and leveling the playing field for urban youths. Yet, none of these studies have examined whether participation in AP shaped whether and what kinds of college students attended. And, these studies have only just begun to look at effects among African American, Latino/a, and low-income youth where, in general, results are inconsistent but more promising with even small sample sizes. The quite significant predictive power of AP examination scores at the school and student level is also being interpreted as evidence that high quality AP curriculum may offer significant advantages, particularly for low-income students. But, these studies also illustrate the methodological complexity of identifying the potential payoffs to the current investment in AP using cross-sectional data sets. Studies to date have not adequately addressed four central problems that researchers must contend with that currently limit the ability of studies to come to conclusions about the effects of AP: (a) selection effects, (b) school effects, (c) proxy and measurement effects, and (d) issues of generalizability of results.

## Problems in Identifying the Effects of Advanced Placement

*Selection Effects*  Perhaps the most important, but often unaddressed problem that occurs when estimating the effect of AP courses, as well as advanced coursework more generally, is that students who complete higher level courses are students who may be the most motivated to attend college and who have done well in previous courses—a group that currently is highly self-selected. Indeed, the idea that participation in AP courses is a marker of a student's motivation was the justification colleges originally gave for giving AP preference in college admission. Researchers have tried to address for this problem by statistically controlling for prior achievement, a student's demographic and family background characteristics, and high school coursework. But, this is simply inadequate. A student who, on entering high school has the same achievement level as another student but who chooses or is chosen to take an AP class is not comparable to her or his counterparts who do not.[3]

Selection effects are just as problematic in disentangling whether passing AP examinations matters. Consider Dougherty and his colleagues' (2006) finding that students who took AP courses and passed exams were more likely than students who took AP courses and did not take the exam to graduate from college. The prevalent interpretation of this finding is that AP course quality matters—implying that students who took and passed exams had higher quality AP courses than students who took the course but did not pass. But, without directly addressing the selection problem, we don't know whether this is a quality effect or a selection effect. A student with the same entering test scores who took an AP class in the same school and decided not to take the exam must be different in some unmeasured respects or have had a different experience than students who decided not to take the exam in ways that would shape their performance in college independent of their AP course experience.

**School Effects** Dougherty, Meller, and Jian (2006) did recognize the selection problem that occurs within schools, and currently this is the only study that tried to explicitly address selection effects by examining whether the percentage of students in a high school who took and passed an AP examination was associated with performance in college. The logic behind such an approach is that if AP is simply sorting students and, thus, identifying the college outcomes of the best students in the school, the average college performance of students from that high school would not be different from that of similar students in high schools that did not have as many students passing AP examinations. Intuitively this approach makes sense, and is an approach that we used in a modified form in this chapter. The problem with using this method in a cross-sectional data set, without broader measures of the quality of the high school independent of AP, is that is hard to disentangle whether this result means that mastering AP curriculum matters or that students who go to a high quality school that delivers high performance for their students (as indicated by high AP pass rates) will do better in college. Dougherty and his colleagues included some measures of the characteristics of high schools but only had a pre-high school measure of test performance (8th grade test scores). Without a measure of high school test performance, we don't know whether the association between a high school's average AP test performance and the average college performance of its students would have been equally strong if the researchers had included any measure of high school test performance such as average SAT or ACT scores. Students with similar eighth grade achievement who went to schools in which high numbers of students took and passed AP exams might do better than comparable students who attended schools with poor AP performance because their experience in the curriculum across the board was of higher quality—a method of identifying overall school effects using AP results but not an adequate method to identify the effects of AP performance independent of the overall quality of the school. There is evidence that school quality is an important predictor of AP test performance and that high school quality shapes college performance (Betts & Morell, 1999). In one study of minority student success on AP exams, Burton and her colleagues (2002) found that teachers whose minority students had better than expected test scores on AP calculus and literature examinations tended to work in higher SES schools and in schools where teachers gave higher ratings to the quality of the pre-AP curriculum and pre-AP academic skill levels of their students. This makes sense in that better prepared students may be more likely to pass AP examinations. It makes it difficult to interpret cross-sectional differences across high schools in the association between their students' AP performance and their students' performance in college.

**Proxy Effects** The problem of school effects is simply that, without substantial controls for school quality, average AP participation and examination performance may simply be standing in as a proxy measure of overall school quality. Jay Matthews (2006) has made the argument that AP participation is a proxy variable in defending *Newsweek's* use of AP participation rates in ranking U.S. high schools. While the use of proxy measures may be defensible when used to rank schools or when used as an indicator of whether a student is willing to work hard, the fact that AP participation and AP examination performance can be a proxy variable severely complicates identifying the independent effect of the program. Students do not randomly participate in AP courses. They tend to participate in AP courses after engaging in more rigorous coursework prior to AP (e.g., honors courses) and in concert with their AP participation. The finding of Klopfenstein and Thomas (2006) and Adelman (2006) suggests that without controls for curriculum both prior to and concomitant with their AP courses, studies may substantially overestimate the effects of AP participation.

A similar issue of proxy effect occurs when interpreting the strong association between AP examination performance and college performance. As Geiser and Santelices (2004) point out, a student's score on an AP examination in a content area may simply represent a measure of content knowledge that would be associated with college performance regardless of AP participation. Advanced Placement examination performance may also be a measure of a student's work ethic, and general ability to prepare and perform on external exams that may be an important measure of whether students can perform well in college regardless of the quality of their AP curriculum. Addressing these problems will become increasingly important as researchers try to follow up on the initial findings that AP examination scores matter for success in college. This is not just a problem of proxy effects. It is also a problem of missing data because researchers do not have an independent measure of a student's content knowledge in non-AP courses. For example, one could compare measures of the content knowledge of students in AP mathematics courses versus alternative fourth year mathematics courses. But without equivalent measures of the performance on non-AP students, we don't know the extent to which the strong association between AP test performance and college outcomes represents the effect of AP coursework or differences between students in their level of mastery of their high school coursework that would lead to differences in college performance regardless of AP.

**Generalizability of Results** Issues of student selection, general school quality, and proxy effects are all problems that make it difficult to obtain unbiased estimates of the effects of AP participation and test performance on outcomes.

A final important issue is the extent to which prior findings on the effect of AP participation are generalizable as the program expands, particularly to urban and less advantaged districts that are the primary targets of policy. First, will the program maintain quality as it expands? And, second, will AP have the same effect on students who come to the AP courses with less prior academic training, who may not be eligible for the most selective colleges, and who may have lower educational aspirations and support for their school work at home? While the first question is about implementation, the second question is whether AP will have differential effects on students who have traditionally not participated in the program. One perspective is that the benefits of AP will be lower for students with less prior preparation and in lower quality instructional environments (Dougherty et al., 2006; Lichten, 2000; National Research Council, 2002). If it is passing AP examinations and not taking AP courses that matters, then simply enrolling more students without getting them to pass the test will not provide them with benefits; and there is strong evidence that students with less prior preparation are significantly less likely to pass AP exams (Burton et al., 2002; Dougherty et al., 2006).

Another perspective is that AP may be beneficial for first-generation college students, particularly in schools without an existing strong college preparation program (Camera et al., 2000). When estimating an effect of a program such as AP, the effect should be estimated off of the counterfactual: what would happen in the absence of the treatment? The marginal effect of AP is the effect of being in an AP course over and above what curriculum students would be exposed to otherwise. In higher achieving schools, we might expect that the marginal effect on the quality of instruction and the content students are exposed to might be small if, in the absence of AP, students would be exposed to high quality teaching and content that was aligned with college expectations. In the absence of AP, higher performing high schools might have teachers who would be more likely to align their courses with college content and would be more likely to offer their students rigorous 4th year courses, such as 4th year mathematics. In lower and midperforming schools, however, the difference in quality between AP classes and students' counterfactual might be more significant if, in the absence of the AP course, students may be less likely to participate in more advanced coursework (e.g. fourth year mathematics) and if their teachers are less likely to push students to college standards. In addition, as discussed above, AP may have positive impacts in opening access to 4-year and particularly more selective 4-year colleges for urban and minority students.

Addressing these sets of methodological problems is daunting but not insurmountable. The simplest yet most difficult and expensive approach would be to mount a randomized experiment. Randomly assigning students to AP courses would address selection effects because it is only through random assignment that we can be assured that there are no unmeasured differences between treatment and control groups that may shape subsequent results. The difficulties of such an approach might be quite significant. It might be difficult to convince parents, students, and schools to agree to random assignment given the current climate in which AP is seen as a significant advantage in college admissions for the top students without an alternative treatment option. Most importantly, it is unclear what treatment and control conditions students should be randomized to. There has been little research that has tried to disentangle whether there are differential benefits to taking one AP course versus multiple AP courses and how those effects may differ by course content (e.g., English versus mathematics). A second question is: What is the appropriate counterfactual? Should we compare participation in AP courses to what would be offered in the school in the absence of AP (e.g., where current graduation requirements often lead to lower participation in advanced mathematics and science)? Or, should the effect of AP be estimated off of the effect of taking those same subjects and levels (e.g., English literature, calculus, or physics) in non-AP courses?

Another approach is to use methods and develop data sets that are explicitly designed to inform the current policy debate and that approach the problem from multiple dimensions. Tai and Sadler's studies of the predictors of student performance in introductory science courses, for example, provide a promising approach to getting inside the black box of AP to understand whether students' experiences in AP courses are actually different, how they are different, and whether those differences matter for college performance (Sadler & Tai, 2001; Tai et al., 2005). While their methods do not explicitly address selection effects, understanding how students' instructional experiences are associated with early college performance provides a mechanism for disentangling AP effects. A third option is for researchers to begin using methods that address selection effect into courses and that pay particular attention to general school effects. Quasi-experimental methods to address selection effects, such as propensity score modeling and instrumental variable models, do provide approaches to addressing selection effects with some benefits and limitations. There is not space in this chapter to go into detail on these methods and their general approaches. An important issue, however, is that using cross-sectional data when selection occurs on unmeasured variables, as in AP, becomes problematic. Methods like propensity score analysis, which has become an increasingly popular approach in educational research to addressing selection bias using quasi-experimental research, only effectively address selection on measured characteristics (Heckman & Hotz, 1989; Luellen, Shadish, & Clark, 2005; Rubin, 1997). Looking at changes across time is a particularly advantageous approach. In the remainder of this chapter we illustrate the importance of paying attention to issues of selection, the logic of such an approach, and the advantages of a longitudinal comparison by examining the effect of expanding AP participation on college enrollment in a large urban school system that serves predominantly African American and Latino youth.

## Estimating the Effect of Advanced Placement on Improving College Attendance in the Chicago Public Schools

Since 2004, researchers at the Consortium on Chicago School Research (CCSR) have tracked the postsecondary experiences of successive cohorts of graduating students from Chicago Public Schools (CPS) and examined the relationships among high school preparation, support, college choice, and postsecondary outcomes (Roderick et al., 2006). Drawing on an extensive database on CPS students and high schools, the project links together information on students' high school experiences including their coursework, achievement test scores, and grades with a postsecondary tracking system that identifies whether and where students enroll in college.[4]

Chicago presents an ideal setting to study the effects of expanding AP participation in an urban district. Chicago Public Schools (CPS) has been at the vanguard of expanding AP participation. In the mid-1990s, CPS raised graduation requirements to require all students to take a college preparatory curriculum.[5] Chicago Public Schools also began to promote AP and IB programs in neighborhood high schools. From 1998 to 2004, the number of CPS students taking AP courses grew from 1,746 to 3,239. Changes in the core graduation requirements applied to all students. Increases in AP offerings were not uniformly distributed across schools, reflecting differences in principals' decisions about where to invest school funds. Table 14.1 shows changes between 1998 and 2003 (the two cohorts we focus of in this illustration) in the proportion of graduating seniors who took an AP course. Schools are categorized into three groups based on the extent of their AP expansion. This dramatic expansion of AP provides an important opportunity to examine the effect of the program on students who have traditionally not participated in AP coursework (predominantly minority and low-income students in an urban school system) and in particular the effect of AP participation in shaping college enrollment. None of the 17 high schools which dramatically expanded their AP course offering during this period was a magnet (e.g., selective enrollment) high school. Did the expansion of AP, particularly in those schools that invested in this strategy, lead to more positive college enrollment for these students? A central argument in this chapter is

**TABLE 14.1**

**Seniors with at Least One AP Course, by Changes in AP Course Enrollment**

| Proportion of Graduating Seniors with at Least One AP Course | 1998 | 2003 |
|---|---|---|
| CPS total | 16.4% | 29.6% |
| High change (17 schools) | 15.6% | 40.3% |
| Mid change (14 schools) | 15.0% | 27.3% |
| Low change (15 schools) | 19.4.% | 21.7% |

*Note.* This table only includes CPS high schools that were open at both time points and were not alternative high schools. In 1998, only one of the high schools in the study was considered a magnet selective high school and that school is included as a low-change school. Seniors are students who graduated and were not enrolled in special education or alternative high schools. Charter high schools were excluded from the analysis.

that the answer to that question will differ significantly by whether researchers pay attention to student selection and school effects. To illustrate this point, we contrast how estimates from a cross-sectional analysis of the association between AP participation and college enrollment compare to estimates from an analysis that looks at changes across time in college enrollment at the school level; an approach that allows researchers to pay attention to student selection into AP courses and high school quality effects.

*Cross-Sectional Analysis: Are Students Who Participate in AP More Likely to Attend a 4-Year College and Attend More Selective Colleges?* Table 14.2 shows the results of a Hierarchical Linear Model (HLM) analysis for the odds of two college outcomes: (a) whether a student enrolled in a 4-year college within the year after graduation [log odds of college versus no college], and (b) whether a student who enrolled in a 4-year college enrolled in a selective or more selective college versus a somewhat or less selective 4-year college. Thus, the first outcome looks at the odds of enrolling in a 4-year versus a 2-year college or no college within the year after high school graduation. The second set of outcomes examines the selectivity level of 4-year colleges students enrolled in, coded by Barron's selectivity ratings, only among students who enrolled in 4-year college. The model was estimated for all CPS graduates in the 1998 and 2003 cohorts who attended a high school that existed in both time periods and that had at least one

**TABLE 14.2**

**Summary of Estimated Effects of Enrollment in One or More AP courses and Cohort on Odds of Attending a 4-Year College and Attending a Selective or More Selective College**

| Log Odds of Attending | 4-Year college | | | Selective or More Selective College Among 4-Year College Goers | | |
|---|---|---|---|---|---|---|
| | Coefficient | Odds ratio | *t*-statistic | Coefficient | Odds ratio | *t*-statistic |
| **Level 1: Student** | | | | | | |
| Intercept | −3.19 | | 23.73 | -5.30 | | 16.67 |
| Advanced Placement | .50 | 1.65 | 7.52 | .50 | 1.65 | 5.25 |
| Cohort 03 | −.38 | .68 | 6.29 | −.17 | .85 | 2.01 |
| N schools | 46 | | | 35 | | |
| N students | 17,449 | | | 15,314 | | |

AP class in either time period.[6] When estimating results by the selectivity of a college for those students who attended 4-year colleges, the sample is further restricted to schools that sent 12 or more students to a 4-year college.[7]

Advanced Placement course participation is identified from course codes on high school transcripts. For each outcome, Table 14.2 presents the estimated association between participation in one or more 11th or 12th grade AP courses and the log odds of enrollment controlling for: (a) *demographic and neighborhood characteristics,* race/ethnicity, gender, and measures of the average SES and poverty concentration of the student's census block; (b) *high school choice,* whether a student attends a high school outside his or her attendance boundary; (c) *pre-AP (10th grade) achievement* measured by a student's average reading and mathematics percentile rank on the Test of Achievement Proficiency (TAP) at 10th grade and cumulative sophomore GPA; (d) pre-AP coursetaking measured by the number of honors courses students enrolled in prior to 10th grade; and (e) *average high school characteristics* as measured by the average 10th grade TAP percentile rank, SES composition, and racial composition of the graduating class at the school (see Appendix A). The model does not include controls for non-AP course taking in the senior year such as advanced mathematics and science courses because very few CPS students in nonselective high schools took a 4th-year mathematics or science course. Thus, in Table 14.2, the effect of AP represents the effect of taking any upper level courses above the CPS graduation requirements.

Controlling for students' prior grades, test scores, and pre-AP course taking, AP participation is strongly associated with the likelihood of attending a 4-year college and attending a selective or more selective 4-year college. The odds of enrolling in a 4-year college are 1.65 higher for students who took one or more AP courses. Translating this into predicted probabilities, we estimate that taking one or more AP courses was associated with an increase of 12 percentage points in the chances of enrolling in a 4-year college controlling for students' background and pre-AP 10th grade high school performance. Participation in an AP course is similarly associated with a significant increase in the 4-year college goers that they will attend a selective or more selective college (odds ratio 1.65).

Note that the coefficient on the dummy variable (Cohort 03) that compares the adjusted odds of college enrollment between the 1998 and 2003 cohorts is negative for both college outcomes. Thus, in these high schools, the percentage of students attending 4-year colleges and selective or more selective colleges, adjusted for their students' demographic characteristics and 10th grade high school performance, declined during this period. This decline is most likely attributed to two factors. First, during this period, CPS opened several new magnet high schools that attracted the highest performing students away from neighborhood high schools. The fact that the most college-oriented students are less likely to be in the 2003 versus 1998 cohort in our sample schools suggests that these cross-sectional estimates

might underestimate the effect of AP expansion in shaping the college behavior of students within these schools since the most college-oriented students might be selecting out of these schools. Second, test scores rose substantially during this period. Higher achieving students, as reflected in the significant coefficient on TAP scores, are more likely to attend college. Thus, after accounting for the rise in test scores, the adjusted trend is negative on both college outcomes.

Comparing AP to non-AP participants within the same high school suggests that AP participation is associated with more positive college outcomes for students. This finding illustrates the central problem of cross-sectional analyses of AP participation even with substantial controls. Within these schools, students who might be more oriented toward college may be selecting into AP coursework. Thus, it is unclear the extent to which the coefficient on AP means that students who take AP are more likely to attend 4-year colleges or whether those students who are more likely to attend 4-year colleges enroll in AP. The dramatic expansion of AP in Chicago, however, and the fact that rates of expansion differed across schools provides an opportunity to address selection effects. In those schools identified as having a high change in AP participation, the percentage of seniors who had taken an AP course increased from 15.6 to fully 40.3%. In addition, the effect of AP participation did not appear to differ across cohorts; for example, when the model presented in Table 14.2 is estimated separately for the 1998 and 2003 cohorts the coefficient on AP is quite similar. If AP shapes students' likelihood of enrolling in college and is not simply identifying the students within high schools that are planning to go to college, and if the relative association between AP participation and each of the college outcomes remained similar as more students participated, then college outcomes should improve as schools increase their proportion of students taking AP courses. We would expect, moreover, that these changes would be most marked in those schools that dramatically increased their AP enrollment.

***Modeling the Effect of Changes in AP Enrollment at the School Level on College Outcomes and Adjusting for General System and School Improvements*** To be explicit, changes in AP enrollment within high schools create an important opportunity to examine how AP enrollment may shape college going patterns in a high school. Differences in the opportunity to participate in AP across time means that, among students with similar characteristics, we will observe dramatic differences in the likelihood of taking AP depending upon what year a student entered high school and what CPS high school they attended. This administrative variation lends itself to more advanced selection modeling such as propensity score modeling, because we can identify students who might have similar propensities for AP in each time period but who have different access and participation rates across time and across schools. Presenting a full propensity score analysis is beyond the scope of this chapter. For the purpose of this illustration, we present a more basic analysis by simply modeling changes in college enrollment by the extent of expansion of AP at the school level. This basic approach to testing whether increases in AP enrollment was associated with improved college outcomes is close to Dougherty and his colleagues' (2006) approach to addressing selection effects. The difference, however, is that rather than simply estimating school level rates of enrollment cross-sectionally, longitudinal analysis allows us to look at changes in student outcomes in the same high schools across time, and address differences in school effects.

While longitudinal analysis increases researchers' ability to address school effects, longitudinal estimates must also adjust for any other general improvements in the performance of students in that high school unrelated to AP participation. The problem with looking at changes across time is that the benefits of AP may be overstated if there are broader changes in the high school that might lead to improved student performance, regardless of AP. In Chicago, there are two changes that complicate the analysis. First, as noted, in the 1990s CPS changed its graduation requirements which means that the 2003 graduating class was held to more rigorous graduation requirements than the 1998 graduates. In addition, test scores were rising in CPS throughout this period and this might lead students to do better in high school. This problem is addressed in two ways. First, the model is estimated to compare changes in college enrollment rates in schools that rapidly expanded AP participation (high change schools) to the general trend in the system as estimated by trends in schools that didn't expand AP participation. Since all schools were subject to changes in graduating requirements and more general changes in high school policies, overall improvements in college participation rates should be captured by trends in college participation in low and medium change schools. Second, the model can further adjust for any general improvements in the performance of students in a high school unrelated to AP participation by controlling for differences across time in the characteristics of the student body, 10th grade test scores, and sophomore level GPA. Thus, if the schools that saw increased AP expansion were more generally improving faster than other schools because schools that were adopting AP were attracting a more highly qualified student body or had more reform oriented principals, we would expect those improvements to be reflected in the 10th grade performance in that school as measured by test scores and sophomore GPA.

For simplicity in this illustration, schools are grouped by the overall change in the percentage of their students taking AP over the two periods (see Table 14.1). Low change schools were those in which there was less than a 10 percentage point change in the percentage of graduating seniors who had taken at least one AP classes. Medium change schools were those that experienced an increase of between 11 to 18 percentage points in the percentage of graduates who had taken one or more AP courses. High

change schools ranged from 20 to a fully 43 percentage point change in the percentage of students taking at least one AP class. Estimates of the school-wide change were derived from a two-level HLM where students across time were nested within schools (see appendix B). The model controlled for the demographic characteristics and socioeconomic characteristics of the student body and the students' school performance pre-AP as measured by sophomore GPA and 10th grade achievement test scores.

Table 14.3 shows the unadjusted predicted probability of attending a 4-year college for each of the subgroups of schools and the adjusted difference in the odds of each outcome. In estimating changes in college outcomes across the two cohorts, the coefficient on the level 2 intercept represents the adjusted change from 1998 to 2003 for low change schools, the excluded group. The coefficient is negative (-.291) which suggests that students in low change schools were less likely between 1998 and 2003 to enroll in a 4-year college after adjusting for their 10th grade test scores, demographic characteristics, and early high school performance—a negative system-wide trend. The coefficients reported in Table 14.3 for medium change and high change schools represent the difference in the change in the odds between that group of schools and the low change schools between 1998 and 2003. As demonstrated in the unadjusted trends in the college going rates, both medium and low change schools experienced small declines in the percentage of their graduates attending a 4-year college in the year after graduation.

Students in high change schools were, however, more likely to enroll in a 4-year college in 2003 than in 1998. Thus, despite the opening of the magnet schools and after adjusting for prior test scores and early high school performance, schools that had dramatic increases in AP participation rates did experience improvements in the proportion of students enrolling in 4-year colleges. The size of this effect, unlike the cross-sectional analysis, is quite moderate. Despite the dramatic expansion of participation in AP in high change schools, high change schools experienced moderate increases in the unadjusted enrollment in 4-year colleges (4 percentage points) among their graduates compared to a small decline in 4-year college enrollment for medium and low change high schools. This finding holds up after adjusting for changes over time in student body composition and the performance of 10th graders. The odds ratio of 1.27 for high change schools means that, on average, the change in the odds of enrolling in a 4-year college between 1998 and 2003 was .27 times higher in high versus low change ap schools, a difference that is statistically significant.

Table 14.3 also presents the observed change and estimated differences across schools in the change in the odds of attending a selective or more selective among students who attended 4-year colleges in school. Here the results are promising but exploratory because the sample of schools had to be limited to high schools that sent enough students to 4-year colleges to model differences across time in college type. On average, high change schools experienced

**TABLE 14.3**
**Effect of One or More AP Courses on Odds of Attending a 4-Year College and Attending a Selective or More Selective College Adjusted for General System and School Improvements**

| | Observed College Outcomes | | | | | |
|---|---|---|---|---|---|---|
| | 1998 | 2003 | Unadjusted Change | Adjusted Coefficient | Adjusted odds ratio | t-ratio |
| **4-Year College (n = 46)** | | | | | | |
| Low change | 30% | 27% | −3.0% | | | |
| *(intercept Cohort 03 vs. 98)* | | | | −.291 | .747 | 7.14 |
| Medium change | 38% | 34% | −4.0% | | | |
| *(estimated difference from change in low change schools)* | | | | −.005 | 1.00 | .000 |
| High change | 31% | 35% | +4.0% | | | |
| *(estimated difference from change in low change schools)* | | | | .262 | 1.27 | 1.96 |
| **Selective or More Selective College Given 4-Year College Enrollment (n = 35)** | | | | | | |
| Low change | 35% | 39% | +4.0% | | | |
| *(intercept Cohort 03 vs. 98 )* | | | | −.049 | .95 | .49 |
| Medium change | 37% | 39% | +2.0% | | | |
| *(estimated difference from change in low change schools)* | | | | −.045 | .95 | .18 |
| High change | 33% | 43% | +10.0% | | | |
| *(estimated difference from change in low change schools)* | | | | .144 | 1.15 | .51 |

*Note.* See appendix B.

larger improvements than low- to medium change schools in the percentage of graduates attending a selective or more selective 4-year college among those graduates who attended 4-year colleges. The percentage of 4-year college goers attending a selective or more selective high school increased by 10% in high change schools versus 4% in our low change AP high schools. These differences are not statistically significant in the multivariate model. Looking only at school level changes in this reduced sample, however, results in estimates with very low power. The 95% confidence interval on the odds ratio for high change schools is .662 to 2.015. Thus, looking at school averages, while intuitively an appealing approach to addressing selection problems and school effects, is problematic because of the significant reduction of power in the model.

***Discussion*** In this section, we presented analysis from the Chicago Postsecondary Transition Project to illustrate potential approaches to and the importance of addressing selection and school effects when estimating the effects of Advanced Placement. The focus of the analysis was in an area where there has been little prior research: Is there evidence that expanding participation in AP in urban high schools is associated with increases in the likelihood of attending a 4-year college and in shaping the odds of attending a selective or more selective college? On the glass half full side, these results are promising. Even after accounting for improvements in students' entering test scores and sophomore year performance, schools in the high change AP group experi-

enced significant improvements in the percentage of students attending 4-year colleges. Results on college selectivity are less conclusive and demonstrate the difficulties of studying college attendance in urban school systems where in many high schools very few students attend 4-year colleges. At the same time, the very moderate improvements in college going in the cross-time analysis stand in stark contrast to the cross-sectional results where there is no attention to selection effects and underscores the importance of paying attention to selection effects when estimating the benefits of expanding participation in advanced coursework.

**Conclusion**

In their seminal study, Powell, Farrar, and Cohen (1985) characterized the American high school as a "Shopping Mall" in which most students took watered down, nonrigorous courses, and students chose from a variety of extracurricular and elective courses intended to meet minimum student interest and reward students for seat time. Educational historians generally agree that curriculum "diversity," watered down standards, and lack of attention to student learning that these authors identified as so pervasive in American high schools was largely the method that high schools used in the postwar period to move more and more students to graduation—essentially trading off academic standards for equal access to schooling and the credentialing it afforded (Powell et al., 1985; Ravitch, 1983). Yet, in a portent assessment, Powell and his colleagues (1985) came to the conclusion that high school reforms, such as requiring more academic courses, would not be enough to reform high schools in the absence of strong external incentives:

> educational requirements cannot substitute for real economic and social incentives for study. If many demanding and rewarding jobs awaited well-educated high school graduates, lots of students would work harder. If college and university entrance requirements were substantial, many students who now idle through the college track would step on the gas. (p. 304)

Over the ensuing two decades, the incentives that these authors referred to changed substantially. The economy stepped on the gas. Many students, predominantly higher income students and their families, began to demand more of their high school and changed their behavior. The growth of Advanced Placement was accompanied by concomitant increases in the proportion of students taking advanced coursework and more college oriented sequences (U.S. Department of Education, 2003 ). It has also been accompanied by an increasing scramble for entrance into competitive colleges and what some have called an education "arms" race (Marklein, 2006). These trends have created a significant shift in the nature of high school education for many students. While the 11th and 12th grades have traditionally been seen as a time for finishing up high school and a time of adolescent social experience with proms, dances, and entry into work, increasingly the 11th and 12th grades have become a time of ratcheting up of academic work and as a time of intense preparation for college and involvement in college search and application.

In this changed social environment AP stepped into a policy void. Even without research evidence, students received strong signals that AP would be advantageous. Many districts gave students extra GPA credits, colleges explicitly gave extra preference to AP students, and admission directors were quite explicit that they "wanted to see AP courses" on students' transcripts. It did not seem to matter to most students and their parents that there was little evidence that these courses were educationally superior, nor is there evidence that would suggest that these students did better in college because of their participation in AP. What parents and students hoped is that these courses themselves would get these students into their college of choice and into educational environments that would most likely provide higher quality college educations.

While these behaviors are not surprising, the fact that there is little strong and consistent evidence that AP participation improves college performance is a concern for policy. Advanced Placement coursework is no longer just seen as a means for advantaged, highly qualified students to look better on applications to elite universities. Advanced Placement program incentives have now been included in federal legislation, are supported by states, and are being advanced in many urban districts as a core strategy for improving college access for low-income and minority students, for increasing college preparedness, and reducing the minority achievement

gap. As we saw in this literature review, there has been little research on whether and how AP shapes college access for minority, low-income and first generation college students. There is limited and inconsistent evidence of some positive effects of scoring well on AP examinations, versus simply taking AP courses, for minority students though it is unclear what that indicator means. The good news is that researchers and funders have begun to pay attention to our limited research understanding of a program that is now affecting high numbers of American students. In this chapter, we have tried to highlight the methodological issues researchers must grapple with as they try to understand the effect of AP participation in shaping students' college performance. We have also tried to highlight critical areas where research is most needed. We end this chapter by highlighting four specific areas of research need.

*How Does AP Shape College Access Versus College Performance?* In this chapter, we identified two mechanisms by which AP participation may shape college performance for low-income and minority and urban students: (a) by increasing the likelihood of attending a 4-year college and of attending more selective 4-year colleges, and (b) by increasing students' college readiness and making it more likely that students will do better within the colleges they attend. Without jointly considering these two effects, researchers might actually underestimate and misunderstand the effect of AP participation. Researchers have begun to pay attention to the question of whether AP participation shapes college performance within colleges, but have not paid adequate attention to whether AP participation affects students' likelihood of attending different colleges and the extent to which these effects might accrue benefits.

*What Is Different about AP Courses and Do Those Differences Matter?* Given the high rates of AP participation in suburban school systems, it is quite surprising that students do not seem to benefit from participation. One hypothesis is that the students who are selecting into these courses would have done well in college regardless and that colleges were right in using AP as a mechanism to identify the most motivated students (the selection effect). Another hypothesis is that these students, in the absence of AP, might have had a high quality curriculum that would have laid the basis for positive performance regardless—thus assuming that curriculum matters but that the curriculum in AP does not differ substantially from what students get in their upper level courses in higher performing school systems. We hypothesized that this might not be true in urban school systems where differences in content and instructional foci might be quite different in AP and non-AP courses. A key area for research then is to get inside the black box of AP and non-AP coursework to understand differences in content coverage, instructional methods, and students' work effort and motivation that might explain whether AP courses differ from non-AP coursework and whether those difference matter for student performance later on.

*How Do AP Effects Differ by Students' Prior Level of Skills, the Colleges Students Choose to Attend, and their High School Contexts?* Increasing basic levels of college readiness is a high priority in urban school systems. When students leave high school with very low levels of college readiness and poor levels of qualification, they are unlikely to be able to attend 4-year colleges and be successful once there. The AP program was not, however, intended to address this problem. It was designed to serve students who already were "college-ready." In this respect, AP being advanced as a strategy for improving college readiness may be a mismatch between the most prevalent policy problem and the adopted solution. We do not have evidence, however, to evaluate this claim. Urban students are not a homogenous group. Advanced Placement may play a central role in filling in a critical gap for students who have met basic levels of college readiness but need transitional skills and content as well as the motivation and confidence to achieve. But for students who lack basic levels of college readiness, we don't know whether AP is a match to their skills needs. The critical question may not be: Can AP make up for deficits students bring to the course? The question may be: What would 11th and 12th grade curricula look like that would effectively prepare students who are at high risk of difficulty in the college transition? This third area requires that we investigate how AP effects may differ by urban students' prior levels of preparation, prior coursework, and what colleges they choose to attend. It also requires that we examine more broadly what sets of skills students will require in order to meet their needs for "college preparedness" and what alternatives to AP would look like.

*How Does AP Shape Teacher Practice and the Pre-AP curriculum?* An increasingly popular argument being advanced for AP is that the AP program will lead teachers to raise their expectations of their students and that AP courses push high schools to make changes to the pre-AP curriculum so that students are getting ready for the rigors of AP. This is an appealing argument. Yet, there is little research evidence to support this argument or to evaluate how the AP program is viewed by teachers and may shape their practice. Addressing this question would require a longitudinal analysis of schools pre- and post-AP adoption to chart these potential effects. It is an area where both qualitative and quantitative research is needed in order to test hypotheses and identify effects. Ultimately, however, the research questions we have identified are not only about identifying the effects of AP. Rather, what is needed is a broader understanding and research base that will allow policymakers and educators to grapple with the complex questions of what it will take to change the high school curriculum and teacher practice in ways that build college readiness, what it means to prepare students for college and for different kinds of colleges, and what role curriculum and instruction effects play in shaping college access and performance and urban and racial/ethnic minority students.

## Notes

1. This Department of Education Initiative "The Advanced Placement Incentive Program" is included under the No Child Left Behind Act; see http://www.ed.gov.

2. The authors attribute the positive effect of AP science courses for Hispanic students not to a differential effect of AP on Hispanics but to a specific program in Texas that was aimed at providing support for Hispanic students in the sciences and which promoted AP participation in the sciences.

3. Our discussion of selection effects focuses on student selection. There may also be a teacher selection effect. It makes sense that the "best" teachers are selected to teach more advanced courses. Thus we don't know how much of the effect of these courses simply reflect individual teacher effects that would have occurred even in the absence of a particular coursework title.

4. The CCSR database includes complete administrative records on all students including high school transcripts and achievement test scores. Socioeconomic status indicators were developed by geo-coding students' addresses and using 2000 Census block data. College participation was identified using data from the National Student Clearinghouse (NSC), a nonprofit college tracking system, and is part of a larger tracking project of the CPS (Roderick et al., 2006). The selectivity of a student's college was identified using Barron's selectivity rankings. We estimate that NSC tracking data misses up to 5% of CPS graduates who enroll in college (Roderick et al., 2006).

5. The CPS graduation requirements specify 4 years of English, a mathematics sequence of algebra, geometry, and advanced algebra/trigonometry, 3 years of laboratory science, and 3 years of social science.

6. Because this study examined within school changes in AP offerings, the analysis is restricted to students who attended a high school that existed in both time periods (n = 46) and which enrolled at least 12 students in one AP class in either time period, thus excluding very low performing high schools. Because of high rates of transfer in Chicago schools, a school may have seniors who took an AP course in another school. We use the cutoff of 12 because this is the minimum number of students that would comprise an AP class. Dropping schools that were not operating in 1998 and 2003 or that did not offer an AP course in either year excludes 13 schools and 2,543 students. This leaves 46 high schools with a total enrollment of 9,129 graduates in 1998 and 8,665 graduates in 2003 (17,794 total students).

7. In schools with very low 4-year college attendance rates, it makes it difficult to estimate change in the types of college students attend. In fully 25% of the sample high school (12 schools), which already excluded some of the lowest performing school in the city, fewer than 12 students attended a 4-year college. In these schools, small differences in college choice (e.g. a change of two students attending a selective college) will produce significant changes in the likelihood among 4-year college goers of attending selective or more selective colleges. When estimating results by the selectivity of a college, then, the study had to adjust the sample further to examine only schools in which 12 or more students attended a 4-year college.

## References

Achieve, Inc. (2005). *Rising to the challenge: Are high school graduates prepared for college and work. A study of recent high school graduates, college instructors and employers.* Washington, DC: Peter D. Hard.

ACT. (2004). *Crisis at the core: Preparing all students for college and work* (ACT Research Report Series). Iowa City, IA: Author.

ACT. (2005). *Courses count: Preparing students for postsecondary success* (ACT Policy Report). Iowa City, IA: Author.

Adelman, C. (1999). *Answers in the tool box: Academic intensity, attendance patterns, and bachelor's degree attainment.* Washington, DC: U.S. Department of Education.

Adelman, C. (2006). *The toolbox revisited: Paths to degree completion from high school through college*. Washington, DC: U.S. Department of Education.

Alexander, K. L., & Pallas, A. M. (1984). Curriculum reform and school preformance: An evaluation of new basics. *American Journal of Education, 92,* 391–420.

American Diploma Project. (2004). *Ready or not: Creating a high school diploma that counts.* Washington, DC: Achieve.

Angus, D. L., & Mirel, J.E. (1999). *The failed promise of the American high school: 1990 to 1995.* New York: Teachers College Press.

Berkner, L., Chavez, L., & Carroll, C. (1997). *Access to postsecondary education for the 1992 high school graduates* (NCES 98-105). Washington, DC: U.S. Government Printing Office.

Berkner, L., He, S., Cataldi, E. F., & Knepper, P. (2002). *Descriptive summary of 1995–96 beginning postsecondary students: Six years later.* Washington, DC: National Center for Education Statistics.

Betts, J., & Moreel, D. (1999). The determinants of undergraduate grade point average: The relative importance of family background, high school resources, and peer group effects. *Journal of Human Resources, 34*(2), 268–293.

Bishop, J. (1990) Incentives for learning: Why American high school students compare so poorly to their counterparts overseas. *Research in Labor Economics, 11,* 17–51.

Breland, H. M., & Oltman, P. K. (2001). *An analysis of advanced placement (AP) examinations in economics and comparative government and politics* (Research Report no 2001-4). New York: College Board.

Bryk, A. S., Lee, V. E., & Holland, P. B. (1993). *Catholic schools and the common good.* Cambridge, MA: Harvard University Press.

Burton, N., Whitman, N. B., Yepes-Baraya, M., Cline, F., & Myung-in Kim R. (2002). *Minority student success: The role of teachers in Advanced Placement (AP) course*s (Research Report No. 2002-08 ETS RR-02-17). New York: College Board.

Camera, W., Dorans, N. J., Morgan, R., & Myford, C. (2000). Advanced placement: Access not exclusion. *Educational Policy Analysis Archives, 8.* Retrieved from http://eepa.asu.edu/eepa/v8n40.html

Casserly, P. L. (1986). *Advanced placement revisited.* New York: College Board.

Chen, X. (2005). *First generation students in postsecondary education: A look at their college transcripts.* (NCES 2005-171). Washington, DC: National Center for Education Statistics.

College Board. (2005). *Advanced placement report to the nation.* New York: Author. Retrieved from http://www.collegeboard.com

College Board. (2006). *Frequently asked questions about the AP program.* New York: Author. Retrieved from http://www.collegeboard.com

Dougherty, C., Mellor, L., & Jian, S. (2005). *The relationship between advanced placement and college graduation.* Austin: University of Texas at Austin, The National Center for Educational Accountability.

Dougherty, C., Mellor, L., & Jian, S. (2006). *Orange juice or orange drink? Ensuring that "advanced courses" live up to their label.* Austin: University of Texas at Austin, the National Center for Educational Accountability.

Dougherty, K. J. (1996). Opportunity to learn standards: A sociological critique. *Sociology of Education. 69,* 40–65

Education Commission of the States. (2000). *Advanced placement courses and examinations—State level policies.* Denver CO: Author.

Geiser, S., & Santelices, V. (2004). *The role of advanced placement and honors courses in college admissions.* Berkeley, CA: University of California Berkeley, Center for Studies in Higher Education. Retrieved from http://ishi.lib.berkeley.edu/cshe/

Greene, J. P., & Winters, M. (2005). *Public high school graduation and college readiness. College readiness rates:1991–2002* (Education working paper 8). New York: Manhattan Institute.

Heckman, J., & Hotz, V. (1989). Choosing among alternative nonexperimental methods for estimating the impact of social programs: The case of manpower training. *Journal of American Statistical Association, 84*(408), 862–874.

Horn, L., & Carroll, C. D. (2001). *High school academic curriculum and the persistence path through college: Persistence and transfer behavior of undergraduates 3 years after entering 4-year institutions.* Washington, DC: National Center for Education Statistics.

Kilgore, S. B., & Pendleton, W. W. (1993). The organizational context of learning: Framework for understanding the acquisition of knowledge. *Sociology of Education, 66,* 63–97.

Kirsch, I., Braum, H., & Sum, A. (2007). *America's perfect storm: Three forces changing our nation's future.* Princeton, NJ: Policy Evaluation and Research Center, Policy Information Center, Educational Testing Service.

Klopfenstein, K. (2004). The advanced placement expansion of the 1990's: How did traditionally underserved students fare? *Education Policy Analysis Archives, 12*(68). Retrieved from http://eepa.asu.edu/eepa/v12n68

Klopfenstein, K., & Thomas, M. K. (2006). The link between advanced placement experience and early college success. (available at k.klopfenstein@tcu.edu)

Lee, V. E., Burkham, D.T., Chow-Hoy, T., Smerdon, B. A., & Geverdt, D. (1998). *High school curriculum structures: Effects on coursetaking and achievement in mathematics for high school graduation* (Working Paper No. 98-09). Washington, DC: U.S. Department of Education, Office of Educational Research and Improvement.

Lee, V. E., & Bryk, S. (1988). Curriculum tracking as mediating the social distribution of high school achievement. *Sociology of Education, 61,* 78–94.

Lee, V. E., & Smith, J. B. (1995). Effects of high school restructuring and size on early gains in achievement and engagement. *Sociology of Education, 68,* 241–270.

Lee, V. E., Smith, J. B., & Croninger, R. G. (1995). Another look at high school restructuring: More evidence that it improves student achievement and more insight into why (pp. 1–10). *Issues in Restructuring Schools.* Madison, WI: University of Wisconsin, Center on Organization and Restructuring of Schools.

Lee, V. E., Smith, J. B., Perry, T. E., & Smylie, M. A. (1999). *Social support, academic press, and student achievement: A View from the middle grades in Chicago.* Chicago, IL: Consortium on Chicago School Research.

Lichten, W. (2000). Whither advanced placement? *Education Policy Analysis Archives, 8*(9). Retrieved from http://eepa.asu.edu/eepa/v8n29.html

Luellen, J., Shadish, W., & Clark, M. (2005). Propensity scores: An introduction and experimental test. *Evaluation Review, 29*(6), 530–558.

Marklein, M. B. (2006, March 30). Advanced coursework: An "arms race" among students. *USA Today,* 2D.

Matthews, J. (2006, May 8). Why AP matters. *Newsweek,* 63–64.

McPartland, J. M., & Schneider, B. (1996). Opportunities to learn and student diversity: Prospects and pitfalls of a common core curriculum. *Sociology of Education, 69,* 66–81.

Morgan, R., & Ramist, L. (1998). *Advanced placement students in college: An investigation of course grades at 21 colleges.* New York: The College Board.

National Governors Association Center for Best Practices. (2005a). *Getting it done: Ten steps to a state action agenda.* Retrieved from http://www.nga.org/Files/pdf/05warnerguide.pdf

National Governors Association Center for Best Practices. (2005b). *A profile of state action to improve America's high schools.* Retrieved from www.nga.org/Files/pdf/0507edstateprofiles.pdf

National Research Council. (2002). *Learning and understanding: Improving advanced study of mathematics and science in U.S. high schools.* Committee on Programs for Advanced Study of Mathematics and Science in American High Schools. J. P. Gollub, M.W. Berthenal, J. B. Labov, & P. C. Curtis (Eds.). Washington, DC: National Academy Press.

Pallas, A. M. (1988). School climate in American high schools. *Teachers College Record, 89,* 4, 541–554.

Pallas, A. M., & Alexander, K. L. (1983). Sex differences in quantitative SAT performance: New evidence on the differential coursework hypothesis. *American Educational Research Journal, 20*(2), 165–182.

Planty, M., Bozick, R., & Ingels, S. J. (2006). *Academic pathways, preparation and performance—A descriptive overview of the transcripts form the high school graduating class of 2003-04* (NCES 2007-316). Washington, DC: U.S. Government Printing Office.

Powell, A. G. (1996). Motivating students to learn, an American dilemma. In S. H. Fuhrman & J. O'Day (Eds.), *Rewards and reform: Creating educational incentives that work* (pp. 19–59). San Francisco, CA: Jossey-Bass.

Powell, A. G., Farrar, E., & Cohen, D. K. (1985). *The shopping mall high school: Winners and losers in the educational marketplace.* Boston, MA: Houghton-Mifflin.

Purkey, S., & Smith, M. (1983). Effective schools: A review. *Elementary School Journal, 85,* 353–389.

Ravitch, D. (1983). *The troubled crusade: American education 1945–1980.* New York: Basic Books.

Roderick, M. (2006). *Closing the aspirations-attainment gap implications for high school reform: A commentary from Chicago.* New York: MDRC.

Roderick, M., Nagaoka, J., Allensworth, E., Stoker, G., Correa, M., & Coca, V. (2006). *From high school to the future: A first look at Chicago public school graduates. (College enrollment, college preparation, and graduation from four-year colleges.).* Chicago, IL: Consortium on Chicago School Research.

Rose, H., & Betts, J. (2001). *Math matters: The links between high school curriculum, college graduation, and earnings.* San Francisco, CA: Public Policy Institute of California.

Rubin, D. (1997). Estimating causal effects from large data sets using propensity scores. *Annals of Internal Medicine, 127*(8), 757–763.

Rutter, M., Maughan, B., Mortimore, P., & Outston, J. (1979). *Fifteen thousand hours: Secondary schools and their effects on children.* Cambridge, MA: Harvard University Press.

Sadler, P. M., & Tai, R. H. (2001). Success in introductory college physics: The role of high school preparation. *Science Education, 85,* 111–136.

Sebring, P. A. (1987). Consequences of differential amounts of high school coursework: Will the new graduation requirements help? *Educational Evaluation and Policy Analysis, 9,* 259–273.

Shouse, R. C. (1996). Academic press and sense of community: Conflict and congruence in American high schools. *Research in Sociology of Education and Socialization, 11,* 173–202.

Stevenson, D. L., Schiller, K. S., & Schneider, B. (1994). Sequences of opportunity for learning. *Sociology of Education, 67,* 184–198.

Tai, R. H., Sadler, R. M., & Loehr, J. F. (2005). Factors influencing success in introductory college chemistry. *Journal of Research in Science Teaching, 42*(9), 987–1012.

Turner, S. E. (2004). Going to college and finishing college: Explaining different educational outcomes. In C. M. Hoxby (Ed.), *College choices: The economics of where to go, when to go, and how to pay for it* (pp. 13–62). Chicago, IL: University of Chicago Press.

U.S. Department of Education. (2003). *The condition of education. 2003* (NCES 2003-067). Washington, DC: Author.

U.S. Department of Education, National Center for Education Statistics. (2004a). *The condition of education,* 2004 (NCES 2004-007). Washington, DC: U.S. Government Printing Office.

U.S. Department of Education, National Center for Education Statistics. (2004b). *The digest of education statistics, 2003* (NCES 2004-025). Washington, DC: U.S. Government Printing Office.

Walberg, H. J., & Shanahan, T. (1983). High school effects on individual students. *Educational Researcher, 12*(7), 4–9.

Warburton, E. C., Bugarin, R., & Nuñez, A. M. (2001). *Bridging the gap: Academic preparation and postsecondary success of first-generation students* (NCES 2001-153). Washington, DC: National Center for Education Statistics.

**APPENDIX A**
**Variables, Means, and Standard Deviations for Analysis of College Outcomes 1998 and 2003 Cohorts Combined**

| Variable | Definition | Sample for Log Odds of Enrolling In a 4-Year College | | Sample for Log Odds of Enrolling in a Selective or More Selective College Given Enrollment in a 4-Year College | |
|---|---|---|---|---|---|
| | | Mean | S.D. | Mean | S.D. |
| Advanced placement | (0,1) enrolled in one or more Advanced Placement courses junior or senior year | .23 | .42 | .40 | .49 |
| Sophomore core GPA | Unweighted Grade Point Average in core (English, Mathematics, Science, Social Studies, and Foreign Language) 9th and 10th grade | 2.31 | .91 | 2.78 | .87 |
| Average TAP scores | Average percentile rank, reading and mathematics,10th grade Test of Achievement Proficiency | 47.23 | 21.93 | 58.86 | 20.93 |
| Average TAP Scores Quadratic Effect | Square of AVGTAP to account for nonlinearity | 2712.14 | 2237.88 | 3902.34 | 2443.89 |
| No. honors courses 10th grade | Number of honors taken in core subjects 9th and 10th grade (pre-AP) | 1.54 | 2.59 | 2.63 | 3.05 |
| Cohort 03 | 0 = 1998 cohort, 1= 2003 cohort | .49 | .50 | .47 | .50 |
| Male | 0 = female, 1 = male | .40 | .49 | .37 | .48 |
| White | 1 if student's race /ethnicity is coded as on school records as White (including other ethnic) | .14 | .34 | .18 | .38 |
| Asian | 1 if race/ethnicity is Asian | .07 | .25 | .13 | .33 |
| Latino | 1 if race/ethnicity is Hispanic | .36 | .48 | .26 | .44 |
| Attend assigned high school | Whether a student attends a high school other than assigned neighborhood high school | .36 | .48 | .22 | .42 |
| Neighborhood concentration of poverty | Mean poverty in census block group (reversed coded) measured by % of families above poverty level and % of adults males employed) | .08 | .69 | −.03 | .67 |
| Neighborhood social composition | Mean social status in census block group based on % of employed persons 16 years or older who are managers or executives and mean level of education of people over 18 | −.25 | .76 | −.005 | .76 |

## APPENDIX B
## Modeling Changes in the Log Odds of Enrollment in College Outcomes by the Level of a School's Growth in AP Participation 1998 to 2003

The analysis was conducted as a two level Hierarchical Linear Model where student across time were nested within schools. At level 1, then, we obtain an estimate of the change in the log odds of each college outcome adjusted for difference across students and cohorts in the demographic characteristics of the student body and the entering test scores and sophomore level performance of students. The level 1 model is:

### Level 1: Student in School k for Both Cohorts

$$\log\left(\frac{P}{1-p}\right) = \beta_0 + \beta_1 Cohort03 + \beta_2 \text{ 10th grade TAP scores} + \beta_3 TAP^2 + \beta_4 \text{ GPA 10th grade} + \beta_5 \text{ Latino} +$$

$$\beta_6 \text{ White/other} + \beta_7 \text{ Asian} + \beta_8 \text{ Gender} + \beta_9 \text{ High school chooser}$$

The variables are described in appendix A. Notice that level 1 does not designate whether a graduate took an AP course. This is because we want to estimate the change in the odds of our college outcome by the school level change in the participation of AP students not by whether a particular student took an AP course. At level 2 we then model both the intercept (adjusted baseline 1988 log odds) and the coefficient on Cohort 03 (adjusted change in the log odds from 1998 to 2003) as a function of the racial composition of the school and the extent of change in AP participation.

### Level 2: School

$$\beta_0 = \alpha_{00} + \alpha_{01} \text{ Medium change AP school} + \alpha_{02} \text{ High change AP school} + \alpha_{03} \text{ Percent White}$$
$$+ \alpha_{04} \text{ Percent Black} + \alpha_{05} \text{ Percent Hispanic} + \alpha_{06} \text{ Percent Asian}$$
$$\beta_1 = \alpha_{10} + \alpha_{11} \text{ Medium change AP school} + \alpha_{12} \text{ High change AP school}$$
$$\beta_2 \, \beta_9 = fixed$$

In this model, low change schools are excluded. Thus $\alpha_{00}$ is the adjusted estimated outcome for students in low-change school in 1998 and $\alpha_{01}$ and $\alpha_{02}$ estimate difference between medium and low and medium and high change schools respectively in their pre-AP expansion (1998) college outcomes. $\alpha_{10}$ estimates the adjusted change from 1998 to 2003 in the log odds of each college outcome in low change school (our excluded group) and $\alpha_{11}$ and $\alpha_{12}$ estimates the difference in the change between low and medium and low and high change schools. $\alpha_{12}$ provides our program effect, it represents the extent to which schools that rapidly expanded AP increased their college outcomes over and above that experienced in low change AP school.

# Part V

## Schooling and Educational Equity

# 15

# Socioeconomic Status

## *Its Broad Sweep and Long Reach in Education*

Doris R. Entwisle, Karl L. Alexander, and Linda S. Olson

Studies of the social inequality *in* schooling or *because* of schooling began with the Coleman Report (Coleman et al., 1966), which responded to Section 402 of the Civil Rights Act of 1964. It said:

> The Commissioner shall conduct a survey and make a report to the President and the Congress…concerning the lack of availability of equal educational opportunities for individuals by reason of race, color, religion, or national origin in public educational institutions at all levels in the United States, its territories and possessions, and the District of Columbia. (p. iii)

Focusing attention on six racial and ethnic groups, the survey addressed four major questions: (a) the extent of racial and ethnic segregation in public schools; (b) whether the schools offer equal educational opportunities to these groups in terms of school characteristics like library size, teacher characteristics, and so on; (c) how much students of various groups learn as measured by standardized test performance; and (d) whether relationships exist between students' achievement and the kinds of schools they attend. Over 700 pages in length, the Report, dated July 2, 1966, analyzed over 645,504 "instruments returned."

The Report's major conclusion (p. 304) was a bombshell. It announced that the proportion of variance in students' achievement accounted for by "school facilities," like school and teacher characteristics, is "vanishingly small," but large contributions come from "student body characteristics," that is, from students' family backgrounds and related factors; that is, socioeconomic status. This conclusion, so different from what was expected, triggered a shower of reanalyses that culminated several years later in Mosteller and Moynihan's (1972) reaffirmation of the Report's major findings.

Many large studies since the Coleman Report (e.g., Jencks & Phillips, 1998; Lee, 2002) continue to show gaps in achievement favoring richer children over their poorer counterparts, or favoring Whites over Blacks. These gaps, visible even for children in the earliest grades, get larger with age. Because of this "fan spread," even a slight edge in achievement in the early years predicts greater gaps with age (Alexander, Entwisle, & Bedinger, 1994; Alexander, Entwisle, & Dauber, 2003; Consortium for Longitudinal Studies, 1983; Ensminger & Slusarcick, 1992; Entwisle & Hayduk, 1982, 1988; Harnqvist, 1977; Husén & Tuijnman, 1991; Kerckhoff, 1993; Kraus, 1973; Luster & McAdoo, 1996).

No doubt, as we will discuss in more detail later, reasons for this persistence in stratification are multiple. First, the average socioeconomic status (SES) of the school where children begin first grade is probably not much different from the average SES of the school where they finish. Second, parents' plans for their children's education are in place long before high school, and these plans—or the lack of them—tend to reflect parents' own social structural locations. Third, the basic curriculum in reading and reckoning is cumulative, especially in the early years. Starting in first grade, reading and math skills are built up step by step, and doing well one year helps children do well the next, not only because they know more to start with, but also because their doing well leads parents and teachers to hold high expectations for them. In fact, over four decades ago, noting the persistence in children's achievement levels, Bloom (1964) wrote: "All subsequent learning in the school is affected and in large part determined by what the child has learned…by the end of grade 3" (p. 110; see also Husén, 1969; Kraus, 1973). Still, no national study in the United States has yet directly linked school experience in the primary grades to educational outcomes in young adulthood, although Kerckhoff (1993) shows such long-term ties in Great Britain.

Subsequent to the Coleman Report, and perhaps because of continuing skepticism about its validity, sociologists investigated mainly the organization of high schools, how curriculum tracking relates to inequalities in test scores or years of completed education (e.g., Sewell & Hauser, 1975). The many fewer studies along the same lines in elementary schools focused on ability grouping within classrooms. Most such research in the 1970s, however, dealt with educational achievement as a stepping stone to status attainment; that is, with social stratification more generally (see Sewell & Hauser, 1975). In this tradition, family SES was essentially modeled as a unitary force, as an attribute indicating the quality of the home environment. The mechanism(s) or processes by which its effects on schooling came about, for the most part, were not on the agenda.

Except for the cross-cultural work in "child socialization" and early work in sociolinguistics, other researchers did not pay much attention to SES either. Writing about the survival of people in urban slums from a "cross-cultural perspective," however, Hess (1970) contrasted the life circumstances of the middle class to those of the "lower class" urban poor. He saw aspects of American social structure as significant in the *early* acquisition of behavior, given the extreme contrasts between the lives of the poor and the middle class (see pp. 464–465). He also recognized that middle-class parents have more facility in dealing with ideas and in verbalizing motives and that parents orient children toward roles in society based on their own class position. Moreover, in the laboratory he showed that in teaching their 4-year-old children, welfare mothers employed strategies different from those of professional mothers. Mothers on welfare describe school to their 4-year-old children in terms of the school's authority system rather than, like professional mothers, in terms of the child's problems with learning (Hess & Shipman, 1965). Also, lower status parents teach children to be passive, and their language is directive rather than oriented toward problem solving.

In these same early years, developmental sociolinguists took a different approach, trying to link cultural and regional differences between dialects to differences in children's school success. Early on, some U.S. researchers attributed cognitive deficits to dialect differences. Bernstein's (1967, 1971) group in the UK likewise pointed to "restricted" codes as characteristic of lower-class parents' speech in contrast to the "elaborated" codes characteristic of middle-class parents. Restricted codes were thought to undercut lower-class children's cognitive development (Bernstein, 1967, 1971) in much the same way as dialect differences.

The "dialect" and "code" approaches were soon and soundly rejected, however, especially in the face of Lambert and MacNamara's (1969) brilliant studies. In Montreal, Francophone (lower class) children consistently did poorly in school compared to Anglophone (middle class) children, and language differences were presumed to be at issue. However, when middle-class Anglophone children were schooled entirely in French speaking schools starting in kindergarten, by fourth grade these children did just as well in all school subjects as their counterparts who attended English-speaking schools (Lambert & Tucker, 1972). This work made it clear that the correlates of social class rather than language structure hobble poorer children's learning in school. Around the same time in the United States, research on placebo effects in education, especially the studies

directed at teachers' higher expectations for middle-class children, suggested other ways social class effects could be mediated. Rist's (1970) ethnography of a kindergarten class, for instance, describes classroom seating patterns with the poorest (worst-dressed) children seated at a table the most distant from the teacher, and the better-dressed seated successively closer.

## Thematic Perspectives

In the 1970s, research on SES and children's schooling was redirected and reformulated by Bourdieu's ideas about "cultural capital" and by Elder's use of life course models. Even when not explicitly referenced, these two advances underlie much of the current U.S. research on SES and schooling.

Pierre Bourdieu (Bourdieu & Passeron, 1977) proposed that social inequalities are maintained through parents' cultural capital. Among many other things, this concept implies that the more parents share the school's standards, the easier it is for parents to help their children do well in school. Cultural capital includes most of what is implied by "taste." It recognizes socially stratified linguistic patterns, like those Hess noted earlier, but embraces much more, such as parents' "savvy" about the workings of schools and society, children's exposure (or lack of it) to "high culture" like classical music and art, and parents' worldviews and outlook as bound up with their social class positions. Like Hess, Bourdieu emphasizes how parents' social roles lead to differences in problem solving strategies and expectations about children's social roles. His ideas underlie a series of insightful studies in sociology (see especially, Lareau, 1996, 2002).

A shift to life course studies, the other major advance, is best represented by Elder's (1974) *Children of the Great Depression*. This particular work and its extensions generally side-step issues of schooling but use social class as a fulcrum to explain not only change in a wide range of outcomes like level of schooling, but also outcomes such as worldviews, marriage timing, and the likelihood of "success" more generally. The book emphasizes how changes in family circumstances brought about by historical events (the Depression) affect human development over the long term. The core assumption of the life course perspective—that developmental processes and outcomes are constantly changing and shaped by the life trajectories children follow—has increasingly directed attention to cultural identities and SES as *bundles* of variables that impact children's life trajectories, including their schooling. Elder was among the earliest to examine the impact of social change on development over the life course and to emphasize plasticity in behaviors and attitudes throughout life (Elder, 1998).

The idea that long-term trajectories are key to understanding educational outcomes is now a dominant theme in school attainment research in the United States (Oakes, 1985; Stevenson, Schiller, & Schneider, 1994). For example, we now know that adolescents more often fail a grade if their mothers are on welfare early in the child's life (Furstenberg, Brooks-Gunn, & Morgan, 1987), or that economically disadvantaged children in first grade are more likely to drop out of school in adolescence (Alexander, Entwisle, & Kabbani, 2003; Ensminger & Slusarcick, 1992; Reynolds, 1992), or that SES in first grade can be a better predictor of status at age 22 than first-grade test scores (Entwisle, Alexander, & Olson, 2005).

The best evidence so far on the benefits of a longitudinal approach to schooling, however, comes from long-term follow-ups of randomized experiments evaluating preschools (e.g., Barnett, 1995; Darlington, Royce, Snipper, Murray, & Lazar, 1980; Lazar & Darlington, 1982) and of participants in the Panel Study of Income Dynamics (Garces, Thomas, & Currie, 2002). Compared to their control-group counterparts without preschool, low-income children who attended the Perry Preschool in the 1960s were less likely to be retained in grade or placed in special education as they progressed up through the grades. They had higher achievement scores at age 14, and their advantage continued into adulthood: they have higher literacy scores at age 19, and by age 27 more of them have high school degrees or a GED (71% versus 54%), more earned at least $2,000 per month (29% versus 7%), more owned their own homes (36% versus 13%), and more had stayed off welfare (41% versus 20%) (Schweinhart, Barnes, & Weikart, 1993). Still, exactly how preschooling or additional income early in life improves children's life chances is hard to specify. The wide range of studies that have begun to tackle these issues are the focus of the next section.

## Socioeconomic Status and the Family Context

To review the full range of influences correlated with parents' status and class standing that could affect children's schooling is a much larger task than this chapter can undertake. Our review is necessarily selective, and to start, a few words are needed about "social class."

The terms *social class* or *socioeconomic status* are used almost interchangeably in developmental research. Social class comparisons often involve "middle class," as compared with "working class/blue collar" or "disadvantaged/poverty." "Poverty" implies family income at or below the federal government's poverty line, most often judged by whether children are eligible for subsidized meals at school. The U.S. poverty rate, based solely on money income, is updated annually to reflect changes in the Consumer Price Index and is adjusted for family size. For example, the poverty threshold for a family of four was $8,414 in 1980, $17,029 in 1999 (Table 681, U.S. Census Bureau, 2001). According to the 2007 figures, it is now $20,614 for a family of four (Table 688, U.S. Census Bureau, 2007). Eligibility for subsidized meals at school is either "full" for children in families with incomes equal to 130% or less of the current poverty level, or "partial" for those with incomes from 131% to 180% of poverty level. More generally, "social class" or "SES" can be measured by even one variable,

like parent income or education level, or job prestige level, either alone or in some combination. These definitions tend to be specific to each study unless they are based entirely on poverty status (Entwisle & Astone, 1994).

A great deal of effort is currently devoted to specifying the correlates of a child's social class or SES—things other than parent income or education—that could be important for schooling. In this connection note that race/ethnicity and SES overlap: 34% of African American children and 29% of Hispanic children were in the lowest 20% of the population as the 21st century began (Lee & Burkam, 2002).

Most people in the United States have only a fuzzy recognition of status boundaries, perhaps because of the American ethic of egalitarianism. Language, however, signals social status even for persons who will not consciously admit status boundaries, and it defines the character of social relations between people as well. A listener can correctly judge the social class of a speaker from 10 to 15 seconds of recorded speech (Harms, 1961). Teachers use such cues to distinguish middle-class children from children whose families are variously labeled "blue collar," "working class," "disadvantaged," or "poor" (Williams, 1970).

Language differences are not easily ignored even when people try very hard to do so. Such judgments, at a level that may be below a teacher's awareness, *can* bias other judgments. Bikson (1974) showed, for example, that teachers "hear" sentences spoken by Anglo children to be of the same length as sentences spoken by minority group children despite the fact that the sentences spoken by the minority group children are about twice as long as those spoken by Anglo children. Such unconscious biases may lead a teacher to expect one child to learn to read easily and expect another child to have difficulty in learning to read. Such status-linked judgments also can have far-reaching consequences, especially early in a child's school career, because such judgments, even when unconscious, cause a child to sense that he or she is held in low or high esteem. Moreover, social differentiations of speech and of nonverbal cues like body language are primary and ever-present.

***Things Money Can Buy*** Probably the most researched correlate linked to social class is income. Study after study links it and other measures of family economic status to the amount of schooling children obtain (e.g. Elder, 1974; Garfinkel & McLanahan, 1986; Haveman & Wolfe, 1994; McLoyd, 1989, 1990). There is no doubt that family income can predict much of the variance in school outcomes. For example, we know that children living in poverty for at least one year are 6% less likely than those not raised in poverty to graduate from high school (Haveman & Wolfe, 1994). Moreover, the strong relationship between family income and children's school outcomes begins early. Children from advantaged homes arrive at first grade with their verbal and math skills at a higher level than those of children from disadvantaged homes (Huston, 1994; Lee & Burkam, 2002; Smith, 1972; West, Denton, & Germano-Hausken, 2000).

Books, games, computers, family trips to museums, zoos, science centers, historical sites, and sporting events, summer camp attendance and tutoring as well as the purchase of bicycles, musical instruments, and hobby equipment are often mentioned as resources that higher SES families are better able to provide (Heyns, 1978; Saxe, Guberman, & Gearhart, 1987; Schneider & Coleman, 1993; Entwisle & Alexander, 1995), and data are consistent with the coupling of economic resources and these kinds of learning materials in higher SES homes (Entwisle, Alexander, & Olson, 1997). Baltimore children on meal subsidy in 1990, for example, were less likely to have a daily newspaper, magazines, encyclopedias, or an atlas in the home, and also less likely to have a computer than those not on subsidy (38% versus 17%). During the first few grades, children on subsidy were also less likely than those not on subsidy to go to state or city parks, the zoo or science center, fairs or carnivals, or to take trips or vacations. But none of these resources by itself is essential, and in her monograph *Things Money Can't Buy*, Mayer (1997) makes a strong case that income by itself, or material goods that money can buy, is not the main factor explaining the correlation between family income and children's success in school—money does not buy either the material or psychological well-being that children require to succeed. Mayer points out that doubling low income families' income would reduce the dropout rate only from 17.3% to 16.1%, perhaps because things families purchase as their incomes increase—cars, restaurant meals—are not what help children do well. In fact, things that can help children in school, like books and family trips, cost so little that it is the family's "taste" rather than money income that governs family activities. Children's opportunities *are* unequal, but income inequality is not the primary reason. Children do better in school because they have parents who love to do math or to read and who have other *noneconomic* characteristics. Income is a good indicator of family lifestyles, consumption patterns, and cultural or social opportunities, however.

Heyns (1978) earlier saw income as the means through which families express their willingness to commit resources directly to children, and emphasized the importance of cultural activities, independent of family income, for children's schooling.

***Correlates of Income and Education*** A substantial body of research now demonstrates the many ways that class-related family resources other than money influence schooling. For example, compared to working-class parents, middle-class parents more often advocate for their children at school (Baker & Stevenson, 1986; Hess, 1970; Lareau, 1987, 1992, 2002; Useem, 1991), and seek out stronger schools and academic programs (Entwisle, Alexander, & Olson, 2006). Middle-class parents also give their children a sense of entitlement, telling them that teachers can be questioned or that school personnel will be helpful (Hess & Shipman, 1965; Lareau, 1987, 2002). Social class provides parents with unequal resources to comply with teachers' requests for parental participation. Thus, even though middle-class and working-class parents tend to have the same educational values, working-class parents are more likely to turn over responsibilities for education to teachers, while middle-class parents see education of their children as a joint enterprise with teachers. Middle-class parents also read more to their children, more often initiate contact with teachers, attend more school events, and consort with other children's parents more often than do working-class parents. In fact, the class position of parents predicts their overall level of school involvement.

Resources in neighborhoods are another dimension of family SES (see Sampson, 1992; Wilson, 1987). Research on neighborhoods and children's schooling so far relates mainly to poverty, often taking the form of qualitative studies of parenting styles that facilitate children's cognitive growth (see Brooks-Gunn, Duncan, & Aber, 1997a, 1997b). For instance, Furstenberg et al. (1999) find that some poor families in Philadelphia who are not able to move to better neighborhoods nevertheless manage to send their adolescents to parochial schools. Even among these highly disadvantaged families, parents with a little more education tend to have more positive social networks and more institutional connections in the neighborhood than those with less education. *Only about one tenth* of the variation in academic competence, even among severely disadvantaged adolescents in Philadelphia, is explained by low family income, welfare dependence, or low parent education. Furstenberg et al. (1999) say "Psychological competence [of parents] is part of the picture, but not as important as social resources that connect the child to the community" (p. 132). Like Lareau (1987), they emphasize the role of social class in promoting access to other social institutions.

Neighborhoods can also influence children through other means (Entwisle, Alexander, & Olson, 1997). With family SES taken into account, gains that Baltimore children make on achievement tests over summer periods when schools are closed are significantly higher in neighborhoods where poverty rates were lower. Controlling on students' meal subsidy level and parents' education, children's achievement gains in summers correlate positively with the percentage of families above the poverty line in their neighborhoods and inversely with schools' meal subsidy rates. In other words, when the resources provided by the school are cut off, the resources in neighborhoods can in part replace them.

Other recent research brings us back to the importance of class-related features of speech and language, reminiscent of the early work on speech as a signal of social class differences. Lareau (2002) emphasizes parents' use of reasoning rather than directives. Hart and Risley (1995) note that professional parents speak over 2,000 words per hour to their toddlers; this compares to 600 words per hour spoken by parents on welfare to their toddlers. By age 4 a typical child of professionals would have heard 45 million words compared to 13 million for welfare children. Middle-class parents are also more likely than working-class parents to start conversations or to use language in ways that provide entrée to the larger world (see Rothstein, 2004).

Language relates to SES differences in childrearing patterns as well. Working- class toddlers get two reprimands for every expression of encouragement by parents, while toddlers of professionals get an average of six encouragements per reprimand (Hart & Risley, 1995). Similarly, in middle school, parents' use of encouragement and praise predicts favorable track placements (Dornbusch & Glasglow, 1995).

Some of the earlier research is especially revealing about social class differences in how parents teach problem solving, such things as generating and testing hypotheses, willingness to defer solutions, ability to verbalize crucial elements in a problem, and general tolerance of uncertainty. In several studies of verbal interaction between mothers and their children as mothers attempt to guide the children in solving problems, compared to lower-class mothers, middle-class mothers take more actions that will help their children to become successful problem solvers (Bee, Van Egeren, Streissguth, Nyman, & Leckie,1969; Hess & Shipman, 1965; Rackstraw & Robinson, 1967). Bee et al. note that the middle-class mother allows her child to work at his or her own pace, offering general structuring suggestions on how to search for a problem's solution and telling the child what he or she is doing that is *correct*. The lower-class mother, by contrast, makes more controlling and disapproving comments, and makes more highly specific suggestions that do not emphasize basic problem-solving strategies. In trying to solve problems, positive instances are more helpful than negative instances. When the middle-class mother emphasizes what is correct, she effectively blocks off a number of alternatives whose exploration would be fruitless. Hess and Shipman (1965) also note that lower-class mothers do not permit their children enough time to formulate alternative hypotheses. Middle-class mothers show more tentativeness and see more alternatives to explain behavior. Middle-class mothers are also more receptive and responsive to their children's questions, tend to evade questions less, and to give more accurate and more informative answers (Rackstraw & Robinson, 1967). Middle-class speakers are also more apt to use mitigating forms: "You might want to…," "I would do…," "Perhaps we should…," rather than "Do this" or "Don't do that."

The imprint of status and class standing runs much deeper than parents knowing the ropes of the local school system or their use of language, however. Parents' expectations for their children, which are derived from their own worldviews, correlate strongly with SES and predict the specific actions taken to help children learn. Compared to parents with lower expectations, those who expect their first graders to get high marks read to their children more, see the child's school records more often, ensure that their children borrow books from the library in summer, and take their children on more summer trips (see Entwisle, Alexander, & Olson, 1997, 2000). All these examples differ across social class boundaries (see Lareau, 2002). Moreover, parents who

have high expectations encourage their children to have high expectations for themselves (Entwisle & Hayduk, 1982), and children with higher expectations take part more often in class, by raising their hands, for example (Entwisle & Webster, 1972). Parents' expectations are an important source of consistency in children's social contexts. For example, parents' expectations for how far their children will go in school persist: at ages 6 and 13, $r = .49$; at ages 6 and 16, $r = .44$ (Entwisle et al., 1997).

Most of the research covered so far pertains to the home context and early schooling. A natural question is the extent to which SES resources early in life predict outcomes over the long term. The next section reviews some evidence on this question. Much of the evidence comes from the Beginning School Study (BSS), one of the first longitudinal studies to examine the long-term impact of early school experiences.

## The Beginning School Study

Initiated in 1982, the Beginning School Study (BSS) followed 790 students randomly selected from Baltimore public schools, from the beginning of first grade (age 6) up to the present (age 28). Two-thirds of these students were on meal subsidy when their formal schooling began (see Entwisle, Alexander, & Olson, 1997 for a fuller description of the BSS sample and study design).

***Timing of SES Resources*** To estimate the long-term impact of socioeconomic status (SES) early in life on children's ultimate school attainment, information on the BSS panel collected at age 6 (beginning first grade) was used to forecast educational attainment at age 22 for a randomly selected panel of Baltimore students (Entwisle, Alexander, & Olson, 2005). Their model can be represented by one equation (see Figure 15.1 with SES taken as a measure of the social resources available to children as they start first grade). (In this example, SES is a composite of both parents' education level, both parents' occupational status, plus the child's eligibility for meal subsidy.) Other independent predictors in the equation are race, gender, parent psychological support, neighborhood poverty level, the child's temperament/disposition, and two indicators of the child's cognitive skills (a standardized test score composite and a composite of first grade marks in reading and math, see Figure 15.1).[1] This equation states that children's educational attainment by age 22 varies directly in response to the eight variables measured at age 6: race, gender, family SES, neighborhood, parents' psychological support, temperament/disposition, and cognitive skills (Duncan, Brooks-Gunn, Yeung, & Smith, 1998; Entwisle et al., 1997; Furstenberg, Cook, Eccles, Elder, & Sameroff, 1999; Hart, Atkins, & Fegley, 2003; Sampson, Morehoff, & Gannon-Rowley, 2002; Wilson, 1996).

Many attainment studies use measures obtained in adolescence to predict educational attainment in adulthood (see e.g., Haveman & Wolfe, 1994), but in the age

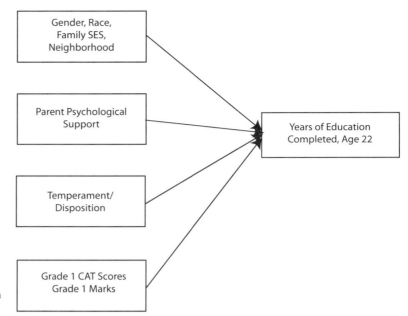

**Figure 15.1** Conceptual model of grade 1 predictors of years of education completed at age 22.

6 model described above, effects of predictors measured at age 6 are assessed 16 years later. Assessing the effect of students' individual social resources *before they could have been much affected by the experience of schooling* identifies SES resources present when schooling starts and distinguishes these resources from those produced by the school. Estimating separate effects for SES and parents' psychological support before school begins has the advantage of separating the psychological capital of parents as a resource from their SES as a resource (Entwisle & Alexander, 1996). (Note that the influence of SES is measured *net* of the influence of other variables in the equation, such as test scores.)

When children start first grade their SES, race, gender, and neighborhood are predetermined. Parents' initial expectations for their children's school performance crystallize either prior to or concurrent with entry into first grade (see Entwisle et al., 1997; Entwisle & Hayduk, 1982; Finn & Cox, 1992). Demographics and family resources are known to influence children's development prior to first grade and to predict children's earliest standardized test scores and marks. Children's temperament/disposition also can predict their cognitive status by first grade (see Entwisle et al., 2005).

For the panel of Baltimore students, the model estimates the contribution of students' SES *when they start school* to their educational attainment and level of schooling 16 years later (age 22), controlling for sex, race, and other predictors in the equation. By age 22, about half of the panel had either dropped out or obtained a high school degree, and the rest had gone on to postsecondary schooling, either subbaccalaureate or 4-year college. By age 22, then, we have a complete picture of the paths children took upon finishing compulsory education and then over the years immediately after leaving high school.

The model in Figure 15.1, estimated by OLS, explains 42% of the variance in educational attainment by age 22. All the age 6 variables (except test scores) *directly* predict years of school completed.

Table 15.1 shows that by age 22, female students have higher educational attainment than their male peers. Also, African Americans are doing better than Whites, and living in a poor neighborhood undercuts schooling (standardized coefficient of -.11). The latter effect is comparable in size to that of every other predictor except family SES. Family SES has by far the largest direct path (standardized coefficient of .40), and so stands out as the most powerful predictor of the amount of education 6-year-olds in this panel attained by age 22.

***Comparison with a High School Model*** The next question is whether the size of the SES coefficient estimated with

**TABLE 15.1**
**OLS Regression Model to Explain Effects of Demographic, Parental, and Personal Predictors on Educational Attainment at Age 22**

|  | Years of Education at Age 22 | | | |
|---|---|---|---|---|
| Gender | .10* | .10* | .10* | .10* |
| Race (African American, White) | .06+ | .08* | .09* | .10* |
| Family SES Index | .42* | .42* | .41* | .40* |
| Poor/Non-Poor Neighborhood | −.11* | −.11* | −.12* | −.11* |
| Parent Psychological Support Index | .21* | .14* | .12* | .11* |
| Temperament/Disposition |  | .17* | .15* | .13* |
| Composite CAT Score, Spring 1983 |  |  | .06 | .02 |
| Composite Marks, End Grade 1 |  |  |  | .09+ |
| R² | .39 | .42 | .42 | .42 |

*Note.* Standardized Regression Coefficients, N = 521. Estimates are weighted to account for attrition in the sample between grade 1 and age 22 (sample attrition is 20%).
+ $p \le .10$. * $p \le .05$.

data secured at age 6 is the same as the size of a coefficient estimated with data secured later in life. A highly similar study of high school sophomores' attainment 15 years later (Alexander & Eckland, 1975) shows a much smaller direct effect of SES (.14) and their model explains only a little more variance in attainment (44% versus 42%) than the first-grade model does. One difference between the two models is that Alexander and Eckland include several more predictors, variables like class rank and curricular choices in high school, which can be seen as intermediate outcomes. In fact, much of the influence of SES in the Alexander and Eckland model flows *through* variables like class rank and curricular choices, showing that school processes are an important link between family SES level and ultimate educational attainment. The importance of this comparison of the two models is that we see in the second model how SES is converted into other resources as children go though school. In the high school model, SES even has a *smaller direct path* to educational attainment than do the school-related variables like educational expectations or curriculum.

The difference in the size of direct effect of SES (.40 versus .14), depending on whether data are secured at age 6 or in adolescence, bears directly on questions of model specification raised by Haveman and Wolfe (1994) and Alexander and Cook (1982). The direct path coefficient for SES in the high school model is far smaller than the *total* effect of SES, which is the sum of the *direct path and all the indirect paths*, and these examples suggest why. Much of the influence of SES is converted to other school outcomes like rank in class or curricular choices as children progress through school.

Many different kinds of studies now suggest that supplementing SES resources early in life, even before preschool, is very effective for boosting attainment (e.g., Barnett, 1995; Gomby, Larner, Stevenson, Lewit, & Behrman, 1995). We see why: SES resources present early in life are continuously being converted into other resources, like class standing or achievement, and probably many other things not included in the high school model, perhaps problem-solving strategies, self-confidence, not being held back, and so on.

The two models presented above that compare the direct impact of SES measured at age 6 to its direct impact when measured in high school make a strong case for supplementing children's SES resources as early in life as possible. Students' achievement in high school necessarily reflects SES influence on earlier outcomes.

In what has been said up to here, SES has been taken to signify a measure of *each child's* home context, parents' SES assets, and its correlates. Children's other main social context is the school, and schools *as institutions* respond to the SES of their individual students. Curriculum tracks or "ability" groups, for example, often turn out to be mainly "SES groups." Likewise, a curriculum track labeled "college preparatory" in a low SES school may have little in common with a track by the same name in a high SES school. The next section looks into how students' SES relates to

school organization, how schools are organized relative to the average SES of their student bodies.

## SES and Within School Tracks

Following the Coleman Report, sociologists and others concerned with equity in schooling turned, as we said, mainly to studies of curriculum tracking and course taking. The evidence is clear that poor children are disproportionately placed in low ability groups in elementary schools and in non-college-bound tracks in high schools, and further that these placements in lower tracks and ability groups lead to lower achievement and negative attitudes and behaviors (Kao & Thompson, 2003). Moreover, even within tracks, low-income students disproportionately take low level and remedial classes related to low-skill jobs. While tracking practices in high school became less standardized toward the end of the 20th century (Lucas, 1999), they are still much in evidence in the United States.

The large majority of U.S. middle schools also track students (Braddock, 1990), but research on tracking in middle schools is less extensive than that in high schools (e.g., Eccles, Midgley, & Adler, 1984; Eccles, Midgley, Wigfield, et al., 1993; Feldman & Elliott, 1990; Reynolds, 1992). Still, in middle school many students are first aware of formal tracking, a key organizational change for them (Braddock, Wu, & McPartland, 1988; Hoffer, 1992, 1994). Middle school tracks generally have effects like those attributed to high school tracks, in that students in low tracks tend to learn less than those in high tracks (Catsambis, 1992; Fulgini, Eccles, & Barber, 1995; Hallinan, 1992).[2] Whether middle school tracking affects *ultimate* outcomes is not altogether clear except that taking algebra and (usually) a foreign language in middle school are prerequisites for most college tracks in high school. Many low-income or minority group parents, who tend not to have gone to college themselves, are unaware of this critical fork in the road. Often, schools are reluctant to inform parents and students about track placements and their potential effects (Eccles & Harold, 1996). As a consequence then, often low SES parents are not informed or misinformed about tracking.

Despite the generally held view that the United States possesses a more "open" system than does Great Britain, the similarities between middle school choices in the United States and the British 11+ exams is plain (Entwisle, Alexander, & Olson, 2006). All in all, tracking and course taking patterns work to the overall disadvantage of low-income students in high school and middle school. What is not generally recognized, however, is that practices in elementary school not generally seen as "tracking" *are* probably much more harmful for low-income or minority students, and they feed into the middle school tracks. These practices include retention, special education, and ability grouping within classrooms, especially in first grade. Each of these administrative decisions effectively creates a "track" and the evidence is overwhelming that students who are retained,

Doris R. Entwisle, Karl L. Alexander, and Linda S. Olson

placed in special education, or in low ability groups are of lower SES than children not so placed.

Research *directly* on curriculum tracking, grade-school retention, and special education placement from a school organizational perspective is rare. For this reason, we will draw heavily on the Baltimore Beginning School Study (BSS) in what follows. Much of the information on retention and special education tracking presented here is from Entwisle, Alexander, and Olson (1997) and Alexander, Entwisle, and Dauber (2003).

For the most part, elementary schools have a simple flat plan of organization—a string of self-contained classrooms with individual teachers—so their structure has prompted relatively little sociological research. Nevertheless, because elementary schools reflect the characteristics of the neighborhoods in which they are located, the BSS showed that primary school students were tracked *between* schools by SES (Dauber, Alexander, & Entwisle, 1993; Entwisle & Alexander, 1993). Then, first grade children were held back or placed in special education. Thus, tracks were created *within* schools, but these groupings were not perceived as tracks. Nevertheless, these tracks presented different and lesser curricula, and poor or disadvantaged children were much more likely to occupy these tracks than were better-off children.

***Grade Retention*** When the Beginning School Study started, there were only rough estimates of the number of children held back (retained) each year in the United States because there were no national data on grade retention until the early 1990s. However, using Census data, Hauser and his colleagues (Hauser, 2001; Hauser, Pager, & Simmons, 2000; Heubert & Hauser, 1999) identified children who are a year or more older than was typical for their grade in school and then focus on patterns of overage enrollments. Combining complex information from several sources, Hauser (2001, p. 160) estimated a cumulative retention rate through middle school (ages 12–14) of about 17 to 18% for children who began school in the late 1980s. For certain children, mainly those of low SES, however, rates were much higher. To give an example, Bianchi (1984), using Census data, estimated retention rates for students in poverty households, where the head is a high school dropout, at about 50% for boys and 40% for girls. Likewise, among National Educational Longitudinal Study (NELS88; Smith-Maddox, 1999) eighth graders in the lowest SES quartile, over 31% were held back versus about 8% of children in the highest quartile (National Center for Education Statistics, 1990). Similarly, by the sixth year of the BSS, among low SES students, 59% of the boys and 43% of the girls had been retained at least once.

Early studies of grade retention also suggested that rates vary inversely with age, with first graders showing the highest rates. For 15 states for which data were available, first grade retention averages over 11%, and retentions are around 7% per year for grades 2 through 6 (Shepard & Smith, 1989). Grade specific rates in the 7 to 8% range for elementary children are consistent with cumulative retention rates on the order of 50% in many areas of the country. Beginning School Study data reflected the same patterns: over 17% of BSS first-graders were held back (23% of low SES students), a rate more than twice that for any later year (see also Fine, 1991).

The causes and consequences of retention are not well understood, mainly because most research on retention ignores children's preretention status even though students who are retained have many problems *before* retention.[3] About 84% of BSS first-graders who were retained were on meal subsidy, compared to 63% of those who were not retained. Also, compared to never-retained, the average reading comprehension scores of first-graders who would be retained later that year were about one standard deviation lower than those of other children when they began first grade. Retainees were more likely than the never retained to come from a one-parent than a two-parent home (58% versus 39%) and their mothers were less likely to have completed high school. Retainees were also absent about 50% more often, less popular with peers, less involved in classroom activity, and less well-behaved in class. The scheduling of BSS children's retentions matched the severity of their difficulties: those with the lowest California Achievement Test scores at the beginning of first grade were held back that year, those with the next lowest scores were held back in their second year, and so on (Alexander et al., 1994; see also Reynolds, 1992; Shepard & Smith, 1989). In the BSS panel, by the end of third grade, 43% of those on subsidy had been retained compared with only 17% of students not on subsidy.

From the perspective of school organization, retention effectively creates a separate school track for multiple reasons and has unintended consequences for children. First, retained children are separated from their age mates, moved away from their peer group. Second, retained children are "off-time" in the rigidly age-graded system of the elementary school, usually permanently. Also, compared to their classmates, grade repeaters are taller, heavier, and have fewer deciduous teeth. For example, the average BSS girl in fourth grade who had been retained once, was 7 pounds heavier (about 10%) than her "on-time" classmates. Additionally, by taking the same grade twice, retained children are exposed to a less advanced curriculum than their agemates. Because they are often assigned to the lowest reading group before being retained, they are doubly disadvantaged in reading (Alexander, Entwisle, & Legters, 1998). Lastly, retained children often have incomplete school records because they miss testing sessions and move more often. Of four California Achievement Tests routinely involving BSS children in the first 2 years of school, 44% of retainees missed at least one test compared to only 9% of the other children. Missing tests creates gaps in school records that put retained students at a further disadvantage, because these gaps in themselves are a kind of "labeling."

It is also important to point out that higher retention rates allow schools to look better on standardized tests because the least capable students (those who are retained) take easier tests than their age-mates who are promoted. First grade repeaters who would take Grade 2 level tests if they were on time, take Grade 1 achievement tests in their second year of school after they have been retained, for instance. Schools also have a better looking profile on standardized tests when retained students miss tests or their tests are "lost," because then proportionately more low scores are left out of the school average.

To summarize, the Beginning School Study showed that the largest percentage of children who will ever be retained are retained in their first and second years of school. Grade retention effectively placed children in a curriculum track that slowed down their academic development. With no national data on retention at the time, neither the public nor policy analysts appreciated how prevalent early retention was or how misleading evaluations of its effects were, especially for low income students.

***Special Education Placement*** Special education placement is less common than retention but still far from rare (Heller, 1982; Karweit, 1992; Leinhardt & Pallay, 1982). Following the passage of Public Law 94-142 in 1975, the proportion of children in federally funded special education programs jumped from about 8% of public school students to just under 12% by 1992 to 1993 (U.S. Department of Education 1995, p. 346). In 2003 to 2004, the rate was almost 14%, and children with mild learning handicaps showed the biggest jump between 1976 to 1977 and 2001 to 2002. The proportion of learning disabled rose from 1.8% to 6.0% of the total enrollment in public schools (U.S. Department of Education, 2006).

Children with special learning needs can be placed in separate classes, but the majority are now mainstreamed for all but 1 or 2 hours a day. Even so, special education is a "track" that is obvious to students and to teachers, and the consequences of being placed in special education can be almost as serious as the consequences of retention. Also, most children placed in special education tend to remain there for their school careers (Edgar, Heggelund, & Fisher, 1988; Walker et al., 1988).

From the Beginning School Study, we learned that special education placement was often the next step taken if retention is not effective in getting children up to satisfactory performance levels at the start of elementary school. Of the 42 first-grade retainees who remained in Baltimore schools for at least 8 years, 38 were also in special education for that entire period (Alexander et al., 1994).

***Multiple Tracks*** Analysts generally treat retention, special education, and ability-grouping as three isolated events, but ignoring children's placement in multiple tracks could easily disguise or misrepresent the effects of placements. For a child to be in a low reading group, and then retained, is a different experience from being placed only in a low reading group.

The large majority of BSS students (69%) had no low placements in first grade (Entwisle & Alexander, 1993; Alexander & Entwisle, 1996b); however, this percentage varied by SES—39% of low SES students had at least one low placement compared with 29% of higher SES students. Overall, 22% were in the lowest reading group, 16% were held back at year's end, and 13% received special education services. The other side of the coin is that over half (53%) of higher SES students were in the highest reading group compared with only a third (32%) of the low SES students. Also, 21% of low SES students were retained in first grade compared with only 6% of the higher SES group. Of those who experienced any of these placements, over half (60%) had one low placement, but 48% of low SES students compared with only 18% of higher SES students had multiple low placements.

The multiple low placements were in all possible combinations. For example, almost three fourths of children in low first grade reading groups were eventually held back, half of them in first grade. By the end of the sixth grade, 35% of those who had been in low first grade reading groups were retained a second time. In comparison, *none* of the children in high reading groups repeated first grade and 88% did not repeat any grade. Children in low groups in first grade were also more likely than other children to receive special education services later: more than half the children in low reading groups in first grade were receiving special education services in sixth grade, compared to only 6% of children in the high group in first grade (Alexander & Entwisle, 1996b).

Change in reading group level from one grade to the next could signal lack of reliability in initial assignments, because BSS children in both the lowest and highest first grade reading groups were found at *all* second grade reading levels. Just 45% of BSS children remained in the same level of reading group in first and second grade, with 34% predicted to stay in the same group by chance alone. Movement between years is generally downward, however. While 87% of BSS first-graders were in high or middle groups, only 69% of those same children were in high or middle groups in second grade. The lowest group enlarged the most—from 13% to 31%. The downward trend in group placement between years is partly a consequence of the high rate of retention in first grade. That is, when the least successful students are retained, the "low" group in second grade must be filled from the ranks of the children left to choose from (those who are promoted). In this way, a high retention rate has implications for children *not* retained by consigning more of them to lower reading groups in the following years. Altogether, 37% of BSS children were in a low reading group in year one or year two, or both.

Prior to BSS, only a few studies in the United States followed a single cohort of children from first grade up through the later grades (e.g., Ensminger & Slusarcick, 1992; Pedersen, Faucher, & Eaton, 1978; Stroup & Robins, 1972), but all find evidence of long-term consequences of early tracking. *Other things equal*, BSS children's first grade reading group rank predicted their standardized achievement scores in reading and math at least up to the fourth grade (see Pallas, Entwisle, Alexander, & Stluka, 1994). Children's reading group rank had larger effects on their test scores than their reading marks did, and some rank effects on scores also were direct, that is, independent of marks (see Entwisle et al., 1997, p. 90).

The tracks within schools created by retention and special education are especially problematic because these "tracks" are far below the level of public consciousness. The majority of retention and special education assignments are made early in children's school careers, actually in the first 2 years, when their full significance may not be appreciated. By the end of second grade, for example, roughly one quarter (27%) of BSS children had either been held back or placed in special education. The evidence is now overwhelming that retention is a significant correlate of high school dropout (see e.g., Allensworth & Nagoka, chapter 20 this volume; Cairns, Cairns, & Neckerworth, 1989; Ensminger & Slusarcick 1992; Roderick, 1994; Rumberger, 2001).

***School Calendars[4]*** Long summer vacations may exacerbate early tracking related to children's socioeconomic status. Results from the Beginning School Study (BSS) also examined growth in children's achievement during the academic year and summer months. Scores that come from tests given at the start and end of the *academic* year (September to June) show that children's annual gains in test scores have two components. Between September and June, children who come from low SES homes gain as much on standardized tests as do children from higher SES homes (Entwisle et al., 1997; see Table 3.1). More specifically, in *winters* over the first 5 years of school, BSS children from low SES homes gained a total of 193 points on CAT tests of verbal comprehension while those from higher SES homes gained about the same amount—191 points. (In math, gains are 186 points for each SES subsample, respectively, over the same five winter periods.) During winter periods when school was in session the low SES and higher SES children thus gained the same amounts on standardized tests. In *summers*, by contrast, the *total* gains in verbal comprehension over the same 5-year period are only 1 point for the low SES but 47 points for the higher SES children (summer math gains total 8 points for low SES and 25 points for higher SES children, respectively). During summers when school is closed, higher SES youth continue to gain in reading and in math but lower SES children do not.

The idea that SES predicts children's learning mainly over the summer when school is closed is not new and has been demonstrated in nationally representative data as well as in localized samples (e.g., see Borman & Boulay, 2004; Downey, von Hippel, & Broh, 2004; Entwisle & Alexander, 1992, 1994; Entwisle, Alexander, & Olson, 1997; Cooper, Borman, & Fairchild, chapter 21 this volume; Heyns, 1978; Murnane, 1975). The "summer learning" data show that SES resources have episodic effects. Thus, not only the nature of SES resources but the presence of *other* resources

can make a difference in evaluating the impact of SES resources. When school is in session, resources children need for learning are available to everyone, so all children gain. In the summer, however, without the benefit of school resources, low SES students stop gaining. The resources available to them from their homes and neighborhoods are not sufficient to promote their continued growth, while high SES students who have plentiful resources at home continue to gain. This information is important for social and educational policy because it shows that resources from *other* entities like the school can replace resources lacking in the family, at least over the elementary years and earlier, judging from the Perry Preschool and other randomized experiments on preschool. It may be important to work out the boundary conditions on this substitutability. The comparison of the grade 1 and high school models in the last section would argue that high school is a much less optimum time to supplement SES resources than are the preschool years.

## SES Differences Between Schools

Family SES, as we have just seen, predicts track placement and functioning within schools. It also predicts differences between schools. A school's SES—the collective SES of the student body—has as much impact on achievement growth of high school students as does their family SES (Rumberger & Palardy, 2005). We suspect that SES tracking between schools far surpasses within-school tracking as a force affecting schooling.

Elementary schools appear to have the same general structure because the topics covered in their curricula look much the same across grades and across schools. With the exception of grouping within classes, as we have noted, society perceives them as "untracked"—one program fits all. However, the BSS provided considerable evidence showing SES differences between public schools in Baltimore. The elementary schools there and elsewhere (see Kahlenberg, 2006), differ strongly by the average family SES level of their student bodies.

The small size of elementary schools in Baltimore and elsewhere, plus curriculum focused on basic academic skills, helps support the myth that not until middle school does "tracking" begin. Quite the opposite is true, however. In Baltimore, the variation in SES level *between* elementary schools actually outstripped that between secondary schools. In 1990 to 1991, for example, the proportion of Baltimore children participating in the subsidized meal program varied across *all* elementary schools on average from 5% to 100%, but varied only from 8% to 65% across high schools (Baltimore City Public Schools, 1991). This greater SES variation across elementary schools is mainly a consequence of their small catchment areas which differ sharply by family income level. Neighborhoods differ in terms of the SES of the families that inhabit them and therefore the elementary schools within these neighborhoods also differ by SES.

The correspondence between average SES levels of neighborhoods and schools in Baltimore can be seen in data on the average number of students on meal subsidy in a school and measures of neighborhood SES. The rank order correlations in first grade between meal subsidy level of students across schools and neighborhood indicators are as follows: average school subsidy level correlates .86 with median household income of the neighborhood, .66 with percentage of workers in the neighborhood with high status jobs, and .83 with neighborhood poverty level.

BSS students who lived in the better-off neighborhoods began school with higher test scores than students who lived in the poorer neighborhoods. Of the 20 schools randomly selected to participate in the BSS, the school with the fewest (11%) students on meal subsidy enrolled children whose average California Achievement Test score in reading comprehension at the beginning of first grade was 302 and average math concepts score was 316. However, in the school with most students (90%) on meal subsidy, reading scores averaged 265 (37 points lower, about 0.9 SD's) and math scores averaged 273 (43 points lower, about 1.3 SD's). The rank-order correlations between the percentage of first grade students on meal subsidy in the 20 BSS schools and students' average reading and math California Achievement Test scores when they began first grade are .65 in reading and .72 in math.

The achievement test differences across BSS schools when children began first grade enlarged as they progressed up through the grades. By the end of year 5, the difference in standardized test scores between children in the highest and lowest SES schools was 66 points in reading and 48 points in math.

The figures for *all* Baltimore City elementary schools show these same patterns during the period of the Beginning School Study (see Baltimore City Public Schools, 1988). In schools with 50% or fewer students on meal subsidy, children were reading at grade level 3.19 by the end of Grade 2 and at over one year above grade level (7.15) by the end of Grade 5. In schools where 89% or more of students were on subsidy, children were reading at half a year below grade level at the end of Grade 2, and slightly below grade level at the end of grade 5. The gap in reading achievement between the highest and lowest SES schools in Baltimore increased between the end of Grade 2 and Grade 5 from about two-thirds of a grade level to one and one-third grade levels 3 years later.

Other studies also reveal strong patterns of SES stratification across elementary schools. One of the earliest was the Coleman Report (1966) based on a nationwide sample of over 400,000 children, which documented greater school-to-school variability in standardized test scores for children in their elementary years (grades 1, 3, 6) than for children in their secondary years (grades 9 and 12). In fact, variation across schools in reading scores is almost 60% greater at grade 3 than at Grade 12 and in math over 100% greater. Similar stratification by SES characterizes schools in Britain where, as here, primary schools are also much smaller

than secondary schools. Teachers' salaries, the proportion of oversize classes, expenditures for fuel and the like, all vary *more* across primary schools than do the equivalent indices across secondary schools (Central Advisory Council for Education, 1967, pp. 618–619).

***Socioeconomic Stratification and School Contexts*** That students' track placement in high school is not simply a consequence of their prior achievement or ability is well-known (Alexander, Cook, & McDill, 1978; Heyns, 1978; Jencks et al., 1972). The perceived single curriculum of the elementary school, however, has tended to conceal tracking between elementary schools. This variation in SES of the student body, not surprisingly, is associated with differences in how elementary schools function, as most parents know. In fact, parents of BSS children used many strategies to get their children into "high SES" schools. In the poorest areas especially, they turned to private (mainly parochial) schools. Similar findings were reported by Furstenberg and colleagues (1999) in Philadelphia. To place children into better schools, some parents resorted to stating that a child was living at one address (perhaps that of an aunt) while actually living at another.

From the Beginning School Study, we learned that this parental concern was justified because not only do the marks teachers give, but also teachers' ratings of children's noncognitive traits, correspond to the SES level of the student body. When first-grade teachers rated BSS students' temperament/disposition, in the school where only 11% of children were on meal subsidy, they rated pupils about one standard deviation higher than did teachers in the school where 90% of children were on subsidy. The rank-order correlation (inverse) between school meal subsidy level and teachers' average ratings of students' temperament/disposition is .71. Moreover, in schools with high percentages of children on subsidy, some children were rated "off the scale," that is, three SDs below their school's mean on temperament/disposition. No student was rated off the scale in the more affluent schools.

The picture involving SES and school functioning becomes more distinct the longer children are in school. Less than half (47%) of BSS children who started first grade in a school where more than 90% of children were on subsidy had reached fifth grade 5 years later because 53% had either been retained or designated to receive special education services. By contrast, 77% of those who started first grade in schools where 50% or less of the children were on subsidy were in fifth grade 5 years later.

Clearly, *where* children started elementary school effectively placed them on a track. Baltimore School Study children of high SES had relatively high test scores as they entered first grade and were grouped together. Children of low SES levels had relatively lower test scores in first grade, and they were grouped together. The same schools then reported the highest and lowest scores at the end of elementary school. For BSS children, correlations are .41 and .55 respectively, between initial California Achievement

Test scores in reading and math in the fall of first grade and scores on higher levels of the same tests at the end of elementary school.

The stratified outcomes *later* in the educational pipeline also can be forecast surprisingly well from the stratification patterns visible in elementary school (see also Alexander & Entwisle, 1996b; Kerckhoff, 1993). Baltimore School Study children with the highest test scores at the end of elementary school were more likely to take algebra and a foreign language in middle school, and so to get the needed prerequisites to move into college preparatory programs in high school. Those with low scores at the end of elementary school were not found in these courses (Dauber, Alexander, & Entwisle, 1996). For example, 62% of BSS children placed in the lowest reading group in one first grade classroom took "low level" English in sixth grade. Likewise, 51% of the children retained in first grade are in "low math" in sixth grade.

### Socioeconomic Stratification and School Transitions
We discussed earlier the BSS teachers' perceptions of children's noncognitive attributes correlated with the SES level of the school the children attend. This section takes up a different set of issues: the variation in the organizational structure of elementary schools associated with SES of the student body.

Elementary schools (N = 118) in Baltimore in 1982 generally had grade structures that covered five or six grades plus kindergarten and perhaps prekindergarten, but at least 10 other organizational patterns existed (K–3; PK–K; PK–2, PK–3; 3–5, 4–6, 1–5; K–8; PK–8; K–12). One serious problem with nonstandard grade structures is that they require students to make "extra" transitions. For example, children in PK–2 or PK–3 schools had to transfer to another elementary school to complete grades 3, 4, and 5. In Baltimore the elementary schools with nonstandard grade patterns had proportionately more children on subsidy (80% versus 67%), and most of these schools (10 out of 14) were located in the poorest Baltimore City neighborhoods (over 40% of residents in poverty). Making extra school transitions was thus a burden imposed more often upon low than upon higher SES children. School transitions are difficult hurdles for children of all ages (Alexander, Entwisle, & Dauber, 1994; Anderman & Mueller, chapter 13 this volume; Eccles, 2004; Hamre & Pianta, chapter 3 this volume; Simmons & Blyth, 1987; Vernon-Feagans, Gallagher, & Kainz, chapter 11 this volume). Among BSS students, retention rates over the first 5 years of school were significantly higher (50% versus 35%) for students who did not stay in the same elementary school throughout the 5-year period (Entwisle et al., 1997).

Another kind of transition is also more common for low than for higher SES youth. Low SES families tend to move often, and these moves often require children to transfer between schools at times that interfere with their schooling (McLanahan & Sandefur, 1994). Nationally, in 1994, among families with annual incomes less than

$10,000, 30% had attended three different schools by 3rd grade compared to 10% of children with annual incomes over $25,000 (see Rothstein, 2004). School moves can have other negative consequences. Teachman and colleagues (Teachman, Paasch, & Carver, 1996) reported that *all* of the benefits of attending Catholic schools for youth in the NELS88 sample can be explained by the negative relationship between family moves and attendance at parochial schools.

Baltimore School Study data revealed similar patterns. Of those who made two or more school moves in their elementary years, 88% were on meal subsidy compared to 65% of those who did not move. In addition, these moves were made *within* the school year almost twice as often as in the summer (between school years). In Year 4 of the study, for example, of 92 within-system moves, 57 (62%) were within-year transfers (see Entwisle et al., 1997).

Off-time moves are difficult because children must adjust to a new neighborhood, new school, new teacher, new classmates, and a new physical plant with few or no institutional supports to help. Even orderly transitions like that from elementary to middle school are disruptive and challenging, but because these moves are expected, the school and family are at least partially mobilized to smooth the student's way, with allowances made for need to readjust to new rules and a new curriculum. It is hard for teachers to accommodate students who make unscheduled moves in the middle of the year, however. The curriculum and the pace at which it is covered usually differ from one school to the next (Barr & Dreeben, 1983). Also, new students disrupt the teaching schedule and create a feeling of restlessness and upheaval in the classroom. With many students coming and going all year long, as happens in poverty areas, teachers find it necessary almost continuously to "reteach," "backtrack," and in other ways try to catch up new students to the class (Lash & Kirkpatrick, 1990).

The links between meal subsidy, household moves, and deficits in school performance are clear. Baltimore School Study children who moved two or more times within the system *began* first grade with California Achievement Test scores from 25% to 50% of a standard deviation below those of children who did not move later on. Those who moved the most also started school with other serious problems. Conduct marks at the beginning of first grade for *future* frequent movers (3 or more moves), for example, were low: 45% needed improvement versus 20% of the children who did not move. Even in the first year the frequent movers were absent more (18 days compared to 12), and retention rates over the first 5 years of school were significantly higher (50% versus 35%) for those who moved.

Data on household moves, daunting as they are, still fail to capture the full complexity of poor children's school transitions. The mobility histories of the BSS youth in just one school, where grade structure (PK–3) required that students move after third grade to complete elementary school, show that of the 69 BSS youngsters who started first grade in this school, where the meal subsidy rate was over 90%, less than one-fifth went through their elementary years in a completely orderly way (see Entwisle et al., 1997).

### School-to-School Tracks

Kerckhoff's (1993) longitudinal analysis of British schooling shows that SES patterns persist from infant school to points in life well past secondary school (age 23). Little of the research on middle or high school transitions in the United States at this time focused on the ways in which school organizational structures or student SES levels mesh over transitions between schools (Alexander & Entwisle, 1996a; Becker, 1987). Still, when children enter or leave a school, effects of SES tend to be most apparent (see Dauber et al., 1996; Simmons & Blyth, 1987). At the beginning of middle school, for example, the SES background of BSS youth predicted placements in math better than it predicted changes in placements during the middle school years. Why? Probably because higher SES parents were more effective as advocates for their children (Lareau, 1987), and were more aware of the tracking in middle school. Fifth-grade test scores, marks, and retention histories, which all correlate with SES, as well as SES itself, predicted placement decisions for BSS youth at the start of middle school.

An earlier transition into first grade may be even more telling because SES predicts children's cognitive status when they start school (Duncan, Brooks-Gunn, et al., 1998). As we said, children from disadvantaged homes start kindergarten with lower cognitive skills than their better-off counterparts (Lee & Burkam, 2002). They have much smaller vocabularies than children from higher SES homes (Hart & Risley, 1995; U.S. Department of Education, 2003). These deficits put children from low SES families at higher risk for retention in first grade than children from better off families (Alexander, Entwisle, & Dauber, 2003; Reynolds 1992; Shepard & Smith, 1989; Zill, 1996).

Whether tracking effects are cumulative, that is, whether tracks mesh over transitions, cannot be fully addressed with the BSS data, but retention in elementary school predicted remedial placements of BSS students in middle school, and those in remedial tracks learned less than did those in other tracks due to a less demanding curriculum (Entwisle, Alexander, & Olson, 2006). Also, high middle school tracks led to a college track in high school, while remedial tracks were much less likely to do so.

### Summary of Lessons from BSS

To summarize decades of research on the BSS, children's academic histories start long before age 6, and are carried along in more ways than by test scores or marks. The "sorting and selecting" by SES into elementary school tracks or preschools sets the stage for placements that follow (e.g., Alexander, Entwisle, & Dauber, 1994; Ensminger & Slusarcick, 1992; Entwisle & Alexander, 1993; Entwisle, Alexander, & Olson, 1997; Entwisle & Hayduk, 1988; Kerckhoff, 1993; Peterson, DeGracie, & Ayabe, 1987; Stroup &

Robins, 1972). First grade track assignments, for example, predict test scores and dropout in middle school (Alexander, Entwisle, & Horsey, 1997; Cairns et al. 1989; Ensminger & Slusarcick, 1992; Lloyd, 1978). Other things equal, low SES children are more often in "low" tracks in elementary school, whether in low ability groups, retention or receiving special education services (Alexander, Entwisle, & Dauber, 1994; Bianchi, 1984; Entwisle & Alexander, 1988). By middle school, family SES was also converted into a tracking advantage: In high SES middle schools, higher family SES increased the odds of BSS students getting into an advanced track rather than a "regular" track by almost 5 to 1, while prior test scores increased the odds by 3 to 1 (Entwisle, Alexander, & Olson, 2006).

The idea of an ongoing envelope surrounding the path of attainment is useful for determining the points at which a trajectory may be modified (see Alexander, Entwisle & Dauber, 2003; Alexander, Entwisle & Horsey, 1997; Kerckhoff, 1993). The channeling force of trajectories is *not* constant over the entire schooling period. Baltimore School Study research suggests that family SES produces more deflections at educational transition points, such as at the beginning of first grade, when middle school begins or ends, or when students apply for college, rather than from year-to-year (Dauber et al., 1996; Entwisle & Alexander, 1993). Altering a trajectory is most effective at the start, however, when children begin school, because initial trajectories tend to persist (Entwisle, Alexander, Cadigan, & Pallas, 1987; Lazar & Darlington, 1982). Also, parents' expectations boost achievement gains more over first grade than later (Duncan et al., 1998; Entwisle, Alexander, & Olson, 1997, 2004; Entwisle & Hayduk, 1982). Schools are highly selective by SES, and in the BSS panel, between-school tracking effects far exceed within-school tracking effects (Entwisle, Alexander, & Olson, 2006).

We need more research on students' and parents' knowledge about SES tracking, especially in the preschool and elementary years. Informed decisions by parents presuppose familiarity with all the options, knowledge of both the short- and long-term consequences of placements, and open lines of communication between parents and schools. However, parents' input into placement decisions is not necessarily "good news" (Gamoran, 1992). Unless knowledge about school differences in program quality is distributed across all families, parent input may actually increase educational inequality (see Baker & Stevenson, 1986; Lareau, 1987).

### Outlook for the Future

Research on schools and schooling in the United States has probably overemphasized the importance of individual choices and underemphasized the role of institutional arrangements. Curriculum tracking in high schools may be on the wane (Lucas, 2001) but tracking in preschools and elementary schools is probably accelerating because of the growing inequality in family incomes. Also important is the tendency to gloss over early SES tracking, and to mislabel it as a "retention problem" or as a "minority problem" or "as a school readiness problem."

The American educational system is often perceived as more "open" than the British. Coleman (1993), for example, characterized the U.S. educational system as one with little or no differentiation at any stage, with all children exposed to the same educational environment. Still, we see SES matching of elementary schools with neighborhoods, SES tracking by way of retention and special education in elementary schools, and the strong persistence of educational trajectories starting at age 6. Also, although there are exceptions (see Rosenbaum, 2001), U.S. research on school tracking overlooks possible ways that *early* tracking may affect the substantial fraction of youth not bound for 4-year colleges. The largely buried systems of tracking within and between elementary schools, especially retention, that channel noncollege bound students along separate pathways need to be made more transparent.

Retention in elementary school, far more than academic performance, predicts school dropout (Alexander, Entwisle, & Kabbani, 2001; Cairns et al., 1989; Ensminger & Slusarcick, 1992). It also predicts placement in remedial sections in middle school (Entwisle, Alexander, & Olson, 2006), which is another step toward dropout. Aside from dropouts, 85% of BSS youth in remedial sections in middle school did not go on to *any* form of postsecondary education. In predicting age 22 educational attainment of BSS panel members, retention, middle school tracks, tracking in high school, and SES all proved more important than early test scores. School tracking channels students, opening doors for some, closing doors for others (e.g., Oakes, 1988, 1989–1990). As in Kerckhoff's (1993) study in Great Britain, SES tracking in the BSS panel started at the beginning of elementary school, and persisted across levels of schooling.

From our perspective, patterns of SES tracking are imposed on schools by forces both external and internal to the school. For instance, the test score advantage of higher SES children when they start school, together with the SES clustering of neighborhoods and grade schools, comes from outside the school. Socioeconomic status tracking within schools comes from the high correlation between SES and test scores inside the school. Whether youth are tracked by scores, ability groups, retention, or special education placement, they are tracked by SES as well.

Countering these strong trends, about 40 American school districts now are trying to employ SES as a factor in student assignment (see Kahlenberg, 2006). In LaCrosse, Wisconsin, for instance, no elementary school can have less than 15% or more than 45% of students eligible for meal subsidy. It is important that SES integration can achieve racial integration as a by-product because, as Kahlenberg says, the learning deficits that accompany racial segregation are partly offset by reducing SES segregation (Orfield, 1978). Much of course depends on the details of individual integration plans. Kahlenberg (2006) explains: "Proponents of socioeconomic integration should be under no illusion that

conservatives will support such plans as a matter of public policy…many conservatives do not like plans promoting socioeconomic integration any more than they like policies aimed at racial integration" (p. 4). Our own opinion is that SES integration will lead to higher levels of achievement the earlier it is undertaken, preferably in preschool.

Some commentators forecast declines in social inequality over the 21st century (Gamoran, 2001). The likelihood of this reduction, we think, depends on attenuating the *early* influence of SES on children's preschooling. Debate in the past has centered on whether poverty affects children's schooling through parents' altered norms and "tastes" for nonnormative behavior (e.g., welfare dependence, chronic joblessness, and the like), or whether poverty affects children for structural reasons, through continuing social and economic disadvantage (Tienda, 1991). This dichotomy may be off the mark, however, because the resources schools provide seem sufficient to prompt the same amount of growth in children of *all* SES levels, and sometimes even greater growth by poor children when schools are in session (Downey et al., 2004).

***Timing of SES Resources*** Questions about when in children's lives social resources matter most are not new, nor are they the exclusive province of academics. In 1949, Rogers and Hammerstein put folk wisdom to song in *South Pacific*:

You've got to be taught
Before it's too late
Before you are six, or seven, or eight.

Still, scientific reassurance about benefits from preschools has been a long time coming, whether from the Perry Preschool Project, the Panel Study of Income Dynamics, or Reynolds's Chicago Study. A majority of children are now enrolled in early childhood programs (in Head Start, preschools, nursery schools, prekindergarten, and other programs). But in these schools, tracking by SES is the rule (see U.S. Department of Education, 2006, Table 2.8). Of the 57% of 3- to 5-year-olds enrolled in early childhood education in 2005, for instance, in all ethnic groups the nonpoor children outnumbered the poor: White 61% versus 45%; Black 68% versus 65%; Hispanic 48% versus 36%. Generally, program quality in preschools tends to correlate with SES (see Currie, 2001).

The lack of preschool facilities for disadvantaged youngsters prior to kindergarten is a major way that tracking by family income takes an early hold upon children from disadvantaged backgrounds. We believe a few extra test points conferred by attending a good preschool could help protect economically disadvantaged children against low placements or retention in the first couple of grades (see Entwisle, 1995), because a number of longitudinal studies show that less advantaged children do profit from preschool (e.g., the Head Start evaluations by Consortium, 1983; Lazar & Darlington, 1982; Reynolds, Wang, & Walberg, 2001).

Moreover, a number of randomized studies now confirm that attending preschool away from home helps children before they start first grade (see Barnett, 1995).

Sawhill (1999) estimates that universal preschool would translate into higher academic achievement, higher rates of high school graduation, better health for participants, lower crime rates, and less dependence on welfare, which would save the government $13,000 to $19,000 per child above the cost of sending that child to preschool. The original Head Start programs were exceedingly variable in content, even in the ages of the children they enrolled, but for this very reason the benefits children derived from these programs are strong testimony to the importance of school attendance per se rather than to the details of programs or settings.

To wait until high school to counteract effects of SES segregation is to wait too long. Children start school with positive views of themselves. At age 6 it is hard to measure what would correspond to a child's self-image, but in first grade the academic self-images of BSS students were unrelated to their parents' economic resources. This seeming sturdiness of young children's self-images, however, is soon tested by school organizational patterns. In first grade, children's marks, instructional level, and first grade placements like retention all reflect the SES patterns of their school. More children are held back in schools where children are of low SES, and marks are lower on average, so eventually these low marks and other school evaluations undermine students' self-image. Baltimore School Study children retained in first grade, for instance, had less favorable self-images than nonretained children by middle school (Alexander, Entwisle, & Dauber, 1994).

Society confuses uneven growth trajectories with a reduced ability to grow. Even though BSS children of all SES levels gained the same amount on standardized tests when school was in session, parents and teachers of children in low SES schools held lower expectations for those children. Also, teachers gave those children lower marks than higher SES children, and many more of the lower SES children were held back.

Of the many ways to improve the school climate in poor neighborhoods, we believe the main one is to correct the mistaken public perception that elementary schools are falling down on the job. Children's families and the public at large need to be made aware that the early deficits in test scores of poor children as they start first grade come from the lack of resources *before* first grade. Compelling evidence in Atlanta (Heyns, 1978), Baltimore (Entwisle, Alexander, & Olson, 1997), and nationally (Downey et al., 2004) shows that *when schools are in session* they tend to offset SES differences in test score gains. During the school year, low SES children gain as much from attending elementary school as higher SES children do—schools are counteracting family disadvantage when children are attending school.

How can this be in the face of the evidence reviewed earlier about variation in school quality related to SES? Downey et al. (2004) explain the paradox as follows: Low

SES children in "disadvantaged" schools get a bigger boost from attending a low SES school than the boost higher SES children get from attending a high SES school, despite the (probably) poorer quality of the lower SES schools, because of the *extreme* lack of resources in their home environments.

We have come a long way since the Coleman report, if not in improving children's life chances, at least in beginning to understand how SES fits into the picture. Even the timing issue—when SES resources matter most—has been a challenge. The evidence on negative effects of retention and special education placement in the Lazar and Darlington (1982) reanalysis of Head Start evaluations was largely overlooked until recently, as was the evidence showing that in first grade low SES children get more of a boost when school is in session than do high SES children. A key development, now in the wings, is school integration by SES. That trend, plus the emphasis on preschooling, can bode well for the future.

We believe the optimum approach for improving the life chances of disadvantaged children is to provide more preschools. It is rare for a policy decision that involves education to be as firmly grounded in scientific evidence as is the long-term value of preschool *and* its economic efficiency. Investment in preschooling, as we have said, confers benefits far into adulthood. The softer side of this policy, less often noticed, is its potential for increasing children's sense of well-being, and what that could mean for the functioning of schools and families.

**Author Note**

Preparation of this chapter was supported by the National Science Foundation #SES-0451711, Spencer Foundation #200600005, and a Mellon Fellowship to Doris Entwisle.

**Notes**

1. See Entwisle, Alexander, and Olson (2005) for a fuller description of this analysis.
2. See Hoffer (1992, 1994). Overall, grouping by ability does not appear to be an improvement over mixed groupings.
3. See Allensworth and Nagoaka (chapter 20 this volume).
4. For additional studies on school calendars and academic achievement, see Harris, Borman, and Fairchild (chapter 21 this volume).

**References**

Alexander, K. L., & Cook, M. A. (1982). Curricula and coursework: A surprise ending to a familiar story. *American Sociological Review, 47,* 626–640.

Alexander, K. L., Cook, M. A., & McDill, E. L. (1978). Curriculum tracking and educational stratification. *American Sociological Review, 43,* 47–66.

Alexander, K. L., & Eckland, B. K. (1975). Contextual effects in the high school attainment process. *American Sociological Review, 40,* 402–416.

Alexander, K. L., & Entwisle, D. R. (1996a). Educational tracking during the early years: First grade placements and middle school constraints. In A. C. Kerchoff (Ed.), *Generating social stratification: Toward a new research agenda* (pp. 83–113). Boulder, CO: Westview Press.

Alexander, K. L., & Entwisle, D. R. (1996b). Early schooling and educational inequality: Socioeconomic disparities in children's learning. In J. Clark (Ed.), *James S. Coleman* (pp. 63–79). Hampton, England: Falmer Press.

Alexander, K. L., Entwisle, D. R., & Bedinger, S. D. (1994). When expectations work: Race and socioeconomic differences in school performance. *Social Psychology Quarterly, 57,* 283–299.

Alexander, K. L., Entwisle, D. R., & Dauber, S. L. (1994). *On the success of failure: A reassessment of the effects of retention in the primary grades.* New York: Cambridge University Press.

Alexander, K. L., Entwisle, D. R., & Dauber, S. L. (2003). *On the success of failure: A reassessment of the effects of retention in the primary grades* (2nd ed.). New York: Cambridge University Press.

Alexander, K. L., Entwisle, D. R., & Horsey, C. (1997). From first grade forward: Early foundations of high school dropout. *Sociology of Education, 70,* 87–107.

Alexander, K. L., Entwisle, D. R., & Kabbani, N. (2001). The dropout process in life course perspective: Early risk factors at home and school. *Teachers College Record, 103,* 760–822.

Alexander, K. L., Entwisle, D. R., & Kabbani, N. (2003). Grade retention, social promotion, and "Third Way" alternatives. In A. J. Reynolds, M. C. Wang, & H. J. Walberg (Eds.), *Early childhood programs for a new century* (pp. 197–238). Washington, DC: Child Welfare League of America.

Alexander, K. L., Entwisle, D. R., & Legters, N. (1998, August). *On the multiple faces of first grade tracking.* Paper presented at the annual meeting of the American Sociological Association, San Francisco, CA.

Baker, D. P., & Stevenson, D. L. (1986). Mothers' strategies for children's school achievement: Managing the transition to high school. *Sociology of Education, 59,* 156–166.

Baltimore City Public Schools. (1988). *School profiles: School year 1987–88.* Baltimore, MD: Office of the Superintendent of Public Instruction.

Baltimore City Public Schools. (1991). *Maryland school performance program report, 1991, school system and schools—Baltimore City.* Baltimore, MD: Author.

Barnett, W. S. (1995). Long-term effects of early childhood care and education on disadvantaged children's cognitive development and school success. *The Future of Children, 5,* 25–50.

Barr, R., & Dreeben, R. (1983). *How schools work.* Chicago: University of Chicago Press.

Becker, H. (1987). *Addressing the needs of different groups of early adolescents* (Report No. 16). Baltimore, MD: Johns Hopkins University, Center for Research on Elementary and Middle Schools.

Bee, H., Van Egeren, L. F., Streissguth, A. P., Nyman, B. A., & Leckie, S. (1969). Social class differences in maternal teaching strategies and speech patterns. *Developmental Psychology, 1,* 726–734.

Bernstein, B. (1967). Elaborated and restricted codes: An outline. *International Journal of Applied Linguistics, 33,* 126–133.

Bernstein, B. (1971). A sociolinguistic approach to socialization: With some reference to educability. In J. Gumperz & D. Hymes (Eds.), *Directions in sociolinguistics* (pp. 465–497). New York: Holt, Rinehart & Winston.

Bianchi, S. M. (1984). Children's progress through school: A research note. *Sociology of Education, 57,* 184–192.

Bikson, T. K. (1974). *Minority speech as objectively measured and subjectively evaluated.* Paper presented at the American Psychological Association meeting, New Orleans, LA.

Bloom, B. B. (1964). *Stability and change in human characteristics.* New York: Wiley.

Borman, G. D., & Boulay, M. (2004). *Summer learning: Research, policies, and programs.* Mahwah, NJ: Erlbaum.

Bourdieu, P., & Passeron, J.C. (1977). *Reproduction in education, society, culture.* Beverly Hills, CA: Sage.

Braddock II, J. H., Wu, S. C., & McPartland, J. (1988). *School organization in the middle grades: National variations and effects* (Report No. 24). Baltimore, MD: Johns Hopkins University, Center for Research on Elementary and Middle Schools.

Braddock, J. (1990). Tracking the middle grades: National patterns of grouping for instruction. *Phi Delta Kappan, 71,* 445–449.

Brooks-Gunn, J., Duncan, G., & Aber, J. L. (1997a). *Neighborhood poverty: Context and consequences for children* (Vol. 1). New York: Russell Sage.

Brooks-Gunn, J., Duncan, G., & Aber, J. L. (1997b). *Neighborhood poverty: Context and consequences for children* (Vol. 2). New York: Russell Sage.

Cairns, R. B., Cairns, B. D., & Neckerman, H. J. (1989). Early school dropout: Configurations and determinants. *Child Development, 60,* 1437–1452.

California Achievement Test. (1979). *California achievement tests: Norms tables, level 18, forms C and D.* Monterey, CA: CTB/McGraw Hill.

Catsambis, S. (1992, March). *The many faces of tracking middle school grades: Between- and within-school differentiation of students and resources.* Paper presented at the Society for Research on Adolescence Meeting, Washington, DC.

Central Advisory Council for Education. (1967). *Children and their primary schools.* London: Her Majesty's Stationery Office.

Coleman, J. S. (1993). Foreword. In A. C. Kerckhoff (Ed.), *Diverging pathways: Social structure and career deflections* (pp. xiii–xvii). New York: Cambridge University Press.

Coleman, J. S., Campbell, E. Q., Hobson, C. J., McPartland, J., Mood, A., Weinfeld, F. D., & York, R. L. (1966). *Equality of educational opportunity.* Washington, DC: U.S. Government Printing Office.

Consortium for Longitudinal Studies. (1983). *As the twig is bent: Lasting effects of preschool programs.* Hillsdale, NJ: Erlbaum.

Currie, J. (2001). Early childhood education programs. *Journal of Economic Perspectives, 15,* 213–238.

Darlington, R. B., Royce, J. M., Snipper, A. S., Murray, H. W., & Lazar, I. (1980). Preschool programs and later school competence of children from low-income families. *Science, 208,* 202–204.

Dauber, S. L., Alexander, K. L., & Entwisle, D. R. (1993). Characteristics of retainees and early precursors of retention in grade: Who is held back? *Merrill-Palmer Quarterly, 39,* 326–343.

Dauber, S. L., Alexander, K. L., & Entwisle, D. R. (1996). Tracking and transitions through the middle grades: Channeling educational trajectories. *Sociology of Education, 69,* 290–307.

Dornbusch, S. M., & Glasgow, K. L. (1995). The structural context of family-school relations. In A. Booth & J. F. Dunn (Eds.), *Family-school links* (pp. 35–44). Mahwah, NJ: Erlbaum.

Downey, D. B., Von Hippel, P. T., & Broh, B. (2004). Are schools the great equalizer? Cognitive inequality during the summer months and the school year. *American Sociological Review, 69,* 613–635.

Duncan, G. J., Brooks-Gunn, J., Yeung, W. J., & Smith, J. K. (1998). How much does childhood poverty affect the life chances of children? *American Sociological Review, 63,* 406–423.

Eccles, J. S. (2004). Schools, academic motivation, and stage-environment fit. In R. M. Lerner & L. Steinberg (Eds.), *Handbook of adolescent psychology* (2nd ed., pp. 125–153). New York: Wiley.

Eccles, J. S., & Harold, R. D. (1996). Family investment in children's and adolescents' schooling. In A. Booth & J. F. Dunn (Eds.), *Family school links* (pp. 3–34). Mahwah, NJ: Erlbaum.

Eccles, J. S., Midgley, C., & Adler, T. (1984). Grade-related changes in the school environment: Effects on achievement motivation. In J. G. Nicholls (Ed.), *The development of achievement motivation* (pp. 283–331). Greenwich, CT: JAI Press.

Eccles, J. S., Midgley, C., Wigfield, A., Buchanan, C. M., Reuman, D., Flanagan, C., & MacIver, D. (1993). Development during adolescence: The impact of stage–environment fit on young adolescents' experience in school and families. *American Psychologist, 48,* 90–101.

Edgar, E., Heggelund, M., & Fisher, M. (1988). A longitudinal study of graduates of special education preschools: Educational placement after preschool. *Topics in Early Childhood Special Education, 8,* 61–74.

Elder Jr., G. H. (1974). *Children of the great depression: Social change in life experience.* Chicago: University of Chicago Press.

Elder Jr., G. H. (1998). The life course and human development. In W. Damon & R. M. Lerner (Eds.), *Handbook of child psychology: Vol.*

*1. Theoretical models of human development* (pp. 939–991). New York: Wiley.

Ensminger, M. E., & Slusarcick, A. L. (1992). Paths to high school graduation or dropout: A longitudinal study of a first-grade cohort. *Sociology of Education, 65,* 95–113.

Entwisle, D. R. (1995). The role of schools in sustaining benefits of early childhood programs. *The Future of Children, 5,* 133–144.

Entwisle, D. R., & Alexander, K. L. (1988). Factors affecting achievement test scores and marks received by Black and White first graders. *The Elementary School Journal, 88,* 449–471.

Entwisle, D. R., & Alexander, K. L. (1992). Summer setback: Race, poverty, school composition, and mathematics achievement in the first two years of school. *American Sociological Review, 57,* 72–84.

Entwisle, D. R., & Alexander, K. L. (1993). Entry into schools: The beginning school transition and educational stratification in the United States. *Annual Review of Sociology, 19,* 401–423.

Entwisle, D. R., & Alexander, K. L. (1994). Winter setback: School racial composition and learning to read. *American Sociological Review, 59,* 446–460.

Entwisle, D. R., & Alexander, K. L. (1995). A parent's economic shadow: Family structure versus family resources as influences on early school achievement. *Journal of Marriage and the Family, 57,* 399–409.

Entwisle, D. R., & Alexander, K. L. (1996). Further comments on seasonal learning. In A. Booth & J. F. Dunn (Eds.), *Family-school links: How do they affect educational outcomes?* (pp. 125–136). Mahwah, NJ: Erlbaum.

Entwisle, D. R., Alexander, K. L., Cadigan, D., & Pallas, A. M. (1987). Kindergarten experience: Cognitive effects or socialization? *American Educational Research Journal, 24,* 337–364.

Entwisle, D. R., Alexander, K. L., & Olson. L. S. (1997). *Children, schools and inequality.* Boulder, CO: Westview Press.

Entwisle, D. R., Alexander, K. L., & Olson. L. S. (2000). Summer learning and home environment. In R. D. Kahlenberg (Ed.), *A notion at risk: Preserving public education as an engine for social mobility* (pp. 9–30). New York: Century Foundation Press.

Entwisle, D. R., Alexander, K. L., & Olson. L. S. (2004). The first grade transition in life course perspective. In J. T. Mortimer & M. J. Shanahan (Eds.), *Handbook of the life course* (pp. 229–250). New York: Kluwer Academic/Plenum.

Entwisle, D. R., Alexander, K. L., & Olson. L. S. (2005). First grade and educational attainment by age 22: A new story. *American Journal of Sociology, 110,* 1458–14502.

Entwisle, D. R., Alexander, K. L., & Olson. L. S. (2006). Educational tracking within and between schools: From first grade through middle school and beyond. In A. Huston & M. Ripke (Eds.), *Developmental contexts in middle childhood* (pp. 173–197). New York: Cambridge University Press.

Entwisle, D. R., & Astone, N. M. (1994). Some practical guidelines for measuring youth's race/ethnicity and socioeconomic status. *Child Development, 65,* 1521–1540.

Entwisle, D. R., & Hayduk, L. A. (1982). *Early schooling: Cognitive and affective outcomes.* Baltimore, MD: Johns Hopkins Press.

Entwisle, D. R., & Hayduk, L. A. (1988). Lasting effects of elementary school. *Sociology of Education, 61,* 147–159.

Entwisle, D. R., & Webster Jr., M. (1972). Raising children's performance expectations. *Social Science Research, 1,* 147–158.

Feldman, S. S., & Elliott, G. R. (1990). *At the threshold: The developing adolescent.* Cambridge, MA: Harvard University Press.

Fine, M. (1991). *Framing dropouts: Notes on the politics of an urban public high school.* Albany, NY: State University of New York Press.

Finn, J. D., & Cox, D. (1992). Participation and withdrawal among fourth-grade pupils. *American Educational Research Journal, 29,* 141–162.

Fulgini, A. J., Eccles, J. S., & Barber, B. L. (1995). The long-term effects of seventh-grade ability grouping in mathematics. *Journal of Early Adolescence, 15,* 58–89.

Furstenberg Jr., F. F., Brooks-Gunn, J., & Morgan, S. P. (1987). *Adolescent mothers in later life.* New York: Cambridge University Press.

Furstenberg Jr., F. F., Cook, T. D., Eccles, J., Elder Jr., G. H., & Sameroff, A. (1999). *Managing to make it.* Chicago: University of Chicago.

Gamoran, A. (1992). The variable effects of high school tracking. *American Sociological Review, 57,* 812–828.

Gamoran, A. (2001). American schooling and educational inequality: A forecast for the 21st century [Special issue]. *Sociology of Education,* 135–153.

Garces, E., Thomas, D., & Currie, J. (2002). Longer-term effects of head start. *Poverty Research News, 6,* 3–5.

Garfinkel, I., & McLanahan, S. S. (1986). *Single mothers and their children: A new American dilemma.* Washington, DC: Urban Institute Press.

Gomby, D. S., Larner, M. B., Stevenson, C. S., Lewit, E. M., & Behrman, R. E. (1995). The long-term outcomes of early childhood programs: Analysis and recommendations. *The Future of Children, 5,* 6–24.

Hallinan, M. T. (1992). The organization of students for instruction in the middle school. *Sociology of Education, 65,* 114–127.

Harms, L. S. (1961). Listener judgments of status cues in speech. *Quarterly Journal of Speech, 47,* 164–168.

Harnqvist, K. (1977). Enduring effects of schooling: A neglected area in educational research. *Educational Researcher, 6,* 5–11.

Hart, B., & Risley, T. R. (1995). *Meaningful differences in the everyday experience of young American children.* Baltimore, MD: Brookes.

Hart, D., Atkins, R., & Fegley, S. (2003). Personality and development in childhood. *Monographs of the Society for Research in Child Development, 68,* 1–108.

Hauser, R. M. (2001). Should we end social promotion? Truth and consequences. In G. Orfield & M. Kornhaber (Eds.), *Raising standards or raising barriers? Inequality and high stakes testing in public education* (pp. 151–178). New York: Century Foundation.

Hauser, R. M., Pager, D. I., & Simmons, S. J. (2000, October). *Race-ethnicity, social background, and grade retention.* Paper presented at the National Invitational Conference "Can Unlike Children Learn Together? Grade Retention, Tracking, and Grouping," Alexandria, VA.

Haveman, R. H., & Wolfe, B. L. (1994). *Succeeding generations: On the effects of investments in children.* New York: Russell Sage Foundation.

Heller, K. A. (1982). Effects of special education placement on educable mentally retarded children. In K. A. Heller, W. H. Holtzman, & S. Messick (Eds.), *Children in special education: A strategy for equity* (pp. 262–299). Washington, DC: National Academy Press.

Hess, R. D. (1970). Social class and ethnic influences on socialization. In P. H. Mussen (Ed.), *Carmichael's manual of child psychology* (pp. 457–558). New York: Wiley.

Hess, R. D., & Shipman, V. C. (1965). Early experience and the socialization of cognitive modes in children. *Child Development, 36,* 869–888.

Heubert, J. P., & Hauser, R. M. (1999). *High stakes: Testing for tracking, promotion, and graduation.* Washington, DC: National Academy Press.

Heyns, B. (1978). *Summer learning and the effects of schooling.* New York: Academic.

Hoffer, T. B. (1992). Middle school ability grouping and student achievement in science and mathematics. *Educational Evaluation and Policy Analysis, 14,* 205–227.

Hoffer, T. B. (1994, August). *Cumulative effects of secondary school tracking on student achievement.* Paper presented at the annual meeting of the American Sociological Association, Los Angeles.

Husén, T. (1969). *Talent, opportunity and career.* Stockholm, Sweden: Almqvist & Wiksell.

Husén, T., & Tuijnman, A. (1991). The contribution of formal schooling to the increase in intellectual capital. *Educational Researcher, 20,* 17–25.

Huston, A. C. (1994). Children in poverty: Designing research to affect policy. *Social Policy Report, Society for Research in Child Development, 8,* 1–12.

Jencks, C., & Phillips, M. (1998). The Black–White test score gap: An introduction. In C. Jencks & M. Phillips (Eds.), *The Black–White test score gap* (pp. 1–54). Washington, DC: Brookings Institution Press.

Jencks, C., Smith, M., Ackland, H., Bane, M. J., Cohen, D., Gintis, H., et al. (1972). *Inequality: A reassessment of the effect of failure and schooling in America*. New York: Basic Books.

Kahlenberg, R. D. (2006). *A new way on school integration*. New York: Century Foundation Press.

Kao, G., & Thompson, J. S. (2003). Racial and ethnic stratification in educational achievement and attainment. In K. Cook & J. Hagen (Eds.), *Annual review of sociology* (Vol. 29, pp. 417–442). Palo Alto, CA: Annual Reviews.

Karweit, N. (1992). Retention policy. In M. Alkin (Ed.), *Encyclopedia of educational research* (pp. 1114–1118). New York: Macmillan.

Kerckhoff, A. C. (1993). *Diverging pathways: Social structure and career deflections*. New York: Cambridge Press.

Kraus, P. E. (1973). *Yesterday's children*. New York: Wiley.

Lambert, W. E., & MacNamara, J. (1969). Some cognitive consequences of following a first-grade curriculum in a second language. *Journal of Educational Psychology, 60*, 86–96.

Lambert, W. E., & Tucker, G. R. (1972). *The St. Lambert program of home-school language switch, grades K through five*. Montreal, Canada: McGill University.

Lareau, A. (1987). Social class differences in family-school relationships: The importance of cultural capital. *Sociology of Education, 60*, 73–85.

Lareau, A. (1992). Gender differences in parent involvement in schooling. In J. Wrigley (Ed.), *Education and gender equality* (pp. 207–224). London: Falmer Press.

Lareau, A. (1996). Assessing parent involvement in schooling: A critical analysis. In A. Booth & J. F. Dunn (Eds.), *Family school links* (pp. 57–64). Mahwah, NJ: Erlbaum.

Lareau, A. (2002). Invisible inequality: Social class and child rearing in Black families and White families. *American Sociological Review, 67*, 747–776.

Lash, A. A., & Kirkpatrick, S. L. (1990). A classroom perspective on student mobility. *Elementary School Journal, 91*, 171–191.

Lazar, I., & Darlington, R. (1982). Lasting effects of early education: A report from the Consortium for Longitudinal Studies. *Monographs of the Society for Research in Child Development, 47*, ix–139.

Lee, J. (2002). Racial and ethnic achievement gap trends: Revising the progress toward equity. *Educational Researcher, 31*, 3–12.

Lee, V., & Burkam, D. T. (2002). *Inequality at the starting gate: Social background differences in achievement as children begin school*. Washington, DC: Economic Policy Institute.

Leinhardt, G., & Pallay, A. (1982). Restrictive educational settings: Exile or haven? *Review of Educational Research, 54*, 557–578.

Lloyd, D. N. (1978). Prediction of school failure from third-grade data. *Educational and Psychological Measurement, 38*, 1193–1200.

Lucas, S. R. (2001). Effectively maintained inequality: Education transitions, track mobility, and social background effects. *American Journal of Sociology, 106*, 1642–1690.

Lucas, S. R. (1999). *Tracking inequality: Stratification and mobility in American high schools*. New York: Teachers College Press.

Luster, T., & McAdoo, H. (1996). Family and child influences on educational attainment: A secondary analysis of the High/Scope Perry preschool data. *Developmental Psychology, 32*, 26–39.

Mayer, S. E. (1997). *What money can't buy: Family income and children's life chances*. Cambridge, MA: Harvard University Press.

McLanahan, S. S., & Sandefur, G. (1994). *Growing up with a single parent: What hurts, what helps*. Cambridge, MA: Harvard University Press.

McLoyd, V. (1989). Socialization and development in a changing economy: The effects of paternal income and job loss on children. *American Psychologist, 44*, 293–302.

McLoyd, V. C. (1990). The impact of economic hardship on Black families and children: Psychological distress parenting, and socioemotional development. *Child Development, 61*, 311–346.

Mosteller, F., & Moynihan, D. P. (1972). *On equality of educational opportunity*. New York: Vintage.

Murnane, R. J. (1975). *The impact of school resources on the learning of inner city children*. Cambridge, MA: Ballinger.

National Center for Education Statistics. (1990). *Dropout rates in the United States: 1989*. (NCES 90-659). Washington, DC: U.S. Department of Education, Office of Educational Research and Improvement.

Oakes, J. (1985). *Keeping track: How schools structure inequality*. New Haven, CT: Yale University Press.

Oakes, J. (1988). Tracking in mathematics and science education: A structural contribution to unequal schooling. In L. Weis (Ed.), *Class, race and gender in American education* (pp. 106–125). Albany, NY: SUNY Press.

Oakes, J. (1989–1990). Opportunities, achievement and choice: Women and minority students in science and mathematics. *Review of Research in Education, 16*, 153–222.

Orfield, G. (1978). *Must we bus? Segregated schools and national policy*. Washington, DC: Brookings Institution Press.

Pallas, A. M., Entwisle, D. R., Alexander, K. L., & Stluka, M. F. (1994). Ability-group effects: Instructional, social or institutional? *Sociology of Education, 67*, 27–46.

Pedersen, E., Faucher, T. A., & Eaton, W. W. (1978). A new perspective on the effects of first-grade teachers on children's subsequent adult status. *Harvard Educational Review, 48*, 1–31.

Peterson, S. E., DeGracie, J. S., & Ayabe, C. R. (1987). A longitudinal study of the effects of retention/promotion on academic achievement. *American Educational Research Journal, 27*, 107–118.

Rackstraw, S. J., & Robinson, W. P. (1967). Social and psychological factors related to variability of answering behavior in five-year-old children. *Language and Speech, 10*, 88–106.

Reynolds, A. J. (1992). Grade retention and school adjustment: An explanatory analysis. *Educational Evaluation and Policy Analysis, 14*, 101–121.

Reynolds, A. J., Wang, M. C., & Walberg, H. J. (2001). *Early childhood programs for a new century*. Washington, DC: Child Welfare League of America, Inc.

Rist, R. (1970). Student social class and teacher expectations: The self-fulfilling prophecy in ghetto education. *Harvard Educational Review, 40*, 411–451.

Roderick, M. (1994). Grade retention and school dropout: Investigating the association. *American Educational Research Journal, 31*, 729–759.

Rosenbaum, J. (2001). *Beyond college for all: Career paths for the forgotten half*. New York: Russell Sage Foundation.

Rothstein, R. (2004). *Class and schools*. Washington, DC: Economic Policy Institute.

Rumberger, R. W. (2001, January). *Why students drop out of school and what can be done*. Paper prepared for the Civil Rights Project at Harvard University's Graduate School of Education and Achieve. Cambridge, MA.

Rumberger, R. W., & Palardy, G. J. (2005). Does segregation still matter? The impact of student composition on academic achievement in high school. *Teachers College Record, 107*, 1999–2045.

Sampson, R. J. (1992). Family management and child development: Insights from social disorganization theory. In J. McCord (Ed.), *Advances in criminology theory: Vol 3. Fact, frameworks, and forecasts* (pp. 63–93). New Brunswick, NJ: Transaction.

Sampson, R. J., Morenoff, J. D., & Gannon-Rowley, T. (2002). Assessing "neighborhood effects": Social processes and new directions in research. *Annual Review of Sociology, 28*, 443–478.

Sawhill, I. (1999). Kids need an early start: Universal preschool education may be the best investment Americans can make in our children's education–and our nation's future. *Blueprint Magazine*, (Fall) 37–39.

Saxe, G. B., Guberman, S. R., & Gearheart, M. (1987). Social processes in early number development (Serial No. 216). *Monographs Social Research Child Development*. Malden, MA: Blackwell.

Schneider, B. L., & Coleman, J. S. (1993). *Parents, their children, and schools*. Boulder, CO: Westview.

Schweinhart, L. J., Barnes, H. V., & Weikart, D. P. (1993). *Significant benefits: The High Scope/Perry preschool study through age 17*. Ypsilanti, MI: High Scope Educational Research Foundation.

Sewell, W. H., & Hauser, R. M. (1975). *Education, occupation, and earnings*. New York: Academic.

Shepard, L. A., & Smith, M. L. (1989). *Flunking grades: Research and policies on retention*. London: Falmer Press.

Simmons, R. G., & Blyth, D. A. (1987). *Moving into adolescence: The impact of pubertal change and school context*. Hawthorn, NY: Aldine de Gruyter.

Smith, M. S. (1972). Equality of educational opportunity: The basic findings reconsidered. In F. Mosteller & D. Moynihan (Eds.), *On equality of educational opportunity* (pp. 230–342). New York: Vintage Books.

Smith-Maddox, R. (1999). The social networks and resources of African American eighth graders: Evidence from the National Educational Longitudinal Study of 1988. *Adolescence, 34*(133), 169–183.

Stevenson, D. L., Schiller, K. S., & Schneider, B. (1994). Sequences of opportunities for learning. *Sociology of Education, 67*, 184–198.

Stroup, A. L., & Robins. L. N. (1972). Elementary school predictors of high school dropout among black males. *Sociology of Education, 45*, 212–222.

Teachman, J. D., Paasch, K., & Carver, K. (1996). Social capital and dropping out of school early. *Journal of Marriage and the Family, 58*, 773–783.

Tienda, M. (1991). Poor people and poor places: Deciphering neighborhood effects on poverty outcomes. In J. Huber (Ed.), *Macro-micro linkages in sociology* (pp. 244–262). Maberry, CA: Sage.

U.S. Census Bureau. (2001). *Statistical abstract of the United States: 2001*. Washington, DC: Author.

U.S. Census Bureau. (2007). *Statistical abstract of the United States: 2007*. Washington, DC: Author.

U.S. Department of Education. (1995). *The condition of education 1995*. (Technical Report No. NCES 95-273). Washington, DC: U.S. Department of Education, National Center for Education Statistics.

U.S. Department of Education. (2003). *Digest of educational statistics*. Retrieved from http://nces.ed.gov/programs/digest/d03

U.S. Department of Education. (2006). *The condition of education 2006*. (NCES 2006-071). Washington, DC: U. S. Government Printing Office, National Center for Educational Statistics.

Useem, E. L. (1991). Student selection into course sequences in mathematics: The impact of parental involvement and school policies. *Journal of Research on Adolescence, 1*, 231–250.

Walker, D. K., Singer, J. D., Palfrey, J. S., Orza, M., Wenger, M., & Butler, J. (1988). Who leaves and who stays in special education: A 2-Year follow-up study. *Exceptional Children, 54*, 393–402.

West, J., Denton, K., & Germino-Hausken, E. (2000). *America's kindergartners: Findings from the Early Childhood Longitudinal Study, Kindergarten Class of 1998–99, Fall 1998*. (NCES 2000-070). Washington, DC: U.S. Department of Education, National Center for Education Statistics.

Williams, F. (1970). Psychological correlates of speech characteristics: On sounding disadvantaged. *Journal of Speech and Hearing Research, 13*, 472–488.

Wilson, W. J. (1987). *The truly disadvantaged: The inner city, the underclass, and public policy*. Chicago: University of Chicago Press.

Wilson, W. J. (1996). *When work disappears: The world of the new urban poor*. New York: Knopf.

Zill, N. (1996). Family change and student achievement: What we have learned, what it means for schools. In A. Booth & J. Dunn (Eds.), *Family-school links: How do they affect educational outcomes?* (pp. 139–174). Mahwah, NJ: Erlbaum.

# 16

# Expectations, Stereotypes, and Self-Fulfilling Prophecies in Classroom and School Life

*CLARK MCKOWN, ANNE GREGORY, AND RHONA S. WEINSTEIN*

Schools are a critical context for children's development (Rutter & Maughan, 2002; Rutter, Maughan, Mortimore, Ouston, & Smith, 1979; Weinstein, 2002). The events and relationships that unfold over the approximately 15,000 hours children spend in elementary and secondary schools influence many facets of development. Children acquire knowledge and skills that reflect the core mission of schools. In addition, as the chapters in this volume so comprehensively review, what happens in schools can have a profound influence on children's views about themselves as learners, their motivation to work hard and learn, their persistence in the face of failure, and their behavior and mental health. We know that children generally begin school enthusiastic about learning and that over the course of their school careers, children's engagement declines (Eccles & Midgley, 1990). This decline is particularly striking for girls in some areas such as mathematics and for members of academically stereotyped ethnic groups (Graham, 2001). Declines in engagement, particularly for girls and ethnic minorities, naturally raises the question of what characteristics of school and classroom life may contribute to these declines, and what may be done prevent this decline.

Perhaps reflecting the profound complexity of classroom and school life, a large number of school-related influences on children's development have been investigated, including teacher–student relationships (Hamre & Pianta, chapter 3 this volume; Wentzel, chapter 6 this volume), classroom goal structures (Urdan, chapter 7 this volume), school climate (Battistich, chapter 8 this volume), parent involvement (Pomerantz & Moorman, chapter 25 this volume), and curriculum and instruction (Slavin & Madden, chapter 27 this volume). This partial list reflects a fraction of the possible mechanisms through which schools influence children's development. This chapter focuses on a specific dimension of the school experience—adults' beliefs about children's abilities and the mechanisms through which those beliefs propagate self-fulfilling prophecies. We focus in particular

on teacher expectations and broadly held ethnic stereotypes about academic ability, which are two types of belief that can influence children's development.

In this chapter, we briefly review what is known about teacher expectancy and stereotype threat effects. We compare and contrast these two phenomena, underscoring the importance of integrating these largely disparate literatures. We discuss the broad range of situational cues in classrooms and schools that may communicate expectations and stereotypes to children and we describe the range of developmental outcomes that may be affected by these cues. We conclude by describing promising intervention strategies to reduce the negative effects of these social influence processes on children's development. Throughout, we will draw a connection between these two forms of self-fulfilling prophecy and the well-documented ethnic achievement gap (Jencks & Phillips, 1998).

## A Brief Overview of Research on Self-Fulfilling Prophecies

How might beliefs—both individual teacher beliefs and broadly held ethnic stereotypes about ability—affect children's development? In this section, we discuss two interrelated processes of social influence through which beliefs about ability shape children's behavior, particularly their academic achievement. In pursuing this integrative discussion, we hold these premises: (a) teachers, like other professionals, are a part of and influenced by the broader cultural context; (b) within contemporary American society, many believe that men and women and individuals from different ethnic groups have different levels of talent (Bobo, 2001; Dovidio & Gaertner, 2004); (c) teacher education, district and school policies, and curriculum also shape beliefs about children's ability; and (d) both cultural and educational beliefs can influence teacher expectations about ability or permeate the schooling environment such that these beliefs can be acted upon, by teachers or students alike, with potent consequences for children.

***Interpersonal Expectancy Effects*** For more than half a century, social scientists have closely examined the varied ways our expectations about individuals and about groups influence the targets of those expectations (for reviews, see Brophy, 1983, 1998; Good & Nichols, 2001; Jussim & Harber, 2005; Rosenthal, 2003: Weinstein, 2002). First described by sociologist Robert K. Merton (1948), the self-fulfilling prophecy is a process by which a perceiver's beliefs, when acted upon, shape a target's behavior. Merton's classic article underscored intraindividual, interpersonal, and societal self-fulfilling prophecies, which implied that self-fulfilling prophecies could result not only from transactions between a perceiver and a target but also from transactions between situations and targets. The most intense area of empirical inquiry on interpersonal expectancy effects has been the relationship between teacher expectations about ability and student achievement.

Rosenthal and Jacobson (1968) provided the first empirical test of teacher expectancy effects. In their field study in an elementary school, teachers were told that some of their students were "early bloomers." Students were randomly assigned to this expectancy induction. Rosenthal and Jacobson (1968) found children in the positive expectancy induction condition performed better at year-end (an effect seen in the early grades) than their classmates, who were equivalent except that they had not been the target of an induced high expectation. Although the Rosenthal and Jacobson (1968) study has been criticized on methodological grounds (e.g., Snow, 1995), several hundred experimental studies have been conducted that demonstrate the effects of induced expectancy effects. Meta-analyses suggest that in the context of experimental studies of expectancy effects on achievement or IQ confirm that under controlled laboratory conditions, expectations cause self-fulfilling prophecies (Jussim & Harber, 2005; Raudenbush, 1984; Rosenthal & Rubin, 1978; Smith, 1980).

Teacher expectancy effects have also been demonstrated in naturalistic studies. These studies typically assess teacher expectations early in the academic year and student achievement at year-end. Analyses examine whether teacher expectations in the fall are predictive of year-end achievement. Many naturalistic studies control for prior achievement, which answers the important question of whether teacher expectations in the fall are predictive of year-end achievement for students with a similar prior record of achievement. For example, Jussim (1989) studied the relationship between teacher expectations and year-end achievement in a sample of Michigan sixth graders by measuring teacher expectations early in the school year, and gathering data on prior-year and year-end achievement. He found that teacher expectations about student ability predicted student grades and achievement scores in mathematics after controlling for the effects of prior student achievement differences. Naturalistic studies consistently find that teacher expecta-

tions are predictive of year-end achievement for students with similar achievement histories. The overall effect size of expectancy effects in these studies is more modest than in experimental studies (Rosenthal & Rubin, 1978), but is statistically significant and consistent across a large number of studies. Furthermore, there are conditions, which we describe in greater detail below, in which expectancy effects are quite strong (Brattesani, Weinstein, & Marshall, 1984; Kuklinski & Weinstein, 2001).

Although offering substantial evidence of teacher expectancy effects, these studies say nothing about the mechanisms through which teacher expectations influence student achievement. Brophy and Good (1970) provided the first classroom observational evidence that teachers treat high- and low-expectancy students very differently and proposed a model for understanding both direct and indirect pathways of influence (see also Brophy, 1983; Brophy & Good, 1974). Teachers form expectations about students and those expectations then affect children through two distinct mediating pathways. The teacher may provide more challenging learning opportunities for children for whom she has high expectations and less challenging learning opportunities for children for whom she has low expectations. Differential exposure to a stimulating curriculum, accorded partially on the basis of the teacher's expectations, can affect what students learn, causing student academic performance to conform to the teacher's expectations.

Teacher expectations can also affect student achievement indirectly, mediated by student perceptions of teacher expectancy behaviors. Research studies have documented a long list of teacher behaviors that can be accorded differentially to students—behaviors that reflect the emotional climate of the teacher–student relationship, instructional approaches, quality and valence of performance feedback, and opportunities for student response (Rosenthal, 1993). If children perceive these cues about what is expected of them, this knowledge of the teacher's expectations can, in turn, shape student beliefs about their own abilities, and lead them to perform in the direction of the teacher's expectations.

In the 1970s and 1980s, Weinstein and her colleagues began investigating from the students' (rather than the observers') point of view, whether children were aware of differential treatment, what teacher behaviors communicated high and low expectations, and what were the implications of such awareness. To evaluate this question, they developed the Teacher Treatment Inventory (TTI) in which students independently rated the frequency of a variety of teacher behaviors toward a hypothetical high- and low-achieving student. Weinstein and colleagues found that in deciphering teacher expectations, children attended to (a) the amount of negative feedback and teacher directives; (b) the extent to which teachers require students to adhere to rules; and (c) the extent to which teachers explicitly express high expectations and give students choices and opportunities, with high achievers perceived to be favored with less negativity, fewer rules, and more privileges (Weinstein, Marshall, Brattesani,

& Middlestadt, 1982; Weinstein, Marshall, Sharp, & Botkin, 1987; Weinstein & Middlestadt, 1979).

The study of student perceptions of teacher behaviors that communicate expectations has yielded a rich understanding of expectancy processes. First, it showed that children as young as first graders are aware of and can reliably report teacher behavior that communicates expectations (Weinstein, Marshall, Brattesani, et al., 1982; Weinstein, Marshall, Sharp, & Botkin, 1987; Weinstein & Middlestadt, 1979). In fact, elementary school children make rapid judgments about what teachers expect on the basis of fleeting slices of verbal and nonverbal behavior (Babad, Bernieri, & Rosenthal, 1991). Second, it demonstrated that across the elementary school years, students' perceptions of their teachers' expectations become more correlated with teacher expectations, suggesting greater sensitivity to teacher cues with age (Weinstein et al., 1987). Third, student perceptions of teacher behavior, aggregated at the classroom level, are informative about the extent to which individual teachers treat high and low achievers differently. The more teachers treat high and low achievers differently, the clearer is the message about what teachers expect. In classrooms where teachers treat high and low achievers very differently, students are more likely to know what the teacher expects of themselves and their classmates. In those classrooms, student self-expectations and teacher expectations are more strongly correlated, particularly among older elementary-aged children (Kuklinski & Weinstein, 2001). Furthermore, when teacher expectancy cues are more salient, those cues affect student self-perceptions. Finally, the research findings suggest that in classrooms in which teacher expectancy cues are salient, the relationship between teacher expectations and year-end achievement is stronger than in classrooms where those cues are not as salient (Brattesani et al., 1984).

Some of the work on teacher expectancy effects has examined the important question of whether teacher expectations contribute to ethnic, income, and gender differences in achievement. For example, if teachers hold higher expectations for White than for Black students or for boys than for girls in math, then those differential expectations could contribute to group differences in achievement. Rist (1970) conducted an ethnographic study of an elementary school classroom and observed that students were assigned to ability group based largely on clues from their dress and manner about their social class background, with low-income students assigned to remedial, low-quality reading instruction and high-income students assigned to more advanced reading groups. Research on the relationship between child characteristics and teacher expectations since Rist's study has not found a clear association between group membership and expectations, with estimates from meta-analyses concluding that teacher expectations are only weakly associated with child ethnicity and gender (Dusek & Joseph, 1983).

There is, however, evidence that teacher expectations can contribute to educational inequality. Channouf, Man-

gard, Baudry, and Perny (2005) varied information about student social class and family background given to middle school teachers and measured teachers' judgments about the appropriate student track. They found that teachers held lower expectations of students from lower socioeconomic backgrounds than their similarly talented peers from higher socioeconomic classes. In a cross-sectional naturalistic study that included measures of teacher expectations, student attitudes toward learners, and classroom behavioral observations, Parsons, Kaczala, and Meece (1982) found that teachers treat boys and girls differently, and that in some classrooms, there are particularly noteworthy differences in teacher treatment toward boys and girls.

Similarly, McKown and Weinstein (2008) found in two independent samples that the relationship between child ethnicity and teacher expectations (controlling for prior achievement) is greater in classrooms that are more ethnically diverse and in which students report greater differential treatment by teachers. Furthermore, the quality of the relationship between students and teachers appears to vary systematically by ethnicity, with White students generally enjoying more positive relationships with their teachers than Black and Latino/a students (Hughes, Gleason, & Zheng, 2005; Saft & Pianta, 2001; Skiba, Michael, Nardo, & Peterson, 2002). The functional use of group membership, including differential teacher treatment toward children on the basis of gender or ethnicity, may create differences in academic self-concept, academic achievement (McKown & Weinstein, 2008), and intergroup prejudices (Brown & Bigler, 2002). These varied findings all suggest children from academically stereotyped ethnic groups may bear the burden of lower expectations. Those lower expectations can in turn exacerbate achievement gaps between children from different ethnic groups (Jussim, Eccles, & Madon, 1996; McKown & Weinstein, 2002).

More recent research has investigated the influence of teacher expectations and student achievement at the classroom level rather than an individual level. This work addresses the question of how students fare with teachers who generally hold low expectations for their students compared to teachers who generally hold high expectations for their students. In a New Zealand study of elementary-aged students, Rubie-Davies (2006) found that across one school year, in classrooms where teachers hold generally lower expectations, student reading and math self-concept declined. In contrast, in classrooms where teachers held generally higher expectations, student reading and math self-concept increased. Consistent with earlier work by Weinstein and colleagues, these findings suggest that teacher expectations can serve to create a classroom climate that is greater than the sum of the individual teacher–student relationships.

Several general conclusions can be drawn from the work on teacher expectancy effects. First, teacher expectancy effects can indeed lead to self-fulfilling prophecies. Although much of the research has concentrated on the question of whether teacher expectancy effects are real, we feel that it is more important to understand the conditions (individuals or groups, environments, and their interaction) under which expectancy effects are heightened or minimized. The exploration of these contextual moderators of expectancy effects, although still in its infancy, suggests in some settings, for some teachers, and for some subgroups of children, teacher expectancy effects are more powerful (Weinstein, 2002; Weinstein, Gregory, & Strambler, 2004; Weinstein & McKown, 1998). Second, children are good at appraising what teachers expect of them. Thus, beyond the direct effects of differential curricular exposure or practice on children's development, the indirect pathway of *interpreted* expectancy cues is vitally important to pursue. Finally, links between interpersonal expectancy effects and group achievement inequalities have barely been explored. To locate and prevent interpersonal expectancy effects that contribute to group academic inequalities requires a deep understanding and close examination of the settings in which those expectations are formed and expressed. Advances in research on interpersonal expectancy effects are marked by an embrace by researchers of ecological perspectives that place individuals and groups within their complex and nested environmental settings (McKown, 2005; Weinstein, 2002; Weinstein & McKown, 1998).

***Stereotype Threat***  With a more recent empirical history and derived from the work by Allport (1954) on prejudice and Goffman (1963) on stigma, research on stereotype threat has focused on the effects of broadly held stereotyped group expectations on the targets of those stereotypes (Aronson & Steele, 2005; Steele & Aronson, 1995). Research on stereotype threat in K-12 schools is sparse. However, the existing research, predominantly conducted with college students, has implications for children's performance in school. Stereotype threat is defined as an individual's concern, evoked by a situational cue, that her behavior may be judged in relation to a negative societal stereotype about a group to which she belongs (Major & O'Brien, 2005; Steele, 1997; Steele & Aronson, 1995). This concern can lead targets of stereotypes to confirm the stereotype in a self-fulfilling prophecy. Stereotype threat occurs under very specific conditions. First, a student must have a stigmatized identity, defined as an identity that is devalued by society. Recent survey and experimental research (Bobo, 2001; Dovidio & Gaertner, 2004) suggests that African American and Latino/a intellectual ability remains devalued in American society. Girls' abilities are still questioned in the areas of mathematics and science (Spelke, 2005). Second, the stigmatized student must be aware of the prevailing beliefs and attitudes about his or her stigmatized identity (McKown & Weinstein, 2003). Third, those beliefs and attitudes must be domain-specific and valenced. For example, the stereotype that African Americans are not intellectually capable is domain specific with regard to intellectual ability as well as negatively valenced in its reference to lack of ability.

The final condition is that a person's stigmatized identity must be made salient by a situational cue so that a student from a stereotyped group believes the stereotype might

be used to judge his or her behavior (Steele, 1997). Steele and Aronson (1995), for example, conducted a series of experiments in which they asked African American and European American college students to take a difficult test. They assigned students to different testing conditions. In one set of experiments, some students were told that the test would be diagnostic of their ability; other students were told that the test was a challenging problem-solving task. In other experiments, students were randomly assigned either to indicate their ethnicity or not before taking the test. They found that when African American students took the test under conditions in which their stigmatized identity was made salient, they performed worse than under conditions in which their stigmatized identity was not made salient. In general, research on stereotype threat has identified four kinds of stereotype threat cues, including describing a performance situation as diagnostic of ability (e.g., McKown & Weinstein, 2003, Study 2; Steele & Aronson, 1995, Experiment 1), making participants think about self-relevant stereotyped identity (e.g., Ambady, Shih, Kim, & Pittinsky, 2001), telling participants directly that people in their group perform worse on a task (e.g., Leyens, Desert, Croizet, & Darcis, 2000), and exposing participants to stereotype relevant words before performing a task. Sometimes, those words are presented consciously (e.g., Dijksterhuis & van Knippenberg, 1998) and other times, they are presented subliminally (e.g. Bargh, Chen, & Burrows, 1996).

The lion's share of stereotype threat studies have examined the effects of stereotype threat conditions on academic test performance. However, a growing body of work suggests that stereotypes can shape behavior across a wide range of outcome domains. Since the early stereotype threat experiments, over a hundred published studies have applied this construct to different groups including women (Spencer, Steele, & Quinn, 1999), men (Koenig & Eagly, 2005), elders (Chasteen, Bhattacharyya, Horhota, Tam, & Hasher, 2005), and children (e.g., Ambady et al., 2001; McKown & Weinstein, 2003). In addition, stereotype threat studies have examined a range of outcomes beyond achievement, including athletic performance (Beilock & McConnell, 2004; Stone, 2002), job performance (Farr, 2003), and social sensitivity (Koenig & Eagly, 2005).

The mechanism through which stereotype threat conditions affect target performance remains unclear. Wheeler and Petty (2001) argued that either affective or cognitive processes are likely to mediate the effects of stereotype threat conditions on performance. One potential affective mediator is anxiety, although evidence for the anxiety hypothesis has been mixed. In terms of cognitive processes, situational cues may make stereotyped behaviors cognitively accessible. Called an "ideomotor" response, this increase in cognitive accessibility may then lead targets to enact the stereotyped behavior (see review by Wheeler & Petty, 2001). Supporting the ideomotor hypothesis, stereotype-consistent behavior has been shown to follow conscious and subliminal priming conditions (DeMarree, Wheeler, & Petty, 2005). For instance, activation of positive stereotypes of the elderly has been linked to faster walking time among the elderly (Hausdorff, Levy, & Wei, 1999). This theory has not been examined with children in the lab setting or in the naturalistic context of school. In a recent review, Aronson and Steele (2005) argued that the weight of evidence suggests that stereotype threat conditions cause cognitive overload, which affects memory and problem-solving processes. Regardless of whether emotional or cognitive factors represent the process linking stereotype cues and performance, most researchers feel that targets need not be aware of stereotype threat cues for those cues to affect targets' behavior. In other words, stereotype threat can operate out of conscious awareness.

Virtually all stereotype threat studies have been true experiments focused on adults. The consistency of the effect across studies and investigators suggests that this is a robust phenomenon, at least among higher achieving college students. Furthermore, the emphasis of the stereotype threat literature on the testing context strongly suggest that the conditions of testing, including the way tests are described can affect student performance not because of student effort or ability, but because concern about being judged stereotypically interferes with performance. The subset of stereotype threat studies that focused on children suggest that children may be susceptible to stereotype threat effects as early as elementary school (Ambady et al., 2001; McKown & Weinstein, 2003).

In summary, stereotype threat is a form of self-fulfilling prophecy that is induced by situational cues that signal to members of stereotyped groups that they may be judged stereotypically. The phenomenon has been replicated many times, suggesting it is a robust phenomenon. Stereotype threat can be induced through a number of apparently subtle events preceding a performance task. Finally, stereotype threat appears to function on a large variety of groups about which a stereotype is made salient, and it can affect outcomes in a wide range of behavioral domains. Although little research on stereotype threat has examined children or the operation of stereotype threat in naturalistic contexts, it seems likely that situational cues that signal to students that their intellectual ability is devalued because of their group membership may be negatively affected by this social process.

### Synthesis: Expectancy Effects and Stereotype Threat

*Overlapping Instances of Self-Fulfilling Prophecies*    Research on teacher expectancies and stereotype threat describes processes through which beliefs about the other propagate self-fulfilling prophecies. When those expectations are negative, the self-fulfilling prophecy has the potential to harm students. When they are positive, they have the potential to promote the development of talent. As a result, both have critical implications for educational practices and policies. Despite these similarities, it is striking that scholarly work on interpersonal expectancy effects on the one hand and stereotype threat on the other have developed in parallel, with little intersection between the

theories or empirical work. Given the relevance of both processes to schooling and children's development, it is critical to offer an integrated account of interpersonal expectancy and stereotype threat effects to guide further theory development, empirical research, and most importantly, educational policy and practices. Here, we forge an integration of these two phenomena: focusing on differences, commonalities, developmental considerations, and the advantages of an integrative focus.

*Differences*    There are situations that clearly reflect either interpersonal expectancy effects or stereotype threat and there are situations that reflect both processes. A teacher who holds higher expectations for an average-performing student because the student is likeable and hard working may create a positive self-fulfilling prophecy that is not shaped by stereotypes. In that case, an interpersonal expectation, not stereotype threat, shapes the student's achievement. In contrast, a student who is taking a test that has been characterized as diagnostic of ability may become concerned about being judged stereotypically and perform poorly. In that case, stereotype threat, but not interpersonal expectancies, shapes student academic performance.

There are several key differences between the two processes. Interpersonal expectancy effects involve the influence of an individual's expectations on another person's behavior; stereotype threat involves the influence of broadly held stereotypes and situational cues on stereotyped group members. In the interpersonal expectancy process, there *must* be a perceiver who actively expects a particular outcome from a target. In stereotype threat, situational cues initiate the effect. Thus, there need not be a perceiver involved for stereotype threat to occur. In interpersonal expectancies, the perceiver's expectations *may* be shaped by stereotypes—for example, a math teacher's expectations about a particular girl may be influenced by the teacher's belief that girls are not good at math. However, interpersonal expectations are not limited to stereotypes. In stereotype threat, the influential expectation is by definition a stereotype. The mechanisms of action are also partially distinct: Teacher expectations shape the instructional opportunities and support teachers give students, which directly and indirectly affect student learning and achievement. In contrast, with stereotype threat, situational cues signal to students that their intellectual ability may be devalued because of their group membership, which leads them to underperform. Children's awareness of teacher expectations may or may not affect their response to the expectation. In stereotype threat, children *must* be aware of broadly held stereotypes, although it is important to note that under threat conditions, they may not be consciously aware that a stereotype is being applied to them.

*Similarities*    Despite differences between the two phenomena, important similarities bind them, as a real-world example illustrates. Imagine a teacher who believes that a third-grade girl with strong math skills will do badly in math. This appears to be a straightforward interpersonal expectancy situation: An individual teacher holds a belief about the ability of an individual student. However, now imagine that this student is aware that many people believe that girls are not good at math. Furthermore, she has detected cues that the teacher thinks she is bad at math. As she sits down to do a math assignment, she becomes concerned that the teacher will judge her performance through the lenses of a stereotype about girls' math ability. Her mind goes blank. She performs poorly on the assignment even though she has the skill to succeed. Her poor performance reflects a self-fulfilling prophecy. Was this an interpersonal expectancy effect or stereotype threat? On the one hand, the teacher's expectation, expressed in the relationship between teacher and student, propagated a chain of events leading to poor performance. On the other hand, the student was concerned about being judged on the basis of a stereotype, and this concern interfered with her performance.

Thus, in some situations, stereotype threat and interpersonal expectancy processes operate indivisibly. When an interpersonal expectation reflects a broader stereotype, the belief may affect the target of the belief through multiple pathways. The low expectation could lead the teacher to provide this student with fewer and less rigorous learning opportunities, directly affecting her learning and performance. The student may read overt and subtle behavioral cues that signal to the student that the teacher does not think much of the student's abilities, in turn shaping the student's self-expectations, engagement in math, and math achievement. This reflects an indirect expectancy effect. Finally, reading the expectancy cues, the student may wonder, consciously or not, whether the teacher's low expectations reflect a general belief about girls' math ability, which may lead her to become concerned about being judged by the teacher in terms of the stereotypes. This concern may negatively affect the student's performance via stereotype threat.

***Developmental Considerations*** Interpersonal expectancy effects and stereotype threat may depend, in part, on targets' understanding of others' beliefs about them. In terms of stereotype threat, for an individual to be concerned that another will judge that person stereotypically, the person must, by definition, be aware of the broadly held societal stereotypes that are commonly applied to his or her group. In the moment-to-moment of stereotype threat situations, targets may not be consciously aware that their behavior is shaped by concern about stereotypes. Nonetheless, awareness of broadly held stereotypes is necessary for those stereotypes to be threatening (McKown & Weinstein, 2003). In terms of teacher expectancy effects, students do not have to be aware of a teacher's expectations to be affected by those expectations—differential exposure to challenging curriculum can shape student learning and achievement even if the student is totally unaware of what the teacher expects. However, we know that when students are aware of the teacher's expectations, this can affect student self-

concept and motivation, which can in turn affect school engagement and learning (Brattesani et al., 1984; Kuklinski & Weinstein, 2001). Thus, children's awareness of the expectations of others plays an important role in interpersonal expectancy and stereotype threat processes (McKown & Weinstein, 2002).

The way that interpersonal expectancy and stereotype threat processes affect children thus partially depends on children's ability to infer others' beliefs and intentions. We know from the developmental literature that children's ability to infer others' beliefs and intentions changes considerably with age (Perner & Wimmer, 1985). We would thus expect children's ability to accurately infer others' expectations and stereotypes to change with age, which in turn would affect the manner in which expectations and stereotypes affect children. In the realm of teacher expectancies, Weinstein et al. (1987) found that between first and fifth grades, children become more accurate at estimating teacher expectations. In addition, Brattesani et al. (1984) found that the more children perceive differential teacher treatment toward high- and low-achieving students, the more strongly teacher expectations predicted student achievement. Together, these findings suggest that even young children actively interpret expectancy cues, their ability to infer teacher expectations becomes more accurate with age, and perceptions of ability cues play an important role in determining the magnitude of expectancy effects.

Few studies have examined stereotype threat in children. Ambady et al. (2001) found that making ethnicity salient can affect the test performance of elementary and middle-school aged children. In their study, children were randomly assigned to an ethnicity prime, a gender prime, or a neutral prime condition before taking a math test. Younger children colored pictures of Asian children either eating with chopsticks (ethnicity prime), playing with dolls (gender prime), or coloring a landscape (control condition). Older children filled out questionnaires that focused either on ethnicity, gender, or the outdoors (control condition). When a positively academically stereotyped identity (Asian ethnicity) was primed, younger and older children performed well on a test. In contrast, when a negatively academically stereotyped identity (gender) was primed, younger and older children performed poorly on the same test. Furthermore, children exhibited stereotype activation in each condition. This suggests that explicit identity priming can activate stereotypes and affect the academic achievement of even young children.

How might age-related changes in social cognitive development affect children's response to stereotype threat conditions? McKown and Weinstein (2003) found that between the ages of 6 and 10, children developed dramatically increased awareness of broadly held stereotypes. For children who are aware of broadly held stereotypes and who are from academically stereotyped ethnic groups (African American and Latino), when a test is described as diagnostic of ability, children perform worse than when the same test is described as a problem-solving test. When children are not aware of broadly held stereotypes, the conditions of testing do not produce stereotype threat effects. This suggests that awareness of broadly held stereotypes is a necessary condition for situational cues to induce stereotype threat. By the age of 8, half the children in their sample were aware of broadly held stereotypes, such as the stereotype that Blacks are less intellectually capable than Whites. Increasing awareness of others' expectations and of stereotypes may also increase the potency of teacher expectations for members of stereotyped ethnic groups. In study that included a sample of 6- to 10-year-olds, McKown and Weinstein (2002) found that older elementary-aged children from stereotyped ethnic groups were more likely to confirm teacher underestimates, rather than overestimates, of ability in their academic performance.

These studies lead to some general conclusions about the role of social cognitive development in interpersonal expectancy and stereotype threat processes. First, consistent with a constructivist view of development, children actively interpret environmental cues about others' expectations and stereotypes. Second, in middle childhood, the ability to make inferences about others' mental states becomes more sophisticated with age. The studies reviewed above suggest that as children traverse middle childhood, their ability to infer others' expectations and stereotypes moves from inaccurate and underdeveloped to accurate and detailed. Finally, efforts to intervene to reduce any negative effects of stereotypes and expectations or, in the case of positive expectations, to enhance their benefits should account for age-related differences in children's appraisals of expectancy- and stereotype-relevant environmental cues.

***Advantages of an Integrative Focus*** A careful examination of both social influence processes side by side suggests important intersections between the phenomena. Interpersonal expectations can be shaped by stereotypes and propagate self-fulfilling prophecies via stereotype threat. Conversely, stereotype threat processes are in theory not limited to performance or test situations—the quality of the teacher–student relationships may induce stereotype threat, shaping achievement and motivation. The vast majority of stereotype threat experiments conducted so far have examined the role of testing situations on student performance. It remains an open question how and when social life in school—beyond the conditions of testing—signals to students that their intellectual ability is valued or devalued because of their group membership. It is highly likely that situations other than tests communicate to students that their intellectual ability may be discounted because of their group membership, affecting motivation and learning. Thus, by examining both processes side by side, we may gain a broader view of the range of situations in which both processes affect student learning and achievement, the processes through which those situations affect students, and the moderating role of individual characteristics and environments.

## The Social Ecology of Expectations and Stereotypes

The social complexity of classrooms and schools often is viewed by researchers as "noise" to be controlled (Shinn & Toohey, 2003). With a few exceptions (e.g., Weinstein, 2002), this is the stance taken by investigators examining teacher expectancy effects and stereotype threat. The question most expectancy and stereotype threat research seeks to answer is, if you subtract other sources of social influence from school, how much do teacher expectations and societal stereotypes influence children? An alternative view is that the very social complexity of the schools contains as yet unidentified events that signal to students what is expected of them. Viewed in this way, the complexity of the social context of schooling contains a system of signs and signals, some deliberate and some implicit, about expectations and stereotypes. In this section, we discuss the critical role of individual and contextual factors in communicating expectations and magnifying or diminishing the effects of teacher expectations and stereotype threat.

In identifying the breadth of events that communicate expectations and stereotypes and that moderate their effects, we adopt an ecological perspective (Bronfenbrenner, 1977; Eccles & Roeser, chapter 2 this volume; Kelly, 1987; Weinstein, 2002). Ecological theory suggests that social processes operating within individuals, in intimate interpersonal interactions, within organizations and institutions, and in society at large interact with and shape individual behavior. The vast majority of research on interpersonal expectancy effects and stereotype threat has focused on teacher–student dyads (expectancy effects) and on a narrow range of situational cues preceding a performance task (stereotype threat). To identify a more complete set of events that signal expectations and stereotypes, the lens of inquiry needs to widen to include qualities of settings, institutions, broad social norms, and social policies. An ecological framework may guide investigators to conduct such work systematically and rigorously. With advances in methodological strategies for evaluating the influences of settings on individuals, a rigorous science of social ecologies is within our grasp.

### Research Findings on Contextual and Individual Moderators of Self-Fulfilling Prophecies

*Perceived Differential Teacher Treatment and Achievement Cultures* Classroom practices that make each student's place in the achievement hierarchy highly visible to all may communicate important information to students about expectations and stereotypes, in turn magnifying the effects of teacher expectations and stereotype threat. Supporting this general proposition, Brattesani et al. (1984) and Kuklinski and Weinstein (2001) found that teacher expectations were more strongly related to year-end achievement (controlling for prior achievement) in classrooms in which students reported that teachers treated high and low achievers differently. In those classrooms where teacher expectations were highly visible to all, expectancy effects were more powerful. What does this imply about how to reduce negative expectancy effects and promote talent equitably? Weinstein (2002) argued strongly that school cultures of achievement affect the extent to which expectations constrain or support achievement, and that schools whose staff view student talent in a differentiated way, who provide varied niches of opportunity for students to express their talent and learn, who create opportunities for challenging instruction for all students, not a limited few, and that incorporate reflective professional development practices may create a positive expectancy climate in which more children benefit from the positive power of expectations to develop talent.

*Within-Class Ability Grouping*  Within-class ability grouping may provide important information to students about expectations. It is likely that in addition to communicating expectations, within-class ability grouping magnifies the power of expectations to shape student achievement. One quasi-experimental study (Smith, Jussim, Eccles, Van-Noy, Madon, & Palumbo, 1998) suggests that the effects of self-fulfilling prophecies are more powerful where students were grouped by ability in the classroom, particularly for low-ability group students. These findings suggest again that some classroom practices make each student's place in an achievement hierarchy highly salient to others. Furthermore, when the achievement hierarchy is highly salient and student talent is defined narrowly, teacher expectations may affect student achievement more strongly, particularly for low-achieving students.

*Teacher Susceptibility to Biased Expectations*  So far, we have examined the social settings in which teacher expectations may be more potent, focusing on the classroom as the unit of analysis. Are there teacher characteristics that might make it more likely that teacher expectations will be biased, inflexible, and influential? Using experimental methods, Hazelrigg, Cooper, and Strathman (1991) investigated personality correlates of biased expectations. They found that college students with a strong need for social influence were more likely to create expectancy effects in an experimental context. Similarly, Babad and Inbar (1981) investigated teacher susceptibility to biasing information about students. They found that teachers who were more conventional, who conformed to social rules, who were concerned about authority, and whose supervisors judged them to be more dogmatic, were more likely to be biased in their judgments of students. Thus, the teacher's disposition can affect the likelihood of strongly held expectations.

*Student Susceptibility to Expectations and Stereotypes*  Some students are more susceptible to expectancy effects than others. Experimental work with college students suggests that people who have a high need for approval are more likely to conform to others' expectations (Hazelrigg et al., 1991). Whether this is so among school-aged children and youth remains an open question. Beyond personality

characteristics, stigmatized group membership appears to be a risk-factor for expectancy confirmation. Madon, Jussim, and Eccles (1997) found that students with a history of low achievement are more susceptible to self-fulfilling prophecies. Jussim et al. (1996) found that African American students and students from low socioeconomic backgrounds were more susceptible to teacher expectancy effects. Similarly, McKown and Weinstein (2002) found that African American students and older girls with regard to math were particularly susceptible to negative self-fulfilling prophecies. More work is sorely needed to understand child characteristics that magnify or attenuate the effects of teacher expectations on children's achievement.

In the case of stereotype threat, no research we are aware of has examined contextual moderators, but some research has evaluated individual vulnerability. By definition, being the member of a stigmatized group is a risk factor for stereotype threat. However, not all members of stigmatized groups respond the same to stereotype threat situations. There are several individual characteristics that are likely to moderate the effects of stereotype threat conditions on behavior. The more a stereotyped individual cares about performance in the stereotyped domain (Steele, 1997), the more the individual identifies with the stereotyped group (Aronson & Steele, 2005), and the more the individual expects that others will use stereotypes to judge him or her (Brown & Pinel, 2003; Mendoza-Denton, Downey, Purdie, Davis, & Pietrzak, 2002), the more likely he or she is to be vulnerable to stereotype threat. In some of the only work on susceptibility to stereotype threat among children, McKown and Weinstein (2003) found that stereotype threat only affected cognitive task performance of children from stereotyped groups when they were aware of broadly held stereotypes.

**Other Potential Contextual and Individual Moderators of Self-Fulfilling Prophecies**  An important direction for future research and reflective practice is to explore what commonplace classroom events may, even inadvertently, communicate to students that their intellectual ability is devalued. We focus in the following review on classroom climates and events that are likely to signal important information about teacher expectations and stereotypes, all of which require further investigation.

*Racial and Gender Climate*  One contextual factor that may communicate important information to students particularly about stereotypes is the overall racial and gender climate of the school. The stereotype threat literature suggests that concern about being judged on the basis of a stereotype is the main factor driving stereotype threat effects on academic performance and behavior. If this is so, the racial climate, defined as the aggregate racial attitudes of participants in a setting, may affect the likelihood that individual participants in that setting will be affected by stereotype threat. In ethnically heterogeneous schools, the more children and adults in a school endorse racial stereotypes and prejudices, the more likely children are to experience being the target of a stereotype (Brown & Bigler, 2005; McKown & Weinstein, 2003) and the more likely they are to be concerned about being judged on the basis of a stereotype. The converse is likely to be true as well. In settings characterized by high aggregate levels of egalitarian racial attitudes, the threat posed from racial stereotypes is likely to be lower, lessening their effect on student learning. This hypothesis suggests that the racial climate of the classroom, where the bulk of interpersonal interactions that intersect with performance contexts occur, is a critical aspect of climate. If racial climate is related to student experience of stereotype threat, then a range of intervention strategies are available to teachers to reduce prejudice and therefore the likelihood of stereotype threat (Bigler, Jones, & Lobliner, 1997; McKown, 2005; Paluck & Green, 2009; Pfeifer, Brown, & Juvonen, 2007).

*Functional Use of Group Membership* Related to the racial and gender climate are classroom practices that increase status differences between members of different groups. For example, the functional use of group membership to organize instruction or daily routines may signal important information about the status of individual group members. Bigler et al. (1997) found that when teachers used novel groupings (blue and yellow T-shirts) to organize daily activities such as having children line up for recess, children quickly developed group biases that favored their own group and denigrated the other group. By extension, functional groupings in school may signal to students what teachers and society expect. In schools, many functional groups cleave along ethnic lines. Imagine an ethnically heterogeneous high school in which honors and AP courses are populated largely by European American students and general education and remedial classes are populated by ethnic minority children. Many students in this school are aware that the different academic tracks reflect different expectations about student capabilities and that the different tracks are populated by members of different ethnic groups. In this school, expectations about individual students are communicated by functional grouping. Because the functional grouping divides children from different ethnic groups into academic groups with different status, this practice may also signal to students that ethnic stereotypes about academic ability are used to make judgments about student course assignment.

*Perceptions of Fairness* When students believe that unfair treatment relates to their ethnicity or gender, the climate may induce stereotype threat. School climate research has shown that adolescents' perceptions of the clarity and fairness of rules at their school are associated with better behavior in schools (Gottfredson, Gottfredson, & Hybl, 1993; Welsh, 2000) and lower school crime and violence (Mayer & Leone, 1999), when controlling for risk factors such as school rates of poverty (Gottfredson, Gottfredson, Payne, & Gottfredson, 2005). Gregory and Weinstein (2008)

showed that the more high school students perceived teacher fairness, care, and academic expectations, the less defiant and more cooperative they were with teachers. Additional research is needed to understand the cumulative effects of the multiple school environments faced by high schoolers as they traverse multiple classrooms. Similarly, it would be helpful to understand the protective effects of sustained interactions with teachers that students believe are fair. The experience of multiple teachers as fair and nondiscriminatory may have positive and cumulative effects on the development of adolescent behavior. Broad social climate factors such as perceived fairness may communicate behavioral and academic expectations and shape students' behavior and academic performance.

*Instructional Practices and Goal Structures* Other instructional practices may affect the salience of status and ability in the classroom, which may in turn affect the strength of expectancy effects. Competitive or performance-oriented instructional practices may heighten the clarity and power of expectations and stereotypes in the classroom. Johnson and Johnson (1999) describe competitive instructional practices as "forced, salient, and obtrusive comparisons" among students. In competitive classrooms, a limited number of students can obtain a goal, and it is highly visible who wins and who loses. Grading on a forced curve reflects a competitive instructional practice. Limited entry into highly academically rewarding honors courses also reflects a kind of competitive instructional practice. It seems likely that the more competitive the school and classroom, the clearer the signals about what is expected of each student. In addition, competitive instructional practices may, like diagnostic test instructions, make students from stereotyped groups concerned that they will be judged on the basis of a stereotype.

Similarly, teachers create goal structures through practices that communicate the achievement goals that are most valued. In some classes, public demonstration of competence or *performance* is valued; in others, the private attainment of specific academic skills or *mastery* is valued (Ames, 1992; Urdan, 2004). These practices may overlap with competitive instructional practices. For example, public posting of grades and other indications of performance may signal to students that public performance of competence is valued more than mastery of skills. The goal structure of classrooms has mainly been measured by surveying student perceptions of the instructional climate, leaving many questions about what teacher practices that might be visible to an outside observer signal to students that performance goals are salient (Urdan, 2004). It is likely that whatever these practices are, they highlight ability cues, thus magnifying the effects of teacher expectations. And it is also likely that performance goal structures, like diagnostic test instructions, may lead to stereotype threat.

*Teacher and Student Theories of Intelligence* Dweck and colleagues have demonstrated that people vary in the extent to which they believe intelligence is a fixed entity or a malleable quality of individuals. People with "entity" theories of intelligence tend to view failure as proof that they are not intelligent and so do not persist as much at challenging tasks (Dweck, 1999). In contrast, children with "incremental" theories of intelligence believe that hard work is key to being smart, and they tend to persist in the face of failure. Similarly, Rosenholtz and Simpson (1984) argued that teachers can create classrooms that are "unidimensional" or "multidimensional" in the way student talent is defined. In unidimensional classrooms, student talent is narrowly defined and achievement hierarchies are highly visible. In contrast, in multidimensional classrooms, talent is valued across multiple performance dimensions and classrooms are more equitable. It is likely that teacher practices communicate to children the teacher's theory of intelligence and the "dimensionality" of intelligence. In classrooms in which entity theories or unidimensional views prevail, children may view failure as proof that they are not smart. The heightened sense of academic risk may magnify the salience of expectancy cues and may induce stereotype threat for students from academically stereotyped groups.

***Future Direction: Mapping the Diversity of Signals*** We have outlined briefly some of what is known about events that signal to students what teachers and society expect. We have also described other features of classroom life that may communicate expectations and stereotypes. The interpersonal expectancy and stereotype threat literatures have brought into clear focus the proximal events that propagate self-fulfilling prophecies. What is less well known is the full array of factors, situation in relation to society, that communicate expectations and stereotypes, and magnify their effects. It also remains unclear whether factors that magnify the power of expectations and stereotypes operate in conjunction—are expectancy effects particularly potent in settings in which several contextual moderators are present simultaneously? Reducing the negative effects of stereotypes and expectancy effects requires identifying and deeply understanding a fuller range of social processes that signal our beliefs about one another and shape the development of talent.

## Self-Fulfilling Prophecies across Multiple Domains of Child and Youth Functioning

Research on expectancy processes and stereotype threat has focused on the effects on children's achievement, but implications for the developing child go beyond academics. First, the effects of teachers' academic expectations and stereotype threat may "spill over" from the academic domain to other domains of functioning, including children's mental health, self-esteem, and identity development (Reddy, Rhodes, & Mulhall, 2003; Roeser, Eccles, & Sameroff, 2000). Substantive research on nonacademic domains suggests that examining such spillover may capture the cross-domain and far-reaching effects of academic expectations and stereotype

threat. Second, it is also possible that expectations and stereotypes may be formed about nonacademic attributes, such as student behavior and personality. Thus, these processes may reach into the behavioral domain. For example, teachers may communicate expectations or stereotypes about aggression, leading students to behave aggressively.

### *Nonacademic Effects of Academic Expectations and Stereotypes*

*Mental Health* The negative effects of expectancy and threat processes in the academic domain may spill over into the domain of mental health. In the social science statement that accompanied the appellants' briefs in the landmark court decision of Brown versus Board of Education, Clark, Chein, and Cook (1952/2004) described children's emotional responses to school segregation and prejudice, such as self-hatred and depression. Since then, studies of African Americans have focused on the negative mental health consequences of perceived discrimination in middle childhood through adolescence. African American 10- to 12-year-olds who report frequent victimization by discriminatory acts are likely to exhibit symptoms of depression (Simons et al., 2002). Similarly, African American seventh and eighth graders who perceive teachers as treating them more harshly and judging them more negatively because of their race are more angry and depressed (Wong, Eccles, & Sameroff, 2003). African American high school students who have more encounters with discrimination report higher internalizing symptoms (Clark, Coleman, & Novak, 2004). Awareness of biased treatment may increase hopelessness and helplessness in the face of uncontrollable forces, which have been linked to children's depression (Kaslow, Adamson, & Collins, 2000) and anxiety (Vasey & Ollendick, 2000).

*Self-Esteem and Identity* For children from academically stereotyped groups, academic stereotypes and low teacher expectations appear either to erode children's sense of self-worth or their identification with school. For example, in the face of negative academic performance feedback, attributing the negative feedback as arising from prejudice may protect self-esteem (Major, Kaiser, & McCoy, 2003). Major and colleagues (2003) asked undergraduates to imagine being denied entrance into a course. Those who were told that the rejection might be due to the professor's sexist attitudes were less likely to blame themselves for the rejection. Explaining academic adversity as a product of prejudice protects self-esteem. However, the costs of this strategy—discounting the value of school—may be great for members of stereotyped groups (Steele, 1997). Thus, targets of frequent prejudice face a dilemma—experience negative feedback as threatening and remain invested in academics or discount negative feedback as prejudicial and disidentify with school. It remains unclear whether these same attributional mechanisms protect the self-worth of children and adolescents and help them reject the negative messages of low academic expectations (Major & Vick, 2005).

A meta-analytic review showed that African Americans, a group that faces discrimination, have higher self-esteem than Whites (Twenge & Crocker, 2002). Low-achieving students who are met with low teacher expectations and stereotype threat may disengage from the academic domain and rely on other domains to develop a positive sense of self (Crocker, Brook, Niiya, & Villacorta, 2006; Steele, 1997). Schmader, Major, and Gramzow (2001) study defensive detachment from the academic domain through two processes—devaluing and discounting. Devaluing includes detaching self-esteem from achievement success or failure. Discounting includes dismissing the validity of the evaluation, which threatens a sense of self. Schmader et al. (2001) found that for African American undergraduates, broad beliefs about ethnic injustices were linked to greater discounting of the academic domain and devaluing of academic feedback. Ultimately, this may lead to "disidentification" from school (Steele, 1997) and to dropping out of school (Fine, 1991) as strategies to protect against negative effects of unfair treatment and low achievement.

***Effects of Behavioral Expectations and Stereotypes*** Although it has received less attention than academic expectations, nonacademic expectations and stereotypes may affect children's functioning in the corresponding nonacademic domain. Harris, Milich, Corbitt, Hoover, and Brady (1992) conducted one of the few studies with children that used experimental manipulation to examine behavioral self-fulfilling prophecies. In their study, children were randomly assigned to an expectancy induction. Some children were told that an unacquainted peer was in a special behavior problems class, disrupts the classroom, and acts silly. Others were told the name and the grade of the peer. The study showed that negative expectancies were associated with greater rejection and negative social interactions during a play session. Children reduced their involvement with and had greater negative affect toward stigmatized playmates who had been labeled as behavior problems. These findings reveal how adult labels about behavior can affect how children are viewed, can shape the nature of interactions, and can affect targets' behavior. This most clearly applies to stigmatizing labels such as "emotionally disturbed," "special needs," or "hyperactive" (Hinshaw, 2005, 2006).

The effects of stereotype threat on behavior have yet to be examined with children and adolescents. However, research with undergraduates on stereotypes and athletic performance suggests that athletic performance can be affected when racial stereotypes are primed (Stone, Lynch, Sjomeling, & Darley, 1999). White participants had depressed performance on a golf task when instructed that the task was diagnostic of natural athletic ability, and Black participants performed worse when instructed that their performance was diagnostic of athletic intelligence (Stone et al., 1999).

How behavioral expectations and stereotype threat operate in classrooms is understudied. Yet classroom environments are unlikely to be exempt from race-based and gender-based stereotypes about behavior. Gender stereotypes about behavior include boys as unruly or aggressive and girls as passive and compliant (Murphy et al., 200). Racial stereotypes of students as aggressive and defiant are also of concern (Sagar & Schofield, 1980), as reflected, for example, in the common media portrayal of African Americans as criminals (Mastro & Stern, 2003).

Indeed, research on teacher perceptions of behavior, conducted largely with elementary-aged students, suggests that teachers are more likely to hold negative judgments of ethnic minority students than White students. In one study, for example, compared to ethnic minority teachers, White kindergarten teachers were more likely to report having conflict with their ethnic minority students (Saft & Pianta, 2001) and report overall higher rates of student difficulty in following directions (Rimm-Kaufman, Pianta, & Cox, 2000). These trends in teacher perception may be reflected in racial patterns in discipline referrals. Teachers disproportionately sanction African American adolescents for uncooperative, disruptive, and defiant behavior (Gregory & Weinstein, 2008). In a path analysis explaining the disproportionate sanctioning of Black students, McCarthy and Hoge (1987) found that, despite Black and White students' similar self-reports of misconduct, teachers' evaluation of the students' demeanor explained a significant amount of the association between race and teacher punishments. In a large study of urban middle schools in the Midwest, Skiba and colleagues (Skiba, Michael, Nardo, & Peterson, 2000) found that reasons for suspension of African American students were more subjective than reasons for suspension of White students.

Although adults' racial stereotypes may contribute to the targeting of certain racial groups for discipline in schools, students' responses to stereotyping may also contribute to disciplinary patterns. Students may fulfill the prophecy of negative behavioral expectations by rejecting teacher authority and school rules that are seen as unfair and discriminatory. In an ethnography of black masculinity in an elementary school, Ferguson (2000) argued that many fifth and sixth grade African American boys regain power and a positive sense of self by acting out. Students obtain power in the hallways by assuming the identity of feared Black males. Externalizing behavior might be reinterpreted as a coping mechanism by which Black male students are asserting a "right to respect" (Spencer, Noll, Stoltzfus, & Harpalani, 2001). Research with adolescents and adults offers some initial evidence to support the link between adolescent externalizing behavior and perceived unfair treatment. Urban African American adolescents' perceptions of discriminatory treatment predicted defiance of teacher authority (Gregory & Weinstein, 2008) and an increase in violent acts from ninth grade to young adulthood (Caldwell, Kohn-Wood, Schmeelk-Cone, Chavous, & Zimmerman, 2004). In adult studies, authorities perceived as unfair obtain less cooperation and are seen as less legitimate (Tyler, 2006). Children and adolescents who perceive unfair treatment may similarly dismiss adult authority.

In sum, research on how stereotype threat and expectancy processes in the academic domain affect mental health, identity, and behavior as children's growth unfolds across time and across microclimates in school is in its infancy. Future work should examine how expectancy and situational threats to identity interact with individual coping styles and critical dimensions of the school contexts to affect mental health. In addition, future research should include a closer examination of the ways in which individual characteristics and social context moderate the effects of perceived discrimination in the academic domain, which can set some students on a negative behavioral trajectory in school, while others strive to disprove the expectations (Major & O'Brien, 2005; Sanders, 2006; Weinstein, 2002), and still others internalize the negative expectancy beliefs (Kuklinksi & Weinstein, 2001).

## Implications for Intervention

What effective strategies are available to reduce the negative consequences of expectations and stereotypes? What promising approaches might be employed and evaluated? How might a broad view of the social ecology of schools be enlisted to enhance existing approaches? We review interventions that focus on teacher and student beliefs and behaviors, and setting characteristics. We conclude by suggesting additional promising intervention strategies.

### *Targeted Interventions with Teachers and Students*

*Changing Teacher Beliefs and Behavior*    A crucial place to address expectations and stereotypes is with teachers themselves. A particularly important target of intervention is teacher behavior that communicates powerful expectations. For the past 30 years, a staff development program, Teacher Expectations and Student Achievement (TESA), has sought to change the overt and subtle expectancy messages teachers communicate in their interactions with students (Cantor, Kester, & Miller, 2000). In TESA workshops, teachers learn how to structure their classrooms for equity, to offer effective praise, to engage students respectfully, and to understand the meaning of nonverbal teacher behavior. Outcomes of the intervention have been uneven, with several studies showing little or no academic gains among low-achieving students (Fisher, 1995; Gottfredson, Marciniak, & Birdseye, 1995). Increased positive interactions with students, a result of the TESA training (Steeg, 1982), may not translate into achievement gains if other structural features of the classroom are not addressed (e.g., ability grouping, tracking, exposure to high-level course work).

Research on nonverbal communications provides important clues about why explicit behavioral interventions might change teacher awareness and some controllable behavior, while not changing other behaviors that continue to communicate expectations. Babad and colleagues have found

that biased teachers unwittingly communicate expectations through nonverbal cues (Babad, Bernieri, & Rosenthal, 1989). Changing overt expectancy behaviors may be less challenging than changing less controllable nonverbal behaviors that convey expectations. To address these more intractable expectancy cues, Babad (1990) used actual data collected in his participating teachers' classrooms to raise consciousness about their behavior. He identified gaps between student and teacher perspectives. Seventh graders in his study tended to perceive that teachers offered high achievers more emotional support than low achievers. In the treatment condition, teachers discussed student perceptions of differential treatment. Half of the small sample of teachers demonstrated a lack of openness to the feedback in the intervention. Perhaps constrained by the small sample size, the intervention did not show significant change in student reports of differential emotional support in the classroom.

Evaluative feedback may be a particularly powerful mechanism through which stereotyped expectations are communicated. When adults from stereotyped groups receive negative performance feedback, this can raise a question of whether the feedback is an expression of a stereotype (Cohen, Steele, & Ross, 1999). Based on this observation, Cohen and Steele (2002) developed a strategy they call "wise" feedback in which teachers provided critical feedback while reducing the potential for stereotype threat. In an experimental study with Black and White undergraduates, they found that feedback that communicated both high standards and assurance of student competence lowered mistrust of the evaluator as biased (Cohen, Steele, & Ross, 1999). In a similar study, women performed better on a science task when they received critical yet reassuring feedback as compared to simply critical feedback (Cohen & Steele, 2002). The gap in test performance between African Americans and Whites was eradicated on an exam when they were told the test was developed to be racially fair (Brown, 2001) and designed as a problem solving challenge, not as a diagnostic tool (Steele & Aronson, 1995). Although conducted with college students, these interventions suggest that seemingly simple changes to teacher practices hold promise for raising the achievement of stigmatized children and adolescents.

*Shaping Children's Beliefs*    Student beliefs about ability may affect student susceptibility to expectations and stereotypes. In a 12-week, randomized experiment, Rappaport and Rappaport (1975) found that inducing positive expectations in 5- and 6-year olds had larger effects on achievement gains than inducing positive expectations with the teacher only. The results of their intervention trial suggest that praise and positive predictions about future achievement might change students' own self-expectation and academic motivation.

Another strategy is to teach students ideas about intelligence that reduce the impact of stereotype threat conditions on test performance. Good, Aronson, and Inzlicht (2003) assigned mentors to seventh graders in a low income, rural school with a majority Latino/a enrollment. In addition to a control condition, mentors were asked to communicate specific ideas about intellectual ability and the causes of failure. One group of mentors taught their mentees that intelligence is not fixed and can develop through hard work and support. Other mentors encouraged mentees to attribute their difficulties to the normative hardship of entering junior high and not to their own stable, internal deficits. A third group of mentors combined messages about intelligence and attributions. Mentors and mentees worked together and completed web-based projects that reinforced the assigned educational message. The gender gap in math performance on a standardized test was reduced in all three conditions, compared to the control condition. Overall, the sample of predominately Black and Latino/a students in the intervention conditions had higher reading achievement on a standardized test compared to students in the control condition. This intervention suggests that equipping students with healthy ideas about ability and the causes of academic success is an important way to reduce the effects of stereotype threat.

In a more recent study, Cohen, Garcia, Apfel, and Master (2006) conducted a field experiment to lessen the effects of stereotype threat among middle school students. Students were randomly assigned to complete a self-affirmation exercise or a control writing exercise. They found that affirming important values led to improved grades for African American students while not having a negative effect on European American academic performance. This suggests that self-affirmation boosted resistance to stereotype threat among students from stereotyped groups.

In academically heterogeneous classrooms, children develop status differences that may exacerbate achievement differences between high and low-status students. Cohen and Lotan (1995) address this problem with a particular strategy for equalizing status in academically heterogeneous classrooms. Their intervention aimed to equalize participation among high and low-status students during an elementary school classroom activity. Teachers were trained to give specific, task relevant, and public feedback focusing on low-status students' competencies and to talk about how multiple abilities are needed to complete the activity. Observations of the interactions in the cooperative activities showed that when teachers used status-equalizing strategies, low-status students participated at higher rates than similar students in classrooms in which teachers did not implement these strategies. They also found that the use of status-equalizing messages was not associated with lower participation of high-status students. Teacher messages about competency can have positive ripple effects among students, shifting how they interact with one another.

The more children are racially prejudiced or hold stereotypic views, the more likely children from stereotyped groups will feel judged stereotypically. In theory, therefore, aggregate classroom- and school-level racial attitudes may affect the likelihood that students will experience stereotype threat. A number of classroom-based interventions attempt to reduce children's prejudice. Although the prejudice reduction interventions are grounded in theoretical traditions other than expectancy and stereotype processes (McKown, 2005), they offer insights into effective methods to improve the racial climate, potentially reducing the prevalence of stereotype threat. Methods of reducing prejudice in schools include teaching children to recognize differences within out-groups and recognize similarities between members of different groups (Aboud & Fenwick, 1999; Katz & Zalk, 1978) and structuring intergroup contact to maximize interdependence through cooperative learning strategies in which each student's success is contingent upon the success of others in his or her work group (e.g., Aronson & Patnoe, 1997; Slavin & Cooper, 1999) and minimize status differences (Cohen & Lotan, 1995). Prejudice-reduction curricula have also been incorporated into classrooms (Gabelko & Michaelis, 1981). For example, a 10-week, classroom-based program, "Facing History and Ourselves," examines intergroup conflict through material on the Holocaust and the Armenian genocide. It has shown some success in lowering middle school students' prejudice (Shultz, Barr, & Selman, 2001).

Ongoing work on the development of children's thinking about and response to race and racism is likely to yield additional strategies for reducing prejudice (Killen & McKown, 2005; Quintana & McKown, 2008). It remains an open question whether reducing prejudice in schools will reduce prevalence of stereotype threat and thus increase academic equity. However, research suggests that cooperative learning reduces student prejudice and increases student achievement, and that achievement gains are particularly robust for children from academically stereotyped ethnic groups (Slavin & Madden, 2001). It is possible that the *reason* that students from stereotyped groups benefit so greatly from cooperative learning is that reduced prejudice reduces students' exposure to stereotype threat situations. Whether this is so is an important question for future research. If this hypothesis is confirmed, then a broad range of school-based prejudice reduction strategies may be enlisted to promote student achievement and equity (McKown, 2005).

### School-Wide Interventions

*Integrative Perspective*   Good and Nichols (2001) proposed a multimodal expectancy intervention to raise the reading performance of first grade ethnic minority students. With teachers, they suggested professional development focused on how teacher behavior and emotions communicate expectations. They posited that teachers need to be able to give students corrective feedback that does not communicate a belief in lowered student potential. They also argued that small class sizes may increase teachers' interactions with individual students, thereby increasing the flexibility in teacher perceptions of low-achieving students. They also emphasized that warm, welcoming, and well-maintained school buildings communicate that students are honored and valued. Few interventions have put these recommendations into practice and evaluated their effects.

In an exception to this general rule, Weinstein and colleagues (Weinstein, Madison, & Kuklinski, 1995; Weinstein, Soulé et al., 1991) engaged in a collaborative intervention with the ninth grade students, administrators, and teachers in a midsized urban high school. The focus of their work included multiple aspects of the ecology of the ninth grade and the classroom and school environments. With a team of teachers and administrators in a regular consultation group, they reviewed scientific evidence about the negative effects of low expectations. Together, they developed strategies to improve the expectancy climate of the classroom and the school. They sought to expand the number of students across the achievement hierarchy who were exposed to challenging work that reflected high expectations. Despite the initial pessimism of teachers and perceived obstacles to change (Weinstein et al., 1995), they created opportunities for exposure to high-level coursework for a broader range of students. For example, enrollment in AP classes was expanded and ninth grade classes were detracked. They also targeted students themselves when they instituted additional academic supports and opportunities for students to reflect on their process of learning.

In their 2-year evaluation following students to the end of 10th grade, they documented a shift in teacher perceptions from a focus on student deficit to a focus on student strengths and potential (Weinstein, 2002; Weinstein, Madison, & Kuklinski, 1995). They used an archival sample of comparable ninth graders to assess the effects of the intervention on student achievement and behavior (Weinstein, Soulé et al., 1991). Program students had higher grade point averages and fewer disciplinary referrals at the end of the first year of the program. By the end of the 10th grade, a greater percentage of program students remained in the school than the comparison cohort. Noteworthy is that the program students did not have significantly higher grades than the comparison group at the end of 10th grade. Increased enrollment in more challenging college-bound courses may have masked improvements in academic performance.

*Increasing Exposure to High-Level Coursework* Children from academically stereotyped ethnic groups are typically overrepresented in low-track classes. Those classes, characterized by slow pacing, remedial material, and excessive control may widen racial and socioeconomic gaps in achievement (Oakes, 2005). Detracking initiatives rest on the premise that exposure to high-level coursework and to high-achieving peers will raise the achievement of traditionally underperforming students. Individual subject matter classes have been detracked (Mason, Schroeter, Combs, & Washington, 1992) as have entire grade levels (Oakes & Wells, 1996). Mason and colleagues (1992) found that opening an eighth grade prealgebra class to average-achieving general math students led both the high-achieving and the average-achieving math students

to make greater gains in math. In addition, the average-achieving math students were more likely to enroll in more advanced math classes in high school. Similar results were found in the "Algebra Project," which enrolls eighth graders of all abilities in algebra to prepare them for advanced course sequences in high school (Silva & Moses, 1990). They changed the curriculum to increase students' conceptual understanding of algebra and the relevance of mathematics to students' everyday life. They aimed to shift teachers' roles from "weeding out" students to cultivating students' potential. An evaluation of the program showed that detracked eighth grade students performed higher on achievement tests and enrolled in advanced high school mathematics courses compared to eighth graders who did not participate in the program (West & Davis, 2005). The underlying mechanisms that fostered growth have not been identified. Thus, it is unknown whether changes in teacher expectations, students' academic self-concept, exposure to high-level coursework, or affiliation with high-achieving peers fostered the achievement growth.

School-wide detracking efforts often include the elimination of remedial, low-tracked classes, the addition of supplemental academic supports, and the addition of instructional strategies specifically designed for academically heterogenous groups (Oakes & Wells, 1996). Recent research has demonstrated that methodical detracking from middle school through high school is linked to a narrowing of the racial achievement gap and an overall raising of achievement for all (Burris, Welner, & Wiley, 2006). In a suburban district with 20% African American and Latino/a student enrollment, a 10-year detracking effort began in the middle school and, by 2004, had reached the 10th grade (Burris et al., 2006). Their efforts have yielded promising results. Burris et al (2006) found that compared to tracked students with similar aptitude and demographic characteristics, the detracked students had six times the odds of attaining a New York State Regents diploma, which can only be achieved after passing exams in eight core subject areas.

In sum, as this chapter has outlined, teacher expectations and academic stereotypes operate in the social ecology of schools. In the universe of school reform efforts, relatively few interventions have been designed, implemented, and evaluated to reduce the negative consequences of low expectations and stereotypes. Promising interventions have targeted single aspects of stereotype and expectancy processes such as teacher instructional practices and the quality of teachers' evaluative feedback. Other interventions have targeted the students' themselves. Interventions targeting student beliefs or teacher practices have not yet been designed to attend to the broader social environment that might communicate those expectations and stereotypes. School level interventions, such as detracking, have tended to focus on exposing more students to high-level coursework. However, the structural reform of detracking has been criticized for ignoring the processes of stratification which can occur within classrooms (Cohen & Lotan, 1995; Weinstein, 1996). In the face of a substantial body of evidence that expectations and stereotypes matter and that they operate in complex social contexts, comprehensive approaches at altering patterns and practices associated with expectancy communication are warranted. The field awaits expectancy enhancement interventions focused on reframing multiple organizational features, including rigid and inflexible ability grouping, student attributions for failure, school-wide racial attitudes, peer achievement hierarchies, teacher stereotypes, the conditions of testing, and the nature of evaluative feedback.

## Summary and Conclusions

Individual teacher expectations and broadly held stereotypes about talent play an important role in children's lives. The literatures on teacher expectancy effects and stereotype threat each describe a distinct chain of events, occurring in schools, though which beliefs about ability affect the targets of those beliefs. Based in interpersonal expectancy theory, the literature on teacher expectations describes correlations between student characteristics and teacher expectations, between teacher expectations and teacher verbal and nonverbal behavior towards students, between student appraisals of and response to expectancy cues, and processes through which expectations shape student achievement. Based on social psychological theories of stigma and the self, the literature on stereotype threat describes the ways in which situational cues make broadly held academic stereotypes salient in the mind of the target, and the process through which that experience impairs performance in a stereotyped domain.

The research on interpersonal expectancy effects and stereotype threat share many strengths and many opportunities for further development. In both realms, we know a great deal about the proximal events that make expectations and stereotypes salient, particularly teacher behaviors and testing situations. On the other hand, there are likely many other situational cues that communicate to students what is expected of them or their group. Our understanding remains limited in terms of the role of child and setting characteristics in moderating the effects of expectations and stereotypes on children's development. In addition, most of the evidence about expectancy effects and stereotype threat has focused on academic outcomes, with intriguing evidence of influences across a range of functional domains highlighting the importance of investigating the behavioral and emotional consequences of expectations and stereotypes.

There are strengths and opportunities for development that are particular to the interpersonal expectancy effects literature. Teacher expectancy effects have been evaluated through true experiments in highly controlled laboratory conditions, field experiments, and naturalistic longitudinal studies in which teacher expectations are correlated with later achievement, controlling for prior achievement. The breadth of methodologies employed to evaluate teacher expectancy effects leads to reasonably firm conclusions

about the causal impact and overall effect size of teacher expectancy effects. Nonetheless, in our opinion, too little research on teacher expectancy effects has examined characteristics of children, teachers, classroom settings, and school contexts more broadly construed that may set the stage for stronger or weaker expectancy effects (Weinstein, 2002). This noteworthy lack of attention, particularly to social context, exists despite early recognition in the field that not all teachers create self-fulfilling prophecies. Furthermore, although even the most skeptical researchers acknowledge that teacher expectancy effects are real and that they can be powerful (Jussim & Harber, 2005), very little work has been done to intervene to enlist the power of teacher expectations for students' greater good.

Similarly, there are strengths and opportunities that are particular to the stereotype threat literature. Stereotype threat has largely been studied using true experiments conducted in controlled settings. A strength of this research is the causal inference that such designs permit. Furthermore, the phenomenon appears quite robust across age groups, stereotyped identity, stereotype threat cue, and stereotype domain (academic or nonacademic). The experimental evidence thus suggests that stereotype threat is a consistent, real, and potentially powerful phenomenon. Little attention has yet been paid to stereotype threat in naturalistic contexts, however, so it is difficult to know whether and how much stereotype threat affects student achievement. Noteworthy exceptions include two field experiments conducted in schools evaluating the effects of stereotype threat reduction interventions on student achievement, both of which suggest that when steps are taken to lessen stereotype threat, students from stereotyped groups reap substantial benefit. A second area for future research is the identification of school setting conditions that magnify or attenuate the strength of stereotype threat effects. A final area for clarification is a specific account of what psychological mechanism mediates the effects of stereotype threat cues and performance. Probably the best conclusion from the current state of the evidence is that stereotype threat is likely to affect student test performance. How large the effect, which individuals are most susceptible, and what naturalistic nontesting circumstances create stereotype threat remain open questions.

Our hope is that both of these important strands of research might inform one another, that we may come to a full and useful understanding of the conditions of schooling that set in motion self-fulfilling prophecies, and that we may use that understanding to promote student achievement and equity. We believe that scholars and practitioners who jointly draw upon what we know about stereotype threat and expectancy effects will contribute greatly to understanding the modes of self-fulfilling prophecies that can shape classroom and school life. Such an integrative perspective may better lend itself to the development of strategies for pervasively altering classroom structures to reduce negative self-fulfilling prophecies and promote greater equity.

## Author Note

Work on this chapter was supported by a William T. Grant Scholar's Award to Clark McKown.

## References

Aboud, F. E., & Fenwick, W. (1999). Exploring and evaluating school-based interventions to reduce prejudice. *Journal of Social Issues, 55,* 767–786.

Allport, K. G. (1954). *The nature of prejudice.* Cambridge, MA: Addison-Wesley.

Ambady, N., Shih, M., Kim, A., & Pittinsky, T. L. (2001). Stereotype susceptibility in children: Effects of identity activation on quantitative performance. *Psychological Science, 12,* 385–390.

Ames, C. (1992). Classrooms: Goals, structures, and student motivation. *Journal of Educational Psychology, 84,* 261–272.

Aronson, E., & Patnoe, S. (1997). *The jigsaw classroom: Building cooperation in the classroom* (2nd ed.). New York: Longman.

Aronson, J., & Steele, C. M. (2005). Stereotypes and the fragility of academic competence, motivation, and self-concept. In A. J. Elliot & C. S. Dweck (Eds.), *Handbook of competence and motivation* (pp. 436–456). New York: Guilford.

Babad, E. Y. (1990). Measuring and changing teachers' differential behavior as perceived by students and teachers. *Journal of Educational Psychology, 82,* 683–690.

Babad, E. Y., Bernieri, F., & Rosenthal, R. (1989). Nonverbal communication and leakage in the behavior of biased and unbiased teachers. *Journal of Personality and Social Psychology, 56,* 89–94.

Babad, E. Y., Bernieri, F., & Rosenthal, R. (1991). Students as judges of teachers' verbal and nonverbal behavior. *American Educational Research Journal, 28,* 211–234.

Babad, E. Y., & Inbar, J. (1981). Performance and personality correlates of teachers' susceptibility to biasing information. *Journal of Personality and Social Psychology, 40,* 553–561.

Bargh, J. A., Chen, M., & Burrows, L. (1996). Automaticity of social behavior: Direct effects of trait construct and stereotype activation on action. *Journal of Personality and Social Psychology, 71,* 230–244.

Beilock, S. L., & McConnell, A. R. (2004). Stereotype threat and sport: Can athletic performance be threatened? *Journal of Sport and Exercise, 26,* 597–609.

Bigler, R. S., Jones, L. C., & Lobliner, D. B. (1997). Social categorization and the formation of intergroup attitudes in children. *Child Development, 68,* 530–543.

Bobo, L. (2001). Racial attitudes and relations at the close of the twentieth century. In N. J. Smelser, W. J. Wilson, & F. Mitchell (Eds.), *America becoming: Racial trends and their consequences* (pp. 264–301). Washington, DC: National Academy Press.

Brattesani, K. A., Weinstein, R. S., & Marshall, H. H. (1984). Student perceptions of differential teacher treatment as moderators of teacher expectation effects. *Journal of Educational Psychology, 76,* 236–247.

Bronfenbrenner, U. (1977). Toward an experimental ecology of human development. *American Psychologist, 32,* 513–531.

Brophy, J. E. (1983). Research on the self-fulfilling prophecy and teacher expectations. *Journal of Educational Psychology, 75,* 631–661.

Brophy, J. E. (Ed.). (1998). *Advances in research on teaching: Vol. 7. Expectations in the classroom.* Greenwich, CT: JAI Press.

Brophy, J., & Good, T. (1970). Teachers' communication of differential expectations for children's classroom performance: Some behavioral data. *Journal of Educational Psychology, 61,* 365–374.

Brophy, J., & Good, T. (1974). *Teacher–student relationships: Causes and consequences.* New York: Holt, Rinehart, & Winston.

Brown, C. S., & Bigler, R. S. (2002). Effects of minority status in the classroom on children's intergroup attitudes. *Journal of Experimental Child Psychology, 83,* 77–110.

Brown, C. S., & Bigler, R. S. (2005) Children's perceptions of discrimination: A developmental perspective. *Child Development, 76,* 533–553.

Brown, J. L. (2001). Performance expectations are not a necessary mediator of stereotype threat in African American verbal test performance. *Dissertation Abstracts International, 61*(11-B), 6184.

Brown, R. P., & Pinel, E. C. (2003). Stigma on my mind: Individual differences in the experience of stereotype threat. *Journal of Experimental Social Psychology, 39,* 626–633.

Burris, C. C., Welner, K. G., & Wiley, E. W. (2006, April). *Closing the achievement gap by detracking high school classes.* Paper presented at the American Educational Research Association, San Francisco, CA.

Caldwell, C. H., Kohn-Wood, L. P., Schmeelk-Cone, K. H., Chavous, T. M., & Zimmerman, M. A. (2004). Racial discrimination and racial identity as risk or protective factors for violent behaviors in African American young adults. *American Journal of Community Psychology, 33,* 91–105.

Cantor, J., Kester, D., & Miller, A. (2000). Amazing results! Teacher expectations and student achievement (TESA) follow-up survey of TESA-trained teachers in 45 states and the District of Columbia. Retrieved from http://streamer.lacoe.edu/TESA/

Channouf, A., Mangard, C., Baudry, C., & Perney, N. (2005). The effect of salient social stereotypes on academic tracking decisions. *European Review of Applied Psychology, 55,* 217–223.

Chasteen, A. L., Bhattacharyya, S., Horhota, M., Tam, R., & Hasher, L. (2005). *Experimental Aging Research, 31,* 235–260.

Clark, K. B., Chein, I., & Cook, S. W. (2004). The effects of segregation and the consequences of desegregation: A (September 1952) social science statement in the Brown v. Board of Education of Topeka Supreme Court case. *American Psychologist, 59,* 495–501. (Original work published 1952)

Clark, R., Coleman, A. P., & Novak, J. D. (2004). Brief report: Initial psychometric properties of the everyday discrimination scale in black adolescents. *Journal of Adolescence, 27,* 363–368.

Cohen, E. G., & Lotan, R. A. (1995). Producing equal-status interaction in the heterogeneous classroom. *American Educational Research Journal, 32,* 99–120.

Cohen, G. L., Garcia, J., Apfel, N., & Master, A. (2006). Reducing the racial achievement gap: A social-psychological intervention. *Science, 313*(5791), 1307–1310.

Cohen, G. L., & Steele, C. M. (2002). A barrier of mistrust: How negative stereotypes affect cross-race mentoring. In J. Aronson (Ed.), *Improving academic achievement: Impact of psychological factors on education* (pp. 303–327). San Diego, CA: Academic Press.

Cohen, G. L., Steele, C. M., & Ross, L. D. (1999). The mentor's dilemma: Providing critical feedback across the racial divide. *Personality and Social Psychology Bulletin 25,* 1302–1318.

Crocker, J., Brook, A.T., Niiya, Yu, & Villacorta, M. (2006). The pursuit of self-esteem: Contingencies of self-worth and self-regulation. *Journal of Personality, 74,* 1749–1771.

DeMaree, K. G., Wheeler, S. C., & Petty, R. E. (2005). Priming a new identity: Self-monitoring moderates the effects of nonself primes on self-judgments and behavior. *Journal of Personality and Social Psychology, 89,* 657–671.

Dijksterhuis, A., & van Knippenberg, A. (1998). The relation between perception and behavior, or how to win a game of trivial pursuit. *Journal of Personality and Social Psychology, 74,* 865–877.

Dovidio, J. F., & Gaertner, S. L. (1998). On the nature of contemporary prejudice: The causes, consequences, and challenges of aversive racism. In J. L. Eberhardt & S. T. Fiske (Eds.), *Confronting racism: The problem and the response* (pp. 3–32). Thousand Oaks, CA: Sage.

Dovidio, J. F., & Gaertner, S. L. (2004). Aversive racism. In M. P. Zanna (Ed.), *Advances in Experimental Social Psychology, 36,* 1–52.

Dusek, J. B., & Joseph, G. (1983). The bases of teacher expectancies: A meta-analysis. *Journal of Educational Psychology, 75,* 327–346.

Dweck, C. (1999). *Self-theories: Their role in motivation, personality, and development.* Philadelphia, PA: Psychology Press.

Eccles, J. S., & Midgley, C. (1990). Changes in academic motivation and self-perception during early adolescence. In R. Montemayor, G. Adams, & T. P. Gullotta (Eds.), *From childhood to adolescence: A transitional period? Advances in adolescent development: An annual book series* (Vol. 2., pp. 134–155). Thousand Oaks, CA: Sage.

Farr, J. L. (2003). Introduction to the special issue: Stereotype threat effects in employment settings [Special issue]. *Human Performance, 16*, 179–180.

Ferguson, A. A. (2000). *Bad boys: Public school and the making of Black masculinity.* Ann Arbor: University of Michigan Press.

Fine, M. (1991). *Framing dropouts: Notes on the politics of an urban public high school.* Albany, NY: SUNY Press.

Fisher, P. E. S. (1995). An investigation to determine if TESA training has an effect on student achievement among third-grade students in Cabell County Schools. *Dissertation Abstracts International, 57*(06), 2289. (UMI No. 9635063)

Gabelko, N. H., & Michaelis, J. U. (1981). *Reducing adolescent prejudice: A handbook.* New York: Teachers' College Press.

Goffman, E. (1963). *Stigma: Notes on the management of spoiled identity.* Englewood Cliffs, NJ: Prentice-Hall.

Good, C., Aronson, J., & Inzlicht, M. (2003). Improving adolescents' standardized test performance: An intervention to reduce the effects of stereotype threat. *Applied Developmental Psychology, 24*, 645–662.

Good, T. L., & Nichols, S. L. (2001). Expectancy effects in the classroom: A special focus on improving the reading performance of minority students in first grade classrooms. *Educational Psychologist, 36*, 113–126.

Gottfredson, D. C., Gottfredson, G. D., & Hybl, L.G. (1993). Managing adolescent behavior: A multiyear, multischool study. *American Educational Research Journal, 30*, 179–215.

Gottfredson, D. C., Marciniak, E. M., & Birdseye, A. T. (1995). Increasing teacher expectations for student achievement. *Journal of Educational Research, 88*, 155–163.

Gottfredson, G. D., Gottfredson, D. C., Payne, A. A., Gottfredson, N. C. (2005). School climate predictors of school disorder: Results from a national study of commitment to prevention and schools. *Journals of Research in Crime and Delinquency, 42*, 412–444.

Graham, S. (2001). Inferences about responsibility and values: Implication for academic motivation. In F. Salili & C. Y. Chiu (Eds.), *Student motivation: The culture and context of learning* (pp. 31–59). (Plenum series on Human Exceptionality). Dordrecht, Netherlands: Kluwer Academic.

Gregory, A., & Weinstein, S. R. (2008). The discipline gap and African Americans: Defiance or cooperation in the high school classroom. *Journal of School Psychology, 46*, 455–475.

Harris, M. J., Milich, R., Corbitt, E. M., Hoover, D. W., & Brady, M. (1992). Self-fulfilling effects of stigmatizing information on children's social interaction. *Journal of Personality and Social Psychology, 63*, 41–50.

Hausdorff, J. M., Levy, B. R., & Wei, J. Y. (1999). The power of ageism on physical functioning of older persons: Reversibility of age-related gait changes. *Journal of the American Geriatrics Society, 47*, 1346–1349.

Hazelrigg, P. J., Cooper, H., & Strathman, A. J. (1991). Personality moderators of the experimenter expectancy effect: A reexamination of five hypotheses. *Personality and Social Psychology Bulletin, 17*(5), 569–579.

Hinshaw, S. (2005). The stigmatization of mental illness in children and parents: Developmental issues, family concerns, and research needs. *Journal of Child Psychology and Psychiatry, 46*, 714–734.

Hinshaw, S. (2006). *The mark of shame: Stigma and mental illness and an agenda for change.* New York: Oxford University Press.

Hughes, J. N., Gleason, K. A., & Zhang, D. (2005). Relationship influences on teachers' perceptions of academic competence in academically at-risk minority and majority first grade students. *Journal of School Psychology, 43*, 303–320.

Jencks, C., & Phillips, M. (Eds.). (1998). *The Black-White test score gap.* Washington, DC: Brookings Institution.

Johnson, D. W., & Johnson, R. T. (1999). *Learning together and alone: Cooperative, competitive, and individualistic learning.* Boston: Allyn & Bacon.

Jussim, L. (1989). Teacher expectations: Self-fulfilling prophecies, perceptual biases, and accuracy. *Journal of Personality and Social Psychology, 37*, 469–480.

Jussim, L., Eccles, J. S., & Madon, S. (1996). Social perception, social stereotypes, and teacher expectations: Accuracy and the quest for the powerful self-fulfilling prophecy. *Advances in Experimental Social Psychology, 28*, 281–388.

Jussim, L., & Harber, K. D. (2005). Teacher expectations and self-fulfilling prophecies: Knowns and unknowns, resolved and unresolved controversies. *Personality and Social Psychology Review, 9*, 131–155.

Kaslow, N. J., Adamson, L. B., & Collins, M. H. (2000). A developmental psychopathology perspective on cognitive components of child and adolescent depression. In A. J. Sameroff, M. Lewis, & S. M. Miller (Eds.), *Handbook of developmental psychopathology* (2nd ed., pp. 491–510). Kluwer Academic.

Katz, P. A., & Zalk, S. R. (1978). Modification of children's racial attitudes. *Developmental Psychology, 14*, 447–461.

Kelly, J. (1987). An ecological paradigm: Defining mental health consultation as a preventive service. *Prevention in Human Services, 4*(3–4), 1–36.

Killen, M., & McKown, C. (2005). How integrative approaches to intergroup attitudes advance the field. In M. Killen & C. McKown (Eds.), *Children's and adolescents' intergroup attitudes about race and ethnicity* [Special issue]. *Journal of Applied Developmental Psychology, 26*, 616–622.

Koenig, A. M., & Eagly, A. H. (2005). Stereotype threat in men on a test of social sensitivity. *Sex Roles, 52*, 489–496.

Kuklinski, M., & Weinstein, R. S. (2001). Classroom and developmental differences in a path model of teacher expectancy effects. *Child Development, 72*, 1554–1578.

Leyens, J. P., Desert, M., Croizet, J. C., & Darcis, C. (2000). Stereotype threat: Are lower status and history of stigmatization preconditions of stereotype threat? *Personality and Social Psychology Bulletin, 26*, 1189–1199.

Madon, S., Jussim, L., & Eccles, J. (1997). In search of the powerful self-fulfilling prophecy. *Journal of Personality and Social Psychology, 72*, 791–809.

Major, B., Kaiser, C. R., & McCoy, S. K. (2003). It's not my fault: When and why attributions to prejudice protect self-esteem. *Personality and Social Psychology Bulletin, 29*, 772–781.

Major, B., & O'Brien, L. T. (2005). The social psychology of stigma. *Annual Review of Psychology, 56*, 393–421.

Major, B., & Vick, S. B. (2005). The psychological impact of prejudice. In J. F. Dovidio, P. Glick, & L. A. Rudman (Eds.), *On the nature of prejudice: Fifty years after Allport* (pp. 155–172). Malden, MA: Blackwell.

Mason, D. A., Schroeter, D. D, Combs, R. K., & Washington, K. (1992). Assigning average-achieving eighth graders to advanced mathematics classes in an urban junior high. *Elementary School Journal, 92*, 587–599.

Mastro, D. E., & Stern, S. R. (2003). Representations of race in television commercials: A content analysis of prime-time advertising. *Journal of Broadcasting and Electronic Media, 47*, 638–647.

Mayer, M. J., & Leone, P. E. (1999). A structural analysis of school violence and disruption: Implications for creating safer schools. *Education and Treatment of Children, 22*, 333–356.

McCarthy, J. D., & Hoge, D. R. (1987). The social construction of school punishment: Racial disadvantage out of universalistic process. *Social Forces, 65*, 1101–1120.

McKown, C. (2005). Applying ecological theory to advance the science and practice of school-based prejudice reduction interventions. *Educational Psychologist, 40*, 177–189.

McKown, C., & Weinstein, R. S. (2002). Modeling the role of child ethnicity and gender in children's differential response to teacher expectations. *Journal of Applied Social Psychology, 32*, 159–184.

McKown, C., & Weinstein, R. S. (2003). The development and consequences of stereotype consciousness in middle childhood. *Child Development, 74*, 498–515.

McKown, C., & Weinstein, R. S. (in press). Teacher expectations, classroom context, and the achievement gap. *Journal of School Psychology.*

Mendoza-Denton, R., Downey, G., Purdie, V. J., Davis, A., & Pietrzak, J. (2002). Sensitivity to status-based rejection: Implications for African

American students' college experience. *Journal of Personality and Social Psychology, 83*, 896–918.

Merton, R. K. (1948). The self-fulfilling prophecy. *The Antioch Review, 8*, 193–210.

Oakes, J. (2005). *Keeping track of inequality* (2nd ed.). New Haven, CT: Yale University Press.

Murphy, P. A., Devine, P. G., Valian, V., Harper, K. D., DeAngelis, T., & Dowdy, Z. R. (2000). Prejudice, discrimination, and stereotyping. In M. H. Davis (Ed.), *Annual editions: Social psychology 2000/2001* (4th ed., pp. 126–147). Guilford, CT: Dushkin/Mcgraw-Hill.

Oakes, J., & Wells, A. S. (1996). *Beyond the technicalities of school reform: Policy lessons from detracking schools.* Los Angeles, CA: UCLA Graduate School of Education and Information Studies.

Paluck, E. L., & Green, D. P. (in press). Prejudice reduction: What works? A review and assessment of research and practice. *Annual Review of Psychology.*

Parsons, J. E., Kaczala, C. M., & Meece, J. L. (1982). Socialization of achievement attitudes and beliefs: Classroom influences. *Child Development, 53*, 322–339.

Perner, J., & Wimmer, H. (1985). "John thinks that Mary thinks…" Attribution of second-order beliefs by 5- to 10- year-old children. *Journal of Experimental Child Psychology, 39*, 437–471.

Pfeifer, J., Brown, C., & Juvonen, J. (2007). Teaching tolerance in schools: Lessons learned since Brown v. Board of Education about the development and reduction of children's prejudice. *Social Policy Report: Giving Child and Youth Development Away, 21*, 3–25.

Quintana, S. M., & McKown, C. (Eds.). (in press). *Handbook of race, racism, and the developing child.* Hoboken, NJ: Wiley.

Rappaport, M. M., & Rappaport, H. (1975). The other half of the expectancy equation: Pygmalion. *Journal of Educational Psychology, 67*, 531–536.

Raudenbush, S. W. (1984). Magnitude of teacher expectancy effects on pupil IQ as a function of the credibility of expectancy induction: A synthesis of findings from 18 experiments. *Journal of Educational Psychology, 76*, 85–97.

Reddy, R., Rhodes, J. E., & Mulhall, P. (2003). The influence of teacher support on student adjustment in the middle school years: A latent growth curve study. *Development and Psychopathology, 15*, 119–138.

Rimm-Kaufman, S. E., Pianta, R. C., & Cox, M. J. (2000). Teachers' judgments of problems in the transition to kindergarten. *Early Childhood Research Quarterly, 15*, 147–166.

Rist, R. (1970). Student social class and teacher expectations: The self-fulfilling prophecy in ghetto education. *Harvard Educational Review, 40*, 411–451

Roeser, R. W., Eccles, J. S., & Sameroff, A. J. (2000). School as a context of early adolescents' academic and social-emotional development: A summary of research findings. *The Elementary School Journal, 100*, 443–471.

Rosenholtz, S. J., & Simpson, C. (1984). Classroom organization and student stratification. *Elementary School Journal, 85*, 21–37.

Rosenthal, R. (1993). Interpersonal expectations: Some antecedents and some consequences. In P. D. Blanck (Ed.), *Interpersonal expectations: Theory, research, and applications* (pp. 3–24). New York: Cambridge University Press,

Rosenthal, R. (2003). Covert communications in laboratories, classrooms and the truly real world. *Current Directions in Psychological Science, 12*, 151–154.

Rosenthal, R., & Jacobson, L. (1968). *Pygmalion in the classroom: Teacher expectation and pupils' intellectual development.* New York: Holt Rinehart & Winston

Rosenthal, R., & Rubin, D. B. (1978). Interpersonal expectancy effects: The first 345 studies. *Behavioral and Brain Sciences, 1*, 377–415.

Rubie-Davies, C. M. (2006). Teacher expectations and student self-perceptions: Exploring relationships. *Psychology in the Schools, 43*, 537–552.

Rutter, M., & Maughan, B. (2002). School effectiveness findings: 1979–2002. *Journal of School Psychology, 40*, 451–475.

Rutter, M., Maughan, B., Mortimore, P., Ouston, J., & Smith, A. (1979).

*Fifteen thousand hours: Secondary schools and their effects on children.* Cambridge, MA: Harvard University Press.

Saft, E. W., & Pianta, R. C. (2001). Teachers' perceptions of their relationships with student: Effects of child age, gender, and ethnicity of teachers and children. *School Psychology Quarterly, 16*, 125–141.

Sagar, A. H., & Schofield, J. W. (1980). Racial and behavioral cues in Black and White children's perceptions of ambiguously aggressive acts. *Journal of Personality and Social Psychology, 39*, 590–598.

Sanders, M. G. (2006). Overcoming obstacles: Academic achievement as a response to racism and discrimination. *The Journal of Negro Education, 66*, 83–93.

Schmader, T., Major, B., & Gramzow, R. H. (2001). Coping with ethnic stereotypes in the academic domain: Perceived injustice and psychological disengagement. *Journal of Social Issues, 57*, 93–111.

Schultz, H. L., Barr, D. L., & Selman, R. L. (2001). The value of a developmental approach to evaluating character development programmes: An outcome study of facing history and ourselves. *Journal of Moral Education, 30*, 1–27.

Shinn, M., & Toohey, S. M. (2003). Community contexts of human welfare. *Annual Review of Psychology, 54*, 427–459.

Silva, C. M., & Moses, R. P. (1990). The Algebra Project: Making middle school mathematics count. *Journal of Negro Education, 59*, 375–391.

Simons, R. L., Murry, V., McLoyd, V., Kuei-Hsiu, L., Cutrona, C., & Conger, R. D. (2002). Discrimination, crime, ethnic identity, and parenting as correlates of depressive symptoms among African American children: A multilevel analysis. *Development and Psychopathology, 14*, 371–393.

Skiba, R., Michael, R. S., Nardo, A. C., & Peterson, R. (2002). The color of discipline: Sources of racial and gender disproportionality in school punishment. *Urban Review, 34*, 317–342.

Slavin, R. E., & Cooper, R. (1999). Improving intergroup relations: Lessons learned from cooperative learning programs. *Journal of Social Issues, 55*, 647–663.

Slavin, R. E., & Madden, N. A. (2001, April). *Reducing the gap: Success for all and the achievement of African American students.* Paper presented at the Annual Meeting of the American Educational Research Association, Seattle, WA.

Smith, A. E., Jussim, L., Eccles, J., VanNoy, M., Madon, S., & Palumbo, R. (1998). Self-fulfilling prophecies, perceptual biases, and accuracy at the individual and group levels. *Journal of Experimental Social Psychology, 34*, 530–561.

Smith, M. (1980). Teacher expectations. *Evaluation in Education, 4*, 53–55.

Snow, R. E. (1995). Pygmalion and intelligence? *Current Directions in Psychological Science, 4*, 169–171.

Spelke, E. S. (2005). Sex differences in intrinsic aptitude for mathematics and science? A critical review. *American Psychologist, 60*, 950–958.

Spencer, M. B., Noll, E., Stoltzfus, J., & Harpalani, V. (2001). Identity and school adjustment: Revisiting the "acting White" assumption. *Educational Psychologist, 36*, 21–30.

Spencer, S. J., Steele, C. M., & Quinn, D. M. (1999). Stereotype threat and women's math performance. *Journal of Experimental Social Psychology, 35*, 4–28.

Steeg, J. L. (1982). Behavioral and attitudinal changes of teachers toward low achieving students as a result of the TESA program. *Dissertation Abstracts International, 43*(2-A), 425.

Steele, C. M. (1997). A threat in the air: How stereotypes shape intellectual identity and performance. *American Psychologist, 52*, 613–629.

Steele, C. M., & Aronson, J. (1995). Stereotype threat and the intellectual test performance of African Americans. *Journal of Personality & Social Psychology, 69*, 797–811.

Stone, J. (2002). Battling doubt by avoiding practice: The effects of stereotype threat on self-handicapping in white athletes. *Personality and Social Psychology Bulletin, 28*, 1667–1678.

Stone, J., Lynch, C. I., Sjomeling, M., & Darley, J. M. (1999). Stereotype threat effects on black and white athletic performance. *Journal of Personality and Social Psychology, 77*, 1213–1227.

Twenge, J. M., & Crocker, J. (2002). Race and self-esteem: Meta-analyses comparing Whites, Blacks, Hispanics, Asians, and American Indians and comment on Gray-Little and Hafdahl. *Psychological Bulletin, 128*, 371–408.

Tyler, T. R. (2006). Psychological perspectives on legitimacy and legitimation. *Annual Review of Psychology, 57*, 375–400.

Urdan, T. (2004). Predictors of academic self-handicapping and achievement: Examining achievement goals, classroom goal structures, and culture. *Journal of Educational Psychology, 96*, 251–264.

Vasey, M. W., & Ollendick, T. H. (2000). Anxiety. In A. J. Sameroff, M. Lewis, & S. M. Miller (Eds.), *Handbook of developmental psychopathology* (2nd ed., pp. 511–530). Dordrecht, the Netherlands: Kluwer Academic.

Weinstein, R. S. (1996). High standards in a tracked system of schooling: For which students and with what educational supports? Section 3: Higher standards. *Educational Researcher, 25*, 16–19.

Weinstein, R. S. (2002). *Reaching higher: The power of expectations in schooling.* Cambridge, MA: Harvard University Press.

Weinstein, R. S., Gregory, A., & Strambler, M. J. (2004). Intractable self-fulfilling prophecies fifty years after Brown v. Board of Education. *American Psychologist, 59*, 511–520.

Weinstein, R. S., Madison, S. M., & Kuklinski, M. R. (1995). Raising expectations in schooling: Obstacles and opportunities for change. *American Educational Research Journal, 32*, 121–159.

Weinstein, R. S., Marshall, H. H., Brattesani, K. A., & Middlestadt, S. E. (1982). Student perceptions of differential teacher treatment in open and traditional classrooms. *Journal of Educational Psychology, 74*, 678–692.

Weinstein, R., Marshall, H., Sharp, L., & Botkin, M. (1987). Pygmalion and the student: Age and classroom differences in children's awareness of teacher expectations. *Child Development, 58*, 1079–1093.

Weinstein, R. S., & McKown, C. (1998). Expectancy effects in "context": Listening to the voices of students and teachers. In J. Brophy (Ed.), *Advances in research on teaching: Vol. 7* (pp. 215–242). *Expectations in the classroom.* Greenwich, CT: JAI Press.

Weinstein, R., & Middlestadt, S. (1979). Student perceptions of teacher interactions with male high and low achievers. *Journal of Educational Psychology, 71*, 421–431.

Weinstein, R. S., Soulé, C. R., Collins, F., Cone, J., Mehlhorn, M., & Simontacchi, K. (1991). Expectations and high school change: Teacher-researcher collaboration to prevent school failure. *American Journal of Community Psychology, 19*, 333–364.

Welsh, W. (2000). The effects of school climate on school disorder. *Annals, AAPSS, 567*, 88–107.

West, M. W., & Davis, F. E. (2003). Research related to the Algebra Project's intervention to improve student learning in mathematics. Retrieved from http://www.algebra.org/

Wheeler, C. S., & Petty, R. E. (2001). The effects of stereotype activation on behavior: A review of possible mechanisms. *Psychological Bulletin, 127*, 797–926.

Wong, C. A., Eccles, J. S., & Sameroff, A. (2003). The influence of ethnic discrimination and ethnic identification on African American adolescents' school and socioemotional adjustment. *Journal of Personality, 71*, 1998–1232.

# 17

# The Schooling of African American Children

*STEPHANIE J. ROWLEY, BETH KURTZ-COSTES, AND SHAUNA M. COOPER*

The schooling of African American[1] children has taken center stage in a number of school reform debates, from the *Brown vs. Board of Education* school desegregation legislation to the current No Child Left Behind (NCLB; 2002) policy. Many of these policies were developed to try to address the decades of exclusion of African Americans from mainstream educational institutions, the negative effects of widespread neighborhood racial segregation, and institutional racism (J. Lee, 2006). Although these efforts have resulted in some reduction in Black–White achievement gaps (Perie, Grigg, & Donahue, 2005), it is still the case that African American students underperform compared to their White peers, even after socioeconomic factors are taken into account (Chatterji, 2006; Fryer & Levitt, 2005; J. Lee, 2006). A number of factors related to the achievement gap have been identified, including racial differences in parenting, access to resources, and social factors; among these, differential schooling experiences have emerged as both a significant factor in the achievement of African American children and a promising arena for intervention (Fryer & Levitt, 2005; Hanushek & Rivkin, 2006; Jencks & Phillips, 1998).

The ways in which schooling affects African American students are complex. Although the same factors that are associated with school performance in other groups predict achievement outcomes in African Americans—small class sizes, responsive teachers, and parental involvement, for example (Ferguson, 1991; Hill & Craft, 2003; Taylor, Clayton, & Rowley, 2004; Wigfield, Eccles, Schiefele, Roeser, & Davis-Kean, 2006), African American students are less likely than European American students to have access to these resources, and a number of schooling practices (e.g., tracking and high stakes testing) negatively affect African American children disproportionately (Madaus & Clarke, 2001). Moreover, African American students bring a unique set of experiences and preferences with them to school, necessitating close examination of race-differentiated ex-

periences (e.g., discrimination) as well as the interaction between home and school environments.

This chapter examines the effects of schooling on the development of African American children. Although we acknowledge the widely known deficits in the performance of African American students, the achievement gap is not the focus of the chapter. Details of the achievement gap and the factors that have been found to reduce it are well detailed elsewhere (e.g., Fryer & Levitt, 2005; Jencks & Phillips, 1998). Instead of framing the experiences of African Americans in terms of these deficits, we attempt to provide a broad, ecological perspective on the school-related factors affecting African Americans. It is the case that most of the research in this area describes African Americans in terms of their differences from European Americans, so some comparison is inevitable. We make every attempt, though, to also include points of strength, contextualize differences, and highlight factors that uniquely affect this group. We discuss the influence of school structural factors (i.e., school quality, racial segregation, and school climate), learner characteristics (i.e., achievement motivation, racial identity, gender, and culture), social influences (i.e., racial discrimination and perceived racial stereotypes), and home–school connections on developmental outcomes for this group. Although the majority of this work focuses on achievement-related outcomes, we include other outcomes such as mental health, self-concept, and social competence where relevant. Following these substantive sections we discuss strengths and weaknesses of the current literature and make suggestions for future research.

## School Context

As is aptly chronicled in other sections of this *Handbook*, the aspects of schooling that influence development go well beyond curriculum and pedagogy (Cole-Henderson, 2000; Wigfield et al., 2006; Wilkins, 2006). Children's ability to learn, the development of their self-concept, and their social development are heavily influenced by a number of school structural factors. Recent research shows that the school context in which most African American students are growing and developing is quite different than the context of students of other ethnic backgrounds. The sections that follow detail the differential school environments in which African American students tend to find themselves and the effects of those environments on learning and development.

*Segregation*   Despite accounts of increasing diversity in the United States, American schools are now more segregated than they were in the late 1970s (Frankenberg, Lee, & Orfield, 2003; Orfield & Lee, 2006). Although nearly 40% of American school students are from ethnic minority groups, White students, on average, still attend schools with student bodies that are 80% White (Orfield & Lee, 2006). After the Supreme Court authorized segregated neighborhood schools in 1991, the demographic face of American schools changed dramatically. Orfield and Lee (2006) noted that whereas 66% of African American students attended majority non-White schools in 1991, 73% did in 2003. The Harvard Civil Rights Project calls these "apartheid schools" (Frankenberg et al., 2003; Orfield & Lee, 2006). These highly segregated schools differ from integrated schools in a number of ways. They tend to have high concentrations of poor students, low quality teachers, very low test scores, and little access to advanced coursework (Frankenberg et al., 2003; Lee, 2004; Orfield & Lee, 2006; Owens & Sunderman, 2006; Wilkins, 2006).

School segregation affects students in several ways. Despite attention in the 1940s and 1950s to the unequal resources associated with education in predominantly African American schools, recent research shows that poor quality facilities, inadequate materials, and poorly trained teachers are still more likely to be found in schools with large African American enrollments than in majority White schools (Orfield & Lee, 2006; Wilkins, 2006). Teachers in highly segregated schools tend to have different goals for students than those in integrated or predominantly White schools, and these differing goals are reflected in teaching strategies and expectations. Madaus and Clarke (2001) found that teachers in schools with high concentrations of African American and Latino students were more concerned about improving test scores and reported more teaching to the test than teachers in more racially integrated schools. These authors suggested that this concern might lead to rigid teaching practices and reductions in creativity, conceptual learning, and student motivation. In one study, degree of racial segregation was associated with school dropout and reduced educational aspirations (Cutler & Glaeser, 1997; see also Lee, 2004). Interestingly, these effects were stronger for Blacks than for non-Blacks. It is not surprising, then, that school segregation is a consistent contributor to the Black–White achievement gap (Card & Rothstein, 2006; Lee, 2004) or that the achievement gap closed most

significantly between the 1970s and 1990s when American schools were most integrated (Madaus & Clarke, 2001).

A number of highly successful predominantly African American and predominantly poor schools have been identified, which illustrates that racial composition of a particular school is not the issue (Hoover, 1992; Wilkins, 2006). Instead, inequities in funding, teacher quality, and expectations drive the negative effects of segregation (Lee, 2004). Therefore, programs that simply aim to desegregate schools may not accomplish significant change without attention to these deeper issues. Indeed, researchers have suggested that tracking within integrated schools has created racial differences in the schooling experiences of students in such schools (Losen & Orfield, 2002).

*Tracking*   Even within integrated schools, African American students tend to experience a very different context from Whites and Asian Americans because of tracking. Oakes (2005) considers tracking to be "second generation" segregation. Although African American students constitute 17% of the American school system, they represent 33% of those enrolled in special education classes and just 8% of those identified as gifted (Losen & Orfield, 2002). Parrish (2002) used data from the U.S. Department of Education to calculate risk ratios reflecting the likelihood of each major racial group, relative to European Americans, being identified as mentally retarded or emotionally disturbed. Using this method, he found that African American students are three times as likely as non-African Americans to be labeled mentally retarded and two times as likely to be labeled emotionally disturbed. Moreover, Asian Americans and Latinos tend to be underidentified as mentally retarded relative to European Americans. In addition, Black students receiving special services are less likely than Whites to be educated in fully inclusive classrooms and are more likely to be in separate settings (Fierros & Conroy, 2002). Card and Rothstein (2006) found that even within the most racially integrated schools, African American students are less well represented than European and Asian Americans in the most advanced classes, thereby rarely benefiting from the most challenging curricula. In response to public debate on the negative effects of tracking on students of color, a number of organizations have pushed for detracking and greater use of mixed-ability grouping (Oakes, 2005). However, studies of American secondary schools show that although rigid ability-group tracking with segregation of students is no longer prevalent, more subtle tracking still occurs. Even in cases where students have some choice in class selection, African American and Latino students in integrated schools are overrepresented in lower tracks, and segregated schools tend to have disproportionate numbers of low-level courses. This segregation within integrated schools has been associated with poorer long term outcomes and pressure from other African American students to underachieve (Tyson, Darity, & Castellino, 2005).

A number of scholars have tried to explain the overrepresentation of African American students in special education classes. One suggestion is that teachers and administrators are biased against African American students and are therefore more apt to refer them for special education services (Meyer & Patton, 2001). For example, Neal, McCrary, and Webb-Johnson (2001) found that children whose behavior reflects certain African American cultural trappings, such as speaking African American vernacular English, needing more sensory stimulation, and having more stereotypical appearance, are more likely to be referred for special education. The somewhat subjective nature of a special education designation makes it particularly easy for biased teachers and administrators to overrefer African American students. Many special education diagnoses are in the vague "learning disabled" category and use one-time IQ tests for placement (Hilliard, 2000). The recent emphasis on high-stakes testing complicates this matter even further. When schools are faced with the possibility of losing resources because of poor student performance, they may refer students for special education services so that the students can receive special accommodations when taking year-end exams (e.g., extra time). African American students, who tend to do poorly on standardized exams, may therefore be more likely to be referred for special education services, even when it is not warranted. Studies show that teachers and school psychologists feel mounting pressure from administrators to refer poorly performing students for special education (Fielding, 2004). The combination of poor quality teaching and emphasis on testing in schools with large numbers of African American students make these results particularly disconcerting.

The underrepresentation of African American students in gifted courses is nearly as troubling as their overrepresentation in special education classrooms. Gifted courses represent the most challenging and intellectually engaging curricula and often require teachers to receive additional training (Gallagher, 2000). Ford (1998) noted that many teachers fail to refer African American students for gifted programs because of narrow views about the nature of intelligence. Darity and his colleagues found that while 30 to 40% of students in North Carolina in 2000 were African American, only 10% of the students identified as gifted were African American (Darity, Castellino, Tyson, Cobb, & McMillen, 2001). Less than 15% of the schools studied had representation of African American and Latino students in gifted courses that closely approximated their enrollment at the school. A school district on Long Island was able to substantially narrow the Black–White achievement gap by offering advanced curricula to students who would ordinarily be in lower level classes (Oakes, 2005). These results suggest that ending tracking and offering African American students higher quality curricula might improve social and academic outcomes for African American students.

***Teacher Qualifications*** In addition to being clustered in lower level courses, African American students are more likely than European Americans to be taught by underqualified teachers—those who are either uncertified or are not teaching in the field in which they were trained (Goldhaber, Perry, & Anthony, 2004). Harris and Ray (2003) found that in Michigan teachers of African American students are less likely than teachers of European American students to be certified. Nearly 15% of teachers in schools that are 70% or more African American are not board certified in their main subject versus just 3% of those in schools with less than 10% African American enrollment. Advanced Placement (AP) teachers in North Carolina schools with high African American and Latino populations are less likely to be teaching in-field than AP teachers in majority White schools (Darity et al., 2001). Ferguson (1991) found similar results in a study of 900 schools in Texas, where race makeup of schools was related to teachers' scores on a standardized skills assessment. Moreover, he found that teacher skill accounted for more than 25% of the Black–White achievement gap in Texas. The combination of high rates of racial segregation and school poverty make African American students prime targets for poor quality teaching.

***School Climate*** In addition to these structural factors, psychological aspects of the school context are important influences on the development of African American students. School climate is a multidimensional construct that includes fairness and equity, discipline practices, sharing of resources, support from teachers, and school safety (Anderson, 1982; Loukas & Robinson, 2004; Roeser, Eccles, & Sameroff, 2000). Although a number of studies have shown that the extent to which the environment is supportive and equitable can affect the school experiences of all students (Eccles, Wigfield, & Schiefele, 1998; Roeser & Eccles, 1998; Vieno, Perkins, Smith, & Santinello, 2005), there is also evidence that African American students tend to perceive a less supportive school climate, including more teacher bias, inequitable discipline by school authorities (e.g., higher rates of school suspensions and expulsions), as well as unfair use of law enforcement by school authorities (Ruck & Wortley, 2002; Utley, Kozleski, Smith, & Draper, 2002). Additionally, African American and Hispanic students are more likely than White students to perceive that their schools are unsafe (Griffith, 1996; National Center for Educational Statistics, 2007). Given that African American youth are likely to perceive their school environments as unsafe, unsupportive, and inequitable, school climate is consequential in understanding their school experiences.

Brown and Jones (2004) found that African American high school students who perceived fairness and equality in their school environment reported more positive academic engagement than those who perceived an inequitable school and classroom climate. These perceptions of inequity also have implications for whether African American students participate in school extracurricular activities (Phelan, Yu, & Davidson, 1994). In addition to proximal influences on achievement, school participation (e.g., school clubs and organizations) may also threaten long-term educational trajectories, including college acceptance.

Brody, Dorsey, Forehand, and Armistead (2002) found

that both classroom rules and student involvement predicted higher self-control, a factor that has been associated with positive educational outcomes for African American youth. Moreover, this longitudinal study of African American families and children suggested that classroom organization and rule clarity were indirectly linked with child adjustment (e.g., depressive symptoms, aggression) through their influence on self-regulatory behaviors. Other studies have similarly linked more positive school climate to lower levels of externalizing (Kuperminc, Leadbeater, Emmons, & Blatt, 1997) and greater efficacy beliefs (Kuperminc, Leadbeater, & Blatt, 2001) among African American students.

Another aspect of school climate that shapes the schooling experiences of African American youth is school disciplinary practices. State-wide and local data show that African American students, particularly males, are more likely to receive disciplinary action (e.g., expulsions, suspensions) than European American students (Davis & Jordan, 1994; Gregory, 1997; Skiba, Michael, Nardo, & Peterson, 2002). These disciplinary actions both detract from the available opportunities to learn and threaten the long-term educational trajectories of African American youth (Townsend, 2000). As Cairns and Cairns (1994) noted, many youth who are classified in school records as dropouts are, in fact, "throw outs"; that is, after multiple expulsions, youth have missed so much school that they are unable to keep up with classmates academically. Moreover, students who experience repeated disciplinary actions develop identities and activities that are incompatible with academic success (Fields, 2004).

Research with students of various racial/ethnic and socioeconomic backgrounds suggests that the extent to which one feels secure at school predicts academic success and school engagement (Kuperminc et al., 2001; Whitlock, 2006). African American students, particularly those from low socioeconomic backgrounds, are more likely than Whites to attend schools with higher crime rates. The extent to which a student feels safe within the school environment is a predictor of not only educational outcomes (Leventhal & Brooks-Gunn, 2004), but also behavioral problems (T. Y. Marsh & Cornell, 2001) and school attendance (Bowen & Bowen, 1999). School safety has also been associated with engagement in sexual activity, which is both a predictor and outcome of academic difficulties (Moore, Manlove, Glei, & Morrison, 1998). In addition, schools that are welcoming and secure encourage parent–school involvement (McKay, Atkins, Hawkins, Brown, & Lynn, 2003).

As a whole, the literature suggests that although the same variables tend to predict outcomes similarly regardless of ethnicity, African American students are disproportionately exposed to unhealthy school contexts. Moreover, patterns of residential segregation have led to concentrated, overlapping spheres of risk that are unique to African Americans. Even within integrated schools, African American students tend to be concentrated in lower tracks with less engaging curricula than European and Asian American students. Despite the gravity of some of these statistics, it is still the case that many schools serve African American students well, and that many African American students excel (Education Trust, 2008). More systematic research on the factors leading to systemic change and success among schools serving African American students, though, is still in order.

## Learner Characteristics

African American children bring with them to school a host of skills, abilities, and interests that shape their school experiences. Thus, the influence of schooling on children's development depends, in part, on these learner characteristics. In this section we explore learner characteristics (motivation, racial identity, culture, and gender) that moderate the influence of school on the development of African American children.

*Achievement Motivation* Expectancy-value theories of motivation posit the centrality of expectations and values: In order to be motivated to act, an individual must believe in his or her ability to achieve a goal (i.e., the individual believes that effort will lead to success) and must value the goal (Eccles & Wigfield, 2002). Our review of motivation in African American youth is organized around those two themes.

A large body of literature indicates that African American children and adolescents, on average, view themselves as competent to succeed in school. Graham (1994) summarized approximately 140 studies that had examined achievement motivation in African American children and adolescents. Few reliable race differences were noted in her review; her summary showed that, on average, African American children and adolescents have positive self-regard, report adaptive causal attributions, and have healthy need for achievement and expectancy of success. In the last two decades, most researchers studying motivation in African Americans have used within-race rather than race-comparative designs, and more research has focused on self-esteem and academic self-concept than attributions, expectancy of success, or need for achievement. This more recent work has substantiated Graham's conclusions that on average, African American children and adolescents have healthy self-esteem and academic self-concept (Cokley, 2002; Gray-Little & Hafdahl, 2000; Greene & Way, 2005; Morgan & Mehta, 2004; Okeke, Howard, Kurtz-Costes, & Rowley, 2008). Thus, overall, the literature supports the contention that African American youth, on average, hold competency beliefs that would support healthy achievement striving. Results regarding the valuing of achievement are less straightforward.

Theorists from several traditions have argued that healthy competence beliefs may be insufficient to enhance the motivation of African American youth in academic settings because school experiences lead these youth to devalue educational attainment and academic excellence. One such approach, coming primarily from social psychology, has focused on "disidentification." Steele (1992) suggested that because of negative stereotypes about the academic abilities of African Americans, Black youth disidentify with academics; that is, in order to maintain healthy self-esteem in the face of negatively biased academic evaluations, their self-esteem becomes detached from academic performance. Youth whose self-esteem is not tied to external evaluations of academic ability are buffered from academic feedback that might be racially biased (Crocker & Major, 1989; Major & Schmader, 1998).

Research in self-perceptions of competence with predominantly White samples has shown a robust relationship between academic self-concept and achievement that increases with age to high levels in high school (Marsh & Yeung, 1997; Wigfield & Eccles, 1994). Longitudinal data have supported a bidirectional relationship between self-concept and performance: Positive beliefs enhance motivation, thereby resulting in improved performance, and high performance, on the other hand, is accurately reflected in high self-perceptions (Marsh & Craven, 2006; Marsh, Trautwein, Luedtke, Koeller, & Baumert, 2005; Marsh & Yeung, 1997). Thus, the self-perceptions about academic skills that youth bring to the school setting moderate their school experiences, with schooling resulting in greater academic gains for those youth who have positive self-beliefs.

Research using both survey methods and experimental designs has provided some evidence that African American students are more psychologically disengaged from the academic domain than their European American counterparts. In two experiments, Major and her colleagues (Major, Spencer, Schmader, Wolfe, & Crocker, 1998) gave bogus performance feedback to African American and European American college students, measuring students' self-esteem both before and after feedback was received. The self-esteem of European American students declined after failure feedback and increased after success feedback. In contrast, the self-esteem of African American students did not change.

In two studies using data from the National Educational Longitudinal Study (NELS), Osborne (1995, 1997) found that self-esteem was related to academic performance among European American and Hispanic students in the sample and for African American girls, but that correlations decreased from eighth to 12th grade for African American boys. However, in a reanalysis of the same data, Morgan and Mehta (2004) found somewhat different results. Their regression analyses indicated a significant relationship between academic self-concept and school achievement for both Black and White youth, with the relationship stronger among Whites than Blacks. Although they did not report a gender by race interaction, the race differences seemed primarily due to White girls, who had a .675 increase in academic self-concept for each standard deviation increase in achievement. Those coefficients were .43, .41, and .38 for White males, Black males, and Black females, respectively, corroborating other recent research that showed positive relationships between academic self-concept and

achievement in Black boys and girls (Saunders, Davis, Williams, & Williams, 2004). Morgan and Mehta (2004) also tested the relationship between academic self-concept and general self-esteem, and found no racial differences in the relationship. Moreover, in contrast to Osborne's (1995, 1997) results, Morgan and Mehta found no race or sex differences in the relationship between self-esteem and academic achievement between eighth and 12th grade. Similar results (i.e., no race or ethnic differences in the relationship between self-esteem and achievement) have been found with college students (Crocker, Luhtanen, Cooper, & Bouvrette, 2003).

A weaker relationship between measures of self-worth and achievement among African American students compared to White students may be due to a devaluing of the academic domain, or it may result from discounting of feedback (Major, Spencer, et al., 1998). The research to date supports the contention that African American students may discount feedback that they perceive as biased, yet most Black youth continue to value academic excellence. Thus, schooling experiences—particularly experiences of racial discrimination—may lead to disidentification in a small percentage of African American youth, while a majority of their peers remain invested in school and view successful achievement as desirable.

Although researchers have assessed disidentification, few studies have explicitly related disidentification to motivation or other outcomes, and long term effects of disidentification are not clear. In other words, it is unclear whether youth whose self-esteem is unrelated to their achievement are less motivated in the school setting and ultimately benefit less from school than youth whose self-esteem is tied more tightly to academic outcomes. A second limitation of this research is that disidentification has been typically viewed by theorists in a trait-like manner rather than as a state. However, it is likely that context plays a heavy role, particularly in the discounting of performance outcomes. Discounting negative feedback is far more likely to occur when students perceive that the teacher is biased—and such discounting may be adaptive—than when teachers are perceived as fair. Additional research is needed to elucidate the relationship between self-beliefs and achievement among African American youth, to determine the mechanisms that might drive this relationship (e.g., devaluing versus discounting; the extent to which teacher and school characteristics shape these processes), and to determine the motivational and developmental consequences.

The disidentification literature has posited the centrality of both expectancy (i.e., self-perceptions) and values in understanding the achievement motivation of African Americans. Other perspectives are focused more tightly on the degree to which educational attainment is valued (Fordham & Ogbu, 1986; Mickelson, 1990). One of the most widely cited of these perspectives has been Ogbu's cultural–ecological perspective (1988), which asserts that the academic performance of African American students is an adaptation to limited social and economic choices.

Ogbu (1988) argued that because of their perceptions of limited opportunities, African American students devalue traditional modes of education and academic success. As an adaptive response to racial and social inequalities, African American students develop an *oppositional cultural identity* and view academic success as characteristic of European culture or "acting White" (Ogbu, 1988, 1992). According to this perspective, social conditions and school experiences lead African American youth to believe they must choose between peer acceptance (with low achievement) and academic success accompanied by peer rejection (Peterson-Lewis & Bratton, 2004; Wilson, Cooke, & Arrington, 1997).

Although the concepts of oppositional identity and Acting White have been widely discussed in the popular media as an explanation for the achievement gap, empirical support for these ideas is weak. Two studies using data from the National Educational Longitudinal Study (NELS) found that high-achieving African American adolescents did not report more academic peer pressure than their European American counterparts (Ainsworth-Darnell & Downey, 1998; Cook & Ludwig, 1998), and in a sample of African American high school students, strong academic performance was not detrimental to the social relationships of students (Horvat & Lewis, 2003). Successful students in these studies did not disengage or underachieve in order to maintain their ties with African American peers. Conversely, other research has shown that both African American and European American youth are sometimes stigmatized by peers for excelling academically (e.g., Kinney, 1993; Tyson et al., 2005).

The oppositional culture idea has also been contested by evidence suggesting that a strong African American identity is associated with academic engagement and success. Spencer, Noll, Stoltzfus, and Harplani (2001) found that African American middle school students who reported more Eurocentric beliefs had lower academic achievement than students with more Afrocentric beliefs. Other studies have also suggested that, consistent with the historical valuing of education as the means to escape the deeply rooted social and political disenfranchisement that originated in slavery, African American youth place high value on academic success (Cokley, 2003; Ford & Harris, 1996; Solorzano, 1992).

Noting the seeming inconsistency between positive reported attitudes toward education, yet a relative lack of academic engagement and success among African American youth, Mickelson (1990) differentiated between "abstract" and "concrete" values. She hypothesized that in a generalized, abstract manner, African Americans place a high value on academic success. However, because of ongoing racial discrimination, such as racially discriminating pay scales and glass ceilings in promotion decisions, African American youth accurately recognize that educational success will have smaller pay-offs for them than for Whites. Mickelson (1990) argued that the "attitude-achievement paradox," as she called it, can be understood by recogniz-

ing that although Blacks value education in the abstract, the limited opportunity structure leads to negative concrete values and less academic engagement. Mickelson (1990) found support for these hypotheses in a sample of over 1,000 high school seniors. Rowley (2000) extended this research by showing that African American students who had low levels of concrete values (i.e., more awareness of discrimination) and high levels of abstract values tended to also have high rates of academic achievement.

Much of the research and theory summarized above is based on comparisons between Blacks and Whites. Within each racial group, substantial individual and developmental differences characterize children's motivational beliefs and school experiences (e.g., Ford & Harris, 1996; Graham & Long, 1986; Tracy & Erkut, 2002). Relatively little research has examined normative development of academic motivation and individual differences in African American students; where such development has been studied, it usually parallels the processes found with youth of other racial/ethnic backgrounds (Ramey, Lanzi, Phillips, & Ramey, 1998; Seidman, Allen, Aber, Mitchell, & Feinman, 1994; Valeski & Stipek, 2001). For example, Seidman and his colleagues (1994) found that self-esteem, academic efficacy, GPA, and class preparation all declined over the transition to middle school, but that these declines were similar for White and Black youth. Seidman, Aber, Allen, and French (1996) also found declines in GPA, but not self-concept, across the transition to high school, again with similar patterns across racial groups. Ethnicity does play a role in these transitions in that students tend to have more difficult transitions when moving to a more diverse environment, which is likely to be the case for students of color (Seidman et al., 1996).

As with majority youth, African American students who have positive experiences at school, who feel supported by their teachers, and who have expectations of success that are also shared by school personnel are likely to remain motivated and engaged (Midgley, Maehr, et al., 2000; Phelan et al., 1994; Wigfield et al., 2006). Although theorists are not in agreement regarding the relationships between self-appraisals and motivation among Black youth, this research area has demonstrated that motivation is interwoven within personal and racial identity, to which we now turn.

***Racial Identity*** Race is one of the many social identities that may influence the lives of children and adolescents (Cross & Fhagen-Smith, 2001). In this section, we consider ways in which racial identity influences the schooling experiences of African American youth and ways that schooling shapes development through its impact on racial identity.

A great deal of research focuses on how racial identity, or the significance and meaning of race to one's self-concept, influences the lives of African American youth (Cross & Fhagen-Smith, 2001; Sellers, Rowley, Chavous, Shelton, & Smith, 1997). Much of this research has shown that, due to social racial inequities (e.g., racism and discrimination), a healthy racial identity is an important aspect of development for African American youth (Cross & Fhagen-Smith, 2001). Moreover, racial identity is associated with positive outcomes for African American youth at various developmental stages (Chavous et al., 2003; Cross, 1995; Phinney & Chavira, 1992; Rowley, Sellers, et al., 1998; Smith, Walker, Fields, Brookins, & Seay, 1999; Spencer, Cunningham, & Swanson, 1995).

According to Chavous et al. (2003), researchers have focused on racial identity as a way of understanding how youth perceive and respond to their academic contexts. Feelings of belonging and affirmation of one's racial group are positively associated with a range of motivational factors, including classroom engagement and behavior, academic self-efficacy, academic aspirations, and educational attainment (Chavous et al., 2003; O'Connor, 2001; Oyserman, Harrison, & Bybee, 2001; Taylor, Casten, Flickinger, Roberts, & Fulmore, 1994; Thomas et al., 2003). Several studies have found that pride in one's racial group (i.e., private regard) is associated with positive achievement outcomes for both children and adults (e.g., Bowman & Howard, 1985; Chavous et al., 2003; Wong, Eccles, & Sameroff, 2003). A strong connection to one's racial group and positive views about African Americans are associated with positive school adjustment. In addition, some studies have shown that more assimilationist (e.g., endorsement of mainstream beliefs) beliefs are associated with less positive school adjustment for youth of color (Sellers, Chavous, & Cooke, 1998; Spencer et al., 2001). By and large, these findings suggest that attachment to one's ethnic group positively influences African American students' classroom behaviors, beliefs, and attitudes.

Little research has explored the mechanisms by which racial identity influences academic outcomes, but one possibility is self-esteem and other self-beliefs. Racial identity is associated with more positive self-views in African American youth, ranging from preadolescence through early adulthood (Phinney & Chavira, 1992; Rowley et al., 1998; Thomas, Townsend, & Belgrave, 2003). Phinney and Chavira (1992) found that racial identity was positively associated with self-esteem across a 3-year period for Asian American, African American, and Latino adolescents. Presumably, one's sense of belonging to one's racial/cultural group fosters a positive social identity that enhances personal identity. These positive self-views, in turn, lead to positive developmental outcomes and schooling experiences of African American children and adolescents. As is the case for majority youth, African American youth with more positive self-views are more engaged, more confident in their academic abilities, and have higher academic aspirations than those with less positive self-views (Campbell, Pungello, & Miller-Johnson, 2002; Davis, Johnson, Cribbs, & Saunders, 2002). Thus, racial identity may influence schooling experiences through its positive contribution to minority youth's self-esteem and overall self-concept. A strong racial identity may be a risk factor, however, in educational settings in which racial stereotypes are endorsed (Okeke et al., 2008; Yip, 2008).

*African American Culture and Schooling* A number of scholars have noted that culture and schooling are tightly linked (Boykin, 1983; Okagaki, 2001; Rogoff, 2003). Culture affects the way that knowledge is gained, whether achievement outcomes are valued, and the ways in which individuals interact with important agents within the school (Boykin, 1983; Gallimore & Goldenberg, 2001; Okagaki, 2001). African American culture is often at odds with the mainstream culture of most American schools (Boykin, 1983; Pai, Adler, & Shadiow, 2006). African American families tend to be characterized by high levels of movement, multiple and simultaneous sources of sensory stimulation (e.g., music, conversation), and a communalistic orientation that privileges group efforts over individual activities. American schools, on the other hand, tend to focus on individualism, competition, and physical restraint.

A number of studies demonstrate that African American students learn best in school contexts that support these cultural inclinations. For example, allowing African American students to move during story reading and a subsequent recall task yields better scores than low movement contexts (Boykin & Cunningham, 2001). Studies also show that although most students prefer cooperative learning opportunities to individualistic experiences, African American students prefer working in a group to a higher degree than students of other ethnic groups (Dunn et al., 1990; Ellison, Boykin, Tyler, & Dillihunt, 2005). In addition, African American students perform better on mathematics and reading activities when learning in a communal context (seated together, sharing materials) than when assigned to individual learning or peer tutoring conditions (Dill & Boykin, 2000; Hurley, Boykin & Allen, 2005). Highlighting the cultural underpinnings of these results are other studies showing that although communalistic and cooperative learning contexts (see Serpell, Boykin, Madhere, & Nasim, 2006 for a description of the difference) benefit both African American and European American students, African American students benefit to a greater degree than Whites (Boykin & Bailey, 2000; Serpell et al., 2006). High levels of movement have been shown to have a salutary effect on the cognitive performance of African American students, but a negative effect on the performance of White students (Allen & Boykin, 1991; Boykin & Bailey, 2000).

The differing cultural preferences of African American students have several implications for their development. First, teachers rate students who exhibit mainstream cultural behaviors as more motivated and view traditional African American cultural behaviors negatively (Boykin & Cunningham, 2001; Neal et al., 2001). Second, African American students tend to like high achieving peers who embody these cultural values over peers who enact mainstream cultural orientations (Marryshow, Hurley, Allen, Tyler, & Boykin, 2005; Sankofa, Hurley, Allen, & Boykin, 2005), leading to a potential mismatch between the values of African American students and those of the school. Finally, extreme differences between home and school environments might cause confusion for young children about why behavior deemed typical and acceptable at home is viewed as deviance and misbehavior at school (A. R. Taylor, 1991).

Language differences may also serve as a point of discontinuity between African American students' home and school environments. Some accounts suggest that as many as 80% of African American families use some form of African American Vernacular English (AAVE) at home (Lippi-Green, 1997). An analysis of differences between AAVE and Standard English is beyond the scope of this chapter. The primary issue in terms of schooling experiences is that African American children frequently come to school with a set of internalized grammatical, syntactic, and pragmatic language tools that differ from those in the classroom (Washington & Craig, 2002). Teachers, even African American teachers, tend to view AAVE speakers more negatively than those who speak Standard English (Tauber, 1997). AAVE is viewed as incorrect, sloppy language rather than a dialect formed from a unique African and American experience (Siegel, 2006). Language discontinuity may also dampen academic engagement in AAVE users as repeated correction of language from teachers leads to increased cognitive monitoring and anxiety about speaking (Delpit, 2003). Students may become frustrated with basic attempts at communications that are corrected, and reduce help-seeking or proximity-seeking behaviors with teachers (Delpit, 2003; Siegel, 2006).

In some cases, African American students may use language as a marker of identity. Speakers of AAVE may be frustrated at the realization that their linguistic (and cultural) style is denigrated while styles associated with middle class White students are privileged (Siegel, 2006). Fordham (1999) found that African American adolescents sometimes use AAVE and slang as a way to resist what they see as the racist school establishment, adopting what Ogbu (1999) calls oppositional language frames. Students felt that they were unfairly forced to use Standard English and to abandon AAVE; therefore, they used AAVE to demonstrate their cultural pride.

Implications of language discontinuity can be far-reaching. There is clear evidence that AAVE use is associated with poorer standardized test scores, even after accounting for indicators of family economic status (Charity, Scarborough, & Griffin, 2004). It also appears that students coming with a strong AAVE register are at risk for low motivation, reluctant engagement, and frustration (Fordham, 1999; Ogbu, 1999; Siegel, 2006). Interventions aimed at teaching awareness of linguistic components of AAVE and the inclusion of AAVE in instruction show that negative attitudes toward AAVE use, and the resultant declines in student performance and motivation, can be significantly reduced when teachers and students are informed of the history and foundations of AAVE (Siegel, 2006; Wolfram, Adger, & Schilling, 1999). This awareness may also aid students' ability to shift between AAVE and Standard English, a skill associated with improved academic performance (Craig & Washington, 2004).

These findings underscore recent calls for culturally sensitive schooling that reduces the cultural discontinuities between African American students' home and school environments (Boykin & Bailey, 2000). Although the results robustly support these contentions, they are mostly conducted with low-income samples of elementary school students in urban settings. Little is known about cultural variation within African American homes across different contexts or endorsement of these cultural values in middle class African American homes. In addition, few studies of cultural continuity for middle and high school students exist. Finally, little of this research acknowledges the agency of the children and families involved. Boykin and Ellison (1995) suggest that students and families have some control over the extent to which they buy into the culture of the classroom and the extent to which they are able to negotiate the balance between home values and school values. It is thus possible that parents may socialize their children in ways that allow them to participate successfully in mainstream schools while maintaining ties to the African American community.

***Gender and Schooling*** Although both African American boys and girls are at risk for school difficulties, the schooling experiences and related outcomes of African American boys have taken center stage in recent discussions of race and schooling. Major newspapers have run series chronicling the plight of African American men (e.g., Eckholm, 2006) and literature reviews and research articles have recounted the academic difficulties of African American male students (e.g., Davis, 2003; Noguera, 2003; Roderick, 2003; Swanson, Cunningham & Spencer, 2003). By numerous indices, African American girls are more successful in school than African American boys. African American boys are more likely than girls to be suspended or expelled from school, are more likely to be retained a grade, have lower grades, have less positive attitudes toward school, are less likely to complete high school, and less likely to attend college (Peter & Horn, 2005; Roderick & Camburn, 1999; Saunders et al., 2004; Wilds, 2000).

Both cultural and structural explanations have been posited for these gender differences. On the cultural side, it has been suggested that African American males devalue education and develop an oppositional identity in response to perceived discrimination (Cokley, 2002; Osborne, 1995, 1997). Similarly, one study found that African American boys were less likely than their female peers to report that they admired, respected, or wanted to be like peers who were academically successful (Graham, Taylor, & Hudley, 1998).

Structural explanations for African American males' relatively poor performance have also been offered. Teachers of African American boys tend to view them as academically and behaviorally deviant (Davis, 2003; Frazier-Kouassi, 2002) and treat them differently in the classroom as early as kindergarten (Slaughter-Defoe & Richards, 1994 as cited in Davis, 2003; Simpson & Erickson, 1983). For example, Simpson and Erickson (1983) found that African American boys receive more teacher criticism than any other group. Honora (2003) found that Black boys, as compared to Black girls, perceive these negative attitudes and distrust teachers. Thus, Black boys may disproportionately suffer from the negative effects of low teacher expectations, disciplinary actions, and lack of support. Some scholars have pointed to the importance of family and community support in offsetting these negative influences (Hrabowski, Maton, & Greif, 1998).

Although it appears that both cultural and structural explanations are important pieces to this puzzle, very little research examines the interaction of cultural and structural factors. Does oppositional identity appear only in certain school contexts where African American males are devalued? Ferguson (2003) demonstrated that African American students' school behavior and engagement is predicted by teacher support and perceptions of high expectations. Research using a transactional approach showing the dynamic relationship between schools and individuals is in order. Such research could clarify how students' educational values are perceived by teachers, leading to differential treatment, and how differential treatment influences students' values and behaviors.

Although this focus on African American boys is clearly warranted, some have cautioned that African American girls also perform significantly less well than their European American counterparts, yet receive less explicit attention in the literature (Frazier-Kouassi, 2002). Research suggests that African American females are more socially isolated in racially mixed classrooms than African American males (Grant, 1984) and receive less teacher and peer attention (Irvine, 1986). For example, Irvine (1986) found that whereas Black boys receive negative attention in the classroom because of misbehavior, Black girls in the upper elementary grades received less academic feedback from teachers than did African American boys. African American girls may be particularly vulnerable in the areas of math and science (Reid & Roberts, 2006). The literature suggests that the unique experiences of African Americans lead to problems not simply explained by gender, but by the intersection of race and gender. Additional research is needed to disentangle race and gender effects.

## Social Influences

In an attempt to illuminate the role of race in the schooling of African American youth, a great deal of the literature has discussed how racial discrimination (Brown & Jones, 2004; Mickelson, 1990; Taylor et al., 1994; Wong et al., 2003) and negative racial stereotypes (Steele, 1992) impact the schooling of African American youth. Indeed, some scholars have argued that these social influences play a significant role in the achievement gap between African American and European American youth (Farkas, 2003; McKown & Strambler, 2008; Mickelson, 2003; O'Connor, 2001).

*Racial Discrimination and the Schooling of African American Youth* A growing number of studies have documented the ill effects of racial discrimination on African American children and adolescents (e.g., Caldwell, Kohn-Wood, Schmeelk-Cone, Chavous, & Zimmerman, 2004; Harris-Britt, Valrie, Kurtz-Costes, & Rowley, 2007; Neblett, Phillip, Cogburn, & Sellers, 2006). These studies indicate that African American students are more likely than students of other ethnicities to perceive racial discrimination, particularly experiences occurring in educational settings (Fisher, Wallace & Fenton, 2000; Rosenbloom & Way, 2004).

The preponderance of the literature linking perceived discrimination with schooling experiences can be classified into two groups—individual (e.g., Wong et al., 2003) and group-based racial discrimination (e.g., Mickelson, 1990; Ogbu, 1988). While the former deals with personal experiences with racial discrimination, the latter addresses racial discrimination aimed at one's racial group (Ruggiero & Taylor, 1995). In this section, we discuss how both types of discrimination may influence the schooling and development of African American youth.

*Individual Experiences with Racial Discrimination* A small body of research examines the consequences of perceived racial discrimination on the schooling and development of African American youth. Whereas some literature suggests that awareness of racial discrimination may be a positive motivational factor (Bowman & Howard, 1985; Rowley, 2000; Sanders, 1997), direct experiences with racial discrimination negatively influence the motivation and classroom-related behaviors of African American adolescents (e.g., Cooper, 2005; Fisher et al., 2000; Phelan et al., 1994; Rosenbloom & Way, 2004; Wong et al., 2003).

Perceiving racial discrimination in the school environment may have an adverse effect on African American students' sense of belonging to the school community. Wong et al. (2003) found that perceived peer and teacher discrimination was associated with increased achievement motivation and academic performance as well as increases in problem behaviors among African American youth as they progressed from seventh to ninth grade. Perceived discrimination has also been associated with declines in school participation and a more hostile learning environment (Phelan et al., 1994; Rosenbloom & Way, 2004).

The effects of racial discrimination on psychological functioning are of particular importance when discussing the schooling of African American children and adolescents (Cooper, McLoyd, Wood, & Hardaway, 2008). Both longitudinal (e.g., Dubois, Burk-Braxton, Swenson, Tevendale, & Hardesty, 2002; Sellers, Caldwell, Schmeelk-Cone, & Zimmerman, 2003), and cross-sectional investigations (e.g., Harris-Britt et al., 2007; Romero & Roberts, 2003) have indicated that experiences with discrimination adversely influence mental health functioning. Thus, racial discrimination not only has a direct impact on schooling experiences, but, also indirectly influences schooling through its effect on youth's psychological well-being.

*Perceptions of Group-Based Racial Discrimination* Some studies have indicated that African American youths' perceptions of discrimination aimed at their racial group have important implications for their academic motivation, school engagement, and subsequent academic outcomes (Mickelson, 1990; Steele, 1992). As noted earlier, although African American youth have a strong belief in the general utility of education, they are also aware that the value of education is limited by racial discrimination (Mickelson, 1990; Rowley, 2000).

Several studies have related awareness of discrimination against African Americans to achievement-related outcomes. In their study examining the effects of perceptions of discriminatory job ceiling on adolescents' academic performance, Taylor et al. (1994) found that African American adolescents who perceived potential barriers to job success were less likely to endorse the importance of school than those perceiving fewer potential barriers to job success. Brown and Jones (2004) found that perceptions of bias within the school context were related to lower academic values. This investigation also indicated that African American students who perceived that school and classroom practices were fair to all students were more likely to have positive educational outcomes than those perceiving a biased environment. Thus, perceptions of group-based discrimination may adversely influence the educational outcomes and school experiences.

*Race-Related Stereotypes* Stereotypes are widely held beliefs about the attributes of members of a social group. A common stereotype in the United States is that African Americans are intellectually inferior to European- and Asian Americans (Devine & Elliott, 1995; Krueger, 1996). Because of the myriad ways in which intellectual ability is salient within the school setting, race-related stereotypes are part of the backdrop of the schooling of African American children. In this section, we explore three ways in which stereotypes in the context of school experiences shape the development of African American children: teacher bias, children's stereotypes, and performance decrements due to stereotype threat.

*Teacher Bias* In the decades following Rosenthal and Jacobson's classical work (1968) on teacher expectations, hundreds of studies examined expectancy effects. Overall, this body of research speaks clearly to the power of expectations in shaping the behavior of others. This phenomenon—called the Pygmalion effect—is predicated on the assumption that teachers' expectations, or in this case, race stereotypes about cognitive ability, cause them to treat students in different ways that serve to undermine student behavior, motivation, beliefs, and achievement, which cause the teachers' negative expectations to become a self-fulfilling prophecy. Rosenthal (1994) identified four classes of behaviors that mediate teacher expectancy effects: affect (teachers treat "special" students with greater warmth); input/effort (teachers teach more material and

more difficult material to "special" students); output (teachers give special students more opportunity to participate); and feedback (teachers provide more informative feedback to special students than to others).

Two meta-analyses from the 1980s concluded that teachers' expectations of White students were consistently higher than their expectations of children of color (Baron, Tom, & Cooper, 1985; Dusek & Joseph, 1983). Although more recent research has yielded mixed findings (see Ferguson, 2003, for a summary), overall, research indicates that (a) teacher behaviors, including subtle, nonverbal behaviors, are related to their expectations of students (Rosenthal, 1994); (b) children are aware of teacher expectations (e.g., Weinstein, Marshall, Sharp, & Botkin, 1987); (c) teacher expectations—of both classroom behavior problems and academic performance—are frequently related to social class and race (Ferguson, 2003; Madon et al., 1998); and (d) the influence of teacher bias is greater among African Americans than among Whites (Jussim, Eccles, & Madon, 1996).

Jussim and his colleagues (Jussim & Harber, 2005; Jussim, Harber, Crawford, Cain, & Cohen, 2005) have argued that self-fulfilling prophecies occur because teachers are accurate in their perceptions of ability, and that the actual cumulative effects of teachers' biased expectations are relatively small. Nonetheless, teacher biases related to stigmatized groups may have more far-reaching implications than for nonstigmatized groups (Jussim et al., 1996; Madon, Jussim, & Eccles, 1997). Tracking that results from low teacher expectations is an example of an outcome that could affect a student's entire academic career. Some scholars have found that the overrepresentation of African American children in special education courses and underrepresentation in accelerated honors courses is, in part, a function of low teacher expectations (Darity et al., 2001; Meyer & Patton, 2001; Neal et al., 2001). Results of the Baltimore study indicate that school grades may be especially powerful in shaping student trajectories early on: Children's average report card mark in grade 1 was a strong predictor of school dropout by grade 9 (Alexander, Entwisle, & Kabbani, 2001). Alexander and colleagues argue that school dropout is a process that unfolds over the course of a student's school trajectory. Teacher bias that causes a child to associate school with failure and reprimands at the point of school entry may initiate a set of experiences for children that lead to lowered motivation, less attachment to school, and eventual dropout. Thus, a relatively small bias early on may lead to a large effect over time (Farkas, Grobe, Sheehan, & Shuan, 1990; Ferguson, 2003).

In addition to assignment of grades and recommendations regarding course placement, teachers shape the school environment through their expression of enthusiasm about and selection of academic topics, subtle and overt messages about student qualities, and level of involvement with students. Some theorists have argued that the quality of teacher–student relationships may have a more detrimental effect on the development of African American children than teachers' expectations (McKown & Strambler, 2008). European American students, on average, report more positive relationships with teachers than do African American students, and teacher involvement is related to student engagement even with prior achievement controlled (Hughes, Gleason, & Zhang, 2005; Tucker et al., 2002). Teacher bias in the early grades may influence the child without the student's awareness that differential treatment is linked to race. African American students' awareness of race-related academic stereotypes will be discussed in the next section.

*Awareness of Racial Stereotypes*  To date, relatively little research has examined the development of children's awareness or endorsement of race stereotypes and even less research has focused on academic race stereotypes. McKown and Weinstein (2003) conducted two studies that examined what they termed "stereotype consciousness," or children's awareness of the stereotypes of others. Racial stereotypes were simulated by vignettes about a land inhabited by two types of people (the Greens and the Blues). Results indicated that children's stereotype awareness increases markedly between the ages of 6 and 10, and at every age, children from stigmatized groups (i.e., African Americans and Latinos) were more likely than those from nonstigmatized groups (i.e., Whites and Asians) to be aware of stereotypes. This research illustrated developmental changes in children's stereotype consciousness; however, it is unclear to what extent children and adolescents themselves endorse stereotypes or believe that stereotypes are widely held.

A recent study of academic stereotype endorsement in children in grades 4, 6, and 8 showed that both African American and European American youth endorsed traditional race academic stereotypes (Rowley, Kurtz-Costes, Mistry, & Feagans, 2007). Participants rated the academic abilities of Blacks and Whites in reading, writing, mathematics, and science using a 100-point scale. Both Whites and Blacks reported in-group biases in grade 4 (i.e., each race reported their own group as better than the other), but sixth and eighth graders reported traditional academic stereotypes favoring Whites.

Hudley and Graham (2001) also found evidence that youth endorse traditional race stereotypes regarding academic abilities. Their study used a peer nomination procedure in two studies to examine young adolescents' stereotypes. Middle school students were asked to choose which of a set of photos of African American, Latino, and White boys and girls matched a series of descriptions. Whereas photos of girls of all ethnicities were consistently chosen to fit descriptions of high-achieving students, adolescents were most likely to choose photos of ethnic minority boys (i.e., Latino or African American) as academically disengaged. Gender and ethnic differences in responses occurred in both studies. For example, when given high-achieving descriptions, African American girls chose African American and Anglo girls with equal frequency, whereas Latina and Anglo girls chose White girls most

often. These results indicate that by middle school, students endorse race academic stereotypes for boys, but not girls.

African American children who are aware of the academic race stereotypes of others might develop negative beliefs about their own academic abilities or might become disengaged from school, placing greater value and interest in other activities such as athletic prowess rather than academic achievement. Little research has examined whether stereotype awareness leads to lower perceived competence and academic disengagement. In contrast, a substantial body of research has examined the phenomenon of "stereotype threat"; the idea that whether or not an individual endorses a stereotype, priming of membership in a stigmatized group can hurt performance (e.g., Steele & Aronson, 1995).

Most stereotype threat research has been conducted with young adults, sometimes focusing on gender or sports stereotypes as well as race stereotypes. A few studies have focused on race stereotype threat in children. McKown and Weinstein (2003, Study 2) asked children to write as many letters of the alphabet as possible in 45 seconds starting backwards from "Z." Half of the children were assigned to a stereotype threat condition in which they were told that the alphabet test was diagnostic of cognitive ability. The other half were told that the tasks would help the experimenters understand how children learn. As hypothesized, African American and Latino children in the threat condition who were aware of stereotypes scored lower than the other groups.

Conclusions about research in this area must be tempered with the caveat that very little research has addressed race academic stereotypes in children and adolescents. Nonetheless, the extant studies suggest that although teacher bias influences children already at the point of school entry, children only become aware of race stereotypes later. By early adolescence African American youth are aware of race academic stereotypes; this awareness likely hinders their academic performance in some school situations (Rowley et al., 2007).

*Home–School Collaborations*  Although this chapter has focused predominantly on direct influences of school experiences, it is also important to acknowledge less proximal school-related influences on the development of African American youth. One area of importance is the relationship between home and school. A number of scholars have noted that the effects of schooling on development are mitigated, to some degree, by the relationship between the family and school (e.g., Eccles & Harold, 1996). The nature of family–school relations can influence a range of developmental outcomes. Although it is clear that family–school relationships affect all children in some similar ways, a fair amount of research has been dedicated to demonstrating some of the unique aspects of these relationships for African American students (e.g., Hill & Craft, 2003; Hill et al., 2004).

Studies of elementary school students show that increased parent–school involvement is related to greater academic achievement, increased student efficacy, and fewer behavior problems for African American children (Hill & Craft, 2003; Reynolds, 1999). Scholars suggest that when parents are involved in their children's schooling they communicate the importance of doing well in school, are better able to coordinate home teaching efforts with school curriculum, and like their children's teachers better (Epstein & Dauber, 1991). Results of studies with older children tend to be more mixed. In general, greater involvement and monitoring at home relate to better grades and motivation for middle and high school students, but parents frequently only communicate with teachers when there is a problem, leading to a negative relationship between involvement and performance (Hill et al., 2004). Moreover, some differences in relationships across ethnic groups have been found. Hill and colleagues (2004) found that parent–school involvement was similarly related to fewer school behavior problems and aspirations for European Americans and African Americans in their sample of high school students, but was only related to change in achievement from sixth to ninth grade (modestly, but positively) for African American students. Other research has shown that parent school involvement predicted high school grades similarly (and positively) for European Americans and African Americans (Keith et al., 1998).

On the whole this research suggests that parent involvement improves the schooling experiences of African American youth and that these effects are similar to effects in other ethnic groups. Little research, though, has examined the ways in which African American parents negotiate race-related interactions with teachers. Lareau and Horvat (1999), for example, suggest that when African American parents are confrontational with teachers in response to perceived discrimination, teachers are less supportive of the children. More subtle attempts to monitor and engage teachers (strategies often adopted by middle class parents) were more beneficial to teacher–student relationships. More research on parents' negotiation of race in the school context and the effects of this negotiation on children is needed.

## Implications for Future Research

Considerable progress has been made in building a strong science of the development of African American children in schools, yet much work remains. Much of the research that has been conducted to date is based on a deficit approach that is neither culturally sensitive nor accurate in portraying the many strengths and resiliencies of ethnic minority children and families (cf. Slaughter-Defoe et al., 2006). Moreover, much of the research is not methodologically strong. To take one example: The extant literature reviewed on cultural differences in learning styles largely appeared in book chapters or nonrefereed journals, and much of this writing was strictly theoretical without empirical substantiation.

Because most 20th century research on African American children and families used a deficit approach that focused on populations at risk (Slaughter-DeFoe et al., 2006),

little is known about normative developmental processes in middle class African American families. This limitation has been addressed to some degree by new, large, nationally representative data sets (e.g., NELS, Early Childhood Longitudinal Study) and publicly available studies with ethnically and economically diverse samples (e.g., Maryland Adolescent Development in Context Study). Still, much of what is known about the effects of schooling on children's development has been established with White samples, and it is unclear to what extent the results are applicable to African Americans. For example, a rich body of research has analyzed gender differences in math performance, attitudes, and values among White children (e.g., Bleeker & Jacobs, 2004; Eccles et al., 1998; Tiedemann, 2000). However, it is unclear whether teachers and parents hold the same gender stereotypes about math for African Americans as for European Americans, and whether the performance and behavioral choices of African American boys and girls reflect traditional gender stereotypes (cf. Kurtz-Costes, Rowley, Harris-Britt, & Woods, 2008).

Another consequence of this deficit view is that very little research exists on successful schooling of African American students. A number of successful interventions aimed at improving academic and social outcomes for African American youth have been described; for example, Boykin's talent development model (Boykin, 2000), Comer's school development program (1987), Robert Moses's algebra project (Moses & Cobb, 2001), and Slavin's cooperative learning (Slavin & Cooper, 1999), but less work has identified personal and familial sources of resilience for African American students in schools.

A related issue is the lack of attention to context in the development of African American students. Many studies of African American students include relatively little information about the social context in which the participants reside and fail to report the racial and economic composition of the schools and neighborhoods under study. Moreover, large bodies of literature are dedicated to the study of African American children in urban contexts, while less research has covered the situation of African American students in rural (see Brody et al., 2002, for an exception) and suburban settings (see Lareau, 2003, for an exception). Therefore, discussions of normative development in African American students are frequently based on a narrow range of contexts or without regard for context.

Research that addresses ethnic variation within "African American" samples also is needed. Recent research has examined differences between African American youth and Black (African and Afro-Caribbean) immigrants. Ogbu (1992) suggests that experiences and beliefs of African American families, who came to the United States involuntarily through slavery, and Black immigrant families, who came voluntarily in search of better educational and occupational opportunities, should be quite different. Indeed, findings show that youth from Black immigrant families tend to look similar to other voluntary immigrants, such as European or Asian immigrants, in terms of their strong focus on academic achievement. Tseng (2006) found that Afro-Caribbean first and second generation college students took college courses with stronger mathematics and science content than those of third or greater generational status. This pattern was similar to those of other immigrant groups. Moreover, unlike most African Americans, Afro-Caribbeans hold self-views that are shaped by both race and national identities (Hall & Carter, 2006; Waters, 2001). Waters (1994) found that Afro-Caribbeans who identified more strongly with their home country tended to have more optimistic views about opportunities and perceived less discrimination than their counterparts who identified as Black American. Very little research has explored the educational situation of immigrants from African countries, and almost no work focuses on normative development of Black immigrant children and families. Crude measures of race and ethnicity used in most social science research probably lead to these youth being categorized as African American.

Future research on schooling and African American child development should be guided by contemporary conditions and concerns. The effects of the accountability movement on African American students must be better understood. National and state-level mandates for accountability in the last decade are affecting numerous aspects of schooling, including distribution of resources to schools, teaching practices, instructional time, and parents' enrollment decisions for their children. Research is needed to examine the effects of accountability measures on African American students, who are overrepresented in schools that do not meet federal standards.

Whereas normative research with middle class African American children, adolescents, and families is sparse, investigations regarding the schooling of mixed race children are even rarer. Given the changing demographics of the United States, research with mixed race children is likely to be increasingly important, particularly research with children who share African American and Latino heritage.

## Conclusion

Overall, this review points to a pattern of vulnerability and underdevelopment of African American students in American schools. Racial segregation, biased tracking, low expectations, and differential treatment negatively affect African American students across social, emotional, physical, and academic outcomes. Although policy has certainly been instituted to address some of these inequities, more can be done to reduce segregation, make accountability efforts less harmful for low-income African American students, and improve methods for identifying African American students for gifted and special education services.

This review also noted points of resilience in the lives of African American students. Positive racial identity and parent involvement can buffer the negative effects of a caustic school environment. In addition, many African American students attend schools with supportive teachers, involved parents, and large numbers of successful students.

Research in student resilience and school reform is needed to help researchers and practitioners reverse the pernicious achievement gap so that supportive contexts and student success are the norm.

## Notes

1. The term *African American* will be used throughout the chapter to refer to Black youth living in the United States. Distinguishing among Blacks from different ethnic backgrounds (e.g., African immigrants, Black Carribbeans) is beyond the scope of this chapter. Many sources, such as the Census Bureau and major repositories of educational statistics, do not make these distinctions within reports and so it would be difficult to effectively draw comparisons. We will attempt to make these distinctions when information is provided within individual studies that are reviewed.

## References

Ainsworth-Darnell, J. W., & Downey, D. D. (1998). Assessing the oppositional culture explanation for racial/ethnic differences in school performance. *American Sociological Review, 63*, 536–553.

Alexander, K. L., Entwisle, D. R., & Kabbani, N. S. (2001). The dropout process in life course perspective: Early risk factors at home and school. *Teachers College Record, 103*, 760–822.

Allen, B., & Boykin, A. W. (1991). The influence of contextual factors on Afro-American and Euro-American children's performance: Effects of movement opportunity and music. *International Journal of Psychology, 26*, 373–387.

Anderson, C. S. (1982). The search for school climate: A review of the research. *Review of Educational Research, 52*, 368–420.

Baron, R., Tom, D. Y. H., & Cooper, H. M. (1985). Social class, race, and teacher expectations. In J. B. Dusek (Ed.), *Teacher expectancies* (pp. 245–259). Hillsdale, NJ: Erlbaum.

Bleeker, M. M., & Jacobs, J. E. (2004). Achievement in math and science: Do mothers' beliefs matter 12 years later? *Journal of Educational Psychology, 96*, 97–109.

Bowen, N. K., & Bowen, G. L. (1999). Effects of crime and violence in neighborhoods and schools on the school behavior and performance of adolescents. *Journal of Adolescent Research, 14*, 319–342.

Bowman, P. J., & Howard, C. (1985). Race-related socialization, motivation, and academic achievement: A study of Black youths in three-generational families. *Journal of the American Academy of Child Psychiatry, 24*, 134–141.

Boykin, A. W. (1983). On task performance and Afro-American children. In U. R. Spencer (Ed.), *Achievement and achievement motives* (pp. 324–371). Boston, MA: Freeman.

Boykin, A. W. (2000). The talent development model of schooling: Placing Students at promise for academic success. *Journal of Education for Students Placed at Risk, 5*(1&2), 3–25.

Boykin, A. W., & Bailey, C. (2000). The role of cultural factors in school relevant cognitive functioning: Synthesis of findings on cultural contexts, cultural orientations, and individual differences (Report No. 42). Washington, DC: Center for Research on the Education of Students Placed At Risk (CRESPAR), Howard University.

Boykin, A. W., & Cunningham, R. T. (2001). The effects of movement expressiveness in story content and learning context on the analogical reasoning performance of African American children. *Journal of Negro Education, 70*, 72–83.

Boykin, A. W., & Ellison, C. M. (1995). The multiple ecologies of Black youth socialization: An Afrographic analysis. In R. L. Taylor (Ed.), *African American youth: Their social and economic status in the United States* (pp. 93–128). Westport, CT: Praeger.

Brody, G. H., Dorsey, S., Forehand, R., & Armistead, L. (2002). Unique and protective contributions of parenting and classroom processes to the adjustment of African American children living in single-parent families. *Child Development, 73*, 274–286.

Brown, W. T., & Jones, J. M. (2004). The substance of things hoped for: A study of the future orientation, minority status perceptions, academic engagement and academic performance of Black high school students. *Journal of Black Psychology, 30,* 248–273.

Cairns, R. B., & Cairns, B. D. (1994). *Lifelines and risks: Pathways of youth in our time.* New York: Cambridge University Press.

Caldwell C., Kohn-Wood, L., Schmeelk-Cone, K., Chavous, T., & Zimmerman, M. (2004). Racial discrimination and racial identity as risk factors for violent behaviors in African American young adults. *American Journal of Community Psychology, 33,* 91–105.

Campbell, F. A., Pungello, E. P., & Miller-Johnson, S. (2002). The development of perceived scholastic competence and global self-worth in African American adolescents from low-income families: The roles of family factors, early. *Journal of Adolescent Research, 17,* 277–302.

Card, D., & Rothstein, J. (2006). *Racial segregation and the Black–White test score gap* (NBER Working Paper 12078). Cambridge, MA: National Bureau of Economic Research.

Charity, A. H., Scarborough, H. S., & Griffin, D. M. (2004). Familiarity with school English in African American children and its relation to early reading achievement. *Child Development, 75,* 1340–1356.

Chatterji, M. (2006). Reading achievement gaps, correlates, and moderators of early reading achievement: Evidence from the Early Childhood Longitudinal Study (ECLS) kindergarten to first grade sample. *Journal of Educational Psychology, 98,* 498–507.

Chavous, T. M., Bernat, D. H., Schmeelk-Cone, K., Caldwell, C., Kohn-Wood, L., & Zimmerman, M. A. (2003). Racial identity and academic attainment among African American adolescents. *Child Development, 74,* 1076–1090.

Cokley, K. O. (2002). Ethnicity, gender, and academic self-concept: A preliminary examination of academic disidentification and implications for psychologists. *Cultural Diversity and Minority Psychology, 8,* 378–388.

Cokley, K. O. (2003). What do we know about the motivation of African American students? Challenging the "anti-intellectual" myth. *Harvard Educational Review, 73,* 524–558.

Cole-Henderson, B. (2000). Organizational characteristics of schools that successfully service low-income urban African American students. *Journal of Education for Students Placed at Risk, 5*(1–2), 77–91.

Comer, J. P. (1987). New Haven's school–community connection. *Educational Leadership, 44,* 13–16.

Cook, P. J., & Ludwig, J. (1998). The burden of "acting White:" Do Black adolescents disparage academic achievement? In C. Jencks & M. Phillips (Eds.), *The Black-White test score gap* (pp. 375–400). Washington, DC: Brookings Institution Press.

Cooper, S. M. (2005). *Racial socialization, perceptions of school discrimination and the educational outcomes of African American male and female adolescents* (Unpublished doctoral dissertation). University of Michigan, Ann Arbor, MI.

Cooper, S. M., McLoyd, V., Wood, D., & Hardaway, C. (2008). The mental health consequences of racial discrimination for African American adolescents. In S. Quintana & C. McKown (Eds), *Handbook of race, racism and the developing child* (pp. 278–312). New York: Wiley.

Craig, H. K., & Washington, J. A. (2004). Grade-related changes in the production of African American English. *Journal of Speech, Language, and Hearing Research, 47,* 450–463.

Crocker, J., Luhtanen, R. K., Cooper, M. L., & Bouvrette, A. (2003). Contingencies of self-worth in college students: Theory and measurement. *Journal of Personality and Social Psychology, 85,* 894–908.

Crocker, J., & Major, B. (1989). Social stigma and self-esteem: The self-protective properties of stigma. *Psychological Review, 96,* 608–630.

Cross, W. E., Jr. (1995). Oppositional identity and African American youth: Issues and prospects. In W. D. Hawley & A. W. Jackson (Eds.), *Toward a common destiny: Improving race and ethnic relations in America* (pp. 185–204). San Francisco, CA: Jossey-Bass.

Cross, W. E., Jr., & Fhagen-Smith, P. (2001). A life-span developmental model of racial identity. In C. J. Wijeyesinghe & B. W. Jackson (Eds.), *Reflections on racial identity development: Essays on theory, practice and discourse* (pp. 243–270). New York: New York University Press.

Cutler, D. M., & Glaeser, E. L. (1997). Are ghettos good or bad? *Quarterly Journal of Economics, 112,* 827–872.

Darity, W. Jr., Castellino, D., Tyson, K., Cobb, C., & McMillen, B. (2001). *Increasing opportunity to learn via access to rigorous courses and programs: One strategy for closing the achievement gap for at-risk and ethnic minority students.* Report prepared for the North Carolina Department of Public Instruction. Retrieved from http://www.ncpublicschools.org/docs/ec/development/gifted/increasingopportunities.pdf.

Davis, J. E. (2003). Early schooling and academic achievement of African American males. *Urban Education, 38,* 515–537.

Davis, J. E., & Jordan, W. J. (1994). The effects of school context, structure, and experiences on African American males in middle and high school. *Journal of Negro Education, 63,* 570–587.

Davis, L. E., Johnson, S., Cribbs, J. M., & Saunders, J. (2002). A brief report: Factors influencing African American youth decisions to stay in school. *Journal of Adolescent Research, 17,* 223–234.

Delpit, L. (2003). Educators as "seed people" growing a new future. *Educational Researcher, 32,* 14–21.

Devine, P., & Elliott, A. (1995). Are racial stereotypes really fading? The Princeton trilogy revisited. *Personality and Social Psychology Bulletin, 21,* 1139–1150.

Dill, E. M., & Boykin, A. W. (2000). The comparative influence of individual, peer tutoring, and communal learning contexts on the recall of African American children. *Journal of Black Psychology, 26,* 65–78.

DuBois, D. L., Burk-Braxton, C., Swenson, L. P., Tevendale, H. D., & Hardesty, J. L. (2002). Race and gender influences on adjustment in early adolescence: Investigation of an integrative model. *Child Development, 73,* 1573–1592.

Dunn, R., Gemake, J., Jalai, F., Zenhausen, R., Quinn, P., & Spiridakis, J. (1990). Cross-cultural differences in learning styles of elementary-age students from four ethnic backgrounds. *Journal of Multicultural Counseling and Development, 18,* 68–93.

Dusek, J. B., & Joseph, G. (1983). The bases of teacher expectancies: A meta-analysis. *Journal of Educational Psychology, 75,* 327–346.

Eccles, J. S., & Harold, R. D. (1996). Family involvement in children's and adolescents' schooling. In J. S. Eccles & R. D. Harold (Eds.), *Family-school links: How do they affect educational outcomes?* (pp. 3–34). Hillsdale, NJ: Erlbaum.

Eccles, J. S., & Wigfield, A. (2002). Motivational beliefs, values, and goals. *Annual Review of Psychology, 53,* 109–132.

Eccles, J. S., Wigfield, A., & Schiefele, U. (1998). Motivation to succeed. In W. Damon & N. Eisenberg (Vol. Ed.), *Handbook of child psychology: Vol. 3. Social, emotional, and personality development* (5th ed., pp. 1017–1095). New York: Wiley.

Eckholm, E. (March 20, 2006). The plight deepens for Black Men. *New York Times,* A1.

Education Trust. (2008). *Dispelling the myth.* Retrieved from http://www2.edtrust.org/edtrust/dtm.

Ellison, C. M., Boykin, A. W., Tyler, K. M., & Dillihunt, M. L. (2005). Examining classroom learning preferences among elementary school students. *Social Behavior and Personality, 33,* 699–708.

Epstein, J. L., & Dauber, S. L. (1991). School programs and teacher practices of parent involvement in inner-city elementary and middle schools. *The Elementary School Journal, 91,* 289–305.

Farkas, G. (2003). Racial disparities and discrimination in education: What do we know, how do we know it, and what do we need to know? *Teachers College Record, 105,* 1119–1146.

Farkas, G., Grobe, R. P., Sheehan, D., & Shuan, Y. (1990). Cultural resources and school success: Gender, ethnicity, and poverty groups within an urban school district. *American Sociological Review, 55,* 127–142.

Ferguson, R. F. (1991). Racial patterns in how school and teacher quality affect achievement and earnings. *Challenge, 2,* 1–35.

Ferguson, R. F. (2003). Teachers' perceptions and expectations and the Black–White test score gap. *Urban Education, 38,* 460–507.

Fielding, C. (2004). Low performance on high-stakes test drives special education referrals: A Texas survey. *The Educational Forum, 68,* 126–132.

Fields, B. (2004). Breaking the cycle of office referrals and suspensions: Defensive management. *Educational Psychology in Practice, 20,* 103–115.

Fierros, E. G., & Conroy, J. E. (2002). Double jeopardy: An exploration of restrictiveness and race in special education. In D. Losen & G. Orfield (Eds.), *Racial inequity in special education* (pp. 39–70). Cambridge, MA: Harvard Education Press.

Fisher, C. B., Wallace, S. A., & Fenton, R. E. (2000). Discrimination distress during adolescence. *Journal of Youth and Adolescence, 29,* 679–695.

Ford, D. Y. (1998). The underrepresentation of minority students in gifted education: Problems and promises in recruitment and retention. *Journal of Special Education, 32,* 4–14.

Ford, D. Y., & Harris, J. J. III (1996). Perceptions and attitudes of Black students toward school, achievement, and other educational variables. *Child Development, 67,* 1141–1152.

Fordham, S. (1999). Dissin' "the standard": Ebonics as guerrilla warfare at Capital High. *Anthropology and Education Quarterly, 30,* 272–293.

Fordham, S., & Ogbu, J. U. (1986). Black students' school success: Coping with the burden of "acting White." *The Urban Review, 18,* 176–206.

Frankenberg, E., Lee, C., & Orfield, G. (2003). *A multiracial society with segregated schools: Are we losing the dream?* Cambridge, MA: Harvard Civil Rights Project. (ERIC Document Reproduction Service No. ED. 472347)

Frazier-Kouassi, S. (2002). Race and gender at the crossroads: African American females in school. *African American Research Perspectives, 8,* 151–162.

Fryer, R. G., & Levitt, S. D. (2005). *The black-white test score gap through third grade* (NBER Working Paper no. 11049). Cambridge, MA: National Bureau of Economic Research.

Gallagher, J. J. (2000). Unthinkable thoughts: Education of gifted students. *Gifted Child Quarterly, 44,* 5–12.

Gallimore, R., & Goldenberg, C. (2001). Analyzing cultural models and settings to connect minority achievement and school improvement research. *Educational Psychologist, 36,* 45–56.

Goldhaber, D., Perry, D., & Anthony, E. (2004) The national board for professional teaching standards (NBPTS) process: Who applies and what factors are associated with NBPTS certification? *Educational Evaluation and Policy Analysis, 26,* 259–280.

Graham, S. (1994). Motivation in African Americans. *Review of Educational Research, 64,* 55–117.

Graham, S., & Long, A. (1986). Race, class, and the attributional process. *Journal of Educational Psychology, 78,* 4–13.

Graham, S., Taylor, A. Z., & Hudley, C. (1998). Exploring achievement values among ethnic minority early adolescents. *Journal of Educational Psychology, 90,* 606–620.

Grant, L. (1984). Black females' "place" in desegregated classrooms. *Sociology of Education, 57,* 98–111.

Gray-Little, B., & Hafdahl, A. R. (2000). Factors influencing racial comparisons of self-esteem: A quantitative review. *Psychological Bulletin, 126,* 26–54.

Greene, M. L., & Way, N. (2005). Self-esteem trajectories among ethnic minority adolescents: A growth curve analysis of the patterns and predictors of change. *Journal of Research on Adolescence, 15,* 151–178.

Gregory, J. F. (1997). Three strikes and they're out: African American boys and schools' responses to misbehavior. *International Journal of Adolescence and Youth, 7,* 25–34.

Griffith, J. (1996). Relation of parental involvement, empowerment, and school traits to student academic performance. *Journal of Educational Research, 90*(1), 33–41.

Hall, S. P., & Carter, R. T. (2006). The relationship between racial identity, ethnic identity, and perceptions of racial discrimination in an Afro-Caribbean descent sample. *Journal of Black Psychology, 32,* 155–175.

Hanushek, E. A., & Rivkin, S. G. (2006). School quality and the Black-White achievement gap (NBER Working Paper 12651). Cambridge, MA: National Bureau of Economic Research.

Harris, D., & Ray, L. (2003). *No school left behind? The distribution of teacher quality in Michigan's public schools* (Policy report). East Lansing: Educational Policy Center, Michigan State University.

Harris-Britt, A., Valrie, C., Kurtz-Costes, B., & Rowley, S. J. (2007). Perceived racial discrimination and self-esteem in African American youth: Racial socialization as a protective factor. *Journal of Research on Adolescence, 17,* 669–682.

Hill, N. E., Castellino, D. R., Lansford, J. E., Nowlin, P., Dodge, K. A., Bates, J. E., & Petit, G. (2004). Parent academic involvement as related to school behavior, achievement, and aspirations: Demographic variations across adolescence. *Child Development, 75,* 1491–1509.

Hill, N. E., & Craft, S. (2003). Parent–school involvement and children's school performance: Mediated pathways among African American and Euro-American children. *Journal of Educational Psychology, 95,* 74–83.

Hilliard, A. (2000). Excellence in education versus high-stakes standardized testing. *Journal of Teacher Education, 51,* 293–304.

Honora, D. (2003). Urban African American adolescents and school identification. *Urban Education, 38,* 58–76.

Hoover, M. E. R. (1992). The Nairobi Day School: An African American Independent School, 1966–1984. *Journal of Negro Education, 61,* 201–210.

Horvat, E. M., & Lewis, K. S. (2003). Reassessing the "burden of 'acting white'": The importance of peer groups in managing academic success. *Sociology of Education, 76,* 265–280.

Hrabowski, F. A., Maton, K. I., & Greif, G. (1998). *Beating the odds: Raising academically successful African American males.* New York: Oxford University Press.

Hudley, C., & Graham, S. (2001). Stereotypes of achievement striving among early adolescents. *Social Psychology of Education, 5,* 201–224.

Hughes, J. N., Gleason, K. A., & Zhang, D. (2005). Relationship influences on teachers' perceptions of academic competence in academically at-risk minority and majority first grade students. *Journal of School Psychology, 43,* 303–320.

Hurley, E. A., Boykin, A. W. & Allen, B. A. (2005). Communal versus individual learning of a math-estimation task: African American children and the culture of learning contexts. *The Journal of Psychology, 6,* 513–527.

Irvine, J. J. (1986). Teacher–student interactions: Effects of student race, sex, and grade level. *Journal of Educational Psychology, 78,* 14–21.

Jencks, C., & Phillips, M. (1998). *The Black–White test score gap.* Washington, DC: Brookings Institution Press.

Jussim, L., Eccles, J., & Madon, S. (1996). Social perception, social stereotypes, and teacher expectations: Accuracy and the quest for the powerful self-fulfilling prophecy. In M. P. Zanna (Ed.), *Advances in experimental social psychology* (Vol. 28, pp. 281–388). San Diego, CA: Academic Press.

Jussim, L., & Harber, K. D. (2005). Teacher expectations and self-fulfilling prophecies: Knowns and unknowns, resolved and unresolved controversies. *Personality and Social Psychology Review, 9,* 131–155.

Jussim, L., Harber, K. D., Crawford, J. T., Cain, T. R., & Cohen, F. (2005). Social reality makes the social mind: Self-fulfilling prophecy, stereotypes, bias, and accuracy. *Interaction Studies, 6,* 85–102.

Keith, T. Z., Keith, P. B., Quirk, K. J., Sperduto, J., Santillo, S., & Killings, S. (1998). Longitudinal effects of parent involvement on high school grades: Similarities and differences across gender and ethnic groups. *Journal of School Psychology, 36,* 335–363.

Kinney, D. A. (1993). From nerds to normals: The recovery of identity among adolescents from middle school to high school. *Sociology of Education, 66,* 21–40.

Krueger, J. (1996). Personal beliefs and cultural stereotypes about racial characteristics. *Journal of Personality and Social Psychology, 71,* 536–548.

Kuperminc, G. P., Leadbeater, B. J., & Blatt, S. J. (2001). School social climate and individual differences in vulnerability to psychopathology among middle school students. *Journal of School Psychology, 39,* 141–159.

Kuperminc, G. P., Leadbeater, B. J., Emmons, C., & Blatt, S. J. (1997). Perceived school climate and difficulties in the social adjustment of middle school students. *Applied Developmental Science, 1*, 76–88.

Kurtz-Costes, B., Rowley, S. J., Harris-Britt, A., & Woods, T. A. (2008). Gender stereotypes about mathematics and science and self-perceptions of ability in late childhood and early adolescence. *Merrill Palmer Quarterly, 54*, 386–410.

Lareau, A. (2003). *Unequal childhoods: Class, race, and family life.* Berkeley: University of California Press.

Lareau, A., & Horvat, E. M. (1999). Moments of social inclusion and exclusion: Race, class, and cultural capital in family-school relationships. *Sociology of Education, 72*, 37–53.

Lee, C. (2004). *Racial segregation and educational outcomes in metropolitan Boston.* Cambridge, MA: The Civil Rights Project at Harvard University.

Lee, J. (2006). *Tracking achievement gaps and assessing the impact of NCLB on the gaps: An in-depth look into national and state reading and math outcome trends.* Cambridge, MA: The Civil Rights Project at Harvard University.

Leventhal, T., & Brooks-Gunn, J. (2004). A randomized study of neighborhood effects on low-income children's educational outcomes. *Developmental Psychology, 40*, 488–507.

Lippi-Green, R. (1997). What we talk about when we talk about Ebonics: Why definitions matter. *Black Scholar, 27*, 7–11.

Losen, D., & Orfield, G. (2002). *Racial inequality in special education.* Cambridge, MA: Harvard Civil Rights Project.

Loukas, A., & Robinson, S. (2004). Examining the moderating role of perceived school climate in early adolescent adjustment. *Journal of Research on Adolescence, 14*, 209–233.

Madaus, G., & Clarke, M. (2001). *The adverse impact of high stakes testing on minority students: Evidence from 100 years of test data.* (ERIC Document Reproduction Service No. ED. 450183)

Madon, S., Jussim, L., & Eccles, J. (1997). In search of the powerful self-fulfilling prophecy. *Journal of Personality and Social Psychology, 72*, 791–809.

Madon, S., Jussim, L., Keiper, S., Eccles, J., Smith, A., & Palumbo, P. (1998). The accuracy and power of sex, social class, and ethnic stereotypes: A naturalistic study in person perception. *Personality and Social Psychology, 24*, 1304–1318.

Major, B., & Schmader, T. (1998). Coping with stigma through psychological disengagement. In J. K. Swim & C. Stangor (Eds.), *Prejudice: The target's perspective* (pp. 219–241). San Diego, CA: Academic Press.

Major, B., Spencer, S., Schmader, T., Wolfe, C., & Crocker, J. (1998). Coping with negative stereotypes about intellectual performance: The role of psychological disengagement. *Personality and Social Psychology Bulletin, 24*, 34–50.

Marryshow, D., Hurley, E. A., Allen, B. A., Tyler, K. M., & Boykin, A. W. (2005). Impact of learning orientation on African American children's attitudes toward high-achieving peers. *American Journal of Psychology, 118*, 603–618.

Marsh, H. W., & Craven, R. G. (2006). Reciprocal effects of self-concept and performance from a multidimensional perspective. *Perspectives on Psychological Science, 1*, 133–163.

Marsh, H. W., Trautwein, U., Luedtke, O., Koeller, O., & Baumert, J. (2005). Academic self-concept, interest, grades, and standardized test scores: Reciprocal effects models of causal ordering. *Child Development, 76*, 397–416.

Marsh, H. W., & Yeung, A. S. (1997). Causal effects of academic self-concept on academic achievement: Structural equations models of longitudinal data. *Journal of Educational Psychology, 89*, 41–54.

Marsh, T. Y., & Cornell, D. G. (2001). The contribution of student experiences to understanding ethnic differences in high-risk behaviors at school. *Behavioral Disorders, 26*, 152–163.

McKay, M. M., Atkins, M. S., Hawkins, T., Brown, C., & Lynn, C. J. (2003). Inner-city African American parental involvement in children's schooling: Racial socialization and social support from the parent community. *American Journal of Community Psychology, 32*(1/2), 107–114.

McKown, C., & Strambler, M. J. (2008). Social influences on the ethnic achievement gap. In S. M. Quintana & C. McKown (Eds.), *Handbook of race, racism, and the developing child* (pp. 366–397). Hoboken, NJ: Wiley.

McKown, C., & Weinstein, R. S. (2003). The development and consequences of stereotype-consciousness in middle childhood. *Child Development, 74*, 498–515.

Meyer, G., & Patton, J. M. (2001). On the nexus of race, disability, and overrepresentation: What do we know? Where do we go? On point… Brief discussions of critical issues in urban education. (ERIC Document Reproduction Service No. ED. 462587)

Mickelson, R. A. (1990). The attitude-achievement paradox among Black adolescents. *Sociology of Education, 63*, 44–61.

Mickelson, R. A. (2003). When are racial disparities in education the result of racial discrimination? A social science perspective. *Teachers College Record, 105*, 1052–1086.

Midgley, C., Maehr, M. L., Gheen, M. H., Hruda, L., Marachi, R., Middleton, M., et al. (2000). *The transition to high school study; Report to participating schools and districts.* Retrieved from http://www.umich.edu/~pals/hs_feedback_report.PDF

Moore, K. A., Manlove, J., Glei, D. A., & Morrison, D. R. (1998). Nonmarital school-age motherhood: Family, individual, and school characteristics. *Journal of Adolescent Research, 13*, 433–457.

Morgan, S. L., & Mehta, J. D. (2004). Beyond the laboratory: Evaluating the survey evidence for the disidentification explanation of Black–White differences in achievement. *Sociology of Education, 77*, 82–101.

Moses, R., & Cobb, C. (2001). *Radical equations: Civil rights from Mississippi to the Algebra Project.* Boston, MA: Beacon Press.

Moses, R. P., & Cobb, C. E. (2002). *Radical equations: Math literacy and civil rights.* Boston, MA: Beacon Press.

National Center for Education Statistics. (2007). *Indicators of school crime and safety: 2007* (NCES 2008–021). Washington, DC: U.S. Department of Education.

Neal, L. I., McCrary, A. D., & Webb-Johnson, G. (2001). The effects of African American movement styles on teachers' perceptions and reactions. *Journal of Special Education, 37*, 49–57.

Neblett, E. W., Jr., Philip, C. L., Cogburn, C. D., & Sellers, R. M. (2006). African American adolescents' discrimination experiences and academic achievement: Racial socialization as a cultural compensatory and protective factor. *Journal of Black Psychology, 32*, 199–218.

Noguera, P. A. (2003). The trouble with black boys: The role and influence of environmental and cultural factors on the academic performance of African American males. *Urban Education, 38*, 431–459.

Oakes, J. (2005). *Keeping track: How schools structure inequality* (2nd ed.). New Haven, CT: Yale University Press.

O'Connor, C. (2001). Making sense of the complexity of social identity in relation to achievement: A sociological challenge in the new millennium [Special issue]. *Sociology of Education*, 159–168.

Ogbu, J. U. (1988). Cultural diversity and human development. *New Directions for Child Development, 42*, 11–28.

Ogbu, J. U. (1992). Adaptation to minority status and impact on school success. *Theory into Practice, 31*, 287–295.

Ogbu, J. U. (1999). Beyond language: Ebonics, proper English, and identity in a Black-American speech community, *American Educational Research Journal, 36*, 147–184.

Okagaki, L. (2001). Triarchic model of minority children's school achievement. *Educational Psychologist, 36*, 9–20.

Okeke, N. A., Howard, L., Kurtz-Costes, B., & Rowley, S. J. (2008). *Academic race stereotypes, academic self-concept, and race centrality in African American youth.* Manuscript submitted for publication.

Orfield, G., & Lee, C. (2006). *Racial transformation and the changing nature of segregation.* Cambridge, MA: The Civil Rights Project at Harvard University.

Osborne, J. W. (1995). Academics, self-esteem, and race: A look at the underlying assumptions of the disidentification hypothesis. *Personality and Social Psychology Bulletin, 21*, 449–455.

Osborne, J. W. (1997). Race and academic disidentification. *Journal of Educational Psychology, 89*, 728–735.

Owens, A., & Sunderman, G. L. (2006). *School accountability under NCLB: Aid or obstacles for measuring racial equity?* Cambridge, MA: The Civil Rights Project at Harvard University.

Oyserman, D., Harrison, K., & Bybee, D. (2001). Can racial identity be promotive of academic efficacy. *International Journal of Behavioral Development, 25,* 379–385.

Pai, Y., Adler, S. A. & Shadiow, L. K. (2006). *Cultural foundations for education.* Upper Saddle River, NJ: Pearson Education.

Parrish, T. (2002). Racial disparities in the identification, funding, and provision of special education. In D. Losen & G. Orfield (Eds.), *Racial inequity in special education* (pp. 15–38). Cambridge, MA: Harvard Education Press.

Perie, M., Grigg, W., & Donahue, P. (2005). *The Nation's Report Card: Reading 2005* (NCES 2006-451). U.S. Department of Education, National Center for Education Statistics. Washington, DC: U.S. Government Printing Office.

Peter, K., & Horn, L. (2005). *Gender differences in participation and completion of undergraduate education and how they have changed over time* (NCES 2005-169). U.S. Department of Education, National Center for Education Statistics. Washington, DC: U.S. Government Printing Office.

Peterson-Lewis, S., & Bratton, L. M. (2004). Perceptions of "acting Black" among African American teens: Implications of racial dramaturgy for academic and social achievement. *Urban Review, 36,* 81–100.

Phelan, P., Yu, H. C., & Davidson, A. L. (1994). Navigating the psychosocial pressures of adolescence: The voices and experiences of high school youth. *American Educational Research Journal, 31,* 415–447.

Phinney, J. S., & Chavira, V. (1992). Ethnic identity and self-esteem: An exploratory longitudinal study. *Journal of Adolescence, 15,* 271–281.

Ramey, S. L., Lanzi, R. G., Phillips, M. M., & Ramey, C. T. (1998). Perspectives of former head start children and their parents on school and the transition to school. *Elementary School Journal, 94,* 311–327.

Reid, P. T., & Roberts, S. K. (2006). Gaining options: A mathematics program for potentially talented at-risk adolescent girls. *Merrill-Palmer Quarterly, 52,* 288–304.

Reynolds, A. J. (1999). Educational success in high-risk settings: Contributions of the Chicago Longitudinal Study. *Journal of School Psychology, 37,* 345–354.

Roderick, M. (2003). What's happening to the boys? Early high school experiences and school outcomes among African American male adolescents in Chicago. *Urban Education, 38,* 538–607.

Roderick, M., & Camburn, E. (1999). Risk and recovery from course failure in the early years of high school. *American Educational Research Journal, 36,* 303–344.

Roeser, R. W., & Eccles, J. S. (1998). Adolescents' perceptions of middle school: Relation to longitudinal changes in academic and psychological adjustment. *Journal of Research on Adolescence, 8,* 123–158.

Roeser, R. W., Eccles, J. S., & Sameroff, A. J. (2000). School as a context of early adolescents' academic and social-emotional development: A summary of research findings. *The Elementary School Journal, 100,* 443.

Rogoff, B. (2003). *The cultural nature of human development.* New York: Oxford University Press.

Romero, A. J., & Roberts, R. E. (2003). The impact of multiple dimensions of ethnic identity on discrimination and adolescents' self-esteem. *Journal of Applied Social Psychology, 33,* 2288–2305.

Rosenbloom, S. R., & Way, N. (2004). Experiences of discrimination among African American, Asian American, and Latino adolescents in an urban high school. *Youth and Society, 35,* 420–451.

Rosenthal, R. (1994). Interpersonal expectancy effects: A 30-year perspective. *Current Directions in Psychological Science, 3,* 176–179.

Rosenthal, R., & Jacobson, L. (1968). *Pygmalion in the classroom,* New York: Holt, Rinehart, & Winston.

Rowley, S. J. (2000). Profiles of African American college students' educational utility and performance: A cluster analysis. *Journal of Black Psychology, 26,* 3–26.

Rowley, S. J., Kurtz-Costes, B., Mistry, R., & Feagans, L. (2007). Social status as a predictor of race and gender stereotypes in late childhood and early adolescence. *Social Development, 16,* 150–168.

Rowley, S. J., Sellers, R. M., Chavous, T. M., & Smith, M. A. (1998). The relationship between racial identity and self-esteem in African American college and high school students. *Journal of Personality & Social Psychology, 74,* 715–724.

Ruck, M. D., & Wortley, S. (2002). Racial and ethnic minority high school students' perceptions of school disciplinary practices: A look at some Canadian findings. *Journal of Youth and Adolescence, 31,* 185–195.

Ruggiero, K. M., & Taylor, D. M. (1995). Coping with discrimination: How disadvantaged group members perceive the discrimination that confronts them. *Journal of Personality and Social Psychology, 68,* 826–838.

Sanders, M. (1997). Overcoming obstacles: Academic achievement as a response to racism and discrimination. *Journal of Negro Education, 66,* 83–93.

Sankofa, B. M., Hurley, E. A., Allen, B. A., & Boykin, A. W. (2005). Cultural expression and Black students' attitudes toward high achievers. *Journal of Psychology: Interdisciplinary and Applied, 139,* 247–259.

Saunders, J., Davis, L., Williams, T., & Williams, J. H. (2004). Gender differences in self-perceptions and academic outcomes: A study of African American high school students. *Journal of Youth and Adolescence, 33,* 81–90.

Seidman, E., Aber, J. L., Allen, L., & French, S. E. (1996). The impact of the transition to high school on the self-esteem and perceived social context of urban poor youth. *American Journal of Community Psychology, 24,* 489–515.

Seidman, E., Allen, L., Aber, J. L., Mitchell, C., & Feinman, J. (1994). The impact of school transitions in early adolescence on the self-system and perceived social context of poor urban youth. *Child Development, 65,* 507–522.

Sellers, R. M., Caldwell, C. H., Schmeelk-Cone, K. H., & Zimmerman, M. A. (2003). Racial identity, racial discrimination, perceived stress, and psychological distress among African American young adults. *Journal of Health and Social Behavior, 44,* 302–317.

Sellers, R. M., Chavous, T. M., & Cooke, D. Y. (1998). Racial ideology and racial centrality as predictors of African American college students' academic performance. *Journal of Black Psychology, 24,* 8–27.

Sellers, R. M., Rowley, S. A. J., Chavous, T. M., Shelton, N. J., & Smith, M. A. (1997). Multidimensional inventory of Black identity: A preliminary investigation of reliability and construct validity. *Journal of Personality and Social Psychology, 73,* 805–815.

Serpell, Z., Boykin, A. W., Madhere, S., & Nasim, A. (2006). The significance of contextual factors on African American students' transfer of learning. *Journal of Black Psychology, 32,* 418–441.

Siegel, J. (2006). Language ideologies and the education of speakers of marginalized language varieties: Adopting a critical awareness approach. *Linguistics and Education, 17,* 157–174.

Simpson, A. W., & Erickson, M. T. (1983). Teachers' verbal and nonverbal communication patterns as a function of teacher race, student gender and student race. *American Educational Research Journal, 20,* 183–198.

Skiba, R. J., Michael, R. S., Nardo, A. C., & Peterson, R. L. (2002). The color of discipline: Sources of racial and gender disproportionality in school punishment. *Urban Review, 34,* 317–342.

Slaughter-Defoe, D. T., Garrett, A. M., & Harrison-Hale, A. O. (2006). Our children too: A history of the Black Caucus of the Society for Research in Child Development, 1973–1997. *Monographs of the Society for Research in Child Development, 71,* 1–211.

Slavin, R. E., & Cooper, R. (1999). Improving intergroup relations: Lessons learned from cooperative learning programs. *Journal of Social Issues, 55,* 647–663.

Smith, E. P., Walker, K., Fields, L., Brookins, C., & Seay, R. C. (1999). Ethnic identity and its relationship to self-esteem, perceived efficacy and prosocial attitudes in early adolescence. *Journal of Adolescence, 22,* 867–880.

Solorzano, D. G. (1992). An exploratory analysis of the effects of race, class, and gender on student and parent mobility aspirations. *Journal of Negro Education, 61,* 30–44.

Spencer, M. B., Cunningham, M., & Swanson, D. P. (1995). Identity as coping: Adolescent African-American males' adaptive responses to high-risk environments. In H. W. Harris, H. C. Blue, & E. E. Griffith (Eds.), *Racial and ethnic identity: Psychological development and creative expression* (pp. 31–52). New York: Routledge.

Spencer, M. B., Noll, E., Stoltzfus, J., & Harplani, V. (2001). Identity and school adjustment: Revisiting the "Acting White" assumption. *Educational Psychologist, 36,* 21–20.

Steele, C. M. (1992). Race and the schooling of African Americans. *The Atlantic Monthly, 269,* 68–78.

Steele, C. M., & Aronson, J. (1995). Stereotype threat and intellectual test performance of African Americans. *Journal of Personality and Social Psychology*, 69, 797–811.

Swanson, D. P., Cunningham, M., & Spencer, M. B. (2003). Black males' structural conditions, achievement patterns, normative needs, and "opportunities." *Urban Education, 38,* 608–633.

Tauber, R. T. (1997). *Self-fulfilling prophecy: A practical guide to its use in education*. Westport, CT: Praeger.

Taylor, A. R. (1991). Social competence and the early school transition: Risk and protective factors for African-American children. *Education and Urban Society*, 24, 15–26.

Taylor, L. T., Clayton, J., & Rowley, S. J. (2004). Academic socialization: Understanding parental influences on children's school-related development in the early years. *Review of General Psychology, 8,* 163–178.

Taylor, R. D., Casten, R., Flickinger, S. M., Roberts, D., & Fulmore, C. D. (1994). Explaining the school performance of African-American adolescents. *Journal of Research on Adolescence, 4,* 21–44.

Thomas, D. E., Townsend, T. G., & Belgrave, F. Z. (2003). The influence of cultural and racial identification on the psychosocial adjustment of inner-city African American children in school. *American Journal of Community Psychology, 32*(3–4), 217–228.

Tiedemann, J. (2000). Parents' gender stereotypes and teacher's beliefs as predictors of children's concept of their mathematical ability in elementary school. *Journal of Educational Psychology*, 92, 144–151.

Townsend, B. L. (2000). The disproportionate discipline of African American learners: Reducing school suspensions and expulsions. *Exceptional Children, 66,* 381–391.

Tracy, A. J., & Erkut, S. (2002). Gender and race patterns in the pathways from sports participation to self-esteem. *Sociological Perspectives, 45,* 445–466.

Tseng, V. (2006). Unpacking immigration in youths' academic and occupational pathways. *Child Development*, 77, 1434–1445.

Tucker, C. M., Zayco, R. A., Herman, K. C., Reinke, W. M., Trujillo, M., Carraway, K. et al. (2002). Teacher and child variables as predictors of academic engagement among low-income African American children. *Psychology in the Schools, 39,* 477–488.

Tyson, K., Darity, W. Jr., & Castellino, D. R. (2005). It's not "a Black thing": Understanding the burden of acting White and other dilemmas of high achievement. *American Sociological Review, 70,* 582–605.

Utley, C. A., Kozleski, E., Smith, A., & Draper, I. L. (2002). Positive behavior support: A proactive strategy for minimizing behavior problems in urban multicultural youth. *Journal of Positive Behavior Interventions, 4,* 196–207.

Valeski, T. N., & Stipek, D. J. (2001). Young children's feelings about school. *Child Development, 72,* 1198–1213.

Vieno, A., Perkins, D. D., Smith, T., & Santinello, M. (2005). Democratic school climate and sense of community in school: A multilevel analysis. *American Journal of Community Psychology*, 36, 327–341.

Washington, J. A., & Craig, H. K. (2002). Morphosyntactic forms of African American English used by young children and their caregivers. *Applied Psycholinguistics, 23*, 209–231.

Waters, M. C. (1994). Ethnic and racial identities of second-generation Black immigrants in New York City. *International Migration Review, 28,* 795–820.

Waters, M. C. (2001). Growing up West Indian and American: Gender and class differences in the second generation. In N. Foner (Ed.), *Islands in the city: West Indian migration to New York* (pp. 237–256). Berkeley: University of California Press.

Weinstein, R. S., Marshall, H. M., Sharp, L., & Botkin, M. (1987). Pygmalion and the student: Age and classroom differences in children's awareness of teachers' expectations. *Child Development, 58,* 1079–1093.

Whitlock, J. L. (2006) Youth perceptions of life at school: Contextual correlates of school connectedness in adolescence. *Applied Developmental Science, 10,* 13–29.

Wigfield, A., & Eccles, J. S. (1994). Children's competence beliefs, achievement values, and self-esteem: Changes across elementary and middle school. *Journal of Early Adolescence, 14,* 107–138.

Wigfield, A., Eccles, J. S., Schiefele, U., Roeser, R. W., & Davis-Kean, P. (2006). Development of achievement motivation. In W. Damon (Series Ed.) & N. Eisenberg (Volume Ed.), *Handbook of child psychology: Vol. 3. Social, emotional, and personality development* (6th ed., pp. 933–1002) New York: Wiley.

Wilds, D. J. (2000). *Minorities in higher education, 1999–2000. Seventeenth annual status report.* Washington, DC: American Council on Education.

Wilkins, A. (2006). Yes we can: Telling truths and dispelling myths about race and education in America. Retrieved from http://www2.edtrust.org/NR/rdonlyres/DD58DD01-23A4-4B89-9FD8-C11BB072331E/0/YesWeCan.pdf

Wilson, M. N., Cooke, D. Y., & Arrington, E. G. (1997). African American adolescents and academic achievement: Family and peer influences. In R. D. Taylor & M. C. Wang (Eds.), *Social and emotional adjustment and family relations in ethnic minority families* (pp. 145–155). Mahwah, NJ: Erlbaum.

Wolfram, W., Adger, C. T., & Christian, D. (1999). *Dialects in schools and communities.* Mahwah, NJ: Erlbaum.

Wong, C. A., Eccles, J. S., & Sameroff, A. (2003). The influence of ethnic discrimination and ethnic identification on African American adolescents' school and socioemotional adjustment. *Journal of Personality, 71*(6), 1197–1232.

Yip, T. (2008). Everyday experiences of ethnic and racial identity among adolescents and young adults. In S. M. Quintana & C. McKown (Eds.), *Handbook of race, racism, and the developing child* (pp. 182–202). Hoboken, NJ: Wiley.

# 18

# Parental and School Influences Promoting Academic Success among Latino Students

*Rosario Ceballo, Marisela Huerta, and Quyen Epstein-Ngo*

Several recent demographic trends highlight the importance of focusing on Latinos' educational attainment. First and foremost, Latinos comprise the fastest growing ethnic minority group in the United States (Marotta & Garcia, 2003). According to estimates by the U.S. Census Bureau (2007), there were approximately 44 million Hispanics living in the United States in 2007, representing nearly 15% of the total U. S. population. While the U.S. Census uses the term *Hispanic*, we prefer and will instead employ the term *Latino* for the rest of this chapter. Despite our use of the single term *Latino*, it is important to note at the outset that Latinos can be of any race, and they constitute a highly heterogeneous group of people. Within the category of "Latino," we are referring to people who trace their ethnic heritage to Mexico, Central and South America, or the Caribbean. Needless to say, there is tremendous diversity among Latino families with regard to immigration histories, socioeconomic status, acculturation levels, English language proficiency, and sociocultural values. To date, Mexicans comprise the largest Latino subgroup in the United States (64%), followed by those of Central and South American descent (13%), and then Puerto Ricans (9%) (U.S. Census Bureau, 2007).

A second reason to carefully scrutinize Latinos' educational attainment rests on the fact that our nation will increasingly depend upon Latinos in the work force. More and more, employers will need to fill positions from the rising numbers of working-age Latino adults and the educational success of Latinos is intricately bound to the occupational skills they will have to offer. Finally, Latinos are overrepresented among those living in poverty. While Latinos constitute about 15% of the total U.S. population, 22% of Latinos are living in poverty (U.S. Census Bureau, 2007). Moreover, Latino youth (under 18) are much more likely than non-Latino White children to live in poverty. Living in poverty is accompanied by a host of detrimental consequences related to poor physical health, strained psychological well-being, and generally restricted occupational and life choices. Educational attainment and,

more specifically, a college degree offer poor, working class Latinos a viable route for upward mobility, an important step toward eradicating long-standing social and economic inequalities.

By many accounts, the educational attainment of Latinos in the United States is disturbingly low. Although Latino educational attainment has improved over the last decade, discrepancies continue to exist. For instance, 2005 data gathered by the National Center for Educational Statistics (2007) indicated that Latino students were among the most likely to attend high-poverty schools. Further, Latino students were more likely to drop out of school compared to African American and European American students (National Center for Educational Statistics [NCES], 2007). While only 11% of non-Latino Whites over the age of 25 years had not obtained a high school diploma, a full 40% of Latinos had not yet received their high school diplomas; and whereas 61% of non-Latino, White high school graduates enrolled in college, only 45% of Latinos did so in 2007 (U.S. Census Bureau, 2007).

Scholars have proposed a number of explanations to account for the scholastic underachievement of Latino youth. Poverty and economic disadvantage have long been associated with poor academic achievement (Ackerman, Brown, & Izard, 2004; Brown & Low, 2008), and poverty rates among Latino families are disproportionately high, even for those families with an employed adult living in the home. As previously noted, Latino children are overrepresented among children living in poverty. Whereas 8% of non-Latino White children live in poverty, a full 29% or over three times more Latino children live below the poverty line (U.S. Census Bureau, 2007). Relying upon the National Education Longitudinal Study (NELS) for a nationally representative sample of Latino high school students, Battle (2002) found that socioeconomic status was a stronger predictor of adolescents' academic performance than family structure (single parent vs. two parent households). Other factors, closely intertwined with poverty, serve as barriers and obstacles to scholastic achievement, such as limited English language proficiency, attendance at large underfunded schools, institutional practices of racism within schools (e.g., tracking), and parental reliance on migratory employment (Arellano & Padilla, 1996; Okagaki & Frensch, 1998).

Two theoretical views explain race- and class-based discrepancies in academic achievement, specifically proposing explanatory frameworks for the underachievement of racial minority groups in the United States. John Ogbu (1981, 1986, 1992) was the greatest proponent of the cultural–ecological theory. According to Ogbu, educational systems present racial minorities with institutional barriers, blocking access to real educational and economic opportunities. In response to an unfair and biased system, racial minorities may reject normative socialization patterns and instead, develop alternative beliefs and behaviors in opposition to majority European American culture. Hence, there may be less parental pressure for children to achieve academically because parents are aware of the lack of economic opportunity for racial minority youth and of the existence of job ceilings and other discriminatory employment practices. Similarly, as Latino students are themselves exposed to stressful and limiting experiences associated with poverty and discrimination, they may develop a sense of fatalism about their future educational prospects.

For far too many families, our current institutions of public education constitute an unequal and unjust two-tiered system. "The system of public education in the United States, financed primarily by community property taxes, has resulted in a two-tiered institution: One tier is well-equipped and maintained and serves mostly suburban, middle-class children, and another contains run-down and decaying schools in which there is generally a lack of everything but problems" (Lott, 2002, p. 104). At their worst, our schools function as institutional vehicles for perpetuating social roles based on profound race and class based inequalities (Stanton-Salazar, 1997). From this perspective, institutional and individual discriminatory practices collectively work to discourage parents from participating in schools and learning about school-based goals and procedures for guiding their children towards academic success.

A second theoretical model is based on a sociocultural framework. According to models of cultural discontinuity, the manner in which children learn is embedded and shaped by their daily experiences in a cultural setting (Moreno, 2002). Scholars have thus attributed racial gaps in educational achievement as reflecting the lack of congruence between Latino cultural practices in the home and the norms of a majority culture followed at school. The lack of congruence is predicated upon different sociocultural norms, customs, and ways of thinking and communicating. As would be expected then "these cultural differences lead to development of different sets of cognitive and social behavioral repertoires" (Okagaki, Frensch, & Gordon, 1995, p. 162). It is therefore parents' lack of knowledge about the American educational system that results in their

providing less effective support and guidance for their children's schooling—not a lack of interest in education or failure to value the importance of an education. From this vantage point, Latino immigrants who are newly arrived in this country present a particularly vulnerable population because of discontinuities in language, cultural practices, and social norms.

Historically, deficit approaches guided the work on ethnic minority educational outcomes. The manner and degree to which Latino families and homes differed from European American, high-income homes explained the "deficiencies" in Latino families that led to children's inferior educational performance (Alva, 1991; Moreno, 2002; Stevenson, Chen, & Uttal, 1990). More specifically, scholastic underachievement was attributed to cognitive and linguistic deficits, low expectations, the absence of intellectually stimulating home environments, poor self-esteem, lack of achievement motivation, and difficulties in delayed gratification. Despite the overall academic underachievement of Latino youth, some Latino children, even some from highly impoverished homes, do succeed academically against the odds. The literature on resiliency and people's ability to overcome adversity is vast, covering a broad expanse of stressful life conditions, from chronic medical diseases to life-threatening traumatic events. While very little of this work is specifically done with Latino populations, identification of factors that promote academic resilience may be quite pertinent to Latino students. For example, researchers have identified high self-esteem as a protective factor that is not simply a byproduct of academic success (Spencer, Cole, DuPree, Glymph, & Pierre, 1993; Werner, 1993). Additionally, emotionally responsive parenting combined with structure and the agency to make certain choices contribute to children's academic competence (Egeland, Carlson, & Sroufe, 1993; Reese, Kroesen, & Gallimore, 2000; Werner, 1993). Until recently, the long-standing scholarly focus on the academic underachievement of Latinos suppressed work on the strengths and resources of academically successful Latino children. More studies have begun to approach research from the opposite perspective, investigating factors that promote the academic success of Latino students and their academic resiliency (Arellano & Padilla, 1996; Cabrera & Padilla, 2004; Ceballo, 2004; Gandara, 1995; Rodriguez, 1996).

This chapter will present a review of the literature on Latinos' academic achievement in the United States from a resiliency perspective. We are not interested in chronicling deficits or ways in which Latinos lack attributes possessed by their European American counterparts. Rather, we highlight those protective factors that researchers have identified as mediating Latino paths to academic success. While our chapter is organized by topic areas, we also attend to different developmental time periods within these general research areas and focus on Latino education from the elementary school years through high school. For practical reasons, we address those areas of research related to promoting the academic success of Latino students that have received the most attention in the literature and about which we, therefore, have the most accumulated knowledge. The remainder of this chapter will address the relations between Latino children's academic achievement and both parental factors (like parents' educational values, parental school involvement, and generational status) and school factors (such as standards and expectations, teacher characteristics, academic mentors, and racial discrimination). We conclude by highlighting two examples of successful, school-based programs that have advanced the educational attainment of Latino students in rural and urban settings.

## Family Influences on School Performance

We begin with an examination of the ways in which parental beliefs and behavior influence Latino children's school performance. More specifically, we will review parents' educational values, parental school involvement, and the generational status of Latino students and their parents.

*Educational Values* One of the most pernicious myths about Latino families is that they neither value educational achievement nor aspire to higher education. In our opinion, this myth is based on ethnocentric presumptions that all families "should" behave like European American, middle class families; moreover, it is rooted in deficit-based models, reflecting a grave misunderstanding of Latino family values. The high value that Latino parents place on the importance of education for their children is a consistent and long-standing research finding, and Latino youth frequently attest to hearing repeated parental messages about the importance of education (Arellano & Padilla, 1996; Cabrera & Padilla, 2004; Ceballo, 2004; Gandara, 1995; Garcia Coll et al., 2002; Delgado-Gaitan, 1992; Okagaki & Frensch, 1998; Okagaki, Frensch, & Gordon, 1995; Plunkett & Bamaca-Gomez, 2003; Steinberg, Dornbusch, & Brown, 1992). Gandara (1995) conducted a retrospective study of 50 Mexican Americans from poor families who obtained PhD, MD, or JD degrees from well-regarded American universities. Although their parents had few resources and very limited formal education themselves, they offered their children tremendous verbal support and encouragement for educational pursuits. Thus, for many Latino immigrant parents, an American education represents the ticket to fulfilling the American Dream of upward mobility for the next generation (Arellano & Padilla, 1996).

The strong belief in the value of education can be so uniform among Latino parents that some researchers have found a lack of variance when measuring this variable (Alva, 1991; Okagaki, Frensch, & Gordon, 1995). Among a sample of 1,000 African American, European American, and Latina mothers and elementary school-age children, Latina mothers rated the importance of school grades and homework higher than their European American counterparts (Stevenson et al., 1990). Further, these Latina mothers were enthusiastic about their children's education and held high academic expectations for their children. Among Mexi-

can American parents of 33 academically high-achieving and 49 low-achieving fourth and fifth grade students, there were no significant group differences between these parents' beliefs in the primacy of education (Okagaki, Frensch, & Gordon, 1995). Additionally, most of these parents believed they should help children with schoolwork and once again, there were no group differences on their reported frequency for helping children with homework. Virtually the same results were reported by Alva (1991). Taken together, these findings attest to the consistency with which Latino parents hold educational attainment in high regard.

In comparison to European American parents, research indicates that Asian American parents hold higher academic expectations for their children and place greater emphasis on the role of effort, as opposed to innate ability, in accounting for scholarly achievement (Okagaki & Frensch, 1998). Accordingly, in comparison to Latino parents, Okagaki and Frensch (1998) found that Asian American parents' responses to their children's grades were not as related to their perceptions about their children's ability. In their study of Mexican American, high and low achieving elementary school age children, the parents of high achievers were more likely to be concerned and upset by grades of Cs and Ds from their children, and they expressed greater confidence in their ability to help their children excel academically (Okagaki, Frensch, & Gordon, 1995).

*Parental School Involvement* Among European American, middle- to upper-income families, greater parental expectations about academic attainment, parental monitoring, and parental involvement in children's schoolwork and school setting are predictive of higher cognitive abilities and academic performance (Crouter, MacDermid, McHale, & Perry-Jenkins, 1990; Desimone, 1999; Hoover-Dempsey & Sandler, 1997; Okagaki & Frensch, 1998). In a nationally representative sample of over 24,000 adolescents and their parents (using NELS data), Desimone (1999) found that traditional measures of parental involvement (e.g., discussions about school, rules about homework, parent–teacher organization [PTO] attendance, and school contact and volunteering) were better predictors of achievement for European American and middle-income students than for African American, Latino, and low-income students. It is worth noting that across all racial and socioeconomic groups, students' perceptions of parental involvement mattered more than parents' report of their involvement. Also relying on a National Education Longitudinal Study (NELS) sample of 2,107 Latino and 9,787 European American eighth graders, Valadez (2002) reported ethnic differences, similar to Desimone's (1999) findings, on the effects of parental involvement on achievement in advanced mathematics. Whereas parental participation in PTO meetings, parental school involvement (e.g., visiting classes, attending school meetings, and talking to teachers), and monitoring of children's school behavior (e.g., homework supervision and TV restrictions) all had positive effects on European American children's math performance, they had no impact on the academic performance of Latino students.

Alternatively, other findings point to the importance of parental efforts to support education within the home, with parent–child discussions about school. Using a subsample of NELS data focusing solely on 1,714 Mexican American eighth graders and parents, Keith and Lichtman (1994) reported that parent–child discussions about school activities, programs, and plans were significantly related to better school performance for children. Not surprisingly, however, they found that parents with higher levels of education and income were more likely to engage in such discussions with their children. By the same token, Valadez (2002) reported that parent–child discussions about school were also important predictors of enrollment in algebra and advanced math classes for Latino students. A caveat to these findings is introduced by Desimone's (1999) results with the same data set. She found that students' reports about discussions with parents on school related matters was a significantly better predictor of academic achievement for European American and middle-income students than for Asians, African Americans, Latino, and low-income students.

Despite the strong value Latino parents place on educational achievement, they often report feeling ill-equipped to help their children with specific school assignments and tasks. Stevenson and colleagues (1990) found that Latino mothers did not feel as capable in providing their children with assistance on schoolwork when compared to African American and European American mothers. Similarly, Okagaki and Frensch (1998) reported that Latino parents were not as confident as European American parents in their ability to help their children succeed in school. Yet in this study of 109 Latino (primarily Mexican) and 91 European American parents, Latino parents did not differ from European American parents in the frequency of their efforts to help their children with schoolwork. Although Martinez and colleagues (2004) similarly found no significant differences in the frequency of providing parental help with homework between Latino and non-Latino parents, the Latino parents reported more difficulty helping their children with homework. Like many parents, Latino parents believe that they should help their children with schoolwork and typically provide assistance for as long as they are able (Okagaki et al., 1995; Reese et al., 1995; Stevenson et al., 1990).

While Latino parents believe it is important to help children with schoolwork at home, they are not highly engaged in school-based activities. For example, not a single one of the 50 professionally educated Mexican Americans in Gandara's (1995) study described their parents as actively involved in their school or as being in frequent, regular contact with their teachers. For predominantly poor Latino parents there are many understandable barriers that prevent support for their children's education from assuming the more conventional mode of engaging in frequent contact with teachers and school personnel. For instance, Latino parents may have limited educational backgrounds themselves, little proficiency with English, rigorously demanding

or atypical work schedules, and problems with transportation or child care (Delgado-Gaitan, 1992; Garcia Coll et al., 2002; Plunkett & Bamaca-Gomez, 2003). Indeed, it is a testament to the tenacity of Latino parents' belief in the importance of education that they maintain their faith in education despite their cultural distance from American schools.

In view of what is often seen as a lack of parental involvement in children's schooling among Latino parents, many scholars have proposed explanations to account for this behavior. Latino parents may, for example, feel unwelcome in their children's schools. Some schools have few Latino staff or personnel who can speak Spanish with Spanish-speaking parents. Further, our society tends to stigmatize, distance, and blame people who are poor, and poor parents are painfully aware of how they may be viewed by middle class professionals. Lott (2002) contends that the typical response to poor people is one of "distancing, that is, separation, exclusion, devaluation, discounting, and designation as 'other,' and that this response can be identified in both institutional and interpersonal contexts" (p. 100). With specific regard to education, Lott (2001) illustrates how many teachers subscribe to dominant, stereotypical beliefs about low income, racial minority parents. Teachers tend to view poor parents as uncaring about their children's education, unqualified to provide practical assistance, and discouraging of academic achievement. Thus, when low-income parents do interact with school professionals and take steps to be "involved" in schools, they may be ignored, dismissed, or disrespected (Lott, 2001).

Drawing on Coleman's theory of social capital, Valadez (2002) highlights the way that knowledge of cultural rules and practices allow middle- and upper-income parents to effectively negotiate with school personnel and systems. In contrast, impoverished Latino parents often lack knowledge about American school norms, rules, expectations, and cultural scripts that are often not explicit. Understandably then, when Latino parents do interact with schools, they are often disempowered and rendered ineffective in facilitating their children's schooling. Conversely, Gandara (1995) underscores the kinds of social capital that low-income Latino parents may possess—even those parents like the ones in her study who had an average of only 4 to 5 years of formal schooling:

> Low-status parents may, in fact, have considerable cultural capital of the sort valued by the schools; however, in a society with racist tendencies, this may not always be evident to school personnel...they supported the aims of the school and nurtured their children's aspirations. Yet they would no doubt have been viewed by the schools, like most poor parents, as in need of "parent education...." The best strategy may sometimes be for parents to support the school's mission from a distance. Greater contact between parents and schools does not necessarily breed better understanding. (pp. 47–48)

Zambone and Alicea-Saez (2003) underscore the potential conflict between Latino cultural values and the more "traditional" practices of school involvement for parents. For many Latinos, a cultural value of *respeto* professes that people in positions of authority, such as physicians, lawyers, and teachers should be treated with great respect. Ironically then, Latino parents may not become involved in schools due to a respect of and fear of encroaching upon knowledgeable school professionals. In an ethnographic study of 32 poor, Mexican and Central American parents with kindergarteners, Reese and colleagues (1995) conducted an in-depth analysis of how parents believe they should prepare their young children for formal schooling. Only rarely did these parents promote reading or academically-oriented activities when asked how they should prepare their children for school. Instead, these parents spoke about the importance of *educación*. The term *educación* carries with it a multitude of rich inferences, encompassing moral values and good upbringing as well as academic learning. The two concepts are inextricably intertwined, so much so that you cannot have one without the other. "Virtually without exception, the parents see their primary responsibility being the moral upbringing of the child. Similarly, beliefs about the need to guide children along the 'good path,' [*el buen camino*], to teach children to respect their parents, and to maintain family unity are expressed by parents of both academically successful and unsuccessful children" (Reese, Balzano, Gallimore, & Goldenberg, 1995, p. 73). Still, once their children began kindergarten, the majority of parents reported assisting their children with school tasks and focusing on academically-oriented activities at home.

Conversely, like Gandara (1995), Lopez (2001) offers a staunch critique of accepting a categorization of Latino parents as "uninvolved." It is already clear that parental involvement is often defined as those strategies typically seen among European American and middle income families. As such, our expectation of parental involvement in schooling is framed through a lens tinted by race and social class. As evidence, Lopez presents a case study of a Mexican family where the parents work as migrant farm workers and have five academically successful children. At first glance, many might assume that the parents are "uninvolved" because they do not attend school meetings, volunteer in their children's schools, or provide assistance with schoolwork. However, Lopez contends that these parents inculcated the value of education in their children by having a broader sense of involvement in their children's lives. Via the medium of hard work and the belief in giving their children a strong work ethic, these parents gave their children first-hand experience working in the fields. They did so in order that their children would understand that they had a choice to make—they could either work hard in the fields or they could work hard at school to qualify for different kinds of employment in the future. Far from being "uninvolved," these parents were highly involved in teaching their children life lessons about the work available to unskilled and poorly educated people, the value of money, and the enormous opportunities only offered to them by working hard at school. Similarly, the professionals in Gandara's (1995) study emphasized their

family's hard work ethic and were acutely "aware of the kind of work their parents did…and the near legendary way in which they performed this work" (pp. 111–112).

Clearly, as Garcia Coll and colleagues (2002) note, an explicit focus on school-based, parental activities restricts the construct of parental involvement to a unidimensional concept. While Latino parents do not employ an arsenal of strategies for conventional parent–school involvement, we concur with Lopez (2001), as he illustrated with a single case study, that Latino parents do nonetheless contribute to their children's schooling in positive yet different ways. Qualitative and ethnographic research has been particularly helpful with the effort to broaden notions of parental involvement by identifying and illuminating other strategies practiced by Latino parents in support of their children's educational efforts (Arellano & Padilla, 1996; Auerbach, 2006; 2007; Ceballo, 2004; Gandara, 1995; Lopez, 2001; Menard-Warwick, 2007; Sy, 2006). These strategies do not mirror the parental practices we would expect to see in upper-class and middle-class homes; rather, they are consistent with the socioenvironmental context with which poor, ethnic minority parents must contend. Latino children in migrant families are perhaps the most vulnerable and most likely to slip through the cracks of our educational system. Each year, anywhere from 3 to 5 million families, largely Latino, move across the country, following farm-based employment (Menchaca, 2003). Migrant children may transfer schools as much as three times per year. Not surprisingly, they have the lowest high school graduation rate of any population group. Acknowledging the hazards that migrant farm work poses for their children's education, some parents express their support for their children's education by sacrificing financial needs and employment to stop migrating. For example, a participant in Ceballo's (2004) study explained:

> To show me that they thought education was important, we stopped migrating during the school year. Because we used to migrate to the northern states starting like April and then we would come back home right around October…. that went on until fourth grade, and then they stopped migrating so that I wouldn't miss school. (p. 180)

In a retrospective study of 30 academically successful Mexican college students, Arellano and Padilla (1996) found that all students reported a great deal of parental involvement and investment in their education. Parental support included talking to their children about school progress; modeling and encouraging literacy in the home, often reading to their children in Spanish; enforcing rules regarding the completion of homework; and making personal sacrifices so that their children did not have to work and could focus on their studies. While the students who lived in the poorest families did not have parents who could provide academic assistance, they did, instead, offer moral, spiritual, and emotional forms of support and assistance to their children. In a similar retrospective qualitative study of 10 Puerto Rican and Mexican college students who came from poor families and were attending Yale University, Ceballo (2004) found that the students frequently described their parents as engaging in an array of nonverbal expressions of support for their educational goals. Although their parents could not provide direct assistance with more difficult high school homework, they found other ways to express unconditional support and commitment for their children's education. They would, for example, excuse their children from chores and other tasks if they had schoolwork to do or they would go out of their way to limit disruptions in noisy, often overcrowded homes so children could study. Participants in Ceballo (2004) and Gandara's (1995) studies provide two illustrative examples of the potency of such unconventional support for education:

> My sister was trying to do some homework and she was trying to find the definition of "fortnight" and dad didn't know exactly what it was and couldn't find it in the small dictionary that we had…we didn't have a telephone in those days, but he went and knocked on doors of people that he thought would have dictionaries to get them up so they could find a definition of "fortnight" for him. (Gandara, 1995, p. 40)

> (My mother) would type things for me sometimes. That was really remarkable because think of how strange that could be for a person that doesn't speak English as well as I do… to type so carefully and look at each letter. (Ceballo, 2004, p. 181)

*Generational Status* Scholars have reported conflicting findings with regard to Latinos' educational attainment across successive generations. Using a Census Bureau sample of European American, Latino, and Asian respondents ages 14 to 24, Rong and Grant (1992) reported that Latinos have lower levels of educational attainment across all generations but each successive generation of Latinos in the United States reached higher educational levels. Additionally, they found that for all ethnic groups, children of immigrants attained significantly more schooling than immigrants. The authors proposed two interpretations for their results with Latino families. The findings may be attributable to rising levels of acculturation among students or to schools' greater accommodation of minority cultures. Conversely, other models indicate that Latinos' educational attainment does not increase with successive generations (Kao & Tienda, 1995). Further, Zsembik and Llanes (1996) contend that the array of conflicting results is due to the way in which scholars aggregate Latinos from different nationalities into one homogenous group for analysis. Zsembik and Llanes limited their sample to persons of Mexican descent using data from the Panel Study of Income Dynamics (PSID) and found that educational gains stalled in the second generation (native born children with at least one immigrant parent) for Mexican Americans. Mexican immigrants completed significantly fewer years of schooling than second generation Mexican Americans, but second and third generation (native born children of two U.S. born parents) Mexican Americans completed an equivalent number of years of schooling. In short, a pattern of upward intergenerational educational mobility did not apply to Mexican American families.

Immigrant status and limited English language proficiency may be markers of particular vulnerability for poor educational outcomes among Latinos. Interestingly, Stanton-Salazar and colleagues (Stanton-Salazar, Chavez, & Tai, 2001) reported that when Spanish dominant Latinos were compared to English proficient Latinos, Spanish dominant immigrant students reported significantly less interpersonal openness. Moreover, 68% of the Spanish dominant group of high school students did not report a desire for academic support and assistance. A lack of trust may inhibit many Latino students from engaging in help-seeking behaviors with teachers and other school personnel. In a study of 384 10th grade Mexican American students, stress related to language issues was the most powerful discriminator of high versus low performance on tests of reading, language, and math achievement skills (Alva, 1991). Additionally, Alva (1991) found that linguistic competence was more important in predicting standardized tests than classroom grades, suggesting that standardized test performance may require a higher level of language competence than classroom performance, even among students who do not require English as a Second Language (ESL) instruction. Once again, these findings indicate that immigrant students with limited English language proficiency face particularly elevated risks for academic problems.

Conversely, other studies report good academic outcomes among students from immigrant families. On the whole, these studies compare Latinos to other racial minority groups and cluster Latinos from many different nationalities into one group. In a study of over 1,000 adolescents from Latino, East Asian, Filipino, and European American backgrounds, Fuligni (1997) reported that adolescents from immigrant families (where neither parent or student was U.S.-born or where the student was U.S.-born but one of the parents was not) received higher grades in math and English than their peers from native families (both student and parent was U.S.-born) where English was spoken more frequently in the home. Moreover, adolescents from immigrant families indicated a higher value for schooling and reported expending greater amounts of time and effort on school endeavors in comparison to native born students with native born parents. For adolescents from immigrant families, their strong scholarly motivation was encouraged and shared by both parents and peers. Additionally, gender differences appeared, such that girls from immigrant families performed better academically than boys. Fuligni (1997) concludes that "adolescents from immigrant families seem to share their parents' belief that education is the most important route to their success in this country" (p. 362).

Despite the enormous heterogeneity of Latinos, commonalities among cultural values and traditions among Latino subgroups are evident. The first, most commonly noted cultural value among Latino families is the importance of *familismo,* valuing family unity, closeness, and familial duty, with families often incorporating large interconnected networks of extended family members and close friends. This value is often set in contrast to Western values of autonomy and individualization. For example, European American adolescents are often depicted as spending as little time with their families as possible, preferring to spend their time socializing with peers, participating in extracurricular activities, and working at part-time jobs (Fuligni, Tseng, & Lam, 1999). Other cultural values attributed to Latinos include a commitment to a sense of community and strong religious affiliations. Among traditional Latino families, authority within families tends to be hierarchical and strict gender role norms may be practiced. However, recent evidence indicates that gender roles may be more flexible and contemporary than previously thought (De Leon, 1996). Thus, caution against depicting stereotypes of Latinas as passively submissive and Latinos as aggressive and authoritarian is more than warranted.

Large studies of immigrant versus nonimmigrant families have explored the transmission of cultural values across generations. In general, Latino adolescents display stronger values and expectations regarding their obligations to assist, respect, and support their families in comparison to European American adolescents (Fuligni et al., 1999). Moreover, a curvilinear relation was found in that moderate acceptance of family obligations had the strongest association with academic success, as compared to adolescents with the greatest and weakest endorsements for familial obligations. Among Mexican American families, Phinney and colleagues (Phinney, Ong, & Madden, 2000) did not find discrepancies in values of family obligation between parents and children across generational cohorts.

*Summary*  Despite pervasive myths about Latino families who do not value educational achievement nor aspire to higher education, numerous scholarly works have found the opposite to be true (Arellano & Padilla, 1996; Cabrera & Padilla, 2004; Ceballo 2004; Gandara 1995; Okagaki & Frensch, 1998; Okagaki et al., 1995; Steinberg et al., 1992). Part of this misconception may be attributed to hegemonic norms around what constitutes parental involvement in their children's schoolwork and school settings. In fact, ethnographic and qualitative studies have presented a broader and more nuanced picture of just how very involved Latino parents are in promoting their children's commitment to educational pursuits (Arellano & Padilla, 1996; Auerbach, 2006, 2007; Ceballo 2004; Gandara, 1995; Lopez, 2001; Menard-Warwick, 2007; Sy, 2006).

With regard to generational status, scholars have reported conflicting findings in Latinos' educational attainment across successive generations. While some scholars have found evidence for higher educational attainment with each successive generation of Latinos (Rong & Grant, 1992), others argue that the inconsistent aggregation of Latinos from different nationalities masks intragroup differences in generational academic achievement (Zsembik & Llanes, 1996). To more fully understand the experiences of different

generational cohorts, it is imperative that future research heed Tseng's (2006) call to "unpack" the immigration experience, attending specifically to immigration-related constructs like language acquisition/proficiency, acculturative stress, and dynamic cultural values or family roles.

## School Influences on Academic Performance

We now turn to a discussion of school characteristics, as well as some successful strategies employed by schools and intervention programs, that are illustrative of efforts aimed at promoting the educational success of Latinos. Theoretically, research on the influence of school factors among Latinos is guided primarily by two frameworks: an ecological model and an academic resilience perspective. Bronfenbrenner's (1986) ecological model emphasizes the need to understand developmental processes as a function of the child's interactions and experiences across multiple contexts, including the school environment (see Eccles & Roeser, chapter 2 this volume). Grounded in this framework, researchers naturally explore the complex interrelations between family-school-community factors. Despite environmental adversities, Latino students can possess educational resiliency, demonstrating the potential for high academic achievement (Plunkett & Bámaca-Gomez, 2003). An academic resiliency perspective underscores the support that children receive from significant people in their lives in fostering academic success (Alfaro, Umaña-Taylor, & Bámaca, 2006). Teachers, parents, community leaders, and friends are all possible sources of academic support and encouragement. Moreover, this approach takes the academic potential of racial minority children as a given, shifts the focus away from risk markers, and seeks to identify both proximal and distal factors that are linked to children's high academic motivation and functioning. As would be expected, these two theoretical frameworks are quite compatible and do not present mutually exclusive approaches. Whereas numerous studies report on factors contributing to high school and college drop out patterns among Latino students, in this section we have chosen to focus on school-related characteristics and processes that promote academic success among Latino youth.

*School Standards and Expectations*  Another imperative in understanding a child's ecological world is to understand what parts of a child's school context can be enhanced to promote academic success and well-being. In the final report of the Department of Education's Hispanic Dropout Project, Secada and colleagues (1998) identified five school characteristics that were particularly important in promoting resiliency and academic achievement among Latino students. One characteristic displayed by effective schools was high academic and behavioral standards for all of their students. In other words, teachers and administrators believed that their students could achieve at a high academic level and that they could maintain the behaviors necessary to be successful in school. In conjunction with high academic expectations, effective schools were able to clearly communicate their standards to students. Not only were they able to communicate high standards, but school staff provided students with the support and resources necessary to successfully meet the high standards. Similarly, Scribner and Reyes (1999) found that high performing schools have teachers who value students and care about what their students learn. Inherent in this, these authors suggest, is the ability of teachers to believe that Latino students can succeed, to empower their students, and to provide them with opportunities for learning. Another characteristic of successful schools is that they encouraged their students to think about college and career options for the future. In short, school teachers and staff members both plant the visions and expectations of a college education while simultaneously facilitating students' college-bound goals in practical ways.

Rosenthal and Jacobson's (1968) classic groundbreaking study demonstrated the potent impact of teachers' expectations and biases upon students' performance and achievement. Schools set the foundation for children's future academic trajectories. When teachers believe that their students are capable of achieving, students often respond, in turn, by rising to meet these expectations (Zambone & Alicea-Sáez, 2003). This is perhaps especially true for Latina girls, for whom positive student–teacher bonding can be particularly beneficial for academic achievement. Using a nationally representative sample of over 10,000 adolescents, Crosnoe and colleagues (Crosnoe, Johnson, & Elder, 2004) found that the link between students' positive views about teachers and higher grades was strongest among Latina girls compared to European Americans and boys. If, on the other hand, teachers believe students are neither bright nor capable of learning certain material, students will internalize this message and all too frequently come to accept this assessment of their abilities. Hence, high expectations coupled with genuine caring and respect for students can have a powerfully positive effect on Latino students (Katz, 1999).

In a sense, teachers are "institutional gatekeepers," responsible for assessing students' levels of ability or achievement and establishing their likely academic trajectories (Cooper, Denner, & Lopez, 1999). Consequently, teachers influence whether children are tracked into higher or lower level reading and math groups in elementary school. Latino children, in particular, are disproportionately tracked into lower level reading and math classes, vocational tracks, and special education classes (Cooper et al., 1999; Meece & Kurtz-Costes, 2001). As they move into middle school and high school, children who were in lower level classes continue on to remedial, noncollege prep courses, leaving them in a disadvantaged position when it is time to consider college options. While tracking and "gifted" programs are beneficial to some Latinos, we agree with Gandara (1995) that for most Latinos, such programs erect institutional barriers to academic advancement by unfairly lowering the expectations for the majority of "ungifted" students. A

highly illustrative example of the power of teachers' expectations is provided in a quote from one of the participants in Gandara's (1995) study:

> One teacher had an amazing impact on me…. She had always taught honors, and she ended up with us, and this class was a mistake. We got assigned to her and we weren't honors students, and she was mad. She let us know the first day of class that there was a mistake and she was going to do everything in her power to change it. So she hoped that within two or three weeks we would have a different teacher. We were all scared. It was hard. Quiet. Silent.
>
> She couldn't get her schedule fixed…and so she came in and said, "Well, I'm not going to teach this class any different than I would an honors class." And so we were all on our best behavior, it was just kind of set up that we had to prove ourselves. It was a literature course; that led to my interest in English. We read Wordsworth, Thoreau, and Emerson, and…I made As in that course and she liked me a lot. And she encouraged me. She didn't tell me to go to college, she just said, "You're diligent." (pp. 113–114)

In some schools, students' excessive absenteeism was sometimes used as reason for suspension or placement in remedial tracks (Secada et al., 1998). Teachers and administrators assumed Latino students and their parents were not interested in having challenging content presented in the classroom. However, when asked, both students and parents said that they wanted and expected challenging classroom curricula. Their frustration came when their desire for challenging, interesting, and relevant materials went unmet. Among a sample of 107 Latino adolescents in Los Angeles, Chin and Kameoka (2002) found that age attenuated Latino students' educational expectations such that older children reported less optimism. The authors interpret these findings as resulting from students' increasing exposure to systemic obstacles to educational achievement, such as experiences with discrimination and "the tracking of students into classes in which there are tacitly lower expectations" (p. 459). There is little doubt that the messages students receive at school about their academic potential and future career options are a strong predictor of students' academic motivation and educational/occupational expectations (Alfaro et al., 2006; Chin & Kameoka, 2002).

***Teacher Characteristics*** Not surprisingly, positive teacher–student interactions have a beneficial impact on the academic performance of Latino students (Brewster & Bowen, 2004; Szalacha, Marks, Lamarre, & Garcia Coll, 2005). Teacher support includes students' feelings that they are listened to, cared about, respected, and encouraged. Brewster and Bowen (2004) surveyed 633 Latino middle and high school students who were identified as "at risk of school failure" by school personnel and other community professionals. Their results indicated that support from teachers was not only associated with students' positive feelings about school and perceived meaningfulness of school but also with fewer incidences of problem behaviors at school (e.g., absenteeism, consistent tardiness to class, fighting, not completing homework, etc.). Moreover, these effects were present even when accounting for demographic differences and the effects of parental support. Both teacher support and parental support were significant predictors of school meaningfulness, supporting an ecological model of the importance of multiple social systems (e.g., family and school) on students' school engagement.

Secada and colleagues (1998) found that teachers who successfully worked with and engaged Latino high school students distinguished themselves from less successful teachers by their willingness to frame students' academic, social, and psychological background as a source of strength. They used students' experiences and backgrounds as points upon which additional competencies could be built. In contrast, teachers who were not as successful at engaging Latino youth tended to use students' disadvantaged backgrounds as explanations for their lower levels of achievement and inability to achieve. Likewise, Scribner and Reyes (1999) proposed that in order for schools to facilitate the academic success of Latino children, teachers need to consider and make use of students' cultural background. Teachers must be willing to revise lesson plans to accommodate the knowledge and learning styles of Latino populations. In their review, Iglesias and Fabiano (2003) note that patterns of communication in bilingual families create discourse styles and content knowledge that is different from English speaking children and families. Further, Montano and Metcalf (2003) concur that current school curriculums promote cultural and linguistic discontinuity for Latino students. Thus, Secada and colleagues (1998) recommend that teachers teach content in an interesting, culturally relevant, and challenging manner and provide the necessary support for students to understand the material.

Whereas teachers must communicate high expectations to their students, teachers themselves must, in turn, receive the professional development necessary to employ effective teaching strategies for Latino students. Institutions that train teachers must prioritize training that encompasses an understanding of Latino cultural values, strengths, and the many systemic barriers facing Latino families including the far-reaching ramifications of poverty, institutionalized racism, and other societal factors that influence Latino children's academic achievement (Brewster & Bowen, 2004; Lott, 2001). Some scholars advise educators to actively prepare student teachers to work with Latino families in ways that accommodate the daily lives, knowledge, and learning styles of specific Latino groups. Professional training of this kind would assist teachers in using students' cultural background as an asset in the classroom (Lopez, 2001; Montano & Metcalf, 2003; Scribner & Reyes, 1999). Brewster and Bowen (2004) refer to this as a "strength-based perspective" (p. 64). Teachers in many schools where Latino students are successful make concerted attempts to effectively communicate with Latino families (Secada et al., 1998). Such teachers often make tremendous efforts to ensure that parents know how their children are doing in school and to provide par-

ents with important information about college and career opportunities (Scribner & Reyes, 1999).

***Academic Mentors and Role Models*** In their Department of Education report, Secada and colleagues (1998) determined that successful schools made efforts to connect their Latino students to adults who would mentor and actively guide them. In keeping with an academic resiliency model, providing Latino adolescents with meaningful mentoring relationships in a school setting facilitates students' general and academic self-confidence, sense of school belonging, and knowledge of college and career options. When asked why they stayed in school despite having friends who had dropped out, students frequently pointed to teachers or other adults in the school who had taken a special interest in them and encouraged them to have future goals (Secada et al., 1998). Further, teacher support for and encouragement of participation in extracurricular activities is associated with better academic outcomes among Latino students (Martinez, DeGarmo, & Eddy, 2004). Supportive and involved teachers may promote Latino students' sense of school belonging, a predictor of academic performance for Latino students across several studies (Gonzalez & Padilla, 1997; Sánchez, Colon, & Esparza, 2005). We cannot underestimate the important role of faculty mentors and role models for all students, and especially for Latino students who often come from poor homes with parents who may not have much knowledge about the American educational system.

Academically successful Latino students are often quick to acknowledge the faculty mentors and role models who took a particular interest in them and who guided their careers towards a college education (Arellano & Padilla, 1996; Cabrera & Padilla, 1995; Ceballo, 2004). Among 384 Mexican American 10th graders, Alva (1991) found that college preparation was the most powerful discriminator between those students with good versus poor grades. Latino students often depend on teachers and mentors to inculcate them with what Cabrera and Padilla (2004) refer to as a "culture of college." The term encompasses the knowledge of things that will guide students toward a college education, such as scholastic achievement tests (SATs), extracurricular activities, the college application process, fee waivers, and financial aid. Without such concrete and practical knowledge about the steps required for college admission, many bright, motivated, and hard working Latino students from poor families will view a high school degree as the finishing line.

Once Latino students enroll in college, the need for academic mentoring and support hardly diminishes. Compared to their European American counterparts, Latino college students face higher levels of academic and financial stress during their college years (Quintana, Vogel, & Ybarra, 1991). On college campuses across the nation, the number of Latino faculty is quite small. Zambone and Alicea-Saez (2003) note that 89% of college faculty are European American. "Because faculty construct the curriculum, determine the quality of learning experiences in the classroom, and serve as mentors and advisors, the culture of higher-education institutions typically reflects a White, male, middle-class orientation" (Zambone & Alicea-Saez, 2003, p. 69). It is critical, therefore, that institutional sources of support and personnel are culturally sensitive and competent at all levels of the educational system. Without such cultural acceptance and support, students are less likely to achieve.

In sum, Zambone and Alicea-Sáez (2003) outline several suggestions for colleges and universities that are committed to the academic advancement of Latino students; their recommendations appear equally useful and applicable to elementary and secondary schools. These recommendations include: diversifying the faculty, employing Latinos in leadership positions, funding and developing programs to recruit and retain Latino students, establishing a community that values and respects cultural diversity, and providing integrated social, academic, and financial support services. With ever increasing rates of racial diversity in our country's student population, a lack of corresponding diversity among teachers presents a serious problem for our school system.

***Ethnic Identity and Racial Stereotypes in the Schools*** Compounding the challenges facing poor Latino youth in their educational pursuits is the existence of negative racial stereotypes that can filter into school settings and contexts. Like other racial minorities, Latinos face negative cultural stereotypes that depict them as less cognitively capable and intelligent than European Americans (Steele, 1997). Even worse, "derogatory cultural stereotypes represent Latinos as illegal immigrants who prefer to work at menial jobs, driving down wages while driving up the cost of public social services…young Latino males in particular are perceived as unintelligent, extremely violent and antisocial, with little personal ambition" (Hudley & Graham, 2001, p. 203). Demonstrating the saliency and tenacity of such stereotypes among 197 African American, Latino, and European American early adolescents, Hudley and Graham (2001) presented adolescents with scenarios of high or low achieving students and asked them to choose one of 12 photos that best matched the hypothetical student's description. The photos varied by race (African American, Latino, and European American) and gender. Girls were significantly chosen more often to match scenarios of an academically achievement oriented student. All students, even Latinos themselves, overwhelmingly selected racial minority males, especially Latinos, to match depictions of low-achievement striving students. Further, the authors cited evidence that even preschool children have internalized such negative and degrading racial stereotypes. How can such publicly shared social conceptions not influence the self-concept, academic performance, and school behavior of Latino children and adolescents?

Experiences of discrimination and cultural alienation are bound to present unique stressors for Latino students. In a sample of 564 6th through 12th graders, Martinez and colleagues (2004) reported that compared to non-Latino students, Latino students experience higher institutional obstacles to school success, including experiences with discrimination, less access to resources, and feeling unwelcome at school. These structural barriers were related to academic grades and drop out rates. Accordingly, among 277 Latino students, experiences with discrimination were the most frequently mentioned obstacle to school involvement (Valencia & Johnson, 2006). Even more troubling, Steele and colleagues (1997) have provided evidence that racial minorities disengage and underachieve in academic tasks when racial stereotypes are made salient. Consequently, racially stereotyped groups may "psychologically disengage their feelings of self-worth from their academic outcomes" (Schmader, Major, & Gramzow, 2001, p. 94). The majority of work on racial identity and discrimination experiences has focused on Latino students in college settings. In one study of 30 successful, Mexican American college students, a strong sense of affiliation with their Latino identity was a consistent source of strength and pride (Arellano & Padilla, 1996). Among 45 Mexican American and Puerto Rican Ivy League college students, Ethier and Deaux (1990) similarly reported that the majority of students identified being Latino as an important part of their identity. Moreover, for Latino male college students, the strength of their ethnic identity served as a buffer from experiences of discomfort with their ethnicity.

The role that ethnic identity plays in anyone's life will vary in saliency and degree in different contexts. However, students' adjustment will inevitably depend upon the specific educational context and setting involved. This point was highlighted by Schneider and Ward's (2003) study of 35 Latino students attending a medium-sized, state university. In this setting, Latinos with high ethnic identification were less adjusted than less-identified Latinos. Moreover, perceived support mediated the relation between ethnic identification and college adjustment, suggesting that highly identified Latinos were less adjusted, in part, because they perceived lower support in a university where Latinos were highly underrepresented.

***Summary*** Taken together, many of the school characteristics discussed in this section (e.g. high expectations, teachers' reliance on culturally relevant instruction, academic mentoring, and support for coping with discrimination) are interdependent and combine to promote success and achievement among Latino youth. All of the things we have discussed thus far, however, are based on a common understanding that many of the schools in our country are grossly underfunded. Many public schools lack necessary teaching supplies and even sufficient space for all of their students (Montano & Metcalf, 2003). Therefore, policies, curricular advancements, and teacher training initiatives must be accompanied by concrete improvements in the physical structures (e.g., clean and safe buildings) and material resources (e.g., textbooks and computers) that are desperately needed in many public American schools.

## Examples of Successful School Programs

In order to make more tangible the ways in which school factors come together to create academic environments that support and promote Latino academic achievement, we will examine two studies which have looked at effective school-based models and interventions. Scholars have found that rural and migrant Latino populations face especially elevated risks for academic failure (Riggs & Greenberg, 2004); hence, our first example will focus on a program serving Latinos in a rural, predominantly European American Mormon community. Diversi and Mecham (2005) created and evaluated an after-school program for Latino high school students in a rural town in northern Utah. The town's population of Latinos had more than tripled between 1990 and 2000, most of whom were recent immigrants from Central Mexico with low levels of formal education and a limited grasp of the English language. The local schools were inundated with a burgeoning population of Latino immigrants whom they were ill-equipped to educate and counsel. Many of the children were tracked into low-level or special education classes due to difficulties with the English language. Those students who may have had some level of proficiency in reading English did not always have the comprehension necessary to understand what they were reading or what was expected in their homework. Consequently, some teachers believed that students were lazy and unwilling to complete their homework assignments (Diversi & Mecham, 2005).

Widespread miscommunication between the school and parents occurred frequently. Teachers complained about the lack of involvement from Latino parents and were particularly frustrated when parents did not attend scheduled parent–teacher conferences. The school attempted to communicate information to parents by having the information that was sent home translated into Spanish. However, many of the poorly educated immigrant parents were unable to read in their own language and so were still unable to make use of and respond to the information sent home by the schools. While administrators and teachers expected Latino parents to be more involved, the parents believed that the education of their children lay exclusively in the power and authority of the school personnel (Diversi & Mecham, 2005).

In response to these challenges, the authors created an after-school mentoring and tutoring program geared toward improving the academic achievement of the Latino adolescents and learning more about how their experiences at school informed their identity and goals for the future (Diversi & Mecham, 2005). The mentoring program consisted of 50 eighth and ninth graders who worked with 20 mentors. Most of the participants were failing classes or having behavioral issues in school, and all had little or no fluency in English. Mentors were primarily White, female college students, but among the most involved with three Latino males. The students and mentors met twice a week for 1.5 hour sessions to work on, "homework, tests, school

projects, and acculturation issues, with a focus on increasing students' awareness of biculturalism" (p. 34). In addition to the after-school sessions, students and mentors attended activities outside of school as well. Diversi and Mecham (2005) report on experiences from the first 2 years of this after-school mentoring program.

When the authors reviewed the Latino youths' thoughts about the program, three themes emerged. First, students felt more successful in school because they were now able to complete their school work with the help and support of their mentors. The mentors not only encouraged and helped students complete their homework, but they followed up with them to see how they were doing in school. Second, students had fun and felt respected during their time in the program. The adolescents were able to relax and also form bonds of camaraderie with their mentors and the other students in the program. One student commented about the fair treatment that all of the students received from their mentors and program staff. A third theme was that students felt their mentors helped to make their lives better overall by being models of successful and responsible adults. The adolescents felt that their participation in the program helped them to avoid problem behaviors and to aspire to get good grades in order to graduate from high school. Most importantly, students' overall GPA increased during their participation in the after-school program and these improvements were sustained for over a year. In the second year of the program, the students' average GPA went from 1.95 to 2.45 between the first and third trimesters. Youth who terminated their participation in the program prematurely experienced declines in grades (Diversi & Mecham, 2005). Thus, the authors suggest that "close collaboration between youth and adult mentors could be a realistic alternative for the immigration challenges that American schools and society will be facing in this new century" (p. 39).

The second example is provided in a study conducted by Conchas (2001) who examined Latino school engagement at Baldwin High School, an urban, predominantly racial minority school in the western United States. Specifically, Conchas (2001) was interested in Baldwin High School's Medical Academy, a program within the school designed for students interested in health related careers and specifically targeted for students who were at risk for dropping out of school. Baldwin High School serves a low-income, racially diverse student body of about 1,800 students (65% African American, 20% Asian American, 10% Latino, with over 50% eligible for free or reduced lunch). In addition to the Medical Academy, Baldwin High also had a Graphics Academy that was closely associated with Advanced Placement course offerings in five subject areas. That is, most of the students who were enrolled in Advanced Placement courses at the school were also enrolled in the Graphics Academy. The administrators and teachers at Baldwin High hoped to create a number of smaller, career focused programs in order to provide students with more intimate educational settings.

Outside of the Medical Academy, students were keenly

aware of the racial stratification within the school's tracking system. Latino students perceived that most lower level courses were primarily composed of African American and Latino students while higher level courses, including Advanced Placement courses, were dominated by Asian American and European American students. In fact, Latinos made up only 4% of the students in the Advanced Placement Program despite the fact that Latinos composed 10% of the overall school population. Moreover, Latino students who were academically successful enough to be tracked into the Advanced Placement Program did not associate with other Latinos, particularly those outside of their programs. Thus, less successful Latino students felt that their higher achieving peers dismissed and ignored them, while the more academically successful Latinos felt isolated from others in their ethnic group. Although successful in their scholastic pursuits, Latinos in the AP Program experienced higher levels of stress, alienation, and depression (Conchas, 2001).

In contrast, the Medical Academy emphasized cooperative learning and attempted to bridge classroom learning with experiential learning (i.e., students were also required to and supported in gaining work and volunteer experiences as well as career exploration opportunities). At the Medical Academy, teachers worked collaboratively in an interdisciplinary approach to link course materials across various disciplines and met regularly to discuss strategies for improving the academic success of individual students. The program also worked hard to provide extensive support and tutoring services to students and to maintain communication between teachers and families. In fact, "every teacher knew each student by name" (p. 494). Further, teacher involvement did not end with school success. Rather, teachers were involved in multiple aspects of their students' school experiences, and the Academy provided activities throughout the year that promoted a sense of community and highlighted program successes.

As a result, Latino students in the Medical Academy felt strong ties to each other and to the other students in their program, regardless of racial and ethnic differences. Sense of community was strongly emphasized, and students were encouraged to help and support each other by learning and working cooperatively. The students' team learning styles were supported and modeled by their teachers' team teaching styles. Another unique aspect of the Medical Academy was that students were encouraged to talk about the racial disparities in their school. Not only were students aware of the disproportionate number of African American and Latinos in lower level tracks, but they also talked about it. Students were able to discuss and critique school-based structures and processes that impede academic success for racial minorities. In learning together and talking about racial issues directly, students were able to challenge their own prejudices and dispel myths that they may have had about peers with ethnic and racial backgrounds different from their own. Among a group of at-risk adolescents on the verge of dropping out of school, the Medical Academy graduated 93% of its class in 1998 (the other 7% moved out of the district or enrolled in another high school), and 91% of the graduating students went on to college.

## Conclusions and Future Directions for Research

Large, quantitative studies focusing solely on Latino samples will facilitate greater and more accurate comparisons across different Latino nationalities. Much of the work, to date, has used qualitative and ethnographic methodologies with small sample sizes. Well designed studies that explore within-group differences among Latinos will provide rich sources of data that avoid a reliance on European Americans as the norm and a retreat to deficit-based explanations (Meece & Kurtz-Costes, 2001). Not only should researchers turn their attention to intragroup variation among Latinos, but studies must also explore hypotheses about Latinos' educational outcomes that are theoretically driven. Similar to past research on African American children, race-comparative paradigms do little but document outcome differences between Latinos and other racial groups, thus evading the more sophisticated questions about process-oriented mechanisms that lead to various academic outcomes (Garcia Coll, et al., 1996; McLoyd, 1990). Simplistic comparisons of Latinos with other racial groups like European Americans do not foster a deeper understanding about the meaning of differences and instead curtail "the development of a rich, meaningful, and culturally anchored knowledge base" (McLoyd, 1990, p. 264).

Relatedly, researchers studying Latinos' educational performance must expand their gaze beyond school walls to include familial, cultural, and contextual factors that contribute to the academic trajectories of Latino children. Okagaki (2001) highlighted the importance of attending to the links between child, family, and school in order to understand the role of each in children's academic performance. Garcia Coll et al. (1996) posit that the interaction of social class, culture, ethnicity, and race must be placed at the center of theoretical models, rather than their typical peripheral location. Moreover, the gender gap in academic achievement among Latino students is in need of much greater attention. Whereas Latina females are more likely to finish high school and to have higher grade point averages than their male counterparts (Coley, 2001; Marotta & Garcia, 2003; Sanchez, Colon, & Esparza, 2005), researchers have offered little to explain these gender disparities—sometimes referring to the possible roles of cultural values and gender role socialization among Latino families. Accordingly, many researchers speculate about the influence of Latino cultural values in post hoc interpretations of empirical findings. It is imperative that future work directly examine the role of Latino cultural values (e.g., *familismo*, *respeto*) in the educational trajectories of Latino students and thereby move the field beyond easy-to-make, post hoc attributions to "culture." Additionally, an expansion of ecological frameworks can incorporate more process-oriented variables that capture the tone and nature of interactions between students and their parents, teachers, or peers.

Research that joins quantitative and qualitative methodologies in a purposeful and skillful manner, similar to that conducted by Phinney and Haas (2002), is sorely needed. Qualitative research is especially pertinent in uncovering the richness of meaning and interpretations that people attribute to their own behaviors and situations. More generally, both quantitative and qualitative research is needed to address the following kinds of topics among Latino students: the relation between educational values, occupational expectations, and explanations for poverty and wealth in our country; rural as well as urban school characteristics associated with academic achievement; individual and family factors that moderate the relation between poverty/economic stress and academic adjustment; the influence of peer and sibling relationships in scholastic performance; the relation between out-of-school activities and school engagement; and the impact of racial stereotypes and discrimination on school experiences, academic effort, and sense of school belonging.

Academic researchers, teachers, school personnel, and policy makers have all heralded the benefits of parental involvement, as assessed in the most traditional sense (Desimone, 1999: Lopez, 2001). Indeed, increasing parental involvement has emerged as a popular focus of policies and interventions, in part, because it is seen as relatively malleable. In some cases, federal funding for educational intervention programs requires a programmatic emphasis on parental involvement. Yet, this new focus of educational reform ignores research demonstrating that impoverished, racial minority parents do not get "involved" in the same ways that European American, middle-class parents are involved in children's schooling. The reasons for this difference are various and understandable if we attend to the context of financial and social stressors in the lives of poor, racial minority parents. More systematic work should explore culturally consistent ways in which poor, Latino parents demonstrate support for their children's academic work. Starting from a resiliency perspective, we should "begin to identify the unique ways that marginalized parents are *already* involved in their children's education, and search for creative ways to capitalize on these and other subjugated forms of involvement" (Lopez, 2001, p. 434).

In studying 50 Mexican American doctors, lawyers, and academics from impoverished backgrounds, Gandara (1995) highlighted the importance of the historical period in which her subjects came of age. All of her participants received their college and graduate degrees during the 1960s and 1970s. Structured educational opportunities had opened up for many minorities after the passing of major civil rights legislation. Indeed, colleges and universities were actively recruiting racial minorities and government sponsored financial aid was widely available. Despite their ambition and commitment to hard work, even these students needed to have doors opened to educational opportunity. American institutions of higher learning remain, to this day, bastions of privilege for children of middle and upper class families. Although some children from impoverished families are able to obtain a college education, they do so in disproportionately small numbers. More often than not, poor children are blocked from the opportunities that avail themselves to those with college degrees. Current political attacks on affirmative action policies only serve to gravely worsen the prospects of higher education for many Latinos.

## Author Note

The authors wish to thank Professors Tabbye Chavous, Jacquelynne Eccles, Judith Meece, and Abigail Stewart for their thoughtful and constructive feedback on an earlier version of this chapter.

## References

Ackerman, B., Brown, E., & Izard, C. (2008). The relations between contextual risk, earned income, and the school adjustment of children from economically disadvantaged families. *Developmental Psychology, 40*, 204–216.

Alfaro, E. C., Umaña-Taylor, A. J., & Bámaca, M. Y. (2006). The influence of academic support on Latino adolescents' academic motivation. *Family Relations: Interdisciplinary Journal of Applied Family Studies, 55*, 279–291.

Alva, S. A. (1991). Academic invulnerability among Mexican-American students: The importance of protective resources and appraisals. *Hispanic Journal of Behavioral Sciences, 13*, 18–34.

Arellano, A. R., & Padilla, A. M. (1996). Academic invulnerability among a select group of Latino university students. *Hispanic Journal of Behavioral Sciences, 18*, 485–507.

Auerbach, S. (2006). "If the student is good, let him fly": Moral support for college among Latino immigrant parents. *Journal of Latinos and Education, 5*, 275–292.

Auerbach, S. (2007). From moral supporters to struggling advocates: Reconceptualizing parent roles in education through the experience of working-class families of color. *Urban Education, 42*, 250–283.

Battle, J. (2002). Longitudinal analysis of academic achievement among a nationwide sample of Hispanic students in one- versus dual-parent households. *Hispanic Journal of Behavioral Sciences, 24*, 430–447.

Brewster, A. B., & Bowen, G. L. (2004). Teacher support and the school engagement of Latino middle and high school students at risk of school failure. *Child & Adolescent Social Work Journal, 21*, 47–67.

Bronfenbrenner, U. (1986). Ecology of the family as a context for human development: Research perspectives. *Developmental Psychology, 22*, 723–742.

Brown, E., & Low, C. (2008). Chaotic living conditions and sleep problems associated with children's responses to academic challenge. *Journal of Family Psychology, 22*, 920–923.

Cabrera, N. L., & Padilla, A. M. (2004). Entering and succeeding in the "culture of college": The story of two Mexican heritage students. *Hispanic Journal of Behavioral Sciences, 26*, 152–170.

Ceballo, R. (2004). From barrios to Yale: The role of parenting strategies in Latino families. *Hispanic Journal of Behavioral Sciences, 26*, 171–186.

Chin, D., & Kameoka, V. A. (2002). Psychosocial and contextual predictors of educational and occupational self-efficacy among Hispanic inner-city adolescents. *Hispanic Journal of Behavioral Sciences, 24*, 448–464.

Coley, R. J. (2001). *Differences in the gender gap: Comparisons across racial ethnic groups by education and work* (Policy Information Report). Princeton, NJ: Educational Testing Service.

Conchas, G. Q. (2001). Structuring failure and success: Understanding the variability in Latino school engagement. *Harvard Educational Review, 71*, 475–504.

Cooper, C. R., Denner, J., & Lopez, E. M. (1999). Cultural brokers: Helping Latino children on pathways toward success. *The Future of Children, 9*, 51–57.

Crosnoe, R., Johnson, M. K., & Elder, G. H. J. (2004). Intergenerational bonding in school: The behavioral and contextual correlates of student–teacher relationships. *Sociology of Education, 77*, 60–81.

Crouter, A. C., MacDermid, S. M., McHale, S. M., & Perry-Jenkins, M. (1990). Parental monitoring and perceptions of children's school performance and conduct in dual- and single-earner families. *Developmental Psychology, 26*, 649–657.

De Leon, B. (1996). Career development of Hispanic adolescent girls. In B. J. Ross Leadbeater & N. Way (Eds.), *Urban girls: Resisting stereotypes, creating identities* (pp. 380–398). New York: New York University Press.

Delgado-Gaitan, C. (1992). School matters in the Mexican American home. *American Educational Research Journal, 29*, 495–513.

Desimone, L. (1999). Linking parent involvement with student achievement: Do race and income matter? *Journal of Educational Research, 93*, 11–31.

Diversi, M., & Mecham, C. (2005). Latino(a) students and Caucasian mentors in a rural after-school program: Towards empowering adult-youth relationships. *Journal of Community Psychology, 33*, 31–40.

Egeland, B., Carlson, E., & Sroufe, L. A. (1993). Resilience as a process. *Development and Psychopathology, 5*, 517–528.

Ethier, K., & Deaux, K. (1990). Hispanics in ivy: Assessing identity and perceived threat. *Sex Roles, 22*, 427–440.

Fuligni, A. J. (1997). The academic achievement of adolescents from immigrant families: The roles of family background, attitudes, and behavior. *Child Development, 68*, 351–363.

Fuligni, A. J., Tseng, V., & Lam, M. (1999). Attitudes toward family obligations among American adolescents with Asian, Latin American, and European backgrounds. *Child Development, 70*, 1030–1044.

Gandara, P. (1995). *Over the ivy walls: The educational mobility of low-income Chicanos.* Albany, NY: SUNY Press.

Garcia Coll, C., Akiba, D., Palacios, N., Bailey, B., Silver, R., DiMartino, L. et al. (2002). Parental involvement in children's education: Lessons from three immigrant groups. *Parenting: Science and Practice, 2*, 303–324.

Garcia Coll, C., Lamberty, G., Jenkins, R., McAdoo, H. P., Crnic, K., Wasik, B. H., & Garcia, H. V. (1996). An integrative model for the study of developmental competencies in minority children. *Child Development, 67*, 1891–1914.

Gonzalez, R., & Padilla, A. M. (1997). The academic resilience of Mexican American high school students. *Hispanic Journal of Behavioral Sciences, 19*(3), 301–317.

Hoover-Dempsey, K. V., & Sandler, H. M. (1997). Why do parents become involved in their children's education? *Review of Educational Research, 67*, 3–42.

Hudley, C., & Graham, S. (2001). Stereotypes of achievement striving among early adolescents. *Social Psychology of Education, 5*, 201–224.

Iglesias, A., & Fabiano, L. C. (2003). Bilingual Latino students: The contexts of home and school. In V. I. Kloosterman (Ed.), *Latino students in American schools: Historical and contemporary views* (pp. 79–94). Westport, CT: Praeger.

Kao, G., & Tienda, M. (1995). Optimism and achievement: The educational performance of immigrant youth. *Social Science Quarterly, 76*, 1–19.

Katz, S. R. (1999). Teaching in tensions: Latino immigrant youth, their teachers, and the structures of schooling. *Teachers College Record, 100*, 809–840.

Keith, P. B., & Lichtman, M. V. (1994). Does parental involvement influence the academic achievement of Mexican-American eighth graders? Results from the national education longitudinal study. *School Psychology Quarterly, 9*, 256–273.

Lopez, G. R. (2001). The value of hard work: Lessons on parent involvement from an (im)migrant household. *Harvard Educational Review, 71*, 416–43 .

Lott, B. (2002). Cognitive and behavioral distancing from the poor. *American Psychologist, 57*, 100–110.

Lott, B. (2001). Low-income parents and the public schools. *Journal of Social Issues, 57*, 247–259.

Marotta, S. A., & Garcia, J. G. (2003). Latinos in the United States in 2000. *Hispanic Journal of Behavioral Sciences, 25*, 13–34.

Martinez, C. R., DeGarmo, D. S., & Eddy, J. M. (2004). Promoting academic success among Latino youth. *Hispanic Journal of Behavioral Sciences, 26*, 128–151.

McLoyd, V. C. (1990). Minority children: Introduction to the special issue. *Child Development, 61*, 263–266.

Meece, J. L., & Kurtz-Costes, B. (2001). Introduction: The schooling of ethnic minority children and youth. *Educational Psychologist, 36*, 1–7.

Menard-Warwick, J. (2007). Biliteracy and schooling in an extended-family Nicaraguan immigrant household: The sociohistorical construction of parental involvement. *Anthropology & Education Quarterly, 38*, 119–137.

Menchaca, V. D. (2003). Ensuring success for Latino migrant students. In V. I. Kloosterman (Ed.), *Latino students in American schools* (pp. 129–138). Westport, CT: Praeger.

Montano, T., & Mecalfe, E. L. (2003). Triumphs and tragedies: The urban schooling of Latino students. In V. I. Kloosterman (Ed.), *Latino students in American schools* (pp. 139–151). Westport, CT: Praeger.

Moreno, R. P. (2002). Teaching the alphabet: An exploratory look at maternal instruction in Mexican American families. *Hispanic Journal of Behavioral Sciences, 24*, 191–205.

National Center of Educational Statistics. (2007). *Status and trends in the education of racial and ethnic minorities.* Washington, DC: U.S. Department of Education, Office of Educational Research and Improvement.

Ogbu, J. U. (1981). Origins of human competence: A cultural-ecological perspective. *Child Development, 52*, 413–429.

Ogbu, J. U. (1986). The consequences of the American caste system. In U. Neisser (Ed.), *The school achievement of minority children: New perspectives* (pp. 19–56). Hillsdale, NJ: Erlbaum.

Ogbu, J. U. (1992). Understanding cultural diversity and learning. *Educational Researcher, 21*, 5–14.

Okagaki, L. (2001). Triarchic model of minority children's school achievement. *Educational Psychologist, 36*, 9–20.

Okagaki, L., & Frensch, P. A. (1998). Parenting and children's school achievement: A multiethnic perspective. *American Educational Research Journal, 35*, 123–144.

Okagaki, L., Frensch, P. A., & Gordon, E. W. (1995). Encouraging school achievement in Mexican American children. *Hispanic Journal of Behavioral Sciences, 17*, 160–179.

Phinney, J. S., & Haas, K. (2002). The process of coping among ethnic minority first-generation college freshmen: A narrative approach. *The Journal of Social Psychology, 135*, 707–726.

Phinney, J. S., Ong, A., & Madden, T. (2000). Cultural values and intergenerational value discrepancies in immigrant and non-immigrant families. *Child Development, 71*, 528–539.

Plunkett, S. W., & Bamaca-Gomez, M. Y. (2003). The relationship between parenting, acculturation, and adolescent academics in Mexican-origin immigrant families in Los Angeles. *Hispanic Journal of Behavioral Sciences, 25*, 222–239.

Quintana, S. M., Vogel, M. C., & Ybarra, V. C. (1991). Meta-analysis of Latino students' adjustment in higher education. *Hispanic Journal of Behavioral Sciences, 13*, 155–168.

Reese, L., Balzano, S., Gallimore, R., & Goldenberg, C. (1995). The concept of educación: Latino family values and American schooling. *International Journal of Educational Research, 23*, 57–79.

Reese, L., Kroesen, K., & Gallimore, R. (2000). Agency and school performance among urban Latino youth. In R. D. Taylor & M. C. Wang (Eds.), *Resilience across contexts: Family, work, culture, and community* (pp. 295–332). Mahwah, NJ: Erlbaum.

Riggs, N. R., & Greenberg, M. T. (2004). Moderators in the academic development of migrant Latino children attending after-school programs. *Applied Developmental Psychology, 25*, 349–367.

Rodriguez, N. (1996). Predicting the academic success of Mexican American and White college students. *Hispanic Journal of Behavioral Sciences, 18*, 329–342.

Rong, X. L., & Grant, L. (1992). Ethnicity, generation, and school attainment of Asians, Hispanics, and non-Hispanic whites. *The Sociological Quarterly, 33*, 625–636.

Rosenthal, R., & Jacobson, L. (1968). *Pygmalion in the classroom: Teacher expectation and pupils' intellectual development.* New York: Holt, Rinehart, & Winston.

Sánchez, B., Colon, Y., & Esparza, P. (2005). The role of sense of school belonging and gender in the academic adjustment of Latino adolescents. *Journal of Youth and Adolescence, 34*, 619–628.

Schmader, T., Major, B., & Gramzow, R. H. (2001). Coping with ethnic stereotypes in the academic domain: Perceived injustice and psychological disengagement. *Journal of Social Issues, 57*, 93–111.

Schneider, M. E., & Ward, D. J. (2003). The role of ethnic identification and perceived social support in Latinos' adjustment to college. *Hispanic Journal of Behavioral Sciences, 25*, 539–554.

Scribner, J. D., & Reyes, P. (1999). Creating learning communities for high-performing Hispanic students: A conceptual framework. In P. Reyes, J. D. Scribner, & A. Paredes Scribner (Eds.), *Lessons from high-performing Hispanic schools: Creating learning communities* (pp. 188–210). New York: Teachers College Press.

Secada, W. G., Chavez-Chavez, R., Garcia, E., Munoz, C., Oakes, J., Santiago-Santiago, I., et al. (1998). *No more excuses: The final report of the Hispanic dropout project.* Washington, DC: U.S. Department of Education.

Spencer, M., Cole, S. P., DuPree, D., Glymph, A., & Pierre, P. (1993). Self-efficacy among urban African-American early adolescents: Exploring issues of risk, vulnerability, and resilience. *Development and Psychopathology, 5*, 719–739.

Stanton-Salazar, R. (1997). A social capital framework for understanding the socialization of racial minority children and youths. *Harvard Education Review, 67*, 1–40.

Stanton-Salazar, R. D., Chavez, L. F., & Tai, R. H. (2001). The help-seeking orientations of Latino and non-Latino urban high school students: A critical-sociological investigation. *Social Psychology of Education, 5*, 49–82.

Steele, C. (1997). A threat in the air: How stereotypes shape intellectual identity and performance. *American Psychologist, 52*, 613–629.

Steinberg, L., Dornbusch, S. M., & Brown, B. B. (1992). Ethnic differences in adolescent achievement: An ecological perspective. *American Psychologist, 47*, 723–729.

Stevenson, H. W., Chen, C., & Uttal, D. H. (1990). Beliefs and achievement: A study of Black, White, and Hispanic children. *Child Development, 61*, 508–523.

Sy, S. R. (2006). Family and work influences on the transition to college among Latina adolescents. *Hispanic Journal of Behavioral Sciences, 28*, 368–386.

Szalacha, L. A., Marks, A. K., Lamarre, M., & Garcia Coll (2005). Academic pathways and children of immigrant families. *Research in Human Development, 2*, 179–211.

Tseng, V. (2006). Unpacking immigration in youths' academic and occupational pathways. *Child Development, 77*, 1434–1445.

U.S. Bureau of the Census. (2007). *2005–2007 American Community Survey 3-year estimates: Hispanic or Latino origin by specific origin.* Retrieved from http://factfinder.census.gov/servlet/ACSSAFFPeople?_submenuId=people_10&_sse=on.

Valadez, J. R. (2002). The influence of social capital on mathematics course selection by Latino high school students. *Hispanic Journal of Behavioral Sciences, 24*, 319–339.

Valencia, E. Y., & Johnson, V. (2006). Latino students in North Carolina: Acculturation, perceptions of school environment, and academic aspirations. *Hispanic Journal of Behavioral Sciences, 28*, 350–367.

Werner, E. (1993). Risk, resilience, and recovery: Perspectives from the Kauai longitudinal study. *Development and Psychopathology, 5*, 503–515.

Zambone, A. M., & Alicea-Sáez, M. (2003). Latino students in pursuit of higher education: What helps or hinders their success? In V. I. Kloosterman (Ed.), *Latino students in American schools* (pp. 63–77). Westport, CT: Praeger.

Zsembik, B. A., & Llanes, D. (1996). Generational differences in educational attainment among Mexican Americans. *Social Science Quarterly, 77*, 363–374.

# 19

# Schooling, Cultural Diversity, and Student Motivation

*Revathy Kumar and Martin L. Maehr*

The 1983 report, *A Nation at Risk,* highlighted American students' poor academic performance in comparative studies and called for major educational reforms. Twenty-five years later, the academic achievement of children—particularly minority children—in the United States remains a major concern, one that Gloria Ladson-Billings addressed before the American Educational Research Association (Ladson-Billings, 2006). She raised perennial questions that confound families, practitioners, educational researchers, and policymakers alike: Why the high levels of school dropout among urban students? Why do factors like race and class remain strong predictors of achievement? These questions are particularly relevant as large-scale immigration into the United States continues and educational institutions find themselves hard pressed to understand and meet the demands of a racially, ethnically, and economically diverse student population.

In this chapter we explore factors that motivate adolescents from diverse backgrounds to select certain academic choices over others. We specifically examine how sociocultural background affects cultural minority students' motivation for achievement and how school culture fosters or undermines this motivation. Students' cultural groups profoundly influence their thoughts, feelings, motives, and behavior. They also help students locate themselves in relation to other cultural groups within a pluralistic society. To gain a clear understanding of the cognitions and motivations that influence cultural minority adolescents' learning and development, we review the work of researchers from different disciplines and analyze their research from a choice-and-decision theory perspective.

Throughout the chapter we stress the following three components as critical to understanding motivation as a situated process: (a) potential to succeed or fail and the value students place on succeeding at a task; (b) availability of options from which choices are made and the major role of sociocultural factors in framing action options from which students choose; and (c) how purposes that the context

provides and the student adopts change the "rules" that guide decision making. We conclude by suggesting ways that schools' academic and social cultures can be modified to assist teachers in meeting the challenges of cultural diversity and ensuring adaptive outcomes for all students in a culturally pluralistic society.

By way of definition, we use the terms *minority* and *minority group status* in conjunction with ethnicity, race, and culture to denote groups that experience powerlessness and discrimination (Greenfield & Cocking, 1994) within dominant, mainstream White society. In this chapter *ethnicity* refers to an individual's membership in and psychological attachment to a group sharing a common heritage based on nationality, language, and culture (Phinney, 2003). Sometimes based on phenotypic group characteristics, ethnicity also includes a racialized component referred to as *racial identity* (Chavous et al., 2003) and *racial-ethnic identity* (Altschul, Oyserman, & Bybee, 2006). *Culture* is a multifaceted construct indicating shared value, belief, and behavior scripts among a group of people and transmitted through socialization across generations. In contrast to the ascribed nature of ethnicity and race, culture is a learned behavior that varies across and within ethnic and racial groups. While overlap exists among constructs of ethnicity, race, and culture, the concepts are not synonymous (Parke & Buriel, 2006). Immigrant status adds a further layer of complexity to motivations underlying academic choices and decisions of minority adolescents (Portes & Rumbaut, 2001; Tseng, 2006). *Minority group, cultural minority group, ethnic or racial minority,* and *immigrant minority* are used interchangeably, when appropriate, in the remaining sections of this chapter.

## A Decision-Theory Model of Motivation

This chapter is guided by a decision-theory model of motivation. That is, motivation can be treated as a decision process in which individuals essentially "choose" to act in one way or another. A decision-theory perspective provides an integrative and useful framework for examining the effect of sociocultural influences on motivation, and thus achievement, in school settings.

Decision theory builds on the assumption that action represents a choice made from a set of perceived options. This theory represents a contextually situated understanding of achievement motivation that furthers our understanding of culture's immediate and enduring influences on motivation and achievement.

Early motivational research on decision making was conducted primarily in laboratories, where, in studies of decision making, perceived options are characterized in terms of the likely value of pursuing a course of action and the probability of success or failure in doing so (Atkinson, 1957; Kahneman, 2003). Atkinson suggested that enduring motivational orientations ("hope of success" and "fear of failure") held by the individual could profoundly influence decision making. More specifically, he proposed that in achievement situations the value of succeeding was an inverse function of the difficulty of the task or the probability of success or failure in performing it. However, he and his colleagues paid little attention to either the situated nature of these two orientations or the reality that choices and options for action in the real world are significantly framed by social norms; group expectations and the feelings, actions, and thoughts of significant persons and groups.

The modern expectancy-value theories (Feather, 1988; Wigfield & Eccles, 2000, 2001), grounded in real-world achievement tasks, improve on Atkinson's theory, proposing that expectations for success and value are positively, not inversely, related (Feather, 1988). Eccles and colleagues provide a more nuanced conceptualization of expectancy and value, linking them to an array of psychological and sociocultural determinants (Wigfield & Eccles, 2000). They conceptualize subjective task value in terms of *attainment value*—extent to which the task provides opportunities to fill basic needs of autonomy, relatedness and competence; *intrinsic value*—inherent pleasure gained from engaging in a task; *utility value*—task's instrumental value in achieving short- and long-term goals; and *cost*—what must be relinquished as a consequence of engaging the task.

Values, according to Eccles and colleagues, are linked to stable self-schema and identity constructs; therefore choices do not necessarily result from conscious and rational decision-making processes (Eccles, 1987). Thus, despite availability, individuals may not actively consider all available options (Eccles, 2005). Wigfield and Eccles (1992) incorporate three major components in their general expectancy-value model of achievement choices: the social world (cultural milieu), cognitive processes (perceptions and attributions), and motivational beliefs (task value and expectancy).

Of particular relevance to understanding cultural minority students' motivation in expectancy-value theory is the critical role that culturally embedded, subjective task value

plays in shaping individuals' values and expectations—and, consequently, options they choose or eliminate.

### Subjective Culture and Perceived Options

In his treatment of *subjective culture,* a group's characteristic way of perceiving its social environment, Triandis (1972) demonstrates that shared norms play a critical role in determining the range of options individuals perceive as available for a particular decision (p. 339). According to Triandis, cognitive structures of beliefs, norms, ideals, and values are particularly important in defining subjective culture. By providing group members with an understanding of values such as autonomy and freedom and knowledge about their obligations to self and others, subjective culture leads individuals to select a course of action, thus shaping their behavior.

Adolescents' subjective culture—including beliefs about parents' academic and behavioral expectations, occupational aspirations, and normative attributions for success and failure in school (e.g., Hess, Chang, & McDevitt, 1987; Jodl et al., 2001; Lamborn, Mounts, Steinberg, & Dornbusch, 1991; Stevenson & Lee, 1990)—shapes their behavioral choices, as well as their motivational orientation toward learning and achievement. Immigrant and minority adolescents may find such choices difficult when aspects of family subjective culture conflict with mainstream culture. Recently, the value that various cultures place on autonomy, agency, and freedom to choose has come under considerable scrutiny (e.g., Kagitcibasi, 1996; La Guardia, Ryan, Couchman, & Deci, 2000; Markus & Kitiyama, 1991).

*Cultural Perspectives on Autonomy*   In their seminal comparative work on cognition and motivation among individuals from Western and Eastern cultures, Markus and Kitiyama (1991) emphasize the autonomous nature of the individual Western self as opposed to the relatively malleable Eastern self attuned to intragroup role obligations. More recently, other scholars have also sought to understand how perspectives on autonomy influence motivation; how understandings of autonomy differ by culture, and how orientations toward autonomy change with prolonged exposure to other cultures.

The Western emphasis on autonomy and choice in decision making is borne out by the fundamental assumption of all sociocognitive achievement motivation theories: Individuals have an inherent need for independence, personal agency, responsibility, and control (Ames, 1992; Bandura, 1989, 1997, 2001; Deci, Vallerand, Pelletier, & Ryan, 1991; Ryan & Deci, 2000). In summarizing the essentials of *self-efficacy theory,* Bandura asserts that "efficacy beliefs play a key role in shaping the course lives take by influencing the type of activities and environments people choose to get into…. Thus, by choosing and shaping environments, people can have a hand in what they become" (Bandura, 2001, pp. 10–11).

The basis for self-determination theory and theories that focus specifically on autonomy, choice, and intrinsic/

extrinsic motivation is learning that stems from an internal need to achieve personal goals. These approaches share the assumption that people value and engage in activities they find personally satisfying (Deci et al., 1991). As Deci and his colleagues demonstrate, individuals experience a sense of self-determination and intrinsic motivation when they choose a course of action rather than when they are externally controlled. Iyengar and Lepper (1991) demonstrated the culturally situated nature of choice in intrinsic motivation by studying Asian American and European American elementary school children's motivations to engage in tasks involving personal choice rather than choice made for them by mothers or experimenters. More recent research among first-, second-, and third-generation immigrant adolescents to the United States (Fuligni, 1998) suggests that individuals' identity, attitudes, values, behaviors, and their perceived subjective cultures, vary as a function of intercultural contact. With each passing generation, immigrants' cultural values are likely to become more aligned with host-culture values (Fuligni, Witkow, & Garcia, 2005; Portes & Rumbaut, 2001; Tseng, 2006; Waters & Jimenez, 2005). In a comparative study of immigrant and U.S.-born adolescents, Fuligni (1998) reported that third-generation Mexican, Filipino, and Chinese immigrants were likely to expect autonomy at an earlier age than first-generation immigrants, suggesting that sustained, continuous intercultural contact makes later generations more likely to share the beliefs and expectations of their European American peers.

Researchers who assess the relative importance of choice and autonomy, whether through intergenerational comparisons among immigrant adolescents, or comparisons among mainstream and immigrant students, implicitly assume that autonomy and personal choice are not highly valued cultural attributes among immigrants from collectivist countries. Self-determination theorists refute this assumption and state that, in conjunction with the need for competence and relatedness (Baumeister & Leary, 1995), people of all cultures share a basic psychological need for autonomy (Ryan & Deci, 2000). Chirkov, Ryan, Kim, and Kaplan (2003) report that in both individualistic and collectivistic cultures *relative autonomy,* experience of volition and the self-endorsement of one's actions (p. 107), is positively related to well-being. Self-determination theorists label this willingness to follow expert advice in making choices and decisions *reflective* autonomy (Koestner & Losier, 1996) and distinguish it from *reactive* autonomy, a propensity to resist external influences. Relative autonomy coheres with Kagitcibasi's (1996) assertion that autonomy does not necessarily mean distancing oneself from others. However, Western thought conflates the different—though related—dimensions of agency and relatedness. Thus interdependent orientation is often thought to exclude autonomy because it emphasizes relatedness. Research examining the child-rearing practices of Chinese (Lin & Fu, 1990), Korean (Cha, 1994), and Turkish (Kagitcibasi, Sunar, & Bekman, 1988) parents points to parental values that actually combine autonomy and relatedness.

Scholars familiar with Eastern cultures (Misra & Agarwal, 1985; Salili, 1996; Saraswathi & Ganapathy, 2002) suggest that when personal and group goals are synchronous, individuals in collectivistic cultures such as India and China pursue *social achievement motivation* that rewards both self and in-group. Parallels exist between Eastern scholars' conception of social achievement motivation and self-determination theorists' definition of reflective autonomy. Therefore, while reasonable to conclude that autonomy is essential for adolescents' psychological well-being, the definition and interpretation of autonomy seems to be culturally bound.

Further research is required to better understand both the meaning and interpretation of *choice* and *autonomy* in different cultures. However, an extensive review of extant literature suggests that adolescents from collectivistic cultures begin to conceptualize autonomy, choice, and control differently upon immigration to individualistic cultures such as the United States. Moreover, parents and children differ in understanding these motivational constructs, a circumstance that often leads to intergenerational conflicts (Szapocznik & Kurtines, 1993) and maladaptive adjustment.

*Choices and Options Defined by the Subjective Culture of Teachers and Peers*   Choices and options cultural minority students perceive as available are often shaped by the subjective culture of teachers and peers. This subjective culture may reflect deep societal ambivalence toward minorities and immigrants (Suarez-Orozco & Suarez-Orozco, 2002). O'Connor (1999) uses the term *reflection* to describe how adolescents' multiple social identities are experienced as a consequence of how they interpret and make meaning of these identities. She uses *refraction* to describe how cultural positionings and interpretations of these identities by others (e.g., teachers and peers) in the context shape adolescent experience. Students' beliefs about themselves are influenced by teachers' attitudes toward them and the ways in which teachers' expectations of particular students are communicated. If teachers view cultural minority students as lazy, less intelligent, and more prone to get into trouble, such expectations are likely to have a profound effect on students' motivations and the academic choices they make.

That these are not students' unfettered motivational and behavioral choices has been repeatedly illustrated in research examining the influence of teacher expectations on students' course selections and performance (e.g., Alvidrez & Weinstein, 1999; Eccles & Wigfield, 1985; Jussim, 1989; Smith et al., 1998). Teachers' low expectations, particularly of minority and poor students, limit students' options and future career opportunities (Oakes, 1985; Rist, 2000).

The importance of considering individuals and group subjective cultures within culturally diverse contexts is supported by studies on acculturation patterns of immigrant minorities to host cultures (Bourhis, Moise, Perreault, & Senecal, 1997). Bourhis and colleagues examined both the orientation adopted by the immigrant group within mainstream cultural settings and the orientation adopted by members of the mainstream population toward specific immigrant minority groups. Mainstream members are likely to adopt a segregationist orientation toward immigrants whose culture differs considerably from their own. How members of ethnic and minority immigrant groups are included or excluded within society are reflected in patterns of ethnic group relations in schools (Montreuil & Bourhis, 2001). The effect of subjective culture on students' friendship patterns and school involvement is evident: Friendship patterns are based on the inclusion or exclusion of a student's racial, ethnic, or national group within American society. Thus, as subjective cultures determine and define what is acceptable, unacceptable, tolerable, or desirable in social contexts, predicting motivation and learning among students could be improved by incorporating subjective culture into the motivation equation.

***Possible Selves and Perceived Options***  Possible selves serve as personal objectives or orientations that build bridges between where one is and where one wants to be. Giving structure and meaning to the future, they encourage individuals to invest energy in and focus attention on realizing goals. In the process, individuals are mindful of their options and careful of the action choices they make (Markus & Ruvolo, 1989). Thus, possible selves suggest different ways of being and doing that reflect available perceived options.

The realm of possible selves available may vary in culturally pluralistic societies, demarcating choices available for members of dominant and subordinate cultural groups in society. For example, middle-class adolescents from the dominant group may see their future opening up, with unlimited options waiting to be claimed. However, this may not be the case for adolescents from devalued minority groups. These adolescents are often likely to perceive impediments—internal (within the individual), external (features of the social context), or both—that curtail their future aspirations.

Because they provide a sense that the self is mutable, positive possible selves can facilitate optimism and belief that change is possible (Markus & Nurius, 1986). It is equally likely that possible selves can be negative. Thus minority youth exposed to images of a low-achieving in-group renders incongruent a successful academic possible self (Thomas, Townsend, & Belgrave, 2003). Societal expectations of minority youth have a profound effect on their possible self-expectations—witness young African American males' adoption of a hyper-masculine persona in response to teachers' perceptions that African American youth are potentially aggressive (Spencer, 1999).

Adolescents are well aware that schools, colleges, and workplaces are not "level playing fields" and that not everyone has the same career opportunities. They see a striking disparity in the number of minorities in leadership positions in the United States (Jaret, 1995; Waters & Eschbach, 1995). This awareness is likely to influence both the future selves

adolescents aspire to and the beliefs and behaviors associated with the present self.

Qualitative interviews with seventh-grade adolescents indicate that, as compared with African American boys from more affluent backgrounds, low-income African American boys did not have a clear vision of what their future held, nor were they cognizant of the path they needed to follow to succeed in life (Kumar, 2003). If academic aspirations are beyond the realm of possibilities, adolescents may motivationally withdraw from school (Oyserman, Bybee, Terry, & Hart-Johnson, 2004).

***Cultural Differences, Perceived Options, and Free and Forced Choices***  Neither physical nor intellectual ability nor personal preferences account fully for the choices individuals make. The implicit or explicit expectations of significant groups also frame the action options from which persons choose or from which they deviate at heavy cost. This is often the case for immigrant adolescents whose membership in social and cultural groups within family and immigrant community is juxtaposed with membership in mainstream social groups such as school and peers. Students' difficulty or ease in decision making is also a consequence of the differences in perceived action options within the "culture in school" and the "culture of the home or neighborhood."

A great deal of sociocultural, socioeconomic, and generational diversity exists among the home cultures of immigrant and minority children and adolescents (Fuligni, 1998; Portes & Rumbaut, 2001; Portes & Zhou, 1993; Suarez-Orozco & Suarez-Orozco, 2002). Some experience insurmountable differences between home and school cultures. Others negotiate, though at great psychological cost, the boundaries between them even when norms and behavior expectations are dissonant. Still others, despite differences in communication styles, values, and beliefs, may adjust to and succeed in school (Phelan, Davidson, & Yu, 1998). In the following paragraphs we examine these three possibilities in more detail.

Sociocultural factors associated with educational attainment include, among others, ethnicity (Rumberger & Larson, 1998), parental education and socioeconomic status (Glick & White, 2003), and U.S. birth versus immigrant birth in country of origin (Zhou, 1997). As mentioned, some students find cultural differences irreconcilable; over time these differences interfere with their ability to adjust to school environments, escalate into academic problems (Arunkumar, Midgley, & Urdan, 1999; Erikson, 1987; Heath, 1990; Kumar, 2006; Lafromboise, Hardin, Coleman, & Gerton, 1993; Okagaki, 2001; Phelan et al., 1998; Tharp, 1989), and, eventually, failure (Erikson, 1987). Tharp and his colleagues (Reese & Gallimore, 2000; Trueba, 1988; Weisner, Gallimore, & Jordan, 1988) demonstrate how home–school dissonance interferes with learning by examining the experience of Native Hawaiian students in traditional American schools. Changes in classroom structure that incorporated the group learning centers and peer collaboration that paralleled their community's emphasis on sharing and cooperation facilitated adjustment to school. Similar findings are reported with other immigrant and minority groups (Heath, 1990).

Students who experience cultural dissonance often feel devalued and socially marginalized in school and are perceived as uncooperative and unmotivated. Even if these students know schooling is necessary for future opportunities, feelings of hopelessness (Arunkumar et al., 1999) and inadequacy (LeCompte & Dworkin, 1991) prevent them from succeeding in school. These students often lack both access to relevant information and the knowledge needed to obtain information that permits them to make informed educational choices and decisions (Phelan et al., 1998). Furthermore, though many immigrant students have family environments that support achievement (Fuligni, 1998; Suarez-Orozco & Suarez-Orozco, 2002), poor immigrant parents lack the resources to provide the instrumental support adolescents need to make educational choices that ensure future success (Okagaki & Frensch, 1998). Therefore, action options available to immigrant adolescents may be unclear, limiting, and confusing.

The second group of students manages to negotiate sociocultural borders between home and school and achieve academic success, though such success often exacts a heavy psychological price (Phelan et al., 1998). Studies involving academically successful immigrant adolescents from different ethnic groups—students of Japanese descent and recent Mexican immigrants (Matute-Bianchi, 1986), Punjabi high school students (Gibson, 1988), Chinese (Chao, 2001), and other Asian American students (Schneider & Lee, 1990)—demonstrate that despite deep-seated cultural differences, they navigate school and peer contexts. The academic success of recent foreign-born immigrants who migrated as children or adolescents (Rumbaut, 1997), and straddle two culturally disparate worlds, is attributed to their social capital; a deliberate choice to assimilate specific aspects of mainstream culture beneficial to personal advancement (Gibson, 1988; Portes & Zhou, 1993). Also of importance is their *planful competence;* that is, intellectual investment in school, self-confidence based on school performance relative to other students, and consistency in attending school (Dinovitzer, Hagan, & Parker, 2003). Though this second group achieves academic success, students experience dissonance because they feel excluded by their peers; they resist, as best they can, the forces of cultural assimilation (Gibson, 1988). Academic success for these students stems from the support of family and community culture: high parental expectations; a close-knit, supportive community; and cultural values stressing the importance of education and effort to overcome adversity (Okagaki & Frensch, 1998; Pearce, 2006).

For the third, and sizeable group, cultural differences become a source of opportunity. These adolescents find that exposure to multiple cultural perspectives and contrasting systems of thought and affect enrich their own worldview and increase the action options they perceive as available. Adolescents from several immigrant groups fall into this

category, among them children of Eastern European political refugees; those who are culturally and phenotypically similar to the mainstream population (Portes & Zhou, 1993); and—depending on school context—minority adolescents from middle class backgrounds. These adolescents have the support of highly educated parents who can navigate the complexities of the American educational system with ease while continuing to honor and maintain traditional values (Kumar, 2005; Phelan et al., 1998). Thus, these adolescents feel integrated in both traditional community and mainstream culture (Berry, Phinney, Sam, & Vedder, 2006). Moreover, community connections and supports ensure a solid buffer even when they encounter less-than-optimal classroom and school environments.

***Summary*** A decision theory perspective provides a framework within which we can examine how individuals' action choices and perceived options are shaped by individual and contextual factors. Examining individuals' cognitions and perceptions from this perspective indicates that the action choices individuals make and the options perceived as available are informed by their subjective cultures and those of significant others in the context. Second, perceived availability of choices is determined by the nature and content of individuals' projected possible selves, which are limited by their sociocultural backgrounds. Finally, conflicting expectations of those significant to cultural minority adolescents influence these adolescents' behavioral choices, options, and consequent decisions.

## Motivational Consequences and Behavioral Decisions in Achievement Situations: A Function of Available Options

Choice in achievement tasks, persistence during those tasks, and vigor in carrying them out are behavioral markers of motivation. Achievement-related beliefs, values, and goals are determinants of motivation. Current models of achievement motivation focus on answering questions such as "Can I do this activity?" (Bandura, 1989), "Do I want to do this activity?" (Wigfield & Eccles, 2001), and "What do I need to do to succeed?" (Pintrich & Zusho, 2001). As they seek to understand answers to these questions, motivational theorists have relied primarily on European American samples (Graham, 1994). However, the past few years have witnessed a gradual shift in motivational literature as researchers become mindful that motivation is, in part, a function of perceived opportunities determined by sociocultural factors. Though the possibility for inquiry is broad, our present discussion of motivational outcomes and behavioral decisions is limited to cultural minority students' perceived opportunities and options.

***Perceptions of Blocked Opportunities, Racial–Ethnic Identity, and Educational Choices*** Poor school performance and lack of motivation among minority youth are often attributed to blocked opportunities and limited options.

In his now-famous cultural ecological theory, Ogbu (1987) maintains that subordinate status of minority students, or *involuntary minorities*, directly affects academic motivation and aspiration. For example, African American and other involuntary minority students are often devalued in school and feel vulnerable in the classroom. Stifled educational opportunities and the prospect of limited access to economic resources as adults alienate these adolescents from school. They see the decision to fail in school as the only viable option, because they are motivated to demonstrate solidarity with their group. Cultural minority students, particularly involuntary minority students who have educational goals at odds with group norms, are forced to choose between the two. Attaining one goal often precludes the attainment of the other (Fordham, 1988; Matute-Bianchi, 1986; Suarez-Orozco & Suarez-Orozco, 2002).

Rejecting school and the educational values associated with it are direct consequences of the anger, distrust, and alienation that these students experience (Biafora et al., 1993). Spending a greater part of the day, every day, in an environment they neither like nor value is stress-provoking. The cumulative effect of such stress—their subjective culture at odds with school culture—and their perception that school does not contribute meaningfully to their future selves often motivate these students to drop out of school (Delgado-Gaitan, 1988).

Many sociologists and social and developmental psychologists contest Ogbu's interpretation of the relationship between minority students' ethnic and racial identification and academic motivation and performance. Sociologists attribute poor school performance and educational disengagement among poor and minority adolescents to devaluing of education arising from perceived structural barriers (Mickelson, 1990) rather than the need for oppositional identities. O'Connor (1999) critiques extant literature for presenting a simplistic picture of how individuals perceive social opportunity structure and mobility, and for relying on a single social identity, such as race, to understand determinants of academic engagement and performance. This critique is particularly salient as evidence indicates substantive variation among African American adolescents in their perceptions of how race, class, and gender affect "getting ahead" in American society (Ford, 1992; O'Connor, 1999).

Research emerging from social and developmental psychology (e.g., Oyserman, Coon, Kemmelmeier, 2003; Rowley, Sellers, Chavous, & Smith; 1998; Spencer, 1999) also suggests that involuntary minority status does not automatically translate into oppositional identity. These researchers argue that a strong identification with one's group has beneficial effect. It is associated with higher self-esteem (Crocker, Luthanen, Blaine, & Broadnax, 1994), better mental health (Phinney & Chavira, 1995; Sellers, Caldwell, Schmeelk-Cone, & Zimmerman, 2003), and acts as a buffer against the negative effect of perceived discrimination on adolescents' academic self-concepts and school achievement (Altschul et al., 2006; Wong, Eccles, & Sameroff, 2003). According to Spencer and her colleagues,

"the problem with acting White (Fordham & Ogbu, 1986) and assumptions about minority youths' achievement efforts (e.g., Ogbu, 1987) is that these perspectives lack a dynamic integration of context character, cultural traditions, developmental status, and diverse responsive adaptations" (Spencer, Noll, Stoltfuz, & Harpalani, 2001, p. 25). Spencer found that high Eurocentric values are associated with low achievement patterns, low self-efficacy scores, and low self-esteem scores. A reactive Afrocentric racial identity (superficial, fadlike use of cultural icons) is also associated with low achievement, but strong Afrocentric identity that also acknowledges positive aspects of other cultural traditions and achievements is positively related to academic excellence and healthy self-esteem. The need to protect self-worth as an explanation for the relative low performance of African American and Hispanic adolescents as compared to White adolescents is demonstrated by Graham and colleagues as well (Graham & Hudley, 2005; Graham, Taylor, & Hudley, 1998; Taylor & Graham, 2007).

Findings from cross-discipline research point to the difficulties that minority adolescents encounter in schools. Most choices adolescents are forced to make—the development of an oppositional identity, disengagement from school because of perceived barriers to positive possible futures, or the selection of negative alternative pathways to protect self-worth—are maladaptive. However, a strong ethnic identity that values academic achievement decreases minority adolescents' vulnerability to the negative effect of cultural and institutional discrimination.

***Lost Opportunities: Decisions in Response to Stereotype Threat*** Drawing on studies of *stereotype threat*, Steele (1997) suggests that such awareness of negative perceptions about one's sociocultural group is sufficient to undermine achievement. This is because negative stereotypes about one's group can be a plausible interpretation of something one does or for a situation one is in. Thus the stereotype is relevant to self-definition (Steele, 1997, p. 616). Negative stereotypes ("Blacks are lazy" or "girls are bad at math") convey attributional information resulting in long-term negative motivational and psychological consequences for group members (Reyna, 2000; Schemander, 2002; Steele & Aronson, 1995).

Students from minority cultural groups who identify with academic achievement in early school years may disidentify when repeatedly accosted with stereotype threat. Steele (1997) concluded that schools can be particularly stressful contexts for adolescents from devalued groups if they perceive that their capabilities are implicitly or explicitly questioned. Attributions associated with stereotypes impose obstacles to success for stigmatized children and adolescents because attributions regarding the stigmatized group's intellectual capacity are seen by group members and others as being relatively stable, internal, and uncontrollable qualities. Such attributions impair cognitive functioning as stigmatized group members focus energy and efforts on protecting self-worth. Thus internal, stable, and uncontrollable ascriptions associated with low-ability stereotype—and not the stereotype per se—are detrimental to academic motivation and performance (Reyna, 2000).

Davis, Aronson, and Salinas (2005) conducted an experimental study demonstrating that racial-identity status attitudes, as those described by Cross (1991), moderate intellectual performance in high-, medium-, and low-stereotype threat conditions. A strong internalized racial identity, they found, is protective in low-stereotype threat conditions but not in high-stereotype threat conditions. Their findings suggest that racial-ethnic identity could function as both a risk and a protective factor.

Stereotype threat limits available action options for devalued minority students. In order to protect self and experience self-affirmation, the two motivational consequences of experiencing stereotype threat, students can either avoid a situation or strive to disprove the ability stereotypes associated with group membership. Both options are maladaptive outcomes in the long run. Students often respond to this threat by disassociating from school contexts, downplaying the importance of succeeding in school, and minimizing expended effort (Steele, 1997). Other students may choose to disconfirm the stereotype. Failing this, they may drop out (Osborne & Walker, 2006). While students' final decision to drop out may be a volitional one, the motivational and emotional responses to stereotype threat—disidentification with academic achievement and a detachment of their self-esteem from academic experiences (Winston, Eccles, Senior, & Vida, 1997)—seldom result from conscious deliberation.

### Motivational Hazards of Living up to the Model-Minority Label

Asian immigrants are often touted as *model minorities*, those who have achieved academic and economic success in the United States through hard work and talent (Sue & Kitano, 1973; Zhou & Xiang, 2005). As model minorities, these adolescents are seen as compliant, respectful, better prepared, more motivated, and excellent math and science students, despite the cultural barriers they face (Kim, 2004; Pearce, 2006; Zhou & Xiang, 2005). Positive academic perceptions of Asian American adolescents act as a protective factor, helping them achieve academic success (Lee, 1996) despite income and employment inequities that Asian American immigrants often face.

Research indicates that middle-class Asian American adolescents from educated families attending schools in affluent neighborhoods endorse the model-minority stereotype (Lew, 2004, 2006; Kumar, 2005). These primarily first- and second-generation adolescents are privy to community networks that provide important economic and social resources necessary for informed academic and occupational decisions (Lew, 2006). This association between close community ties and motivation to succeed academically is echoed not only in studies of other Asian American immigrant groups, but also in many studies involving first- and second-generation immigrants from other countries (Caplan, Choy, & Whitmore, 1992; Fuligni et al., 2005; Gibson, 1988; Portes & Rumbaut, 2001; Suarez-Orozco & Paez,

2002; Waters, 1999; Zhou & Bankston, 1998). The added boost that high-achieving first- and second-generation affluent Asian American students enjoy—one that other first- and second-generation high achieving immigrant adolescents do not—is internalization of the model-minority stereotype as self-defining and consequently self-affirming. As Smith et al. (1998) observe, susceptibility to self-fulfilling prophecies can benefit targets.

By the same token, low-performing and socially marginalized Asian American adolescents are at a greater disadvantage. As members of the model minority group, these adolescents are set up for failure because parents accept this model-minority stereotype and hold unrealistic academic expectations for their children (Kumar, 2005). Further, many low-performing, model-minority adolescents are reluctant to seek academic support because they feel ashamed of their poor performance and inability to fulfill the stereotype. This results in such maladaptive motivational outcomes as self-handicapping and cheating (Karabenick & Newman, 2006; Ryan & Pintrich, 1997). Finally, as they seek social acceptance from peers and reject the "nerd" image associated with the stereotype, they engage in rebellious behavior (Lee, 1996) antithetical to Asian American model-minority conduct.

The model-minority stereotype does not account for the variation of nationality, language, religion, culturally valued beliefs and behaviors, and reasons for immigration (Kitano, 1981). It also denies the poverty and lack of opportunity in school and community that many endure. As Lee (1996) concludes in *Unraveling the "Model Minority" Stereotype*,

> The model minority stereotype is dangerous because it tells Asian Americans and other minorities how to behave. The stereotype is dangerous because it is used against other minority groups to silence claims of inequality. It is dangerous because it silences the experiences of Asian Americans who can/do not achieve model minority success. And finally, the stereotype is dangerous because some Asian Americans may use the stereotype to judge their self-worth. (p. 125)

### Motivational Consequences of Social Exclusion

In school, cultural minority students often experience social exclusion related to group membership. Though exclusion can be particularly debilitating during the adolescent years when the psychological need for acceptance and support from peers is heightened (Brendt, 1979; Newman & Newman, 2001), adolescents have the cognitive complexity to realize that social identity operates differently in different social contexts. It can be the source of bonding and closeness in one context and of alienation and rejection in another. Adolescents may find that, while belonging to a minority cultural group can be a powerful source of support (Kumar, 2005), it creates distance between them and mainstream peers. With their capacity for reflective thinking, adolescents are better able to understand social relationships and the implications of belonging to one group or another. As they become aware of status hierarchy of the groups in their schools, they recognize how others view their group.

Group membership acts as the lens through which individuals in a culturally pluralistic society view each other. Thus social categorization as a minority, both by self and by others within the school context, increases the probability of stereotyping, ethnocentrism, intergroup clashes, and competition (Hogg, 2005; Tajfel, 1978; Tajfel & Turner, 1979). In fact, cultural minority students in more integrated school environments report that they experience higher exclusion and ostracism than students in more homogenous school environments. Ethnic and numerical minority adolescents within school contexts are at greater risk of suffering peer harassment that adversely affects their self-appraisal, emotional well-being, school performance (Graham & Juvonen, 2002), and sense of school belonging (Goodenow & Grady, 1993).

The disrupted intergroup relationships in schools and ostracism of Arab and Middle Eastern origin students after 9/11 demonstrate the maladaptive consequences of social exclusion (Ajrouch, 2000; Kumar, 2003; Zine, 2001). It exacts a toll on students' feelings about school, valuing of self, achievement motivation, and academic achievement. Social exclusion was correlated with increased aggressive and antisocial behavior (Twenge, Baumeister, Tice, & Stueke, 2001), procrastination (Twenge, Catanese, & Baumeister, 2002), poor performance on IQ and GRE tests (Baumeister, Twenge, & Nuss, 2002), and diminished intrinsic motivation (Deci et al., 1991).

Patterns of such exclusion highlight the vital role that schools play in helping adolescents understand how racial, ethnic, national, and cultural differences are socially constructed and the important consequences each has for interpersonal relationships, motivation, involvement in school, and overall well-being.

*Summary* Cultural minority adolescents are often at risk for problematic motivations and maladaptive action choices—the consequence of school exclusion experiences, perceptions that schooling and education cannot help them access blocked economic opportunities, fear of fulfilling low-ability stereotypes, or fear of not fulfilling model-minority stereotypes. Schools and teachers increasingly encounter these challenges as America's student population becomes more diverse.

In an effort to address such challenges and advance the education of *all* students, one group of researchers has proposed changes to school policies and practices based on the achievement goals students pursue. We turn now to an examination of achievement goals; situate them within the context of other goals students pursue, and examine implications for the education of cultural minority students.

## Goals, Goal Orientation, and the Decision Making Process

The study of goals developed through research in cognition, personality, and motivation (detailed discussions in Austin & Vancouver, 1996). This section focuses primarily on achievement goal theory, a social cognitive motivation theory. We use this framework to examine the role goals play in initiating choices and framing behavior in academic achievement contexts. However, achievement goals cannot be understood in isolation from other goals or from the cognitive and affective responses that result from pursuing these goals. Therefore, we also consider the work of other theorists, including goal content theorists (Ford, 1992; Wentzel, 1989).

*Achievement Goal Theory* Achievement goal theory emerged in the 1980s when several researchers (e.g., Ames, 1992; Dweck & Leggett, 1988; Grant & Dweck, 2003; Maehr & Midgley, 1991; Midgley, 1993; Nicholls, 1984) attempted to understand why students engaged in academic behavior and how they perceived the purpose of schooling emphasized in schools and classrooms. Achievement goal theory focuses on *why* students engage in certain behaviors and why they choose one course of action over another in learning situations (Anderman & Maehr, 1994; Maehr, 1984). It views decision-making variables as a dynamic process involving varied components of self and how these components—individually and jointly—operate in decision-making process situations, contexts, and sociocultural circumstances.

Central to achievement goal theory are two goals: *mastery goal* and *performance goal*. Each embodies an integrated belief system examining why students engage in achievement behavior (Pintrich, 2000). Mastery-focused students believe that the primary reason for schoolwork is to learn, improve, and be challenged; performance-focused students believe the primary purpose of schoolwork is to appear smarter than classmates, demonstrate ability, compare favorably with others in class, or avoid looking incompetent (Anderman & Maehr, 1994; Nicholls, 1984). These purposes have different effects on choices in achievement situations, as well as actions and outcomes that follow.

Some achievement-goal theorists have sought to incorporate into mastery- and performance-goal orientations the approach-avoidance distinction that exists in earlier achievement motivation literature (Atkinson, 1957; Elliot; 1999; Elliot & Covington, 2001; Lewin, Dembo, Festinger, & Sears, 1944; McClelland, Atkinson, Clark, & Lowell, 1953; Pintrich, 2000). Still others (Wolters, 2003) emphasize the need to incorporate work-avoidance into the framework of achievement goal theory.

*The Selves Embedded in Achievement Goal Orientation* Achievement goal orientations assign a central role to self-processes that have direct consequences for the self. All three achievement goal orientations—mastery, performance-approach, and performance-avoid goals—are differentially associated with self-worth contingencies (Dweck, 1999). Nicholls (1984) labels performance goals *ego goals,* using the term *ego-orientation* to indicate that this orientation encourages individuals to compare self with others either to enhance or protect self-worth.

However, recent incorporation of distinctions between performance-approach and performance-avoid goals takes into account the need for self-enhancement associated with approach and the feelings of threat-to-self associated with avoid. Thus, performance-approach goals are associated with self-enhancing behaviors, performance-avoid goals are associated with self-protecting behaviors.

This distinction has received mixed support in empirical research. Self-handicapping strategies (Midgley & Urdan, 2001) and fear of failure (Elliot & Church, 1997) positively related to both performance-*avoid* and performance-*approach* goals. One can argue from Tesser's self-evaluation model (2003) that the underlying motives for both performance goal orientations are to maintain positive self-evaluations when engaging in social comparison. If students have difficulty maintaining positive evaluations through the self-enhancement afforded by performance approach orientations, they may revert to self-protection by adopting a performance avoid orientation. Adopting a mastery goal orientation, on the other hand, directs attention away from the self toward the task at hand. Here too the self is implicated, but directed toward self-improvement (Kumar & Maehr, 2007).

*Beliefs and Behaviors Associated with Achievement Goal Orientations*   In general, a mastery goal-orientation is associated with adaptive motivational processes and positive cognitive (Elliot & McGregor, 2001; Meece, Blumenfeld, & Hoyle, 1988; Middleton & Midgley, 1997; Wolters, 2004), affective (Kaplan & Maehr, 1999; Kumar, 2006; Midgley, Anderman, & Hicks, 1995; Roeser, Midgley, & Urdan, 1996; Turner, Thorpe, & Meyer, 1998), and behavioral (Karabenick & Newman, 2006; Ryan & Pintrich, 1997) outcomes.

Elliot and Harackewicz (1996) suggested that both mastery goals and performance-approach goals "engender a host of affective and perceptual-cognitive processes that facilitate task engagement" (p. 462). However, the pattern of relations for performance-approach orientation is less uniform among outcomes (Bong, 2001; Church, Elliot, & Gable, 2001; Ryan & Pintrich; 1997; Wolters, 2004). Several studies indicate maladaptive outcomes, and others find no relation or positive relations (see Midgley, Kaplan, & Middleton, 2001). Performance-avoid orientation was associated with a more negative pattern of outcomes, among them increased test anxiety, lower efficacy, lower intrinsic motivation and lower exam performance among college (Elliot & Harackiewicz, 1996; Elliot, McGregor, & Gable, 1999) and middle school students (Middleton & Midgley, 1997; Skaalvik, 1997). Research also indicates that students may endorse more than one achievement goal. In general, high mastery goals coupled with either high or low performance goals are equally adaptive (Pintrich, 2000).

*Personal Achievement Goals within the Context of Multiple Personal Goals*   The effect of personal achievement goals on learning and development cannot be examined in isolation. Several factors, including other goals, influence whether adolescents pursue achievement goals and, if so, what kind. Ford (1992) detailed a goals taxonomy divided broadly into *intrapersonal* (desired within person outcomes) and *interpersonal* (desired relationship between person and environment) goals. This taxonomy includes social relationship goals such as *social responsibility, superiority, equity, resource acquisition,* and *resource provision* (Ford, 1992). The relative importance and salience of personal achievement goals and how they help or hinder learning are best understood within the context of the salience and significance of students' other goals (Wentzel, 1994, 2003).

Multiple goals and the intentional actions they initiate become increasingly important as individuals better articulate their conception of self in relation to context. Researchers, in turn, are more aware of the need to examine how adolescents' social goals relate to academic goals (Ryan, 2001; Urdan & Maehr, 1995). Brandtstadter (2006) suggests that, in addition to developmental factors that inform personal goals, other cultural and historical factors shape and constrain these goals, determining whether they are within the realm of possibility. This process influences cultural minority students' selection of goals and the extent to which they coincide or conflict with cultural demands.

The belief that behavior stems from multiple goals, is selected from alternative options, and is constrained by individuals' representations of social rules and conventions resonates with the choice and decision theory focus of this chapter. To understand motivations that influence the learning and development of cultural minority adolescents, we need to examine the effect of interrelationships among the multiple goals these adolescents pursue in terms of relative importance (Wright & Brehm, 1989), intensity (Locke & Latham, 1990), valence and relevance (Ford, 1992), and action choices.

*Decision Making in the Context of Multiple Goals*   Choosing a course of action in a multigoal context likely depends on perceived or available action options that depend on what others in the group expect and promote. Options are also determined by the hierarchy of importance among goals pursued, as well as the compatibility among and alignment of desired goals (Ford, 1992). As Dodge, Asher, and Parkhurst (1989) point out, "often environmental and personal constraints prevent the accomplishment of multiple goals. Priorities must be evaluated and compromises must be reached. Even important goals must be sacrificed occasionally" (p. 122). In other words, goals need to be coordinated (Pintrich & Shunk, 2002), and if attempts to achieve one goal impede another, the goals' relative importance must be weighed and consequences of behavioral options considered. As a result, choice—a concept central to both motivation and decision making—can be severely curtailed.

Researchers caution that goal conflict is problematic and emphasize the importance of goal alignment for involvement, commitment, and intellectual creativity (Ford, 1992;

Wentzel, 1989). However, when individuals consider various combinations of social and academic goals, they may actually be compatible and aligned, clearly delineating the appropriate action and behavior. However, negative motivational, affective, and long-term learning and developmental consequences may result from aligned but maladaptive goals.

As we examine the relation between cultural minority adolescents' achievement-goal orientations and other motivations in achievement contexts, several factors require consideration: (a) behavior is usually guided by multiple goals simultaneously; (b) these goals may or may not be hierarchical in terms of importance and relevance; (c) the activation of one goal does not preclude the activation of other goals (Ford, 1992); (d) goals may be aligned or in conflict with other goals (Wentzel, 1989); (e) while individuals may have multiple goals, only a few are activated based on subjective task value (Eccles, 2005), salience, availability, and accessibility in memory (Higgins, 1987).

For example, what achievement goal orientation is compatible with cultural minority adolescents' need for parental approval? How salient are achievement goals when adolescents disengage from school and learning? The achievement goal orientations—mastery, performance-approach, or performance-avoid—that they favor depend somewhat on whether these goals also meet other goal(s).

*Cultural Minority Students' Achievement-Goal Orientation in the Context of Other Goals And Motivations* Only recently have researchers begun to explore this issue among minority and immigrant groups in the United States. Studies have examined differences in African American and White students' goal orientation (Freeman, Gutman, & Midgley, 2002; Midgley, Arunkumar, & Urdan, 1996), suggesting that mastery goals proved adaptive for students from both groups. However, performance-goal oriented African Americans were more likely than their White counterparts to opt out of higher-level mathematics classes (Gutman, 2006) and engage in self-handicapping strategies (Midgley et al., 1996), giving credence to the argument that performance-oriented African Americans must navigate stereotype threat.

Much work regarding Asian and Asian American students' motivation has been conducted within the motivational attribution theory framework and has focused on differences in effort and ability attributions for success and failure. Attribution theory of motivation grew from fundamental questions asked in achievement situations and the answers they provide. These attributions, in turn, affect future motivations and reasons for engaging in tasks. Attributing success or failure to ability or effort has a profound effect on individuals' feelings about their capabilities and competences, consequent affective reactions, and future behaviors (Weiner, 1985).

Comparative research among Asians, Asian Americans, and non-Asians' attributions of success indicates that, unlike non-Asians, Asians and Asian Americans attribute academic success and failure primarily to effort (Eaton & Dembo, 1997; Grant & Dweck, 2001; Hess et al., 1987; Holloway, 1988; Stevenson & Lee, 1990). However, in studies where effort attributions are significantly associated with Asian Americans achievement, the effects are relatively small (Zusho, 2004). In comparative studies, as a group, Asian American students displayed higher levels of fear of failure, endorsed performance-avoidance goals, and displayed more anxiety but better math performance than White students (Zusho, Pintrich, & Cortina. 2005). Kumar (2005) reports similar findings with a sample of Asian Indian middle and high school adolescents. Inability to meet parental expectations and fulfill the model-minority stereotype was related to Asian Indian adolescents' adoption of maladaptive achievement goal orientations and heightened feelings of home–school dissonance. These findings suggest that the avoidance dimension of achievement-goal orientation—whether mastery or performance—is probably high among Asian American adolescents.

*Summary* This section examines adaptive and maladaptive consequences of different personal achievement-goal orientations—mastery goals, performance-approach goals, and performance-avoid goals—as the reasons that students choose certain behaviors in achievement situations. We further emphasize the need to adopt a multiple-goal perspective when examining cultural minority students' action choices and behavioral decisions.

## School as a Context for Expanding Action Options

Both the poor performance of U.S. students and the gap that persists between mainstream and minority students remain sources of national concern. The two issues are related. If a major segment of America's student population underperforms, the country cannot compete successfully in the international arena. However, a review of literature exploring cultural determinants of achievement motivation suggests that we can take positive measures to improve education quality so that minority and mainstream students have the opportunity for healthy development. Indeed most research examining education, learning, and development concludes with a call for change in school policies and practices.

Educational researchers from across disciplines propose improvements to school policies and programs, though they do so at different levels. Psychologists focus on interactions among teachers, counselors, and students; sociologists are more likely to examine larger societal and organizational structures (Dornbusch, Glasgow, & Lin, 1996). Multicultural education and social cognitive theories of motivation share a common vision for redefining and transforming schools to enhance their effectiveness (Kumar, 2003). Multicultural educationists base school-reform proposals on an understanding of education as antiracist, comprehensive, pervasive, and rooted in social justice (Nieto, 2002, p. 125). Achievement goal theorists base school-reform proposals on an understanding of education as a process of progressing, growing in understanding, and equipping children to become lifelong learners (Maehr & Midgley, 1996, p. 110). Though the stated purposes differ, they are complementary. Informed decisions about changes in school policies and practices that serve the needs of a pluralistic student body require us to examine the common themes that emerge from research in different disciplines.

Before examining suggested changes to school policies and practices, we explore three existing practices and policies consistently cited as impediments to students' development, regardless of background.

***Curricular Tracking Curtailing Choices***  Curricular tracking and ability grouping, particularly in math and science courses, is a common structural feature of most American secondary schools (Oakes, 1985). Research regarding the practice suggests that it is seldom in students' best interest and does not promote equality. Tracking contributes to hostile relationships between student groups and separates them along ethnic and social-class lines. Often, children are tracked on tenuous grounds. Students are selected and sorted based on socioeconomic status, race, or ethnicity. A disproportionate number of low socioeconomic status and disadvantaged minority students are tracked into low ability, less cognitively challenging, non-college-bound courses (Oakes, 1985).

As mentioned earlier, teachers' expectations are likely to be influenced by their personal beliefs and stereotypes— their subjective cultures (Madon, Jussim, Eccles, 1997). Oakes, Selvin, Karoly, & Guiton (1991) found that Asian American students were more likely to be assigned to advanced courses than were Hispanic students, even when their test scores were equivalent.

The differential opportunity structure results in diminished academic aspirations and motivation and disengagement from school among lower-tracked students. Eliminating the tracking process is a necessary first step in transforming pedagogy and creating equitable learning conditions for all students.

***No Child Left Behind Policy***  The No Child Left Behind Act (NCLB; 2001) aims to close the achievement gap that parallels race and class. To its credit, this policy has brought the uneven achievement of poor and minority students—both in large urban schools and in suburban and rural schools—into our national consciousness. However, the complicated rules mandated by NCLB, coupled with its unrealistic goals, have made it difficult for schools to provide the kind of education students need (Berliner, 2006; Darling-Hammond, 2006). Ironically, as all these scholars point out, the NCLB policy of requiring schools to demonstrate adequate yearly progress through test scores has created incentives to neglect those who need the most help—the poor and minority students.

Darling-Hammond (2006) provides a detailed analysis of the problems and unintended consequences that have resulted from the implementation of this policy. These include accountability provisions that create punitive counterincentives. NCLB encourages high dropout and pushout rates for low-achieving students (poorly performing students are removed from school to improve average test scores), creates obstacles for meeting individual needs of students, and discourages authentic assessments that cultivate higher-order thinking. In other words, NCLB fails to recognize the importance of developing school policies and practices grounded in well-researched educational theories.

***Zero-Tolerance Policy***  Zero-tolerance policy represents federal efforts to restrict firearms and substance use and to support suspension and expulsion for violation of the policy (Casella, 2003). Studies examining punitive measures as a means of ensuring that students comply with school policies suggest that these measures do little to reduce student substance abuse (Kumar, O'Malley, & Johnston, 2005; Munro & Midford, 2001).

The consequences of the zero-tolerance policy are particularly negative for poor and minority students. For example, poor Latino and African American youth are more likely to be involved in fights due to the high rates of neighborhood violence, social isolation, and diminished job opportunities (Anderson, 1999). There is growing evidence within the psychological literature, too, that both Latino and African American boys perceive the school climate as hostile and teachers as unfair and unsupportive (Spencer, 1999) and that harsh discipline is disproportionately used on African American and Latino boys as part of the zero-tolerance policy (Taylor & Graham, 2007).

## School Reforms in Policies and Practices Based on Theoretically Grounded Empirical Research

School restructuring requires changes in the patterns of roles, relationships, expectations, and responsibilities among school administrators, teachers, students, and parents—people jointly engaged in promoting the development of students. In the following sections we examine changes to school policies and practices that can be initiated based on multicultural education and achievement goal theory perspectives.

***Social Reconstructionist Perspective on School Reforms***
Using a social reconstructionist multicultural perspective, many multicultural educationists (Banks, 2002; Cochran-Smith, 1995; Darling-Hammond, 2006, Delpit, 2006; Gay, 2000; Ladson-Billings, 2006; Sleeter, 2001) call for the dismantling of current school policies that promote inequality and advocate policies and practices such as equity pedagogy and culturally responsive teaching. These, they believe, empower students to acquire the knowledge and skills necessary to function effectively and thoughtfully in society.

Social reconstructionist reforms to NCLB policy call for resources and incentives to develop, recruit, and retain high-quality teachers who possess both the content and pedagogical knowledge to teach in schools that serve cultural minority students, rather than focusing on test scores and punishing low-achieving schools. They suggest allowances for interdisciplinary teaching, a focus on authentic assessment that includes critical thinking and performance rather than low-level, multiple-choice tests employed in state-mandated standardized tests. To make NCLB an effective tool that enhances learning and performance for all students, schools should be evaluated in terms of their ongoing contribution to students' learning progress (Darling-Hammond, 2006). Realizing the vision of multicultural education through equity pedagogy and culturally responsive teaching requires transformation of school culture so that students are empowered, validated, and included.

### Transformation of School and Classroom Cultures Based on Achievement Goal Theory

Relative to other social cognitive theories of motivation, achievement goal theory focuses on creating learning environments that facilitate cognitive skills development by promoting adaptive motivations. Achievement goal theory defines as *mastery focused* school practices that encourage intellectual development through effort and engagement in challenging activities, and terms *performance-focused those* school practices in which comparison and competition are the norm (Ames, 1992; Maehr & Midgley, 1991, 1996).

Ames's work on classroom goal structures (1992) and Maehr and Midgley's work on transforming school cultures (1996) detail critical facets of classrooms and schools that determine whether they are mastery-focused or more performance focused. Ames suggests that students would be better-served if teachers engage in instructional practices that are meaningful and challenging, actively solicit participation in classroom decisions, minimize social comparisons, and adopt criterion- rather than norm-referenced evaluation techniques (see Maehr & Midgley, 1996; Meece, Anderman, & Anderman, 2006). These suggestions are echoed by research emerging from such social cognitive theories of motivation as expectancy-value theory (Wigfield & Eccles, 2000).

Such reforms would eliminate many practices associated with the policies discussed earlier. They would require moving away from ability-grouping practices; a careful review of what initiatives ensure that no child is left behind; and careful examination of the effects of suspension and expulsion on adolescents' learning, behavior, and healthy development.

### Mastery-Focused Learning Environments for Culturally Pluralistic Classrooms

Feelings of inclusion are enhanced in mastery-focused environments because the setting is designed to minimize competition and avoid threatening students with social comparison. At the heart of a mastery-focused education is the belief that people work together, collaborate, and help each other. This environment creates a community of learners in an atmosphere of mutual

respect and is likely to encourage students and teachers to be less judgmental of others whose ideas, values, and cultural norms are different from theirs (Kumar, 2003). As demonstrated in a multilevel growth curve study examining students' experiences of home–school dissonance across the transition from elementary to middle school, teachers' reported mastery-focused middle school practices were associated with a decrease in feelings of home–school dissonance. In addition, students who perceived middle school classrooms as more performance- and less mastery-focused than elementary classrooms, reported an increase in their feelings of dissonance (Kumar, 2006). These findings are not surprising, considering that performance-focused environments tend to elicit greater self-consciousness (Roeser, Midgley, & Urdan, 1996). Such an environment calls into question personal ability or the ability of one's social group, evokes stereotypes about one's group, and places minority students at greater risk for experiencing a stereotype threat and feeling vulnerable and inadequate.

Mastery-focused environments are validating because the tasks and activities students engage in are personally relevant and meaningful for students (Blumenfeld, 1992; Meece, 1991). Mastery-focused learning environments require teachers to employ a variety of instructional strategies that account for different ways of learning and understanding. For example, in culturally pluralistic classrooms, teachers take into account students' cultural background and prior experiences when planning lessons (Ames, 1992). In sum, mastery-focused learning environments foster a situation in which there is equal respect for learners' backgrounds, the learning process embraces a range of needs and interests, and the integrity of every learner is sustained.

## Conclusion

The primary purpose of school reform is to successfully educate *all* students. To do this we must eliminate policies and practices that create roadblocks for students' progress. For schools to meet the challenge of forming today's students into tomorrow's responsible and productive citizens, meeting the needs of a culturally diverse student body must take priority. If children are to grow up confident that they can contribute to society, we must educate them in a supportive environment that does not threaten self-worth or question abilities. To realize the goal of education for all students, we need to cultivate mastery-focused educational institutions where cultural diversity is an opportunity to grow and not a problem to solve.

## References

*A nation at risk.* (1983, April). Retrieved January 19, 2010, from U.S. Department of Education website: http://www.ed.gov/pubs/NatAtRisk/risk.html

Ajrouch, (2000). Place, age, and culture: Community living and ethnic identity among Lebanese American adolescents. *Small Group Research, 21,* 447–469.

Altschul, I., Oyserman, D., & Bybee, D. (2006). Racial-ethnic identity in mid-adolescence: Content and change as predictors of academic achievement. *Child Development, 77,* 1155–1169.

Alvidrez, J., & Weinstein, R. S. (1999). Early teacher perceptions and later student academic achievement. *Journal of Educational Psychology, 91,* 731–746.

Ames, C. (1992). Classrooms: Goals, structures, and student motivation. *Journal of Educational Psychology, 84,* 261–271.

Anderman, E. M., & Maehr, M. L. (1994). Motivation and schooling in the middle grades. *Review of Educational Research, 64,* 287–309.

Anderson, E. (1999*). Code of the street: Decency, violence, and the moral life of the inner city.* New York: Norton.

Arunkumar, R., Midgley, C., & Urdan, T. (1999). Perceiving high or low home-school dissonance: Longitudinal effects on adolescent emotional and academic well being. *Journal of Research on Adolescence, 4,* 441–466.

Atkinson, J. W. (1957). Motivational determinants of risk-taking behavior. *Psychological Review, 64,* 359–372.

Austin, J. T., & Vancouver J. B. (1996). Goal constructs in psychology: Structure, process, and content. *Psychological Bulletin, 120,* 338–375.

Bandura, A. (1989). Social cognitive theory. In R. Vasta (Ed.), *Annals of child development* (Vol. 6, pp. 1–60). Greenwich, CT: JAI Press.

Bandura, A. (1997). *Self efficacy: The exercise of control.* New York: Freeman.

Bandura, A. (2001). Social cognitive theory: An agentic perspective. In S. T. Fiske, D. L. Schacter, & C. Zahn-Waxler (Eds.), *Annual review of psychology* (Vol. 52, pp. 1–26). Palo Alto, CA: Annual Reviews.

Banks, J. A. (2002). *An introduction to multicultural education.* Boston, MA: Allyn & Bacon.

Baumeister, R. F., & Leary, M. R. (1995). The need to belong: Desire for interpersonal attachments as a fundamental human motivation. *Psychological Bulletin, 117,* 497–529.

Baumeister, R. F., Twenge, J. M., & Nuss, C. K. (2002). Effects of social exclusion on cognitive processes: Anticipated aloneness reduces intelligent thought. *Journal of Personality and Social Psychology, 83,* 817–827.

Berliner, D. C. (2006). Our impoverished view of educational research. *The Teachers College Record, 108,* 949–995 I

Berry, J. W., Phinney, J. S., Sam, D. L., & Vedder, P. (2006). Immigrant youth: Acculturation, identity, and adaptation. *Applied Psychology: An International Review, 55,* 303–332.

Biafora, Jr., F. A., Warheit, G. J., Zimmerman, R. S., Gil, A. G., Apospori, E., & Taylor, D. (1993). Racial mistrust and deviant behaviors among ethnically diverse Black adolescent boys. *Journal of Applied Social Psychology, 23,* 891–910.

Blumenfeld, P. C. (1992). Classroom learning and motivation: Clarifying and expanding goal theory. *Journal of Educational Psychology, 84,* 272–281.

Bong, M. (2001). Between- and within-domain relations of academic motivation among middle and high school students: Self-efficacy, task-value, and achievement goals. *Journal of Educational Psychology, 93,* 23–34.

Bourhis, R, Y., Moise, L. C., Perreault, S, & Senecal, S. (1997). Towards an interactive acculturation model: A social psychological approach. *International Journal of Psychology, 32,* 369–386.

Brandtstader, J. (2006). Action perspectives on human development. In R. M. Lerner & W. Damon (Series Eds.) & R. M. Lerner (Vol. Ed.), *Handbook of child psychology: Vol. 1. Theoretical models of development* (6th ed., pp. 516–568). New York: Wiley.

Brendt, T. J. (1979). Developmental changes in conformity to peers and parents. *Developmental Psychology, 22,* 444–449.

Caplan, N., Choy, M. H., & Whitmore, J. K. (1992). Indochinese refugee families and academic achievement. *Scientific American, 2,* 36.

Casella, R. (2003). Zero tolerance policy in schools: Rationale, consequences, and alternatives. *Teachers College Record, 105,* 872–892.

Cha, J. H. (1994). Aspects of individualism and collectivism in Korea. In U. Kim & H.C. Triandis (Eds.), *Individualism and collectivism: Theory, method, and applications. Cross-cultural research and methodology series* (Vol. 18, pp. 157–174). Thousand Oaks, CA: Sage.

Chao, R. K. (2001). Extending research on the consequences of parenting style for Chinese Americans and European Americans. *Child Development, 72,* 1832–1843.

Chavous, T. M., Bernat, H. D., Schmeelk-Cone, K., Caldwell, C. H., Kohn-Wood, L., & Zimmerman, M. A. (2003). Racial identity and academic attainment among African American adolescents. *Child Development, 74,* 1076–1090.

Chirkov, V., Ryan, R. M., Kim, Y., & Kaplan, U. (2003). Differentiating autonomy from individualism and independence: A self-determination theory perspective on internalization of cultural orientations and well-being. *Journal of Personality and Social Psychology, 84,* 97–109.

Church, M., Elliot, A., & Gable, S. (2001). Perceptions of classroom environment, achievement goals, and achievement outcomes. *Journal of Educational Psychology, 93,* 43–54.

Cochran-Smith, M. (1995). Color blindness and basket making are not the answers: Confronting the dilemmas of race, culture, and language diversity in teacher education. *American Educational Research Journal, 32,* 493–522.

Crocker, J., Luthanen, R., Blaine, B., & Broadnax, S. (1994). Collective self-esteem and psychological well-being among White, Black, and Asian college students. *Personality and Social Psychology Bulletin, 20,* 503–513.

Cross, W. E. (1991). *Shades of Black: Diversity in African American identity.* Philadelphia: Temple University.

Darling-Hammond, L. (2006). No child left behind and high school reform. *Harvard Educational Review, 76,* 642–667.

Davis III, C., Aronson, J., & Salinas, M., (2005). Shades of threat: Racial identity as a moderator of stereotype threat. *Journal of Black Psychology, 32,* 399–417.

Deci, E. L., Vallerand, R. J., Pelletier, L. G., & Ryan, R. M. (1991). Motivation and education: The self-determination perspective. *Educational Psychologist, 26,* 325–346.

Delgado-Gaitan, C. (1988). The value of conformity: Learning to stay in school. *Anthropology and Education Quarterly, 19,* 354–379.

Delpit, L. (2006). Lessons from teachers. *Journal of Teacher Education, 57,* 220–232.

Dinovitzer, R., Hagan, J., & Parker, P. (2003). Choice and circumstance: Social capital and planful competence in the attainments of immigrant youth. *Canadian Journal of Sociology, 28,* 463–488.

Dodge, K. A., Asher, S., & Parkhurst, J. T. (1989). Social life as goal coordination task. In C. Ames & R. Ames (Eds.), *Research on motivations in education* (Vol. 3, pp. 107–135). New York: Academic Press.

Dornbusch, S. M., Glasgow, K. L., & Lin, I. C. (1996). The social structure of schooling. *Annual Review of Psychology, 47,* 401–429.

Dweck, C. S. (1999). *Self theories: Their role in motivation, personality, and development.* Philadelphia, PA: Taylor & Francis.

Dweck, C. S., & Leggett, E. L. (1988). A social cognitive approach to motivation and personality. *Psychological Review, 95,* 256–273.

Eaton, M. J., & Dembo, M. H. (1997). Differences in the motivational beliefs of Asian American and non-Asian students. *Journal of Educational Psychology, 89,* 433–440.

Eccles, J. S. (1987). Gender roles and women's achievement related decisions. *Psychology of Women Quarterly, 11,* 135–172.

Eccles, J. S. (2005). Subjective task value and the Eccles et al. model of achievement-related tasks. In A. J. Elliot & C. S. Dweck (Eds.), *Handbook of competence and motivation* (pp. 105–121). New York: Guilford.

Eccles, J., & Wigfield, A. (1985). Teacher expectations and student motivation. In J. Dusek (Ed.), *Teacher expectancies* (pp. 185–217). Hillsdale, NJ: Erlbaum.

Elliot, A. J. (1999). Approach and avoidance motivation and achievement goals. *Educational Psychologist, 34,* 169–189.

Elliot A. J., & Church, M. A. (1997). A hierarchical model of approach and avoidance achievement motivation. *Journal of Personality and Social Psychology, 72,* 218–232.

Elliot, A. J., & Covington, M. V. (2001). Approach and avoidance motivation. *Educational Psychology Review, 13,* 93–92.

Elliot, A. J., & Harackiewicz, J. M. (1996). Approach and avoidance achievement goals and intrinsic motivation: A mediational analysis. *Journal of Personality and Social Psychology, 70,* 461–475.

Elliot, A. J., & McGregor, H. A. (2001). A 2 × 2 achievement goal framework. *Journal of Personality and Social Psychology, 80,* 501–519.

Elliot, A. J., McGregor, H., & Gable, S. (1999). Achievement goals, study strategies, and exam performance: A mediational analysis. *Journal of Experimental Social Psychology, 91,* 549–463.

Erikson, F. (1987). Transformation and school success: The politics and culture of educational achievement. *Anthropology and Education Quarterly, 18,* 335–356.

Feather, N. T. (1988). Values, valences, and course enrollment: Testing the role of personal values within an expectancy-value framework. *Journal of Educational Psychology, 8,* 381–391.

Ford, M. E. (1992). *Human motivation: Goals, emotions, and personal agency beliefs.* Newbury Park, CA: Sage.

Fordham, S. (1988). Racelessness as a factor in Black students' school success: Pragmatic strategy or pyrrhic victory? *Harvard Educational Review, 58,* 54–84.

Fordham, S., & Ogbu, J. U. (1986). Black students' school success: Coping with the "burden of acting White." *The Urban Review, 18,* 176–206.

Freeman, K. E., Gutman, L. M., & Midgley, C. (2002). Can achievement goal theory enhance our understanding of the motivation and performance of African American young adolescents? In C. Midgley (Ed.), *Goals, goal structures, and patterns of adaptive learning* (pp. 175–204). Hillsdale, NJ: Erlbaum.

Fuligni, A. J. (1998). The adjustment of children from immigrant families. *Current Directions in Psychological Science, 7,* 99–103.

Fuligni, A. J., Witkow, M., & Garcia, C. (2005). Ethnic identity and the academic adjustment of adolescents from Mexican, Chinese, and European backgrounds. *Developmental Psychology, 41,* 799–811.

Gay, G. (2000). *Culturally responsive teaching: Theory, research, and practice.* New York: Teachers College Press.

Gibson, M. (1988). *Accommodation without assimilation: Sikh immigrants in American high schools.* Ithaca, NY: Cornell University Press.

Glick, J. E., & White, M. J. (2003). The academic trajectories of immigrant youth: analysis within and across cohorts, *Demography, 40,* 759–783.

Goodenow, C., & Grady, K. E. (1993). The relationship of school belonging and friends values to academic motivation among urban adolescent students. *Journal of Experimental Education, 62,* 60–71.

Graham, S. (1994). Motivation in African Americans. *Review of Educational Research, 64,* 55–117.

Graham, S., & Hudley, C. (2005). Race and ethnicity in the study of motivation and competence. In A. J. Elliot & C. S. Dweck (Eds.), *Handbook of competence and motivation* (pp. 392–413). New York: Guilford.

Graham, S., & Juvonen, J. (2002). Ethnicity, peer harassment, and adjustment in middle school: An exploratory study. *Journal of Early Adolescence, 22,* 173–199.

Graham, S., Taylor, A., & Hudley, C. (1998). Exploring achievement values among ethnic minority early adolescents. *Journal of Educational Psychology, 91,* 606–620.

Grant, H., & Dweck, C. S. (2001). Cross-cultural response to failure: Considering outcome attributions with different goals. In F. Salili, C. Y. Chiu, & Y. Y. Hong (Eds.), *Student motivation: The culture and context of learning* (pp. 203–247). New York: Kluwer Academic/Plenum.

Grant, H., & Dweck, C. (2003). Clarifying achievement goals and their impact. *Journal of Personality and Social Psychology, 85,* 541–553.

Greenfield, P. M., & Cocking, R. R. (1994). *Cross-cultural roots of minority child development.* Hillsdale, NJ: Erlbaum.

Gutman, L. M. (2006). How student and parent goal orientations and classroom goal structures influence the math achievement of African Americans during the high school transition. *Contemporary Educational Psychology, 31,* 44–63.

Heath, S. B. (1990). The children of Trackton's children: Spoken and written language in social change. In J. W. Stigler, R. A. Shweder, & G. Herdt (Eds.), *Cultural psychology: Essays on comparative human development* (pp. 426–520). New York: Cambridge University Press.

Hess, R. D., Chang, C. M., & McDevitt, T. M. (1987). Cultural variations in family beliefs about children's performance in mathematics:

Comparisons among People's Republic of China, Chinese-American, and Caucasian-American families. *Journal of Educational Psychology, 79,* 179–188.

Higgins, E. T. (1987). Self-discrepancy: A theory relating self and affect. *Psychological Review, 94,* 319–340.

Hogg, M. A. (2005). Fringe dwellers: Processes of deviance and marginalization in groups. In D. Abrams, M. A. Hogg, & J. M. Marques (Eds.), *The social psychology of inclusion and exclusion* (pp. 191–210). New York: Psychology Press.

Holloway, S. D. (1988). Concepts of ability and effort in Japan and the United States. *Review of Educational Research, 58,* 327–345.

Iyengar, S. S., & Lepper, M. R. (1991). Rethinking the value of choice: A cultural perspective on intrinsic motivation. *Journal of Personality and Social Psychology, 76,* 349–366.

Jaret, C. (1995). *Contemporary racial and ethnic relations.* New York: HarperCollins College.

Jodl, K. M., Michael, A., Malanchuk, O., Wong, E., Eccles, J. S., & Sameroff, A. (2001). Parents' role in shaping early adolescents' occupational aspirations. *Child Development, 72,* 1247–1265.

Jussim, L. (1989). Teacher expectations: Self-fulfilling prophecies, perceptual biases, and accuracy. *Journal of Personality and Social Psychology, 57,* 469–480.

Kagitcibasi, C. (1996). The autonomous-relational self: A new synthesis. *European Psychologist, 1,* 180–186.

Kagitcibasi, C., Sunar, D., & Bekman, S. (1988). *Comprehensive school education project: Final report.* Ottawa, Ontario: IRDC.

Kahneman, D. (2003). A perspective on judgment and choice: Mapping bounded rationality. *American Psychologist, 58,* 697–720.

Kaplan, A., & Maehr, M. L. (1999). Achievement goals and student well-being. *Contemporary Educational Psychology, 24,* 330–358.

Karabenick, S. A., & Newman, R. S. (Eds.). (2006). *Help seeking in academic settings: Goals, groups, and contexts.* Mahwah, NJ: Erlbaum.

Kim, C. (2004). Imagining race and nation in multiculturalist America. *Ethnic and Race Studies, 27,* 987–1005.

Kitano, H. H. (1981). Asian-Americans: The Chinese, Japanese, Koreans, Filipinos, and Southeast Asians. *Annals of the American Academy of Political and Social Science, 454,* 125–138.

Koestner, R., & Losier, G. F. (1996). Distinguishing reactive versus reflective autonomy. *Journal of Personality, 64,* 465–494.

Kumar, R. (2003). Multicultural education and achievement goal theory. In M. L. Maehr & P. R. Pintrich (Eds.), *Advances in motivation and achievement: Vol. 13. Motivating students, improving schools* (pp. 137–157). Greenwich, CT: Jai Press.

Kumar, R. (2005). The Asian Indian Hindu adolescent in America: Religious identity and the need to belong. In M. L. Maehr & S. Karabenick (Eds.), *Advances in motivation and achievement: Vol. 14. Religion and motivation* (pp. 347–371). Greenwich, CT: Jai Press.

Kumar, R. (2006). Students' experiences of home-school dissonance: The role of school academic culture and perceptions of classroom goal structures. *Contemporary Educational Psychology, 31,* 253–279.

Kumar, R., & Maehr, M. L. (2007). Cultural interpretations of achievement motivation: A situated perspective. In F. Salili (Ed.), *Culture, motivation and learning: a multicultural perspective* (pp. 43–66). Charlotte, NC: Information Age Publishing, Inc.

Kumar, R., O'Malley, P. M., & Johnston, L. D. (2004). Policies and practices regarding alcohol and illicit drugs among American secondary schools and their association with student alcohol and marijuana use. *Youth, Education, and Society* (Occasional Paper No. 5). Ann Arbor, MI: Institute for Social Research.

Ladson-Billings. G. (2006). From the achievement gap to the education debt: Understanding achievement in U.S. schools. *Educational Researcher, 35,* 3–12.

Lafromboise, T., Coleman, H. L. K., & Gerton, J. (1993). Psychological impact of biculturalism: Evidence and theory. *Psychological Bulletin, 114,* 395–412.

La Guardia, J. G., Ryan, R. M., Couchman, C., & Deci, E. L. (2000). Within-person variations in attachment style and their relations to psychological need satisfaction. *Journal of Personality and Social Psychology, 79,* 367–384.

Lamborn, S. D., Mounts, N. S., Steinberg, L., & Dornbusch, S. M. (1991). Patterns of competence and adjustment among adolescents from authoritative, authoritarian, indulgent, and neglectful families. *Child Development, 62,* 1049–1065.

LeCompte, M. D., & Dworkin, A. G. (1991). *Giving up on school: Student dropouts and student burnouts.* Newbury Park, CA: Corwin Press.

Lee, S. J. (1996). *Unraveling the "model minority" stereotype: Listening to Asian American youth.* New York: Teachers College Press.

Lew, J. (2004). The "other" story of model minorities: Korean American high school dropouts in an urban context. *Anthropology & Education Quarterly 35,* 303–323.

Lew, J. (2006). Burden of acting neither white nor black: Asian American identities and achievement in urban schools. *The Urban Review, 38,* 335–352.

Lewin, K., Dembo, T., Festinger, L., & Sears, P. S. (1944). Level of aspiration. In J. Hunt (Ed.), *Personality and behavior disorders* (pp. 333–378). New York: Ronald Press.

Lin, C. Y. C., & Fu, V. R. (1990). A comparison of child rearing among Chinese, immigrant, Chinese, and Caucasian American parents. *Child Development, 61,* 429–433.

Locke, E. A., & Latham, G. P. (1990). *A theory of goal setting and task performance.* Englewood Cliffs, NJ: Prentice-Hall.

Madon, S., Jussim, L., & Eccles, J. (1997). In search of the powerful self-fulfilling prophecy. *Journal of Personality and Social Psychology, 72,* 791–809.

Maehr, M. L. (1984). Meaning and motivation: Toward a theory of personal investment. In C. Ames & R. Ames (Eds.), *Research on motivation in education* (pp. 115–144). New York: Academic Press.

Maehr, M. L., & Midgley, C. (1991). Enhancing student motivation: A school-wide approach. *Educational Psychologist, 26,* 399–427.

Maehr, M. L., & Midgley, C. (1996). *Transforming school cultures.* Boulder, CO: Westview.

Markus, H. R., & Kitiyama, S. (1991). Culture and self: Implications for cognition, emotion, and motivation. *Psychological Review, 98,* 224–253.

Markus, H., & Nurius, P. (1986). Possible selves. *American Psychologist, 41,* 954–969.

Markus, H., & Ruvolo, A. (1989). *Possible selves: Personalized representations of goals.* Hillsdale, NJ: Erlbaum.

Matute-Bianchi, M. E. (1986). Ethnic identities and patterns of school success and failure among Mexican-descent and Japanese–American students in a California high school: An ethnographic analysis. *American Journal of Education, 95,* 233–255.

McClelland, D., Atkinson, J. W., Clark, R. A., & Lowell, E. L. (1953). *The achievement motive.* New York: Appleton-Century Crofts.

Meece, J. L. (1991). The classroom context and students' motivational goals. In M. L. Maehr & P. Pintrich (Eds.), *Advances in motivation and achievement* (Vol. 7, pp. 261–286). Greenwich, CT: JAI Press.

Meece, J. L., Anderman, E. M., & Anderman, L. H. (2006). Classroom goal structure, student motivation, and academic achievement. *Annual Review of Psychology, 57,* 487–503.

Meece, J. L., Blumenfeld, P. C., & Hoyle, R. (1988). Students' goal orientations and cognitive engagement in classroom activities. *Journal of Educational Psychology, 80,* 514–523.

Mickelson, R. A. (1990). The attitude-achievement paradox among Black adolescents. *Sociology of Education, 63,* 44–61.

Middleton, M., & Midgley, C. (1997). Avoiding the demonstration of the lack of ability: An under-explored aspect of goal theory. *Journal of Educational Psychology, 89,* 710–718.

Midgley, C. (1993). Motivation and middle level schools. In P. Pintrich & M. L. Maehr (Eds.), *Advances in motivation and achievement: Vol. 8. Motivation in the adolescent years* (pp. 219–276). Greenwich, CT: JAI.

Midgley, C., Anderman, E. M., & Hicks, L. (1995). Difference between elementary and middle school teachers and students: A goal theory approach. *Journal of Early Adolescence, 15,* 90–113.

Midgley, C., Arunkumar, R., & Urdan, T. (1996). "If I don't do well tomorrow, there's a reason." Predictors of the use of self-handicapping strategies in middle school. *Journal of Educational Psychology, 3,* 323–334.

Midgley, C., Kaplan, A., & Middleton, M. (2001). Performance approach goals: Good for what, for whom, and under what circumstances, and at what cost? *Journal of Educational Psychology, 93,* 77–86.

Midgley, C., & Urdan. T. (2001). Academic self-handicapping and achievement goals: A further examination. *Contemporary Educational Psychology, 26,* 61–75.

Misra, G., & Agarwal, R. (1985). The meaning of achievement: Implication for a cross-cultural theory of achievement motivation. In I. R. Lagunes & Y. H. Poortinga (Eds.), *From a different perspective: Studies of behavior across culture.* (pp. 250–276). Amsterdam, the Netherlands: Swets & Zeitlinger.

Montreuil, A., & Bourhis, R. Y. (2001). Majority acculturation orientations toward "valued" and "devalued" immigrants. *Journal of Cross-Cultural Psychology, 32,* 698–719.

Munro G., & Midford, R. (2001). "Zero tolerance" and drug education in Australia. *Drug and Alcohol Review, 20,* 105–109.

Newman B. M., & Newman, P. R. (2001). Group identity and alienation: Giving the we its due. *Journal of Youth and Adolescence, 30,* 515–538.

Nicholls, J. G. (1984). Achievement motivation: Conceptions of ability, subjective experience, task choice, and performance. *Psychological Review, 91,* 328–346.

Nieto, S. (2002). *Language, culture, and teaching: Cultural perspectives for a new century.* Mahwah, NJ: Erlbaum.

No Child Left Behind Act. (2001). Retrieved January 19, 2010, from U.S. Department of Education website: http://www.ed.gov/policy/elsec/leg/esea02/107-110.pdf

Oakes, J. (1985). *Keeping track: How schools structure inequality.* New Haven, CT: Yale University Press.

Oakes, J., Selvin, M. J., Karoly, L., & Guiton, G. (1991). *Educational matchmaking: Toward a better understanding of curriculum and tracking decisions.* Santa Monica, CA: Rand.

O'Connor, C. (1999). Race, class, and gender in America: Narratives of opportunity among low-income African American youths. *Sociology of Education, 72,* 137–157.

Ogbu, J. U. (1987). Variability in minority school performance: A problem in search of an explanation. *Anthropology and Education Quarterly, 18,* 312–334.

Okagaki, L. (2001). Triarchic model of minority children's school achievement, *Educational Psychologist, 36,* 9–20.

Okagaki, L., & Frensch, P. A. (1998). Parenting and children's schooling achievement: A multiethnic perspective. *American Educational Research Journal, 35,* 123–144.

Osborne, J. W., & Walker, C (2006). Stereotype threat, identification with academics, and withdrawal from school: Why the most successful students of color might be most likely to withdraw. *Educational Psychology, 26,* 563.

Oyserman, C., Bybee, D., Terry, K., & Hart-Johnson, T. (2004). Possible selves as road maps. *Journal of Research on Personality, 38,* 130–149.

Oyserman, D., Coon, H. M., & Kemmelmeier, M. (2002). Rethinking individualism and collectivism. Evaluation of theoretical assumptions and meta-analyses. *Psychological Bulletin, 128,* 3–72.

Parke, R. D., & Buriel, R. (2006). Socialization in the family: Ethnic and ecological perspectives. In R. M. Lerner & W. Damon (Series Eds.) & R. M. Lerner (Vol. Ed.), *Handbook of child psychology: Vol. 1. Theoretical models of development* (6th ed., pp. 429–504). New York: Wiley.

Pearce, R. R. (2006). Effects of cultural and social structural factors on the achievement of White and Chinese American students at school transition points. *American Educational Research Journal, 43,* 75–101.

Phelan, P. K., Davidson, A. L., & Yu, H. C. (1998). *Adolescents' worlds: Negotiating family, peer, and school.* New York: Teachers College Press.

Phinney, J. S. (2003). *Ethnic identity and acculturation.* Washington, DC: American Psychological Association.

Phinney, J. S., Chavira, V., & Tate, J. D. (1996). The effect of ethnic threat on ethnic self-concept and own group ratings. *Journal of Social Psychology, 133*, 469–478.

Pintrich, R. R. (2000). Multiple goals, multiple pathways: The role of goal orientation in learning and achievement. *Journal of Educational Psychology, 92*, 544–555.

Pintrich, P. R., & Schunk, D. H. (2000). *Motivation in education: Theory, research, and applications* (2nd ed.). Upper Saddle River, NJ: Merrill-Prentice Hall.

Pintrich, P. R., & Zusho, A. (2001). The development of academic self-regulation: The role of cognitive and motivational factors. In A. Wigfield & J. S. Eccles (Eds.), *Development of achievement motivation* (pp. 250–284). Orlando, FL: Academic Press.

Portes, A., & Rumbaut, R. G. (2001). *Legacies: The story of immigrant second generations.* Berkeley: University of California Press.

Portes, A., & Zhou, M. (1993). The new second generation: Segmented assimilation and its variants. *Annals of the American Academy of Political and Social Science, 530*, 74–96.

Reese, L., & Gallimore, R. (2000). Immigrant Latinos' cultural model of literacy development: An evolving perspective on home-school discontinuities. *American Journal of Education, 108*, 103–134.

Reyna, C. (2000). Lazy, dumb, or industrious: When stereotypes convey attribution information in the classroom. *Educational Psychology Review, 12*, 85–110.

Rist, R. (2000). HER classic: Student social class and teacher expectations: The self-fulfilling prophecy in ghetto education. *Harvard Educational Review, 70*, 257–301.

Roeser, R., Midgley, C., & Urdan, T. (1996). Perceptions of the school psychological environment and early adolescents' psychological and behavioral functioning in school: The mediating role of goals and belonging. *Journal of Educational Psychology, 88*, 402–422.

Rowley, S. J., Sellers, R. M., Chavous, T. M., & Smith, M. A. (1998). The relationship between racial identity and self-esteem in African American college and high school students. *Journal of Personality and Social Psychology, 74*, 715–724.

Rumbaut, R. G. (1997) Assimilation and its discontents: Between rhetoric and reality. *International Migration Review, 31*, 923–960.

Rumberger, R. W., & Larson, K. A. (1998). Toward explaining differences in educational achievement among Mexican American language minority student. *Sociology of Education, 71*, 68–93.

Ryan, M. R. (2001). The peer group as a context of development of young adolescent motivation and achievement. *Child Development, 72*, 1135–1150.

Ryan, A. R., & Pintrich, P. R. (1997). Should I ask for help? The role of motivation and attitude in adolescents' help-seeking in math class. *Journal of Educational Psychology, 89*, 329–341.

Ryan, R. M., & Deci, E. L. (2000). Self-determination theory and facilitation of intrinsic motivation, social development, and well-being. *American Psychologist, 55*, 68–78.

Salili, F. (1996). Learning and motivation: An Asian perspective. *Psychology and Developing Societies, 8*, 55–81.

Saraswathi, T. S., & Ganapathy, H. (2002). The Hindu world view of child and human development: Reflections in contemporary parental ethnotheories. In H. Keller, Y. Poortinga, & A. Scholmerich (Eds.), *Between biology and culture: Perspectives on ontogenetic development* (pp. 79–88). Cambridge, England: Cambridge University Press.

Schemander, T. (2002). Gender identification moderates stereotype threat effects on women's math performance. *Journal of Experimental Social Psychology 38*, 194–201.

Schneider, B., & Lee, Y. (1990). A model of academic success: The school and home environment of East Asian students. *Anthropology and Education Quarterly, 21*, 358–377.

Sellers, R. M., Caldwell, C. H., Schmeelk-Cone, K. H., & Zimmerman, M. A. (2003). Racial identity, racial discrimination, perceived stress, and psychological distress among African American young adults. *Journal of Health and Social Behavior, 43*, 302–317.

Skaalvik, E. M. (1997). Self-enhancing and self-defeating ego orientation: Relations with task and avoidance orientation, achievement, self-perceptions, and anxiety. *Journal of Educational Psychology, 89*, 71–81.

Sleeter, C. E. (2001). Preparing teachers for culturally diverse schools: Research and the overwhelming presence of Whiteness. *Journal of Teacher Education, 52*, 94–123.

Smith, A. E., Jussim, L., Eccles, J., VanNoy, M., Madon, S., & Palumbo, P. (1998). Self-fulfilling prophecies, perceptual biases, and accuracy at the individual and group levels. *Journal of Experimental Social Psychology, 3*, 530–561.

Spencer, M. B. (1999). Social and cultural influenced on school adjustment: The application of an identity-focused cultural perspective. *Educational Psychologist, 34*, 43–57.

Spencer, M. B., Noll, E., Stoltzfus, J., & Harpalini, V. (2001). Identity and school adjustment: Revisiting the "acting White" hypothesis. *Educational Psychologist, 36*, 21–30.

Steele, C. M. (1997). A threat in the air: How stereotypes shape intellectual identity and performance. *American Psychologist 52*, 613–629.

Steele, C. M., & Aronson, J. (1995). Stereotype threat and the intellectual test performance of African Americans. *Journal of Personality and Social Psychology, 69*, 797–811.

Stevenson H. W., & Lee, S. Y. (1990). *Contexts of achievement* (Vol. 55). Chicago, IL: University of Chicago Press.

Suarez-Orozco, M., & Paez, M. (2002). *Latinos: Remaking America.* Berkeley: University of California Press.

Suarez-Orozco, C., & Suarez-Orozco, M. M. (2002). *Children of immigration.* Cambridge, MA: Harvard University Press.

Sue, S., & Kitano, H. L. (1973). Stereotypes as a measure of success. *Journal of Social Issues, 29*, 83–98.

Szapocznik, J., & Kurtines, W. M. (1993). Family psychology and cultural diversity: Opportunities for theory, research, and application. *American Psychologist, 48*, 400–407.

Tajfel, H. (1978). *Differentiation between social groups: Studies on social psychology of intergroup relations.* London: Academic Press.

Tajfel, H., & Turner, J. C. (1979). An integrative theory of intergroup conflict. In W.G. Austin & S. Worschel (Eds.), *The social psychology of intergroup relations* (pp. 33–47). Monterrey, CA: Brooks/Cole.

Taylor, A. Z., & Graham, S. (2007). An examination of the relationship between achievement values and perceptions of barriers among low-SES African American and Latino Students. *Journal of Educational Psychology, 99*, 52–64.

Tesser, A. (2003). Self-evaluation. In M. A. Leary & J. P. Tanjney, (2003). *Handbook of self and identity* (pp. 275–290). New York: Guilford.

Tharp, R. (1989). Psychocultural variables and constants: Effects on teaching and learning in schools. *American Psychologist, 44*, 349–359.

Thomas, D., Townsend, T., & Belgrave, F. (2003). The influence of cultural and racial identification on the psychosocial adjustment of inner-city African American children in school. *American Journal of Community Psychology, 32*, 217–228.

Triandis, H. C. (1972). *The analysis of subjective culture.* New York: Wiley.

Trueba, H. T. (1988). Culturally based explanations of minority students' academic achievement. *Anthropology and Education Quarterly, 19*, 270–287.

Tseng, V. (2006). Unpacking immigration in youths' academic and occupational pathways. *Child Development, 77*, 1434–1445.

Turner, J. C., Thorpe, P. K., & Meyer, M. K. (1998). Students' report of motivation and negative affect: A theoretical and empirical analysis. *Journal of Educational Psychology, 90*, 758–771.

Twenge, J. M., Baumeister, R. F., Tice, D. M., & Stueke, T. S. (2001). If you can't join them beat them: Effects of social exclusion on aggressive behavior. *Journal of Personality and Social Psychology, 81*, 1058–1069.

Twenge, J. M., Catanese, K. R., & Baumeister, R. F. (2002). Social exclusion causes self-defeating behavior. *Journal of Personality and Social Psychology, 83*, 606–615.

Urdan, T. C., & Maehr, M. L. (1995). Beyond a two-goal theory of motivation and achievement: A case for social goals. *Review of Educational Research, 65*, 213–243.

Waters, M. C. (1999). *Black identities: West Indian immigrant dreams and American realiti*es. New York; Cambridge, MA: Russell Sage Foundation/Harvard University Press.

Waters, M. C., & Eschbach, K. (1995). Immigration and ethnic and racial inequality in the United States. *Annual Review of Sociology, 21,* 419–446.

Waters, M. C., & Jimenez, T. R. (2005). Assessing immigrant assimilation: New empirical and theoretical challenges. *Annual Review of Sociology, 31,* 105–125.

Weiner, B. (1985). An attribution theory of achievement motivation and emotion. *Psychological Review, 92,* 548–573.

Weisner, T. S., Gallimore, R., & Jordan, C. (1988). Unpackaging cultural effects on classroom learning: Native Hawaiian peer assistance and child-generated activity. *Anthropology and Education Quarterly, 19,* 327–252.

Wentzel, K. R. (1989). Adolescent classroom goals, standards of performance, and academic achievement: An interactionist perspective. *Journal of Educational Psychology, 81,* 131–142.

Wentzel, K. R. (1994). Relation of social goal pursuit to social acceptance, and perceived social support, *Journal of Educational Psychology, 86,* 173–182.

Wentzel, K. R. (2003). Sociometric status and adjustment in middle school: A longitudinal study. *Journal of Early Adolescence, 23,* 5–28.

Wigfield, A., & Eccles J. (1992). The development of achievement task values: A theoretical analysis. *Developmental Review, 12,* 265–310.

Wigfield, A., & Eccles, J. S. (2000). Expectancy-value theory of motivation. *Contemporary Educational Psychology, 25,* 68–81.

Wigfield, A., & Eccles, J. S. (2001). The development of competence beliefs, expectancies for success, and achievement values from childhood through adolescence. In A. Wigfield & J. S. Eccles (Eds.), *Development of achievement motivation* (pp. 92–120). Orlando, FL: Academic Press.

Winston, C., Eccles, J. S., Senior, A. M., & Vida, M. (1997). The utility of an expectancy/value model of achievement for understanding academic performance and self-esteem of African-American and European

American adolescents. *Zeitschrift Fur Padagogische Psychologie, 11,* 177–186.

Wolters, C. (2003). Understanding procrastination from a self-regulated learning perspective. *Journal of Educational Psychology, 95,* 179–187.

Wolters, C. A. (2004). Advancing achievement goal theory: Using goal structures and goal orientations to predict students' motivation, cognition, and achievement. *Journal of Educational Psychology 96,* 236–250.

Wong, C. A., Eccles, J. & Sameroff, A. (2003). The influence of ethnic discrimination and ethnic identification on African American adolescents; school adjustment and emotional adjustment. *Journal of Personality, 71,* 1197–1232.

Wright, R. A., & Brehm, J. W. (1989). Energization and goal attractiveness. In L. A. Pervin (Ed.), *Goal concepts in personality and social psychology* (pp. 77–92). Hillsdale, NJ: Erlbaum.

Zhou, M. (1997). Segmented assimilation: Issues, controversies and recent research on the new second generation. *International Migration Review, 31,* 975–1008.

Zhou, M., & Bankston, C. L. III (1998). *Growing up American: How Vietnamese children adapt to life in the United States.* New York: Russell Sage Foundation.

Zhou, M., & Xiang, Y. S. (2005). The multifaceted American experiences of the children of Asian immigrants: Lessons for segmented assimilation. *Ethnic and Racial Studies, 28,* 1119–1152.

Zine, J. (2001). Muslim youth in Canadian schools: Education and the politics of religious identity. *Anthropology and Education Quarterly, 32,* 399–423.

Zusho, A. (2004). *Culture, self, and goals: An investigation into the motivational processes of bicultural Asian American and Anglo American college students* (Unpublished doctoral dissertation). University of Michigan, Ann Arbor.

Zusho, A., Pintrich, P. R., & Cortina. K. S. (2005). Motives, goals, and adaptive patterns of performance in Asian American and Anglo American students. *Learning and Individual Differences, 15,* 141–158.

# Part VI

**School Organization and Educational Policy**

# 20

# Issues in Studying the Effects of Retaining Students with High-Stakes Promotion Tests

## *Findings from Chicago*

ELAINE ALLENSWORTH AND JENNY NAGAOKA

The practice of retaining students in grade has changed dramatically over the past two decades. Traditionally, the decision to hold students back was made by teachers and parents about individual students, based on a holistic appraisal of the child's school performance. Beginning in the 1980s, the accountability movement brought a dramatic shift in the practice of grade retention. Increasingly, policies at the state and district levels mandated grade retention for students who failed to meet specific criteria for promotion.[1] Grade retention under such conditions is on a much larger scale, and is qualitatively different from traditional grade retention. In this chapter, we discuss what is known about traditional and mandated retention and the issues involved in studying their short- and long-term academic and social outcomes.[2]

## The Rationale behind Retention

The traditional structure of elementary schools in the United States organizes students in grades by their age. Students are promoted based on completion of a year of school, rather than mastery of academic skills. There have always been exceptions to this pattern—students singled out to repeat or skip a grade based on particularly low or high academic skills and other criteria such as social maturity, absenteeism, and behavior (Alexander, Entwisle, & Dauber, 1994; Dauber, Alexander, & Entwisle, 1993; Jimerson, Carlson, Rotert, Egeland, & Sroufe, 1997; Smith & Shepard, 1988). In fact, it is estimated that about one-third of students are retained at some point in school.[3] Yet, under traditional retention, students are usually held back no more than once before high school. Thus, while 30% of students have ever been retained, each year the vast majority of students (about 95%) are promoted to the subsequent grade despite wide differences in ability and maturity. The practice of promoting students despite weak academic skills has been termed *social promotion*, and it has been widely criticized.

Social promotion is seen as having a number of negative consequences for students and for society.[4] Many people believe that because students are promoted for simply persisting through a grade, the practice provides little incentive to work hard and learn expected skills and knowledge. Colleges and businesses have pointed to social promotion as one of the main reasons high school graduates lack adequate preparation and require remedial training. Retaining students in grade until they master defined skills seems an obvious solution. It is generally seen as preferable to social promotion by both teachers and the public (Byrnes, 1989; Byrnes & Yamamoto, 1986; Christman & Pugh, 1989; Johnson, Arumi, & Ott, 2006; Tomchin & Impara, 1992).

Grade retention is generally viewed as a response to academic problems, giving students more time to mature and learn the skills expected at their grade level. Advocates note that students struggle in subsequent grades if they have not learned expected skills. They also suggest there may be social–emotional benefits to an extra year in grade; by allowing students to raise their skills relative to their peers, it may improve their self-concept (Finlayson, 1977; Gottfredson, Fink, & Graham, 1994; Pierson & Connell, 1992; Plummer & Graziano, 1987; Scott & Ames, 1969; Tomchin & Impara, 1992). It may also allow students time to mature physically, emotionally, and socially, which could prevent social and learning problems later on (Graue & DiPerna, 2000; Karweit, 1991; May & Welch, 1984; Novak, 1965).

## Concerns about Retention

Promoting students with weak academic skills is perceived as problematic by both school practitioners and the general public; however, educational researchers have voiced great concern about the consequences of retaining students in grade (American Educational Research Association, 2000; Heubert & Hauser, 1999; House, 1998; McCoy & Reynolds, 1999; National Association of School Psychologists, 2003; Reynolds, 1992). Many of their concerns focus on students' social-emotional well-being, although there are also concerns about its effectiveness at improving students' academic skills and its adverse effects on high school graduation. In addition, there are concerns about the fairness of the practice, as male, minority, and low-income students are disproportionately affected (Cosden, Zimmer, & Tuss, 1993; Jackson, 1975; Karweit, 1999; Mantzicolopos, 2003; Mantzicolopos, Morrison, Hinshaw, & Carte, 1989).

The most commonly expressed concern is that holding students back in grade for academic reasons can have negative affective consequences. The term *social promotion* implies that educators promote students with concern for their long-term social adjustment over their concern for educational progress. In fact, even teachers who believe that holding students back improves their long-term chances of academic success often worry that retention may have a negative impact on students' self-esteem (Byrnes, 1989; Jacob, Stone, & Roderick, 2004; Plummer & Graziano, 1987; Tomchin & Impara, 1992). Grade retention may stigmatize students in the eyes of their peers or teachers. Retained students are older than others in their class, and this may become increasingly problematic as students age and begin taking on adult responsibilities (Grissom & Shepard, 1989; Holmes & Saturday, 2000; Roderick, 1994). Retained students will have to stay in school a year longer than their age-mates, remaining in school while peers enter adult roles. For these reasons, there is concern that retention leads students to be more likely to drop out of school.

Furthermore, there is doubt about the degree to which retaining students in grade actually leads to stronger academic growth. While it does provide students with an additional year of instruction—if students remain in school through graduation—retention may slow down the pace of students' academic progress. It may be easier for students to master repeated material, but they may learn more if exposed to higher-level material in the subsequent grade. As discussed below, research on the academic effects of retention is contradictory, in part, because of conflicting views about what retention should do—improve the rate of learning, improve students' achievement relative to their peers, or simply provide an extra year of education.

***Issues Surrounding Promotion Standards and Grade Retention*** Recently, policies that mandate retention have emerged out of the movement for schools to be more accountable for student learning and do something about low achievement and lax standards (Byrnes, 1989; Labaree, 1984). These policies provide a mechanism for school districts to appear responsive to poor student performance. Standards for promotion can be implemented quickly and at a low short-term cost, even though the long-term costs are estimated to be high (Alexander et al., 1994; Center for Policy Research in Education [CPRE], 1990). The call for ending social promotion had reached the highest levels of government; in the late 1990s—President Clinton urged in his 1997 State of the Union address that schools use tests to make promotion decisions (Clinton, 1998).

Promotion standards are based on the rationale that students should progress only if they have mastered the skills expected at their grade level. By setting standards and signaling that achievement matters, policymakers hope that students will work harder and teachers and parents will pay attention to the needs of the lowest-performing students (Schwager, Mitchell, Mitchell, & Hecht, 1992). With the right test, alignment of course content should also lead to better exposure of students to appropriate material, providing greater opportunity to learn (Cohen, 1996; Darling-Hammond, 1996). These last benefits should accrue to students regardless of whether they are retained in grade by the standards. All students should experience positive effects in terms of motivation, alignment of the curriculum, and readiness to learn in the testing grade.

Unlike teacher-initiated retention decisions, which are generally based on multiple indicators of students' maturity and performance, promotion criteria generally include no more than a few indicators of performance. Often, single scores on standardized tests are used. Such tests provide a clear criterion for promotion, and a clear standard towards which students and teachers can strive. However, there is concern about the appropriateness of the use of standardized tests to make retention decisions. There are also concerns regarding adverse effects on classroom instruction and on student engagement that arise with policy-mandated retention.

Reliance on one measure of performance, instead of a holistic appraisal of a student, has inherent problems with respect to fairness and appropriateness. Using one test score to evaluate a student's learning will always have measurement error. Thus, when a single test is used to determine a promotion decision, some students will be retained despite having the requisite skills, and others will be promoted despite lacking them. However, most of the students incorrectly promoted or retained because of measurement error will have true skills that are close to the test-score cutoff, and second-chance testing may reduce the occurrence of inappropriate retention. More problematic is that retention decisions are based only on the skills being tested. Students who are adept in other areas, be it other subject areas or social maturity levels, will be required to repeat them because they were lacking the specific skills being tested for grade promotion. The use of test scores as promotion criteria is particularly complicated for students eligible for special education or bilingual services.[5] For these reasons, the practice of using single test scores for promotion decisions has been widely condemned by national education organizations and research review panels as a misuse of testing (American Educational Research Association, 2000; National Association of School Psychologists, 2003).

In addition, using test scores as promotion criteria may have an adverse impact on classroom instruction. In their efforts to help more students reach the criteria, teachers may spend more time on test preparation and on the specific skills students need to pass the test. As a result, these policies may result in significant narrowing of the curriculum and less focus on intellectually challenging work (Au, 2007; Bryk, 2003; Linn, 1993; Madaus, 1988; Mehrens, 1998; Newmann, Bryk, & Nagaoka, 2001). Research on test-based accountability generally finds that teachers react to accountability programs by altering their content coverage and assessment methods so that they are aligned with the test, and that they increase time on test preparation (Darling-Hammond & Wise, 1985; Firestone, Mayrowetz, & Fairman, 1998; Jones, Jones, & Hardin, 1999; Koretz, Barron, Mitchell, & Stecher, 1996; McNeil & Valenzuela, 2001; Rosenholtz, 1987; Smith, 1991; Urdan & Paris, 1994). While some students may benefit from the narrowing of focus, the impact of any changes in instruction and curriculum affect all students, even those not at risk of retention.

The high-stakes testing environment and the threat of retention may also have an impact on students' engagement in school. Low-achieving students may become disengaged if they feel that the promotional standards are out of their reach (Betts & Costrell, 2001; Lee, Smith, Perry, & Smylie, 1999; Wheelock, Bebell, & Haney, 2000). The high-stakes testing environment may also have an effect on high-achieving students; by focusing attention on the lowest-achieving students and narrowing the curriculum, high-achieving students may become less challenged and less engaged in school.

Finally, there are concerns that such policies hold the wrong people accountable—children are accountable for their own performance, rather than their teachers or schools. The policies operate under the assumption that a primary reason for students' underperformance is a lack of motivation and effort, and that students will be able to respond to incentives to improve their performance. Because these policies do not address problems of poor instruction, or poor school capacity, opponents suggest that they are unlikely to have substantial long-term effects on achievement (Picklo & Christenson, 2005). Instead, they punish children that have the misfortune of attending a low-quality school or classroom.

## Methodological Issues in Research on Traditional Retention

Research on the effects of traditional retention on student achievement is abundant; there are also a substantial number of studies on its effects on educational attainment and social–emotional outcomes. However, there are conflicting views about the conclusions that can be drawn from this large body of work. The disagreement across studies arises, in part, because they use different methodologies or make different assumptions about how retention should affect student achievement. In addition, the effects of retention seem to depend on how it is implemented. For example, the grade level at which students are retained seems to matter, with the most positive effects documented in the upper-primary grades, and the most adverse effects found in the middle-school grades (Alexander et al., 1994; Holmes, 1989;

Holmes & Matthews, 1984; Jimerson, 2001). Estimates are more likely to be positive where there are support services for retained students, and seem to depend on preretention achievement and economic status (Holmes, 1989).

Three prominent meta-analyses by Holmes and Matthews (1984), Holmes (1989), and Jimerson (2001) each concluded that overall, the evidence showing adverse effects of retention on achievement and social–emotional outcomes greatly outweighed the evidence showing positive effects. Most scholars concur with this view; however, their work has been criticized for the overrepresentation of methodologically weak studies and their misinterpretation of the results of these studies (Alexander et al., 1994; Jimerson, 2001; Reynolds, 1992). Whether this criticism is valid has been the subject of considerable debate (Alexander et al., 1994; Hauser, 2001; Shepard, Smith, & Marion, 1996). Few studies on retention satisfactorily deal with the methodological problems inherent in this work.

Here, we identify three broad ways in which the research on retention differs in methods and assumptions. First, the point at which achievement effects are estimated depends on how retention as an intervention is framed—should retention be a strategy for improving learning, or for bringing students' achievement in line with grade-level norms? Researchers who believe the former compare retained students to same-age peers who have been promoted; those who believe the latter compare retained students to same-grade peers who started school a year later. The second methodological issue concerns the comparability of test scores and other student outcomes across grades and across ages. The third issue is the ability of researchers to construct adequate comparison groups of retained and promoted children without regard for selection bias. Very few studies address this issue satisfactorily.

***Same-Grade versus Same-Age Comparisons*** Most research on the effects of retention on academic achievement use one of two strategies for constructing comparison groups: same-grade comparisons or same-age comparisons. Each strategy addresses a different legitimate question. The same-grade comparisons tell us if retained students are performing closer to grade-level norms than they were before retention. The same-age comparisons tell us if retention has improved students' rate of learning.[6]

The same-grade studies compare students who are experiencing a grade for the second time with classmates who are experiencing it for the first time. This shows the effects of having an extra year of instruction as an intervention for underperforming students. If the goal of retention is to bring low-performing students' achievement closer to grade-level expectations, then this is the appropriate comparison. However, these comparisons will inevitably show positive retention effects on achievement. Indeed, it is hard to imagine that students' achievement would not improve with an entire year of additional instruction.[7] Thus, same-grade comparisons could be viewed as too easy of a standard for judging retention.

The same-age studies compare retained students to their promoted classmates who moved on to the next grade. This allows for the examination of the counterfactual—whether retained students would have learned at the same rate had they been promoted instead of repeating a grade. If they learn at a faster rate by being promoted, then the value of retention for learning is questionable. It suggests that the benefit seen with same-grade retention is simply a result of more instructional time, which is an intervention that does not have to include retention. But this comparison could also be viewed as unfair. Because the comparison group has been exposed to more advanced material than the retained group, it is difficult for the retained group to show equal skills. Students tend to show higher-level skills when exposed to higher-level material (Cohen, Raudenbush, & Ball, 2003; Natriello, Pallas, & Alexander, 1989; Stein & Lane, 1996). Thus, same-age comparisons tend to favor promotion. For this reason, same-age comparisons could be viewed as too difficult of a standard for judging retention.

### Problems with the Comparability of Outcome Indicators
A second problem in retention studies is the comparability of outcome indicators between students in different grades (for same-age comparisons), and students of different ages (for same-grade comparisons). Same-age comparisons of test scores are often affected by comparability issues across grades, particularly if tests are not equated across levels. For example, Chicago used the Iowa Tests of Basic Skills (ITBS) and, until 2002, used grade equivalents (GE) to make retention decisions. Across test-levels, comparability issues in the GE are particularly acute at the extremes of the score distribution. In general, students at the lower end of the distribution receive higher scores simply by taking a higher level of the test, leading to negative estimates of the effects of retention (Bryk, Thum, Easton, & Luppescu, 1998; Easton et al., 2000). In addition, course grading changes as students move across grades, and social–emotional outcomes are affected by changes in school structure as students move from elementary to middle to high school. Thus, comparison of students in different grades is problematic for these indicators. Within the same grade, a number of social–emotional outcomes are affected by age and maturity, making it difficult to disentangle the effects of retention versus the effects of age. In the higher grades, delinquent behaviors, course skipping, and dropout are more common among older students, making same-grade comparisons difficult. Even standardized tests can vary in their difficulty from one year to another, making same-grade comparisons problematic if current year scores are compared to scores in the previous year and test forms are not equated (Rosenkranz, 2002).

### Adequacy of Comparison Groups for Avoiding Selection Bias
Finally, studies differ in the extent to which they are able to address selection effects that bias estimates of retention. Many of the initial studies of retention, including those in the meta-analyses of Holmes, were severely limited by

their lack of a valid comparison group for retained students. Studies conducted more recently have been more sensitive to the need to construct adequate comparison groups and to estimate retention using statistical adjustments for prior differences between groups (e.g., Alexander et al., 1994; Peterson, DeGracie, & Ayabe, 1987; Reynolds, 1992). However, neither statistical adjustment for previous performance, nor matching on defined characteristics, may completely address selection. Measured characteristics alone might not explain why one student is retained and another is promoted. For example, teachers are more likely to retain students who have high absence rates, but high absence rates can lead to less learning and a higher likelihood of leaving school. Thus, absences can cause a spurious relationship between retention and learning or dropout. A multitude of other factors could also cause spurious relationships (e.g., poor social or emotional skills, low motivation, family disruption), leading to difficulty in establishing a causal relationship between retention and academic outcomes.

One particularly salient issue in constructing the comparison group arises from the time point at which initial comparisons are made. Many studies only compare student outcomes in the years after retention. This assumes that the retained and comparison groups were equal to begin with on the outcome measure. If there was already a gap in the outcome measure prior to retention, as there often is, this difference would be falsely attributed to retention. An alternative is to construct the control groups based on initial levels of the outcome, for example, in the year prior to retention. Alternatively, one could look for changes in the gap between retained and comparison students after retention, compared to their levels prior to retention. However, these techniques may introduce bias into estimates because of regression to the mean. Students tend to be retained after a bad year, and we would expect that they would follow that particularly poor performance with a better year.[8] This "rebound" after a particularly bad year would then be misinterpreted as a benefit of retention. An alternative would be to compare students on the indicator for several years prior to retention. However, this is generally not feasible, especially when looking at early-grade retention.

### Some Consistent Findings about the Effects of Traditional Retention
Much of the existing research on traditional retention suffers from these inherent methodological issues, so it does not provide a clear answer about whether retention is beneficial or harmful. However, there are some consistent findings. It seems that the effects of retention depend on context, including the grade level at which retention occurred, the degree to which retention was a common practice in the grade, and the availability of supplemental supports (although these effects may be confounded with those of retention). Retention does not seem to increase students' rate of learning—same-age comparisons consistently show either no effects or adverse effects of retention on achievement growth. However, retention does change the comparison group to younger students, which can be

beneficial for students' grades and confidence. By providing extra instructional time, retained students are brought closer to grade-level performance in the retained year. However, this achievement boost diminishes over time, so that several years after being retained, retained students' achievement is again well below grade-level expectations (Alexander et al., 1994; Holmes, 1989; Jimerson et al., 1997; Mantzico-poulos & Morrison, 1992; Peterson et al., 1987). There is also consistency in conclusions about retention effects on educational attainment—retained students are more likely to drop out of school before graduation than students who are not retained in grade (Alexander, Entwisle, & Dauber, 2003; Alexander, Entwisle, & Horsey, 1997; Alexander, Entwisle, & Kabbani, 2001; Allensworth, 2005a; Grissom & Shepard, 1989; House, 1998; Jimerson, 1999, 2001; Roderick, 1994; Rumberger, 1995).

## Research on Policy-Mandated Retention versus Traditional Retention

The vast majority of research on retention is on traditional, teacher-initiated retention. This research may not be applicable to retention under high-stakes testing because of the different context in which grade retention occurs. Both the basis of the retention decision, and students' experiences with retention, are qualitatively different. In addition, the research focus should be broader when studying the effects of policy-mandated retention because of its potential effects on nonretained students.

While individual teachers may use test scores to make decisions about retaining students in grade under traditional retention, their decisions are based on many additional sources of information, such as student attendance, grades and behavior, and are likely to be more subjective, based on their own attitudes about retention and their perceptions of the student. With high-stakes testing, decisions are based on an objective criterion, usually test scores. Thus, the retention decision under high-stakes testing may be less appropriate for the child because it does not consider a broad range of indicators about that student. Yet, because the retention criterion is explicit and objective, policy-mandated retention might also be more equitable than traditional retention which tends to incorporate teachers' biases, and results in higher retention rates among males and racial/ethnic minorities.[9]

The experience of retention itself may also be quite different when mandated, compared to traditional retention, both in terms of its social–psychological effects on students, and the instructional responses of teachers and schools. For example, the explicit criteria for promotion under high-stakes testing might lead students to internalize failure more when retained, rather than blaming their school or teacher. This might lead to a lower academic self-concept, but it also may lead them to be more open to instructional help. Alternatively, with mandated retention, students may be less likely to feel singled out or unfairly punished. If retention is relatively common in a school, the stigma associated with being held back may not be as strong. In terms of instructional responses, teachers may be more likely to tailor instruction to a group of retained students than they would to a single retained student. Thus, when we study mandated retention, we need to consider the specific context in which the retention occurred; this could vary considerably across different schools and teachers.

Besides taking into account the different contexts of mandated retention, the research focus should be broader when studying the effects of retention under high-stakes testing versus teacher-initiated retention. Retention under high-stakes testing is part of a larger strategy and its effects are not expected to occur just with the students retained (Caterall, 1989; Mehrens, 1998; Roderick & Engel, 2001). All students may be motivated to work harder under the threat of grade retention. Likewise, all students will be affected by changes in teacher behavior associated with pressure to prepare students to pass the high-stakes test. Both of these effects should be seen in grades that are subject to testing standards. Achievement should also improve in the grades that follow testing requirements, as they should contain fewer students with poor academic skills and require less time reviewing remedial material.

Policies mandating retention often include extended instructional time through tutoring, after school, or summer school programs for students who are at risk of being retained or who have been retained. This is a promising strategy; expanding learning opportunities has been linked to improved student achievement (Cooper, Nye, Kelly, Lindsay, & Greathouse, 1996; Cooper, Charlton, Valentine, & Muhlenbruck, 2000; Denham & Lieberman, 1980; Fisher & Berliner, 1985; Levin & Tsang, 1987; Smith, 1998). While these programs are an integral part of the policy, if research is considering the effect of the retained year rather than the policy as a whole, the effect of these supplemental programs should be measured independently of the retention experience. Simply comparing promoted students to students who were not only retained, but participated in additional interventions, could bias interpretation of the specific effects of retention.

Research on retention effects under high-stakes testing faces some of the same methodological issues as with traditional retention, including issues of same-age versus same-grade comparisons and problems of test equating. However, estimating a counterfactual and constructing control groups under high-stakes testing are problematic in different ways. Selection bias is much less problematic when studying mandated retention because of the objective criteria on which decisions are made. As long as the retention criteria are implemented consistently, there should be no spurious factors affecting the relationship of retention with student outcomes. However, because such policies could have motivational and instructional effects on all students, it is difficult to construct a counterfactual to policy retention; there is no comparison group that was not affected by the policy. In the rest of this chapter we demonstrate the ways in which we dealt with these issues to study retention under high-stakes testing in Chicago.

## The Policy to End Social Promotion in Chicago

In 1996, Chicago began an ambitious new initiative aimed at ending social promotion in the third, sixth and eighth grades. Promotional test-score cutoffs were based on grade equivalent (GE) scores on the Iowa Tests of Basic Skills (ITBS) in reading and math. Those students who did not meet the standard in the spring of the year were required to attend a very structured summer school program with small class sizes, focused on improving skills in reading and math so that students could pass the promotion standard (Roderick, Engel, & Nagaoka, 2003). At the end of summer, students were retested. Those who passed the test were promoted with their original cohort, and those who did not were retained. Besides summer school, Chicago also brought additional resources to retained students and students at-risk of being retained through an after-school tutoring program. Other than that, the district gave little structure to the retained year and left decisions about how to group retained students and develop instructional strategies to principals. Most students received few extra supports or alternative interventions (Stone, Engel, Nagaoka, & Roderick, 2005). Thus, in Chicago, the educational experience of retention amounted to going through the grade a second time.

While a clear theory of action underlying the Chicago policy was not clearly articulated at its conception, we can identify three mechanisms for improvement embedded in the Chicago Policy: (1) the *threat* of retention; (2) *extended* instructional time; and (3) *retention* itself. The three mechanisms were enacted largely on an economic view of education: by creating incentives to change the behavior of students, parents, and teachers, and increasing time on task, school performance will improve. The first component, the threat of retention, was intended to motivate students to work hard, encourage parents and teachers to pay attention to students at risk, and compel teachers to teach basic skills. The second mechanism, extended instructional time through after school and summer programs, was designed to help low-achieving students learn enough to pass standards. The third mechanism, a second time through the grade, was intended to provide additional instruction for students who were not ready to move on to the next grade. Because the policy could have affected students through any of these three mechanisms, the study of the policy was much broader than a study of the effects of retention, and the effects of retention have to be considered within the broader impacts of the other two components.

*Studying the Chicago Policy*   At the start of the policy, the Consortium on Chicago School Research at the University of Chicago (CCSR) took on the challenge of studying its effects. Melissa Roderick led these efforts, bringing in different researchers to study particular aspects of the policy. The authors of this chapter were members of this large research team. The goal was not just to determine whether the policy worked, but how it worked.

This project used multiple methods and a variety of longitudinal data sources to study the different aspects of the policy. The CCSR had access to a longitudinal database on Chicago students' yearly test scores and administrative records. The administrative data were used to follow students' paths across grades, while the testing data allowed us to look for changes in students' growth trajectories. In addition, CCSR has been surveying Chicago teachers, principals, and students in sixth through 10th grades since 1994 to measure school climate and instructional practices. Student survey data could be tied to test score data to determine whether the policy had different effects on students based on their probability of meeting the promotion criteria.

In addition to quantitative data, a longitudinal qualitative study followed 100 low-achieving sixth- and eighth-grade students in five elementary schools from the year before they took the test to the retained or promoted year. Besides interviewing the students, the researchers asked their teachers for written assessments of the students, and interviewed their teachers. The researchers also conducted an evaluation of the summer school program (Summer Bridge) which included classroom observations in 12 schools throughout the summer, and a supplementary survey of sixth and eighth graders and teachers who participated in summer school in 1999. Because of the wide scope of this project, and the many sources of data available to study the policy, a complex portrait of the policy emerged.

*The Effects of the Threat of Retention*   The threat of retention was intended to motivate students to work hard, encourage parents and teachers to pay attention to students at risk, and compel teachers to make sure students learn basic skills. To study whether this was the case, CCSR researchers compared students' and teachers' reports about motivation, support, and instruction on surveys administered well before the policy, to reports on surveys after the policy was in place.

The surveys showed that the policy generally had a positive impact on increasing teacher and parental support, and on motivation for low-achieving students. The vast majority of teachers felt the policy had made parents more concerned about their child's progress, that the policy made them more sensitive and responsive to students' needs, and focused their instructional efforts (Jacob et al., 2004). Students in sixth and eighth grades, particularly low-achieving students at risk of retention, reported higher levels of academic support from teachers and parents after the policy was in place. These changes in teacher support were corroborated by qualitative interviews of low-achieving sixth and eighth graders (Roderick & Engel, 2001). Students also reported increased work effort, increased support from teachers, and more participation in after-school programs for help with schoolwork. In most cases, students' reports were confirmed by teachers in their assessments of students' behavior. Furthermore, teachers appeared to use the policy as a tool to spur student work effort.

One concern raised by critics of high-stakes testing is that such programs place too much pressure on students by raising expectations and standards without concomitant increases in support (Lee et al., 1999). However, CCSR researchers found the opposite—not only did support increase, but teachers did not raise their expectations for course performance. In fact, high-achieving students reported lower levels of academic press in the postpolicy period than in prepolicy years. Thus, students experienced increases in social support without increases in academic expectations.

*Effects on Instruction*    Teachers also changed the content of their instruction as a result of the promotion standards, in ways that could be viewed as both beneficial and problematic. Not surprisingly, time on test preparation increased substantially after the introduction of the high-stakes testing program, almost doubling from approximately 10.5 to over 20 hours a year (Jacob et al., 2004). Teachers also aligned what they taught to focus on the skills tested on the ITBS. Seventh- and eighth-grade teachers in the lowest-performing schools were more likely to cover mathematics topics at grade level, rather than below grade level. Seventh and eighth grade teachers at all schools spent more time teaching reading comprehension versus other language arts activities. Thus, the expected changes in instructional practices did occur, but with contradictory effects on rigor. Pacing in mathematics improved, but the curriculum was narrowed to emphasize those topics covered on the ITBS, and more class time was devoted to practicing test-taking skills.

*The Effects of Extended Instructional Time*    A critical part of the policy was providing students at risk of retention with extended instructional time through summer school and after school programs.[10] While these programs were a key component of the policy to end social promotion, they were distinct from the retention experience. Almost all students who were eventually retained participated in these extra supports, but many students received these supports and then were able to pass the promotion standard. Thus, their effects on achievement should not be confounded with the effects of retention, which affected a much smaller group of students.

Teachers and principals welcomed these supports; over 90% of principals and 85% of teachers felt that the summer school and after school programs had positive effects on students. Students also reacted positively to the environment of summer school with its small classes and personal attention. They described summer school as a positive learning environment in which they were expected to work hard and where teachers supported their efforts. Students also reported higher levels of academic press and support from their teachers in the summer than these same students did during the school year (Roderick et al., 2003). These positive reports were reflected in test score improvements. Students who attended summer school, particularly sixth and eighth graders, had significant test score gains at the end of the summer, even after adjusting for regression to

the mean (Roderick et al., 2003). The effects of the after school tutoring program were more mixed. While there was a clear association in the third grade between after school participation and achievement gains, there were weaker effects in the sixth grade, and no effects in the eighth grade (Smith, Roderick, & Degener, 2005).

***The Overall Effects of the Policy on Student Achievement***    Given the generally positive reactions to the policy in terms of increased support and effort, and extension of instructional time, we would expect to see improvements in student achievement after implementation of this policy. Indeed, test scores rose significantly during the period after 1996, particularly in the sixth and eighth grades (Bryk, 2003; Roderick, Nagaoka, Bacon, & Easton, 2000). The percentage of sixth graders with test scores below the promotional cutoff decreased from 37% in 1995, the year before the policy took effect, to 14% in 1999; results were similar for eighth graders (Roderick et al., 2000).

The positive effects of the policy on support, effort, and instructional time complicate the study of the effects of retention itself by requiring us to study its effects within the context of improving achievement overall. Furthermore, effects attributable to the policy need to be differentiated from any potential effects of other policies and demographic changes occurring simultaneously. Decentralization policies from prior years particularly were still likely having positive effects on student achievement over this time period (Bryk, 2003). Furthermore, some of the improvements in test scores certainly were due to testing effects rather than real gains in student learning (e.g., trying harder, taking practice tests). The first step in understanding the effects of retention on achievement was to determine the degree to which the overall policy (i.e., the cumulative effects of retention, motivation, extra support, changes in instruction and instructional time) resulted in improvements in learning. Following this, we look at the specific effects of retention.

The overall policy effects on achievement were estimated using growth curve modeling that identified test score increases in the grades subject to the policy above those predicted from a student's prior growth trajectory. Policy effects were derived by comparing the size of the value-added in the grades subject to promotion standards, comparing pre- and postpolicy cohorts (Roderick, Jacob, & Bryk, 2002). In the third grade, there was little evidence of positive effects in reading, with slight positive effects in mathematics. The lowest-achieving schools even showed declines in the learning growth of third graders with beginning test scores close to grade level. There was evidence of positive effects in the sixth and eighth grades, with policy effects being larger in the second and third year of the policy. In the sixth and eighth grades, the average gain in student achievement was approximately one-third to one-half of a year's learning higher in post- versus prepolicy cohorts. These findings suggest that the policy mechanisms that occurred prior to retention had positive effects on student achievement, at least in the sixth and eighth grades. Still, it is possible that the effects found in sixth and eighth grades did not reflect real gains in learning, but simply reflect students taking the test more seriously, or the rise in test preparation. When a single test is used for accountability, school systems often experience increases in scores on that test that are often short lived and are not generalizable to other measures of performance (Amrein & Berliner, 2002; Bryk, 2003; Klein, Hamilton, McCaffrey, & Stecher, 2000; Koretz, 1999; Koretz & Barron, 1998; Linn, 2000).

*The Effects of Mandated Retention on Student Achievement* High-stakes testing has an impact on all students, but retention is only experienced by a subset of students. The central argument for grade retention is that retained students do better than if they were promoted because they have the opportunity to catch up and master material, rather than continue to struggle in the next grade. These students should also continue to show improvements in learning in subsequent grades because their understanding is at the expected level for their grade. Thus, the achievement gains of a student retained in third grade should be greater than a similar student who was promoted to fourth grade; the following year the retained student should show better gains from third to fourth grade than the promoted student shows from fourth to fifth grade. For this reason, we argue that same-age comparisons, rather than same-grade comparisons, are most appropriate when evaluating the effects of retention (Nagaoka & Roderick, 2004; Roderick & Nagaoka, 2005).

To avoid selection bias in our study of retention effects, we used a regression discontinuity design, taking the sharp discontinuity in the probability of retention created by the single cutoff score to construct a comparison group of nonretained students.[11] We compared students who scored just below the test-score cutoff in reading at the end of summer (the below-cutoff group), the majority of whom were retained, to students whose scores were just above the cutoff at the end of the summer (the above-cutoff group), the majority of whom were promoted. Both groups experienced the benefits of summer school and enhanced motivation and preparation for the test, and would likely be similar in their pre- and postachievement growth in the absence of retention. Thus, the achievement growth of students in our above-cutoff group provides an estimate of the counterfactual of how retained students would have performed had they been promoted.

We addressed the issue of the lack of comparability of the GE metric across test levels and forms by conducting an extensive equating study that converted ITBS test scores to a logit metric using Rasch models that were comparable across time and across test levels and forms. This is particularly important when evaluating the effects of retention because, two years after failing to meet the test score cutoff, students were in several different grades (two grades below their age-appropriate counterparts, one grade below, or on grade level).

The simplest method of estimating retention effects is to compare the one-year achievement growth of students during the year after retention. However, because the groups are defined on the basis of one test score, the results could be biased by regression to the mean, as discussed earlier in this chapter. Therefore, we used data on students' entire test score histories to model students' growth curves; this minimizes error associated with performance on any one test, and any testing effects based on the high stakes placed on that test. To obtain these estimates, we used three-level hierarchical generalized linear models (HGLM) with years nested within students nested within schools (Roderick et al., 2003). Estimating students' growth curves in HGLM has three advantages (Bryk & Raudenbush, 2002). First, it allows us to estimate students' growth curves even if they are missing test scores. Second, it allows us to adequately deal with the nested structure of the data. Third, it allows us to explicitly model differences in achievement growth across students and control for differences in the achievement growth of students by their demographic characteristics and their school.

We estimated several variations of the basic model. The first variation used a regression discontinuity design to avoid possible selection bias by basing comparisons on test scores, rather than actual promotion decisions. In the next variation, we compared the achievement growth of promoted and retained youth by their actual experience of retention—whether, 2 years after the promotion test grade, they were promoted, experienced a full year of retention and remained one grade below their age counterparts, experienced two retentions, were placed in special education, or were initially retained but later rejoined their age group. These models provided a direct examination of the effects of the retained year, but also introduced the potential for selection bias. The third variation, an instrumental variables approach, confirmed that our results were not affected by selection bias.[12] This approach took advantage of the existence of factors that affected retention which were independent of a students' own motivation and achievement to determine retention effects, including the wide variation across six region offices in their willingness to grant retention waivers, the use of a strict test-score cutoff and across-year variation in the retention of third-grade students.

In our first comparison, the regression discontinuity design, we calculated test score gains from the year before the promotion test grade (e.g., the fifth grade score to study retention in sixth grade) to avoid problems with regression to the mean. In this comparison, third graders in the below-cutoff group, those who were predominantly retained by the policy, had slightly larger 2-year learning gains after second grade (until the year after retention) than their counterparts in the above-cutoff group who narrowly passed the test-score cutoff in reading (most of whom went on to fourth grade). These small gains, however, were short-lived. The achievement growth of the below-cutoff group across three years (from second grade to two years after the promotion test) was not statistically different from the above-cutoff group. For sixth graders, we found negative effects of retention. Sixth graders in the below-cutoff group had a roughly 6% lower learning gain over 2 years (one year after the promotion test) than students in the above-cutoff group. This gap continued one year later, two years after the promotion test.

The first comparison could be considered a conservative estimate of the effects of retention. Not all students in the below-cutoff group were retained at the end of the summer, many students who were retained later rejoined their classmates, and many were placed in special education. Thus, our estimates of the effects of retention are based on the average achievement growth of students who did not reach the promotional cutoff, but who had very different experiences after summer school. When we examine learning gains by students' actual retention experiences, rather than whether they were just above or below the cutoff, we introduce the possibility of selection bias. However, among third graders, we obtained the same results as in the first comparison. The achievement growth of third graders who experienced a full year of retention was slightly, but not significantly, greater than their low-achieving counterparts who were promoted at the end of the summer. After 2 years, there was no significant difference in the achievement growth of third graders who experienced a full year of retention and those who were promoted. In sixth grade, the second comparison showed a larger decline in learning for retained sixth graders than the first comparison. Sixth graders who experienced a full year of retention gained 31% less than promoted students in the first year of retention, and 24% less in the second year.

The two-stage instrumental-variables models, which further removed the possibility of selection bias, showed slightly more negative retention effects than the regression-discontinuity models. In the third grade, retention was not associated with a difference in achievement, even in the first year after retention. In the sixth grade, the effects of retention on achievement were consistent with the negative findings of the second comparison. Even after modeling for selection effects, retained sixth graders experienced achievement growth nearly 21% lower than promoted students.

Thus, in the third grade, we found no evidence that retention led to greater achievement growth two years after the promotional standard. In the sixth grade, we found that retention was associated with *lower* achievement growth. Our findings are consistent with other research using same-age comparisons to examine traditional teacher-initiated retention, which tends to find either no effect or adverse effects of retention on achievement growth (Alexander et al., 2003; Holmes, 1989; Holmes & Matthews, 1984; Jimerson, 2001). It is also consistent with research on traditional retention in that the effects were most adverse among older students. These similarities suggest some commonalities in the effects of mandated retention, compared with traditional retention. One of the limitations of our examination of the effects of retention on achievement

was our inability to determine its effect on eighth-grade achievement. To look at the impact of retention on eighth graders, we turned to a different outcome—student dropout from high school.

*The Effects of Mandated Retention on Student Dropout*     Consistently, research on teacher-initiated retention has shown that retained students are much more likely to drop out than students at the expected grade for their age, and that they tend to drop out at earlier ages (e.g., Alexander et al., 2001; Grissom & Shepard, 1989; Roderick, 1994; Rumberger, 1995). Therefore, opponents of the Chicago policy were concerned that it would lead more students to drop out. Proponents argued, however, that the benefits associated with promotion standards—increased motivation, more attention to low-skilled students, better alignment of instruction with standards—should counter any adverse effects of retention. Thus, the policy could have had contradictory effects, aggravating dropout rates by retaining students, yet lowering dropout rates by improving achievement.

The sudden implementation of the policy allowed for a good comparison to estimate retention effects without selection bias—we could compare cohorts subject to the policy to cohorts in earlier years that were not subject to the policy. However, we needed to discern the specific effects of retention on dropout net of any improvements in achievement or other system-wide changes occurring postpolicy. This called for a mixed-methods approach which modeled retention effects separately from achievement effects, and took into account selection factors regarding who was retained (Allensworth, 2005a).

Initial comparisons of dropout rates across the cohorts showed very little change, despite large increases in the percentage of eighth graders retained.[13] Dropout rates had been declining slightly across the last three cohorts not subject to the eighth-grade promotional standard, and while they did not continue to decline with the first two cohorts subject to the policy, they remained at the same level as the last prepolicy cohort. Dropout rates then declined slightly with the third cohort subject to the promotional standard, and fell considerably with the fourth postpolicy cohort. The lack of a large increase in dropout rates, along with the improvements in the later cohorts, might suggest that mandated retention had no harmful effects. Such a perspective, though, ignores the possibility that other policies might have affected dropout rates at the same time, and that dropout rates should have improved simply because of rising achievement levels among students—improvements that may not be fully attributable to the policy.

Confidence in the results of studies on the retention–dropout relationship has been limited by the degree to which these studies have been able to control spurious factors. If students are retained because of unobserved characteristics, which also make them more likely to drop out, the retention effect is overestimated. The advantage of studying this relationship in a high-stakes testing environment is that the vast majority of students were retained solely on the basis of their eighth-grade test score. However, even with this criterion there was the possibility of selectivity effects when studying the Chicago policy because of some discrepancies in implementation.[14]

If achievement had not increased dramatically with the policy, it would be possible to calculate the retention effect by comparing very low-achieving postpolicy students who were at high risk of retention to those with similar achievement prepolicy who were at low risk. However, because of the rise in achievement, such groupings would not be equivalent in terms of students' achievement relative to cohort peers. It was also not possible to look at the effect of retention by simply controlling for student achievement, because under the policy, retention and achievement became correlated.[15] Therefore, distribution of their shared variance became problematic. In addition, the context of testing changed postpolicy, and this could have altered the relationship between achievement and dropping out. Thus, the high-stakes environment created unique problems for creating appropriate comparison groups.

The latter problems were addressed by using a different measure of achievement than students' observed eighth-grade test score, and closely examining the achievement–dropout relationship pre- and postpolicy to be sure that it was correctly specified. Instead of using students' one eighth-grade test score as the measure of achievement, as with our analysis of retention effects on third and sixth graders, we used a measure of latent achievement based on students' history of performance on the ITBS from grades 3 through 8. The relationship of latent achievement with dropping out in prepolicy cohorts was compared to that in postpolicy cohorts to determine if the relationship had changed. So that retention effects would not be confounded in these comparisons, only students *not retained* in the eighth grade were included. The relationship was found to be the same, suggesting that the latent achievement measure could be used as a control variable across cohorts, if prepolicy cohorts were included in the analysis. This allowed the achievement–dropout relationship to be properly controlled postpolicy to calculate the retention effect.[16] If retention increased the chances that students would drop out, more low-achieving students should have dropped out after high-stakes testing was introduced, since so few of these students were retained prior to the policy and so many were retained after the policy. But there should not be any difference in the pre- to postpolicy dropout rates of students whose achievement put them at little risk of retention.

This is exactly what happened. Virtually no students with above-average achievement were retained in eighth grade postpolicy, and among these students, pre- and postpolicy dropout rates remained unchanged. Dropout rates did change, however, among low-achieving students. The lower students' test scores were, the higher their probability of retention, and the greater the discrepancy between prepolicy and postpolicy dropout rates—for each

10 percentage point rise in retention, dropout rates were about one percentage point larger. This discontinuity in the achievement–dropout relationship between high- and low-achieving students provided strong initial evidence that retention had an adverse effect on students' likelihood of graduating (Allensworth, 2005a).

Two-stage instrumental-variable models were used to confirm the existence of a retention effect. These took advantage of year-to-year changes in the cutoff score, and the sudden implementation in the first year, to create an instrument of retention to substitute for actual retention. These models showed a clear and strong effect of retention on dropout, with students retained by the policy about 12% more likely to drop out by age 17 than students not retained by the policy (Allensworth, 2005a ).

The estimates from the selection models were somewhat high, however, because they incorporated the effects of school selection—retained students were less likely to attend higher-quality schools than students not retained. Better estimates were obtained through hierarchical generalized linear models (HGLM), which nested students within schools to discern the effects of retention. These models had the potential of incorporating selection bias into the estimates, but comparison with different types of two-stage selection models showed that they did not. The HGLM showed retention effects of 9.9 percentage points under the promotion policy.

Retention rates rose with the policy, and retention increased the likelihood of students dropping out. Yet, dropout rates did not rise. The reason for this was the countervailing trend of rising achievement. It is difficult to say to what extent improvements in achievement resulted from the high-stakes testing program versus other policy changes. However, it is possible to estimate the total achievement effect on dropout rates as a means of determining the maximum beneficial effect. Using estimates from the HGLM, the postpolicy increase in achievement should have lowered dropout rates among retained students by as much as 3.3 percentage points, from 44.0% to 40.7%, and among nonretained students by about 2 percentage points. The adverse effect on dropout due to retention was larger than the beneficial effect of higher achievement for students retained by the policy. However, because the proportion of students retained by the policy was just a small fraction of the total, small improvements in dropout associated with higher achievement among nonretained students more than balanced the higher risk of dropping out among the group of students retained by the policy.

Previous research has shown that students who are old-for-grade are particularly likely to drop out at early grades. However, this relationship has been confounded with spurious factors. To examine the timing of dropping out, a discrete-time event history analysis was performed using HGLM, predicting the hazard of dropping out from age 15 to age 17. Consistent with studies of traditional retention, these models showed that prepolicy retention was particularly associated with dropping out at early ages—students retained prepolicy were 26 percentage points more likely to drop out at age 15, 22 percentage points more likely to drop out at age 16, and 20 percentage points more likely to drop out at age 17 than nonretained students. But among postpolicy students, dropout rates among retained students were about 3.5 percentage points higher than those of promoted students at all ages. Students were not more likely to drop out immediately upon retention by the promotional standard (i.e., within the next year or two), but their likelihood of dropping out was elevated throughout their remaining years in school (Allensworth, 2005a).

Not all students faced the same likelihood of being retained by the promotion standard; therefore, changes in dropout rates varied across subgroups of students (Allensworth, 2004). Students that had already been retained in grade at an earlier point in school were particularly vulnerable to failing the eighth-grade promotion standard and being retained in grade for a second time. Over a quarter of the students already old-for-grade by age 13 were held back by the promotion standard, while less than 1% of the old-for-grade students in prepolicy cohorts were held back in eighth grade. These students already were likely to drop out, and being retained more than once made them even more likely to do so; by age 19, 78% had dropped out of school. The policy also exacerbated racial differences in dropout rates. After the policy, dropout rates improved among all but African American students as achievement levels improved among all students, but retention rates rose the most among African American students.

Retention resulting from testing did not have as large an impact on dropping out as would be expected based on studies of teacher-initiated retention; the effect was about one-third the size. Retention resulting from high stakes testing also did not affect the timing of dropping out, but it elevated students' risk of dropping out for the remainder of their time in school. These differences in retention effects between traditional and mandated retention may have been due to differences in context, but also because the effects of unobserved characteristics were removed to a greater extent than in studies on teacher-initiated retention.

***Capacity of Schools*** The picture that emerges from these studies is that Chicago's initiative largely depended on increasing instructional time and providing strong incentives for teachers to change who they pay attention to and what they teach. There was, however, little incentive in the policy for teachers and schools to focus on the basic technology of instruction—how they teach. Indeed, one reading of our findings is that ending social promotion offered a solution that did little to challenge teachers. The policy indicated that the problem was that students were not motivated enough and the solution to low performance was to create incentives to work harder and focus on basic skills. This approach may have addressed one struggle educators were facing in their classroom, but in a way that provided little to guidance or reason to improve instruction. In interviews, teachers seldom answered that they were doing anything to

change their instructional approach to help students at-risk of retention (Jacob et al., 2004).

Our evaluation of Chicago's summer school program provides an example of how instructional capacity matters in how well teachers are able to respond to students' needs. The evaluation concluded that summer school was effective in producing short-term test score gains, particularly in the sixth and eighth grades. Even with its highly structured approach, however, learning gains in summer school varied widely across schools. Higher-achieving elementary schools were able to mount much more effective programs than lower-achieving schools, even after controlling for differences across schools in the characteristics of students who attended the program. For example, the summer reading test score gain for an average third grader was nearly three times larger if a student attended summer school in a school that had high achievement during the school year than if that same student attended summer school in a low-achieving elementary school. Teachers in these high-achieving schools were more positive about the learning environment in summer school and reported paying more attention to the needs of individual students (Roderick, Engel, & Nagaoka, 2003).

Analysis of classroom observation data similarly found significant variation in classroom effects (Roderick, Engel, & Nagaoka, 2003). Even with its mandatory curriculum, there were large differences in the quality of instruction and resultant learning gains. Students of teachers who had "tailored instruction"—meaning they not only delivered the curriculum, but had meaningful and constructive interactions with students, taught topics in multiple ways, and individualized instruction—experienced significantly greater learning gains in summer school than students of teachers who simply followed the curriculum. Unfortunately, only about 20% of summer school classrooms had tailored instruction (Roderick et al., 2003).

Not surprisingly, retention rates were highly concentrated in specific schools. In 1998, there were 416 schools in Chicago in which more than 20 third-grade students were retained under the policy, but less than a quarter of those schools had 50% of the retained third graders (Nagaoka & Roderick, 2004). In the 100 schools with the highest retention rates, 42% of their test-eligible third graders were retained. Students retained in the eighth grade were even more concentrated, with 61% attending just 100 schools.

The lack of attention to improving teaching capacity became most evident in the one arena where technical solutions were most needed—for the lowest performing students and the schools that did not have the instructional capacity to use the policy to motivate students and target instruction. In general, those students who were retained by the policy were those who for various reasons of personal, family, or school capacity could not raise their test scores during the school year and summer. These students were concentrated in schools and classrooms which demonstrated the least capacity to serve their needs, and many of them had special emotional, family, or learning issues. This became obvious in qualitative interviews (Roderick & Engel, 2001). Students who went a second time through the same grade at the same school that had low instructional capacity, and lacked adults who paid attention to the other issues affecting their engagement in schooling, did not see higher learning gains.

As we look back on the theory of action for retention in Chicago, we see that the responsibility of determining how to respond to the incentives rested entirely on individuals: teachers, students, and their parents. The school system did not provide support to change the school structure or direction to teachers on how to improve their instructional practice and remediate students' skills. Students with serious barriers to achievement, and those without access to good teachers, were the least likely to benefit from the policy. The policy didn't deal with improving capacity. As a result, after the first few years, improvements in test scores leveled off.[17] It looks as if the policy reached the limits of what it could do just by improving motivation and focusing attention on low-achieving students.

**Implications for Studying Retention under High-Stakes Testing**

The study of retention is fraught with difficult methodological issues, from finding appropriate comparison groups to comparing outcomes across students in different grades and different ages. Inconsistency in the conclusions of research on retention arises, in part, from problems in appropriately addressing these issues. But inconsistency also arises because of the very different perspectives that exist regarding what retention is supposed to achieve. The methods used to study retention are determined by what one thinks retention should accomplish. This can be seen in debates regarding the evidence on traditional retention, and in the ways that one might approach studying mandated retention. For example, if we believe that a retention policy is simply meant to keep students from advancing without requisite skills, then we should test its effectiveness by examining whether more students are advancing with grade-level skills. But if we believe that the goal of retention is to motivate students to work harder so that they are not actually retained, then we need to know if achievement improved among all students, not just those who experienced retention.

The study of retention in the context of high-stakes testing raises a number of issues beyond those that exist with traditional retention, which we have highlighted in this chapter. When retention is used in a high-stakes testing environment, it has an impact on all students in all schools, not just those who are retained. If we had just looked at retention in our study of the Chicago policy, we would have missed the motivational issues and how they had an impact on achievement across the system. Most importantly, we also could have confused the positive effects of the after school and summer school programs, and the changes in instruction, motivation and support, with the effect of the retained year, and come to a very different conclusion about the effects of retention itself.

When people talk about retention under high-stakes testing, they are often not solely talking about retention itself. It is natural to ascribe the overall outcomes of a retention policy to the defining element of the policy—retention. However, there is retention and there is "retention-plus." Retention under high-stakes testing is rarely done in complete isolation. It is frequently accompanied by efforts to increase instructional time and provide additional supports for students who have been retained or who are at risk of being retained. In Chicago, the policy was very front-loaded with motivational effects, an after school program and a summer school program—all designed to get students to pass the promotion standards and avoid retention. Older students seemed to benefit the most from these supports, while also facing the most adverse effects from retention. If we were not clear about the specific effects of the various components of a retention policy, then we would have made incorrect conclusions about the effects of different interventions (e.g., standards versus instructional supports versus retention). Efforts to replicate the policy could fail if those components that worked well are left off in favor of components that were not successful. Retention was not an effective strategy, but the threat of retention and some of the accompanying instructional changes and supports were beneficial for some groups of students.

The complexity of high-stakes testing policies and their potential effects suggests that simple studies of their effectiveness are not sufficient. If we just looked at whether the policy worked or did not work across all students—which is often the aim of studies using experimental methods—we would not know what it was that worked with the policy, and what did not work. We would also be unable to distinguish high-stakes testing policy effects from other changes that were occurring in the school system over the same time period, such as school-level accountability. Besides the implementation of school-level accountability policies, there were improvements in the stability of system leadership, reduction in conflicts with the teachers' union, large improvements in school infrastructure, and continuing improvements in schools resulting from earlier decentralization reforms. When studying something as methodologically difficult as retention, using multiple methods was essential for understanding the effects of different components of the policy on the school system as a whole, and its effects on individual students.

It is clear that testing and accountability are powerful levers affecting school practices and student achievement. But grade retention itself does not appear to be an effective intervention. In the long run, moving urban school systems to higher levels of performance must ultimately involve building the capacity of schools. This will require an understanding of how accountability and incentives can be used to push instruction and build strong systems of supports for teachers and schools to mount effective strategies that increase students' engagement in school and ability to learn.

## Notes

1. In 2005, 12 states had policies that directed state boards or local education authorities to enact test performance criteria for promotion in specific grades. Numerous local school districts have also enacted promotion policies, including New York, Baltimore, Philadelphia, and Chicago.

2. The focus of this chapter is on policy-mandated retention. A good overview of issues surrounding traditional grade retention is Alexander, Entwisle, and Dauber (2003).

3. Estimates range from 20 to 50% (Jimerson, 2001; NASP, 2003). About 30% of students are old-for-grade by age 14 (Roderick, 1995).

4. A summary of the arguments for ending social promotion can be found in a guide produced by the U.S. Department of Education (1999).

5. Reviews of the issues can be found in Allington and McGill-Franzen (1992), National Research Council (1997, 2000).

6. For comparisons of results that use these different methods see Alexander et al. (2003), Holmes (1989), Karweit (1999), Mantzicolopous and Morrison (1992), Peterson et al. (1987), and Reynolds (1992).

7. It is possible for same-grade comparisons to show no effect of retention if the comparisons are made relative to a fixed standard (e.g., achievement at grade level norms). In this case, students' achievement may increase, but not to the level of the standard, and not be considered an improvement.

8. This issue is discussed in the dialogue between Alexander et al. (1994, 2003) and Shepard and Smith (1998). What Shepard and Smith see as regression to the mean, Alexander and colleagues suggest is the successful intervention of retention—reversing deterioration in students' performance seen in the retained year. Either interpretation is plausible with the data.

9. Hauser (2001) documents differences in retention by gender and race. In Chicago, we found that retention under high stakes testing was equitably applied by gender, once adjustments were made for initial achievement, because of adherence to test score cutoffs (Roderick et al., 1999).

10. The voluntary after school program funded an additional hour of literacy and mathematics instruction 3 or 4 days a week for 20 or more weeks during the school year. It served up to 30% of all Chicago elementary school students (Smith, Roderick, & Degener, 2005).

11. Shadish, Cook, and Campbell (2002) give a general explanation of this method.

12. We used a derivation of the two-stage least squares approach called two-stage probit which simultaneously estimates the probability of retention and postretention achievement gains (see Roderick & Nagaoka, 2005).

13. Dropouts were defined using a cohort method, following students from age 13 to age 17 and coding students as dropouts if they officially dropped out, transferred to an alternative school, were expelled, or no longer enrolled with no record of a valid transfer (see Allensworth, 2005b).

14. Of those students who passed the eighth-grade test in spring or summer 1998, 0.2% were retained, and of those who failed in both spring and summer 11% were promoted.

15. The prepolicy relationship between achievement and retention was small (-.05) compared to postpolicy (-.32).

16. It is not possible to discern the extent to which retention, rather than achievement, encouraged dropping out using only postpolicy data because of collinearity among retention, achievement, and dropping out, and the nonlinear relationships among them postpolicy.

17. Between 1997 and 2002 the percentage of students in the grades that scored at or above national norms increased, however, after 2002 the scores showed little improvement.

## References

Alexander, K. L., Entwisle, D. R., & Dauber, S. L. (1994). *On the success of failure: A reassessment of the effects of retention in the primary grades*. Cambridge, England: Cambridge University Press.

Alexander, K. L., Entwisle, D. R., & Horsey, C. (1997). From first grade forward: Early foundations of high school dropout. *Sociology of Education, 70*, 87–107.

Alexander, K. L., Entwisle, D. R., & Kabbani, N. (2001). The dropout process in life course perspective: Early risk factors at home and school. *Teachers College Record, 103*, 760–822.

Allensworth, E. M. (2004). Graduation and dropout rates after implementation of high-stakes testing in Chicago's elementary schools: A close look at students most vulnerable to dropping out. In G. Orfield (Ed.), *Dropouts in America: Confronting the graduation rate crisis* (pp. 157–180). Cambridge, MA: Harvard Educational Press.

Allensworth, E. M. (2005a). Dropout rates after high-stakes testing in elementary school: A study of the contradictory effects of Chicago's efforts to end social promotion. *Educational Evaluation and Policy Analysis, 27*, 341–364.

Allensworth, E. M. (2005b). *Graduation and dropout trends in Chicago: A look at cohorts of students from 1991 through 2004*. Chicago, IL: Consortium on Chicago School Research.

Allington, R. L., & McGill-Franzen, A. (1992). Unintended effects of educational reform in New York. *Educational Policy, 6*(4), 397–414.

American Educational Research Association. (2000). *AERA position statement concerning high stakes testing in pre K-12 education*. Washington, DC: Author.

Amrein, A. L., & Berliner, D. C. (2002). High-stakes testing, uncertainty, and student learning. *Education Policy Analysis Archive, 10*, 1–70.

Au, W. (2007) High-stakes testing and curricular control: A qualitative metasynthesis. *Educational Researcher, 36*, 258–267.

Betts, J. R., & Costrell, R. (2001). Incentives and equity under standards-based reform. In D. Ravitch (Ed.), *Brookings papers on education policy* (pp. 9–74). Washington, DC: Brookings Institution.

Bryk, A. S. (2003). No child left behind, Chicago style. In P. E. Peterson & M. R. West (Eds.), *No child left behind? The politics and practice of school accountability* (pp. 242–269). Washington, DC: Brookings Institution.

Bryk, A. S., & Raudenbush. (2002). *Hierarchical linear models: Applications and data analysis methods*. Thousand Oaks, CA: Sage.

Bryk, A. S., Thum, Y. M., Easton, J. Q., & Luppescu, S. (1998). *Academic productivity of Chicago Public Schools: A technical report*. Chicago: Consortium on Chicago School Research.

Byrnes, D. A. (1989). Attitudes of students, parents, and educators toward repeating a grade. In L. A. Shepard & M. L. Smith (Eds.), *Flunking grades: Research and policies on retention* (pp. 108–131). Philadelphia: Falmer Press.

Byrnes, D., & Yamamoto, K. (1986). View on grade repetition. *Journal of Research and Development in Education, 20*, 14–20.

Caterall, J. S. (1989). Standards and dropouts: A national study of tests required for graduation. *American Journal of Education, 98*, 1–34.

Center for Policy Research in Education. (1990). *Repeating grades in school: Current practice and research evidence* (CPRE Policy Briefs). New Brunswick, NJ: Author.

Christman, J. B., & Pugh, W. C. (1989). Implementing a systemwide promotion policy: Dilemmas for principals and teachers in urban schools. *The Journal of Negro Education, 58*, 163–176.

Clinton, W. J. (1998). State of the Union address. *Public Papers of the Presidents of the United States: William J. Clinton, 1998* (Book I, pp. 112–121, 2 vols). Washington, DC: U.S. Government Printing Office.

Cohen, D. K. (1996). Rewarding teachers for student performance. In S. H. Furman & J. A. O'Day (Eds.), *Rewards and reform: Creating educational incentives that work* (pp. 60–112). San Francisco, CA: Jossey-Bass.

Cohen, D. K., Raudenbush, S. W., & Ball, D. L. (2003). Resources, instruction, and research. *Educational Evaluation and Policy Analysis, 25*, 119–142.

Coley, R. J. (1995). *Dreams deferred: High school dropouts in the United States*. Princeton, NJ: Educational Testing Service.

Cooper, H., Charlton, K., Valentine, J. C., & Muhlenbruck, L. (2000). Making the most of summer school: A meta-analytic and narrative review. *Monographs of the Society for Research in Child Development, 65*, 1–127.

Cooper, H., Nye, B., Lindsay, J., & Greathouse, S. (1996). The effects of summer vacation on achievement test scores: A narrative and meta-analytic review. *Review of Educational Research, 66*, 227–268.

Cosden, M., Zimmer, J., & Tuss, P. (1993). The impact of age, sex, and ethnicity on kindergarten entry and retention decisions. *Educational Evaluation and Policy Analysis, 15*, 209–222.

Darling-Hammond, L. (1996). Beyond bureaucracy: Restructuring schools for high performance. In S. H. Furman & J. A. O'Day (Eds.), *Rewards and reform: Creating educational incentives that work* (pp. 144–192). San Francisco, CA: Jossey-Bass.

Darling-Hammond, L., & Wise, A. E. (1985). Beyond standardization: State standards and school improvement. *The Elementary School Journal, 85*, 315–336.

Dauber, S. L., Alexander, K. L., & Entwisle, D. R. (1993). Characteristics of retainees and early precursors of retention in grade: Who is held back? *Merrill-Palmer Quarterly, 39*, 326–343.

Denham, C., & Lieberman, A. (Eds.). (1980). *Time to learn.* Washington, DC: U.S. Department of Education, National Institute of Education.

Easton, J. Q., Rosencranz, T., Bryk, A. S., Jacob, B. A., Luppescu, S., & Roderick, M. (2000). *Annual CPS test trend review, 1999.* Chicago, IL: Consortium on Chicago School Research.

Finlayson, H. J. (1977). Nonpromotion and self-concept development. *Phi Delta Kappan, 54*, 205–206.

Firestone, W. A., Mayrowetz, D., & Fairman, J. (1998). Performance-based assessment and instructional change: The effects of testing in Maine and Maryland. *Educational Evaluation and Policy Analysis, 20*, 95–113.

Fisher, C. W., & Berliner, D. C. (Eds.). (1985). *Perspectives on instructional time.* New York: Longman.

Gottfredson, D. C., Fink, C. M., & Graham, N. (1994). Grade retention and problem behavior. *American Educational Research Journal. 31*, 761–784.

Graue, M. E., & DiPerna, J. (2000). Redshirting and early retention: Who gets the "gift of time" and what are its outcomes? *American Educational Research Journal, 32*, 509–534.

Grissom, J. B., & Shepard, L. A. (1989). Repeating and dropping out of school. In L. A. Shepard & M. L. Smith (Eds.), *Flunking grades: Research and policies on retention* (pp. 34–36). London: Falmer Press.

Hauser, R. M., (2001). Should we end social promotion? Truth and consequences In G. Orfield & M. L. Kornhaber (Eds.), *Raising standards or raising barriers: Inequality and high-stakes testing In public education* (pp. 151–178). New York: Century Foundation.

Heubert, J. P., & Hauser, R. M. (1999). *High stakes: Testing for tracking, promotion and graduation.* Washington, DC: National Academy Press.

Holmes, C. T. (1989). Grade level retention effects: A meta-analysis of research studies. In L. A. Shepard & M. L. Smith (Eds.), *Flunking grades: Research and policies on retention* (pp. 16–33). London: Falmer Press.

Holmes, C. T., & Matthews, K. M. (1984). The effects of nonpromotion on elementary and junior high school pupils: A meta-analysis. *Review of Educational Research, 54*, 225–236.

Holmes, C. T., & Saturday, J. (2000). Promoting the end of retention. *Journal of Curriculum and Supervision, 15*, 300–314.

House, E. R. (1998). *The predictable failure of Chicago's student retention program.* Boulder, CO: University of Colorado-Boulder.

Jackson, G. B. (1975). The research evidence on the effects of grade retention. *Review of Educational Research, 45*, 613–635.

Jacob, R. T., Stone, S., & Roderick, M. (2004). *Ending social promotion in Chicago: The response of teachers and students.* Chicago, IL: Consortium on Chicago School Research.

Jimerson, S. R. (1999). On the failure of failure: Examining the association between early grade retention and education and employment outcomes during late adolescence. *Journal of School Psychology, 37*, 243–272.

Jimerson, S. R. (2001). Meta-analysis of grade retention research: Implications for practice in the 21st century. *School Psychology Review, 30*, 420–437.

Jimerson, S. R., Carlson, E., Rotert, M., Egeland, B., & Sroufe, A. L.

(1997). A prospective, longitudinal study of the correlates and consequences of early grade retention. *Journal of School Psychology, 35*, 3–25.

Johnson, J., Arumi, A. M., & Ott, A. (2006). *Reality check 2006: Is support for standards and testing fading?* (No. 3). New York: Educational Insights, Public Agenda. Retrieved from http://www.publicagenda.org/reports/reality-check-2006-issue-no-3

Jones, M. G., Jones, B. D., & Hardin, B. (1999). The impact of high-stakes testing on teachers and students in North Carolina. *Phi Delta Kappan, 81*, 199–203.

Karweit, N. L. (1991). *Repeating a grade: Time to grow or denial of opportunity?* Baltimore, MD: Center for Research on Effective Schooling for Disadvantaged Students, John Hopkins University.

Karweit, N. L. (1999). *Grade retention: Prevalence, timing and effects.* Baltimore, MD: Center for Research on Effective Schooling for Disadvantaged Students, John Hopkins University.

Klein, S. P., Hamilton, L. S., McCaffrey, D. F., & Stecher, B. M. (2000). *What do test scores in Texas tell us?* Santa Monica, CA: RAND.

Koretz, D. (1999). *Foggy lenses: Limitations in the use of achievement tests as measures of educators' productivity.* Paper presented at National Academy of Sciences Conference, Devising Incentives to Promote Human Capital, Irvine, CA.

Koretz, D. M. & Barron, S. I., (1998). *The validity of gains in scores on the Kentucky instructional results information system (KIRIS).* Santa Monica, CA: RAND.

Koretz, D. M., Barron, S. I., Mitchell, K. J., & Stecher, B. M. (1996). *Perceived effects of the Kentucky instructional results information system.* Santa Monica, CA: RAND.

Labaree, D. F. (1984). Setting the standard: Alternative policies for student promotion. *Harvard Educational Review, 54*, 67–87.

Lee, V. E., Smith, J. B., Perry, T. E., & Smylie, M. A. (1999). *Social support, academic press and student achievement: A view from the middle grades in Chicago.* Chicago, IL: Consortium on Chicago School Research.

Levin, H. M., & Tsang, M. C. (1987). The economics of student time. *Economics of Education Review, 6*, 357–364.

Linn, R. L. (1993). Educational assessment: Expanded expectations and challenges. *Education Evaluation and Policy Analysis, 15*, 1–16.

Linn, R. L. (2000). Assessments and accountability. *Educational Researcher, 29*, 4–16.

Madaus, G. F. (1988). The influence of testing on the curriculum. In L. Tanner (Ed.), *Critical issues in curriculum, NSSE yearbook, part 1* (pp. 83–121). Chicago, IL: University of Chicago Press.

Mantzicopoulos, P. (2003). Flunking kindergarten after Head Start: An inquiry into the contribution of contextual and individual variables. *Journal of Educational Psychology, 95*, 268–278.

Mantzicopoulos, P., & Morrison, D. C. (1992). Kindergarten retention: Academic and behavioral outcomes through the end of second grade. *American Educational Research Journal, 29*, 182–198.

Mantzicopoulos, P., Morrison, D. C., Hinshaw, S. P., & Carte, E. T. (1989). Nonpromotion in kindergarten: The role of cognitive, perceptual, visual-motor, behavioral, achievement, socioeconomic, and demographic characteristics. *American Educational Research Journal, 26*, 107–121.

May, D. C., & Welch, E. L. (1984). The effects of developmental placement and early retention on children's later scores on standardized tests. *Psychology in the Schools, 21*, 381–385.

McCoy, A. R., & Reynolds, A. J. (1999). Grade retention and school performance: An extended investigation. *Journal of School Psychology, 37*, 273–298.

McNeil, L. M. & Valenzuela, A. (2001) The harmful impact of the TAAS system of testing in Texas: Beneath the accountability rhetoric. In M. Kornhaber & G. Orfield (Eds.), *Raising standards or raising barriers? Inequality and high stakes testing in public education* (pp. 127–150). New York: Century Foundation.

Mehrens, W. A. (1998). Consequences of assessment: What is the evidence? *Education Policy Analysis Archive, 6*(13). Retrieved from http://www.olam.ed.asu.edu.epaa.v6n13.html.

Nagaoka, J., & Roderick, M. (2004). *Ending social promotion in Chicago:*

*The effects of retention*. Chicago, IL: The Consortium on Chicago School Research.

National Association of School Psychologists. (2003). *Position statement on using large scale assessment for high stakes decisions*. Bethesda, MD: Author.

National Research Council. (1997). *Improving schooling for language-minority children: A research agenda*. Committee on Developing a Research Agenda on the Education of Limited-English-Proficient and Bilingual Students. D. August & K. Hakuta (Eds.), Commission on Behavioral and Social Sciences and Education. Washington, DC: National Academy Press.

National Research Council. (2000). *Testing English-language learners in U.S. schools: Report and workshop summary*. Committee on Educational Excellence and Testing Equity. K. Hakuta & A. Beatty (Eds), Board on Testing and Assessment, Center for Education. Washington, DC: National Academy Press.

Natriello, G., Pallas, A. M., & Alexander, K. (1989). On the right track? curriculum and academic achievement. *Sociology of Education, 62,* 109–118.

Newmann, F. M., Bryk, A. S., & Nagaoka, J. (2001). *Authentic intellectual work and standardized tests: Conflict or coexistence?* Chicago, IL: Consortium on Chicago School Research.

Novak, E. L. (1965). Sharing personal and professional experiences of nonpromotion with an elementary principal. *Theory into Practice, 4,* 114–116.

Peterson, S. E., DeGracie, J. S., & Ayabe, C. R. (1987). A longitudinal study of the effects of retention/promotion on academic achievement. *American Educational Research Journal, 24,* 107–118.

Picklo, M., & Christenson, S. L. (2005). Alternatives to retention and social promotion. *Remedial and Special Education, 26,* 258–268.

Pierson, L. H., & Connell, J. P. (1992). Effect of grade retention on self-system processes, school engagement, and academic performance. *Journal of Educational Psychology, 84,* 300–307.

Plummer, D. L., & Graziano, W. G. (1987). Impact of grade retention on the social development of elementary school children. *Developmental Psychology, 23,* 267–275.

Reynolds, A. J. (1992). Grade retention and school adjustment: An explanatory analysis. *Educational Evaluation and Policy Analysis, 14,* 101–121.

Roderick, M. (1994). Grade retention and school dropout: Investigating the association. *American Educational Research Journal, 31,* 729–759.

Roderick, M. (1995). Grade retention and school dropout: Policy debate and research questions. *Phi Delta Kappa Research Bulletin, 15,* 1–8.

Roderick, M., Bryk, A. S., Jacob, B. A., Easton, J. Q., & Allensworth, E. (1999). *Ending social promotion: Results from the first two years.* Chicago, IL: Consortium on Chicago School Research.

Roderick, M., & Engel, M. (2001). The grasshopper and the ant: Motivational responses of low-achieving students to high-stakes testing. *Educational Evaluation and Policy Analysis, 23,* 197–227.

Roderick, M., Engel, M., & Nagaoka, J. (2003). *Ending social promotion: Results from Summer Bridge.* Chicago, IL: Consortium on Chicago School Research.

Roderick, M., Jacob, B. A., & Bryk, A. S. (2004). Summer in the city: Achievement gains in Chicago's Summer Bridge program.In G. D. Borman & M. Boulay (Eds.), *Summer learning: Research, policies and programs* (pp. 73–102) Mahwah, NJ: Erlbaum.

Roderick, M., & Nagaoka, J. (2005). Retention under Chicago's high-

stakes testing program: Helpful, harmful or harmless? *Education Evaluation and Policy Analysis, 24,* 309–340.

Roderick, M., Nagaoka, J., Bacon, J., & Easton, J. Q. (2000). *Update: Ending social promotion in Chicago: Passing, retention, and achievement trends among promoted and retained students.* Chicago, IL: Consortium on Chicago School Research.

Rozenholtz, S. J. (1987). Education reform strategies: Will they increase teacher commitment? *American Journal of Education, 96,* 534–562.

Rosenkranz, T. (2002). *2001 CPS trend review: Iowa tests of basic skills.* Chicago, IL: Consortium on Chicago School Research. Retrieved from http://www.consortium-chicago.org/publications/p55.html

Rumberger, R. W. (1995). Dropping out of middle school: A multilevel analysis of students and schools. *American Educational Research Journal, 32,* 583–625.

Schwager, M. T., Mitchell, D. E., Mitchell, T. K., & Hecht, J. B. (1992). How school district policy influences grade level retention in elementary school. *Educational Evaluation and Policy Analysis, 14,* 421–438.

Scott, B. A., & Ames, L. B. (1969). Improved academic, personal, and social adjustment in selected primary-school repeaters. *The Elementary School Journal, 69*(8), 431–439.

Shadish, W. R., Cook, T. D., & Campbell, D. T. (2002) *Experimental and quasi-experimental designs for generalized causal inference.* Boston: Houghton Mifflin.

Shepard, L. A., & Smith, M. L. (Eds.). (1989). *Flunking grades: Research and policies on retention.* New York: Falmer Press.

Shepard, L. A., Smith, M. L., & Marion, S. F. (1996). Failed evidence on grade retention. *Psychology in the Schools, 33,* 215–261.

Smith, B. (1998). *It's about time: Opportunity to learn in Chicago's elementary schools.* Chicago, IL: Consortium on Chicago School Research.

Smith, B., Roderick, M., & Degener, S. C. (2005). Extended learning time and student accountability: Assessing outcomes and options for elementary and middle grades. *Educational Administration Quarterly, 41,* 195–236.

Smith, M. L. (1991). Put to the test: The effects of external testing on teachers. *Educational Researcher, 20,* 8–11.

Smith, M. L., & Shepard, L. A. (1988). Kindergarten readiness and retention: A qualitative study of teachers' beliefs and practices. *American Educational Research Journal, 25,* 307–333.

Stein, M. K., & Lane, S. (1996). Instructional tasks and the development of student capacity to think and reason: An analysis of the relationship between teaching and learning in a reform mathematics project. *Educational Research and Evaluation, 2,* 50–80.

Stone, S. I., Engel, M., Nagaoka, J., & Roderick, M. (2005). Getting it the second time around: Student classroom experience in Chicago's Summer Bridge program. *Teachers College Record, 107,* 935–957.

Tomchin, E. M., & Impara, J. C. (1992). Unraveling teacher's beliefs about grade retention. *American Educational Research Journal, 29,* 199–223.

Urdan, T. C., & Paris, S. G. (1994). Teachers' perceptions of standardized achievement tests. *Educational Policy, 8,* 137–156.

U.S. Department of Education. (1999). *Taking responsibility for ending social promotion: A guide for educators and state and local leaders.* Retrieved from: www.edu.gov/PDFDocs/socialprom.pdf

Wheelock, A., Bebell, D., & Haney, W. (2000, November 2). Student self-portraits as test-takers: Variations, contextual differences, and assumptions about motivation. *Teachers College Record.* Retrieved January 18, 2010, from http://www.tcrecord.org ID Number: 10635

# 21

# School Calendars and Academic Achievement

HARRIS COOPER, GEOFFREY BORMAN, AND RON FAIRCHILD

Contrary to popular mythology, the standard 9-month school calendar is not the result of an agrarian economy in early America. In fact, summers played a critical role in the early years of U.S. public education when young students living in both urban and rural communities frequently attended school during the summer months. During the 19th century, it was common for public schools in America to include summer terms, and many schools were closed during the spring and fall (Gold, 2002). This arrangement reflected a true agrarian calendar, as it freed children in rural communities to assist with planting and harvesting. However, as compulsory public education grew during the late 1800s and families became more mobile, often moving from rural to urban communities, state and county officials gradually began an effort to standardize the school calendar to the 180-day, nine-month school year that remains prevalent to this day.

By the early 1900s, most schools had removed summer sessions from their calendars (Association of California School Administrators, 1988). As a result, many children in the early 20th century either held jobs or were idle during the summer months, which became a cause of concern for city dwellers (Dougherty, 1981). The passage of the first child labor law in 1916 meant that school-aged children had little to do during their vacation from school. Community leaders demanded that organized recreational activities be made available for students when school was not in session. The resulting "vacation schools" of the early 20th century offered nonacademic programs and were frequently run by churches, charity organizations, and women's groups in major cities in the Northeast and Midwest (Gold, 2002). As programs grew, they became financed and administered by public education officials, which led to the creation of summer school programs designed specifically for students to earn or recover academic credits over the summer months. Despite some recent efforts to change the American school calendar in order to provide additional opportunities for learning and alleviate overcrowding in schools, only ap-

proximately 10% of U.S. children attend public schools in summer, and summer-related expenditures constitute less than 2% of total school costs (Gold, 2002; National Center for Education Statistics [NCES], 1998).

The empirical study of school calendars followed shortly after calendars were standardized. In 1906, William White, a professor of mathematics at the State Normal School in New Paltz, New York, tested seven students on math computation in June and then retested them in September. Summer loss was reported for computation speed but not accuracy, although no statistical tests were conducted. In 1919, Garfinkel examined the June and September math computation scores of 747 fifth, sixth, and seventh graders. He found a general decrease in both speed and accuracy. Garfinkel also reported comparatively less summer loss for children engaged in summer jobs and concluded "...the child who keeps his brain alert by meeting actual problems of life is in a better position to retain what he has learned than the one who plays or studies" (p. 48). Interest in studying calendar issues was keen in the 1920s, when nine such studies were conducted, but diminished throughout the 1930s, and disappeared entirely between 1937 and 1962.

The modern era of school calendar research began in the mid-1970s. At that time, studies of summer learning loss routinely started to (a) use standardized test scores as academic outcome measures and (b) conform to reporting standards that permitted calculation of estimates of the change in achievement test scores and the cumulating and comparison of results across studies. At the same time, school districts that had modified some schools' calendars to do away with the long summer break began conducting evaluations of the effect of different calendar arrangements by comparing the achievement of students on traditional and modified calendars.

In addition, when attempting to measure how much a student learns over a given year, most educational researchers and the vast majority of contemporary school accountability programs continue to employ annual spring-to-spring or fall-to-fall testing schedules. These methods, though, conflate the academic year, during which student learning benefits from both schools and families, with the summer recess and other breaks in the school calendar, during which only families tend to influence learning. Indeed, exploring the relative and independent contributions of families and schools to educational outcomes, which first received widespread national attention with the publication of *Equality of Educational Opportunity* ("Coleman Report"; Coleman et al., 1966), has long interested educational researchers. By being attentive to the school calendar and any differences between students' in-school and out-of-school learning changes, we gain valuable opportunities to understand more clearly the effects that families and schools have on educational outcomes.

In this chapter, we will examine the impact of school calendars on students' academic achievement. To begin, we provide an answer to the question of whether the long summer vacation that is part of the modern school calendar has detrimental effects on student learning and whether these effects might be different for students from different economic backgrounds. Finding that learning loss does occur over summer and in some areas is more pronounced for children from low socioeconomic status (SES) families, we examine some theoretical accounts for why this might be so. Then, we describe two approaches to avoiding summer learning loss and closing the out-of-school learning gap. First, we examine the effectiveness of summer school programs and describe some current models for delivering summer instruction, especially to children who are struggling in school. Second, we examine the effects on achievement of modified school calendars, in which the long summer break is replaced by multiple shorter breaks through the school year.

## The Effect of Summer Vacation on Achievement Test Scores

What impact does the long summer break have on the learning of children and adolescents? A research synthesis performed by Cooper, Nye, Charlton, Lindsey, and Greathouse (1996) examined the effects of summer vacation on student achievement. These researchers found 39 studies that looked at the effects of summer vacation. As noted above, some of these studies were conducted in the early 20th century and provided only limited statistical data. Still, applying a simple vote count to the results of studies conducted before 1975 indicated that evidence existed for summer learning loss in math computation skills and spelling. After 1975, 13 studies were found that provided enough information for use in a meta-analysis. The meta-analysis indicated that summer learning loss equaled at least one month of instruction. On average, children's achievement test scores were about one month lower when they returned to school in fall than when students left in spring.

The meta-analysis also found differences in the effect of summer vacation on different skill areas. Consistent with the early studies, summer loss was more pronounced for math computation skills and spelling than for other tested skill areas. The explanation of this result may rest on the common characteristic that both computation and spelling skills involve the acquisition of factual and procedural knowledge whereas other skill areas, especially learning math concepts, solving math problems, and reading comprehension, are more conceptual. Without practice, facts and procedural skills may be most susceptible to forgetting (e.g., G. Cooper & Sweller, 1987).

The meta-analysis also suggested that summer loss was more pronounced for math overall than for reading overall. Cooper et al. (1996) speculated that children's home environments might provide more opportunities to practice reading skills than to practice mathematics.

In addition to the influence of subject area, the meta-analysis also examined numerous differences among students as possible moderators of the effect of summer vacation. Overall, neither the student's sex nor ethnicity appeared to have a consistent influence on summer learning loss. Likewise, the meta-analysis revealed little evidence to suggest that a student's IQ had an impact on the effect of summer break. However, a study by Sargeant and Fidler (1987) provided some evidence suggesting children with learning disabilities are more susceptible to summer learning loss.

Family economics was also examined as an influence on what happens to children's knowledge and skills over summer. The meta-analysis revealed that all students, regardless of the resources in their home, lost roughly equal amounts of math skills over summer. However, substantial differences in summer learning loss for reading were related to family economics. On some measures, middle-SES children showed gains in reading achievement over summer but children from low-SES families showed losses. Reading comprehension scores of both income groups declined, but more so for less-wealthy students. Again, the authors speculated that income differences could be related to differences in opportunities to practice and learn reading skills over summer, with more books and reading opportunities available for middle-SES children.

Cooper et al. (1996) noted several difficulties in studying summer learning loss that might influence the precision of results. First, studies varied in how much instructional time was contained within the summer vacation interval. No study measured achievement on the very last and very first days of the school year. So, to the extent that the testing interval differs from the vacation interval, studies may underestimate the extent of the summer loss.

Second, studies use a variety of metrics to measure learning loss, from raw change, to standardized change (e.g., expressed in standard deviation units), to change in percentile rank against norming groups, to changes in grade level equivalence (GLE) scores. These metrics have implications for how change is to be interpreted, with the absolute change measures likely revealing the most interpretable effects. This is because GLE scores should take average changes within the norming group into account over any designated period of time. For example, an average raw score of 50 on a test given at the end of fifth grade might receive a normed GLE score of 5.9. However, an average raw score of 45 on the same test at the start of the sixth grade would receive a normed GLE score of 6.0. Thus, GLE score may "norm out" some summer loss, as measured by absolute achievement.

***The Link between Summer Learning and Educational Inequality*** As suggested by the Cooper et al. (1996) meta-analysis, the summer achievement loss seems to have a particularly deleterious effect on the reading achievement of students from low-SES backgrounds. While middle-SES children's reading scores showed slight gains during the summer months, low-SES children's scores showed declines of over two months of grade-level equivalency. As a result, low-SES children's reading skill levels fall approximately 3 months behind those of their middle-SES peers—a difference equivalent to about a third of the typical amount of learning that takes place during a regular school year.

More recent analyses of seasonal learning based on the national Early Childhood Longitudinal Study, Kindergarten (ECLS-K) data set have revealed similar findings. First, Downey, von Hippel, and Broh (2004) concluded that nearly every gap between minority and White groups and between SES groups grew faster during the summer after kindergarten than during the kindergarten and first grade school years. Similar to the result from the previous synthesis of the summer learning literature by Cooper et al. (1996), Downey and his colleagues estimated that the reading achievement level of a low-SES child with a household income below $40,000 fell 2.5 months behind the achievement level of a higher-SES child with a household income of $100,000 or greater. Second, Burkam, Ready, Lee, and LoGerfo (2004) also found a social stratification in summer learning for young children between kindergarten and first grade. However, their results suggested that the relationship between SES and children's summer learning is not linear. Instead, the most important summer learning differences were those separating the very advantaged and very disadvantaged children from the highest and lowest quintiles of the SES distribution.

The large and persistent achievement gaps between minority poor students and White middle-SES students are enduring national problems. Recent evidence suggests that these gaps tend to separate advantaged and disadvantaged students when they begin their formal schooling (Lee & Burkam, 2002). Further, a meta-analysis by Phillips, Crouse, and Ralph (1998) and the work of Entwisle, Alexander, and Olson (1997) provide evidence that the gaps expand as students proceed through school.

The widening of achievement gaps as students proceed through school would seem, quite naturally, to implicate the schools and to lend support to the contentions of researchers such as Bowles and Gintis (1976) that schools magnify existing inequities by reinforcing outside sources of disadvantage. However, the data from the longitudinal

Beginning School Study (BSS), collected by Doris Entwisle and Karl Alexander of Johns Hopkins University, suggest the summer learning deficits of low-SES children *accumulate* over the elementary-school years (Entwisle et al., 1997). By middle school, these summer reading differences plus a relatively small initial achievement lag at the beginning of first grade produced a cumulative lag of 2 years in reading achievement. Because the data also suggest that lower- and higher-SES children learned at essentially the same rate while in school, the Beginning School Study suggests that the widening of the gaps is explained almost entirely by the compounded deficits that result from these SES-based summer learning differences.

***The Effects of Summer Vacation on Student Health and Well-Being*** It is important also to briefly mention that, in addition to fewer learning opportunities, lower-SES youth are also at risk of experiencing setbacks in their overall health and nutrition during the summer months, and this can influence learning as well as their overall well-being. Food scarcity during the summer months is a significant health issue for lower-SES children in the United States. According to the U.S. Department of Agriculture (Food Research and Action Center, 2002), only one in five children who participate in federally subsidized meals during the regular school year also participate in such programs over the summer months. In addition, during the summer, when many children typically lack access to a nutrition program similar to the one they participated in during the school year, research demonstrates that children regress on measures of health, such as percent of body fat and body mass index (Caballero, 2004). Von Hippel, Powell, Downey, and Rowland (2007) found that the body mass index of children grew faster and more variably during summer vacation than during the kindergarten and first-grade school years. Furthermore, the difference between school and summer growth rates was especially large for three at-risk subgroups: African American children, Hispanic children, and children who were already overweight at the beginning of kindergarten. This research suggests that while schools' diet and exercise policies may be less than ideal, summer vacation may play more of a role than school environments in contributing to early childhood obesity.

## Theories Explaining Seasonal Learning Patterns

Entwisle, Alexander, and Olson's (2000) faucet theory provides an explanation for the seasonal patterns in learning. When school is in session, the resource faucet is turned on for all children, and all experience relatively equal gains; when school is not in session, the school resource faucet is turned off. During the summer, low-wealth families cannot make up for the resources schools provide and their children's achievement plateaus or declines. On the other hand, middle-class families can make up for the school's resources to a considerable extent and their children's growth continues, though perhaps at a slower pace than during the school year. These apparent compensatory effects of schools belie widely held beliefs about the failures of school systems burdened by high-poverty enrollments. Because there is good evidence suggesting that school-year learning rates are similar for students from across varying socioeconomic backgrounds, researchers such as Entwisle and Alexander (1992) have argued that schools may be doing a better job than they have been given credit for or, as Downey et al. (2004) suggested, that the schools may serve as a "great equalizer."

Other researchers have advanced four principal frameworks for understanding summer learning deficits. The first model is linked to the theoretical work of economists, most notably Becker (1981) and Becker and Tomes (1986), who have promulgated *investment models*. Building on developmental learning theories, which have identified age-specific techniques of promoting cognitive growth, social scientists have also investigated the relationship between parental behaviors and children's achievement growth (Entwisle et al., 1997; Heyns, 1978; Mayer, 1997). A third approach, rooted in educational and status attainment research, focuses on parental psychological attributes and their effects on children's summer achievement growth (Entwisle et al., 1997). Finally, educational researchers and evaluators have studied the effectiveness of summer school, extended school year programs, and other modifications of the school calendar as practical methods for preventing summer achievement losses and for continuing the cognitive development that takes place during the school year.

***The Investment Model***   The investment model grew out of economic theory, which has been applied to the development of human capital among children. Becker (1981) and others have asserted that parents invest both human and other forms of wealth in the development of their children. Human wealth takes the form of time spent with children and the parents' own levels of human capital. Other forms of wealth take the form of income and assets, which affect not only the goods and services parents can purchase. According to this theory, the greater the value of parental resources the larger the investment in children and the greater the children's educational attainment (Haveman, Wolfe, & Spaulding, 1991).

Researchers have diverged in their interpretations of the importance of material wealth, or economic resources, in developing the human capital of children. For instance, McLanahan (1985) noted an approximate 15% increase in the likelihood of high school graduation for each $10,000 increase in family income (McLanahan, 1985). This model suggested a linear relationship between economic resources and educational outcomes. In contrast, Mayer (1997) found that the shape of the relationship between financial resources and achievement growth was that of a threshold. Once children's basic material needs were met, achievement growth no longer responded to further monetary investment. Mayer's findings represent a clear departure from McLanahan's concern about the importance of economic

resources, but they do not dispel the notion that economic resources play an important role in producing educational outcomes. Rather, Mayer's findings point to the importance of considering measures that distinguish between parental expenditures and other types of parental resources.

***Techniques for Promoting Cognitive Growth during Summers***   Heyns (1978) devoted her attention to measuring the relationship between various summer activities and achievement growth. She found a strong positive relationship between summer achievement gains and the frequency with which children read books or visited the library during the summer (Heyns, 1978). The effect size was similar for African American and White students and was robust to controls for family income. Of all the activities Heyns studied, she found that encouraging more reading held the most promise for combating summer achievement losses. However, these effects of reading explained no more than about 10% of the variance in summer achievement growth. Kim (2004) found that regardless of race, socioeconomic level, or previous achievement, students who read four more books over the summer months scored higher on fall reading comprehension tests than their peers who had read one or no books over the summer. Furthermore, there were no significant differences in achievement based on which type of books children read.

Mayer (1997) found statistically significant achievement effects associated with two measures of parenting practices. The strongest predictor in Mayer's study combined a measure of hours per day of parental television watching with a measure of the frequency with which parents read to their children. Mayer weighted television watching negatively and reading positively in order to produce a "TV-Read Index." This index was positively associated with achievement growth in both reading and math (Mayer, 1997). Taken together, these findings suggest that all parents, regardless of their socioeconomic status level, can take action in order to promote their children's learning during the summer.

***Parental Psychological Resources***   Findings from the BSS led Entwisle and colleagues to conclude that parental expectations for their children's academic success are equal in importance to parental SES, and that these two factors are statistically independent in their effects on summer achievement growth. Unfortunately though, parental expectations are not evenly distributed among children of different SES levels. According to BSS measures of parental expectations prior to the first grade, parents of low SES tended to have lower expectations for their children's first-year reading and math grades, as well as lower expectations for their children's subsequent educational attainment, independent of the family's SES group. Parental expectations were correlated with actual reading grades and reading instructional level, the conduct and work habit appraisals of teachers, and eighth-grade course placements (Entwisle et al., 1997). Despite the less frequent incidence of high expectations among parents of low SES, the Entwisle et al. (1997) findings demonstrate that parental expectations matter for disadvantaged children. Across status groups, higher parental expectations were positively associated with academic self-esteem and students' own reading expectations, and were negatively related to problems including absences and referrals for academic problems (Entwisle et al., 1997).

Furthermore, children of parents with high expectations were more likely to engage in activities associated with summer achievement growth. Entwisle et al. also found a positive correlation between parents' expectations and their appraisals of the socioemotional status of their children. Combined with Mayer's finding concerning the linkage between positive appraisals and parental nurturing, this result suggests that parents with higher expectations may also be more nurturing of their children than other parents. These findings suggest the importance of considering parental expectations as a factor that may promote summer learning. Parental expectations can have a direct impact on school success, as well as indirect impacts through their effects on activities and behaviors that promote learning. Thus, from a methodological standpoint, these findings point to the importance of creating separate measures of parental expectations and parental activities, and of exploring the various connections between expectations and activities.

***Calendar Modifications***  Finally, educators and educational policymakers have suggested that summer school, extended school year programs, and other modifications of the school calendar could provide practical methods for preventing summer achievement losses and for continuing the cognitive development that takes place during the school year. The existence of summer learning loss and the research presented can be used to argue for increasing students' access to summer learning opportunities. These might include extending the school year, expanding access to summer schools, and/or incorporating additional learning activities into summer recreation and camp experiences. It can also be used to argue for adopting changes in the school calendar, perhaps by modifying it to do away with the long summer break. However, the existence of summer learning loss could not ipso facto be taken to mean that summer programs or an extended school year are effective interventions, nor that modified calendars that redistribute vacations throughout the year produce higher achievement among students than the traditional school calendar. Rather, the impacts of these interventions and innovations need to be evaluated on their own merits. Now, we turn to an in-depth examination of two of these calendar interventions.

## Summer School

***History and Goals of Summer School***  Although keeping children and adolescents off the street provided the initial impetus for summer school, by the 1950s educators realized that summer schools could furnish opportunities to remediate or prevent learning deficits (Austin, Rogers, &

Walbesser, 1972). Because the wealthy were able to hire tutors for their children, the educational summer programs made available through schools largely served students from disadvantaged backgrounds.

***Summer School to Redress Academic Deficiencies***  There are four types of summer programs meant to remediate learning deficits. First, some summer programs are meant to help students meet minimum competency requirements for graduation or grade promotion. Second, students who fail a particular course during the regular academic year use summer school as an opportunity to retake the course. Third, federal law requires school districts to offer summer programs for students who qualify for special education services. Fourth, a desire to break the cycle of poverty has led to the use of federal funds to establish summer programs for disadvantaged youth. These summer programs focus on both the prevention and remediation of learning deficiencies.

***Summer School for Nonremedial Purposes***  James B. Conant's (1959) book *The American High School* recommended that summer opportunities be provided not only for students who were struggling in school but also for those who needed more flexible course schedules or who sought enriched educational experiences. This would be accomplished by providing summer opportunities to take courses routinely given during the school year. Conant suggested students who were heavily involved in extracurricular activities or who worked after school could use summer school as a way to lighten their academic burden without delaying their graduation. Students who wished to graduate early could use summer school to accelerate their credit accumulation.

***Alternatives to Summer School***  In addition to formal summer school programs, many school districts, community-based nonprofit groups, and faith-based organizations provide camps and other types of informal learning programs during the summer months that offer a range of activities designed to help students catch up, get ahead, and develop new skills that will support higher levels of student achievement and youth development. In fiscal year (FY) 2005, Congress appropriated just under $1 billion for after school programs, the majority of which offered programs both during the summer and the regular school year. The focus of the 21st century Community Learning Centers program, reauthorized under Title IV, Part B, of the No Child Left Behind Act (2001), is to provide expanded academic enrichment opportunities for children attending low performing schools. Tutorial services and academic enrichment activities are designed to help students meet local and state academic standards in subjects such as reading and math. In addition, funded programs provide youth development activities; drug and violence prevention programs; technology education programs; art, music, and recreation programs; counseling; and character education to enhance the academic component of the program (U.S. Department of Education, 2005).

Summer vacation also has been embraced as an ideal time to provide specialized programs for students with academic gifts and other talents. These programs often involve offering advanced instruction that goes beyond the typical course of study. At the high school level, the content of these courses might be based on college-level curricula. Other programs take students with special talents to college during summer and provide in-residence programs.

***Research Examining the Effects of Summer School*** A research synthesis reported by Cooper, Charlton, Valentine, and Muhlenbruck (2000) used both meta-analytic and narrative procedures to integrate the results of 93 evaluations of summer school. The 54 reports from which effect sizes could be obtained described 52 separate summer school programs. A total of 477 comparisons were made between students before and after attending summer school or between students who did and did not attend summer school. About 33,500 students participated in all. Documents appeared between the years 1963 and 1995. Thirty-seven of the documents described programs that had as a goal the remediation of learning deficiencies. Three studies evaluated programs meant solely to prevent at-risk high school students from dropping out or to prevent "culturally deprived" kindergartners from falling behind in first grade. The remaining studies were divided among programs with the goal of acceleration and programs with other or multiple goals. Because of substantial differences in study characteristics, programs with the three different goals were examined separately. The main meta-analysis related to programs with the goal of remediation of learning deficiencies. Among these, participants were drawn from all grade levels and both low-SES and middle-SES families.

The authors offered five principle conclusions from their research synthesis. First, they concluded that summer school programs focused on lessening or removing learning deficiencies had a positive impact on the knowledge and skills of participants. Overall, students completing remedial summer programs were shown to have scored about one-fifth of a standard deviation higher than the control group on outcome measures. This conclusion was based on the convergence of numerous estimates of summer school effects. Lipsey and Wilson (1993) cataloged the effect sizes from 181 meta-analyses of different educational interventions and found the middle 20% of effects varied between .25 standard deviations and .49 standard deviations difference between intervention and comparison students. By this standard then, the summer school effect would be considered below average. Borman and D'Agostino (1996) examined the impact of regular school year Title I programs on the achievement of participants. These authors integrated the results of 17 federal summaries of local evaluations encompassing the test scores of over 41 million students. Their results, based largely on comparisons of students' preprogram and postprogram scores, revealed an average

difference between test scores of .11 standard deviations. By this standard the summer school effect would be large. However, the authors cautioned that the overall impact of summer school should be viewed as an average effect found across a diverse group of programs evaluated with a wide variety of methods. There was great variation around the mean. The overall estimate of effect might guide policy decisions at the broadest level but local officials could find effects quite different from the overall finding. Generally however, both the overall confidence intervals and those associated with specific categories of programs suggested it was likely that most summer school programs would find positive effects.

A second central finding of the meta-analysis was that summer school programs focusing on acceleration of learning or on nonremedial goals had a positive impact on participants roughly equal to programs that focused on remediation. However, while the overall effect was significantly different from zero, there were only seven such evaluations, so the meta-analysts could not examine the robustness of these findings across methodological, student, program, and outcome variations.

A third finding was that summer school programs had more positive effects on the achievement of middle-SES students than on students from low-SES backgrounds. The authors speculated that summer programs in middle-class school districts might have had better resources available. Alternatively, Heyns (1978) suggested that SES differences in summer school outcomes might occur because "programs are less structured and depend on the motivation and interest of the child" (p.139). A study comparing students' access to out-of-school time learning found great disparities based on income. More affluent children received enrichment programs while lower-SES children received only remediation, regardless of whether they needed it (Littell & Wynn, 1989). Finally, even though an SES difference did exist, the authors made three additional points. First, while the effect of summer school was larger for middle-SES students, the estimates of summer school's impact on lower-SES students were still significantly different from zero. Second, the few evaluations of summer programs for children of migrant workers indicated these programs had clear positive effects. And finally, if summer programs are targeted specifically at disadvantaged students they can serve to close the gap in educational attainment between rich and poor.

A fourth finding of the Cooper et al. (2000) meta-analysis was that remedial summer programs had larger positive effects when the program was run for a small number of schools or classes or in a smaller community. They found that analyses examining the influence of the size of the community, and the number of schools and classrooms, all revealed results that favored smaller programs. However, even the largest programs showed positive average effects that were significantly different from zero. The authors speculated that small programs might give teachers and administrators greater flexibility to tailor class content and instruction to the specific needs of the students they served and to their specific context. Small programs also may make planning easier, and may remove roadblocks to the efficient use of resources. As a caution to this interpretation, the authors pointed out that the size-related program variables might also be related to the socioeconomic background of the community being served, with larger programs serving less wealthy communities. If this is the case then economics might be the underlying causal factor, not local control.

Finally, the meta-analysis found that summer programs that provided small group or individual instruction produced the largest impact on student outcomes. For example, summer programs that operated in classes with less than 20 students revealed a positive effect of .38 standard deviations while classes larger than 20 students revealed positive effects of .24 standard deviations. Further, those evaluations that solicited comments about the positive aspects of summer school often revealed teachers believed small group and individual instruction were among the program's strengths.

In addition to the five principle conclusions, there were five other conclusions Cooper et al. (2000) felt could be drawn from the research synthesis, but with less confidence. First, summer programs that required some form of parent involvement produced larger effects than programs without this component. The types of parent involvement required in the summer programs included conferences with teachers, observing their child in class, and reading at home. Second, remedial summer programs may have a larger effect on math than on reading achievement. Cooper et al. (2000) specu-lated that control students in summer school evaluations likely received less practice in math than in reading. Third, the achievement advantage gained by students who attend summer school appeared to diminish over time. However, students who do not attend summer programs may receive similar programs during the school year that may diminish the difference between summer attendees and nonattendees. Fourth, remedial summer school programs had positive effects for students at all grade levels, although the effects were most pronounced for students in early primary grades and secondary school than for students in middle grades. Cooper et al. (2000) suggested the greatest achievement gains might be expected in the earliest and latest grades because these teachers placed the greatest emphasis on instruction in subject matter. Summer school in the middle years may place more emphasis on the teaching of study skills that eventually, but not immediately, have an impact on a diffuse set of outcome measures.

Fifth, the meta-analysis revealed summer programs that underwent careful scrutiny for treatment fidelity, including monitoring of attendance and instruction, might produce larger effects than unmonitored programs. These associa-tions may be due to the impact that surveillance had on the rigor with which programs were delivered.

Finally, two findings of the meta-analysis deserve mention because they were not found to be associated with program effectiveness. First, there was inconsistent evidence regarding whether or how the achievement label given to students (e.g., "underachieving," "at risk") was associated with the amount of benefit students derived from remedial summer programs. Second, summer school remedial programs that required attendance appeared no less effective than programs that were voluntary. It may be that compulsory attendance requirements were associated with student performance levels that were most likely to benefit from summer school activities.

In sum then, the major findings of the meta-analysis suggest that summer programs focusing on remedial or ac-celerated learning have a positive impact on the knowledge and skills of participants. Although all students benefited from remedial summer school, students from middle-SES homes showed larger positive effects then students from disadvantaged homes. Remedial programs had larger effects when the program was relatively small and when instruction was provided in small groups.

Still, Cooper et al. (2000) recognized the need for much more research on summer school effects. In particular they noted that future research needs to replicate some of their more tentative findings, especially the U-shaped relationship between summer program effects and grade level and the effect of student SES. Also, the persistence of summer school effects over time requires greater re-search attention. Finally, the meta-analysts pointed out that more studies employing random assignment of students to summer school conditions were needed using multiple comparison groups and embedding qualitative research methods so the casual and mediating mechanisms could be better understood.

### Can Summer Learning Programs Prevent the Accumu-lation of Summer Learning Losses and the Widening of SES-Based Achievement Gaps?

The combination of findings from the Cooper et al. (2000) meta-analysis of summer school effects and from Alexander, Entwisle, and Olson's Beginning School Study and, more recently, from the analyses of Downey et al. (2004) of the national Early Childhood Longitudinal Study (ECLS) data, have important implications for educational equality. If summer learning differences, compounded year after year, are an impor-tant cause of widening achievement gaps, could a series of yearly summer learning programs for disadvantaged students prevent the gap from widening? If we were to extrapolate across multiple summers the findings of Coo-per et al. (1996) regarding the one-year effects of summer vacation on lower-SES and middle-SES students' reading outcomes and the Cooper et al. (2000) results concerning one-year effects of summer school, the achievement growth trajectories would appear as those depicted in Figure 21.1. This figure shows the hypothetical reading achievement outcomes of lower-SES and middle-SES students over the first 5 years of formal schooling, kindergarten through grade 4, and across four summers.[1]

As suggested by the findings of Entwisle et al. (1997), this figure illustrates the cumulative widening of the achievement gap between SES groups of summer program

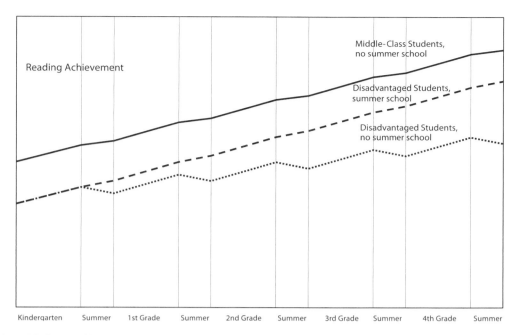

**Figure 21.1** A model of seasonal learning differences and summer school effects for disadvantaged students.

nonattendees. Alternatively, expanding on the findings of Cooper et al. (2000) for the one-year effect of summer school, the figure suggests that lower-SES students who are provided with summer programs year after year may be able to keep pace with the achievements of middle-SES students. To achieve absolute equality, additional interventions are needed, either to bridge the gap separating low- and middle-SES students when they begin their formal schooling or to accelerate the school-year growth of low wealth students. However, if the repeated effect of summer school is similar to the one-year effect found by Cooper and colleagues, summer school may be a key intervention through which educators can prevent the cumulative widening of the reading achievement gap.

Although this notion is provocative, the achievement trends displayed in Figure 21.1 remain largely hypothetical. We need more and better data to reach definitive policy conclusions regarding longitudinal trends in students' seasonal learning outcomes and the role that various types of summer learning opportunities may play in reducing the achievement gaps. It was only recently that researchers examined empirically the effects of a multiyear summer learning program. As a practical response to Entwisle and Alexander's findings from their Baltimore-based study of seasonal learning, Borman and Dowling (2006) conducted a 3-year study on the effects of a multiyear summer learning program, Teach Baltimore, in preventing the cumulative effect of summer learning losses, and promoting longitudinal achievement growth. Designed as a randomized field trial, the study randomly assigned 438 kindergarten and first-grade students from high-poverty schools to three consecutive summers of intervention. Longitudinal outcomes for the summer program participants were contrasted to those for 248 children randomized into a no-treatment

control condition. Multilevel growth models revealed no intention-to-treat effects of assignment to the multiyear summer learning program.

However, student attendance patterns at the voluntary program were variable across the 3 years that the intervention was offered. Maximum likelihood mixture models, which estimated the effects of the treatment for compliers, revealed statistically significant effects on learning across all three literacy domains tested for those students who attended the Summer Academy at an above average rate across two or more of the three summers that it was offered. Relative to their control-group counterparts, treatment compliers held advantages of 40% to 50% of one grade level on the final posttests. Therefore, Borman and Dowling (2006) provided some evidence that with good attendance, proactive and preventative summer learning programs can prevent summer achievement loss. Specifically, summer learning programs for disadvantaged students which begin early, before students have had the opportunity to fall so far behind as to be threatened with retention, can help prevent the growth in the achievement gap.

***Some Current Models of Summer Instruction*** There are several models of state and local interventions that respond directly to the research on the importance of early and consistent access to summer learning opportunities. The New Mexico Kindergarten Plus program designed to provide summer learning programs to children entering kindergarten and first grade began in 2003 as a 3-year pilot program administered in four school districts: Albuquerque, Gadsden, Gallup-McKinley, and Las Cruces. During the 2003–2004 school year, 260 students participated across all four districts and in 11 high-poverty schools. Despite wide variations in programs and results, a number of positive outcomes were observed, including: positive assessment trends on the Dynamic Indicator of Basic Early Literacy Skills (DIBELS), particularly in letter naming and word sound fluency; decreases in students classified with delayed skills in the prekindergarten project in the Gadsden School District; and strengthened social maturity and greater parental involvement (New Mexico Office of Accountability, 2005).

Founded in Boston in 1992, Building Educated Leaders for Life (BELL) is a community-based, nonprofit organization designed to increase the educational opportunities and achievements of children living in low-income communities. BELL Accelerated Learning Summer Program is a comprehensive 6-week academic program that provides intensive academic instruction; educational, cultural, artistic, and recreational activities; guest speakers; community service; and field trips. BELL serves more than 7,000 underperforming elementary school children, grades K-6, in Boston, New York City, Washington, DC, and Prince George's and Montgomery counties in Maryland. Children entering the program perform between 6 months and 2 years below grade level. The average yearly household income of a BELL scholar is $16,047 and 87% of children qualify for free or reduced price lunch. More than 95% of scholars are African American or Latino. BELL scholars gain an average of 6 months' grade-equivalent skills in reading and math. Scholars move closer to their peers, performing at the 50th and 42nd percentiles in reading and math by the end of the program, compared to the 43rd and 31st percentiles when the program began. Eighty-three percent of parents reported improvement in scholars' self-esteem, motivation to learn, and ability to work well with others (BELL, 2005).

A recent randomized study of the BELL Summer program conducted by the Urban Institute and Mathematica found that children in the BELL treatment group gained about a month's worth of reading skills more than their counterparts in the comparison group during the summer (Capizzano & Chaplin, 2006). Over 1,000 elementary school children who applied to BELL summer programs in New York and Boston in 2005 were randomly chosen to be in either a treatment group that was selected to participate in the BELL summer program, or a comparison group that was not. Independent researchers collected student reading tests (Gates-MacGinitie) and student and teacher surveys.

The study found modest, yet notable increase in reading skills for a 6-week program and evidence of positive impacts on the degree to which parents encouraged their children to read. No impacts were found on academic self-perceptions or social behaviors. Overall, this study provides scientifically rigorous evidence regarding the ability of the BELL summer program to improve the reading skills of low-performing elementary school children. Few out-of-school time programs have produced evidence of effectiveness when evaluated in such a rigorous manner. The results are of particular importance given the longstanding public policy focus on raising achievement levels of low-SES students.

The Montgomery County Public Schools' Extended Learning Opportunities (ELO) program is a 20-day voluntary, half-day summer program first implemented during the summer of 2002 with the goal of enhancing instruction and student achievement in the 18 elementary schools in Montgomery County, Maryland receiving Title I federal funds. The overall ELO initiative also includes an extended day component during the school year. The program is available to all current and new rising Kindergarten through fifth graders at any of the district's Title I schools. In 2003, 5,406 students registered for the program, representing 75% of the eligible population. Sixty-seven percent of ELO students participate in the free- and reduced-price meals system. ELO serves a diverse student body, including: 0.3% American Indian, 9.9% Asian American, 26.6% African American, 9.4% White, and 53.8% Hispanic. In 2003, students who attended the program for 16 or more days had the highest improvement in both reading and mathematics when compared to students who attended less than 5 days or did not attend at all. Improvements were statistically and educationally significantly only for fourth graders in the second year of the program, but all groups benefited academically as a result of participation (Montgomery County Public Schools, Office of Shared Accountability, 2004).

The Energy Express summer program began in West Virginia in 1994 with two sites in two counties and 13 college students mentoring 85 children. Since then, Energy Express has grown dramatically. By 2004, there were 87 sites in all counties in West Virginia with 3,334 children enrolled. Energy Express programs run for 3.5 hours a day for 6 weeks and serve rising first through sixth graders. For a site to qualify, more than 50% of the children in a school community must be eligible for free- or reduced-price meals. Seventy percent of participants are eligible for free- and reduced-priced meals. Twenty percent receive special education services. Over the years, the program has documented that participants experience gains in letter/word identification, comprehension and fluency, and broad reading as measured on pre- and postsummer reading achievement measures. In addition, the organization has served more than 191,500 nutritious meals and children have received almost 20,000 take-home books (Energy Express, 2005).

Summer Scholars (Denver, CO) is a year-round community literacy initiative partnering with 19 Northeast Denver elementary schools. The program works to improve the reading skills of elementary school students in an area affected by high rates of poverty and many related social problems. Classroom teachers and principals recruit students to participate in the Summer Scholars program by inviting the students they feel would benefit from additional help in reading and writing. In 2002, 1,253 elementary school students were recruited to participate in the program, and the majority of students served were in grades first through third. The average student was 8.5 years old. The majority of participants were either Latino or African American, and 26% came from Spanish-speaking households. One third lived with single mothers, most students were eligible for the federal free lunch program. One third of the participants were returning students, and a quarter had siblings who had participated in the program in previous years. More than half of the students scored below the "proficient" level on the Colorado Student Assessment Program or were at risk of not being proficient by third grade. In addition, 111 third and fourth graders (8.9% of total students) were required by the Denver Public School System to attend Summer Scholars. In 2002, 78.5% of second graders and 82.4% of third graders who participated in the program improved by at least one level on the Developmental Reading Assessment (Summer Scholars, 2005).

These programs provide examples of a wide variety of models currently in use for delivery of summer instruction to children who are struggling in school and come from low wealth backgrounds. Although varying in rigor, each provides evidence of the effectiveness of the approach.

## Modified School Calendars

*Alternatives to the Traditional School Calendar* Suggestions for change in the traditional school calendar can be grouped into two types. The first involves an *extended school year* that increases the number of days children spend in school. The most frequent argument for increasing the number of school days is the potential to increase student learning. These arguments are supported by international comparisons showing that the number of days American students spend in school lags behind most other industrialized nations. For example, the National Education Commission on Time and Learning (1994) reported that most students in the United States spend between 175 and 180 days in school each year while students in Japan spend 240 days in school. Implicit in this argument is the notion that increased time on task would result in increased knowledge acquisition.

Arguments against extending the school year generally take no issue with the theory of time-on-task but do question whether more school time truly translates into more task time. For example, the National Educational Association (1987) questioned whether additional time in school might simply lead to additional fatigue for students. Others have suggested that if only a few days are added to the school calendar, no change will result in the amount of material taught to students. Unless additional time is accompanied by changes in teaching strategy and curricula, the added time may not be used productively (Karweit, 1985). Related to this argument is the notion that adding, for example, five or six days to a school year represents only a 3% increase in school time. Hazleton and colleagues (Hazleton, Blakely, & Denton, 1992), based on work by Karweit (1984), suggested that 35 extra days would be needed to produce a noticeable change in student achievement. Thus, opponents

of extending the school year ask whether money might not more effectively be spent on improving the quality of instruction or reducing class size.

A second form of calendar change involves an arrangement in which children might or might not attend school for more days but the long summer vacation disappears. This is often referred to as *year-round schooling* but we will refer to it as a *modified school calendar.* Modified calendars have been especially popular in school districts where there is a great need for additional school space and classrooms because it can increase the number of students a particular school facility can accommodate (Shields & Oberg, 2000). By using a modified calendar, children can be placed in alternate vacation sequences and the building can be in use year-round. The strategy is called *multitracking.* When all children in a school are on the same modified calendar, it is called *single tracking.*

### Current Use of Modified Calendars in the United States

In school year 2004–2005, over 2.28 million students in 47 states attended over 3,200 schools that operated without the long summer break (National Association for Year-Round Education, 2006). About three-quarters of these students attended elementary schools with the remainder equally divided between middle and high school students. The state with the largest number of students in modified calendar schools was California, followed by Arizona, Hawaii, Nevada, and Kentucky. It is not irrelevant that these states were experiencing the largest population growth rates in the country.

### Arguments for and against Modified Calendars
First and foremost, proponents of modified school calendars point to the possible negative impact of summer vacations on learning as a rationale for calendar change. They suggest that children learn best when instruction is continuous. The long vacation breaks the rhythm of instruction, leads to forgetting, and requires that significant time be spent on review of material when students return to school in the fall. Opponents of modified calendars (SummerMatters.com, 2006) are skeptical about the alleged benefits of modified calendars. First, they suggest that shorter, more frequent school breaks might actually create more opportunities to forget things and, therefore, increase the need for time spent on review. Second, they claim that changing the calendar diverts attention from the real problems in education, such as ineffective teaching methods, lack of parental involvement, and the need for curriculum restructuring. Finally, they point to a study by Mitchell and Mitchell (2005) that examined a large California school district using a multitracked modified calendar. The researchers found that different tracks served students with different average achievement levels and economic and ethnic backgrounds. Poorer performing tracks were associated with fewer teacher resources (e.g., teachers with less experience). Thus, intentionally or not, multitracking could lead to educational inequities even within the same school.

Advocates of modified calendars counter by suggesting that such schedules not only prevent summer learning loss but also provide multiple, shorter breaks for children who are struggling in school. Teachers who see a student struggling on the traditional calendar may be frustrated by their limited ability to forcefully intervene until summer. Three or 4-week breaks that occur after 9 or 12 weeks of instruction might provide an opportunity for more timely remedial activities. Proponents point to positive examples that include schools making remedial, enrichment, and acceleration classes available to students during the multiple breaks. Opponents counter that remedial intersessions will be of limited effectiveness because they force students who already may have bad attitudes toward school to be exposed to more of the same type of failing instructional techniques.

### Research Examining School Calendar Effects on Achievement

Cooper, Valentine, Charlton, and Barnett (2003) presented the results of a meta-analysis of studies that looked at the impact of modified school calendars on academic achievement. They used data from 39 evaluations conducted in different school districts. Documents were published or prepared between the years 1973 and 2000. Most of the districts were in the southern half of the United States (where most modified calendar schools are located) and the vast majority involved elementary schools, with a few also including middle and high schools. Most outcome measures were standardized tests and most evaluations included measures of both reading and math achievement.

First, these reviewers reported that the quality of evidence available on modified school calendars was generally of very poor quality. They noted that for ethical and political reasons it is virtually impossible to conduct an experimental study of calendar variations. Natural experiments, in which a school district (a) had many more families wishing to have their child attend school on a modified calendar than could be enrolled in the school, and (b) used a random lottery to choose which students would be enrolled in the modified calendar school was absent from the research literature. Further, 59% of evaluations made no attempt to match students who attended modified calendar schools and their traditional calendar counterparts, beyond choosing a similar school in the same school district.

Cooper et al. (2003) reported that, even within this weak inferential framework, the evidence from the meta-analysis revealed ambiguous results. A vote-count of evaluations conducted in 58 different school districts from which the direction of the calendar comparison could be discerned revealed that 62% of the districts reported students in the modified calendar program outperformed students in the traditional calendar program. The estimated effect size from the vote count suggested that students from modified calendar schools outperformed traditional calendar students by about one twenty-fifth of a standard deviation. Among 39 school districts that provided enough information to permit direct calculation of effect sizes, the results suggested

students from modified calendar schools outperformed traditional calendar students by about one-twentieth of a standard deviation. When only school districts that attempted some statistical or matching control of preexisting student differences were examined the average weighted effect size was roughly the same.

These are very small effects. However, Cooper et al. (2003) went on to point out that these evaluations might underestimate the effect on achievement of modified calendars because there might be more vacation days for modified calendar schools during fall and winter. Therefore, an achievement test given to all students on the same day in May or June will mean modified calendar students had received less instruction during that academic year. For example, Stripling (1994) reported that students on the modified calendar in the Waco (Texas) Independent School District had 14 fewer days of instruction at the time of statewide testing than the comparison group of students attending traditional calendar schools.

Also, most evaluations looked at the impact of school calendars for only a single academic year. If the causal mechanism underlying the impact of the modified calendar is that it prevents or lessens summer learning loss, and therefore requires less class time spent on review, then it is reasonable to expect that the effect would be cumulative over multiple years of exposure. For example, students in elementary schools will be exposed to the modified calendar for 5 or 6 years. Therefore, over the course of an elementary school education the impact of the modified calendar might be a quarter standard deviation or more.

Cooper et al. (2003) found four studies that examined cumulative effects of modified calendars. Kneese (2000) compared the fall and spring scores of students in modified and traditional calendar schools during the students' second and third years in the modified calendar program. She found significantly greater gains favoring the modified calendar during student's second year in the program but not during the third year. Stripling (1995) compared achievement in reading and mathematics for students who had been on the modified calendar for only 1 year and those who had been on the modified calendar for 2 years. Students who had been on the modified calendar for 1 year had slightly more favorable achievement levels, while those who had been on the modified calendar for 2 years showed slightly less favorable achievement levels when compared to traditional calendar students. Bechtel (1991) compared yearly gain scores for students who had been on modified calendars for either 1, 2, or 3 years to traditional calendar students and found diminishing gains over time. Students who had been on modified calendars for 3 years performed no differently from traditional calendar students. Cason (1995) found an opposite effect; reading and math scores in modified calendar schools improved significantly after the second year, relative to traditional calendar schools. These findings suggest no additive positive effect of modified calendars. However, because most of the studies looking at cumulative effects were begun when the modified calendar was first instituted at the school, it is possible that the schools were improving their new instructional delivery system over the years. This would weigh against finding a cumulative, additive effect.

Opponents of modified calendars have argued that the availability of intersessions, rather than doing away with the long summer break, could be the causal mechanism underlying any positive effect of a modified calendar. Cooper et al. (2003) suggested that it would be difficult to test this assertion because students attending traditional calendar schools have access to summer school programs just as students on modified calendars have access to added instruction during intersessions. The Cooper et al. (2003) meta-analysis identified 15 districts that explicitly indicated intersession instruction was available. Their results were compared to evaluations that did not mention intersessions and might or might not have offered them. This rough test revealed that districts stating they offered intersessions reported slightly more positive effects, although these effects were statistically significant under only one of four testing models.

*District, Student, and Program Variations that Might Influence Calendar Effects*   The meta-analysis revealed few other moderators of the overall calendar effect. The most reliable moderator was the socioeconomic composition of the community served by the modified calendar school. The average students from lower-SES communities who attended a modified calendar school outperformed their traditional calendar counterparts by about one fifth of a standard deviations. McMillan (2001) also found lower achieving students in modified calendar schools outperformed their traditional calendar counterparts. Taken together, these findings suggest that the modified calendar may have its greatest impact on students struggling in school or from disadvantaged homes.

While the positive impact of modified calendars for lower-SES students appears promising, it is important to point out that in many instances the impetus for adoption of modified calendars in low-wealth school districts has not been based on its effect on achievement. Rather, modified calendars have been adopted primarily to accommodate demographic changes and evidence suggests modified calendars are falling disproportionately on some disadvantaged population groups; for example, the poor and English language learners (Quinlan, George, & Emmett, 1987). If this is so, the argument could be made that this innovation is being used as an alternative to providing higher quality facilities to already disadvantaged populations (Orellana & Thorne, 1998).

The meta-analysis revealed three other moderating variables that were worth noting but were of limited generalizability. Therefore, they should not be taken as indicators of what might be revealed in future evaluations. First, suburban and rural modified calendar programs found larger effects than urban programs. Programs implemented in smaller communities might have been more success-

ful because patrons had more input into the program's implementation.

Second, effect sizes from single-track schools were somewhat larger than those from multitrack schools. There is little reason to expect that the instruction received by students in single-track and multitrack systems would be very different. However, multitracking often requires classrooms to shift location and this can be a disruption for students and teachers. Also, teaching specialists' energies might be drained on a multitrack system because they often are needed year-round. Further, multitrack systems are typically more controversial, perhaps diminishing community and parent support.

Finally, the meta-analytic result examining the impact of the students' grade level on calendar effects provided some indication of significantly better achievement for elementary than secondary students on modified calendars when compared to traditional calendar students.

## Conclusion

In this chapter, we have reviewed evidence suggesting that learning loss over summer is a real phenomenon and that children from low-SES families are more likely to experience summer learning loss in reading than are children from middle class homes. All children lose math skills. Further, we found evidence that summer learning loss may accumulate over time. We reviewed several theories that suggest the summer loss might be attributable to the relative lack of learning resources available to students over summer, and that these learning resources, or lack thereof, are related to the availability of more general resources associated with family wealth and parent availability. During summer vacations, young elementary school children from low-SES families show small losses, while more advantaged groups make academic gains. During the school year, learning rates are roughly equal, although lower-SES children continue to lose ground academically over time, because they gain little or nothing during summer months, while higher-SES children continue to grow. Then, we reviewed the rationale for summer learning programs and the evidence for their effectiveness. This research reveals that summer programs are generally effective and suggests ways to implement more effective programs. However, while summer school may help to address inequities in achievement if programs are made available to low-SES students, overall the data suggest that summer school programs are not equally benefiting low- and middle-SES students. Middle-SES students have benefited more from summer school, though the mechanisms through which this occurs are still a matter of speculation. We briefly described several current models of effective summer learning programs. Finally, we reviewed the pros and cons of modified school calendars and showed that the cumulative evidence for their effect on academic achievement was far from rigorous and revealed only small effects. However, we pointed out that modified calendar research (a) may have permitted less instructional time in modified calendar schools before the intervention effect was assessed and (b) may show larger effects for low wealth students.

There are numerous implications of school calendar research for educational policies. First, educational policymakers could simply choose to live with the diminished learning opportunities and skills decay that accompany the present school calendar. They could accept the argument that, rather than increase the amount of time students spend in school, or rearrange the calendar, it makes more sense, both from an economic and pedagogical viewpoint, to improve the way we use school time. However, policymakers who take this position also must address whether or not schools and society are obligated to remedy the inequities in learning opportunities, and the consequent differences in achievement, that the current school calendar creates for children at risk for failure. They must also state why an optimal pedagogical strategy ought not to include both alternative calendars *and* more efficient use of time.

Second, the summer vacation findings might help direct the efforts of summer enrichment and remedial programs. Specifically, a focus on math instruction would seem to be needed most when options for summer programs are limited. Alternatively, if summer programs have the purpose of mitigating inequities across income groups then a focus on reading instruction for lower income students would seem to be most beneficial. Further, summer programs appear to have larger positive effects when the program is run for a small number of schools or classes and when the classes themselves have fewer students. Small programs and classes may give teachers and administrators greater flexibility to tailor class content and instruction to the specific needs of the students they serve.

Finally, current evidence, based on less-than-optimal research designs, indicates modified calendars have at best a very small positive impact on achievement. However, proponents of modified calendars can find encouragement in a few findings. First, a case can still be made that the effect of calendar modification on achievement is cumulative. A well-designed, longitudinal study is needed to test this hypothesis. Second, there is evidence that modified calendar programs do noticeably improve achievement for economically disadvantaged or poorachieving students.

We hope the research covered herein, and the exercise of placing the several lines of research side-by-side, will serve to heighten public and policymaker awareness of issues related to school calendars and achievement. We concur that numerous important school reforms are needed to ensure that all children achieve to their full potential. However, calendar issues can easily be overlooked because they form the diffuse background in which other reforms are carried out. To fully understand children's ability or inability to achieve their full potential, we must consider not only what children experience in school but also what they experience while out of school, and how those experiences are patterned and interrelate.

## Notes

1. Informed by the findings of Burkam and Lee (2002), this figure also depicts a significant SES-based inequality in achievement outcomes at the beginning of kindergarten.

## References

Alexander, K. L., Entwisle, D. R., & Olson, L .S. (2007). Summer learning and its implications: Insights from the Beginning School Study. *New Directions in Youth Development, 114,* 11–32.

Association of California School Administrators. (1988). *A primer on year-round education.* Sacramento, CA: Author.

Austin, G. R., Rogers, B. G., & Walbesser, H. H. (1972). The effectiveness of summer compensatory education: A review of the research. *Review of Educational Research, 42,* 171–181.

Bechtel, R. E. (1991). A study of academic growth in third grade students and its relationship to year-round education (Doctoral dissertation, Pepperdine University, 1991). *Dissertation Abstracts International, 52-07,* 2404.

Becker, G. S. (1981). *A treatise on the family.* Cambridge, MA: Harvard University Press.

Becker, G. S., & Tomes, N. (1986). Human capital and the rise and fall of families. *Journal of Labor Economics, 4,* 1–39.

Building Educated Leaders for Life (BELL) Accelerated Learning Summer Program. (2005, March). Retrieved from http://www.summerlearning.org/programs/docs/BELL.pdf

Borman, G. D., & D'Agostino, J. V. (1996). Title I and student achievement: A meta-analysis of federal evaluation results. *Educational Evaluation and Policy Analysis, 18,* 309–326.

Borman, G. D., & Dowling, N. M. (2006). The longitudinal achievement effects of multi-year summer school: Evidence from the Teach Baltimore randomized field trial. *Educational Evaluation and Policy Analysis, 28,* 25–48.

Bowles, S., & Gintis, H. (1976). *Schooling in capitalist America.* New York: Basic Books.

Burkam, D. T., Ready, D., Lee, V. E., & LoGerfo, L. F. (2004). Socialclass differences in summer learning between kindergarten and first grade: Model specification and estimation. *Sociology of Education, 77,* 1–31.

Caballero, B. (2004). Obesity prevention in children: Opportunities and challenges. *International Journal of Obesity, 28,* S90–S95.

Capizzano, J., & Chaplin, D. (2006). *Impacts of a summer learning program: A random assignment study of Building Educated Leaders for Life (BELL).* Washington, DC: The Urban Institute. Retrieved from http://www.urban.org/url.cfm?ID=411350

Cason, C. B. (1995). The impact of year-round school on student achievement, student/teacher attendance, and discipline. *Dissertation Abstracts International, 56–11,* 4262.

Coleman, J. S., Campbell, E. Q., Hobson, C. J., McPartland, J., Mood, A. M., Weinfeld, F. D., et al. (1966). *Equality of educational opportunity.* Washington, DC: U.S. Government Printing Office.

Coleman, R. W., & Freehorn, C. L. (1993, February). *A comparative study of multi-track year-round education and the use of relocatables.* Paper presented at the meeting of the National Association for Year-Round Education, San Diego, CA.

Conant, J. B. (1959). *The American high school.* New York: McGraw-Hill.

Cooper, G., & Sweller, J. (1987). Effects of schema acquisition and rule automation on mathematical problem-solving transfer. *Journal of Educational Psychology, 79,* 347–362.

Cooper, H., Charlton, K., Valentine, J. C., & Muhlenbruck, L. (2000). *Making the most of summer school.* Malden, MA: Blackwell.

Cooper, H., Nye, B., Charlton, K., Lindsay, J., & Greathouse, S. (1996). The effects of summer vacation on achievement test scores: A narrative and meta-analytic review. *Review or Educational Research, 66,* 227–268.

Cooper, H., Valentine, J. C., Charlton, K., & Barnett, A. (2003). The effects of modified school calendars on student achievement and school community attitudes: A research synthesis. *Review of Educational Research, 73*, 1–52.

Dougherty, J. W. (1981). *Summer school: A new look.* Bloomington, IN: Phi Delta Kappa.

Downey, D. B., von Hippel, P. T., & Broh, B. A. (2004). Are schools the great equalizer? Cognitive inequality during the summer months and the school year. *American Sociological Review, 69*, 613–635.

Energy Express. (2005, March). Retrieved from http://www.summerlearning.org/programs/docs/Energy_Express.pdf

Entwisle, D., & Alexander, K. (1992). Summer setback: Race, poverty, school composition, and mathematics achievement in the first two years of school. *American Sociological Review, 57*, 72–84.

Entwisle, D. R., Alexander, K. L., & Olson, L. S. (1997). *Children, schools, and inequality.* Boulder, CO: Westview.

Entwisle, D. R., Alexander, K. L., & Olson. L. S. (2000). Summer learning and home environment, In R. D. Kahlenberg (Ed.), *A notion at risk: Preserving public education as an engine for social mobility* (pp. 9–30). New York: Century Foundation Press.

Food Research and Action Center. (2002). *Hunger doesn't take a vacation: Summer nutrition status report.* Washington, DC: Author.

Garfinkel, M. A. (1919). The effect of the summer vacation on ability in the fundamentals of arithmetic. *Journal of Educational Psychology, 10*, 44–48.

Gold, K. M. (2002). *School's in: The history of summer education in American public schools.* New York: Lang.

Haveman, R., Wolfe, B., & Spaulding, J. (1991). Childhood events and circumstances influencing high school completion. *Demography, 28*, 133–157.

Hazelton, J. E., Blakely, C., & Denton, J. (1992). *Cost effectiveness of alternative year schooling.* Austin, TX: Educational Economic Policy Center, University of Texas, Austin.

Heyns, B. (1978). *Summer learning and the effects of schooling.* New York: Academic Press.

Karweit, N. (1984). Time-on-task reconsidered: Synthesis of research on time and learning. *Educational Leadership, 41*, 32–35.

Karweit, N. (1985). Should we lengthen the school term? *Educational Researcher, 14*, 9–15.

Kim, J. (2004). Summer reading and the ethnic achievement gap. *Journal of Education for Students Placed at Risk, 9*, 169–188.

Kneese, C. (2000). *Year-round learning: A research synthesis relating to student achievement.* San Diego, CA: National Association for Year-Round Education.

Lee, V. E., & Burkam, D. T. (2002). *Inequality at the starting gate: Social background differences in achievement as children begin school.* Washington, DC: Economic Policy Institute.

Lipsey, M. W., & Wilson, D. B. (1993). The efficacy of psychological, educational, and behavioral treatment: Confirmation from meta-analysis. *American Psychologist, 48*, 1181–1209.

Littell, J., & Wynn, J. (1989). *The availability and use of community resources for young adolescents in an inner-city and a suburban community.* Chicago, IL: Chapin Hall Center for Children.

Mayer, S. E. (1997). *What money can't buy: Family income and children's life chances.* Cambridge, MA: Harvard University Press.

McLanahan, S. (1985). Family structure and the reproduction of poverty. *The American Journal of Sociology, 90*, 873–901.

McMillan, B. J. (2001). A statewide evaluation of academic achievement in year-round schools. *Journal of Educational Research, 95*, 67–74.

Mitchell, R. E., & Mitchell, D. E. (2005). Student segregation and achievement tracking in year-round schools. *Teachers College Record, 107*, 529–562.

Montgomery County Public Schools, Office of Shared Accountability. (2004, January). *2003 summer evaluation of the Extended Learning Opportunities (ELO) program evaluation report.* Retrieved from http://www.mcps.k12.md.us/departments/accountability/pdf/evaluation/elo2002.pdf

National Association for Year-Round Education. (2006). Statistical summary, 2005. Retrieved from http://www.nayre.org/

National Center for Education Statistics. (1998). *The condition of education 1998* (ED Publication No. NCES 98-013). Washington, DC: U.S. Government Printing Office.

National Education Association. (1987). *What research says about extending the school day/year: Proposals and results.* Washington, DC: Author.

National Educational Commission on Time and Learning. (1994). *Prisoners of time: Schools and programs making time work for students and teachers.* Washington, DC: U.S. Government Printing Office. (ERIC Document Reproduction Service No. ED 366115)

New Mexico Office of Accountability. (2005, January). *The New Mexico kindergarten plus pilot program: Initial findings and recommendations.* Retrieved from http://www.state.nm.us/clients/dfa/Files/OEA/Kindergarten%20Plus%20Year%20One%20Report.pdf

Orellana, M. F., & Thorne, B. (1998). Year-round schools and the politics of time. *Anthropology & Education Quarterly, 29*(4), 446–472.

Phillips, M., Crouse, J., & Ralph, J. (1998). Does the Black–White test score gap widen after children enter school? In C. Jencks & M. Phillips (Eds.), *The Black–White test score gap* (pp. 229–272). Washington, DC: Brookings Institution Press.

Quinlan, C., George, C., & Emmett, T. (1987). *Year-round education: Year-round opportunities. A study of year-round education in California.* Sacramento, CA: California State Department of Education, Special Studies and Evaluation Reports Unit. (ERIC Document Reproduction Service No. ED282272)

Sargent, L. R., & Fidler, D. A. (1987). Extended school year programs: In support of the concept. *Education and Training in Mental Retardation, 22*, 3–9.

Shields, C. M., & Oberg, S. L. (2000). *Year-round schooling: Promises and pitfalls.* Lanham, MD: Scarecrow Press.

Stripling, R. (1994). *The effectiveness and efficacy of year-round education in the Waco Independent School District, 1993–1994.* Waco TX: Waco Independent School District.

Stripling, R. (1995). *The effectiveness and efficacy of year-round education in the Waco Independent School District, 1994–1995.* Waco TX: Waco Independent School District.

SummerMatters.com. (2001). *What research says.* Retrieved from http://www.summermatters.com/reviews.htm

Summer Scholars. (2005, March). Retrieved from http://www.summerlearning.org/programs/docs/Summer_Scholars.pdf

U.S. Department of Education. (2005). *21st century community learning centers—Funding status.* Retrieved from http://www.ed.gov/programs/21stcclc/funding.html

von Hippel, P. T., Powell, B., Downey, D. B., & Rowland, N. (2007). The effect of school on overweight in childhood: Gains in children's body mass index during the school year and during summer vacation. *American Journal of Public Health, 97*, 796–802.

# 22

# Developmental and Educational
# Role of Recess in School

*ANTHONY PELLEGRINI AND DANIELLE DUPUIS*

The psychologist interested in peer relations during middle childhood is hard pressed to find a venue to observe naturally occurring peer interactions. One of the few, yet understudied, places that this can be done with relative efficiency is on the school playground during the recess period (Hart, 1993). The recess period is similar to free playtime for preschool children. In both places we have a relatively large sample of children, located in one place, engaging in spontaneous and relatively unstructured peer interactions. Further, in both places children develop and learn important social skills and take a break from the more structured classroom regimens.

In light of this it is interesting that the school recess period is currently being drastically eliminated or cut from the school day across the United States and the United Kingdom. The typically stated reason for this policy is that recess is counterproductive to traditional educational aims. For example, it is often stated that having recess takes time away from teaching more basic skills in an already very limited and crowded school day. Thus, limiting recess time and reallocating that time to instruction, on the assumption that this will maximize school performance, is one proffered solution to limited instructional time.

In this chapter we will argue that the recess period actually maximizes cognitive dimensions of school performance. Further, the recess period affords opportunities for children to learn and develop skills associated with two key "developmental tasks" of middle childhood (Waters & Sroufe, 1983): Peer relations and adjustment to full day, formal schooling. It is important to stress, as we will later in this chapter, that peer relations in school are empirically related to more traditional measures of school performance (Coie & Dodge, 1998). But first, we provide a brief historical and theoretical background to the debate surrounding the role of recess and breaks from work during the school day.

## Some Historical and Theoretical Debate

*Work Is Good—Play Is Bad* Questioning the role of recess in the primary school educational day is similar, we think, to the ways in which children's play and leisure have been questioned by some educators. Play, like what goes on at recess, is often seen as a force opposing work: Work is viewed as good and play is not. Some trace this dichotomy to the Puritan/Calvinistic ethic in America and much of the Anglo Saxon world (e.g., Sutton-Smith, 1997; Tawney, 1926/1969). Break times, leisure, and play are viewed as "slothful." Sloth, remember, is one of the seven deadly sins, portrayed in many Medieval (before the Reformation, per se) and Renaissance paintings. Thus, we cannot "blame" Calvinism or the Protestant work ethic primarily for devaluing play and leisure in relation to work.

Correspondingly, the positive role of labor and work was certainly stressed by explicitly anti-Christian theorists, most notably Karl Marx (1867/1906). Marx stated that one's labor, realized as one's place in the means of production, defined and formed one's consciousness. Further, benefits that accrued without the individual engaging in labor was frowned upon in Marx's notion of the "unearned increment." That is, the value of work over less visibly "productive" activities has a long history and has had appeal to a very wide audience. Bertrand Russell (1932/1972) referred to this bias as the "cult of efficiency."

While Russell's argument is not aimed at children and schools per se but at the role of leisure and breaks from work for adults in modern industrial society (early 20th century), his notion of "idleness" is close to our conceptions of recess and play—"a capacity for light-heartedness and play" (p. 24). He suggested that the workday be reduced (remember this was published in 1932) so that people would have more time to spend in leisure activities, such as playing games, dancing, listening to music, and going to the cinema. The benefit associated with this extension of leisure, for Russell, was that people such as teachers or physicians might choose to learn more about their professions, and people in general might learn more about allied fields or volunteer in public causes. All of this would, he argued, make the world a better and indeed a *more productive* place.

There are also developmental implications of Russell's view of leisure. Specifically, and as will be explicated later in this chapter, the view advanced by Russell was that the benefits associated with leisure and play were "immediate," not deferred until a later developmental period. That is, leisure, like play during childhood, is beneficial to that period of development, for both children and adults, where the leisure activities were exercised; they were not postponed to a later period.

By contrast, a more common stance, at least in much of developmental psychology, is to attribute importance to "early experience" and posit that the benefits associated with play and leisure during childhood are "deferred" until adulthood; for example, the roles that children enact in dramatic play are practice for the skills associated with those roles in adulthood. A nonpsychological variant of his notion can be found in Thomas Hughes's (1895) praise for the moral instruction afforded by game playing in childhood. In his book, *Tom Brown's School Days*, Hughes (echoing Wellington after he had defeated Napoleon at Waterloo in 1812) talked about the moral and social lessons learned when young boys engaged in games played on the fields of Rugby School. Hughes saw the social skills learned while playing games as similar to those needed to lead men in battle: The lessons learned on the playing fields at Rugby were generalized to Waterloo.

The realist might say (and rightly so) that discussions of play and school recess must be conducted in light of the world of real school policy. That is, parents, educators, and politicians are concerned about children's academic achievement as well as their safety in schools. Where they raise concerns that recess may interfere with safety and learning, those concerns must be addressed. This has lead to recess being diminished or eliminated in the United States and Britain.

***The Place of Recess in the School Day***  Documentation of the place of recess in the school day is very spotty, possibly reflecting the low regard for recess in both the school and academic community. One early "national survey" was conducted by the National Association of Elementary School Principals (NAESP) in 1989. This survey was sent to the state superintendents of education of all 50 states plus the District of Columbia.

It is important to recognize that this survey is technically not strong but it is the only data from this period of which we are aware. Responses from 47 states were received. Results indicated that "recess," in some form, was held in 90% of the cases and of those cases, 96% had one or two

recess periods daily. In 75% of the cases recess lasted 15 to 20 minutes each. Importantly, we do not know the form that recess took. It could have been a physical education class or a more traditional free play period on the playground. Data from this survey should be interpreted very cautiously given the limitations associated with the selectively of the sample and the unknown psychometric properties of the survey.

In 1997 a longitudinal study of children and families was conducted and in this nationally representative survey, time budgets of elementary school children's school day (grades 1–5) was presented (Roth, Brooks-Gunn, & Linver, 2003). Time spent in recess was included in this survey and they found that 6.8% of children's school day or about 26 minutes a day was spent in recess and the longer the school days the more time was spent in recess. Specifically, with school days of 6, 6½, and 7 hours duration, the corresponding time spent in recess was 23, 25, and 31 minutes. Further, older children had less recess time than younger children: In grades 1 and 2, 3, and 4 and 5 recess periods were, respectively, 28, 29, and 23 minutes. Most surprisingly, there was a relation between recess time and children's poverty status: Children above poverty status, relative to those at or below poverty status, had close to twice as much of their time for recess (7.2 % vs. 4.3% of their school day). We will return to some of these results when we discuss policy implications.

There is a similar trend in the United Kingdom for recess to be diminished and the motivations appear similar to those at work in the United States: concern with achievement. In a well-designed, nationally representative survey of recess, or break time as it is called in Britain, Blatchford and Sumpner (1998) asked about changes in recess across the 5 years between 1990 and 1991, and 1995 and 1996. They found that 38% and 35% of junior (7–11 years of age) and secondary schools (11–16 years of age), respectively, had reduced duration of the lunchtime recess break and 26% of the infant schools (5–7 years of age) reported reduction. Similarly, reductions were reported for the afternoon recess period: 12, 27, and 14% of infant, junior, and secondary schools, respectively, reported the elimination of that recess period! Like the U.S. case presented above, as students get older, they have less recess time.

These data clearly indicate that recess holds a marginal place in the school curriculum.  Like Russell, we argue that there is not enough leisure time in school in the form of recess. We will present developmental theory and data suggesting that recess time actually helps students adjust to school and learn in the traditional sense.

## Development in Schooling: A Metamorphic View

The idea that development can serve as a guide to schooling is, of course, not a new one. Perhaps the most visible translation of a developmental model for schools comes in the form of developmentally appropriate practices from the

National Association for the Education of Young Children (NAEYC, 1992). This document is a manifesto for the ways in which young children should be taught. Specifically, it lists instructional practices for infants, toddlers, pre-schoolers, and primary school students; for example, the authors stress the importance of play for preschoolers and the foundational role of primary school experiences for subsequent learning.

Most traditional approaches to schooling, such as the NAEYC policy, view children as "imperfect adults" (Bateson, 1981, 2005; Kagan, 1971) and the role of education is to move children along the path to adulthood. This is not to say that children are not viewed as qualitatively different from adults. From this teleological view, children's thinking is described as a progression from less to more differentiated, or developed, and by what it is they cannot do. This view of development highlights the importance of early experience as a determinant of adult behavior. The benefits of education from this orientation are conceptualized as "deferred": A skill is built in childhood and the benefits are reaped in adulthood in the form of enhanced skill development.

A contrasting view has been presented by Pat Bateson (1981, 2005; see also Pellegrini, Dupuis, & Smith, 2007), whose "metamorphic" view of development considers those "immature" behaviors characterizing childhood as advantageous to the niche of childhood, rather than something imperfect which need to be overcome. Like the metamorphosis of a tadpole into a frog or a caterpillar into a butterfly, the characteristics and behaviors of the young child are well suited to the period of childhood per se and may not be especially relevant to adult related skills. The benefits reaped from these behaviors are immediate, rather than deferred. These behaviors are not something directly shaped into adult-relevant skills. For example, the sucking behavior of infants is certainly relevant to feeding during infancy but not related to feeding behaviors later in life (Bateson & Martin, 1999).

The metamorphic view posits that "immature" behaviors characteristic of childhood, like play, are important to childhood per se and the benefits of play are reaped during that period (Bateson, 2005; Bjorklund & Pellegrini, 2000; Pellegrini et al., 2007). The clearest example of such an "immediate benefits" view of play relates to locomotor play. The cardiovascular and physical fitness benefits of play in childhood are immediate and do not relate to adult cardiovascular health (Pellegrini & Smith, 1998).

Dave Bjorklund and Tony Pellegrini (Bjorklund & Pellegrini, 2000) used this notion of the immediate value of "immature" behavior in applying the cognitive immaturity hypothesis to children's play—suggesting that these processes are not inferior variants of adult behavior but instead specific adaptations to the niche of childhood that enable young children to effectively learn skills and behaviors important for that period per se. For example, children's overestimation of their own social skills enables them to persevere at tasks even though, by adult standards, they are not doing it very well. This perseverance may lead to self-perceived success which may, in turn, lead to higher self-perceived competence and help with learning complicated skills and strategies. At root, this view of development highlights the importance of the notion that natural selection works on different periods of development, not only on adulthood. After all, in order to live to reproduce in adulthood, one must adapt to and survive childhood!

The construct of a "developmental task" is important in identifying those behaviors and skills which are crucial to each developmental period (Sroufe, Egelund, & Carlson, 1999; Waters & Sroufe, 1983). Developmental tasks vary with age; for example, impulse control during the preschool period and peer group membership and adjustment during the early primary school years. Mastering the skills necessary for membership in one's school peer group and feeling efficacious in this area should provide a basis for adjustment to school (Pellegrini, Kato, Blatchford, & Baines, 2002). We suggest that children's facility with social games is a candidate for an important developmental task as children make the transition to formal schooling.

***Recess and Social Development*** Children's social behavior is important for their success and adjustment to school (Coie & Dodge, 1998). Children with poor peer relations in school, for example, typically become disaffected with school and begin to disengage from school and affiliate with other disaffected children, resulting in dropping out of school and antisocial behavior (Coie & Dodge, 1998). In this section we examine an important aspect of children's social behavior at recess: games.

Games, like recess, surprisingly, have not received extended empirical attention from psychologists or educators for a number of years. We say surprisingly because at least one influential theorist (Piaget, 1968) suggested that games have important implications for children's social and cognitive development. Correspondingly, there have been repeated calls since the 1950s in the developmental literature for more research on games (e.g., Gump & Sutton-Smith, 1955; Hart, 1993; Rubin, Fein, & Vandenberg, 1983; Sutton-Smith, 1971). Yet, neither the 1998 nor the 2006 *Handbook of Child Psychology* volume on social and personality development (Eisenberg, 1998, 2006), has a single reference in the subject index to games or games with rules, down from the rather sparse six references in the 1983 *Handbook* (Hetherington, 1983)!

While there are a number of possible reasons for the recent neglect of research on children's games, it clearly is consistent with the theme that scholars, like many school systems in the United States and Britain, do not take children's play and games seriously. Another reason for this neglect may relate to availability of and access to a research sample of young children at a time when they typically engage in games (i.e., elementary school). Compare the ease with which infants and preschool children can be observed in university laboratory schools and the massive amount of research on the modal forms of play for children of these ages, sensorimotor and fantasy play. Elementary school children, on the other hand, are less accessible for study and proffer fewer opportunities for observations of peer interaction because much of their school day is tightly scheduled around regimens of solitary and sedentary academic work (Pellegrini & Blatchford, 2000).

Observations of children at recess are an excellent venue to examine children's competence because interaction with peers at recess is both motivating and demanding for children—two necessary conditions for a reliable and valid assessment of social competence, where social competence is defined rather globally as children's adjustment to the various developmental tasks, such as developing control of one's emotions, learning to make friends, and adjusting to school across the life span (Waters & Sroufe, 1983). That is, children typically enjoy recess and games, and to successfully engage in games requires a fair level of social and cognitive sophistication (Piaget, 1965). For example, children must know the rules of the games and subordinate their personal views and desires to those rules and to the positions of their peers. That they enjoy these interactions (possibly because they are self-selected) motivates them to exhibit the high levels of competence required to participate in the games. Children's engagement in playground games with their peers then should provide opportunities to learn and develop social skills as well as provide valid insight into their competence.

Before proceeding, it is important to differentiate play and games as they are sometimes confused, possibly because they share some design features. For example, both play (e.g., fantasy play) and games (e.g., soccer) are rule governed. The rules governing games, however, are a priori and codified, whereas the rules governing play are flexible, negotiated by players in different ways, and not set in advance. For example, in a play episode where two children are pretending to cook a meal, they can negotiate rules and roles regarding what is to be cooked (e.g., "Let's cook *stew*. No, let's make a *cake*") and how it is to be cooked ("*I* want to be the cook now"). Once these issues are agreed upon, play behavior is consistent with the rules for the theme and the roles, until the rules or roles are challenged. At that time they are typically renegotiated (Fein, 1981; Garvey, 1990). Indeed, more time is typically spent negotiating and renegotiating roles and rules in play than in play itself (Garvey, 1990; Sachs, Goldman, & Chaille, 1984).

Games, on the other hand, are guided by explicit rules that are set in advance and violations of these rules usually result in some form of sanction, not renegotiation (Garvey, 1990). So, for example, in a game of basketball, a child running with the ball without dribbling would be told by peers to forfeit the ball. Because games require following a priori rules they are not typically observed in children until the primary school years. Further, there are reliable gender differences in games. Following Piaget (1965) and others, boys, more than girls, prefer to engage in competitive games outdoors (Harper & Sanders, 1975; Pellegrini, 1992a, 2004; Pellegrini, Kato, et al., 2002; Thorne, 1993).

*Some Data* We present data from a longitudinal study of first graders attending two public schools in Minneapolis (Pellegrini, Kato, et al., 2002). The sample consisted of 78 children (30 males and 48 females), with a mean age of 77 months. Most of the children in the sample were lower socioeconomic status (as judged by their receiving free or reduced lunch) and for approximately 40% of the sample, Spanish was the first language. A total of four research associates worked on this project, all of whom were female graduate students. Logistically, each of two research associates was assigned to separate schools to conduct behavioral observations. To minimize bias, research associates did not interview or test the children they observed.

We predicted that being facile with games on the school playground at recess should predict adjustment to the very earliest school years because game facility is an indicator of children's engagement in one important dimension of the school day. Being engaged in this context with peers should generalize to school adjustment in first grade because, as a developmental task for this period, it is an indicator of children's sense of efficacy in the very early grades of school. Children attribute great importance to having peers with whom to interact at recess. Being good at games at recess seems to be an important part of enjoying school and peers at school.

Game facility was defined here (Pellegrini, Kato, et al., 2002) using multiple informants and formats. These individual measures were aggregated to maximize construct validity (Cronbach, 1971). First, and most generally, game facility was also defined observationally as the percent of total time observed engaged in games across the entire school year, where games were generally coded as chase games (e.g., tag), verbal games (e.g., jump rope/chanting), and ball games (e.g., basketball). Second, and also using direct observations, we indexed the number of children in the focal child's immediate peer group while on the playground. This idea of facility is derived from the ethologically oriented work on group centrality and dominance (Chance, 1967; Pellegrini, Roseth, et al., 2007; Vaughn & Waters, 1981). Most dominant individuals are leaders and are sought after, central in the group, and attended to by peers. Children want to be around leaders for a number of reasons. For example, by affiliating with leaders youngsters may learn valuable social skills from and form alliances with them. Thus, number of individuals surrounding an individual is an observational indicator of leadership status.

All direct observation used focal child sampling and continuous recording rules (Pellegrini, 2004). Specifically, focal children were identified daily from a randomized list of all children for whom we had informed consent. Each focal child was followed for 3 minutes and her or his behavior was recorded continuously for that entire period. Each child was observed minimally once a month.

Game facility was also assessed in terms of peer nominations (e.g., Who's good at games?) and teacher ratings of children's facility with games (e.g., Good at games?), each conducted during the fall and spring of the school

**TABLE 22.1**
**Intercorrelations between Indicators of Game Facility**

|                     | 2      | 3      | 4      |
|---------------------|--------|--------|--------|
| Observed games(1)   | .60**  | .29**  | .24**  |
| Group size(2)       |        | .32**  | .28**  |
| Peer nominations(3) |        |        | .35**  |
| Adult ratings(4)    |        |        |        |

** $p < .01$.

year. Children whose first language was Spanish were interviewed by a native speaker of Spanish using translated protocols. The intercorrelations between each of these variables are displayed in Table 22.1.

School adjustment, too, was defined from different perspectives and aggregated into one score. Specifically, during the fall and spring of children's first grade year they were asked to rate 12 questions concerning how they felt about school (e.g., Going to school makes me happy. School is boring.): yes, not sure, no. Correspondingly, teachers rated children's adjustment to school during the fall and spring of the year on an instrument derived, in part, from Ladd and Profilet's (1996) Child Behavior Scale (e.g., Coping well with school. Has friendly and responsive relationship with teacher.). The aggregate of children's and teachers' responses comprised our measure of school adjustment.

Results from this one-year longitudinal study showed that game facility predicted end-of-year school adjustment, after statistically controlling children's social competence and adjustment at the start of the school year. The separate regression models for boys and girls are displayed in Table 22.2. Game facility was a predictor of adjustment for boys, but not for girls.

Boys used their facility with games as a way in which they could achieve and maintain competence with their peers and to adjust to the demands of formal schooling. This finding is consistent with the assumption that the social rules and roles that children learn in one niche (with their peers on the school playground) should predict competence in related niches, with their peers in first grade. Both niches are similar to the extent that they encourage rule-governed behavior and cooperative interaction with peers, all in the larger context of school. These relations, however, held only for boys, not for girls. This finding is consistent with

**TABLE 22.2**
**Regression Models Predicting Boys' and Girls' School Adjustment**

| Variable Entered     | Order Entered | Df | t-value | p-value |
|----------------------|---------------|----|---------|---------|
| **Boys**             |               |    |         |         |
| Time1 adjustment     | 1             | 1  | 1.01    | .31     |
| Time 1 game facility | 2             | 2  | 2.54    | .01     |
| **Girls**            |               |    |         |         |
| Time1 adjustment     | 1             | 1  | .23     | .82     |
| Time 1 game facility | 2             | 2  | 1.82    | .08     |

the view that male groups are hierarchic and competence in these groups is often judged by ability to compete and lead (Blatchford, Bains, & Pellegrini, 2003; Maccoby, 1998; Maccoby & Jacklin, 1987; Pellegrini, 2004).

That game facility predicted boys' school adjustment is a very important finding for educational policy makers. Games probably provide opportunities to learn and practice the skills necessary for effective social interaction, such as turn taking and subordinating behavior to socially defined rules, with peers in an important socialization context, early schooling.

While these results do reinforce earlier research where children's peer relations in school predicted adjustment to school and school success (e.g., Ladd, Kochenderfer, & Coleman, 1996), they also extend this earlier work in that the majority of the students in our work were low-income children. It is well known that children, and again boys especially, from economically disadvantaged groups have difficulty adjusting to and succeeding in school (e.g., Greenfield & Suzuki, 1998, pp. 1094–1101; Heath, 1983). We have demonstrated that their success in one part of the first grade school day (games at recess) can predict more general school adjustment. The mechanisms by which this happens, however, are not clearly understood and are worthy of further study.

***Recess and Attention in the Classroom***　In this section we address a more proximal effect of recess on children's cognitive performance in school by examining the experimentally manipulated effect of varying recess timing regimens on children's attention to controlled classroom tasks. Attention is a measure that is consistent with theories suggesting that breaks from concentrated schoolwork should maximize performance. Following the notion of massed vs. distributed practice (Ebbinghaus, 1885/1964; James, 1901), children should be less attentive to classroom tasks during longer, compared to shorter, seatwork periods (e.g., Stevenson & Lee, 1990). Briefly, massed vs. distributed practice posits that individual performance is maximized when efforts are "distributed" across number of trials, rather than "massed" into one or fewer trails. For example, a child given a total of 100 spelling words to memorize will do better if he studies the words in 10 separate 10 minute sessions rather than in two 50 minute sessions.

Research in the area of massed vs. distributed practice is also interesting to the extent that the effects are robust across all age groups (e.g., Ebbinghaus, 1885/1964; James, 1901; Kausler, Wiley, & Phillips, 1990; Toppino, Kasserman, & Mracek, 1991)! Consequently, the current practice of reducing the duration of the recess period as students get older is not consistent with theory. While it may seem intuitive that children need less time at recess with age, policy should be backed by theory and data.

Following Stevenson and Lee's (1990) anecdotal attributions of the role of recess in Asian children's achievement, we designed a series of experiments to test the effects of recess breaks on children's classroom behavior after recess. In the studies reported below, attention and inattention were measured in terms of children's looking/ not looking at either their seatwork or, in cases when the teacher was reading to them, at the teacher. Additionally, children's fidgeting and listlessness was also coded as a measure of *in*attention while children did their seatwork. While this measure of attention was less differentiated than others, such as skin conductivity or heart rate, it was practical for classroom research, yet it is a valid indicator of more general school achievement (Johnson, McGue, & Iacano, 2005).

The effects of recess timing on children's attention to classroom work was examined, following the design used by Smith and Hagan (1980), where recess timing was defined as the amount of time *before* recess that children are forced to be sedentary (or are deprived of social and physical play) and attend to class work. This type of regimen typifies most elementary school classrooms (Minuchin & Shapiro, 1983). The school in which this research was conducted allowed the researchers to manipulate the times that children went out for recess as well as children's seatwork before and after recess.

The children enrolled in this public elementary school were from varied socioeconomic and ethnic backgrounds. In all of the cases, the children in each of the grades were systematically exposed to different schedules for recess timing. On counterbalanced days they went out to recess either at 10 a.m. or at 10.30 a.m. Before and after each recess period children were read an experimentally manipulated male-preferred (with male characters) or a female-preferred (with female characters) book. During this time we coded their attention/inattention to the task.

In this first study, to our knowledge, to address directly this issue of outdoor recess activity and postrecess attention, it was found that third grade children's attention before recess was lower than it was after recess, especially for boys, thus suggesting that recess facilitates attention (Pellegrini & Davis, 1993). Those findings, however, were limited to the extent that we did not control the pre- and postrecess task used to assess children's attention. Specifically, these results may have been due to the fact that attention was related to the gender role stereotypicality of the tasks on which the children worked. Specifically, in the Pellegrini and Davis (1993) study children's class work often involved listening to a story. Because the researchers did not systematically manipulate or control the stories read, it may have been the case that some of the stories read were more preferred by girls. Thus, their attention may have been related to the task, not the effect of recess. In the next series of experiments this confound was removed by systematically varying gender-preference of tasks before and after recess.

In Experiment 1 of a new series of experiments, the effects of outdoor recess timing on the classroom behavior of boys and girls in grades K (~ 5 years old), 2 (~ 7 years old), and 4 (~9 years old) were examined (Pellegrini, Huberty, & Jones, 1995). As in all experiments in this series, recess timing varied by 30-minutes. Children's attention/inatten-

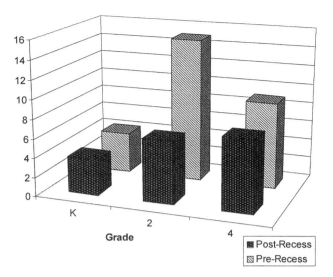

**Figure 22.1** Inattention pre- and post-recess, Experiment 1.

tion was assessed before and after recess on male-preferred and female-preferred books.

In Experiment 1, the prerecess results supported the suppositions of Stevenson and Lee (1990), who proposed that children are less attentive during long compared to short work periods. That is, children were generally more attentive after recess than before recess and older children, relative to younger children, were more attentive. For example, fourth grade children's mean attention scores were greater during the short deprivation time, relative to the long deprivation time. Figure 22.1 displays the prerecess and postrecess *inattention* for grades K, 2, and 4. Note that at each grade level the children were more *inattentive* before than after recess.

Further, it was found that boys' and girls' attention was influenced by the gender-role stereotypicality of the story. For example, fourth grade boys in the long deprivation condition were more attentive to male-preferred stories and less attentive to female-preferred stories while the pattern was reversed for the girls. This finding is consistent with the extant literature on gender preference for stories (e.g., Monson & Sebesta, 1991).

Results from this experiment should be interpreted cautiously primarily because of the small sample size (20 children/grade and 10 children/sex within each grade) and because there was only one classroom at each grade level. Replication is clearly needed to assure that the results are not aberrational (Lykken, 1968), especially when the results have implications for school policy.

In Experiment 2, the same outdoor recess timing and attention procedures were used as in Experiment 1; second and fourth graders (one classroom for each grade) were studied in the same school as in Experiment 1. The results from Experiment 2, similar to those from Experiment 1, revealed that children's task attention is affected by recess timing and that timing interacted with dimensions of the task as well as children's age and gender. Children generally,

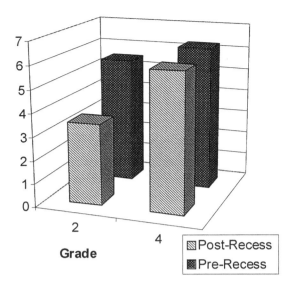

**Figure 22.2** Inattention pre- and post-recess, Experiment 2.

but especially second graders, were more attentive after recess. In Figure 22.2, the pre- and postrecess inattention scores are displayed.

In Experiment 3, students in two fourth grade classrooms were studied and the same recess timing paradigm was employed. The recess period was indoors, however. The same experiment was conducted with two separate intact classrooms. Such a design was chosen because of the relatively small samples involved in each classroom. This procedure minimizes the probability of obtaining aberrant results if similar results are obtained in both samples, thus replicating each other. The results from this experiment are similar to those from other experiments: Attention was greater after the recess period than it was before the break in classroom 2. The result from the indoor recess study was similar to the outdoors results: Children are generally more attentive to classroom work after recess than before. Whether recess

is indoors or outdoors does not seem to matter. In Figure 22.3, these results are displayed with prerecess and postrecess scores of inattention for the two classrooms. Again, note that in both cases, inattention is lower after recess, as displayed in Figure 22.3.

The message from this research is clear. Breaks between periods of intense work seem to maximize children's attention to their class work. More speculatively, it is probably this increased attention that is partially responsible for the positive relations between recess and performance on achievement tests (Pellegrini, 1992b).

What we really still need to know, however, is the effect of different recess regimens on attention. A first step in this direction was already presented, as we found that indoor recess periods, like outdoor periods, seemed to be effective facilitators of children's attention to class work. This result is consistent with mass vs. distributed practice as the mechanism responsible for the effects of recess on attention. From this view, the nature of the break is less important than having a break per se. To more thoroughly examine this explanation, researchers should examine different types of breaks after periods of intense cognitive work. For example, does watching a short and entertaining video or listening to music for a short period facilitate attention? Further, do these effects vary with age? Researchers, however, need to consider the possibility that different aspects of recess regimens will have different optima for different outcome measures (Bateson, personal communication, July, 2005). Frequent, well timed breaks may affect attention, while social dimensions of the recess period are probably more important for social competence and more general school adjustment.

Bjorklund's cognitive immaturity hypothesis provides some general guidance here (Bjorklund & Pellegrini, 2000). The theory suggests that breaks for preschool and young primary school children should be "playful" and unstructured. Providing time for children to interact with peers or materials on their own terms, that is, with minimal adult direction, should maximize attention to subsequent tasks. With older children and adults, merely providing breaks between periods of intense work might suffice to maximize attention. The research on massed vs. distributed practice with adults supports this view.

Another crucial aspect of the recess period that needs further research is the duration of the recess period. Should it be 10 minutes, 20 minutes, 30 minutes, or more? We simply do not know. Answers to this question have obvious implications for school policy and scheduling. We explored the issue of recess duration with a sample of preschool children (age 4–5 years) (Holmes, Pellegrini, & Schmidt, 2006). Procedurally, children had "circle time" and were read a story before recess. Then they went outdoors for recess periods of 10, 20, or 30 minutes. When they returned to their classrooms they again sat in a circle and listened to a story read to them by their teachers. Attention was recorded and coded (using scan sampling and instantaneous recording procedures) for whether the child was gazing in the direction of the book or the teacher reading the book.

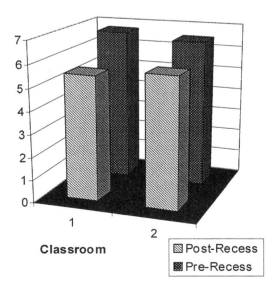

**Figure 22.3** Inattention pre- and post-recess, Experiment 3.

Consistent with earlier work with older elementary school children reported above, attention was greater following the recess period and girls were more attentive than boys to classroom tasks in all conditions. Thus it seems reasonable to conclude that recess breaks help children attend to classroom tasks.

Regarding the differing durations of recess periods, we found that attention to classroom tasks was greatest following the 20- and 10-minute outdoor play periods whereas the 30-minute period resulted in higher rates of inattention. These findings are consistent with anecdotal evidence from the United Kingdom that stated that children become bored with recess after too long a period, and thus longer periods may become counterproductive (Blatchford, 1998). This work needs to be replicated as it represents only one short term study with a relatively small sample. The duration of the recess periods is clearly important because it is one of the persistent questions posed to us by parents and teachers. How long should the recess be? Should its duration vary with children's age? Clearly at this point we only have hints and are not sure.

**Policy Implications**

Theory and data presented in this chapter provide support for the positive role of recess in the school curriculum. In this section we will briefly review the findings presented in this chapter and use these results to make suggestions that might be used to inform school policy. While some of the findings we present are more robust in terms of having empirical support for policy, we will also make more recommendations that are not directly supported, but are suggested, by our findings.

At a basic level and robust level, providing breaks over the course of the instructional day facilitates primary school children's attention to classroom tasks. That these results were obtained using well-controlled field experiments (e.g., recess deprivation periods and classroom attention tasks were experimentally manipulated) and replicated should provide confidence in the findings. While we are not clear on the mechanisms responsible for these results, we are rather confident that providing breaks during the school day maximizes students' attention to class work.

Additionally, these studies also demonstrated the effects of both indoor and outdoor recess periods on attention and thus provide insight into the role of a relatively sedentary break period on subsequent attention. This finding is especially important for policy because educators sometimes use indoor recess as an alternative to outdoor breaks. This may be due to the fact that teachers or playground supervisors are reluctant to go outdoors during inclement weather or they may be sensitive to the possibility of lawsuits related to injuries on playground equipment. Our results provide support into the efficacy of indoor breaks.

The facilitative effect of both indoor and outdoor on attention to class work is relevant to the often recommended role of physical education as a replacement for recess. Recess periods are sometimes replaced by physical education classes following the questionable logic that physical education, and its associated vigorous behavior, enable children to "blow off steam" that accumulates after prolonged periods of sedentary behavior. Once "released," children are then able to concentrate on class. The idea of "blowing off steam" is rooted in Spencer's (1873) surplus energy theory, an early evolutionary theory of behavior, suggesting that humans as well other "higher" animals have a "surplus of energy" from their phylogenetic past because their current niches no longer require them to hunt or forage (Evans & Pellegrini, 1997). This theory, like other hydraulic theories, is *not valid*. For example, and perhaps most basically, children, and other animals, will often be active well beyond the point of the depletion of any surplus (however that is defined), frequently to the point of exhaustion (Evans & Pellegrini, 1997).

Thus the idea of using any form of physical exercise, such as a gym class, instead of recess should be dismissed. Indeed even the Council on Physical Education for Children (2001) recommends against this practice. Physical education is instructional, adult led, and skill building. Recess on the other hand is not, or at least should not be, adult led or skill oriented. Recess then, is more like play and physical education is instructional. Providing children with a physical education class as a substitute for recess, does not serve the same purpose (Council on Physical Education for Children, 2001; Pellegrini, 2005).

This conclusion is supported on a number of fronts. First, and at the level of theory, both the cognitive immaturity hypothesis and massed vs. distributed practice theory suggest that after periods of intense instruction children need breaks from this instruction. A physical education class is another form of instruction and thus would not provide the sort of break needed to maximize instruction. Further, physical education classes typically do not provide the variety of rich opportunities for peer interaction that recess does. The research presented above pointed to the importance of peer interaction for both social and cognitive outcomes.

Our longitudinal observations of children's games at recess during their first year of full time schooling also reinforce the importance of relative unstructured peer interaction for development. Child initiated games with peers are both motivating and demanding for children and consequently they maximize children's use of complex social cognitive strategies that are important in other dimensions of schooling, and life.

These results have also been replicated with both an inner city London sample (Blatchford et al., 2003) and an inner city Minneapolis sample (Pellegrini, Kato, et al., 2002), both of which were very diverse. These findings demonstrated that the games that young children play in the playground at recess (i.e., during their first years in school) are related to not only school adjustment but also to dimensions of social competence, such as cooperative behavior and peer popularity (Blatchford et al., 2003; Pellegrini, Kato, et al., 2002). In Britain, as in the United States, what children do in the playground at recess has "educational value" to the extent that children's participation in games predicts school adjustment and social competence (Blatchford et al., 2003). This evidence should inform policy and be used to guide those policy makers and politicians seeking to diminish or eliminate recess from the school curriculum.

That the two studies of games reviewed above, in London and Minneapolis, each contained culturally diverse samples is relevant to the finding cited above that American primary school children at or below poverty level, relative to children above, had less recess time (Roth et al., 2003). Without speculating about how this state of affairs came about, our results clearly indicate that the social games played by poverty level children at recess help them adjust to school (Blatchford et al., 2003; Pellegrini, Kato, et al., 2002). Games may be one way in which children are able to feel good about being in school: They're good at the games they play at recess, so school, at some level, is a happy place for them. While clearly educators cannot stop there, they can, and should, try to build a transfer from this positive experience to other dimensions of school.

Of course, the generalizability of our results, like all research, is limited to our specific samples. Even with that said, we are relatively confident in the results as they are consistent with theory and were replicated across a number of studies and sites. Both of these conditions are important in minimizing Type I error.

From these results we can now speculate a bit. We suggest that American children's school days and school years should be lengthened. Indeed, school superintendents in the state of Minnesota are currently trying to lengthen the school year in an effort to improve achievement. Such a policy would bring the total number of hours American children attend school in a year closer to the number of hours spent in school in other countries in the world. This increase should have the corresponding benefit of increasing achievement. We stress however, that longer school days and years should have a corresponding increase in breaks per day. Indeed, the national survey presented above showed that recess time was related to duration of the school day: The longer the day, the more recess.

Additionally, a longer school day and year would ensure that children have a safe place while their parents are at work. Children would be in school, learning and interacting with their peers, rather at home, unsupervised, or in expensive after-school care. The need for children and adolescents for a safe and stimulating haven while parents are at work is felt by all segments of our society. For example, the increase of latchkey children means that youngsters are unsupervised and more likely, relative to supervised children, to engage in undesirable behavior (Steinberg, 1986). Further, the benefits associated with increased time in school, such as with compulsory kindergarten, are especially important for economically disadvantaged families who cannot afford quality childcare (Phillips & Stipek, 1993; Stipek, 2002). It is important, however, that these programs provide opportunities for "developmentally appropriate practices,"

such as opportunities to interact with peers as they typically do at recess.

In short, recess is indeed an important part of the school day. In the current environment where the virtues of "evidence based practice" are extolled, we have demonstrated that the evidence does indeed support this claim. What is not supported by the evidence is the elimination of recess.

## Author Note

We acknowledge comments of Pat Bateson as well as those of anonymous reviewers on earlier drafts of this paper.

## References

Bateson, P. P. G. (1981). Discontinuities in development and changes in the organization of play in cats. In K. Immelmann, G. Barlow, L. Petrinovich, & M. Main (Eds.), *Behavioral development* (pp. 281–295). New York: Cambridge University Press.

Bateson, P. P. G. (2005). Play and its role in the development of great apes and humans. In A. D. Pellegrini & P. K. Smith (Eds.), *The nature of play: Great apes and humans* (pp. 13–26). New York: Guilford.

Bateson, P. P. G., & Martin, P. (1999). *Design for a life: How behaviour develops.* London: Cape.

Bjorklund, D. F., & Pellegrini, A. D. (2000). Child development and evolutionary psychology. *Child Development, 71*, 1687–1708.

Blatchford, P. (1998). *Social life in school.* London: Falmer.

Blatchford, P., Baines, & Pellegrini, A. D. (2003). The social context of school playground games: Sex and ethnic differences and changes over time after entry into junior school. *British Journal of Developmental Psychology, 21*, 481–505.

Blatchford, P., & Sumpner, C. (1998). What do we know about break time? Results from a national survey of break time and lunch time in primary and secondary schools. *British Educational Research Journal, 24*, 79–94.

Chance, M. R. A. (1967). Attention structure as a basis for primate rank order. *Man, 2,* 503–518.

Coie, J. D., & Dodge, K. A. (1998). Aggression and antisocial behavior. In N. Eisenberg (Ed.), *Manual of child psychology: Vol. 3. Social, emotional, and personality development* (pp. 779–862). New York: Wiley.

Council on Physical Education for Children. (2001). Recess in elementary schools: A position paper from the National Association for Sport and Physical Education. Retrieved from http://eric.ed.uiuc.edu/naecs/position/recessplay/html

Cronbach, L. J. (1971). Validity. In R. L. Thorndike (Ed.), *Educational measurement* (pp. 443–507). Washington, DC: American Council on Education.

Ebbinghaus, H. (1964). *Memory.* New York: Teachers College Press. (Original work published 1885)

Eisenberg, N. (Ed.). (1998). *Manual of child psychology: Vol. 3. Social, emotional, and personality development.* New York: Wiley.

Eisenberg, N. (Ed.). (2006). *Handbook of child psychology: Vol. 3. Social, emotional, and personality development.* New York: Wiley.

Evans, J., & Pellegrini, A. D. (1997). Surplus energy theory: An endearing but inadequate justification for break time. *Educational Review, 49*, 229–236.

Fein, G. G. (1981). Pretend play in childhood: An integrative review. *Child Development, 52*, 1095–1118.

Garvey, C. (1990). *Play* (2nd. ed.). Cambridge, MA: Harvard University Press.

Greenfield. P. M., & Suzuki, L. K. (1998).Culture and human development: Implications for parenting, education, pediatrics, and mental health. In I. E. Sigel & K. A. Renninger (Eds.), *Handbook of child psychology: Vol. 4. Child psychology in practice* (pp. 1059–1109). New York: Wiley.

Gump, P. V., & Sutton-Smith, B. (1955). The "It" role in children's games. *The Group, 17,* 3–8.

Harper, L., & Sanders, K. (1975). Preschool children's use of space: Sex differences in outdoor play. *Developmental Psychology, 11,* 119.

Hart, C. (1993). Children on playgrounds: Applying current knowledge to future practice and inquiry. In C. Hart (Ed.), *Children on playgrounds* (pp. 418–432). Albany, NY: SUNY Press.

Heath, S. (1983). *Ways with words.* New York: Cambridge University Press.

Hetherington, E. M. (Ed.), *Handbook of child psychology: Vol. 4. Socialization, personality and social development.* New York: Wiley.

Holmes, R., Pellegrini, A., & Schmidt, S. (2006). The Effects of different recess timing regimens on children's classroom attention. *Early Child Development and Care, 176,* 735–744.

Hughes, T. (1895). *Tom Brown's school days.* Cambridge, England: Riverside Press.

James, W. (1901). *Talks to teachers on psychology: And to students on some of life's ideals.* New York: Holt.

Johnson, W., McGue, M., & Iacano, W. G. (2005). Disruptive behavior and school grades: Genetic and environmental relations in 11-year-olds. *Journal of Educational Psychology, 97,* 391–405.

Kagan, J. (1971). *Change and continuity in infancy.* New York: Wiley.

Kausler, D., Wiley, J., & Phillips, L. (1990). Adult age differences in memory for massed and distributed actions. *Psychology and Aging, 5,* 530–534.

Kessen, W. (Ed.). (1975). *Childhood in China.* New Haven, CT: Yale University Press.

Ladd, G. W., Kochenderfer, B. J., & Coleman, C. C. (1996). Friendship quality as a predictor of young children's early school adjustment. *Child Development, 67,* 1103–1118.

Ladd, G. W., & Profilet, S. M. (1996). The Child Behavior Scale: A teacher-report measure of young children's aggression, withdrawn, and prosocial behaviors. *Developmental Psychology, 32,* 1008–1024.

Lykken, D. (1968). Statistical significance in psychological research. *Psychological Bulletin, 70,* 151–159.

Maccoby, E. E. (1998). *The two sexes: Growing up apart, coming together.* Cambridge, MA: Harvard University Press.

Maccoby, E., & Jacklin, C. (1987). Gender segregation in childhood. In H. Reese (Ed.), *Advances in child development* (Vol. 20, pp. 239–287). New York: Academic.

Marx, K. (1906). Das *capital* (Vol. 1). Chicago: Charles Kerr. (Original work published 1867)

Minuchin, P., & Shapiro, E. (1983). The school as a context for social development. In E. M. Hetherington (Ed.), *Manual of child psychology* (Vol. 4. pp. 197–274). New York: Wiley.

Monson, D., & Sebesta, S. (1991). Reading preferences. In: J. Flood, J. Jensen, D. Lapp, & J. Squire (Eds.). *Handbook of research on teaching the English language arts* (pp. 664–673). New York: Macmillan.

National Association for the Education of Young Children. (1992). *Developmentally appropriate practice in early childhood programs serving infants, toddlers, younger preschoolers.* Washington, DC: Author.

Pellegrini, A. D. (1992a). Preference for outdoor play during early adolescence. *Journal of Adolescence, 15,* 241–254.

Pellegrini, A. D. (1992b). Kindergarten children's social cognitive status as a predictor of first grade success. *Early Childhood Research Quarterly, 7,* 565–577.

Pellegrini, A. D. (2004). Sexual segregation in childhood: A review of evidence for two hypotheses. *Animal Behaviour, 68,* 435–443.

Pellegrini, A. D. (2005). *Recess: Its role in development and education.* Mahwah, NJ: Erlbaum.

Pellegrini, A. D., & Blatchford, P. (2000). *The child at school: Interactions with peers and teachers.* London: Arnold.

Pellegrini, A. D., & Davis, P. (1993). Relations between children's playground and classroom behaviour. *British Journal of Educational Psychology, 63,* 88–95.

Pellegrini, A. D., Dupuis, D., & Smith, P. K. (2007). Play in evolution and development. *Developmental Review, 27,* 261–276.

Pellegrini, A. D., Huberty, P. D., & Jones, I. (1995). The effects of recess timing on children's playground and classroom behaviors. *American Educational Research Journal, 32,* 845–864.

Pellegrini, A. D., Kato, K., Blatchford, P., & Baines, E. (2002). A short-term longitudinal study of children's playground games across the first year of school: Implications for social competence and adjustment to school. *American Educational Research Journal, 39,* 991–1015.

Pellegrini, A. D., Roseth, C., Milner, S., Bohn, C., Van Ryzin, M., Vance, N., et al. (2007). Social dominance in preschool classrooms. *Journal of Comparative Psychology, 121,* 54–64.

Pellegrini, A. D., & Smith, P. K. (1998). Physical activity play: The nature and function of a neglected aspect of play. *Child Development, 69,* 577–598.

Phillips, D., & Stipek, D. (1993). Early formal schooling: Are we promoting achievement or anxiety? *Applied and Preventative Psychology, 2,* 141–150.

Piaget, J. (1968). *The moral judgment of the child.* New York: Free Press.

Roth, J. L., Brooks-Gunn, J., & Linver, M. R. (2003). What happens during the school day? Time diaries from a national sample of elementary school teachers. *Teachers College Record, 105,* 317–343.

Rubin, K. H., Fein, G., & Vandenberg, B. (1983). Play. In E. M. Hetherington (Ed.), *Handbook of child psychology: Vol. 4. Socialization, personality and social development* (pp. 693–774). New York: Wiley.

Russell, B. (1972). *In praise of idleness and other essays.* New York: Simon & Schuster. (Original work published 1932)

Sachs, J., Goldman, J., & Chaille, L. (1984). Planning in pretend play. In A. Pellegrini & T. Yawkey (Eds.), *The development of oral and written language in social context* (pp. 119–128). Norwood, NJ: Ablex.

Smith, P. K., & Hagan, T. (1980). Effects of deprivation on exercise play in nursery school children. *Animal Behaviour, 28,* 922–928

Spencer, H. (1873). *Principles of psychology* (Vol. 1). New York: Appleton.

Sroufe, L. A., Egelund, B., & Carlson, E. A. (1999). One social world: The integrated development of parent-child and peer relationships. In W. A. Collins & B. Laursen (Eds.), *Relationships as developmental contexts. The Minnesota symposia on child psychology* (Vol. 30, pp. 241–261). Mahwah, NJ: Erlbaum.

Steinberg, L. (1986). Latchkey children and susceptibility to peer pressure. *Developmental Psychology, 22,* 433–439.

Stevenson, H. W., & Lee, S. Y. (1990). Concepts of achievement. *Monographs for the Society for Research in Child Development* (Serial No. 221), *55*(1–2).

Stipek, D. (2002). At what age should children enter kindergarten? A question for policy makers and parents. *Social Policy Report, 16*(2), 3–16.

Sutton-Smith, B. (1971). A syntax for play and games. In R. Herron & B. Sutton-Smith (Eds.), *Child's play* (pp. 298–310). New York: Wiley.

Sutton-Smith, B. (1997). *The ambiguity of play.* Cambridge, MA: Harvard University Press.

Tawney, R. H. (1969). *Religion and the rise of capitalism.* Harmondsworth, England: Penguin. (Original work published 1926)

Thorne, B. (1993). *Gender play: Boys and girls in school.* Buckingham, England: Open University Press.

Toppino, T. C., Kasserman, J. E., & Mracek, W. A. (1991). The effect of spacing repetitions on the recognition memory of young children and adults. *Journal of Experimental Child Psychology, 51,* 123–138.

Vaughn, B. E., & Waters, E. (1981). Attention structure, sociometric status, and dominance: Interrelations, behavioral correlates, and relationships to social competence. *Developmental Psychology, 17,* 275–288.

Waters, E., & Sroufe, L. A. (1983). Social competence as developmental construct. *Developmental Review, 3,* 79–97.

# 23

# Protect, Prepare, Support, and Engage

## *The Roles of School-Based Extracurricular Activities in Students' Development*

BONNIE L. BARBER, MARGARET R. STONE, AND JACQUELYNNE S. ECCLES

Going to school involves much more than formal class-room education for the majority of students. The broader school environment can offer a range of opportunities for students to find their niche and invest their energies in endeavors such as sports, music, or student government. The earliest examinations of the effects of such participation comprised research in sociology and leisure studies concerned with the apparent benefits of extracurricular activities for future educational attainment (e.g., Hanks & Eckland, 1976; Holland & Andre, 1987; Otto & Alwin, 1977; Spady, 1970), with little attention to the processes whereby activity participation enhanced development for students (Brown, 1988). Though relatively neglected in studies of child and adolescent development, school-based extracurricular activities have attracted increasing attention in research (Mahoney, Larson, & Eccles, 2005). Current investigations are exploring the factors that attract young people to participate, the barriers they encounter and overcome in order to persist, and the array of benefits out-of-school activities provide. There is growing interest in the developmental consequences of extracurricular activities for youth, fueled by increasing recognition of the possible role of such activities in both promoting school achievement and preventing school dropout and school disengagement (Eccles, Barber, Stone, & Hunt, 2003). However, recent reviewers have observed that the scientific research base pertaining to school-based activity participation has been limited (Eccles & Gootman, 2002; Feldman & Matjasko, 2005). There has been far less research on the developmentally facilitative processes one might find in constructive leisure activities than on those manifest in other contexts such as family and school. Nevertheless, it is becoming clear that structured leisure activities are important, with mounting evidence that participation in school and community-based activity facilitates healthy development (e.g., Eccles & Barber, 1999; Eccles & Gootman, 2002; Larson, 2000; Mahoney & Cairns, 1997; Marsh

& Kleitman, 2002; Roth, Brooks-Gunn, Murray, & Foster, 1998; Youniss & Yates, 1997).

The lack of research on extracurricular activities relative to that on other key developmental contexts is particularly surprising given the high rates of extracurricular participation found among students. For example, 70% of students in the National Longitudinal Study of Adolescent Health reported participating in at least one school-based activity (Feldman & Matjasko, 2005). This rate is consistent across a number of other studies, despite measuring activity participation in different ways (e.g., Eccles & Barber, 1999; Mahoney, Schweder, & Stattin, 2002). Sports are the most commonly reported activities, followed by the performing arts (Eccles & Barber, 1999; Feldman & Matjasko, 2007; Zill, Nord, & Loomis, 1995). Girls tend to participate in more types of activities, while boys are most likely to play sports (Eccles & Barber, 1999; Feldman & Matjasko, 2007; Mahoney & Cairns, 1997). Youth from lower SES families participate in most school-based extracurricular activities at lower rates that higher SES youth (Feldman & Matjasko, 2007; Mahoney, Harris, & Eccles, 2006; Pedersen & Seidman, 2005; Zill et al., 1995), but there is evidence that the participation benefits may be more pronounced for these youth (Mahoney & Cairns, 1997). Given the prevalence of extracurricular activities in the daily lives of youth, it is important to understand their role in successful development and healthy adjustment.

This chapter summarizes the research on school-based extracurricular activities and their connection to adolescents' social and emotional development. First, an outline of the conceptual approaches guiding the study of the effects of activities is provided, including a review of research on the influences of activities on student behavior, attitudes, achievement, and adjustment. Second, an examination of the theoretical and methodological approaches used in this research is presented, which highlights a number of proposed mechanisms whereby extracurricular activity participation exerts its effects. The strengths and limitations of existing research are considered, and the chapter concludes with suggestions for further research and educational policy applications.

## The Impact of Extracurricular Activity Participation on Development

As in much developmental research, there are varied approaches to examinations of the impact of extracurricular activities on youth. A broad array of outcomes has been examined, ranging from problem prevention to promotion of engagement and initiative. One branch of the work on activities has focused on the role of participation in risk reduction. Such studies have been concerned with whether activity participation is related to lower rates of risk behavior and delinquency, substance use, and school dropout. A second, large, and growing set of studies has examined the impact of extracurricular activity participation on a broad range of skills and attitudes with an eye toward preparation for successful transition to adulthood. The final and somewhat more recent cluster of research on activities has focused on the opportunities provided by activities for optimizing development and enjoyment.

***Risk Reduction and Problem Prevention*** One area to be considered in extracurricular activity research is the extent to which participation may protect youth from risk and harm. Studies in this area examine the extent to which those who participate in activities manifest fewer problems than those who do not. A smaller group of studies go further, examining longitudinal patterns that suggest long-term reduction of harm.

*Risk Behavior and Delinquency* Activity participation has been found to be associated with lower levels of problem behavior in adolescence (Elliot & Voss, 1974; Mahoney, Larson, Eccles, & Lord, 2005). Feldman and Matjasko's comprehensive review (2005) evaluated the evidence for this protective role of participation, and highlighted a number of studies linking participation to less delinquency. For example, Mahoney and his colleagues have documented the link between extended participation in extracurricular activities during high school, and reduced rates of criminal offending, particularly for high risk youth (Mahoney, 2000; Mahoney & Cairns, 1997).

*Substance Use* The evidence for extracurricular participation as protective against substance use is more equivocal. Participation in activities that provide the opportunity for service predicts lower rates of drinking and drug use in adolescence (Dawkins, Williams, & Guilbault, 2006; Eccles & Barber, 1999; Youniss, McLellan, Su, & Yates, 1999; Youniss, Yates, & Su, 1997) and young adulthood (Barber, Eccles, & Stone, 2001). More cumulative years of participation predict less marijuana and other drug use

(Darling, 2005). Amount of time spent participating in activities is also related to substance use: in general more time participating is related to less smoking, drinking, and drug use (Mahoney, Harris, & Eccles, 2006; Zill et al., 1995). There is some evidence, however, that sports involvement is not unambiguously positive. Some studies have found that sports participation predicts higher delinquency (Fauth, Roth, & Brooks-Gunn, 2007) and greater substance use (Barber et al., 2001; Fauth et al., 2007).

*School Dropout* Activity participation is related to lower rates of dropping out of school (Zill et al., 1995). More specifically, sports participation has been shown to predict a lower likelihood of school dropout and higher rates of college attendance, particularly for low achieving and male athletes from blue-collar families (Deeter, 1990; Feldman & Matjasko, 2005; Holland & Andre, 1987; McNeal, 1995). A likely mechanism that holds participants in school is attachment to the activity that is based at school. We have found that school engagement is higher among activity participants (Eccles & Barber, 1999). The next section details the links between participation in extracurricular activities and positive educational outcomes.

***Achievement, School Attachment, and Attainment*** Although activities may help to reduce risks for students, Pittman reminds us that being problem-free is not the same as being fully prepared (Pittman, Irby, Tolman, Yohalem, & Ferber, 2002). We generally hope for more for our youth than simply a lack of delinquency and substance use. In addition to considering the potential problems that can be prevented in youth, developmental scientists consider youth as resources to be developed (Lerner, 2001). Alongside the prevention of problems, students need key opportunities for growth and help in navigating the primary tasks of adolescence, including acquiring education and other experiences needed for adult work roles, resolving issues of identity, and becoming increasingly autonomous. Of central importance with regard to this chapter's place in this volume is the role of school-based extracurricular activities as complementary to the academic curriculum in pursuit of the accomplishment of a range of developmental tasks.

School-sponsored activities such as sports and performing arts are important contexts that can support or undermine these developmental goals (Barber, Eccles, & Stone, 2001). Previous research has suggested that school activities link students to the larger society of the school (Entwisle, 1990), and that these experiences are positively related to adolescents' feelings of school competence, efficacy, and academic achievement (Holland & Andre, 1987; Marsh & Kleitman, 2002). School-based activities also offer opportunities that regular classroom activities may not, including initiative, identity work, and engagement (Dworkin, Larson, & Hansen, 2003; Fraser-Thomas, Côté, & Deakin, 2005; Larson, 2000; Larson, Hansen, & Moneta, 2006), increasing the likelihood that students will feel connected to their school (Feldman & Matjasko, 2005). It should not be surprising, therefore, that participation predicts academic achievement and educational attainment.

*School Attachment and Engagement*   We have argued that although a sense of belonging at school can result from a number of personal and social contextual factors, extracurricular activities are an especially likely path to school attachment, particularly for those youth who do not excel academically (Eccles et al., 2003). Participation in extracurricular activities can facilitate connections in the school context that satisfy adolescents' developmental need for social relatedness, competence, and autonomy. Activities also contribute to one's identity as a valued member of the school community. In turn, a strong attachment to one's school can facilitate the internalization of other aspects of the schools' agenda—such as those related to academics. In support of this idea, research has documented the connections between activity participation and higher achievement and aspirations (e.g., Barber et al., 2001; Cooper, Valentine, Nye, & Lindsay, 1999; Darling, 2005; Darling, Caldwell, & Smith, 2005; Eccles & Barber, 1999; Eccles et al., 2003; Mahoney & Cairns, 1997; Mahoney, Cairns, & Farmer, 2003; Mahoney, Lord, & Carryl, 2005; Marsh, 1992, 1993; Marsh & Kleitman, 2002).

*Academic Achievement*   Participation in organized activities has been shown to be positively related to academic performance, with students participating in activities such as sports, performing arts, service learning, and academic clubs receiving better grades than their nonparticipating peers (Broh, 2002; Crosnoe, 2001; Eccles et al., 2003; Guest & Schneider, 2003; Marsh & Kleitman, 2003). These relations generally hold up even when key variables are controlled, including family background and both prior achievement and scores on standardized aptitude tests. Several researchers have documented that benefits seem to be especially pronounced for sports (e.g., Barber, Eccles, & Stone, 2001; Mahoney & Cairns, 1997; Marsh, 1993; Marsh & Kleitman, 2002). For example, in National Educational Longitudinal Study (NELS) data, sport participation was related to numerous positive academic indicators (Marsh & Kleitman, 2003).

*Educational and Occupational Attainment*   A long research tradition in sociology has focused on the beneficial link between adolescents' extracurricular activities and their future educational attainment, occupation, and income (Hanks & Eckland, 1976; Holland & Andre, 1987; Otto, 1975, 1976; Otto & Alwin, 1977; Spady, 1970). In our research, we have found that participation in sports, school-based leadership and spirit activities, and academic clubs predicted increased likelihood of being enrolled full-time in college at age 21 (Eccles et al., 2003). Participation in extracurricular and service learning activities has also been linked to better job quality, more active participation in the political process and other types of volunteer activi-

ties, continued sport engagement, and better mental health during young adulthood (Barber et al., 2001; Marsh, 1992; Perkins, Jacobs, Barber, & Eccles, 2004; Youniss, McLellan et al., 1999).

***Optimal Development and Engagement***   Although preparation for adult roles is useful and important, scholars have argued that we need to provide more than that for youth. If adolescents are often bored and unmotivated (Larson, 2000), then they need something in which to become engaged. Organized activities offer that opportunity (Abbott & Barber, 2007). Extracurricular activities provide a forum for the development of initiative and engagement in challenging tasks, and allow participants to express their talents, passion, and creativity (Agnew & Petersen, 1989; Csikszentmihalyi, 1990; Csikszentmihalyi & Kleiber, 1991; Haggard & Williams, 1992; Kleiber, 1999; Kleiber, Larson, & Csikszentmihalyi, 1986; Larson, 2000; Larson & Kleiber, 1993; Larson & Richards, 1989). Sport psychologists have been describing the crucial role of enjoyment in sports participation and motivation for some time (see Scanlan, Babkes, & Scanlan, 2005 for a review). The opportunity for mastery development in optimally challenging activities and persistence in the pursuit of goals are proposed as crucial aspects of sport participation that can result in enjoyment (Duda & Ntounumis, 2005; Scanlan et al., 2005).

Similarly, initiative is proposed as a central aspect of activity involvement affording optimal development (Larson, 2000). In working toward achieving an activity-related goal, students are likely to use skills such as planning, time management, problem solving, and contingency thinking over a period of time (Larson et al., 2005). Therefore, school-based extracurricular activities may challenge adolescents, and time spent in such activities may enhance the development of initiative (Larson, 2000). To test this connection, Larson and his colleagues have developed the Youth Experience Survey (YES) 2.0 that has allowed them to map the developmental experiences of youth participating in organized activities (Hansen, Larson, & Dworkin, 2003; Larson et al., 2006). In one of their recent studies, comparing different organized activities, arts and sports activities were reported by adolescents as providing more experiences related to initiative than other activities, and all organized activities examined offered more opportunities for initiative than core school classes did.

***The Importance of Patterns of Participation***   Most of the studies summarized so far have compared participants to nonparticipants, often in sports activities, or have pooled all types of activities. However, there is a growing number of more complex approaches to the conceptualization of "activity participation," including number of activities, duration, intensity, participation profiles, and breadth. Generally, there is a positive relation between number of activities and outcomes for students (Feldman & Matjasko, 2005). For example, Gilman (2001) found that participating in more activities predicted higher school satisfaction. Fredricks and Eccles (2006a, 2007) have documented positive linear relationships between the number of activities and school belonging, grades, educational expectations, and adjustment. In our own research, the total number of clubs and activities has predicted greater attachment to school, higher GPA, increased likelihood of college attendance, and lower rates of substance use (Barber & Eccles, 1997; Barber, Stone, & Eccles, 2005). The number of sports teams on which a student played also predicted increased likelihood of college attendance and higher GPA. Such results were also consistent with Marsh and Kleitman's (2002, 2003) evidence that higher levels of athletic participation were associated with greater benefits.

Some research has taken an approach focused on stability or *duration* of involvement. Results indicate that continuity of participation across the years predicts positive development, including better grades, psychological resilience, and school belonging (Darling, 2005; and for duration of school club participation, but not sports, Fredricks & Eccles, 2006a), and higher educational attainment in young adulthood (e.g., Mahoney et al., 2003; Zaff, Moore, Papillo, & Williams, 2003). Stability, or continuity, of sport team participation has been shown to predict greater attachment to high school, particularly for those most invested in sports (Barber & Hunt, 2004; Eccles et al., 2003).

In some quarters, there has been rising concern with the amount of time youth spend in structured activities. Thus, another focus of activity research, given this overscheduling worry, has been to consider the *intensity* of involvement, or amount of time spent participating. Results generally indicate that the more time spent in structured extracurricular activities, the greater the achievement, connection to school, and adjustment of the students (Cooper et al., 1999; Mahoney, Harris, & Eccles, 2006; Marsh & Kleitman, 2002; Roth, Linver, Gardner, & Brooks-Gunn, 2007). More time spent in an activity also predicts higher self-concept and fewer problem behaviors, and reporting more positive peer group characteristics, even after controlling for prior levels of these indicators (Roth et al., 2007). A few studies have found a leveling off of benefits at the highest levels of participation (Cooper et al., 1999; Zill et al., 1995), but even so, there remains a developmental advantage to the highest-level participants compared to those students who did not participate at all. Darling (2005) has reported that more time spent on activities also buffered adolescents from the negative effects of life events on academic aspirations and drug use.

Furthermore, there has been a recent call to consider the *patterns or profiles* of participation; in other words, the ways that students combine multiple activities, or not (Feldman & Matjasko, 2007). For example, while some students play on a sport team or two, and others spend their time in academic clubs, still others combine different types of activities. In fact, Feldman and Matjasko (2007) found that multiple activity portfolios were the most common profiles of participation, with 43% of students engaged in more than

one type of activity, and of those in multiple activities, patterns including a sport were the most common. This study also highlighted the challenge to researchers examining the effects of distinct portfolios, as they identified 26 different combinations of 2, 3, 4, and 5 activity type portfolios in the nationally representative Adolescent Health data set.

Another way to study the role of activities in the lives of youth is to construct an index of *breadth*, or eclectic participation. We have found that the extent of participation across a broad range of activity domains (number of different types of activities) such as music, art, sports, leadership, and community service predicted greater school attachment, higher GPA, and greater likelihood of college attendance, even after controlling for academic aptitude (Barber & Eccles, 1997; Barber et al., 2005; Fredricks & Eccles, 2006a, 2006b). In follow-up analyses motivated by the current interest in overscheduling, we have tested for both the linear and quadratic (leveling off) effects of breadth of involvement in grade 10 on number of years of education attained in later life. The linear effect was significant, and the quadratic was not. Greater breadth, or eclectic participation across a range of 3 or more activities, predicted more years of education, net of math and verbal aptitude and mother's education (adjusted $M = 15.1$ years) than participation in only one activity domain ($M = 14.8$ years), which in turn was better than no activity participation (adjusted $M = 14.1$ years).

***Summary*** A majority of youth participates in some kind of organized activity, and research to date suggests numerous potential benefits of that involvement. Through extracurricular activities, students are offered opportunities for learning and healthy development at school outside of their formal classroom settings. A range of tests of key patterns of participation by and large shows that more participation is better than less participation, which is in turn better than none. How these activities structure and facilitate the developmental experiences of students is the focus of the next section.

## Developmental Properties of Activities

There is adequate descriptive data to suggest that organized activities may be beneficial in establishing healthy pathways for adolescents. The lines of research summarized above clearly suggest the profound potential that activities may have for furthering the development of participants. Unfortunately, research on developmental outcomes has often, in effect, conceived of activities as a commodity whose good effects may be related simply to exposure or "dosage." In the past, researchers rarely examined the sequelae of participation in extracurricular programs that afford higher and lower levels of developmentally facilitative opportunities. However, given the growing evidence for the benefits of activity participation, a number of scholars have turned their attention to explaining the associations between activity involvement and these outcomes. The methodology for this research has moved from primarily descriptive correlational work identifying concurrent links between activities and development, to more predictive, longitudinal research. Key advances in this field have involved longitudinal studies testing specific theoretically based hypotheses about the mechanisms likely to explain the association between activity participation and healthy development. Although comprehensive high-quality research assessing the impact of different aspects of extracurricular activity experiences is scarce (Eccles & Gootman, 2002; Larson, 2000), some progress certainly has been made in understanding the potential reasons that activity participation facilitates healthy development.

As yet, there is no overarching theory integrating all the mechanisms that have been proposed by scholars working in the area of extracurricular activity participation. Research on extracurricular activities has been guided by several theoretical approaches, and lies at the interface between person–environment fit frameworks and ecological approaches. Person–environment fit frameworks have focused on the match between the attributes of the students, including their identities and motivations, and the characteristics of the activities in which they participate. Ecological approaches have considered the features of the activity contexts that might prevent problems and facilitate positive development. Such studies often consider the features common to activities that may account for their benefits. Among such features are the involvement of adult leaders, and affiliation with prosocial peers. In this review, we focus on three properties of activities that have been shown to foster positive development in research from the two theoretical perspectives mentioned above: the extent to which activities (a) are identity enhancing, (b) facilitate connections to positive peers, and (c) open doors to relationships with supportive adults at school.

***Identity Enhancement in a Conventional and Valued Endeavor*** Voluntary participation in discretionary activities fosters assessment and clarification of one's talents, values, and motivations (Erikson, 1963). More rigidly structured arenas of participation such as school, work, and religion may provide less freedom to explore and express identity options than do discretionary activities. Therefore, voluntary participation in discretionary extracurricular activities provides an opportunity for adolescents to be personally expressive and to communicate to both themselves and others that "this is who I am" (Barber et al., 2005; Coatsworth, Sharp, Palen, Darling, Cumsille, & Marta, 2005). Eccles and her colleagues refer to this aspect of activities as attainment value; that is, the value of an activity to demonstrate that one is the kind of person one most hopes to be. The opportunity to both express and refine one's identity is a key aspect of socioemotional development during adolescence, and activity participation offers a meaningful and constructive domain for such work. Coatsworth and his colleagues have provided evidence from three countries of a broad range of activities that youth consider to be "self-defining," which

include organized activities such as sports, performing arts, religious and altruistic activities (Coatsworth et al., 2005). Within those activities, it appears that greater personal expressiveness of activities predicts lower delinquency (Palen & Coatsworth, 2007), and explains the link between activity participation and adolescent wellness (Coatsworth, Palen, Sharpe, & Ferrer-Wreder, 2006). More specifically, with reference to school belonging, activities also contribute to one's identity as a valued member of the school community. Such links to school likely result in the findings that activity participants have higher academic focus (Marsh & Kleitman, 2002) and reduced likelihood of dropping out (Mahoney & Cairns, 1997).

The process can be described using sport as an example activity. Engaging in sports allows one to demonstrate that one is an athlete or a jock and to explore whether being an athlete or a jock is an identity that feels compelling. Engaging in sports should also facilitate the internalization of an identity as an athlete or a jock. To the extent that one both develops a jock identity and engages in sports, one is likely to pick up other characteristics associated with the athletic peer culture in one's social world. We have explored these connections in our research, and have found clear links between high school social identities and activities (Barber et al., 2005; Eccles & Barber, 1999).

Youniss and Smollar (1985) have argued that adolescents develop a social sense of self as well as an individual and autonomous sense of self during adolescence. In addition, Brown and colleagues have suggested that adolescents develop socially construed representations of their peers' identities, or "crowd" identities, which serve not only as preexisting, symbolic categories through which they can recognize potential friends or foes, tormenters, collaborators, or competitors (Brown, Mory, & Kinney, 1994), but also provide public identities for themselves that are recognized and accepted by peers (Stone & Brown, 1998). Some recent research (Horn, 2006) also provides evidence that peers perceive their classmates as appropriate or inappropriate for roles in certain activities (e.g., student council and cheerleading) depending upon their social identity. These social identities have been linked to both positive and risky outcomes (Barber, Eccles, & Stone, 2001; Brown, Dolcini, & Leventhal, 1997), but there has been very little research on whether self-perceptions of belonging to particular social "crowds" in high school might influence one's experiences in particular activities. Of central importance from a person–environment fit perspective, we need to know if those students who perceive themselves to be "jocks" or "princesses" tend to benefit most from participating in activities such as sports or cheerleading that validate their self-images and foster integration into relevant social traditions.

In our recent work in this area, we have found that, in keeping with our expectations regarding both additive and contingent effects, consistency between one's identity and one's activities predicts better functioning than does inconsistency. For example, those self-perceived jocks who were not involved in school sports had lower GPAs and felt more socially isolated than those who were involved in school sports (Barber et al., 2005). Similarly, dropping out of sports appears to undermine attachment to school for those who highly value sports. Consistent with a person–environment fit framework, we have found that those students who placed a high value on sports in 10th grade and were no longer involved in sports in the 12th grade suffered the most dramatic decline in attachment to school. Those athletes who had not placed high value on sports in 10th grade and were no longer involved in sports in 12th grade did not experience this decline in school attachment (Barber, Jacobson, Horn, & Jacobs, 1997). Thus, the extent to which sports were more central to one's identity influenced the connection between participation and school attachment (Barber et al., 2005). Guest and Schneider (2003) have demonstrated that such links are also context-dependent, with athletic identity being a stronger predictor of higher achievement in lower class and middle class schools, compared to upper class schools, because the meaning of being athletic differs across these contexts.

***Peer Networks*** Extracurricular activities also help adolescents meet their need for social relatedness, connecting youth to constructive peer networks (e.g., Barber et al., 2005). Involvement in a school organization or sport links an adolescent to a set of similar peers, provides shared experiences and goals, and can reinforce friendships between peers. To the extent that one spends a lot of time in these activity settings with the other participants, it is likely that one's friends will be drawn from among the other participants. It is also likely that the collective behaviors of this peer group will influence the behaviors of each member. Thus, some of the behavioral differences associated with activity participation may be a consequence of the behavioral differences of the peer groups and of the peer cultures associated with these different activity clusters (Eccles et al., 2003; Fredricks & Eccles, 2005; Mahoney, 2000). For example, adolescents who play on teams together or work together on projects or performances are likely to spend a substantial amount of time together, developing new friendships; sharing experiences; discussing values, goals, and aspirations; and coconstructing activity-based peer cultures and identities. Our previous research has found significant relations between friendship network characteristics and activity participation (Barber et al., 2005; Blomfield & Barber, 2008; Fredricks & Eccles, 2005). Adolescents in extracurricular activities generally have more academic friends and fewer friends who skip school and use drugs than adolescents who do not participate in activities (Eccles & Barber, 1999). In turn, having more academic and fewer risky friends predicts other positive outcomes for adolescents (Fredricks & Eccles, 2005). Conversely, being part of a peer network that includes a high proportion of youth who engage in and encourage risky behaviors predicts increased involvement in risky behaviors and decreased odds of completing high school and going to college. Patterson and colleagues (Patterson, Dishion, & Yoerger, 2000)

have documented a pattern wherein early involvement with deviant peers is associated with more "mature" forms of deviance, such as risky sexual behavior, substance abuse, and crime. Such a dynamic makes it imperative to understand how some activities facilitate membership in positive peer networks while others facilitate membership in more problematic peer networks (Blomfield & Barber, 2008; Dishion, Poulin, & Burraston, 2001). The critical mediating role of peer affiliations in the link between extracurricular activities and youth outcomes has also been documented by Eder and Parker (1987), Kinney (1993), and Youniss, McLellan, et al. (1999). Similarly, the mechanism proposed by Mahoney (2000) to effect the moderation of antisocial behavior patterns was beneficial peer associations. This research indicated that it was critical for participants at high risk for criminal offending (based on earlier antisocial patterns) that their peer group also participated in school activities.

***Activity Participation and Connections with Adults*** Another mechanism through which activities can influence positive development is the interpersonal and institutional supports created by participation. Most activities involve public participation that may help adults recognize and support the students who occupy these roles. Structured extracurricular activities provide adolescents with access to caring nonfamilial adults, who are often teachers or counselors acting as coaches and leaders. Coaches, club advisors, and other involved adults often invest a great deal of time and attention in these young people, acting as teachers, mentors, friends, and problem solvers (e.g., Youniss & Yates, 1997). This investment provides adolescents with a range of social developmental opportunities, establishes supportive networks of adults and adolescents, integrates adolescents into adult-sponsored culture, and allows them to achieve positive recognition (e.g., Camino, 2000; Fletcher & Shaw, 2000; Youniss, Yates, & Su, 1997). With the right adults, such contact is likely to have positive effects on development, particularly during adolescence. For example, Mahoney, Schweder, and Stattin (2002) found that participation in after-school activities is linked to lower levels of depressed affect primarily for those youth who perceived high social support from their activity leader. Similarly, the evaluation work on mentoring has documented the positive power of a good mentor in the lives of adolescents living in risky neighborhoods (Rhodes & Spencer, 2005). Our research also supports this idea (Eccles et al., 2003), with school-sport participants reporting closer connections to adults at school.

***The Character and Quality of Activities*** In addition to these three key mechanisms whereby extracurricular activities may afford positive developmental opportunities, scholars have suggested other factors that are important to consider in evaluating the quality of experiences in activities for adolescents. Larson (2000) stressed the importance of activities being both voluntary and requiring concerted engagement over time so that participants can learn the skills associated with taking initiative. Eccles and Gootman (2002), in their report on community-based activities for youth from the National Research Council, reiterated these criteria and added the following characteristics: opportunities to do things that really matter to the organization and the community in which the adolescents live (e.g., service activities and leadership activities); opportunities to learn quite specific cognitive, social, and cultural skills; opportunities to form close social relationships with nonfamilial adults; clear and consistently reinforced positive social norms and rules; and practices that both respect the adolescents' growing maturity and expertise and foster strong bonding of the adolescents with prosocial community institutions. Hansen and Larson (2007) articulate several amplifiers of developmental experiences in activities: amount of time spent in the activity, involvement in a leadership role, and ratio of adults to youth. Future research needs to consider more of these attributes in attempting to explain the benefits of some activities, and the ineffectiveness of others.

**Methodological Issues**

The growing evidence for the benefits of participation in extracurricular activities is encouraging, with a major caveat: We often do not know to what extent the "effects" are attributable to the characteristics of the youth who nominate for and stay in the programs. One of the major challenges to those studying extracurricular activities is, thus, the issue of "selection effects." In this section, we examine the characteristics of youth, their families, and their communities that predict initial and continued participation in various types of organized activities.

***Do Activities Attract Young People with Particular Skills, Interests, and Backgrounds?***

*Human Capital* Numerous sources of differences between participants are evident in the literature on extracurricular activity participation. We focus briefly here on attributes at three different levels: youth, family, and culture. Such youth characteristics as gender, ethnicity, socioeconomic status background, and earlier participation history have been shown to have an impact on participation in school-based activities (Antshel & Anderman, 2000; Videon, 2002). More "psychological" individual attributes (e.g., motivation, self-concept, aptitude, and social competence) have also been shown to predict which adolescents choose to take up activities, whether they are likely to persist, and how much they benefit (e.g., Eccles, Barber, & Jozefowicz, 1998; Stone, Barber, & Eccles, 2001). Over the past 25 years, Eccles and her colleagues have developed and tested a model of the motivational and social factors influencing such achievement goals and behaviors as educational and career choices, recreational activity selection, and the allocation of effort across various achievement-related activities (see Eccles, 1987; Eccles et al., 1983; Meece, Eccles, Kaczala, Goff, & Futterman, 1982). The model

links achievement-related choices such as whether or not to participate in sports or activities directly to two sets of beliefs: the individual's expectations for success in and sense of personal efficacy for, the various options, and the importance or value the individual attaches to the choices available.

For example, consider activity participation decisions. The model predicts that people will be most likely to participate in activities that they think they can master and that they value. Expectations for success depend on the confidence the individual has in his or her abilities and on that person's estimations of the difficulty of the activity. These beliefs have been shaped over time by the student's experiences and subjective interpretation of those experiences (e.g., does the person think that her or his successes are a consequence of high ability or lots of hard work?). Likewise, the value of a particular activity to the individual is assumed to be influenced by several factors. For example, does the adolescent enjoy doing the sport or activity? Does the activity validate the adolescent's identity? Is the activity seen as instrumental in meeting one of the individual's long- or short-range goals? Furthermore, the assumption that achievement-related decisions, such as the decision to try out for the marching band or to switch to the school newspaper rather than nominate for student government, are made from among a wide variety of choices; each has both long-range and immediate effects. Consequently, the choice is often between two or more positive options or between two or more options with both positive and negative aspects. For example, the decision to join the swim team is typically made in the context of other important decisions such as whether to compete for a place in the school play or get an after-school job.

Over the last several years, we have been conducting longitudinal work to investigate how useful the model is in predicting involvement in sports, social activities, instrumental music, and academic subjects. The model works very well in each of these activity domains. It is especially powerful in predicting individual differences in participation in voluntary leisure type activities like sports. The evidence supporting the power of expectancies and values as both directly effecting participation decision and as mediating gender differences in behavioral choices in domains such as sports is quite strong (Eccles, Barber, & Jozefowicz, 1998). Positive self-beliefs, clearly defined interests, and a tendency to perceive the usefulness of activities characterize those youth who choose to participate, and we see these attributes as important considerations in efforts to estimate the benefits of activities. Not only might these qualities predict who will participate, but they themselves may be important third variables useful in explaining differences between activity participants and nonparticipants, depending on the "outcome" domains tested. In addition to directing choices about selecting activities, self beliefs predict persistence in activities (Barber et al, 2005). Consistent with the Eccles expectancy-value model, ratings of enjoyment, perceived importance, and self-concept of ability in sports predict persistence in sports (Barber, Jacobson, Eccles, & Horn, 1997). We imagine that similar processes may operate in nonathletic extracurricular activities. Those who enjoy and value activities are more likely to maintain participation, whereas those who find the experience irrelevant, boring, or lacking in challenge may opt out. Thus, psychological attributes of the participants are likely to be important predictors of continued participation, and in turn may influence program "outcomes." Such methodological issues can compromise study results, and can thus limit our ability to test effects of participation.

*Social and Physical Capital* We also need to take an interest in the function of social capital—an attribute that is differentially distributed across individuals. For example, research on the function of peer relationships of youth in organized activities (Loder & Hirsch, 2003; Persson, Kerr, & Stattin, 2007) suggests that peer groups may play an especially salient role not only in recruitment and retention, but also in the effectiveness of participation. Mahoney's research on at-risk males (Mahoney, 2000) also suggests that individuals may not benefit from activity participation unless they also have a peer network that participates in activities. The demonstrated importance of peer relationships in adolescence means that this issue is appealing to consider as a subtle and yet malleable selection factor, and an opportunity for research that could be used to inform practice and improve youth supports under varying conditions.

Family characteristics, including parental behaviors and attitudes (e.g., opportunity provision, involvement, and encouragement), as well as social class, have been shown to predict initiation and continuity of participation in extracurricular activities (Fletcher, Elder, Mekos, 2000; Videon, 2002). Families clearly differ in levels of interest in organized activities for their children and in their ability to provide opportunities and encouragement for participation. As an economic perspective would suggest, families must make decisions about the allocation of their time and financial resources to various competing and worthwhile ends. They must also decide which sacrifices of competing opportunities they are willing to make to obtain any particular benefit (Foster, 2002). Among families living above the poverty line, some have very limited resources beyond the provision of necessities while others enjoy more discretionary funds and time. Income, the specific earning-power of each parent, parental employment, family configuration, and family size are crucial determinants for constraints such as these.

However, there are also differences in the extent to which families value activities, in the kinds of activities they value, and in the goals they have for such participation. In more general terms, families differ in the value they place on present and future goods, on their attitudes toward equity for siblings (Foster, 2002) and the entitlements accruing from differential ability (e.g. musical or athletic talent). Both developmental and economic perspectives would probably confirm that families make decisions about such

issues as providing parental chauffeur service for activity participation or the money to rent a musical instrument in light of numerous cost–benefit calculations. The result is that financial and transportation constraints continue to reduce the participation levels and continuation of youth from families who do not enjoy affluence (Newman, Lohman, Newman, Myers, & Smith, 2000). Some less obvious features of adolescent experience that are correlated with disadvantage and have an impact on participation relate to relatively frequent residential transitions and family structure changes (Olive, 2003).

Communities reflect macrolevel effects of socioeconomic disadvantage. The National Research Council (NRC) report on youth programs (Eccles & Gootman, 2002) suggests that insufficient access to programs in low- to moderate-income communities is the most serious and long-standing challenge to national efforts to support youth development with after-school programs. It has been estimated that in some urban areas programs can only meet the needs of one quarter of youth who need and want organized after-school activity options (U.S. General Accounting Office, 1997).

*Culture and Inclusion* Multiple studies have offered an understanding of the role of community and cultural contexts in family process and the development of young people (Lamborn, Dornbusch, & Steinberg, 1996). For example, Furstenberg and colleagues found in their extensive study on relatively less advantaged families that a family with high-functioning parents with good parenting strategies could facilitate the positive development of their children no matter where they lived, but the sheer accumulation of risks in less advantaged households and communities was definitely related to patterns of outcomes (Furstenberg, Cook, Eccles, Elder, & Sameroff, 1999). Nevertheless, community and cultural contexts are often neglected in research on activity participation (for a recent exception that focuses on neighborhoods, see Fauth et al., 2007).

Further, ethnic background and sexual orientation are characteristics that are rarely considered in activity participation research (Rodriguez, Morrobel, & Villarruel, 2003; Russell & Andrews, 2003). This is problematic, insofar as both factors are known to have an impact on well-being and identity development. One recent study of a sample of Latino/a youth (Borden, Perkins, Villarruel, Carleton-Hug, & Stone, 2006) found that participation was often dependent on barriers related to resources, family, culture, religion, and outside responsibilities. Darling (2005) found that European American youth were most likely to participate, relative to Hispanic, African American, and Asian youth, especially in sports. Researchers believe that nationality, immigrant history, generational status (Umana-Taylor & Fine, 2001) national subgroup, and skin color (Rodriguez et al., 2003) are all underresearched, but play important roles in the adjustment of Latino/a youth. Other researchers point out that sexual orientation, gender, and child-bearing can have a tremendous impact on adolescent well-being, as well as the activity opportunities adolescents have and their experiences within activities (Eccles & Gootman, 2002; Russell & Andrews, 2003). It seems logical to expect that any developmental benefits of activities would be contingent on the willingness and capacity of activity leaders to engage with the differing characteristics of the entire target population as well as their families.

***How Much of an Activity's Benefit Is Attributable to the Young People Who Participate?*** Scholars interested in the effects of activities (as well as those who study other potentially beneficial experiences) have pointed out that activity participation may not be a cause of positive adaptation, but rather a result or marker of preexisting positive characteristics and developmental assets (Mahoney, 2000). It is clear that more motivated, competent, and socially advantaged youth are more likely to select opportunities to participate in activities, and to choose to continue their participation. To what then should we attribute good "outcomes" for extracurricular activity participants?

*Activities: "Markers" or Promoters of Well-Being?* The importance of the issue of selection effects is related to both practical concerns and to basic theoretical and methodological challenges. When interpreting apparent effects in research, it is important not to overestimate the effects of activities. Youth with a relatively large store of preexisting assets are likely to experience relatively positive outcomes with or without activities. Therefore, we should not automatically interpret positive sequelae in the lives of asset-rich youth who participate as being the result of their participation. Further, some of the same factors that are associated with activity participation are also, in themselves, associated with positive outcomes (e.g., parental support and involvement).

This theoretical and practical challenge is made more complicated by the tendency for resources and risk factors to occur in correlated "packages" of "developmental constraints" operating at biological, behavioral, and societal levels (Cairns, 1996). This phenomenon can be illustrated by the example of a student from an advantaged background whose physical competence, family support, and intelligence are coupled with private music lessons, relationships with peers who encourage academic engagement, constructive experiences in the school orchestra, and a positive identity based on her achievements. Clearly, positive outcomes cannot be fairly attributed to any one of the correlated developmental assets she enjoys. Because assets do not appear to be independent, numerous researchers and theorists have suggested that development must be viewed "organismically," "ecologically," or "holistically," such that any one asset (or risk) can only be seen to have an effect in the context of its relationship and its bidirectional transactions with other asset and risk systems (Barber, Stone, Hunt, & Eccles, 2005; Bronfenbrenner, 1979; Cairns, 1996; Cairns & Cairns, 1994; Ford & Lerner, 1992; Mahoney, 2000).

Risk factors may be seen to collaborate against numerous young people who do not enjoy a coherent system of social

capital enjoyed by the hypothetical student in our example. However, some research has suggested that activity participation might forestall the effects of correlated risks. Many disadvantaged participants may be most likely to benefit from youth programs because they have few other supports (Marsh, 1992; Marsh & Kleitman, 2002). Mahoney and Cairns have shown, for example, that school activity participation may be associated with reduced levels of both dropping out and criminal behavior for at-risk youth (Mahoney, 2000; Mahoney & Cairns, 1997; Mahoney et al., 2003).

***For Whom Do Activities Afford Developmental Benefits?*** The benefits of activity participation may be stronger for some subgroups of youth than for others. Two approaches to this question seem promising: (a) examining issues related to the starting point for youth on the outcomes of interest, and how those levels influence findings related to outcomes; and (b) considering the fit of program demands and opportunities with youth resources and interests.

*Pretest Scores as Starting Points* Divorce intervention research by Wolchik provides a model for considering youth characteristics in evaluating activity participation effects. Using pretest scores on targeted outcomes (e.g., internalizing and externalizing), Wolchik has found that child characteristics moderate program effects. A number of pretest by intervention condition interactions emerge— most often indicating greater impact for those most in need (Wolchik, Sandler, et al. 2002; Wolchik, West, Westover, & Sandler, 1993; Wolchik, Wilcox, Tein, & Sandler, 2000). This approach may be fruitful for evaluating the effects of activity involvement. We know little about differential benefits of activity participation, but when subgroup differences are considered, social disadvantage emerges as crucial. Students from lower SES families and those at greater risk for dropping out benefit more from school-based extracurricular activity participation than those from advantaged backgrounds (Mahoney & Cairns, 1997; Marsh, 1992). Analytic strategies that include pretest levels of assets or risks not only as control variables but also in interaction terms with activity participation, can identify groups who benefit more from a program.

*Fit of Program to Youth* Developmental researchers have found that problems in psychological adjustment are sometimes related to a mismatch between the needs of individuals and the environmental context in which they develop (Eccles, Midgley, et al., 1993). We believe that activity–person mismatch may lead not only to attrition and lack of motivation for activities, but also to reduced benefits for those whose developmental needs are not met by specific programming. Evidence of benefit, or competent behavior, is most likely to occur when the resources of the individual are a fit with environmental demands (Huebner, 2003). Further, as noted above, we have found that the benefits of activities are sometimes contingent on adolescent self-beliefs.

*Summary* Because of such moderating effects, we want to assert that selection effects and the selection mechanisms that produce such effects cannot be viewed only as simple control variables. Instead, we view selection mechanisms as involving transactions between the characteristics of individuals and the specific characteristics and developmental opportunities provided by the activities. For instance, an after-school sports program that has hair-length requirements (as mentioned in Eckert, 1989) becomes a participation or attrition problem only in relation to (and mismatch with) youngsters whose peer group values alternative grooming styles. Similarly, after-school activities that allow youngsters who must care for younger siblings to bring the siblings to the program can provide a beneficial match in communities and cultures where this family pattern is a norm, but would not be relevant in other communities.

We need more research on activity participation for adolescents that considers preexisting characteristics of participants in longitudinal studies. Such studies should be designed to test notions about the qualities of activities that are believed to enhance developmental outcomes, using methods dedicated to separating out confounds of selection bias. In addition to understanding the characteristics that should be *controlled for* in analyses, there is also a need to examine these characteristics as possible *moderators* of program impact. Although much research indicates general benefits of activity participation for youth, few scholars in this area have examined how the relations vary in different subgroups. When differences are considered, social disadvantage is one youth attribute that emerges as crucial.

## Conclusions and Implications for Policy

In this chapter, we have reviewed the existing literature on the relation of school-based extracurricular activities to students' development, outlined the most prevalent concerns about methodological issues in this body of research, and suggested viable and important future directions for this area of study. We have tried to make clear the historical roots of this research area, as well as its promise for our future understanding of social development within the context of schools. There has been tremendous growth in the area of study over the last 10 to 15 years, after a long hiatus. It is very exciting and gratifying to see this growth in theories, studies, and methods. But more work is needed.

We understand that we are asking for more complex models explaining how activities might be beneficial, but we think it is imperative for the advancement of the field to initiate multicomponent and multilevel modeling of activity effects. Because of the challenge involved in testing "what works" for youth (Dryfoos, 1990), it has been difficult to examine the specifics about "why" particular activities work. We are proposing a focus on the developmental contexts offered in activities, a focus that could facilitate and enhance future decision making. With such insight into extracurricular activities, policymakers may be in a better position to recommend funding directions when

faced with budget cuts or surpluses. Through informed and intentional change in activity contexts, we can maximize the potential for supporting youth who experience varying conditions of life. It is through such methods that we are most likely to facilitate substantial improvement in the quality engagement of youth in activities that enhance their development.

As we think more about the policy implications of this field of research, it is important to put what we have reviewed into a larger context. The last 15 years have seen the growth of interest in both in and out of school activities for positive youth development. In fact, we have seen the emergence and growth of the new field of positive youth development. The amount of support from the federal government for youth programs has growth exponentially, as have pressures to evaluate the effectiveness of both in and out of school based youth programs. Similar interest has grown in other countries as well, both in funding such programs and in evaluating their effectiveness. We of course find this expansion in interest and funding very promising.

But, as noted earlier, many youth, particularly youth living in poor communities and neighborhoods, still have quite limited access to high quality programs. At the same time, as school budgets have been cut, the availability in schools of extracurricular activities has declined, leaving many youth with little opportunity to participate in well-designed programs. Thus, at the policy level, there is great need for more coordinated efforts between schools, communities, and funding agencies to increase the number and range of high quality programs available to young people, particularly to young people living in poor, underresourced neighborhoods in both rural and urban areas. We now know a great deal about the general characteristics of programs that are likely to have a positive impact on youth's development. We also know how hard it is for such programs to be sustained in poor communities and poor schools. School budgets are very tight and schools are under great pressure to focus on academic achievement. Administrators in community-based programs have to navigate a complex funding environment just to keep their programs running—distracting them from the very important business of providing high quality programs with a stable core of staff members.

Lest we leave you with a pessimistic view of youth programming, it is very important to acknowledge all of the many educators and policy makers who have dedicated their lives to improving the opportunities for youth to participate in meaningful and effective extracurricular activities both in and out of schools. As noted above, this country has seen a major increase in interest in such programs—interest in both research and program development. Youth have responded with enthusiasm, seeking out such programs in large numbers. Programs become filled as soon as they become available. Schools are rethinking decisions to cut extracurricular programs and they are exploring ways to work more effectively with community based organizations to meet the needs of all youth. But we have a ways to go! And it is an exciting time to do research in this area.

# References

Abbott, B. D., & Barber, B. L. (2007). Not just idle time: Adolescents' developmental experiences provided by structured and unstructured leisure activities. *The Australian Educational and Developmental Psychologist, 24,* 59–81.

Agnew, R., & Petersen, D. M. (1989). Leisure and delinquency. *Social Problems, 36,* 332–350.

Antshel, K. M., & Anderman, E. M. (2000). Social influences on sports participation during adolescence. *Journal of Research & Development in Education, 33,* 85–94.

Barber, B. L., & Eccles, J. S. (1997, April). *Student council, volunteering, basketball, or marching band: What kind of extracurricular involvement matters?* Paper presented at the biennial meeting of the Society for Research on Child Development, Washington, DC.

Barber, B. L., Eccles, J. S., & Stone, M. R. (2001). Whatever happened to the Jock, the Brain, and the Princess? Young adult pathways linked to adolescent activity involvement and social identity. *Journal of Adolescent Research, 16,* 429–455.

Barber, B. L., & Hunt, J. (2004, October). *Motivation for sports and school: Linkages between athletic participation and academic outcomes in the U.S.* Paper presented at the Australian Psychological Society, Sydney, Australia.

Barber, B. L., Jacobson, K. C., Eccles, J. S., & Horn, M. C. (1997, April). *"I don't want to play any more": When do talented adolescents drop out of competitive athletics?* Paper presented at the biennial meeting of the Society for Research on Child Development, Washington, DC.

Barber, B. L., Jacobson, K. C., Horn, M. C., & Jacobs, S. L. (1997, August). *Social and individual factors that predict adolescents' school attachment during high school.* Paper presented at the seventh EARLI conference, Athens, Greece.

Barber, B. L., Stone, M. R., & Eccles, J. S. (2005). Adolescent participation in organized activities. In K. Moore & L. H. Lippman (Eds.), *Conceptualizing and measuring indicators of positive development: What do children need to flourish?* (pp. 133–146). New York: Springer.

Barber, B. L., Stone, M. R., Hunt, J., & Eccles, J. S. (2005). Benefits of activity participation: The roles of identity affirmation and peer group norm sharing. In J. L. Mahoney, R. W. Larson, & J. S. Eccles (Eds.) *Organized activities as contexts of development: Extracurricular activities, after-school and community programs* (pp. 185–210). Mahwah, NJ: Erlbaum.

Blomfield, C. J., & Barber, B. L. (2008, March). *Risks linked to Australian adolescents' extracurricular activity participation: Is the relationship mediated by peer attributes?* Paper presented at the biennial meeting of the Society for Research on Adolescence, Chicago.

Borden, L. M., Perkins, D. F., Villarruel, F. A., Carleton-Hug, A., & Stone, M. R., (2006). Challenges and opportunities to Latino youth development: Increasing meaningful participation in youth development programs. *Hispanic Journal of Behavioral Sciences, 28,* 187–208.

Broh, B. A. (2002). Linking extracurricular programming to academic achievement: Who benefits and why? *Sociology of Education, 75,* 69–91.

Bronfenbrenner, U. (1979). *The ecology of human development: Experiments by nature and design.* Cambridge, MA: Harvard University Press.

Brown, B. B. (1988). The vital agenda for research on extracurricular influences: A reply to Holland and Andre. *Review of Educational Research, 58,* 107–111.

Brown, B. B., Dolcini, M. M., & Leventhal, A. (1997). Transformations in peer relationships at adolescence: Implications for health-related behavior. In J. Schulenberg, J. L. Maggs, & K. Hurrelmann (Eds.), *Health risks and developmental transitions during adolescence* (pp. 161–189). New York: Cambridge University Press.

Brown, B. B., Mory, M. S., & Kinney, D. (1994). Casting adolescent crowd in a relational perspective: Caricature, channel, and context. In R. Montemayor, G. R. Adams, & T. P. Gullota (Eds.), *Advances in adolescent development: Vol. 5. Personal relationships during adolescence* (pp. 123–167). Newbury Park, CA: Sage.

Cairns, R. B. (1996). Socialization and sociogenesis. In D. Magnusson (Ed.), *The lifespan development of individuals: Behavioral, neurobiological, and psychosocial perspectives: A synthesis* (pp. 277–295). New York: Cambridge University Press.

Cairns, R., & Cairns, B. (1994). *Lifelines and risks: Pathways of youth in our time.* New York: Cambridge University Press.

Camino, L. A. (2000). Youth–adult partnerships: Entering new territory in community work and research. *Applied Developmental Science, 4,* 11–20.

Coatsworth, J. D., Palen, L. A., Sharpe, E. H., & Ferrer-Wreder, L. (2006). Self-defining activities, expressive identity, and adolescent wellness. *Applied Developmental Science, 10,* 157–170.

Coatsworth, J. D., Sharp, E. H., Palen, L. A., Darling, N., Cumsille, P., & Marta, E. (2005). Exploring adolescent self-defining leisure activities and identity experiences across three countries. *International Journal of Behavioral Development, 29,* 361–370.

Cooper, H., Valentine, J. C., Nye, B., & Lindsay, J. J. (1999). Relationship between five after-school activities and academic achievement. *Journal of Education Psychology, 91*(2), 369–378.

Crosnoe, R. (2001). The social world of male and female athletes in high school. *Sociological Studies of Children and Youth, 8,* 87–108.

Csikszentmihalyi, M. (1990). *Flow.* New York: Harper.

Csikszentmihalyi, M., & Kleiber, D. A. (1991). Leisure and self-actualization. In B. L. Driver, P. J. Brown, & G. L. Peterson (Eds.), *Benefits of leisure* (pp. 91–102). State College, PA: Venture.

Darling, N. (2005). Participation in extracurricular activities and adolescent adjustment: Cross-sectional and longitudinal findings. *Journal of Youth and Adolescence, 34,* 493–505.

Darling, N., Cadwell, L. L., & Smith, R. (2005). Participation in school-based extracurricular activities and adolescent adjustment. *Journal of Leisure Research, 37,* 51–76.

Dawkins, M., Williams, M., & Guilbault, M. (2006). Participation in school sports: Risk or protective factor for drug use among Black and White students? *Journal of Negro Education, 75,* 25–33.

Deeter, T. E. (1990). Remodeling expectancy and value in physical activity. *Journal of Sport and Exercise Psychology, 12,* 83–91.

Dishion, T. J., Poulin, F., & Burraston, B. (2001). Peer group dynamics associated with iatrogenic effects in group interventions with high-risk young adolescents. In D. W. Nangle & C. A. Erdley (Eds.), *The role of friendship in psychological adjustment* (pp. 79–92). San Francisco, CA: Jossey-Bass/Pfeiffer.

Dryfoos, J. G. (1990). *Adolescents at risk: Prevalence and prevention.* New York: Oxford University Press.

Duda, J. L., & Ntoumanis, N. (2005). After-school sport for children: Implications of a task-involving motivational climate. In J. R. W. Larson & J. S. Eccles (Eds.), *Organized activities as contexts of development: extracurricular activities, after-school and community programs* (pp. 311–330). Mahwah, NJ: Erlbaum.

Dworkin, J. B., Larson, R., & Hansen, D. (2003). Adolescents' accounts of growth experiences in youth activities. *Journal of Youth and Adolescence, 32,* 17–26.

Eccles, J. S. (1987). Gender roles and women's achievement-related decisions. *Psychology of Women Quarterly, 11,* 135–172.

Eccles, J., Adler, T. F., Futterman, R., Goff, S. B., Kaczala, C. M., Meece, J. L., et al. (1983). Expectations, values and academic behaviors. In J. T. Spence (Ed.), *Perspective on achievement and achievement motivation* (pp. 75–146). San Francisco, CA: W. H. Freeman.

Eccles, J. S., & Barber, B. L. (1999). Student council, volunteering, basketball, or marching band: What kind of extracurricular involvement matters? *Journal of Adolescent Research, 14,* 10–43.

Eccles, J. S., Barber, B. L., & Jozefowicz, D. (1998). Linking gender to educational, occupational, and recreational choices: Applying the Eccles et al. model of achievement-related choices. In W. B. Swann, J. H. Langlois, & L. C. Gilbert (Eds.), *Sexism and stereotypes in modern society: The gender science of Janet Taylor Spence* (pp. 153–192). Washington DC: American Psychological Association.

Eccles, J. S., Barber, B. L., Stone, M., & Hunt, J. (2003). Extracurricular activities and adolescent development. *Journal of Social Issues, 59,* 865–890.

Eccles, J. S., & Gootman, J. A. (2002).*Community programs to promote youth development.* Washington, DC: National Academy Press.

Eccles, J. S., Midgley, C., Buchanan, C. M., Wigfield, A., Reuman, D., & Mac Iver, D. (1993). Developmental during adolescence: The impact of stage/environment fit. *American Psychologist, 48,* 90–101.

Eckert, P (1989*). Jocks and burnouts: Social categories and identity in the high school.* New York: Teacher College Press.

Eder, D., & Parker, S. (1987). The cultural production and reproduction of gender: The effect of extracurricular activities on peer-group culture. *Sociology of Education, 60,* 200–213.

Elliott, D., & Voss, H. (1974) *Delinquency and dropout.* Lexington, MA: D. C. Heath.

Entwisle, D. R. (1990). Schools and the adolescent. In S. Feldman & G. Elliot (Eds.), *At the threshold: The developing adolescent* (pp. 197–224). Cambridge, MA: Harvard University Press.

Erikson, E. H. (1963). *Childhood and society.* New York: Norton.

Fauth, R. C., Roth, J. L., & Brooks-Gunn, J. (2007). Does the neighborhood context alter the link between youth's after-school time activities and developmental outcomes? A multilevel analysis. *Developmental Psychology, 43,* 760–777.

Feldman, A. M., & Matjasko, J. L. (2005). The role of school-based extracurricular activities in adolescent development: A comprehensive review and future directions. *Review of Educational Research, 75,* 159–210.

Feldman, A. M., & Matjasko, J. L. (2007). Profiles and portfolios of adolescent school-based extracurricular activity participation. *Journal of Adolescence, 30,* 313–322.

Fletcher, A. C., Elder, G. H. Jr., & Mekos, D. (2000). Parental influences on adolescent involvement in community activities. *Journal of Research on Adolescence, 10,* 29–48.

Fletcher, A. C. & Shaw, R. A. (2000). Sex differences in associations between parental behaviors and characteristics and adolescent social integration. *Social Development, 9,* 133–148.

Ford, D. H., & Lerner, R. M. (1992). *Developmental systems theory.* Newbury Park, CA: Sage.

Foster, E. M. (2002). How economists think about family resources and child development. *Child Development, 73,* 1904–1914.

Fraser-Thomas, J. L., Côté, J., & Deakin, J. (2005). Youth sport programs: An avenue to foster positive youth development. *Physical Education and Sport Pedagogy, 10,* 19–40.

Fredericks, J. A., & Eccles, J. S. (2005). Developmental benefits of extracurricular involvement: Do peer characteristics mediate the link between activities and youth outcomes. *Journal of Youth and Adolescence, 34,* 507–146).

Fredericks, J. A., & Eccles, J. S. (2006a). Extracurricular involvement and adolescent adjustment: Impact of duration, number of activities, and breadth of participation. *Applied Developmental Science, 10,* 132–146.

Fredericks, J. A., & Eccles, J. S. (2006b). Is extracurricular activity participation associated with beneficial outcomes? Concurrent and longitudinal relations. *Developmental Psychology, 42,* 698–713.

Furstenberg, F. F., Cook, T. D., Eccles, J., Elder, G. H., & Sameroff, A. (1999). *Managing to make it: Urban families and adolescent success.* Chicago: University of Chicago Press.

Gilman, R. (2001). The relationship between life satisfaction, social interest and frequency of extracurricular activities among adolescent students. *Journal of Youth and Adolescence, 30,* 749–767.

Guest, A., & Schneider, B. (2003). Adolescents' extracurricular participation in context: The mediating effects of schools, communities, and identity. *Sociology of Education, 76,* 89–109.

Haggard, L. M., & Williams, D. R. (1992). Identity affirmation through leisure activities: Leisure symbols of the self. *Journal of Leisure Research, 24,* 1–18.

Hanks, M. P., & Eckland, B. K. (1976). Athletics and social participation in the educational attainment process. *Sociology of Education, 49,* 271–294.

Hansen, D. M., Larson, R. W., & Dworkin, J. B. (2003). What adolescents learn in organized youth activities. *Journal of Research on Adolescence, 13,* 25–55.

Holland, A., & Andre, T. (1987). Participation in extracurricular activities in secondary school: What is known, what needs to be known? *Review of Educational Research, 57,* 437–466.

Horn, S. (2006). Group status, group bias, and adolescents' reasoning about the treatment of others in school contexts. *International Journal of Behavioral Development, 30,* 208–218.

Huebner, A. J. (2003). Positive youth development: The role of competence. In F. Villarruel, D. Perkins, L. Borden, & J. Keith (Eds.), *Community youth development: Practice, policy, & research* (pp. 341–357). Thousand Oaks, CA: Sage.

Kinney, D. A. (1993). From nerds to normals: The recovery of identity among adolescents from middle school to high school. *Sociology of Education, 66,* 21–40.

Kleiber, D. A. (1999). *Leisure experience and human development: A dialectical interpretation.* New York: Basic Books.

Kleiber, D. A., Larson, R., & Csikszentmihalyi, M. (1986). The experience of leisure in adolescence. *Journal of Leisure Research, 18,* 169–176.

Lamborn, S. D., Dornbusch, S. M., & Steinberg, L. (1996). Ethnicity and community as moderators of the relations between family decision making and adolescent context. *Child Development, 67,* 283–301.

Larson, R. W. (2000). Toward a psychology of positive youth development. *American Psychologist, 55,* 170–183.

Larson, R. W., Hansen, D. M., & Moneta, G. (2006). Differing profiles of developmental experiences across types of organised youth activities. *Developmental Psychology, 42,* 849–863.

Larson, R., & Kleiber, D. (1993). Free time activities as factors in adolescent adjustment. In P. Tolan & B. Cohler (Eds.), *Handbook of clinical research and practice with adolescents* (pp. 125–145). New York: Wiley.

Larson, R., & Richards, M. (Eds.). (1989). The changing life space of early adolescence [Special issue]. *Journal of Youth and Adolescence, 18,* 501–626.

Lerner, R. (2001). Promoting promotion in the development of prevention science. *Applied Developmental Science, 5,* 254–257.

Loder, T., & Hirsch, B. (2003). Inner-city youth development organizations: The salience of peer ties among early adolescent girls. *Applied Developmental Science, 7,* 2–12.

Mahoney, J. L. (2000). School extracurricular activity participation as a moderator in the development of antisocial patterns. *Child Development, 71,* 502–516.

Mahoney, J. L., & Cairns, R. B. (1997). Do extracurricular activities protect against early school dropout? *Developmental Psychology, 33,* 241–253.

Mahoney, J. L., Cairns, B. D., & Farmer, T. W. (2003). Promoting interpersonal competence and educational success through extracurricular activity participation. *Journal of Educational Psychology, 95,* 409–418.

Mahoney, J. L., Harris, A. L., & Eccles, J. S. (2006). Organized activity participation, positive youth development, and the over-scheduling hypothesis. *Social Policy Report, 20,* 3–31.

Mahoney, J. L., Larson, R. W., & Eccles, J. S. (2005). *Organised activities as contexts of development: Extracurricular activities, after-school and community programs.* Mahwah, NJ: Erlbaum.

Mahoney, J. L., Larson, R. W., Eccles, J. S., & Lord, H. L. (2005). Organized activities as developmental contexts for children and adolescents. In J. L. Mahoney, R. W. Larson, & J. S. Eccles (Eds.), *Organized activities as contexts of development: extracurricular activities, after-school and community programs* (pp. 3–22). Mahwah, NJ: Erlbaum.

Mahoney, J. L., Lord, H., & Carryl, E. (2005). An ecological analysis of after-school program participation and the development of academic performance and motivational attributes for disadvantaged children. *Child Development, 76,* 811–825.

Mahoney, J. L., Schweder, A. E., & Stattin, H. (2002). Structured after-school activities as a moderator of depressed mood for adolescents with detached relations to their parents. *Journal of Community Psychology, 30,* 69–86.

Marsh, H. (1992). Extracurricular activities: Beneficial extension of the traditional curriculum or subversion of academic goals? *Journal of Educational Psychology, 84,* 553–562.

Marsh, H. W. (1993). The effects of participation in sport during the last two years of high school. *Sociology of Sport Journal, 10*, 18–43.

Marsh, H. W., & Kleitman, S. (2002). Extracurricular school activities: The good, the bad, and the non-linear. *Harvard Educational Review, 72*, 464–514.

Marsh, H. W., & Kleitman, S. (2003). School athletic participation: Mostly gain with little pain. *Journal of Sport and Exercise Psychology, 25*, 205–228.

McNeal, R. B. (1995). Extracurricular activities and high school dropouts. *Sociology of Education, 68*, 62–80.

Meece, J. L., Eccles, J., Kaczala, C. M., Goff, S. B., & Futterman, R. (1982). Sex differences in math achievement: Toward a model of academic choice. *Psychological Bulletin, 91*, 324–348.

Olive, E. (2003). The African American child and positive youth development. In F. Villarruel, D. Perkins, L. Borden, & J. Keith (Eds.), *Community youth development: Practice, policy, & research* (pp. 27–46). Thousand Oaks, CA: Sage.

Otto, L. B. (1975). Extracurricular activities in the educational attainment process. *Rural Sociology, 40*, 162–176.

Otto, L. B. (1976). Extracurricular activities and aspirations in the status attainment process. *Rural Sociology, 41*, 217–233.

Otto, L. B., & Alwin, D. (1977). Athletics, aspirations and attainments. *Sociology of Education, 50*, 102–113.

Palen, L. A., & Coatsworth, J. D. (2007). Activity-based identity experiences and their relations to problem behaviour and psychological well-being in adolescence. *Journal of Adolescence, 30*, 721–737.

Patterson, G., Dishion, T., & Yoerger, K. (2000). Adolescent growth in new forms of problem behavior: Macro- and micro-peer dynamics, *Prevention Science, 1*, 3–13.

Pedersen, S., & Seidman, E. (2005). Contexts and correlates of out-of-school activity participation among low-income urban adolescents. In J. L. Mahoney, R. W. Larson, & J. S. Eccles (Eds.), *Organized activities as contexts of development: extracurricular activities, after-school and community programs* (pp. 85–146). Mahwah, NJ: Erlbaum.

Perkins, D. F., Jacobs, J. E., Barber, B. L., & Eccles, J. S. (2004). Childhood and adolescent sports participation as predictors of participation in sports and physical fitness activities during young adulthood. *Youth & Society, 35*, 495–520.

Persson, A., Kerr, M., & Stattin, H. (2007). Staying in or moving away from structured activities: Explanations involving parents and peers. *Developmental Psychology, 43*, 197–207.

Pittman, K., Irby, M., Tolman, J., Yohalem, N., & Ferber, T. (2002). *Preventing problems, promoting development, encouraging engagement: Competing priorities or inseparable goals?* Washington, DC: The Forum of Youth Investment.

Rhodes, J., & Spencer, R. (2005). Someone to watch over me: Mentoring programs in the after-school lives of children and adolescents. In J. Mahoney, R. Larson, & J. Eccles (Eds.), *Organized activities as contexts of development: Extracurricular activities, after-school and community programs* (pp. 419–435). Mahwah, NJ: Erlbaum.

Rodriguez, M., Morrobel, D., & Villarruel, F. A. (2003). Research realities and a vision of success for Latino youth development. In F. Villarruel, D. Perkins, L. Borden, & J. Keith (Eds.), *Community youth development: Practice, policy, & research* (pp. 47–78). Thousand Oaks, CA: Sage.

Roth, J., Brooks-Gunn, J., Murray, L., & Foster, W. (1998). Promoting healthy adolescents: Synthesis of youth development program evaluations. *Journal of Research on Adolescence, 8*, 423–459.

Roth, J., Linver, M. R., Gardner, M. M., & Brooks-Gunn, J. (2007). *Intensity of participation in organized activities and adolescent development: The role of peer and school processes.* Paper presented at the biennial meetings of the Society for Research in Child Development, Boston.

Russell, S. T., & Andrews, N. (2003). Adolescent sexuality and positive youth development. In F. A. Villarruel, D. F. Perkins, L. M. Borden, & J. G. Keith (Eds.), *Community youth development: Practice, policy, and research* (pp. 146–161). Thousand Oaks, CA: Sage.

Scanlan, T. K., Babkes, M. L., & Scanlan, L. A. (2005). Participation in sport: A developmental glimpse at emotion. In J. L. Mahoney, R.W. Larson, & J. S. Eccles (Eds.), *Organized activities as contexts of development: Extracurricular activities, after-school and community programs* (pp. 275–311). Mahwah, NJ: Erlbaum.

Spady, W. (1970). Lament for the letterman: Effect of peer status and extracurricular activities on goal and achievement. *American Journal of Sociology, 75*, 680–702.

Stone, M. R., Barber, B. L., & Eccles, J. S. (2001). *How to succeed in high school by really trying: Does activity participation benefit students at all levels of social competence?* Paper presented at the biennial meetings of the Society for Research in Child Development, Minneapolis.

Stone, M. R., & Brown, B. B. (1998). In the eye of the beholder: Adolescents' perceptions of peer crowd stereotypes. In R. Muuss (Ed.), *Adolescent behavior and society: A book of readings* (5th ed., pp. 158–169). Boston: McGraw-Hill College.

U.S. General Accounting Office. (1997). Welfare reform: Implications of increased work participation for child care. Washington, DC: U.S. General Accounting Office.

Umana-Taylor, A. J., & Fine, M. A. (2001). Methodological implications of grouping Latino adolescents into one collective ethnic group. *Hispanic Journal of Behavioral Sciences, 23*, 347–362.

Videon, T. M. (2002). Who plays and who benefits: Gender, interscholastic athletics, and academic outcomes. *Sociological Perspectives, 45*, 415–444.

Wolchik, S. A., Sandler, I. N., Millsap, R. E., Plummer, B. A., Greene, S. M., Anderson, E. R. et al. (2002). Six-year follow-up of preventive interventions for children of divorce: A randomized controlled trial. *Journal of the American Medical Association, 288*, 1874–1881.

Wolchik, S. A., West, S. G., Westover, S., & Sandler, I. N. (1993). The children of divorce parenting intervention: Outcome evaluation of an empirically based program. *American Journal of Community Psychology, 21*, 293–331.

Wolchik, S. A., Wilcox, K. L., Tein, J. Y., & Sandler, I. N. (2000). Maternal acceptance and consistency of discipline as buffers of divorce stressors on children's psychological adjustment. *Journal of Abnormal Child Psychology, 28*, 87–102.

Youniss, J., McLellan, J. A., Su, Y., Yates, M. (1999). The role of community service in identity development: Normative, unconventional, and deviant orientations. *Journal of Adolescent Research, 14*, 248–261.

Youniss, J., & Smollar, J. (1985). *Adolescent relations with mothers, fathers, and friends.* Chicago: University of Chicago Press.

Youniss, J., & Yates, M. (1997). *Community service and social responsibility in youth.* Chicago: University of Chicago Press.

Youniss, J., Yates, M., & Su, Y. (1997). Social integration: Community service and marijuana use in high school seniors. *Journal of Adolescent Research, 12*, 245–262.

Zaff, J. F., Moore, K. A., Papillo, A. R., & Williams, S. (2003). Implications of extracurricular activity participation during adolescence on positive outcomes. *Journal of Adolescent Research, 18*, 599–630.

Zill, N., Nord, C. W., & Loomis, I. S. (1995). *Adolescent time use, risky behaviour, and outcomes: An analysis of national data.* Rockville, MD: Westat.

# 24

# After-School Program Participation
# and Children's Development

*Joseph L. Mahoney, Maria E. Parente, and Edward F. Zigler*

There has been increasing awareness that how children spend their time during the hours following school dismissal has consequences for their schooling and development. As a result, research on the risks and benefits of a variety of after-school activities has rapidly expanded. Like other organized activities such as school-based extracurricular activities or community-based youth organizations, after-school programs (ASPs) operate outside of the school day and are characterized by structure and opportunities to build competencies (Mahoney, Larson, & Eccles, 2005). Different from some other organized activities, ASPs tend to serve elementary and middle-school school-age children (ages 5–14), provide service for most afternoons during the school week, and offer a curriculum that includes nutrition, academic activities (e.g., homework assistance), and non-academic activities (e.g., physical recreation, arts, music, clubs) (Grossman et al., 2002; Kane, 2004; Welsh, Russell, Williams, Reisner, & White, 2002). Moreover, a salient objective of ASPs is to provide a safe and adult-supervised environment for children whose parents are working during the hours following school dismissal. This service permits parents to work without worrying about their children's well-being during the afternoon.

This chapter reviews research evidence concerning two main propositions suggested by the broader literature on participation in organized activities and children's development (e.g., Lauer, Akiba, Wilkerson, et al., 2006; Mahoney et al., 2005; National Research Council and Institute of Medicine, 2002; Vandell, Pierce, & Dadisman, 2005). First, participation in ASPs can influence the school-related success and well-being of the whole child, including: academic performance and the motivational attributes that support cognitive growth; interpersonal competencies and social relationships; psychological well-being; and physical health. Second, the extent to which participation in ASPs has positive consequences for schooling and development requires that characteristics of the child, features of the program, and the broader ecological settings of which the

child is a part (e.g., family, school, and neighborhood) be considered and assessed over time. Both propositions underscore the need for a bioecological perspective to development (Bronfenbrenner & Morris, 2006) to understand relations between ASP participation and children's schooling and development.

The chapter is divided into three main sections that follow this introduction. The first section discusses implications of a bioecological perspective for conceptualizing, planning, and conducting research concerned with the impact of ASP participation on children's development. The second section reviews the research on ASP participation and children's school-based adjustment and development from a bioecological perspective. The final section offers conclusions and directions for research, practice, and policy concerning ASP participation and children's schooling and development based on the existing research. Readers interested in first learning about the historical and political influences affecting the growth of ASPs in America are directed to Mahoney, Parente, and Zigler (2010).

## A Bioecological Perspective to the Study of After-School Programs

Because ASPs represent a common developmental experience for millions of American children, scientists, practitioners, and policymakers have become increasingly interested in whether and how participation affects children's development. Considerable interest has focused on the extent to which ASPs may confer benefits for children's functioning in the classroom. To answer this question, we begin by outlining some basic assumptions about the developmental process that follows from a bioecological perspective. This perspective has been helpful in conceptualizing developmental consequences of children's involvement in a variety contexts (e.g., family, school, neighborhood), including ASPs (e.g., Durlak, Mahoney, Bohnert, & Parente, in press; Mahoney, Lord, & Carryl, 2005; Riggs & Greenberg, 2004a;

Vandell & Posner, 1999). We then discuss the implications of the bioecological perspective for planning and conducting research/evaluation studies concerning whether and how ASP participation impacts children's development.

## Key Tenets of a Bioecological Perspective to Development

Most modern theories of child development share a basic proposition: Development occurs as part of a complex process involving a system of interactions within the individual and between the individual and the environmental contexts of which he or she is part, over time (e.g., Bronfenbrenner & Morris, 2006; Magnusson & Stattin, 1998). The general implication of this proposition is that to understand best how any particular experience—such as a child participating in an ASP—affects the developmental process, characteristics of the child and the ecologies in which the child develops must be studied in an integrated and temporal manner (Zigler, 1998).

In his seminal work, Bronfenbrenner (1979) described the child's ecology in terms of a set of nested levels. He labeled ecologies where face-to-face interactions between the child and the environment take place the *microsystem*. The child's direct involvement in the school classroom, ASP, peer group, family, and neighborhood are examples of microsystems. The combinations of microsystems that encapsulate the child's direct experiences across settings were referred to as the *mesosystem*. At the level of the mesosystem, the developmental consequences associated with involvement in any one microsystem (e.g., the school) are seen as relative to the child's experience in other microsystems (e.g., the family, the peer group). In other words, these proximal ecologies are assumed to have reciprocal and synergistic influence on the developmental process such that the impact of one setting can only be understood with reference to the others. At a more distal level, the term *exosystem* refers to ecologies that the child may not be involved in directly but, nonetheless, may influence his or her development indirectly by affecting the conditions of the microsystems (e.g., conditions at a parent's workplace could influence the family microsystem). Finally, the term *macrosystem* represents the broadest level of influence in this framework and encompasses aspects such as culture or federal policy that both affect and are affected by the combinations of ecologies described previously.

Although Bronfenbrenner's earlier work specified that development involves a dynamic interplay within and across levels of the child's ecologies, attention to the biological contributions and child's own role in the developmental process was limited. However, more recent versions of the bioecological theory of human development emphasize that all characteristics of the child—biological, psychological, social, and emotional—must be considered to understand the developmental process (e.g., Bronfenbrenner & Morris, 2006). In this more recent view, the child is seen as an active and purposeful agent in the developmental process;

characteristics of the whole child both affect and are affected by the interactions that occur within and across the nested levels of the ecologies in a reciprocal fashion across development. This underscores the general assumption guiding most modern developmental theories: Development "happens" through a process of systemic interactions within and between the individual and the environment over time (cf., Cairns, Elder, & Costello, 1996; Magnusson & Stattin, 1998; Zigler, 1963).

Bronfenbrenner and Morris (2006) noted that person–context interactions occurring at the microsystem level were of special importance. Although more distal ecologies influence the type and quality of interactions that occur within the microsystem, development is directly influenced by the moment-to-moment pattern of exchange between the individual and his or her surroundings. Whether, and to what extent, these proximal exchanges facilitate development in a positive direction depends partly on what scholars have to referred to as "stage–environment fit" (e.g., Eccles & Midgley, 1989; Eccles, Midgley, Wigfield, et al., 1993). According to stage–environment fit theory, the development of any given behavior or attribute depends on the degree of match between a child's existing abilities, characteristics, and interests and the opportunities afforded to him or her in the immediate social environment. Fit is optimal when the environmental features experienced are structured according to the child's current needs and developmental level. A mismatch in fit reflects asynchrony between the type or amount of stimulation in the environment and the child's existing abilities or motivations. One implication is that simultaneous attention to the developmental trajectory of the child and the structure, stimulation, and opportunities in the environment are needed to understand how any microsystem affects schooling and development. A second implication is that, to maintain a good stage–environment fit, microecologies must be adjusted over time to reflect the child's increasing maturity and changing needs and interests.

## Implications for Understanding After-School Program Impacts

In conceptualizing whether and how ASP participation may affect children's development, there are at least two broad implications that follow from the bioecological perspective described above. First, *developmental impacts related to ASP participation should be relative* to the following: (1) characteristics of the individual child considered including the competencies, background, and developmental needs that he or she brings to the program context and the proximal psychosocial experiences that occur therein; (2) features of the program context, including how well the opportunities provided by the program match the characteristics, interests, and needs of the developing child (i.e., the person-stage-environment fit); and (3) linkages between the child's experiences in the ASP context and other ecological settings that affect, and are affected by such participation including, for example, the family, school, alternative after-school settings, and the broader neighborhood conditions in which the child and program are situated.

Second, *multiple domains of children's adjustment may be affected by ASP participation*. Different from the research on organized after-school activities for adolescents that has been concerned with a broad array of developmental outcomes (e.g., Mahoney, Vandell, Simpkins, & Zarrett, 2009), the stated goals and measured outcomes from several recent, large-scale ASP evaluations have focused on children's academic skills (e.g., Huang, Gribbons, Kim, Lee, & Baker, 2000; U.S. Department of Education, 2003a; Welsh et al., 2002). The focus on academic outcomes may reflect current funding targets, a view that ASPs, particularly those serving poor children in low-income areas, should emphasize remedial learning opportunities to boost the achievement of students who are struggling during the school day, or a response to the debate surrounding the academic benefits of ASPs (Mahoney & Zigler, 2006).

Regardless of the reason, that the large-scale studies of ASPs have often focused on academic goals is reminiscent of the narrowly defined cognitive goals (i.e., to raise IQ) that have been used to determine the success of early intervention programs such as Head Start (e.g., Henrich, 2004; Phillips & Styfco, 2006). On this score, it is noteworthy that some of the most significant benefits of participation in these programs have been conceived of (e.g., Raver & Zigler, 1997; Zigler & Trickett, 1978) and observed to occur in areas of children's psychosocial well-being (e.g., Currie & Duncan, 1995; Lattimore, Mihalic, Grotpeter, & Taggart, 1998; Schweinhart, Barnes, Weikart, et al., 1993). Indeed, with respect to children's development, success in school, and eventual efficacy in the work force, some recent work indicates that social–emotional competence is as, or more, important than traditional measures of intellectual functioning (e.g., Gormley, Phillips, Newmark, & Perper, in press); Heckman, 2005; Zigler & Styfco, 2005; but see Duncan, Downsen, Claessens, et al., 2007). Moreover, consistent with the view that different domains of child functioning are integrated and coeffecting, programs focused on making improvements in one domain (e.g., social competence) can sometimes also improve other domains (e.g., academic performance) (e.g., Durlak, Weissberg, & Pachan, in press). Accordingly, to achieve a more complete understanding of ASP impacts requires that attention be given to the developing child as a whole across cognitive, psychological, social-emotional, relationship-based, and physical domains. In addition, assessments of child functioning in these areas need to be made both within the program context itself and the interrelated ecologies where program impacts are likely to transfer over time (e.g., the school classroom) (cf., C. S. Mott Foundation Committee on After-school Research and Practice [Mott-CARP; 2005]).

These two implications raise methodological issues for the planning, design, and conduct of research and evaluations aimed at understanding whether and how ASPs affect children's development within and beyond the school setting. These include: (1) the need to specify conceptual links between program goals, features, and outcomes, and (2) the selection of an appropriate research design or evaluation strategy to gauge the impact of ASP participation on children's development over time.

## Conceptualizing and Measuring After-School Program Impacts: Important Considerations

Conceptualizing how and why ASPs affect children's development necessitates a theory describing program goals, how and why program elements are assumed to produce change leading to the attainment of those goals, and the timeframe under which the change process will occur. A logic model is often developed for this purpose because it provides a concise depiction of program inputs (i.e., the exact features of the program), what features of the model the inputs are assumed to impact, and the order and timing in which developmental processes are anticipated to be (e.g., Reynolds, 1998, 2005). Constructing a detailed logic model necessitates attention to several model components: The rationale for the program, its goals, and desired impact must be specified. The various resources (physical, social, and material) needed/available to accomplish the goals must be described. A theoretical rationale for all program inputs (i.e., the features and content of the program) must be provided. A theory of change must be specified to describe the developmental processes that program inputs will impact to achieve the desired goals (e.g., Chen & Rossi, 1987; Weiss, 1997). The ways in which the program features and outcomes will be operationalized and measured to gauge progress toward the anticipated goals must be described, and a determination must be made of what outcomes will be observed and when they are anticipated to occur.

Figure 24.1 provides a depiction of relations between several basic components typically included in a logic model (adapted from Mott-CARP, 2005). We emphasize that this is neither an actual logic model nor is it suitable for use to evaluate a specific program. An actual logic model cannot be depicted in a simple diagram because, among other things, it requires greater detail with respect to the specific content of each component represented (e.g., program features, outcomes, etc.) along with a detailed specification of the theory of change (i.e., the process by which program inputs affect children's development and culminate in the attainment of program goals). For examples of well-specified logic models see those developed for the Parents as Teachers (2006) and Emotional Literacy (Brackett & Rivers, in press) programs. Mott-CARP (2005) provide particular suggestions for specifying program components and indicators relevant to ASPs.

A number of more general points concerning the use of logic models for research and evaluation of ASPs are in order. First, although the bioecological perspective implies that a broad array of developmental outcomes may be impacted through participation in ASPs, it does not follow that involvement in any given program can or should af-

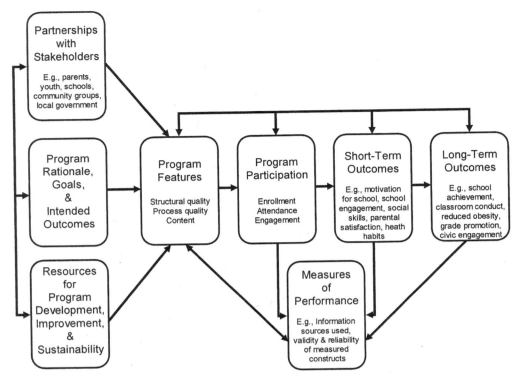

**Figure 24.1** Relations between basic components typically included in a logic model that may be considered in afterschool program research. Adapted from Mott-CARP, 2005.

fect all possible outcomes—at least not all at once or to the same degree. Accordingly, the selection of desired program goals should be prioritized. In doing so, simultaneous attention should be given to the developmental needs of the participants, the values and interests of those who have a stake in the program, and the feasibility of attaining such goals given the existing resources of the program. It is also essential that the magnitude of impact expected be carefully considered. For example, Kane (2004) suggested that ASP participation will often produce small effects on children's development (at least in the short-term) because participants spend little time in the ASP context relative to some other settings (e.g., the school day classroom, the family). The overselling of ASP impacts—particularly those expected to occur in the short-term (e.g., over the space of one school year) or in newly developed programs—may lead to false conclusions concerning the (in)effectiveness of such programs (Mahoney & Zigler, 2006).

A second, and related point that follows from the bio-ecological perspective is that ASPs are themselves changing and dynamic entities. As programs mature, their goals, personnel, participants, and resources often change. As a result, a program's level of implementation must be taken into account when considering program impacts. In the classic volume, *Experimental and Quasi-Experimental Designs for Research*, Campbell and Stanley (1966) distinguished between process and outcome phases of evaluation. The former concerns whether the program is delivering services in the manner intended as specified by program theory and goals; the latter assesses whether the program is achieving

its intended outcomes or impact. *Program fidelity*—the extent that program features are being carried out as planned and delivered to all participants in a consistent manner—is at the heart of a process evaluation. Recent evaluations of ASPs indicate that it takes time, often several years, for programs to be fully implemented and achieve fidelity (Love, Eliason Kisker, Ross, et al., 2002; Walker & Abreton, 2002; Welsh et al., 2002). Therefore, a principal tenet in evaluation research is to hold off conducting outcome evaluations until "the program is proud" (Campbell & Stanley, 1966).

Third, the certainty of conclusions concerning the impact of ASP participation on children's development depends, in part, on the performance indicators chosen. Performance indicators are the particular measures used to gauge program functioning and assess effectiveness (Little, DuPree, & Deich, 2002). It is generally important that the indicators chosen capture the full range of program goals detailed in the logic model and that they demonstrate sound psychometric properties (i.e., reliability, validity). Although this information is basic knowledge for scholars trained in research methodology and evaluation, it is not always familiar to those providing ASP services. In recent years, a large number of ASP performance measures have been developed and are freely available via the Internet. However, information concerning the rationale, item and scale development, validation, psychometric properties, or utility of such measures is rarely given.

Fourth, Figure 24.1 specifies participation as a distinct component in the logic model that can be subdivided into enrollment, attendance, and engagement (Weiss, Little, &

Bouffard, 2005). *Enrollment* is the most basic aspect of participation and refers to whether or not a child is involved in the program. The majority of research on ASPs has relied on enrollment to assess participation because it is cost effective and relatively easy to measure (Simpkins, Little, & Weiss, 2004). However, enrollment provides little information concerning individual variability in the child's participation experience and scholars have suggested that, beyond "being present," the benefits are also likely to depend on attendance and engagement (Bartko, 2005; Mahoney, Lord, & Carryl, 2005a; Weiss et al., 2005).

*Attendance* refers to how much time children spend in ASPs. Attendance is often operationalized in terms of intensity/dosage (i.e., how many days a child attends an ASP over a specified time interval) and duration (i.e., the longevity and stability of a child's ASP attendance over a specified time interval). It appears to be important to include measures of attendance. Indeed, some evidence suggests that consistent attendance (i.e., more than 1 or 2 days in an average week) may be required to derive significant program-related benefits (e.g., Kane, 2004; Simpkins et al., 2004). Similarly, studies of duration indicate that benefits are more apparent when ASP attendance is sustained for a year or longer (Simpkins et al., 2004; Welsh et al., 2002). Attendance rates have also been observed to be low in newly developing programs and to increase as programs mature (Kane, 2004; Mahoney & Zigler, 2006; Welsh et al., 2002).

Although attendance provides a better understanding of participation than does enrollment, the extent to which children are *engaged* in the program while attending is also important (e.g., Bartko, 2005; Mahoney et al., 2005b; Weiss et al., 2005). Consistent with the ecological perspective's emphasis on direct person-context interactions, *engagement* refers to the child's active participation, both psychologically and behaviorally in the central activities of the proximal environment (Mahoney, Parente, & Lord, 2007). Engagement is characterized by relatively high amounts of attention, interest, effort, and enjoyment that occur during the process of learning and acquiring skills (Larson, 2000; Weiss et al., 2005). In contrast, apathy, boredom, inattentiveness, or passivity are characteristic of a lack of engagement. Although a considerable literature exists on the link between engagement during school and the development of social and educational success (e.g., NRC-IOM, 2004; Newmann, 1992), few studies have focused on engagement in ASPs. However, the available research indicates both that engagement can be measured reliably at the person or program level and that such measures are predictive of program outcomes (Mahoney, Lord, et al., 2005b; Mahoney, Parente, et al., 2007: Vandell, Shernoff, Pierce, et al., 2005).

Finally, like some initial evaluations of early childcare education programs (Westinghouse Learning Corporation, 1969) and early studies of structured after-school activities for adolescents (e.g., Holland & Andre, 1987), many of the studies on ASPs have been concerned primarily with outcomes. However, following decades of research on early childcare settings (e.g., NRC-IOM, 2000) and more recent work on organized out-of-school activities for adolescents (e.g., Mahoney, Vandell, et al., 2009), it is now recognized that features of the ASP context affect the quality of children's experiences while participating and help to explain the direction and magnitude of program impacts (e.g., NRC-IOM, 2002; Vandell, Reisner, Brown, Dadisman, et al., 2004). We review this literature below, but the essential message is that while participation in ASPs has been associated with academic and social benefits for participants, involvement in ASPs that operate poorly has been linked to low school grades, relatively high levels of internalizing and externalizing behavior problems in the school classroom, and long-term antisocial behavior and criminality (e.g., Mahoney, Stattin, & Lord, 2004; Pierce, Hamm, & Vandell, 1999; Rosenthal, & Vandell, 1996). Accordingly, to understand how and why ASPs affect children's development requires that program outcomes be interpreted with regard to program features.

## Important Features of After-School Programs

When conceptualizing important ASP features, Vandell, Reisner, Brown, and colleagues (Vandell, Reisner, Brown, Dadisman, et al., 2005; Vandell, Reisner, Brown, Pierce, et al., 2004) emphasize the importance of studying structural dimensions, process quality, and program content. Structural dimensions of ASPs include: physical characteristics of the ASP environment (amount of space, furnishings); the number of children served (ratio of children to staff, overall program size); characteristics of the staff and administration providing service (educational background, training, prior experience working with young people, skills); material resources (amount of diversity of learning materials and equipment); financial resources for sustainability and improvement, as well as ties between the program, stakeholders, and external agencies (parents, host schools, community organizations, local and state governments). These structural elements are assumed to affect child outcomes, at least indirectly, because they define the types and ranges of opportunities that children can experience in the program context (National Institute of Child Health and Development [NICHD] Early Child Care Research Network, 2004).

*Process quality and program content features* involve "face-to-face" exchanges between the child and the program environment and are likely to have a direct impact children's development. Process and content features include: adult-child and peer-to-peer interactions (which may also be influenced by adults) occurring in the program context; the social climate and organization of the program; expectations communicated to the child with respect to behavior and skill development; the types of activities provided; the manner in which they are conducted; and the extent to which they represent opportunities for children to promote social, cognitive, and physical competencies (e.g., Mahoney, Parente, et al., 2007; Vandell, Reisner,

Brown, Pierce, et al., 2004; Walker, Marczak, Blyth, & Borden, 2005).

Research suggests that the qualifications and training of adults who provide the program services and the relationships that children have with these adults are critical to process quality (e.g., Foley & Eddins, 2001; Intercultural Center for Research in Education [ICRE] & National Institute of Out of School Time [NIOST], 2005). In Bronfenbrenner's bioecological model, human development is substantively affected by the pattern of interchanges that occur in social relationships within microsystems. Accordingly, beyond material resources, the social climate and quality of learning opportunities provided by ASPs depend greatly on the program staff and have been shown to influence the extent to which attending children will benefit from ASP participation (e.g., Mahoney & Stattin, 2000; NRC-IOM, 2002; Pierce, Bolt, & Vandell, in press; Pierce, Hamm, & Vandell, 1999; Rosenthal & Vandell, 1996).

Although there is some level of agreement about which program features are important, questions concerning how ASPs should be organized to optimally facilitate children's development remain. For example, while some research has shown that various structural and process features tend to be significantly correlated within programs (e.g., Mahoney, Parente, et al., 2007; Vandell, Reisner, Brown, Dadisman, et al., 2005) very little is known about how the different features interact or complement one another, whether they form a cohesive whole (e.g., Smith, Peck, Denault, Blazevski, & Akiva, in press), or which ones are most important to facilitate particular aspects of children's development (Mahoney, Lord, et al., 2005b).

Moreover, the combinations of features most important for children's development may differ according to the child's characteristics (e.g., age, race/ethnicity, socioeconomic background) (Durlak, Weissberg, & Pachan, in press). For instance, several national and large-scale studies have documented declining rates of ASP attendance from childhood to adolescence (Capizzano, Tout, & Adams, 2000; Grossman, Price, Fellerath, et al., 2002; U.S. Department of Education, 2003a). Consistent with the notion of "stage–environment fit" discussed earlier, scholars have suggested that, to maintain attendance, programs need to operate in a manner consistent with the developmental status and interests of the participants (e.g., Grossman et al., 2002; Lauver, Little, & Weiss, 2004; NRC-IOM, 2002). Specifically, this work suggests that ASPs may be more attractive to adolescents when they offer flexible schedules that acknowledge youth are likely to have competing interests during the out-of-school hours; provide a diversity of activities that both differ from the school day and resonate with adolescents' interest in developing marketable skills; allow for participation in community- and service-learning activities and for students to become involved in the paid labor force; provide for greater autonomy and increasing opportunities for youth to take leadership roles as they mature; and ensure that staff are able to relate well to the youth served.

## Assessment Tools to Study After-School Program Features

A variety of ASP assessment tools and related standards have been developed in recent years to assess whether such programs provide features likely to promote the positive development of participating children (e.g., Tolman, Pittman, Yohalem, Thomases, & Trammel, 2002; Yohalem, Pittman, & Wilson-Ahlstrom, 2004). These measures vary with respect to their theoretical origins, purpose, scope, and method of data collection (for a detailed examination and comparison of common instruments see Yohalem and Wilson-Ahlstrom, 2009, in press). For example, the goals of these instruments range from implementing a national improvement and accreditation system for ASPs (National School-Age Care Alliance, 1998), to creating city-wide standards for improving ASP quantity and quality (e.g., Boston After-school Quality Initiative, Kansas City Youth Net Standards, New York State Afterschool Network, Standards for Baltimore After-school Opportunities), to assessment protocol designed for use across a broad range of ASP settings (e.g., Foundations Quality Assurance System, Promising Practices Rating System, School-Age Care Environment System, Youth Program Quality Assessment). Despite such variability, Yohalem et al. (2004) identified a number of commonalities across these measures. As shown in Table 24.1, these basic features correspond well with developmental contexts known to facilitate positive youth development identified by the National Research Council and Institute of Medicine (NRC-IOM, 2002).

Although a consensus is emerging around several basic elements of ASP quality, this area of study is still in its infancy. Research on the stability and change in different facets of quality over time, the comparability of information gained about quality from various instruments when employed to study different types of ASPs, the general utility of these instruments for gauging program improvement efforts, and the applicability of these measures for use with diverse populations are some important areas for future research.

## Research Designs to Evaluate After-School Program Impacts

"Do after-school programs have any impact on participants?" The basic question can be addressed through a myriad of research designs (e.g., experimental, quasi-experimental and econometric, qualitative, and ethnographic). Each of these designs has particular strengths and limitations; however, the experimental design has been viewed as the "gold standard" to assess program impacts (e.g., Rossi, 1997; Shadish, Cook, & Campbell, 2002). A main strength of the experimental design is that, under optimal conditions, it offers a solution to the problem of selection bias by creating a control group that is randomly denied access to the program and a treatment group that is randomly granted access to the program (Heckman & Smith, 1995).

**TABLE 24.1**
**Features of After-School Program Quality**

| Yohalem et al. (2004) | NRC-IOM (2002) |
| --- | --- |
| **Opportunities for Youth** | • Physical and psychological safety and security |
| • Positive relationships | • Structure that is developmentally appropriate, with clear expectations for behavior as well as for increasing opportunities to make decisions, to participate in governance and rule-making, and to take on leadership roles as one matures and gains more experience |
| • Safety and belonging | |
| • Exploration and skill building | |
| • Meaningful involvement | |
| • Expression/reflection | • Emotional and moral support |
| • Service and work | • Opportunities to experience supportive adult relationships |
| **Staff Practices** | • Opportunities to learn how to form close, durable relationships peers that support and reinforce healthy behaviors |
| • Youth as partners | • Opportunities to feel a sense of belonging and being valued |
| • Safe, fair environment | • Opportunities to develop positive social values and norms |
| • Supportive relationships | • Opportunities for skill building and mastery |
| • Personalized participation | • Opportunities to develop confidence in one's abilities to master one's environment (a sense of personal efficacy) |
| • Learning opportunities/intentional skill-building | |
| • Continuity within/across program settings | • Opportunities to make a contribution to one's community and to develop a sense of mattering |
| **Organizational Policies and Structures** | • Strong links between families, schools, and broader community resources |
| • Consistent, safe, inviting environment | |
| • High quality staffing | |
| • Effective leadership and management | |
| • Range of diverse, interesting, skill-building activities | |
| • Meaningful linkages with community | |
| • Youth involvement | |

*Source:* National Research Council and Institute of Medicine, Committee on Community-Level Programs for Youth. (2002). *Community programs to promote youth development.* In J. Eccles & J. A. Gootman (Eds.), *Board on Children, Youth, and Families, Division of Behavioral and Social Science and Education* (pp. 90–91). Washington, DC: National Academy Press. Reprinted with permission.
Yohalem et al. (2004). Copyright © 2004 President and Fellows of Harvard College. Reprinted with permission from Harvard Family Research Project (www.hfrp.org).

As a result, the randomization of participants can provide for high internal validity and allow conclusions concerning cause and effect. Perhaps because of this, results derived from experimental research can provide compelling evidence to policymakers—particularly in the current political zeitgeist. Indeed, the Department of Education's Institute for Educational Sciences regards experimental designs as the primary means from which to discern the effectiveness of social and educational programs (e.g., U.S. Department of Education and Institute Educational Sciences, 2003b). Some research on ASPs has followed an experimental design (e.g., U.S. Department of Education, 2003) as have studies in the larger area of research concerning children's and adolescents' participation in organized after-school activities (e.g., NRC-IOM, 2002).

However, in recent years, a number of scholars have raised questions concerning whether randomized control trials are likely to provide the best information about program impacts (e.g., Heckman & Smith, 1995; McCall & Green, 2004). Common challenges associated with experimental evaluations of social programs are listed in Table 24.2. These concerns suggest that whether this approach represents a standard that is "gold" or "brass" depends on many factors, not the least of which is a potential trade-off between higher internal validity and lower external validity and generalizability. However, it should be noted that some of these challenges may be more likely when the randomization occurs at the individual level (e.g., assigning individual children to participate or not to participate in ASPs). As a result, interest in group-level experimental

designs that randomly assign social units (e.g., programs) has increased rapidly (e.g., Bloom, Richburg-Hayes, & Black, 2005; Raudenbush, Martinez, & Spybrook, 2005). This approach is promising insofar as randomization at the program level often can reduce problems associated with treatment diffusion (also referred to cross-over or contamination) and may help to alleviate ethical concerns that surround the withholding of treatment or services to populations in need. In line with the ecological perspective, group-level randomization can also generate information concerning the impact of attending ASPs that operate in a similar fashion but are located in different environments or

**TABLE 24.2**
**Common Challenges Facing Experimental Evaluations of Social Programs**

• Ethical concerns regarding the denial of access to program services that may confer benefits to participants
• Potentially low external validity and generalizable findings as a result of the selective willingness of programs or participants who agree to be involved in experimental evaluations
• Difficulty in implementing and carrying out randomized trials in applied settings, including maintaining the integrity of treatment and control groups
• Diffusion of treatment, or cross-over of experimental conditions, resulting either from the inadvertent application of the treatment to the control/comparison group or the inadvertent failure to apply the treatment to persons assigned to receive it
• Potential effects of the randomization procedure on participant motivation and behavior as a result of awareness of the condition to which they are assigned
• Lack of sensitivity to evaluating treatment provided at the individual level

serve different populations of children. Similarly, impact comparisons between programs operating at different stages of maturity can also be undertaken in group-level experimental designs (e.g., Love et al., 2002).

While experimental designs can be effective for probing causal relations and theories, program effects can also be inferred from quasi-experimental designs that are effective in accounting for possible selection bias and those that systematically test presumed causal mechanisms and expected program-outcome associations over time. One example is the regression–discontinuity design discussed by Cook and Campbell (1979). This approach was employed in a study evaluating cognitive impacts associated with the universal prekindergarten (pre-K) program in Oklahoma (Gormley, Gayer, Phillips, & Dawson, 2005). Gormley and colleagues used the birthday cut-off qualification for enrollment in pre-K to identify treatment and control groups. Children who just made the cut-off and enrolled in the pre-K program (treatment) were compared to similar children who just missed the cut-off and did not enroll (controls). This approach was found to be effective in alleviating preexisting differences between comparison groups and therefore increasing the certainty of conclusion concerning the impact of attending pre-K programs. Although ASPs do not necessarily have age-related enrollment cut-offs, many are oversubscribed and place children on waiting lists based on the timing of enrollment application receipt. In this case, a parallel procedure could be employed. Participants whose application are just in time and are allowed to enroll could be compared to those whose application are just late and are placed on a waiting list.

A second example is the empirically validated Confirmatory Program Evaluation (CPE) approach developed by Reynolds (1998, 2005). Confirmatory Program Evaluation

is appropriate for conducting theory-driven research on social and education programs such as ASPs and is in line with the earlier emphasis on building logic models to conceptualize the process by which programs are assumed to impact participant adjustment. In the CPE framework, the strength of causal inference in quasi-experimental design increases under the following conditions: (a) the outcome measures are gathered antecedent to program involvement; (b) the program effect size remains adequate after controlling for relevant sources of selection bias; (c) the dosage effects (e.g., program attendance) can be identified after controlling for relevant sources of selection bias; (d) the effects can be specifically related to hypothesized subsets of persons or to targeted outcome measures; (e) the consistency of program effects can be demonstrated across sites or subgroups that are hypothesized not to differ; and (f) the appropriate comparison groups are available.

With reference to the last aspect of CPE—the choice of appropriate comparison groups—research on ASPs must be sensitive to the fact that, although different after-school care contexts may be physically distinct, they are not necessarily independent in terms of a child's experience. It is estimated that 40% of school age children of employed mothers do not have a primary after-school care arrangement; instead most children experience multiple arrangements during the course of a week or even in the space of one afternoon (Capizzano et al., 2000; Hofferth, Brayfield, Diech, & Holcomb, 1991; Kleiner, Nolin, Chapman, 2004). Figure 24.2 presents a conceptual model of the after-school ecology that highlights common after-school arrangements children experience (cf. Vandell & Posner, 1999). This model emphasizes that each arrangement can vary in terms of its physical setting, social environment, types of activities offered, and extent of child involvement over time.

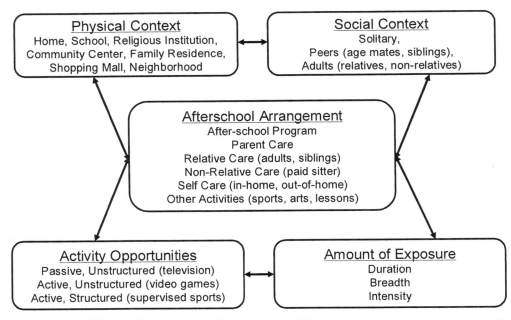

**Figure 24.2** A conceptual model of the afterschool ecology. A child may be involved in one or several after-school arrangements. The impact of participation should be relative to the amount of exposure a child has to alternative afterschool arrangements, the physical and social contexts in which they occur, and the activity-related opportunities they provide. Adapted from Vandell & Posner (1999). Reprinted with permission.

In designing research and evaluation of ASPs, consideration of these alternative after-school care contexts is necessary for at least two reasons. First, they provide a specific basis from which to compare the impact of ASP participation. The impact of ASPs may be most apparent when compared to children whose arrangements lack adult supervision and opportunities for skill building (e.g., self-care; Mahoney & Parente, 2009; Posner & Vandell, 1994). By contrast, impacts may be less apparent when compared to arrangements that offer an adult-supervised context and structured, skill-building activities (e.g., other organized after-school activities). Second, because children who participate in ASPs often have more than one arrangement, a child's *pattern* of involvement across different after-school care arrangements may be required to accurately characterize the after-school ecology and gauge the impact of ASP participation. For example, experiencing a mixed pattern of care involving both structured after-school activities and self-care (i.e., an after-school arrangement where the child is not under the direct supervision of an adult for extended periods of time) is associated with different social-academic outcomes than experiencing either one as a primary arrangement (e.g., Mahoney, Lord, et al., 2005b; Pettit, Laird, Bates, & Dodge, 1997).

Finally, implicit throughout this section is the need for research and evaluations of ASPs to follow a longitudinal design. Whether the goal is to monitor program development or understand the process by which participation affects children's development, it is difficult to envision how either can be achieved without repeated assessments of program functioning and persons over time. However, this does not require that one always apply a long-term perspective requiring a life-span design. The frequency of assessments, particular measures included at each wave, and longevity of the investigation are matters that must be determined on the basis of theory concerning the timing of the expected change process. A considerable amount of this work must be done at the planning stage—in longitudinal research one cannot go back in time to correct mistakes due to a lack of forethought. Thereafter, evaluations must be conducted under a timeframe that will yield the strongest scientific evidence. Speed is the enemy of good science. The rush to initiate, conduct, and complete evaluations has led to premature conclusions concerning program impacts that have threatened to eliminate or cripple ASPs and other social-educational programs in recent history (Mahoney & Zigler, 2006).

## Research on After-School Program Participation and Developmental Outcomes

In this section we review the research and evaluation literature involving regional, state, or national samples that have considered the impact of ASP participation on children's development. We include both published studies that underwent external peer review and nonpublished reports that provided sufficient information concerning sampling, methodology, and analyses. Among these studies, the review is restricted in several ways: First, we concentrate on ASPs serving school-age children between the ages of 5 and 14 years. This age range encompasses the majority of ASP participants and the literature concerning organized after-school activities for older adolescents is described elsewhere (e.g., Mahoney, Vandell, et al., 2009). Second, given the topic of this volume, emphasis is placed on studies of ASPs that are school-based or those relating ASP participation to indicators of children's well-being in the school environment. Third, in most cases, we focus on studies that are longitudinal and follow either a quasi-experimental or experimental design that includes information on the adjustment of a well-defined comparison group(s) of children who do not participate in ASPs. Exceptions are made for those cross-sectional studies focused on understudied populations of children or associations between ASP features and children's development. Fourth, in some cases, multiple reports from the same investigation were available, particularly for large-scale evaluations with annual progress reports. In these instances, unless the individual reports address substantively different aspects of the ASPs or related outcomes, we focus on the most comprehensive one. Finally, we concentrate on findings that are statistically significant. Although other criteria (e.g., effect sizes, cost–benefit ratio) provide important information on the impact of ASP participation, few of the studies reviewed provided this information directly. We return to this issue in the final section of the chapter.

***Description of Available Research Studies*** Forty-three investigations satisfied the above requirements. Owing to space limitations, the sample characteristics, program descriptions, research designs, outcomes compared, and significant findings for the 36 quasi-experimental and seven experimental studies considered are provided in Mahoney, Parente, and Zigler (2009) or by request from the first author. Noting that some studies did not report on every aspect of interest, this body of research has the following characteristics:

- Quasi-experimental (84%)
- Economically disadvantaged samples or those selecting children with preexisting social-academic adjustment problems (70%)
- Samples drawn from urban (66%) or regionally diverse areas (23%)
- Samples of children who are primarily Black (22%), Hispanic (14%), Black and Hispanic (22%), White (17%), culturally diverse (14%), or other (11%)
- Samples of elementary school students (65%) or a mix of elementary and middle school students (28%)
- Programs located in public schools (49%) or a mix of public and private schools and community-based programs (39%)
- Programs in their first 3 years of maturity (68%)
- Comparisons of program participants to a general group

of nonparticipants in the same schools or sampled areas (81%)

- Focus on outcomes related to academic performance (77%) or social-emotional functioning (63%)

Accordingly, in drawing conclusions from the impact studies reviewed, the reader should be aware that knowledge concerning ASP participation and children's development is rather limited in the following respects: samples including Asians, Native Americans, or children from immigrant families and those with limited English proficiency; middle-income or suburban youth; programs that have matured for four or more years; comparisons of program participants to children in specific alternative after-school arrangements.

### After-School Program Participation and Children's School-Related Outcomes

Prior reviews of the ASP literature have noted mixed findings concerning the association between participation and indicators of children's academic and social development (e.g., Durlak & Weissberg, 2007; Grossman et al., 2002; Lauer et al., 2006; NICHD Early Child Care Research Network, 2004; Vandell & Posner, 1999). It has been argued that the discrepant findings result from variability in research designs, sample characteristics, and program features across the studies and that a bioecological systems perspective to development helps to clarify the conditions under which participation is associated with benefits (e.g., Mahoney, Lord, et al., 2005b; Vandell & Posner, 1999). From this vantage point, we discuss the studies that have focused on academic and psychosocial outcomes, aspects of physical health, and time use with reference to person, program, and contextual factors.

*Standardized Measures of Academic Achievement*   Among the studies reviewed, the most common academic outcomes are achievement test performance in reading and math, school grades, school attendance, and student or teacher reports of school-related effort, motivation, or attachment. The majority of studies examining standardized measures of *reading achievement* have found that ASP participation is associated with increased performance (e.g., Bergin, Hudson, Chryst, & Resetar, 1992; Bissell et al., 2002; Chase & Clement, 2000; Cosden, Morrison, Albanese, & Macias, 2001; Huang et al., 2000; Knutson, 2005; Lord & Mahoney, 2007; Mahoney, Lord, et al., 2005b; Morris, Shaw, & Perney, 1990; Riggs & Greenberg, 2004b; Ross, Lewis, Smith, & Sterblin, 2002). A lesser number of studies did not find a significant relation between ASP participation and increased scores on reading achievement assessments (e.g., Anderson-Butcher, 2002; Foley & Eddins, 2001; Lauver, 2002; NICHD Early Child Care Research Network, 2004; Posner & Vandell, 1994; U.S. Department of Education, 2003; Welsh et al., 2002). None of the studies reviewed reported a significant decline or iatrogenic (i.e., unintended negative) effect in reading associated with ASP participation.

Results are less consistent for various measures of *math-ematics achievement*. About half of studies that assessed mathematics achievement showed a significant positive association between ASP participation and standardized achievement gains in math (e.g., Chase & Clement, 2000; Cosden et al., 2001; Finn-Stevenson, Ginicola, & Yekelchik, 2005; Foley & Eddins, 2001; Huang et al., 2000; Riggs & Greenberg, 2004b; Welsh et al., 2002). However, nearly as many studies did not find a significant relation (e.g., Anderson-Butcher, 2002; Lauver, 2002; NICHD Early Child Care Research Network, 2004; Posner & Vandell, 1994; Prenovost, 2001; U.S. Department of Education, 2003), and one study found that ASP participants had significantly poorer mathematics achievement compared to children in mother care (Vandell & Corasaniti, 1988). Concerning the negative results from this final study, the authors explain that program quality was often questionable (e.g., many children were served by small numbers of staff who received minimal training, the number of age appropriate activities available were limited).

*Moderators of Associated After-School Programs' Effects On Standardized Achievement*   Individual and contextual factors help to explain the discrepant findings concerning ASP participation and reading and mathematics achievement. First, with respect to the greater consistency in associated benefits for reading vs. mathematics achievement, it should be noted that several studies targeted samples with reading deficits or programs emphasizing literacy development over mathematics (Bergin et al., 1992; Bissell et al., 2002; Morris et al., 1990; Prenovost, 2001; Riggs & Greenberg, 2004b; Ross et al., 2002). After-school programs that focus on children's mathematical skills have been more apt to find significant gains in mathematics achievement (e.g., Finn-Stevenson et al., 2005; Welsh et al., 2002). The implication is that ASP research and evaluation should anticipate and assess only those outcomes that are consistent with a program's theory, goals, and content.

Second, the majority of studies that have reported positive associations involve samples that are economically disadvantaged or targeted high risk subgroups of children (i.e., low English proficiency, immigrant families, history of low achievement). In some cases the associated achievement benefits apply only to these high risk groups (e.g., Knutson, 2005). The few studies involving middle-income and economically heterogeneous samples have been less apt to find achievement gains for ASP participants (e.g., NICHD Early Child Care Research Network, 2004; Pettit et al., 1997; Vandell & Corasaniti, 1988).

Although it may be tempting to conclude that achievement-related benefits of ASP participation are exclusive to disadvantaged children, it would be premature and potentially erroneous to draw such a conclusion on the basis of the limited research available. For example, earlier work on the cognitive and academic benefits associated with early childhood educational programs suggested that gains in these areas were most apparent for disadvantaged children. However, recent studies show that such benefits are also quite apparent for children from middle-income families (e.g., Barnett, Brown, & Shore, 2004; Schulman & Barnett, 2005) and that a mix of disadvantaged and more affluent children in the same program is linked to cognitive benefits for disadvantaged children without compromising the adjustment of the more affluent participants (Kahlenberg, 2001). Related, a policy lesson learned from early childhood educational programs providing universal coverage is that they struggle to survive when funding targets are focused primarily on programs serving disadvantaged populations. Targeting funding to serve disadvantaged children appears to both stigmatize the recipients and constrain political and constituent support for such programs. Funding targets for the main source of federal support for ASPs (i.e., the 21st Century Community Learning Centers [21CCLCs]) are focused on low-income populations. Accordingly, much more needs to be known about outcomes related to ASP participation for nonpoor children.

Third, achievement-related gains of ASP participation depend on both structural and process quality. For example, Foley and Eddins (2001) found that associated benefits in achievement were linked to lower child-to-staff ratios, staff holding a 4-year degree, or those who were school day teachers, and programs with low rates of staff turnover (see also, ICRE & NIOST, 2005). Moreover, several studies report that such gains are most apparent for those students with regular program attendance (e.g., Cosden et al., 2001; Foley & Eddins, 2001; Huang et al., 2000; Riggs & Greenberg, 2004b; Ross et al., 2002; Welsh et al., 2002) and those who are highly engaged in program activities while attending (Mahoney et al., 2005b). Indeed, uncertainty concerning different aspects of ASP quality has been a limitation of several recent investigations (e.g., Mahoney, Lord, et al., 2005a, 2005b; Mahoney & Zigler, 2006; NICHD Early Child Care Research Network, 2004; Posner & Vandell, 1999; Vandell & Corasaniti, 1988). The implication is to examine a process that connects structural and process features of ASPs with facets of children's participation and their developmental outcomes. Studies of early childhood programs have carried out this type investigation (e.g., NICHD Early Child Care Research Network, 2002). Although several current studies of ASPs have the capacity to examine this process, little research is currently available (Mahoney, Parente, et al., 2007). Fourth, specifying comparison groups also helps to clarify the discrepancy. For instance, Mahoney, Lord, et al. (2005b) found that associated reading achievement gains were greatest when ASP participants were compared to children whose after-school arrangements involved a combination of self/sibling care and relative care. Fifth, program maturity has been linked positively to achievement gains in at least two studies (Knutson, 2005; Welsh et al., 2002).

*After-School Programs, Student Grades, School Attendance, and Motivation*  Some studies have reported increased *school grades* in various academic subjects such as reading (Bergin et al., 1992), mathematics (Finn-Stevenson et al., 2005; Schinke, Cole, & Poulin, 2000), science and fine arts (Smith & Zhang, 2001), or social studies (U.S. Department of Education, 2003). However, more often, studies do not report a significant association between ASP participation and school grades (e.g., Cosden et al., 2001; Huang et al., 1995; Lauver, 2002; Lord & Mahoney, 2007; Mahoney, Lord, et al., 2005b; Mahoney, Parente, et al., 2007; Posner & Vandell, 1994; U.S. Department of Education, 2003). Two studies have found ASP participation was negatively related to student grades (Morrison et al., 2000; Vandell & Corasaniti, 1988).

As with achievement, program features, participation levels, and research methodology help to explain the inconsistent findings on school grades. For instance, program features appear to moderate the relationship. Pierce et al. (1999) found that program staff negativity (i.e., staff showing negative behavior and affect toward children such as anger, impatience, or general dislike) predicted lower math and reading grades and that a large number of diverse program activities (i.e., physical, social, and cognitive activities) related to lower reading grades for boys. In terms of participation, the retrospective study of Pettit et al. (1997) found that moderate amounts of weekly activity-oriented care was positively associated with students' GPAs, but that high amounts of the same activities predicted lower GPAs; however, Finn-Stevenson et al. (2005) found no relationship between attendance and school grades. Pettit et al. also found that GPA was lower for students in self care alone than for students in a combination of self care and activity-oriented care. More generally, Mahoney, Lord, et al. (2005b) suggested that creating reliable coding schemes for student school grades can be challenging (particularly when report cards from multiple schools or school districts are involved) and that they represent a more subjective and global account of teacher perceptions of student ability compared to standardized achievement test performance. Finally, like achievement, one should not anticipate an impact in student grades unless this is part of the goal of the program and activities likely to produce the outcome are central to the program.

Several studies report that ASP participation is associated with better *school attendance* in one or more respects (i.e., more days attended, fewer days absent, fewer suspensions, less tardiness; e.g., Anderson-Butcher, 2002; Finn-Stevenson et al., 2005; Foley & Eddins, 2001; LoSciuto, Hilbert, Fox, Porcellini, & Lamphear, 1999; Schinke et al., 2000; U.S. Department of Education, 2003; Welsh et al., 2002). However, the amount of attendance gained is variable across these studies (Durlak & Weissberg, 2007) and at least three investigations (Bissell et al., 2002; LaFrance et al., 2001; Lauver, 2002) did not find this association to be significant. Overall, related gains in school attendance appear largest for students with regular and durable ASP attendance (e.g., Anderson-Butcher, 2002; Prenovost, 1999; Welsh et al., 2002) and those in later elementary and middle school (e.g., Foley & Eddins, 2001; Schinke et al., 2000). Aspects of program structural quality (i.e., number of staff, staff education, lower turnover) (Foley & Eddins, 2001), program maturity (Welsh et al., 2002), and whether participation is voluntary (LaFrance, 2001) have also been associated with increased school attendance. In addition, at least one study (Huang et al., 2000) has shown that increased school attendance partially mediates the relation between ASP participation and academic achievement gains.

Finally, studies consistently report that ASP participation is related to increases in aspects of children's *school-related effort, motivation, or attachment* (e.g., Bissell et al., 2002; Chase & Clement, 2000; Cosden et al., 2001; Huang et al., 2000; Mahoney, Lord, et al., 2005b; Mahoney, Parente, et al., 2007; Morrison et al., 2000; Pierce & Shields, 1998; Prenovost, 2001; Schinke et al., 2000) as well as parents' involvement in children's schooling (e.g., Chase & Clement, 2002; Morrison et al., 2000; U.S. Department of Education, 2003). Some evidence suggests that the gains depend on the child's level of engagement in the ASP (e.g., Mahoney, Lord, et al., 2005b) and may be strongest for children with low English proficiency (Cosden et al., 2001). Although these psychological aspects are sometimes viewed as "soft" indicators of academic success, they are directly associated with children's academic performance (Zigler, Bennett-Gates, Hodapp, & Henrich, 2002), and disadvantaged children are more likely to be deficient in them relative to their more affluent counterparts (Gruen & Zigler, 1968; Malakoff, Underhill, & Zigler, 1998). On this score, most of the studies reporting positive associations in this area have involved low-income samples. In addition, these aspects are frequently conceived of as early indicators of educational success. Over time, they may evolve into more traditional indicators of academic performance and educational attainment.

*After-School Programs and Psychosocial Outcomes*   The most common psychosocial outcomes studied are externalizing and disruptive behaviors in the school classroom, criminal offending and substance use, school-based peer relations and interpersonal competencies, and psychological and emotional well-being. To begin, several investigations have found an overall decline in *externalizing/disruptive behaviors* or improvements in children's social conduct in the classroom for ASP participants compared to nonparticipants (e.g., Finn-Stevenson et al., 2005; Garza Fuentes & LeCaptaine, 1990; Gottfredson, Gerstenblith, Soulé, Worner, & Lu 2004; Morrison et al., 2000) or to children in self-care more specifically (e.g., Marshall et al., 1997; Posner & Vandell, 1994). Three studies found no relationship (e.g., Lord & Mahoney, 2007; NICHD Early Child Care Research Network, 2004; Ross et al., 1992); however, these studies focused primarily on programs aimed at promoting academic skills or those with variable quality.

Some of the findings pertaining to psychosocial development are qualified by person or program features. For example, Pierce et al. (1999) found that boys had lower levels of aggression in the classroom when they attended ASPs

with staff who were more positive and attended programs scheduling a fewer number of activities. This same study found that girls' aggression in the classroom was lower when peer interactions in the program context were less negative. Similarly, the ICRE & NIOST (2005) evaluation of 78 ASPs in Massachusetts showed that children's social behavior and peer relations improved in relation to program features (i.e., better relationship with host school, higher percentage of certified teachers, and more space). Finally, few studies have looked at ASP attendance in relation to externalizing behaviors and the findings are not consistent. Specifically, Pettit et al. (1997) found that a moderate attendance rate was most indicative of low externalizing behavior problems in the classroom, but Riggs (2006) reported a linear, negative association between program attendance and behavior problems.

Because antisocial behaviors such as *crime and substance use* are most prevalent in later adolescence, few of the studies reviewed assessed these outcomes. Nonetheless, those that have tend to find a significant decline both in actual drug use or attitudes toward the use of illicit substances (e.g., Gottfredson et al., 2004; LoSciouto et al., 1999; Pierce & Shields,1988) and rates of criminal arrests/recidivism (e.g., LaFrance et al., 2001; Myers et al., 2000) for ASP participants compared to nonparticipants. In terms of ecological factors, Gottfredson et al. (2004) found reductions in delinquent and antisocial behaviors were most marked for children attending ASPs that emphasized social skills and character development. Additionally, in an evaluation of an ASP serving adjudicated Black males the associated reductions in criminal offending were more evident for participants who attended the program on a voluntary basis (LaFrance et al., 2001).

However, one exception to the substance use-related benefits comes from the national evaluation of the 21st-Century Community Learning Centers (21CCLCs) (U.S. Department of Education, 2003b). Stated findings from the middle school sample of this evaluation indicated that ASP participants increased in their drug use and buying/selling of drugs compared to nonparticipants. However, because baseline differences were not fully accounted for (i.e., ASP participants were at higher social and demographic risk than nonparticipants at baseline) and comparison groups did not remain intact due to cross-over of condition, the stated findings from this study remain a source of controversy (Mahoney & Zigler, 2006).

With some exceptions (e.g., Lauver, 2002; Vandell & Corasaniti, 1988), investigations considering *peer relations and interpersonal competence* tend to report benefits associated with ASP participation. In a study of highly disadvantaged children, Mahoney, Lord et al. (2005a) found that, over time ASP participants increased significantly in their popularity and peer acceptance in the classroom compared to nonparticipants. With respect to program features, this same investigation showed that children attending ASPs observed to be highly engaging demonstrated greater social competence in the classroom relative to similar children attending programs that were less engaging (Mahoney, Parente, et al., 2007). Similarly, in a study of migrant Latino children, Riggs (2006; Riggs, Bohnert, Guzman, & Davidson, in press) found ASP participants had relatively high social competence when they attended an ASP regularly and Morrison et al. (2000) reported that ASP participants showed increased adaptive responses (i.e., assertiveness) to peer conflicts compared to nonparticipants. Finally, Gottfredson et al. (2004) showed that increases in positive peer relationships (i.e., fewer peer drug models) mediated the associated decline in delinquent and antisocial behaviors for ASP participants vs. nonparticipants.

Finally, although *psychological and emotional well-being* involves a diverse set of behaviors, the evidence across subareas suggests that ASP participants increase in their well-being relative to their nonparticipating counterparts. This includes associated declines in internalizing behaviors such as anxiety and depression (e.g., Finn-Stevenson et al., 2005; Marshall et al., 1997), better emotional adjustment and more positive psychological states while participating (e.g., Posner & Vandell, 1999; Vandell, Shernoff, Pierce, et al., 2005), and improvements in self-efficacy and social-academic self-concept (e.g., Cosden et al., 2001; Garza Fuentes & LeCapitaine, 1990). Again, some of these relations depend on features of the ASP investigated. For example, Pierce et al. (1999) found that boys showed relatively high levels of internalizing problems when the program featured high amounts of negative peer interactions and when the number of activities was high. Likewise, Rosenthal and Vandell (1996) found that ASPs with high enrollment rates (i.e., a large group size) had poorer social climates and were perceived by the participants (particularly boys) as offering low emotional support and autonomy.

*After-School Programs and Physical Health*   Despite the fact that physical recreation, nutrition, and to a lesser extent health education are common components of ASPs, a paucity of research has considered the impact of participation on children's physical health. One exception is a study of child obesity by Mahoney, Lord, et al. (2005a). In a disadvantaged sample of children with a high prevalence of obesity, results showed that, over time, children who became regular participants in ASPs developed a significantly lower body mass index (BMI) and were less likely to be clinically obese than similar children who did not participate in ASPs regularly. The magnitude of difference increased with program attendance. This is consistent with the limited research conducted on adolescents' participation in organized activities and overweight/obesity status (Elkins, Cohen, Koralewicz, & Taylor, 2004). It also resonates with the time use findings of Vandell, Pierce, et al. (2005) showing that ASP participants were more physically active and less apt to be snacking than nonparticipants. The lower levels of snacking behavior were evident for participants even during nonprogram hours of operation suggesting that ASPs may help to promote a healthier lifestyle with respect to food and activity choices.

*After-School Programs and Time Use*   A few studies have found that ASP participation is associated with different patterns of children's after-school time use and activities. Relative to their nonparticipating counterparts, ASP participants have been found to spend more of their time after school interacting with peers and adults; participating in organized activities such as sports, arts, and community service; and engaged in academic activities such as tutoring, reading/writing/science, and homework (Marshall et al., 1997; Posner & Vandell, 1994; 1999; Vandell, Shernoff, Pierce, et al., 2005; U.S. Department of Education, 2003). These same studies find that ASP participants spend less time watching television, snacking, unoccupied, involved in unstructured outdoor activities, performing household chores, participating in recreation centers, and involved in parent or sibling care. Although this work has not tended to connect the differences in time use to outcomes, it is plausible that the increased time in social and academic enrichment activities, healthier dietary behaviors, and greater activity levels of ASP participants may help to explain many of the findings reviewed above.

***Summary of Studies Reviewed***   Studies of the predictive associations between children's participation in ASPs and their subsequent academic and psychosocial adjustment indicate that these programs are important contexts of development. The types of experiences that children have in ASPs can influence both academic and psychosocial success in the school setting and beyond. In most cases, the quasi-experimental and experimental studies show that ASP participation is related to significant positive growth and development. However, not all studies find significant benefits for each and every outcome. Moreover, a very small number of investigations suggest that ASP participation can be a risk factor for lower achievement or social behavior problems when program quality is poor or in question.

Consistent with a bioecological perspective to development, the extent to which ASP participation leads to positive developmental outcomes depends on child and family characteristics, program features, and broader ecological conditions. With respect to child and family characteristics, positive outcomes were most apparent for children from low-income families and those with preexisting adjustment problems (e.g., low English proficiency, low achievement, history of adjudication). However, because few of the studies considered middle-income samples or subgroups of highly competent children, it is difficult to draw conclusions concerning the benefits ASPs for children at low risk for academic or psychosocial problems. Another individual difference, attendance dosage, was related to the magnitude of academic-related benefits in several studies (few studies of social outcomes assessed dosage-related effects). Indeed, in some cases, academic benefits were not observed *unless* children attended the ASPs regularly (cf., Kane, 2004). Although studied infrequently, other aspects of participation (engagement, duration of involvement) also tend to predict positive outcomes.

Studies examining links between program features and related outcomes indicate that the benefits associated with ASP participation depend on the characteristics of the program considered. Structural dimensions such as fewer numbers of children served by the program (i.e., a smaller program size) and lower child-to-staff ratios, higher levels of staff education or proportion of certified teachers, and process dimensions such as more positive social interchanges between/among staff and peers in the program context or observed levels of program engagement in program activities predict positive growth in children's academic or social functioning. Accordingly, program quality is likely to have a significant influence on whether and how ASPs impact children's development.

On this score, it is noteworthy that efforts to improve the quality of ASPs have been undertaken and with apparent success. Hall and Cassidy's (2002) evaluation of North Carolina's school-age care accreditation initiative involved 28 sites and determined pre- and posttest program quality from three assessment tools (i.e., SACERS, Caregiver Interaction Scale, and Human Relationships Keys of Quality scale). Beginning with training workshops for ASP staff and followed by 9 months of ongoing program support, the overall quality of the ASPs improved significantly from pre- to posttest. Improvements were most evident for ASPs that were unlicensed programs, had lower child-to-staff ratios (i.e., quality improvements were most apparent for staff providing service for a smaller number of children), and led by staff directors with lower levels of education at baseline. The importance of staff training and quality is underscored in other sizable evaluations of ASPs (Finn-Stevenson et al., 2005).

Comparison of ASP participants to a heterogeneous group of nonparticipants has been the most common research design employed. However, in some cases, the associated benefits of participating in ASPs have been shown to vary according to the alternative after-school arrangements to which they are compared. In low-income samples, there is evidence to suggest that program-related academic and social benefits are most apparent when ASP participants are compared to children in self-care. In addition, children with a combination of ASP and self-care may have superior academic performance than children in self-care alone. The associated buffering effect of ASPs is likely caused by the heightened risks of self-care for poor children living in dangerous environments. The program-related benefits may be diminished or masked entirely when ASP participants are compared to children in other adult supervised arrangements (e.g., parent care) or those participating in alternative organized after-school activities (i.e., sports, lessons, clubs).

## Conclusions and Future Directions

In recent decades, ASPs have become increasingly prevalent and popular in the United States. These programs now provide a significant source of childcare through the provision of a safe environment and adult supervision for children during the hours following school dismissal while their parents work. Moreover, from the early 1990s to the present, research on the associated impact of ASP participation for children's development has grown. This research suggests that ASP participation is often linked to benefits for children's academic and social competencies in the school setting and beyond it. This appears to be particularly true for children from low-income areas and those in need of social and academic supports. However, not all studies have found benefits associated with ASP participation. Moreover, those studies that have reported benefits for participants in some areas do not necessarily report improvements in all domains considered.

Consistent with a bioecological perspective, whether positive outcomes were observed across the studies reviewed depended significantly on the quality of programming provided in relation to the needs and interests of the children served. Coupled with evidence that the current supply of ASPs does not meet the demand for ASPs (e.g., Mahoney, Parente, & Zigler, 2009), and that a high child-to-staff ratio in existing programs is associated with poor outcomes for children, one basic conclusion is that we need more resources to develop high quality ASPs in the United States. Expanding the federal investment in the 21CCLCs would begin to address the problem of availability. However, 21CCLC funds provide a temporary source of support (3 years with the possibility of extending the use of funds to 5 years). As such, additional investments at the state and local levels are critical to building and maintaining such programs or improving their quality (Hall & Cassidy, 2002). To facilitate these efforts, additional research is needed to understand better the myriad of factors involved in developing quality ASPs and sustaining them over time (Holleman, Sundius, & Bruns, in press; Paisano-Trujillo, 2005).

Another basic conclusion is that we need to prepare and develop the after-school workforce so that they are able to provide high quality programming. Several models of staff development are now being developed and tested. For example, led by Professors Joseph Mahoney and Deborah Vandell, the University of California's Department of Education has initiated a Certificate in After-School Education (CASE) program (University of California, Irvine Department of Education, 2009). The long-term goal of CASE is to prepare after-school educators to promote positive youth development through high quality programming. To earn a certificate, participants must complete five quarter-long (10-week) courses that combine classroom instruction with fieldwork. The classroom instruction includes content-focused courses (e.g., literacy, math, tutoring, youth sports, arts, and technology), principles of after-school learning and youth development, basic knowledge in child and adolescent development, and multicultural education. These in-class experiences are blended with at least 70 hours of hands-on experience working in local ASPs under the supervision of experienced leaders. Enrollment in the

CASE program is open to UCI students and ASP staff and adults in the surrounding communities though university extension.

Based on the impact studies reviewed in this chapter, the bulk of knowledge concerning ASP participation and children's development comes from short-term investigations of low-income children from specific minority groups. Studies of certain racial/ethnic groups (i.e., Asians, Native Americans) and immigrant families are scarce and much more needs to be known about middle-income and affluent children's experiences in these programs. In addition, the majority of research has studied programs in their early years of maturity. To the extent that program maturity positively influences aspects such as program quality and participant attendance, then little is known about the potential range and magnitude of positive impacts that may result from regular participation in mature programs that are of high quality. More generally, while studies considering how program features may affect program-related impacts have been increasing, much more research on the long-term processes by which particular program characteristics relate to individual differences in children's program experiences and how those experiences translate into developmental changes is needed.

It should also be pointed out that most of the literature reviewed focused on statistical significance as the indicator of ASP impacts. Significance is important. But, effect sizes provide information on the magnitude of associated benefits. This information is critical for gauging the practical benefits of social programs (McCartney & Rosenthal, 2000). Because effect sizes tended not to be reported in the studies reviewed, it is difficult to draw conclusions about the degree of benefits linked to ASP participation. However, two recent meta-analyses have considered effect sizes for out-of-school program participation and young people's academic achievement (Lauer et al., 2006) and social adjustment (Durlak, Weissberg, & Pachan, in press). Overall, these studies find that program participation tends to be positively associated with academic and social competencies and that the effect sizes are of small-to-moderate magnitude depending on both the outcome assessed and the person- and program-level features considered. Nonetheless, for policymakers, of potential greater interest than either statistical significance or effect sizes is whether the program is cost effective. Cost-benefit analyses have rarely been undertaken in ASP research.

Finally, in terms of promoting children's schooling and educational development, ASPs are viewed increasingly as contexts that can complement the learning experiences that occur during the school day. This viewpoint represents a departure from the notion that ASPs should be mere extensions of the traditional school day. The content of ASPs reviewed in this chapter (see also Durlak, Mahoney, et al., in press) supports a conclusion that ASPs need not resemble school day instruction in order to yield academic or social benefits for participating children. Indeed, Mahoney, Parente, et al. (2007) showed that ASPs devoting

more time to enrichment and recreation activities and less time to homework were observed to be highly engaging. The engagement of the program was, in turn, significantly and positively related to multiple aspects quality and to the participants' school motivation and social competence in the classroom. However, perhaps owing to the rapid growth of ASPs in recent years, the goals of these programs have not always been integrated well with those of schools and the relationship between host schools and ASPs is sometimes one of antipathy. As suggested by a bioecological perspective, providing the most comprehensive educational opportunities for children requires an approach that aligns the activities of schools and ASPs with the needs of those served.

Overall, a large-scale approach to developing and sustaining ASPs is needed that attends to the issues of quality, the importance of careful evaluation, effectively integrates the child's school and after-school experiences, provides for early and school-age child care and education that meets the needs of working families, and is economically feasible. To this end, we conclude by highlighting one promising model—the School of the 21st Century (21C) (Henrich, Ginicola, & Finn-Stevenson, 2006). Conceptualized and developed by Edward Zigler and Matia Finn-Stevenson in 1988, the 21C model has been implemented in over 1,300 schools nationwide making it the largest whole school reform effort that has been mounted in our nation. The basic components of 21C include: guidance and support for parents, early care and education, school-aged childcare (i.e., before/after-school programs), health education and services, networks and training for childcare providers to ensure quality programming, and information and referral services. A guiding principle of 21C is universal access to these services for all children, regardless of family income. The model has been effectively implemented statewide in Kentucky and Arkansas is rapidly moving to statewide implementation.

In addition to integrating the goals of schools and programs with the needs of children and families, the 21C model is sensible both from a child development perspective and economic standpoint. In terms of providing for quality programs that can serve large numbers of children, public schools have the organizational structure and experience in place to coordinate services on a large scale, manage program quality and provide for the training needs of staff, are universally available, and allow for continuity in services for children and families across development (Henrich et al., 2006). Further, the 21C model is fiscally realistic and sustainable. 21C funding comes from a combination of Title I with ESEA, 21CCLC grants, state subsidization through money sent to local school districts, and parent fees that are calibrated to family income. Parent fees for the school-age care component turn a profit for the host schools that is used to defray other costs including scholarships for children from families who cannot afford to pay enrollment fees. Evaluations of the 21C model indicate that this model can be implemented effectively on a large scale, is received favorably by parents, students, schools, and communities, and associated with academic and social benefits for participating children (Finn-Stevenson et al., 2005).

## References

Anderson-Butcher, D. (2002). *An evaluation report for the Cap City Kids program: Phase two*. Columbus, OH: Center for Learning Excellence, Ohio State University.

Barnett, W. S., Brown, K., & Shore, R. (2004). The universal v. targeted debate: Should the United States have preschool for all? *Preschool Policy Matters* (Issue 6). Retrieved from http://nieer.org/resources/policybriefs/6.pdf

Bartko, W. T. (2005). The A-B-Cs of engagement in out-of-school programs. In H. B. Weiss, P. M. D. Little, & S. M. Bouffard (Issue Eds.) & G. G. Noam (Editor-in-Chief), *New directions in youth development: Vol. 105. Participation in youth programs: Enrollment, attendance, and engagement* (pp. 109–120). San Francisco, CA: Jossey-Bass.

Bergin, D. A., Hudson, L. M., Chryst, C. F., & Resetar, M. (1992). An after-school intervention program for educationally disadvantaged young children. *The Urban Review, 24,* 203–217.

Bissell, J., Dugan, C., Ford-Johnson, A., & Jones, P. (2002). *Evaluation of the YS-CARE After School Program for California Work Opportunity and Responsibility to Kids (CALWORKS): 2002*. Irvine, CA: Department of Education, University of California-Irvine.

Bloom, H. S., Richburg-Hayes, L, & Black, A. R. (2005). Using covariates to improve precision: Empirical guidance for studies that randomize schools to measure the impacts of educational interventions. Retrieved from http://www.wtgrantfoundation.org/usr_doc/2005_Cluster_parameter_November_2005new.pdf

Brackett, M. A., & Rivers. S. E. (in press). What is emotional literacy? In M. A. Brackett & J. P. Kremenitzer (Eds.), *Emotional literacy in the classroom: Upper elementary*. Portchester, NY: National Professional Resources.

Bronfenbrenner, U. (1979). *The ecology of human development: Experiments by nature and design*. Cambridge, MA: Harvard University Press.

Bronfenbrenner, U., & Morris, P. (2006). The bioecological model of human development. In W. Daman & R. M. Lerner (Editors-in-Chief) & R. M. Lerner (Vol. Ed.), *Handbook of child psychology: Vol 1. Theoretical models of human development* (pp. 793–828). Hoboken, NJ: Wiley.

Cairns, R. B., Elder, G. H., Jr., & Costello, E. J. (Eds.). (1996). *Developmental science*. Cambridge, England: Cambridge University Press.

Campbell, D. T., & Stanley, J. C. (1966). *Experimental and quasi-experimental designs for research*. Chicago, IL: Rand McNally.

Capizzano, J., Tout, K., & Adams, G., (2000). *Child care patterns of school-age children with employed mothers*. Washington, DC: The Urban Institute.

Chase, R. A., & Clement, D. (2000). *Hmong youth pride: Outcomes evaluation summary*. St. Paul, MN: Wilder Research Center.

Chen, H., & Rossi, P. (1987). The theory-driven approach to validity. *Evaluation and Program Planning, 10,* 95–103.

Cook, T. D., & Campbell, D. T. (1979). *Quasi-experimental design and analysis issues for field settings*. Boston, MA: Houghton Mifflin.

Cosden, M., Morrison, G., Albanese, A. L., & Macias, S. (2001). When homework is no home work: After school programs for homework assistance. *Journal of Educational Psychology, 36,* 211–221.

C. S. Mott Foundation Committee on After-School Research and Practice. (2005). *Moving toward success: Framework for after-school programs*. Retrieved from http://www.publicengagement.com/Framework/images/framework_61505.pdf

Currie, J., & Duncan, T. (1995). Does Head Start make a difference? *American Economic Review, 85,* 341–364.

Duncan, G. J., Dowsen, C. J., Claessens, A., Magnusson, K., Huston, A. C., Klebanov, P., et al. (2007). School readiness and later achievement. *Developmental Psychology, 43,* 1428–1446.

Durlak, J., Mahoney, J. L., Bohnert, A. M., & Parente, M. E. (in press). Developing and improving after-school programs to enhance youth's personal growth and adjustment: A special issue of AJCP. *American Journal of Community Psychology.*

Durlak, J. A., & Weissberg, R. P. (2007). *The impact of after-school programs that promote personal and social skills*. Chicago, IL: Collaborative for Academic, Social, and Emotional Learning.

Durlak, J. A., Weissberg, R. P., & Pachan, M. (in press). A meta-analysis of after-school programs that seek to promote personal and social skills in children and adolescents. *American Journal of Community Psychology.*

Eccles, J. S., & Midgley, C. (1989). Stage/environment fit: Developmentally appropriate classrooms for early adolescents. In R. E. Ames & C. Ames (Eds.), *Research on motivation in education* (Vol. 3, pp. 139–186). San Diego, CA: Academic Press.

Eccles, J. S., Midgley, C., Wigfield, A., Buchanan, C. M., Reuman, D., Flanagan, C., et al. (1993). Development during adolescence: The impact of stage-environment fit on young adolescents' experiences in schools and in families. *American Psychologist, 48,* 90–101.

Elkins, W. L., Cohen, D. A., Koralewicz, L. M., & Taylor S. N. (2004). After school activities, overweight, and obesity among inner city youth. *Journal of Adolescence, 27,* 181–189.

Finn-Stevenson, M., Ginicola, M., & Yekelchik, A. (2005). *Evaluation of the Child and Family Learning Centers—21CCLC grant at Independence, MO public schools: 2004–2005 report*. New Haven, CT: Zigler Center in Child Development and Social Policy, Yale University.

Foley, E. M., & Eddins, G. (2001). *Preliminary analysis of Virtual Y After-School Program participants' patterns of school attendance and academic performance: Final evaluation report program year 1999–2000*. New York: National Center for Schools and Communities, Fordham University.

Garza Fuentes, E., & LeCapitaine, J. E. (1990). The effects of a primary prevention program on Hispanic children. *Education, 110,* 298–303.

Gormley, W. T., Gayer, T., Phillips, D., & Dawson, B. (2005). The effects of universal pre-K on cognitive development. *Developmental Psychology, 41,* 872–884.

Gormley, W. T., Phillips, D. A., Newmark, K., & Perper, K. (in press). Socio-emotional effects of early childhood education programs in Tulsa. *Child Development.*

Gottfredson, D. C., Gerstenblith, S. A., Soulé, D. A., Worner, S. C., & Lu, S. (2004). Do after school programs reduce delinquency? *Prevention Science, 5,* 253–266.

Grossman, J. B., Price, M. L., Fellerath, V., Jucovy, L. Z., Kotloff, L. J., Raley, R., et al. (2002). *Multiple choices after school: Findings from the Extended-Service Schools Initiative*. Philadelphia, PA: Public/Private Ventures.

Gruen, G., & Zigler, E. (1968). Expectancy of success and the probability learning of middle-class lower-class, and retarded children. *Journal of Abnormal Psychology, 73,* 343–352.

Hall, A. H., & Cassidy, D. J. (2002). An assessment of the North Carolina School-Age Accreditation Initiative. *Journal of Research in Child Education, 17,* 84–96.

Heckman, J. J. (2005). A broader view of what education policy should be. In N. F. Watt, C. Ayoub, R. H. Bradley, J. E. Puma, & W. A. LeBoeuf (Eds.), *The crisis of youth mental health: Early intervention programs and policies* (pp. 3–26). Portsmouth, NH: Greenwood.

Heckman, J. J., & Smith, J. A. (1995). Assessing the case for social experiments. *Journal of Economic Perspectives, 9,* 85–110.

Henrich, C. C. (2004). Head Start as a national laboratory. In E. Zigler & S. J. Styfco (Eds.), *The Head Start debates* (pp. 517–532). Baltimore, MD: Brooks.

Henrich, C. C., Ginicola, M. M., & Finn-Stevenson, M. (2006). *The School of the 21st Century is making a difference: Findings from two research studies*. New Haven, CT: Yale University, School of the 21st Century Program.

Hofferth, S. L., Brayfield, A., Diech, S., & Holcomb, P. (1991). National childcare survey: 1990. (Report No. 91-5). Washington, DC: Urban Institute.

Holland, A., & Andre, T. (1987). Participation in extracurricular activities in secondary school: What is known, what needs to be known. *Review of Educational Research, 57*, 437–466.

Holleman, M. A., Sundius, M. J., & Bruns, E. J., (in press). Building opportunity: Developing city systems to expand and improve after school programs. *American Journal of Community Psychology.*

Huang, D., Gribbons, B., Kim, K. S., Lee, C., & Baker, E. L. (2000). *A decade of results: The impact of the LA's BEST after school enrichment initiative on subsequent student achievement and performance.* Los Angeles, CA: University of California at Los Angeles, Graduate School of Education & Information Studies, Center for the Study of Evaluation.

Intercultural Center for Research in Education and the National Institute on Out-of-School Time. (2005). *Pathways to success for youth: What counts in after-school?* Massachusetts After-School Research Study (MARS) report. Boston, MA: United Way of Massachusetts Bay.

Kahlenberg, R. (2001). *All together now: Creating middle-class schools through public school choice.* Washington, DC: Brookings Institution Press.

Kane, T. J. (2004). *The impact of after-school programs: Interpreting the results of four recent evaluations.* Retrieved from http://www.wtgrantfoundation.org/usr_doc/After-school_paper.pdf

Kleiner, B., Nolin, M. J., & Chapman, C. (2004). *Before- and after-school care, programs and activities of children in kindergarten through eighth grade: 2001* (NCES 2004-008). Washington, DC: U.S. Department of Education, National Center for Education Statistics.

Knutson, K. A. (2005). *CHAMPS after-school program outcome evaluation year three: FY2005.* Coral Springs, FL: Author.

LaFrance, S., Twersky, F., Latham, N., Foley, E., Bott, C., & Lee, L. (2001). *A safe place for healthy youth development: A comprehensive evaluation of the Bayview Safe Haven.* San Francisco, CA: BTW Consultants & LaFrance Associates.

Larson, R. W. (2000). Toward a psychology of positive youth development. *American Psychologist, 55,*170–183.

Lattimore, C. B., Mihalic, S. F., Grotpeter, J. K., & Taggart, R. (1998). *Blueprints for violence prevention, book four: The Quantum Opportunities Program.* Boulder, CO: University of Colorado at Boulder, Center for the Study and Prevention of Violence.

Lauer, P. A., Akiba, M., Wilkerson, S. B., Apthorp, H. S., Snow, D., & Martin-Glenn, M. L. (2006). Out-of-school-time programs: A meta-analysis of effects for at-risk students. *Review of Educational Research, 76,* 275–313.

Lauver, S. C. (2002). *Assessing the benefits of an after-school program for urban youth: An impact and process evaluation.* Philadelphia, PA: Author.

Lauver, S. C., Little, P. M. D., & Weiss, H. (2004). *Moving beyond the barriers: Attracting and sustaining youth participation in out-of-school time programs.* Retrieved from http://www.hfrp.org/content/download/1098/48603/file/issuebrief6.pdf

Little, P., Dupree, S., & Deich, S. (2002). *Documenting progress and demonstrating results: Evaluating local out-of-school time programs.* Cambridge, MA and Washington, DC: Harvard Family Research Project and The Finance Project.

Lord, H., & Mahoney, J. L. (2007). Neighborhood crime and self care: Risks for aggression and lower academic performance. *Developmental Psychology, 43,* 1321–1333.

LoSciuto, L., Hilbert, S. M., Fox, M. M., Porcellini, L., & Lamphear, A. (1999). A two-year evaluation of the Woodrock Youth Development Project. *Journal of Early Adolescence, 19,* 488–507.

Love, J. M., Eliason Kisker, E., Ross, C. M., Schochet, P. Z., Brooks-Gunn, J., Paulsell, D., et al. (2002, June). *Making a difference in the lives of infants and toddlers and their families: The impacts of Early Head Start.* Princeton, NJ: Mathematica Policy Research. Retrieved from http://www.mathematica-mpr.com/publications/PDFs/ehsfinal-summ.pdf

Magnusson, D., & Stattin, H. (1998). Person-context interaction theories. In W. Damon (Series Ed.) & R. M. Lerner (Vol. Ed.), *Handbook of child psychology: Vol. 1. Theoretical models of human development* (5th ed., pp. 685–759). New York: Wiley.

Mahoney, J. L., Larson, R. W., & Eccles, J. S. (2005). *Organized activities as contexts of development: Extracurricular activities, after-school and community programs.* Mahwah, NJ: Erlbaum.

Mahoney, J. L., Lord, H., & Carryl, E. (2005a). After-school program participation and the development of child obesity and peer acceptance. *Applied Developmental Science, 9,* 202–215.

Mahoney, J. L., Lord, H., & Carryl, E. (2005b). An ecological analysis of after-school program participation and the development of academic performance and motivational attributes for disadvantaged children. *Child Development, 76,* 811–825.

Mahoney, J. L., & Parente, M. E. (2009). Should we care about adolescents who care for themselves? What we've learned and what we need to know about youth in self-care. *Child Development Perspectives, 3,* 189–195.

Mahoney, J. L., Parente, M. E., & Lord, H. (2007). After-school program engagement: Developmental consequences and links to program quality and content. *The Elementary School Journal, 107,* 385–404.

Mahoney, J. L., Parente, M. E., & Zigler, E. F. (2010). Appendix of studies reviewed. Retrieved from http://www.gse.uci.edu/jmahoney/Mahoney.Parente.Zigler.Appendix.Final.pdf

Mahoney, J. L., Parente, M. E., & Zigler, E. F. (2009). After-school programs in America: Origins, growth, popularity, and politics. *Journal of Youth Development, 4*(3).

Mahoney, J. L., & Stattin, H. (2000). Leisure activities and adolescent antisocial behavior: The role of structure and social context. *Journal of Adolescence, 23,* 113–127.

Mahoney, J. L., Stattin, H., & Lord, H. (2004). Unstructured youth recreation center participation and antisocial behavior development: Selection influences and the moderating role of antisocial peers. *International Journal of Behavioral Development, 28,* 553–560.

Mahoney, J. L., Vandell, D. L., Simpkins, S. D., & Zarrett, N. R. (2009). Adolescent out-of-school activities. In R. M. Lerner & L. Steinberg (Eds.), *Handbook of adolescent psychology*: Vol. 2. *Contextual influences on adolescent development* (3rd ed., pp. 228–267). Hoboken, NJ: Wiley.

Mahoney, J. L. & Zigler, E. F. (2006). Translating science-to-policy under the No Child Left Behind Act of 2001: Lessons from the national evaluation of the 21st-Century Community Learning Centers. *The Journal of Applied Developmental Psychology, 27,* 282–294

Malakoff, M. E., Underhill, J. M., & Zigler, E. (1998). Influence of inner-city environment and head start experience on effectance motivation. *American Journal of Orthopsychiatry, 68,* 630–638.

Marshall, N., Coll, C. G., Marx, F., McCartney, K., Keefe, N., & Ruh, J. (1997). After-school time and children's behavioral adjustment. *Merrill-Palmer Quarterly, 43,* 497–514.

McCall, R. B., & Green, B. L. (2004). Beyond methodological gold standards of behavioral research: Considerations for practice and policy. *Social Policy Report, 18*(2), 1–19.

McCartney, K., & Rosenthal, R. (2000). Effect size, practical importance, and social policy for children. *Child Development, 71,* 173–180.

Morris, D., Shaw, B., & Perney, J. (1990). Helping low readers in grades 2 and 3: Volunteer tutoring program. *The Elementary School Journal, 91,* 133–150.

Morrison, G. M., Storino, M. H., Robertson, L. M., Weissglass, T., & Dondero, A. (2000). The protective function of after-school programming and parent education and support for students at risk for substance abuse. *Evaluation and Program Planning, 23,* 365–371.

Myers, W. C., Burton, P., Sanders, P. D, Donat, K. M., Cheney, J., Fitzpatrick, T. et al. (2000). Project Back-on-Track at 1 year: A delinquency treatment program for early-career juvenile offenders. *Journal of the American Academy of Child & Adolescent Psychiatry, 39,* 1127–1134.

National Institute of Children's Health and Development (NICHD), Early Child Care Research Network. (2002). Child-care structure, process, and outcome: Direct and indirect effects of child-care quality on young children's development. *Psychological Science, 13,* 199–206.

National Institute of Children's Health and Development (NICHD), Early Child Care Research Network. (2004). Are child development outcomes related to before- and after-school care arrangements?

Results from the NICHD Study of Early Child Care. *Child Development, 75*, 280–295.

National Research Council and Institute of Medicine, Committee on Community-Level Programs for Youth. (2002). *Community programs to promote youth development.* J. Eccles & J. A. Gootman (Eds.), Board on Children, Youth, and Families, Division of Behavioral and Social Science and Education. Washington, DC: National Academy Press.

National Research Council and Institute of Medicine. (2004). *Engaging schools: Fostering high school students' motivation to learn.* Committee on Increasing High School Students' Engagement and Motivation to Learn. Board on Children, Youth, and Families, Division of Behavioral and Social Sciences and Education. Washington, DC: National Academies Press.

National School-Age Care Alliance. (1998). *The NSACA standards for quality school-age care.* Hollis, NH: Puritan Press.

Newmann, F. (1992). *Student engagement and achievement in American secondary schools.* New York: Teachers College Press.

Paisano-Trujillo, R. (2005, September 22–23). Out-of-school time: A critical setting for promoting positive youth development. In A-M. Chung (Facilitator), *Developing and evaluating after school systems.* Symposium paper presented at the After School Evaluation Symposium, Washington, DC.

Parents as Teachers. (2006). *Parents as teachers logic model.* Retrieved from http://www.opfibti.org/pat/resources/PAT%20Logic%20Model.pdf

Pettit, G. S., Laird, R. D., Bates, J. E., & Dodge, K. A. (1997). Patterns of after-school care in middle childhood: Risk factors and developmental outcomes. *Merrill-Palmer Quarterly, 43*, 515–538.

Phillips, D., & Styfco, S. (2006). Child development research and public policy: Triumphs and setbacks on the way to maturity. *Child development and social policy: Knowledge for action* (pp. 11–27). Washington, DC: American Psychological Association.

Pierce, K. M., Bolt, D. M., & Vandell, D. L. (in press). Specific features of after-school program quality: Associations with children's functioning in middle childhood. *American Journal of Community Psychology.*

Pierce, K. M., Hamm, J. V., & Vandell, & D. L. (1999). Experiences in after-school programs and children's adjustment in first-grade classrooms. *Child Development, 70*, 756–767.

Pierce, L. H., & Shields, N. S. (1988). The Be a Star community-based after-school program: Developing resiliency factors in high-risk pre-adolescent youth. *Journal of Community Psychology, 25*, 175–183.

Posner, J. K., & Vandell, D. L. (1994). Low-income children's after-school care: Are there beneficial effects of after-school programs? *Child Development, 65*, 440–456.

Posner, J. K., & Vandell, D. L. (1999). After-school activities and the development of low-income urban children: A longitudinal study. *Developmental Psychology, 35*, 868–879.

Prenovost, J. K. E. (2001). *A first-year evaluation of after-school learning programs in four urban middle schools in the Santa Ana Unified School District.* Irvine, CA: Author.

Raudenbush, S. W., Martinez, A., & Spybrook, J. (2005). *Strategies for improving precision in group-randomized experiments.* Retrieved from http://epa.sagepub.com/cgi/content/abstract/29/1/5

Raver, C. C., & Zigler, E. F. (1997). Social competence: An untapped dimension in evaluating Head Start's success. *Early Childhood Research Quarterly, 12*, 363–385.

Reynolds, A. J. (1998). Confirmatory program evaluation: A method for strengthening causal inference. *American Journal of Evaluation, 19*, 203–221.

Reynolds, A. J. (2005). Confirmatory program evaluation: Applications to early childhood interventions. *Teachers College Record, 107*, 2401–2425.

Riggs, N. R. (2006). After-school program attendance and the social development of rural Latino children of immigrant families. *Journal of Community Psychology, 34*, 75–87.

Riggs, N. R., Bohnert, A. M., Guzman, M. D., & Davidson, D. (in press). Examining the potential of community-based after-school programs for Latino youth. *American Journal of Community Psychology.*

Riggs, N. R., & Greenberg, M. T. (2004a). After-school youth development

programs: A developmental-ecological model of current research. *Clinical Child and Family Psychology Review, 7*, 177–190.

Riggs, N. R., & Greenberg, M. T. (2004b). Moderators in the academic development of migrant Latino children attending after-school programs. *Applied Developmental Psychology, 25*, 349–367.

Rosenthal, R., & Vandell, D. L. (1996). Quality of care of school-aged child-care programs: Regulatable features, observed experiences, child perspectives, and parent perspectives. *Child Development, 67*, 2434–2445.

Ross, S. M., Lewis, T. L., Smith, L., & Sterblin, A. (2002). *Evaluation of the Extended-Day Tutoring Program in Memphis City Schools: Final report to CRESPAR.* Retrieved from http://www.hfrp.org.

Rossi, P. H. (1997). Advances in quantitative evaluation, 1987–1996. In D. Rog & D. Fournier (Eds.), *New directions for program evaluation* (Vol.76, pp. 57–68). San Francisco, CA: Jossey-Bass.

Schinke, S. P., Cole, K. C., & Poulin, S. R. (2000). Enhancing the educational achievement of at-risk youth. *Prevention Science, 1*, 51–60.

Schulman, K., & Barnett, W. S. (2005). *The benefits of prekindergarten on middle-income children, NIEER policy report.* New Brunswick, NJ: Rutgers University. Retrieved from http://nieer.org/resources/policyreports/report3.pdf

Schweinhart, L., Barnes, H., Weikart, D., Barnett, W. S., & Epstein, A. S. (1993). Significant benefits: The High/Scope Perry Preschool study through age 27. *Monographs of the High/Scope Educational Research Foundation Number 10.* Ypsilanti, MI: High/Scope Press.

Shadish, W. R., Cook, T. D., & Campbell, D. T. (2002). *Experimental and quasi-experimental design for generalized causal inference.* Boston, MA: Houghton-Mifflin.

Simpkins, S. C., Little, P. M. D., & Weiss, H. B. (2004). *Understanding and measuring attendance in out-of-school programs.* Retrieved from http://www.gse.harvard.edu/hfrp/projects/after-school/resources/issuebrief7.html

Smith, C., Peck, S. C., Denault, A-S., Blasevski, J., & Akiva, T. (in press). Quality at the point of service: Profiles of practice in after-school settings. *American Journal of Community Psychology.*

Smith, D. W., & Zhang, J. J. (2001). *Shaping our children's future: Keeping a promise in Houston communities: Year 4 evaluation of the Mayor's After-school Achievement Program (ASAP).* Houston, TX: University of Houston.

Tolman, J., Pittman, K., Yohalem, N., Thomases, J., & Trammel, M. (2002). *Moving an out-of-school agenda: Lessons across cities.* Takoma Park, MD: Forum for Youth Investment.

University of California—Irvine, Department of Education. (2009). UCI undergraduate certificate in after-school education. Retrieved from http://www.gse.uci.edu/case/case_program.php

U.S. Department of Education. (2003a). *When schools stay open late: The national evaluation of the 21st Century Learning Centers Program, first year findings.* Washington, DC: Author.

U.S. Department of Education and Institute Educational Sciences. (2003b). *Random assignment in program evaluation and intervention research: Questions and answers.* Retrieved from http://www.ed.gov/offices/IES/NCEE/qa.html

Vandell, D. L., & Corasaniti, M. A. (1988). The relation between third graders' after-school care and social, academic and emotional functioning. *Child Development, 59*, 868–875.

Vandell, D. L., Pierce, K. M., & Dadisman, K. (2005). Out-of-school settings as a developmental context for children and youth. In R. Kail (Ed.), *Advances in child development* (Vol. 33, pp. 43–77). Oxford, England: Elsevier.

Vandell, D. L., & Posner, J. K. (1999). Conceptualization and measurement of children's after-school environments. In S. L. Friedman & T. Wachs (Eds.), *Measuring environments across the lifespan: Emerging methods and concepts* (pp. 167–196). Washington, DC: American Psychological Association.

Vandell, D. L., Reisner, E. R., Brown, B. B., Dadisman, K., Pierce, K. M., Lee, D., et al. (2005). *The study of promising after-school programs: Examination of intermediate outcomes in year 2.* Retrieved from http://www.wcer.wisc.edu/childcare/statements.html

Vandell, D. L., Reisner, E. R., Brown, B. B., Pierce, K. M., Dadisman, K., & Pechman, E. M. (2004). *The study of promising after-school programs: Descriptive report of the promising programs.* Retrieved from http://www.wcer.wisc.edu/childcare/statements.html.

Vandell, D. L., Shernoff, D. J., Pierce, K. M., Bolt, D. M., Dadisman, K., & Brown, B. B. (2005). Activities, engagement, and emotion in after-school programs. In H. B. Weiss, P. M. D. Little, & S. M. Bouffard (Issue Eds.) & G. G. Noam (Editor-in-Chief), *New directions in youth development: Vol. 105. Participation in youth programs: Enrollment, attendance, and engagement* (pp. 121–129). San Francisco, CA: Jossey-Bass.

Walker, J., Marczak, M., Blyth, D., & Borden, L. (2005). Designing youth development programs: Toward a theory of developmental intentionality. In J. L. Mahoney, R. W. Larson, & J. S. Eccles (Eds.), *Organized activities as contexts of development: Extracurricular activities, after-school and community programs* (pp. 399–418). Mahwah, NJ: Erlbaum.

Walker, K., & Abreton, A. (2002). *Working together to build Beacon Centers in San Francisco: Evaluation findings from 1998–2000. Theory of change process.* Public/Private Ventures. Retrieved from http://www.ppv.org/pdffiles/beacons.pdf

Weiss, C. (1997). Theory-based evaluation: Past, present, and future. *New Directions in Program Evaluation, 76,* 41–56.

Weiss, H. B., Little, P. M. D., & Bouffard, S. M. (2005). More than just being there: Balancing the participation equation. In H. B. Weiss, P. M. D. Little, & S. M. Bouffard (Issue Eds.) & G. G. Noam (Editor-in-Chief), *New directions in youth development: Vol. 105. Participation in youth programs: Enrollment, attendance, and engagement* (pp. 15–31). San Francisco, CA: Jossey-Bass.

Welsh, M. E., Russell, C. A., Williams, I., Reisner, E. R., & White, R. N. (2002). *Promoting learning and school attendance through after-school programs: Student-level changes in educational performance across TASC's first three years.* Washington, DC: Policy Studies Associates.

Westinghouse Learning Corporation. (1969). *The impact of Head Start: An evaluation of the effects of Head Start on children's cognitive and affective development* (Vols. 1 & 2). Report to the Office of Economic Opportunity. Athens, OH: Author.

Yohalem, N., Pittman, K., & Wilson-Ahlstrom, A. (2004). Getting inside the black box to measure program quality. *The Evaluation Exchange, 10*(1), 6–7.

Yohalem, N., & Wilson-Ahlstrom, A. (in press). Inside the black box: Assessing and improving quality in youth programs. *American Journal of Community Psychology.*

Yohalem, N., Wilson-Ahlstrom, A., with Fischer, S., & Shinn, M. (2009). *Measuring youth program quality: A guide to assessment tools* (2nd ed.). Washington, DC: The Forum for Youth Investment, Impact Strategies.

Zigler, E. F. (1963). Metatheoretical issues in developmental psychology. In M. Marx (Ed.), *Theories in contemporary psychology* (pp. 341–369). New York: Macmillan.

Zigler, E. F. (1998). A place of value for applied and policy studies. *Child Development, 69,* 532–542.

Zigler, E. F., Bennett-Gates, D., Hodapp, R., & Henrich, C. (2002). Assessing personality traits of individuals with mental retardation. *American Journal on Mental Retardation, 107,* 181–193.

Zigler, E. F., & Styfco, S. J. (2005). Epilogue. In N. F. Watt, C. Ayoub, R. H. Bradley, J. E. Puma, & W. A. LeBoeuf (Eds.), *The crisis in youth mental health: Early intervention programs and policies* (pp. 347–372). Portsmouth, NH: Greenwood.

Zigler, E. F., & Trickett, P. K. (1978). IQ, social competence, and evaluation of early childhood intervention programs. *American Psychologist, 33,* 789–798.

# 25

# Parents' Involvement in Children's Schooling

## *A Context for Children's Development*

EVA M. POMERANTZ AND ELIZABETH A. MOORMAN

Since the late 1990s, there have been numerous calls for parents to become more involved in children's schooling. Perhaps most prominent is the U.S. federal government's No Child Left Behind Act of 2002 in which increasing parents' involvement is one of six targeted areas for reform. Such calls are also visible in schools all over the United States as indicated by the presence of Parent–Teacher Associations (PTAs). The calls for parents' involvement in children's academic lives are based on a wealth of evidence showing that the more parents take part in school activities such as parent–teacher conferences and school open houses, the more children flourish academically in that they enjoy their schoolwork, are engaged in it, and earn good grades (for reviews, see Hill & Taylor, 2004; Pomerantz, Grolnick, & Price, 2005). The evidence comes from research that has focused largely on linking the *extent* of parents' involvement to children's academic functioning. Such research has been critical in establishing that parents need to be involved in children's schooling. However, the "more-is-better" framework used to date neglects a number of factors that are important to understanding the effects on children of parents' involvement.

In this chapter, we move away from such a framework by arguing that parents' involvement in children's schooling is best viewed as a context for children's development in that it may create an environment that launches children onto either a positive or negative trajectory. We make the case that what is key to understanding the effects on children of parents' involvement is not so much the extent of parents' involvement, but the resources it provides to children. As Epstein and Van Voorhis (2001) have argued with regards to the time children spend on homework, it is "more than minutes." In fact, contrary to what is often assumed, more involvement on parents' part may not always be better for children. We begin by providing a definition of parents' involvement in children's schooling. We then review the evidence emerging from research linking the extent of

parents' involvement to children's academic functioning. Drawing from models of how parents' involvement shapes children's academic functioning, we argue that when parents become involved in children's academic lives, they create an environment that may have benefits or costs for children dependent on the resources parents provide. Research supportive of this perspective is reviewed. The advantages of treating parents' involvement in children's schooling as a context for children's development are then discussed.

## Defining Parents' Involvement

Drawing on several diverse lines of theory and research, Grolnick and Slowiaczek (1994) define parents' involvement in children's schooling as parents' commitment of resources to the academic area of children's lives. Although a number of meaningful distinctions have been drawn between different forms of such commitment (e.g., Epstein, 1987b; Grolnick & Slowiaczek, 1994; Hickman, Greenwood, & Miller, 1995; Ritblatt, Beatty, Cronan, & Ochoa, 2002), following several investigators (Becker & Epstein, 1982; Hoover-Dempsey & Sandler, 1997; Izzo, Weissberg, Kasprow, & Fendrich, 1999), we make the broad distinction between involvement based at school and that based at home. We use this distinction because it is a concrete, parsimonious one that may be employed easily by researchers, policy makers, educators, and parents. As such, it allows for continuity across these often separate, albeit related, stake holders in children's lives. Moreover, the distinction between involvement on the school front and that on the home front is of import because the two forms of involvement may represent two distinct ways that parents become involved in children's schooling. It may also be essential to understanding the effects on children of parents' involvement, as the two may differ in the types of resources they provide for children, thereby often having different effects on children (see below).

398

***School-Based Involvement*** School-based involvement represents practices on the part of parents that require their making actual contact with the school. Practices in this vein include, but are not limited to, being present at general school meetings, talking with teachers (e.g., attending parent–teacher conferences and initiating contact with teachers), attending school events (e.g., open houses and science fairs), and volunteering at school. In the United States, parents most commonly become involved on the school front through their presence at general school meetings and parent–teacher conferences, which national surveys indicate are attended by at least two thirds of parents (U.S. Department of Education, 2006). Such involvement increases with socioeconomic status and educational attainment, with other forms of school-based involvement also increasing with socieoeconomic status and educational attainment (U.S. Department of Education, 2006). For example, volunteering at school is more common among more educated (e.g., 54 to 62% in 2003) than less educated parents (e.g., 16 to 40% in 2003) and among European American (e.g., 48% in 2003) than African American (e.g., 32% in 2003) and Hispanic (e.g., 28% in 2003) parents (U.S. Department of Education, 2006) . Parents' school-based involvement may also include involvement at a higher level, such as being a member of the school board and attending school board meetings. However, in line with the majority of extant research (for some exceptions, see Eccles & Harold, 1996; Epstein, 1987b), we do not focus on parents' involvement at such a level. Although it may have benefits, the direct impact on children may be relatively minor because parents and children may have only limited interactions in this context. Moreover, only a very small proportion of parents—5 to 6%—appear to become involved in high-level activities on the school front (Ritblatt et al., 2002).

***Home-Based Involvement*** Home-based involvement represents parents' practices related to school that take place outside of school, usually, albeit not always, in the home. Such practices can be directly related to school, including, among other things, assisting children with school-related tasks, such as course selection and homework (e.g., creating a quiet place for children to study and helping children complete homework), responding to children's academic endeavors (e.g., choices about the topic of a school project and performance on a test), and talking with children about academic issues (e.g., what happened in school and the value of doing well in school). National surveys in the United States indicate that parents' involvement on the home front as manifest in assisting with homework is relatively frequent with 70% of parents helping children at least once a week, regardless of parents' socioeconomic status, educational attainment, or ethnicity (U.S. Department of Education, 2006). Also characteristic of parents' home-based involvement is engaging children in intellectual activities (e.g., reading books with children and taking them to the museum) that are not directly related to school per se, but are likely to foster children's academic development. Grolnick and

Slowiaczek (1994) label this cognitive–intellectual involvement. Based on national surveys, in the United States this form of involvement is most frequently manifest in visiting the library with children (e.g., 50% in 2003), but also occurs fairly frequently in terms of taking children to plays (e.g., 36% in 2003) and museums or historical sites (e.g., 22% in 2003), with such involvement somewhat more common among more educated, wealthier, non-Hispanic parents (U.S. Department of Education, 2006). It is of note that parents' involvement on the home front may sometimes be tied to their involvement on the school front. For example, parents may discuss with children at home what they learned at a parent–teacher conference.

## Effects of Parents' Involvement

Since the early 1980s, much theoretical and empirical attention has been directed toward understanding the role of parents' involvement in children's academic functioning; that is, children's motivational beliefs (e.g., perceptions of competence and intrinsic versus extrinsic motivation), engagement (e.g., effort exerted in school and attention paid to teacher), and performance (e.g., grades and achievement test scores). This endeavor is evident itself in two bodies of research which have covered families from diverse backgrounds with children mainly in preschool through middle school (for research on families with children in high school, see Brown, Mounts, Lamborn, & Steinberg, 1993; Gonzalez, Holbein, & Quilter, 2002; Taylor, 1996). In one line of research, the focus has been on the effects of parents' naturally occurring involvement. Investigators have generally measured the extent of a variety of forms of parents' involvement in children's schooling using parents', teachers', and children's reports. The associations of such reports with children's academic functioning, as assessed with children and teachers' reports as well as school records, have then been examined, mostly concurrently, but also longitudinally. In a second line of research, using a variety of designs (e.g., pre- and postassessment and experimental and matched control groups), investigators have examined the effects on children's academic functioning of interventions that are intended to promote parents' involvement in children's schooling (e.g., a booklet of academic activities for parents to encourage children's reading and a contract between staff, parents, and children pledging involvement on the part of parents). As will be apparent from our review of these two lines of research, they yield fairly different conclusions.

### *Research on Parents' Naturally Occurring Involvement*
*School-Based Involvement* There is now a wealth of research linking parents' involvement on the school front to children's academic functioning (e.g., Culp, Hubbs-Tait, Culp, & Starost, 2000; Grolnick & Ryan, 1989; Hill, 2001; Keith et al., 1993; Miliotis, Sesma, & Masten, 1999). The findings of the studies examining the effects of parents' school-based involvement are fairly consistent with the

notion that such involvement is beneficial for children. Much of the research has revealed concurrent associations between heightened school-based involvement on parents' part and enhanced academic functioning on children's part. For example, Stevenson and Baker (1987) using a nationally representative sample linked teachers' reports of parents' involvement in school activities with teachers' reports of children's performance in school and the extent to which children performed up to their ability during the elementary through high school years. Similarly, focusing on mainly middle-class European American families, Grolnick and Slowiaczek (1994) showed that teachers' and children's reports of parents' involvement in school activities (e.g., parent–teacher conferences and open houses) were associated with early adolescents' motivational beliefs (e.g., perceptions of competence and intrinsic versus extrinsic motivation) and grades in school. The benefits of parents' involvement are also evident among families of other backgrounds (e.g., d'Ailly, 2003; Jeynes, 2003, 2005). For example, Hill and Craft (2003) found that middle-class African American mothers' involvement in school activities (as reported by mothers and teachers) was associated with enhanced academic engagement and achievement among children during their kindergarten years.

More notably, longitudinal research indicates that parents' school-based involvement foreshadows children's later academic functioning (e.g., Grolnick, Kurowski, Dunlap, & Hevey, 2000; Hill, Castellino et al., 2004; Miedel & Reynolds, 1999). For example, in a study of low-income, ethnically diverse families, mothers' reports of their involvement on the school front (e.g., presence at parent–teacher conferences and volunteering in the classroom) when children were in kindergarten predicted heightened literacy skills among children during the elementary school years, even after adjusting for children's literacy skills during kindergarten (Dearing, Kreider, Simpkins, & Weiss, 2006). In a similar vein, also focusing on low-income, ethnically diverse families, Izzo and colleagues (Izzo et al., 1999) found that during the elementary school years, parents' participation in school activities foreshadowed heightened math achievement among children 2 years later, taking into account children's earlier achievement. In a study of early adolescents, parents' reports of their school-based involvement (e.g., attendance at school open houses and volunteering in the classroom) predicted increased grades 2 years later among both European American and African American children, adjusting for their earlier grades (Gutman & Eccles, 1999).

*Home-Based Involvement*    There is much research consistent with the notion that parents' involvement on the home front has positive effects on children's academic functioning (e.g., Hickman et al., 1995; Hill et al., 2004; Kurdek & Sinclair, 1988). This is particularly true for parents' practices that are not related directly to school; that is, practices related to children's intellectual enrichment. For example, in their study of mainly middle-class families of European

descent, Grolnick and Slowiaczek (1994) found that such involvement (e.g., reading the newspaper with children and taking children to the library) as reported by children was positively associated with motivational beliefs and grades among children during the early adolescent years. In fact, parents' cognitive–intellectual involvement foreshadows children's perceptions of competence and their grades in reading among children following the transition to junior high, even after adjusting for children's earlier standing on these dimensions (Grolnick et al., 2000). In their longitudinal research with mainly middle-class parents of European descent, Senechal and Lefevre (2002) demonstrated that the more exposed children were to reading during the kindergarten years, the better children's subsequent reading skills (e.g., receptive language and phonological awareness) in third grade (for similar results among low-income ethnically diverse families, see Raikes et al., 2006).

Unfortunately, the effects of parents' home-based involvement in activities that are directly related to school are less clear. Several studies looking at such involvement among European American and African American parents find little evidence of a link with children's academic functioning (e.g., Halle, Kurtz-Costes, & Mahoney, 1997; Hill & Craft, 2003). In his (1989) meta-analysis, Cooper found that correlations between parents' involvement in children's homework and children's achievement ranged from −.22 to +.40. Studies since then have not yielded a more consistent picture (e.g., Pezdek, Berry, & Renno, 2002; Shumow & Lomax, 2002). Indeed, several concurrent investigations of families from diverse backgrounds reveal that parents' assistance with homework is associated with poor performance in school among children (e.g., C. Chen & Stevenson, 1989; Cooper, Lindsay, & Nye, 2000; Georgiou, 1999). Although it is possible that this reflects the negative effects of parents' assistance with homework, research conducted by Pomerantz and Eaton (2001) suggests that this is unlikely. In this research with lower- and middle-class European American families, children's poor performance in school predicted mothers' heightened assistance with homework 6 months later. Importantly, once children's initial achievement was taken into account, mothers' assistance predicted an increase in children's achievement over time. This implies that parents assist children who are having difficulty with homework, which then improves how these children do in school. Thus, it is likely that the findings of concurrent investigations reflect a tendency for parents to respond to children's poor performance in school with increased assistance. However, even some longitudinal research has failed to find positive effects of parents' assistance when adjusting for children's prior achievement (Levin et al., 1997).

*Summary and Conclusions*    In sum, the research on parents' involvement on the school front is fairly consistent in suggesting that such involvement benefits the academic functioning of children from multiple backgrounds. Unfortunately, the research on parents' involvement on the home front yields a less consistent picture. On the one hand, similar to parents' school-based involvement, parents' home-based practices geared toward children's intellectual enrichment not directly related to school foreshadow enhanced academic functioning. On the other hand, parents' home-based involvement directly linked to school does not always have such benefits—in fact, it sometimes appears to have costs. The ambiguity regarding parents' home-based involvement raises particular concern, because on a day-to-day basis this is the most frequent form of involvement for many parents (Ritblatt et al., 2002). As we will argue later, considering parents' involvement as a context for children's development may also provide insight into the inconsistency, given that such a perspective, unlike the traditional more-is-better framework, takes into account the resources provided by parents' involvement, as well as the fit of such resources with children's needs.

***Research on Interventions to Promote Parents' Involvement*** Although the research on the effects of parents' naturally occurring involvement in children's academic lives suggests that it often, albeit not always, has positive effects, the research on the effects of interventions to promote parents' involvement is less clear. In 1992, White, Taylor, and Moss conducted a meta-analysis of the effects of programs intended to promote parents' involvement in the context of early intervention programs, such as Head Start, for disadvantaged, at risk, and handicapped children. The large majority of studies focused on parents' home-based involvement in terms of parents teaching children developmental skills, such as motor, language, and self-help skills. In the context of predicting children's cognitive abilities, when the internal validity of the studies was high, the effect sizes of early intervention programs with parental involvement were about the same as those of programs without parental involvement. Moreover, although there were not many internally valid studies manipulating parental involvement in the context of early intervention programs, when parental involvement was manipulated, there was little evidence that it was beneficial for children. Since White and colleagues' (1992) meta-analysis, there has been little research contradicting their conclusions.

Meta-analyses examining the effects of programs to promote parents' involvement in children's schooling during the elementary and middle school years also do not provide overwhelming support for the benefits of such programs (Cooper, Charlton, Valentine, & Muhlenbruck, 2000; Mattingly, Prislin, McKenzie, Rodriguez, & Kayla, 2002). In 2002, Mattingly and colleagues conducted a meta-analysis of programs designed to promote parents' involvement (mostly home-based, but some school-based). Although the 17 studies using a pre- and postintervention design yielded positive effects of such programs across a variety of outcomes (e.g., children's achievement and parents' attitudes toward school), this was not the case for the 14 studies using a design in which the intervention was compared to an unmatched or matched control group. If

anything, these more internally valid studies yielded negative effects of intervention programs aimed at increasing parents' involvement. However, as Mattingly and colleagues (2002) emphasize, these findings must be interpreted with caution due to serious methodological problems in many of the studies conducted to date.

A somewhat more positive picture is painted by a meta-analysis on the effects of summer programs for remediation of learning deficiencies with parental involvement components (e.g., volunteering in the classroom, observing in the classroom, and attending parent–teacher conferences) (Cooper, Charlton, et al., 2000). In this meta-analysis, such programs had larger positive effects on children's academic performance than did similar programs without parental involvement components. However, Cooper and colleagues (2000) emphasize caution in drawing conclusions from these findings because there were only eight programs with parental involvement components and there was "great variation in the effect estimates" (p. 74) among these programs.

*Summary and Conclusions* In sum, the research on interventions designed to promote parents' involvement in children's schooling yields a less positive view of the effects of parents' involvement than does the research on parents' naturally occurring involvement. Because such interventions are often targeted at children with learning difficulties, it might be assumed that their ineffectiveness lies not in the interventions themselves, but rather the children whom they are designed to serve. However, parents' naturally occurring involvement in children's schooling appears to have the same positive effects on children with learning difficulties as their counterparts without such difficulties (Patrikakou, 1996). On the one hand, the ineffectiveness of interventions is problematic because intervention studies provide the optimal window into causation by manipulating parents' involvement. On the other hand, as Mattingly and colleagues (2002) argue, there has not been enough internally valid research on the effectiveness of interventions designed to promote parents' involvement to draw firm conclusions about the influence of such interventions. In addition, parents who are naturally involved in children's academic lives may be involved in a different manner from parents who have been induced to be involved. Thus, as discussed later when we suggest that parents' involvement serves as a context for children's development, understanding the environment created by parents' involvement may be crucial to understanding why intervention programs have generally not succeeded in improving children's academic functioning.

## Parents' Involvement as a Developmental Context

The research conducted within the more-is-better framework has been accompanied by models to explain why parents' heightened involvement in children's schooling is beneficial for children's academic functioning. Two major sets of models have been proposed: skill development models and motivation development models. In their aim to explain why more involvement on parents' part is better for children, these models have generally assumed that by becoming involved in children's academic lives, parents create positive environments for children rich in skill- and motivation-related resources. Following our review of the two sets of models, we discuss why this is not always the case. In this context, we propose that parents' involvement can indeed create environments that provide children with such resources, but parents' involvement can also create environments that are devoid of them, sometimes even detracting from the skills and motivation children already possess. As such, parents' involvement in children's academic lives may act as a developmental context in which children may either thrive or suffer, which may account for some of the inconsistencies highlighted earlier in the effects of parents' involvement on children's academic functioning.

### Models of Parents' Involvement

*Skill Development Models*    In what we label *skill development models*, parents' involvement fosters skill-related resources which subsequently enhance children's achievement. By skill-related resources we mean cognitive skills, such as receptive language capability and phonological awareness, and meta-cognitive skills, such as planning, monitoring, and regulating the learning process. A number of reasons have been put forth as to why parents' involvement may enhance children's skills. First, when parents are involved in children's schooling, they may gain knowledge about how and what children are learning in school; such information may aid parents in helping children to build skills (Baker & Stevenson, 1986). Second, parents may gain accurate information about children's abilities when they are involved in children's academic lives. Holding such information may enable parents to assist children in a manner that fosters maximal skill development (Connors & Epstein, 1995; Epstein, 1987b). Third, even when parents are not informed about children's learning and abilities in school, their home-based involvement may provide children with opportunities to learn from practice and instruction (Senechal & LeFevre, 2002). Fourth, Epstein (1983) has argued that parents' involvement on the school front is valuable because when teachers believe parents are involved, they give the children of these parents heightened attention toward developing their skills.

*Motivation Development Models*    The central idea behind *motivation development models* is that parents' involvement provides children with a variety of motivation-related resources (e.g., positive perceptions of competence, investment in school, and intrinsic motivation), which foster children's engagement in school and subsequently their achievement. First, when parents are involved in children's academic lives, they highlight the value of school to children, which allows children themselves to view school as valuable (e.g., Epstein, 1988; Hill & Taylor, 2004).

Children may internalize the value of school over time; as a consequence, their academic engagement may be driven by intrinsic or autonomous (e.g., enjoyment or personal importance) rather than extrinsic or controlled (e.g., avoidance of shame or rewards) forces (Grolnick & Slowiaczek, 1994). Second, parents' involvement in children's schooling is an active strategy for tackling school and its challenges. Grolnick and Slowiaczek (1994) have argued that by being involved, parents are modeling an approach to school in which they take control of the situation, often to create positive change. Such an approach may communicate to children that they also have control over their performance in school. Third, parents' involvement in children's academic lives may heighten children's familiarity with school tasks, which may lead children to see themselves as academically competent (Grolnick & Slowiaczek, 1994).

*Summary and Conclusions*    The two central sets of models are both aimed at explaining why parents' involvement in children's schooling benefits children, but the two differ in their focus on the underlying mechanism responsible for the benefits—*skill* development versus *motivation* development. It is likely that parents' involvement enhances children's academic functioning through both forms of development (see Grolnick & Slowiaczek, 1994). Parents' involvement may provide resources that simultaneously cultivate children's skills and motivation. Moreover, when parents aid children in developing their academic skills, children benefit in terms of their motivation. For example, children can develop skills that lead them to feel competent and in control in algebra when parents provide them with useful strategies for solving algebra problems. The reverse may also be true: To the extent that parents' involvement may enhance children's motivation, it may enhance their skills. Thus, when parents cultivate intrinsic motivation in children for reading, for instance, children may so enjoy reading that they exert heightened effort in this area, thereby improving their reading skills. Regardless of the precise mechanism posited to underlie the benefits of parents' involvement, both sets of models make the assumption that parents' involvement provides children with resources that lead children to flourish academically.

### Parents' Involvement as a Resource Providing or Depleting Environment    Although parents' involvement may often be characterized by positive qualities that provide children with skill- and motivation-related resources, this is not always the case. In fact, although parents' involvement is often positively associated with dimensions of authoritative parenting, such as warmth and structure, and negatively associated with dimensions of authoritarian parenting (e.g., Culp et al., 2000; Grolnick & Ryan, 1989; Juang & Silbereisen, 2002; Steinberg, Lamborn, Dornbusch, & Darling, 1992), the size of the associations (e.g., *r*s range in absolute value from .02 to .46) indicates that there is variability among parents. Although many parents are involved in children's schooling in a positive manner, many are not.

Indeed, the term *helicopter parenting* has been used by the popular press to characterize parents who are highly involved in children's schooling and highly controlling in this context (e.g., Kantrowitz & Tyre, 2006). Moreover, research examining distinct characteristics of parents' involvement, such as the extent to which it is associated with parents' affect or an orientation toward mastery yield evidence of almost no association. Pomerantz, Wang, and Ng (2005a) found correlations of .19, *p* < .10, and .14, *ns*, between the frequency with which mothers reported assisting children with homework across a 2-week period and the frequency with which mothers reported experiencing positive and negative affect, respectively, in their interactions with children over the same period. In fact, in the analyses that looked at mothers' affect on the days that they provided assistance, mothers actually reported heightened negative affect, although their positive affect was the same, compared to days they did not provide assistance. In the same sample, these investigators (Pomerantz, Ng, & Wang, 2006) found that the frequency with which mothers provided homework assistance was not associated (*r* = .16, *ns*) with their orientation toward mastery (i.e., helping children to understand the work and encouraging children to figure it out on their own) while providing such assistance.

Given such findings, it is quite likely that parents differ in how they become involved in children's academic lives with some parents creating an environment that promotes skill and motivation development among children and some parents failing to create such an environment (see Pomerantz et al., 2006; Pomerantz, Wang, et al., 2005a, 2005b). To the extent that parents' involvement in children's academic lives creates an environment that enhances children's skills and motivation, children may benefit from parents' involvement as specified in the models put forth to date. However, to the extent that parents' involvement does not create such an environment, children may not benefit. In fact, they may suffer if their parents' involvement detracts from the skill- and motivation-related resources that they already possess. Parents' involvement may thus create a developmental context in which children are launched onto either a positive or negative trajectory of academic functioning as they make their way through school.

Consistent with the proposal that how parents are involved in children's schooling matters, Darling and Steinberg (1993) have argued that the effects of parents' practices on children are determined by the style in which such practices are used. In regard to parents' involvement practices, we focus on four qualities of parents' style that have emerged as important in theory and research on parenting (see Darling & Steinberg, 1993; Dix, 1991; Eccles, 1983; Maccoby & Martin, 1983; Pomerantz, Grolnick et al., 2005; Pomerantz, Wang, et al., 2005b): the degree to which parents' involvement is autonomy-supportive versus controlling, structured versus chaotic, focused on the process of learning versus the ability or performance of children, and characterized by positive versus negative affect. As we will argue below, each of these qualities is

likely to influence how parents' involvement contributes to children's skill and motivation development and in turn their academic functioning (see Pomerantz, Grolnick et al., 2005; Pomerantz, Wang, et al., 2005b). We now turn to reviewing the evidence for the effects on children's academic functioning of how parents become involved in their academic lives. The research on the quality of parents' involvement has mainly been conducted on middle-class families of European descent. Although more research is clearly needed, the small amount of research conducted on families from other backgrounds has yielded findings similar to those described below (e.g., Bean, Bush, McKenry, & Wilson, 2003; Brody & Flor, 1997; d'Ailly, 2003; McGroder, 2000; Simpkins, Weiss, McCartney, Kreider, & Dearing, 2006; Wang, Pomerantz, & Chen, 2007).

*Controlling versus Autonomy-Supportive Involvement* There is an extensive body of theory and research on multiple forms of parental autonomy support and control (for reviews, see Grolnick, 2003; Pomerantz & Ruble, 1998a; Rollins & Thomas, 1979; Steinberg, 1990). Here, we draw on Deci and Ryan's (1987) self-determination theory (see also Grolnick & Ryan, 1989; Ng, Kenney-Benson, & Pomerantz, 2004) in defining autonomy support as allowing children to explore their own environment, initiate their own behavior, and take an active role in solving their own problems. In contrast, controlling behavior is defined as the exertion of pressure by parents to push children toward particular outcomes (e.g., doing well in school) by regulating children through such methods as commands, directives, love withdrawal, or restrictions. In the context of parents' school-based involvement, autonomy-support and control may take a variety of forms. For example, when visiting children's classroom during a school open-house, parents may be autonomy supportive by allowing or encouraging children to show them around or controlling by directing the tour themselves. On the home front, autonomy-supportive involvement may include supporting children in making their own decisions about what courses they take, whereas controlling involvement may include dictating what courses children take.

When parents' involvement in children's academic lives is characterized by autonomy-support rather than control, children's academic functioning may benefit. In line with the notion that parents' involvement enhances children's achievement through skill development, autonomy-supportive involvement provides children with the experience of solving challenges on their own, enabling children to develop skills that enhance their achievement (e.g., Ng et al., 2004; Nolen-Hoeksema, Wolfson, Mumme, & Guskin, 1995; Pomerantz & Ruble, 1998b). In contrast, when parents' involvement is controlling, children do not have the experience of solving challenges on their own. Consistent with motivation development models, when parents support children's autonomy, they allow children to take initiative, leading children to feel that they are in charge and capable of controlling their surroundings (e.g., Deci & Ryan, 1985;

Grolnick, Deci, & Ryan, 1997). Such feelings heighten children's intrinsic interest, leading them to be engaged with their environment. Conversely, when parents attempt to control children, they may deprive children of feeling that they are autonomous, effective agents, thereby undermining children's motivation.

There is a wealth of evidence consistent with the notion that parents' autonomy support enhances children's academic functioning, whereas parents' control inhibits it (for reviews, see Grolnick, 2003; Pomerantz, Grolnick, et al., 2005). These effects appear to begin early in children's lives and extend into the adolescent years. A number of studies, mostly but not entirely on middle-class European American families, have shown that the more autonomy-supportive and less controlling parents are, the more positive children's perceptions of their academic competence (e.g., Grolnick & Ryan, 1989; Grolnick, Ryan, & Deci, 1991; Steinberg, Lamborn, Darling, Mounts, & Dornbusch, 1994; Wagner & Phillips, 1992) and attributions for their academic performance (Pomerantz & Ruble, 1998b). Children of such parents are also intrinsically rather than extrinsically motivated in the school context (e.g., d'Ailly, 2003; Ginsburg & Bronstein, 1993; Grolnick & Ryan, 1989). They demonstrate heightened persistence in the face of challenge (Nolen-Hoeksema et al., 1995) and engagement in self-regulated learning strategies (Wang et al., 2007). Mothers' controlling behavior, particularly appeals to authority, with 4-year-old children predicts not only children demonstrating poor school readiness a year or two later, but also children doing poorly in school 8 years later (Hess & McDevitt, 1984). Notably, the link between children's views of their parents as autonomy supportive rather than controlling and children's enhanced achievement is accounted for, in part, by their elevated perceptions of competence, intrinsic motivation, and engagement in school (Grolnick, Ryan, & Deci, 1991; Steinberg, Elmen, & Mounts, 1989).

The little research that has focused on the extent to which parents' involvement in children's academic lives per se is autonomy-supportive versus controlling paints a similar picture. Middle-class European American parents adopting an autonomy-supportive rather than controlling orientation toward assisting elementary and middle school children with homework by refraining from assisting with work when children do not need it but assisting when they do, have children who do well in school in terms of their grades as well as their standardized test scores (Cooper, Lindsay, et al., 2000). In a similar vein, Steinberg and colleagues (1992) demonstrated that parents' involvement in adolescents' schooling (e.g., assisting with homework and attending school programs), as reported by adolescents from a variety of ethnic backgrounds, is more beneficial over time for adolescents' achievement when administered by parents whom children perceive as authoritative (i.e., high in autonomy support, structure, and warmth) versus authoritarian (i.e., high in control and structure and low in warmth).

*Structuring versus Chaotic Involvement*   Another important dimension of parenting, albeit one that has received less attention than parents' autonomy support versus control, is the extent to which parents' create a structured versus chaotic environment for children. Parents' structure entails their provision of a systematic framework oriented toward the development of children's competence through clear and consistent guidelines, expectations, and rules for children (Grolnick et al., 1997; Grolnick & Ryan, 1989; Skinner, Johnson, & Snyder, 2005). Parents' structure also involves predictable consequences for children's actions and clear feedback to children in which the relations between children's actions and outcomes are apparent. In contrast, parents can provide a chaotic environment for children in which guidelines, expectations, and rules for children are unclear and inconsistent as well as arbitrary, thereby obscuring the pathway from children's behavior to desired outcomes (Skinner et al., 2005). Structure may manifest itself in school-based involvement when in the context of volunteering in the classroom, parents provide clear expectations for their children's work habits at school. An example of structured involvement on the home front is that parents have clear and consistent rules about when children need to complete their homework.

Parents' structure versus chaos may contribute to children's academic functioning by shaping both children's skills and motivation. When parents provide a structured environment for children, children come to learn what the standards are and how to meet them, which may assist children in developing skills that are useful to doing well in school. In contrast, a chaotic environment may give children little information relevant to developing such skills. Consistent with motivation development models, parents' structure may also provide motivation-related resources (Grolnick et al., 1997; Grolnick & Ryan, 1989; Skinner et al., 2005). When expectations and guidelines are clear and consistent, children can foresee the effects of their actions, allowing them to develop a sense of control understanding. In contrast, when parents create an environment that is haphazard, unpredictable, or chaotic, children do not have a basis from which to be or feel effective.

In general, when parents create structured rather than chaotic environments, children experience enhanced academic functioning (for a review, see Pomerantz, Grolnick, et al., 2005). For example, in one of the first studies to examine the role of parents' structure in children's academic functioning, Grolnick and Ryan (1989) employed structured interviews with middle-class European American parents, and found that the more structure (e.g., clear and consistent provision of rules, expectations, and guidelines for children) parents provided to early adolescent children, the more children felt in control of their performance in school, although they did not actually do better in school. In a similar vein, in a study conducted on mainly middle-class European American families, Skinner and colleagues (2005) showed that the more structure (e.g., clear expectations for children and following through on promises) and the less chaos parents and children reported parents as providing (e.g., unpredictable reactions when children get in trouble and frequent changing of the rules), the more children felt in control and were engaged in school.

Research focusing on the quality of parents' assistance and instruction, as reflected in the extent to which parents structure the task and coordinate their activity to children's activity and needs, demonstrates similar positive effects of parents' structure on children's academic functioning. In several studies, the quality of parents' assistance and instruction has been related to children's academic functioning (e.g., Pianta, Smith, & Reeve, 1991). For example, Pianta, Nimetz, and Bennett (1997) showed that among low-income European American and African American families the more that mothers' instructions to preschool children involved teaching, including an initial orienting instruction and well-timed hints, the better children's academic functioning in terms of their work habits and competence during kindergarten. Similarly, the more structured low-income mothers' instruction when children were 3.5 years old, the higher children's IQ at 5 years old, and the better their achievement in first and third grades (Englund, Luckner, Whaley, & Egeland, 2004).

*Process versus Person Focused Involvement* Several lines of recent theory and research suggest that the extent to which parents focus on the process of learning versus innate ability or performance is an important dimension of parenting (e.g., Dweck & Lennon, 2001; Gottfried, Fleming, & Gottfried, 1994; Hokoda & Fincham, 1995; Pomerantz et al., 2006). We refer to this dimension of parents' involvement as process- versus person-focused (see Dweck & Lennon, 2001). However, other labels, such as mastery- versus performance-orientation (Hokoda & Fincham, 1995; Pomerantz et al., 2006) and task endogeny versus exogeny (Gottfried et al., 1994) have been used in a similar vein. When parents adopt a process-focused orientation, they emphasize the importance and pleasure of effort and learning (Gottfried et al., 1994; Kamins & Dweck, 1999; Mueller & Dweck, 1998; Pomerantz et al., 2006). Parents with a person-focused orientation, in contrast, emphasize the importance of stable attributes, such as intelligence, and performance (Gottfried et al., 1994; Kamins & Dweck, 1999; Mueller & Dweck, 1998; Pomerantz, Grolnick, et al., 2005). An example of a process- versus person-focus orientation in the context of school-based involvement is when volunteering in the classroom and witnessing children at work there, parents comment on children's effort rather than on their ability. In the context of home-based involvement, while helping children with homework, parents focus children on learning rather than performance.

When parents adopt a process- rather than a person-focus orientation in the context of their involvement in children's academic lives, they may enhance children's performance in school through skill and motivation development. In terms of skill development, part of being involved in a process-focused manner includes highlighting the importance of ef-

fort or learning which is likely to engage the development of skills important to achievement (Pomerantz et al., 2006). In contrast, when parents' involvement is person focused, little attention may be directed to effort and learning, because importance is placed on the attributes children already possess. Thus, such involvement may not provide children with an opportunity for developing skills important to achievement. In line with motivation development models, the emphasis on effort and learning of parents' process-focused involvement may lead children to be motivated for intrinsic reasons such as mastery (see Hokoda & Fincham, 1995; Mueller & Dweck, 1998). However, when parents are person focused, children may come to concentrate on demonstrating their intelligence (see Mueller & Dweck, 1998), which may eventually lead them to be extrinsically motivated.

There is a growing body of research, relying almost exclusively on middle-class European American samples, consistent with the idea that parents' process-focused involvement provides children with resources that enhance their academic functioning. For example, Mueller and Dweck (1998) had an unknown adult give elementary school children either process-focused praise (i.e., "You must have worked hard at these problems") or person-focused praise (e.g., "You must be smart at these problems") in the laboratory. Children given process-focused praise were more likely to view ability as malleable, adopt mastery over performance goals, and to attribute their failure to effort instead of ability than were children given person focused praise. Children given process-focused praise also persisted to a greater extent, expressed more positive affect, and performed better in the face of failure. Similarly, in another study, when preschool children imagined their teachers giving them process-oriented criticism (i.e., "Maybe you could think of another way to do it."), they were less likely than their counterparts to imagine person oriented criticism (e.g., "I am very disappointed in you") to draw negative conclusions about their abilities from their failure, experience negative affect, and to give up (Kamins & Dweck, 1999).

The effects of parents' process and person-focused practices are similar to those documented for experiments. Using observational methods in the context of a laboratory task with qualities similar to those of homework, Hokoda and Fincham (1995) reported that middle-class European American mothers who reacted to their elementary school children's performance oriented behavior (e.g., concentrating on how much time is left) with process focused practices ("That's okay; you did your best") were particularly likely to have mastery-oriented children (see also Gottfried et al., 1994). Research in which mainly middle-class European American mothers reported daily on their responses to elementary- and middle-school children's academic successes found that when mothers refrained from using person focused praise, 6 months later, children held an incremental view of ability and embraced challenging tasks (Kempner & Pomerantz, 2003). In research examining the extent to which mothers are process focused in the context of their assistance with homework, among mainly middle-class European American families, such a focus was beneficial over time for children's academic functioning as reflected in their perceptions of competence and mastery orientation, but only for children initially perceiving their academic competence in negative terms (Pomerantz et al., 2006).

*Involvement Characterized by Positive versus Negative Affect*  As Dix (1991) has emphasized, parenting is an inherently affective endeavor (see also Larson & Gillman, 1999). This may be particularly true of parents' involvement in children's schooling. On the positive side, parents may become involved in children's academic lives to establish a sense of connectedness with them (Pomerantz, Wang, et al., 2005a). Thus, when involved in children's schooling, many parents may attempt to maintain positive affect by making their interactions with children enjoyable, loving, and supportive. On the negative side, despite attempts to be positive in their involvement in children's academic lives, parents may experience negative affect in part because children experience negative affect around academic activities (Fuligni, Yip, & Tseng, 2002; Leone & Richards, 1989), leading parents to become irritated and annoyed or even hostile and critical (Pomerantz, Wang, et al., 2005a). Parents' positive versus negative affect may manifest itself in school-based involvement in a variety of ways. For example, parents may express enjoyment rather than irritation while talking to children's teachers or volunteering in children's classroom. On the home front, parents may be supportive and caring, rather than hostile and critical, during conversations with children about their day at school or while assisting children with homework.

When parents' involvement is characterized by more positive than negative affect, they may provide children with motivation-related resources that promote achievement in school (see Estrada, Arsenio, Hess, & Holloway, 1987; Hokoda & Fincham, 1995; Nolen-Hoeksema et al., 1995; Pomerantz, Wang, et al., 2005a). By keeping their involvement enjoyable and loving, parents may convey to children that although schoolwork can be frustrating, it is an enjoyable endeavor, thereby fostering an intrinsic orientation in which mastery is valued. However, when parents are involved in an irritable, critical manner, they may convey that doing schoolwork is an unpleasant task. Parents' positive affect may also signal parents' support of children during times of difficulty, enabling children to confront challenge constructively (see Estrada et al., 1987; Nolen-Hoeksema, 1987; Pomerantz, Wang, et al., 2005a). In contrast, parents' negative affect may lead children to experience their parents as a hostile force that they need to please. Parents' positive affect may also directly foster positive affect in children that counters the negative affect they often experience in the homework context (Pomerantz, Wang, et al., 2005a). Fredrickson (1998, 2001; see also Lyubomirsky, King, & Diener, 2005) argues that the experience of positive emotions may create openness to novel ideas and courses of action which may foster enhanced skills and subsequently achievement among children.

The research to date is consistent with the idea that parents' affect plays a role in children's academic functioning. In laboratory research in which mainly middle-class European American children just entering elementary school and their mothers worked on an unsolvable task, when mothers' expressed negative affect (e.g., hostility and criticism) toward children during this task, children were less persistent in the face of challenge in the laboratory and school (Nolen-Hoeksema et al., 1995). Also looking mainly at middle-class European Americans, Hokoda and Fincham (1995) found similar effects of mothers' negative affect (e.g., pouting and anger) in their laboratory research with elementary school children. These investigators also demonstrated that children exhibited less of a helpless orientation when mothers responded with positive affect (e.g., enjoyment and laughter) to tasks that were particularly difficult for children. Using mothers' daily reports of their affect, Pomerantz and colleagues (2005a) showed in a mainly middle-class European American sample that when mothers experienced low positive affect (i.e., fun and love) and high negative affect (i.e., irritation and annoyance) in their interactions with children on days they assisted children with homework, children were less mastery oriented and intrinsically motivated in school 6 months later. Moreover, in a low-income, ethnically diverse sample, Simpkins and colleagues (2006) found that the more mothers characterize their relationship with their kindergarten children as warm, the more children's achievement benefits when mothers are involved in their academic lives on the school front. Although not directly assessing parents' affect, Grolnick and colleagues examined what they labeled parents' personal involvement in children's schooling; that is, children's perceptions of their parents as supportive of their academic endeavors. Such involvement was associated with children's perceptions of competence and grades in school during the junior high school years (Grolnick et al., 2000; Grolnick & Slowiaczek, 1994). Moreover, parents' personal involvement enables the maintenance over the transition to junior high school of children's grades in the area of reading (Grolnick et al., 2000).

*Summary and Conclusions*  There is much evidence consistent with the developmental-context idea that the manner in which parents become involved in children's schooling plays a role in children's academic functioning. When parents are involved in an autonomy-supportive manner, provide structure, focus on the process of learning, or express positive affect, children benefit, presumably because of the skill- and motivation-related resources that parents provide when involved in such ways. However, children's academic functioning suffers when parents are controlling, create a chaotic environment, focus on children's attributes or performance, or express negative affect in the context of their involvement. Under such conditions, children may experience costs because parents' involvement inhibits children's development of skill- and motivation-related resources. This challenges the widely held idea that more involvement on parents' part is always better for children. Indeed, parents' involvement in children's schooling may not always be accompanied by the skill- and motivation-related resources assumed in models of the effects on children of parents' involvement.

## The Advantages of Considering Parents' Involvement as a Developmental Context

Considering parents' involvement in children's schooling as a context for children's development in which children are provided with the resources to either excel or fail as they make their way through school has several key advantages. First, such a developmental context framework has the potential to explain the discrepancies in the effects of parents' school- and home-based involvement, as well as the discrepancies in the effects of parents' naturally occurring and intervention fostered involvement. Second, when parents' involvement is treated as a developmental context, general notions of development can be applied. One such particularly relevant notion is the fit between what children bring to their interactions with parents and what children themselves bring (Pomerantz, Wang, et al., 2005b). Third, treating parents' involvement as a context for children's development suggests that parents' involvement may create an environment that contributes not only to academic functioning among children, but also emotional and social functioning. We now turn to discussing each of these advantages of treating parents' involvement as a context for children's development. In doing so, we outline directions for future research on parents' involvement in children's schooling using the developmental-context framework.

### Implications for Understanding Inconsistencies in the Effects of Parents' Involvement

*School-Based versus Home-Based Involvement* When parents' involvement in children's schooling is treated as a developmental context in which parents create environments either rich in needed resources or devoid of them, a window is provided into why there are discrepancies in the effects of parents' involvement on the school and home fronts. In fact, there are several possibilities for such discrepancies that emerge from the developmental-context framework. For one, the environment that parents create through their involvement on the school and home fronts may be quite different in terms of the resources it provides.

On the school front, the events in which parents become involved are often structured in a manner that facilitates parents providing children with skill- and motivation-related resources. Many school-based events, such as school open houses, festivals, plays, and bake sales are designed by school personnel to be enjoyable for families. As such, they may capitalize on parents' desire to become involved in children's academic lives to establish a sense of connectedness with them. Moreover, such events often place little

emphasis on children's performance. Because of their low demands on time, they also place little pressure on parents. As a consequence, parents may find it relatively easy to be autonomy-supportive, focused on the process of children's learning, and affectively positive in their interactions with children. Even when school-based events are not enjoyable, are focused on children's performance, and involve some pressure on parents, as may be the case for parent–teacher conferences, parents may become positively involved in children's academic lives, because school personnel provide guidance to parents about how to do so. For example, when parents learn at a parent–teacher conference that children are not doing well in reading, teachers may give advice on how to provide structured assistance with reading homework.

In contrast, on the home front, although it may be easy for parents to provide skill- and motivation-related resources when their involvement revolves around activities that are not directly related to school (e.g., reading to children and taking them to the museum), this may be difficult when parents' involvement revolves around activities directly related to school (e.g., assisting with homework and responding to performance). Such involvement may be viewed by parents as more important to children's performance than are other forms, leading it to frequently be driven by parents' belief that it is their obligation to become involved, their attempts to remedy children's poor performance, or their feelings that their own self-worth is contingent on children's performance (Levin et al., 1997; Pomerantz & Eaton, 2001; Pomerantz, Wang, et al., 2005a). As a consequence, parents may sometimes feel pressured, frustrated, and overly concerned with children's performance in the context of their home-based involvement directly related to school. This may cause this form of parents' involvement to be controlling, chaotic, person-focused, and characterized by negative affect (see Grolnick, Gurland, DeCourcey, & Jacob, 2002; Pomerantz & Eaton, 2001; Pomerantz, Wang, et al., 2005a) more often than are other forms. Indeed, when parents feel pressure to ensure children perform up to standards, they exert heightened control over children (Grolnick et al., 2002; Gurland & Grolnick, 2005). Negative involvement may also arise because parents experience themselves as lacking the skills to constructively assist children, often because of changes in pedagogy since parents were in school. In the context of their involvement in children's schooling on the home front, such an experience may cause parents to become frustrated and even provide incorrect information (Hoover-Dempsey, Bassler, & Brissie, 1992; Kay, Fitzgerald, Paradee, & Mellencamp, 1994; Levin et al., 1997).

Parents' involvement on the home front in activities directly related to school may also be negative because children may find a number of such activities disagreeable. As a consequence, many parents may not become involved in a manner that provides children with needed resources. Regardless of their achievement level, children frequently experience negative affect while doing homework (Fuligni et al., 2002; Leone & Richards, 1989). As noted earlier, this negative affect may influence how parents become involved in assisting children. It may not only funnel down to parents so that they also experience negative affect (Pomerantz, Wang, et al., 2005a), but also lead parents to become more controlling as they attempt to contain children's negative affect. Moreover, parents are particularly likely to assist children with homework when children are uncertain about how to do the work (Pomerantz & Eaton, 2001) and become frustrated (Pomerantz, Wang, et al., 2005a). Research by Pomerantz and colleagues (2005a) suggests that a major reason mothers experience heightened negative affect on days they help children with homework is because children are frustrated with their homework. Children's frustration may also increase the chances that mothers are controlling, unable to focus on the learning process, and provide a chaotic environment for children.

In line with the more-is-better framework, the issues we have raised suggest that parents' heightened involvement on the school front may generally create an environment for children that fosters their skill and motivation development. In contrast, consistent with the developmental-context framework, parents' involvement on the home front may not always create such an environment. Although some parents may become involved in activities directly related to school on the home front in a manner that cultivates children's skills and motivation, this may not be the case for other parents; in fact, as we have just highlighted, some parents' involvement on the home front may even inhibit children's development along these lines. It is thus not surprising that research has yielded consistent positive effects on children of parents' school-based involvement, but not of their home-based involvement. It is of note that the effects of parents' home-based involvement may be particularly strong because not only is this the most frequent form of parents' involvement (Ritblatt et al., 2002), but also likely to entail more interaction between parents and children than does parents' school-based involvement. As a consequence, there may be greater opportunity for the environment created by parents' home- (vs. school-) based involvement to enhance or detract from children's skill- and motivation-related resources. It may be that forms of parents' involvement on the home front directly related to school that do not involve heightened interaction (e.g., setting up a schedule for children to do their homework and being available for questions) may not be heavily dependent on how parents become involved, and thus the effects may not be as contingent on the quality of parents' involvement.

*Naturally Occurring versus Intervention-Fostered Involvement*   The ineffectiveness of interventions designed to promote parents' involvement may be due to the quality of involvement induced by such interventions. Unfortunately, because such interventions have emerged from the more-is-better framework, rather than the developmental-context framework, they often focus on the quantity instead of quality of parents' involvement. As a consequence, many interventions may not produce involvement among parents that provides skill- and motivation-related resources to children. Indeed, it is quite possible that parents who become involved on their own generally do so in a more positive manner than those who need prodding (see Zellman & Waterman, 1998). Moreover, as White and colleagues (1992) emphasize, parents need to feel empowered, but intervention programs may actually leave them feeling just the opposite, often heightening feelings of pressure and frustration among parents. Because interventions are often designed to boost children's achievement through parents' involvement, parents may also become overly focused on children's performance and their role in promoting it. For example, in one intervention intended to highlight children's effort to children and parents, parents were told regularly not only about children's effort but also about children's performance (Fantuzzo, Davis, & Ginsburg, 1995). Moreover, parents were provided with a list of celebration activities and required to report back about how they celebrated children's efforts and performance. As with parents' naturally occurring involvement, the pressure, frustration, and concern with children's performance that may be induced by interventions may produce involvement that creates an environment that actually inhibits the development of children's skills and motivation.

This may be further compounded by the fact that the majority of involvement that is promoted by interventions is on the home front where it is not only more difficult for parents to become involved in a resource-facilitating manner, but there is much interaction between parents and children. Indeed, as noted earlier in our review of the effects of interventions to promote parents' involvement, the most effective interventions have been in the context of remedial summer school programs which, unlike many other interventions, focus on parents' school-based, rather than home-based, involvement (Cooper, Charlton, et al., 2000).

*Future Directions*   The window provided by the developmental-context framework into the discrepancies yielded by research on parents' involvement in children's schooling suggests several key directions for future research. Perhaps most notably, the research on parents' home-based involvement directly related to school is relatively inconsistent. This is troubling given that for many parents this is the most frequent form of their involvement in children's schooling (Ritblatt et al., 2002). The dearth of research may reflect the difficulty in finding effects of parents' involvement on this front, particularly for activities directly related to school. Moreover, when such effects are found they may often be negative which is inconsistent with the more-is-better framework. Elucidation of the role of parents' home-based involvement in children's schooling demands research that treats such involvement as a developmental context in that it focuses on how parents become involved. Indeed, several investigators (Cooper, Lindsay, et al., 2000; Epstein, 1983; Pomerantz et al., 2006; Pomerantz, Wang, et al., 2005a) have called for research on parents' assistance with homework to take into account how parents provide assistance. The research to date which has done so has shown that the quality of parents' assistance matters (e.g., Cooper, Lindsay, et al., 2000; Pomerantz et al., 2006; Pomerantz, Wang, et al., 2005a). Additional research examining this issue is needed, however. In this endeavor, an understanding of how parents' involvement provides a context for children's development could be gained by taking both a micro- and macroanalytic approach to understand the immediate and delayed effects of parents' home-based involvement on the development of children's skills and motivation.

In their meta-analysis of intervention programs, Mattingly and colleagues (2002) point out serious methodological problems in many of the studies conducted to date that need to be addressed. The developmental-context framework highlights another major problem: Attention has not been given to the resources intervention-fostered involvement provides children. Intervention programs should not be designed simply to increase parents' involvement; they should also be designed to enhance the quality of parents' involvement so that parents may foster the development of children's skills and motivation. Such an endeavor involves understanding the factors that lead parents to engage in resource-providing involvement. Although we have suggested a number of such factors (e.g., empowering parents, ensuring they do not feel pressured, and focusing them on children's learning), very few have actually received empirical attention (for an exception, see Grolnick et al., 2002).Thus, future research should first comprehensively examine the factors that lead parents to become involved in children's schooling in an autonomy-supportive, structured, process-focused, and positively affective manner. Subsequently, knowledge about these factors can be used to design interventions that assist parents in becoming involved in a manner that benefits children.

***Implications for a Moderated Model of Parents' Involvement*** Treating parents' involvement in children's schooling as creating an environment varying in the extent to which it provides children with resources suggests that the resources children bring to their interactions with parents may be of import. Pomerantz, Wang, and Ng (2005b) proposed that as a consequence of a variety of influences (e.g., peer socialization and cognitive abilities), children may come to their interactions with parents differing in their competence experiences, with such experiences reflecting their need for skill- and motivation-related resources. Children with negative competence experiences (e.g., perceiving themselves as lacking the ability to do well in school or receiving poor grades in school) are likely to lack the skills and motivation to do well, whereas their counterparts with positive experiences (e.g., perceiving themselves as possessing the ability to do well in school or receiving high grades in school) may possess such resources. Pomerantz and colleagues (2005b) thus suggest that although most children may benefit from parents' involvement in their academic lives when it is character-

ized by resource-providing qualities, the benefits may be moderated by children's competence experiences.

Children with negative competence experiences may be particularly sensitive to the quality of parents' involvement because they have a heightened need to develop skills and motivation (Pomerantz, Wang, et al., 2005b). Thus, such children may derive particular benefit when parents' involvement in their academic lives is autonomy supportive, structured, process-focused, or affectively positive. Through skill and motivation development, such resource-providing parental involvement may foster gains in academic functioning among children who have negative competence experiences. Unfortunately children with negative competence experiences may be particularly vulnerable when parents' involvement is controlling, chaotic, person-focused, or affectively negative, because it deprives them of the resources of which they are in so much need. In contrast, children with positive competence experiences may not be as sensitive to how parents become involved as they already possess skill- and motivation-related resources, and thus do not need their parents to provide such resources.

Although focused almost entirely on middle-class European American families, research supports the notion that children with negative competence experiences are more sensitive than are children with positive experiences to how parents become involved. Children with negative experiences are particularly likely to benefit when parents are involved in their academic lives in an autonomy-supportive rather than a controlling manner. In one study of mainly middle-class European American families, mothers' responses to their elementary and middle school children's failure in a variety of areas including the academic were assessed with a daily checklist (Study 2, Ng et al., 2004). Mothers' autonomy-supportive responses (i.e., discussing children's failure with them) predicted increased performance and their controlling responses (i.e., reprimanding children for their failure or punishing children for their failure) predicted decreased performance more for low- than high-achieving children the next day and 6 months later. In another study (also of mainly middle-class European American families), mothers' involvement with their elementary school children was observed in the laboratory in the context of a challenging task designed to reflect the homework situation (Study 1, Ng et al., 2004). Over the course of their interactions with children, mothers' autonomy support predicted enhanced subsequent performance and their control predicted diminished subsequent engagement more for low- than high-achieving children.

A similar pattern is evident for mothers' process-focused involvement in children's schooling. In a daily telephone interview, Pomerantz and colleagues (2006) examined mainly middle-class European American mothers' process orientation (i.e., encouraging children to understand their work and to do their work on their own) in the context of their assistance with elementary and middle school children's homework. When mothers adopted a process orientation, children with negative perceptions of their academic competence were more likely than children with positive perceptions to benefit 6 months later in terms of their perceptions of competence, thereby narrowing the difference over time in such perceptions. In addition, children initially perceiving themselves as lacking competence experienced gains over time in their mastery orientation when mothers were process oriented. Notably, children with negative perceptions of competence were no less mastery oriented than were their counterparts with positive perceptions if their mothers were process oriented.

When mothers' involvement in children's academic lives is characterized by positive affect, children with negative competence experiences also appear to be particularly likely to benefit. Pomerantz and colleagues (2005a) used the daily interview method to examine mainly middle-class European American mothers' affect on the days their elementary and middle school children had homework. In this study, the focus was on children's competence experiences as manifested in helplessness (i.e., frustration and giving up) in the academic context. When mothers' affect was positive on days children had homework, children demonstrating high levels of helplessness experienced heightened mastery orientation 6 months later to a greater extent than did children demonstrating low levels of helplessness. The benefit was to such an extent that when mothers were particularly high in positive affect, helpless children's mastery orientation was not lower than that of children who were not helpless.

The heightened sensitivity of children with negative competence experiences to parents' involvement in their schooling is noteworthy because these are often the children who are in particular need of aid. As Cooper, Charlton and colleagues (2000) note, parents' involvement may be most beneficial when parents adjust it to children's competence experiences (see also Pomerantz et al., 2006). All of the research to date on the moderating role of children's competence experiences has focused on home-based involvement directly linked to school. It will be important to determine if a similar pattern exists for other forms of parents' involvement. However, the moderating role of children's competence experiences suggests that one reason parents' home-based involvement directly linked to school may not have the same positive effects as other forms of parents' involvement is because its effects are contingent to a larger extent on what children bring to the interaction (see Pomerantz et al., 2006; Pomerantz, Wang, et al., 2005a). This may be particularly true given the heightened interaction between parents and children that occurs in the context of such involvement.

*Future Directions* Adopting the perspective that the effects on children of parents' involvement in their academic lives depends on what children bring to their interactions with parents suggests important directions for future research. Most notably, research might go beyond children's competence experiences to examine the moderating role of other factors that have the potential to influence children's

skill- and motivation-related resources. For example, a common theme in studying parents' involvement in children's schooling has been its effects among families with children at risk for achievement problems because of their families' socioeconomic status, educational attainment, or ethnicity (e.g., Anderson & Keith, 1997; Dearing et al., 2006; Englund et al., 2004; Gutman & Eccles, 1999; Hill et al., 2004). Hill and colleagues (2004) suggest that parents' involvement in children's schooling may be more beneficial for African American than European American children because African American children are more likely to live in environments characterized by forces that detract from their academic life. The same may be true of children growing up in poor, uneducated families. In line with this idea, parents' involvement sometimes matters more for African American than European American children (e.g., Hill et al., 2004); there is also evidence that parents' involvement plays a particularly large role in the achievement of children with relatively uneducated parents (Dearing et al., 2006; Dearing, McCartney, Weiss, Kreider, & Simpkins, 2004). A fruitful direction for future research is to examine if these heightened benefits of parents' involvement are due to children's heightened need for skill- and motivation-related resources.

Other factors also influence children's skill- and motivation-related resources, and thus may moderate the effects on children of parents' involvement. For one, children's age may shape their need for skill-related resources. As children become older, parents generally decrease their involvement in children's schooling (e.g., Cooper, Lindsay, et al., 2000; Dearing, McCartney, et al., 2006; Pomerantz, Wang, et al., 2005a; U.S. Department of Education, 2006). This may be due to the fact that with age, children develop the skills necessary for doing their schoolwork independently. For example, children may become increasingly skilled at planning, monitoring, and regulating their learning process. Given such developments, parents' involvement may become less effective as children progress through the school system. However, this may depend on the form of involvement: perhaps all children need their parents to show interest in their lives by inquiring about school, but with age, children no longer need their parents to sit down and help them go through their homework problem by problem. In a somewhat different vein, girls may have more skill- and motivation-related resources than do their male counterparts. Girls outperform boys in terms of grades; they are also more self-disciplined and mastery-oriented in the academic context than are boys (e.g., Duckworth & Seligman, 2006; Kenney-Benson, Pomerantz, Ryan, & Patrick, 2006). Thus, future research might test the possibility that boys benefit more than do girls from parents' involvement in their academic lives because of boys' relatively impoverished skill- and motivation-related resources.

***Implications for Extending the Effects of Parents' Involvement beyond Academic Functioning*** Given that improving children's learning is one of the most central goals of educational policy, the central reason for heightening parents' involvement in children's academic lives has generally been that of boosting children's achievement (for some exceptions, see Eccles & Harold, 1996; Epstein, 1990). In line with this concern, the large majority of the research to date on parents' involvement in children's schooling has focused on its effects on children's academic functioning. Enhancing such functioning is clearly an endeavor of much import. On the individual level, as children make their way into adulthood, heightened academic functioning provides important opportunities for pursuing higher education and ultimately a choice of careers that can afford a high quality of life (Hill et al., 2004; Young & Friesen, 1992). On the societal level, developing children's academic skills is beneficial for national advancement because such skills are often important to areas (e.g., technology, science, and education) critical to the successful operation of society.

A number of investigators have argued that the educational setting is an important context for the development of children's emotional functioning (Eccles, Lord, Roeser, Barber, & Jozefowicz, 1997; Ladd, 1996; Noddings, 2003; Roeser & Eccles, 2000; Rudolph, 2005), as well as social functioning (Noddings, 2003; Slavin, 1996; Slavin & Cooper, 1999). As an extension of the educational setting, parents' involvement in children's academic lives may also shape such functioning among children (Pomerantz et al., 2006; Pomerantz, Wang, et al., 2005a). Indeed, treating parents' involvement in children's schooling as a context for children's development suggests that parents' involvement may create an environment contributing to not only children's academic functioning, but also emotional and social functioning. The resources that parents may provide by becoming involved in children's academic lives may promote positive functioning among children outside of the academic arena. We now turn to discussing how parents' involvement in children's schooling may contribute to children's emotional and social functioning.

*Emotional Functioning*    To the extent that parents provide children with a resource-rich environment through their involvement in children's schooling, parents' involvement may be a significant school-related context for the development of children's emotional functioning (Pomerantz et al., 2006; Pomerantz, Wang, et al., 2005a). For one, the enhanced skills and subsequent achievement that parents' involvement fosters may improve children's emotional functioning as children respond positively to their success. Children's basic competencies, such as intelligence, appear to foster emotional resiliency in children encountering adversity (for a review, see Masten & Coatsworth, 1998). Moreover, there is a strong association between children's achievement in school and their emotional functioning, with some evidence suggesting that when children do well in school, they experience reductions in emotional distress (e.g., X. Chen & Li, 2000; Roeser,

Eccles, & Sameroff, 1998). Second, many of the motivational resources provided by parents' involvement may improve not only academic functioning, but also emotional functioning among children. Indeed, positive perceptions of competence, an orientation toward mastery, and heightened engagement in school, particularly when it is accompanied by persistence, are associated with dampened emotional distress, often over time, among elementary and middle school children (e.g., Cole, Martin, Peeke, Seroczynski, & Fier, 1999; Nolen-Hoeksema, Girgus, & Seligman, 1992; Pomerantz & Rudolph, 2003; Roeser et al., 1998; Rudolph, 2005). Third, parents' involvement in children's schooling may directly provide children with affective resources that foster positive emotional development beyond the school arena (see Pomerantz et al., 2006; Pomerantz, Wang, et al., 2005a, 2005b).

To date, there has been relatively little research linking parents' involvement in children's schooling to children's emotional functioning. However, the research is generally consistent with the notion that parents' involvement serves as an important context for the development of children's emotional functioning (e.g., Grolnick et al., 2000). For example, examining low-income ethnically diverse families, Shumow and Lomax (2002) reported that parents' heightened involvement mainly on the school front (e.g., attendance at school events and talking to children's teacher), was associated with heightened self-esteem among adolescents. Hill and Craft (2003) demonstrated that the more middle-class European American and African American parents were involved in kindergarten children's school activities (as reported by mothers and teachers), the better children's emotion regulation skills. On the home front, mainly middle-class European American mothers' heightened assistance with homework predicts elementary and middle school children's negative emotional functioning (i.e., experience of negative emotions, depressive symptoms, and anxiety symptoms) over 6 months, even after adjusting for their earlier negative emotional functioning (Pomerantz et al., 2006).

The little research taking the quality of parents' involvement into account extends the idea that parents' involvement plays a role in children's emotional functioning, by suggesting that parents must be involved in a resource-providing manner. Kenney-Benson and Pomerantz (2005) created a situation in the laboratory designed to mirror the homework situation. Middle-class European American elementary school children whose mothers were involved in the task in an autonomy-supportive manner were less vulnerable to depressive symptoms than were their counterparts whose mothers were involved in a controlling manner. This was accounted for by the tendency for children with autonomy-supportive mothers to report feeling less external pressure to meet perfectionistic standards than did children with controlling mothers. In addition, among mainly middle-class families of European descent, children perceiving their academic competence negatively are particularly likely to benefit in terms of their positive, but not negative, emotional functioning over 6 months when their mothers assist with their homework in a process-oriented manner (Pomerantz et al., 2006). Moreover, in mainly middle-class European American families, children's positive emotional functioning suffers over 6 months when mothers accompany their assistance with high negative and low positive affect (Pomerantz, Wang, et al., 2005a).

*Social Functioning* The resources that parents' involvement in children's schooling can provide may also enhance children's social functioning; that is, it may improve their behavioral conduct (e.g., following the rules in school and refraining from aggressive behavior) and relationships with their peers. First, the academic skills and motivation that children develop when their parents are positively involved in their academic lives, along with the ensuing enhanced achievement, may place children in a leadership role in which they take positive initiative in the classroom with their peers, refraining from violating classroom norms. Such behavior may foster positive peer relationships because not only do children become role models, but they also engage in positive interactions with their peers. Second, beyond these resources, secure attachment between parents and children and parental care for children may be communicated when parents' are positively involved in their children's academic lives (Grolnick & Slowiaczek, 1994). The positive relationship between parents and children may serve as a model for children in developing relationships with others, thereby promoting positive relationships with peers (e.g., Bowlby, 1988; Cohn, 1990).

Evidence for the idea that parents' involvement in children's schooling plays a role in children's social functioning comes from a number of studies on the issue. Several studies focusing on families from a variety of backgrounds have linked parents' involvement in children's schooling to decreased behavior problems (e.g., acting out, delinquency, and substance abuse) among children (e.g., Jenkins, 1995; Reynolds, Weissberg, & Kasprow, 1992b; Scheer, Borden, & Donnermeyer, 2000; but see also, Stewart, 2003). For example, among a Head Start sample of mainly low-income African American families, parents' home-based involvement (e.g., creation of a space for learning activities and provision of learning opportunities in the community) as reported by parents at the beginning of the school year, predicted diminished classroom behavior problems among children as reported by teachers at the end of the school year (Fantuzzo, McWayne, Perry, & Childs, 2004; see also Hill & Craft, 2003). A similar relation has been established for early adolescents, for whom parents' involvement in seventh grade on both the school (e.g., contact with teachers and attendance at school open-houses) and home fronts (e.g., assistance in choosing classes and discussion with children about what they are doing in school) predicts decreased school behavior problems in eighth grade among middle but not lower class children (Hill et al., 2004). Several studies have also found that the more involved parents are in children's schooling, the more positive children's social

skills. In one such study of mainly low-income African American families, parents' involvement on both the school (e.g., creation of opportunities to get to know children's teachers and participation in parent education programs at school) and home (e.g., provision of educational materials and routine reviewing of school work) fronts was associated with kindergarten children's social skills that contribute to successful interaction with peers (McWayne, Hampton, Fantuzzo, Cohen, & Sekino, 2004). It is of note that parents' heightened involvement sometimes is associated with dampened social functioning (e.g., Izzo et al., 1999). For example, in a mainly middle-class European American sample, Grolnick and colleagues (2000), found that increases in parents' school involvement across the transition to junior high school were associated with increased acting out behaviors among children. It could be the case that parents heighten their involvement on the school front when children experience social difficulties, often in response to calls from school personnel (Grolnick et al., 2000; Izzo et al., 1999).

As is the case for academic and emotional functioning, how parents become involved in children's schooling appears to be important for children's social functioning. Reynolds and colleagues (1992a) assessed the extent of low-income, ethnically diverse parents' school-based involvement when children were in kindergarten by having teachers report on the frequency with which it occurred. The quality of parents' school-based involvement was reflected in teachers' reports of their satisfaction with such involvement as well as how constructive it was. Teachers' ratings of the quality of parents' involvement was a stronger predictor of children's behavior problems (e.g., acting out behavior and poor relations with peers) one year later than the extent of such involvement after adjusting for children's earlier behavioral problems. Focusing on low-income ethnically diverse families, Izzo and colleagues (1999) also showed that the quality of parent–teacher interactions (i.e., teachers' perceptions that they have a constructive relationship with parents and sufficient contact with them) predicted over time more positive social skills among elementary school children, adjusting for their earlier social skills. In a similar vein, among junior high school students from mainly middle-class European American families, what Grolnick and Slowiaczek (1994) call parents' personal involvement in children's schooling—that is, children's perceptions of their parents as supportive of their academic endeavors—predicts decreased acting out behavior among children. This is particularly notable given that changes in the extent of parents' school and cognitive-intellectual involvement did not predict such behavior (Grolnick et al., 2000). Taken together, these findings highlight the importance of examining the role of the quality of parents' involvement in children's social functioning.

*Future Directions* The research to date examining the role of the quality of parents' involvement in children's emotional and social functioning presents a picture quite similar to that yielded by the research on the role of the quality of parents' involvement in children's academic functioning: It appears that quality matters; in fact, the evidence suggests that quality trumps quantity. However, the research on the link between parents' involvement in children's schooling and children's emotional and social functioning is quite sparse compared to that on the link between parents' involvement and children's academic functioning. Thus, quite simply, an important direction for future research is to look at the effect of the extent as well as the quality of diverse forms of parents' involvement on children's emotional and social functioning, particularly over time. In this context, it will be critical to identify the mechanisms by which parents' involvement in children's schooling shapes children's emotional and social functioning. We have suggested the importance of skill- and motivation-related resources in the academic arena, as well as of the direct effects of positive affect and relations with parents. However, there may well be other mechanisms. For example, it has been suggested that by being involved in children's academic lives, parents establish relationships with school personnel as well as other parents from which they learn important information about behavioral expectations; they then communicate this information to children (e.g., Epstein, 1987a; Hill & Taylor, 2004). Future research will also need to establish that it is really parents' involvement in the academic arena and not other arenas, such as the social one, that drive the effects. It is quite likely that parents who are involved in children's academic lives may also be involved in other areas of their lives.

***Summary and Conclusions***   In sum, treating parents' involvement in children's schooling as a context for children's development in which parents either provide children with important resources or fail to do so has a number of important advantages. We highlighted the benefits of the developmental-context framework for resolving the discrepancies in prior work on parents' involvement in children's schooling. In addition, we argued that such a framework extends the role of parents' involvement in children's development in two key ways. First, in line with Parent × Child models of development, it suggests that the resources children bring to their interactions with parents are essential to fully understanding how parents' involvement will affect children's subsequent functioning. Second, to the extent that parents' involvement in children's academic lives provides children with fundamental resources it may influence children's functioning beyond the academic arena. Taken together, these advantages of the developmental-context framework paint a more complex and extensive, as well as more consistent, portrait of the role of parents' involvement in children's development than does the more-is-better framework. In doing so, the developmental-context framework sets the agenda for a second phase of research that moves beyond simply linking the extent of parents' involvement to children's academic functioning.

## Conclusions

Given the evidence that parents' involvement in children's schooling plays a positive role in children's academic functioning, calls for increasing parents' involvement will surely continue. There is much evidence to justify such calls. However, there is also much evidence to suggest that calls for increasing parents' involvement must be accompanied by attention to the *quality* of parents' involvement. Environments need to be created for parents in which they are able to provide children with skill- and motivation-related resources through their involvement in children's school lives. In such an endeavor, sensitivity to the type of involvement being encouraged (school- versus home-based), the children receiving the involvement, and parents' reasons for becoming involved will be needed. Moreover, parents may need information about how to become involved in a positive manner. Promoting positive involvement among parents has the potential to enhance not only children's academic functioning, but their emotional and social functioning as well. As a consequence, much effort should be made to assist parents, particularly of struggling children, to become positively involved in children's schooling.

## Author Note

Work on this chapter was supported by grant #R01 MH57505 from NIMH.

## References

Anderson, E. S., & Keith, T. Z. (1997). A longitudinal test of a model of academic success for at-risk high school students. *Journal of Educational Research, 90,* 259–268.

Baker, D. P., & Stevenson, H. W. (1986). Mothers' strategies for children's school achievement: Managing the transition to high school. *Sociology of Education, 59,* 156–166.

Bean, R. A., Bush, K. R., McKenry, P. C., & Wilson, S. M. (2003). The impact of parental support, behavioral control, and psychological control on the academic achievement and self-esteem of African American and European American adolescents. *Journal of Adolescent Research, 18,* 523–541.

Becker, H. J., & Epstein, J. L. (1982). Parent involvement: A study of teacher practices. *Elementary School Journal, 83,* 85–102.

Bowlby, J. (1988). *A secure base: Parent–child attachment and healthy human development.* New York: Basic.

Brody, G. H., & Flor, D. L. (1997). Maternal psychological functioning, family processes, and child adjustment in rural, single-parent, African American families. *Developmental Psychology, 33,* 1000–1011.

Brown, B. B., Mounts, N., Lamborn, S. D., & Steinberg, L. (1993). Parenting practices and peer group affiliation in adolescence. *Child Development, 64,* 467–482.

Chen, C., & Stevenson, H. W. (1989). Homework: A cross-cultural examination. *Child Development, 60,* 551–561.

Chen, X., & Li, B. (2000). Depressed mood in Chinese children: Developmental significance for social and school adjustment. *International Journal of Behavioral Development, 24,* 472–479.

Cohn, D. A. (1990). Child–mother attachment of six-year-olds and social competence at school. *Child Development, 61,* 152–162.

Cole, D. A., Martin, J. M., Peeke, L. A., Seroczynski, A. D., & Fier, J. (1999). Children's over- and underestimation of academic competence: A longitudinal study of gender differences, depression, and anxiety. *Child Development, 70,* 459–473.

Connors, L. J., & Epstein, J. L. (1995). Parents and school partnerships. In M. H. Bornstein (Ed.), *Handbook of parenting: Vol. 4. Applied and practical parenting* (pp. 437–458). Hillsdale, NJ: Erlbaum.

Cooper, H. (1989). *Homework*. White Plains, NY: Longman.

Cooper, H., Charlton, K., Valentine, J. C., & Muhlenbruck, L. (2000). Making the most of summer school: A meta-analytic and narrative review. *Monographs of the Society for Research in Child Development*, 65(1).

Cooper, H., Lindsay, J. J., & Nye, B. (2000). Homework in the home: How student, family, and parenting-style differences relate to the homework process. *Contemporary Educational Psychology*, 25, 464–487.

Culp, A. M., Hubbs-Tait, L., Culp, R. E., & Starost, H. (2000). Maternal parenting characteristics and school involvement: Predictors of kindergarten cognitive competence among Head Start children. *Journal of Research in Childhood Education*, 15, 5–17.

d'Ailly, H. (2003). Children's autonomy and perceived control in learning: A model of motivation and achievement in Taiwan. *Journal of Educational Psychology*, 95, 84–96.

Darling, N., & Steinberg, L. (1993). Parenting style as context: An integrative model. *Psychological Bulletin*, 113, 487–496.

Dearing, E., Kreider, H., Simpkins, S., & Weiss, H. B. (2006). Family involvement in school and low-income children's literacy: Longitudinal associations between and within families. *Journal of Educational Psychology*, 98, 653–664.

Dearing, E., McCartney, K., Weiss, H. B., Kreider, H., & Simpkins, S. (2004). The promotive effects of family educational involvement for low-income children's literacy. *Journal of School Psychology*, 42, 445–460.

Deci, E. L., & Ryan, R. M. (1985). *Intrinsic motivation and self-determination in human behavior*. New York: Plenum.

Deci, E. L., & Ryan, R. M. (1987). The support of autonomy and the control of behavior. *Journal of Personality and Social Psychology*, 53, 1024–1037.

Dix, T. (1991). The affective organization of parenting: Adaptive and maladaptive processes. *Psychological Bulletin*, 110, 3–25.

Duckworth, A. L., & Seligman, M. E. (2006). Self-discipline gives girls the edge: Gender in self-discipline, grades, and achievement test scores. *Journal of Educational Psychology*, 98, 198–208.

Dweck, C. S., & Lennon, C. (2001). *Person vs. process focused parenting: Impact on achievement motivation*. Paper presented at the Society for Research on Child Development, Minneapolis, MN.

Eccles, J. S. (1983). Expectancies, values and academic behaviors. In J. T. Spence (Ed.), *Achievement and achievement motives* (pp. 75–146). San Francisco: W.H. Freeman.

Eccles, J. S., & Harold, R. D. (1996). Family involvement in children's and adolescents' schooling. In A. Booth & J. F. Dunn (Eds.), *Family–school links: How do they affect educational outcomes?* (pp. 3–33). Mahwah, NJ: Erlbaum.

Eccles, J. S., Lord, S. E., Roeser, R. W., Barber, B. L., & Jozefowicz, D. M. (1997). The association of school transitions in early adolescence with developmental trajectories through high school. In J. Schulenberg, J. L. Maggs, & K. Hurrelmann (Eds.), *Health risks and developmental transitions during adolescence* (pp. 283–320). New York: Cambridge University Press.

Englund, M. M., Luckner, A. E., Whaley, G. J. L., & Egeland, B. (2004). Children's achievement in early elementary school: Longitudinal effects of parental involvement, expectations, and quality of assistance. *Journal of Educational Psychology*, 96, 723–730.

Epstein, J. L. (1983). Longitudinal effects of family-school-person interactions on student outcomes. In A. Kerckhoff (Ed.), *Research in sociology of education and socialization* (Vol. 4, pp. 101–128). Greenwich, CT: JAI Press.

Epstein, J. L. (1987a). Toward a theory of family-school connections: Teacher practices and parent involvement. In K. Hurrelman, F. X. Kaufmann, & F. L. Sel (Eds.), *School intervention: Potential and constraints* (pp. 121–136). Berlin: Walter de Gruyter.

Epstein, J. L. (1987b). What principals should know about parent involvement. *Principal*, 66, 6–9.

Epstein, J. L. (1988). How do we improve programs for parental involvement? *Educational Horizons*, 66, 75–77.

Epstein, J. L. (1990). School and family connections: Theory, research, and implications for integrating sociologies of education and family. *Marriage and Family Review*, 15, 99–126.

Epstein, J. L., & Van Voorhis, F. L. (2001). More than minutes: Teachers' roles in designing homework. *Educational Psychologist*, 36, 181–193.

Estrada, P., Arsenio, W. F., Hess, R. D., & Holloway, S. D. (1987). Affective quality of the mother–child relationship: Longitudinal consequences for children's school-relevant cognitive functioning. *Developmental Psychology*, 23, 210–215.

Fantuzzo, J. W., Davis, G. Y., & Ginsburg, M. D. (1995). Effects of parent involvement in isolation or in combination with peer tutoring on student self-concept and mathematics achievement. *Journal of Educational Psychology*, 87, 272–281.

Fantuzzo, J. W., McWayne, C., Perry, M. A., & Childs, S. (2004). Multiple dimensions of family involvement and their relations to behavioral and learning competencies for urban, low-income children. *School Psychology Review*, 33(4), 467–480.

Fredrickson, B. L. (1998). What good are positive emotions? *Review of General Psychology*, 2, 300–319.

Fredrickson, B. L. (2001). The role of positive emotions in positive psychology: The broaden and build theory of positive emotions. *American Psychologist*, 56, 218–226.

Fuligni, A. J., Yip, T., & Tseng, V. (2002). The impact of family obligation on the daily activities and psychological well-being of Chinese American adolescents. *Child Development*, 73, 302–314.

Georgiou, S. (1999). Parental attributions as predictors of involvement and influences on child achievement. *British Journal of Educational Psychology*, 69(3), 409–429.

Ginsburg, G. S., & Bronstein, P. (1993). Family factors related to children's intrinsic/extrinsic motivational orientation and academic performance. *Child Development*, 64, 1461–1474.

Gonzalez, A. R., Holbein, M. F. D., & Quilter, S. (2002). High school students' goal orientations and their relationship to perceived parenting styles. *Contemporary Educational Psychology*, 27, 450–470.

Gottfried, A. E., Fleming, J. S., & Gottfried, A. W. (1994). Role of parental motivational practices in children's academic intrinsic motivation and achievement. *Journal of Educational Psychology*, 86, 104–113.

Grolnick, W. S. (2003). *The psychology of parental control: How well-meant parenting backfires*. Hillside, NJ: Erlbaum.

Grolnick, W. S., Deci, E. L., & Ryan, R. M. (1997). Internalization within the family: The self-determination theory perspective. In J. Grusec & L. Kuczynski (Eds.), *Parenting and children's internalization of values: A handbook of contemporary theory* (pp. 135–161). New York: Wiley.

Grolnick, W. S., Gurland, S. T., DeCourcey, W., & Jacob, K. (2002). Antecedents and consequences of mothers' autonomy support: An experimental investigation. *Developmental Psychology*, 38, 143–154.

Grolnick, W. S., Kurowski, C. O., Dunlap, K. G., & Hevey, C. (2000). Parental resources and the transition to junior high. *Journal of Research on Adolescence*, 10, 465–488.

Grolnick, W. S., & Ryan, R. M. (1989). Parent styles associated with children's self-regulation and competence in school. *Journal of Educational Psychology*, 81, 143–154.

Grolnick, W. S., Ryan, R. M., & Deci, E. L. (1991). Inner resources for school achievement: Motivational mediators of children's perceptions of their parents. *Journal of Educational Psychology*, 83, 508–517.

Grolnick, W. S., & Slowiaczek, M. L. (1994). Parents' involvement in children's schooling: A multidimensional conceptualization and motivational model. *Child Development*, 64, 237–252.

Gurland, S. T., & Grolnick, W. S. (2005). Perceived threat, controlling parenting, and children's achievement orientations. *Motivation and Emotion*, 29, 103–121.

Gutman, L. M., & Eccles, J. S. (1999). Financial strain, parenting behaviors, and adolescents' achievement: Testing model equivalence between African American and European American single- and two-parent families. *Child Development*, 70, 1464–1476.

Halle, T. G., Kurtz-Costes, B., & Mahoney, J. L. (1997). Family influences on school achievement in low-income African-American children. *Journal of Educational Psychology, 89,* 527–537.

Hess, R. D., & McDevitt, T. M. (1984). Some cognitive consequences of maternal intervention: A longitudinal study. *Child Development, 55,* 2017–2030.

Hickman, C. W., Greenwood, G., & Miller, D. (1995). High school parent involvement: Relationships with achievement, grade level, SES, and gender. *Journal of Research and Development in Education, 28,* 125–134.

Hill, N. E. (2001). Parenting and academic socialization as they relate to school readiness: The roles of ethnicity and family income. *Journal of Educational Psychology, 93,* 686–697.

Hill, N. E., Castellino, D. R., Lansford, J. E., Nowlin, P., Dodge, K. A., Bates, J. E., et al. (2004). Parent-academic involvement as related to school behavior, achievement, and aspirations: Demographic variations across adolescence. *Child Development, 75,* 1491–1509.

Hill, N. E., & Craft, S. A. (2003). Parent–school involvement and school performance: Mediated pathways among socioeconomically comparable African American and Euro-American families. *Journal of Educational Psychology, 95,* 74–83.

Hill, N. E., & Taylor, L. C. P. (2004). Parental school involvement and children's academic achievement: Pragmatics and issues. *Current Directions in Psychological Science, 13,* 161–164.

Hokoda, A., & Fincham, F. D. (1995). Origins of children's helpless and mastery achievement patterns in the family. *Journal of Educational Psychology, 87,* 375–385.

Hoover-Dempsey, K. V., Bassler, O. C., & Brissie, J. S. (1992). Explorations in parent–school relations. *Journal of Educational Research, 85,* 287–294.

Hoover-Dempsey, K. V., & Sandler, H. M. (1997). Why do parents become involved in their children's education? *Review of Educational Research, 67,* 3–42.

Izzo, C. V., Weissberg, R. P., Kasprow, W. J., & Fendrich, M. (1999). A longitudinal assessment of teacher perceptions of parent involvement in children's education and school performance. *American Journal of Community Psychology, 27,* 817–839.

Jenkins, P. H. (1995). School delinquency and school commitment. *Sociology of Education, 68,* 221–239.

Jeynes, W. H. (2003). A meta-analysis: The effects of parental involvement on minority children's academic achievement. *Education and Urban Society, 35,* 202–218.

Jeynes, W. H. (2005). A meta-analysis of the relation of parental involvement to urban elementary school student academic achievement. *Urban Education, 40,* 237–269.

Juang, L. P., & Silbereisen, R. K. (2002). The relationship between adolescent academic capability beliefs, parenting, and school grades. *Journal of Adolescence, 25,* 3–18.

Kamins, M. L., & Dweck, C. S. (1999). Person versus process praise and criticism: Implications for contingent self-worth and coping. *Developmental Psychology, 35,* 835–847.

Kantrowitz, B., & Tyre, P. (2006, May 22). The fine art of letting go. *Newsweek,* 48–64.

Kay, P. J., Fitzgerald, M., Paradee, C., & Mellencamp, A. (1994). Making homework work at home: The parent's perspective. *Journal of Learning Disabilities, 27,* 550–561.

Keith, T. Z., Keith, P. B., Troutman, G. C., Bickley, P. G., Trivette, P. S., & Singh, K. (1993). Does parent involvement affect eighth-grade students achievement? Structural analysis of national data. *School Psychology Review, 22,* 474–496.

Kempner, S., & Pomerantz, E. M. (2003). *Mothers' use of praise in their everyday interactions with their children: The moderating role of children's gender.* Paper presented at the Society for Research on Child Development, Tampa, FL.

Kenney-Benson, G. A., & Pomerantz, E. M. (2005). The role of mothers' use of control in children's perfectionism: Implications for the development of children's depressive symptoms. *Journal of Personality, 73,* 23–46.

Kenney-Benson, G. A., Pomerantz, E. M., Ryan, A., & Patrick, H. (2006). Sex differences in math performance: The role of how children approach school. *Developmental Psychology, 42,* 11–26.

Kurdek, L. A., & Sinclair, R. J. (1988). Relation of eighth graders' family structure, gender, and family environment with academic performance and school behavior. *Journal of Educational Psychology, 80,* 90–94.

Ladd, G. W. (1996). Shifting ecologies during the 5–7 year period: Predicting children's adjustment to grade school. In A. Sameroff & M. Haith (Eds.), *The five to seven year shift* (pp. 363–386). Chicago, IL: University of Chicago Press.

Larson, R. W., & Gillman, S. (1999). Transmission of emotions in the daily interactions of single-mother families. *Journal of Marriage and the Family, 61,* 21–37.

Leone, C. M., & Richards, M. H. (1989). Classwork and homework in early adolescence: The ecology of achievement. *Journal of Youth and Adolescence, 18,* 531–548.

Levin, I., Levy-Shiff, R., Appelbaum-Peled, T., Katz, I., Komar, M., & Meiran, N. (1997). Antecedents and consequences of maternal involvement in children's homework: A longitudinal analysis. *Journal of Applied Developmental Psychology, 18,* 207–227.

Lyubomirsky, S., King, L., & Diener, E. (2005). The benefits of frequent positive affect: Does happiness lead to success? *Psychological Bulletin, 131,* 803–855.

Maccoby, E. E., & Martin, J. (1983). Socialization in the context of the family: Parent child interaction. In E. M. Hetherington (Ed.), *Handbook of child psychology: Vol. 4. Socialization, personality, and social development* (4th ed., pp. 1–101). New York: Wiley.

Masten, A. S., & Coatsworth, J. D. (1998). The development of competence in favorable and unfavorable environments: Lessons from research on successful children. *American Psychologist, 53,* 205–220.

Mattingly, D. J., Prislin, R., McKenzie, T. L., Rodriguez, J. L., & Kayzar, B. (2002). Evaluating evaluations: The case of parent involvement programs. *Review of Educational Research, 72,* 549–576.

McGroder, S. M. (2000). Parenting among low income, African American single mothers with preschool-age children: Patterns, predictors, and developmental correlates. *Child Development, 71,* 752–771.

McWayne, C., Hampton, V., Fantuzzo, J., Cohen, H. L., & Sekino, Y. (2004). A multivariate examination of parent involvement and the social and academic competencies of urban kindergarten children. *Psychology in the Schools, 41*(3), 363–377.

Miedel, W. T., & Reynolds, A. J. (1999). Parent involvement in early intervention for disadvantaged children: Does it matter? *Journal of School Psychology, 37,* 379–402.

Miliotis, D., Sesma, A. J., & Masten, A. S. (1999). Parenting as a protective process for school success in children from homeless families. *Early Education and Development, 10,* 111–133.

Mueller, C. M., & Dweck, C. S. (1998). Praise for intelligence can undermine children's motivation and performance. *Journal of Personality and Social Psychology, 75,* 33–52.

Ng, F. F., Kenney-Benson, G. A., & Pomerantz, E. M. (2004). Children's achievement moderates the effects of mothers' use of control and autonomy support. *Child Development, 75,* 764–780.

Noddings, N. (2003). *Happiness and education.* New York: Cambridge University Press.

Nolen-Hoeksema, S. (1987). Sex differences in unipolar depression: Evidence and theory. *Psychological Bulletin, 101,* 259–282.

Nolen-Hoeksema, S., Girgus, J. S., & Seligman, M. E. (1992). Predictors and consequences of childhood depressive symptoms: A 5-year longitudinal study. *Journal of Abnormal Psychology, 101,* 405–422.

Nolen-Hoeksema, S., Wolfson, A., Mumme, D., & Guskin, K. (1995). Helplessness in children of depressed and nondepressed mothers. *Developmental Psychology, 31,* 377–387.

Patrikakou, E. N. (1996). Investigating the academic achievement of adolescents with learning disabilities: A structural modeling approach. *Journal of Educational Psychology, 88,* 435–450.

Pezdek, K., Berry, T., & Renno, P. A. (2002). Children's mathematics achievement: The role of parents' perceptions and their involvement in homework. *Journal of Educational Psychology, 94,* 771–777.

Pianta, R. C., Nimetz, S. L., & Bennett, E. (1997). Mother–child relationships, teacher–child relationships, and school outcomes in preschool and kindergarten. *Early Childhood Research Quarterly*, *12*, 263–280.

Pianta, R. C., Smith, N., & Reeve, R. (1991). Observing mother and child behavior in a problem solving situation at school entry: Relations with classroom adjustment. *School Psychology Quarterly*, *56*, 1–16.

Pomerantz, E. M., & Eaton, M. M. (2001). Maternal intrusive support in the academic context: Transactional socialization processes. *Developmental Psychology*, *37*, 174–186.

Pomerantz, E. M., Grolnick, W. S., & Price, C. E. (2005). The role of parents in how children approach school: A dynamic process perspective. In A. J. Elliot & C. S. Dweck (Eds.), *The handbook of competence and motivation* (pp. 259–278). New York: Guilford.

Pomerantz, E. M., Ng, F., & Wang, Q. (2006). Mothers' mastery-oriented involvement in children's homework: Implications for the well-being of children with negative perceptions of competence. *Journal of Educational Psychology*, *98*, 99–111.

Pomerantz, E. M., & Ruble, D. N. (1998a). The multidimensional nature of control: Implications for the development of sex differences in self-evaluation. In J. Heckhausen & C. S. Dweck (Eds.), *Motivation and self-regulation across the life-span* (pp. 159–184). New York: Cambridge University Press.

Pomerantz, E. M., & Ruble, D. N. (1998b). The role of maternal control in the development of sex differences in child self-evaluative factors. *Child Development*, *69*, 458–478.

Pomerantz, E. M., & Rudolph, K. D. (2003). What ensues from emotional distress? Implications for competence estimates. *Child Development*, *74*, 329–346.

Pomerantz, E. M., Wang, Q., & Ng, F. F. (2005a). Mothers' affect in the homework context: The importance of staying positive. *Developmental Psychology*, *41*, 414–427.

Pomerantz, E. M., Wang, Q., & Ng, F. F. (2005b). The role of children's competence experiences in the socialization process: A dynamic process framework for the academic arena. In R. Kail (Ed.), *Advances in child development and behavior* (Vol. 33, pp. 193–227). San Diego, CA: Academic Press.

Raikes, H., Pan, B., Luze, G., Tamis-LeMonda, C. S., Brooks-Gunn, J., Constantine, J., et al. (2006). Mother–child book reading in low-income families: Correlates and outcomes during the first three years of life. *Child Development*, *77*, 924–953.

Reynolds, A. J., Weissberg, R. P., & Kasprow, W. J. (1992a). Prediction of early social and academic adjustment of children from the inner-city. *American Journal of Community Psychology*, *20*, 599–624.

Reynolds, A. J., Weissberg, R. P., & Kasprow, W. J. (1992b). Prediction of early social and academic adjustment of children from the inner city. *American Journal of Community Psychology*, *20*, 599–624.

Ritblatt, S. N., Beatty, J. R., Cronan, T. A., & Ochoa, A. M. (2002). Relationships among perception of parent involvement, time allocation, and demographic characteristics: Implication for policy formation. *Journal of Community Psychology*, *30*, 519–549.

Roeser, R. W., & Eccles, J. S. (2000). Schooling and mental health. In A. J. Sameroff, M. Lewis, & S. M. Miller (Eds.), *Handbook of developmental psychopathology* (2nd ed., pp. 135–156). Dordrecht, Netherlands: Kluwer Academic.

Roeser, R. W., Eccles, J. S., & Sameroff, A. (1998). Academic and emotional functioning in early adolescence: Longitudinal relations, patterns, and prediction by experience in middle school. *Development and Psychopathology*, *10*, 321–352.

Rollins, B. C., & Thomas, D. L. (1979). Parental support, power, and control techniques in the socialization of children. In W. R. Burr, R. Hill, F. I. Nye, & I. L. Reiss (Eds.), *Contemporary theories about the family* (pp. 317–364). New York: Free Press.

Rudolph, K. D. (2005). A self-regulation approach to understanding adolescent depression in the school context. In T. Urdan & F. Pajares (Eds.), *Educating adolescents: Challenges and strategies* (Vol. 4, pp. 33–64). Greenwich, CT: Information Age.

Scheer, S. D., Borden, L. M., & Donnermeyer, J. F. (2000). The relationship between family factors and adolescent substance use in rural, suburban, and urban settings. *Journal of Child and Family Studies*, *9*, 105–115.

Senechal, M., & LeFevre, J. (2002). Parental involvement in the development of children's reading skill: A five year longitudinal study. *Child Development*, *73*, 445–460.

Shumow, L., & Lomax, R. (2002). Parental efficacy: Predictor of parenting behavior and adolescent outcomes. *Parenting: Science and Practice*, *2*, 127–150.

Simpkins, S. D., Weiss, H. B., McCartney, K., Kreider, H. M., & Dearing, E. (2006). Mother–child relationship as a moderator of the relation between family educational involvement and child achievement. *Parenting: Science and Practice*, *6*, 49–57.

Skinner, E., Johnson, S., & Snyder, T. (2005). Six dimensions of parenting: A motivational model. *Parenting: Science and Practice*, *5*, 175–235.

Slavin, R. E. (1996). Research on cooperative learning and achievement: What we know, what we need to know. *Contemporary Educational Psychology*, *21*, 43–69.

Slavin, R. E., & Cooper, R. (1999). Improving intergroup relations: Lessons learned from cooperative learning programs. *Journal of Social Issues*, *55*, 647–663.

Steinberg, L. (1990). Autonomy, conflict, and harmony in the family relationship. In S. Feldman & G. R. Elliott (Eds.), *At the threshold: The developing adolescent* (pp. 255–277). Cambridge, MA: Harvard University Press.

Steinberg, L., Elmen, J. D., & Mounts, N. S. (1989). Authoritative parenting, psychosocial maturity, and academic success among adolescents. *Child Development*, *60*, 1424–1436.

Steinberg, L., Lamborn, S. D., Darling, N., Mounts, N. S., & Dornbusch, S. (1994). Over-time changes in adjustment and competence among adolescents from authoritative, authoritarian, indulgent, and neglectful homes. *Child Development*, *65*, 754–770.

Steinberg, L., Lamborn, S. D., Dornbusch, S. M., & Darling, N. (1992). Impact of parenting practices on adolescent achievement: Authoritative parenting, school involvement, and encouragement to succeed. *Child Development*, *63*, 1266–1281.

Stewart, S. D. (2003). Nonresident parenting and adolescent adjustment: The quality of nonresident father–child interaction. *Journal of Family Issues*, *24*, 217–244.

Taylor, R. D. (1996). Adolescents' perceptions of kinship support and family management practices: Association with adolescent adjustment in African American families. *Developmental Psychology*, *32*, 687–695.

U.S. Department of Education. (2006). *Parent and family involvement in education: 2002–03; and the parent survey* (Parent:1999) and *the parent and family involvement in education survey* (PFI: 2003 of the nation household education surveys programs). Washington, DC: National Center for Education Statistics.

Wagner, B. M., & Phillips, D. A. (1992). Beyond beliefs: Parent and child behaviors and children's perceived academic competence. *Child Development*, *63*, 1380–1391.

Wang, Q., Pomerantz, E. M., & Chen, H. (2007). The role of parents' control in early adolescents' psychological functioning: A longitudinal investigation in the United States and China. *Child Development*, *78*, 1592–1610.

White, K. R., Taylor, M. J., & Moss, V. D. (1992). Does research support claims about the benefits of involving parents in early intervention programs? *Review of Educational Research*, *62*, 91–125.

Young, R. A., & Friesen, J. D. (1992). The intentions of parents in influencing the career development of their children. *Career Development Quarterly*, *40*, 198–207.

Zellman, G. L., & Waterman, J. M. (1998). Understanding the impact of parent school involvement on children's educational outcomes. *Journal of Educational Research*, *91*, 370–380.

# Part VII

## School-Based Interventions

# 26

# The Yale Child Study Center School Development Program[1]

*JAMES P. COMER*

The School Development Program (SDP) is a clinical service and research unit of the Yale Child Study Center, which is associated with the Child Psychiatry Department of the Yale School of Medicine. The work of the SDP, which began in 1968, is based on the belief that school experiences, guided by child development principles, have the potential to prevent behavioral, academic, and mental health problems. The initial piloting of the SDP led to the creation of a framework and process model for applying child and adolescent development principles to all aspects of the school experience in a way that improves school functioning and outcomes. The principles of the process also can be applied to practice and policy issues throughout the various levels of the education enterprise—schools, districts, staff preparatory institutions, local and state education authorities, community organizations, parents, and all other people and programs influencing schooling.

The chapter begins with a brief presentation of my experiences in schools that served as the inspiration for the SDP. I then discuss the development of the SDP program, including the pilot program in the late 1960s. The second half of the chapter includes a discussion of the refinement of the SDP model and the evaluations of its effects on schools, teachers, and students. To date, the SDP model has been implemented in over 1,000 schools across the United States (Comer, 2004). The chapter ends with a presentation of the implications of the research on the SDP for school-reform efforts, teaching practices, and educational policy.

## Background of the School Development Program

The SDP grew out of my obsession with the question of why my four siblings and I, who are Black, were successful in a predominantly White, working class to upper middle class school system and why my three best Black friends, equally intelligent, were not. These differences were in spite of the fact that our parents had similar jobs as domestic workers and steel mill laborers. Why was the same all-White teach-

ing staff, which my friends found unsupportive, reasonably to strongly supportive, with only a few exceptions, of my siblings and me?

The questions intensified during my internship at St. Catherine's Hospital in my hometown of East Chicago, Indiana, where I observed my friends engaged in a downhill course in life, while my siblings and I were headed toward professional careers. This experience contributed to my abandoning a plan to become a general practitioner of medicine and to a period of deep reflection and exploration about issues of race, class, the reality of "access to opportunity," implications of a changing economy for individuals without an education, and, finally, the critical role of child rearing and development to the prevention of school and life problems.

During this period of reflection and exploration, I served in the U.S. Public Health Service (USPHS), earned an MPH at the University of Michigan, and received training in adult and child psychiatry at the Yale University School of Medicine. Each experience contributed to the eventual form and function of the SDP. It was during this period that I began to realize that the difference between my educational and life outcome and that of my three friends was the better quality of developmental experiences that I received at home and through my family's social networks. Thus, my next question became whether good schools could provide similar quality experiences for young people who do not receive adequately supportive experiences at home. The opportunity to pursue this question arose almost immediately.

The Yale Child Study Center (CSC) has a long history of consultation in public schools in the interest of learning more about children in schools and in the promotion of good child rearing, development, and mental health. The CSC was concerned that too many theories from disciplines other than education and psychology were being applied in schools without the understanding of how schools work and how academic learning takes place. Another CSC concern was whether it was appropriate to use therapeutic methods for children who were often referred for school-related problems. Would a school-based preventive psychiatry approach be more appropriate and more effective?

About the time I finished my training at the Center, Dr. Albert Solnit, then director, invited me to lead an inquiry-intervention team in a collaborative pilot project with the New Haven Public School System. Our task was to work (live in) full time in two elementary schools for a year, learn how they work, and develop, with the school stakeholders, an effective way to improve staff, parent, and student performance in school.

We were open to a variety of perspectives. Still, we were most influenced by child psychiatry because it brings a biopsychosocial perspective to understanding human behavior or performance. Importantly, all five of our intervention team members had social and behavioral science backgrounds. We believed that schooling for young people that focuses on development and academic learning could prevent behavior and mental health problems, and promote positive mental health. My clinical experiences at the CSC provided valuable knowledge and skills that influenced our work in the schools. These several influences greatly shaped our conceptualization of the way schooling can positively affect students' development and learning as well as informed our intervention.

### Conceptualization of the School Development Program

While our understanding deepened as we worked, from the beginning, our SDP team believed that child development and academic learning are inextricably linked and that, in fact, academic learning is largely a product of development. There are many development pathways, but growth along six (social-interactive, psycho-emotional, moral-ethical, physical, linguistic, cognitive-academic) are critically important in promoting children's self-expression and regulation, academic learning, and life management capacities.

In an effort to understand the many influences on child development and learning, we conceptualized the child as enmeshed in at least three networks that influenced school performance—the primary social network of the family; the secondary network of work, school, health and social services, and recreational organizations; and the tertiary network of practice and policy opinion leaders and decision makers. An understanding of the development of a child in the process of movement in and through these three networks facilitates the creation of an effective school intervention.

*Primary Social Network* The primary social network is probably the most powerful source of influence. It is comprised of parents or caretakers, along with their kin, friends, and organizations to which they have a sense of belonging. Parents are the carriers of the values, attitudes, and behaviors that are characteristic of the network. Children are greatly influenced by their experiences in this network. The forces in this network that influence development and learning are probably stronger than in any other later-in-

life network or condition. This is the case because, at birth, children are essentially a bundle of biological potentials and energies, driven by a developmental imperative, but so underdeveloped and dependent that they will die without the support of people around them.

The innate capacities of relatedness and aggression, the drive for attachment, and the presence of a caretaker, constitute the major survival arrangement. Through interactions between the child and the caretaker, the attachment and bonding process takes place. The child begins to identify with, imitate, and internalize the values, attitudes, and behaviors of parents and other caretakers. It is the caretakers, at the critical developmental pathways, and through many activities, who shape a child's expressive and survival energies as well as maintain and enhance the developmental imperative to grow healthily, achieve competences, and form important relationships with others.

*Secondary or Services Network* The school is a part of the secondary or services network of families and children. Bronfenbrenner's (1979) ecological model of development provides a foundation to understand the role of this network. As defined by Garbarino and Abromowitz (1992), Bronfenbrenner's model contains multiple levels, each exerting influence on one another and on the individual (in this case, children in schools). Children who experience a seamless transition between reasonably well-functioning homes and schools have the best chance to build on early developmental progress. When families have values, attitudes, and behaviors that are similar to the school or secondary social network; the children gain what is necessary to be successful in school simply by growing up and interacting with their parents or caretakers. Such children and families usually feel that they belong in the school.

Children who are marginal to the mainstream, especially children from low-income and minority families, often do not feel a sense of belonging in the school or in other secondary social networks (e.g., health centers, libraries, recreation programs). As a result, they are at greater risk for school and life failure (Comer, 1980). Nonmainstream families whose values, attitudes, and behaviors have greater overlap with mainstream culture can often gain what is necessary to be successful in the mainstream. My own childhood experience provides a useful example. I had the same socioeconomic background as my three best friends. My parents, however, had life goals, styles, and skills that were different from those of my friends' parents.[2]

As a domestic worker with ambition, my mother Maggie had the opportunity to observe and employ mainstream child-rearing knowledge and skills at work and at home. My father was a leader in a reasonably well functioning church community. The church culture was supportive of the culture of the societal mainstream. This combination of experiences provided us with the values, attitudes, and behaviors necessary to function in school and in other secondary networks or mainstream institutions.

Returning to my own schooling experiences, one incident illustrates how differences in the home environment can lead to different outcomes in school. My fourth-grade teacher devised a library usage contest that required us to obtain a library card and read and report on as many books as possible during the first semester. I read the most books and won the contest. My three friends, the only other Black students, were the only ones in the class who did not read any books. My teacher, who was not a racist, but who was frustrated, said, "If you three little colored boys don't want to be like the rest of us, you should not come to our school!" Already not feeling a sense of belonging in the setting, they experienced a direct expression of rejection from their teacher, an important authority figure. If she had understood that these were the grandchildren and great-grandchildren of sharecroppers and tenant farmers, and that they were intimidated by mainstream institutions, she would have helped them participate in the library contest.

In this and many other ways, my friends were not able to elicit a positive response from adult caretakers and authority figures in the school, which limited their ability to form a positive emotional attachment to the people and the academic program of the school. Despite the fact that they were intelligent and able, they experienced low levels of school success that eventually led to a downhill course in school and in life.

As children begin to fail to meet the expectations of school, they often act up and act out in a struggle for power with school staff or authority figures (Comer, 1980). They often turn away from the accepted standards of achievement and behavior and seek membership in groups, both in and out of school, that do not value school learning. Accordingly, they do not develop the personal discipline, aspirations, and skills necessary for school success, and they do not grow along the developmental pathways important for success in today's economy and society. Once these troublesome habits are established, they begin a downward trajectory that is very difficult to change (Comer, 1980). These were some of the multiple and interacting influences we identified in the school settings during our pilot years, and addressed during our full intervention.

*Tertiary Social Network* The tertiary social network comprises policy and practice decision makers and trend-setters whose attitudes about and actions in employment, education, housing, health, and other areas have an effect on conditions in families and schools or the primary and secondary networks. The policy and practice decision makers act from political, economic, social, faith, and advocacy group venues or the tertiary social network. When decisions made in the tertiary network emphasize secondary and primary social networks, children from vulnerable families are less likely to be prepared for school and, as such, more likely to have a downhill course in school and in life (Comer, 1980).

Prior to the 1950s, school failure or leaving for any reason was less of a problem than it is today. Most heads of household could earn a living without completing elementary school and, until the late 1960s, without a high school or postsecondary education. They were able to take care of themselves and their families and were more likely to contribute to their neighborhoods and communities in ways that made these areas safe and supportive of the development of their children. As science and technology were applied to all aspects of community life, however, education gradually became a requirement to obtain a living wage job (Comer, 2004). Further, good development was necessary to obtain an education. The education enterprise did not make the adjustments necessary to enable educators to provide the support for development in schools that was now more difficult to obtain outside of schools.

High mobility and rapid visual communication (i.e., television and now video games) contributed greatly to a breakdown in the sense of community and belonging that once supported families and the development of their children. Potentially harmful information that once was provided and limited by the important people in their primary networks, as mature and responsible adults deemed appropriate, began to go directly to children, often in stimulating and sometimes provocative formats. The breakdown in a sense of community, along with a decline of work that did not require a formal education, the reduction in low-skill jobs, the growth of an underground economy, and other factors contributed to the rapid growth of an underclass that is less able to provide what children need to grow and to succeed in school and in life (Comer, 2004).

The students in our pilot schools were from families that were most severely affected by historical conditions and contemporary changes in the nature of the economy that began to occur in the 1960s. The influences from the tertiary networks were powerful, and we had little control over them. We suspected, however, that the proximal or school-based influences were much more powerful than most people had imagined. We also suspected that they could be managed so as to recreate critical aspects of natural communities and thereby improve students' development and learning. My own sense that this could be the case came from my experience with milieu therapy during my psychiatry training. I was impressed that the beliefs fostered by a group in which each individual wanted to belong could have a powerful influence on individual behavior.

The question was whether we could modify the school to approximate the influences of well functioning families and communities. James Coleman and colleagues (1966) made the point that low-income children lack social capital, and they provided research evidence suggesting that schools could not make a difference. Ron Edmonds (1982), however, presented research showing that schools with certain characteristics that were largely supportive of student growth were effective. His effective schools' research, however, did not demonstrate how to help dysfunctional schools become well functioning and effective.

The work of our School Development Program (SDP) was designed to consider the major influences on schooling and to develop a way to minimize the impact of negative influences, create social capital, and promote desirable influences at a level that would promote positive development and academic learning. This approach led to our SDP framework and process model.

***Refinement of SDP Model*** During the first year of our pilot project in 1968 and 1969, we hypothesized that the underlying problem in low-performing schools was that too many of the students were not adequately prepared or had developed in a way that did not enable them to meet the expectations of school people. On the other side, most school people, through no fault of their own, were not prepared to help their students develop to the level necessary for school success. The challenge was to help close the gap for both. However, in 1968, there was little, if any, comprehensive school reform research. Our five-member Child Study Center intervention team used our discipline-based knowledge and skills.

In *School Power: Implications of an Intervention Project* (Comer, 1980), I describe the challenges that we faced as we tried to change the life of schools based on knowledge of child development and public health. We discovered one child who was being seen by seven different support staff who did not talk to each other. Multiple community organizations were trying to help the schools, but they were contributing to the confusion. There was an absence of student intake, transfer, and transition procedures based on the developmental needs of the students. Much frustration, anger, and conflict were created by these conditions. As a result, the school climate and culture could not support good teaching, development, or learning.

We knew that children develop best in environments in which the interactions between students and adults are informed by the understanding that development and learning are inextricably linked. Thus, our first focus had to be on improving the school climate and eventually creating a culture that facilitated student development. We found that we had to help staff and parents simultaneously to "think and do" development. Based on our theory of change, we expected good teaching and learning to follow.

We discovered, however, that lectures about child rearing and development were not enough to promote the effective application of child development principles in the classroom or on the school level. Mandating change based on these principles, without creating the conditions that would make it possible, was not useful at all; it was even counterproductive. Helping teachers and administrators apply developmental principles on a one-to-one or small-group basis was more useful but affected too few people. We needed a systemic process that pulled the energies and abilities of all the participants together in a goal-directed way.

We used a pathway metaphor to explicitly and implicitly indicate that the central task of schooling is to support student development in the service of academic learning and preparation for adult life. The pathway metaphor is based on the theories and empirical research of several scholars (see Comer, 2005). In order to allow us to create the conditions

in which these tasks or goals could be reached, we back-mapped to design a building process that would achieve this end. Nevertheless, many of the parents had experienced educational failure themselves and were apprehensive about education theory and practice.

We took these complex and sometimes intimidating findings and figured out a way to communicate them effectively to teachers and parents. What emerged during our meetings with parents and teachers was a set of case studies that resonated with people and an idea that proved to be powerful over the years. This idea is that child development, not learning theory, is the foundational science of education. As we say, children who develop well, learn well. Talking about the impact of development on their child's schooling helps parents enable their children to make the transition from home to school, from the primary social network to the secondary or services network. This approach proved much more effective than mandate and lecture.

***Nine Elements in School Reform Process Model*** The nine-element framework and school reform process model we created, which eventually produced coordinated and productive interactions, grew out of our responses to the day-to-day challenges and opportunities in the two pilot elementary schools. The nine elements include three mechanisms, three operations, and three guidelines. They individually and collectively address what we call the three critical operations and functions in a school—organization and management, development and appropriate interactions among all the participants, and instruction. When these basic school tasks are carried out well, it is possible to create well functioning schools even in very difficult environments. When these three functions are not addressed well, low performing schools are the usual outcome.

The three mechanisms or teams for management of the SDP are the: (a) School Planning and Management Team (SPMT), (b) Parent Team (PT), and (c) School-Staff Support Team (SSST). All three teams are involved in the following operations: (a) the creation and implementation of a Comprehensive School Plan (CSP), (b) staff development, and (c) assessment and modification of the CSP. Underlying all aspects of the SDP are the three relationship guidelines: No fault problem solving, consensus decision making, and collaboration. Each of these nine elements is described below, beginning with the relationship guidelines.

*Relationship Guidelines* The greatest challenge to working well together is our powerful human tendency to be defensive, to attack or fight when we perceive an attack, or to withdraw rather than resolve disagreements. When bad feelings are not open and strongly expressed, they often seethe just below the surface. Enormous energy is discharged, without improving living conditions or opportunities for the adults or the students.

Thus, the first relationship guideline, *no fault problem solving,* was designed to address this troublesome behavior. Some argue that this relational guideline is the most important element. It asks all involved not to point the finger of blame, but rather to focus on preventing or solving relationship and performance problems. This guideline reduces the need for defensiveness and promotes civil problem-solving discussions. Some feel that it provides a sense of freedom from attack and an incentive not to attack others. It does not mean that individuals are not accountable for their performance or behavior. In practice, it works to make people more responsible for their own behavior and performance because of our need for a sense of inclusion, which is enhanced by group expectations.

*No fault problem solving* is also thought of as the most difficult element with which to live. The impulse to attack is great and, to make this element work, colleagues must help each other. One administrator spoke of a potential argument in which one teacher told the other that what she said was not very "Comerlike" (*no fault*). The other reminded her that what she did was not very "Comerlike" either. By invoking the expectation, rather than trying to win the war, they were able to laugh and save their energy for real work. Admittedly, this is not easy.

The second relationship guideline, *consensus decision making*, is guided by the developmental needs of the students. Decisions made in schools sometimes contribute to the formation of cliques and the quest for power, rather than to meeting the needs of students. By focusing on student needs, discussions have a strong reference point that makes it more difficult to get lost in personal staff and parent biases and desires. Nobody has to be right or wrong, and there is no need for a commitment to doing it "my way." There is a willingness first to try the approach that most agree appears best for students, but also to try later what others believe if the majority approach does not work. The idea is that another approach may emerge later, as people work to implement the first approach.

In this way, there are no winners or losers as well as fewer struggles for power with related bad feelings. There are no losers to say, "You won, you do it." It is everybody's decision and everybody's task. Cooperation is more likely because it is all about the students, rather than about winning and losing.

In one school, students running and making noise were a particular problem in one area of the building, and the teachers had been blaming each other and the students, rather than acting together. In thinking about how to address the problem, they talked about the impulsiveness of students as well as the need for students to experience agreement among the school authority figures. As planned, with the next few incidents, several teachers at that end of the hall immediately appeared at the door, and one reminded the students of the danger and the expectation. Problem solved—for a while. An "old school tale" suggests why such incidents must be addressed often. One student who had been reminded about the rule against running replied, "Oops, Ms. Jones, my head remembered, but my feet forgot."

We now understand the power of impulse to override the self-regulation ability of the young, which argues for the need of the adults to provide ongoing support. Additionally, this developmental understanding enables teachers to realize that the misbehaving student is not deliberately "ruining their day." This perspective relies on a developmental understanding rather than on moral judgments. Approaching everyday issues in this way reduces anger and rage because the perspective gives meaning to the effort of helping students manage their behavior. Moreover, it allows adults to appreciate their part in enabling student growth and improving behavior.

The third relationship guideline, *collaboration*, becomes more possible when there is decreased conflict among and between adults and students. Collaboration improves communication, decreases fragmentation, and creates a "we're all in this together" spirit. We originally referred to this component as "no paralysis" to make the point that the teams should not paralyze the principal or person with the legal responsibility for school outcomes but that the principal should not ignore the input of the teams or group. Because this is not a problem once a spirit of collaboration is established, we decided that *collaboration* was a more appropriate name for this guideline than *no paralysis*. A spirit of collaboration made joint projects, team teaching, and parent–staff cooperation more possible and more useful to students.

Working together, these three relationship guidelines make it possible for teams to carry out operations. As the operations are carried out, the guidelines permeate all school activities and positively influence behavior and performance. An improved school climate or environment as well as improved behavior and academic outcomes strengthen the willingness of participants to live by the guidelines. At the outset of our school reform process, we help schools understand that it takes time and effort to learn and eventually incorporate these relationship guidelines in everyday interactions. We ask many people to give up longstanding ways of behaving that are important to them, especially when the behaviors are counterproductive. More than once, schools that later became enthusiastic supporters of our model almost voted it out in the beginning. Again, participants must help each other to work in accordance with these guidelines.

### Managing the SDP: The Three Teams

*School Planning and Management Team (SPMT)*    The SPMT mechanism is the major decision-making body in the school and the engine of the process model. It sets in motion and regulates the interactive process that structures or frames all school activities. As the relationship guidelines become more ingrained in the culture of a school, the team becomes more effective. When the work of this team is carried out adequately, it helps create a desirable school culture and environment. The SPMT enables all the adults to interact well with each other and with the students. As a result, students can identify with, imitate, and internalize the values, attitudes, and behaviors that are most productive.

Desirable behavior and good academic learning are valued most.

An example is useful here. An 11-year-old transfer student was about to start a fight because someone accidentally stepped on his foot during a classroom exercise. He had transferred three times during the previous semester and had to fight his way to acceptance at the previous schools. A male classmate in the school (which was in its third year of implementing our process) said, "Hey man. We don't do that in *this* school!" The expression of the teacher and other students supported the no-fighting expectation. The would-be fighter readily accepted this different way of living and dropped his fists. He did not have to fight for respect, belonging, or inclusion. While the adults helped establish the expectation, the students, through attachment and bonding, identification, imitation, and internalization, had become its carriers.

The SPMT is composed of the administrator(s), teachers, parents, professional support staff such as social workers and others, and nonprofessionals such as the custodian. They are all selected by their respective colleagues. In this way, every voice in the school is represented at the decision-making table. We found that the team was most effective when made up of no more than 12 to 15 people. This arrangement addresses what is now known to be one of the major reasons that 50% of new teachers leave the profession in 5 years—a sense that they are powerless to influence the conditions in their work environment (National Commission on Teaching and America's Future, 2003).

The major task of the SPMT is to manage the implementation of the SDP process. It does so directly and through permanent and ad hoc subcommittees. It establishes the school goals and is responsible for creating the Comprehensive School Plan (CSP) needed to achieve them. The subcommittee work informs, and is acted on, by the SPMT. This prevents program fragmentation, duplication, conflict, and the waste of psychological energy that is usually found in dysfunctional schools (Noblit, Malloy, & Malloy, 2001).

In many schools, members of the support staff are involved primarily after student problems occur, and many parents do not have meaningful roles. Our other teams, the Parent Team and the School Staff Support Team, overcome this problem by involving parents and support staff in supporting the implementation of the Comprehensive School Plan created by the SPMT. Because the CSP is designed to help create a positive school climate or culture and an academic program that promotes development and learning, parents and support staff are involved in the most central work of the school in an integrated and important way.

*The Parent Team (PT)*   Involvement of the Parent Team helps to restore the almost seamless movement from home to school communities that existed prior to the 1960s, when children were often involved in networks of caring adults at home and sometimes home and school. In the SDP "recreated community," there is less student acting-up behavior

and good support for growth along the critical developmental pathways—social-interactive, psychoemotional, moral-ethical, and cognitive-academic growth and development. Staff control and student rebellion cycles are less likely. Students who feel a sense of belonging take more responsibility for their own behavior. The framework provides an opportunity for all of the adults to be supportive. Often, however, parent and staff beliefs and attitudes must change to make effective parent participation possible.

In many low-income schools, parents often lack a high level of education or often had difficult school experiences themselves. They hope that the school will better serve their children, but often fear that it will not. They sometimes feel intimidated by school people and threatened by the school's expectations of themselves and their children. Additionally, such families are often under economic and social stress. As a result, there is often a reluctance to get involved in the work of the school.

For these and other reasons, during our first year, only 15 parents turned out for the school Christmas party. Three years later, with no significant change in the demographics, more than 400 parents, relatives, and friends attended the same event. All of the SDP components contributed to this change, but the social program of the CSP probably contributed the most. Parents joined with staff in implementing this program and gained an important sense of ownership of the work of the school. Our program facilitator helped the parents gain the skills and confidence needed to interact with the staff and fully support school activities.

In the SDP, we help the entire school community interact with parents in a way that makes them feel like welcomed partners in education. It is important that teachers and administrators come to understand the way that parental involvement facilitates student development in school and, simultaneously, facilitates teaching and student learning. This alleviates many of the concerns that teachers may have about involving parents (Epstein & Becker, 1982).

The parent team is open to all parents, and an effort is made to involve all the different identifiable groups in a community. Initially, the parents who presented themselves through concern about problems or with an interest in helping were invited to serve on the team. With the success of each activity, the number of members grew. In schools that already had a Parent Teacher Association (PTA) or other established groups, to avoid duplication and rivalry, the members of these groups became our SDP Parent Team. We helped them work in ways consistent with our approach.

The Parent Team selects representatives to serve on the School Planning and Management Team, thereby providing the parent community with a voice. Three levels of parent participation evolved. The first level is the group of parents who turn out for events. Most parents participate at the first level—attending activities on the school social calendar. The calendar is an aspect of the social component of the comprehensive school plan.

In the initial project, some parents worked at the second level as paid assistants and helped in classrooms and with field trips, in the cafeteria, and with other activities. These were the core members of the Parent Team. Their engagement and knowledge about the school encouraged others to get involved. Some schools continue this level with and without pay. Parents at level two are involved with the staff to create social activities that help develop a positive school climate or environment. The third level of participation is decision making as members of the SPMT.

Through the work of the team, parents often design programs to strengthen their own child-rearing knowledge and skills. In some cases, the programs prepare them for future work opportunities. Many parents who worked in the schools gained knowledge, skills, and confidence that enabled them to obtain jobs that they would not have aspired to previously. Some went back and finished high school, or equivalent programs. A few went on to finish college, and at least one earned a master's degree. The children of such parents benefited. About 20 years ago, 15 parents from the original program returned for a television interview about SDP. They attributed their later successes to the school staff, positive school climate, productive learning conditions, strong role models, and to the opportunity to be more helpful to their own children.

*School Staff Support Team (SSST)* Initially this group was called the Mental Health Team. The intent was to bring mental health knowledge and skills into schools in a way that might prevent more severe mental health and behavior problems. Another intent was to promote good mental health and student success in school. Because of the stigma often attached to mental health work, and because our focus was on improving the school environment, it was more useful to have the name reflect the function—the School Staff Support Team. The SSST, comprising social workers, psychologists, special education teachers, nurses, and other helping professional, focused on helping individuals and groups of students as well as helping adults create a school climate and culture that promoted good development, desirable behavior, and improved academic learning.

An SSST member serves on the SPMT and other key committees to help participants think about child development issues reflected in behavior and learning and to guide their work accordingly. For example, in our pilot schools, knowledge that little children cannot sit very long helped the staff change the format of assemblies in a way that overcame disruptive student–staff interactions harmful to both and to the overall climate of the school. Although it was probably not new knowledge, the team members helped the staff think about when and how to apply it. As each application of the development mindset reduces relationship problems, awareness of and the tendency to "think and do" development spreads throughout a building until it is a part of the culture.

The team brought together the helping professionals who were working separately. This reduced the fragmentation of services that had probably made them less effective, even useless and wasteful, in the first place. The referrals and

case management became more effective. The team not only worked with students, but also helped staff think about how developmental capacities impeded or facilitated student behaviors and how they could be helpful. Teachers were delighted to be able to respond to troublesome behaviors in ways that promoted student attachment and bonding and growth as well as helped students identify positively with the staff and the program of the school.

Early in our work, a panel of psychiatrists advised our major foundation supporter that the students had been traumatized in a way that would require one-on-one therapy, not simply environmental change and support for development. Interestingly, in the early 1980s, because they were being sued to provide high-cost residential care services, the New Haven School System surveyed all schools to determine the level of need and cost. Our two pilot schools were the only two in the district that had not made any referrals for such services. We were not able to fully explore the meaning of this finding, but we believe that it suggests that, when students receive good support for development, precursors of mental health problems do not go on to become serious clinical conditions.

In high-stress communities, some SDP participants find the SSST to be useful more often than the SPMT. The principal of PS 46 in New York City, Carmen Gonzalez (2004), has described a staggering number of severe problems ranging from tardiness and attendance to bullying and vision and medical emergencies. She employed her professional support group, the SSST (called the Child Study team in their building), to manage the many challenges. This permitted the teaching and learning functions to be carried out without significant interference. As a result of the systematic way that they worked, in 2002, this elementary school had the highest percentage of students in New York City that moved from the lowest ranks of achievement to the highest.

### Operations of the SDP

*The Comprehensive School Plan (CSP)* The CSP is an important operation. It is created by, and is the most important task of, the SPMT. Through its two components, one social and the other academic, it addresses instructional, curricular, relationship, and child development issues in a school.

The social component of the Comprehensive School Plan was designed to help create a good school climate. It is carried out by a subcommittee appointed by the SPMT. We included all the social activities on a school calendar—holiday celebrations, beginning- and end-of-year activities, and others. Previously given as "fun breaks" from the stress of academic work, they were reconceptualized as opportunities to promote desirable interactions among parents, students, and staff. The intent of these activities was to enable the adults to promote student development along the social-interactive, psychoemotional, moral-ethical, physical, linguistic, and cognitive-academic pathways. The academic program of the CSP is also carried out by a subcommittee appointed by the SPMT. Whatever curriculum and instruction program exists in a school is implemented through this operation.

As a school improves, the staff is usually able to integrate all four of the focus areas, curricular, instructional, relational, and developmental, into all activities. It is an easy next step to use science fairs and other academic activities to support both academic achievement and healthy interactions that promote growth along the developmental pathways.

While the SPMT can be likened to an engine, the Comprehensive School Plan is somewhat like a steering wheel. It is informed by data from periodic assessment activities, and modification or adjustment of the plan and its implementation is in response to these assessment findings. Most importantly, the plan is centered on promoting young people's learning and development and not on the adults' turf and bureaucratic issues. The school management teams utilize assessment data and staff development forums to refine the Comprehensive School Plan. All activities proposed from inside and outside a school are expected to help create a culture that promotes child development and academic achievement. The SDP is not, in and of itself, an instructional program. However, it affects the curriculum and instructional program in a powerful way. By creating a good school environment or culture, overall staff performance (attitudes, behavior, and instruction) improves. Through healthy interactions with adults in a good environment, students become amenable to learning. In even modestly difficult school environments, or environments not geared to supporting adults or students, good academic achievement is less likely.

It is important to point out that the SDP does not use a particular curriculum or instruction method and was not designed to raise test scores. By creating an environment that enables adults to support student development and by facilitating good staff development, improved teaching and learning and test scores come about; regardless of the kind of instructional programs. Nonetheless, we do address some instructional issues. We have created instruction-related programs that promote curriculum alignment, help nonreaders become readers, and enable teacher study groups to learn about innovative teaching models (Joyner, Ben-Avie, & Comer, 2004). In sum, these instructional components were added because we repeatedly found that instructional problems create significant behavior and relationship problems, negatively affecting the school climate and interfering with support for student development.

As we became more certain that lack of preparation for school interfered with academic learning, we became more intentional in addressing areas of student underdevelopment. Our SPMT created a program designed to give nonmainstream students the kind of experiences that many mainstream children gain simply by growing up with their parents. It was a part of our Comprehensive School Plan and was called the Social Skills Curriculum for Inner City Children.

The Social Skills Curriculum for Inner City Children

program integrated the teaching of basic academic skills, social skills, and appreciation of the arts and athletics. It was carried out through activity units in politics and government, business and economics, health and nutrition, and leisure and spiritual time. While all the elements of the SDP contributed, the Social Skills Curriculum was particularly effective in facilitating a 7-month jump in the nationally standardized achievement tests scores. The pilot schools that were initially ranked 32nd and 33rd in achievement eventually were ranked 3rd and 4th in New Haven.

While the Social Skills Curriculum for Inner City Children does not exist in the original format in the schools now using the SDP model, there are activities in place that are designed to serve the same purpose. The Comer Carolina Coalition, a network of SDP schools in North and South Carolina (Hart, McLaughlin, Ennis, & Stone, 2004), designed activities that allow the staff to help children develop and gain the skills needed for school success. Many of the SDP elements used to change the whole school environment are modified and used in classrooms. For example, the kindergarten and first grade students in some schools sit four to a table. They work as a team, each having rotating, one-week task assignments of facilitator, timekeeper, and so on. As they carry out their tasks, the adult staff helps them gain social interaction, collaboration, consensus decision making, problem solving, and other capacities.

*Staff Development*   In many school districts, staff development is a central office responsibility and, when carried out at the building level, supervisors or building-level administrators and support staff provide it. Building-level staffs often do not influence the content or format; thus, these efforts are sometimes not very useful in meeting school needs. The SDP framework facilitates staff input through the SPMT's implementation of the Comprehensive School Plan. Staff development is tied to the goals articulated in the plan, the first operation, and outcome findings and needs identified through the third operation, the assessment process.

Our SDP has created instruments that are used by schools to learn more about who their students are as well as the students' developmental needs (Emmons, 2004). The in-service staff development program is tied closely to the identified needs. There is in-school training from colleagues, as well as from district level and other resources, as deemed needed by the staff. Our SDP training helps the staff integrate child and adolescent development principles into all academic and social interactions. Staff development relative to the implementation of our SDP model will be discussed below in the section on training.

*Assessment and Modification*   The School Planning and Management Team's assessment and modification of the Comprehensive School Plan are data driven, using the districts' academic achievement findings and our own climate and implementation scales. Our clinical and field observations complement statistical measures, and formal and informal use of these data takes place in all planning for students and the school.

We began our work with the notion that accountability is probably more effective when it stems from internal, goal-based assessments than from measures imposed from outside a school. Our experience suggests that, in schools where there is a sense of belonging and inclusion, fostered by cooperative and collaborative goal setting and participation, individuals and groups take greater responsibility for their own contribution to program outcomes. Thus, the assessment and modification activities involve all the participants and are tied to school goals. The findings help the staff plan, implement, reflect on outcomes, and make program adjustments. This kind of assessment is simultaneously a powerful staff development process, probably more powerful than didactic staff development approaches.

We believe that education should be preparation for life and not just the accumulation of academic knowledge and skills. Taking a developmental perspective, schools plan experiences that help young people begin to gain capacities that will help them become adults who are able to take care of themselves, their families, and their communities. High level academic achievement alone does not guarantee well functioning adults. In Sternberg's (2003) words, "students can become content experts who nevertheless do not use their expertise in the search for a common good" (p. 5). For this reason, he calls for an "augmented conception of expertise" that teaches children to think wisely. From our origin in 1968, this was the intent of the SDP.

The major focus of the assessment and modification operation is on the CSP and on test scores as the primary indicator of the impact of SDP implementation. We also assess the quality of the SDP implementation through student and staff observation measures. Additionally, we are looking for behavioral and developmental indicators that could be reliable predictors of adequate preparation for good adult life performance.

***Dissemination of the SDP Model*** Our SDP team completed work in the pilot schools in 1984. Shortly thereafter, we were asked by several schools and districts to help them implement our program. Over the next 6 years, we used this opportunity both to field test the model and to experiment with training approaches to disseminate our process in 12 schools in various parts of the country. A consistent pattern emerged of remarkable improvements in students' learning and development once schools implemented our process (Comer, 1988b). With success and greater visibility, we were able to obtain support to design a major dissemination program.

While all 12 schools showed social and academic achievement gains, our "one man band" approach could not be sustained and, therefore, could not have a deep impact on the districts involved. A major dissemination effort required more staff and codification of our work in a way that made a training program necessary and possible. Additionally, by the 1990s, numerous school improvement programs were beginning to show that the test scores of poor children could be raised. New research showed that some schools were doing well despite high levels of poverty, often without special programs. Policy and opinion leaders began to call for bringing successful models to scale (McDonald et al., 1999).

Our field test work suggested that the notion of models as products that could be imposed or reproduced was not a useful way to think about the school improvement and scale challenge. We found each district and school to be different in ways that had to be taken into account. We suspected that, when schools do well in situations that one would not predict, it is because of a chance collection of gifted staff people with an intuitive ability to create an environment that supports the developmental needs of students as well as reasonably good instruction (Haycock, 2006). Nevertheless, chance and unusual gifts are not good enough.

We believe that all school people need to have the capacity for self-improvement, assisted as necessary by carriers of a knowledge base that enables them to apply child development and pedagogical principles to all aspects of schooling. Our training had to help new groups engage in a process that created conditions that would promote self-improvement rather than "buy off the shelf" a prepackaged school change product. We believe that our national system(s) of education can improve significantly only when all educators are trained in this way.

We used a trainer-of-trainer approach. Our Yale Child Study Center staff were involved in providing theory and practice findings to partners and districts called coordinators. The person(s) in a district responsible for establishing the SDP process locally is called a facilitator. To overcome the problem of distance, and to address the lack of connection between districts and preparatory programs, we worked with several schools of education across the country. We merged our knowledge and experience in the application of child and adolescent development principles with their knowledge of curriculum, instruction, and assessment to create good school environments or cultures. Our partners, in turn, helped schools and districts learn to implement the model. In some cases, our partners eventually took primary responsibility for helping district facilitators to gain the attitudes, knowledge, and skills needed to implement the model in schools. The university partners often tied their own institutions more closely to local districts. The partnerships they formed with school districts helped them to be more responsive to district needs and to the kind of experiences their own preservice teachers needed to become effective educators.

Until recently, most of the training was carried out at the Yale Child Study Center. Recently, three of our longtime and very effective partners established regional training centers (Hart et al., 2004). Additionally, SDP national faculty, who were recruited to work with us after they retired from successful programs, train participants in districts that are unable to send their staff to national or regional trainings.

Five training modules introduce teachers, administrators,

parents, school board members, and other policy makers to our school reform process. These modules include training about the kind of organization and management needed to carry out meaningful change, deepen knowledge of development, and involve students in support of their own development and learning. The modules are as follows: The 101 and 102 Academies, the Principal's Academy, the Developmental Academy, and the Comer Kids' Academy. Training for the three instructional strategies, Essentials of Literacy, Balanced Curriculum, and Teachers Helping Teachers, is integrated into the adult-oriented academies. These instructional modules are designed to address the same three activity areas targeted by the SDP process—organization and management, student development, and the development of all participating adults, and instruction. The intentions of the Comer Kids' Academy are to use the interests and needs of students to support their development. We also collaborate with the initiative launched by my colleague at Yale, Edward Zigler. The School of the 21st Century was conceptualized by Zigler as an approach to the national childcare challenge (Zigler & Finn-Stevenson, 1989).

The 101 Academy introduces teachers, administrators, support staff, and others to the nine components of the SDP and the six developmental pathways. Trainers at the academy also discuss how schools might use the model to pull together under one umbrella the often fragmented activities in their home districts and schools to improve the school's overall functioning and thereby focus more intentionally and effectively on student development and learning. The 102 Academy, which is designed for schools that have implemented the process for at least one year, is structured to encourage participants to reflect on their experiences. The academy deepens participants' understanding of how to better apply child development principles in practice.

The Developmental Academy is designed primarily for teachers. It helps them infuse developmental principles in their instructional strategies. The Principal's Academy helps school leaders appreciate how the governance and management components connect with the instructional and developmental components as well as the framing and facilitating nature of SDP.

The Yale CSC SDP faculty provided the initial training. Because they were also coordinators helping district and other coordinators and facilitators on the front lines, they were able to shape the training to the needs of school staffs. They were aware of the difficulty involved in taking theory to practice and continually made adjustments accordingly. As practicing and retired practitioners joined our national faculty, our ability to translate theory and research into practice improved.

Since the late 1980s, through training and with the support of our SDP staff, district facilitators were able to establish the SDP process in over 1000 schools. The nine elements sometimes have different names, but the same structure, function, and goals are expected. Because the model is otherwise open, rather than prescriptive, and encourages participant creativity, programs can look very dif-

ferent but achieve similar outcomes. However, a continuing problem has been the level of "buy in" and continuity.

### Evaluation of the SDP Model
*Long-Term Outcomes from the Pilot Program*  The two New Haven pilot elementary schools initially ranked 32nd and 33rd in academic achievement of the 33 schools in the city. Eleven years later, with the same target population, they ranked third and fifth in academic achievement. There was marked improvement in parent, staff, and student relationships after 2 years, but little academic gain until 8 years later. Additionally, they were the only two schools in which there was not a direct correlation between the socioeconomic level of the students and the nationally standardized tests used citywide. They had the best attendance in the city, and there were no serious behavior problems. One school also had no teacher turnover for 13 years. After a change in leadership, there was little to no training of new staff, and the quality of implementation of the process gradually declined, as did the test scores.

We had one natural experiment. The students from one of our pilot schools attended a junior high school that also served a neighboring elementary school. The students from our pilot achieved at a significantly higher rate on standardized tests than did their neighbors. This was the case throughout the middle school period. They also had fewer problem behaviors, and they were more often school leaders (Cauce, Comer, & Schwartz, 1987).

*Dissemination Studies*  There have been approximately 12 combined qualitative and quantitative external evaluations focusing on how the SDP model influences student outcomes as well as the mechanisms of change. Almost all suggested that the SDP had a favorable impact on structures and processes important to improving school environment, student, and staff performance. Additionally, there were two major external experimental design studies and the meta-analysis discussed below.

One evaluation study (Wong, Oberman, Mintrop, & Gamson, 1996) found that usually the first outcome of the implementation of the SDP or Comer Process was improved school organization. They also found that the SDP schools were better organized to deal with the tasks that they must perform and the issues that they have to address. This finding supported our own observations. Several studies (Noblit, Malloy, & Malloy, 2001; Springfield et al., 1995) found that the process contributes to staff member feelings of empowerment and ownership. They also found that the process reduced teacher isolation. Turnball, Fiester, and Wodatch (1997), Noblit et al. (2001), and Payne (1994) found that the SDP structures clearly provide support for change. They suggested that the major reason was the effective flow of information made possible by the process.

Many studies report that SDP schools showed improved social climate, better relationships, and greater feelings of safety (Cook, Murphy, & Hunt, 2000; Millsap et al., 2000). Several researchers found that SDP had a positive impact on student attitudes toward education and improved overall student behavior at school (Cook et al., 2000; Wong et al., 1996). One study found that students at the SDP schools reported better anger control, greater disapproval of misbehavior, and less acting out behavior than did their counterparts in control schools (Cook et al., 2000).

*Experimental Studies*   Two experimental or random assignment research design studies were conducted, one in Chicago, Illinois, and one in Prince George's County, Maryland (Cook, Habib, et al., 1999; Cook, Murphy, et al., 2000). The findings in Chicago showed positive outcomes in the SDP or Comer schools, including implementation of the process, improved social and academic climates, reductions in negative behaviors, and improved academic achievement. Students who were in the Comer schools for three or more consecutive years caught up with and passed their counterparts in math on the Iowa Test of Basic Skills by grade 8. Students in the SDP or Comer Schools began about three points behind students in the control schools on the grade 5 tests, but by grade 8, they had improved more than four more points to outperform students in the control schools. The difference between the two groups increased over time in both the climate and academic achievement areas in favor of the SDP schools.

The results of this study drew the following comment from Cook, Murphy, and colleagues (2000):

> The data suggest that the Comer program caused positive changes in two socially important sets of outcomes: (1) standardized test scores and (2) beliefs, feelings, and behaviors relevant to disruptive and illegal behaviors. It is rare for a single study to show changes in both of these domains, which are so central to current discussions of the need for school reform, particularly in the impacted inner-city areas. (p. 589)

The Prince George's County data are difficult to interpret because contextual factors led to contamination. Some schools in the control group used key components of the intervention, while some in the experimental group strongly resisted change (Comer & Haynes, 1999). Contamination most likely contributed to the finding that there were no significant differences between SDP and control schools on school climate or student outcomes. Cook, Habib, et al. (1999) acknowledge that there was wide variation in implementation within the experimental and control schools and that schools with more Comer-like procedures, regardless of official assignment, tended to have "positive changes in social behavior and psychological adjustment" (p. 579). Similarly, Emmons (2004) reported that the quality of program implementation correlates strongly with academic achievement and social performance measures.

Reflecting on our work in the late 1990s, during the dissemination phase, it appeared that about one third of the schools make high levels of environmental improvement as well as student developmental and academic achievement gains. About one third make modest gains, and about one

third make no gains (Comer, 2004). This pattern cannot be attributed to socioeconomic levels because some of the lowest-income schools have made extraordinary gains, equaling and surpassing high-income schools. We hypothesized that school success is determined by the degree of "buy in" and that the pattern of "buy in" is influenced by teacher and administrator early preparation and by the level of district support for a focus on child development in the service of academic learning.

A reasonably small but persistent number of building-level resistors can prevent "buy in." Because school culture is an important motivator of students, staff, and parents, limited gains take place in such situations. Additionally, we had schools that improved dramatically over a 3- to 5-year period, only to decline swiftly when a new district leader who did not believe in the model was selected. Similar problems occurred when several new teachers joined the staff and were not trained. We had suspected that district-level leadership and district-wide support for a child and adolescent development focus would promote more rapid and greater teacher "buy in." These problems led to our district-wide application of the model and to our interest in helping preparatory programs to encourage future educators to think of themselves and to work as child developers. I present the achievement outcomes in our system- or district-wide programs in the section below.

*District-Wide Studies*   These studies were a particular focus within our overall dissemination effort. The purpose was to determine whether district-wide leadership support could improve or hasten "buy in" at the building level. The model was used system- or district-wide in five districts: Westbury Union Free School District (New York), Asheville City Schools and Hertford County Public Schools (North Carolina), The City of Orange Public Schools (New Jersey), and Community School District 17 (New York). Significant academic gains were made in all five schools.[3]

Asheville, North Carolina, was the only district with demographics that permitted a racial comparison. The most important outcome in Asheville is that, over a 5-year period, 1999 to 2003, after SDP was introduced, the gap in reading and mathematics proficiency between Black and White elementary school students was almost completely closed on the state achievement test by the fifth grade. There was a gain in proficiency in each year over the previous year in third through fifth grade. The following is an excerpt from an article by Barbara Blake in *The Asheville Citizen Times* from August 26, 2003 reporting the progress:

> The most significant improvement was seen at Hall Fletcher Elementary, where the gap between African-American and white students in third grade were 33.3 percent in math in 2001–02, and only .07 percent last year. A gap of 28.8 percent in reading in 2001–02 dropped to 6.7 percent in 2002–03. (Ray, 2004, p. 91)

Of particular interest, the majority White students were of greater affluence than in many communities. Importantly, their proficiency improved as well over this time frame. Additionally, the teachers were about 80% White. This district did not focus on race or class challenges. Rather, it focused on integrating child and adolescent development principles in all aspects of school life. These results suggest that support for development is probably a more important determinant of outcomes than is race or social class (Ray, 2004).

We found that district level leadership hastened "buy in." Governance and management and human issues, from retirement, movement of leadership for various reasons, or illness and death, however, made it difficult to sustain change even where there was good district and development of "buy in." Over the years, in several places where replacement staff were open to change and received training, gains were sustained. We found, however, that the pool of people willing and ready to focus on child and adolescent development in the service of learning was too small. This suggests the need for such a focus in all staff preparatory programs. Our current program and policy interest is in the preparatory program area.

***Strengths and Weaknesses of the SDP Model*** Our major weakness is probably our greatest strength. We are criticized most for not being an instructional program. However, the Borman, Hewes, Overman, and Brown (2003) meta-analysis shows that our SDP was only one of three of the 29 comprehensive school reform programs studied in which empirical evidence demonstrated improved test scores. This finding supports our theory of change, that improved school culture with a focus on student and staff development contributes powerfully to improved academic outcomes as long as the instructional program is adequate. Our work suggests that poor academic learning is due as much (or more) to student underdevelopment than to instruction. Again, underdeveloped students tend not to be motivated to learn and, therefore, are less amenable to "exposing themselves to unaccustomed experiences" (Pinner, 1962, p. 960) that are at the heart of learning. Students who are developing well will learn because development and learning are inextricably linked. Thus, the underlying problem in schools is that most educators are not prepared to build on prior support for development or to continue the process in school. This is particularly harmful for students whose out-of-school support, for whatever reason, is not strong. All instructional programs are less effective than they could be under these circumstances.

Instruction in dysfunctional schools is like sowing seeds on cement; modestly achieving schools are like seeds on unplowed clay. The work of the SDP is like plowing the soil and providing the nutrients needed to help seedlings grow. The instructional program, and all other activities and resources in a school, have a reasonable chance of being effective in a well functioning school or district.

A major strength of the SDP is that it is a framework or set of organizing principles that facilitates synchronous application of child and adolescent development principles in a way that simultaneously improves school climate, facilitates positive adult–child interactions, and promotes student development as well as development among all other program participants. To do so, unlike most other school improvement models, it focuses primarily on improving the environment and climate in a way that promotes a culture that supports academic learning. It promotes a sense of inclusion and enthusiasm that many others in education call "soft stuff" or a waste of time. However, this focus prepares and motivates students for academic learning and increases the effectiveness of all instructional programs.

Our SDP focus on student development taps into an imperative that is stronger than that for academic learning, but when integrated, facilitates it. It may be the only comprehensive school reform approach that simultaneously provides parents, staff, and students with the skill sets that make future school and life success more likely.

Additionally, the SDP is a framework or tool that is respectful of staff knowledge and skill, while helping them to help themselves become more effective. It is not a magic pill or treatment. It promotes individual and organizational growth among all the participants. Once the process is internalized, growth is experienced in an organic way, and school communities expand their capacity for self- and building-level change and improvement. The SDP promotes creativity within self-made boundaries and is modified through self- and group-study and assessment. With careful attention to the training of new participants, and periodic renewal among all, the SDP process makes continual and sustained growth possible. It does not promote an "anything goes" spirit. Instead, the SDP promotes a willingness to build on effective practice and to modify less effective practices, as indicated by assessment and reflection.

Some believe that it is too slow and difficult. Initially, this was a weakness. Currently, most schools can expect social and academic changes in one to two years. The implementation of SDP, however, is not a quick fix. Moreover, it moves many people out of their comfort zones and promotes resistance among some. As mentioned above, we are sometimes almost voted out in some schools, and sometimes actually voted out, before the process takes hold. Yet, our experience suggests that once a staff member takes the time to learn and internalize the model, the effects last longer and become organic in a way that is less likely with prescriptive programs.

Another "good problem" or weakness is that, once successful, some claim that their leadership, not the SDP, was responsible, even when a school was not successful previously. The claim is partially true. We want the schools to feel ownership of their effort and outcomes, but also to understand that they have become more effective because they are using the SDP as a tool, and it is the tool that helps them help students develop and learn. The "I did it" response usually means that the leaders do not fully understand the SDP principles or process. We have observed that such schools lose their gains in time as a result. If school improvement rests on the hard work and personality of the leader, we are left with the impossible task of finding an enormous number of remarkable leaders. The SDP provides a framework and principles that most reasonably intelligent and effective people can use to be successful.

Finally, it has the weakness of all models. It cannot be sustained without extensive "buy in" or acceptance of developmental principles and knowledge of how to use them in practice. For all of us, it is very difficult to modify practice when what we are being asked to do was not a part of our initial professional development and not a part of the way that we have been working. Indeed, we are being asked to give up what once, in many cases, received praise. Change is all the more difficult when it is not easy initially and when strong support and training for the different practice is not readily available. Many parents, educators, and the education enterprise as a whole remain skeptical. With this current level of skepticism, even good implementation and outcomes are not convincing to those who have not directly observed the remarkable change that occurs within young people. We have been told, "But that (high performance) can't happen with *our* kids!"

***Implications for School Reform*** The major implication of our SDP experience is that the key adult persons in all three networks in which children live, parents, school people, opinion leaders, and policy makers, should be able to create an environment that will help students develop and learn. There are important implications for theorists and researchers as well. Because schools, with a 3 million-person workforce, are specifically charged with the education mission and strategically located in the lives of students, they are in the best position to inform and influence all of the others. Thus, I will discuss what our work suggests can and should be done to support the preparation and practice of administrators and teachers.

Because of the traditional focus on curriculum, instruction, assessment, and resource utilization, most preparatory institutions are not able to help their students create environments that promote child development and academic learning in practice. The strong integration of development and pedagogy into theory, research, and practice is rare. The knowledge and skills needed for such integration and application must be moved from places where they now reside into preparatory institutions or programs and, from there, into education practice.

Widespread "buy in" and change cannot take place on a large scale or be sustained through action research projects such as the SDP. The skills and knowledge needed to create supportive school environments and to apply child and adolescent behavior principles must be built into the fabric of teacher and administrator preparation nationwide. Once a sufficiently large pool of educators understand and apply developmental principles in practice, they can then help students, parents, community organizations, researchers, opinion leaders, and policy makers understand and use the principles to support schools through their respective and related work.

Out-of-school programs and people are important to child and youth development but are not as well positioned or as potentially powerful as are schools. The intense, goal-oriented, longer duration, and continuous teacher and staff interactions with students in school are likely to have a much greater impact on student development than the necessarily more fragmented and probably less continuous interactions that students will have with adult teachers, coaches, and others in nonschool settings. Additionally, schools are in a better position to make adjustments to meet student needs.

Development and learning are incremental processes that take place best over a sustained period, from preschool through the 12th to the 16th year (or to maturity). With schools organized to promote student development, community organizations with similar goals can work hand-in-hand with schools in a mutually beneficial way. Collaboration between schools and community agencies along these lines would broaden the support for the development that young people need to experience in their schools and communities.

Our society should do much more to help parents gain the knowledge and skills needed to rear their children in a way that supports their development from birth forward. Support for parents and their efforts to promote development could be strengthened through schools' focus on development that works back into homes and communities. This focus would help to connect students and their families to mainstream opportunities.

Such changes will not be easy. Inertia, from many sources, is massive. The way underdevelopment or underachievement is related to many of our nation's most pressing social problems is not apparent to most. Even where there is interest in the connection, there is doubt that attention to underdevelopment can adequately address these problems. Thus, while there is a sense of urgency about the need to improve education, there is not strong support for a major focus on child and adolescent development.

Frustration and the promise of a quick fix make us vulnerable to fads, gimmicks, and non-child-centered reforms rather than the application of developmental principles. Further, the increased use of test scores as evidence of school effectiveness is moving us away from rallying our efforts to promote students' developmental needs. Even before the national focus on test scores, the media made little effort to understand schooling. Thus, there is little exploration of what it will actually take to prepare students to become lifelong learners, workers, family members, and citizens. Nevertheless, there are a few hopeful signs.

Several major educational organizations, including the Association of Supervisors and Curriculum Developers (ASCD) and the National Council for Accreditation of Teacher Education (NCATE), have called attention to the need to promote the whole child and possibly create new accreditation standards that require administrators and teachers to demonstrate their ability to apply child development principles in practice. At least one state has passed legislation requiring school staff to have child development and mental health promotion knowledge and skills. Some districts are working with new teachers facing organizational, management, and child development challenges.

Some state departments of education are beginning to explore ways to help school staff acquire child development application knowledge and skills. This movement can eventually help preparatory programs focus on providing opportunities to help educators make "child developer" a part of their professional identity, a part of what is required to be a teacher. As a result, their resistance to using such principles will decrease.

An infrastructure or framework for change is needed. I have made the argument that something close to the Agricultural Extension Service that was used to make a major shift to science-based farming a century ago, against great inertia and resistance, could be useful in education. The Extension Service brought new knowledge and skills about farming from public and private sources to farmers through university-based and other agencies. The agents, and eventually more successful farmers, helped policy makers and the public understand the need for change.

One aspect of our current SDP work, the University Partners Program, is a tiny pilot model of how an Extension Service might work in education. We are working with several university, school district, and policy-maker groups to explore ways to incorporate the application of child and adolescent development principles into day-to-day education practice.

## Summary and Conclusions

The Yale Child Study Center School Development Program is a school improvement process model as well as a set of principles relative to child and adolescent development and growth in school. The project began as a response to the question of why some low-income minority group students did well in school, while too many others did not. Additionally, it was an effort to determine whether a positive mental health approach could be as or more effective than direct therapeutic efforts with children demonstrating learning and behavior problems in school.

The pilot project initiated in 1968 resulted in a nine-element change model that is still at the core of all SDP work. When implemented well, the nine elements of our school reform process model help school people and systems organize and manage in a way that creates a good environment or culture, promotes student and adult growth and development, and facilitates continuous improvement in instruction and learning. The successful pilot was field tested and then disseminated in over 1,000 schools. Multiple studies demonstrate the effectiveness of the SDP. These findings support the initial belief that development and learning are inextricably linked as well as support the theory that creating school environments that support student development leads to students' improvement in academics and behavior.

When we began our work, it was widely believed that such students could not do well in school. Parents, students, and staff in such schools were often drowning in a sea of hopelessness and despair. In 1994, (the late) James Coleman, a University of Chicago sociologist and an educator researcher, quizzically mentioned to me that the people in the SDP schools in Chicago were very enthusiastic. I say "quizzically" because, at the time, hope and enthusiasm were uncommon in many low-income schools, and the connection between good school climate and achievement in such settings had not yet been fully explained or accepted. The role of the environment in promoting development and academic achievement remains greatly underappreciated.

The major implication of the SDP, our successes, and limitations, is that, in a supportive environment or culture, all students can learn at an acceptable level. Such environments, however, are not natural; they must be created. To make this possible for all students nationwide, all teachers and administrators should be prepared to create supportive environments that will promote student development in the service of academic learning and improved behavior. Because this would be a massive change against many sources of resistance, a national infrastructure, similar to what was used to improve American agriculture, will be needed to significantly improve the quality of education nationwide.

## Notes

1. This chapter primarily draws on research by James Comer and, therefore, is written in the first person.
2. I wrote about my growing up experiences in Maggie's American Dream (see Comer, 1988a).
3. For further information about the model in the five districts, see http://www.schooldevelopmentprogram.org/about/achievements.html.

## References

Borman, G. D., Hewes, G. M., Overman, L. T., & Brown, S. (2003). Comprehensive school reform and student achievement: A meta-analysis. *Review of Educational Research, 73*(2), 125–230.
Bronfenbrenner, U. (1979). *The ecology of human development.* Cambridge, MA: Harvard University Press.
Cauce, A., Comer, J., & Schwartz, D. (1987). Long-term effects of a systems-oriented prevention project. *American Journal of Orthopsychiatry, 57,* 127–131.
Coleman, J. S., Campbell, E., Hobson, C., McPartland, J., Mood, A., Weinfeld, R., et al. (1966). *Equality of educational opportunity.* Washington, DC: U.S. Government Printing Office.
Comer, J. P. (1980). *School power: Implications of an intervention project.* New York: Free Press.
Comer, J. P. (1988a). *Maggie's American dream: The life and times of a black family.* New York: New American Library.
Comer, J. P. (1988b). Educating poor minority children. *Scientific American, 259,* 42–49.
Comer, J. P. (2004). *Leave no child behind: Preparing today's youth for tomorrow's world.* New Haven, CT: Yale University Press.
Comer, J. P. (2005). Child and adolescent development: The critical missing focus in school reform. *Phi Delta Kappan, 86*(10), 757–763.
Comer, J. P., & Haynes, N. M. (1999). The dynamics of school change: Response to the article, "Comer's School Development Program in

Prince George's County, Maryland: A theory-based evaluation," by Thomas D. Cook et al. *American Educational Research Journal, 36*(3), 599–607.

Cook, T. D., Habib, F., Phillips, M., Settersten, R. A., Shagle, S. C., & Degirmencioglu, S. M. (1999). Comer's School Development Program in Prince George's County, Maryland: A theory-based evaluation. *American Educational Research Journal, 36*(3), 543–597.

Cook, T. D., Murphy, R. F., & Hunt, H. D. (2000). Comer's School Development Program in Chicago: A theory-based evaluation. *American Educational Research Journal, 37*(2), 535–597.

Edmonds, R. (1982). Programs of school improvement: An overview. *Educational Leadership, 40*(3), 4–11.

Emmons, C. (2004). Assessing system reform: How do you know that the Comer process is making a difference in your school or district? In E. T. Joyner, M. Ben-Avie, & J. P. Comer (Eds.), *Dynamic instructional leadership to support student learning and development* (pp. 215–239). Thousand Oaks, CA: Corwin Press.

Epstein, J. L., & Becker, H. J. (1982). Teachers' reported practices of parent involvement: Problems and possibilities. *The Elementary School Journal, 83*(2), 103–113.

Garbarino, J., & Abromowitz, R. H. (1992). The ecology of human development. In J. Garbarino (Ed.), *Children and families in the social environment* (pp. 11–33). New York: Aldine de Gruyter.

Gonzalez, C. (2004). Schools in society. In J. P. Comer, E. T. Joyner, & M. Ben-Avie (Eds.), *Six pathways to healthy child development and academic success* (pp. 25–28). Thousand Oaks, CA: Corwin Press.

Hart, A. H., McLaughlin, M., Ennis, E., & Stone, W. S. (2004). Systemic reform: We started with one school. In E. T. Joyner, M. Ben-Avie, & J. P. Comer (Eds.), *Dynamic instructional leadership to support student learning and development* (pp. 29–36). Thousand Oaks, CA: Corwin Press.

Haycock, K. (2006). No more invisible kids. *Educational Leadership, 64*(3), 8–42.

Joyner, E. T., Ben-Avie, M., & Comer, J. P. (Eds.). (2004). *Dynamic instructional leadership to support student learning and development.* Thousand Oaks, CA: Corwin Press.

McDonald, J. P., Hatch, T., Kirby, E., Ames, N., Haynes, N. M., & Joyner, E. T. (1999). *School reform behind the scenes: How ATLAS is shaping the future of education.* New York: Teachers College Press.

Millsap, M. A., Chase, A., Obdeidallah, D., Perez-Smith, A., Brigham, N., & Johnston, K. (2000). *Evaluation of Detroit's Comer schools and families initiative: Final report.* Cambridge, MA: Abt.

National Commission on Teaching and America's Future. (2003). *No dream denied: A pledge to America's children.* Washington, DC: Author.

Noblit, G. W., Malloy, W. W., & Malloy, C. E. (2001). *The kids got smarter: Case studies of successful Comer Schools.* Cresskill, NJ: Hampton Press.

Payne, C. M. (1994). *The Comer School Development process in Chicago: An interim report.* Evanston, IL: Northwestern University, Center for Urban Affairs and Policy Research.

Pinner, F. (1962). The crisis of the state universities: Analysis and remedies. In J. Adelson & S. Nevitt (Ed.), *The American college: A psychological and social interpretation of the higher learning* (pp. 940–971). New York: Wiley.

Ray, C. P. (2004). A demonstration of Comer-in-the-classroom. In E. Joyner, M. Ben-Avie, & J. P. Comer (Eds.), *Dynamic instructional leadership to support student learning and development* (pp. 83–92). Thousand Oaks, CA: Corwin Press.

Springfield, S., Millsap, M. A., Yoder, N., Brigham, N., Nesselrodt, P., Schaffer, E., et al. (1995). *Urban and suburban/rural special strategies for educating disadvantaged children: Third year report.* Washington, DC: Office of Planning, U.S. Department of Education.

Sternberg, R. J. (2003). What is an "expert student?" *Educational Researcher, 32*(8), 5–9.

Turnball, B., Fiester, L., & Wodatch, J. (1997). *A process is not a program: An early look at the Comer Process in Community School District 13* (Report to the Rockefeller Foundation). Washington, DC: Policy Studies.

Wong, P. L., Oberman, I., Mintrop, H., & Gamson, D. (1996). *Evaluation of the San Francisco Foundation Bay Area school reform portfolio* (Summary report). Stanford, CA: Stanford University.

Zigler, E., & Finn-Stevenson, M. (1989). Child care in America: From problem to solution. *Educational Policy, 3*, 313–329.

# 27

# Success for All

*Prevention and Early Intervention in School-Wide Reform*

Robert E. Slavin and Nancy A. Madden

Despite the constant public outcry about the crisis in American education, every community has one or more outstanding and often widely recognized public schools. Some of these appear to succeed because they serve children of wealthy, well-educated parents, or because they are magnet schools that can screen out unmotivated or low achieving students. However, there are also schools that serve disadvantaged and minority children in inner city or rural locations and, year after year, produce outstanding achievement outcomes. Such schools play a crucial role in reminding us that the problems of our school system have little to do with the capabilities of children; they provide our best evidence that all children can learn. Yet the success of these lighthouse schools does not spread very far. Excellence can be demonstrated in many individual schools but rarely in whole districts or communities. An outstanding elementary school benefits about 500 children, on average. Yet there are millions of children who are placed at risk by ineffective responses to such factors as economic disadvantage, limited English proficiency, or learning difficulties. How can we make excellence the norm rather than the exception, especially in schools serving many at-risk children? How can effective practices based on research and on the experiences of outstanding schools be effectively implemented every day by hundreds of thousands of teachers?

Success for All was designed in an attempt to answer these questions. Born in one Baltimore school in 1987, Success for All is used (as of fall, 2009) in more than 1,000 schools in 48 states, plus schools in Britain, Canada, and Israel. More than 2 million children have attended Success for All schools. These schools are highly diverse. They are in most of the largest urban districts, but also hundreds of rural districts, inner suburban districts, and Indian reservations. Most are Title I school-wide projects with many children qualifying for free lunches, but many are in much less impoverished circumstances. Success for All is by far the largest research-based, whole-school reform model

ever to exist. It is the first model to demonstrate that techniques shown to be effective in rigorous research can be replicated on a substantial scale with fidelity and continued effectiveness.

The purpose of this chapter is to describe Success for All, its rationale, and its research base, as one example of a replicable approach to prevention and early intervention in elementary schools.

## Success for All: Prevention and Early Intervention

With few exceptions, children enter kindergarten with enthusiasm, intelligence, creativity, and an expectation that they will succeed. The first goal of school reform should be to ensure that every child, regardless of home background, home language, or learning style, achieves the success that he or she so confidently expected in kindergarten, that all children maintain their motivation, enthusiasm, and optimism because they are objectively succeeding at the school's tasks. Any reform that does less than this is hollow and self-defeating.

What does it mean to succeed in the elementary grades? The elementary school's definition of success, and therefore the parents' and children's definition as well, is overwhelmingly success in reading. Very few children who are reading adequately are retained, assigned to special education, or given long-term remedial services. Other subjects are important, of course, but reading and language arts form the core of what school success means in the early grades.

When a child fails to read well in the early grades, he or she begins a downward progression. In first grade, some children begin to notice that they are not reading adequately. They may fail first grade or be assigned to long term remediation. As they proceed through the elementary and middle grades, many students begin to see that they are failing at their full-time jobs. When this happens, things begin to unravel. Failing students begin to have poor motivation and poor self-expectations, which lead to continued poor

434

achievement, in a declining spiral that ultimately leads to despair, delinquency, and dropout.

Remediating learning deficits after they are already well established is extremely difficult. Children who have already failed to learn to read, for example, are now anxious about reading, and doubt their ability to learn it. Their motivation to read may be low. They may ultimately learn to read but it will always be a chore, not a pleasure. Clearly, the time to provide additional help to children who are at risk is early, when children are still motivated and confident and when any learning deficits are relatively small and remediable. The most important goal in educational programming for students at risk of school failure is to try to make certain that we do not squander the greatest resource we have: the enthusiasm and positive self-expectations of young children themselves.

In practical terms, what this perspective implies is that schools, and especially Title I, special education, and other services for at-risk children, must be shifted from an emphasis on remediation to an emphasis on prevention and early intervention. Prevention means providing developmentally appropriate preschool and kindergarten programs so that students will enter first grade ready to succeed, and it means providing regular classroom teachers with effective instructional programs, curricula, and professional development to enable them to ensure that most students are successful the first time they are taught. Early intervention means that supplementary instructional services are provided early in students' schooling and that they are intensive enough to bring at-risk students quickly to a level at which they can profit from good quality classroom instruction.

Success for All is built around the idea that every child can and must succeed in the early grades, no matter what this takes. The idea behind the program is to use everything we know about effective instruction for students at risk to direct all aspects of school and classroom organization toward the goal of preventing academic deficits from appearing in the first place; recognizing and intensively intervening with any deficits that do appear; and providing students with a rich and full curriculum to enable them to build on their firm foundation in basic skills. The commitment of Success for All is to do whatever it takes to see that every child becomes a skilled, strategic, and enthusiastic reader by the end of the elementary grades and beyond.

Usual practices in elementary schools do not support the principle of prevention and early intervention. Starting in first grade, a certain number of students begin to fall behind, and over the course of time these students are assigned to remedial programs (such as Title I) or to special education, or are simply retained.

Our society's tacit assumption is that those students who fall by the wayside are defective in some way. Perhaps they have learning disabilities, or low IQs, or poor motivation, or parents who are unsupportive of school learning, or other problems. We assume that since most students do succeed with standard instruction in the early grades, there must be something wrong with those who don't.

Success for All is built around a completely different set of assumptions. The most important assumption is that every child can learn. In particular, every child without organic retardation can learn to read. Some children need more help than others and may need different approaches than those needed by others, but one way or another every child can become a successful reader.

The first requirement for the success of every child is *prevention*. This means providing excellent preschool and kindergarten programs, improving curriculum, instruction, and classroom management throughout the grades, assessing students frequently to make sure they are making adequate progress, and establishing cooperative relationships with parents so they can support students learning at home.

Top-quality curriculum and instruction from age 4 on will ensure the success of most students, but not all of them. The next requirement for the success of *all* students is *intensive early intervention*. This means one-to-one tutoring for primary-grade students having reading problems. It means being able to work with parents and social service agencies to be sure that all students attend school, have medical services or eyeglasses if they need them, have help with behavior problems, and so on.

The most important idea in Success for All is that the school must relentlessly stick with every child until that child is succeeding. If prevention is not enough the child may need tutoring. If this is not enough he or she may need help with behavior or attendance or eyeglasses. If this is not enough a modified approach to reading or other subjects may be needed. The school does not merely provide services to children, it constantly assesses the results of the services it provides and keeps varying or adding services until every child is successful.

***Overview of Success for All Components*** Success for All has somewhat different components at different sites, depending on the school's needs and resources available to implement the program. However, there is a common set of elements characteristic of all.

*Reading Program* Success for All uses a reading curriculum based on research and effective practices in beginning reading (e.g., Adams, 1990), and an appropriate use of cooperative learning (Slavin, 1995; Stevens, Madden, Slavin, & Farnish, 1987).

Reading teachers at every grade level begin the reading time by reading children's literature to students and engaging them in a discussion of the story to enhance their understanding of the story, listening and speaking vocabulary, and knowledge of story structure. In kindergarten and first grade, the program emphasizes development of basic language skills with the use of Story Telling and Retelling (STaR), which involves the students in listening to, retelling, and dramatizing children's literature. Big books as well as oral and written composing activities allow students to develop concepts of print as they also develop knowledge of story structure. Specific oral language experiences are used to further develop receptive and expressive language.

*Reading Roots* (Madden, 1995) is introduced in the second semester of kindergarten. This K-1 beginning reading program uses as its base a series of phonetically regular but meaningful and interesting minibooks and emphasizes repeated oral reading to partners as well as to the teacher. The minibooks begin with a set of "shared stories," in which part of a story is written in small type (read by the teacher) and part is written in large type (read by the students). The student portion uses a phonetically controlled vocabulary. Taken together, the teacher and student portions create interesting, worthwhile stories. Over time, the teacher portion diminishes and the student portion lengthens, until students are reading the entire book. This scaffolding allows students to read interesting literature when they only have a few letter sounds.

Letters and letter sounds are introduced in an active, engaging set of activities that begins with oral language and moves into written symbols. Individual sounds are integrated into a context of words, sentences, and stories. Instruction is provided in story structure, specific comprehension skills, metacognitive strategies for self-assessment and self-correction, and integration of reading and writing.

Spanish bilingual programs use an adaptation of *Reading Roots* called *Lee Conmigo* ("Read With Me"). *Lee Conmigo* uses the same instructional strategies as *Reading Roots*, but is built around shared stories written in Spanish.

When students reach the second grade reading level, they use a program called *Reading Wings* (Slavin, Madden, Chambers, & Haxby, 2009; Madden et al. 2007), an adaptation of Cooperative Integrated Reading and Composition (CIRC) (Stevens, Madden, Slavin, & Farnish, 1987). *Reading Wings* uses cooperative learning activities built around story structure, prediction, summarization, vocabulary building, decoding practice, and story-related writing. Students engage in partner reading and structured discussion of stories or novels, and work toward mastery of the vocabulary and content of the story in teams. Story-related writing is also shared within teams. Cooperative learning both increases students' motivation and engages students in cognitive activities known to contribute to reading comprehension, such as elaboration, summarization, and rephrasing (Slavin, 1995). Research on CIRC has found it to significantly increase students' reading comprehension and language skills (Stevens et al., 1987).

In addition to these story-related activities, teachers provide direct instruction in reading comprehension skills, and students practice these skills in their teams. Classroom libraries of trade books at students' reading levels are provided for each teacher, and students read books of their choice for homework for 20 minutes each night. Home readings are shared via presentations, summaries, puppet shows, and other formats twice a week during "book club" sessions.

Materials to support *Reading Wings* through the sixth grade level (and beyond) exist in English and Spanish. The English materials are built around children's literature and around the most widely used basal series and anthologies. Supportive materials have been developed for more than 100 children's novels and for most current basal series (e.g., Houghton Mifflin, Scott Foresman, Harcourt, Macmillan, Open Court). The upper-elementary Spanish program, *Alas para Leer*, is built around Spanish-language novels and basal series.

Beginning in the second semester of program implementation, Success for All schools usually implement a writing/language arts program based primarily on cooperative learning principles (see Slavin, Madden, & Stevens, 1989/90).

Students in grades 1 and up are regrouped for reading. The students are assigned to heterogeneous, age-grouped classes most of the day, but during a regular 90-minute reading period they are regrouped by reading performance levels into reading classes of students all at the same level. For example, a reading class taught at the 2–1 level might contain first, second, and third grade students all reading at the same level. The reading classes are smaller than homerooms because tutors and other certificated staff (such as librarians or art teachers) teach reading during this common reading period.

Regrouping allows teachers to teach the whole reading class without having to break the class into reading groups. This greatly reduces the time spent in seatwork and increases direct instruction time, eliminating workbooks, dittos, or other follow-up activities which are needed in classes that have multiple reading groups. The regrouping is a form of the Joplin Plan, which has been found to increase reading achievement in the elementary grades (Slavin, 1987).

*Quarterly Reading Assessments*   At 9-week intervals, reading teachers assess student progress through the reading program. The results of the assessments are used to determine who is to receive tutoring, to change students' reading groups, to suggest other adaptations in students' programs, and to identify students who need other types of assistance, such as family interventions or screening for vision and hearing problems.

*Reading Tutors*   One of the most important elements of the Success for All model is the use of tutors to promote students' success in reading. One-to-one tutoring is the most effective form of instruction known (see Slavin, Karweit, & Madden, 1989; Wasik & Slavin, 1993). Most tutors are certified teachers with experience teaching Title 1, special education, or primary reading. Often, well-qualified paraprofessionals also tutor children with less severe reading problems. Tutors work one-on-one with students who are having difficulties keeping up with their reading groups. The tutoring occurs in 20-minute sessions during times other than reading or math periods.

In general, tutors support students' success in the regular reading curriculum, rather than teaching different objectives. For example, the tutor generally works with a student on the same story and concepts being read and taught in the regular reading class. However, tutors seek to identify learning problems and use different strategies to teach the same skills. They also teach metacognitive skills beyond those taught in the classroom program. Schools may have as many as six or more teachers serving as tutors depending on school size, need for tutoring, and other factors.

During daily 90-minute reading periods, certified teacher-tutors serve as additional reading teachers to reduce class size for reading. Brief forms are used by reading teachers and tutors to communicate about students' specific problems and needs and they meet at regular times to coordinate their approaches with individual children.

Initial decisions about reading group placement and the need for tutoring are based on informal reading inventories that the tutors give to each child. Subsequent reading group placements and tutoring assignments are made based on curriculum-based assessments given every 8 weeks, which include teacher judgments as well as more formal assessments. First graders receive priority for tutoring, on the assumption that the primary function of the tutors is to help all students be successful in reading the first time, before they fail and become remedial readers.

*Preschool and Kindergarten*    Most Success for All schools provide a half-day preschool or a full-day kindergarten for eligible students. The preschool and kindergarten programs focus on providing a balanced and developmentally appropriate learning experience for young children. The curriculum emphasizes the development and use of language. It provides a balance of academic readiness and nonacademic music, art, and movement activities in a series of thematic units. Readiness activities include use of language development activities and Story Telling and Retelling (STaR), in which students retell stories read by the teachers. Reading instruction begins during the second semester of kindergarten.

*Family Support Team*    Parents are an essential part of the formula for success in Success for All. A Family Support Team (Haxby, Lasaga-Flister, Madden, & Slavin, 1999) works in each school, serving to make families feel comfortable in the school and become active supporters of their child's education as well as providing specific services. The Family Support Team consists of the Title I parent liaison, vice-principal (if any), counselor (if any), facilitator, and any other appropriate staff already present in the school or added to the school staff.

The Family Support Team first works toward good relations with parents and to increase involvement in the schools. Family Support Team members may complete "welcome" visits for new families. They organize many attractive programs in the school, such as parenting skills workshops. Most schools use a program called "Raising Readers" in which parents are given strategies to use in reading with their own children. Family support staff also helps introduce a social skills development program called "Getting Along Together," which gives students peaceful strategies for resolving interpersonal conflicts.

The Family Support Team also intervenes to solve problems. For example, they may contact parents whose children are frequently absent to see what resources can be provided to assist the family in getting their child to school. Family support staff, teachers, and parents work together to solve school behavior problems. Also, family support staff members are called on to provide assistance when students seem to be working at less than their full potential because of problems at home. Families of students who are not receiving adequate sleep or nutrition, need glasses, are not attending school regularly, or are exhibiting serious behavior problems, may receive family support assistance.

The Family Support Team is strongly integrated into the academic program of the school. It receives referrals from teachers and tutors regarding children who are not making adequate academic progress, and thereby constitutes an additional stage of intervention for students in need above and beyond that provided by the classroom teacher or tutor. The Family Support Team also encourages and trains parents and other community members to fulfill numerous volunteer roles within the school, ranging from providing a listening ear to emerging readers to helping in the school cafeteria.

*Program Facilitator*    A program facilitator works at each school to oversee (with the principal) the operation of the Success for All model. The facilitator helps plan the Success for All program, helps the principal with scheduling, and visits classes and tutoring sessions frequently to help teachers and tutors with individual problems. He or she works directly with the teachers on implementation of the curriculum, classroom management, and other issues, helps teachers and tutors deal with any behavior problems or other special problems, and coordinates the activities of the Family Support Team with those of the instructional staff.

*Teachers and Teacher Training*    The teachers and tutors are regular certified teachers. They receive detailed teachers' manuals supplemented by 3 days of in-service at the beginning of the school year, followed by classroom observations and coaching throughout the year. For classroom teachers of grades 1 and above and for reading tutors, training sessions focus on implementation of the reading program (either Reading Roots or Reading Wings), and their detailed teachers' manuals cover general teaching strategies as well as specific lessons. Preschool and kindergarten teachers and aides are trained in strategies appropriate to their students' preschool and kindergarten models. Tutors later receive two additional days of training on tutoring strategies and reading assessment.

Throughout the year, additional inservice presentations are made by the facilitators and other project staff on such topics as classroom management, instructional pace, and cooperative learning. Facilitators also organize many informal sessions to allow teachers to share problems and problem solutions, suggest changes, and discuss individual children. The staff development model used in Success for All emphasizes relatively brief initial training with extensive classroom follow-up, coaching, and group discussion.

*Special Education* Every effort is made to deal with students' learning problems within the context of the regular classroom, as supplemented by tutors, who evaluate students' strengths and weaknesses and develop strategies to teach in the most effective way. In some schools, special education teachers work as tutors and reading teachers with students identified as learning disabled as well as other students experiencing learning problems who are at risk for special education placement. One major goal of Success for All is to keep students with learning problems out of special education if at all possible, and to serve any students who do qualify for special education in a way that does not disrupt their regular classroom experience (Slavin, 1996).

None of the elements of Success for All are completely new or unique. All are based on well-established principles of learning and rigorous instructional research. What is most distinctive about them is their school-wide, coordinated, and proactive plan for translating positive expectations into concrete success for all children. Every child can complete elementary school a confident, strategic, and joyful learner and can maintain the enthusiasm and positive self-expectations they had when they came to first grade. The purpose of Success for All is to see that this vision can become a practical reality in every school.

## Research on Success for All

One of the guiding principles in the development of Success for All is an emphasis on rigorous evaluation. The elements of the program are themselves derived from current research on reading and writing, on early childhood, second language learning, and special education, and on parent involvement, professional development, and school change, among many others. However, it is not enough for a program to be based on good research: it must also be rigorously and repeatedly evaluated in many schools over meaningful periods of time in comparison to similar control schools.

Success for All is arguably the most extensively evaluated school reform model ever to exist. Experimental-control comparisons have been made by researchers at 18 universities and research institutions other than Johns Hopkins, both within the United States and in five other countries. Taken together, more than 50 studies have compared Success for All and control schools on individually administered standardized tests and on state accountability measures.

*Independent Reviews* A number of independent reviews of research on comprehensive school reform and reading programs have all concluded that Success for All is among the most successfully evaluated of programs. Success for All has been cited as one of only two elementary comprehensive designs that met the highest standards for research given in a review of 22 programs done by the Compre-

hensive School Reform Quality Center at the American Institutes for Research (CSRQ, 2005). The CSRQ review identified 31 "convincing" studies of Success for All, 10 for Direct Instruction, and no more than 6 for any other program. The same conclusion was reached in an earlier AIR review (Herman, 1999) and in studies commissioned by the Fordham Foundation (Traub, 1999) and the Milliken Family Foundation (Schacter, 1999). A meta-analysis of research on 29 comprehensive school reforms by Borman, Hewes, Overman, and Brown (2003) listed Success for All among three CSR models with "strongest evidence of effectiveness."

*Longitudinal Studies* Longitudinal experiments evaluating SFA have been carried out since the earliest program implementations in Baltimore and Philadelphia. Later, third-party evaluators at the University of Memphis, Steven Ross, Lana Smith, and their colleagues, added evaluations in many districts across the United States. Studies focusing on English language learners in California have been conducted by researchers at WestEd, a federally funded regional educational laboratory. Each of these evaluations compared Success for All schools to comparison schools on measures of reading performance, starting with cohorts in kindergarten or in first grade and following these students as long as possible (details of the evaluation design appear below). Several studies were able to follow Success for All schools for many years. Data comparing matched SFA and traditional control schools on individual reading measures have been collected from schools in many U.S. districts, and other studies have compared Success for All to a variety of alternative reform models, have compared full and partial implementations of SFA, and have made other comparisons. Most recently, a 3-year national randomized experiment involving 41 schools has compared SFA and control schools. In addition, there have been many studies involving group-administered standardized tests including both national norm-referenced tests and state criterion-referenced tests used in state accountability programs. Experimental-control comparisons have also been carried out in Canada, England, Australia, and Israel.

The largest number of studies has compared the achievement of students in Success for All schools to that of children in matched comparison schools using traditional methods, including locally developed Title I reforms.

A common evaluation design, with variations due to local circumstances, was used in a foundational set of Success for All evaluations carried out by researchers at Johns Hopkins University, the University of Memphis, and WestEd. Each Success for All school was matched with a control school that was similar in poverty level (percent of students qualifying for free lunch), historical achievement level, ethnicity, and other factors. Schools were also matched on district-administered standardized test scores given in kindergarten or on Peabody Picture Vocabulary Test (PPVT) scores given by the evaluators in the fall of kindergarten or first grade.

The measures used in these evaluations were as follows:

1. *Woodcock Reading Mastery Test.* Three Woodcock scales, Word Identification, Word Attack, and Passage Comprehension, were individually administered to students by trained testers. Word Identification assesses recognition of common sight words, Word Attack assesses phonetic synthesis skills, and Passage Comprehension assesses comprehension in context. Students in Spanish bilingual programs were given the Spanish versions of these scales.
2. *Durrell Analysis of Reading Difficulty.* The Durrell Oral Reading scale was also individually administered to students in grades 1 through 3 in some studies. It presents a series of graded reading passages which students read aloud, followed by comprehension questions.
3. *Gray Oral Reading Test.* Comprehension and passage scores from the Gray Oral Reading Test were obtained in some studies from students in grades 4 and 5.

Analyses of covariance with pretests as covariates were used to compare raw scores in all evaluations, and separate analyses were conducted for students in general and, in many studies, for students in the lowest 25% of their grades at pretest.

Each of the evaluations summarized in this chapter follows children who began in Success for All in first grade or earlier, in comparison to children who had attended the control school over the same period. Students who start in SFA after first grade are not considered to have received the full treatment (although they are of course served within the schools).

## Reading Outcomes

### National Randomized Evaluation of Success for All   The definitive evaluation of the reading outcomes of Success for All was a U.S. Department of Education-funded evaluation (Borman et al., 2005a, 2005b; Slavin, Madden, Cheung, et al., 2006) involving 41 Title I schools throughout the United States. Schools were randomly assigned to use Success for All or to continue with their existing reading programs in grades K-2. At the end of the three-year study, children in the Success for All schools were achieving at significantly higher levels than control students on all three measures, using conservative hierarchical linear modeling analyses with school as the unit of analysis. In effect sizes (difference in adjusted posttests divided by unadjusted standard deviations), the differences were ES = +0.38 for Word Attack, ES = +0.23 for Word Identification, and ES = +0.21 for Passage Comprehension. This study is of particular importance for several reasons. First, the use of random assignment to conditions eliminates selection bias (the possibility that schools that chose SFA might have been better schools than the control schools). Random assignment has become extremely important in program evaluation as the U.S. Department of Education has virtually required randomized designs and emphasized this design element in its What Works Clearinghouse reviews of effective programs. Second, the large sample size allows for the use of hierarchical linear modeling (HLM), which uses the school as the unit of analysis. This is the appropriate analysis for school-wide interventions (all previous studies used the student as the unit of analysis). Third, the size of the evaluation is of great importance for the study's policy impact. In small studies, there is always the possibility that researchers can ensure high-quality implementations. Cronbach et al. (1980) called this the "superrealization" of a program's impact, where the program is evaluated at a level of quality far beyond what could be achieved at a large scale. In the Slavin et al. (2006) study, implementation of SFA was actually found to be of lower quality than that typical of SFA schools. A study on such a large scale is a good representation of the likely policy effect, or what would be expected if a district or state implemented the program on a broad scale. For example, the Slavin et al. (2006) findings imply that if many schools serving African American or Hispanic students experienced Success for All, the minority–White achievement gap (about 50% of a standard deviation on the National Assessment of Educational Progress) would be reduced by half.

***Matched Longitudinal Studies***   In the 1990s, researchers at Johns Hopkins University and other research institutions carried out a series of longitudinal matched studies to evaluate Success for All. A common design and set of measures were used for these studies, as noted above. Schools in 13 districts across the country were involved.

The results of the matched experiments evaluating Success for All are summarized in Figure 27.1 for each grade level, 1 through 5, and for follow-up measures into grades 6 and 7. The analyses average cohort means for experimental and control schools. A cohort is all students at a given grade level in a given year. For example, the grade 1 graph compares 68 experimental to 68 control cohorts, with cohort (50–150 students) as the unit of analysis. In other words, each bar is a mean of scores from more than 6,000 students. Grade equivalents are based on the means, and are only presented for their informational value. No analyses were done using grade equivalents.

Combining across studies, statistically significant ($p = .05$ or better) positive effects of Success for All (compared to controls) were found on every measure at every grade level from 1 through 5 (Slavin & Madden, 1993). For students in general, effect sizes averaged around a half standard deviation at all grade levels. Effects were somewhat higher than this for the Woodcock Word Attack scale in first and second grades, but in grades 3 through 5 effect sizes were more or less equivalent on all aspects of reading. Consistently, effect sizes for students in the lowest 25% of their grades were particularly positive, ranging from ES = +1.03 in first grade to ES = +1.68 in fourth grade. Again, cohort-level analyses found statistically significant differences favoring

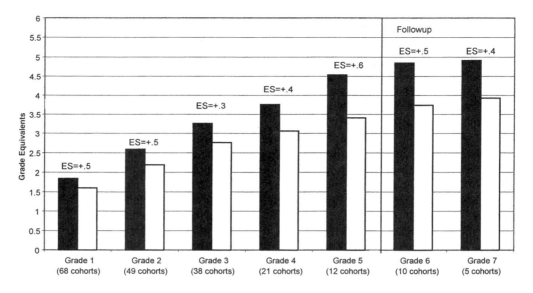

**Figure 27.1** Comparison of Success for All and control schools in mean reading grade equivalents and effect sizes 1988–1999.

low achievers in Success for All on every measure at every grade level. A follow-up study of Baltimore schools found that positive program effects continued into grade 6 (ES = +0.54) and grade 7 (ES = +0.42), when students were in middle schools.

### Long-Term Outcomes

Borman and Hewes (2003) carried out a longitudinal study of children from five Success for All and five control schools in Baltimore. They located children city wide who had attended these schools in first grade and remained from 1 to 6 (mean = 3.8 years). At posttest, students who had been promoted each year would have been in the eighth grade, having been out of a Success for All school for at least 3 years.

Long-term differences were found on achievement, retentions, and special education placements. In achievement, former SFA students still scored significantly better than controls on standardized, district-administered CTBS reading scores (ES = +0.29, p<.001). Surprisingly, there was also a small difference favoring the former SFA students in math (ES = +0.11, p<.05), even though mathematics was not part of the intervention.

Students in Success for All schools were far less likely to have been retained in elementary school. Nine percent of SFA students and 23% of control students had been retained at least once by fifth grade (ES = +0.27, p<.001). Similarly, control students spent 50% more time in special education, on average, than SFA students (ES = +0.18, p<.001).

The importance of the Borman and Hewes (2003) study is in its finding that at entry to high school, former Success for All students were in much better shape than control students. The best predictors of high school success are reading achievement and avoidance of retention and special education placements. Success for All students were substantially higher on all of these measures.

### The Success for All Middle School

The Success for All Middle School was evaluated in a national study by Slavin, Daniels, and Madden (2005). In this study, reading results at the school level from 2001 to 2004 were obtained from state websites. Analyses compared achievement gains on state high-stakes reading measures in SFA middle schools to those in matched comparison schools.

In all of the seven school pairs, students in the SFA Middle Schools gained more on their state reading assessments than did students in comparison schools. In many cases, these differences were striking. For example, at Tahola School, a K-12 school primarily serving Native American students in rural Washington State, the Success for All seventh graders gained 95.5 percentage points, to 100% of students meeting standards on the Washington Assessment of Student Learning (WASL). The comparison school gained 18.4 percentage points, while the state average gained 20.7 percentage points. Similarly, seventh graders at Richards Middle School in rural Missouri gained 31.5 percentage points in students passing the Missouri Assessment Program (MAP) Reading Scale, while a matched control school gained 10.3 points and the state declined by 2.4 points.

Recognizing the problems inherent in averaging across different state measures, it is still interesting to note that across the seven SFA schools, students gained an average of 24.6 percentage points on state reading tests, far better than the gain of 2.2 percentage points in matched control schools and the average gain made by middle schools in their respective states, 4.2 percentage points.

Table 27.1 summarizes the gains in each SFA school, its matched control, and its state.

### Success for All and English Language Learners

The education of English language learners is at a crossroads. On one hand, research on bilingual education continues to

**TABLE 27.1**
**Gains in Percent of Students Passing State Reading Tests in Success for All and Control Middle Schools, 2001 to 2004**

| School (State) | Measure | Grades tested | Gains in Percent Passing | | |
|---|---|---|---|---|---|
| | | | SFA | Control | State |
| Washington | WASL | 7 | +95.5 | +18.4 | +20.7 |
| Missouri | MAP | 7 | +31.5 | +10.3 | +2.4 |
| Indiana—pair 1 | ISTEP | 6, 8 | +9.0 | +0.5 | +7.0 |
| Indiana—pair 2 | ISTEP | 6, 8 | +15.5 | +4.0 | +7.0 |
| Mississippi | MCT | 6, 7 | +5.8 | +2.3 | +8.1 |
| Arizona | AIMS | 8 | +3.0 | −12.0 | −6.0 |
| Louisiana | LEAP | 8 | +12.0 | −8.0 | −5.0 |
| Means* | | | +24.6 | +2.2 | +4.2 |

* Means across different state assessments should be interpreted cautiously.

show that children who are initially taught in their home language and then transitioned to English ultimately read as well or better in English than children taught only in English (National Academy of Sciences, 1998; Slavin & Cheung, 2005). Despite these findings, political pressure against bilingual education, most notably in California's Proposition 227, has mounted in recent years, based largely on the fact that Latino/a children perform less well than Anglo children on achievement tests, whether or not they have been initially taught in Spanish.

While language of instruction is an essential concern for children who are acquiring English, the *quality* of instruction (and corresponding achievement outcomes) is at least as important, whatever the initial language of instruction may be. There is a need for better programs for teaching in the home language and then transitioning to English, and for better programs for teaching English language learners in English with support from English as a second language strategies. Both development and research on Success for All have focused on both of these issues.

Six studies have evaluated adaptations of Success for All with language minority children (see Cheung & Slavin, 2005; Slavin & Madden, 1999). Three of these evaluated *Éxito Para Todos* ("Success for All" in Spanish), the Spanish bilingual adaptation, and three evaluated a program adaptation incorporating strategies for English as a second language.

*Bilingual Studies* One study compared students in *Éxito Para Todos* to those in a matched comparison school in which most reading instruction was in English. Both schools served extremely impoverished, primarily Puerto Rican student bodies in inner-city Philadelphia. Not surprisingly, *Éxito Para Todos* students scored far better than control students on Spanish measures. More important was the fact that after transitioning to all-English instruction by third grade, the *Éxito Para Todos* students scored significantly better than controls on measures of *English* reading. These differences were significant on Word Attack, but not on Word Identification or Passage Comprehension.

An evaluation of *Éxito Para Todos* in California bi-

lingual schools was reported by Livingston and Flaherty (1997), who studied three successive cohorts of students. On Spanish reading measures, *Éxito Para Todos* students scored substantially higher than controls in first grade (ES = +1.03), second grade (ES = +0.44), and third grade (ES = +.23). However, the second and third grade differences almost certainly understate the true effects; the highest-achieving students in the bilingual programs were transitioned early to English-only instruction, and the transition rate was twice as high in the *Éxito Para Todos* classes as in the controls.

A large study in Houston compared LEP first graders in 20 schools implementing *Éxito Para Todos* to those in 10 control schools (Nunnery et al., 1996). As an experiment, schools were allowed to choose Success for All/*Éxito Para Todos* as it was originally designed, or to implement key components. The analysis compared three levels of implementation: high, medium, and low. None of the *Éxito Para Todos* programs were categorized as "high" in implementation because a bilingual teacher shortage made it impossible to hire certified teachers as Spanish tutors, a requirement for the "high implementation" designation. Medium implementation schools significantly exceeded their controls on all measures (mean ES = +0.24). Low implementers exceeded controls on the Spanish Woodcock Word Identification and Word Attack scales, but not on Passage Comprehension (mean ES = +.17).

One additional study evaluated Bilingual Cooperative Integrated Reading and Composition (BCIRC), which is closely related to *Alas Para Leer*, the bilingual adaptation of Reading Wings. This study, in El Paso, Texas, found significantly greater reading achievement (compared to controls) for English language learners in grades 3 through 5 transitioning from Spanish to English reading (Calderón, Hertz-Lazarowitz, & Slavin, 1998).

*ESL Studies* Three studies have evaluated the effects of Success for All with English language learners being taught in English. In this adaptation, English as a second language (ESL) strategies (such as total physical response) are integrated into instruction for all children, whether or not they are limited in English proficiency. The activities of ESL teachers are closely coordinated with those of other classroom teachers, so that ESL instruction directly supports the Success for All curriculum, and ESL teachers often serve as tutors for LEP children.

The first study of Success for All with English language learners took place in Philadelphia. Students in an Asian (mostly Cambodian) Success for All school were compared to those in a matched school that also served many Cambodian-speaking children. Both schools were extremely impoverished, with nearly all children qualifying for free lunches.

At the end of a 6-year longitudinal study, Success for All Asian fourth and fifth graders were performing far ahead of matched controls. On average, they were 2.9 years ahead of controls in fourth grade (median ES = +1.49), and 2.8 years ahead in fifth grade (median ES = +1.33). Success for All Asian students were reading about a full year above grade level in both fourth and fifth grades, while controls were almost 2 years below grade level. Non-Asian students also significantly exceeded their controls at all grade levels (see Cheung & Slavin, 2005; Slavin & Madden, 1999).

The California study described earlier (Livingston & Flaherty, 1997) also included many English language learners who were taught in English. Combining results across three cohorts, Spanish-dominant English language learners performed far better on English reading measures in Success for All than in matched control schools in first grade (ES = +1.36) and second grade (ES= +0.46), but not in third grade (ES = +0.09). As in the bilingual evaluation, the problem with the third grade scores is that many high-achieving children were transitioned out of the ESL designation in the Success for All schools, reducing apparent experimental–control differences. Corresponding effect sizes for students who spoke languages other than English or Spanish were +0.40 for first graders, +0.37 for second graders, and +0.05 for third graders.

An Arizona study (Ross, Nunnery, & Smith, 1996) compared Mexican-American English language learners in two urban Success for All schools to those in three schools using locally developed Title I reform models and one using Reading Recovery. Two SES school strata were compared, one set with 81% of students in poverty and 50% Hispanic students and one with 53% of students in poverty and 27% Hispanic students. Success for All first graders scored higher than controls in both strata. Hispanic students in the high-poverty stratum averaged 3 months ahead of the controls (1.75 vs. 1.45). Hispanic students in the less impoverished stratum scored slightly above grade level (1.93), about one month ahead of controls (1.83).

The effects of Success for All for language minority students are not statistically significant on every measure in every study, but the overall impact of the program is clearly positive, both for the Spanish bilingual adaptation, *Éxito Para Todos,* and for the ESL adaptation. What these findings suggest is that whatever the language of instruction may be, student achievement in that language can be substantially enhanced using improved materials, professional development, and other supports.

***Success for All and Special Education*** The philosophy behind the treatment of special education issues in Success for All is called "neverstreaming" (Slavin, 1996). That is, rather than waiting until students fall far behind, and are assigned to special education, and then may be mainstreamed into regular classes, Success for All schools intervene early and intensively with students who are at risk to try to keep them out of the special education system. Once students are far behind, special education services are unlikely to catch them up to age-appropriate levels of performance. Students who have already failed in reading are likely to have an overlay of anxiety, poor motivation, poor behavior, low self-esteem, and ineffective learning strategies that are likely to interfere with learning no matter how good special education services may be. Ensuring that all students succeed in the first place is a far better strategy, if it can be accomplished. In Success for All, the provision of research-based preschool, kindergarten, and first grade reading, one-to-one tutoring, and family support services are likely to give the most at-risk students a good chance of developing enough reading skills to remain out of special education, or to perform better in special education than would have otherwise been the case.

The data relating to special education outcomes clearly support these expectations. Several studies have focused on questions related to special education. One of the most important outcomes in this area is the consistent finding of particularly large effects of Success for All for students in the lowest 25% of their classes. While effect sizes for students in general have averaged around + 0.50 on individually administered reading measures, effect sizes for the lowest achievers have averaged in the range of +1.00 to +1.50 across the grades. In the longitudinal Baltimore study only 2.2% of third graders averaged 2 years behind grade level, a usual criterion for special education placement. In contrast, 8.8% of control third graders scored this poorly. Baltimore data also showed a reduction in special education placements for learning disabilities of about half (Slavin et al., 1992). A longitudinal study following Baltimore children to eighth grade found that students who had been in control schools had spent 50% more time in special education, on average, than those who had been in SFA schools (Borman & Hewes, 2003). A study of two Success for All schools in Ft. Wayne, Indiana found that over a 2-year period 3.2% of Success for All students in grades K-1 and 1-2 were referred to special education for learning disabilities or mild mental handicaps. In contrast, 14.3% of control students were referred in these categories (Smith, Ross, & Casey, 1994).

Taken together, these findings support the conclusion that Success for All both reduces the need for special education services (by raising the reading achievement of very low achievers) and reduces special education referrals and placements. Both of these outcomes have significant consequences for long-term costs of educating students placed at risk.

Another important question concerns the effects of the program on students who have already been assigned to special education. Here again, there is evidence from different sources. In the study comparing Reading Recovery and Success for All described above, it so happened that first graders in special education in the Reading Recovery group were not tutored, but instead received traditional special education services in resource rooms. In the Success for All schools, first graders who had been assigned to special education were tutored one-to-one (by their special education teachers) and otherwise participated in the program in the same way as all other students. As noted earlier, special education students in Success for All were reading substantially better (ES = +.77) than special education students in the comparison school (Ross, Smith, Nunnery, & Sterbin, 1995). In addition, Smith et al. (1994) combined first grade reading data from special education students in Success for All and control schools in four districts: Memphis, Tennessee, Ft. Wayne, Indiana, Montgomery, Alabama, and Caldwell, Idaho. Success for All special education students scored substantially better than controls (mean ES = +.59).

***Embedding Technology in Success for All***  In recent years, the Success for All Foundation has added two technology tools to its early reading programs, and studies of these additions find them to be effective in improving students' reading performance. Reading Reels, used in kindergarten and first grade classes, provides appealing video content to supplement Reading Roots. This includes animations to teach letter sounds, puppet skits to teach sound blending, and live action skits to teach vocabulary. In a study in which schools in Hartford, Connecticut were randomly assigned to use SFA either with or without Reading Reels, students who experienced the videos performed significantly better on the Woodcock Word Attack scale than those who did not experience Reading Reels (Chambers, Cheung, Madden, Slavin, & Gifford, in press).

The second technology enhancement is called *Alphie's Alley*. It is designed for use in SFA tutoring. *Alphie's Alley* helps tutors assess their students, plan their instruction, and provide them with compelling, animated presentations and practice opportunities. Embedded in the content are professional development videos in which experienced tutors demonstrate tutoring strategies. A study involving 25 SFA schools randomly assigned children in tutoring (and their tutors) to tutoring with or without *Alphie's Alley*. In schools that used the program as intended, *Alphie's Alley* students scored significantly better than students given usual paper-and-pencil tutoring on the Woodcock Letter-Word Identification and Word Attack scales as well as DIBELS Fluency (Chambers, Abrami, Tucker et al., 2005).

A third randomized study evaluated outcomes in schools that used both *Reading Reels* and *Alphie's Alley*. Students who received tutoring and experienced both embedded technology interventions scored substantially better than tutored SFA students who did not experience the technology on the Woodcock Letter-Word and Word Attack scales and the Gray Oral Reading Test Fluency and Comprehension scales. Students who were not tutored, and therefore experienced *Reading Reels* but not *Alphie's Alley*, also scored better than non-tutored SFA students who did not experience the videos on Woodcock and Gray reading measures (Chambers, Slavin, et al., 2005).

These studies suggest that using multimedia content embedded in teachers' lessons along with Success for All can significantly enhance learning for children. This type of application, in which technology supplements instead of replacing teachers' instruction, may help teachers reinforce content and skills through visual as well as auditory pathways. The positive findings have led the Success for All Foundation to include both *Reading Reels* and *Alphie's Alley* as standard components of Reading Roots.

**Conclusion**

The results of evaluations of dozens of Success for All schools in districts in all parts of the United States clearly show that the program increases student reading performance. A large, national randomized evaluation found clear positive effects of the program, compared to a control group. Across 50 matched studies done by dozens of researchers, Success for All students learned significantly more than matched control students. Significant effects were not seen on every measure at every grade level, but the consistent direction and magnitude of the effects show unequivocal benefits for Success for All students. Effects on district-administered standardized tests and criterion-referenced tests used in state accountability programs reinforce the findings of the studies using individually administered tests. Large impacts have been seen on the achievement of limited English proficient students in both bilingual and ESL programs, and on both reducing special education referrals and improving the achievement of students who have been assigned to special education.

The Success for All evaluations have used reliable and valid measures, in particular individually administered tests that are sensitive to all aspects of reading: comprehension, fluency, word attack, and word identification. Positive effects on state accountability assessments and on other standardized measures have also been documented many times. Performance of Success for All students has been compared to that of students in similar control schools, who provide the best indication of what students without the program would have achieved. Replication of high-quality experiments in such a wide variety of schools and districts is extremely unusual. As noted earlier, reviews of research by the American Institutes for Research (Herman, 1999), Borman et al. (2003), the Comprehensive School Reform Quality Center (2005), and the Fordham Foundation (Traub, 1999) all found Success for All to be one of only two or three comprehensive elementary reform models to have rigorous, frequently replicated evidence of effectiveness.

An important indicator of the robustness of Success for All is the fact that schools stay with the program. In 2006, the median school used SFA for 6 years. When schools do drop the program, it is usually due to a district decision (forced by policy changes or funding cuts), not a school decision. Hundreds of Success for All schools have survived changes of superintendents, principals, facilitators, and other key staff, major cuts in funding, and other serious threats to program maintenance.

The research summarized here demonstrates that comprehensive, systemic school-by-school change can take place on a broad scale in a way that maintains the integrity and effectiveness of the model. The schools we have studied are typical of the larger set of schools currently using Success for All in terms of quality of implementation, resources, demographic characteristics, and other factors. Program outcomes are not limited to the original home of the program. The widely held idea based on the RAND study of innovation (Berman & McLaughlin, 1978, 1990) that comprehensive school reform must be invented by school staffs themselves is certainly not supported in research on Success for All. While the program is adapted to meet the needs of each school, and while school staffs must agree to implement the program by a vote of 80% or more, Success for All is an externally developed program with specific materials, manuals, and structures. The observation that the program can be implemented and maintained over considerable time periods and can be effective in each of its replication sites certainly supports the idea that every school staff need not reinvent the wheel.

## Author Note

Portions of this chapter are adapted from Slavin, R. E., Madden, N.A., Chambers, B., & Haxby, B. (2009). *Two million children: Success for all* (2nd ed.). Thousand Oaks, CA: Corwin. Reprinted with permission.

## References

Adams, M. J. (1990). *Beginning to read: Thinking and learning about print.* Cambridge, MA: MIT Press.

Berman, P., & McLaughlin, M. (1978). *Federal programs supporting educational change: A model of education change: Vol. 8. Implementing and sustaining innovations.* Santa Monica, CA: RAND.

Borman, G., & Hewes, G. (2003). Long-term effects and cost effectiveness of Success for All. *Educational Evaluation and Policy Analysis, 24*(2), 243–266.

Borman, G. D., Hewes, G. M., Overman, L. T., & Brown, S. (2003). Comprehensive school reform and achievement: A meta-analysis. *Review of Educational Research, 73*(2), 125–230.

Borman, G. D., Slavin, R. E., Cheung, A., Chamberlain, A., Madden, N., & Chambers, B. (2005a). Success for All: First year results from the national randomized field trial. *Educational Evaluation and Policy Analysis, 27*(1), 1–22.

Borman, G., Slavin, R. E., Cheung, A., Chamberlain, A., Madden, N. A., & Chambers, B. (2005b). The national randomized field trial of Success for All: Second-year outcomes. *American Educational Research Journal 42*(4), 673–696.

Calderón, M., Hertz-Lazarowitz, R., & Slavin, R. E. (1998). Effects of bilingual cooperative integrated reading and composition on students making the transition from Spanish to English reading. *Elementary School Journal, 99*(2), 153–165.

Center, Y., Freeman, L., Mok, M., & Robertson, G. (1997, March). *An evaluation of Schoolwide Early Language and Literacy (SWELL) in six disadvantaged New South Wales schools.* Paper presented at the annual meeting of the American Educational Research Association, Chicago.

Chambers, B., Cheung, A., Madden, N., Slavin, R. E., & Gifford, R. (in press). Achievement effects of embedded multimedia in a Success for All reading program. *Journal of Educational Psychology.*

Chambers, B., Slavin, R. E., Madden, N. A., Abrami, P. C., Tucker, B. J., Cheung, A., et al. (2005). *Technology infusion in Success for All: Reading outcomes for first graders.* Manuscript submitted for publication.

Cheung, A., & Slavin, R. E. (2005a). Effective reading programs for English language learners and other language minority students. *Bilingual Research Journal, 29*(2), 241–267.

Cheung, A., & Slavin, R. E. (2005b). Effective reading programs for English language learners and other language minority students. *Bilingual Research Journal, 29*(2), 241–267.

Comprehensive School Reform Quality Center. (2005). *CSRQ Center report on elementary school comprehensive school reform models.* Washington, DC: American Institutes for Research.

Cronbach, L. J., Ambron, S. R., Dornbusch, S. M., Hess, R. D., Hornik, R. C., Phillips, D. C., et al. (1980). *Toward reform of program evaluation: Aims, methods, and institutional arrangements.* San Francisco, CA: Jossey-Bass.

Haxby, B., Lasaga-Flister, M., Madden, N. A., & Slavin, R. E. (1999). *Success for All family support manual.* Baltimore, MD: Success for All Foundation.

Herman, R. (1999). *An educator's guide to schoolwide reform.* Arlington, VA: Educational Research Service.

Livingston, M., & Flaherty, J. (1997). *Effects of Success for All on reading achievement in California schools.* Los Alamitos, CA: WestEd.

Madden, N. A. (1995). *Reading Roots teacher's manual.* Baltimore, MD: Success for All Foundation.

Madden, N. A., Slavin, R. E., Karweit, N. L., Dolan, L. J., & Wasik, B. A. (1993). Success for All: Longitudinal effects of a restructuring program for inner-city elementary schools. *American Educational Research Journal, 30,* 123–148.

Madden, N., Slavin, R., Morrison, T., Haxby, B., Fitchett, W., & Conway, K. (2007). *The reading wing s3rd edition guide.* Baltimore: Success for All Foundation.

McLaughlin, M. W. (1990). The Rand change agent study revisited: Macro perspectives and micro realities. *Educational Researcher, 19*(9), 11–16.

National Academy of Sciences. (1998). *The prevention of reading difficulties in young children.* Washington, DC: Author.

Nunnery, J., Ross, S., Smith, L., Slavin, R., Hunter, P., & Stubbs, J. (1996, April). *An assessment of Success for All program configuration effects on the reading achievement of at-risk first grade students.* Paper presented at the annual meeting of the American Educational Research Association, New York.

Ross, S. M., Smith, L. J., & Casey, J. P. (1997). Preventing early school failure: Impacts of Success for All on standardized test outcomes, minority group performance, and school effectiveness. *Journal of Education for Students Placed at Risk, 2*(1), 29–53.

Ross, S. M., Smith, L. J., Nunnery, J., & Sterbin, A. (1995). *Fall 1995 teacher survey results for the Memphis City Schools restructuring design.* Memphis, TN: University of Memphis Center for Research in Educational Policy.

Schacter, J. (1999). *Reading programs that work: A review of programs for pre-kindergarten to fourth grade.* Santa Monica, CA: Milken Family Foundation.

Slavin, R. E. (1987). Ability grouping and student achievement in elementary schools: A best-evidence synthesis. *Review of Educational Research, 57,* 347–350.

Slavin, R. E. (1995). *Cooperative learning: Theory, research, and practice* (2nd ed.). Boston: Allyn & Bacon.

Slavin, R. E. (1996). Neverstreaming: Preventing learning disabilities. *Educational Leadership, 53*(5), 4–7.

Slavin, R. E., & Cheung, A. (2005). A synthesis of research on language of reading instruction. *Review of Educational Research, 75*(2), 247–284.

Slavin, R. E., Daniels, C., & Madden, N. A. (2005). The Success for All middle school: Adding content to middle grades reform. *Middle School Journal, 36*(5), 4–8.

Slavin, R. E., Karweit, N. L., & Madden, N. A. (Eds.). (1989). *Effective programs for students at risk.* Boston: Allyn & Bacon.

Slavin, R. E., & Madden, N. A. (1993, April). *Multi-site replicated experiments: An application to Success for All.* Paper presented at the annual meeting of the American Educational Research Association, Atlanta, GA.

Slavin, R. E., & Madden, N. A. (1999). Effects of bilingual and English as a second language adaptations of Success for All on the reading achievement of students acquiring English. *Journal of Education for Students Placed at Risk, 4*(4), 393–416.

Slavin, R. E., & Madden, N. A. (2000). Roots & Wings: Effects of whole-school reform on student achievement. *Journal of Education for Students Placed at Risk, 5*(1&2), 109–136.

Slavin, R. E., & Madden, N. A. (2000). Roots & Wings: Effects of whole-school reform on student achievement. *Journal of Education for Students Placed at Risk, 5*(1&2), 109–136.

Slavin, R. E., & Madden, N. A. (in press). *Two million children: Success for All.* Thousand Oaks, CA: Corwin.

Slavin, R. E., Madden, N. A., Cheung, A., Borman, G. D., Chamberlain, A. & Chambers, B. (2006). *A three-year randomized evaluation of Success for All: Final reading outcomes.* Baltimore, MD: Center for Data-Driven Reform in Education, Johns Hopkins University.

Slavin, R. E., Madden, N. A., Chambers, B., & Haxby, B. (2009). *Two million children: Success for All* (2nd ed.). Thousand Oaks, CA: Corwin.

Slavin, R. E., Madden, N. A., & Stevens, R. J. (1989/90). Cooperative learning models for the 3 R's. *Educational Leadership, 47*(4), 22–28.

Smith, L. J., Ross, S. M., & Casey, J. P. (1994). *Special education analyses for Success for All in four cities.* Memphis, TN: University of Memphis, Center for Research in Educational Policy.

Stevens, R. J., Madden, N. A., Slavin, R. E., & Farnish, A. M. (1987). Cooperative integrated reading and composition: Two field experiments. *Reading Research Quarterly, 22,* 433–454.

Traub, J. (1999). Better by design? A consumer's guide to schoolwide reform. Washington, DC: Thomas Fordham Foundation.

Wasik, B. A., & Slavin, R. E. (1993). Preventing early reading failure with one-to-one tutoring: A best-evidence synthesis. *Reading Research Quarterly, 28,* 178–200.

# 28

# The Talent Development Middle Grades Model

## *A Design for Improving Early Adolescents' Developmental Trajectories in High-Poverty Schools*

DOUGLAS J. MAC IVER, ALLEN RUBY, ROBERT W. BALFANZ, LESLIE JONES,
FRAN SION, MARIA GARRIOTT, AND VAUGHAN BYRNES

## The Rise of Comprehensive School Reform Models

For more than 40 years, the U.S. government has made various attempts to spur improvements in the education received by students living in poverty. For example, the Title I program was started in 1965 to provide a revenue stream for schools serving high percentages of economically disadvantaged students so that the schools might provide targeted compensatory educational services to these students. Evaluations of Title I during the 1970s and 1980s showed only small, short-term program impacts on student achievement except in the rare schools where the targeted educational services for eligible students funded by Title I—such as individual pull-outs—were carefully orchestrated to cohere with and support a regular education program of solid curriculum and instruction (for a review, see Rowan & Guthrie, 1989). Fortunately, important changes in the Title I legislation in 1988 made it possible for high-poverty schools—in which 75% or more of the students are living in poverty—to opt for "school-wide models" of Title I service delivery that blend Title I funds and personnel with the school's other funds and personnel in order implement whole-school reforms that seek to improve, coordinate, and integrate the school's compensatory and regular education instructional programs for all students (Rowan, Barnes, & Camburn, 2004). The hope was for high-poverty schools to develop or adopt more comprehensive (and less fragmentary) models for instructional improvement that would stimulate an integrated and strategic set of school-wide reforms to all key aspects of the school's educational program including curriculum, instruction, organization, professional development, and parent involvement (Desimone, 2002; Wong & Meyer, 1998).

The nation's interest in comprehensive school reform was further heightened by the founding of the New American Schools (NAS) Development Corporation in 1991 which solicited contributions from businesses and foundations and then awarded grants to fund the development of 11 "break the mold" designs for whole-school reform (Berends, Bodilly, & Kirby, 2002). Meanwhile, grants from the U.S. Department of Education and from major foundations supported the creation of several additional comprehensive school reform models, including a federal educational research and development center grant that made it possible for the Center for the Social Organization of Schools at Johns Hopkins University to launch the Talent Development Middle Grades Model (TDMG) in 1994 (see next section). Congress's enthusiasm for whole-school reform was further demonstrated by changes in 1994 in Title I legislation to allow majority-poverty schools (50% or more of the students live in poverty) to join high-poverty schools in using Title 1 funds to engage in comprehensive reform. As a result of all these investments in comprehensive reform, by 1997 there were more than 9,000 schools using Title I funds to support whole-school reforms (Wang, Wong, & Kim, 1999).

Massive growth in the number of schools adopting whole-school reform models was spurred by Congress's enactment of the Comprehensive School Reform (CSR) program that provided additional money to the states to support schools that adopted such models. With this program's funds, states invested $35 million in CSR in 1998, $136 million in 1999, $157 million in 2000; $225 million in 2001, and over $265 million a year in 2002, 2003, and 2004. The program was gradually discontinued starting in 2005 with the program's awards to schools dropping to $211 million in 2005; $65 million in 2006; only $5 million in 2007 (U.S. Department of Education, 2007b). However, a significant number of schools continue to adopt or sustain CSR models nationally using Title I, school, or district funds, or using funding provided by their state or by a foundation.

The founders of the NAS initiative initially sought to bring comprehensive reforms to a broad spectrum of the nation's public schools (Glennan, 1998). However, because the bulk of the federal CSR program funding stream was reserved for schools that served majority-poverty or high-poverty student populations, these types of schools were ultimately much more likely than schools serving more economically advantaged student populations to adopt a whole school reform model. The average poverty rate of a school receiving at least 1 year of CSR funding was 82% (U.S. Department of Education, 2007c) and these schools were mainly located in urban (60%) and rural (28%) areas (U.S. Department of Education, 2007a).

Although twice as many elementary schools as middle schools received CSR funding, there was a growing realization during this time period that the comprehensive reform of elementary schools by itself was not enough to ensure the success of students from high-poverty neighborhoods because inadequate schooling during the middle grades was having a profound negative impact on their future prospects. Far too many of these students do not receive high-quality learning opportunities, expert teaching, and supportive learning environments during the middle grades (Balfanz, 2000; Corbett & Wilson, 1997; Juvonen, Le, Kaganoff, Augustine, & Constant, 2004; Wilson & Corbett, 2001). In response, many of these middle grades students become disengaged from school (Balfanz, Herzog, & Mac Iver, 2007; Skinner, Zimmer-Gembek, & Connell, 1998) and their educational achievement levels fall even further behind those of their age mates elsewhere (Balfanz & Byrnes, 2006, Beaton et al., 1996; Hanushek & Rivkin, 2006; Schmidt et al., 1999). The challenge for those seeking to reform high-poverty middle grades schools is to successfully institute reforms that are comprehensive enough to alter the developmental trajectories of these students in ways that increase their odds of attaining the key milestones that many students from middle and upper class backgrounds routinely accomplish: graduating from high school, entering college, and finding a career that pays a living wage.

## Generating and Elaborating a CSR Model for High-Poverty Middle Schools

The Center for Social Organization of Schools (CSOS; 2004) established Johns Hopkins University's Talent Development Middle Grades (TDMG) Program in 1994 to develop a comprehensive whole-school reform model that would enable schools serving high-poverty populations to improve students' developmental trajectories. The curriculum and technical assistance provided by the Program is designed to assist schools to successfully offer high-level classes to all students, provide all teachers with the support and professional development they need to develop deep content knowledge, abandon the pedagogy of poverty (Haberman, 1991), and achieve good teaching that engages students as active and reflective learners in heterogeneous groups that are continually asked to apply their learning to problems of everyday life. Douglas Mac Iver and his colleagues gathered together a multidisciplinary team of experienced middle school educators, research scientists,

teacher coaches, professional and organizational development specialists, and curriculum writers to work with high-poverty middle grades schools in developing and refining the TDMG Model (Balfanz, Ruby, & Mac Iver, 2002; Mac Iver, Ruby, Balfanz & Byrnes, 2003) and to assist these schools in implementing the model and in assessing its impacts on students and teachers.

Schools that embrace the model are assisted to:

1. Adopt a "no-excuses" credo: This is a belief that all students can succeed with a standards-based curriculum and that it is the collective responsibility of the adults and students in the school to overcome obstacles to this success (Wilson & Corbett, 2001);
2. Implement an evidence-based, standards-based instructional program in literacy, mathematics, and science (Mac Iver et al., 2004; Mac Iver & Mac Iver, 2007; Ruby, 2006; Senk & Thompson, 2003);
3. Implement, if they desire, U.S. History (CSOS, 2004) and History of Science (Garriott & Teter, 2007; Teter, Garriott, & Brodowski, 2008) instructional programs based upon the two award winning series, *A History of US* and *The Science Story* (Hakim, 1999, 2004, 2005);
4. Institutionalize multiple tiers of support for teachers that provide them with sustained and focused professional development (Balfanz, Ruby, & Mac Iver, 2002; Cohen & Hill, 2001; Killion, 1999);
5. Provide extra help in reading and mathematics to struggling students during regular school hours (Mac Iver, Young et al., 2001; Ruby & Balfanz, 2006; Ruby 2007a, 2007b);
6. Improve school climate and school-family-community partnerships (Epstein et al., 2002);
7. Create communally organized *structures for caring* (Darling-Hammond, 1997) that give teachers the opportunity to work with a smaller group of students over a longer period of time.

## TDMG's Facilitated Instructional Programs

A team of TDMG curriculum coaches in math, reading/English language arts (RELA), science, and history is assigned to each school. Each curriculum coach assists the school in selecting among TDMG-supported curricular offerings in the subject area of his or her expertise to construct a coherent, standards-based instructional program. Each coach then provides high-quality, monthly grade-specific professional development sessions, which model upcoming activities from the curriculum, develop teachers' content knowledge, demonstrate effective instructional approaches, and provide an opportunity for teachers to engage in collaborative reflective practice. The coaches also provide ongoing in-classroom assistance to teachers that includes peer coaching, team teaching, trouble shooting, and offering advice and encouragement.

***TDMG's School-Wide Adolescent Literacy Program*** Perhaps the biggest challenge faced by middle schools serving high-poverty students is to help their students progress beyond elementary literacy skills and develop proficient reading, writing, communication, and language skills that enable them to learn, pursue postsecondary education, make informed career decisions, contribute to society, and advocate for themselves and others. The TDMG began developing Student Team Literature (STL) in 1995 to meet this challenge by teaching effective reading strategies, extending comprehension skills, and developing fluency in reading and writing.

Student Team Literature (Jones, 1998) is a systematic cooperative learning approach that provides students with explicit instruction in comprehending literature while building their reading fluency and knowledge of the writer's craft. The approach includes teaching strategies for pre-reading, during reading, and after reading to assist students in constructing and extending meaning, and emphasizes vocabulary and literary analysis along with writing, critical thinking, and social skills needed for cooperative learning (Beers, 2008; Mac Iver et al., 2004; Stevens, 2006a). The approach pairs TDMG *Discussion Guides* with high-quality, high-interest, culturally relevant trade books selected by the school's RELA faculty in consultation with their TDMG curriculum coach. Guides are available for over 200 classic and contemporary works of adolescent fiction and nonfiction at a wide variety of reading levels. The guides assist teachers and students as they systematically read and reflect upon themes and topics presented in the literature, and on aspects of "the writer's craft." The guides are used during a cycle of instruction that includes direct teaching and modeling; partner practice, analysis, and discussion; and individual assessment, reflection, and extension activities. The cycle is designed for optimal use during a daily 90-minute period but can be adjusted for shorter periods.

Each book is broken into four or five sections, with each section being the focus of instruction for about one week. Before beginning a section, students learn key vocabulary needed to understand the reading. The teacher pronounces and the students repeat these words, and they work together to identify roots and affixes, build definitions, and use the words in meaningful sentences in which context clues are embedded to signal students' understanding of the denotative and connotative meanings of new vocabulary. Throughout the week, rapid reviews of vocabulary are carried out. If students have trouble with recognizing words or figuring out what they mean, these reviews include help on word recognition skills (Beers, 2003) and vocabulary development strategies (Allen, 1999).

Then, the teacher activates students' prior knowledge regarding the book's content (see Beers, 2003, pp. 73–101). At the beginning of the book, this can be achieved by class discussion of the book's topic, the possible meaning of the book's title, and predictions regarding how the vocabulary words may fit in with the characters, setting, and action. Later on, after sections of the book have been read, students apply their prior knowledge to making predictions as to what will happen in the next section.

After being introduced to both the vocabulary and topic of the book section, students read the section silently. Silent reading allows students to focus on comprehension and not be distracted by the extra demands involved in oral reading, such as achieving appropriate pronunciation, expression, pacing, and volume. Furthermore, the ability to read silently with comprehension is an essential skill that students need in order to thrive in school and in most postacademic careers (RAND Reading Study Group, 2002; Routman, 1998). Nevertheless, silent reading in an STL classroom is often followed by partner reading of the same section or excerpts from it. During partner reading, less able readers and their more able counterparts take turns reading paragraphs aloud to teach other to build fluency. Partner reading gives poor readers and second language learners additional practice, and it gives all students an opportunity to deepen their comprehension and prepare for the guided discussion of the reading that will follow. Partner reading gives students greater incentive to pay attention because each student has only to wait for his partner to read before he gets another turn. This is unlike round robin reading in which *one* student at a time reads aloud to the whole class. All students are taught social skills, such as when and how to correct someone who has made a mistake, to ensure that partner reading goes smoothly. During partner reading, the teacher circulates among pairs to identify problems with fluency that may require the use of additional in-class strategies such as choral or echo reading, or extra help out of class in the Savvy Readers Lab (described later).

The partners (or sometimes, for variety, teams of four) then discuss the reading using questions and graphic organizers from the Guide. Next, they write individual responses to those questions including a justified prediction of what will happen next. Then the students continue to deepen their understanding of the book they are studying through (a) meaningful sentence writing, (b) a minilesson on a specific literary element or device that the author has used, (c) writing in response to a prompt to show understanding of the text and to make connections between the text and students' own experiences, (d) extension research or projects that explore issues and themes in the literature, and (e) peer preassessment in preparation for individual assessments. Guided whole-class discussions are interspersed with these activities in order to draw out and check students' understanding.

Upon completion of a section, students take a comprehension test to assess their understanding of the book so far, a vocabulary pronunciation test, and a word mastery test requiring them to write meaningful sentences for high-frequency words that appear on their vocabulary lists, words that are valuable to have in one's working vocabulary for future use. These end-of-section tests are included in the teachers' edition of each TDMG *Discussion Guide*. In addition, for many books, an end-of-book unit test is available to assess students' overall understanding of the content and vocabulary in the reading. These unit tests take the form of typical standardized reading comprehension and vocabulary tests used in schools. They help students prepare for such tests—while checking their understanding of the reading—without having to abandon daily instruction to engage in disconnected test preparation activities.

Student Team Literature classrooms also feature periodic listening comprehension (LC) and Talent Development writing lessons. During LC lessons, teachers read aloud so that students can hear a fluent reader read and think aloud, practice their own comprehension and listening skills, and learn about key literary devices used by writers of the trade books they are reading. The teacher reads from a work different from the book being read by the class, usually literature written for younger children chosen for its literary richness and relative brevity. Before reading, the teacher introduces the literary element or device to be illustrated. While reading, the teacher pauses to think aloud about what was read (in order to model comprehension strategies) and to ask comprehension questions. Afterward, the teacher holds a class discussion on the literary device, often using a graphic organizer to record student responses.

The writing lessons and activities provide systematic instruction and inspiration for planning, writing, editing, revising, and publishing. Teacher modeling is a key part of these lessons: teachers stand before their students and show them how to approach a writing assignment, as opposed to simply telling them what steps they should take. Students observe as the teacher thinks aloud as she goes through the writing process and considers his or her audience. This gives students a chance to see how mature writers write and to learn new concepts and techniques by example. The lessons also include springboard activities such as role-playing, sensory exercises, and simulations that engage students in the assignment prior to writing and provide them with first-hand experiences, giving them a better understanding of the subject of and audience for the assignment. Depending upon the skills and knowledge needed to complete a given assignment, targeted minilessons help students develop appropriate usage, mechanics, and style. Throughout the writing process, students work in cooperative learning groups that provide them with a caring audience who helps them focus and polish their writing. While groups are meeting, the teacher confers with individual students, discussing and analyzing their writing.

For ease of use, all the materials necessary to carry out STL instruction (such as silent reading, partner reading, partner discussion, prediction, writing prompts, and assessments) are bundled into the Discussion Guides. The teachers' editions contain additional information for the teacher including: (a) a summary of the reading, (b) recommendations for preparing students to read a particular book, (c) questions that lead students to establish expectations regarding what they will read, (d) whole-class discussion questions that build upon prior partner and team discussions, and (e) suggested topics for listening comprehension lessons. With guides written for over 200 pieces of literature,

schools and teachers can choose according to their students' reading levels and areas of interest.

Integral to STL is the use of cooperative learning in teams of four that sometimes function as two partnerships. The teams are heterogeneously organized using two average, one low, and one high level reader. The cooperative segments of STL take advantage of young adolescents' social nature and focus it on academic work (Ares & Gorrell, 2002; Stevens, 2006b). However, since students do not naturally know how to work cooperatively, STL includes explicit instruction in the cooperative social skills. Lessons are provided both on basic skills (such as active listening and staying on task) and complex ones (such as clarifying ideas and negotiating). Explicit instruction in these skills is followed by teacher and student modeling and role playing of them, use of the skills during STL team activities, and teacher monitoring and reinforcing of the skills during partner, team and whole class activities.

*Research on the Impact of STL* Several longitudinal studies have compared the achievement growth for students in schools using STL with those in matched schools not using STL. For example, Mac Iver, Ruby, Balfanz, and Byrnes (2003) conducted a 4-year study of two closely matched fifth through eighth grade middle schools in Philadelphia. The study followed two cohorts of students as they progressed through the middle grades. The STL participants outgrew comparison students on the Stanford 9 Reading Comprehension Test by one quarter of a standard deviation in the first cohort and by .39 standard deviations in the second. Results from Pennsylvania State Standards Assessment (PSSA) provided further confirmation that STL accelerated students' progress in reading; participants outgained comparison students by .35 standard deviations. In another study of middle schools in Philadelphia, Mac Iver, Balfanz, Ruby, Byrnes, Lorentz, and Jones (2004), compared the reading achievement gains across the last 3 years of middle school of 890 Student Team Literature participants from three large nonselective neighborhood schools with those of 662 nonparticipants from three control schools that were matched to the participating schools in racial composition, high poverty status, and past performance before Talent Development began in the district. Student Team Literature participants outgained nonparticipants by 4.3 normal curve equivalents during the last 3 years of the middle grades, an effect size of .29 standard deviations.[1] Ruby, Mac Iver, and Byrnes (2004) took this research one step further by using multinomial logit models to examine the impact of STL on change in students' reading proficiency levels on statewide tests by comparing 1,737 students at 3 high-poverty middle schools in Philadelphia with 9,773 students at 23 similar schools in the district that did not use STL. Students who experienced STL were 73% more likely to overcome a reading deficit during the middle grades as evidenced by moving up from the lowest reading proficiency level between fifth and eighth grade and were 43% less likely to develop a deficit as evidenced by slipping to the lowest reading proficiency level.

Herlihy and Kemple (2005) used a different analytic approach to investigate the impact of the Talent Development Middle School Model on reading achievement in six nonselective, comprehensive middle schools in Philadelphia. Their approach combined an interrupted time series analysis and a comparison schools technique. Thus, they compared the improvements (over the preintervention baseline) in TD schools versus those observed in comparison schools. They found that the Talent Development Model significantly reduced the percentage of eighth graders performing in the bottom quartile in reading achievement only in the second and fifth years of implementation in these schools. The inconsistent pattern of results across different years (positive impacts on reading achievement in some years and no significant impact in others) may reflect the difficulties that these high-poverty urban schools experienced in sustaining reasonable levels of implementation in some classrooms in some years because of high levels of teacher mobility. Issues concerning the sustainability of the TDMG Model will be discussed in a later section.

***TDMG's Mathematics Program***   In 1996, TDMG began developing a mathematics program that combines coherent research-based instructional materials from the University of Chicago School Mathematics Project (UCSMP). These materials include *Everyday Mathematics* in Grades 5 and 6, *Transition Mathematics* in Grade 7, and *Algebra* in Grade 8—or other National Science Foundation-supported middle grades courses of study such as *Mathematics in Context, Connected Mathematics, Mathscape,* and *Math Thematics* with a multitiered teacher support system of sustained professional development and in-class coaching. These standards- and research-based curricula differ from the most commonly used middle grades mathematics programs in many crucial ways (Senk & Thompson, 2003). For example, these curricula:

- Intentionally and systematically build upon the students' prior math knowledge, intuition, and number sense;
- Present students with well-elaborated, varied, and realistic problem situations drawn from everyday life;
- Introduce advanced mathematics topics early and often by including substantial strands featuring geometry, data and statistics, and algebra each year with investigations of these topics becoming more sophisticated in each passing grade;
- Teach students how to use manipulatives (such as pegboards, pegs, and yarn to make broken line graphs) and visual tools (such as rate tables, bar models, and double number lines) to represent mathematical situations and support their thinking, analysis, and problem solving;
- Balance skill development in paper-and-pencil calculation with the development of mathematical intuition, flexible number sense, estimation, mental arithmetic, and prudent use of calculators, spreadsheets, and other technology;
- Feature ongoing informal and formal assessments that

match the types of learning activities in which students are engaged;
- Provide students with a coherent sequence of learning activities designed to help them gradually progress from informal notions and simpler problems to using formal mathematical reasoning and representations to model and solve nonroutine problems;
- Foster students' development of depth of understanding of key conceptual ideas and of proficiency in communicating these understandings through explanations of their thinking, strategies, and solutions and through evaluations or critiques of the mathematical thinking and strategies of others;
- Include extensive instruction on rational numbers and proportional reasoning and the concepts and skills needed to solve problems involving fractions, ratios, rates, percents, and decimals;
- Include regular use of cooperative learning groups.

Teachers were offered multiple tiers of professional development to support their implementation of the specific new mathematics curricula adopted by their school. Three days of summer training were followed by monthly 3-hour workshops on Saturdays. The workshops were grade specific and focused on the unit that would be used during the following month. The instructional facilitators leading the sessions previewed and modeled key activities, reviewed core content knowledge, and discussed appropriate classroom management strategies. In addition, the facilitators provided teachers with an opportunity to discuss with each other what was and was not working in their own classrooms. In all, teachers had access to over 36 hours of professional development per year.

In addition to the monthly professional development sessions, teachers had in-classroom implementation support. Each school was assigned a curriculum coach who spent 1 to 2 days per week in each school working with teachers in their classrooms. Implementation support was nonjudgmental and included modeling, explaining, coteaching, assisting with lesson planning, observing lessons and providing confidential feedback, and working to identify and surmount any obstacles to strong implementation.

*Research on the Impact of TDMG's Mathematics Program*   The impact of the TDMG Mathematics Program on students' achievement growth in mathematics has been evaluated in several longitudinal studies. For example, Mac Iver et al.'s (2003) 4-year-long quantitative case study of two cohorts in two matched middle schools found that students in the school that implemented the TDMG Math program outgrew their peers in the school that did not implement by .21 standard deviation units (on Total Mathematics achievement growth on the Stanford 9 during the first 3 years of middle school) in the first cohort and by .29 standard deviations in the second cohort. Analyses of student growth on the state test, the PSSA Mathematics test, found an even stronger effect of .36 standard deviation units.

Balfanz, Mac Iver, and Byrnes (2006) examined the levels of program implementation attained and the impact of the program on various measures of mathematics achievement in a study comparing three TD schools with three matched comparison schools in the School District of Philadelphia. Implementation levels were measured by an implementation index that combined survey measures from students and from curriculum coaches. Across the 4 years of the study, two-thirds to three-fourths of the classrooms in the TD schools obtained at least a medium-high level of implementation of the program. This suggests that the math teacher support infrastructure that TD established of ongoing professional development and in-classroom coaching was strong enough to withstand the high rates of principal and teacher turnover that occurred during these years. Students in TDMG schools outperformed students from the control schools on multiple measures of mathematics achievement growth during the middle grades. The average effect size by the end of middle school was .24 standard deviation units. In TDMG schools, the entire mathematics achievement distribution shifted upward between fifth and eighth-grade, but remained essentially unchanged in the control schools. The TDMG schools had a 10 percentage point advantage in the percentage of students gaining 5 or more and 10 or more state percentile points on the state's high-stakes mathematics test between fifth and eighth grade. Moreover, the TDMG schools were substantially more successful than the control schools in helping students leave behind the "below basic math skills" achievement category for one of the higher classifications on this test by the time they reached eighth grade.

Herlihy and Kemple (2005) estimated the impact of the TDMG Mathematics program on eighth graders' performance in Philadelphia by comparing the achievement time-series observed in matched sets of comparison schools with the mathematics achievement time-series of six high-poverty, high-minority schools, which began working with the TDMG between 1996 and 1997 and 1998 and 1999. Thus, two interrupted time-series analyses were performed. The first analysis compared eighth grade student performance in TDMG schools with the performance of earlier cohorts of eighth graders in these same schools prior to program implementation. The difference between performance levels in the pre- and postimplementation cohorts is referred to as a "deviation from baseline." The second interrupted time-series analysis computed the deviations from baseline observed in a matched group of non-TDMG schools, a group of comparison schools in the same district that have characteristics similar to those of the TDMG schools. The final step in the analysis computed the differences between the deviations from the baseline in the TDMG schools and the deviations from the baseline in the non-TDMG schools; these differences are the estimated impacts of the TDMG mathematics program. These results showed that TDMG had a positive impact on math achievement that became significant by the third year of implementation and then strengthened further during the next 3 years of implementation. For example, Figure 28.1 plots the deviations from baseline (in normal curve equivalent points) for six TDMG schools and 18 non-TDMG schools on the state's standardized assessment in mathematics. In both the TDMG and non-TDMG, eighth grade performance in mathematics improved over the years but the improvements were significantly greater in TDMG schools than in non-TDMG schools. By implementation year 3, the cumulative improvement was 2.1 normal curve equivalents (NCE) greater in Talent Development schools. By implementation year 4, the cumulative improvement was 2.6 NCEs greater in TDMG schools. By years 5 and 6 of program implementation, the cumulative improvement was 2.9 and 3.4 NCEs greater in TDMG than in non-TDMG schools. The effect size for year 6 of program implementation had reached .23 standard deviation units.

When the Talent Development model began in Philadelphia, 75% of the eighth graders were performing in the bottom quartile on the state assessment in mathematics. Thus, one important goal of Talent Development's mathematics program was to significantly reduce this percentage. Figure 28.2 plots the deviations from baseline in the percentage of eighth graders scoring in the bottom quartile in TDMG and

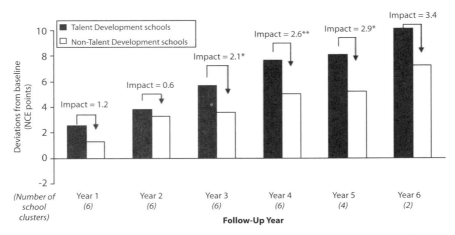

**Figure 28.1** Impacts on state's standardized assessment math NCE for eighth-grade students in early implementing Talent Development Schools. Source: MDRC calculations from individual students' school records from a large, urban school district.

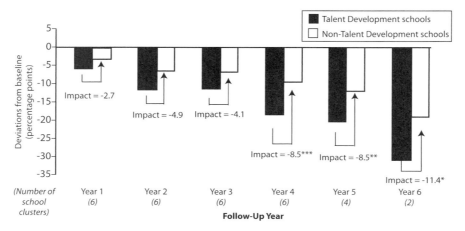

**Figure 28.2** Impact on the percentage of students in the bottom quartile of state's standardized assessment math scores for eighth-grade students in early implementing Talent Development Schools, six-year follow-up results. Source: MDRC calculations from individual students' school records from a large, urban school district.

non-TDMG schools. By year 6 of model implementation, Talent Development schools had reduced the percentage of students scoring in the bottom quartile by over 30 percentage points and this reduction was 11 percentage points (.29 standard deviation units) greater in TDMG schools than non-TDMG schools.

*TDMG's Science Program* The development of the TDMG science program began in fall 1997 at schools already working with TDMG in language arts and mathematics. These schools had made recent large expenditures on science textbooks. TDMG initially supported the use of these texts by (a) helping schools develop an appropriate order of teaching the text's topics (most texts were extremely large and could not be completely taught in 1 year), (b) providing professional development focused on content knowledge to teachers with weak backgrounds in science, and (c) providing supplemental hands-on activities to help students understand the concepts taught.

Within the first 2 years of this support, it became clear that the texts and the form of instruction used with them were not fully engaging students in science. The texts were difficult to read not only because many of the students were reading below grade level but also because they covered a wide range of content and contained much new vocabulary. As a result, students often lost interest when reading on their own or when teachers tried to use reading aloud to ensure better understanding. The texts also proved difficult for the majority of teachers who did not have science backgrounds and who also struggled to keep up with the breadth of content. Because they did not feel comfortable with the content, these teachers primarily had students read the text and answer the chapter questions. The texts did provide some hands-on activities that generated greater student interest but in many cases these were quite simple and not well integrated with the content. The supplemental hands-on activities provided by TDMG were well received because they were more complex and taught the content but there were not enough of them to make a curriculum. A

further constraint on both text and TDMG activities was that schools did not have adequate ordering and reimbursement systems to purchase the various materials from different suppliers needed for the activities.

At this time, a set of new science curricula became available. These were being developed by educational organizations funded by the National Science Foundation. These included the Full Option Science System (FOSS) and the Science Education for Public Understanding Program (SEPUP) developed at the Lawrence Hall of Science, University of California at Berkeley; Science and Technology for Children (STC) developed by the National Science Resources Center (a joint project of the Smithsonian Institutions and the National Academy of Sciences); and Insights developed by the Education Development Center. These curricula took the shape of individual modules each addressing one topic that fell under the category of life science, earth and space science, physical science, or the nature of science. The benefit of the modular approach was that districts and schools could place modules in different grades to conform to the different state and local science standards that were being implemented. The modules were built around a set of hands-on activities that followed a logical progression to teach the topic. The modules took 6 to 8 weeks to teach or, for the more complex ones, 3 to 4 months. As a result, they narrowed the content covered and increased time spent on understanding it. Their focus was not only on doing activities but also planning them and interpreting the results. In this way, they addressed the most common criticism of hands-on activities: that while students typically enjoy such activities, they learn little from them. Since each module came with all the equipment needed to do the module's activities, adoption of the modules was also an easy way to provide each teacher with the equipment needed to use a hands-on approach.

These modules were introduced by TDMG into its partner schools, starting with the lower middle grades and moving up. Student reaction was very favorable. On TDMG-administered surveys, students began to rate their liking of science class higher than any other academic class. Teachers noted that the modules engaged students with weak academic skills who previously had disliked science. But the success of the modules depended heavily on implementation which required that (a) teachers were prepared to teach each lesson, and (b) teachers had first taught the class management procedures needed for cooperative hands-on work. Without these two conditions, student attention wandered and instruction gave way to a focus on classroom control.

Changes began to be made in TDMG professional development to foster these two conditions. During workshops, teachers perform every activity in the module just as they will later lead their students to do in class. In this way, teachers learn what they need to prepare, how students should be organized, and what questions are likely to arise. The content behind each activity is discussed so that teachers know the key concepts to stress. The professional development workshops also provide classroom management techniques. Hands-on science requires students to take on a greater management role, such as planning the activities, picking up materials, using them in a group, keeping the group on task, returning the materials, and discussing the results. If the students don't learn these roles, inattention and even chaos may result. The professional development guides teachers in how to establish cooperative groups, teach social skills for group work, set rotating jobs for the members of each group, arrange the classrooms, and rotate among groups to keep students on task. This focus on what is to be taught in the next lessons and the best practices for teaching it distinguishes both TDMG's science and mathematics workshops from the traditional generic workshops that have failed to change teacher practices and student achievement. During the science workshops teachers are also given two sets of supplemental materials to help them increase students' depth of learning. The first is a set of reading lessons for use with module's readings to assist students comprehend these readings. The second is a set of module-specific homework assignments to provide students with opportunities to practice at home what they are learning in class and share that learning with their families.

To support what was learned in the workshops, a TDMG science facilitator worked with the teacher in their classroom on a weekly basis. Teachers vary in their strengths and weaknesses, and a workshop alone cannot address their individual differences. The facilitator observed the teacher and students in action and helped teachers to adapt what they have learned to the specific conditions and needs of the class through model teaching, coteaching, and critical observation with confidential feedback. The facilitator helped customize the workshop material so that implementation occurs in the desired fashion and inappropriate modifications are avoided. For example, teachers with weaker classroom management skills often replaced student activities with classroom demonstrations, negating the benefits of having students organize and carry out the activity. A facilitator in the classroom observed this modification and the reason

behind it and helped teachers gain the management skills necessary to return to the use of student activities. As the teacher and students become more skilled at this type of instruction, the facilitator advised the teacher on how to further increase the student role.

The science facilitator also has the role of working with the school administration to establish structures to support the change in instructional approach. Timely ordering of materials (both replacements and consumable items) is key to maintaining a hands-on instructional approach and the facilitator helps to establish a formal ordering procedure. For example, each teacher may inventory modules after use and turn in a replacement order to a lead teacher, who then organizes it and turns it in to the staff person responsible for ordering. When the materials arrive, the process is reversed so that restocking of each module occurs. Another important structure is to establish a regular science faculty meeting so that ideas to improve instruction can be raised and technical needs addressed. Facilitators are also in a position to identify science teachers who could take on leadership responsibilities such as training new teachers in the modules. With administration support, these teachers can receive extra professional development and greater responsibilities for maintaining the new curriculum especially after the partnership with TDMG is reduced or ends.

Program implementation at each school was measured by fidelity of implementation scores based on ratings provided by an experienced science facilitator who visited the school each week. For each science class section, the facilitator for a given school rated the frequency of the teacher's use of the recommended modules and instructional practices, the number of science modules taught to the section during the year, and the extent to which the teacher participated in the monthly professional development sessions.

*Research on the Impact of TDMG's Science Program* Ruby (2006) compared the achievement results of a cohort moving from fifth through seventh grade from 1998 through 2001 at three Philadelphia middle schools working with TDMG to three matched control schools and to the districts' 21 schools serving high-poverty, high-minority student populations. Growth in achievement between the end of fourth and the end of seventh grades was measured using the district-given Stanford 9 Science Achievement Test.

In cooperation with the district, the control schools were chosen based on similarities in student poverty levels, student attendance, racial and ethnic makeup of the student body, and previous years' performance on the standardized achievement tests. Two of the three experimental schools had a smaller percentage of White students than their controls. In most cases, the experimental schools' previous year test score averaged slightly higher than their controls. Using growth in test scores rather than absolute scores helped adjust for these modest differences.

Two multivariate analyses were carried out to examine the impact of the TDMG science program on student achievement. The first examined the impact of student exposure to the program on the change in their science achievement test scores between fourth and seventh grades. The second examined the impact on their change in science achievement level between the two grades. The analyses controlled for race/ethnicity, gender, English as a Second Language (ESL), special education status, attendance, and behavior.

The first analysis found that overall students at the treatment schools benefited from the TDMG program gaining about 3.5 scaled points or 2 NCEs more for each year of exposure in comparison to students at the matched control schools (or 2 scaled points and 1.2 NCEs versus students at the 23 district middle schools). When the analysis was further targeted by school, students at two of the schools had significant gains of over 7 points or 4 NCEs per year of exposure while students at one school made no significant gains versus their control school. Interestingly, the latter school also had a low level of implementation of the science program while the other two schools had medium to high levels. A 1 standard deviation change in exposure to the TD science program at schools 2 and 3 led to about a .20 standard deviation greater gain in test score as compared to students in the matched control schools.

The second analysis examined the change in student proficiency levels (below basic vs. basic and above) between the end of fourth grade and the end of seventh grade. At the two experimental schools with medium to high implementation of the TDMG science program, the probability of moving from below basic to basic or above rose 9% for each year a student was in the TDMG program. At the same time, the probability of falling from basic or above to below basic fell 8 to 10% per year.

In addition to looking at student achievement, this study also examined implementation and found that it varied both within and between schools. Within schools, different grades adopted the program to different extents and there were large differences in implementation between schools as well. However, in both cases implementation rose over time. While the study could only analyze the achievement results for one cohort (because the district dropped science testing for later cohorts), analyses of implementation levels indicated an increase for each successive cohort. By the third cohort, all three schools had reached medium to high levels of implementation.

## Providing Individually Targeted Academic Help for Students Who Need Additional Supports beyond the School-Wide Reforms

Despite the substantial positive impacts of TDMG's school-wide instructional programs on student achievement and engagement, there will always be some students who, in order to succeed, need additional supports that are more intensive and individualized. The knowledge and skill gaps and resulting motivational problems that some students bring with them to middle school are simply too vast to resolve without providing the students with special shep-

herding that includes substantial extra doses of targeted instruction, guided practice, and independent practice opportunities delivered by one of the school's most qualified and encouraging teachers. Thus, from the very beginning, the TDMG model has helped participating schools start a Savvy Readers lab for students who struggle with reading and a Computer- and Team-Assisted Mathematics Acceleration lab for students who struggle with mathematics. Each lab is offered as an elective course (with approximately half of the normal class size) for 10 or 20 weeks to provide students with a substantial "extra dose" of intensive and personalized instruction while they continue to attend all of their regular academic classes.

***The Savvy Readers (SR) Lab*** The extra learning opportunities offered in the Savvy Readers Lab help struggling students become proficient at understanding what they read and at acquiring new learning from their reading so that they can begin experiencing more success across the standards-based curriculum in their school. The Lab seeks to liberate these students to become independent readers who assume responsibility for their own learning and who understand and enjoy higher-level books. The SR lab provides explicit instruction and practice in applying a wide variety of powerful reading strategies to various types of narrative and expository reading material.

The SR lab has four major components: (a) instruction in strategic reading, (b) practice of reading strategies, (c) rotation of learning centers, and (d) coaching and in-class support for the SR lab teacher.

*Explicit Instruction in Reading Strategies* At the beginning of each lab period, students receive a minilesson covering a related set of reading strategies. The strategies help them construct meaning while they read; for example, by assisting them to decode unfamiliar words while reading, infer meanings of unfamiliar words, make predictions, monitor understanding while reading, repair comprehension when understanding slows down or stops, and identify and master important new vocabulary. The TD program publishes a comprehensive set of minilessons to go along with each *class-wide book* used in the lab—a book which everyone reads, such as *The Air Down Here, Komodo Dragon,* or *Seedfolks.* The lessons show the teacher how to use the book to introduce and model the reading strategies.

*Practice of Reading Strategies* Each day, students practice applying the reading strategies using a class-wide book or an independent book chosen by the student from the lab's library. Using strategy stickers, students make note of strategies they use as they read and then share their experiences with the class. Students also maintain journals to keep track of progress, respond to reading, and communicate with the teacher.

*Rotation of Learning Centers* For two periods a week, students move to four learning centers where they continue to practice and develop reading and writing strategies independently and in small groups. *Students rotate among a computer center (where they use software to improve reading and vocabulary skills), a listening and recording center (where they listen to books on tape or tape a portion of a book they are reading for the teacher to evaluate), an information resource center (where they engage in independent reading from a variety of books and magazines), and a writing center where students work on writing assignments from their other classes, or assignments specific to the SR lab.* Each writing center is equipped with multiple copies of books designed to inspire writing and give students ideas for writing projects, as well as various reference books useful to writers such as a thesaurus, a dictionary, and rhyming dictionary. Each Savvy Reader Lab also has an independent reading library which includes at least 50 independent reading books spanning a 4-year range of reading levels and five genres to accommodate individual needs and interests. Each book has a pocket at the back containing instructions for four culminating activities. When students finish a book, they select and complete one activity that demonstrates their understanding of and their reactions to the book.

*Coaching and In-Class Support for the SR Lab Teacher* A reading specialist from Johns Hopkins regularly visits each school's lab teacher to provide one-on-one professional development, support, assistance, and useful feedback.

***Quasi-Experimental Research on the Impact of the Savvy Reader Lab*** A quasi-experimental study was conducted in Philadelphia during the 2000–2001 school year to estimate the impact of the Savvy Reader Lab on student achievement. Pre- and postmeasures of reading achievement were available for 43 of the 44 eighth graders who participated in the SR Lab at a middle school in Philadelphia. A comparison sample of eighth graders, with matching prior reading comprehension scale scores from Spring 2000, was drawn from a demographically matched comparison school that did not have a SR Lab. Whenever possible, the selected comparison student was also the same gender as the participant. However, in the few cases where no same-gender match was available, we selected a comparison student of the opposite gender but with the same prior achievement. The resulting groups had identical mean reading comprehension scale scores of 639 (a Grade 5 equivalent score) prior to the intervention.

By sampling eighth graders from another Philadelphia middle school that was demographically similar to the treatment school, we were able to successfully identify a comparison group of students with equal prior achievement to our participants. We then were able to estimate the effect of the SR lab on participants' achievement (when combined with the school-wide STL program) by comparing the scores of the two groups on the spring 2001 administration PSSA reading assessment. SR Lab participants scored 45 scale score points higher on the PSSA reading achievement test for an effect size of .44.

***Computer and Team Assisted Mathematics Acceleration (CATAMA) Lab*** The CATAMA Lab is taught by one of the school's full time, certified, and experienced mathematics teachers, who is viewed by his or her peers as skilled and effective, and who is familiar with the NSF-supported math curriculum being taught at the school. The CATAMA teacher receives intensive initial training and regular follow-up visits from one of TD's CATAMA facilitators who has previously taught the lab and who offer expert assistance and direction. Students usually attend the lab for just one grading period per year. The lab offers a way to accelerate the math learning of a large number of students because it can accommodate 5 classes a day of 16 to 20 students per class with new students taught each grading period. To facilitate instructional focus and integration with the regular classroom, each of the five daily sections of the CATAMA Lab is dedicated to a particular grade/need combination. The first period class, for example, may contain eighth graders struggling in algebra, the second period might address eighth graders with weak basic skills (e.g., multiplying positive and negative numbers), while in the third period sixth graders might need to learn how to move between decimals, fractions, and percentages. Over the course of the year, the lab can serve a broad spectrum of students and typically targets students performing between the 25th and 65th percentiles. The goal with lower-performing students is to raise them to average math performance. The goal with higher-performing students is to provide enrichment that helps prepare them for selective high school programs. Because the lab content varies by grade and by need, students often take the lab more than once over the course of their middle school career.

The CATAMA lab combines the instructional power and flexibility of a strong mathematics teacher (Ma, 1999), the individualized extra-help capabilities of computer-based instruction (Abidin & Hartley, 1998), the motivating and cognitive aspects of peer-assisted learning (Fuchs, Fuchs, Mathes, & Simmons, 1997), and the power of small group and individual tutoring (Wasik & Slavin, 1990). By combining instruction in math concepts as well as skills, the CATAMA lab also avoids the traditional criticism leveled at remediation programs of failing to challenge and motivate students because of repetitive practice of low-level skills (Knapp, 1995).

Each CATAMA class is taught using three main instructional components. *Class begins with the CATAMA teacher providing approximately 15 minutes of whole group instruction that previews skills and concepts students will be working with in their regular classrooms in the near future.* This is done for two purposes. First, it helps the students learn the concepts by giving extra time on each concept. Second, it helps them stay interested and focused in their regular math class. By having some understanding and experience with new concepts before they are introduced in the regular classroom, students will have a better chance of following the material in that class rather than becoming frustrated.

*Class continues with 20 to 30 minutes of individualized computer and peer assisted instruction.* Each CATAMA lab has 10 to 15 networked computers. Students use instructional software tailored to their grade and needs. The software provides preassessments, worked/illustrated examples, structured and tiered problem sets, instant feedback, and quizzes and tests that students need to pass at predetermined levels. Students are paired and then teamed with students at similar skill levels. Peer-assisted learning techniques are taught so that the students can "Ask three before me" or, in other words, first ask their partner, and then their other two teammates if they don't understand something before they ask the teacher. In addition, partners take turns being the "reader" who reads the problem and any instructional tips aloud and the "solver" who inputs the solution. Each student then individually takes the quiz. This is done to encourage students to take time to read problems and consider solutions, rather than just attempt to apply the operation they think the problem is calling for (Kilpatrick, Swafford, & Findell, 2001)

The computer- and peer-assisted learning features of the lab also free up the CATAMA teacher to spend time implementing the third instructional component of the class—*individual and small-group tutoring.* This is where, for example, a student who does not know his or her times tables can get help.

***Experimental Research on the Impact of the CATAMA Lab*** A series of experimental studies have estimated the impact of the CATAMA lab on achievement by giving all the students in the school the same math curriculum in their regular math classes but randomly assigning some students to receive CATAMA as an elective for one semester while assigning the others to receive one of the school's other elective courses. Ruby and Balfanz (2006) reported results for middle grades students (mostly eighth graders) participating in a randomized experiment assessing the impact of the CATAMA Lab on achievement in mathematics. The students were drawn from 3 schools in Philadelphia serving high-minority, high-poverty student populations. Within each regular math class, eligible students (n = 431) were randomly assigned to CATAMA or to a regular elective. All students were pretested and posttested using the CTBS TerraNova mathematics test. As might be expected, the randomization resulted in comparable groups that were not different in pretest achievement, grade, or gender composition. The results show that CATAMA students doubled the test score gains of control students (a gain of 22 scale score points vs. 11 scale score points, p < .01, Effect Size = .26 standard deviations). Subgroup analyses reveal that the CATAMA benefited students regardless of their prior achievement levels. The program also benefited students with both high attendance and low attendance at school, though the high attendance students showed the greatest

gains. Replications of this experiment with 81 Ojibwe students in grades 5 through 8 in Cass Lake, Minnesota (Ruby, 2007b) and with 79 ninth-grade students in Philadelphia (Ruby 2007a) yielded even stronger achievement impacts, with the experimental group outgaining the control group by 20 scale score points in grades 5 through 8 and by 27 scale score points in Grade 9. The effect sizes in the fifth to eighth and ninth grade replication studies were .87 and .68 standard deviations, respectively.

## Summary of TDMG's Instructional Programs

So far, this chapter has summarized TDMG's facilitated instructional programs and extra help labs that seek to ensure that each student has a good year of learning in each major subject during each year of the middle grades—a year featuring coherent, high quality instruction from teachers who are receiving ongoing coaching and professional development to assist them in learning the content knowledge and pedagogical skills they need to make effective use of the curricula and instructional materials in their subject areas. The chapter has also summarized a variety of research studies in high poverty schools that each sought to measure the impacts of a specific program or lab on the learning achieved by participating students. The results of this research suggest that the school-wide instructional programs and the elective extra help labs do positively impact students' learning trajectories and help them begin to close the achievement gaps these students bring with them as they enter the middle grades. The effect sizes ranged from one fifth to two fifths of a standard deviation except for the somewhat larger effect sizes found for the intensive, individualized labs. Traditionally, an effect size of one fifth or two fifths of a standard deviation has been considered small (Cohen, 1988). However, recent research specifically concerned with field studies of educational interventions has found that effect sizes of this magnitude represent serious practical impacts equal to 34 to 133% of a year of learning during the middle grades given the slowing annual achievement growth typically found during these grades (Bloom, Hill, Black, & Lipsey, 2006; Kane, 2004; Keller, 1995). Kane (2004) notes that the national samples used to norm the math SAT 9 found an effect size of .50 when comparing the achievement of fourth and fifth graders; that is, a whole school year of instruction was associated with just one-half of a student-level standard deviation gain in test score. Similar research by Bloom et al. (2006), but with a larger sample of tests and students and grade levels, determined the effect size for the increase in standardized test scores in math for an increase in one grade using six commercially available standardized math tests. They found an effect size of .59 in comparing the achievement of fourth and fifth graders, of .41 when comparing fifth and sixth graders, and of .30 when comparing sixth and seventh graders. When compared to these effect sizes, the size of the TD's effects—increasing student achievement by an additional one- to two fifths of a standard deviation—indicate that the model's instructional programs add a substantial increment to students' achievement growth in the middle grades.

## Schools are About More Than Just Learning

It is not enough, however, just to help students learn more during the middle grades and develop lifelong learning abilities. There are other outcomes in the middle grades that are quite important and that have large impacts on students' well-being and future prospects (Bornstein, Davidson, Keyes, & Moore, 2003). It is currently unfashionable in many districts and states to pay much attention to students' emotional and physical health or to schools' climate or peer culture. Very few districts even try to measure these outcomes systematically. Yet middle grades students in the United States—compared to their peers in other countries—report high levels of emotional and physical problems, extremely negative school climates, and unkind and unsupportive peer cultures (Juvonen et al., 2004; Nishina, Juvonen, & Witkow, 2006). Unfortunately, NCLB has led to high-stakes testing and accountability systems that largely distract schools and districts from considering the well-being of their students holistically or their students' longer-term outcomes across the life course (Juvonen, 2007; Sunderman, 2007). Physical, cognitive, and social-emotional dimensions of well-being—that may be quite predictive of longer term outcomes but that don't have clear and immediate impacts on student's test performance—have been receiving less attention from educators as they have been compelled by heavy-handed accountability to focus increasingly on the narrow and short-term goal of "making AYP this year." As important as it is to improve the learning opportunities and achievement growth of students, such improvements are not enough to ensure their well-being.

## School Organization and Climate Improvement: Establishing Structures for Caring, Positive Behavior Supports, and Productive Partnering

High-poverty middle grades schools are often dysfunctional institutions characterized by debilitating practices, attitudes, and relationships that produce a school climate of alienation, danger, disorder, and despair (Balfanz, 2007; Balfanz, Ruby, & Mac Iver, 2002). To improve such a climate, a school must be helped to implement organizational and interpersonal supports that nurture positive and mutually supportive interpersonal relations among members of the school community.

The TDMG model addresses school climate at several levels. First, TDMG staff assists schools to attain judicious use of communal organization structures such as small learning communities, strategic semidepartmentalization, interdisciplinary teaming, and looping (Balfanz, Ruby, & Mac Iver, 2002; Black 2000; Lincoln, 1998). These *structures for caring* (Darling-Hammond, 1997) give teachers the opportunity to work with a smaller group of students

for longer periods of time, facilitate closer connections with students and their families, and help teachers view students as "my kids" rather than "other people's children."

Five years after the original TDMG model was created, it became clear that these communal organizational structures by themselves were not enough to improve the climate of the most troubled schools in the growing TDMG network. In response, TDMG launched a school-wide climate program that helps teachers and administrators in these schools to establish an orderly climate, reduce disruptive student behaviors, reach out to students in emotional crisis, and promote positive interpersonal relations throughout the school. The program also seeks to change social norms and peer cultures that foster problematic behavior. Specific components of TDMG's High Five climate program address lateness and attendance, acting out in the classroom, disorder outside the classroom, bullying, and school and neighborhood safety issues (Sorrell, 2001; Sorrell & Mac Iver, 2002). In addition, the program stresses positive rewards for good behavior and assists schools in developing small-group and individualized interventions for the most troubled and disruptive students.

The TDMG schools are also encouraged to participate in Johns Hopkins University's National Network of Partnership Schools, which works with schools to develop effective school, family, and community partnerships (Sanders & Epstein, 2000). The network provides schools with support and resources to help create healthy communication and involvement with students' parents and communities.

The TDMG's organizational, climate, and partnership programs—though less directly focused on learning than TDMG's instructional and extra help programs—may be very important in helping keep students in poverty on a trajectory to high school graduation. These structures for caring, positive behavior supports, and school–family partnering practices are key in raising attendance, reducing misbehavior, and marshaling and coordinating the efforts of teachers, families, and other community members to prevent student failure and disengagement. Balfanz, Herzog, and Mac Iver (2007) have shown that attending school less than 80% of the time, poor behavior, or failing a math or English course are early warning flags that identify 60% of the sixth grade students in Philadelphia who will not graduate from the school district on time or will graduate 1 year late.

## Does the TDMG Model Help Keep Students on a Path that Leads to Graduation?

Graduating from high school is a hope and expectation that virtually every parent has for his or her child because failure to graduate has dramatic impacts on the child's future prospects. The prevention literature suggests that school-wide interventions like the TDMG model are the first line of defense against the forces pushing students off the graduation path. With its focus on effective and engaging instruction, substantial extra help, and establishing structures that enhance community and help students and teachers come to really know and care about one another, the TDMG model should reduce the numbers of students who display the early warning signs of chronic poor attendance, poor behavior, or course failures, and should increase the odds that students ultimately graduate. The TDMG model has been existence long enough now to allow us to begin comparing the graduation rates of students who experienced the model during the middle grades with those of comparable students who did not. We estimated the impact of the TDMG model on preventing students from developing sixth grade warning signs of dropout risk and on students' actual graduation rates by comparing the data of 540 students from three schools Philadelphia who experienced the model during their years in the middle grades with the data of 604 students from matched schools that did not experience the TDMG model. The sample includes all students who were sixth graders in Philadelphia's first three TDMG schools in the 1998–1999 school year or who were sixth graders in the three non-TDMG schools that had been selected by the research office of the School District of Philadelphia as the district's most comparable middle schools to serve as control schools. As described in Table 28.1, these six large middle schools mainly serve minority students from low-income families. Overall, the TDMG schools when compared to their control schools served slightly more Blacks (77% vs. 71%), slightly more Asians (7% vs. 4%), fewer White students (3% vs. 12%), and more special education students (19% vs. 10%) than did the control schools but had equal percentages of females (52%), Hispanics (13%), and English language learners (4%).

The first indication that the TDMG model might ultimately increase graduation rates was its impact on reducing the percentage of students who developed chronic poor attendance, low grades, or poor behavior as sixth graders. Table 28.2 shows that TDMG sixth graders were less likely than control sixth graders to develop the early warning signs of high dropout risk that have been identified by Balfanz, Herzog, and Mac Iver (2007). That is, TDMG sixth graders were less likely to display poor attendance habits, get poor or failing math grades, get poor English grades, or receive an out-of-school suspension or unsatisfactory behavior mark.

Past research following an earlier cohort (the 1996–1997 cohort) of 13,000 of Philadelphia's sixth graders during that school year and for seven additional years found that the district's overall graduation rate (on time or 1 year late) was 43% (Balfanz, Herzog, & Mac Iver, 2007). The "nongraduates" include both out-of-district transfers (15%) and those who explicitly dropped out (42%). Some of the transfers may have eventually graduated from another district or from a private school (information on what happened to them after they left the district was not available). The graduation rate for sixth graders with one or more of the early warning signs was only 29%. These overall graduation rates include data from some schools that are more advantaged than our present sample of six high-poverty, high-minority schools that enrolled 1,144 sixth graders. The overall on-time graduation rate in the present sample was 39%. For TDMG students the graduation rate was 45%; whereas the rate for control students was lower at 33%.

Table 28.3 follows the students in the present sample for 6 years after they entered the study as sixth graders at one of the three TDMG schools or one of the three control schools during the 1998–1999 school year. The table indicates what

**TABLE 28.1**
**Demographic Characteristics of Middle Schools in Study Exploring Odds of Graduating on Time (in 2005) for Sixth Graders Who Spent the Middle Grades in TDMG and Non-TDMG Schools**

| Characteristics of School in 1998–1999 | TDMG School A | Control School A | TDMG School B | Control School B | TDMG School C | Control School C |
|---|---|---|---|---|---|---|
| Grade span | 5–8 | 5–8 | 5–8 | 5–8 | 6–8 | 6–8 |
| % Low income students | 86 | 92 | 86 | 92 | 71 | 80 |
| % Minority students | 89 | 71 | 99 | 89 | 89 | 99 |
| Enrollment | 1,116 | 739 | 977 | 902 | 1189 | 755 |

**TABLE 28.2**
**Were TDMG Students as Sixth Graders Less Likely than Control Students to Display Early Warning Signs of Dropout Risk—Low Attendance, Low Math and English Grades, and Bad Behavior?**

| Variable | TDMG (n = 540) | Control (n = 604) | t (df = 1142) |
|---|---|---|---|
| % attending less than 80% of the days | 9% | 18% | −4.39*** |
| Average math mark (A= 4, B = 3, etc.) | 2.4 | 2.0 | 5.07*** |
| % failing math | 6% | 15% | −4.81*** |
| Average English mark | 2.4 | 2.2 | 2.86** |
| % failing English | 7% | 9% | −1.410 |
| % with at least 1 out-of-school suspension | 27% | 34% | −2.471* |
| % with a final "unsatisfactory behavior" mark in at least one class | 36% | 47% | −3.82*** |

* p < .05.  ** p < .01.  *** p < .001.

**TABLE 28.3**
**How Well Did Sixth Graders Enrolled in 1999 in TDMG Schools (T, n = 540) and Control Schools (C, n = 604) Stay on Path to Graduate in 2005 (on time)?**

| % who were in grades … | 2000 | | 2001 | | 2002 | | 2003 | | 2004 | | 2005 | |
|---|---|---|---|---|---|---|---|---|---|---|---|---|
| | T | C | T | C | T | C | T | C | T | C | T | C |
| 6 | 1 | 3 | 0 | <1 | 0 | <1 | 0 | 0 | 0 | 0 | 0 | 0 |
| 7 | **99** | **92** | 4 | 5 | 2 | <1 | <1 | 0 | <1 | 0 | 0 | 0 |
| 8 | | | **96** | **84** | 5 | 10 | 1 | <1 | 1 | 1 | 1 | 0 |
| 9 | | | | 2 | **91** | **80** | 22 | 36 | 9 | 16 | 4 | 5 |
| 10 | | | | | <1 | 1 | **66** | **50** | 13 | 13 | 8 | 9 |
| 11 | | | | | | | <1 | 1 | **44** | **26** | 7 | 6 |
| 12 | | | | | | | | | <1 | 1 | **51** | **40** |
| % who actually graduated | | | | | | | | | <1 | <1 | 45 | 33 |
| Cumulative % who left the District | 0 | 4 | 0 | 9 | 2 | 9 | 11 | 13 | 33 | 44 | 30 | 40 |

*Note.* The percentage of students who were in the expected grade in each following year is in bold.

percentages of students followed the hoped for progression through the middle and secondary grades (i.e., reaching each subsequent grade on time and graduating on time). The table also shows the percentages of students who fell off the path leading to on-time graduation from the district (i.e., those repeating a grade or leaving the district).

As shown in Table 28.3, TDMG students were more likely to stay "on path" than were the control students. For example, 91% of the TDMG students made it to ninth grade on time vs. 80% of the control students. Similarly, 51% of the TDMG students vs. 40% of the control students made it to 12th grade on time.

We used a binary logistic regression to model the difference in the odds of graduating on time for students who had attended a TDMG school or a control school throughout the middle grades. The analysis also took account of the impacts of each student's ethnic group, gender, special education status, and English language learner status on his or her odds of graduating on time (see Table 28.4). The large odds ratio of 1.55 associated with being a TDMG student indicates that—holding ethnic group, gender, special education, and English Language Learner status constant—TDMG students were 55% more likely to graduate on time (versus

**TABLE 28.4**
**Logistic Regression Model Estimating Odds of Graduating on Time for TDMG and Control Students while Adjusting for Differences in the Graduation Rates of Different Subgroups**

| Predictor | Odds Ratio | Parameter | SE | p |
|---|---|---|---|---|
| Asian | 1.87 | 0.63 | .30 | 0.036 |
| Hispanic | 0.83 | -0.18 | .19 | 0.337 |
| White | 0.53 | -0.64 | .27 | 0.019 |
| Female | 1.60 | 0.47 | .12 | 0.000 |
| Special educ. | .87 | -0.14 | .18 | 0.432 |
| English lang. learner | .81 | -0.21 | .37 | 0.569 |
| **TDMG** | **1.55** | **0.44** | **.13** | **0.001** |

falling behind, transferring out-of-district, or dropping out) than were the control students.

## Sustaining Comprehensive Reform in the Middle Grades

The research reported here, along with research on other middle grades reform models such as Turning Points, Making Middle Grades Work, Middle Start, and AIM (e.g., see Juvonen et al., 2004), suggests that middle grades reform models can help students learn more and stay on a path toward graduation by ensuring that they receive the basics of good schooling in the middle grades. This involves providing engaging, meaningful, and challenging curriculum and instruction, delivered by trained and supported teachers, in positive, serious, and safe schools designed to give students the personalized attention they need to succeed in a high-standards learning environment.

Little progress has been made, however, in sustaining such comprehensive reforms for more than half-a-dozen years in the typical middle grades school or district (Herlihy & Kemple, 2004, 2005; Juvonen et al., 2004; Williamson & Johnston, 1999). Teacher, principal, and district leadership turnover; budget, professional development, and staffing reductions; and changing policies, politics, and politicians along with cyclical shifts of attention away from the middle grades to the elementary or high school grades often combine to threaten the sustainability and continuity of middle grades reform efforts. As a result, successfully reformed middle grades schools often see even their most effective, well-implemented reforms dismantled over time.

Even when an instructional reform is not dismantled, its impact can be muted in a given school in a given year if there is a high level of teacher turnover. For example, during each 3-year period between 1998 and 2004, over one-half of the teachers in Philadelphia's high-poverty middle grades schools transferred to other higher-performing, less-troubled district schools, to nondistrict schools, or to other professions; some of those who stayed were assigned to teach a completely different subject or grade level in order to fill one of the schools' many vacancies (Balfanz, Ruby, & Mac Iver, 2002; Ruby 2002; Useem, 2001a, 2001b; Useem & Neild, 2001). These high levels of teacher turnover lead to marked dips in Student Team Literature implementation in some years in some TDMG schools until the replacement teachers were brought up to speed with the training, coaching, and materials they needed to implement the program (Balfanz, Ruby, & Mac Iver, 2002). These fluctuations in implementation led to inconsistent results across years, with positive reading achievement results in some years and no significant differences in reading achievement between TD and control schools in other years.

It is encouraging that some policymakers are awakening to the need to take steps to create more stability and continuity across time in the reforms, leadership, and staff in urban schools. This awakening is partly due to recent reports that document startling turnover in principals in high-poverty middle schools (e.g., Advocates for Children and Youth [ACY], 2007a, 2007b) who are then replaced by inexperienced successors. For example, 90% of the high-poverty schools in Baltimore experienced one or more principal changes in the last 5 years (ACY 2007a). Eighty percent of the schools had two or more principal changes. Half of the schools experienced three or more principal changes during this 5-year period.

Urban districts also experience superintendent/CEO turnover with startling frequency (Hess, 1999). For example, during the most recent 5-year period (2002–2007), Baltimore has had five different CEOs. With such high levels of turnover at the top of urban districts, it is little wonder that many of the most promising whole-school and whole-district reforms are not sustained over time.

Fortunately, there is greater awareness than ever before of the dropout crisis in the United States (see www.gradgap.org for more information). This awareness is increasingly accompanied by an understanding that one key to keeping students on a path that leads to graduation is to implement and sustain comprehensive reforms in the middle grades (Balfanz, 2007). There is therefore reason to hope that more communities will find the means and the will to sustain such reforms.

## How Narrow Testing and Broad Standards Can Sabotage Certain Instructional Reforms

The period from the late 1990s to 2010 has been the heyday of standards and high stakes testing in American education. Disappointing trends in science education in the middle grades during this period highlight the unintended negative consequences that testing and standard-setting decisions can have. Science reform in the middle grades was greatly hampered by the omission of science from the initial testing requirements of No Child Left Behind (NCLB) and by the adoption of science standards that emphasize breadth over depth in most states and districts. No Child Left Behind accountability to date has focused on raising students'

reading and math test scores. As a result, science and other subjects have been neglected in favor of reading and math. Such neglect includes lack of funds to purchase science materials or support science teacher professional development, stealing from science instructional time in order to devote additional time to math or reading instruction or to test preparation activities, and lack of administrative interest in science (Blanc, Useem, & Ruby 2005). This neglect may slowly change as science achievement becomes part of calculating annual yearly progress, but many states have yet to implement science testing.

The national standards movement intended to establish a clear set of learning goals for students to meet by grade or groups of grades. Often this intent included a reduction in the number of these goals so that students would have more time to learn each (as reflected by the slogan "depth over breadth"). But most states and districts have established long lists of science standards for each grade, and breadth has won out. As a result, it is difficult for teachers to spend 6 to 8 weeks on one topic using a module that only covers a small number of standards. Unless states and districts revise both their standards and standardized tests to reward depth of study, pressure continues to favor the use of textbooks that include more topics. As a result, a whole host of wonderful and engaging science modules for the middle grades that were created with support provided by the National Science Foundation continue to be sadly underused in our nation's middle grades schools.

It has been disturbing to see increasing amounts of instructional time in the middle grades devoted to narrow assessment preparation. John Lounsbury, the editor of the *Middle School Journal,* says, "We are in danger of winning the battle of test scores but losing the battle of education" (as cited in Pate, 2001, p. 80). Finding ways to shape the assessments in state accountability systems so that they constitute worthwhile incentive structures for classroom instructional practice in the middle grades is one of the greatest challenges faced by educational policymakers in the 21st century (Mac Iver & Mac Iver, 2008).

### Notes

1. A Normal Curve Equivalent (NCE) is a standard score indicating how a student's performance compares to state-wide norms (on state assessments) or national norms (on national assessments). Scores in the norming population range from 1 to 99 with a mean of 50. The larger NCE gains in STL schools vs. non-STL schools indicate that during the middle grades students in STL schools are catching up to statewide norms in reading faster than are students in the control schools.

### References

Abidin, B., & Hartley, J. R. (1998). Developing mathematical problem solving skills. *Journal of Computer Assisted Learning, 14,* 278–291.
Advocates for Children and Youth (ACY). (2007a). Principal turnover in the Baltimore City Public School System. *Advocates for Children and Youth Issue Brief, 5,* 1–6.
Advocates for Children and Youth (ACY). (2007b). Principal turnover in

Prince George's County public schools. *Advocates for Children and Youth Issue Brief, 5,* 1–3.

Allen, J. (1999). *Words, words, words: Teaching vocabulary in grades 4–12.* York, ME: Stenhouse.

Ares, N., & Gorrell, J. (2002). Middle school students' understanding of meaningful learning and engaging classroom activities. *Journal of Research in Childhood Education, 16,* 263–277.

Balfanz, R. (2000). Why do so many urban public school students demonstrate so little academic achievement? In M. Sanders (Ed.), *Schooling students placed at risk: Research, policy and practice in the education of poor and minority adolescents* (pp. 37–62). Mahwah, NJ: Erlbaum.

Balfanz, R. (2007, May). *What your community can do to end its drop-out crisis: Learnings from research and practice.* Paper presented at the National Summit on America's Silent Epidemic, Washington, DC.

Balfanz, R., & Byrnes, V. (2006). Closing the mathematics achievement gap in high poverty middle schools: Enablers and constraints. *Journal of Education for Students Placed at Risk, 11,* 143–159.

Balfanz, R., Herzog, L., & Mac Iver, D. J. (2007). Preventing student disengagement and keeping students on a graduation path in high-poverty middle-grades schools: Early identification and effective interventions. *Journal of Educational Psychology, 42,* 223–235.

Balfanz, R., Mac Iver, D. J., & Byrnes, V. (2006). The implementation and impact of evidence-based mathematics reforms in high-poverty middle schools: A multi-site, multi-year study. *Journal for Research in Mathematics Education, 37,* 33–64.

Balfanz, R., Ruby, A., & Mac Iver, D. (2002). Essential components and next steps for comprehensive whole-school reform in high poverty middle schools. In S. Stringfield & D. Land (Eds.), *Educating at-risk students: One hundred-first yearbook of the National Society for the Study of Education* (Part 2, pp. 128–147). Chicago, IL: National Society for the Study of Education.

Beaton, A. E., Mullis, I. V. S., Martin, M. O., Gonzalez, E. J., Kelly, D. L., & Smith, T. A. (1996). *Mathematics achievement in the middle school years.* Boston, MA: TIMSS Study Center.

Beers, K. (2003). *When kids can't read: What teachers can do. A guide for teachers 6–12.* Portsmouth, NH: Heinemann.

Berends, M., Bodilly, S. J., & Kirby, S. N. (2002). *Facing the challenges of whole-school reform: New American Schools after a decade.* Santa Monica, CA: RAND.

Black, S. (2000). Together again. *The American School Board Journal, 187,* 40–43.

Blanc, S., Useem, E., & Ruby, A. (2005, July). *Implementation of the science and mathematics core curricula in the middle grades in Philadelphia.* Baltimore, MD: Center for the Social Organization of Schools.

Bloom, H., Hill, C., Black, A., & Lipsey, M. (2006, June). *Effect sizes in education research: What they are, what they mean and why they're important.* Paper presented at the 2006 Research Conference of the Institute of Education Sciences, U.S. Department of Education, Washington, DC.

Bornstein, M. H., Davidson, L., Keyes, C. L. M., Moore, K. A. (Eds.). (2003). *Well-being: Positive development across the life course.* Mahwah, NJ: Erlbaum.

Center for Social Organization of Schools (CSOS). (2004). *Johns Hopkins teaching resource books for* A History of US (Books 1–10). New York: Oxford University Press

Cohen, D. K., & Hill, H. C. (2001). *Learning policy: When state education reform works.* New Haven, CT: Yale University Press.

Cohen, J. (1988). *Statistical power analysis for the behavioral sciences.* Hillsdale, NJ: Erlbaum.

Corbett, H. D. & Wilson, B. L. (1997). *Cracks in the classroom floor: The seventh grade year in five Philadelphia middle schools.* Philadelphia, PA: Philadelphia Education Fund.

Darling-Hammond, L. (1997). *The right to learn: A blueprint for creating schools that work.* San Francisco, CA: Jossey-Bass.

Desimone, L. (2002). How can comprehensive school reform models be successfully implemented? *Review of Educational Research, 72*(3), 433–479.

Epstein, J. L., Sanders, M. G., Simon, B. S., Salinas, K. C., Jansorn, N. R., & Van Voorhis, F. L. (2002). *School, family, and community partnerships: Your handbook for action* (2nd ed.). Thousand Oaks, CA: Corwin Press.

Fuchs, D., Fuchs, L., Mathes, P., & Simmons, D. (1997). Peer-assisted learning strategies: Making classrooms more responsive to diversity. *American Educational Research Journal, 34,* 171–206.

Garriott, M. D., & Teter, C. (2007). *Teacher's quest guide to "Aristotle Leads the Way."* Washington, DC: Smithsonian Books.

Glennan, T. K. (1998). *New American schools after six years.* Santa Monica, CA: Rand.

Haberman, M. (1991). The pedagogy of poverty versus good teaching. *Phi Delta Kappan, 73,* 290–294.

Hakim, J. (1999). *A history of US* (2nd ed., Vols. 1–10). New York: Oxford University Press.

Hakim, J. (2004) *The story of science: Aristotle leads the way.* Washington, DC: Smithsonian Books.

Hakim, J. (2005). *The story of science: Newton at the center.* Washington, DC: Smithsonian Books.

Hanushek, E. A., & Rivkin, S. G. (2006). *School quality and the black-white achievement gap* (Working Paper 12651). Cambridge, MA: National Bureau of Economic Research.

Herlihy, C. M., & Kemple, J. (2004, December*). The Talent Development Middle School Model: Context, components, and initial impacts on students' performance and attendance.* New York: MDRC.

Herlihy, C. M., & Kemple, J. (2005, August). *The Talent Development Middle School Model: Impacts Through the 2002–2003 school year: An update to the December 2004 report.* New York: MDRC.

Hess, F. M. (1999). *Spinning wheels: The politics of urban school reform.* Washington, DC: Brookings.

Jones, L. G. (1998). *Student team literature teachers' manual.* Baltimore, MD: Johns Hopkins University's Center for the Social Organization of Schools.

Juvonen, J. (2007). Reforming middle schools: Focus on continuity, social connectedness, and engagement. *Educational Psychologist, 42,* 197–208.

Juvonen, J., Le, V., Kaganoff, T., Augustine, C. & Constant, L. (2004). *Focus on the wonder years: Challenges facing the American middle school.* Santa Monica, CA: RAND.

Kane, T. (2004). *The impact of after-school programs: Interpreting the results of 4 recent evaluations.* New York: W.T. Grant Foundation.

Keller, D. (1995). *An assessment of national academic achievement growth* (Unpublished doctoral dissertation). University of Delaware, Newark, DE.

Killion, J. (1999). *What works in the middle: Results-based staff development.* Oxford, OH: National Staff Development Council.

Kilpatrick, J., Swafford, J., & Findell, B. (Eds.). (2001). *Adding it up: Helping children learn mathematics.* Washington, DC: National Academy Press.

Knapp, M. S. (1995). *Teaching for meaning in high-poverty classrooms.* New York: Teachers College Press.

Lincoln, R. D. (1998). Looping in the middle grades, *Principal, 78,* 58–59.

Ma, L. (1999). *Knowing and teaching elementary mathematics.* Mahwah, NJ: Erlbaum.

Mac Iver, D. J., Balfanz, R., Ruby, A., Byrnes, V., Lorentz, S., & Jones, L. (2004). Developing adolescent literacy in high poverty middle schools: The impact of Talent Development's reforms across multiple years and sites. In P. R. Pintrich & M. L. Maehr (Eds.), *Motivating students, improving schools: The legacy of Carol Midgley—Advances in motivation and achievement* (Vol. 13, pp. 185–207). Oxford, England: Elsevier.

Mac Iver, D. J., Ruby, A., Balfanz, R., & Byrnes, V. (2003). Removed from the list: A comparative longitudinal case study of a reconstitution-eligible school. *Journal of Curriculum and Supervision, 18,* 259–289.

Mac Iver, D. J., Young, E., Balfanz, R., Shaw, A., Garriott, M., & Cohen, A. (2001). High quality learning opportunities in high poverty middle schools: Moving from rhetoric to reality. In T. Dickinson (Ed.),

*Reinventing the middle school* (pp. 155–175). New York: Routledge Falmer.

Mac Iver, M. A., & Mac Iver, D. J. (2007, April). *The impact of comprehensive school reform with NSF-supported mathematics curricula on urban middle grades student achievement.* Paper presented at the annual meeting of the American Educational Research Association, Chicago, IL.

Mac Iver, M. A., & Mac Iver, D. J. (2008). Middle grades reform. In T. Good (Ed.), *21st century education: A reference handbook* (pp. 304–317). Thousands Oaks, CA: Sage.

Nishina, A., Juvonen, J., & Witkow, M. (2006). Sticks and stones may break my bones, but names will make me sick: The consequences of peer harassment. *Journal of Clinical Child and Adolescent Psychology, 34,* 37–48.

Pate, P. E. (2001). Standards, students, and exploration: creating a curriculum intersection of excellence. In T. S. Dickinson (Ed.), *Reinventing the middle school* (pp. 79–95). New York: Routledge-Falmer.

RAND Reading Study Group. (2002). *Reading for understanding: Toward a R & D program in reading comprehension.* Santa Monica, CA: RAND.

Rowan, B., Barnes, C., & Camburn, E. (2004). Benefiting from comprehensive school reform: A review of research on CSR implementation. In C. T. Cross (Ed.), *Putting the pieces together: Lessons from comprehensive school reform research* (pp. 1–52). Washington, DC: National Clearinghouse for Comprehensive School Reform.

Routman, R. (1998). Selected reading-writing strategies for L. D. and other at-risk students. In C. Weaver (Ed.), *Practicing what we know: Informed reading instruction* (pp. 377–393). Urbana, IL: National Council of Teachers of English.

Rowan, B., & Guthrie, L. F. (1989). The quality of chapter 1 instruction: Results from a study of 24 schools. In R. Slavin (Ed.), *Effective programs for students at risk* (pp. 195–219). Boston, MA: Allyn & Bacon.

Ruby, A. (2002). Internal teacher turnover in urban middle school reform. *Journal of Education for Students Placed At Risk, 7,* 379–406.

Ruby, A. (2006). Improving science achievement at high-poverty urban middle schools. *Science Education, 90,* 1005–1027.

Ruby, A. (2007a, March). *Results from Furness High School CATAMA lab study.* Baltimore, MD: Center for the Social Organization of Schools.

Ruby, A. (2007b, September). *Cass Lake CATAMA results for year 1: 2006–07 school year.* Baltimore, MD: Center for the Social Organization of Schools.

Ruby, A., & Balfanz, R. (2006, June). *Improving math achievement of high-poverty urban middle grade students: Initial results from a randomized experiment for an elective-replacement extra-help math lab (CATAMA).* Paper presented at the Research Conference of the Institute of Education Sciences, U.S. Department of Education, Washington, DC.

Ruby, A., Mac Iver, D., & Byrnes, V. (2004, April). *Improving reading proficiency in high-poverty urban middle schools.* Paper presented at the Annual Meeting of the American Educational Research Association, San Diego, CA.

Sanders, M. G., & Epstein, J. L. (2000). Building school-family-community partnerships in middle and high schools. In M. G. Sanders (Ed.), *Schooling students placed at risk: Research, policy, and practice in the education of poor and minority adolescents* (pp. 339–361). Mahwah, NJ: Erlbaum.

Schmidt, W. H., McKnight, C. C., Jakwerth, P. M., Cogan, L. S., Raizen, S. A., Houang, R. T., et al. (1999). *Facing the consequences: Using TIMSS for a closer look at United States mathematics and science education.* Dordrecht, the Netherlands: Kluwer Academic.

Senk, D., & Thompson, D. (Eds.). (2003). *Standards-based school mathematics curricula: What are they? What do students learn?* Mahwah, NJ: Erlbaum.

Skinner, E. A., Zimmer-Gembeck, M. J., & Connell, J. P. (with commentary by J. E. Eccles). (1998). Individual differences and the development of perceived control. *Monographs of the Society for Research in Child Development, 63*(2–3, Serial No. 254).

Sorrell, A. C. [Producer]. (2001). *The Talent Development Climate Program: Helping middle schools create atmospheres that are safe, nurturing, and positive* [Video and Flyer]. Baltimore, MD: Center for the Social Organization of Schools, Johns Hopkins University.

Sorrell, A. C., Mc Iver, G. J. (2002, April). *Creating a productive learning climate in a disorderly middle school: The pilot test of Talent Development's "High Five" climate program.* Paper presented at the annual meeting of the American Educational Research Association, New Orleans.

Stevens, R. J. (2006a, September). Integrated middle school literacy instruction. *Middle School Journal,* 13–19.

Stevens, R. J. (2006b). Using cooperative learning to integrate middle school reading and language arts instruction. *Research in Middle Level Education Online, 30*(1). Retrieved from www.nmsa.org

Sunderman, G.L. (Ed.) (2007). *Holding NCLB accountable: Achieving accountability, equity, & school reform.* Thousand Oaks, CA: Corwin.

Teter, C. H., Garriott, M. D., & Brodowski, K. (2008). *Teacher's quest guide to accompany "The Story of Science: Newton at the Center."* Washington, DC: Smithsonian Books.

U.S. Department of Education. (2007a). *CSR awards database: Locale summary for all calendar years.* Washington, DC: Author.

U.S. Department of Education. (2007b). *CSR awards database: Multistate funding summaries for each calendar year.* Washington, DC: Author.

U.S. Department of Education. (2007c). *CSR awards database: School demographics for all calendar years.* Washington, DC: Author.

Useem, E. (2001a). New teacher staffing and comprehensive middle school reform: Philadelphia's experience. In V. A. Anfara, Jr. (Ed.), *The handbook of research in middle level education* (pp. 143–160). Greenwich, CT: Information Age.

Useem, E. (2001b, October). *Second-year teachers' experience in Philadelphia's Talent Development Middle Schools.* Philadelphia, PA: Philadelphia Education Fund.

Useem, E., & Neild, R. C. (2001, May). *Teacher staffing in the School District of Philadelphia.* Philadelphia, PA: Philadelphia Education Fund.

Wang, M. C., Wong, K. K., & Kim, J. (1999). The need for developing procedural accountability in Title I schoolwide programs. In G. Orfield & E. H. DeBray (Eds.), *Hard work for good schools: Facts, not fads, in Title I reform* (pp. 175–195). Cambridge, MA: Harvard University, Civil Rights Project.

Wasik, B. A., & Slavin, R. E. (1990). *Preventing early reading failure with one-to-one tutoring: A best evidence synthesis.* Baltimore, MD: Johns Hopkins University Center for Research on Effective Schooling for Disadvantaged Students.

Williamson, R., & Johnston, J. H. (1999, March). Challenging orthodoxy: An emerging agenda for middle level reform. *Middle School Journal,* 10–17.

Wilson, B. L., & Corbett, H. D. (2001). *Listening to urban kids: School reform and the teachers they want.* Albany, NY: SUNY Press.

Wong, K. K., & Meyer, S. J. (1998). Title I schoolwide programs: A synthesis of findings from recent evaluations. *Educational Evaluation and Policy Analysis, 20,* 115–136.

# 29

# The Impact of Concept-Oriented Reading Instruction on Students' Reading Motivation, Reading Engagement, and Reading Comprehension

*Allan Wigfield and John T. Guthrie*

The development of adequate reading comprehension skills is crucial to children's success in school and to other important developmental outcomes. Children who can comprehend well have the opportunity to learn content in many different school subjects; those who read poorly generally make poor academic progress in a variety of academic subject areas (Alvermann & Eakle, 2003; Kirsch et al., 2002). Reading comprehension is a strong predictor of whether children stay in school when the option to drop out at age 16 becomes available to them (Finn, 1989). Therefore, it is essential for all children to develop the ability to comprehend what they read.

Unfortunately, many children and adolescents do not read well. Among U.S. adolescents included in the National Assessment of Educational Progress (NAEP) 2003 report (Donahue, Daane, & Jin, 2005), 68% were at or below the NAEP basic level in reading, which is defined as only partial mastery of the knowledge and skills needed to do the work at a given grade level. Less than 30% were at the NAEP proficient level, which is considered the national goal by 2014 in the No Child Left Behind legislation. The proficient level is defined as having grade-level competencies in subject matter knowledge, ability to apply knowledge, and analytic skills appropriate to the grade level and subject matter being learned. Additionally, surveys show that more than 50% of low-achieving adolescents resist reading, particularly the reading that is done in school (Stipek, 2002). Thus, there is a strong need for new approaches to the teaching of reading comprehension that ensure success and positive motivation for more students.

In this chapter, we discuss the impact of one such program, Concept-Oriented Reading Instruction (CORI), on children's reading motivation, reading engagement, and reading comprehension. A reading comprehension instructional program, CORI merges instruction in science or social studies with reading instruction. The program is designed specifically to enhance children's motivation for

reading, and to increase children's engagement in reading, as fundamental ways of increasing children's reading comprehension.

At the elementary school level, the vast majority of reading programs emphasize the direct instruction of reading strategies. Based on the recommendations of the National Reading Panel (NRP; 2000), reading strategies such as questioning, summarizing, graphic organizing, and predicting are taught with modeling, scaffolding, and guided practice. Investigations that contain experimental comparisons (Rozendaal, Minnaert, Boekaerts, 2005; Souvignier & Mokhlesgerami, 2006) or systematic observations (Taylor, Pearson, Peterson, & Rodriguez, 2003) confirm the benefits of this instruction for reading comprehension. However, none of these studies has shown instructional effects on a standardized test of reading comprehension. Additionally, these programs do not focus to any great extent on students' motivation for reading. The CORI program is distinct from these other reading comprehension programs in its emphasis on motivational support for the strategy instruction and conceptual knowledge growth from text. The CORI program is also distinct because experimental comparisons show benefits for reading motivation, reading strategies, and standardized measures of reading comprehension; we discuss this data later in this chapter.

We organized the chapter in five sections. First, we present our engagement perspective on reading comprehension development, and define reading engagement and reading motivation. Second, we discuss how children's reading motivation links to reading comprehension, by influencing the extent to which children are engaged in reading and read frequently. Third, we discuss changes in children's academic motivation and motivation for reading over the school years, and explanations for the observed changes. Fourth, we describe CORI in some detail, with a special focus on the instructional practices designed to foster children's motivation for reading, because such practices are quite important for fostering children's engagement in reading. Fifth, we present evidence from several studies concerning CORI's effectiveness in enhancing children's reading motivation and comprehension, and explore processes that help explain why CORI has been effective.

## The Engagement Perspective on Reading Comprehension Development

Concept-Oriented Reading Instruction's theoretical grounding is our engagement perspective on reading comprehension development (Guthrie & Wigfield, 2000; see also Baker, Dreher, & Guthrie, 2000; Guthrie, McGough, & Wigfield, 1996). By "engagement" we mean interacting with text in ways that are both strategic and motivated. More broadly, we describe engaged readers as motivated to read, strategic in their approaches to comprehending what they read, knowledgeable in their construction of meaning from text, and socially interactive while reading (Guthrie et al., 1996; Guthrie & Wigfield, 2000; Guthrie, Wigfield, & Perencevich, 2004). Engagement in reading is crucial to the development of reading comprehension skills and reading achievement; we discuss this further later in this chapter. Moreover, engaged reading can compensate for factors such as low levels of family education and low income in the development of children's reading skills (see Guthrie & Wigfield, 2000, for further discussion).

There is evidence in the literature that different instructional practices can increase reading motivation and engagement (Guthrie & Humenick, 2004; Guthrie & Wigfield, 2000). These include such practices as providing interesting texts in classrooms, supporting students' control (or autonomy) over their own learning, giving students opportunities to collaborate with other students, and providing direct instruction in how to use different reading strategies. These and other practices are instantiated by CORI, as we describe in more detail later.

*Engagement* and *motivation* are related terms that sometimes are used interchangeably, so we think it is important to distinguish them at the outset. Engagement is a multidimensional construct that includes behavioral, cognitive, and affective attributes associated with being deeply involved in an activity such as reading (see Fredericks, Blumenfeld, & Paris, 2004; Guthrie, Wigfield, & Perencevich, 2004). In their review of the research on school engagement, Fredericks et al. (2004) defined behavioral engagement as positive conduct, involvement in academic tasks (as indicated by effort and persistence), and participation in various school activities. Emotional engagement encompasses the ways in which students react affectively to classroom activities. Cognitive engagement means the active use of cognitive strategies and other cognitive investments in learning activities.

With respect to reading engagement, we and our colleagues (Guthrie & Wigfield, 2000; Guthrie, Wigfield, & Perencevich, 2004) characterize engaged readers as actively using cognitive strategies in reading, building knowledge while they read, and being socially interactive while read-

ing. Engaged reading is enhanced when the books being read and material discussed involves cognitively rich material with clear content goals for the instruction. Further, social interactions around reading give students opportunities to share with others what they are reading about, thus enhancing their engagement. As Guthrie (2004) put it, "in sum engaged readers are strategic, motivated, knowledge-driven, and socially interactive" (p. 3).

It can be seen from both these definitions that engagement is a broad construct encompassing different aspects; indeed, Fredericks et al. (2004) called it a metaconstruct. By contrast, motivation is a more specific construct that relates to engagement but can be distinguished from it. Motivation is what energizes and directs behavior, and often is defined with respect to the beliefs, values, and goals individuals have in relation to different activities (Eccles & Wigfield, 2002; Wigfield, Eccles, Schiefele, Roeser, & Davis-Kean, 2006). Motivation often is domain specific; in the reading domain, we define reading motivation as follows: "Reading motivation is the individual's personal goals, values, and beliefs with regard to the topics, processes, and outcomes of reading" (Guthrie & Wigfield, 2000, p. 405). Because of its role in directing behavior, choice is an important part of motivation, which often directs individuals' choices regarding activities (Wigfield, Eccles, et al., 2006). Motivation also is important for the maintenance of behavior, particularly when activities are cognitively demanding. Reading is one such activity because it involves many different cognitive skills. These range from processing individual words to generating meaning from complex texts. Further, although reading is required for many school tasks and activities, it is also something students can choose to do or not— "Am I going to read or do something else?" Given these characteristics motivation is especially crucial to reading engagement. Even the reader with the strongest cognitive skills may not spend much time reading if he or she is not motivated to read. In our work, we have focused, in particular, on intrinsic motivation to read, or motivation that comes from inside the person (Guthrie & Wigfield, 2000; Wigfield & Guthrie, 1997). We do so because intrinsic motivation relates to longer-term engagement in learning and use of deeper-level cognitive strategies, among other things (Hidi & Harackiewicz, 2000; Schiefele, 1999).

At the outset of this chapter, it is also important to define reading comprehension. We rely on the definition of the RAND panel, "reading comprehension [is] the process of simultaneously extracting and constructing meaning through interaction and involvement with written language" (National Reading Panel, 2000, p. 11). Thus, the two main aspects of comprehension are understanding what is on the written page (the "extraction" part of the definition) and building meaning from what is on the page (the "construction" part of the definition). Reading comprehension usually is measured by having students read passages and then having them either write about what they learned from the passage, or answer a series of questions about the passage.

## Relations of Reading Motivation to Reading Engagement and Comprehension

Motivation researchers have defined and studied a variety of motivational beliefs, values, and goals that individuals have. Central motivational beliefs include self-efficacy, or one's confidence in one's ability to accomplish different tasks (Bandura, 1997; Schunk & Pajares, 2005; Schunk & Zimmerman, 1997), and the sense of control and autonomy individuals have over their learning (Ryan & Deci, 2000; Skinner, Zimmer-Gelback, & Connell, 1998). Researchers distinguish between intrinsic and extrinsic motivation for different activities, with intrinsic motivation coming from inside the individual and extrinsic motivation coming from outside (e.g., rewards, grades) (Deci & Moller, 2005). Researchers also have discussed different ways in which individuals value activities that they do, including how important they are to the individual, or how useful they might be (Eccles, 2005; Wigfield & Eccles, 2002). Finally, individuals have different kinds of goals and goal orientations for the activities they undertake, such as the goal of increasing one's knowledge or the goal of outperforming others (Elliot, 2005; Pintrich, 2000). Wigfield, Eccles, et al. (2006) and Wigfield and Tonks (2004) provide reviews of the work on these variables from studies of motivation in different areas and specifically in reading.

In our work with CORI, we have focused primarily on building children's self-efficacy for reading, increasing their intrinsic motivation for reading by building their interest in reading, increasing their perceived autonomy or the control they have over their reading, and encouraging social interactions around reading. We chose these aspects of motivation because they are linked to student achievement and are modifiable through various instructional practices (see Guthrie & Humenick, 2004; Guthrie, Wigfield, Barbosa, et al., 2004; Wigfield et al., 2006). We return to these points later.

As noted earlier, motivation influences choice of activities, energy directed to the activity, and level of commitment to the activity (Wigfield, Eccles, et al., 2006); thus, motivation is essential for full engagement in an activity. This point implies that children who are motivated to read likely will read more frequently, and earlier research documents this. We found that children who were more highly motivated to read reported reading more than three times as much as children who were less motivated (Wigfield & Guthrie, 1997). This was particularly true of children who were intrinsically motivated to read. Furthermore, children's reading motivation measured in the fall predicted growth in the amount of reading children did at the end of 3 months. The more highly motivated children increased the amount of reading they did to a greater extent than did less motivated students. It is important to note that these effects were particularly applicable for the children most highly, intrinsically motivated to read. From these and other results, we concluded that children who are moti-

vated (especially those who are intrinsically motivated) to read are more behaviorally engaged in reading.

Being engaged in reading is important because many studies have shown that the amount of reading children do relates strongly to their reading comprehension and achievement, and their knowledge of the world (see Cipielewski & Stanovich, 1992; Guthrie & Wigfield, 2000). Reading amount also relates to the growth over a school year in children's reading comprehension. Thus, increasing children's amount of reading fosters their development of reading comprehension. One major goal of CORI is to increase the amount of children's reading.

*The Development of Achievement Motivation* A large literature exists on how children's motivation develops across the school years (see Eccles, Wigfield, & Schiefele, 1998; Pintrich & Schunk, 2002; Wigfield, Byrnes, & Eccles, 2006, for review). We focus here on change in children's perceptions of competence or efficacy, and change in intrinsic motivation and valuing for learning, some of the motivation constructs central to our efforts in CORI. Many young children tend to have a strong sense of their competence for the different activities they do in school. Children also find most of the activities they do interesting and exciting, so they are enthusiastic about a wide variety of things they do each day at school and value their academic activities. Unfortunately, this optimistic beginning does not last for all children. Children's competence beliefs and intrinsic motivation for learning tend to decline across the elementary school years, especially in academic subject areas like reading and math (Wigfield, Byrnes, & Eccles, 2006). Researchers studying the early development of children's competence beliefs, intrinsic motivation for different subjects (including reading), and valuing of them found that they decrease across the elementary school years (Gottfried, 1990; Gottfried, Fleming, & Gottfried 2001; Jacobs, Lanza, Osgood, Eccles, & Wigfield, 2002; Lepper, Corpus, & Iyengar, 2005; Wigfield et al., 1997). In the Jacobs et al. work the declines of competence beliefs in reading/English were stronger for boys than for girls. Children's extrinsic motivation often increases throughout elementary school and into middle school, sometimes at the expense of their intrinsic motivation (Harter, 1981; Maehr & Midgley, 1996).

Studies looking at reading motivation, in particular, present a somewhat mixed picture. Some show these declines and others do not, but several large-scale studies do show decreases over age in reading attitudes and motivation (see Wigfield, 2000). McKenna, Kear, and Ellsworth's (1995) work on children's attitudes toward reading shows that across the elementary school years children report liking reading less each year. In the National Assessment of Educational Progress (NAEP; Donahue et al., 2005) report, older children reported less enjoyment of reading than did younger children, and many children in middle school become actively resistant to engaging in reading.

Such changes in children's sense of competence and

intrinsic motivation have been explained in two main ways. One explanation focuses on changes that occur within the child (see Wigfield, Byrnes, & Eccles, 2006). Through the school years, children's capacity to understand their own performance increases. They receive more and more feedback about their performance in school, and become much more sophisticated at understanding its meaning. Report card grades, feedback about performance on different school projects and tests, and other evaluative information can lead some children to the realization that they are not as capable as their peers. The realization that one is not as capable as others can decrease intrinsic motivation to learn (Wigfield, 1994).

A second explanation focuses on how certain teaching and evaluation practices contribute to a decline in some children's motivation. A variety of such practices have been discussed (see Ames, 1992; Eccles & Midgley, 1989; Meece, 1994; National Research Council (NRC), 2004; Stipek, 1996, 2002; Wigfield, Byrnes, & Eccles, 2006). We just noted that children get better at interpreting the evaluative information they receive, and they also receive increasing amounts of this information as they go through school. Furthermore, this information gets more specific and focused. For instance, points replace stars and letter grades replace O's for outstanding and S's for satisfactory. Practices that emphasize social comparison among children and excessive competition among them, may lead children to focus too much on how their skills compare to others. Examples of such practices include public evaluations of students, public displays of students' graded work, teachers making direct comparisons of how different students are doing, and competitive activities, such as spelling bees. Such practices can deflate children's competence beliefs, particularly those of children doing less well (Wigfield & Tonks, 2004).

Certain instructional practices can undermine children's intrinsic motivation for learning as well. Instruction that makes few attempts to spark children's interests in different topics can decrease children's intrinsic motivation (Brophy, 2004; Stipek, 1996, 2002). When teachers are overly controlling and do not allow children much choice, intrinsic motivation and autonomy can be stifled (Guthrie, Wigfield, & Perencevich, 2004; Ryan & Deci, 2000). Furthermore, Assor, Kaplan, and Roth (2002) found that when students do not see the relevance of what they are learning to their own values and goals, they are less engaged in learning. We turn next to ways that instructional practices can be changed to foster children's motivation and engagement in reading.

## Fostering Children's Reading Engagement: Concept-Oriented Reading Instruction

Classroom instructional practices that negatively impact children's motivation practices can be changed, and a number of researchers have studied general instructional practices designed to enhance children's motivation in

school (see Ames, 1992; Maehr & Midgley, 1996; NRC, 2004; Stipek, 1996, 2002; Wigfield et al., 2006; Wigfield, Eccles, & Rodriguez, 1998). The National Research Council (2004) reported on engaging schools and listed the following instructional practices as ones that have been shown to enhance students' motivation: (a) having high expectations for all students and helping them to believe they can achieve; (b) emphasizing and providing opportunities for students' active participation in their learning; (c) providing variety in instruction in order that it not become too routine; (d) allowing students control over their own learning; (e) helping students feel connected to their classmates, teachers, and schools; (f) providing all students with challenging work that requires higher-order thinking; (g) giving students opportunities to work together frequently; and (h) connecting learning in meaningful ways to students' lives.

In the reading area, Guthrie and Humenick (2004) did a meta-analysis of experimental studies looking at the effects of different kinds of instructional practices designed to enhance children's intrinsic motivation to read on students' reading comprehension (measured in various ways) and motivation. The study looked at four main practices: (a) providing content goals for instruction; (b) supporting students' autonomy and control over their own learning; (c) using interesting texts and materials in reading instruction; and (d) giving students the opportunity to work with classmates. This list clearly overlaps with the list discussed in the NRC report and by researchers such as Stipek (1996, 2002). Each of these practices had moderate to strong effect sizes (ranging from .48 for collaboration to 1.64 for interesting texts), demonstrating they have an important influence on students' reading comprehension.

This meta-analysis indicated that motivation-supporting practices appear to increase motivation and text comprehension in controlled, primarily laboratory-based studies. However, to date, few studies have shown how such practices may operate together in actual classroom instruction to influence students' motivation and achievement. Our research on CORI addresses this issue, and we begin our discussion of this work with a description of the CORI program.

## Concept-Oriented Reading Instruction (CORI)

Concept-Oriented Reading Instruction is a reading instructional program designed to foster children's reading motivation, engagement, and comprehension (see Guthrie, Wigfield, & Perencevich, 2004, for a detailed portrayal of different aspects of CORI; www.cori.umd.edu presents further information about CORI, including teachers' guides for lesson planning in CORI). As noted earlier, it is based on our engagement model of reading development (Guthrie & Wigfield, 2000), and so focuses on cognitive comprehension strategies, motivational processes, conceptual knowledge, and social interaction during reading.

To date, the effects of CORI have been studied in implementations done in third through fifth grade elementary school classrooms. Earlier implementations (e.g., Guthrie, McGough, & Wigfield, 1996) lasted the full school year, and the most recent implementation lasted for 12 weeks. We focus here primarily on our recent implementation of the 12-week version of CORI in third, fourth, and fifth grade classes, describing the design of the instructional program and practices and summarizing results of several studies of CORI's effects on children's reading comprehension and reading motivation.

### CORI Instructional Practices Supporting Student Motivation

One unique feature of CORI is that students' motivation and engagement are explicitly supported through five instructional practices: (a) using content goals for reading instruction; (b) affording choices and control to students; (c) providing hands-on activities; (d) using interesting texts for instruction; and (e) organizing collaboration for learning from text. The rationale for using several practices to enhance motivation is that changing students' motivation in actual classrooms is a complex process that requires a variety of specific instructional practices. We describe each of these practices in more detail next; see also Guthrie, 2004; Guthrie, Wigfield, Barbosa, et al., 2004 for description of these practices).

Content goals for instruction in reading are instantiated by pairing reading instruction with instruction in either social studies or science. In the most recent implementation, reading comprehension instruction was integrated with science instruction, with a specific focus on the conceptual theme of ecology in life science. We chose life science because we believed it would be appealing to most children.

Knowledge content goals in a subject area such as science, provide motivation for students because they provide a purpose for using different reading comprehension strategies, such as questioning. Students learn about ecological principles and core concepts in ecology, such as predation, reproduction, competition, and defense (see Barbosa & Alexander, 2004 for discussion of the ecological concepts and principles currently being taught in CORI science). In CORI, students learn and perform reading comprehension strategies such as questioning within this meaningful context, which enables students to learn and to use the strategies with greater effort, attention, and interest than in a context devoid of deep, conceptual themes (see also Stipek, 2002, for discussion of the benefits of using rich cognitive content goals in reading instruction).

A second CORI motivational practice consists of optimizing student choice during reading comprehension instruction in the classroom. The optimization process enables students to make decisions and choices about tasks and texts in the classroom that are cognitively appropriate and developmentally productive. Choices must be tailored to students' needs and capabilities. For example, students are given individual choices about which birds or animals to study in depth, and which books to read on the topic. Teachers guide students to match texts to their information needs and reading levels. Such support for autonomy

provides intrinsic motivation, which increases effort and persistence in the challenge of learning and gaining command of reading comprehension strategies (Ryan & Deci, 2000; Skinner, Wellborn, & Connell, 1990). It is important to note that in CORI classrooms all children are given opportunities to choose activities and reading materials, not just the students performing at the highest level.

A third practice is hands-on experiences related to texts and reading activities. The base of CORI is a framework of science inquiry in which students explore ecological issues through observational activities, systematic investigations, and true experiments. Hidi and Harackiewicz (2000), Nolen and Nicholls (1994), and Zahorik (1996) all have argued that such activities are motivating for students in elementary and middle school classrooms. Hands-on CORI activities are connected directly to reading, by having related books in CORI classrooms that connect these activities and are readily available to the students. For example, when students dissect an owl pellet, they become more engaged in their subsequent reading about owls and the food web in which they exist when compared to students doing similar reading without the hands-on experience (Guthrie, Wigfield, Humenick, et al., 2006).

The fourth practice of motivational support in CORI is using an abundance of interesting texts for comprehension instruction. One kind of interesting text is information trade books that possess features such as a table of contents, index, illustrations, bold headings, and a coherent array of subsections. Along with the information texts, a variety of narrative books that relate to the conceptual theme of the unit are provided. The books are chosen carefully to relate to the conceptual theme, vary in difficulty so that students at different reading levels have books they can read, align with the strategies being taught, have features such as illustrations and a writing style that make them attractive to students, and incorporate multimedia on occasion (see Davis & Tonks, 2004, for further details about the book selection process)

Teachers who use CORI are provided with four class sets of books for each student, with each set consisting of two information books, one literary chapter book, and one expressive reading book. In addition, six team sets (one book for each team of four students) are used. In a classroom, interesting texts and other interesting reading materials (e.g., websites) serve a crucial role for facilitating strategy development by enabling students to pursue knowledge goals, exercise choices of subtopics for learning, and satisfy curiosities developed from hands-on experiences.

The fifth practice consists of support for student collaboration with a diversity of reading activities. Students' motivation for using complex comprehension strategies is increased when students are afforded opportunities to share their questions, interesting texts, and information being gained. Rozendaal, Minnaert, and Boekarts (2005) have shown that students given more collaborative opportunities engaged in deeper level processing and were more positively motivated (see also O'Donnell, 2006; Webb &

Palincsar, 1996). In CORI, collaborative activity enables students to clarify their understanding of the core concepts of survival, such as defense, predation, or reproduction, as well as to share other knowledge gained from reading. Teachers provide CORI students with many opportunities to talk with one another about what they are reading, and work together on different kinds of projects.

*CORI Strategy Instruction Practices* In CORI, explicit strategy instruction is provided for a number of reading comprehension strategies that have been shown to be effective in enhancing students' reading comprehension (National Reading Panel, 2000). In grades 3 and 4, the following reading comprehension strategies are emphasized: (a) activating background knowledge; (b) questioning; (c) searching for information; (d) summarizing; (e) organizing graphically; and (f) structuring stories. Each strategy is taught for one week over the first 6 weeks of instruction, and the strategies are systematically integrated with each other in the following 6 weeks. This sequence enables students to gain command of the individual strategies, as well as to fuse them in complex comprehension activities in the classroom. In grade 5, students' monitoring of their comprehension and generating inferences from text are major new strategies that receive strong emphasis during the instructional program.

At all grade levels, the strategies are modeled by the teacher, and scaffolded according to students' needs, with guided practice provided. This approach is similar to the recommendations and practices for multiple strategy instruction described in the NRP report (2000). The strategy instruction emphasizes the attributes of competence in doing the strategy, awareness of when and how to use each strategy, and self-initiation of the strategy to assure sustained self-regulation of effective reading. Thus, in CORI the five practices of motivational support are combined with systematic, explicit instruction in reading comprehension strategies to comprise the CORI context for reading development.

*Implementing CORI* As noted earlier, the most recent implementation of CORI was done with third, fourth, and fifth grade students. The 12-week program began in early fall of the school year and ended before the winter holiday break in December. Instruction was provided for approximately 90 minutes per day, with teachers introducing the different reading strategies instruction in the context of ecological principles. Teachers often started the CORI program with an activity like a walk in the woods, or observation of a plant or animal, and then tied these activities to reading. As children explored books related to the activity, teachers instructed them in the different reading strategies. Other "hands-on" activities were introduced as CORI instruction continued. Along with the direct strategy instruction and motivation support, independent reading also was emphasized in all grades, but especially in fifth grade (see Perencevich, 2004; Sikorski, 2004, for detailed description of how CORI was implemented in third grade

classrooms). A strand of CORI is also devoted to struggling readers at each grade level (Guthrie, 2004). In our current study, CORI was implemented for two consecutive years each in third, fourth, and fifth grades. We next present evidence for CORI's effectiveness using data from the third and fourth grade implementations.

## CORI'S Effects on Children's Reading Motivation, Engagement, and Comprehension

Research on earlier versions of CORI showed that the program has positive effects on children's reading comprehension, strategy use, and motivation (Guthrie, Van Meter, Hancock, et al., 1998; Guthrie, Van Meter, McCann, et al., 1996; Guthrie, Wigfield, & Von Secker, 2000). In an initial study of CORI's effects, we and our colleagues (Guthrie, Wigfield, Perencevich, et al., 1996) implemented CORI for a full year in grades 3 and 5 classrooms in two elementary schools (N = 140). Performance assessments, given in the fall and spring, measured children's reading strategy use and conceptual knowledge gained from reading. Students' reading strategy use and conceptual knowledge gained from reading both increased significantly across the school year, at both grade levels. We further studied CORI's influence on grades 3 and 5 students' reading motivation, using a quasi-experiment design in which we compared the reading motivation of the CORI students to those receiving traditional reading instruction (Guthrie et al., 2000). Students' reading motivation was measured using the Motivations for Reading Questionnaire (MRQ; Wigfield & Guthrie, 1997) that measures different aspects of children's reading motivation. Two aspects of intrinsic motivation (curiosity and involvement) and two of extrinsic motivation (desire for recognition in reading and reading competition) were examined in this study. Children also completed a self-report measure of reading strategy use. The CORI students were higher than students in the traditional instruction classrooms on reading curiosity and strategy use. These studies provided important initial support for CORI's effectiveness.

We turn next to a more detailed description of results from our longitudinal study of our most recent implementations of CORI that we call the Reading Engagement Project. This study was done in several elementary schools in a Maryland school district. Detailed descriptions of the methodology of this study and the measures used can be found in Guthrie, Wigfield, Barbosa, et al. (2004) and Wigfield, Guthrie, Tonks, and Perencevich (2004). We provide a summary of the study's methodology in the next section before describing the results of several substudies within the larger study.

*Reading Engagement Project Overview* This project was a quasi-experimental study conducted with third, fourth, and fifth-grade students; we focus here on results from grades 3 and 4 students because the grade 5 data is still being processed. The project involved each year (from 2001 to 2005) a 12-week implementation of CORI during the fall of the school year, and a 12-week implementation of a Strategy Instruction (SI) based reading comprehension program to teach children different reading strategies known to foster reading comprehension (see further description of SI below). The study had an equivalent groups pretest–posttest design where schools selected by district administrators to be similar on demographic characteristics and previous reading achievement were assigned randomly to either CORI or SI. Children in classrooms in two schools received CORI instruction and children in classrooms in two other schools received SI. The schools each included a diverse group of children both with respect to ethnicity and economic background.

*Procedure*   CORI and SI initially were implemented in third grade, for two consecutive years. In the first year of the third grade implementation, there were 8 CORI teachers and 11 SI teachers. Approximately 150 children received the CORI program and 215 the SI program. In the second year of the third grade implementation, another school was added to the study. Teachers in this school taught the county's reading instruction program, and so we refer to this group of teachers and students as the Traditional Instruction (TI) group. There were nine CORI, 11 SI, and four TI classrooms in the second year. Approximately 155 students received CORI, 220 received SI, and 50 received TI. For fourth grade, there were five CORI teachers, seven SI teachers, and three SI teachers during the first year of implementation.

As noted above, CORI and SI were implemented for 12 weeks each school year, starting in early September and ending in early December. Concept-Oriented Reading Instruction was provided for approximately 90 minutes each day, and included reading strategy instruction; science inquiry focused on ecological issues, concepts, and activities; and support for student motivation. As noted above, students were taught the following reading strategies: activating background knowledge, searching for information, questioning, summarizing, organizing graphically, and identifying story structure. These strategies were selected based on the National Reading Panel's (2000) report of effective strategies for reading comprehension instruction. Each strategy was introduced during one week of instruction during the first 6 weeks of CORI, and combinations of the strategies were introduced in the second 6 weeks. The science inquiry portion of the program focused on ecological concepts of survival, and observational and experimental activities in which the students participated. Motivation support consisted of the five instructional practices discussed above: content goals for instruction (the ecological science concepts), hands-on experiences (the science activities), provision of interesting texts related to the ecological topics, optimizing student choice of reading materials and activities, and supporting students' collaborative activities. Detailed descriptions of the CORI intervention and the instructional practices contained in it can be found in Barbosa and Alexander

(2004), Guthrie (2004), Guthrie, Wigfield, Barbosa, et al. (2004), and Perencevich (2004).

The SI intervention involved instruction in the same reading strategies included in CORI. The SI teachers also taught the same county-based life science objectives (with a heavy emphasis on ecology) and included the same science observations and activities (aquariums) as did the CORI teachers. There was no explicit support for student motivation stipulated in the SI program, although teachers used a variety of practices to motivate their students to read. Guthrie and Taboada (2004) provide a detailed description of the SI program implemented in this project. The TI program consisted of an extensive amount of text interaction with a variety of basal materials and trade books. Strategies such as predicting and activating background knowledge were taught implicitly as appropriate to the text.

*Professional Development*   Teachers learned the CORI and SI models during summer workshops. The CORI teachers participated in a 10-day workshop that included viewing examples of instruction, performing the reading strategies, discussing motivational practices, constructing reading-science integrations, identifying books appropriate for this instruction, and planning their 12-week program using a CORI teacher's guide supplied by the project. The SI teachers participated in a 5-day workshop that included viewing examples of instruction, performing the reading strategies, identifying books appropriate for this instruction, and planning 12 weeks of instruction using an SI teacher's guide supplied by the project. The SI workshop was shorter because teachers did not develop the science activities, motivational practices, or science-reading integrations.

*Measures*   Prior to and following the interventions students completed measures of reading comprehension, reading strategy use, and reading motivation (see Guthrie, Wigfield, Barbosa, et al. 2004 for detailed description of these measures, how they were scored, and their psychometric properties). Reading comprehension was measured by two measures developed by project staff and also by the Gates-MacGinitie Reading Tests. One project-developed comprehension measure involved students reading passages about plants and animals in different ecosystems and then writing about what they learned from them. Students' writing was scored on a 6-level rubric, with each level of the rubric indicating richer comprehension of the materials. A second measure involved students rating the similarity of pairs of words taken from passages the students read; this measure is similar to comprehension measures used by Britton and Gulgoz (1991). The Gates-MacGinitie was added in the second year in order to have a standardized measure of comprehension included in the group of comprehension measures.

Students' motivation for reading also was measured in different ways. Students completed an abbreviated version of the MRQ we developed (Wigfield & Guthrie, 1997). As noted above, the MRQ assesses different aspects of

**TABLE 29.1**
**Sample Items Measuring Different Aspects of Reading Motivation**

| Reading Self-Efficacy | |
|---|---|
| I am a good reader | |
| **Intrinsic Motivation to Read** | |
| Curiosity | I have favorite subjects that I like to read about |
| Reading involvement | I enjoy a long, involved story or fiction book |
| Preference for challenge in reading | If the project is interesting, I can read difficult material |

From the Motivations for Reading Questionnaire, Wigfield, & Guthrie, 1997. With permission.

reading motivation; in this work, we assessed reading self-efficacy and intrinsic motivation to read (defined in this questionnaire as reading curiosity, reading involvement, and preference for challenge in reading). Sample items for each of these constructs are presented in Table 29.1. At the conclusion of the intervention, CORI and SI teachers rated students' reading self-efficacy, intrinsic motivation for reading, and extrinsic motivation for reading.

Students' reading frequency was measured using the Reading Activity Inventory (Wigfield & Guthrie, 1997). This measure assesses students' reports of their frequency of reading different kinds of reading materials in school.

*Pre- and Posttest Measured Students' Actual Strategy Use* The strategies measured included (a) students' activation of their background knowledge with respect to the reading passages used in the text comprehension measure, (b) students' questions about the topics in the packets, and (c) students' skills of searching for information in the packets. Composite measures of strategy use were created for use in the data analyses.

*Implementation Quality* Teacher quality of implementation for both the CORI and SI programs was assessed by videotaping two lessons for each teacher. The videotaped lessons were coded for quality of strategy instruction and implementation of motivational practices. Composite implementation quality scores were created from these codes, and this measure was used as a covariate in some of the analyses reported below.

We next summarize results from several of our published and unpublished studies that assessed how CORI, SI, and TI affected students' reading comprehension and motivation. The first study (Wigfield, Guthrie, Tonks, & Perencevich, 2004) utilized data from the first year of the project to look at changes in children's motivation over time. Tonks, Wigfield, Guthrie, and Perencevich (2004) built on this initial study by looking at CORI's influences on both motivation and reading frequency. They used data from the first year of the fourth grade implementation. In another study (Guthrie, Wigfield, Barbosa, et al., 2004), we analyzed at the classroom level effects of the instructional programs on

children's reading comprehension and reading motivation. This study analyzed data from both third grade implementations. The next study (Guthrie, Wigfield, Humenick, et al., 2006) analyzed in detail how variations in one CORI motivational practice, the use of hands-on activities, influenced third grade children's reading comprehension and motivation. Finally, we present results from a study using data from the fourth grade implementation of CORI that looked at whether reading engagement mediates the effects of instructional practices on students' comprehension and motivation (Wigfield, Guthrie, et al., 2008)

***CORI'S Effects on Students' Motivation and Amount of Reading: Individual Student Level Analyses*** In one of the initial substudies from the larger project, we examined changes in third grade children's motivation for reading, using data from the first year of the project (Wigfield et al., 2004). During that year children received either the CORI instructional program or the SI program. Children's responses to the abbreviated MRQ provided the measures of motivation, and we examined children's reading self-efficacy, curiosity about reading, and preference for challenge in reading.

Using repeated measures of analyses of variance, Wigfield, Guthrie, Tonks, et al. (2004) looked at change in children's self-efficacy, curiosity, and preference for challenge, using the individual child as the unit of analysis. Results showed that children in both groups increased significantly in their self-efficacy. Children experiencing the CORI intervention increased significantly in their reading curiosity and preference for challenging reading materials, whereas children in the SI intervention did not. Thus, this study showed that CORI fosters children's intrinsic motivation to read to a greater extent than does SI, whereas both CORI and SI foster children's self-efficacy for reading.

Tonks, Wigfield, Guthrie, and Perencevich (2004) built on this work by doing similar analyses on students who received CORI and SI instruction in fourth grade. They found that CORI students were higher than SI students in their preference for challenge and involvement in reading at the December posttest. Tonks et al. also looked at the amount of reading children said they did in school. They found that CORI children's amount of reading (as measured by the RAI) increased significantly from pretest to posttest, but SI children's did not. Thus, these studies showed that CORI positively influences children's intrinsic reading motivation and the amount of reading that they do to a greater extent than does SI.

***CORI's Effects on Children's Reading Motivation and Reading Comprehension: Classroom Level Analyses*** We next examined how the different instructional programs included in the Reading Engagement Project influenced third grade children's reading comprehension, reading strategy use, and reading motivation (Guthrie, Wigfield, Barbosa, et al., 2004). The first study in this report was conducted on the first year, third grade children in the CORI implementation. This study used the same sample as that reported by Wigfield et al. (2004), but differed from that study with respect to data analyses, and included measures of reading comprehension and actual strategy use along with measures of students' motivation. Furthermore, the classroom was used as the unit of analysis in this study. We used analysis procedures similar to ones used by Williams et al. (2002), looking first at whether there were instructional group effects on children's scores on the different measures at pretest, and then analyzing the posttest scores separately (see Guthrie, Wigfield, Barbosa, et al., 2004, for detailed descriptions of these analyses).

We found no instructional group differences in reading comprehension, strategy use, or motivation at pretest, indicating that the CORI and SI groups were similar with respect to all the study's measure before the implementation. One-way analyses of covariance with instructional group as the independent variable and teaching implementation quality as the covariate then were done on the posttest data. These analyses showed that CORI students exceeded SI students in reading comprehension (the project-developed text and passage comprehension measures described above), use of reading comprehension strategies, and reading motivation (a composite measure of motivation from the MRQ). The effect sizes were as follows: 1.01 and 1.32 for the two comprehension measures, 1.23 for the strategy use composite, and .98 for reading motivation.

The second study presented in the Guthrie, Wigfield, Barbosa, et al. article (2004) was done on the second year of the third-grade implementation. The Traditional Instruction school was added during this year of the project. We also added the Gates-MacGinitie Reading Tests to the battery of measures in order to have a standardized measure of reading comprehension included in the study. A similar classroom-level analysis strategy was used on the pretest and posttest measures. As in the first study, there were no differences across groups on any of the measures at pretest. Analyses of the posttest data showed that CORI students outperformed TI students, but not SI students, on the project-developed measure of text comprehension (effect size of 2.75), with SI and TI students also not differing. The CORI students outperformed SI and TI students on the Gates-MacGinitie Reading Tests (effect sizes of 1.40 and .71, respectively). The CORI teachers rated their students as higher in reading self-efficacy, intrinsic motivation in reading, and extrinsic motivation in reading than did the SI teachers (effect sizes .95, 1.29, and 1.28, respectively).

These findings showed that reading comprehension instruction that combines reading strategy instruction with support for student motivation, and done in a content area (science), enhanced students' reading motivation and comprehension to a greater extent than did either strategy instruction alone or traditional reading instruction. The design of the two studies presented in the Guthrie, Wigfield, Barbosa, et al. (2004) article was hierarchical, in the following sense. The TI, CORI, and SI groups all spent time reading various texts. The CORI and SI groups received direct strategy instruction on the same set of reading strategies. Only the CORI group received instructional practices specifically designed to support student motivation. We thus conclude that the addition of the motivation supportive practices was crucial in producing the effects. However, we also believe that the motivational supportive practices and the cognitive practices likely interact in complex ways to influence students' comprehension and motivation. For instance, when students have greater control over their learning and choose what they are studying, they may select topics they know something about, and therefore enhance their learning to a greater extent. Reading interesting texts helps students to process information more deeply, leading to richer conceptual understanding.

***Understanding CORI's Effects: The Influence of Stimulating Tasks***   In a recent article, we examined variations in one key CORI instructional practice designed to support students' motivation and how such variation influences children's reading comprehension and motivation (Guthrie, Wigfield, Perencevich, et al., 2006). We focused on the practice of providing children with hands-on activities, in part because teachers have stated that hands-on activities are one of the best ways to maintain and enhance student motivation (Nolen & Nicholls, 1994; Zahorik, 1996). In the reading area, Sweet, Guthrie, and Ng (1998) reported that children's motivation to read increased when they did activities connected to the books they were reading.

Another reason for focusing on hands-on activities was our interest in examining speculations by researchers such as Hidi and Harackiewicz (2000) about how to generate long-term interest from immediate, situational interest children have in a task or activity. Hidi and Harackiewicz proposed that teachers should capitalize on students' situational interest in various classroom activities to generate longer-term interest, because interest relates to deep-level processing of material, and cognitive growth and achievement. Situational interest often is sparked when students engage in different kinds of activities in school, such as hands-on activities (Zahorik, 1996). Hidi and Harackiewicz (2000) and Mitchell (1993) characterized this as the "catch" of students' interest. The catch is not enough to sustain or hold students' motivation, for that to occur the situational interest must be connected to students' more lasting motivation or interests. Although Hidi and Harackiewicz stated the importance of connecting situational interest to longer-term interest and motivation, they provided few specific suggestions for accomplishing this in classroom settings.

We studied the possible links of situational interest to longer-term reading motivation by examining how variations in the number of science inquiry and other activities students performed in the classroom related to their reading comprehension and motivation. The sample for this study was a subsample of third grade children experiencing CORI during the second year of the CORI implementation at that grade level (N = 98). The students were in four CORI classrooms in the two participating schools. In all four classrooms, students did two major hands-on activities, an owl pellet dissection and observations of a predatory diving beetle. They then did a number of follow-up activities after these major activities. Stimulating tasks were defined as students' observations, question generation, drawings, hypothesis formation, and interpretations of findings that were associated with the owl pellet dissection and predator beetle observation; these activities reflected students' engagement in the scientific process.

We proposed that students engaging in more of these activities would likely have a stronger base of situational interest that may be more likely to connect to their longer-term motivation. To test this proposition, we counted the activities students did in the different classrooms. In two classrooms, students performed a significantly greater number of follow-up activities (henceforward called stimulating tasks) than did children in the other two classrooms. Therefore, two instructional groups were created, one that had a higher number of stimulating tasks, and one that had a lower number. An analysis of variance showed that the two groups differed significantly with respect to the number of stimulating tasks that they did. The quality of students' products from the various activities was coded on different rubrics, and an overall measure of the quality of these products was created; we called this variable science process quality.

We then examined relations of the instructional grouping variable, and the quality and quantity of stimulating tasks to students' reading comprehension and reading motivation. Using regression analyses, we found that both the instructional grouping variable and science process quantity and quality variable predicted children's reading comprehension (measured by the Gates McGinitie Reading Tests). These variables also predicted students' intrinsic reading motivation (as measured by teachers' ratings of students' motivation at the end of the intervention). Thus, students in classrooms in which more stimulating tasks were used during CORI instruction had higher reading comprehension and motivation than did CORI students in classrooms with fewer stimulating tasks.

Finally, we examined whether the instructional grouping variable predicted children's reading comprehension when controlling for their reading motivation (done by entering motivation prior to the instructional grouping variable in the analysis). Children's reading motivation significantly predicted their reading comprehension. However, the instructional grouping variable, when entered last in the regression equation, did not directly predict reading comprehension when reading motivation was controlled.

This study provides new information about how engaging in meaningful hand-on activities relates to children's reading motivation. If we assume that the hands-on activities (or stimulating tasks) produce situational interest and the MRQ measures reading motivation at a more general level, the relations between these two variables reflects a connection of situational interest to longer-term motivation. Because our measure of stimulating tasks focused on the

*number* of these activities children did in the classroom, the positive correlation of these measures suggests that when these activities are more frequent children's reading motivation increases. Students experiencing fewer stimulating tasks increased less in intrinsic motivation. Further, because the study occurred in CORI classrooms, teachers were implementing the additional instructional practices designed to foster children's intrinsic motivation to read. These practices, in combination with the stimulating tasks, may also have fostered children's intrinsic motivation to read. Finally, the properties of the stimulating tasks in which the CORI students engaged may also have been crucial to the observed relationship of their frequency to children's reading motivation. These tasks were connected to the books the students were reading in meaningful ways and also to the content goals of the CORI unit. We suggest that such connections may be essential to help the "catch" of a stimulating task lead to the "hold" of longer-term motivation (see Guthrie, Wigfield, Humenick, et al., 2006; Hidi & Harackiewicz, 2000, for further discussion).

***Understanding CORI's Effects: The Role of Students' Engagement in Mediating Instructional Effects*** We examined whether students' engagement mediated the influence of instructional practices on students' reading comprehension, using data from the first year of the fourth-grade implementation of CORI and SI (Wigfield et al., 2008). We proposed that it is not the instructional practices per se that influence students' reading comprehension and motivation, but rather the extent to which these practices promote students' engagement in reading. By looking at the mediating role of students' engagement, we explored one possible process that could explain how motivation supportive practices influence students' comprehension and motivation.

Approximately 400 fourth graders were included in this part of the study, from the same five schools used in the third grade implementation. There were five CORI, seven SI, and three TI teachers for a total of 15 teachers. The treatment groups were equivalent at pretest on the three reading variables of standardized reading comprehension, multiple-text comprehension, and reading comprehension strategies, as well as students' reading motivation, which is a prerequisite of the equivalent groups' pretest–postest design. The measures used included the following: (a) reading comprehension was measured by the Gates-McGinitie Reading Tests and the project-designed text comprehension measure; (b) the reading strategy composite used in the analyses included the measures of students' activation of their background knowledge and questioning described earlier; (c) reading motivation was measured by the abbreviated version of the MRQ described above and a composite measure of self-efficacy and intrinsic motivation was used in the analyses; and (d) reading engagement, a new measure that involved having teachers rate each of their students on different aspects of their engagement (motivational, cognitive, and behavioral). The items from this measure are pre-

**TABLE 29.2**
**Reading Engagement Index**

Items

THIS STUDENT:
  Often reads independently
  Reads favorite topics and authors
  Is easily distracted in self-directed reading
  Works hard in reading
  Is a confident reader
  Uses comprehension strategies well
  Thinks deeply about the content of texts
  Enjoys discussing books with peers

*Note.* Teachers rate each student in their class on this index, using a scale from not true to very true.

sented in Table 29.2. Fidelity of teachers' implementation of CORI and SI again was measured as described above. The analyses described next were done at the classroom level, as we did in the Guthrie, Wigfield, Barbosa, et al. study (2004). We used multivariate analyses of variance on the pretest and posttest measures.

We first looked at correlations of teachers' ratings of engagement to students' reading comprehension and reading strategy use, and we found moderate to strong positive correlations among these variables ($r$'s ranging from .55 to .76). Next, we looked at the effects of the instructional group on children's reading comprehension, reading strategy use, and reading engagement. There were no group differences on any of the measures at pretest. At posttest, students experiencing CORI had significantly higher reading comprehension scores (on both comprehension measures), reading strategy use, and reading engagement than did children in the SI and TI groups. The SI and TI groups did not differ from one another on any of the variables. These results provide an important replication (at a different grade level) of the instructional findings reported earlier from the third-grade studies described earlier.

Finally, as a way to assess whether students' engagement mediated the effect of instructional group on reading comprehension and reading strategy use, we did an analysis of covariance on the comprehension and strategy use measures, using reading engagement as the covariate. The analyses just described established that students' reading engagement relates to their comprehension, and instructional practices relate to students' comprehension; establishing these relations are necessary conditions for the examination of mediation (Baron & Kenny, 1986). Baron and Kenny described mediation using regression analyses; mediation also can be tested using analyses of variance and covariance (G. R. Hancock, personal communication, October 2004). The analyses of covariance we did included reading engagement as the covariate and instructional group as the independent variable. The two measures of reading comprehension and the reading strategy use were the dependent variables. With engagement included in the analysis in this way, the effect of the instructional group on reading comprehension and reading strategy use was not significant.

This is the first study to show that the benefits of CORI

on measures of reading comprehension and reading strategy use are attributable to the effects of these practices on students' levels of engagement in reading during instruction. This is important because the effects on reading comprehension of motivational practices in instructional programs such as CORI could be attributable to a number of different variables, including improved cognitive competency, such as fluency or vocabulary, or other cognitive or social processes. Instead, this study indicates that it was the amount of reading engagement that improved reading comprehension.

The finding that students' engagement mediates the effects of instructional practices provides support to our engagement perspective (Guthrie & Wigfield, 2000), which proposes that classroom practices for reading comprehension instruction increase comprehension via students' level of engagement in reading (that is, the extent to which they are cognitively, motivationally, and socially involved in reading). Given these findings, it is important to continue to study closely the different kinds of instructional practices that increase reading engagement for different children.

## Conclusion

The problem of the decline in children's achievement motivation during the school years is well documented. As discussed earlier, children's motivation determines in a large part their choices of activities to do, involvement with them, and persistence at them. Children's motivation also relates to their engagement in different activities such as reading, and engagement relates to their achievement (Guthrie & Wigfield, 2000). To maintain and increase achievement, it is essential that children's motivation for learning remains high. Unfortunately, many instructional practices that become more prevalent as children progress through school appear to undermine rather than increase children's motivation (Eccles & Midgley, 1989; Stipek, 1996; Wigfield, Eccles, Yoon, et al., 1997).

Literature on instructional practices that can increase rather than undermine children's motivation in school is growing (Ames, 1992; NRC, 2004; Stipek, 1996, 2002; Wigfield, Eccles, & Rodriguez, 1998). Much of the empirical work on change in instructional practices has been done in the math and science subject areas; less is known about effective instructional practices to increase reading engagement. Further, in elementary school reading instruction there is a major shift in instructional emphases from the primary grades (K-2) to the intermediate grades (3-5). According to survey data, and classroom observation studies, teachers at the primary level emphasize phonemic awareness, letter–sound correspondence, word recognition, and fluency (Bauman, Duffy-Hester, & Ro, 2000; Foorman et al., 2006). For comprehension, stories and narrative literature prevail overwhelmingly (Duke, 2000). At the intermediate level, teachers emphasize reading strategies such as questioning, and predicting more fully (Block & Pressley, 2002). Information text is used far more frequently, although it remains a minority of the total time, and writing about text becomes an important element (Cunningham & Hall, 1998). Thus, the cognitive load and text difficulty increase sharply in the intermediate grades putting demands on students' motivation. As cognitive demands increase fewer students may be willing to put in the effort required to meet the higher demands. Therefore, it is imperative to develop and implement instructional programs in reading and other subject areas that can build students' motivation rather than undermine it. As we have discussed, Concept-Oriented Reading Instruction is designed to do that.

Results of the studies reviewed here on CORI's influences on children's motivation, engagement, and comprehension provide compelling evidence that CORI positively influences all three of these critical outcome variables. Compared to children receiving either an instructional program focused on cognitive strategy instruction or traditional reading instruction, CORI students' reading motivation, engagement, and comprehension all were higher at the end of the instructional programs. These results were replicated across several implementations and two grade levels (third and fourth).

We have argued that these results can be attributed in a large part to the motivational practices included in CORI (Guthrie, Wigfield, Barbosa, et al., 2004). These practices are what distinguish CORI from the strategy and traditional reading instructional programs to which we compared CORI. These other programs did not include the motivation-enhancing practices included systematically in CORI. In the other programs without these practices, students were less motivated to read and did not read as well, as assessed by different measures of reading comprehension. Of course, the motivational practices likely interact in complex ways with the strategy instruction practices to influence children's motivation and comprehension; it likely is not the motivation practices alone that produced the effects. It would be interesting in future work to examine solely the impact of the motivational practices to determine their impact on engagement and comprehension.

The motivational practices used in CORI are consistent with the recommendations of motivation theorists, such as Ames (1992) and Stipek (2002), who proposed using a set of several practices to enhance student motivation. What distinguishes the work on CORI from other work in the motivation literature is that CORI practices are specified within a particular set of learning activities in science and reading. It, therefore, is quite feasible to train teachers to use these practices and to modify them for their own unique instructional situations. That is, the practices are concrete and specific enough to be implemented on a daily basis, but they also are not scripted to such an extent that teachers cannot modify them to fit their own instructional needs.

An interesting question is whether all of these instructional practices are needed to foster children's motivation, or whether a subset or even one of the practices would be enough. We believe that generalized, long-term reading motivation is not likely to be substantially increased by a single, focused motivational practice in the classroom,

because children's motivation is complex and multifaceted, and different children likely benefit from different kinds of instructional practices. For instance, some children may be particularly responsive to interesting texts, and others to having autonomy over their own learning. However, it is very likely that these practices interact with each other in complex ways to influence students' motivations, so isolating them may not be productive. For example, autonomy support requires a context because a teacher cannot give choices in a vacuum. Topics, texts, writing activities, groups of students, and other features of the classroom must be present to enable the teacher to afford meaningful choices for students during reading instruction. Similarly, the texts used in CORI may not have been as interesting to students had they not been connected to the hands-on activities.

It is also possible that there are other instructional practices that would further foster children's motivation; some of these are discussed in the motivation literature (Stipek, 1996, 2002). These could be combined with CORI instruction in future research to see if their impact on motivation and comprehension would be stronger than the effects shown in studies to date. However, we suggest that a finite set of instructional supports explicitly targeted to motivational development in reading can facilitate engaged reading and reading comprehension, as demonstrated in the research discussed above. The motivational supportive practices included in this investigation are one set of practices shown to be effective in increasing reading motivation, engagement, and instruction, when combined with reading strategy instruction and text interaction. Thus, we believe these practices provide sufficient support for student motivation (see Guthrie & Alao, 1997 for discussion of necessary and sufficient conditions for fostering students' motivation).

There are several important directions for future research with CORI. One hallmark of this program is the connection of instruction in reading with instruction in a content area; the current implementations of CORI integrate science and reading. Other implementations integrate social studies and reading (see Swan, 2003); to date there has not been much research on the effectiveness of this integration, but it seems quite plausible that such integrations would be successful. Social studies instruction can use various hands-on activities and interesting texts, as well as ways to have students work together and to give them choices in the kinds of activities they do. It would be interesting to see if other reading–content area integrations could be done.

A second important extension would be to different grade levels. Some CORI implementations have been done in the early elementary grades (Swan, 2003), although again there has not been research to evaluate the effectiveness of these implementations. The implementations with younger children face some constraints with respect to the kinds of texts that are available because children's less advanced reading skills limit the kinds of books that are available. Similarly, the kinds of choices children are able to make also are limited to some extent because they may not be ready to make such choices. These constraints do not seem insurmountable, and certainly the other instructional practices such as hands-on activities, collaboration support, and content goals for instruction could be modified for use with younger children.

CORI may be particularly effective in middle school, where book availability is more extensive, peer relations are increasingly important to children, and opportunities for control of their own learning increasingly appeals to children. We have begun a CORI-based intervention study in several middle schools, using science as the content area and focusing on improving children's motivation for and comprehension of science information texts. Preliminary information about this project is available at www.cori. umd.edu.

The research reviewed in this chapter shows that CORI is an effective instructional program for facilitating children's reading motivation, reading engagement, and reading comprehension. This research, and that of other researchers in the motivation field, such as Maehr and Midgley (1996) and Stipek (2002), shows that the observed decline in children's motivation is not inevitable but can be reversed when certain instructional conditions exist. Putting these instructional practices and conditions in place can be done, but poses challenges for schools and school districts as well. There are strengths and limitations in the practical usability of CORI for school applications. CORI is an instructional model, but has been used primarily as a research tool to investigate questions such as whether motivation support during instruction can facilitate reading comprehension. Concept-Oriented Reading Instruction is a model with fundamental principles and features as presented here. It is enriched, in the sense that we used an abundance of books that might not be necessary for a cost-efficient implementation. As a model, CORI has been used by at least several dozen schools, and districts at the grade 1-8 levels, according to the reports of district administrators and teachers. Whether statistically significant advantages have accrued for these schools and children is unknown. To counteract these strengths, CORI is not yet published in a form readily available for schools to purchase. A few schools receive training from a limited number of experienced CORI experts (e.g., Swan, 2003), but a formal professional development system is not available at the time of this writing. Teachers and administrators are advised to consult the book (Guthrie, Wigfield, & Perencevich, 2004) and the website (www.cori.umd.edu) for guidance in understanding the model sufficiently to construct their own applications.

## Author Note

The research on CORI discussed in this chapter was supported by grant 0089225 to John T. Guthrie, Allan Wigfield, and Pedro Barbosa from the National Science Foundation through the Interagency Educational Research Initiative.

The authors thank Eileen Kramer for help in the preparation of this chapter.

## References

Alvermann, D. E., & Eakle, A. J. (2003). Comprehension instruction: Adolescents and their multiple literacies. In A. P. Sweet & C. E. Snow (Eds.), *Rethinking reading comprehension* (pp. 12–29). New York: Guilford.

Ames, C. (1992). Achievement goals and the classroom motivational climate. In D. Schunk & J. Meece (Eds.), *Student perceptions in the classroom* (pp. 327–349). Hillsdale, NJ: Erlbaum.

Assor, A., Kaplan, H., & Roth, G. (2002). Choice is good, but relevance is excellent: Autonomy-enhancing and suppressing teacher behaviours predicting students' engagement in schoolwork. *British Journal of Educational Psychology, 72,* 261–278.

Baker, L., Dreher, M. J., & Guthrie, J. T. (2000). Preface. In L. Baker, J. T. Guthrie, & M. J. Dreher (Eds.), *Engaging young readers: Promoting achievement and motivation* (p. ix). New York: Guilford.

Bandura, A. (1997). *Self-efficacy: The exercise of control.* New York: Freeman.

Barbosa, P., & Alexander, L. (2004). Science inquiry in the CORI framework. In J. T. Guthrie, A. Wigfield, & K. C. Perencevich (Eds.), *Motivating reading comprehension: Concept-oriented reading instruction* (pp. 113–141). Mahwah, NJ: Erlbaum.

Baron, R. M., & Kenny, D. A. (1986). The moderator-mediator variable distinction in social psychological research: Conceptual, strategic, and statistical consideration. *Journal of Personality & Social Psychology, 51,* 1173–1182.

Bauman, J. F., Duffy-Hester, A., & Ro, J. (2000). The first R yesterday and today: U.S. elementary reading instruction practices reported by teachers and administrators. *Reading Research Quarterly, 35,* 338–377.

Block. C., & Pressley, M., (Eds.). (2002). *Comprehension instruction: Research based best practices* (pp. 275–288). New York: Guilford.

Britton, B. K., & Gulgoz, S. (1991). Using Kintsch's computational model to improve instructional text: Effects of repairing inference calls on recall and cognitive structures. *Journal of Educational Psychology, 83,* 329–345.

Brophy, J. (2004). *Motivating students to learn* (2nd ed.). Mahwah, NJ: Erlbaum.

Cipielewski, J., & Stanovich, K. E. (1992). Predicting growth in reading ability from children's exposure to print. *Journal of Experimental Child Psychology, 54,* 74–89.

Cunningham, P., & Hall, D. (1998). Learning in diverse schools and classrooms. In K. R. Harris, S. Graham, & D. Deshler (Eds.), *Teaching every child every day* (pp. 32–76). Cambridge, MA: Brookline Books.

Davis, M. H., & Tonks, S. (2004). Diverse texts and technology for reading. In J. T. Guthrie, A. Wigfield, & K. C. Perencevich (Eds.), *Motivating reading comprehension: Concept-Oriented Reading Instruction* (pp. 143–147). Mahwah, NJ: Erlbaum.

Deci, E. L., & Moller, A. C. (2005). The concept of competence: A starting place for understanding intrinsic motivation and self-determined extrinsic motivation. In A. J. Elliot & C. S. Dweck (Eds.), *Handbook of competence and motivation* (pp. 579–597). New York: Guilford.

Donahue, P. L., Daane, M. C., & Jin, Y. (2005). *The nation's report card: Reading 2003* (Pub. No. NCES 2005453). Washington, DC: National Center for Educational Statistics.

Duke, N. (2000). 3.6 minutes per day: The scarcity of informational texts in first grade. *Reading Research Quarterly, 35,* 202–224.

Eccles, J. S. (2005). Commentary: Studying the development of learning and task motivation [Special issue]. *Learning and Instruction, 15,* 161–171.

Eccles, J. S., & Midgley, C. (1989). Stage/environment fit: Developmentally appropriate classrooms for early adolescents. In R. Ames & C. Ames (Eds.), *Research on motivation in education* (Vol. 3, pp. 139–181). New York: Academic Press.

Eccles, J. S., & Wigfield, A. (2002). Motivational beliefs, values, and goals. *Annual Review of Psychology, 53,* 109–132.

Eccles, J. S., Wigfield, A., & Schiefele, U. (1998). Motivation to succeed. In W. Damon (Series Ed.) & N. Eisenberg (Vol. Ed.), *Handbook of child psychology* (5th ed., Vol. 3). New York: Wiley.

Elliot, A. J. (2005). A conceptual history of the achievement goal construct. In A. J. Elliot & C. S. Dweck (Eds.), *Handbook of competence and motivation* (pp. 52–72). New York: Guilford.

Finn, J. D. (1989). Withdrawing from school. *Review of Educational Research, 59*, 117–142.

Foorman, B., Schatschneider, C., Eakin, M., Fletcher, J., Moats, L., & Francis, D. (2006). The impact of instructional practices in grades 1 and 2 on reading and spelling achievement in high poverty schools. *Contemporary Educational Psychology, 31*, 1–29.

Fredericks, J. A., Blumenfeld, P. C., & Paris, A. H. (2004). School engagement: Potential of the concept, state of the evidence. *Review of Educational Research, 74*(1), 59–109.

Gottfried, A. E. (1990). Academic intrinsic motivation in young elementary school children. *Journal of Educational Psychology, 82*, 525–538.

Gottfried, A. E., Fleming, J. S., & Gottfried, A. W. (2001). Continuity of academic intrinsic motivation from childhood through late adolescence: A longitudinal study. *Journal of Educational Psychology, 93*, 3–13.

Guthrie, J. T. (2004). Differentiating instruction for struggling readers within the CORI classroom. In J. T. Guthrie, A. Wigfield, & K. C. Perencevich (Eds.), *Motivating reading comprehension: Concept-oriented reading instruction* (pp. 173–193). Mahwah, NJ: Erlbaum.

Guthrie, J. T., & Alao, S. (1997). Designing contexts to increase motivations for reading. *Educational Psychologist, 32*, 95–107.

Guthrie, J. T., & Humenick, N. (2004). Motivating students to read: Evidence for classroom practices that increase reading motivation and achievement. In P. McCardle & V. Chabra (Eds.), *The voice of evidence in reading research* (pp. 329–354). Baltimore, MD: Brookes.

Guthrie, J. T., McGough, K., & Wigfield, A. (1996). *Measuring reading activity: An inventory* (Instructional Resource No. 4). Athens, GA: National Reading Research Center.

Guthrie, J. T., & Taboada, A. (2004). Fostering the cognitive strategies of reading. In J. T. Guthrie, A. Wigfield, & K. C. Perencevich (Eds.), *Motivating reading comprehension: Concept-oriented reading instruction* (pp. 87–111). Mahwah, NJ: Erlbaum.

Guthrie, J. T., Van Meter, P., Hancock, G. R., McCann, A., Anderson, E., & Alao, S. (1998). Does concept-oriented reading instruction increase strategy use and conceptual learning from text? *Journal of Educational Psychology, 90*, 261–278.

Guthrie, J. T., Van Meter, P., McCann, A., Wigfield, A., Bennett, L., Poundstone, C., et al. (1996). Growth of literacy engagement: Changes in motivations and strategies during concept-oriented reading instruction. *Reading Research Quarterly, 31*, 306–332.

Guthrie, J. T., & Wigfield, A. (2000). Engagement and motivation in reading. In M. L. Kamil, P. B. Mosenthal, P. D. Pearson, & R. Barr (Eds.), *Handbook of reading research* (Vol. 3, pp. 403–422). Mahwah, NJ: Erlbaum.

Guthrie, J. T., Wigfield, A., Barbosa, P., Perencevich, K. C., Taboada, A., Davis, M. H., et al. (2004). Increasing reading comprehension, motivation, and strategy use through Concept-Oriented Reading Instruction. *Journal of Educational Psychology, 96*, 403–423.

Guthrie, J. T., Wigfield, A., Humenick, N., Perencevich, K. C., Tonks, S., & Barbosa, P. (2006). Influences of stimulating tasks on reading motivation and comprehension. *Journal of Educational Research, 99*, 232–246.

Guthrie, J. T., Wigfield, A., & Perencevich, K. E. (Eds.). (2004). *Motivating reading comprehension: Concept-Oriented Reading Instruction.* Mahwah, NJ: Erlbaum.

Guthrie, J. T., Wigfield, A., Perencevich, K. C., Taboada, A., Humenick, N., Lutz, S., et al. (2006). *A model of the contributions of classroom instruction to students' reading comprehension and reading engagement.* Unpublished manuscript, University of Maryland.

Guthrie, J. T., Wigfield, A., & Von Secker, C. (2000). Effects of integrated instruction on motivation and strategy use in reading. *Journal of Educational Psychology, 92*, 331–341.

Harter, S. (1981). A new self-report scale of intrinsic versus extrinsic orientation in the classroom: Motivational and informational components. *Developmental Psychology, 17*, 300–312.

Hidi, S., & Harackiewicz, J. M. (2000). Motivating the academically unmotivated: A critical issue for the 21st century. *Review of Educational Research, 70*, 151–179.

Jacobs, J., Lanza, S., Osgood, D. W., Eccles, J. S., & Wigfield, A. (2002). Ontogeny of children's self-beliefs: Gender and domain differences across grades one through 12. *Child Development, 73*, 509–527.

Kirsch, I., de Jong, J., Lafontaine, D., McQueen, J., Mendelovits, J., & Monseur, C. (2002). *Reading for change: Performance and engagement across countries. Results from PISA 2000.* Paris: OECD.

Lepper, M. R., Corpus, J. H., & Iyengar, S. S. (2005). Intrinsic and extrinsic motivational orientations in the classroom: Age differences and academic correlates. *Journal of Educational Psychology, 97*, 184–196.

Maehr, M. L., & Midgley, C. (1996). *Transforming school cultures.* Boulder, CO: Westview Press.

McKenna, M. C., Kear, D. J., & Ellsworth, R. A. (1995). Children's attitudes toward reading: A national survey. *Reading Research Quarterly, 30*, 934–956.

Meece. J. L. (1994). The role of motivation in self-regulated learning. In D. H. Schunk & B. J. Zimmerman (Eds.), *Self-regulation of learning and performance: Issues and educational applications* (pp. 25–44). Hillsdale, NJ: Erlbaum

Midgley, C., Feldlaufer, H., & Eccles, J. S. (1989). Student/teacher relations and attitudes toward mathematics before and after the transition to junior high school. *Child Development, 60*, 981–992.

Mitchell, M. (1993). Situational interest: Its multifaceted structure in the secondary school mathematics classroom. *Journal of Educational Psychology, 85*, 424–436.

National Reading Panel. (2000). *Teaching children to read: An evidence-based assessment of the scientific research literature on reading and its implications for reading instruction* (NIH Pub. No. 00-4769). Jessup, MD: National Institute for Literacy.

National Research Council. (2004). *Engaging schools: Fostering high school students' motivation to learn.* Washington, DC: National Academies Press.

Nolen, S. B., & Nichols, J. G. (1994). A place to begin (again) in research on student motivation: Teachers' beliefs. *Teaching and Teacher Education, 10*, 57–69.

O'Donnell, A. M. (2006). The roles of peers and group learning. In P. A. Alexander & P. H. Winne (Eds.), *Handbook of educational psychology* (2nd ed., pp. 781–802). Mahwah. NJ: Erlbaum.

Perencevich, K. C. (2004). How the CORI framework looks in the classroom. In J. T. Guthrie, A. Wigfield, & K. C. Perencevich (Eds.), *Motivating reading comprehension: Concept-Oriented Reading Instruction* (pp. 25–53). Mahwah, NJ: Erlbaum.

Pintrich, P. (2000). An achievement goal perspective on issues in motivation terminology, theory and research. *Contemporary Educational Psychology, 25*, 92–104.

Pintrich, P. R., & Schunk, D. H. (2002). *Motivation in education: Theory, research, and application* (2nd ed.). Columbus, OH: Merrill Prentice Hall.

Rozendaal, J. S., Minnaert, A., & Boekaerts, M. (2005). The influence of teacher perceived administration of self-regulated learning on students' motivation and information processing. *Learning and Instruction, 15*, 141–160.

Ryan, R. M., & Deci, E. L. (2000). Intrinsic and extrinsic motivations: Classic definitions and new directions. *Contemporary Educational Psychology, 25*, 54–67.

Schiefele, U. (1999). Interest and learning from text. *Scientific Studies of Reading, 3*, 257–279.

Schunk, D. H., & Pajares, F. (2005). Competence perceptions and academic functioning. In A. J. Elliot & C. S. Dweck (Eds.), *Handbook of competence and motivation* (pp. 85–104). New York: Guilford.

Schunk, D. H., & Zimmerman, B. J. (1997). Developing self-efficacious readers and writers: The role of social and self-regulatory processes. In J. T. Guthrie & A. Wigfield (Eds.), *Reading engagement: Motivating readers through integrated instruction* (pp. 34–50). Newark, DE: International Reading Association.

Skinner, E. A., Wellborn, J. G., & Connell, J. P. (1990). What it takes to do well in school and whether I've got it: A process model of perceived control and children's engagement and achievement in school. *Journal of Educational Psychology, 82,* 22–32.

Sikorski, M. P. (2004). Inside Mrs. O'Hara's classroom. In J. T. Guthrie, A. Wigfield, & K. C. Perencevich (Eds.), *Motivating reading comprehension: Concept-oriented reading instruction* (pp. 195–224). Mahwah, NJ: Erlbaum.

Skinner, E. A., Zimmer-Gelback, M. J., & Connell, J. P. (1998). Individual differences and the development of perceived control. *Monographs of the Society for Research in Child Development, 63,* v–220.

Souvignier, E., & Mokhlesgerami, J. (2006). Using self-regulation as a framework for implementing strategy instruction to foster reading comprehension. *Learning and Instruction, 16,* 57–71.

Stipek, D. J. (1996). Motivation and instruction. In D. Berliner & R. Calfee (Eds.), *Handbook of educational psychology* (pp. 85–113). New York: Macmillan.

Stipek, D. J. (2002). Good instruction is motivating. In A. Wigfield & J. S. Eccles (Eds.), *Development of achievement motivation* (pp. 309–351). San Diego, CA: Academic.

Swan, E. A. (2003). *Concept-oriented reading instruction: Engaging classrooms, lifelong learners.* New York: Guilford.

Sweet, A. P., Guthrie, J. T., & Ng, M. (1998). Teacher perceptions and student reading motivation. *Journal of Educational Psychology, 90,* 210–224.

Taylor, B. M., Pearson, P. D., Peterson, D. S., & Rodriguez, M. C. (2003). Reading growth in high-poverty classrooms: The influence of teacher practices that encourage cognitive engagement in literacy learning. *Elementary School Journal, 104,* 3–28.

Tonks, S., Wigfield, A., Guthrie, J. T., & Perencevich, K. C. (2004, April) *Effects of two reading instruction programs on children's reading motivation.* Paper presented at the annual meeting of the American Educational Research Association, San Diego, CA.

Webb, N. M., & Palincsar, A. S. (1996). Group processes in the classroom. In D. C. Berliner & R. C. Calfee (Eds.), *Handbook of educational psychology* (pp. 841–873). New York: Macmillan.

Wigfield. A. (1994). Expectancy—Value theory of achievement motivation: A developmental perspective. *Educational Psychology Review, 6,* 49–78.

Wigfield, A. (2000). Facilitating young children's motivation to read. In L. Baker, M. J. Dreher, & J. T. Guthrie (Eds.), *Engaging young readers: Promoting achievement and motivation* (pp. 140–158). New York: Guilford.

Wigfield, A., Byrnes, J. B., & Eccles, J. S. (2006). Adolescent development. In P. A. Alexander & P. Winne (Eds.), *Handbook of educational psychology* (2nd ed., pp. 87–113). Mahwah, NJ: Erlbaum.

Wigfield, A., & Eccles, J. S. (Eds.). (2002). *Development of achievement motivation.* San Diego, CA: Academic Press.

Wigfield, A., Eccles, J. S., & Rodriguez, D. (1998). The development of children's motivation in school contexts. In A. Iran-Nejad & P. D. Pearson (Eds.), *Review of research in education* (Vol. 23, pp. 73–118). Washington, DC: American Educational Research Association.

Wigfield, A., Eccles, J. S., Schiefele, U., Roeser, R., & Davis-Kean, P. (2006). Development of achievement motivation. In W. Damon & N. Eisenberg (Eds.), *Handbook of child psychology* (6th ed., Vol. 3, pp. 933–1002). New York: Wiley.

Wigfield, A., Eccles, J. S., Yoon, K. S., Harold, R. D., Arbreton, A., Freedman-Doan, C., et al. (1997). Changes in children's competence beliefs and subjective task values across the elementary school years: A three-year study. *Journal of Educational Psychology, 89,* 451–469.

Wigfield, A., & Guthrie, J. T. (1997). Relations of children's motivation for reading to the amount and breadth of their reading. *Journal of Educational Psychology, 89,* 420–432.

Wigfield, A., Guthrie, J. T., Perencevich, K., Taboada, A., Klauda, S. L., McRae, S., & Barbosa, P. (2008). The role of reading engagement in mediating the effects of instruction on reading outcomes. *Psychology in the Schools, 45,* 432–445.

Wigfield, A., Guthrie, J. T., Tonks, S., & Perencevich, K. C. (2004). Children's motivation for reading: Domain specificity and instructional influences. *Journal of Educational Research, 97,* 299–309.

Wigfield, A., & Tonks, S. (2004). The development of motivation for reading and how it is influenced by CORI. In J. T. Guthrie, A. Wigfield, & K. C. Perencevich (Eds.), *Motivating reading comprehension: Concept-Oriented Reading Instruction* (pp. 249–272). Mahwah, NJ: Erlbaum.

Williams, J. P., Lauer, K. D., Hall, K. M., Lord, K. M., Gugga, S. S., & Bak, S. J. (2002). Teaching elementary school students to identify story themes. *Journal of Educational Psychology, 94*(2), 235–248.

Zahorik, J., (1996). Elementary and secondary teachers' reports of how they make learning interesting. *Elementary School Journal, 96,* 551–564.

# 30

# Taking "Steps" toward Positive Social Relationships

## A Transactional Model of Intervention

KARIN S. FREY AND SUSAN B. NOLEN

Recent years have seen increased concern about the threat of violence in schools (e.g., Jimerson & Furlong, 2005). Thankfully, such traumatic events are relatively rare. Yet many children are affected by more mundane conditions that nevertheless impact their development, and not incidentally, may be linked to more explosive episodes (Leary, Kowalski, Smith, & Phillips, 2003). A classroom learning environment can suffer a thousand small cuts from disruptive behavior (Fleming et al., 2005) and teachers may spend an inordinate amount of time reacting to unresolved conflicts (Johnson & Johnson, 1996). Children who are not deterred from aggressive, oppositional behaviors follow a developmental trajectory that puts them at risk for substance use, conduct problems, and academic failure (Barker, Tremblay, Nagin, Vitaro, & Lacourse, 2006; Dodge, Greenberg, Malone, & CPPRG, 2008; Fite, Colder, Lochman, & Wells, 2008). Research on victimization also shows links between social, emotional, and academic aspects of development. Those who become chronic targets show decreases in class participation (Buhs, Ladd, & Herald, 2006), attendance, and academic performance (Nishina, Juvonen, & Witkow, 2005; Schwartz & Gorman, 2003), and increases in emotional distress (Hanish & Guerra, 2002; Juvonen, Nishina, & Graham, 2000).

Conversely, developmental trajectories typically show gains in school achievement and standardized test performance when children are protected and social competence is fostered (Wentzel, 2005). A significant body of evidence suggests that school-based prevention and intervention programs can improve school behavior and health while simultaneously achieving gains in grades, test scores, and graduation rates (U.S. Department of Health and Human Services, 2002). Since both antisocial and prosocial behavior patterns are relatively stable between early childhood and late adolescence, such programs may stimulate long-term shifts in developmental trajectories (e.g., Fleming et al., 2005; Lacourse et al., 2002). This chapter describes theory and research related to a universal school program, *Second Step: A Violence Prevention Program* (Committee for Children, 1997a, 1997b, 1997c, 2002).

Universal programs try to address the needs of all, rather than limit their focus to "problem students." All students can benefit from the creation of an ecosystem that supports positive behaviors and redirects negative ones. As we argue in this chapter, individual improvement is unlikely to be sustained unless it is accompanied by supportive changes in the child's social environment. People influence each other and their social contexts through their transactions. Social skill development occurs, or is impeded during interactions with other people. Children, for example, who respond to provocation with emotional outburst and aggression, will have a difficult time learning to moderate their reactions, if they are consistently harassed by classmates. Over time, these interactions shape, and are shaped by the norms and expectations of those social contexts. Socially skilled aggressors may learn to target highly reactive classmates, who are often rejected by peers (Boivin, Hyme, & Hodges, 2001). In some school climates, this will garner approval and status within the group (Vaillancourt, Hymel, & McDougall, 2003). The type and level of skill needed to be seen as socially competent depend on the environment in which those skills are used. Egalitarian, high-spirited exchanges, so appropriate on the playground, will be considered disruptive during a final exam.

Based on this ecological view of social development, school-wide interventions aim to teach prosocial behaviors and change school norms. By making behaviors like negotiation, anger management, and helping others part of the shared expectations of the school, school-wide interventions help create a context in which newly learned skills can be successfully practiced. In this chapter, we propose an ecological model of school-wide intervention that takes into account the transactional relationships among norms, goals, behaviors, and social identities in schools.

## Social Ecology and Transactional Processes

A social ecological approach to development, as illustrated in Figure 30.1, shows individual students embedded within overlapping social microsystems (Bronfenbrenner, 1979) in this case, the peer group, classroom, and school. Arrows indicate some of the potential influences among the individuals and groups. Some students are more influential and have more connections with peers in the class. One is socially isolated. The peer network as a whole influences the individual student through shared beliefs and expectations while individual actions contribute to peer group norms. An analogous set of influences operates between individual students, the teacher, and the peer group.

An example will illustrate how individuals and ecosystems influence each other through transactions over time (Sameroff & MacKenzie, 2003). Consider a classroom in which the peer group norms value aggressive responses to disputes or provocation. Those norms prompt many students to engage in tit-for-tat altercations that sometimes escalate into defiance toward school staff. Unresolved conflicts repeatedly interfere with academic teaching (Johnson & Johnson, 1996). Feeling pressure to recoup that time for academics, the teacher spends less time proactively teaching the norms and skills required to resolve conflicts. Aggressive peer group norms gain strength, and the learning environment continues to erode.

The assumption underlying school-wide prevention is that creating positive social norms and expectations, along with new social-emotional skills and a shared vocabulary for respectfully resolving conflicts, will alter the perceived meaning and value of specific behaviors. As peers and educators shift their view of those behaviors, they will begin to respond in new ways. Transactional processes epitomize what are commonly referred to as beneficent and vicious circles. To the extent that the program alters social norms and environmental responses, motivation to engage in antisocial or positive behaviors may change. Thus, in a successful intervention, social interactions or transactions reflect changes that have occurred throughout the community, and stimulate additional changes within individuals (Sameroff & MacKenzie, 2003).

In this chapter, we use a transactional model of intervention to analyze the effects of *Second Step*. The program draws inspiration from cognitive-behavioral models of social-emotional learning (Crick & Dodge, 1994; Huesmann, 1988; Kendall, 1993). Work on the internal processes that affect social behavior are complemented by research into the effects of social networks on behavior (e.g., Coie et al., 1999; Farmer et al., 2002) and the use of transactional models to examine developmental trajectories (e.g., Caldwell, Rudolph, Troop-Gordon, & Do-Yeong, 2004; Egan & Perry, 1998; Hanish, Martin, Fabes, Leonard, & Herzog, M., 2005). In the following

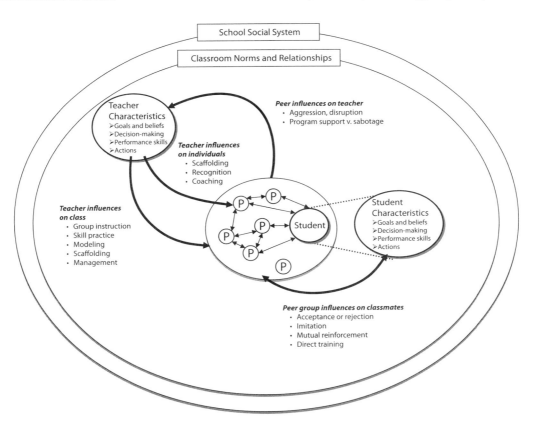

**Figure 30.1** Individual social-cognitions, emotions, and actions are embedded in relationships with teacher and peers that are situated within social systems.

sections, we will first examine the conceptual foundations of the program from the perspective of a transactional intervention model that includes internal processes, group norms, peer interactions, peer group influences on teachers, and teacher influences on peer interactions. We review evaluations of program effectiveness, and consider what these and other studies can tell us about the adequacy of the intervention model.

## A Transactional Intervention Model

Transactional intervention models assume multiple levels of change or stasis. As suggested by Figure 30.1, appreciation of individual change requires an understanding of (a) the thoughts, actions and emotions of individuals; (b) the transactional relationships among individuals; and (c) the collective understanding of social identities and shared norms that underlie all activity with the system. These are the arenas that need to be addressed when undertaking a school-based intervention.

Despite having different social roles, individuals within the class and school systems approach social interactions with commonalities in expectations, values, emotional reactions, and behavioral repertoires. These are based on the normative practices of the social context. Actions take on particular meanings within the values and norms of the social system, but these meanings and values continue to evolve through the ongoing practices and specific transactions of the members. Thus, members are influenced by the actions of others in the group, but also influence norms and values through their own actions and practice (Holland, Lachicotte, Skinner, & Cain, 1998). While transactional models show how feedback loops promote continuity in person—environment transactions, these models can also account for discontinuities in development, since changes in one or two elements of the system may ultimately elicit reciprocal changes in other elements (Sameroff & Chandler, 1975). Presumably, changes that shift the course of development in the individual will be more profound and long-lived if those changes occur in tandem with supportive changes in the social ecology.

### Intervention-Induced Transactional Change 
Sameroff and MacKenzie (2003) describe three types of intervention-induced transactional change: remediation, redefinition, and reeducation. Practices in Second Step create conditions for all three types of change to occur. Remediation refers to direct improvements in problem behaviors—improvements more likely to be sustained if they change related attitudes and behaviors of others. Thus, increased self-regulation and assertiveness on the part of victims may have a transactional effect if perceptions of these children as "easy marks" erode, and bullying declines. If, on the other hand, bullying continues unabated, newly learned assertive responses may be extinguished.

*Second Step* attempts to change social norms by *redefining* behaviors in the classroom and school contexts.

Thus the middle school version of *Second Step* redefines unregulated anger as a loss of control rather than a powerful response to provocation. By itself, redefinition may not result in immediate change. It may lead to increased awareness, however, of personal actions that contribute to peer rejection.

Transactional effects can also be accomplished through *reeducation*, as when teachers are given training in how to coach students in effective conflict resolution strategies. With greater knowledge in how to intervene, teachers are likely to increase their efforts. Those students who receive coaching in effective strategies may subsequently experience fewer peer problems and perceive teachers as able and willing to act.

## The Second Step Program

The aim of the *Second Step* program is to foster the social, emotional, and ethical development necessary for students to lead successful and satisfying lives. Insufficient prosocial motivation or skill contributes to behavior problems, and may also limit the potential of "well-behaved" children to succeed socially and academically (Weissberg & Greenberg, 1998). The developmentally sequenced program was first published in 1985 and updated three times for elementary school and middle school, twice for preschool. School-wide initiatives, classroom lessons, and daily scaffolding from adults teach intrapersonal (e.g., emotion regulation, self-discipline) and interpersonal skills (e.g., empathy, social scripts) along with positive social norms.

The theory and research that lays the foundation for the *Second Step* program provides examples of how transactional change might occur during school-wide interventions. The individual characteristics in Figure 30.1; thoughts, emotions, and actions; influence each other *within* each individual in the social ecology. Research illustrates the dynamic qualities of this internal system, as well as its embedded, socially-situated nature.

### Changing Social Cognitions, Emotions, and Actions 
In order to foster immediate and enduring change, the *Second Step* program attempts to improve behavior and the social-cognitions and emotions believed to underlie that behavior (e.g., Crick & Dodge, 1994; Huesmann, 1988). Research provides evidence of the fluid and simultaneous interplay occurring between an individual's observable actions, "in-the-moment" decision making, and the relatively stable characteristics derived from past actions and experiences (Zelli, Dodge, Lochman, Laird, & CPPRG, 1999). The latter include goals and beliefs, which exercise a strong motivational influence (Huesmann, 1988), and competencies that comprise the individual's repertoire of self-regulatory and performance skills.

### Goals and Beliefs 
As relatively stable characteristics (Burks, Dodge, Price, & Laird, 1999), goals and beliefs are frequent targets of intervention. Goals and belief systems

are coordinated. Relationship-enhancing goals, for example, are most likely when young people have positive views of themselves and others (Salmivalli, Ojanen, Haanpää, & Peets, 2005). Goals embody a person's thoughts and feelings about what is valuable and worthy of pursuit (Jarvinen, & Nicholls, 1996; Rubin & Krasnor, 1986). *Second Step* lessons attend to social goals by providing clear norms for ethical, relationship-enhancing behavior in the context of typical social situations such as negotiating with peers or parents. The norms are concern for safety, fairness, and the feelings of others. Lessons explore how attending to the feelings and justified claims of others promotes self-interest in a broad sense, enabling one to maintain the goodwill and high regard of peers, parents, and teachers. Narrowly self-interested goals are presented as providing short-run benefits (e.g., winning a competition) and long-range costs, such as losing a friend. Positive goals are more likely to be translated into positive actions (Huesmann, 1988) when they are shared with others in the social system.

In line with expectancy-value theory (Eccles, 2005), skill development may influence goal preferences by increasing perceived competence. By teaching social scripts for making friends, resolving conflicts, and managing anger, the program may increase children's feelings of social self-efficacy (Van Schoiack-Edstrom, Frey, & Beland, 2002). Those beliefs may link initial skill development to subsequent situational and mastery goals (Frey, Nolen, Edstrom, & Hirschstein, 2005), providing a conduit for intervention-induced change.

Although the studies we cite focus primarily on the individual, the situated nature of social beliefs is clear. Beliefs held about group norms (Holland et al., 1998), and expected outcomes for aggression (Hubbard, Dodge, Cillessen, Coie, & Schwartz, 2001; Schwartz et al., 1998) are formed through transactions with individuals in the social environment. Attributions of hostility to others may justify retaliation (Huesmann & Guerra, 1997) and often derive from chronic problems in peer relationships (Hubbard et al., 2002; Ladd & Troop-Gordon, 2003).

*Decision-Making Processes* When children interact with one another, each child interprets the other's actions. They construct goals for the specific situation (Troop-Gordon & Asher, 2005), and generate and evaluate possible responses to the other's behavior (Dodge, Pettit, McClaskey, & Brown, 1986). These decision-making processes shape the ways that beliefs influence actions (Zelli et al., 1999), just as decision making is itself shaped by beliefs. *Second Step* starts with an empathy unit that teaches students to notice and interpret contextual and expressive cues to emotional states (Halberstadt, Denham & Dunsmore, 2001). Students learn not to jump to conclusions about the intentions of others. Fostering empathy through emotional understanding is a primary focus. Those able to empathize with others are more prosocial (Eisenberg, et al., 1996) and become less aggressive over time (Hastings, Zahn-Waxler, Robinson, Usher, & Bridges, 2000).

*Self-Regulatory and Performance Skills* Undertaking a selected action requires capabilities that encompass self-regulatory, social-emotional, physical, and cognitive skills. Self-regulatory skills serve as a foundation for a wide range of social, emotional, and achievement outcomes (e.g., Eisenberg, Fabes, Guthrie, & Reiser, 2000; Mischel, Shoda, & Rodriguez, 1989). They enable individuals to sustain goal-directed effort and modulate emotional reactions that might derail progress (Barkley, 1997). Inability to regulate emotions encourages preemptive, nonevaluative processing (Hubbard et al., 2002) that often results in imprudent goals and aggressive actions. An important consideration is that self-regulatory demands increase when individuals attempt unfamiliar social behaviors (Vohs, Baumeister, & Ciarocco, 2005), as students might do during a social-emotional learning program.

Like beliefs, skills and routines are social phenomena. Experimental studies show that social ostracism, for example, diminishes the self-regulatory capabilities of both perpetrators and victims (see review by Vohs & Ciarocco, 2004). Behavior self-regulation can be acquired in the classroom through social modeling, skill rehearsal, and encouragement (Schunk & Zimmerman, 1997). When teaching *Second Step,* educators help students develop appropriate social scripts for specific situations. They model the script and support students' rehearsal it. These *scaffolding* techniques enable skill acquisition by reducing the difficulty of the requisite behavior. They improve the chances that skills will be used by contributing to a classroom community in which self-restraint is valued.

*Actions* Lesson content in *Second Step* reflects the socially embedded nature of the intra- and interpersonal elements described above. The number of ways that these elements might be expressed in action suggests that there are multiple pathways to the development of antisocial or prosocial behavior (Crick & Dodge, 1994). Therefore, the program adopts multiple strategies aimed at discouraging disruptive, relationship-damaging behavior and increasing responsible, relationship-enhancing behavior. The content of *Second Step* lessons provides the template for social interactions within the school ecosystem. Instructors teach children to use the methods during interactions with peers and adults. Instructors are expected to use the same methods when dealing with their students, in order to provide consistent models and to enhance teacher–student relationships. Administrators can use the same template with children referred for problem behavior.

**Adult Leadership** To a greater or lesser extent, all adults in schools are expected to assume leadership positions in respect to students. The mission of adults is to provide guidance, mentoring, redirection of negative behaviors and models of socially responsible, compassionate practices. Like students, educators are not immune to the impact of their own upbringing or the larger culture on their beliefs, goals and skills. We have heard some educators voice the belief that a particularly troublesome child deserves or will benefit from being bullied (Hazler, Miller, Carney, & Green, 2001). Adults with such beliefs may be reluctant to provide the type of protection that high school students perceive as evidence of caring (Astor, Meyer, & Behre, 1999).

***Teacher Roles and Responsibilities*** In most cases, the classroom teacher provides the curriculum to students, and distributes videotaped demonstrations of families using the methods to parents. Lessons make use of direct instruction, discussion, classroom activities, role-playing exercises, self-reflection, live- and videotaped models in order to increase student understanding, comfort, and automaticity in performing skills. Preschool lessons enlist the help of puppets. In later grades, there is more emphasis on self-reflection and discussion. Teacher training, curriculum lesson plans, and the teacher's manual provide guidance on the specific teaching techniques (e.g., role playing), ways to integrate academic and social-emotional learning, and methods of modeling and scaffolding positive behavior throughout the day. Integrating these new social practices into the classroom and school community demonstrates that these new ways to interact are, indeed, normative. This integration may constitute the most influential element of program implementation. Some practices, such as forecasting opportunities to practice specific skills or formally recognizing positive student efforts, are planned in advance. Others make use of teachable moments to scaffold positive efforts and model new norms. Later discussion of teacher implementation evaluations will elaborate on the latter practices.

Teachers have the most contact with students, and probably the most direct influence on students' social behavior (Kallestad & Olweus, 2003). We note, however, that the types of relationships found within the classroom (and illustrated in Figure 30.1) are analogous in many ways to those found within the school ecosystem. Classroom systems relate to each other, with stronger ties between same-grade rooms. Kallestad and Olweus point out that teachers operate in a social network of their peers, and that collegial relationships foster better program implementation.

***Administrator Support of Intervention*** Much like teachers in classrooms, principals are responsible for creating a supportive context for intervention. A study of 544 schools showed that principal support predicted the degree to which prevention programs were integrated into the regular school routine (Payne, Gottfredson, & Gottfredson, 2006). Teacher implementation improves when principals conscientiously implement school-wide procedures. An evaluation of a social-emotional learning curriculum in urban schools revealed that only schools with principal support *and* quality teacher implementation showed decreases in aggression (Kam, Greenberg, & Walls, 2003).

*Second Step* provides resources for administrators wishing to affect multiple aspects of children's environment. Take-home videotapes and family-night presentations show families using the communication, emotion regulation, and problem-solving techniques at home. Plans for family workshops are also available. An administrator's manual provides guidance for (a) encouraging staff buy-in, (b) integrating program concepts with school-wide norms and disciplinary support, and (c) training auxiliary staff such as playground monitors.

*Encouraging Buy-In* Some administrators build staff enthusiasm by creating a demonstration project. One principal personally taught the program to a classroom with a reputation for disciplinary problems. Positive changes in the classroom generated staff enthusiasm for school-wide implementation the following year. Other schools and districts have employed school psychologists or counselors to provide ongoing technical assistance to teachers (e.g., Mehas et al., 1998). Extensive support provided by one middle school principal included "grab and go" kits. Folders of materials and newspaper articles relevant to the week's lessons were placed in each teacher's mailbox, providing tangible assistance and communicating the expectation that all teachers would use them.

Program maintenance is difficult when schools experience high turnover among the teaching and administrative staff. As one elementary counselor recounted, "Teachers say they don't need *Second Step* at this school. That's because they don't know what it was like before we started it." An effective strategy for maintaining long-term enthusiasm and fidelity is to provide evidence of program effectiveness with multiyear data from office referrals, staff surveys, and test results (Noell, Duhon, Gatti, & Connell, 2002).

*Models for Disciplinary Support* Both teachers and administrators have reported using the problem-solving steps when infractions have occurred. Some principals keep program materials in their waiting rooms. Students are expected to identify the problem in neutral terms, and generate possible solutions before seeing the principal. One first-grade teacher created a "*Second Step* corner" in his room. The illustrated lessons cards from previously taught lessons were available for student "teachers" during choice time and for reference after a dispute.

*Staff Training* Effective principals provide ongoing training and mentoring to all members of the school community. Training manuals and videotaped demonstrations of program techniques can help prepare teachers. Administrators may also provide mentoring to teachers who feel uncomfortable with class role-playing exercises, an often omitted aspect of classroom lessons (Kallestad & Olweus, 2003). Many schools and districts find it useful to train an on-site staff person to conduct additional workshops and booster training. Office personnel and school yard monitors are often the first on the scene when altercations occur. Instruction in the vocabulary and problem-solving procedures provides clear expectations to students and scaffolding throughout the school day.

## Evaluation of Second Step Effects on Beliefs and Social Interactions

The Second Step program has been evaluated in a wide variety of geographic locales (American Southwest, Northwest, Midwest, and Northeast; Canada; Europe) and school contexts (urban, suburban, and rural populations; schools situated in housing projects and on military bases). The studied populations represent considerable diversity in ethnicity and economic status. The appendix included at the end of this chapter displays the designs, sample characteristics, measures, and results of Second Step evaluations: Five studies of the elementary program, three of the preschool-kindergarten and two of the middle school/junior high program. Three additional studies evaluate adaptations of the Second Step program.

The quality of the studies varies widely. Only three studies included random assignment of schools to intervention and control groups, thereby providing clear evidence that changes were caused by the program. Five of the studies employ a nonequivalent control group design, common in field situations when random assignment is impossible or unacceptable to school administrators. This raises the possibility that educators most interested in tackling problem behaviors are in the intervention group, thereby "stacking the deck" in favor of positive results. The age-cohort-sequential design (e.g., Holsen, Smith, & Frey, 2008) gets around this problem by comparing pretest results from sixth grade, for example, with the posttest results for students who are in sixth grade one year later. While not as strong as a random-control trial (RCT), the design eliminates the problem of self-selection.

Four other studies have no comparison group. In these studies, participants were assessed before and after program implementation. In these cases, it is difficult to know whether improvements in social-emotional knowledge, for example, are due to the program rather than maturation. In the case of aggression, such designs may work against finding positive results because aggression typically increases from fall to spring (Aber, Jones, Brown, Chaudry, Samples, 1998), and from year to year (Guerra, Huesman, Tolan, Van Acker, & Eron, 1995).

Finally, six of the 12 studies are limited by small samples and a limited number of schools. Only three studies (Frey et al., 2005; Grossman et al., 1997; Holsen et al., 2008) used analyses that account for the commonalities experienced by subjects who are nested in classrooms and schools. Considering these methodological limitations, some conclusions must be tentative. Several studies raise important questions about implementation and contextual factors in intervention.

*Elementary Second Step* Due to the strong methodology, results of two of the elementary school studies are presented in greater detail. Both included randomly assigned groups, sufficient sample sizes distributed in multiple schools, analytic controls for subject nesting, and direct observa-

tions by coders who were blind to condition. In the first of these (Grossman et al, 1997), trained observers coded the social behavior of second and third grade children in three contexts: classroom, cafeteria, and playground. Not surprisingly, all social behaviors occurred most frequently in the cafeteria and playground contexts—4.3 times as much physical aggression as in class, 3.0 times as much verbal aggression, and 2.8 times as much positive social behavior. Controlling for fall pretest observations, results showed posttest group differences in physical aggression and positive social behavior. As shown in Figure 30.2, group differences at the spring posttest reflected a 19% decline in physical aggression in the six intervention schools combined with a 60% increase in the six control schools. Verbal aggression exhibited a similar profile to that of physical aggression, but group differences were not significant. Posttest observations showed increased positive social behaviors in the intervention, but not the control schools.

Observations completed the following fall, after the intervention ceased, indicated a continued downward trajectory among the *Second Step* schools. Physical aggression in the control schools was closer to that of the previous (pretest) autumn. Given the typical yearly cycle of increased springtime aggression (Aber et al., 1998), follow-up observations in the spring would provide a more conclusive test of sustained program effects.

A second study followed second and fourth grade children at 15 schools for 2 years in order to examine behavior,

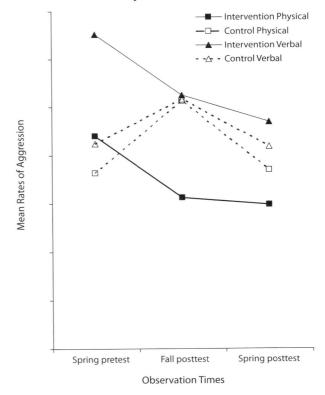

**Figure 30.2** Rates of physical and verbal aggression observed during autumn pretest, spring pretest, and autumn follow-up observations (Grossman et al., 1997). Reprinted with permission. Copyright © 1997 American Medical Association. All rights reserved.

and the thoughts and feelings posited to mediate behavior change (Frey et al., 2005).[1] One year's implementation showed significant declines in teacher reports of antisocial behavior and increases in socially competent behaviors. After 2 years (in grades 3 and 5), we undertook an in-depth examination of children's goals, satisfaction, and dyadic behavior elicited in two socially complex situations. One required that pairs of children agree on a way to divide an array of thank-you gifts consisting of two attractive prizes, a moderately attractive prize, and a relatively unattractive prize. The other situation involved playing what is called a "prisoner's dilemma" game with a partner. In this task, two children from one class and two from another simultaneously made decisions that controlled allocation of money for a year-end class pizza party. For eight trials, each pair of children jointly decided to choose a cooperative or competitive strategy. If both pairs made the cooperative choice on a trial, each class earned $.40. Two competitive choices garnered $.10 for each class. The combination of a competitive and a cooperative response earned $.50 for the class of the competitive pair and $.20 for the class of the cooperative pair.

*Goals, Satisfaction, and Attributions*    Prior to playing the prisoner's dilemma game, children were individually interviewed regarding their most preferred outcome and the reasons for their preference. Using this information, we found that children espoused two types of self-serving goals (one oriented toward outdoing or dominating the other players, and one oriented toward maximum absolute gain). Other children preferred one of two types of prosocial goals (one oriented toward mutual or egalitarian gain, and one oriented toward altruism).

If our model is accurate, we would expect that participants in the Second Step program would have more prosocial goal orientations than those in the control group. Children in the Second Step group were more likely than those in the control group to prefer an egalitarian goal (43.4% and 35.5%, respectively) and less likely to prefer a dominance goal (14.0% and 23.4%). Children in the two groups were equally likely to prefer goals of altruism (9.8%) or maximum gain (32.0%).

Killen and Nucci (1995) point out that moral actions do not entail suppression of self-interest. We considered egalitarian goals to be the most mature, since they provided a fair way of coordinating self-interested goals with those related to relationships and fair play (Dodge, Asher, & Parkhurst, 1989; Ojanen, Grönoos, & Salmivalli, 2005; Troop-Gordon & Asher, 2005). The Second Step program repeatedly stresses that egalitarian behavior supports self-interest in the long run by sustaining social relationships. Students in the intervention group may have responded to this redefinition of self-interest, resulting in a changed perception of the task objectives.

Compared to children in the control group, those in the Second Step group also expected to experience less satisfaction if the game outcome was lopsided in their favor.

Following the prisoner's dilemma game, those in the Second Step group were more likely than their control-group counterparts to cite egalitarian reasons for their satisfaction or dissatisfaction with the outcome. After negotiating with their partners, those in the Second Step group were more satisfied with the prize division. Hypothetical vignettes used to measure attributions of hostile goals and preferred responses to aggression, however, showed no group differences.

*Negotiation Behavior*    Having students work in pairs allowed us to examine dyadic interaction, which was predicted to show group differences in coercive and collaborative behaviors. Behavior coding showed that pairs of children from Second Step classrooms were 42.1% less aggressive than those in the control group during the prize negotiation. Girls in the Second Step group used the most collaborative negotiating strategy 59.2 % more frequently than their counterparts in the control group. Boys asked if their partners agreed 33.3% more than those in the control group—a nonsignificant trend in this case. Pairs of children in Second Step classrooms were 41.1% less likely to require adult intervention in order to complete their negotiations. Effect sizes were modest; *ES* ranged from to .14 to .25. The practical importance for teachers becomes clearer when extrapolated to 25-student classrooms (Abelson, 1985).

Contrary to predictions, no group differences were found in cooperative choices made jointly by student dyads during the prisoner's dilemma game. There were also no group differences in demanding, whiny behavior during negotiations (2.4 events in Second Step pairs versus 2.1 events). We wondered if situations that might have evoked aggression prior to intervention might have elicited lower-level coercive behavior afterwards, an interesting, albeit untested possibility.

A strength of the two studies, the second-by-second observations of behavior by individuals that are "blind" to treatment assignment, is relatively rare in program evaluation. The use of unbiased measures, combined with strong study design and analyses lends considerable support to the conclusions of the two studies: The elementary version of Second Step appears to be a useful tool in the effort to increase positive social development and decrease aggressive and disruptive behavior.

**Preschool Second Step**    Three preschool studies also included direct observations to measure behavior change. These were carried out in quite different school contexts, domestic Marine Corps bases (Thomas, Leidy, Powers, & Holden, 1998) and an urban housing project with African American students (McMahon, Washburn, Felix, Yakin, & Childrey, 2000). All three studies showed improvements in observed classroom behaviors and in social-emotional knowledge. Replications bolster confidence in the results, even though two of the three employed designs lacked a comparison group. Significant changes have been made to the preschool/kindergarten program since these studies were published. The large scale use of "blind" observations in conjunction with randomly assigned control groups would provide the necessary test of program effectiveness.

***Middle School Second Step*** None of the current research on the middle-school program used a random-control design. Conclusions are also limited because evaluators made adaptations made to the program without providing information about fidelity (Domitrovich & Greenberg, 2000; Walker, 2004). Lacking systematic information, we are unable to interpret, for example, disparate results observed between schools (McMahon & Washburn, 2003) or classrooms (Orpinas, Parcel, McAlister, & Frankowski, 1995). The variations noted in this set of studies, however, raise interesting questions about implementation.

Only one study used a comparison group and a substantial sample to test the program as developed (Van Schoiack-Edstrom et al., 2002). In line with predictions regarding program effects on social norms, posttest results showed that students in the intervention group were less accepting of aggression than their cohorts in the control group. They also believed themselves to be more capable at using social-emotional skills such as managing anger and solving social problems. Post hoc analyses suggested that positive changes in social norms were most likely when lessons occurred at least twice a week. This is consistent with recommendations of the developer, but has yet to be explicitly tested. Research that assigns some classrooms to weekly and some to thrice- weekly lessons concentrations would provide important information to educators.

Three of the middle-school studies tested adaptations to the program. Edwards and colleagues (Edwards, Hunt, Meyers, Grogg, & Jarrett, 2005) added material about bullying to the Second Step lessons and evaluated outcomes in all middle schools in a small urban district. Both quantitative and qualitative methods provided encouraging results. This is the first published study that has attempted to examine family participation in program activities. During interviews, 85% of students reported discussing program skills with parents and 65% said parents assisted them with skills, sometimes by engaging in role-playing exercises. This is an important arena for research, especially during adolescence, when parents may appreciate activities that foster positive family bonds. Future research might endeavor to identify factors that encourage family participation. What modes of communication (e.g., take-home videos, joint projects) are effective? Is the topic of bullying particularly likely to foster family participation?

The study by Edwards and colleagues (2005) provides an example of overlaps between specific microsystems. Bronfenbrenner (1979) describes *mesosystemic* influences as ones that occur when one microsystem (e.g., family) influences relationships in another (school). Our model would suggest that direction of influence in this case would be reciprocal. Was the program's apparent success due in part to high levels of parental support? Future research needs to examine how family engagement may contribute to positive

outcomes, and what elements elicit high rates of engagement (e.g., Reid, Eddy, Fetrow, & Stoolmiller, 1999).

Additional research on the middle school program is greatly needed, in particular, large-scale random control studies. Major revisions of the program, subsequent to these studies have added material on bullying and drug resistance strategies.

## Beyond Lessons: Daily Teaching Practices Influence Peer Relations

There is mounting evidence that quality of students' social-emotional relationships within the classroom predicts appropriate classroom engagement (Patrick, Ryan, & Kaplan, 2007). Positive student–teacher relationships in kindergarten contribute to developmental trajectories through eighth grade, with reduced disciplinary infractions, improved work habits, and better grades (Hamre & Pianta, 2001). Beyond the personal relationships they have with individual students, it is evident that many teachers put considerable effort into inspiring, encouraging, and coaching positive peer relationships. Cohen and Lotan (1995), for example, describe how teachers can engineer situations that may enhance a rejected child's social status. Embry (2004) describes brief, evidenced-based practices that teachers can utilize daily. When intervention programs are implemented, educators serve as the primary mediators between program and students (Kallestad & Olweus, 2003). Thus, the success of those programs ultimately depends on the actions of educators, both with respect to providing high quality lessons and fostering a receptive social context.

***Evaluation of Teaching Practices Associated with Second Step*** We are particularly interested in teacher actions that support students' adoption of promoted goals and practices in the ongoing interactions of the classroom. Unfamiliar routines increase demands on self-regulatory capacities (Vohs et al., 2005). Children particularly need assistance when attempting to use new strategies during potentially heated interactions. Using teachable moments, teachers can provide scaffolding for emergent behaviors. Cueing or demonstrating a relevant action reduces the difficulty for the child, indicates when it is appropriately used, and provides an opportunity for a self-reflective pause in high-arousal situations. Recognizing positive efforts helps motivate children to repeat their actions and supports the community's adoption of prosocial goals (Abbott et al., 1998). By scaffolding student behavior in vulnerable moments, teachers may prevent problems from arising and enhance memory for constructive alternatives in the future. The Second Step program also encourages teachers to use classroom events as a springboard for joint problem solving and to integrate lesson content with other subjects. Suggestions for these activities are provided in the curriculum, but ultimately depend on the creativity and commitment of individual teachers.

Qualitative interviews with 15 teachers of Second Step

indicated that most viewed integration into the school day as important for success (Nolen, Frey, Hirschstein, & Sylvester [Edstrom], 1997). A majority were improvising supportive class activities at the end of the first year. Those who reported more daily integration also noted more positive changes in themselves, such as improvements in their anger management or communication skills. Teachers' own social skill development would likely improve the chances of successful intervention.

Quantitative studies of teacher generalization efforts were undertaken using monthly teacher self-reports. These showed moderate-to-strong correlations with observations of teacher behavior (Hirschstein, Van Schoiack-Edstrom, Frey, & Nolen, 2001). Monthly surveys of 89 teachers showed more in-the-moment scaffolding of social-emotional skills when they were assigned to the Second Step intervention group than to the control group (Van Schoiack, 2000). Regardless of group, teachers in the Second Step evaluation who provided more support for social-emotional skills also reported greater social competence among their students, with baseline controlled. Improvements in antisocial behavior, however, were only related to teacher support within the intervention classrooms. Reports of similar behaviors by control-group teachers were not predictive. It may be that in-the-moment prompts that are not accompanied by formal instruction lack a framework sufficient to obtain maximum benefit. Students may not have the relevant vocabulary, or practice in pertinent skills. Lacking formal instruction, they may not have been exposed to discussion of social norms, and why normative behavior is advantageous for all in the long run.

More recent research with a bullying prevention program indicates daily support frequency predicts improvements in playground aggression (Hirschstein, Edstrom, Frey, Snell, & MacKenzie, 2007), and that the type of improvement is specific to the content of support, such as empathy or assertiveness (Frey, Jones, Hirschstein, & Edstrom, in press). In our model, adult's efforts to scaffold and intervene serve to enact the norms that the *Second Step* program endeavors to instill. Such efforts provide visible evidence of systemic change, which is likely to help create a beneficent circle. Perceived school safety is a strong predictor of positive bonds between students and teacher (Crosnoe, Johnson, & Elder, 2004), which support educators' ability to positively influence and mentor students (Wentzel, 2005).

### Examination of Potential Change Mechanisms

Confidence in program effectiveness is indirectly supported when evaluations show effects on possible mechanisms of change as well as on behavioral outcomes (Eddy, Dishion, & Stoolmiller, 1998). In this section we describe secondary analyses that provide support for a transactional perspective on school-based intervention. First we examine how goals and beliefs relate to social behavior. Then we examine how the goals of each member of an interacting dyad relate to observed behavior. The research suggests that dyads and

groups create a behavioral context that is more than the sum of its parts.

### Intraindividual Links between Thought, Emotions, and Actions

*Goals, Attributions, Norms, and Behavior* Analyses of thoughts, feelings, and action measured during our elementary Second Step evaluation (Frey et al., 2005) support our prediction of close links between internal processes and actions. Recall that we measured children's social goals with respect to their preferred outcomes of the prisoner's dilemma game. Although goals vary with the situation, some children will generally prefer relationship-enhancing goals, while others will exhibit a bias toward self-serving goals (Ojanen, Aunola, & Salmivalli, 2007). Despite the specificity of our measurement context, we were impressed that children's goals predicted behavior and attitudes that were measured in different contexts, using different methodologies. As predicted by our model, children who espoused prosocial goals were less likely to endorse either physical or verbal aggression than those who espoused purely self-serving goals. Teacher reports indicated that those with prosocial goals were also more socially competent and less antisocial than self-serving peers.

Troop-Gordon and Asher (2005) point out that the effect of any goal is best understood when considered with other beliefs and objectives. In line with this admonition, we found that the most aggressive attitudes, the lowest social competence, and the most antisocial behavior typified children who preferred self-serving goals *and* tended to interpret ambiguous situations (e.g., being hit by a ball) as the results of hostile intentions. Transactional effects might solidify such beliefs, as when the antisocial behavior of a child with self-serving goals elicits aggressive responses from others.

*Goals and Satisfaction* Goals structure emotional responses to social outcomes by identifying those that are valued and those that disappoint (Crick & Dodge, 1994; Rubin & Krasnor, 1986). In line with previous research (Jarvinen & Nicholls, 1996), we found that children with prosocial goals (altruistic or egalitarian) were more satisfied with the subsequent outcome of the prize division than children with only self-serving goals (absolute or relative gain). They were not more satisfied with the outcome of the prisoner's dilemma game, perhaps reflecting the overall lack of cooperation between dyads. Children with prosocial goals were, however, more likely to cite the well-being of others as a factor in their satisfaction with the outcome.

Program-induced increases in prosocial goals and satisfaction can themselves promote prosocial norms in the classroom. By adopting mutual benefit ("win-win") as their goal in situations with both social and instrumental rewards, children create more opportunities for satisfaction than if they view such proceedings as zero-sum, win-lose propositions. As well as deriving positive emotions from a larger array of beneficial outcomes to oneself and others, children who espouse mutually beneficial goals may engender goodwill and transactional relationships that provide further reinforcement for positive behavior and encourage commitment to prosocial goals (Erdley & Asher, 1999). Our findings are in line with one of the tenets of positive psychology: Thinking beyond oneself is linked to experiencing greater life satisfaction, itself a key social-emotional skill (Seligman, Steen, Park, & Peterson, 2005).

*Peer Contextual Influences* Social interactions of the kind these interventions target do not happen in a vacuum. Peer groups have ongoing histories in which norms, values, and beliefs are developed through social interactions. If aggressive behavior leads to power and status within the group, it is because that behavior has become legitimized within the group over time. Young people who want to belong to the group may take up practices modeled by members with high status, while others may resist group norms by acting against them. The impact of peer influence will vary based on the characteristics and position of the individuals within the group, specific interaction histories (Coie et al., 1999), and characteristics of the social networks in which those interactions occur (Crosnoe & Needham, 2004).

*Dyadic Interactions when Goals Match or Conflict* Both the prize negotiations and the prisoner's dilemma game (Frey et al., 2005) provided complex social contexts for assessing the prosocial and self-interested behavior of the third and fifth grade participants. Children from the same classroom had to coordinate norms of fair play, generosity, and self-interest. They had to maintain a relationship with their partner in order to resolve differences and reach agreement. Within the dyad, partners may or may not have agreed on goals appropriate to the situation. While individuals may consciously or implicitly adopt social goals prior to an interaction, those goals, and the strategies used to

attain them, may change during interaction (Troop-Gordon & Asher, 2006).

When both children in the dyad endorsed prosocial goals for the prisoner's dilemma game, they made more cooperative choices than when both endorsed self-serving goals. Microanalytic observations made while children were negotiating the division of the four thank-you gifts also showed links between prosocial goals and self-restraint. As shown in Figure 30.3, partners who shared prosocial goals were less coercive (demanding and whiny) than other dyads while negotiating a prize division. Those who shared prosocial goals also took the most collaborative approach when negotiating. They made more open-ended inquiries about their partner's preferences. These results support our model and indicate a reassuring consistency between goals and actions during complex social tasks.

Other results were more surprising, indicating that goal concordance may affect the direction as well as magnitude of peer influence. We had anticipated that the actions of some pairs with unshared goals would show evidence of compromise and mutual influence. In others, we expected that one partner's goals would prove more potent, perhaps because of power or position inequalities in the home classroom. In either case, we expected goal conflict to yield behaviors that fell within the range provided by the prosocial and self-serving pairs. Figure 30.3 shows, however, that pairs of children whose goals diverged were the least collaborative, and were equally demanding as pairs of self-serving children. Dyads in this group also made fewer cooperative choices (M = 33%) on the prisoner's dilemma game than those that shared self-serving or prosocial goals (Ms = 37% and 42%, respectively). A possible exception to this pattern may occur with respect to aggression, in which the presence of a cooperative partner may deter escalation. Group differences for this variable, however, were not significant.

Our results are consistent with informal observations

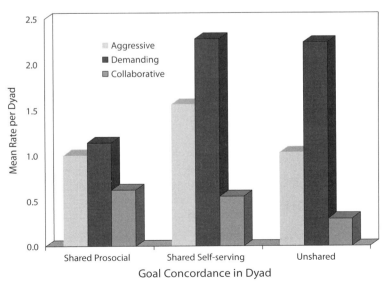

**Figure 30.3** Rates of negotiation behaviors observed in dyads who shared cooperative goals, shared self-interested goals, or were goal-discordant (Nolen et al., 2005). Reprinted with permission.

of partner conflicts during the prisoner's dilemma game. Those espousing prosocial goals sometimes expressed frustration with their inability to influence their partners, even withdrawing from negotiations somewhat. They occasionally criticized self-serving partners for selfishness, or (rarely) for adopting a strategy that would result in less money for all. Self-serving partners appeared oblivious to such arguments and less frustrated with their partners. This could be because they disregarded their partner's position, or because their willingness to ignore their partner's position caused them to prevail more frequently. If this thinking is correct, it may account for the overall self-serving bias in the choices made by pairs. Socially responsible actions are suppressed in egalitarian or communally oriented individuals when they are in relatively powerless positions (Chen, Lee-Chai, & Bargh, 2001).

### Suggested Research on Peer Influences

*Dyadic Processes*   We need additional research to explore these dyadic processes, particularly in regard to children's emotional reactions, sense of self, and peer histories. Our results suggest that negotiations between persons who espouse different value-laden goals may become antagonistic and destructive to the common good, a point not lost on close observers of political discourse. We were nevertheless surprised by the consistently negative association of goal divergence with socially competent behavior. Frustration induced by obstacles to each party's goals may have eroded self-restraint and increased preference for short-term gains (Kramer, McClintock, & Messick, 1986).

An alternative explanation for the poor performance of our goal-discordant pairs is that each one's preferred choices on the prisoner's dilemma game may have threatened the other's identity within the classroom community. Those concerned with peer dominance may have viewed cooperative responses during the game to be appropriate for "losers." Those with egalitarian goals may have felt that their partners' actions threatened their own identities as smart or good people. Perceiving threats to the self predicts more frequent attributions to hostile intent (Dodge & Somberg, 1987). Such conditions may have increased focus on the self, priming children to respond with more self-serving responses.

As Fitzsimmons and Bargh (2004) show, goal states cannot be separated from the context of interpersonal histories. Those histories elicit relationship-specific goal-driven behaviors that bypass conscious awareness. In this case, goal divergence may have simply identified pairs who had preexisting antipathies (Coie et al., 1999; Hubbard, Dodge, et al., 2001; Nangle, Erdley, Zeff, Stanchfield, & Gold, 2004), and were forced by the circumstance to interact with someone they might normally avoid.

The number of possible explanations for our results illustrates the need for further research on how social goals affect and are affected by social interaction. Methodologies that enable investigators to interview children about their goals and perceptions at different point in a social interaction would be especially useful. For example, children could indicate their goals before entering into a situation that can be interpreted as either competitive or cooperative. Afterwards, children could individually view videotapes of the interaction and give retrospective information about their goals and perceptions at different points of the interaction.

*Social Networks*   We could also use additional information about the formation and evolution of social networks. Young children prefer play partners that are similar to themselves on key characteristics (Hanish et al., 2005), and selective association sets transactional processes in motion that affect development. Selective association with aggressive play partners predicts increased conduct problems (Hanish et al., 2005; Snyder et al., 2005).

At school, peer networks tend to be nested within formal groups such as the classroom in elementary school and class (grade) in secondary school. How do formal and informal group memberships interact? Crosnoe and Needham (2004) showed that characteristics of friends (e.g., alcohol use, academic achievement) predict high school behavior problems. Both positive and negative impacts of friends' characteristics are greater when students occupy more central locations in the peer networks. Some of the negative aspects of adolescent friendships, however, are buffered when students perceive the school's teachers to be caring and fair. How else do school-wide conditions moderate microsystem dynamics?

*Peer Status and Power*   Social processes have particular potency when involving valued others. While norms evolve collectively, it is not a consensus. High status students have a greater voice than most in defining "the good" and "the bad." By the end of elementary school, and continuing through secondary school, socially powerful in-groups include a considerable number of aggressive leaders (Rodkin, Farmer, Pearl, van Acker, et al., 2006; Vaillancourt et al., 2003). The actions and appearance of popular or socially dominant students elicit preferential imitation within the confines of their particular cliques and beyond (Farmer et al., 2002). Their positions as popular students may affect how adults and other students interpret their actions. A socially unskilled child who repeatedly disrupted his elementary class was the identified subject of a teacher consultation. Observations indicated that the child's disruptive attempts at humor were virtually identical to the behaviors of a popular and capable class leader. The second young man's remarks were interpreted by the community as attempts to amuse and were enjoyed by teacher and students alike. The less skilled child had an identity as a "troublemaker." His remarks irritated others, who viewed them as expressions of his intention to disrupt the class. Repeated sanctions did not change his behavior, and may have contributed to his ongoing identity as a rejected peer. When the teacher realized the destructive dynamic, her responses to both children changed and the rejected child was ultimately repositioned as an acceptable peer.

Although the teacher and students powerfully shaped the meaning of this young man's behavior, the anecdote also illustrates the powerful effects of peers as models of behavior. Hoping to harness this power, Orpinas and colleagues (1995) adapted the middle school Second Step program to include peer discussion leaders that were chosen by classmates. The exploratory findings in two classrooms provide a cautionary note: Results obtained in one classroom were the best in the study, with boys reporting 51% less aggression at posttest than the control classroom. Reductions in aggression were minimal in the other, perhaps because three of the four students selected by classmates were antisocial leaders. These findings illustrate the need for additional information on how the peer social context may affect school prevention efforts. While the idea of harnessing peer prestige in support of the program is intriguing, greater care and more research are needed before recommendations can be made. Student leaders are not a homogeneous lot. What characteristics define those who are likely to be antagonistic to or supportive intervention programs? Does the enlistment of prosocial leaders have a beneficial effect throughout the student population? Or does identification of the program with a particular social crowd enable other students to discount it's pertinence to themselves?

## Transactional Evolution within Communities of Practice

Although thoughts, emotions, and actions are often studied at the individual level, we have tried to suggest how they are embedded in particular social contexts. Each person's actions and reactions take on meanings within their relationships as peers and as members of "communities of practice" (Lave & Wenger, 1991). These reflect the ongoing social histories of individuals and groups (Coie et al., 1999). Social histories are reflected in norms of the group, and the social identities of its participants. Students within elementary classrooms become more similar to each other with respect to aggression and norms about aggression than to students in other classrooms (Boxer, Guerra, Huesmann, & Morales, 2005). By introducing new practices, Second Step explicitly attempts to shape community values around core prosocial concerns for safety and fairness toward other people.

Integration of prosocial values into the ongoing life of the classroom does more than provide an opportunity for students and teachers to practice behaviors consistent with those values. Classroom communities continually evolve through the joint actions of their members (Holland et al, 1998). If Second Step leads to the enactment of new prosocial goals and strategies, the meaning of particular actions in the community can change. Angry reactions that have been seen as a way to control a situation may be redefined as loss of control. Mutually agreeable resolution to social conflict may become a more desirable goal than prevailing at all costs. In turn, those children who display skills in

newly valued behavior can be positioned as class leaders (Cohen & Lotan, 1995).

Social identities are continually constructed through the interactions of community members (Vadeboncoeur & Portes, 2002). The identity of "rejected child," for example, is created through the interactions of students and teachers, reenacting the values and belief systems. If the community values certain characteristics, say, social adeptness and privilege, children lacking those characteristics will be marginalized through teasing and ostracism. Such actions become mechanisms of social control that further reinforce community values (Chekroun & Brauer, 2002).

The goal of intervention is to inspire positive individual change that is motivated and supported by changes in social ecosystems. When norms shift in the classroom and school communities, individuals have opportunities to experiment with new behaviors and even new identities, a level of transformation that is virtually impossible when change is attempted solely at the individual level. While program activities may focus on individual learning, this is often accomplished through structured interactions with others in the classroom. Individuals change and are changed by the actions of others within a social ecological system. Due to transactional change, changes in individuals can lead to group changes, which motivate and support individual development.

## Needed Research on the Change Process

***Tracking the Change Process*** As the preceding discussion suggests, changes in the evolution of groups and in the trajectories of individual development occur in multiple small steps. Our understanding of the course of those changes is currently very weak, and there is a need for work that repeatedly measures thoughts, feelings, and actions during the change process (Eddy et al., 1998). One example of the kind of information we need is provided by the negotiations during a Second Step evaluation (Frey et al., 2005). As noted earlier, pairs of Second Step students were less aggressive, but no less demanding and whiney than students in the control group. If anything, rates of demanding–whiny statements were slightly, though not significantly, higher in the Second Step group. Could this represent an intermediate step for some children? Using tasks that allowed for multiple assessments might enable investigators to see if aggressive children substitute unpleasant, but less coercive behaviors before expanding their repertoire of positive social behaviors. More detailed descriptions of the change process would tell educators what they might expect during program implementation.

***Developmental Trends and Intervention*** It is also true that school contexts have a long and ongoing history. Newcomers to the school, eager to establish their niche, may be particularly receptive to the accepted practices of their new social environment. Our study of the effects of Second Step on the attitudes of middle school students partially controlled for age across the transition to middle school or junior high school (Van Schoiack-Edstrom et al., 2000). Baseline attitudes were measured in the first and second years of secondary school (grades 6 and 7 for middle school; grades 7 and 8 for junior high). Students at the beginning of their second year in secondary school (grade 7 or 8) were more likely to endorse aggression than students beginning their first year (grade 6 or 7). Neither grade, nor its interaction with year in secondary school were significant, suggesting that immersion in the new milieu helped shift normative beliefs in the direction of those held by older students.

What are the implications of developmental transitions for intervention outcomes? The study results were more consistent in the second year than in the first year of secondary school. Unfortunately, interpretation is complicated by implementation differences. Teachers of returning students taught the lessons at least twice a week—a pattern associated with better outcomes. Was the behavior of teachers a response to perceptions that returning students needed a more concentrated approach? Clearly, there is a strong need for controlled research that examines program efficacy as a function of duration, age, school context, and implementation strategy.

## Summary and Conclusions

A growing body of research indicates that schools can make lasting changes in children's social development. Cognitive-behavioral instruction and environmental support promote protective, prosocial behaviors and mitigate multiple problem behaviors (Greenberg et al., 2003; Wilson, Gottfredson, & Najaka, 2001). Data thus far suggest that the elementary version of the Second Step program is effective when implemented with reasonable integrity. Awaiting random-control trials, results for preschool and middle school versions also offer encouragement. Although most of the cited evaluations examined program effects on individuals, we have attempted to provide a transactional frame from which to view changes during a school-wide intervention. Each intervention occurs in a specific ecological context that can enhance or deter positive change within classroom and school communities. Whether positive changes will "take" ultimately depends on whether transactional changes occur in educator, student, and peer behavior.

As our research shows, actions compatible with prosocial norms are more likely to occur when those norms are shared between interacting peers. Although cultural beliefs often suggest that peers are all-important during adolescence, their influence is moderated by the caring actions of educators (Crosnoe & Needham, 2004). Discussion of the impact of the No Child Left Behind Act on educator stress is pertinent to social-emotional interventions. In parallel with students, educators' beliefs and self-regulatory skills influence their actions within the social context. If they feel that only test scores are valued, teachers may feel tension about devoting time to *Second Step* (Larsen & Samdal,

2007). Teachers who feel burned out by demands placed on them cut back on social intervention (Ransford, 2007). It's also possible that the stress teachers feel may encourage power assertive discipline inimical to caring relationships and positive youth development (Deci & Ryan, 1990).

During our research, we saw many examples of educators' creativity and commitment to their students' well-being. Educators enact changes in norms when they provide daily student support and counter beliefs that adults are oblivious to problems that concern students. The ability of adults to act as a credible source of guidance may hinge on such efforts. As expected from a systems perspective, teachers may view a successful intervention as benefiting themselves as well (Nolen, Horn, Ward, Stevens, & Estacio, 2005), enabling them to enjoy more respectful, caring interactions with their students.

## Note

1. Due to recruitment timing, only 11 of 15 schools were randomly assigned, although all school staffs had to agree to assignment to either group. We discuss findings that were replicated in the randomly controlled subsample and the larger quasi-experimental sample.

## References

Abbott, R. D., O'Donnell, J., Hawkins, J. D., Hill, K. G., Klosterman, R., & Catalano, R. F. (1998). Changing teaching practices to promote achievement and bonding to school. *Journal of Orthopsychiatry, 68,* 542–552.
Abelson, R. P. (1985). A variance explanation paradox: When a little is a lot. *Psychological Bulletin, 97,* 129–133.
Aber, J. L., Jones, S. M., Brown, J. L., Chaudry, N., & Samples, F. (1998). Resolving conflict creatively: Evaluating the developmental effects of a school-based violence prevention program in neighborhood and classroom context. *Development and Psychopathology, 10,* 187–213.
Astor, R. A., Meyer, H. A., & Behre, W. J. (1999). Unowned places and times: Maps and interviews about violence in high schools. *American Educational Research Journal, 36,* 3–42.
Barker, E. D., Tremblay, R. E., Nagin, D. S., Vitaro, F., & Lacourse, E. (2006). Development of male proactive and reactive physical aggression during adolescence. *Journal of Child Psychology & Psychiatry 47,* 793–790.
Barkley, R. A. (1997). Behavior inhibition, sustained attention and executive functions: Constructing a unifying theory of ADHD. *American Psychologist, 121,* 65–94.
Boivin, M., Hymel, S., & Hodges, E. V. E. (2001). Toward a process view of peer rejections and harassment. In J. Juvonen & S. Graham (Ed.), *Peer harassment in school: The plight of the vulnerable and victimized* (pp. 265–289). New York: Guilford.
Boxer, P., Guerra, N. G., Huesmann, L. R., & Morales, J., (2005). Proximal peer-level effects of a small-group selected prevention on aggression in elementary school children: An investigation of the peer contagion hypothesis. *Journal of Abnormal Child Psychology, 33,* 325–338.
Bronfenbrenner, U. (1979). *The ecology of human development: Experiments by nature and design.* Cambridge, MA: Harvard University Press.
Buhs, E. S., Ladd, G. W., & Herald, S. L. (2006). Peer exclusion and victimization: Processes that mediate the relation between peer group rejection and children's classroom engagement and achievement? *Journal of Educational Psychology, 98,* 1–13.
Burks, V. S., Dodge, K. A., Price, J. M., & Laird, R. D. (1999). Internal representational models of peers: Implications for the development of problem behavior. *Developmental Psychology, 35,* 802–810.

Caldwell, M. S., Rudolph, K. D., Troop-Gordon, W., & Do-Yeong, K. (2004). Reciprocal influences among relationship self-views, social disengagement, and peer stress during early adolescence. *Child Development, 75,* 1140–1154.

Chekroun, P., & Brauer, M. (2002). The bystander effect and social control behavior: The effect of the presence of others on people's reactions to norm violations. *European Journal of Social Psychology, 32,* 853–867.

Chen, S., Lee-Chai, A. Y., & Bargh, J. A. (2001). Relationship orientation as a moderator of the effects of social power. *Journal of Personality and Social Psychology, 80,* 173–187.

Cohen, E. G., & Lotan, R. A. (1995). Producing equal-status interactions in the heterogeneous classroom. *American Educational Research Journal, 32,* 99–120.

Coie, J. D., Cillessen, A. H. N., Dodge, K. A., Hubbard, J. A., Schwartz, D., Lemerise, E. A., et al. (1999). It takes two to fight: A test of relational factors and a method for assessing aggressive dyads. *Developmental Psychology, 35,* 1179–1188.

Committee for Children. (1997a). *Second Step: A violence prevention curriculum, grades 1–3* (2nd ed.). Seattle, WA: Author.

Committee for Children. (1997b). *Second Step: A violence prevention curriculum, grades 4–5* (2nd ed.). Seattle, WA: Author.

Committee for Children. (1997c). *Second Step: A violence prevention curriculum, middle–junior high.* (2nd ed.). Seattle, WA: Author.

Committee for Children. (2002). *Second Step: A violence prevention curriculum, preschool/kindergarten* (3rd ed.). Seattle, WA: Author.

Crick, N. R., & Dodge, K. A. (1994). A review and reformulation of social information-processing mechanisms in children's social adjustment. *Psychological Bulletin, 115,* 74–101.

Crosnoe, R., Johnson, M. K., & Elder, G. H. (2004), Intergenerational bonding in school: The behavioral and contextual correlates of student-teacher relationships. *Sociology of Education, 77,* 60–81.

Crosnoe, R., & Needham, B. (2004). Holism, contextual variability, and the study of friendships in adolescent development, *Child Development, 75,* 264–279.

Deci, E., & Ryan, R. (1990). A motivational approach to the self: Integration in personality. In R. Dienstbier (Ed.), *Nebraska symposium on motivation* (Vol. 38, pp. 237–288). Lincoln: University of Nebraska Press.

Dodge, K. A., Asher, S. R., & Parkhurst, J. T. (1989). Social life as a goal coordination task. In C. Ames & R. Ames (Ed.), *Research on motivation in education* (Vol. 3, pp. 107–135). New York: Academic Press.

Dodge, K. A., Greenberg, M. T., Malone, P. S., & CPPRG. (2008). Testing an idealized dynamic cascade model of the development of serious violence in adolescents. *Child Development, 79,* 1907–1927.

Dodge, K. A., Pettit, G. S., McClaskey, C. L., & Brown, M. M. (1986). Social competence in children. *Monographs of the Society for Research in Child Development, 51*(2, Serial No. 213).

Dodge, K. A., & Somberg, D. (1987). Attributional biases in aggressive boys are exacerbated under conditions of threat to self. *Child Development, 58,* 213–224.

Domitrovich, C., & Greenberg, M. (2000). The study of implementation: Current findings from effective programs that prevent mental disorders in school-aged children. *Journal of Educational and Psychological Consultation, 11,* 193–221.

Eccles, J. S. (2005). Subjective task value and the Eccles et al. model of achievement-related outcomes. In A. Elliot, J. Dweck & C. S. Dweck (Eds.), *Handbook of competence and motivation* (pp. 105–121). New York: Guilford.

Eddy, J. M., Dishion, T. J., & Stoolmiller, M. (1998). The analysis of intervention change in children and families: Methodological and conceptual issues embedded in intervention studies. *Journal of Abnormal Child Psychology, 26,* 53–69.

Edwards, D., Hunt, M. H., Meyers, J., Grogg, K. R., & Jarrett, O. (2005). Acceptability and student outcome of a violence prevention curriculum. *Journal of Primary Prevention, 26,* 401–418.

Egan, S. K., & Perry, D. P. (1998). Does low self-regard invite victimization? *Developmental Psychology, 34,* 299–309.

Eisenberg, N., Fabes, R. A., Guthrie, I. K., & Reiser, M. (2000). Dispositional emotionality and regulation: Their role in predicting quality of social functioning. *Journal of Personality and Social Psychology, 78,* 136–157.

Eisenberg, N., Fabes, R. A., Karbon, M., Murphy, B. C., Carlo, G., & Wosinski, M. (1996). Relations of school children's comforting behavior to empathy-related reactions and shyness. *Social Development, 5,* 330–351.

Embry, D. D. (2004). Community-based prevention using simple, low-cost, evidence-based kernals and behavior vaccines. *Journal of Community Psychology, 32,* 575–591.

Erdley, C. A., & Asher, S. R. (1999). A social goals perspective on children's social competence. *Journal of Emotional and Behavioral Disorders, 7,* 156–167.

Farmer, T. W., Leung, M. C., Pearl, R., Rodkin, P. C., Cadwallader, T. W., & Van Acker, R. (2002). Deviant or diverse peer groups? The peer affiliations of aggressive elementary students. *Journal of Educational Psychology, 94,* 611–620.

Fite, P. J., Colder, C. R., Lochman, J. E., & Wells, K. C. (2008). Developmental trajectories of proactive and reactive aggression from fifth to ninth grade. *Journal of Clinical Child and Adolescent Psychology, 37,* 412–421

Fitzsimons, G. M., & Bargh, J. A. (2004). Automatic self-regulation. In R. F. Baumeister & K. D. Vohs (Ed.), *Handbook of self-regulation: Research, theory and applications* (pp. 151–170). New York: Guilford.

Fleming, C. B., Haggerty, K. P., Catalano, R. F., Harachi, T. W., Mazza, J. J., & Gruman, D. H. (2005). Do social and behavioral characteristics targeted by preventive interventions predict standardized test scores? *Journal of School Health, 75,* 342–348.

Frey, K. S., Jones, D. C., Hirschstein, M. K. & Edstrom, L. V. (in press). Teacher support of bullying prevention: The good, the bad, and the promising. In D. L. Espelage & S. M. Swearer (Ed.), *The handbook of bullying in North American schools.* New York: Routledge.

Frey, K. S., Nolen, S. B., Edstrom, L. V., & Hirschstein, M. K. (2005). Effects of a school-based social-emotional competence program: Linking children's goals, attributions and behavior. *Journal of Applied Developmental Psychology, 26,* 171–200.

Greenberg, M. T., Weissberg, R. P., O'Brien, M. U., Zins, J. E., Fredericks, L., Resnik, H., et al. (2003). Enhancing school-based prevention and youth development through coordinated social, emotional, and academic learning. *American Psychologist, 58,* 466–474.

Grossman, D. C., Neckerman, H. J., Koepsell, T. D., Liu, P. Y., Asher, K. N., Beland, K., et al., (1997). Effectiveness of a violence prevention program among children in elementary schools: A randomized controlled trials. *Journal of the American Medical Association, 277,* 1605–1611.

Guerra, N., Huesmann, Tolan, E., Van Acker, R., & Eron, L. D. (1995). Stressful events and individual beliefs as correlates of economic disadvantage and aggression among urban children. *Journal of Consulting and Clinical Psychology, 63,* 518–528.

Halberstadt, A. G., Denham, S. A., & Dunsmore, J. C. (2001). Affective social competence. *Social Development, 10,* 79–119.

Hamre, B. K., & Pianta, R. C. (2001). Early teacher–child relationships and the trajectory of children's school outcomes through eighth grade. *Child Development, 72,* 625–638.

Hanish, L. D., & Guerra, N. (2002). A longitudinal analysis of patterns of adjustment following peer victimization. *Development and psychopathology, 14,* 69–89.

Hanish, L. D., Martin, C. L., Fabes, R. A., Leonard, S., & Herzog, M. (2005). Exposure to externalizing peers in early childhood: Homophily and peer contagion processes. *Journal of Abnormal Child Psychology, 33,* 267–281.

Hastings, P. D., Zahn-Waxler, C., Robinson, J., Usher, B., & Bridges, D. (2000). The development of concern for others in children with behavior problems. *Developmental Psychology, 36,* 531–546.

Hazler, R., Miller, D., Carney, J., & Green, S. (2001). Adult recognition of school bullying situations. *Educational Research, 43,* 133–146.

Hirschstein, M. K., Edstrom, L. V., Frey, K. S., Snell, J. L., & MacKenzie,

E. P. (2007). Walking the talk in bullying prevention: Teacher implementation variables related to initial impact of the *Steps to Respect* program. *School Psychology Review, 36,* 3–21.

Hirschstein, M. K., Van Schoiack-Edstrom, L., Frey, K., & Nolen, S. B. (2001). *The social-emotional learning checklist (SELF-C): Technical report.* Unpublished manuscript, Committee for Children, Seattle, WA.

Holland, D., Lachicotte, W., Skinner, D., & Cain. C. (1998). *Identity and agency in cultural worlds.* Cambridge, MA: Harvard University Press.

Holsen, I., Smith, B. H., & Frey, K. S. (2008). Outcomes of the social competence program Second Step in Norwegian elementary schools. *School Psychology International, 29,* 71–88.

Hubbard, J. A., Dodge, K. A., Cillessen, A. H. N., Coie, J. D., & Schwartz, D. (2001). The dyadic nature of social information processing in boys' reactive and proactive aggression. *Journal of Personality and Social Psychology, 80,* 268–280.

Hubbard, J. A., Smithmeyer, C. M., Ramsden, S. R., Parker, E. H., Flanagan, K. D., Dearing, K. F. et al. (2002). Observational, physiological, and self-report measures of children's anger: Relations to reactive versus proactive aggression. *Child Development, 73,* 1101–1118.

Huesmann, L. R. (1988). An information-processing model for the development of aggression. *Aggressive Behavior, 14,* 13–24.

Huesmann, L. R., & Guerra, N. G. (1997). Children's normative beliefs about aggression and aggressive behavior. *Journal of Personality and Social Psychology, 72,* 408–419.

Jarvinen, D. W., & Nicholls, J. G. (1996). Adolescent's social goals, beliefs about the causes of social success, and satisfaction in peer relations. *Developmental Psychology, 32,* 435–441.

Jimerson, S. R., & Furlong, M. J. (2006). *Handbook of school violence and school safety.* Mahwah, NJ: Erlbaum.

Johnson, D., & Johnson, R. (1996). Conflict resolution and peer mediation programs in elementary and secondary schools: A review of the research. *Review of Educational Research, 66,* 459–506.

Juvonen, J., Nishina, A., & Graham, S. (2000). Peer harassment, psychological adjustment, and school functioning in early adolescence. *Journal of Educational Psychology, 92,* 349–359.

Kallestad, J. H., & Olweus, D. (2003). Predicting teachers' and schools' implementation of the Olweus Bullying Prevention Program: A multilevel study, *Prevention and Treatment, 6,* 3–21.

Kam, C. M., Greenberg, M. T., & Walls, C. T. (2003). Examining the role of implementation quality in school-based prevention using the PATHS curriculum. *Prevention Science, 4,* 55–63.

Kendall, P. C. (1993). Cognitive-behavioral therapies with youth: Guiding theory, current status, and emerging developments. *Journal of Consulting and Clinical Psychology, 61,* 235–247.

Killen, M., & Nucci, L. P. (1995). Morality, autonomy, and social conflict. In M. Killen, & D. Hart (Ed.), *Morality in everyday life: Developmental perspectives* (pp. 52–86). New York: Cambridge.

Kramer, R., McClintock, C. G., & Messick, D. M. (1986). Social values and cooperative response to a simulated resource conservation crisis. *Journal of Personality, 54,* 576–592.

Lacourse, E., Côté, S., Nagin, D. S., Vitaro, F., Brendgen, M., & Tremblay, R. E. (2002). A longitudinal-experimental approach to testing theories of antisocial behavior development. *Development and Psychopathology, 14,* 909–924.

Ladd, G. W., & Troop-Gordon, W. (2003). The role of chronic peer difficulties in the development of children's psychological adjustment problems. *Child Development, 74,* 1344–1367.

Larsen, T. S., & Samdal, O. (2007). Implementing *Second Step*: Balancing fidelity and program adaptation. *Journal of Educational and Psychological Consultation, 17,* 1–29.

Lave, J., & Wenger, E. (1991). *Situated learning: Legitimate peripheral participation.* New York: Cambridge University Press.

Leary, M. R., Kowalski, R. M., Smith, L., & Phillips, S. (2003). Teasing, rejection, and violence: Case studies of the school shootings. *Aggressive Behavior, 29,* 202–214.

McMahon, S. D., & Washburn, J. J. (2003). Violence prevention: An evaluation of program effects with urban African American students. *Journal of Primary Prevention, 24,* 43–73.

McMahon, S. D., Washburn, J. J., Felix, E. D., Yakin, J., & Childrey, G. (2000). Violence prevention: Program effects on urban preschool and kindergarten children. *Applied and Preventive Psychology, 9,* 271–281.

Mehas, K., Boling, K., Sobieniak, S. Sprague, J., Burke, M. D., & Hagen, S. (1998). Finding a safe haven in middle school. *Teaching Exceptional Children, 30*(4), 20–23.

Mischel, W., Shoda, Y., & Rodriguez, M. L. (1989). Delay of gratification in children. *Science, 57,* 358–367.

Nangle, D. W., Erdley., C. A., Zeff, K. R., Stanchfield, L. L., & Gold, J. A. (2004). Opposites do not attract: Social status and behavioral style concordances and discordances among children and the peers who like or dislike them. *Journal of Abnormal Child Psychology, 32,* 425–434.

Nishina, A., Juvonen, J., & Witkow, M. R. (2005). Sticks and stones may break my bones, but names will make me feel sick: The psychosocial, somatic, and scholastic consequences of peer harassment. *Journal of Clinical Child and Adolescent Psychology, 34,* 37–48.

Noell, G. H., Duhon, G. J., Gatti, S. L., & Connell, J. E. (2002). Consultation, follow-up, and implementation of behavior management interventions in general education. *School Psychology Review, 31,* 217–234.

Nolen, S. B., Frey, K. S., Hirschstein, M., & Sylvester (Edstrom), L. (1997, March 26). *Following steps or dancing the dance: Teacher's beliefs, goals and their use of a social-emotional curriculum.* Paper presented at the annual meeting of the American Educational Research Association, Chicago, IL.

Nolen, S. B., Horn, I. S., Ward, C. J., Stevens, R. R., & Estacio, K. (2005). *When worlds collide: Negotiating competing views of teaching across social contexts and the effect on student teachers' motivation to learn.* Paper presented at the biennial meeting of the European Association for Learning and Instruction, Nicosia, Cyprus.

Ojanen, T., Aunola, K., & Salmivalli, C. (2007). Situation-specificity of children's social goals: Changing goals according to changing situations? *International Journal of Behavioral Development, 31,* 232–241.

Ojanen, T., Grönoos, M., & Salmivalli, C. (2005). An interpersonal circumplex model of children's social goals: Links with peer-reported behavior and sociometric status. *Developmental Psychology, 41,* 699–710.

Orpinas, P., Parcel, G. S., McAlister, A., & Frankowski, R. (1995). Violence prevention in middle schools: A pilot evaluation. *Journal of Adolescent Health, 17,* 360–371.

Patrick, H., Ryan, A. M., & Kaplan, A. (2007). Early adolescents' perceptions of the classroom social environment, motivational beliefs, and engagement. *Journal of Educational Psychology, 99,* 83–98.

Payne, A. A., Gottfredson, D., C., & Gottfredson, G. D. (2006). School predictors of the intensity of implementation of school-based prevention programs: Results from a national study. *Prevention Science, 7,* 225–237.

Ransford, C. R. (2007). The role of school and teacher characteristics on teacher burnout and implementation quality of a social-emotional learning curriculum. *Dissertation Abstracts International Section A: Humanities and Social Sciences, 68* (5-A), 1800.

Reid, J. B., Eddy, J. M., Fetrow, R. A., & Stoolmiller, M. (1999). Descriptions and immediate impacts of a preventive intervention for conduct problems. *American Journal of Community Psychology, 27,* 483–517.

Rodkin, P. C., Farmer, T. W., Pearl, R., & Van Acker, R. (2006). They're cool: Social status and peer group support for aggressive boys and girls. *Social Development, 15,* 175–204.

Rubin, K. H., & Krasnor, L. R. (1986). Social-cognitive and social behavioral perspectives on problem-solving. In M. Perlmutter (Ed.), *Cognitive perspectives on children's social and behavioral development* (pp. 1–68). Hillsdale, NJ: Erlbaum.

Salmivalli, C., Ojanen, T., Haanpää, J., & Peets, K. (2005). "I'm O.K. but you're not" and other peer-relational schemas: Explaining individual differences in children's social goals. *Developmental Psychology, 41,* 363–375.

Sameroff, A. J., & Chandler, M. J. (1975). Reproductive risk and the continuum of caretaking causality. In F. D. Horowitz, M. Hetherington, S. Scarr-Salapatek, & G. Siegal (Eds.), *Review of child development research* (Vol. 4, pp. 187–244). Chicago, IL: University of Chicago Press.

Sameroff, A. J., & MacKenzie, M. J. (2003). Research strategies for capturing transactional models of development: The limits of the possible. *Development and psychopathology, 15,* 613–640.

Schick, A., & Cierpka, M. (2005). Faustlos: Evaluation of a curriculum to prevent violence in elementary schools. *Applied and Preventive Psychology, 11,* 157–165.

Schunk, D. H., & Zimmerman., B. J. (1997). Social origins of self-regulatory competence. *Educational Psychologist, 32,* 195– 208.

Schwartz, D., Dodge, K. A., Coie, J. D., Hubbard, J. A., Cillessen, A. H. N., Lemerise, E. A., et al. (1998). Social-cognitive and behavioral correlates of aggression and victimization in boys' play groups. *Journal of Abnormal Child Psychology, 26,* 431–440.

Schwartz, D., & Gorman, A. H. (2003). Community violence exposure and children's academic functioning. *Journal of Educational Psychology, 95,* 163–173.

Seligman, M. E. P., Steen, T. A., Park, N., & Peterson, C. (2005). Positive psychology progress: Empirical validation of interventions. *American Psychologist, 60,* 410–421.

Snyder, J., Schrepferman, L., Oeser, J., Patterson, G., Stoolmiller, M., Johnson, K., et al. (2005). Deviancy training and association with deviant peers in young children: Occurrence and contribution to early-onset conduct problems. *Development and Psychopathology, 17,* 397–413.

Sprague, J., Walker, H., Golly, A., White, K., Myers, D. R., & Shannon, T. (2001). Translating research into effective practice: The effects of a universal staff and student intervention on indicators of discipline and school safety. *Education and Treatment of Children, 24,* 495–511.

Taub, J. (2002). Evaluation of the Second Step violence prevention program at a rural elementary school. *School Psychology Review, 31,* 186–200.

Thomas, M. G., Leidy, B. D., Powers, J., & Holden, M. (1998). *Evaluating violence prevention programs in preschool: Second Step in the United States Marine Corps*, Paper presented at Program Evaluation and Family Violence Research: An International Conference, New Hampshire.

Troop-Gordon, W., & Asher, S. R. (2005). Modifications in children's goals when encountering obstacles to conflict resolution. *Child Development, 76,* 568–582.

U.S. Department of Health and Human Services, Substance Abuse and Mental Health Services Administration. (2002). *SAMHSA model programs: Model prevention programs supporting academic achievement.* Retrieved from www.modelprograms.samhsa.gov

Vadeboncoeur, J. A., & Portes, P. R. (2002). Students "at risk": Exploring identity from a sociocultural perspective. In D. McInerny & S. V. Etten (Eds.), *Sociocultural influences on motivation and learning* (pp. 89–127). Greenwich, CT: Information Age.

Vaillancourt, T., Hymel, S., & McDougall, P. (2003). Bullying is power: Implications for school-based intervention strategies. In M. J. Elias & J. E. Zins (Ed.), *Bullying, peer harassment, and victimization in the schools: The next generation of prevention* (pp. 157–177). New York: Haworth Press.

Van Schoiack, L. (2000). Promoting social-emotional competence: Effects of a social-emotional learning program and corresponding teaching practices in the schools. *Dissertation Abstracts International, 61,* 2689.

Van Schoiack-Edstrom, L., Frey, K. S., & Beland, K. (2002). Changing adolescents' attitudes about relational and physical aggression: An early evaluation of a school-based intervention. *School Psychology Review, 31,* 201– 216.

Vohs, K. D., Baumeister, R. F., & Ciarocco, N. J. (2005). Self-regulation and self-presentation: Regulatory resource depletion impairs impression management and effortful self-presentation depletes regulatory resources. *Journal of Personality and Social Psychology, 88,* 632–657.

Vohs, K. D., & Ciarocco, N. J. (2004). Interpersonal functioning requires self-regulation. In R. F. Baumeister & Vohs, K. D. (Ed.), *Handbook of self-regulation* (pp. 392–410). New York: Guilford.

Walker, H. M. (2004). Commentary: Use of evidenced-based intervention in schools: Where we've been, where we are, and where we need to go. *School Psychological Review, 33,* 398–407.

Weissberg, R. P. & Greenberg, M. T. (1998). School and community competence-enhancement and prevention programs. In. W. Damon (Series Ed.) & I. E. Siegel & K. A. Renniger (Vol. Eds.), *Handbook of child psychology: Vol. 4. Child psychology in practice* (5th ed., pp. 877–954). New York: Wiley.

Wentzel, K. R. (2005). Peer relationships, motivation, and academic performance at school. In A. Elliot, J. Dweck, & C. S. Dweck (Eds.), *Handbook of competence and motivation* (pp. 279–296). New York: Guilford.

Wilson, D. B., Gottfredson, D. C., & Najaka, S. S. (2001). School-based prevention of problem behaviors: A meta-analysis. *Journal of Quantitative Criminology, 17,* 242–272.

Zelli, A., Dodge, K. A., Lochman, J. D., Laird, J., & Conduct Problems Prevention Research Group. (1999). The distinction between beliefs legitimizing aggression and deviant processing of social cues: Testing measurement validity and the hypothesis that biased processing mediates the effects of beliefs on aggression. *Journal of Personality and Social Psychology, 77,* 150–166.

## APPENDIX 30.1
### Summary of *Second Step* Evaluations

| Study | Design | Sample Size | Age Range | Population Characteristics | Measurement & Context | Results of Intervention (compared to control or pretest) |
|---|---|---|---|---|---|---|
| **Studies of the Preschool–kindergarten version of *Second Step*** | | | | | | |
| Thomas, Leidy, Powers, & Holden (1998) | 1: Simple pre & post | 141 | 4–5 | Domestic military bases | Directly observed events | Greater civility (ratio of positive to negative social behaviors) |
| | 2: Non-equivalent control | 136 | 3–5 | Domestic military bases | Social-emotional knowledge | Improved knowledge |
| | | | | | Directly observed events | Greater civility |
| McMahon, Washburn, Felix, Yakin, & Childrey (2000) | Simple pre & post | 109 | 3–7 | Chicago | Directly observed events | Reductions in verbal and physical aggression; disruptive behavior |
| | | | | 78% Black | Social-emotional knowledge | Improved |
| | | | | 100% subsidized lunch | Teacher-rated social competence | No change |
| | | | | | Teacher-rated problem behavior | No change |
| **Studies of the Elementary School version of *Second Step*** | | | | | | |
| Grossman, et al. (1997) | Randomly assigned control | 588 | 6–8 | NW urban & suburban | Directly observed events (playground, class and lunchrooms) | Less physical aggression, more prosocial behavior. Verbal aggression not significant. |
| | | 790 in 12 schools | | 79% White | Teacher-rated social competence | No difference |
| | | | | Low-to-middle income | Teacher-rated problem behavior | No difference |
| | | | | | Parent-rated problem behavior | No difference |
| Frey, Nolen, Edstrom, & Hirschstein (2005) | Randomly assigned control (1) | 703 in 15 schools | 6–11 | NW urban & suburban | *Prisoner's dilemma game* | |
| | | | | | Goal preferences (interview) | More egalitarian, fewer dominating goals |
| | | 393 pairs | | 62% White | Expected satisfaction | Lower for self-serving outcome |
| | | 253 | | 47% subsidized lunch | Post-game satisfaction | No difference |
| | | | | | Satisfaction rationale | More egalitarian |
| | | | | | Joint cooperative choices | No difference |
| | | | | | *Negotiated prize division* | |
| | | | | | Directly observed events | Fewer aggressive and, for girls, more cooperative strategies |
| | | | | | Adult intervention post-negotiation | Less intervention for unresolved conflict |
| | | | | | Satisfaction | Greater satisfaction after prize division |
| | | | | | Hypothetical intent attributions | No difference |
| | | | | | Hypothetical response to aggression | No difference |
| | | | | | Teacher-rated social competence | Higher Year 1, no change Year 2 |
| | | | | | Teacher-rated problem behavior | Lower Year 1, no change Year 2 |

| Study | Design | Sample Size | Age Range | Population Characteristics | Measurement & Context | Results of Intervention (compared to control or pretest) |
|---|---|---|---|---|---|---|
| Schick & Cierpka (2005) | Randomly assigned control | 335 | 6–9 | Heidelberg & Mannheim Germany | Parent-rated internalizing behavior | Less (anxiety/depression) |
| | | | | | Parent-rated externalizing behavior | No difference |
| | | | | | Teacher-rated social competence | No difference |
| Holsen, Smith, & Frey (2008) | Age cohort | 1153 in 11 schools | 11–13 | Norway | Self-rated social competence | Improved, 5th & 6th grade girls |
| | | | | | Self-rated externalizing behavior | Improved, 6th grade boys |
| | | | | | Self-rated internalizing behavior | No differences |
| Taub (2002) | non-equivalent control | 70 in 2 schools | 7–11 | NE rural | Directly observed events (classrooms) | More likely to follow adult direction. Less peer engagement. No differences in bothering students or following rules. |
| | | | | Low income | | |
| | | | | White | Teacher-rated social competence | Higher in intervention group |
| | | | | | Teacher-rated problem behaviors | Lower in intervention group |

**Studies of the Middle School / Junior High version of *Second Step***

| Study | Design | Sample Size | Age Range | Population Characteristics | Measurement & Context | Results of Intervention (compared to control or pretest) |
|---|---|---|---|---|---|---|
| Van Schoiack-Edstrom, Frey, & Beland (2002) | non-equivalent control | 714 | 11–14 | Seattle, Los Angeles & Halifax, Canada | Approval of aggressive behavior: physical, verbal & social exclusion | Less approval of aggression |
| | | | | Ethnically diverse | Perceived difficulty of performing social-emotional skills | Lower perceived difficulty |
| McMahon & Washburn (2003) | Simple pre & post | 86–123 in 2 schools | | Chicago | Self-reported empathy, impulsivity | Improved empathy, not impulsivity Improved |
| | | | | Black | Social-emotional knowledge tests | One school improved, one declined |
| | | | | Low income | Aggression (teacher, peer and self-report) | One school improved, one declined |
| | | | | | Prosocial (teacher & peer-report) Sense of school membership | One school improved, one declined |

**Studies of Adaptations to the *Second Step* Program**

| Study | Design | Sample Size | Age Range | Population Characteristics | Measurement & Context | Results of Intervention (compared to control or pretest) |
|---|---|---|---|---|---|---|
| Orpinas, Parcel, McAlister, & Frankowski (1995) | Three non-equivalent groups: control, program, peer leaders | 210 | 11–12 | Texas 90% Hispanic | Self-reported aggression | No overall differences. Boys' aggression declined in 2 of 4 program classrooms |
| | | | | 50% subsidized lunch | Approval of violent response | Increased more slowly |
| | | | | | Self-efficacy | Improved for anger control, not for resisting peer pressure to fight |
| | | | | | Social-emotional knowledge tests | Improvements in two classrooms only |
| Sprague, Walker, Golly, White, Myers, & Shannon (2001) | Non-equivalent control v. enhanced program | 16 schools | 5–14 8–14 only | Oregon urban & suburban 84% White 45% subsidized lunch | School level disciplinary reports | Fewer disciplinary infractions |
| | | | | | Social-emotional knowledge tests | Greater knowledge |

(*continued*)

**APPENDIX 30.1**
**Continued**

| Study | Design | Sample Size | Age Range | Population Characteristics | Measurement & Context | Results of Intervention (compared to control or pretest) |
|---|---|---|---|---|---|---|
| Edwards, Hunt, Meyers, Grogg, & Jarrett (2005) | Simple pre & post; added material on bullying | 455 in multiple schools | 10–12 | SE urban district ethnically diverse<br><br>72% subsidized lunch | Coping with bullying survey<br>Self-reported behavior<br><br>Social-emotional knowledge tests<br>Teacher-reported behavior<br><br>Acceptability and utility interviews | Improved coping, positive and negative<br>Improved self-reliance, no differences in anxiety or interpersonal relations<br>Knowledge improvements<br><br>Improved grades: respects others; cooperates with peers, teacher<br>96% provided details of using skills, 98% voiced approval of program |

# Contributors

**Karl L. Alexander**
Department of Sociology
The John Hopkins University

**Elaine Allensworth**
Consortium on Chicago School Research
University of Chicago

**Eric M. Anderman**
School of Educational Policy and Leadership
Ohio State University

**Robert W. Balfanz**
Center for Social Organization of Schools
The Johns Hopkins University

**Bonnie L. Barber**
Psychology Department
Murdoch University

**Victor Battistich**
(Deceased)
College of Education
University of Missouri–St. Louis

**Geoffrey Borman**
School of Education
University of Wisconsin – Madison

**Vaughan Byrnes**
Center for Social Organization of Schools
Johns Hopkins University

**Rosario Ceballo**
Department of Psychology
University of Michigan

**Jennifer Coffman**
Center for Developmental Science
University of North Carolina–Chapel Hill

**James P. Comer**
Yale Child Study Center
Yale University

**Carol McDonald Connor**
College of Education
Florida State University

**Harris Cooper**
Department of Psychology
Duke University

**Shauna M. Cooper**
Department of Psychology
University of South Carolina

**Danielle Dupuis**
College of Education and Human Development
University of Minnesota

**Jacquelynne S. Eccles**
Department of Psychology
University of Michigan

**Doris R. Entwisle**
Department of Sociology
The Johns Hopkins University

**Quyen Epstein-Ngo**
Department of Psychology
University of Michigan

**Dorothy L. Espelage**
College of Education
University of Illinois at Urbana-Champaign

**Ron Fairchild**
Center for Summer Learning
The Johns Hopkins University

**Karin S. Frey**
College of Education
University of Washington

**Kathleen C. Gallagher**
Frank Porter Graham Child Development Institute
University of North Carolina–Chapel Hill

**Maria Garriott**
Center for Social Organization of Schools
The Johns Hopkins University

**Jennie Grammer**
Department of Psychology
University of North Carolina–Chapel Hill

**Anne Gregory**
Graduate School of Applied and Professional Psychology
Rutgers University

**John T. Guthrie**
College of Education
University of Maryland

**Jill V. Hamm**
School of Education
University of North Carolina–Chapel Hill

**Bridget K. Hamre**
Curry School of Education
University of Virginia

**Melissa K. Holt**
Center on Adolescence
University of New Hampshire

**Marisela Huerta**
UMACC
University of Michigan

**Leslie Jones**
Center for Social Organization of Schools
The Johns Hopkins University

**Kirsten Kainz**
Frank Porter Graham Child Development Institute
University of North Carolina–Chapel Hill

**Revathy Kumar**
Judith Herb College of Education
University of Toledo

**Beth Kurtz-Costes**
Psychology Department
University of North Carolinae–Chapel Hill

**Douglas J. Mac Iver**
Center for Social Organization of Schools
Johns Hopkins University

**Nancy A. Madden**
Success for All Foundation

**Martin L. Maehr**
School of Education
University of Michigan

**Joseph L. Mahoney**
Department of Education
University of California–Irvine

**Laura McCall**
Department of Psychology
University of North Carolina–Chapel Hill

**Barbara McCombs**
Human Motivation, Learning, and Development Center
University of Denver

**Clark McKown**
Rush Neurobehavioral Center

**Judith L. Meece**
School of Education
University of North Carolina

**Elizabeth A. Moorman**
Department of Psychology
University of Illinois at Urbana-Champaign

**Frederick J. Morrison**
School of Education
University of Michigan

**Christian E. Mueller**
College of Education
University of Memphis

**Jenny Nagaoka**
Consortium on Chicago School Research
University of Chicago

**Susan B. Nolen**
College of Education
University of Washington

**Linda S. Olson**
Sociology Department
John Hopkins University

**Peter Ornstein**
Department of Psychology
University of North Carolina–Chapel Hill

**Maria E. Parente**
Department of Education
University of California–Irvine

**Anthony Pellegrini**
College of Education
University of Minnesota

**Robert C. Pianta**
Curry School of Education
University of Virginia

**Eva M. Pomerantz**
Department of Psychology
University of Illinois at Urbana-Champaign

**V. Paul Poteat**
College of Education
University of Illinois at Urbana-Champaign

**Melissa Roderick**
School of Social Service Administration
University of Chicago

**Robert W. Roeser**
Department of Psychology
Portland State University

**Stephanie J. Rowley**
Department of Psychology
University of Michigan

**Allen Ruby**
Center for Social Organization of Schools
The Johns Hopkins University

**Priscilla San Souci**
Department of Psychology
University of North Carolina–Chapel Hill

**Victoria A. Schaefer**
Westat, Inc.

**Fran Sion**
Center for Social Organization of Schools
The Johns Hopkins University

**Robert E. Slavin**
School of Education
Center for Research and Reform in Education
John Hopkins University

**Ginger Stoker**
Consortium on Chicago School Research
University of Chicago

**Margaret R. Stone**
School of Family and Consumer Science
University of Arizona

**Tim Urdan**
Psychology Department
Santa Clara University

**Lynn Vernon-Feagans**
School of Education
University of North Carolina–Chapel Hill

**Rhona S. Weinstein**
Department of Psychology
University of California–Berkley

**Kathryn R. Wentzel**
College of Education
University of Maryland

**Allan Wigfield**
College of Education
University of Maryland

**Lei Zhang**
School of Education
University of North Carolina–Chapel Hill

**Edward F. Zigler**
Zigler Center in Child Development and Social Policy
Yale University

# Index